Publisher
Richard K. Swadley

Acquisitions and Development Manager
Stacy Hiquet

Managing Editor
Cindy Morrow

Acquisitions and Development Editor
Mark Taber

Production Editor
Carolyn Linn

Editors
Marla Abraham
Kitty Wilson

Editorial Coordinator
Bill Whitmer

Editorial Assistants
Carol Ackerman
Sharon Cox
Lynette Quinn

Technical Reviewers
James A. Armstrong
Sam Kimery
James Pitkow

Marketing Manager
Gregg Bushyeager

Cover Designer
Tim Amrhein

Book Designer
Alyssa Yesh

Director of Production and Manufacturing
Jeff Valler

Imprint Manager
Juli Cook

Manufacturing Coordinator
Paul Gilchrist

Production Analysts
Dennis Hager
Mary Beth Wakefield

Graphics Image Specialists
Tim Montgomery
Dennis Sheehan

Production
Carol Bowers
Michael Brumitt
Elaine Brush
Elaine Crabtree
Judy Everly
Rob Falco
Ayanna Lacey
Stephanie McComb
Chad Poore
Casey Price
Brian-Kent Proffitt
Scott Tullis
Suzanne Tully
Holly Wittenburg

Indexer
Jeanne Clark

Overview

Overview

Appendixes

Contents

Part V Weaving a Web 669

Acknowledgments

Like the intertwining tendrils of the Web, my debt of acknowledgement spreads far and deep.

For the book itself, I thank Mark Taber and the team at Sams Publishing who've given me professional support as well as the freedom to shape my ideas. I thank everyone whose web I've used as an example in this book for their kind permission and for taking the time to answer my questions about their applications. In my writing, I relied on many tools and information sources to research and understand the Web, including Brian Pinkerton's WebCrawler, EINet's Galaxy, the Web Catalog at Centre Universitaire d'Informatique, Richard Bocker's Planet Earth, and the many other tools I describe in the chapters of Part III in this book.

I'd like to thank those who have helped me in my Net adventures and enriched my work by helping it become known and increasing the feedback I receive about it, including Harley Hahn, Oscar Nierstrasz, Brendan Kehoe, Ellie Cutler, Gleason Sackman, Kevin Savetz, Neil Randall, Lou Rosenfeld, and Kevin Hughes. I acknowledge the influence of pioneers in explaining the Internet, Brendan Kehoe and Ed Krol. I thank my fellow Net information surfers—Scott Yanoff, Simon Gibbs, Martijn Koster, Richard Bocker, John Makulowich and the many others whose work continues to contribute to my understanding.

There are many people at Rensselaer Polytechnic Institute who have helped me in my studies. The faculty of the Department of Language, Literature and Communication have directly or indirectly assisted me in many ways. I thank my dissertation advisor, Robert Krull, for understanding why I would take a summer to work on a book. I thank Tersa Harrison and Tim Stephen for their continued guidance in my scholarly growth. I owe a debt of gratitude to Roger Grice for helping me learn about the information development processes and to Elizabeth Keyes and Patricia Search for giving me insights into visual aspects of information layering and structuring—these concepts influenced the weaving methodology I present in Part V. My fellow graduate students in the department have been a source of fun and support. I thank Laura Gurak and Emilie Gould for their help in understanding computer-mediated communication. The staff at Rensselaer's Information Technology Services run a superb Web server, and I thank the RPInfo team for allowing me to contribute information to it.

My work and understanding of the Web itself, as represented in this book, has been influenced and guided by all those whom I've interacted with in my Net activities. I thank the people whose works I include in my CMC Information Sources list. *Computer-Mediated Communication* magazine assistant editors Leysia Palen and Gary Ritzenthaler and everyone participating in the Computer-Mediated Communication Studies Center continue to help me learn. I thank my students in workshops and courses I've taught at the University of Wisconsin-Milwaukee and Rensselaer Polytechnic Institute, whose questions about computers prompted me to think about the needs of new users. I thank everyone on the Net—without you, I'd have a lesser world to explore.

—John December

As always, there are too many people to thank. So I will restrict this list to those who truly contributed.

My deepest gratitude to:

My wife, Heather, for putting up with the sleeplessness and the absences

My daughter Catherine, for her maturity

My daughter Michelle, for her laughter

John December, for sharing the book in the first place

Carrie Pascal, for pitching in when I needed it most

Mark Taber, for actually believing we could finish it

Dave Goodwin, for his encouragement

Keith McGowan, for his patience

The hundreds of creators and developers of the Web and its tools, for obvious reasons

—Neil Randall

About the Authors

John December (decemj@rpi.edu) is a candidate in the Ph.D. program in Communication and Rhetoric at Rensselaer Polytechnic Institute in Troy, New York. He has taught courses in computer science, creative writing, expository writing, and technical communication, and conducted Internet training workshops. Prior to studying at Rensselaer, John earned an M.S. in computer science from the University of Wisconsin-Milwaukee, an M.F.A. in creative writing (Poetry) from The Wichita State University, and a B.S. in mathematics from Michigan Technological University. From 1985 to 1989, he worked as a software developer for the Boeing Company. His poetry has appeared in literary magazines including *Mid-American Review, Sou'wester, Passages North*, and others. Known on the Net for his list of information sources about the Internet and Computer-Mediated Communication, he's also written papers, articles, and book chapters about the Internet and is publisher and editor of *Computer-Mediated Communication Magazine.*

Neil Randall (nrandall@hookup.net) teaches English at the University of Waterloo in Waterloo, Ontario, Canada. He offers courses in professional writing and rhetorical theory, and conducts research in issues surrounding the Internet, computer-mediated communications, and other technological issues. He is the author of *Teach Yourself the Internet: Around the World in 21 Days* (Sams Publishing). He has published articles and reviews in several computer magazines, including *Windows, Compute, Amiga World*, and *Computing Canada*, and is currently a columnist for *PC Gamer* and a contributing editor for *CD-ROM Today* and *Computer Entertainment News*. He writes a weekly newspaper column dealing with computers and has published several related newspaper features.

Thomas Boutell (boutell@netcom.com) keeps the frequently asked questions list (FAQ) for the comp.infosystems.www.* newsgroups and has written a number of other Web-related gimcracks. He became involved with the Web while at Cold Spring Harbor Labs, a biology research laboratory on the East Coast, and has since moved to Seattle where he works for a new firm, Progressive Networks. You can find his home page at the URL http://sunsite.unc.edu/boutell/index.html.

Andrew Dinsdale (aa293@detroit.freenet.org) is an Internet Communications Specialist for DataServ, Inc., a technology integration firm serving the K-12 community. He writes and maintains The Commercial Use (of the Net) Strategies home page, he developed the Web pages for Diversity University MOO, and he contributes to John December's Web-based Computer-Mediated Communication Studies Center.

Laura Lemay (lemay@netcom.com) is a technical writer in northern California who has been a prolific user of and contributor to the Internet for close to eight years. She is the author of *Teach Yourself HTML Web Publishing in a Week,* scheduled to be published by Sams Publishing in December 1994.

Carrie Pascal (clpascal@cantor.math.uwaterloo.ca) is in her final semester at the University of Waterloo, studying English and computer science. She is currently focusing her efforts on examining how humans interact with hypertext and hypermedia systems. She has created and maintains a number of Web pages.

David Woolley (drwool@well.com) created one of the first computer conferencing systems, PLATO Notes, the model for such conferencing software as Lotus Notes, DEC Notes, and the tin newsreader. Today he is a software designer, consultant, and writer, and is involved in a project to set up a Web-based Free-Net in Minneapolis-St.Paul. He is interested in nearly everything.

Introduction

Seldom in human history have people adopted a communications technology so widely and rapidly as Internet users have chosen the Web. Begun in 1991 by developers at the European Laboratory for Particle Physics (CERN) in Geneva, Switzerland, the World Wide Web started as a way to organize and link related information. Through presentations and a demonstrations, the CERN team taught others about their system, and Web use grew among members of scientific communities, researchers, and users of the Internet.

By 1993, the creators of graphical interfaces to the Web like Mosaic had developed a "look and feel" that fueled the Web's popularity even more. By late 1993, the Mosaic browser used with the Web was hailed by John Markoff in the *New York Times* as the "killer app" of the Internet itself. Through its easy-to-use interface, Mosaic revealed a seamless interplay of networked information, a treasure-trove of resources growing more rapidly than the exploding Internet itself.

Some people view the Web and its browsers as a harbinger of an "Information Superhighway." However, the reality of the Web doesn't match the images of a future with 500 TV channels or stereotypes of "hackers" and online subcultures. Instead, the Web exists now and offers opportunities for communication unparalleled in history. As a tool for human expression, the Web displays all the foibles, foolishness, and cacophony people seem destined to create. The Web also has the potential for human brilliance, for fostering sparks of interaction among people that grows into knowledge, perhaps leading to wisdom.

Why This Book?

If you are curious about what global networks may offer, or if you are an experienced Internet traveler, this book gives you information that will help you unleash the power of the World Wide Web. You will learn what the Web is, how to connect to it, how to move through its information spaces, what people do on the Web, the fundamentals of weaving your own web, and what issues the Web and its users face for the future.

- If you are new to computer networks, this book will guide you through the basics of the Web and offer you a reference for future growth.

- If you are in commerce, government, or education and are considering Web-based information and connections among people, this book will expand your awareness of what can be done.

- If you are an experienced Internet traveler, this book will open new insights into the structure and evolution of information spaces.

- If you are an educator, this book can help you define the Network literacy that is right for your students.
- If you are an information publisher, this book presents a method for weaving a web to meet your users' needs.
- If you are in industry, this book will open new avenues for disseminating research, connecting employees, and reaching customers.
- If you are considering the Web as a way to create a community, this book will give you skills in web weaving as well as describe examples of community information systems.
- If you train people in use of the Internet or Web, this book will give you a valuable selection of topics to cover and teach.

Gain an Overview of the Web

The Web itself is a world-wide collection of interconnected hardware, software, and networked systems. Part I of this book delves into the Web's development, history, and basic operation. You'll gain an understanding of the Web in the context of hypermedia and survey the Web in a whirlwind tour of some of its major features.

Find Out How to Connect to the Web

Part II introduces you to the browsers, tools, and connections necessary for you to experience the Web. You'll gain an understanding of the nuts-and-bolts issues of browsers and connecting to the Web, see the variety of browsers available for accessing the Web, and understand the add-ons necessary for multimedia experiences.

Learn How to Navigate the Web

While browsers present a coherent, seamless view into the Web, the problem of making sense of what you find remains. What is important? How does a user find something? Part III presents a full spectrum of skills for using the Web for information discovery and retrieval. You'll learn how the Web's information spaces interconnect, how to use a browser, and all about the many network protocols Web browsers can access. You'll develop skills in navigating and searching for subjects, keywords, and information spaces, and learn how to "surf."

Raise Your Awareness of What the Web Offers

In order to use the Web effectively and also consider how you might contribute your knowledge to it, you need to develop an awareness of the possibilities for Web expression. Part IV surveys dozens of uses in many areas, providing an extensive tour of information and communication applications of the Web. The chapters survey exemplary applications and describe details of the expressive possibilities they offer. You will increase your knowledge of what is "out there" now, with emphasis on the variety and ingenuity of expressions in commerce, entertainment, education, scholarship, research, science, technology, communication, publishing, government, and communities.

Learn How to Weave a Web of Your Own

Just as forming symbols is just one part of the task of writing, there is more to weaving a web that creating files of hypertext markup language code. Part V explains the basics of the hypertext markup language within the context of a method for weaving webs. This web-weaving method includes processes for planning, analysis, design, implementation and development (including publicity) of webs for organizations or individuals, with practical advice on how to serve the needs of a target audience and organize and shape information.

Consider Issues for the Web's Future

Finally, examine some issues important to the future of the Web. Included in Part VI are essays that examine the commercial future of the Web, challenges for information providers and society, the development of communication systems, and the trends in networked information and Web uses.

Unleash the Power of the Web

Perhaps you have heard the term "Information Superhighway." If you have, you might have wondered what it could mean. While not a fulfillment of all the hype associated with this term, the Web today offers an astounding collection of networked information with the potential to become even more extensive and valuable.

The constant growth of the Web creates an important need to gain insight into its tangle of links. As the Web rapidly becomes *the* destination for graphical interfaces to the Net, the focus of user training and the preferred method for perceiving the Net will become the Web. This book aims to unleash the Web's potential by giving you knowledge and skills, introducing expressive possibilities, and providing you with the understanding necessary to take part in the Web's communications revolution.

Typographic Conventions Used in This Book

The term *Web* refers to the global collection of all publicly accessible World Wide Web servers. In lowercase, *web* refers to an collection of hypertext that exists locally on one of these servers. In other words, you can weave a web and connect it to the global Web.

The names of Internet protocols are capitalized when used within the text (for example, Gopher, FTP). In examples of computer interaction or when shown in a Web browser, these terms are presented in lowercase.

Internet addresses, commands, and directory and filenames are set in `monospaced type` to set them off from the rest of the text and clarify, for example, where an address ends and where the rest of the sentence begins.

The World Wide Web Unleashed Support Web

For updates to this book, sample Web pages demonstrating good design, and link to Web applications, interesting Web sites, and Web pages maintained by the book's authors, be sure to visit the **World Wide Web Unleashed Suppost Web** at URL `http://www.rpt.edu/~decemj/works/wwwu.html`

PART

I

Introduction to the World Wide Web

Part I

The standard beginning for a book that deals with a specific topic is to define that topic. If this book were about a word processor, color photography, television, or even the Internet itself, that definition wouldn't present much of a problem. In the case of the World Wide Web, however, definition is almost impossible. Technical definitions are available and are easy enough to reproduce, but deciding on a definition that encompasses all aspects of the Web—its technologies and its social and creative potential alike—is very, very difficult.

Still, that's what Part I of this book attempts: a definition of the Web, followed by a description of the elements contained in that definition; a history of the Web, and of the various ideas, concepts, and technologies the Web incorporates; an overview of the Web, and a guided tour to let you see a portion of what the Web is about.

Like so many other complex ideas, the Web might best be thought of as something that's easy to recognize, even if it's hard to define. But if you want to use the Web to its full potential—searching for specific information and eventually adding your own pages for the world to see—knowing where the Web came from, and what it consists of now, is both necessary and fascinating. Part I offers a guide to that knowledge.

The World Wide Web: Interface on the Internet

by Neil Randall

IN THIS CHAPTER

For any number of historical reasons, the Internet has emerged as a huge, rich source of information accessible only via a series of not-so-friendly interfaces. The basic commands for telnet, FTP, Archie, WAIS, and even e-mail are powerful but unintuitive, and the rapid growth of the Internet's user base has resulted in an increasing number of users who have neither the patience nor the desire to learn the intricacies of these interfaces.

Even those who know them, however, are aware that easier systems can very quickly result in greater productivity, an awareness that has spawned such eminently usable tools as the popular Gopher. But Gopher is limited as an information source by the restrictions of its display; a gopher is primarily a table of contents through which users read or download files, and tables of contents are useful for some but by no means all types of information reservoirs.

Enter the World Wide Web. Conceptualized not long after Gopher itself, the Web began life as a project designed to distribute scientific information across computer networks in a system known as hypertext. The idea was to allow collaborative researchers to present their research complete with text, graphics, illustrations, and ultimately sound, video, and any other means required.

Important ideas within or across publications would be connected by a series of hypertext links (or just "hyperlinks"), much like the information displays made both possible and plentiful through the Macintosh's famous Hypercard program and similar interfaces available on the NeXT, Amiga, X Window, and Microsoft Windows platforms. Users would be able to traverse Internet documents by selecting highlighted items and thereby moving to other, linked documents, and in the case of graphical displays they would see these documents complete with graphics and other multimedia elements.

The World Wide Web project has made possible the idea of accessible and attractive interfaces on the Internet. Using the Web requires an Internet account and a piece of software known as a World Wide Web client, or browser, and it is the browser's task to display Web documents and allow the selection of hyperlinks by the user.

A few browsers exist that require only text-based displays, the most popular of which is the UNIX program Lynx (now available for DOS machines as well). Most, however, run atop graphical user interfaces such as X Window, the Macintosh, Microsoft Windows, NeXTStep, and Amiga. The most popular browser released to date is Mosaic (available for several of these platforms), but many others are available and in development, both as freeware and as commercially available programs.

With a graphical Web browser, you see formatted documents that contain graphics and highlighted hyperlinks. These browsers let you navigate the Internet not by entering commands, but rather by moving the mouse pointer to the desired hyperlink and clicking. Instantly, the World Wide Web software establishes contact with the remote computer and transfers the requested file to your machine, displaying it in your browser as another

formatted, hyperlinked document. You can "surf" the Web by hopping from hyperlink to hyperlink without delving deeply into the contents of any particular document, or you can search the Web for specific documents with specific contents, poring over them as you would a book in the library.

But what *is* the World Wide Web? Where did it come from, and why is it so popular and so potentially important? It is clearly a system of both communication and publication, but how does it work and what can we expect in its future?

These are the questions answered briefly in this chapter and the next four, and examined through a tour in Chapter 6, "The World Wide Web: A Guided Tour." More importantly, however, they're questions explored over the thousand pages of this book, across hundreds of documents on the Web itself, and in magazines, journals, and research reports the world over. The Web is among the most rapidly adopted technological entities of a century that has seen many, and understanding it might be crucial for understanding the next century.

Let's get started.

The Concept of the World Wide Web

The Internet, it is said, is in need of a "killer app." It needs one tool, one program, one application that will take it from being a much-hyped but difficult-to-use linking of computers around the world to being a highly informative, highly usable database and communications tool. The spreadsheet was the killer app for PCs a long time ago, but so far the Net doesn't have one. Some have given "killer app" status to the immensely popular program called Mosaic—see Chapter 10, "The One You Keep Hearing About: NCSA Mosaic," for a lengthy discussion of Mosaic's potential as a killer app—but Mosaic still has its difficulties. The true killer app of the Internet remains somewhere around the corner, and nobody knows if just *one* killer app can handle the Internet's complexity. Until we have one, we simply won't know.

What the Internet does have, however, is a killer *concept*—and the name of that concept is the World Wide Web. In only a few short years of existence, the Web has captured the imagination of data searchers and information surfers alike. Nor is its popularity difficult to understand: The World Wide Web provides the technology needed to offer a navigable, attractive interface for the Internet's vast sea of resources, in much the same way that the toolbar on a word processor screen obscures the intimidating codes that the program actually consists of. Given the Net's history of nearly impenetrable commands and procedures, and the trend in today's software to hide complexity behind usable interfaces, this capability is essential if the Net is become a mainstream set of applications.

But it's important to realize that the Web is a *concept*, not a program, not a system, and not even a specific protocol. It might be more accurate, in fact, to call it an interface, but even that wouldn't be quite right. The most accurate terminology might be meta-interface—an interface that incorporates other interfaces—but words with the word "meta" as a prefix went out of favor sometime during the early nineties. Calling it a tool would be far too restrictive, and calling it a set of applications and interfaces would be reasonably accurate but incredibly clumsy. So let's just stick with "concept," because that's as close as we might be able to get.

The Conceptual Make-up of the Web

Calling the Web a *concept*, however, doesn't answer the question of what the World Wide Web actually *is*. Technically, the Web is nothing more than a distributed hypermedia system (at least, that's what its designers call it, as explained in Chapter 5, "Putting It All Together: The World Wide Web"), but *distributed hypermedia system* is surely no more understandable a term than *concept* itself.

The next four chapters examine the variety of systems that constitute the World Wide Web, of which there are, primarily, three:

- The first is *hypertext*.
- The second is *the Internet* itself.
- And the third is that most overused of 1990s terms, *multimedia*.

Important to keep in mind, however, is that the Web is truly a convergence of these systems, in a way that renders the whole much greater than the sum of the parts.

Right now, though, let's concentrate on defining the World Wide Web, or at least providing a definition that helps understand both its past and its future. To do so, we must turn to the three ideas mentioned above: hypertext, the Internet, and multimedia.

Hypertext is an idea that was introduced way back in the seventies by the sometimes visionary, sometimes flaky, and always provocative Ted Nelson. Hypertext is discussed in Chapter 3, "Hypertext," but the idea is deceptively simple. A hypertext document is one that provides clearly visible links to other documents, and in a hypertext computer environment selecting a link in one document moves you directly to the other. Nelson's idea was to link all the world's information in a huge hypertext system, and the World Wide Web is closer than any other system so far to accomplishing that idea, even though it remains a long, long way from fulfilling Nelson's vision.

The second system inherent in the Web's design is the Internet. Covered more comprehensively in Chapter 2, "The Internet," and in fact through a large array of books on the shelves of libraries and bookstores right now, the Internet is a global system of networked computers that allow user-to-user communication and transfer of data files from one machine to any other on the network.

The Net is the basis of the fictional *matrix* or *web* found in the science fiction of such authors as William Gibson and Bruce Sterling, and the basis, as well, of the Clinton administration's much-hyped information superhighway (or, more properly, Global Information Infrastructure). The World Wide Web, in fact, is the closest thing we have now to approximating any of those fictional or semi-fictional technologies.

It's important to note, however, that *the Web as a system does not require the Internet.* In fact, a distributed information system based on the Web can be constructed on *any* local-area or wide-area network, and in fact such systems are being developed all the time.

But the first two words in *World Wide Web* are "world wide," so it makes little sense to talk about the Web without basing it in the world-wide networking—and the only (relatively) open (relatively) world-wide network now available is the Internet. As a result, we'll build the Internet into our definition.

Hypertext, and the Internet. Nice, but not good enough. There's another concept involved as well: *multimedia.*

Again, multimedia is explored more fully in a short while (Chapter 4, "Multimedia," to be exact), but for now let's just say that, as its name suggests, multimedia combines various presentational technologies in an effort to appeal to as many senses as possible. (Actually, the word should be multimedi*um*—like multipart, multisession, multigerm, and multilane—but we'll let the linguists battle over that one.)

Put a bit more simply, multimedia draws on graphics, sound, animation, and video to create a full, rich computing experience. And for the first time, through browsers like Mosaic, Cello, MacWeb, Viola, and others, the World Wide Web offers a multimedia experience for Internet users.

While certainly in need of further development, the Web already lets information presenters place graphics, sound, and video within the page, and users with a direct, high-speed connection can download them quickly enough to feel as if they're participating in full multimedia. With a 14.4 kbps modem the download process is far too slow, but within the next couple of years high-speed access should be much more available and affordable. The important point is that the groundwork has been laid.

So what is it, then? Let's try this: *The World Wide Web is a convergence of computational concepts for presenting and linking information dispersed across the Internet in an easily accessible way.*

Does this help? Well, maybe. Other definitions of the Web tend to use phrases like "network information delivery system" and "distributed information system" and so forth, and no matter how technically accurate these definitions are they just don't seem very useful, because every term with them needs an individual definition as well. Arguably, so does the rather vague *concept* in our own definition, but we know enough about the word

concept not to need a firm definition. *Concept* is uncertain, volatile, and difficult to grasp, but so is the Web itself—not as a definable computer technology, but rather as a combination of its specifications and its uses. Using the term *concept* might seem like an author's unnecessary avoidance, but anything more precise would almost certainly be outdated within months.

In its initial proposal (discussed in Chapter 5, "Putting It All Together with the Web,") the Web was simply termed "a hypertext project," but it clearly became more than that. What our new definition attempts to do is explain that the Web is a cleverly designed collection of interesting concepts, and allow for the very real possibility that other concepts will soon merge with it.

In fact, this is already happening. Technologies such as WAIS (Wide Area Information Servers) and Archie (the long-lived search engine) are already being programmed into Web-based search tools, and this means that some of the Internet's techniques are already becoming integrated into the Web's conceptual framework. The most successful technologies are those that make its individual components transparent; in the case of the World Wide Web, this seems to be happening early in its history.

The Web contains the technologies necessary to give the Internet a pretty face. Web browsers that take full advantage of these technologies make the Internet easier to use. It's not hard to see where in the history of computing these two crucial ideas—attractiveness and usability—came from. Essentially, the Web and its browsers have done for the Internet in 1994 what the Macintosh did for the personal computer a decade earlier. There were problems with the first Macs from a technological standpoint, and they were written off as toys by the business and computing communities, but they hung on and thrived on the strength of their interface.

Simply put, people could use Macintoshes easily, and that's something that was never true of the IBM PC or its mainframe predecessors. The Mac hid the difficulties of command-line computing under a bunch of objects you could click on with a funny-shaped thing called a mouse, and in doing so it opened computing to the masses. When Microsoft released Windows 3.0 some years later, the iconic, graphic, point-and-click interface (which had originally been developed by Xerox), the masses indeed took over.

Ten years later, graphical World Wide Web browsers such as Mosaic, WinWeb, and MidasWWW offer an interface that has its technological problems, that oversimplifies some important Internet procedures, and that has been called a toy for people who want to glide over the Net rather than delve into it. But just like the Mac, it has thrived because of its interface, and at this time it threatens to overtake all other Internet use, perhaps even the most important Internet tool, electronic mail.

Actually, this comparison between the Mac and the Web isn't quite true, because although the Mac offered just one interface, the Web itself allows all kinds. Its most important interface, however—the graphical, multimedia, point-and-click system offered by Cello and

Mosaic (and others we'll examine in Part II, "Web Browsers and Connections")—is attractive for precisely the same reasons as the Mac and Windows. No matter what its detractors might argue, the World Wide Web offers the Internet to the masses, and that's its true power. No longer do people have to master the vagaries of FTP and Archie and WAIS searching, and as the Web fully develops it should fully incorporate e-mail, newsgroups, telnetting, and other technologies as well.

Different front-ends to the Web will compete for our attention—currently we have Lynx, Viola, Mosaic, Cello, MacWeb, WinWeb, and others—but the principle will remain the same: Link the information, let the users follow whatever path they choose, and once they reach their destination, let them do with the information whatever they please.

It's entirely possible, in fact, that the term "World Wide Web" will become synonymous with the term "Internet," and that's what this book, *The World Wide Web Unleashed,* is largely about. If you wish to master the Internet through the mid- to late-nineties, you can't possibly do so without mastering the Web as well.

Even at this early stage in its development, paying attention to the World Wide Web is crucial. It stands poised to become the basis for the revolution in information and connectivity we've all read about but are still waiting to see. You can browse it, search it, and add your own information to the swiftly expanding sea of Web materials. In many ways, it's there for the taking. Already, the Web has begun to change the face of marketing, customer service, business transactions, education, travel, publishing, information dissemination, and collaborative research. What the Web changes in the future is largely up to us. That, so far, is what makes it so fascinating.

The Internet

2

by Neil Randall

Even though the World Wide Web as a system can operate on any computer network, the Web as we know it is nothing without the Internet. In order to understand the Web's importance, in fact, it is necessary to understand the tools, the fundamentals, and even the history of the Net. But a book about the Web is no place for a fully comprehensive look at the Internet; instead, we'll examine the aspects that are especially pertinent for anyone who wants to know about the Web.

A Very Brief History of the Internet

It's been said often, but it bears repeating once more: The Internet was originally conceived by the U.S. military as a means of ensuring a workable communications system in the event of a strike by enemy missiles or forces. It was the sixties, after all, at the height of the Cold War, when the fear of Soviet attack guided all kinds of military projects. If one central communications location was bombed out of existence, the military wanted to make sure that surviving locations could still talk to one another, and that no communication would be lost.

Because the original network was developed by the Advanced Research Projects Agency of the U.S. military, it was given the name ARPAnet. Eventually, however, as increasing numbers of research institutes and research universities connected themselves to the network, ARPAnet came to handle only this kind of research data while a second network, MILnet, looked after military communications. In the 1980s, the National Science Foundation established NSFnet, linking a half-dozen supercomputers at an extremely high speed that has since been made higher still. NSFnet eventually took over the Internet (as it was now being called) from ARPAnet, and in 1991 the U.S. High Performance Computing Act established the basis for the National Research and Education Network (NREN). NREN's goals are to establish and maintain high-speed, high-capacity research and education networks, while helping to develop commercial presence on the Internet as well.

This last point is immensely important for the World Wide Web, which is rapidly being adopted as a medium of choice for businesses in North America and, increasingly, around the globe. During the Internet's early years, commercial activity was severely constrained by the NSF's "Acceptable Use Policy" (AUP), which directly disallowed any for-profit activities. The AUP has changed somewhat, but more importantly the Internet has taken on different forms and different policies. Although it's not actually stated anywhere, commercial activity is now very much accepted on the Net. Whether or not General Motors will begin to sell its vehicles over the World Wide Web remains to be seen, but already the Web is being used for product ordering and product support—and by very sizeable corporations, too.

The Internet has changed so much, in fact, that during the first half of 1994 the number of domain names for commercial organizations (the com domain) overtook those for educational institutions (the edu domain). In the month ending June 25, over 1,300 new commercial (com) names were registered with the Internet, and the following month saw an additional 1,700. That's a 30 percent jump in just one month! And these businesses aren't just moving onto the Net to do research or e-mail, either; they're there because the Internet offers enormous commercial potential.

To be sure, the Internet is still primarily a research and academic network, at least from the standpoints of creative use and extent of use. There's an enormous amount of activity happening in the educational field as well (with the K-12 area burgeoning), and a great deal involving community and nonprofit issues in addition. That's almost certain to change, however, over the second half of the 1990s. The only question now is whether or not governmental legislation will stop the Internet's amazing growth, and the jury's still very much out on that one.

A Very Basic Knowledge of the Internet

To understand the World Wide Web fully, it's essential to know a few significant Internet issues. Actually, the more you know about the Net, the better you know the Web as well, despite the fact that one of the Web's primary functions is to hide users from the difficulties regarding the interfaces of the Internet's tools. The Web is an important layer of functionality and accessibility riding atop the Net, but without the Net and its horde of concepts, the Web would simply be impossible. You can't have one without....

Some of the major terms and concepts associated with the Net are explained in this section. Arguably, you should know them well before even beginning your Web explorations, but as software like Mosaic, Cello, and Mac Web becomes increasingly popular, this is a bit like asking Windows users to keep their DOS commands in mind. It's just not going to happen. What will unquestionably happen, however, is that things will go wrong while you're cruising the Web, and without a good background knowledge of the Net you may not know what happened or how to proceed.

Domain Names

Every computer on the Internet has an Internet Protocol (IP) address associated with it. IP addresses have four parts, and a typical address looks like this: 198.43.7.85 (that is, four items all separated by periods). Happily, as a World Wide Web user you really don't need to know much about IP addresses, except possibly for getting connected to the Internet in the first place.

What you need familiarity with, however, is the Internet's domain name system (DNS). If you have an Internet account, you're already familiar with DNS: your userid, which originally looked like so much gibberish, contains the domain name for the computer on which your account exists. The U.S. president's e-mail address is president@whitehouse.gov, which contains the *domain name* whitehouse.gov and the

username president. The domain itself is gov, which tells you that it is a government organization (big surprise), while the *subdomain*, whitehouse, tells you which part of government organization this address is attached to (again, big surprise).

Not all domain names are as easy to remember as the president's. Mine, for instance, is nrandall@watarts.uwaterloo.ca, which when analyzed reveals the following: my userid is nrandall (which at least is a whole lot more obvious than some people's userids), and my account is on a machine called watarts (the Arts faculty computer system) at the subdomain uwaterloo (the University of Waterloo), in the domain ca (which stands for the country Canada).

John December, this book's coauthor, has the address decemj@rpi.edu, which is also quite simple. His userid is decemj, the subdomain is rpi (Rensselaer Polytechnic Institute), and the domain is edu, which signifies an educational organization. In your Internet travels, you'll encounter much more complex domain names as well.

Notice the discrepancy between the domain field of my address (ca) and John's (edu). Mine points to a domain location, his to a domain type. The general rule of thumb is this: If a country code is *not* specified, assume the site is in the United States. There is in fact a domain code for the United States—not surprisingly, it's us—but it's rarely used. Similarly, a Canadian or Japanese university could use the edu domain suffix, but that also is rare. The exceptions to this, generally, are found in the net and org domains, and sometimes com, where countries are often unspecified.

Table 1.1 lists the U.S. domains, while Table 1.2 shows some of the many international domains.

Table 1.1. Domain types (usually associated with U.S. addresses).

com	Commercial organizations
edu	Educational institutions
gov	Governmental organizations (except military)
mil	Military organizations
net	Network and service providers
org	Organizations other than those listed above

Table 1.2. A sampling of international domains.

ar	Argentina
au	Australia
at	Austria

be	Belgium
br	Brazil
ca	Canada
cl	Chile
cn	China
cr	Costa Rica
cu	Cuba
cz	Czech Republic
dk	Denmark
ec	Ecuador
eg	Egypt
fi	Finland
fr	France
de	Germany
gr	Greece
hk	Hong Kong
hu	Hungary
in	India
ir	Iran
iq	Iraq
ie	Ireland
il	Israel
it	Italy
jp	Japan
kp	North Korea
kr	South Korea
kw	Kuwait
ly	Libya
my	Malaysia
mx	Mexico
nl	Netherlands
nz	New Zealand
no	Norway

continues

Table 1.2. continued

pa	Panama
pe	Peru
pl	Poland
pt	Portugal
pr	Puerto Rico
ro	Romania
su	Russia
lc	St. Lucia
sa	Saudi Arabia
sn	Senegal
sg	Singapore
sk	Slovakia
sl	Slovenia
za	South Africa
es	Spain
lk	Sri Lanka
se	Sweden
ch	Switzerland
sy	Syria
tw	Taiwan
th	Thailand
tr	Turkey
ua	Ukraine
ae	United Arab Emirates
uk	United Kingdom
us	United States
va	Vatican
ve	Venezuela
vn	Vietnam
zr	Zaire

Domain names affect your use of the World Wide Web in several ways. First, you're very likely to encounter something like a "DNS Lookup Error"; essentially, this means that the "domain name server" on your local computer couldn't translate the name you typed into a legitimate IP address. Practically speaking, it means that the requested file isn't available because the domain name portion of the URL was unrecognizable.

Next, the domain name is, of course, part of the entire filename itself, and you'll find yourself typing domain names plus filenames whenever you request a specific URL address. URLs, or Universal Resource Locators, contain the specific instructions for your Web browser to find and retrieve the file you specify. Clicking on a highlighted hyperlink in a Web document automatically activates the retrieval process (and effectively hides the URL address of the document from you), but Web browsers also allow you to type the URL manually.

Third, by learning domain names you can get a good sense of where you're going on the Web. In Mosaic, for example, when you place the cursor over a link, the URL address for the link appears at the bottom of the screen. It tells you immediately whether the link exists on an educational site, a commercial site, a governmental site, or something else, and this often affects your browsing strategy.

UNIX Filenames

If you want to understand the Internet thoroughly, you *must* develop a knowledge of UNIX. For a variety of reasons, mostly having to do with its strong flexibility and its excellent networking and multiuser capabilities, UNIX has become, in essence, the operating system of the Internet, and in fact all other operating systems must be customized to work with UNIX when they hook into the Net. For the time being, at least, there is no mask over the Net that makes UNIX invisible, although commercial service providers such as America Online are working hard to develop such masks.

To build a World Wide Web site, a good knowledge of UNIX is essential. To simply use the Web, however, you need to know only a tiny portion of it. An increasing number of Web users do their browsing through Macintosh or Microsoft Windows machines, and for them a very limited knowledge of UNIX is necessary. Except for one detail, in fact, they can largely do without its understanding.

That one detail is filenames. It's possible to cruise the Web without ever typing in a UNIX filename, but only if you do your browsing exclusively by clicking on hypertext links. At some point, however, you're almost guaranteed to come across an e-mail message or another document that gives you a URL (Uniform Resource Locator) address, and this almost always represents, or at least contains, a UNIX-like filename. (Actually, the URL isn't a UNIX filename; it's a standard format. But URLs tend to look very much like UNIX filenames, and understanding the filename structure will help you locate specific documents.) In every major browser, you can enter that address to move directly to that page, but if you're not exactly precise in your typing, you'll find yourself unable to get there. That's because of UNIX's complex filename structure.

Unlike, say, DOS filenames, UNIX filenames have virtually no length restriction. If you want to name a file `This_is_an_incredibly_cool.file.man`, go ahead. Of course, conventions do exist (otherwise nobody would be able to find anything), but there's nothing at all like the 8.3-character filename structure of DOS. That's the first thing to keep in mind.

Secondly, UNIX filenames are case-sensitive. The files `OJSimpson.gif`, `OJsimpson.gif`, and `ojsimpson.gif` are all entirely different files. This is something that DOS users typically have considerable difficulty getting to handle efficiently, because DOS is completely case-insensitive. You'll find lots of UNIX filenames that combine lower case, upper case, numbers, and other symbols, and you *must* type them exactly.

Finally, the URL addresses you see will show the complete directory structure for the file. UNIX directories are very much like DOS's, except that they're separated by a forward slash (`/`) rather than a backslash (`\`). Here's a typical UNIX filename, for example: `/u2/ojsimpso/projects/dev_tools/tapp/mango_leaf.tiff`. This simply means that the file `mango_leaf.tiff` can be found in the directory `tapp`, which is a subdirectory of `dev_tools`, which is in turn a subdirectory of `projects`, which is located in the `ojsimpso` subdirectory of the `u2` directory. Not difficult to read, but awfully tricky to type.

On the Web, you'll find this in URL addresses. As already mentioned, these can be typed manually into the Open URL (or similar) dialog box in Web browsers. The following, for example, is the URL to type in when you want to access the support page for my Sams book, *Teach Yourself the Internet: Around the World in 21 Days*:

`http://watarts.uwaterloo.ca/TYI/tyi.html`

Similarly, if you want to access the Table of Contents page for John December's well-known *Internet Tools Summary*, type in the following URL:

`http://www.rpi.edu/Internet/Guides/decemj/itools/toc2.html`

In both cases, you're essentially telling your Web browser to connect to the remote server (that is, the computer where the document resides) and retrieve the specified file. Because you've done this using HTTP (HyperText Transport Protocol), the Web's standard and exclusive protocol, the file will be displayed as hypertext, complete with selectable hyperlinks. Note that both files have the extension `.html`, the standard for a page coded in Hypertext Markup Language (HTML), which is explained in detail in Part V, "Weaving a Web."

FTP—File Transfer Protocol

FTP is both a protocol and a program. As a protocol, it's been around almost as long as UNIX itself, and its function is to ensure a common standard for moving files from one computer to another across a network. As a program, FTP accomplishes these transfers. It enables you to enter file directories on remote machines and retrieve files from those machines or place files in those directories. A full FTP implementation offers a suite of file utilities such as creating directories and renaming and deleting files. Although you can access FTP sites by having an account with a password, the most widely used FTP type for casual users is called "anonymous FTP"; FTP software can be set to allow access to users who offer the word "anonymous" as a login name and their e-mail address as a password.

The World Wide Web makes extensive use of FTP. First, some sites do not have HTTP software in place, so to make their information accessible across the Web they place their HTML documents on FTP servers instead. Second, Web clients such as Lynx, Cello, and Mosaic make FTP connections and perform FTP downloads of files—but not uploads. In the case of sites containing graphics, sound, or video files, many are currently available via FTP only, either through anonymous FTP directly or through Gopher FTP access. FTP access is so common on the Web that you're unlikely to spend more than a few minutes cruising before you encounter an FTP transaction.

Figure 2.1. shows an FTP site as displayed through Mosaic.

FIGURE 2.1.

FTP site in Mosaic, showing extended parsing (includes file sizes).

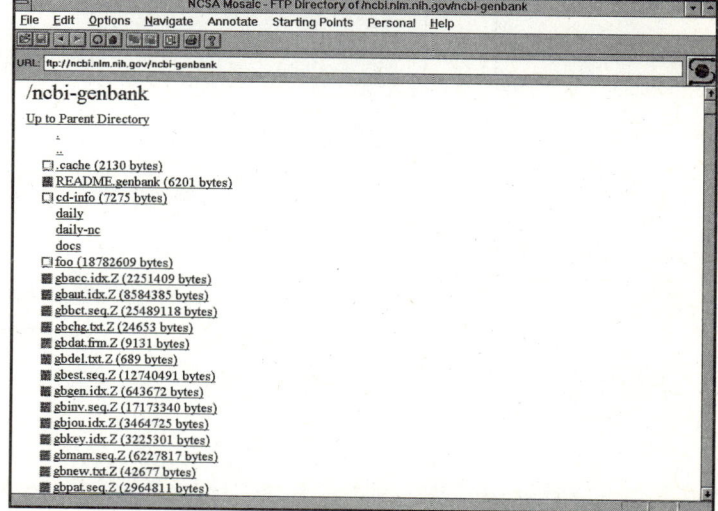

Gopher

Gopher is the best-known interface for the Internet. Developed by the University of Minnesota, Gopher is in fact very much like the World Wide Web, offering a friendly face on such difficult tools as FTP, telnet, Archie, WAIS, Veronica, and others. The main difference is that Gopher is not a hypertext environment. The most common gopher client programs present information in numbered lists instead of hyper-linked documents, with different indicators for different kinds of files (text, sound, search dialogs, etc.). Gopher software for graphical user environments such as X Window, the Macintosh, and Microsoft Windows typically offers the same lists with icons replacing the numbers. The icons offer information as to the type of file or directory you're accessing.

Gophers are directly accessible through the World Wide Web. Often this access is presented in the link itself, but you can use your browser to move to a particular gopher by specifying the gopher:// prefix when you enter a URL address (for example, gopher:// cscns.com). This yields the gopher directory, each item representing a selectable Web link.

Figure 2.2 shows a typical gopher directory listing as seen on the Web.

FIGURE 2.2.

Gopher directory displayed in Mosaic.

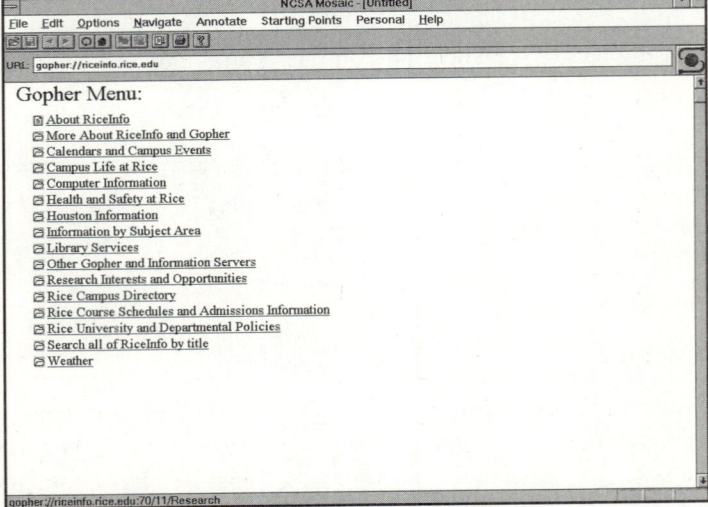

Electronic Mail

It's hard to be on the Internet and not know about electronic mail, but it's easy to overlook the fact that the World Wide Web is mail-enabled to a certain extent. You're not going to find a rich, full-featured e-mail package on the Web, at least not yet, but e-mail plays an important role in the Web's design. Through the use of HTML forms, you can have the readers of your pages submit mail to your address, and users of some browsers can mail directly from within that browser. (XMosaic and Cello are examples.)

Undoubtedly, the use of e-mail in the design of Web pages will increase in both usefulness and frequency. There is one main reason for this: The Web itself is primarily a public medium, while e-mail is primarily a private medium. In order to make full use of the Web even now, you often have to boot up your e-mail program and fire off messages to addresses you discover while browsing Web pages. At some point, a Web browser will probably need to include a strong e-mail feature if it is to be considered complete. Figure 2.3 shows the basic e-mail program contained within Cello.

FIGURE 2.3.

Cello's electronic mail feature.

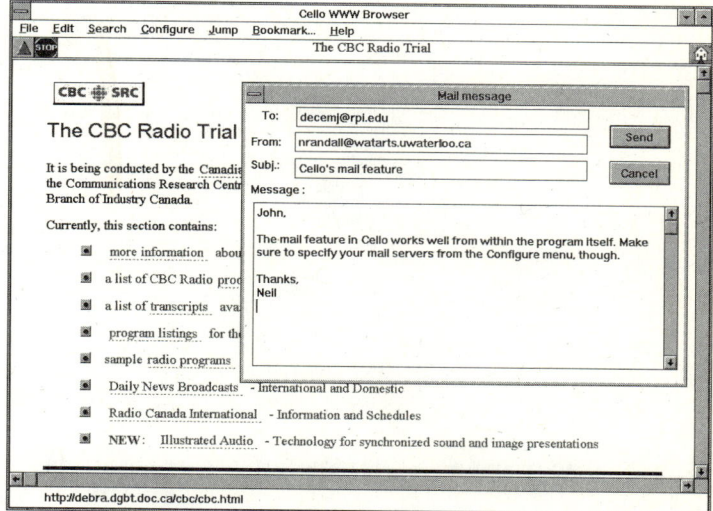

Usenet

Usenet has been in existence for a number of years, as the network through which users communicate in newsgroups. For some Internet users, in fact, Usenet and electronic mail are everything the Net has to offer. Usenet is the focus of any number of Internet stories in the popular press, as newsgroup users appear in stories about online romance, online harassment, the assisting of the unfortunate, and the corruption of the innocent as well. It's a very, very popular tool.

The Web has limited hooks into Usenet, but they exist and they're exploitable. Already in existence are sites that offer newsreader capability, some with graphically rendered subject "threads." It's unclear at this point how the Web will further integrate newsgroups, partly

because they're so popular that it simply may not be necessary to do so. But many Web pages refer to Usenet groups as sources of additional information, so it remains important to know of their existence and their use. Keep in mind, though, that today's Web browsers offer newsreader capability only; at this stage, no browser lets you follow threads, post new messages, filter unwanted topics, or any of the other advanced capabilities of a good news program.

Figure 2.4 shows a Web link to several newsgroups.

FIGURE 2.4.

Link through the World Wide Web to Usenet archives.

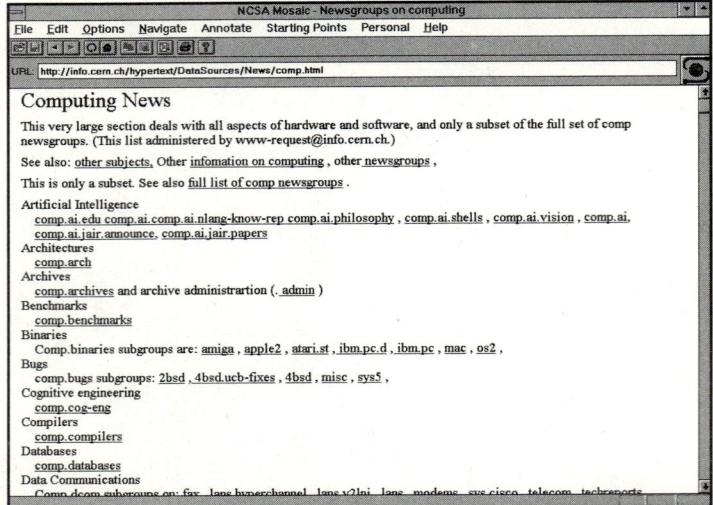

Wide Area Information Servers—WAIS

WAIS is an extremely useful tool that generates and allows you to search through a huge range of databases stored on the Internet. These databases in turn point you to locations on the Net that hold documents containing the keywords you've searched for. Among WAIS's most useful features are its relevance rating of documents—1000 means a direct hit; 100 means a marginal hit—and its ability to build, through a process called "relevance feedback," from one search to another. In other words, you can keep narrowing the search until you find exactly what you want.

The World Wide Web works through WAIS gateways to offer full keyword searching. Several pages feature WAIS searches, and in fact they've become almost the standard for finding specific titles or headings throughout the Web. Typically, WAIS searches on the Web are combined with the HTML feature called "forms," boxes that you fill in by typing text and then you execute by clicking on a button. Fully developed forms allow highly specific searches, and in some cases you can even select the areas of the Net you want searched.

The interesting part is that you often don't know that you're entering a WAIS search. As with other Internet tools, the Web has essentially co-opted the WAIS process, incorporating it into the browsers so that users can access it almost transparently.

Figure 2.5 shows a search form at the top of the screen, and the results of the WAIS search throughout the rest. Notice the relevance ratings beside the items, and note also that each item is a hyperlink to another site or document.

FIGURE 2.5.

Filling in a search form in Mosaic.

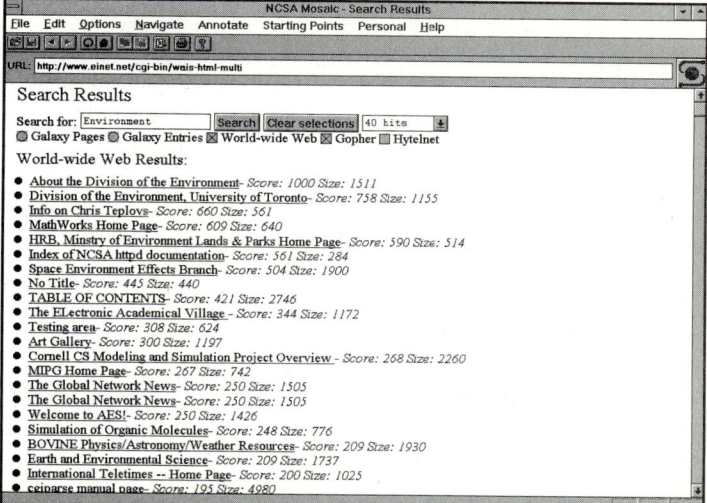

Integration

These aren't the only tools accessible through the World Wide Web. Archie, Veronica, Hytelnet, and a host of others appear in Web pages from a variety of sources, and in many cases the very existence of the Web makes these tools more usable than before. None of this suggests, however, that the Web makes other manifestations of these tools obsolete. As with the newsreading capabilities of the current crop of browsers, the Web's use of the Internet's most important tools is often limited. If you need extensive features on any of these tools, you're likely better off looking elsewhere. For many users, however, the Web's versions of the tools are sufficiently capable.

Remember that the point of the World Wide Web is to offer access to the resources available on the Net. To this end, it has been designed not to replace the existing tools, but rather to integrate them into one appealing and highly usable program, taking advantage of the graphical user interface of today's machines.

There will always be those who prefer the command-line version of FTP, the richness of the feature set of a full Gopher client, and the multiple capabilities of a text- or graphics-based e-mail package. At this point, there seems little chance that any Web browser will ever fully substitute for these. Increasingly, however, the Web will integrate the Internet's tools into its structure to the degree that, for many people, the Web may well *become* the Internet. Not everyone likes that thought, but not everyone likes GUIs, voice-mail, or audio CDs, either. The point is that it's going to happen, and for anyone wishing to stay on top of the Internet, the Web will be an essential and unavoidable concept.

Fortunately, that's far from a bad thing. The Web has received its share of praise and criticism alike, but nobody denies the importance of providing solid, usable access to Internet resources. Personal computers themselves took off when their user interfaces stopped trying to emulate something out of code-level hell, and the Internet as an information provider began its rise when Archie made things findable and Gopher let you get to them. When high-speed access becomes commonly available, there's every reason to suspect that the Web will continue its trend toward becoming the most commonly accessed Internet tool—or tool*kit* — of them all.

Hypertext

3

by Neil Randall

IN THIS CHAPTER

Hypertext is one of those ideas that appeared; rose to prominence by being written about, hyped, and otherwise touted as either a savior or a destroyer; and then seemed to fade away as its promise gave way to the difficulty of actually applying it to anything, or more particularly developing things that it was worth applying to in the first place.

There have been several such ideas in computing, and in some cases the idea has simply been forgotten. But over the years since its introduction, hypertext joined two other concepts, artificial intelligence and speech recognition, in simply refusing to go away. These three ideas were so strong that despite their initial fading, they have begun to reassert themselves in a potentially very big way. Among the three, hypertext has been the most fully developed, at least from the standpoint of people being able to sit at their computers and use it.

The concept of hypertext is disarmingly simple: Use the computer's storage and searching capacity to link documents together and thus let users jump instantly from one piece of information to the next.

A hypertext is a series of documents, each of which displays on the screen a visible link to at least one other document in the set. The link is usually highlighted, either by bold-faced text, reverse text, differently colored text, or underlining. The user "navigates" through a hypertext by selecting these links, typically using either the keyboard or the mouse (although joysticks and touch-screens are certainly possible). The link leads to another document, which in turn offers links to additional documents, and so on. After following five or six links, in fact, the user might not be able to find the way back to the original document, a phenomenon known as becoming "lost in hyperspace."

It's not difficult to see how the concept of hypertext came about. Here's an example. Most of us have read books containing footnotes that contain references to other books. Often—probably because the grass is always greener on the other side—the book mentioned in the footnote sounds more interesting or relevant than the one we're reading. Wouldn't it be nice to simply point to the footnote and magically find that book in our hands?

Essentially, that's what hypertext enables us to do. In a well-constructed hypertext, any significant reference is shown as a link; select that link, and you're suddenly reading the linked document. If the hypertext is indeed well-constructed, the new document will provide a link back to the original document, but often links go only one way. This might be the fault of the hypertext's author, or—in the case of the World Wide Web—of the sheer size of the hypertextual undertaking. Not everything can be linked to everything else.

Vannevar Bush and Ted Nelson

Two names come to mind when considering the origin of hypertext. The first is Vannevar Bush, who way back at the beginning of computer technology (in the July 1945 issue of the *Atlantic Monthly*) published a landmark essay entitled "As We May Think." The other is Ted Nelson, whose fanciful book *Computer Dreams*, published in the late seventies, offered a view of easily accessible information that is still a long way from being in place.

Bush's article has been used to cite the origin of everything from artificial intelligence to multimedia. In fact, it presaged both of these, but neither in particular. Bush was concerned primarily with bringing to the public mind the idea that computers were similar in some respects to the human mind, and that therefore it might be possible to program them to emulate the human mind. Along the way, his article discussed the nature of the dissemination of information, and while hypertext per se doesn't appear in his work, the idea of accessible, computer-organized information speaks quite loudly. Most importantly, however, Bush offered one of the first explorations of computer technology in relation to human thought processes and human information needs, and thus it remains an essential paper.

Nelson thought of computers in anthropormorphic terms long before most people did, and long before the technology suggested the possibilities. *Computer Dreams* is a lot of things to any number of people, but its primary ongoing usefulness is its introduction of the idea that through computer technology we will have access to all the information in the world. Nelson has been alternatively praised and scorned, but through a host of changes in the computer field he has consistently maintained his vision of an information-centered, information-accessible world. His own attempts to realize this world is the Xanadu project, which depending upon whom you listen to is either just around the corner or completely unrealistic. We're not about to make predictions here.

What Nelson did, however, was introduce the term "hypertext." He envisioned a system of information access not much different from what we have today, and there's little doubt that he must cruise the World Wide Web with a knowing smirk and an attitude of "I told you so." He'll also, however, almost certainly wonder why it doesn't work better than it does. What he had in mind seemed somehow much simpler.

Hypercard and Hypermedia

There's little point trying to track down the first hypertext application for personal computers. There is, however, a very real reason to point to the first mass-audience program to allow hypertext creation. That program is Hypercard, which at one point was packaged with every new Macintosh on the shelf.

Hypercard gave cheap, easy hypertext creation facilities to anyone who owned a Mac. Shortly after its introduction, Hypercard "stacks" began to appear, and since the Mac sold well to the artistic and educational communities, these stacks ranged in subject matter across a very broad sphere of human knowledge and experience. Moreover, the stacks were usually made available at no charge, through bulletin boards and other online services, which meant that Mac owners had access to a huge range of hypertext-based information packages. And since Hypercard allowed stack programmers to include graphics and eventually sound and even video, it gave popular birth to a revised concept, "hypermedia."

Hypermedia extends hypertext in two ways. First, it incorporates multimedia (see Figure 3.1) into hypertext documents. Second, it allows graphic, audio, and video elements—rather than just text elements—to become links to other documents or multimedia elements. In other words, with hypermedia you aren't just linking text anymore; instead, you're linking anything the readers can see to anything the author wants them to know. A text link to the Apollo 11 moon landing, for example, might send readers to a text document describing the landing, to a graphic representation of the landing, to a short sound bite of the crew declaring, "The eagle has landed," or to a video showing Neil Armstrong descending the ladder towards the moon. In turn, this link can offer links to other text, graphic, audio, or video elements as well. The combinations are practically unlimited. With the World Wide Web, hypermedia explodes, because any of these elements can also be linked to documents and elements that exist on a computer halfway around the world. But we'll get to that.

Figure 3.1 shows a hypermedia screen from Microsoft Complete Baseball, a CD-ROM product for Windows.

FIGURE 3.1.

Joe Carter's famous winning home run during the 1993 World Series.

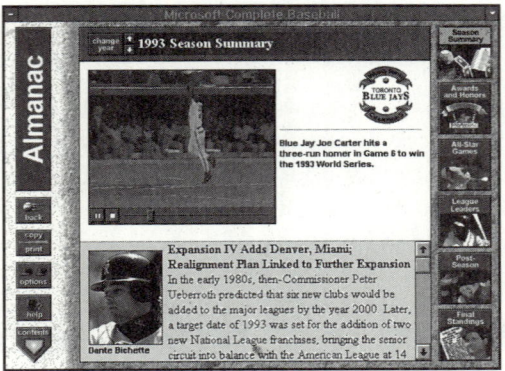

Help Systems

One of the most prevalent and noticeable uses of hypertext has occurred in the help systems for Microsoft Windows and the Macintosh. Windows' help system, for example, has employed hypertext technology for several years, to the extent that the CD-ROM versions of its software base their entire online documentation system around a usable hypertext model. Figure 3.2 shows the hypertext structure of the help system for Word for Windows 6.0, a word processing program, while Figure 3.3 demonstrates a similar structure in the help system of Procomm for Windows 1.0, a communications package.

FIGURE 3.2.

Multipart hypertext screen from Word for Windows 6.0.

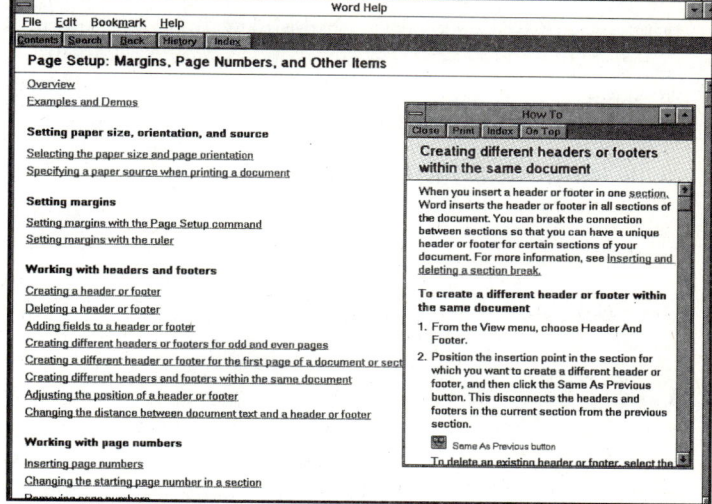

FIGURE 3.3.

Hypermedia graphics display from Procomm for Windows 1.0.

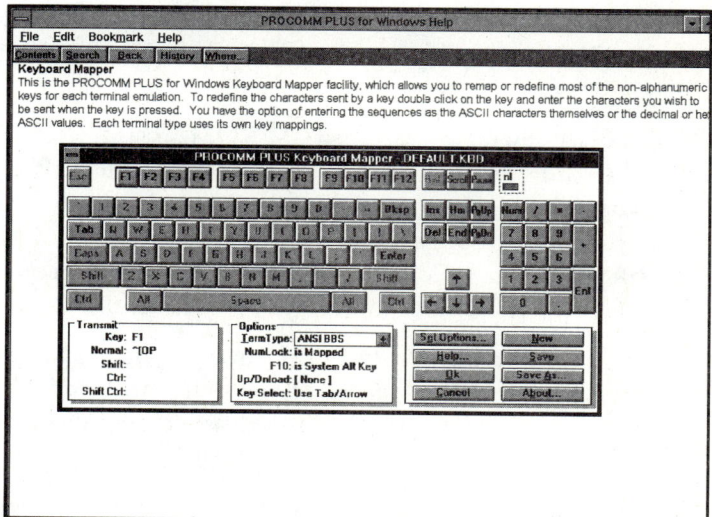

Each link is displayed as an underlined text string or a portion of a graphic. Click on the link, and you're taken to another section of the help system, from where you can click on links to still other sections, or back to the original section. The help system is extremely large in many programs, and these links make it easy to navigate through the descriptions and instructions. For many users, these hypertext systems are easier to use than the printed manuals, because related topics can be accessed quickly. They're simply more effective than the paper-based "see also" instruction.

If you've used the Windows or Mac help system, you'll recognize Mosaic's and Cello's interface instantly. Click on the underlined links, or sometimes on the graphic, to move to a related document or a portion of the same document. It's quick, it's effective, and it's satisfying. But there's one crucial difference: Unlike the help system, these documents are scattered around the world.

Actually, there *is* a help system that exists entirely on Web documents. The help menu in X Mosaic, the Mosaic version for X Window systems, leads you among documents stored on NCSA's systems in Illinois (`http://www.ncsa.uiuc.edu:8001/`). As long as your Internet connection is fast enough, accessing help this way isn't much different from accessing it on your Mac or PC.

CD-ROM

Hypertext and hypermedia have flourished on CD-ROMs, and here we see a direct conceptual link to the idea of accessing information on the Net. CD-ROMs offer enormous storage capabilities (currently about 650 megabytes), and in one sense that's what the Internet offers as well; the challenge for the designers and developers of both is to make all those megabytes accessible in a user-friendly way. Enter hypertext, with its click-and-find mouse controls.

There are clear similarities between CD-ROM and the World Wide Web. Both concepts are proliferating, yet both are very much in their infancy. Both offer the user access to a huge range of detailed information. And both are basing their future around the potential of multimedia, although in this regard CD-ROM has a clear and inevitable lead. CD-ROM can be tailored to the hardware specifications of only one computer type, after all, while the Web is forced to struggle with the conflicting standards of many.

Like the Internet, a typical CD-ROM consists of many, many individual files. These are linked together through the construction of the various programs on the disk, but in the case of information-based CD-ROMs such as encyclopedia and reference tools, users must be presented with a wide range of links for their own individual use.

A product such as Microsoft Bookshelf, for instance—the popular collection of dictionary, thesaurus, mini-encyclopedia, quotation book, and other writing tools—uses hypertext to allow users to maneuver from topic to topic and word to word. Similarly, Compton's Interactive Encyclopedia uses hypertext extensively to link references and ideas among the topics, making the CD-ROM much more easily cross-referenced than a corresponding paper-based encyclopedia.

But these products (and a large and growing number of similar packages) don't just offer text links; also available are hyperlinks among graphic images and audio and video presentations. The best CD-ROMs are full hypermedia systems.

Multimedia

4

by Neil Randall

The World Wide Web is not necessarily a multimedia environment. The original CERN browser, as seen in Figure 4.1, showed text only because it was designed for terminals that were incapable of displaying graphics. A subsequently released Web browser, the well-known Lynx (see Figure 4.2), is similarly without graphics. A standard VT-100 terminal, of course, had nothing to do with sound or video, so those possibilities are out as well.

FIGURE 4.1.

The original CERN browser, with its access via numbers.

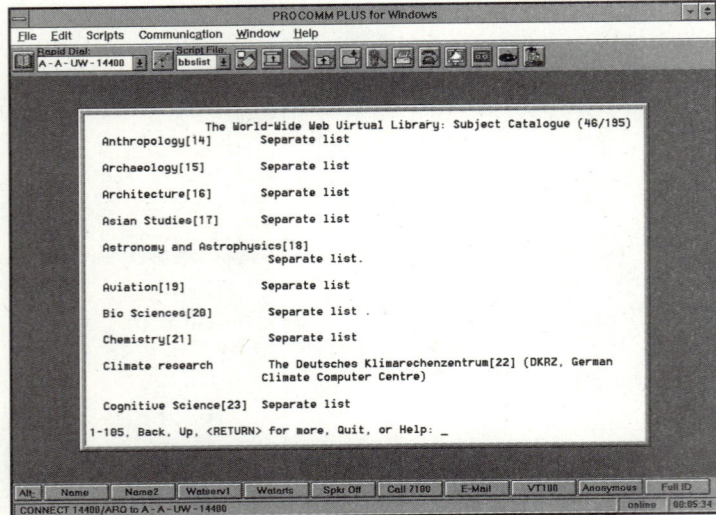

FIGURE 4.2.

Lynx, the popular arrow-key browser.

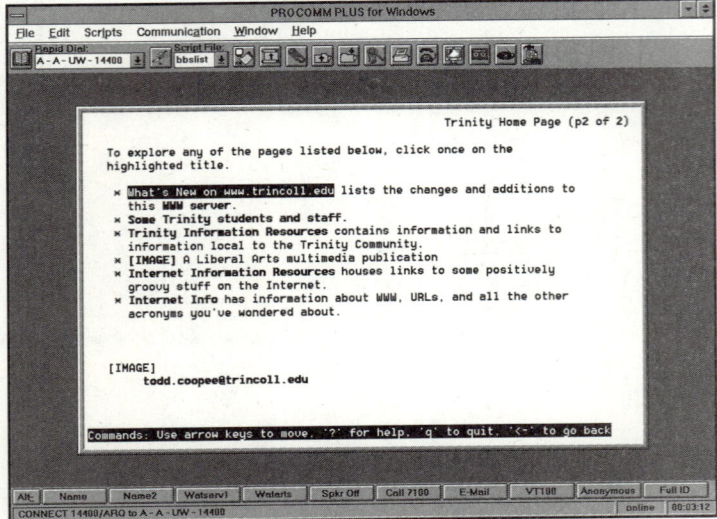

Not until the availability of the later graphical browsers did the Web's multimedia potential demonstrate itself. Mosaic has taken the lead in the browser race, of course, but others, such as Cello (for Windows) and MacWeb (for the Mac) are also multimedia-capable. But in order to understand how these browsers are affecting the concept of exploring the Internet itself, it's helpful to look briefly at the history of multimedia computing, especially as it developed on personal computing systems.

The basic point about multimedia is simple: Barring physical disabilities, we experience the world as a combination of sensory perceptions. So if the world offers visual and auditory information, why can't computers? Presumably computers will one day build in tactility (it's happening already), smell (other than the fried power supply), and taste (edible floppies?). When that happens, we'll have multimedia that goes beyond simply the audio-visual. For now, though, computing is restricted to the visual and audio capabilities offered by movies and television, and it's these two phenomena that multimedia computing is trying to take advantage of.

The Limitations of Text

In the world of computing, anything over five years old is very old, anything over ten years old is ancient, and anything older than that is grounds for both nostalgia and disbelief. It's hard to fathom, when we see computing in the mid-nineties, that the whole idea of graphics on computers was once considered pointless, counter-productive, and to be avoided at almost all costs. Sure, graphics had their use, but only for such applications as medical and other scientific research, and maybe professional publishing. But graphics on a personal computer? Especially one used in business? Not a chance.

When the IBM-PC first shipped in the very early eighties, it offered a text-only display, because that's all a serious computer user needed (according to IBM, that is). Nor was color important, or even desired; the first monitors were monochrome, although there was sometimes a choice between green and amber. Text was all that mattered, because the only perceived uses of business computing were programming (which remains largely text-oriented), word processing (which by definition uses text), spreadsheeting (numbers only), and database management (names, addresses, product numbers, and so forth). Color was merely a distraction; graphics more of one.

Actually, there's more to it than this. In the early eighties, color displays were prohibitively expensive for use with personal computers. But it didn't take long for the lack of color to be deemed a plus among business, academic, and educational users, or for color displays to be denounced as toy-like. Some of this attitude was the result of sour grapes, of course, but color became officially, in some cases, a thing to be avoided.

To be sure, there's still an argument here. You don't need a graphical word processor to write a book (unless you're formatting it yourself, which is a rarity), and you don't need a graphical database management program to keep track of your sales contacts or do relational searches. In fact, most graphical products are considerably slower than their text-only counterparts. But text has its limitations, and this is something the PC line has spent the past decade trying to make up for. Text-only systems simply ignore the fact that information can be provided more effectively in other ways.

Graphics

As any blind or near-blind person can tell us, the world is a visually oriented place. But it took a while for graphics to be accepted on computers for a number of interesting reasons. At first, the hardware didn't exist to support them. But even when graphics became technically feasible, corporate computing cast a dim view on them. Why? Because they weren't seen as necessary.

This might seem strange, but it doesn't take much to see a general bias against graphical representations of material in Western culture. The printed page has long been our most prolific and accepted medium for disseminating important information, and since the invention of the printing press the printed page has been dominated by text. Go to any library—especially an academic library—and browse through the shelves. Very few books have illustrations, and many that do have only technical drawings. When was the last time you read an illustrated novel?

It didn't help, of course, that the first graphics-intensive computer programs were games. North American society has always been phobic about games, objecting to their use in education and utterly forbidding them in the workplace. (There's a fascinating irony here on the pursuit of happiness theme, but never mind.) So as computer graphics became increasingly associated with computer games, the entrenchment towards text-only computing became more concerted.

The biggest culprit was the Commodore 64. Although it wasn't the first computer to offer graphics and sound at a reasonable price—the Apple II could do so with enough add-ons, and the Atari 800 offered arguably better results—the 64 became a huge mainstream hit in the early eighties and made the equation of multimedia and games even stronger. Here was a machine that was compact, inexpensive, and advertised extensively on television; and it displayed graphics, played sound, and even offered reasonably good color. Add these things to the fact that it appealed to home users and kids, and the consensus grew that it was nothing but a toy. I wrote two books and a doctoral thesis on my Commodore 64, but I never managed to convince a single IBM-PC user that it was a computer worth having.

While the 64 crested the wave of its popularity, the IBM-PC slowly began to add graphics. The first kick at the can was CGA, with its four ungodly colors and its total inability to allow animation. Next came EGA, slightly better at 16 colors, but animation was still next to impossible. By the time VGA was introduced, the Atari ST and Commodore Amiga were offering tons of colors and smooth animation, but primarily for these reasons they, too, were considered toys. Or, at best, things that graphics specialists bought.

> **NOTE**
>
> I must emphasize, by the way, that I've owned and liked an Apple II, an Atari 800, a Commodore 64, an Atari ST, a Commodore Amiga, a Macintosh, and several PCs. Just so the rest doesn't sound prejudiced in any way.

The machine that began to signal the acceptance of multimedia was the Macintosh. This is somewhat ironic, since the original Mac had a teeny-tiny monochrome monitor and very little sound to speak of; but because it was seen as a machine for serious artists and, more importantly, serious publishers, it quickly gained a following. Quite simply, it brought a new paradigm to computing, in the form of the graphical user interface (GUI). Because of the Mac's GUI, graphics entered the realm of business computing—not instantly, perhaps, and certainly not without detractors, but they entered, nevertheless. Once business and government organizations saw how quickly users learned the Mac's interface, and how eager computer nonexperts were to use it, they started buying them, which is something that happened very little with the ST and Amiga, both of which had similar interfaces and better multimedia capabilities. Apple was able to market its graphics well, and once the publishing industry adopted the machine, graphical computing was here to stay.

Which is not to say that everyone thought GUIs were great. In fact, many people still don't. And, to be sure, the first Macintosh users put out some of the worst-looking documents ever found on earth, complete with multiple fonts, overly cutesy clip-art, and typographic emphases that would have made any high school newspaper blush in embarrassment. What became important, however, was the concept of direct graphic control. Yes, you could tell WordStar and WordPerfect how to set up your page, but with MacWrite you could see without printing exactly what your decisions would yield. This capability became known as WYSIWYG (what you see is what you get), meaning that you could see on the screen what the printed version would look like.

But, and this is important, the Mac's universe was very much print-oriented. That's why its original screen was black on white; after all, isn't that what a printed page looked like? Although the Mac offered the capability of multimedia, its focus remained squarely on print, which was simply another reason its acceptance began to grow. More importantly, though, it offered a point-and-click interface, with icons that hid program names and mouse procedures that replaced typing. Where the command-line interface relied on users' memories, the GUI relied only on their ability to recognize. That, by itself, made computing available to the masses.

The graphical interface caught on so well that operating system leader Microsoft decided to create one of its own. After a couple of mediocre efforts, and despite the appearance of arguably better interfaces such as GeoWorks, Microsoft Windows 3.0 brought graphical computing to the Intel 80x86 platform (Intel processors or clones run all machines known as IBM compatibles, or simply PCs), and it brought multimedia with it (although DOS-based multimedia had already arrived in the form of games). Windows is now dominant among developers of software for personal computers, a fact that many industry pundits feel is especially unfortunate, partly because Windows is not an operating system per se, but rather a graphical shell that sits atop DOS, a relatively weak operating system to begin with.

Sound and Music

The original IBM-PC was no more interested in sound than it was in graphics. It had sound, but this sound was simple, to-the-point, and efficient. If you did something wrong, the computer beeped. In fact, PCs and their clones still beep today: They beep when you turn them on (one beep means the machine's okay, two means your day's ruined), and they beep when you try to do something DOS doesn't like. It works, it's effective, and it's extremely annoying.

Acceptable sound for personal computers began to appear in the early eighties. Expansion cards for the Apple II offered reasonable sound effects for that machine, while the Atari 800 and the Commodore 64 made music and sound easy to program and effective to use. The Amiga introduced the idea of a dedicated sound chip, and the ST became a favorite of musicians because of its built-in MIDI port. The Macintosh started with very limited sound, but as new models appeared so did improved music and sound capability, until it, too, became a musicians' favorite.

Once again, it was the Mac that made this multimedia feature acceptable. The reason, quite likely, was that the Mac was not a particularly good game machine in the beginning, and even today is not seen an an especially strong gaming computer. By contrast, the Atari 800 and the Commodore 64 were seen by the corporate computing folk as nothing but game machines, and the ST and the Amiga, with their Atari and Commodore names attached, quickly became labelled as game machines as well. People who owned Macs could be taken seriously, even with their mice and icons; people who owned STs and Amigas were primarily seen as game players. Unfair, certainly, but that's the way it happened.

For multimedia computing, sound has been an even harder sell than graphics. Except for business presentations, perhaps, where effective music, digitized speech, and carefully chosen sound effects might help make the point, there seems to be little value to giving a computer the ability to make sounds. In crowded, open-concept offices, graphics don't impose on a neighbor's work, while sound without headphones creates a distraction. Not until the concept of business audio caught on in the early nineties, in fact, was sound considered something to be treated seriously. Even so, its uses remain limited.

But sound is an important feature of multimedia because movies and television, on which multimedia is based, make extensive use of it. Multimedia attempts to mimic both these media (which are themselves multimedia), and sound has attained new importance in related technologies such as the CD-ROM.

Animation and Video

Back in the late seventies, a very simple, very addictive game called Pong appeared on television screens. Actually, it had already been available in arcades, but when it hit the home screen it revolutionized, in its own way, what people did with their TV sets. Pong's graphics were far less sophisticated than those of even the worst TV show, but for the first time people could control what was displayed on the screen. Turn the knob one way, and the bar went up; turn it the other way, and it moved down. You could even put a "spin" on the ball, so Pong quickly became a game of at least some appreciable skill.

A decade and a half later, Pong is small potatoes. Now our TV sets sport video games with graphics realistic enough to be considered by some to be dangerous for young viewers (Mortal Kombat is one such product), and our computer screens offer not only rich animation but equally rich, full-color video. The result has been a growing convergence of the computer with the television, a process that designers have been engaged in ever since computer graphics became a reality.

Animation and video are two separate technologies, but their effects are similar. They offer movement on the computer screen, something that just doesn't happen with spreadsheets or word processors. More importantly, they offer the movement of things that look like people, or at least objects people recognize. In other words, animation and video make computers part of the experience of seeing the world, which all but the sight-impaired rely on every day of their lives. That's what's made the motion picture so fascinating from its beginnings, and what transformed television into the most important (for better or worse) appliance in our houses.

To that end, however, video is significantly better received than animation. Animation is associated with cartoons, and is a drawn representation of the motion we see with our eyes. Video, by contrast, while still only a representation, looks so much like the world we see around us that we've come to accept it as an extension of that world. Put a video camera on someone and the results are called "realistic"; do an animation of someone and people will usually only smile and say, "Pretty good." For general acceptability, video wins hands down.

What's the importance of video to the World Wide Web? If the Internet is an information dissemination system, after all, what does video have to do with it?. First, and very simply, video is an extremely important means of conveying information. Just think, for example, of the Apollo 11 mission in 1969, and the effect the video feeds of the moon landing and moon walk had on us. Had the cameras been unavailable, would we have huddled around the radio listening to the sound of it all? Not likely, given the centrality of video in our lives. More recently, think of the TV coverage given to the O.J. Simpson arrest, that famous (and interminable) overhead view of the multitude of police cars following the van. Would anyone have paid attention to it on radio? Hardly. The only drama the situation presented was the result of the video feed. As a final example, consider the most recent California earthquake disasters. Without video, the extent of the disaster would have been invisible and almost meaningless to anyone not in the immediate area. In all three cases, video provided evidence, and that was what the situation demanded.

Everybody knows that video can be fabricated. Fabrication, in fact, is the central art form of cinematic special effects. But there's something about video that engages the totality of the senses, much more than audio could hope to do. Possibly it has to do with concentration; while it's eminently possible to be doing something visual while listening to the radio, it's almost impossible to accomplish any kind of complex task while watching television. That's why people think nothing of telling you to keep quiet while they're watching TV, but these same people will think nothing of showing you things while you're listening to your favorite symphony. It's also why most people have a very hard time listening to music without simultaneously doing something else, but can watch a movie intently with nothing able to block it out.

Video, in other words, is a crucial technology for information designers whose goal is to fully engage, inform, and entertain. Given that the World Wide Web intends to fulfill all three design goals, its use of video will almost certainly become paramount. There's a catch, however: High-quality video requires high-speed access, and that's something very few people currently have. By the last third of this decade, however, high-speed access should be a given, and Web designers will have the technologies they need to offer full, rich, visually oriented information.

Games

Nothing has pushed the envelope of multimedia technology more than computer games. Since their inception, games have incorporated graphics, sound, and a variety of interactive interfaces, all in an effort to make computer entertainment more enjoyable. While it's been possible for a computer application such as a database program to be acceptable for its underlying technological excellence rather than its appearance and interface, games have been reviewed and bought according to their sensory appeal and their combined ease and realism of play.

The difference between games and applications, of course, is function. If an application is worth using for whatever reason, what it looks like and how easily it handles doesn't matter all that much. Users can be persuaded and even ordered to learn the software because it's good for them or for the company. For games, however, the good-for-you argument doesn't hold. Nobody believes that mastering Wing Commander or Betrayal at Krondor is about to do anything useful for them; they play these games to be solidly entertained. For this reason, multimedia and interface design make all the difference in the world. Offer an exceptional graphics display, superb sound effects, and an interface that makes the experience painless, and you have a possible winner. Offer anything less, and your chances are next to nil.

What does the World Wide Web have to do with games? For one thing, games are starting to appear on the Web, and as access becomes faster and demands stronger, better and more complex games will make their appearance as well. At first, as was the case with the early computers, any game will be happily played, simply because it's an experience different from searching databases. Soon, however, designers of Web-based games will be forced to incorporate the best features of disk- and CD-ROM-based games, especially if they expect anyone to play them. The Web offers the possibility of games with exciting multi-player potential, with players the world over, but by telnetting to MUD (multi-user dungeon/dialog) sites Net users can already get such games. What Web game designers must concentrate on is a combination of world-wide multi-player games with top-notch multimedia capabilities and equally strong interfaces.

There's more, though. As the designers of mainstream computer applications found out, there's a lot to be learned from the people who design computer games. Multimedia tutorials, context-sensitive help, simplified interfaces, and full "customizability" are products of the computer games world, and they've found their way into today's graphically based applications packages. Designers of Web sites can make full use of these and other capabilities as well. The potential for the convergence of solid game design and solid educational design is especially exciting on the Web, and business applications have even stronger potential. A Web-based store, for instance, is essentially a simulation of a store, and designers can make use of the basics of simulation games to help them establish a usable site that invites users to return.

Games continue to push multimedia. If you're a Web designer, ignore them at your own risk.

CD-ROM

CD-ROM threatened to take off as early as the late eighties, but 1993 proved to be its true year of acceptance. Before '93, Mac users had a fair portion of CD-ROMs to choose from, but the emergence of (reasonably) easily installed DOS-based upgrade kits in 1992 made the CD-ROM publishers sit up and take additional notice. The result was the be-

ginning of a flood of products in 1993, with the flood showing every indication of becoming a tidal wave as 1994 draws to a close.

The reason for this growing acceptance is quite simple. Because of its enormous storage capabilities (650 megabytes per disc), CD-ROM let designers make extensive use of sound, music, graphics, animation, and especially video. For the first time it was possible to offer reference works and education and entertainment products that featured a worthwhile smattering of all these technologies. Some products, in fact, became so large that they needed more than one CD-ROM to contain them (one example is the famous horror game, 7th Guest) with even larger products on the horizon (the long-awaited Under a Killing Moon promises four CDs). With the blending of technologies on these packages, CD-ROM became the first stepping stone to the much-hyped fully interactive information superhighway.

As shown earlier in this chapter, CD-ROM is similar to the World Wide Web in many ways. This is nowhere more apparent than in the inherent multimedia design of the two. In fact, it's easy to see how CD-ROMs might replace hard disk storage of Web sites in the near future. With multimedia files taking up enormous amounts of hard disk space, and with recordable CD-ROM in place and dropping in price, it only makes sense that site owners will want their multimedia pages—or at least the multimedia portions of those pages—on inexpensive CD-ROM storage.

Putting It All Together: The World Wide Web

5

by Neil Randall

The Internet, hypertext, and multimedia—three important technologies of the nineties. Bring them all together, and you have the World Wide Web.

The Web is a by-product of the Internet, created because of the Internet's overwhelming size. There is so much information available across the computers and networks that make up the Internet that finding and actually using it is very, very difficult. We live in an age of information, but keep in mind that information—as its name implies—is *formed*. Having access to huge amounts of information is part of the Internet's charm, but perhaps only a small part; more significant is being able to find, view, and make use of this information. The World Wide Web, more than any other Internet concept, allows this to happen.

The first secret of a good Internet browser is making it possible for the user to navigate the Net without having to know, remember, or write down the lengthy and clumsy addresses and filenames which the Net and UNIX need to operate. The second secret is providing not just links from information source to information source, but links that are contextually related.

The Web does both, and this makes it different from any other browsing technology. Gopher, for example, offers a highly usable system of navigation, but its links are primarily to sites, not to contextually related documents or (as the Web makes possible) specific sections of documents. When you enter a Gopher directory, you see a wide range of possibly important information, but you can spend considerable time searching for exactly the document—and exactly the section of the document—you need. A well-constructed Web-based hypertext can make all this seamless, although it must be noted that most Web documents remain far from this ideal.

Through the use of hypertext, the Web can provide access to mountains of information in a very usable way. The primary reason, quite simply, is that the information (or, rather, the links to the information) is provided in a manner with which readers of the language are familiar.

Tables of Contents, headings, paragraphs, lists, and graphic elements make up the pages of books, magazines, and newspapers, and these are the essential elements in an HTML (World Wide Web) page. Gopher's limitation is that it is exclusively list-oriented, while FTP's limitation is that it provides not just lists, but lists of obscure filenames.

Both seem computer-ish, and since the release of the Macintosh "computer-ish" is something computers aren't supposed to be. The Web provides a booklike layer on top of the Net, albeit a book with the less-linear capabilities that hypertext and other computer-ish systems offer, and books with their printed pages remain the most efficient and perhaps the most usable information presentation system we have in place.

A half-millennium of the printed page is not about to be outdone by fifteen years of the scrolling screen, and that's what makes the Web so instantly usable. Its usability will only be enhanced, although its efficiency might not, as it moves towards integrating the multiple media of print with the multiple media of film and television.

History of the Web

The World Wide Web dates back to March, 1989. In that month, Tim Berners-Lee of Geneva's European Particle Physics Laboratory (which is abbreviated as CERN, based on the laboratory's French name) circulated a proposal to develop "a hypertext system" for the purpose of enabling efficient and easy information-sharing among geographically separated teams of researchers in the High Energy Physics community.

The three important components of the proposed system were the following:

- A consistent user interface
- The ability to incorporate a wide range of technologies and document types
- Its "universal readership," that is, anyone sitting anywhere on the network, on a wide variety of different computers, could read the same document as anyone else, and could do so easily

Over a year later, in October 1990, the project was presented anew, and two months later the World Wide Web project began to take shape. Work began on the first line browser (called www), and by the end of 1990 this browser and a browser for the NeXTStep operating system were well on the way. The major principles of hypertext access and reading of different document types had already been implemented.

In March 1991, two years after the presentation of the original proposal, the www line-mode browser saw its first limited network use. Two months later, www was made available more extensively at CERN, and the Web was effectively off and running. That summer saw seminars about the Web, and announcements posted to relevant newsgroups. October 1991 saw the installation of the gateway for WAIS searches (a crucial development for the Web's future as a search as well as a browsing tool), and shortly before the end of 1991 CERN announced the Web to the High Energy Physics community in general.

Essentially, 1992 was a developmental year. The www browser was made available via FTP from CERN, and the Web team presented the Web to a variety of organizations and audiences, but it was the software development efforts of that year that would make it a vitally important time. In January 1993, 50 Web servers were in existence, and at that time the Viola browser was made available for the X Window system. Viola was the early leader in Web browsing technology, offering the first glimpse of the graphical, mouse-based hypertext system originally conceived by the Web proposal.

The Web was on its way. But two other browsers saw daylight at the beginning of 1993, and these proved the most important. CERN's Macintosh browser brought the Mac into the WWW game, and at the same time the Internet community saw its first glimpse of Mosaic. In February, 1993 the first alpha version of X Mosaic (Mosaic for X Window) was released by NCSA (the National Center for Supercomputing Applications in Champaign, Illinois), developed by Marc Andreesen, whose name ranks behind only Berners-Lee's in media popularity surrounding the Web.

In March of 1993, WWW traffic clocked in at 0.1 percent of total Internet backbone traffic. Six months later, the Web began to demonstrate its potential by expanding to a full one percent of backbone traffic. That ten-fold increase became practically the norm for Web access increases, continuing into 1994.

The same ten-fold increase was evident in the number of HTTP servers, which by October 1993 had increased to approximately 500. By the end of 1993, the Web project was beginning to receive technical awards, and articles on the Web and Mosaic (the two were already becoming inextricable) began to appear in publications as prestigious as *The Guardian* and *The New York Times*. By early 1994, in fact, the Web/Mosaic combination had begun to become the sort of media hype that can both make and break a technology. 1993 also saw the release of Cello, an alternative browser, developed by the Legal Information Institute at Cornell University, for users of Microsoft Windows.

1994 saw several important developments. First, work expanded on the development of "secure" Web access, the kind of security needed if real corporate work were to take place across the Web, and if users were ever to provide such details as credit card information.

Second, the licensing of Mosaic to commercial developers took hold, and even less-known browsers such as Cello were seeing licensing potential. NCSA's development of Mosaic took a turn with the departure of Andreesen and others to form the Mosaic Communication Corporation, and the first international World Wide Web conference took place in Geneva.

In July of 1994, CERN began to turn over the Web project to a new group called the W3 Organization, a joint venture between CERN and MIT to develop the Web further. That significant event signals the end of this short history, because it's July, 1994 as I write this. More—much more—anon.

Original CERN Proposal

The original proposal from Tim Berners-Lee outlining the World Wide Web project— actually, a revamped proposal from a little later than the original—is available on the Web itself, at the URL http://info.cern.ch/hypertext/WWW/TheProject.html. As a document predicting the future of a computing resource, it's more than a worthwhile read. As a document outlining a proposed long-term project incorporating both existing and still-to-be-developed computer technologies, a vision of what the World Wide Web could become, it's essential. Nowhere does the proposal suggest that the Web might become as important as it has, but perhaps this is inevitable. Few important inventions have ever had their full effects predicted accurately.

The title of the proposal was "WorldWideWeb: Proposal for a HyperText Project." Note, first of all, that the words "world," "wide," and "web" were, at this stage, joined together as one single word, a usage that is maintained in some instances today but not to a significant degree. But note, also, that the whole venture is described simply as "a hypertext project," not at all as the kind of global networking multimedia concept the Web has become.

Early in the proposal, the authors offer a word about the need for their system: "There is a potential large benefit from the integration of a variety of systems," they state, "in a way which allows a user to follow links pointing from one piece of information to another one. This forming of a web of information nodes rather than a hierarchical tree or an ordered list is the basic concept behind HyperText." Already we have here the word "web," and just as significantly "web" only a couple words away from "information." The way the Web was perceived is essentially the way it was delivered.

The following passage takes the concept still further. I quote it at considerable length here because it remains one of the clearest statements about hypertext, hypermedia, and the Web that exists. It also points out two important facts: Hypertext nodes were seen as being on different machines and different networks, and hypermedia possibilities were part of the original conception.

> The texts are linked together in a way that one can go from one concept to another to find the information one wants. The network links are called a web. The web need not be hierarchical, and therefore it is not necessary to "climb up a tree" all the way again before you can go down to a different but related subject. The web is also not complete, since it is hard to imagine that all the possible links would be put in by authors. Yet a small number of links is usually sufficient for getting from anywhere to anywhere else in a small number of hops.
>
> The texts are known as nodes. The process of proceeding from node to node is called navigation. Nodes do not need to be on the same machine; links may point across machine boundaries. Having a world wide web implies some solutions must be found for problems such as different access protocols and different node content formats. These issues are addressed by our proposal.
>
> Nodes can in principle also contain non-text information such as diagrams, pictures, sound, and animation. The term hypermedia is simply the expansion of the hypertext idea to these other media. Where facilities already exist, we aim to

allow graphics interchange, but in this project, we concentrate on the universal readership for text, rather than on graphics.

It's tempting to copy the entire proposal and go through it in detail, but that's neither practical nor necessary. However, the original goals set by the designers remain of interest today. These, too, appear quite early in the document:

It (the project) will aim:

- To provide a common (simple) protocol for requesting human readable information stored at a remote system, using networks;
- To provide a protocol within which information can automatically be exchanged in a format common to the supplier and the consumer;
- To provide some method of reading at least text (if not graphics) using a large proportion of the computer screens in use at CERN;
- To provide and maintain at least one collection of documents, into which users may (but are not bound to) put their documents. This collection will include much existing data. (This is partly to give us first hand experience of use of the system, and partly because members of the project will already have documentation for which they are responsible);
- To provide a keyword search option, in addition to navigation by following references, using any new or existing indexes (such as the CERNVM FIND indexes). The result of a keyword search is simply a hypertext document consisting of a list of references to nodes which match the keywords;
- To allow private individually managed collections of documents to be linked to those in other collections;
- To use public domain software wherever possible, or interface to proprietary systems which already exist;
- To provide the software for the above free of charge to anyone.

The project will not aim:

- To provide conversions where they do not exist between the many document storage formats at CERN, although providing a framework into which such conversion utilities can fit;
- To force users to use any particular word processor, or mark-up format;
- To do research into fancy multimedia facilities such as sound and video;
- To use sophisticated network authorization systems. Data will be either readable by the world (literally), or will be readable only on one file system, in which case the file system's protection system will be used for privacy. All network traffic will be public.

Little of this needs commentary. It is clear, unambiguous, and important. But it's instructive to read the first and last bullets, the intention to provide a publicly accessible protocol and the insistence that all traffic will be public, and the sheer lack of importance to the project of sound or video, which since that time has become of increasing significance. Clearly, the ideas behind the Web were in place early, but the Web was not seen as the killer concept it has become. Either that, or the authors of the proposal realized what would happen and kept quiet about it, realizing that academic institutions are rarely impressed by inventions with mass appeal.

After these introductory passages, the proposal establishes definitions for browsers and servers, sets milestones, argues the need for personnel, and so forth. There is surprisingly little hard detail on any of these items, but it's also clear that little was necessary. The concept itself drove the proposal, and the only thing at all surprising is that the project wasn't put into place until more than a year later.

How the Web Works: HTTP

Part VI, "Whither the Web: Trends and Issues," offers a detailed explanation of how the World Wide Web operates. Here, we'll take a very brief look at the interactions of Web server and Web document or other Internet protocol, partly for interest and partly because even a short background is helpful when examining Parts II, III, and V.

The most interesting part of the way the Web works is its simplicity. Of course, that might be why it's as powerful as it is. You'd expect a technology like this to have the complexity commensurate with its capabilities, but in fact it doesn't. In fact, as the Web document prepared by CERN (`http://info.cern.ch/hypertext/WWW/Protocols/HTTP/HTTP2.html`) tells us, the transaction takes place in four basic phases, all part of the underlying HTTP (HyperText Transfer Protocol):

- Connection
- Request
- Response
- Close

In the connection phase, the Web client (for example, Mosaic, Cello, Lynx) attempts to connect with the server. This appears on the status line of most browsers in the form "Connecting to HTTP server." If the client can't perform the connection, nothing further happens. Usually, in fact, the connection attempt times out, yielding an explanatory message saying so.

Once the connection to the HTTP server is established, the client sends a request to the server. The request specifies which protocol is being used (including which version of

HTTP if applicable), and it tells the server what object it's looking for and what it how it wants the server to respond. The protocol can be HTTP, or it can be FTP, NNTP (network news transfer protocol), Gopher, or WAIS (the Z39.50 protocol). Included in the request is the *method*, which essentially is the client's command to the server. The most common method is *GET*, which is basically a request to retrieve the object in question.

Assuming the server can fulfill the request (it sends error messages if it can't), it then executes the response. You'll see this phase of the transaction in your browser's status line, usually in the form "Reading Response." Like the request, the response indicates the protocol being used, and it also offers a *reason line*, which appears on the browser's status line. Depending on your browser, you'll see exactly what is going on at this point, usually represented by a "Transferring" message.

Finally, the connection is closed.

At this stage, the browser springs into action again. Effectively, it loads the requested data and displays it, or it saves it to a file or launches a viewer. If the object is a text file, the browser will display it as a nonhypertext ASCII document. If it's a graphic image (such as a GIF file), the browser will launch the graphics viewer specified in its configuration settings. If it's a sound or video file (AU, WAV, MPEG, or other), the browser will launch a similarly configured player. Depending on the type of method specified in the request, the browser might also display a search dialog.

Usually, however, the browser displays an HTML (HyperText Markup Language) document. These are the documents that show the graphics, links, icons and formatting for which the Web has become so famous.

How the Web Works: HTML

HTML is a simplified derivative of SGML, or Standard Generalized Markup Language, which is a code used to make documents readable across a variety of platforms and software. Like SGML, HTML operates through a series of codes placed within an ASCII (that is, text) document. These codes are translated by a World Wide Web client such as Lynx, Mosaic, Cello, Viola, or MacWeb into specific kinds of formats to be displayed on the screen, and on which the user can (in some cases) act.

These items include links, lists, headings, titles, images, forms, and maps. As you might expect, the longer HTML stays around, the more complex it is becoming. The original HTML allowed only text, while later inlined images (graphics that appear on the document) and various types of lists and link types were added, but not until HTML+ were such elements as fill-in forms and clickable maps possible. Not surprisingly, HTML 2.0 promises even more variety, to the extent that HTML might well possess enough features to make serious documentation design possible.

The documents you see on your World Wide Web browser are usually HTML documents. True, the Web can display ASCII files, but they're just plain text files that could be downloaded and opened in any text editor. What makes an HTML file worthwhile is the browser's interpretation of its formatting codes, so that a link appears as a highlighted item, a list appears with associated bullets or numbers, and a graphic appears as the picture it represents. In other words, the World Wide Web would be nothing without HTML.

But HTML is limited, some would say extremely so. Even with HTML+, for example, it's barely possible to place graphics where you want them, and simple items like font selection are constrained as well. Nothing in HTML even approximates the sophistication of the desktop publishing capabilities of today's word processors, and it's a long, long way from offering the design tools of a desktop publishing package like PageMaker or Quark Express. The Web as we see it is still well short of the interest of professional page designers, and as a result many of the pages we see are amateurish, garish, or just downright ugly.

Accessing the Web

The World Wide Web can be accessed through both direct and indirect Internet connections, and through a variety of clients (browsers). Part II, "Web Browsers and Connections," examines the types of connections and how to acquire them, as well as the variety of browsers currently available. Here I'll simply outline the possibilities in a brief explanation of the issues you'll need to consider about Web access.

Indirect and Direct Internet Connections

There are two main types of Internet connection: *indirect* and *direct*. Both types can make use of either modems or existing network cards, and both types range in price from free through very expensive. There are also other ways of describing Net connections (Internet books differ widely on access descriptions), but these two are as effective as any.

The crucial difference between indirect and direct connections is this: With a direct connection, your computer is an individual node on the Internet (or, in some cases, a simulated node). With indirect connection, your computer is simply a terminal on a computer or a network which is itself an individual node on the Internet.

With a direct connection, your computer has its own IP address (See Chapter 2, "The Internet"), and it can be established as a server for FTP, Gopher, News, or the World Wide Web. In turn, you can use software to bring mail and software directly to your computer. Direct access is often necessary if you wish to use programs such as Mosaic for Windows or the Macintosh, as well as the other graphical software available for these machines. It is possible to access this software through some other connection tools, such as PC packages that connect to X Windows servers, but for many users direct access is the only means available.

With an indirect connection, by contrast, you are given disk space and access time on another computer. When you receive mail, the mail stays on that server, and when you transfer files they are stored on that server as well. (You can download this information to your own computer through a variety of means, but that's a separate activity entirely.) With an indirect connection you can't normally use graphical software such as a Web browser, and instead you must rely on the text-based browsers which your server can run.

A Summary of World Wide Web Browsers

Mosaic is the most famous Web browser, but there are many others. Most will be treated in detail in Part II. This section summarizes a selection of them according to their applicable computer platforms. Note that these are the freely available browsers; commercial versions of Mosaic and Cello have been released or are around the corner.

UNIX Clients

Not surprisingly, given the importance of UNIX to the Internet, browsers for UNIX systems have been available longest and are the most plentiful. Here are some of them.

Text Mode UNIX Browsers (Nongraphical)

- CERN's Line Mode Browser—Available for any text-based terminal on the Net, the Line Mode Browser uses a numeric interface.
- Lynx—A full-screen browser for VT100 (or compatible) terminals, Lynx uses the cursor keys for navigation.

Graphical Mode UNIX Browsers

- NCSA Mosaic for X—The most famous client of them all, X Mosaic requires X11/Motif to run, and is full featured and extremely well supported.
- ViolaWWW—Now unsupported, Viola was one of the first graphical browsers.
- Chimera—A browser with an X/Athena interface, Chimera supports both inline images and HTML forms.

Apple Macintosh Clients

- NCSA Mosaic for Macintosh—Released shortly after the original X version, Mac Mosaic offers similar features.
- Samba—Developed by CERN, this client offers basic Web browsing.
- MacWeb—A full-featured client from EINet, MacWeb promises full future support.

Microsoft Windows Clients

- NCSA Mosaic for Windows—The fastest growing Web client, Windows Mosaic is being licensed by several commercial interests.
- Cello—The product of Cornell's Legal Information Institute, Cello offers Windows users a different look and feel.
- WinWeb—This is the Windows version of MacWeb (see above), released shortly before this book was written.

Other Platforms

- NeXTStep WWW Browser-Editor—Available for the NeXTStep operating system, this browser offers both browsing and editing capabilities.
- WWWVM—For VM systems, WWWVM is a full-screen, text-only browser.
- Amiga Mosaic—Although not developed by NCSA, the Amiga version of Mosaic offers similar features.

Uses of the Web

The remainder of Part I and the whole of Part IV, "Exploring the Web," offer glimpses into the wide range of activities currently underway across the World Wide Web. Part IV categorizes existing Web pages according to topic, but that's not the only way to understand what's going on throughout this important global resource. Listed here are the types of tasks being undertaken on the Web, not according to subject matter but rather according to what is being attempted.

Graphical Design of Information

For a long time, book publishers have known the importance of graphical design. So have computer users, of course, as anyone with a word processor and a set of fonts is well aware.

Over networks, however, information has been presented largely as unformatted ASCII, primarily because there were few choices. (ASCII has been an extremely valuable "lowest common denominator," but it is limited.) Exceptions have existed on the Mac, of course, which has had built-in networking since its inception, and more recently on platforms such as NeXTStep, OS/2, and Windows. But over the Internet and other wide area networks, text has been the dominant mode of presentation.

The Web changes that. At least, it changes it if you consider a graphical browser as a default, which is clearly what's happening. Suddenly, information at remote sites can be presented in graphical format, complete with font choices and incorporated drawings, photographs, and other multimedia elements.

The results might have their downside—along the lines of trivial, unnecessary information presented solely because it's possible—but the plus side of the ledger is far more likely. Graphical elements offer different kinds of information, and information providers are researching precisely what that means. We are beginning to see strong uses of charts, diagrams, illustrations, tables, graphics, photographs, maps, flowcharts, and all other kinds of graphical representations as the Web's capabilities increase, and this can only mean an increase in the comprehensibility of the information. Of course, it all has to be done right, but that's another issue. The fact that it's possible means that those who care about their information will figure out how to do it.

Which is not to say that HTML in its current incarnation allows anything like full graphic design. But as HTML moves closer to its progenitor, SGML, it almost undoubtedly will. At that point, we should begin to see exceptionally strong designs.

Dissemination of Research

Dissemination of research was, of course, one of the original purposes of the Internet itself, and more particularly of the Web project at CERN. Today, the Web is being used for this purpose to a certain degree, but perhaps more importantly—for the sake of its mass acceptance, at least—it's being used to make research findings available to the general public. The sheer amount of research available through diligent Web searching is staggering, and much of it is presented so that it's as easily understandable as possible.

This is an important development. As more publicly funded research agencies are called upon to account for their expenditures and activities, they are being forced to come up with increasingly creative ways of making their work known to the public. But booklets and pamphlets distributed through direct mailings are expensive and usually ignored, so getting the word out is difficult.

What better way than the Web? Through a well-designed HTML page, an organization can now demonstrate their activities graphically and comprehensibly, and these pages can be updated inexpensively and frequently as a means of continuing to foster public interest. Organizations like NASA are making extensive use of this kind of public dissemination, and we can expect others to do so as well. Among other things, it's a way of making research timely, enjoyable, and interactive.

Browsing and Ordering of Products

We're already beginning to see product ordering available through the Web, even though discussions continue as to its security for such activities as credit card use. In the near future, "secure" Mosaic will find a variety of releases, and when that happens, expect to see a flurry of Web shopping centers opening up. Until then, you can find a considerable variety of products to order on the Web, ranging from flowers to books to music CDs.

What's the appeal? Very simply, this is home shopping at its most interactive. Unlike home shopping TV stations, you don't have to sit through fifteen descriptions of cubic zirconium rings and bracelets in order to find that elusive Wayne Gretzky undershirt you've been looking for. Shopping on the Web is more like walking into a shopping mall, and in fact *mall* is the name given to many current Web offerings. Just click on the shop you want, turn on the inline graphics to see a picture of the product you're looking for, then go to the order forms page to do the actual ordering.

Client and Customer Support

The World Wide Web's potential for client and customer support is extremely strong. Already, companies like Hewlett Packard and Digital Equipment Corporation are using the Web to make available to their customers such items as technical documents, software patches, and frequently asked questions. The benefits of this approach are obvious. Customers with Web access can take care of their own information needs, resulting in less strain on the supplier's support staff and, quite likely, an improved reception of customer service on the customer's part.

The only danger to this approach is the possibility that the Web will be used as a substitution for person-to-person support. But that's not a danger at all if the Web site offers everything the customer needs, and in many cases that may well be the case. Consider, for example, the possibility of Web-based tutorials offering step-by-step installation procedures for a new piece of equipment, or for that matter how to program your VCR. If it's well designed, it will be better than a tech support phone call because it shows, rather than tells, the customer what to do.

Of course, HTML forms can also be used to provide feedback and questions on products, and these can be posted as well. The idea is to have a place where customers can feel they haven't been forgotten, and where they can learn from the experiences of other customers as well. That's what we're starting to see.

Display of Creative Arts

For some reason, people in the creative arts are often perceived as traditionalists, stodgy and resistant to new technologies. Yes, there are some of those. But throughout history artists have been among the first to adopt new technologies to their own purposes, as witnessed by everything from the printing press to MIDI. And there's every indication that the artistic community is seeing the World Wide Web as yet another medium which they can exploit in order to present their work and link up with other artists.

Already we have online galleries featuring new visual art, collaborative artistic efforts of a kind not previously possible, and presentations of artwork that outsiders are asked to evaluate. Examples of creative writing are springing up all over the Web, including some interactive stories and illustrated texts as well. There are even some preliminary attempts at Web-based drama.

The Web offers artists a couple of very important features. First, it allows an inexpensive way of mounting work. As long as the site is in place, the rest is up to the artist, in a way that differs considerably from standard galleries or the inevitable street corners. Second, everyone posting art on the Web has a built-in global audience, and that's something artists can usually only dream of. Obviously, there are media that will never be entirely suited to Web presentation, but if today's efforts are any indication the Web, all by itself, could lead to a kind of renaissance in both the amount of artwork publicly available and the ability of a mass audience to access and appreciate it.

The Future of the Web

For any technology, it's impossible to predict the future. No sooner are the predictions made than the technology develops unexpected adherents and unforeseen uses. This was the case with gunpowder, with television, with computers, and now with multimedia, on-line services, and the Internet itself. But trends count for something, and the Web has revealed nothing if not a series of trends toward future use. Here are some, presented as ideas to be explored.

■ Full-Scale Publishing

A wide range of publishers have already appeared on the Web. Some have presented samples of publications, others have presented full texts. In the future, there's every reason to expect full publishing efforts on the Web, everything ranging from children's books through advertising-laden magazines. New approaches to design and new accesses to advertisers' wares will have to be considered, but the potential is certainly there. Watch also for newsletters and magazines that will be partially accessible publicly and fully accessible with subscriptions and associated account assignments.

■ Voting

Well, why not? With fill-in forms establishing themselves as perhaps the most important single advance in Internet-based technology, and with the White House and other governments turning to the Net for information dissemination of a variety of kinds, it seems only a matter of time until the Web can be used for voting—maybe not in a presidential election, at least for a while, but certainly for other purposes. Of course, all of this demands common access to huge numbers of people, but the Web need not be the only voting medium. If the idea is to get more people voting on public issues, why not use all public media?

■ Live Interactive Entertainment

Yes, we have television. But television is presentation only, not interaction, and here the Web can make a difference. Why not comedy routines in which Web users participate in skits and jokes? Why not dramatic pieces in which Web users influence the outcome? How about real-time role-playing games? And so on. True, there's a stretch of the imagination to some of this, and all of it has been hyped in the past, but the potential is now global, and that will make a difference.

■ News

The problem with CNN or any other continual news supply is that the news we get is the news they decide we'll get. No matter how comprehensive and fair-minded the programmers might be, we end up hearing a whole slew of news stories we're not interested in, and too little about stories we want to know more about. Here the Web's possibilities are enormous. How about fully customizable news packages, so that if we want to focus on Rwanda, or the Middle East, or a flood or earthquake area, or for that matter the qualifying games among African teams for the 1998 World Cup, we can get the text, audio, and video of whatever subject we want.

■ Distance Education

Obvious, maybe, but no less important for being so. For decades, universities and colleges have been looking for ways of offering courses to students who don't have access to the campus (usually because of physical distance). The Web is beginning to see activity in this regard, and this activity will increase dramatically over the next few years. Watch for full university-level courses to be offered over the Web to all registered students (and perhaps others as well), complete with real-time seminars and exams, and professors' visiting hours. Much more interactive than the audio- or video-taped lectures of today's correspondence courses, Web-based distance education courses will very much be the next best thing to being there. Maybe even better, if it's done right.

■ Distance Presentations

Organizations with high-speed Internet connections might well consider offering multimedia presentations over the Web. These need not be real-time presentations, which eliminates some of the problems presented by desktop conferencing, and they offer the benefit of eliminating travel and accommodation costs, as well as downtime costs, for presentation attendees. Presentations can take full advantage of the Web's multimedia and networking capabilities, and the HTML pages can be quickly redesigned and updated as a result of the presentation. Another benefit is that the presentation can offer links to other information sources, all of which will be updated by the site being linked. The presentation will thus be always up-to-date.

There are other applications: scheduling, interpersonal communication, meetings and conferences, you name it. But the Web is far from the only technology whose future points towards these possibilities, and it remains to be seen if it will overtake, fall behind, or simply incorporate all the rest. What's certain is that the Web is extremely flexible, and that its capabilities haven't begun to be explored. The remainder of *The World Wide Web Unleashed* shows you the present and speculates on the future as well.

The World Wide Web: A Guided Tour

6

by Neil Randall

IN THIS CHAPTER

Now that you know where the Web came from and what it consists of, it's time for a quick tour of what the Web contains. "Quick" is the operative word here, because throughout Part III, "Web Navigation Tools and Techniques," and Part IV, "Exploring the Web," you'll see page after page of worthwhile sites to visit. For now, the idea is to categorize Web pages according to what you might want to see right off the bat, as a means of getting used to the sheer size of the information reservoir that awaits.

There's no attempt here to be comprehensive. That's what the book itself is about, although there's no way it could be comprehensive, either. The Web is growing at such a prodigious rate that keeping track of all the additions is impossible, a fact that we acknowledge freely in this book. This chapter provides a means of getting started, and in many ways Parts III and IV build on these beginnings.

Sites for Getting You Started

If you have no particular goal in mind but just want to browse through the Web to see what it offers, check out some of the sites in this section.

Whether you're just browsing or doing some serious exploring, there are several web sites that serve as a good starting point for connecting to interesting Web resources. Here is just a handful of the best ones.

Starting Points for Internet Exploration

NCSA is the developer of the premier Web client, Mosaic, so it should come as no surprise that it offers a number of worthwhile pages for novice browsers. Two are included in this section, the first of which is the Starting Points for Internet Exploration page (`http://www.ncsa.uiuc.edu/SDG/Software/Mosaic/StartingPoints/NetworkStartingPoints.html`). Included in Mosaic's Starting Points menu, this page takes you to a variety of well-developed places on the Web. Partially because of its placement on Mosaic's own menu, it's an obvious place to begin your exploring.

It isn't perfect, though. For one thing, its first two links (see Figure 6.1) are to CERN's Web Overview and Web Project pages. These are very good pages to visit, but not right off the bat. The Web Project page, for example, offers a wide range of information about the Web itself, but has only limited links to points of general interest. Similarly, the InterNIC InfoGuide link offers extremely useful data for anyone doing research about the Internet, but isn't much from the standpoint of a beginning explorer. Not until further down does this page offer the kinds of exploratory links interesting to a new Web cruiser, and even then there aren't many that don't appear in Mosaic's own menus.

FIGURE 6.1.

The NCSA Starting Points page.

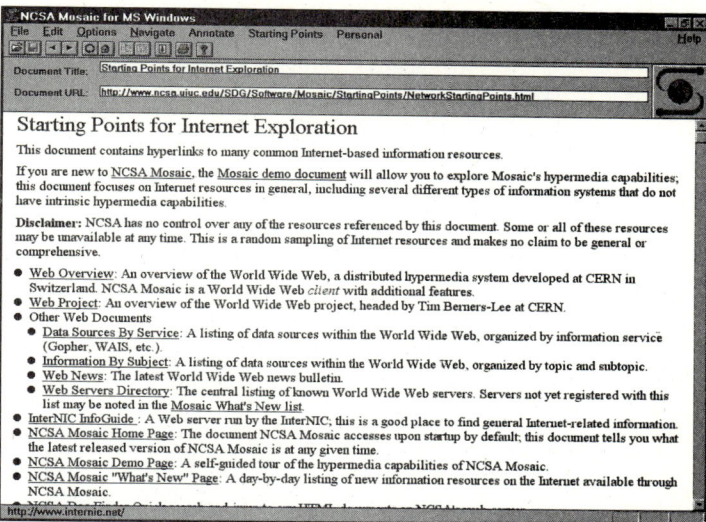

Figure 6.2 shows the result of clicking on one of Starting Points' first links, the Web Servers Directory (`http://info.cern.ch/hypertext/DataSources/WWW/Servers.html`). Arranged geographically, the W3 servers page offers a huge range of useful links, and this is actually more useful for explorers than the original page.

All in all, Starting Points is well worth visiting, but don't expect it to lead you everywhere you wish to go.

FIGURE 6.2.

The W3 servers page, with extended geographical index.

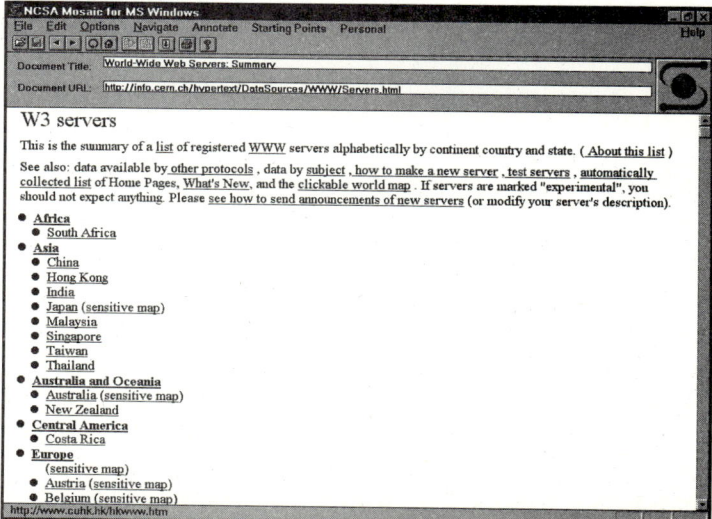

The Whole Internet Catalog

Both a search page and a subject page, The Whole Internet Catalog provides an excellent starting location if you're interested in exploring by topic. From the main page shown in Figure 6.3 (`http://nearnet.gnn.com/wic/newrescat.toc.html`), it's easy to see precisely what to do: Just scroll down the page to the topic you want, click on the appropriate major topic or subtopic, and then watch as the resulting page makes its appearance. The only problem is that it's not always obvious which topics belong in which category, but a reasonably brief period of exploring will help you see what's available throughout.

FIGURE 6.3.

The Whole Internet Catalog home page.

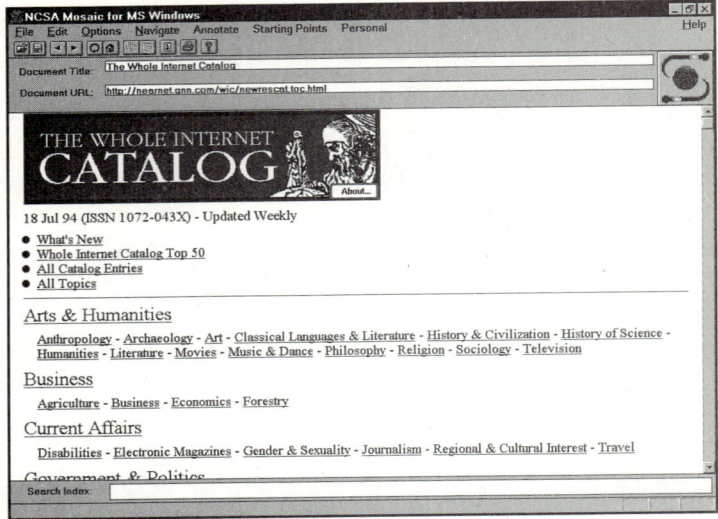

Also available from the catalog is the Whole Internet Catalog Top 50 (`http://nearnet.gnn.com/wic/top.toc.html`). (See Figure 6.4.) From here you can access another good range of topics, and the page also lets you know how many readers have been where you're about to go. It's hard to imagine anyone seeing this page without taking interest in at least one subject area, and more likely several.

The HookUp Mall

As the popularity of the Internet has grown, so has the number of Internet providers, companies who offer Internet connections at monthly rates depending on the kind and amount of access needed. Because these providers quite naturally want to encourage their customers to actually use the Net, they also tend to offer ready access to the best available software. Those offering SLIP and PPP access (see Part II, "Web Browsers and Connections") often include a Web browser (usually Mosaic) as part of the package, and to supplement that offering they establish their own Web page to suit their customers' purposes.

FIGURE 6.4.

The Top 50 Entries from the Whole Internet Catalog.

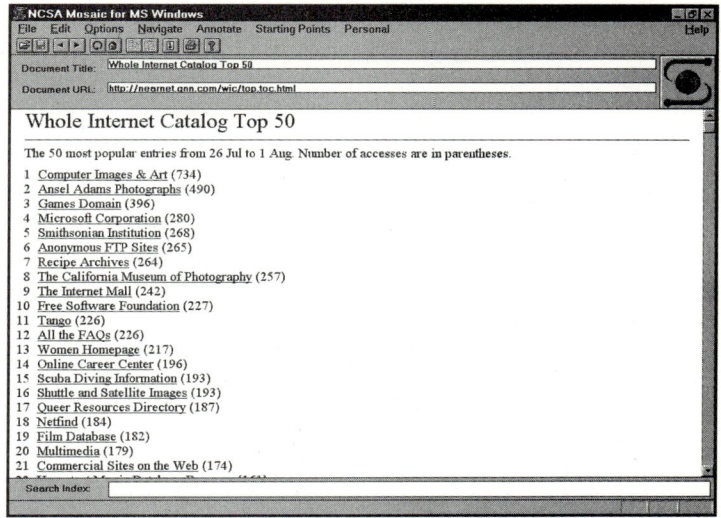

The page shown in Figure 6.5 (`http://hookup.net/mall.html`) is precisely this kind of offering, and although it's typical of a service provider's access pages, this one is very well developed. (It's also the one I access regularly, being a customer of this provider.) Like many offerings on the Web, the page is set up according to the shopping mall metaphor—something that, presumably, we're all very experienced with.

FIGURE 6.5.

HookUp Communications' Mall page.

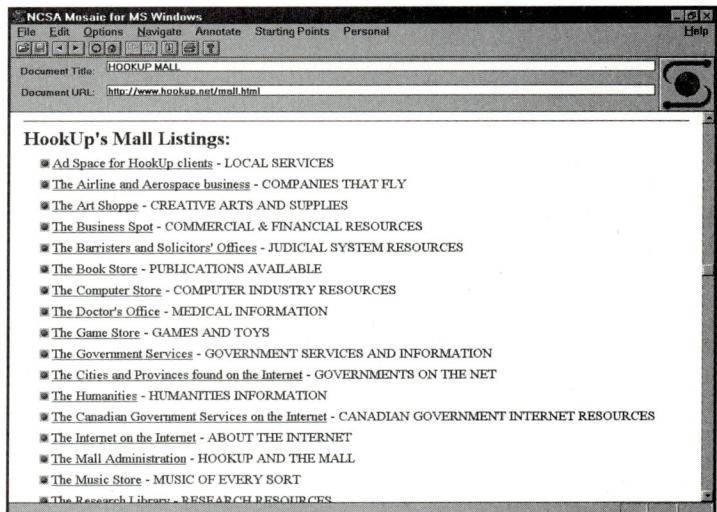

Each links opens to the specific "store," another Web page with additional links. One such store is shown in Figure 6.6 (`http://hookup.net/mall/library.html`). This is the research library area of the mall, with pointers to libraries and library listings. Many of these links lead, in turn, to pages with still more links.

FIGURE 6.6.

The Resource Library store at HookUp.

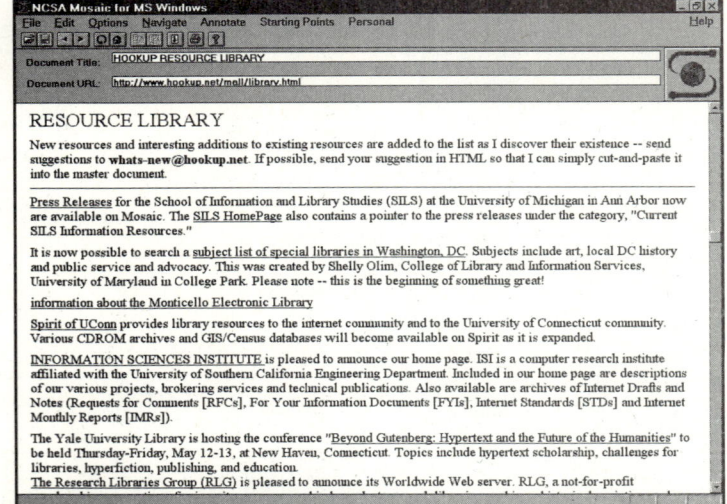

The Scout Report

Updated weekly by InterNIC Information Services, as official an information arm as the Internet has, the Scout Report provides links to sites and services added to the Internet over the preceding seven days. Its usefulness is simple: If you want to keep tabs on what's happening on the Net, this is a very good place to visit regularly. The Web version of the page is a supplement to the e-mail subscription you can also get, the latter being especially helpful for those without easy Web access. But since this book is about the Web, and not the Net in general, it makes sense to show the Web version only.

The Scout Report is actually quite similar to the NCSA What's New Page (see Figure 6.9), except for one important difference. While the Scout Report is less comprehensive than What's New, it includes links to Gopher, FTP, telnet, and other useful Internet sites. By comparison, What's New concentrates on Web sites only.

As Figure 6.7 shows (`http://www.internic.net/scout-report/`), the Scout Report is catalogued by week. Click on any of the weeks, and you get a screen that resembles Figure 6.8 (`http://www.internic.net/scout-report/7-29-94.html`). Shown here are some Gopher, Web, and FTP links, any of which are easily accessible.

FIGURE 6.7.

The InterNIC Scout Report home page.

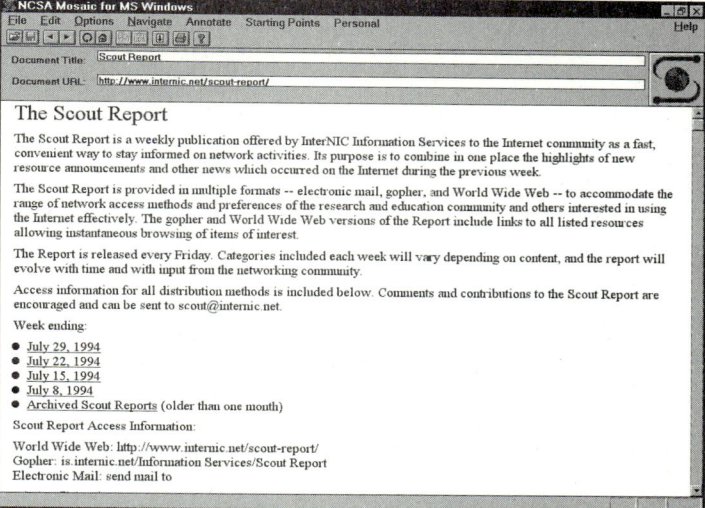

FIGURE 6.8.

A sample Scout Report page showing links to non-WWW sites.

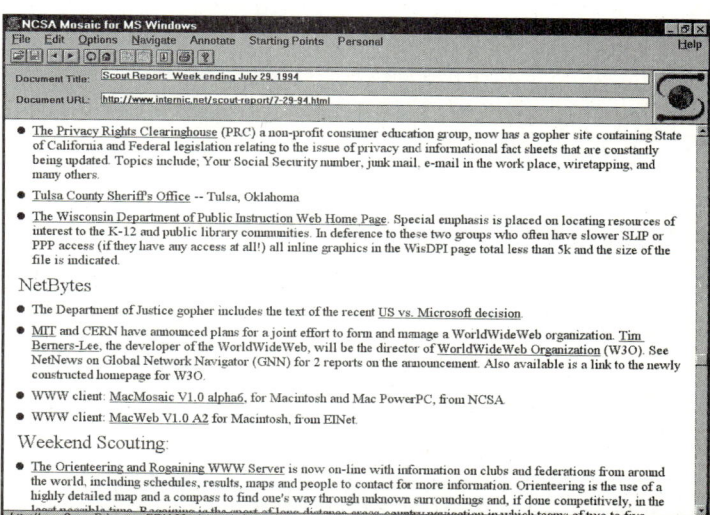

What's New with NCSA Mosaic and the WWW

One of the most heavily accessed resources on the Internet, NCSA's What's New page (`http://www.ncsa.uiuc.edu/SDG/Software/Mosaic/Docs/whats-new.html`) offers links to most, if not all, accessible Web sites. It is not written by the people at NCSA; rather, contributors send a paragraph in HTML format to the page-keepers, who incorporate all paragraphs and add them to a page that grows as the month progresses. In essence, the What's New page offers advertising for Web page designers, and it's an extremely valuable place to tell people about your information center.

Over the past year and a half, the What's New page has grown from a few items a month to hundreds of items per month. In fact, the Web's volume is now the page's only significant problem. For users with slow access—including anyone with a 14.4 kbps modem or less—the What's New page takes far too long to download by the time the month is half over. Beginning in spring 1994, the page began to be updated daily rather than weekly, and the size increased proportionately. To compensate, a provider named Multimedia Ink Designs offers a page called "TOP o WHAT's NEW" (`http://mmink.cts.com/topo.html`), which features only the most recent entries for the page.

Figure 6.9 shows the first screen of a typical What's New page. Figure 6.10 shows the final portions of that page, along with links to the What's New pages for past dates. It's fascinating to look back at where the Web was in mid-1993, to see how much it's grown in the meantime.

FIGURE 6.9.

What's New page for July 29, 1994.

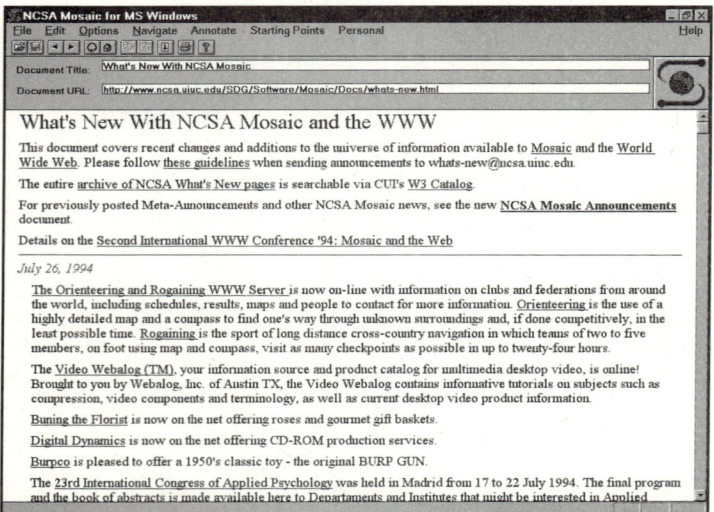

John December's Internet Web Text

Although it might seem a bit self-serving here, it would be inappropriate for *any* tour of the Web not to mention the important work of this book's coauthor, John December. John's Web pages are endlessly useful for anyone wanting to know about the Internet, its tools, or its influence on John's academic research topic: computer-mediated communications.

Figure 6.11 shows John's famous Internet Web Text main page (`http://www.rpi.edu/Internet/Guides/decemj/text.html`), with its well-ordered collection of links to Internet information. Figure 6.12 is one of John's Web-based publishing projects, the current issue of *Computer-Mediated Communications Magazine* (`http://www.rpi.edu/~decemj/cmc/mag/current/toc.html`). This is fascinating reading for anyone interested in the effects of computers and networks (such as the Net and the Web) on human communications, and the fact that you're reading this book probably means that you are.

FIGURE 6.10.

Bottom of What's New page with links to previous dates.

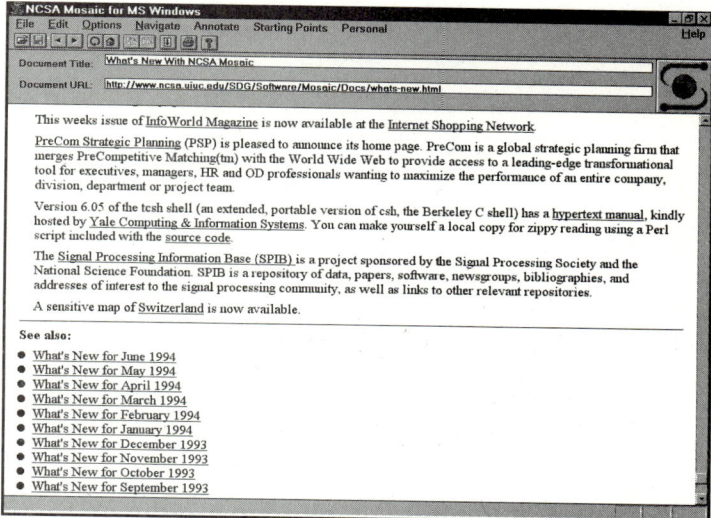

You'll meet John beginning in Part III, "Web Navigation Tools and Techniques." As you can see from these pages, he has a great deal of Web know-how to offer.

FIGURE 6.11.

The Internet Web Text main page.

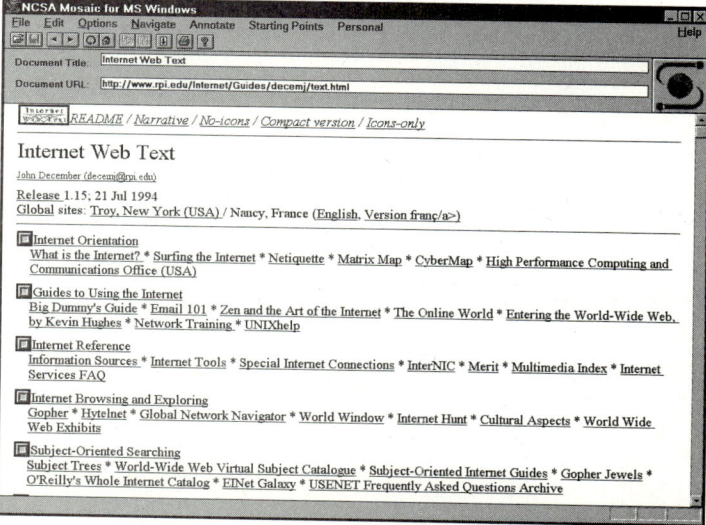

FIGURE 6.12.

The current issue of Computer-Mediated Communication Magazine.

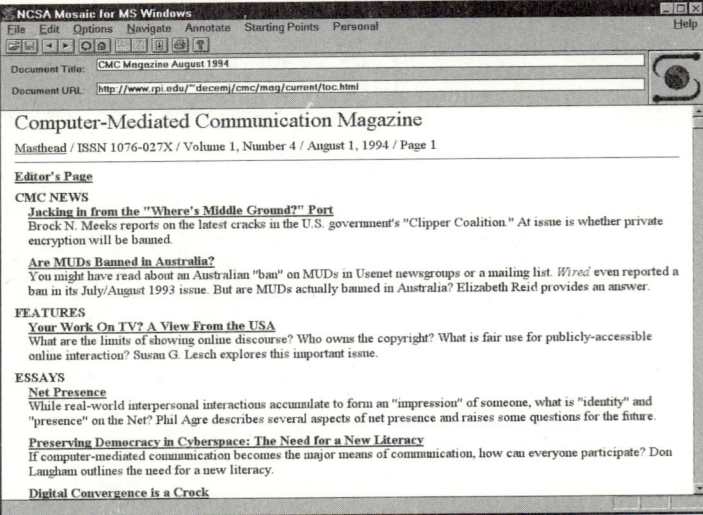

Sites for Conducting a Search

While the World Wide Web is designed to allow point-and-click browsing, with readers moving from point to point more or less as the spirit moves, it's not always convenient or even a good idea to cruise in this manner. Often you need specific information, and you need it fast. For these occasions, the best bet is to turn to one of the Web's search pages. They're accessible and well-designed, and they can get you quickly from no information to tons of information.

Something important to keep in mind, however, is that all search pages work best with browsers that support forms. These include Mosaic 2.0 (for all platforms), MacWeb and WinWeb, and Cello beginning with Version 2. Without forms, the pages are less useful, but they're still worth going to when specific information is sought.

CUI

The CUI W3 Catalog at CERN (`http://cui_www.unige.ch/w3catalog`) is one of the oldest Web search pages available. ("Old" in Web terms means about a year and a half.) As Figure 6.13 shows, when you access the page you're presented with a very simple form, in which you type the topic you're searching for or, if you're more ambitious, a Perl regular expression for advanced searching. The link to Perl offers a help screen for constructing Perl expressions. Once you have your word or expression typed in, you click on the Submit button and the search takes place. As the second-to-the-last link on the page shows, an alternative interface is available for users whose browsing software doesn't support HTML forms (such as Lynx and Version 1 of Cello).

FIGURE 6.13.

The CUI W3 Catalog home page.

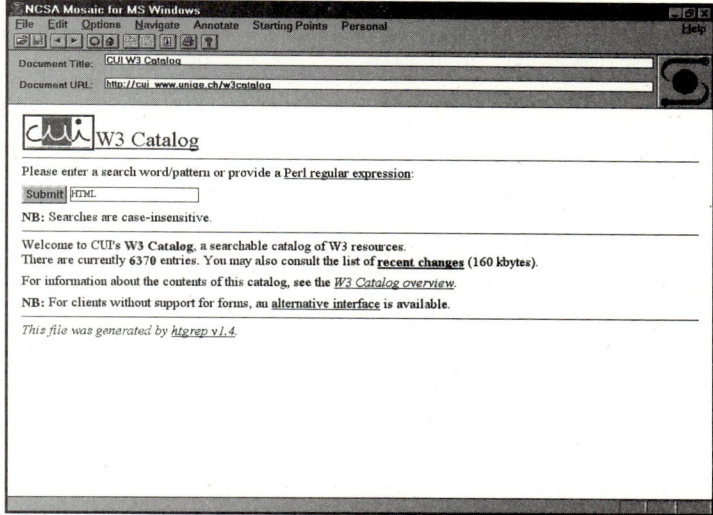

Figure 6.14 displays the results of a CUI search for the term "HTML." At the top of the screen is the same search form as before; below that form are the items the search turned up. The items are in the format of paragraphs with hypertext links, and they're ordered by date, the most recent entries first.

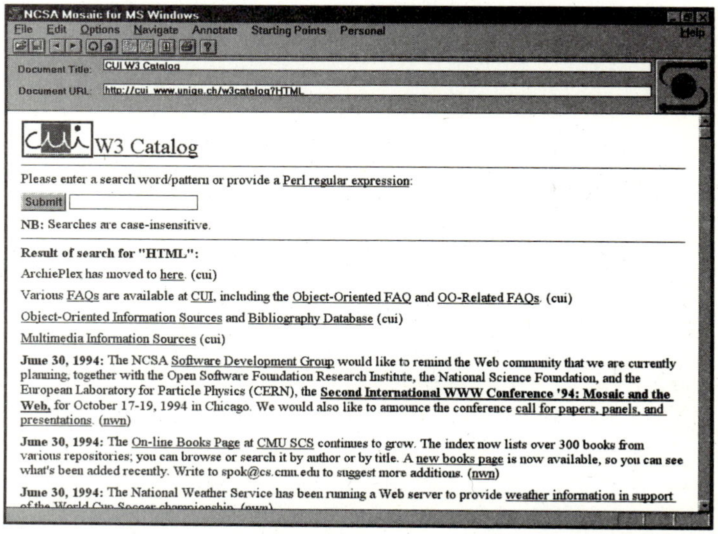

FIGURE 6.14.

The result of a CUI search for "HTML."

EINet Galaxy

The EINet Galaxy is one of the Web's most useful and impressive search tools. It is divided among topic areas (as are other search tools), and at the bottom of the opening screen is a search system that lets you specify where on the Internet you wish to draw your material from. Through a clever use of HTML forms, the Galaxy lets you filter your search requests through Galaxy topics only, through the Web only, through Web and Gopherspace, or some combination. You can also select the number of hits you want to record on your results page.

Figure 6.15 shows the Galaxy home page (`http://www.einet.net/galaxy.html`). Figure 6.16 displays the result of clicking on a subtopic in the Galaxy listing, this time for World Communities. From this page you can access further submenus, or launch a direct search.

FIGURE 6.15.

The EINet Galaxy home page.

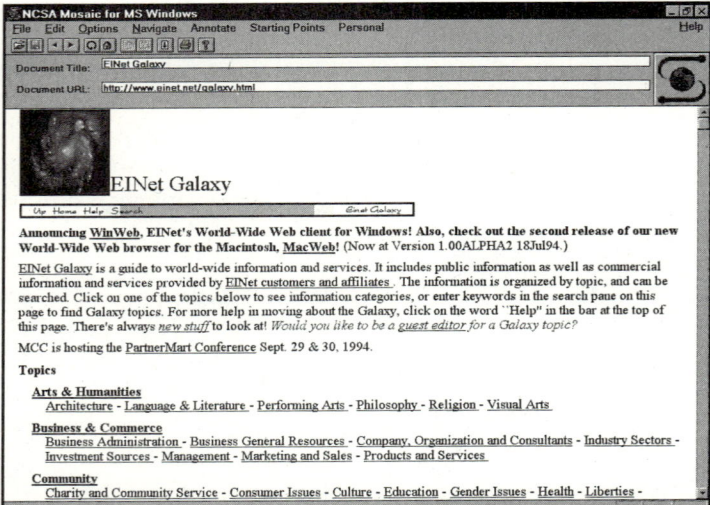

Virtual Library

CERN's Virtual Library offers still another Web search engine, and is available from several pages across the Web. Like the EINet Galaxy, the Library is organized according to topic and subtopic, but the difference is that the subtopic lists on the page aren't as comprehensively listed. The "Agriculture" topic shown in Figure 6.17, for instance (`http://info.cern.ch/hypertext/DataSources/bySubject/Overview.html`), has a smattering of links within it, but to get "Anthropology" information you have to move to a separate list. Still, the Library is an invaluable search tool, and as you might expect from a CERN-developed tool, it makes excellent use of the Web's search capabilities.

FIGURE 6.16.

An EINet Galaxy subpage.

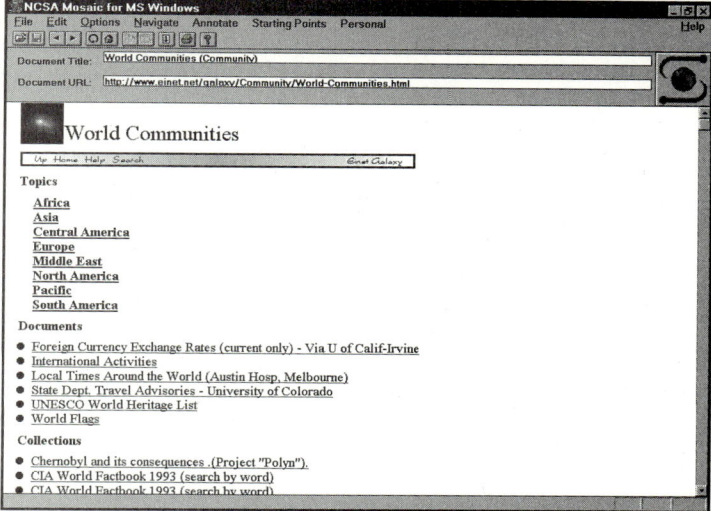

FIGURE 6.17.

The Virtual Library main page.

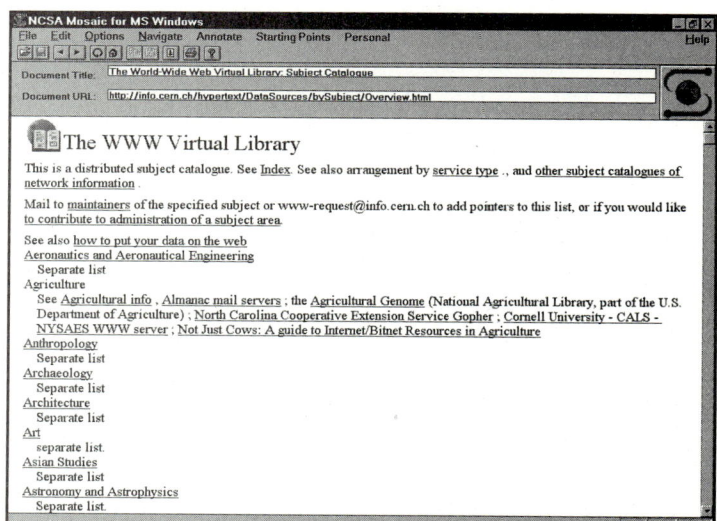

Figure 6.18 (`http://www.actwin.com/WWWVL-Fish.html`) shows the result of clicking on the "Fish" listing from the Library's home page. At this point we've left the CERN pages and gone to a related page on the Net that sports the Library's icon. Information is divided into Web-specific links and other Internet links. It's important that search pages offer all possible resources, since the Web doesn't contain anywhere near the total amount of information available on the Net. There's plenty more out there, in a variety of forms.

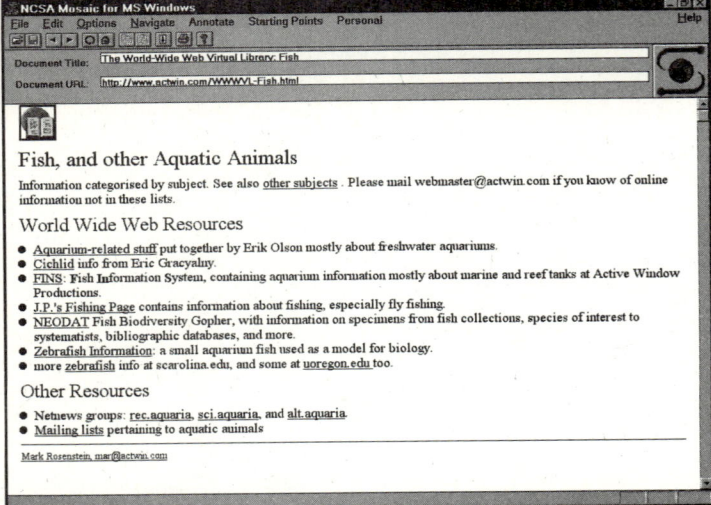

W3 Search Engines Page

The next two figures display an extremely useful Web-based search area called W3 Search Engines. The idea behind this page is to offer the major Internet search tools from one site only, and the effort succeeds marvelously. From here you can search the Web or Gopherspace, you can find Internet users, and you can also locate files on FTP sites. It's essentially one-stop shopping for all your search requirements, and it will quickly become an indispensable toolkit.

Figures 6.19 and 6.20 (`http://golgi.harvard.edu/meta-index.html`) show two portions of the Search Engines page. Along with two links to other search-type pages are forms for CUI and the WWW Worm. (See Figures 6.21 and 6.22.) Figure 6.20 shows the page's ability to search for people, publications, and newsgroup FAQs. As Figure 6.19 shows, this page will work from your local Web server as easily as from Harvard's, and downloading it is recommended.

The World Wide Web Worm

The World Wide Web Worm is a fascinating project. Essentially, it's a piece of software that works its way around the Internet, searching for home pages of all kinds, then collecting these pages in one indexed site. You can then use the Worm's home page to search through the pages it has found, through the forms-based search system shown in Figure 6.21 (`http://www.cs.colorado.edu/home/mcbryan/WWWW.html`). Note that there is no alternative interface; if your browser doesn't support HTML forms, you can't perform searches. (Note also that the reference to MacMosaic shown at the top of Figure 6.21 is no longer accurate.) You can also get a listing of all the home pages it has found, sorted alphabetically by title.

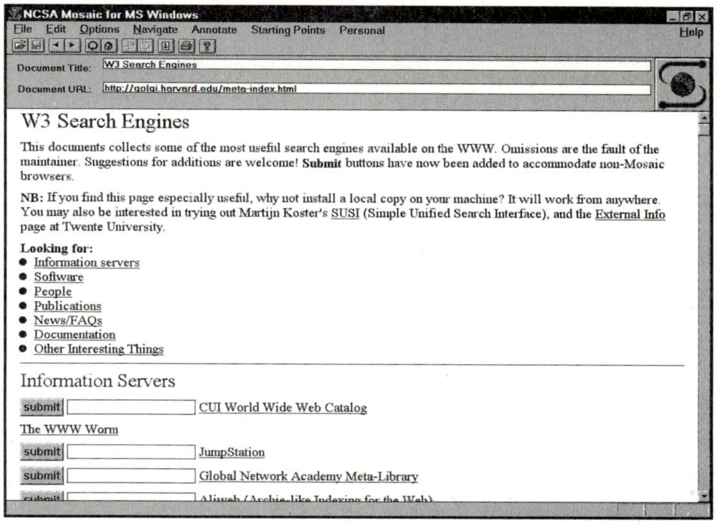

FIGURE 6.19.

Top portion of the W3 Search Engines page.

FIGURE 6.20.

Lower portion of the W3 Search Engines page.

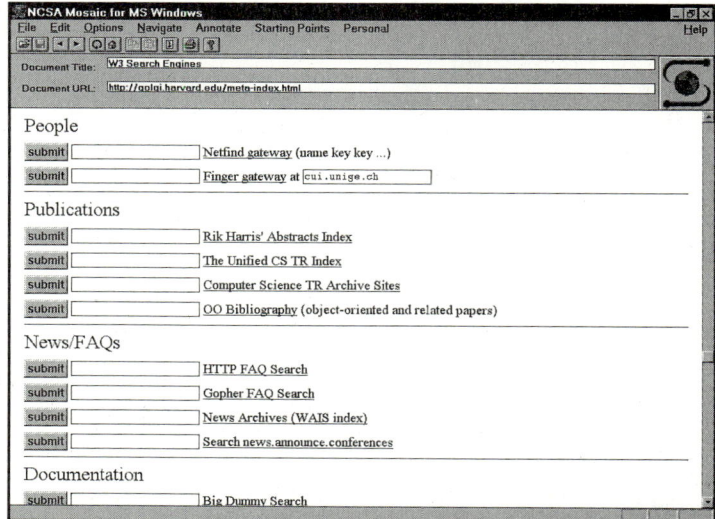

FIGURE 6.21.

Top portion of WWWW home page, showing other search links.

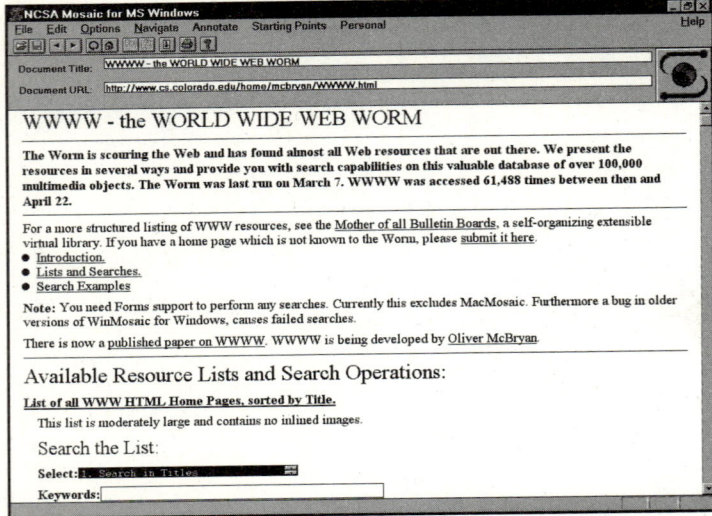

Figure 6.22 shows a lower portion of the WWWW's main page. These are both search forms and examples, and you can customize them as you wish. The idea is to narrow the search as much as possible to avoid coming up with unrelated or unimportant material. The Worm will sift through exactly what you tell it to.

FIGURE 6.22.

Lower portion of WWWW page, with sample searches filled in.

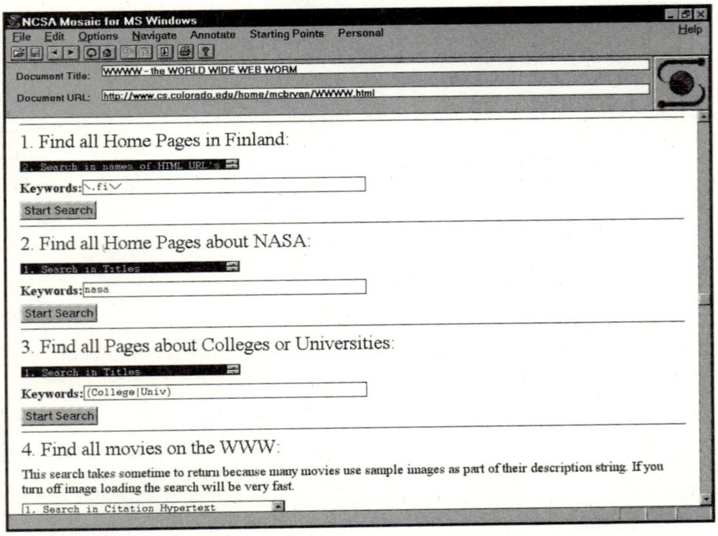

Sites of Exceptional Interest

So much for searching and getting started. Now it's time to move on to a few of the best pages the Web has to offer, pages that have been developed over the course of several months or that have the funding necessary to dedicate extensive design time to them. These are the kinds of pages you'll find yourself using in order to impress not only yourself, but anyone else who wants to know "what this Web stuff is all about."

What makes an exceptional Web page? A number of things, really, but some points simply hit home immediately. First, a great Web page looks good. Second, it offers well-organized pointers to a wide range of sources. Third, it's not just a one-page wonder; it incorporates several interesting pages into its repertoire as well. Fourth, it makes the World Wide Web, and in fact the entire Internet, a more exciting place when you leave than it was when you arrived. These are huge challenges, but they're already being met.

NASA

It's hardly surprising, given the U.S. government's original and continuing interest in the Internet, that a government agency promises to be the best Web site of the lot. Nor is it surprising that NASA has taken up the challenge of becoming that site, because we associate NASA, like the Web, with futurism. What *is* surprising is just how good this site is shaping up to be. For anyone doing research into the U.S. space program, there simply is no better starting point.

Figure 6.23 shows a portion of the NASA home page (`http://www.gsfc.nasa.gov/NASA_home.html`). The central focus, obviously, is the clickable map in the middle of the page; clicking on any of the red dots takes you to the associated NASA Center, which in most cases has a well-developed archive of fascinating information.

As an example, Figure 6.24 is the home page for the famous Kennedy Space Center (`http://www.ksc.nasa.gov/ksc.html`), through which you have access to a wealth of information about current and past NASA missions. From here, you can get everything from the Space Shuttle reference manual through the Center's historical mission archives. Among the most famous of these archives is that for the Apollo 11 mission, a small part of which is shown in Figure 6.25. And despite the rich detail provided in the Kennedy pages, NASA has far more offerings on the Web. One such page, the Langley Research Center's High Performance Computing and Communications K-12 Program (Figure 6.26), provides information about this exciting program as well.

FIGURE 6.23.

NASA home page, showing clickable map of the United States.

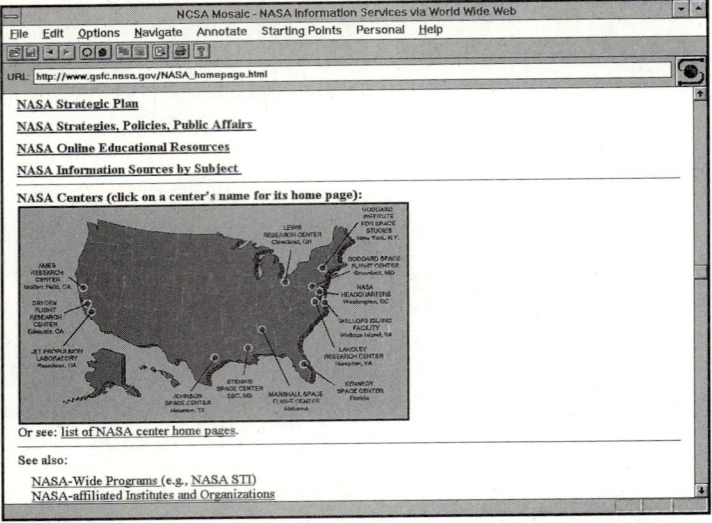

FIGURE 6.24.

Kennedy Space Center home page.

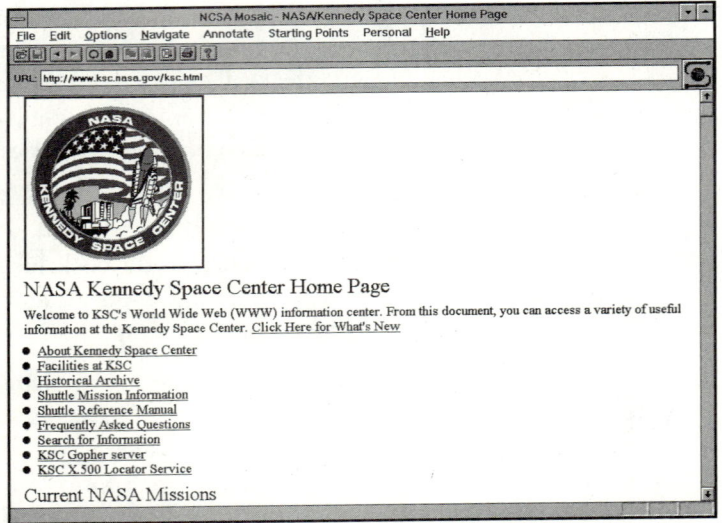

FIGURE 6.25.

Portion of transcript from Apollo 11 mission page.

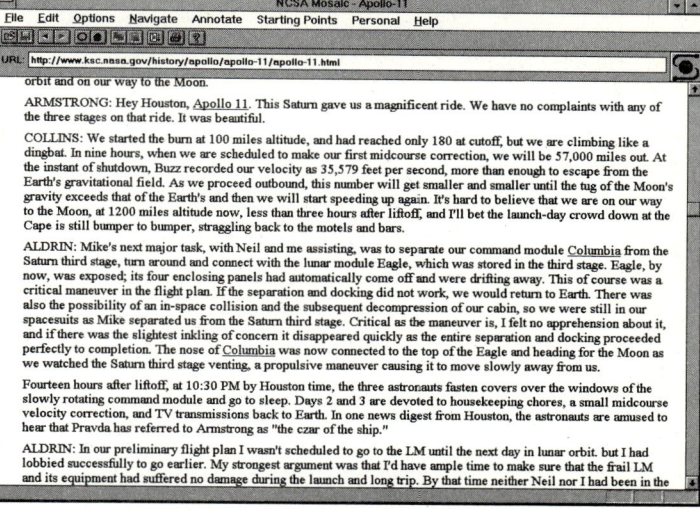

FIGURE 6.26.

Langley Research Center's HPCC K-12 Program page.

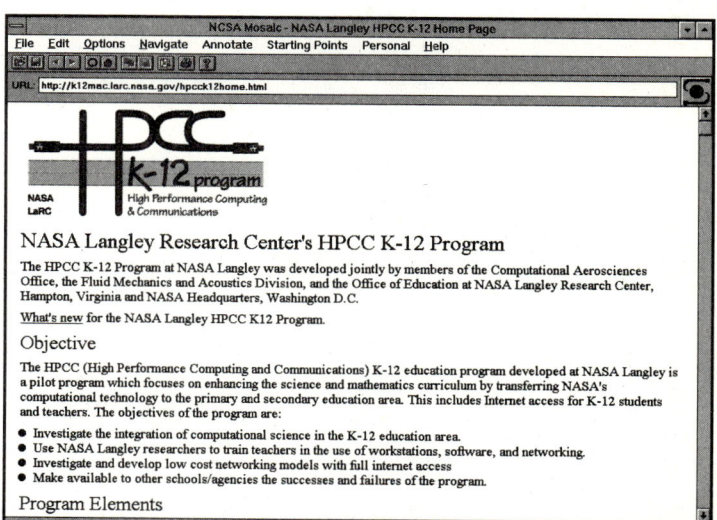

GNN

From the very beginning, the purpose of the Global Network Navigator (GNN) was to provide a colorful, enticing series of pages on the World Wide Web, and to offer not just links but magazine style articles as well. To say that it has succeeded is an understatement, because it remains one of the Web's most popular sites. That popularity is demonstrated by the fact that GNN is mirrored on a variety of computers; the examples shown here, in fact, were taken from one such mirror.

GNN's home page (`http://gnn.interpath.net/gnn/GNNhome.html`), also called the Directory, is deceptively simple. (See Figure 6.27.)

FIGURE 6.27.

GNN's home page, showing links to other departments.

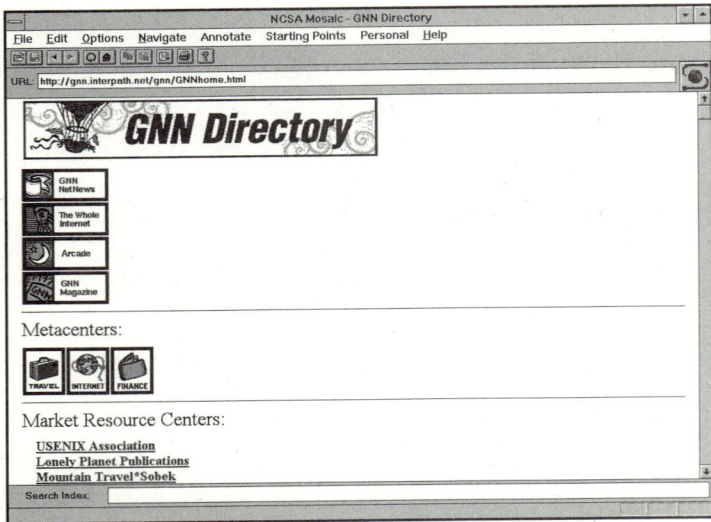

Each of the graphical links leads to entire departments, each with its own subpages and sublinks. The popular Finance Center, shown in Figure 6.28, offers not only fascinating reading in the form of articles, but also links to other finance related pages within GNN and elsewhere on the Net.

The same holds true with the Internet Center (Figure 6.29), with its feature articles and its four linked graphics along the bottom of the page.

FIGURE 6.28.

The Personal Finance Center, with links to Internet resources.

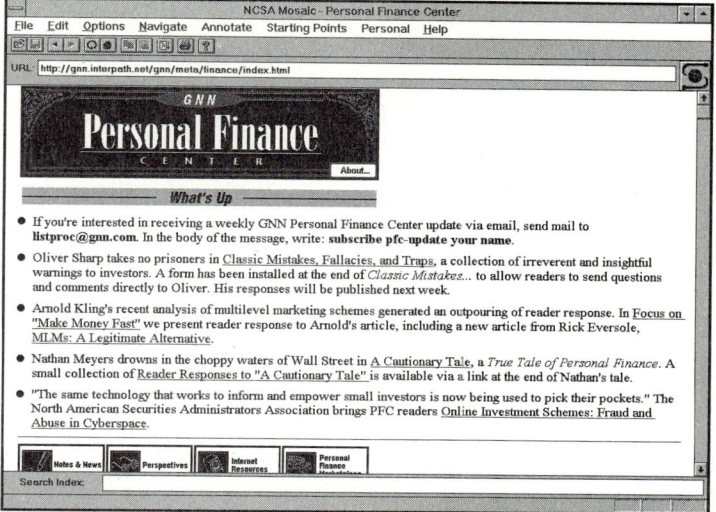

FIGURE 6.29.

GNN's Internet Center, with articles and links.

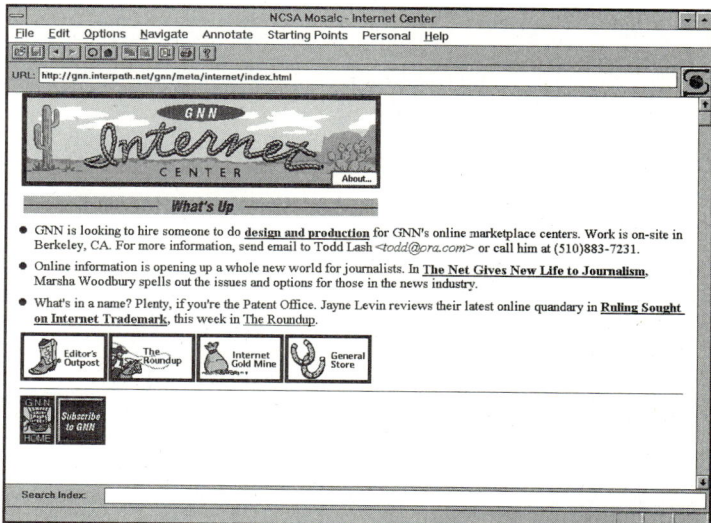

There's a travel center as well, but GNN's entertainment department, called the Arcade (Figure 6.30), is well worth visiting any time you have a few moments. There aren't many sites as nicely designed and superbly developed as the GNN pages. You owe it to yourself to see what they have to offer.

FIGURE 6.30.

The GNN Arcade page, with links to entertainment pages.

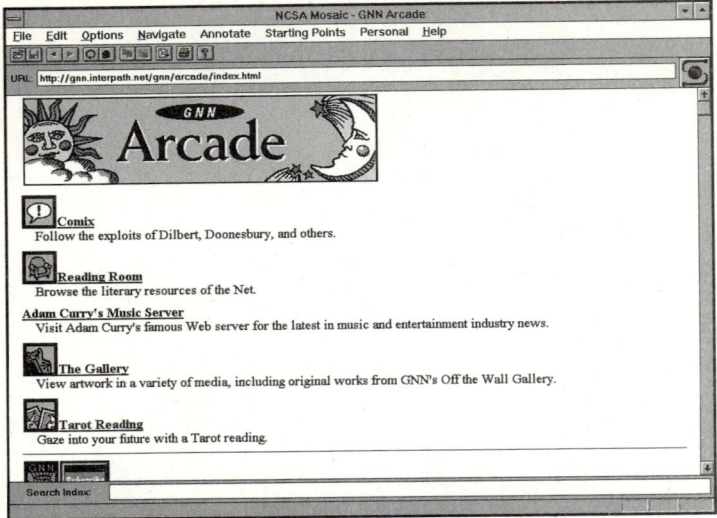

EXPO

Like GNN, Sunsite's EXPO page has been popular almost since its first appearance on the Web. The idea behind the EXPO is to use the Web to offer material in the form of a gallery or exhibition, and to fill each exhibit with as much material as most people would be interested in seeing. Although Figure 6.31 doesn't completely show it, the EXPO home page (`http://sunsite.unc.edu/expo/ticket_office.html`) actually offers several interesting exhibits, all of which are very much worth seeing. From this page you can access the Shuttle Bus, which offers links to all the portions of the exhibits, and further down the page you can even access a book store and a restaurant, complete with graphics and menus.

Figure 6.32 shows a page well inside the Vatican Library exhibit. This page offers graphics of some of the important historical manuscripts in the library. The bordered graphics can be downloaded and viewed, as larger versions, in your own graphics software. Like all exhibits, the details about each artifact aren't comprehensive, but more than enough to help you get started in knowing something about them.

FIGURE 6.31.

The EXPO home page, with links to the Shuttle Bus and exhibits.

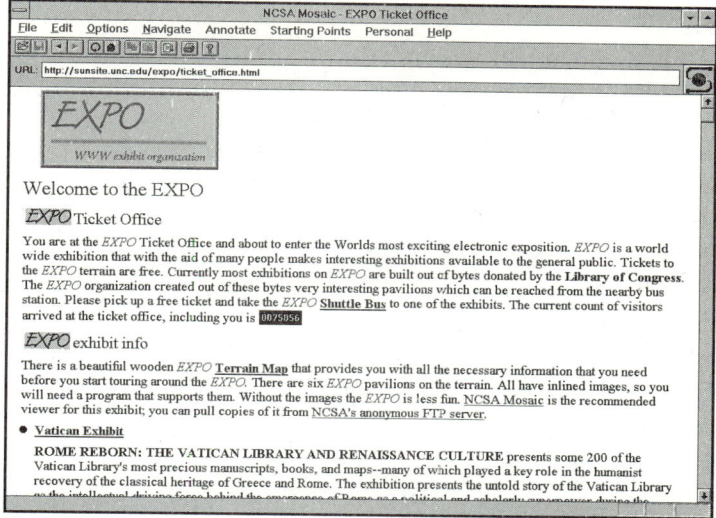

FIGURE 6.32.

A small portion of the Vatican Library exhibit.

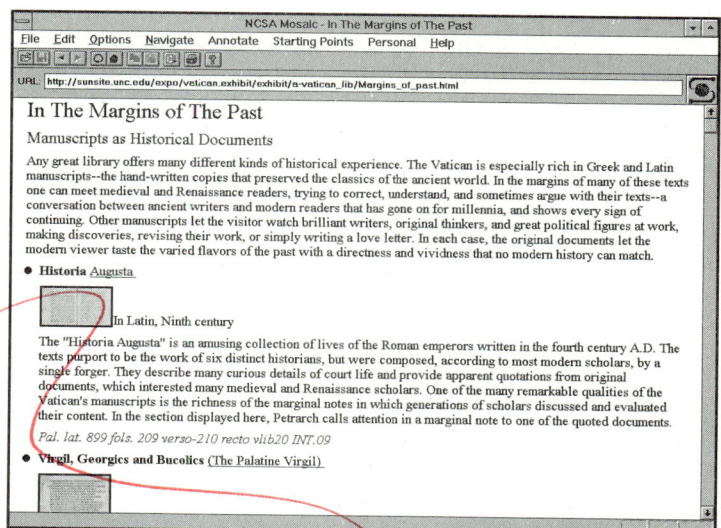

Figures 6.33 and 6.34 show two pages of the Scrolls from the Dead Sea exhibit. The home page offers links to several other pages, one of which (Figure 6.34) shows graphics and data about some of the wooden artifacts found in the area.

FIGURE 6.33.

The Scrolls from the Dead Sea exhibit entrance page.

FIGURE 6.34.

The Wooden Artifacts page from the Dead Sea exhibit.

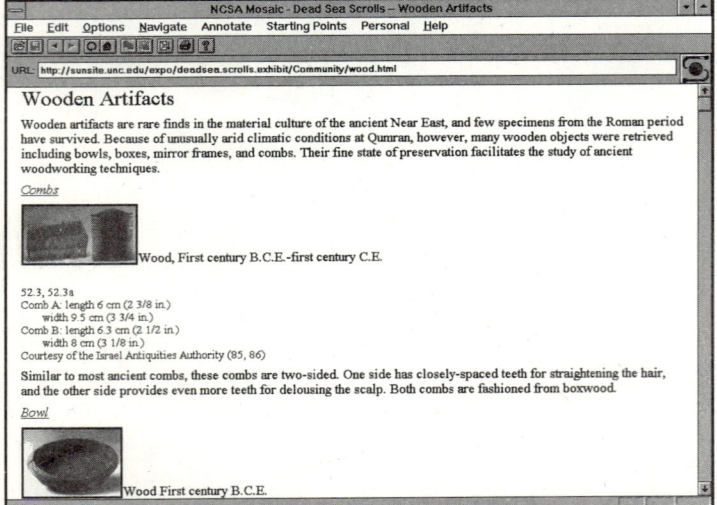

ANIMA

One of the continuing treats in accessing the Web lies in exploring the large and growing collection of art and artists' interests, new examples of which seem to be appearing every week. Although there are many such pages available, one of the most comprehensive collections is ANIMA, the Arts Network for Integrated Media Applications (`http://wimsey.com/anima/ANIMAhome.html`). From here, as Figure 6.35 demonstrates, you can access everything from art galleries through collaborative projects, information maps, and writings about the relationship between art, technology, and interface. Work through these pages, and it's hard to imagine an artist or a nonartist not finding something of possible or exact interest.

FIGURE 6.35.

The ANIMA home page, showing links to other arts resources.

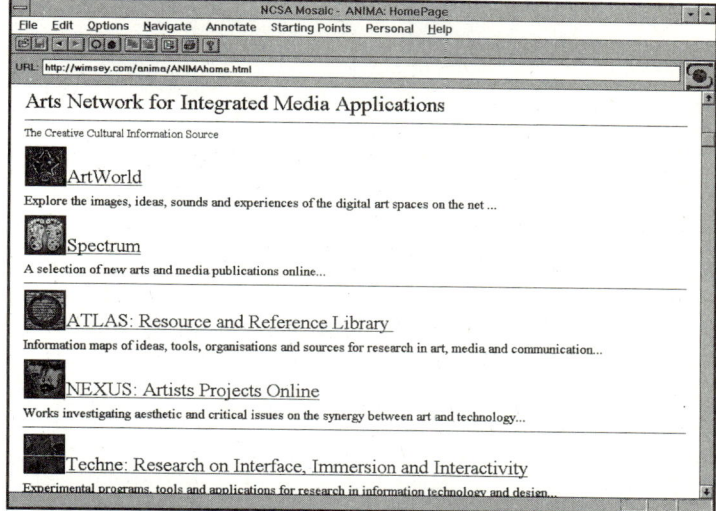

One of the hyperlinks from ANIMA's home page leads to The Web's Edge (`http://kzsu.stanford.edu/uwi.html`), shown in Figure 6.36, which is only one of the increasing number of fascinating contemporary art pages available on the Web. Links from here lead to pages about poetry, zines, journals, and so forth. Other links from ANIMA's pages lead to similar or even more inventive sites, often with displays of digital art, collaborative art, and experimental art, literature, and music.

Cambridge, MA

We're beginning to see several towns and cities placing information on the Web, with entries thus far from places as far apart as Palo Alto (one of the first) through Houston, Austin, Hoboken, Winnipeg, and eastward to London, Berlin, and several other European sites. One of the more recent additions is Cambridge, Massachusetts, whose home page (`http://www.ai.mit.edu/projects/iiip/Cambridge/homepage.html`) is displayed in Figure 6.37. From this page you can read a profile of the city, examine maps, or visit other Web cities. You can also access Senator Ted Kennedy's own page, which lists his current Senate efforts and offers other government-related information as well.

FIGURE 6.36.

The home page for The Web's Edge.

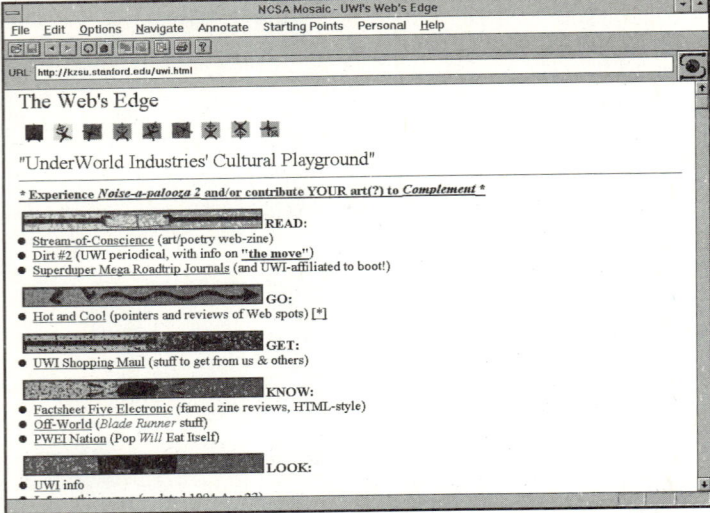

FIGURE 6.37.

City of Cambridge, Massachusetts home page.

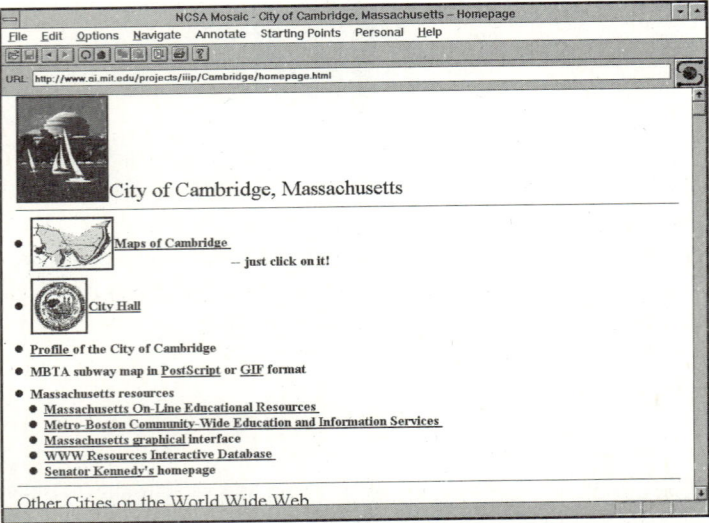

You can also move to the Cambridge City Hall page, which presents a variety of information useful to the city's residents. Among these is a set of pages documenting human rights issues, and one of these, Figure 6.38, is presented in Chinese. Seeing non-Roman alphabets is actually quite unusual on the Web, partly because special software is necessary for Web browser to display them. Here a different technique is used to present the Chinese characters as inline graphics, thereby making them presentable on any browser capable of displaying such graphics.

FIGURE 6.38.

Human rights page in Chinese.

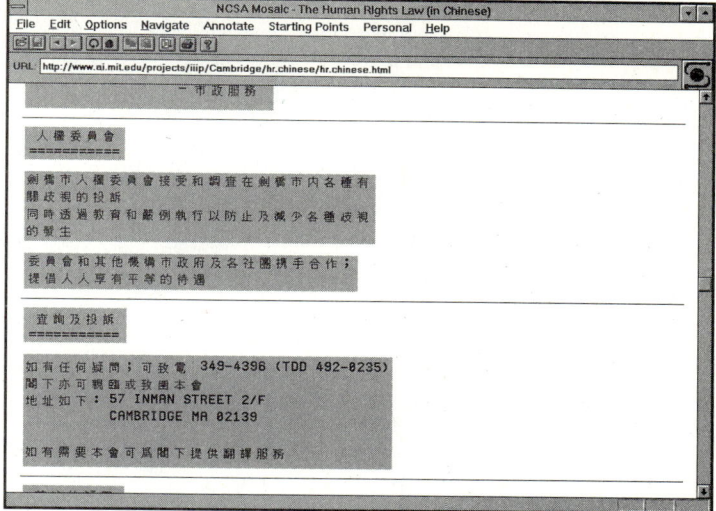

Sites Showing the Web's Advanced Features

The World Wide Web has given the Internet a substantial range of advanced interface features. Three of the most notable are clickable maps, fill-in forms, and multimedia capabilities. Here we finish our short tour of the Web, looking at a couple of examples of the use of each of these features—not necessarily the most elaborate examples, but certainly ones that demonstrate the Web's growing potential. Use of these features will be expanded, and others will be added, but as they stand now they offer enormous possibilities for well-developed sites with excellent interfaces.

Maps

The clickable map has become an increasingly prevalent feature on Web pages. Essentially, these maps work by associating different hyperlinks with corresponding portions of the maps, so that by clicking on a section or point on the map you bring up the linked page. In some cases, in fact, maps are linked to other maps, but it's possible to link maps to other pages, to graphics, to video, or to any other linkable object. We've already seen an example of a clickable map, the NASA home page in Figure 6.21.

Figure 6.39 shows The Virtual Tourist (`http://wings.buffalo.edu/world`), a clickable map of the world that leads you to Web (and other Internet) sites in those portions of the world. In some cases, in fact, they lead to other more focused clickable maps. The Tourist offers an easy method of touring the Web geographically, which for obvious reasons can be extremely useful.

FIGURE 6.39.

The Virtual Tourist main page.

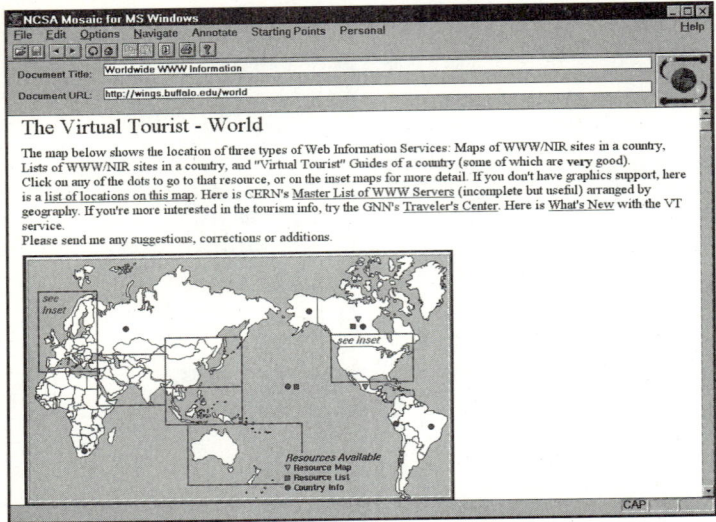

Figure 6.40 demonstrates another use of the clickable map. This is Hewlett Packard's SupportLine page (`http://support.mayfield.hp.com`), in which the idea is for an HP customer to click on the portion of the diagram they'd like to move to. Click on Electronic Digests, for instance, and you can access a large variety of related documents; click on Learning to Navigate, and you're given a tutorial on making your way around. As the Web moves more and more to commercial applications, this use of the clickable map will likely become more frequent.

FIGURE 6.40.

Hewlett Packard's SupportLine page.

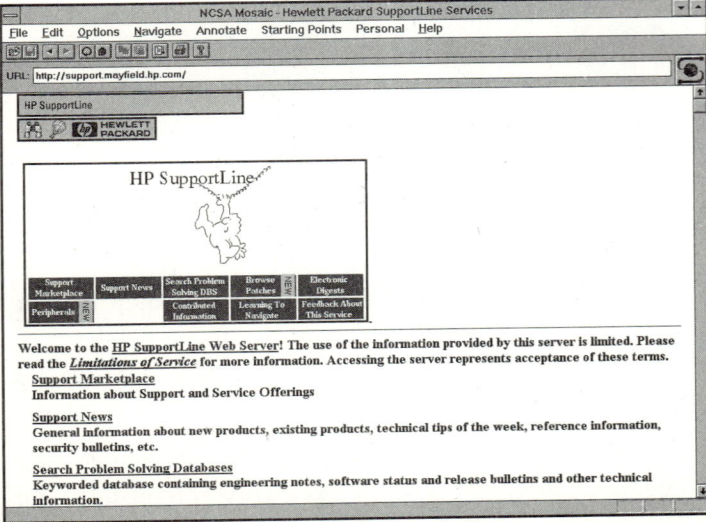

Forms

Beginning with Version 2.0 of Mosaic (all varieties), and then in other clients such as MacWeb and MidasWWW, the Web browsers were capable of displaying fill-in forms. Suddenly, there was yet another way for Net users to interact with the World Wide Web, and a very powerful one at that. A form can be extremely simple, such as the feedback forms available on any number of recent pages, or they can be considerably complex, offering menus with choices and fill-in features such as radio buttons. Combine them, and you can construct an elaborate interactive form, one that will give the providers of these pages all the information they need to conduct their affairs.

Figure 6.41 shows one of the Web's earliest forms of any interest, the order form for Grant's Florist and Greenhouse in Michigan (`http://florist.com:1080/flowers/order-flowers.html`). This is only a portion of this rather lengthy form, which includes spaces for credit card numbers, the address where the flowers are to be sent, and what you want written on the card. Actually Grant's Florist offers another interesting form. In this one, you fill out information to help remind you when to order flowers, and you're automatically notified by e-mail when that day (or a few days previous, if you wish) arrives.

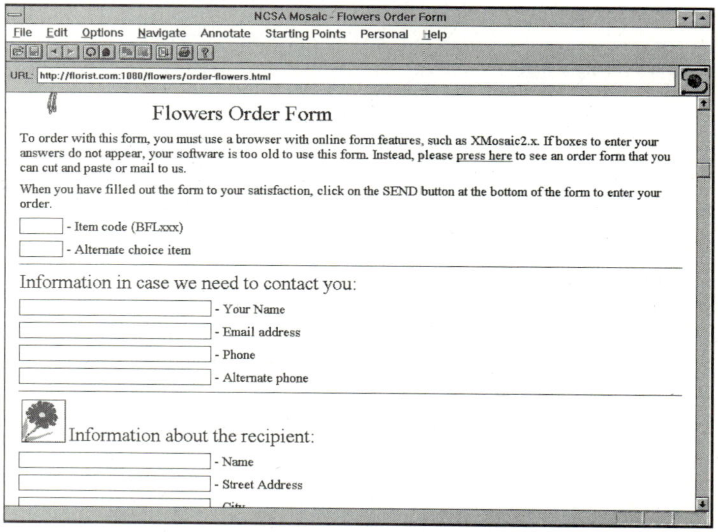

FIGURE 6.41.

Grant's Florist and Greenhouse flowers order form.

Figure 6.42 shows a similar use of a form, this time for a magazine that presents some of its information online. (Very few paper-based magazines publish full editions on the Web.) *ANSWERS* magazine's subscription form (`http://www.service.com/answers/answersorder.html`) requests the usual information about name, address, and so on, as a means of ordering a free copy of the magazine with your subscription. You can also click on a box to request a sample copy only.

Forms have an almost unlimited usefulness on the Web, just as they have in offline life. Expect to see their use increase enormously in the near future.

FIGURE 6.42.

ANSWERS magazine's subscription form.

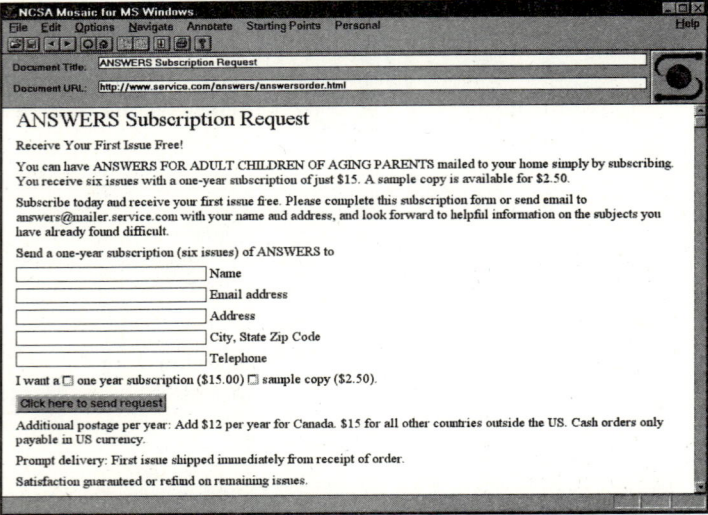

Multimedia

Finally, we move to multimedia. There's a growing amount of multimedia material being made available through the Web, but it's constrained by one major consideration. Multimedia files tend to be large, and unless you have a fast Internet connection you're not likely to get much use out of pages that feature them. If an audio interview takes three hours to download, after all (and this isn't at all uncommon), you're not going to bother with it, and the same goes for a lengthy video segment that you click on early in the evening and then view before you go to bed. The Web's full multimedia capacity is only useful to those with high-speed access, and even then it can be unpleasantly slow. Clearly, easily accessed audio and full-motion video belong to the Web's future, which is why they're being presented last here.

Figure 6.43 shows one of the most ambitious multimedia efforts on the Web, the Internet Multicasting Service (`http://www.cmf.nrl.navy.mil/radio/radio.html`). Thus far, this service consists mainly of Internet Talk Radio, which features audio interviews and other radio-like programming, and Internet Town Hall, with a variety of different broadcasts (including some superb interviews). Access them, but be aware that these files can be huge.

FIGURE 6.43.

The home page for the Internet Multicasting Service.

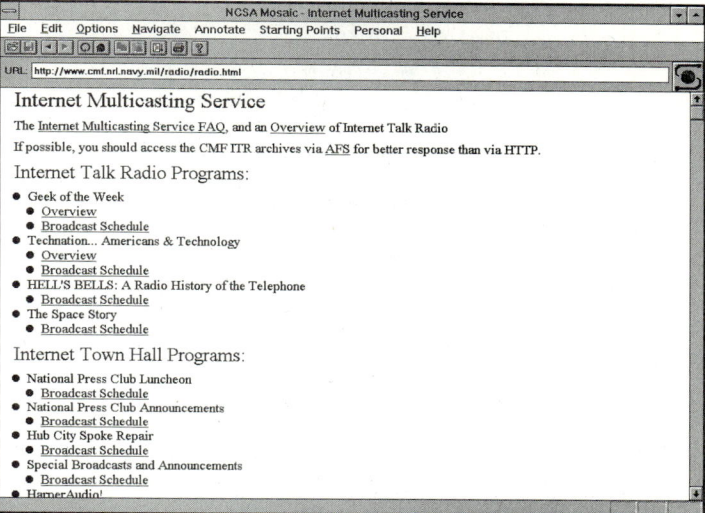

Figures 6.44 and 6.45 are from the Research Projects pages of the Army High Performance Computing Research Center (`http://s1.arc.umn.edu/html/research/research.html`). Figure 6.44 shows a sample large graphics and explanation from one of the projects, including links to video segments of three different resolutions (and three different file sizes). Figure 6.45 shows the main page for the projects, with the links to multimedia pages arranged alphabetically by research discipline.

FIGURE 6.44.

Multimedia page from the AHPCRC projects site.

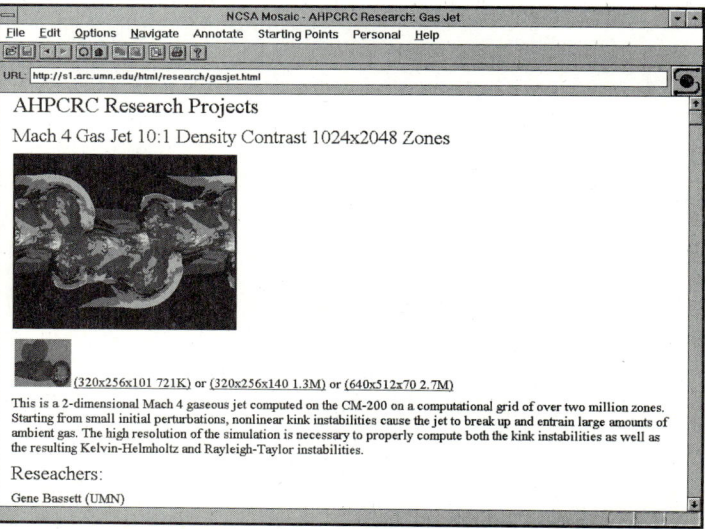

FIGURE 6.45.

The AHPCRC Research Projects home page.

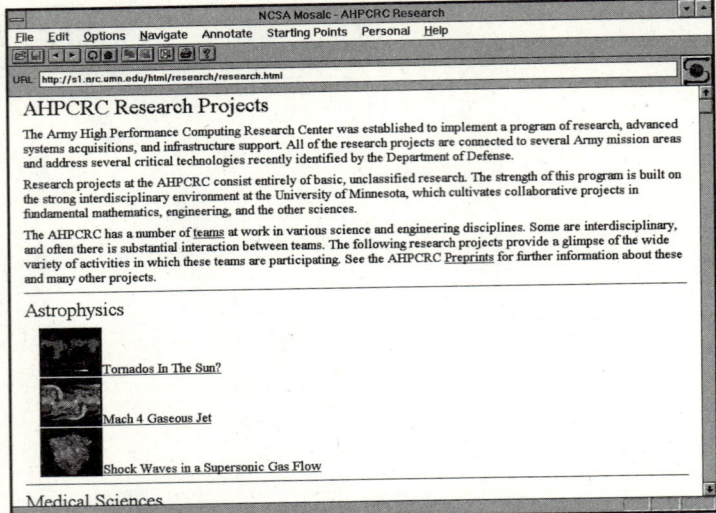

Onwards

This chapter demonstrates a tiny portion of the World Wide Web's offerings, and an equally tiny portion of its potential. Some of the Web sites toured here are among the most popular of them all, while others are indicative of the kind of material the Web has begun to make available. Some of the most thorough sites, as well as some of the most innnovative, informative, and even outrageous, are left to the detailed explorations in Part IV. Even though this has been merely a sampling, from these sites alone you can find practically anything on the Web that interests you.

PART

II

Web Browsers and Connections

The World Wide Web is one thing, while Web browsers are another. For many users, the Web and the browser have become inextricably linked, which is why we hear—and even read—about such nonexistent items as "Mosaic pages." There are Web pages, and there is Mosaic, but there is no such thing as a Mosaic page. Mosaic, like Cello and Lynx and MacWeb and Viola and a host of other such programs, is nothing more than a piece of software that lets you interact with the Web. These programs are called Web *clients* (or *browsers*), and they're the subject of Part II.

No matter which of the three big platforms you work with—UNIX, the Apple Macintosh, or Microsoft Windows—you have multiple clients to choose from. Part II explores several, offering a look at their unique features and presentations, their specific strengths and weaknesses. In addition, this part provides a look at the tools needed to turn the browsers into multimedia presentation programs and a glimpse at tools for the Web that we'll see in the future. Types of Internet access are also discussed, because the kind of access you have determines, to a large degree, the variety of browsers you can use.

World Wide Web Browsers: An Introduction and Gallery

by Neil Randall

IN THIS CHAPTER

In order to use the World Wide Web in any meaningful way, you need a piece of software called a *browser*. Actually, the technical name for these programs is *client*, in keeping with the standard Internet paradigm of client and server, just as the Gopher program you regularly use is called a Gopher client because it allows you to use a Gopher server. But over the brief course of the Web's history, the programs that allow access to its resources have come to be called browsers more often than clients, because browsing is precisely what most Web users seem to do.

Whether or not the Web was originally designed to be browsed rather than engaged is not the point, even though many groups do indeed engage it fully without becoming sidetracked in the process. The Web has become equated with browsing in much the same way as cable TV has become associated with channel-surfing.

The difference between using the Web and engaging the Web is important. As an analogy, let's consider what happens when you enter a library. If you're conducting serious research, you engage the library's resources—its books, its catalogs, its reference tools, its librarians—to help you locate the material you need and to deepen your understanding of the topic under research. But we've all entered libraries where, even if we intended to conduct intensive research, and ended up traversing the shelves, finding books with interesting titles, reading the first few paragraphs of a couple dozen of them, and never coming any closer to our stated research goal. Often, in fact, the experience proved more enjoyable than the research would have been, even if the time could hardly be called productive. This last method is popularly known as browsing the shelves, and it remains one of the most enjoyable things that can happen to you among shelves of books.

Browsing the World Wide Web is much like browsing a library. The Web is filled with documents: Some are highly detailed and extensively researched, some are slick and dazzlingly presented, some are merely signposts on the way to something more useful, and some are the products of amateurs who suddenly have a new way of telling the world about their hobbies. In other words, the Web is a library, and it offers all the variety, all the excitement, all the work, and all the inconsistency that a real library offers.

If you know where you're going on the Web, if you're part of a group that places material on the Web so that others can find it and use it, if you use the Web to help you in your scholarly research, your business dealings, or your scientific collaboration, you don't browse the Web, you *engage* it.

But if you're like the new wave of Web users, who see an interestingly named hyperlink and immediately click, then, without reading the page that appears on their screen, find another interesting link and click again, moving from document to document and computer to computer and possibly never returning to the document from which they started, then you're not engaging the Web, you're *browsing* it. Neither activity is inherently right, and neither is inherently wrong. Both are reality, and designers of client software have come to realize it. And there is, of course, an increasingly significant middle ground.

The most famous single client program in Internet history is *Mosaic*. Arguably, Mosaic has done more to bring public awareness of the Internet than all the e-mail flame wars and all the banned newsgroups in existence. Yet Mosaic is nothing more than one of many Web clients; it is client software that feeds off the thousands of World Wide Web servers, and its only real function is to display the documents it finds in a manner befitting the Web's standards. It's the World Wide Web, not Mosaic, that the mainstream magazines are actually writing about.

Which is not to take anything away from the famous browser. This book, in fact, offers a long, detailed look at Mosaic, giving it an entire chapter (Chapter 10, "The One You Keep Hearing About: NCSA Mosaic") while relegating all the other available browsers to a chapter that is not only shorter, but designed expressly to compare these other Web clients with their headline-making cousin. The reality is that most people who use the Web use Mosaic, and many of those who don't probably use Lynx because they don't have graphical access. The fact that Mosaic exists for the three most important platforms—X Window, the Apple Macintosh, and Microsoft Windows—is reason enough to understand its popularity.

But it's not the only client in existence, not by a long shot. Nor was it the first, not even for a graphical environment. Mosaic is nothing more than a World Wide Web browser that did the things that people wanted from a browser and that appeared at exactly the right time, neither too early for anyone to know what it was all about nor too late to take center stage when center stage was waiting to be taken. It was, in other words, the MTV of its genre.

If you want to understand the World Wide Web thoroughly, there are other client names to get to know. For UNIX itself, there's *Lynx* and the *CERN Line Browser* (or *www*). For X Window, find out about *Viola*, *MidasWWW*, *Chimera*, and *tkWWW*. For the Apple Macintosh, you'll want to know about *MacWeb* and *Samba*. For Microsoft Windows, your alternatives are *Cello*, *WinWeb*, and a growing number of commercially available Web clients. And there are browsers for VMS, NeXT, and the Commodore Amiga as well. These are all Web browsers with their own personalities, their own feature sets, their own strengths, and their own weaknesses. They have the curse of being continually compared with Mosaic, but the comparisons, in many cases, prove to be positive. And some of them avoid some of the well-known problems of the famous browser, everything ranging from bugs causing system crashes to a tendency to consume system memory and hardware resources. Any one of them might be perfect for your needs.

This chapter of *The World Wide Web Unleashed* gives you a brief tour of a tiny portion of the Web, and it does so through many of the browsers that are covered in detail in Chapter 10 and Chapter 11, "Yes, Virginia, There Is a Choice: More Graphical Browsers." You'll see that all the browsers look different from the rest (although some are extremely similar), that each has its peculiar icon or button set and perhaps its own way of displaying hyperlinks and other document characteristics, and that each is inviting or off-putting depending entirely on your preferences for what a browser/client is supposed to do.

As you look at them here, remember at all times that a client's function is to retrieve and display documents from the Web servers around the world and to offer you the ability to change the displays to suit your needs and to bookmark your activity so that you can return to Web locations of importance to you. And even if you're fully committed to one of the browsers before you start, or utterly repelled by another one and refuse to try it, give each browser a quick glance. They're not all here; only X Mosaic is included for that platform (although others are covered in Chapter 11), and Amiga Mosaic and the Windows commercial browsers don't appear here either (but see Chapter 11 again). What are here are some of the best known, and a good sampling of all: three for UNIX, three for Apple's Macintosh, and three for Microsoft Windows.

UNIX Browsers

The first browser available for the World Wide Web was called *www* then, but today it's known as *The CERN Line Browser*. Figure 7.1 shows essentially what the browser looks like, displaying the well-known subject catalog from the Virtual Library, a collection of hyperlinks to Web and Internet resources. Note that there are no graphics, nor will there ever be. This is a text-only client, and it was created purely to demonstrate that hyperlinks could work on a wide area network system.

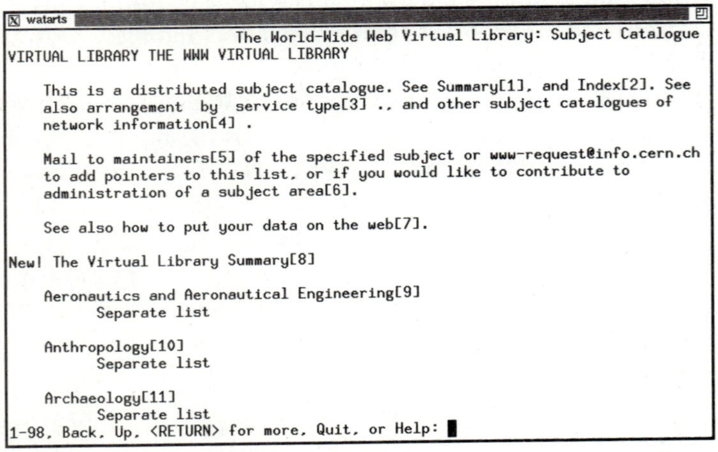

FIGURE 7.1.

The CERN Line Browser, displaying the Virtual Library.

```
X watarts
                                 The World-Wide Web Virtual Library: Subject Catalogue
VIRTUAL LIBRARY THE WWW VIRTUAL LIBRARY

      This is a distributed subject catalogue. See Summary[1], and Index[2]. See
      also arrangement  by  service type[3] .. and other subject catalogues of
      network information[4] .

      Mail to maintainers[5] of the specified subject or www-request@info.cern.ch
      to add pointers to this list, or if you would like to contribute to
      administration of a subject area[6].

      See also how to put your data on the web[7].

New! The Virtual Library Summary[8]

      Aeronautics and Aeronautical Engineering[9]
            Separate list

      Anthropology[10]
            Separate list

      Archaeology[11]
            Separate list
1-98, Back, Up, <RETURN> for more, Quit, or Help:
```

Note the parenthesized numbers appearing at various points in the document (11 in all on this screen). These are the hyperlinks: You don't click on them; your mouse won't work with this browser. Instead, you decide which one you want, then you type in that number and press Return. Off you go, across the Web to the linked document. Or you can press the Return key and go down several screens, finding the subject area you want. One possible choice, Physics, offers a separate list of its own, as shown in Figure 7.2.

FIGURE 7.2.

The CERN Line Browser, displaying a physics-related list.

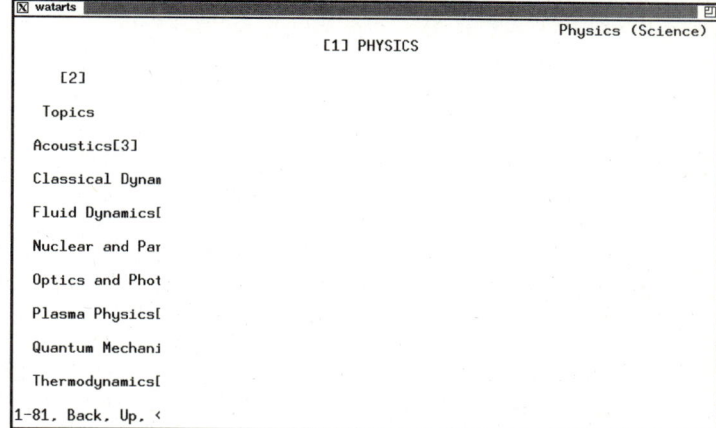

Even though the Line Browser doesn't display graphics, it's hardly useless. In fact, it's better for some kinds of research because there's less chance of becoming sidetracked into areas you had no intention of visiting. Figure 7.3 shows the result of finding a scientific paper on the Web, and something CERN users would routinely do.

FIGURE 7.3.

The CERN Line Browser after loading a scientific paper stored on a Web server.

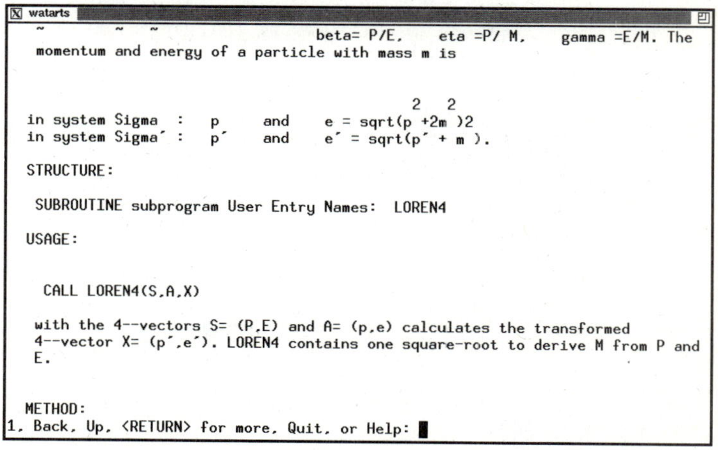

```
X watarts                                                                    凹
   ~      ~    ~              beta= P/E,     eta =P/ M,      gamma =E/M. The
      momentum and energy of a particle with mass m is


                                              2   2
   in system Sigma  :    p      and    e = sqrt(p +2m )2
   in system Sigma´ :    p´     and    e´ = sqrt(p´ + m ).

   STRUCTURE:

     SUBROUTINE subprogram User Entry Names:  LOREN4

   USAGE:


     CALL LOREN4(S,A,X)

   with the 4--vectors S= (P,E) and A= (p,e) calculates the transformed
   4--vector X= (p´,e´). LOREN4 contains one square-root to derive M from P and
   E.


   METHOD:
1, Back, Up, <RETURN> for more, Quit, or Help: █
```

Anything text-based, in fact, works just fine on this browser. Figure 7.4 shows the results of maneuvering through a movie database on the Web, displaying a series of links to the archives of one particular movie-oriented newsgroup on the Internet. It may not look pretty, but the browser serves its purpose, nonetheless.

FIGURE 7.4.

The CERN Line Browser with links to newsgroup archives.

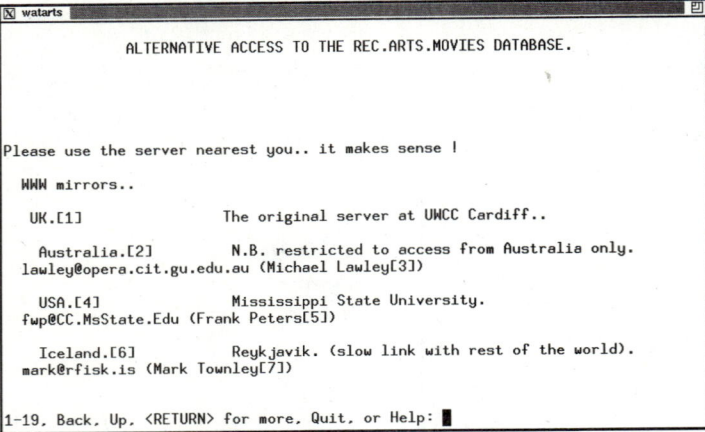

Let's leave the original browser and work with another one, the better known and much more capable *Lynx*. Like the Line Browser, Lynx is a text-only Web client, incapable of displaying graphics or other multimedia elements, although you can configure Lynx to display graphics with an external file viewer. What makes Lynx so interesting—and so usable—is that it makes full use of the VT-100 terminal standard to let you navigate the Web by using little more than the arrow keys, the space bar, and the Return key. As Figure 7.5 shows, the hyperlinks in Lynx (here from the EINet Galaxy listing) appear as bold-faced items, and when you cursor across them they take on a reverse-video appearance. Move to one, then press the right arrow key, and you're on your way to that particular destination.

Moving through the Web, we come to list after list of selectable links. As Figure 7.6 demonstrates, Lynx uses asterisks in place of bullets, and a page like this one is every bit as readable as the same page in a graphical browser. Here we've entered a list dealing with environmental issues, and we've decided to choose an item about "going green."

FIGURE 7.5.

The Lynx client, showing reverse video on the currently selected hyperlink.

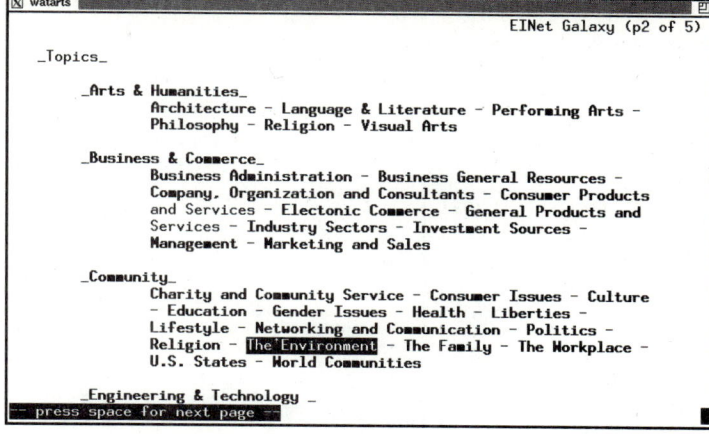

FIGURE 7.6.

Lynx with a full list of hyperlinks.

Choosing this item takes us to the list shown in Figure 7.7. This is primarily a text page, and Lynx displays it clearly and without difficulty. Unfortunately, it can't display the inlined image beside item 12, noting it merely as [IMAGE] and making us wonder what that image might be. This is Lynx's biggest drawback; for displaying only text it's fine, but as soon as the image place-holders begin to appear, the client loses some of its appeal. This is an important point, as more and more Web pages become built around their graphic components.

FIGURE 7.7.

Lynx displaying a text page, with one undisplayable image place-holder.

```
┌─X watarts ───────────────────────────────────────────────────────────── ⊡─┐
│                                              Jalan Hijau: 40 Tips (p3 of 7) │
│ 9. Use cloth towels in the kitchen instead of paper towels. They can       │
│ be re-used after washing.                                                  │
│                                                                            │
│ 10. If your fridge is set too cold and many are 5% colder than they        │
│ need to be - then it's using 25% more electricity. Check it.               │
│                                                                            │
│ 11. Always wait until you have a full load before using the washing        │
│ machine. This saves both water and energy.                                 │
│                                                                            │
│ ON THE ROAD                                                                │
│                                                                            │
│ [IMAGE] 12. Cars are polluters. Limit the use of the car through           │
│ car-pooling. Take turns to fetch children to and from school, music or     │
│ sports or to drive to work.                                                │
│                                                                            │
│ 13. Have one day a week or month - when you leave the car at home and      │
│ take public transport or walk when its a short journey - it's              │
│ healthier! If you must drive, then maintain your car well. A               │
│ well-tuned car with clean filters uses 9% less petrol and that means       │
│ less pollutants in the air.                                                │
│                                                                            │
│ 14. Use unleaded petrol whenever possible & help keep the air clean.       │
│ -- press space for next page --                                            │
└────────────────────────────────────────────────────────────────────────────┘
```

Figure 7.8 shows one area in which Lynx is graphically capable. Taken from a server in Norway, this page contains two downloadable graphics featuring the Oslo City Hall. Lynx displays the size of the graphics and lets you download them to your hard disk. In this way, it's little different from any of the graphical browsers, which also require an external viewer to see noninlined graphics.

FIGURE 7.8.

Lynx displaying downloadable graphics files from Norwegian site.

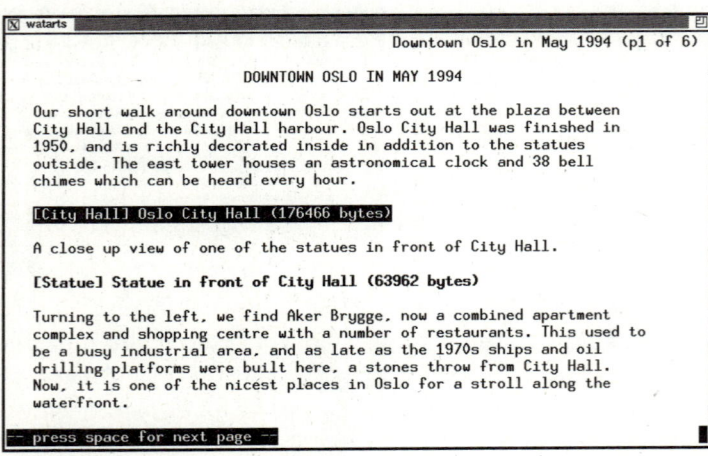

```
┌─X watarts ───────────────────────────────────────────────────────────── ⊡─┐
│                                       Downtown Oslo in May 1994 (p1 of 6)   │
│                          DOWNTOWN OSLO IN MAY 1994                          │
│                                                                            │
│ Our short walk around downtown Oslo starts out at the plaza between        │
│ City Hall and the City Hall harbour. Oslo City Hall was finished in        │
│ 1950, and is richly decorated inside in addition to the statues            │
│ outside. The east tower houses an astronomical clock and 38 bell           │
│ chimes which can be heard every hour.                                       │
│                                                                            │
│ [City Hall] Oslo City Hall (176466 bytes)                                  │
│                                                                            │
│ A close up view of one of the statues in front of City Hall.               │
│                                                                            │
│ [Statue] Statue in front of City Hall (63962 bytes)                        │
│                                                                            │
│ Turning to the left, we find Aker Brygge, now a combined apartment         │
│ complex and shopping centre with a number of restaurants. This used to     │
│ be a busy industrial area, and as late as the 1970s ships and oil          │
│ drilling platforms were built here, a stones throw from City Hall.         │
│ Now, it is one of the nicest places in Oslo for a stroll along the         │
│ waterfront.                                                                 │
│                                                                            │
│ -- press space for next page --                                         █  │
└────────────────────────────────────────────────────────────────────────────┘
```

The last UNIX Web client examined in this chapter is NCSA Mosaic for the X Window System, better known simply as Mosaic, or, for our purposes, X Mosaic. Unlike both the CERN Line Browser and Lynx, X Mosaic is a graphical Web client, one that uses a graphical user interface (Motif in this case) to display Web documents in a formatted manner. Although X Mosaic is capable of showing inline graphics, even a page such as the EINet Galaxy listing in Figure 7.9 shows the effects of formatting. Headings are clear and bold-faced, while each hyperlink demonstrates an equally clear highlighting technique (underlining). Other elements of the program display attractively as well, from the sculpted navigation buttons at the bottom of the screen to the signature spinning globe icon at the top.

FIGURE 7.9.

X Mosaic screen showing list of hyperlinks.

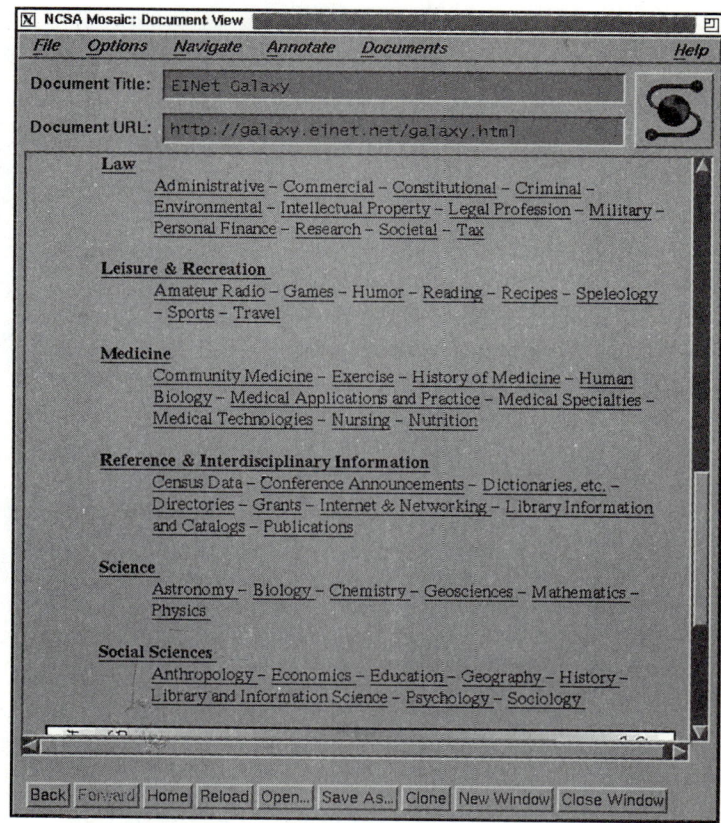

The screen illustrated in Figure 7.10 is an example of why most users prefer graphical browsers. Neither Lynx nor the Line Browser, whatever their other strengths, could display the inline image shown here as the graphic of Jupiter. Unfortunately, *The World Wide Web Unleashed* is not in color, or this page (and many of those that follow) would show this and the other graphical browsers to an even greater advantage.

FIGURE 7.10.

X Mosaic screen displaying an inline image.

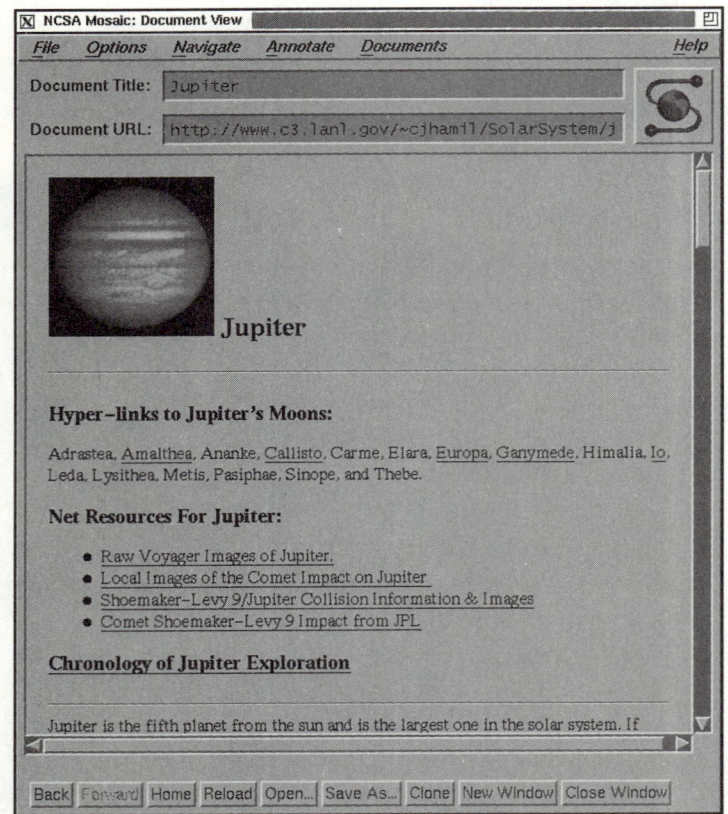

Increasingly, access to graphical browsers is being taken for granted by page designers. Such is the case with the Sense and Perception tutorials shown in Figure 7.11; the reliance on graphics would become even more evident if you were to follow the links further. The small icon at the bottom of this page is admittedly gratuitous (another clear tendency in Web page design), but it, too, has its design appeal.

FIGURE 7.11.

X Mosaic screen showing inline graphic and smaller icon.

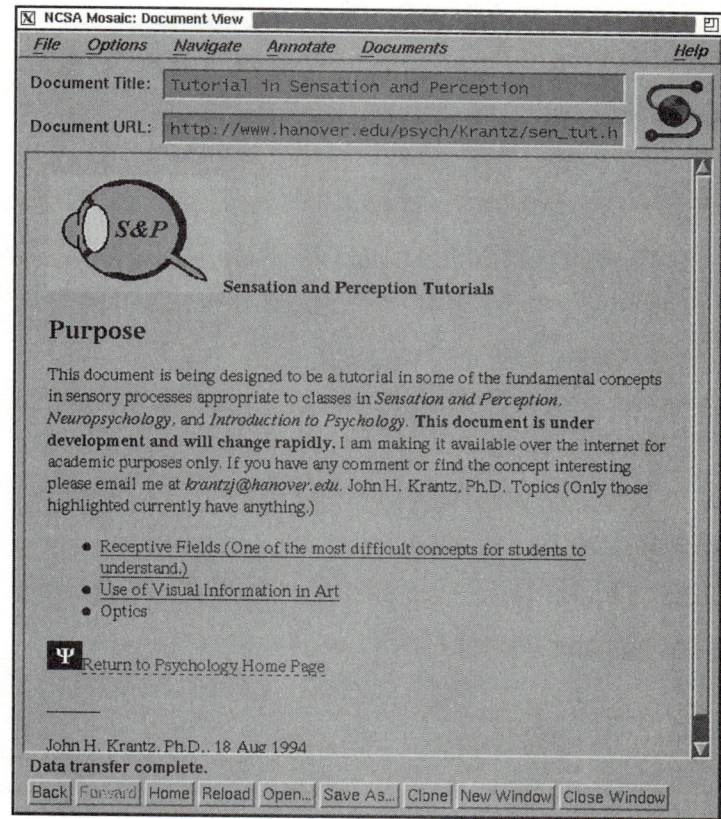

By the time you reach the screen pictured in Figure 7.12, you will see how extensively graphics are figuring in to Web page design, perhaps especially in the entertainment sites. This page is from Switzerland (as evidenced by the .ch in the domain name from the Document URL box), and it offers an entire collection of small inline images. These images, as the page outlines, are actually introductory shots to short videos, which can be displayed by X Mosaic if you've set up the necessary external players properly. (See Chapter 12, "Making It Multimedia: Viewers, Players, and Other Browser Add-Ons.") Note, however, that these video files are *huge*: One is 23 megabytes in size, and even that won't be a long video; 23 megabytes, by the way, would take more than eight hours to download across a 14.4 kbps modem connection.

FIGURE 7.12.

X Mosaic screen showing inline graphics pointing to video files.

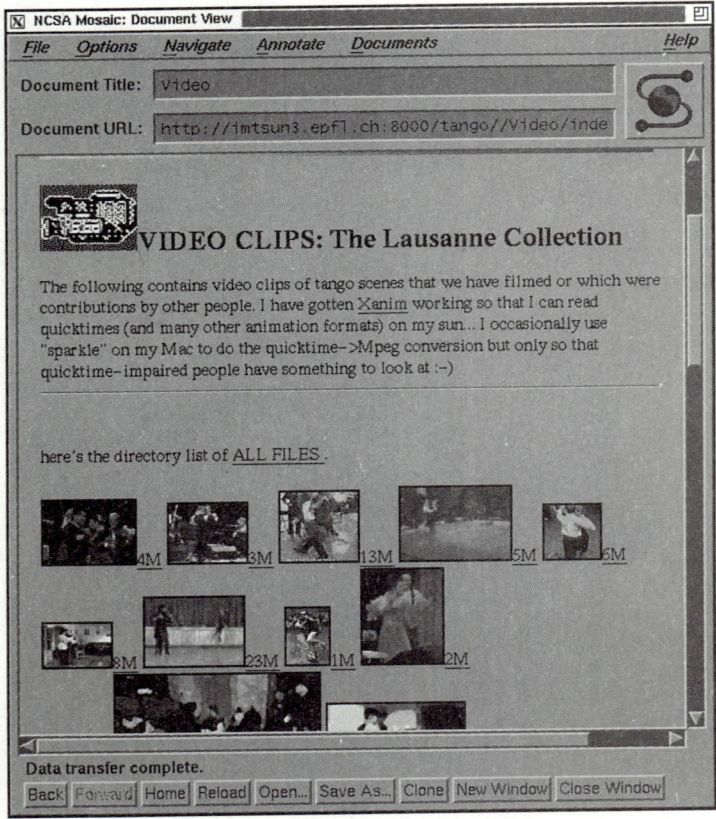

Apple Macintosh Browsers

Three browsers are available for the Macintosh environment, and all three are shown here (and in Chapter 11 as well). The first is Samba, originally known as MacWWW, developed by the same people who brought us the CERN Line Browser. In fact, there are similarities between Samba and the Line Browser, which is to be expected given the fact that both were released shortly after the World Wide Web project began, and both were probably intended to demonstrate how clients might be constructed. Figure 7.13 shows a typical list in Samba.

FIGURE 7.13.

Samba screen showing Hong Kong listing.

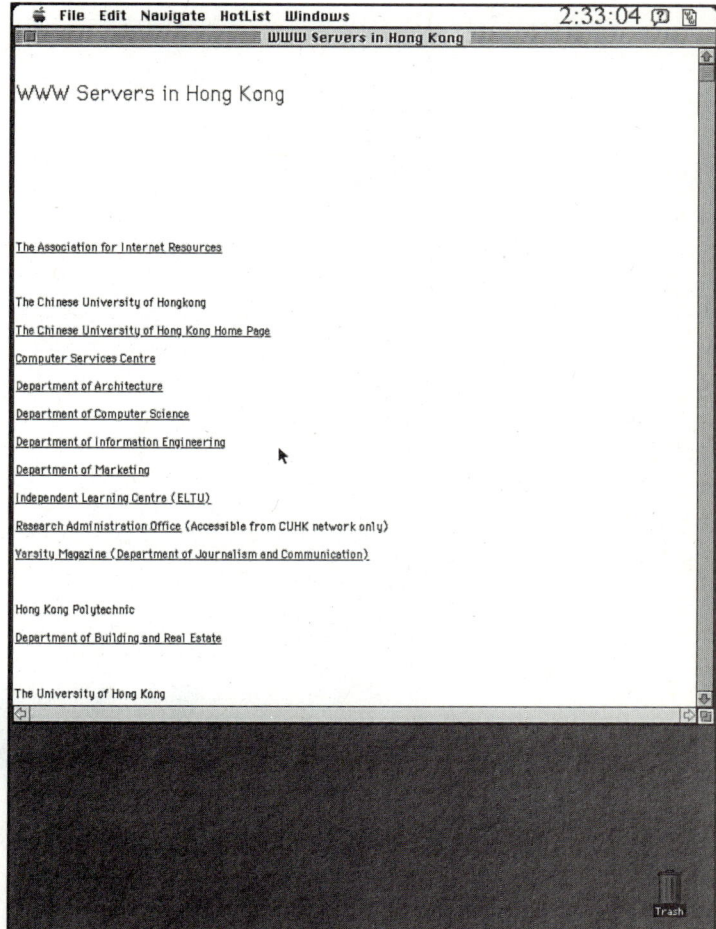

As you move from document to document in Samba, you open new windows. Figure 7.14 shows the result of a series of two accesses past the screen shown in Figure 7.13 (and there are other windows hidden behind these). The result is a fairly messy screen, and in this case an unattractive document appearance as well.

FIGURE 7.14.

Samba screen showing multiple open windows.

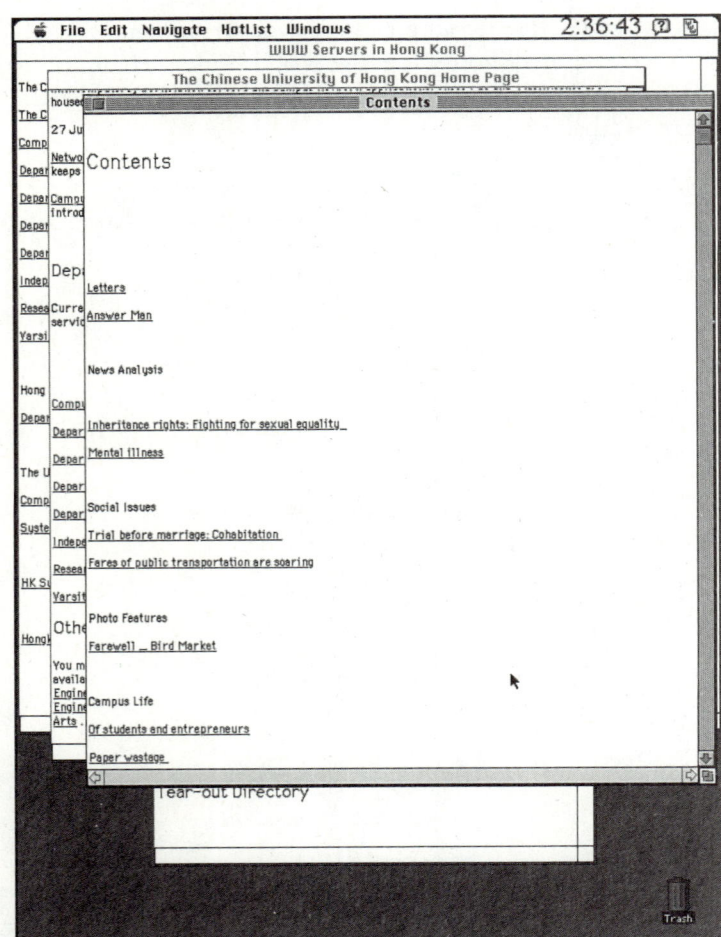

Taken to an extreme, the number of open documents, and their continually changing sizes, renders Samba in some ways unusable. Still, it's a Web browser, and extensive double-clicking allows you to reach the site displayed in Figure 7.15, a text screen that looks as clear as anything we've seen in this browser.

FIGURE 7.15.

Samba screen showing pure text document.

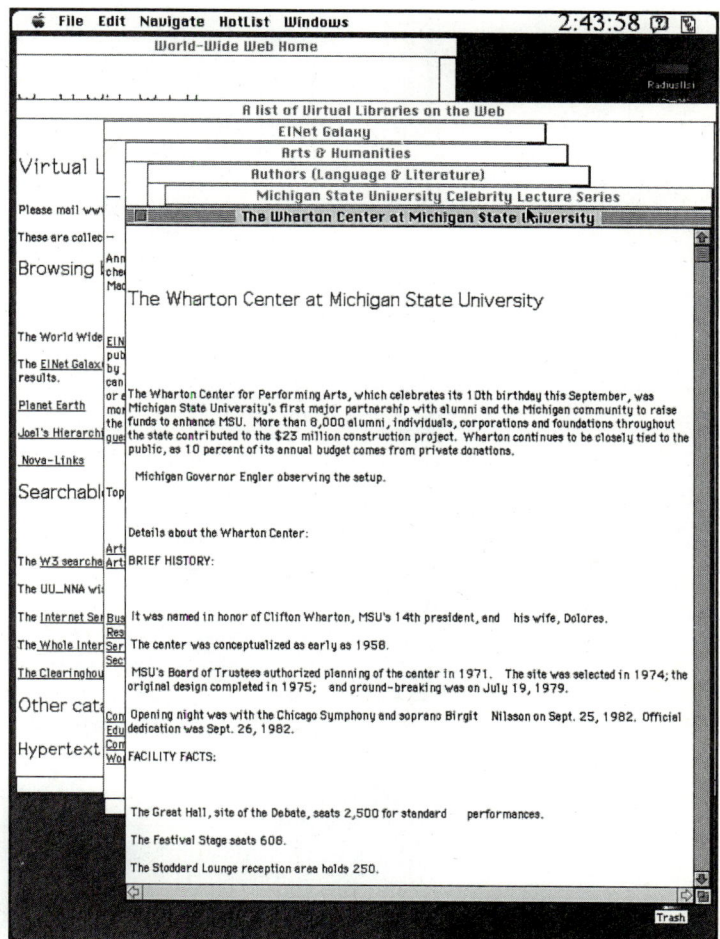

When all the windows are ordered properly, the Samba screen doesn't look all that bad, and it's easy to see where you've been. Figure 7.16 shows a screen with many open documents, and in fact it resembles a graphical Gopher browser rather than a Web browser.

FIGURE 7.16.

Samba screen showing ordered multiple documents.

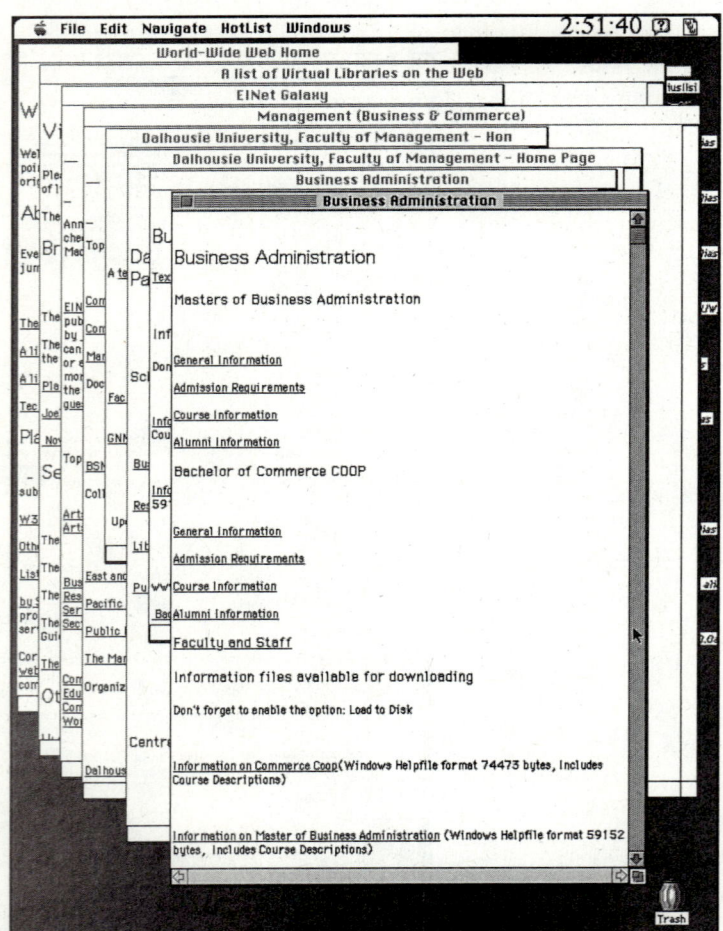

The second Macintosh Web client to appear was NCSA Mosaic for the Apple Macintosh, better known as Mac Mosaic (or just Mosaic, if you're exclusively a Mac user). This is, of course, the Mac counterpart to X Mosaic, and in many ways they're alike. But the appearance of the screen, as shown in Figure 7.17, is significantly different, reflecting the fact that different programming teams are in charge of the different versions. Note the icon bar at the top of Figure 7.17, which replaces X Mosaic's button bar (which was at the bottom). Other differences are evident as well.

FIGURE 7.17.

Mac Mosaic screen showing icon bar and history window.

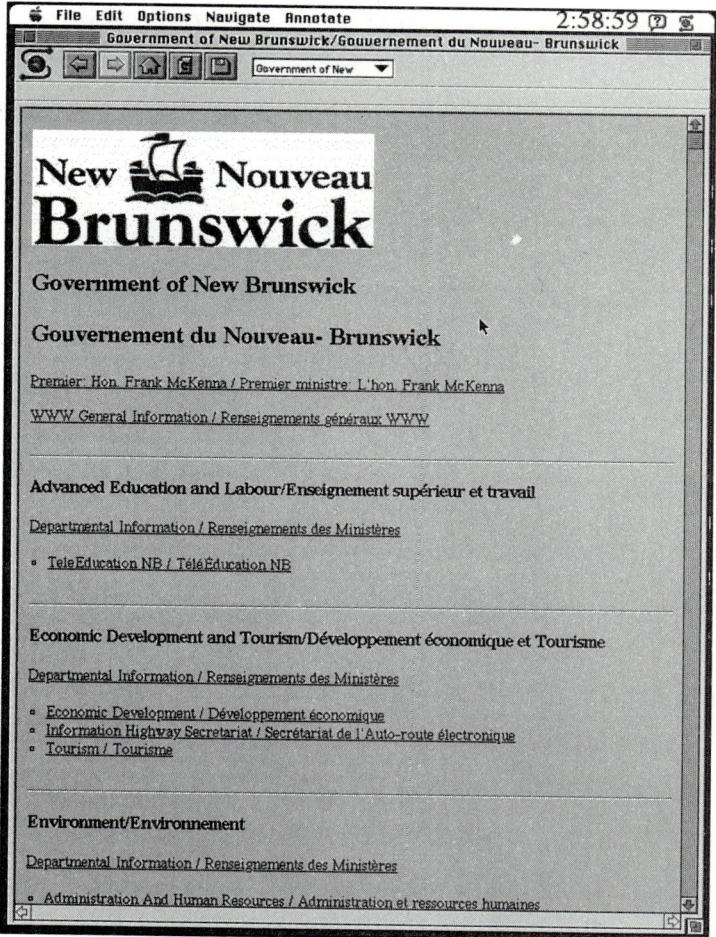

If this book were in color, the Oregon map displayed in Figure 7.18 would be nothing short of eye-catching. As it stands, it's a good demonstration of the "clickable" map finding its way into an increasing number of Web documents that seek to demonstrate a geographic basis. (More such maps appear later in this chapter.) By clicking on one of the cities displayed in outline font, you are taken to a document elsewhere on the Web that contains information about that city. Unfortunately, a graphic like this takes a long time to transfer if you have a slow Internet connection.

FIGURE 7.18.

Mac Mosaic screen with an example of a "clickable" map.

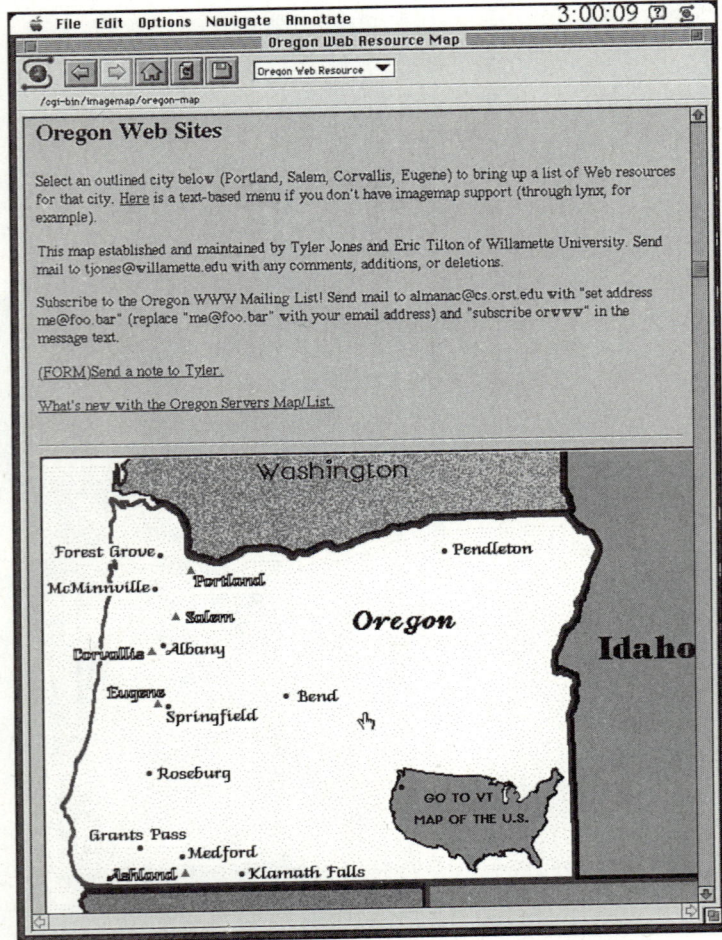

More and more, graphic images are dominating Web documents. The page shown in Figure 7.19 contains not only a striking opening graphic, but creative iconic use as well in the display at the bottom. To maneuver to any of these documents, you need only click on the appropriate icon. This is highly attractive, but possibly unnecessary, and almost unusable by modem connections.

FIGURE 7.19.

Mac Mosaic screen showing extensive use of inline graphics.

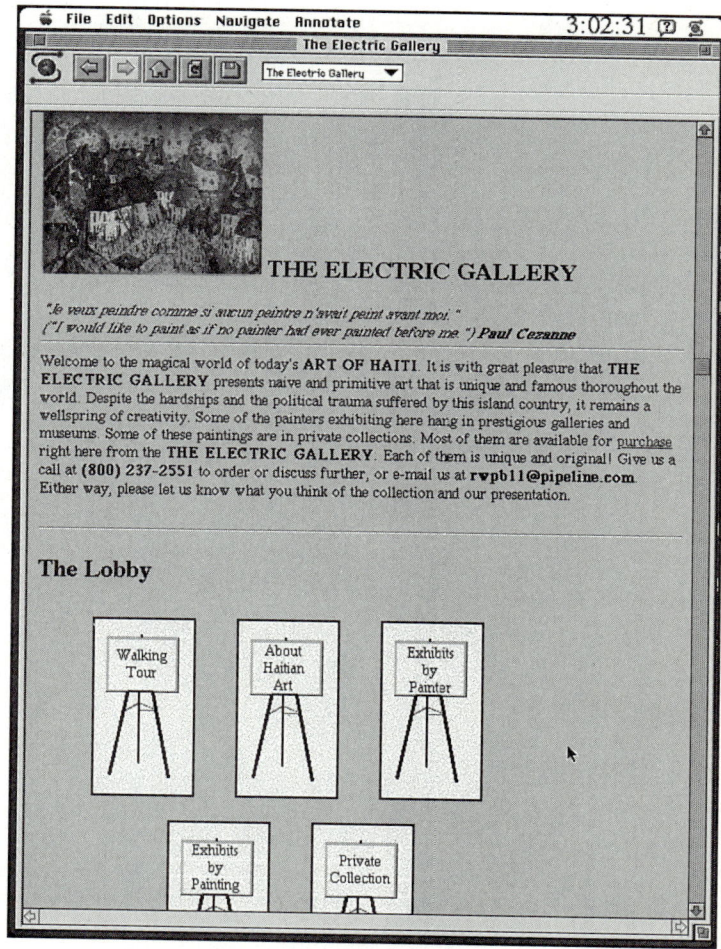

Figure 7.20 is simply a beautifully designed document. By clicking on the musical notes icon you can hear a tune (as long as your Mac and your Mac Mosaic program are configured to play sound files), and each item has its own attractive icon. Expect more such pages as high-speed access increases in the near future.

FIGURE 7.20.

Mac Mosaic screen showing the effects of strong page design.

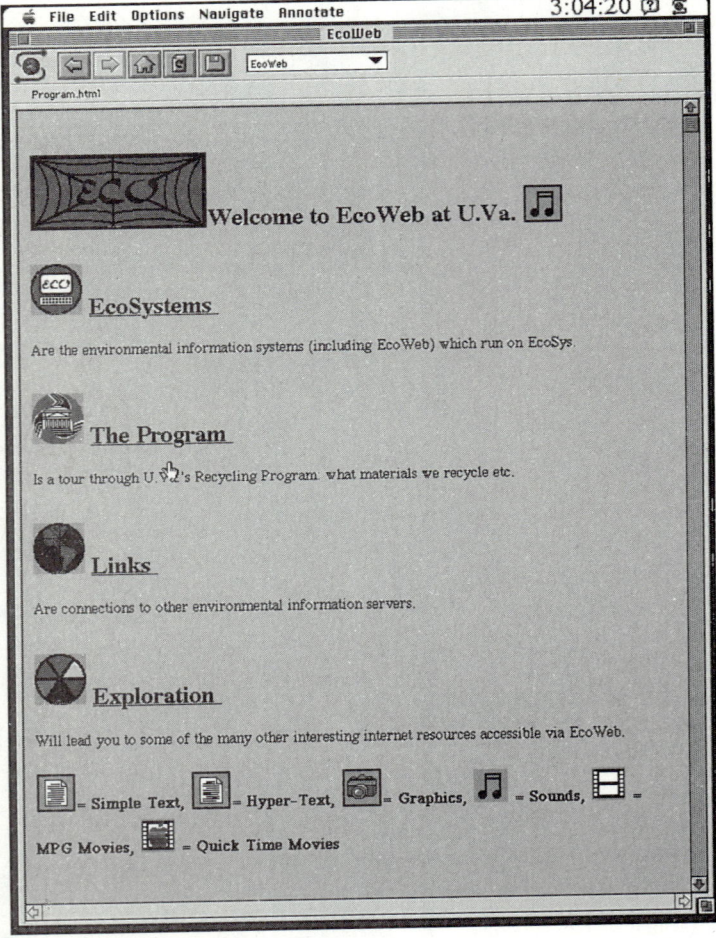

The most recent Macintosh client to be made available is MacWeb. Figure 7.21 shows that this browser is very similar to Mac Mosaic in appearance and is fully capable of displaying whatever graphics Web designers choose to throw at it. The page is from Cornell University's Kids on Campus selection, one of the most creative uses of the clickable graphic on the Internet. As you'd expect, however, it's hopeless for modem users.

FIGURE 7.21.

MacWeb screen showing fascinating graphic design.

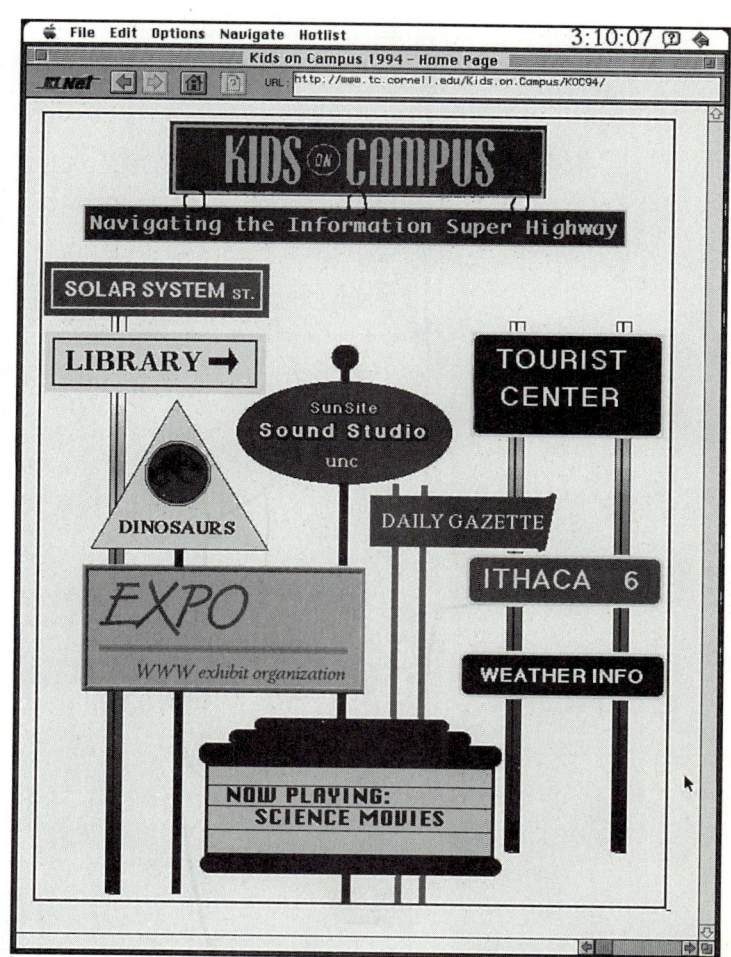

By following a few links from the signs in Figure 7.21, you arrive at the document displayed in Figure 7.22. Each colorful icon leads to a related video, which MacWeb can show if it is configured to use the appropriate external viewer. Note, by the way, how much screen "real estate" MacWeb gives to the actual document; considerably more than Mac Mosaic, in fact.

FIGURE 7.22.

MacWeb screen displaying links to playable videos.

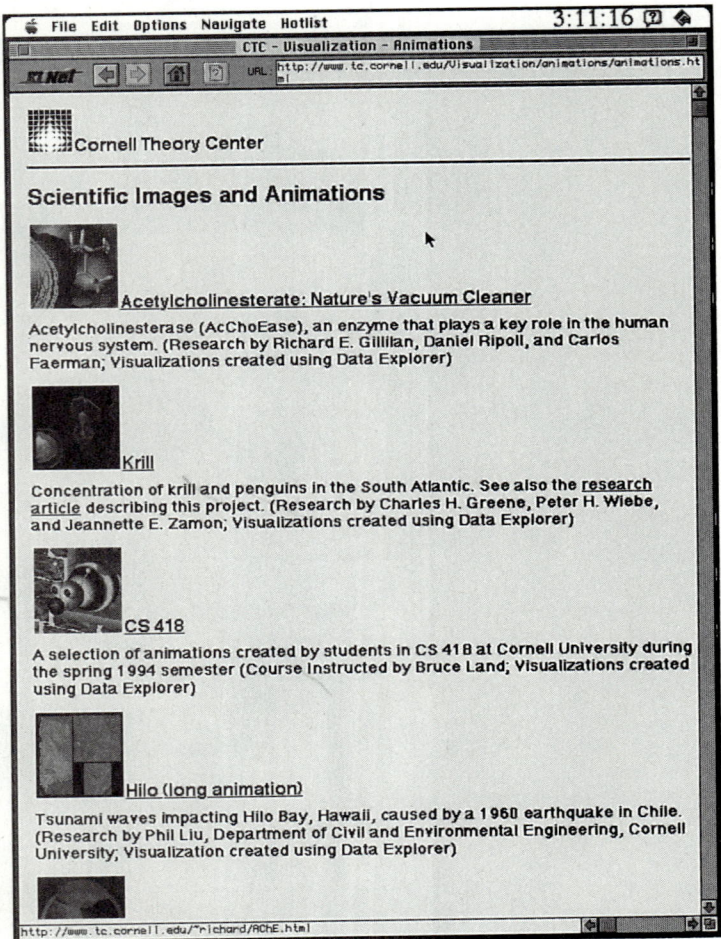

Changing the background color of MacWeb is extremely easy, and in Figure 7.23 it is changed to gray. The page itself is from an excellent collection called The Jerusalem Mosaic; the domain name in the URL box shows the "il" Israel address, meaning that we've transferred the file from Israel itself. There's an increasing number of such informative documents finding their way onto the Web.

FIGURE 7.23.

MacWeb screen showing document from Israel.

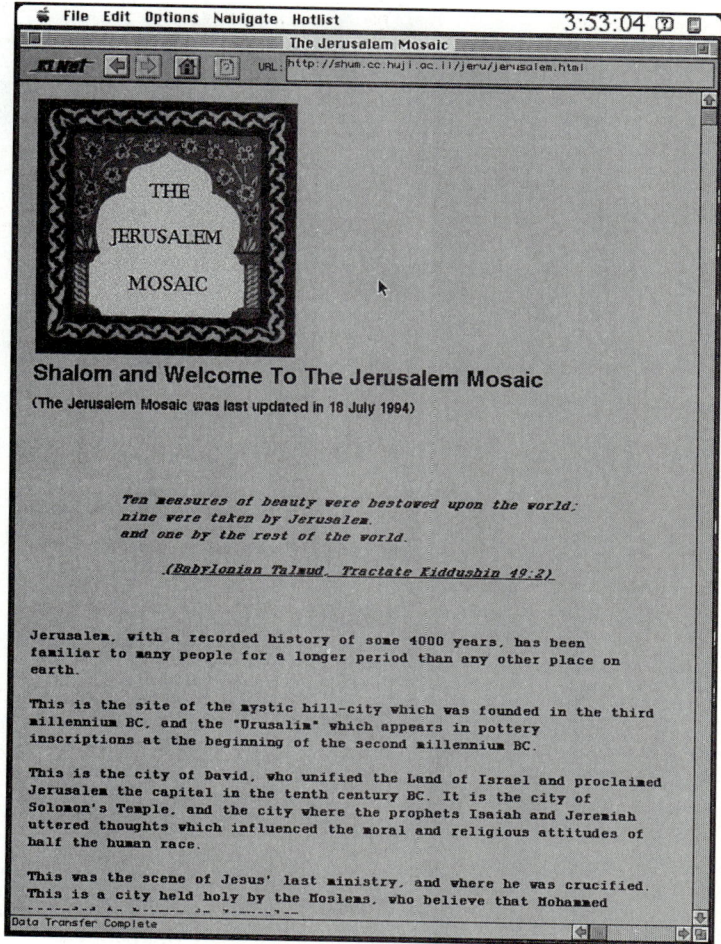

Figure 7.24 shows a document further along the links from The Jerusalem Mosaic in Figure 7.23. Here you can see MacWeb's strong display of inline graphics, both in the picture and the icons at the bottom. Bookmarking the site is possible by simply selecting the Hotlist menu at the top of the screen.

FIGURE 7.24.

MacWeb screen showing document formatting.

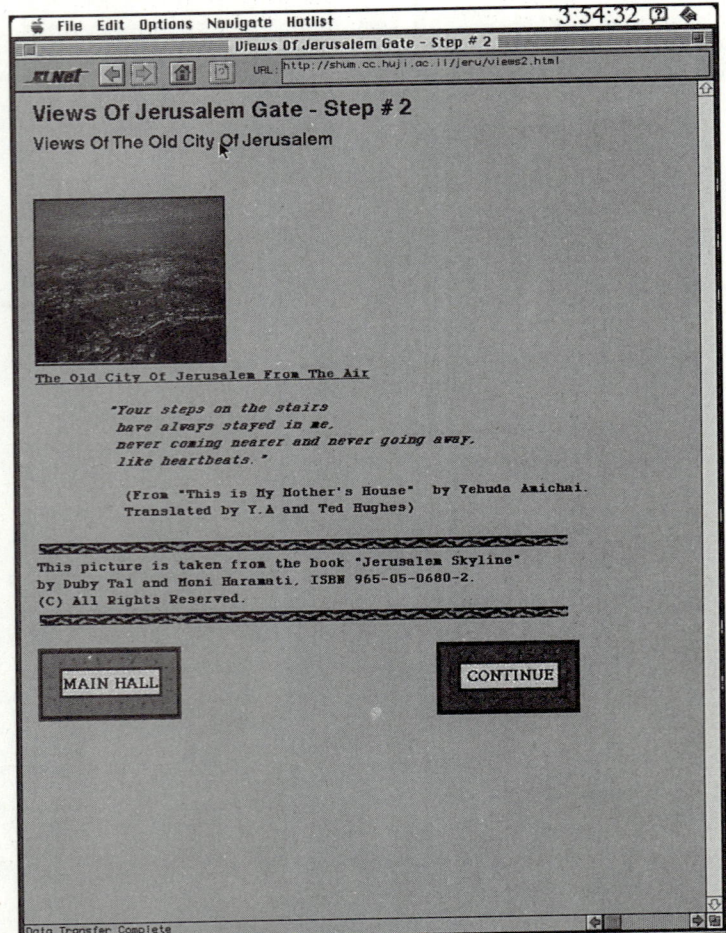

Microsoft Windows Browsers

Although World Wide Web clients for Microsoft Windows have been the last to appear, they've gone far towards catching up to the rest. Two extremely strong candidates are currently available, and a third has just begun and will undoubtedly improve. And commercial browsers are making their appearance as Internet providers begin to tap the vast Windows-user base out there.

We'll start our Windows browser tour with Cello, the favorite of quite a few Windows users, which is available from Cornell University's Legal Information Institute. Figure 7.25 shows that Cello easily handles graphical maps, and that it offers substantial screen space to its documents. This page is The Virtual Tourist, which features a clickable map of the world (and, through the insets, regions as well).

FIGURE 7.25.

Cello screen showing clickable world map.

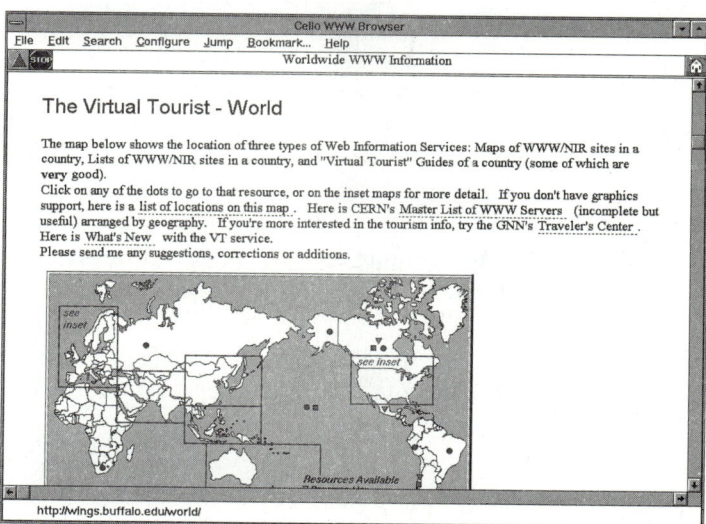

Cello's extraordinary clarity of image is apparent in Figure 7.25. Of course, it helps that the map itself is attractive and crisply designed, but the browser has to be able to display it, and do so quickly. Cello does this, and once again, if this book were in color you'd notice even more about the browser's capabilities.

FIGURE 7.26.

Cello screen showing clear graphical display.

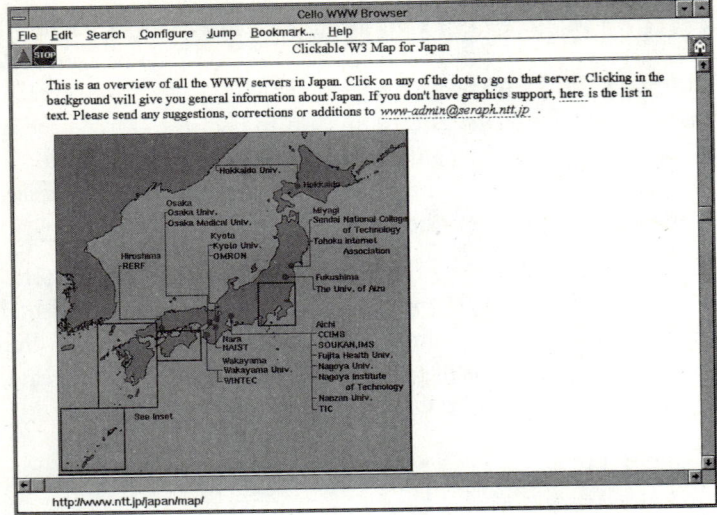

We obviously moved into Japan in Figure 7.26, and in Figure 7.27 we see how the Japanese, despite a very late start, are beginning to design attractive pages for the Web. If Cello were capable of displaying Japanese characters (it's not, but neither is Windows Mosaic, below), we could get even more information. As it stands, this page is clear and informative, and Cello can be configured with an external viewer to play the long sound file displayed near the top. Note also the attractive bullets that come as a Cello default.

FIGURE 7.27.

Cello screen demonstrating default sculpted bullets.

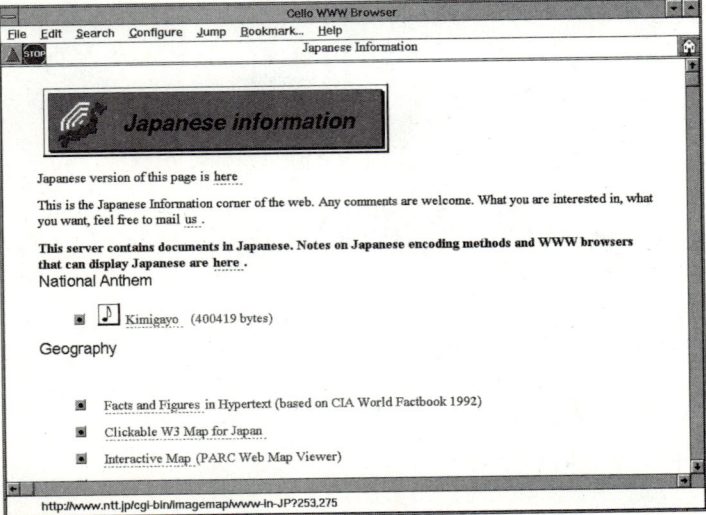

Back to a map display for Figure 7.28, not so much to demonstrate a Cello feature as an intriguing page design. From Xerox PARC (whence comes the graphical user interface concept itself) is a map that, when clicked, zooms in to reveal a closer display. Notice the rivers and political boundaries shown in the map, again rendered crisply by the browser.

FIGURE 7.28.

Cello screen showing innovative map design from Xerox PARC.

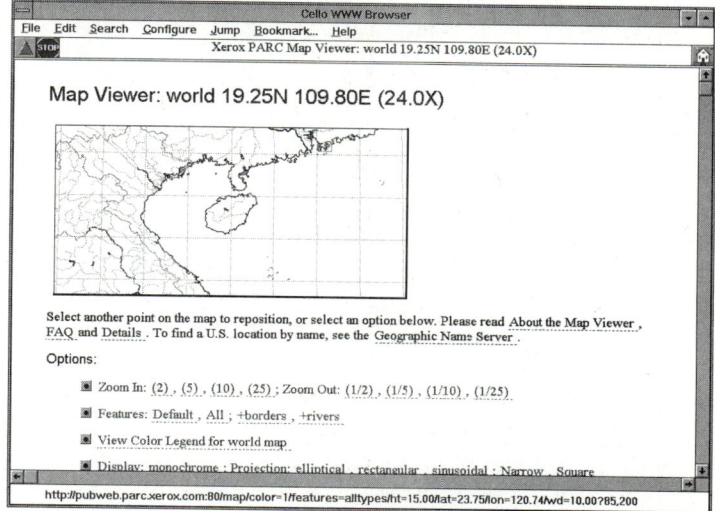

With Figure 7.29, we move to NCSA Mosaic for the Microsoft Windows system, known for our purposes as Windows Mosaic. This program is in high demand among Windows users, although it consumes considerably greater system resources than Cello and, in its latest version, requires the large and not easily available Windows 32-bit extensions in order to run. Still, its popularity is established, and it remains to be seen if the commercial clients will cut into that popularity.

Figure 7.29 shows the City of San Carlos home page in Windows Mosaic, which with its most recent version offers substantially more screen real estate than before. More and more cities and towns are developing Web sites, incidentally, as a means of promoting themselves to the outside world.

FIGURE 7.29.

Windows Mosaic screen showing a city's home page.

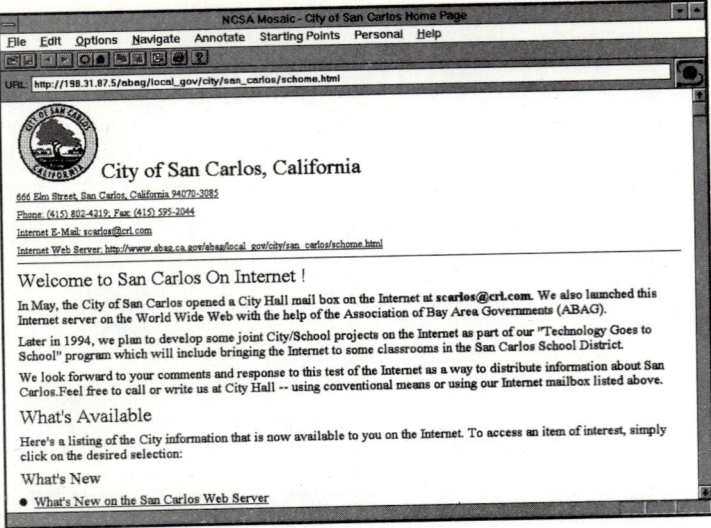

Countries, too, are making themselves known on the Web. Figure 7.30 displays the Singapore government's clear, attractive, and well-organized "online guide," which Windows Mosaic renders well. In fact, as you travel the Web increasingly, you'll come to realize that document writers tend to test their designs exclusively on Mosaic, since some pages display better on it than on Cello or WinWeb.

FIGURE 7.30.

Windows Mosaic, showing Singapore Online Guide.

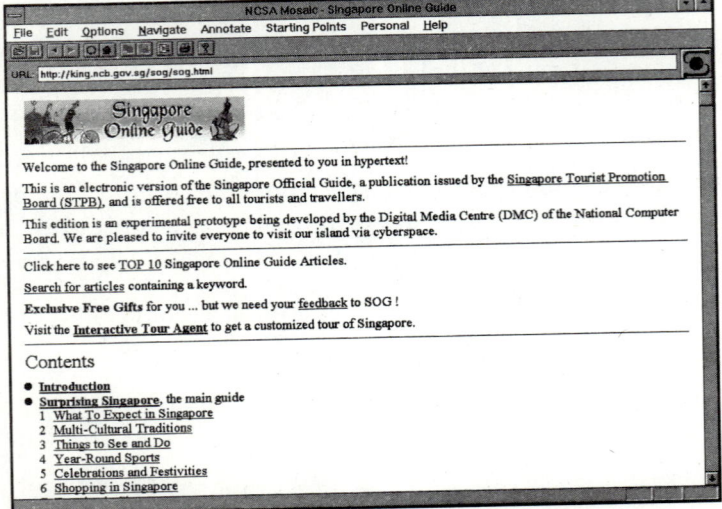

An appealing logo graces the screen in Figure 7.31, and the page is one of many on the Web that offers extensive reading. No specific Windows Mosaic features are shown here, but note that the URL display shows the address only, while the document title appears on the title bar at the top (which is a peculiar feature of Microsoft Windows). Only in the most recent version of Windows Mosaic does the document title *not* appear with the URL address.

FIGURE 7.31.

Windows Mosaic screen showing large inline graphic logo.

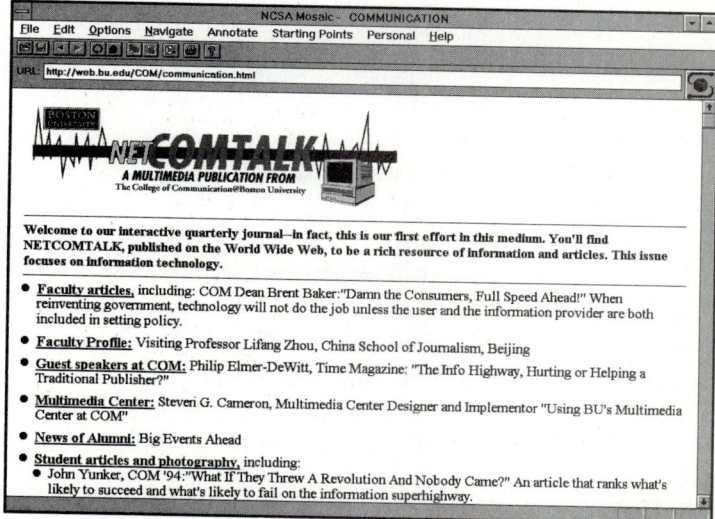

Figure 7.32 demonstrates another extremely creative and appealing page design. This one comes to us out of the U.K., and everything from its logo through its individual icons shows innovation. Windows Mosaic displays it very well indeed. In the menu line of Windows Mosaic is a Personal menu that is entirely customizable from the program's menu editor utility.

FIGURE 7.32.
Windows Mosaic, showing superb Cyber-Town home page.

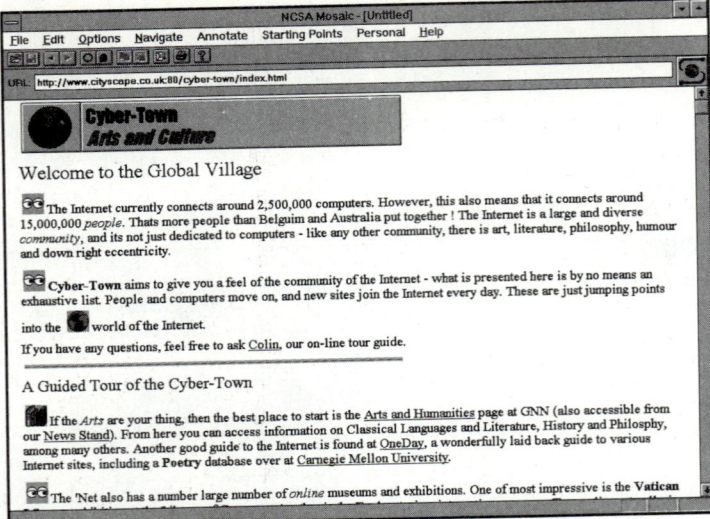

The final browser in our tour is WinWeb, the Windows counterpart to MacWeb, and a client showing all the signs of being in its very first release. As Figure 7.33 shows, the browser displays text pages clearly and well, but the nonunderlined links show up poorly on monochrome displays (which, admittedly, are uncommon among Windows users).

FIGURE 7.33.
WinWeb screen showing small bullets and good alignment.

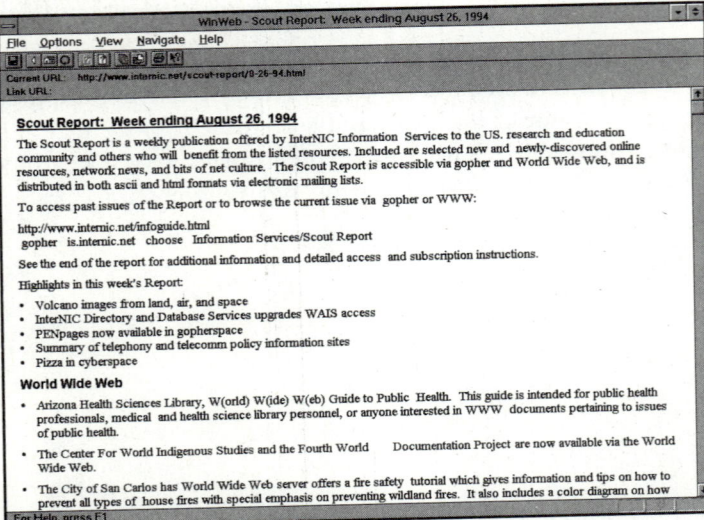

Figure 7.34 demonstrates that WinWeb is fully capable of displaying large graphic images. Unfortunately, in its first version it doesn't recognize that the two bold-faced "Information" lines are actually links, something that renders several Web pages useless. The icon bar is much like Windows Mosaic's, but expected menu items are missing. The page, incidentally, promises some interesting material in the future.

FIGURE 7.34.

WinWeb screen showing unrecognized hyperlinks.

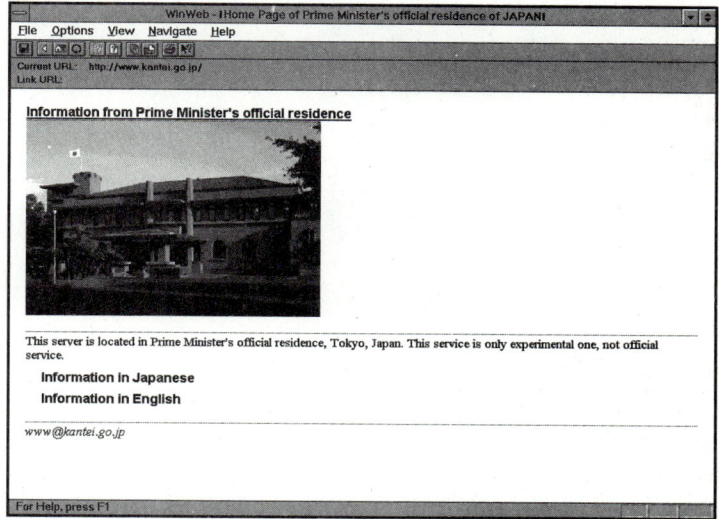

Another demonstration of WinWeb's graphic capability appears in Figure 7.35. Of more interest, however, is the page itself, which is part of a series of pages devoted to the city of Des Moines, Iowa. The graphics here are small versions of huge files that you can download, which together make up a full map of the city. Of course, you could buy one for about three bucks when you get there, but ...

Part II

FIGURE 7.35.

WinWeb screen with large downloadable graphics.

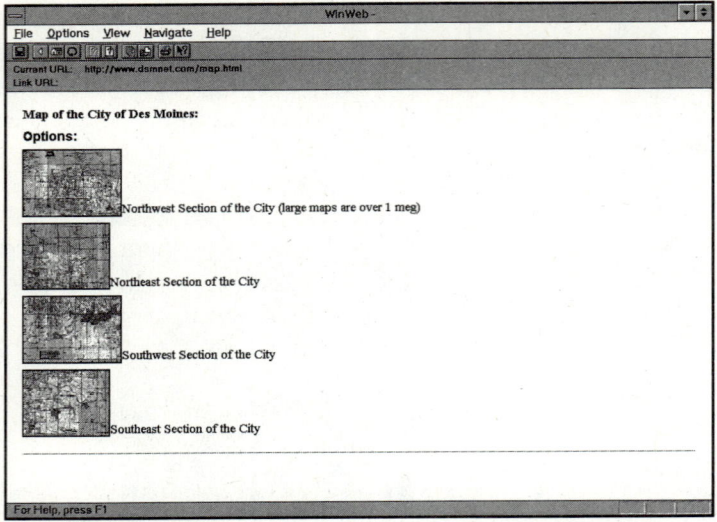

We close our tour of Web clients appropriately, by showing the kind of page that will almost certainly become increasingly visited as the average age of Web users continues to fall. *Vibe Magazine*, perfectly displayed by WinWeb as shown in Figure 7.36, is one of many pages designed to appeal to the twenty-somethings, and there's concern among the older Webbers that this kind of page (and the even more elaborately graphic pages available elsewhere) are simply using up valuable bandwidth. But this page demonstrates that part of the Web's future—a large part, perhaps—lies in entertainment rather than research, and it will be increasingly important for Web client software to be able to handle the challenge.

Besides, I wanted to show the only guy in the world with a smiley for a name.

FIGURE 7.36.

Vibe Magazine displayed on WinWeb.

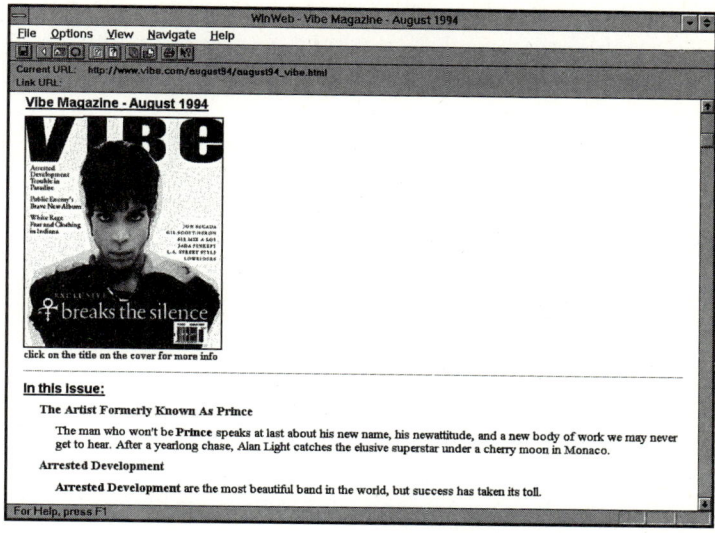

Getting Connected:
Accessing the Web

8

by **Neil Randall**

To connect to the World Wide Web, you need an Internet account. That's probably the most obvious thing this book will say, but it needs saying anyway. The Web is on the Net, and although you could structure a purely local one, or even a company-wide one, it wouldn't be a *world-wide* web. And that's the whole point.

So how do you get an Internet account? There are several ways, all of which are covered briefly in this chapter. (For a much more thorough account, pick up a companion book, *The Internet Unleashed*, from Sams Publishing.) See also Appendix A, which lists Internet service providers in a variety of regions.

Your main choice, however, lies in accessing the Web from within the local area network (LAN) in your organization, or through an Internet service provider via modem. A third choice, only beginning to appear, is to use a commercial online service—CompuServe, America Online, etc.—as a gateway into the Net, or a local bulletin board system (BBS). Finally, there are the cable companies, who are in some cases establishing and even offering Internet access through their systems.

The basic principle of LAN access is this: Your computer is part of an organization's network, in which all computers are wired to each other through a series of hubs and routers and other networking hardware and software. That LAN, in turn, is connected to the Internet, usually through a high-speed line that links either directly to the Internet backbone, or, more commonly, to an Internet service provider, which in turn links to the backbone. Certainly, that's a simplified version of the internetworking chain of being, but for our purposes here, it's workable. (This is a *Web* book, remember.)

Connecting through a modem offers two main varieties. The first is to use a modem to dial into your organization's LAN (called a "dial-in" or "remote" session), and then, through that LAN, into the Net itself. The second, and one becoming increasingly popular and important, is a modem connection to an Internet service provider, which is in turn connected to the Internet.

Actually, the two varieties aren't all that different; in both cases you're moving through one computer—or set of computers—to get to the Internet, but in the latter instance you don't need a LAN account in the first place. In other words, going directly to a service provider makes Internet access possible for anyone with a computer and a modem, not just those who are already hooked up to a network in their offices.

Using one of the commercial services (or a local BBS) for Internet access is a strong possibility, especially if you already have an account with one of these services. In general, however, full Net access is more readily available, and often cheaper, through a commercial Internet provider. For this reason, I devote very limited space to the topic, but if you already belong to one of these services you owe it to yourself to see what your possibilities are.

> **NOTE**
>
> Even more in its infancy is Internet service through your cable TV (CATV) provider. This is an extremely promising category of service because it has the potential to offer high-speed access to any home that has access to cable, and this means millions. The CATV providers also promise super high-speed access for organizations and corporations. Still, this is a beginning service offering, so again this chapter deals briefly with it.
>
> Other access possibilities beckon, such as the long-awaited and now-appearing ISDN (available in an increasing number of regions at a variety of prices), and the fiber optic networks beyond. But this book is concerned with what's here now, so neither CATV nor ISDN will be treated. For the future of the Web, however, these technologies will be crucial. It's impossible to exaggerate the importance of ultra high-speed access to the needs of true multimedia environments.

Access Through a Local Area Network

If you have a computer at work, and you're part of a local area network (usually this means you can send e-mail and perhaps exchange files with your co-workers), you might already have Internet access. Check with your systems or computer services group (often called IS or MIS), and ask them if this is the case.

Increasingly it is, and you might as well take advantage of it. Of course, you'll likely need to go through various channels to establish Net access, but maybe not. Maybe you've been connected all along, and you just haven't known it. If you find out that your organization isn't on the Net, and you're convinced they should be, then make the inquiries you can, request that it be looked into (there are usually standard internal procedures for this sort of request), and do your best to interest others. A good grasp of office politics might be invaluable here.

The point is that you can't establish LAN access to the Net by yourself, unless of course you have absolute authority in systems issues. (I'll assume here that you don't.) Internet access for an organization is expensive, and approval for it must go through the same channels as approval for any other significant expenditure. Chances are, however, that even if your firm isn't on the Net, it's researching the possibilities, and if it's possible you might want to get involved in this process.

If your organization is on the Net but your department is not, and you know very well that your supervisor won't even consider it unless there's a very good reason (they're touchy this way), consider putting together a presentation and even a demonstration of how the Net will help you and your fellow department members. There are a couple ways of doing this.

The easiest is to use *The World Wide Web Unleashed* and its companion book *The Internet Unleashed* as a basis for the presentation, pointing out how important the Net and the Web have become to business and research activities of all kinds.

Of course, there's a large array of Internet books on the shelves of your local bookstore, and many of these will help you as well. Among the most notable are Mary Cronin's *Doing Business on the Internet* and *The Internet Business Guide* by Rosalind Resnick and Dave Taylor, which offers case studies and advice for Internet business activity. And there are business and research chapters in many of the other Internet books as well. Similarly, my own *Teach Yourself the Internet: Around the World in 21 Days* offers two chapters on business-related activity, and points to a number of Net sites dealing with research ventures as well. Another suggestion is to pick up a copy of *Internet World* magazine and order the back issues that deal specifically with business on the Net, and to watch your library and magazine stand for issues of the major computer magazines to see their increasing interest in commercial aspects of the Net.

The other way, if you're really serious about all this, is to take the initiative and get yourself an Internet account from a local service provider. Once it's established, you can use the Net for a few weeks, bookmarking and taking screen shots of the most useful sites and services for your organization. Then, put together a formal presentation using the screen shots (converting them to slides, for instance), your computer and modem, and your account. If it works, and your supervisors listen, you might even be able to recoup your expenses for all of this. Sure it's work, but if you want to be on the Web you might have to expend a fair bit of effort to get there. Not all companies see the benefits of the Internet itself, let alone the Web portion of it.

And remember, getting on the Net doesn't immediately imply Web access. Many firms have e-mail access to the Net, and sometimes Gopher and (restricted) newsgroup access, but Web access requires different software and different goals. When putting together your argument, concentrate on the Web's benefits; if you can't convince yourself, you're certainly not going to convince anyone else. Get into your browser, select your sites carefully, and then show them to the people who can sign the forms.

Still another consideration comes with getting graphical Web access rather than just terminal-based Web access. If you're enchanted by the multimedia capabilities of Mosaic, Cello, or WinWeb/MacWeb, and that's what you want to establish through your LAN, you won't be satisfied with even the best text-mode browser, Lynx. (See Chapter 9, "Browsing Without the Glitz: Nongraphical Web Clients.") It's very capable, but it isn't nearly as pretty. Keep this in mind as you prepare your presentation and demonstration of the Net.

Access Through a Modem

If you're on the Net through a LAN at work, often that LAN is accessible via remote dial-in through a modem. If so, it's possible, as long as both your computer and the LAN have the right software installed, to link to the LAN via modem and access the Internet in that way. This set of connections is far beyond the scope of this book, but again contact your systems group and find out if this kind of access is in place, and, if not, how you might get it established.

Often, such a connection will make your computer a terminal on that network, and you'll be restricted to a text-based "shell" account that lets you send and receive e-mail, exchange files, and (sometimes) read newsgroups. A well-stocked computer will also provide text-based Gopher programs and other Internet tools, and you might also have access to Lynx or another nongraphically based Web browser. Many colleges and universities offer this type of dial-in shell access.

The other kind of modem access is becoming more and more popular as local Internet service providers increase in number. Here, anyone with a computer and a modem can contact the service provider, establish an account for (usually) a monthly fee, and connect to the Internet whenever and for as long as it suits. If you've ever had an account on CompuServe, Prodigy, America Online, or any other commercial online service, you'll recognize this model.

The difference is that the commercial services are based around one proprietary computer, while an Internet account lets you wander around the world's computers. Even this distinction is lessening somewhat, however, as the commercial services scramble to connect their own members to the Net. Leading the way are Delphi, America Online, and CompuServe, but the others will certainly follow suit. In the mid-nineties, the Net is hot stuff.

As you might expect, different Internet providers offer different pricing structures and different types of connections. Increasingly, however, one particular model seems to be gaining dominance. Here, you pay a setup fee to establish an account, and then you pay a flat monthly rate for the type of access you need. Typically, this monthly fee gives you a certain number of access hours, and if you're logged on for more than this number you pay a (relatively) low hourly rate.

Because you want to access the World Wide Web and not just e-mail and newsgroup services, be sure to ask your provider what category of service you'll need. Almost always, this will mean SLIP or PPP dial-in service, or a higher-speed service that doesn't involve modems at all. These higher-speed services usually mean dedicated lines, and are priced for organizations rather than individuals. Normally, a dedicated line will be connected to the organization's internal LAN, in which case see "Access through a Local Area Network," in the preceding section.

NOTE

One type of high-speed service is in place now and will almost certainly plummet in price in the near future. This is ISDN, the long-awaited digital service from telephone companies, and several companies now offer it. At least one U.S. telephone company, Pacific Bell, has promised ISDN services to any Californian who wants it by early 1995. ISDN is covered in more detail in Chapter 13, "Next Year's Catalog: Web Tools of the Future."

SLIP and PPP are the most common protocols for dial-in accounts that support graphical interfaces. SLIP (Serial Line Internet Protocol) is extremely popular for PC users, although it's certainly available for anyone with a UNIX station in their home and for Macintosh users as well. More common for Mac users is PPP (Point to Point Protocol), a newer protocol that offers more security and a more stable connection through a technique known as handshaking.

New versions of SLIP are appearing (particularly CSLIP), but in the PC market SLIP is almost certain to give way to PPP in the very near future. The reason? Windows 4.0 (better known by its famous codename Chicago) ships with Microsoft PPP and a TCP/IP stack, and for better or for worse—and many would say worse—where Windows goes, so goes the PC user and PC standards.

Most services offer both SLIP and PPP as part of their basic package. This is important, because if you want to use a modem to use graphical applications like Mosaic or Cello, you need such a connection. In effect, both SLIP and PPP make it possible for your computer to be an independent "node" on the Internet (see "Indirect Versus Direct Access," later in the chapter), a requirement for using these packages. In a way I keep thinking must sound extremely condescending (but nobody's ever complained), I like to explain to people that SLIP access lets you "slip through" your service provider and directly into the Net. It isn't technically true, but it sure beats trying to explain what Serial Line Internet Protocol means. So far, only one listener has audibly groaned.

Not only do most providers offer SLIP or PPP connections, they also provide you with the software you need to give your own computer SLIP or PPP capabilities. The thing to keep in mind is that your machine and the one you're dialing into must *both* be SLIP- or PPP-enabled. You can buy or download all the SLIP/PPP software in the world, but you still won't be able to access the Net through them if the machine you're dialing into can't handle those protocols. That's why it's important to check what the providers have to offer, and how easy they make it for you to enable your own computer to make these kinds of connections.

In many cases, and increasingly, the service providers don't just provide SLIP/PPP, they also provide a full suite of graphically oriented Internet programs. Common among them are Eudora, the well-known e-mail package for both Windows and Macintosh; a Gopher program and a newsgroup package with a graphical interface; an FTP package; and—almost inevitably—the version of Mosaic your computer needs.

If these aren't provided, as soon as you have your connection you can download them to your machine using your FTP program, or you can get them on disk from a friend, from a computer store (try the shareware and freeware section), from a users' group, or inside any number of current Internet books available in your bookstore. With your SLIP/PPP connection in place, you can install these packages and, sometimes with a bit more configuration, run them without trouble.

In some cases, and increasingly, the service provider will include a suite of Internet tools with your account subscription. For example, one such service—Netcom—makes available a well-designed package called NetCruiser, which includes all the expected tools plus a World Wide Web browser that combines the functionality and appearance of both Mosaic and Cello. Other providers will inevitably follow suit, but make sure that the access you receive lets you download and use other software as well. In other words, before you sign on the dotted line, be certain that your service provider isn't offering some kind of proprietary service, because that's not what the Internet is all about.

Access Through a Commercial Online Service or BBS

Bulletin Board Systems (BBS's) are computers into which users with accounts can dial through a modem. They've been around almost as long as modems have existed, as enterprising or just plain energetic computer owners have long wanted to make it easy for other computer owners to communicate with each other and share programs and other files. Local BBS's are typically run by one person (called a "sysop," or system operator), and the BBS stays in existence only as long as the sysop's energy lasts. Some BBS's have continued for years; others disappear after a few months. To find the phone numbers for local BBS's, check in your newspaper's want ads or at your local computer store.

Larger BBS's are run by several people, and are often either nonprofit or low-profit ventures. Some of them now offer Internet connections, with an increasingly impressive range of features. Again, check with your local computer store for numbers about accessing to these BBS's, or pick up the computer newspapers you'll often find free or cheap at these stores. Try them out, but in many cases be prepared to give them your credit card number. (This is quite safe usually, but many people are hesitant.)

The largest BBS's of all are the commercial online services. The granddaddy of these is CompuServe, but many others have entered the fray. Some of the best-known, in alphabetical rather than chronological order, are America Online, BIX, Delphi, GEnie, and

Prodigy. All of these services are in the process of making Internet access available to their customers on a variety of levels, but the process is proving to be long and difficult. Delphi and BIX offer the most complete service so far, and America Online is the most user-friendly.

From the standpoint of using the Internet, the problem with some of these services is two-fold. First, on the practical level, they cost a lot. Although they advertise their wares at a very low monthly rate (anywhere from about $4.95 through $9.95), that doesn't always get you very much. Check carefully to see how much you'll actually be paying for Internet access.

CompuServe, for instance, charges a certain amount *per message* (about 20 cents) to both send and receive Internet mail, which doesn't sound like a great deal until you consider that joining two or three mailing lists (of the thousands available) can easily result in your receiving 50-100 messages per day. One popular list, for example, net-happenings, generates about 30 messages on the average, and I had to unsubscribe to a list called cybermind and another called sixties-l because I was getting horrendous numbers of mailings. At 50 messages a day, CompuServe would cost $300 per month plus the regular costs, and that's surely not what you had in mind. Other services offer different pricing models, but be absolutely sure you know what you're getting into. It's almost *always* cheaper to go with a local Internet provider. Still, if you're a member of one of these services, find out what they have to offer.

The second problem is a little harder to specify. If the goal of the online service is to open a doorway to the Internet for their customers, and then to let them explore the Net in all its positive and negative aspects, then fine. But if they're trying to establish the Net as just another addition to their service, less fine. Accessing Gopher through America Online, for example, gives nothing of the overwhelming scope of Gopherspace; instead, it simply feels as if you've launched into yet another AOL application. To appreciate what the Net—and hence the Web—has to offer, it's crucial (in my mind, at least) to understand that you're actually switching from computer to computer to computer, all over the world, to access your data and explore what people want you to see. Localize it, and the whole thing starts to mean very little.

Indirect Versus Direct Access

Let me state off the top that Internet access is categorized differently by different people. Sample a bunch of Internet books at your local library, and you'll run into terms like *dedicated access*, *dial-up access*, *remote access*, *terminal access*, *SLIP/PPP access*, and any number of others.

Since *The World Wide Web Unleashed* isn't, once again, a comprehensive guide to the Internet itself, but rather to that portion of the Net known as the Web, my goal is to simplify these details as much as possible, without losing their essential characteristics. For that reason, I'll categorize the major access types as *indirect* and *direct*. These are terms that are coming more and more into prominence, and while they might not be quite as technically accurate as some of the others, they're more than useful enough for our purposes. And from the standpoint of the Mac and Windows users acquiring commercial Net accounts, a group that is growing in size perhaps more than any other, the distinction is the only one that's really necessary.

Indirect Access

Indirect access means that your computer is not directly attached to the Internet. Instead, it is one of many terminals connected to another computer, which is itself attached to the Internet. As a mere terminal, your computer does not have its own IP address, and you cannot perform tasks such as FTPing a file—or downloading e-mail—directly to your hard drive. In other words, your computer is *not* a node on the Internet, and this restricts your activity and your environment to whatever the directly connected computer allows.

Often, this restriction means that you operate from a UNIX *shell* environment. UNIX, the operating system that forms the de facto basis of the Internet, is an immensely powerful and flexible operating system, but its shell environments are difficult for a novice to master and do not provide the graphical interface many personal computer users have grown accustomed to. In fact, UNIX has several graphical environments available—X Window being the one we'll see most often in this book—but a typical shell environment offers only a command-line interface, and an often cryptic one at that.

One of the great benefits of indirect access through UNIX shell environment or any other form of indirect access is that you don't have to worry about finding and downloading new software, nor, in fact, do you have to concern yourself with the computer's operation at all. E-mail packages such as Elm or Pine will be upgraded by the systems people as they become available, as will such essential Internet browsing tools as Gopher. A well-stocked indirect environment will provide you with a host of powerful Internet tools such as an excellent mailer, the most up-to-date Gopher client, a variety of telnet and perhaps FTP possibilities, and two or three newsgroup packages, to name some of the more important. Your only task is to use these tools, not to maintain them on your own.

The major disadvantage of indirect access is that you often can't use the important graphical tools such as Mosaic, Cello, MacWeb, and so on. And those are the tools that are making the most noise. Note that this isn't necessarily the case across LANs, but it is certainly the case for home computer users who purchase an account from a commercial Internet provider. For these users, only direct access is a useful choice.

Direct Access

Direct access means that your computer has its own IP address and is an independent node on the Internet. In effect, you have become another statistic on the Net, one more computer added to the hordes already there. (As a terminal with indirect access, your personal machine wasn't even this significant.) If you wish to establish your computer as an FTP site or, indeed, a World Wide Web site, you can do so. In the latter case, as this book will make clear, you need to do more work than just establishing an IP address, but the point is that it can be done. With indirect access, it can't.

With a direct access Internet account, you FTP files to your own hard disk, rather than to the server's, and your e-mail can appear on your own hard drive as well—again, rather than on the server's. If you create a Web page and store it on your hard drive, you can load it into a browser, click on the links, and be transported to the linked site. With indirect access, by contrast, you typically have to place such a page on the server, because your own machine isn't accessible. Furthermore, while it's true that you're suddenly responsible for maintaining your own Internet software tools, you also have full control over which programs you download, install, and run. If you see an announcement for a new piece of software, or an upgrade to one you already have, simply FTP it to your hard drive, follow the installation procedure, and let fly. Of course, if there are serious bugs in the software (or even a virus), that's your problem and not the systems group's, but such is the price of independence.

Most importantly from the standpoint of users with modem access, direct access means being able to use the graphical tools under constant development for environments such as Windows and the Macintosh. No longer restricted by the text-based interfaces of the UNIX shell, you now have access to e-mail, newsgroup, Gopher, FTP, Archie, WAIS, IRC, and World Wide Web packages that are fully capable of making use of your graphic environment. From a Web user's perspective, this means that you are able to experience, use, and contribute to the Web in all its multimedia glory.

In fact, as mentioned earlier, this strict demarcation between indirect and direct access isn't completely accurate, from a technical point of view. As just one example, SLIP/PPP access gives you your own IP address and the full use of multimedia tools for your environment, but you're not really directly connected to the Net. You're still dependent on a server that is in turn directly connected, and SLIP/PPP in effect only *simulates* a direct connection. (If you don't believe you're not directly connected, try logging in when the server is down for maintenance.) But since the results are the same, who cares? Your machine has a unique IP, you have substantial control over your Internet environment, and you use a multimedia Web browser. Which is, after all, the point.

Browsing Without the Glitz: Nongraphical Web Clients

9

by Carrie Leigh Pascal

IN THIS CHAPTER

```
lynx protocol://host/path/filename
```

where

> protocol: identifies the communications protocol used by the server you are accessing (for example, HTTP, Gopher, FTP or WAIS)

> host: specifies the Internet address of the computer system on which the server you want to access is running

> path *and* filename: identify the directory path and file of interest

If, for example, you want to execute Lynx with NASA's home page, you could type:

```
lynx http://hypatia/gfsc.nasa.gov/NASA_homepage.html
```

Lynx comes up as shown in Figure 9.1.

FIGURE 9.1.

The NASA Home Page in Lynx.

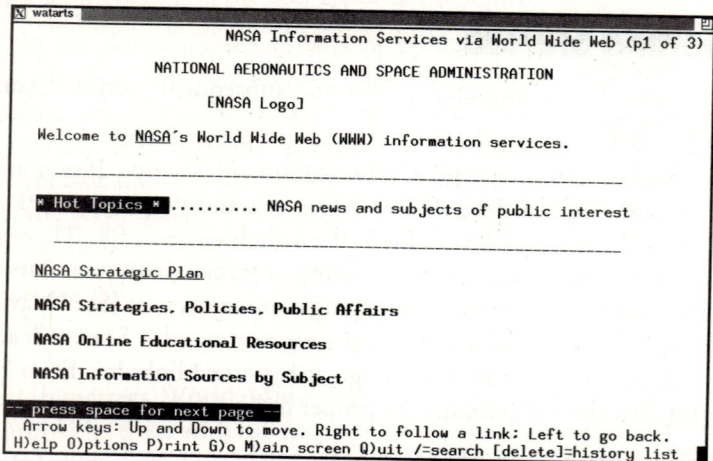

You could also access a specific web page once in Lynx by simply typing the letter **g**. You will be prompted for filename or URL to open, at which point you would enter the protocol, host, path and or filename.

You may want to configure Lynx to execute with the same page all the time. To do so, you must set your home environment variable in UNIX. If you are running ksh, type the following at your UNIX prompt:

```
export www_home=http://hypatia/gfsc.nasa.gov/NASA_homepage.html
```

If you are running csh, type

```
setenv www_home http://hypatia/gfsc.nasa.gov/NASA_homepage.html
```

> **NOTE**
>
> You may replace the above HTTP address with whatever page you would like.

Once your home environment variable is set, when you execute the Lynx command, it will open with whatever page you specified. You can always reset your environment variable by retyping the above command and replacing the URL with a new one. If you choose neither to set a home environment variable, nor to specify a URL or a file name when you execute the Lynx command, Lynx will run with whatever default file was chosen by the administrator of your system.

Leaving Lynx

To exit Lynx, simply type **q**. You will be prompted for confirmation, so type **y** to confirm and **n** if you change your mind. To exit without being prompted for confirmation, type **Q** or **ctrl+d**.

Navigating in Lynx

You may use arrow keys and or the numerical keypad to navigate in Lynx. Do not try using your mouse; it will not work, and may confuse things somewhat. In some UNIX windows, you can always select text with your mouse and change it to reverse video. Doing so while in Lynx, however, may lead you to believe that the text you have selected is a hypertext link, because selected links in Lynx are also represented in reverse video.

The following paragraphs describe how to navigate with the arrow and keyboard keys, and indicate the numpad equivalent in parentheses. See also the Commands section for a list of all Lynx commands.

One Web page may consist of more than one screen. To scroll through a Web page with multiple screens, use the + key (or numpad 3) to move forward one screen and the - key (numpad 9) to move backward one screen. To move from link anchor to link anchor (the highlighted text), use the up and down cursor arrows (numpad 8 and 2, respectively). Do not use the left or right arrow keys to move from anchor to anchor, even if there are multiple links in one line of text. The left and right arrow keys (numpad 4 and 6, respectively) are used to move back and forth between Web pages. That is, they are the equivalent of the Back and Forward commands in Mosaic. Additionally, you may use numpad keys 7 and 1 to return to the top of the current web page or to skip to the bottom.

Link anchors in Lynx will vary depending on your monitor. On a plain, black-and-white monitor, they are represented in bolded text, and they change to reverse video when

selected. Your monitor, of course, may be slightly different. Once you have selected a link with your cursor keys, hit Return or Enter to jump to the destination indicated by the link.

Other keyboard commands may help you chart the web through Lynx. Lynx keeps a list of each site you have visited. You may access this "history list" with the Backspace or Delete keys. You may then scroll through the list and revisit any site by selecting it (again, with your up and down cursor keys) and by hitting Return or Enter. Inside the history list, you may also type **m** to return to the first site you visited.

You may notice on occasion that when you jump to a certain site, the data transfer is extremely slow. This may arise for a number of reasons, but if you do not like staring at the screen while twiddling your thumbs, you may always halt a data transfer by typing **z**. This will stop the transfer completely and will leave you at the site from where you attempted the hypertext jump.

Once in a while, you may encounter a binary file throughout your navigation. You cannot view binary files on screen in Lynx, but you will automatically be prompted to either download the binary file or to cancel the operation altogether. If you select **d** for download, Lynx will transfer the file into a temporary location and offer you a list of options (again, depending on your system setup). The one default option is `save the file to a disk`.

To print, mail, or save a document, type **p** anywhere inside Lynx. The options you receive will depend on the way your system has been set up. You should be able to save the page to a file in any of your directories, print the file, and mail the file to yourself.

Online help is available from anywhere within Lynx. simply type **?** or **H** to access a list of help topics. The Help page shown in Figure 9.2 appears:

FIGURE 9.2.

Lynx Help.

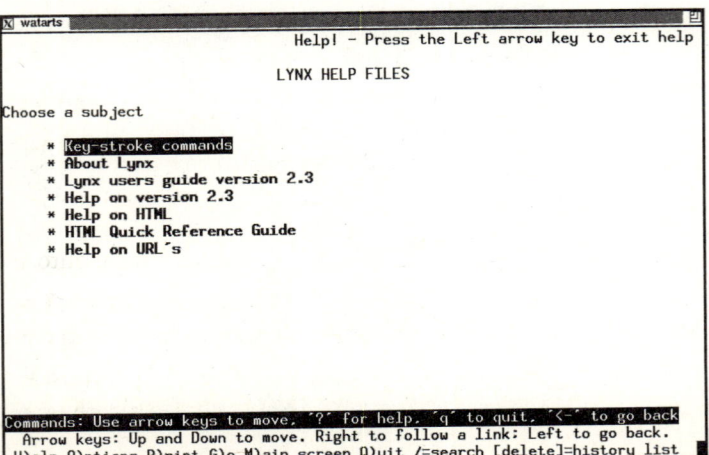

You may also wish to view the online User's Guide. This is available at: `http://www.cc.ukans.edu/lynx_help/Lynx_users_guide.html`.

Lynx Commands

The following is a full list of Lynx commands and their functions. Some of these commands were described in the "Navigating in Lynx" section.

Key Command	Function
↑(numpad = 8)	Move back one link
↓(numpad = 2)	Move forward one link
←(numpad = 4)	Move back one page
→(numpad = 6)	Move forward one page
- (numpad = 9)	Move back one screen
+ (numpad = 3)	Move forward one screen
space bar	Move forward one screen
numpad 7	Jump to the top of the current page
numpad 1	Jump to the end of the current page
/	Enter a search string for the current page (same as "s")
\	Toggle to view the HTML format of the current page
u=	View details about the current page (owner, URL, size, etc.)
Backspace	Access the history list
Delete	Access the history list
?	Access online help
a	Create a bookmark for the current page
b	Jump to the top of the current page (same as numpad 7)
c	Send a comment to the owner of the current page (if an owner exists)
d	Download the current page onto your machine
e	Edit the current page if the editor has been defined through Options and if the page is local
g	Select a URL to open (you must know the fill address of the URL: protocol, host, path, and/or filename)

continues

Key Command	Function
'H'	Access online help
i	Access a Web index, the contents of which depend on your system setup
m	Return to the first page you visited during the current session
n	Search a nonindexed document for keywords
o	Access the options menu
p	Print, mail, or save a file
q	Leave Lynx with confirmation
Q	Leave Lynx without confirmation
r	Remove a bookmark
s	Enter a search string for the current page (same as /)
u	Return to the previous document (same as [27])
v	Access your personal list of bookmarks
z	Abort the current transfer process

Creating Bookmarks in Lynx

Perhaps, throughout your navigation of the Web, you came across a page that you feel you will access often. If so, you may bookmark the page and then access it by calling up your bookmark file and selecting it. Lynx allows you to bookmark in two ways: You may mark an entire document, or you may mark only the link currently selected on the page.

You must have a bookmark file on your machine to create bookmarks (in UNIX, simply create a file titled bookmark_home or something similar in one of your directories). In Lynx, to create a bookmark, type **a**. You will be prompted with:

```
Save D)ocument or L)ink to bookmark file or C)ancel? (d,l,c):
```

Select d to save a link to the document you are currently viewing or l to save the link that is currently selected on the page. Selecting c will cancel the bookmark operation without saving anything.

To call up your list of bookmarks, simply type **v** from inside Lynx. The list of bookmarks you have created will appear, and you may select any of them with your cursor keys.

Setting Options in Lynx

You may configure a number of options in Lynx. To do so, select o from inside Lynx, and a screen listing configurable options appears, as in Figure 9.3.

FIGURE 9.3.

Lynx Options Page.

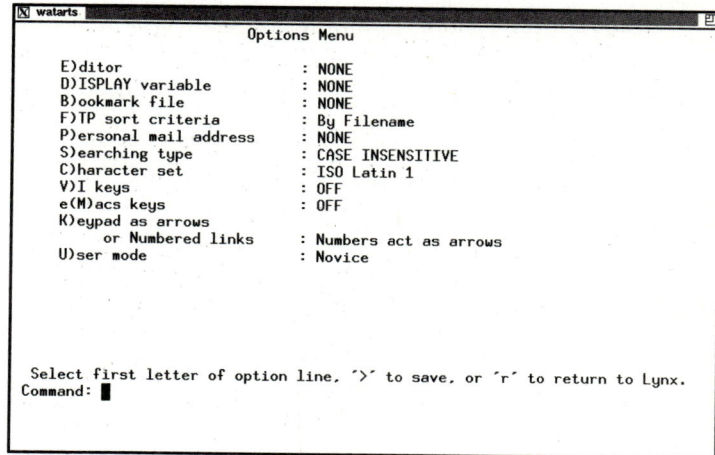

```
watarts                                                                    回
                               Options Menu

        E)ditor                       : NONE
        D)ISPLAY variable             : NONE
        B)ookmark file                : NONE
        F)TP sort criteria            : By Filename
        P)ersonal mail address        : NONE
        S)earching type               : CASE INSENSITIVE
        C)haracter set                : ISO Latin 1
        V)I keys                      : OFF
        e(M)acs keys                  : OFF
        K)eypad as arrows
             or Numbered links        : Numbers act as arrows
        U)ser mode                    : Novice




     Select first letter of option line, '>' to save, or 'r' to return to Lynx.
     Command: █
```

The options are as follows:

Editor	Select the editor you wish to use when editing browsable files and sending mail or comments. Specify the file path name of the editor when possible.
Display variable	Available only on UNIX displays and relevant only to X Window users. This variable is picked up automatically from the environment if it has been previously set.
Bookmark file	Specify the filename and location of your personal bookmark file.
FTP sort criteria	Specify how files should be sorted within FTP listings. Current options include by filename, by size, by type, and by date.
Personal mail address	Specify your mailing address. This will be used when you send files to yourself and will be included as the "From:" address when you mail comments.
Searching type	Specify whether searches should be case sensitive or case insensitive. This affects only searches performed within Lynx.

VI keys	If ON, then lowercase h,j,k and l will map to left, down, up and right arrow keys respectively.
Emacs keys	If ON, the ctrl+p, ctrl+n, ctrl+f and ctrl+b will map to left, down, up, and right arrow keys respectively.
Keypad as arrows or	Allows the options to navigate with numbered links arrow keys or to number every link and then to select a link by typing its corresponding number.
User mode	Choose between Novice (displays two lines of help at the bottom of the screen), Intermediate (turns off the help lines), and Advanced (displays the URL of the currently selected link at the bottom of the screen).
Local execution	If local execution is *not* activated by scripts or links the system administrator, this option allows you to choose Always Off (local execution scripts will never be executed), For Local Files Only (scripts will only be executed if they reside on your machine), and Always On (local execution scripts will always be executed).

Lynx is a powerful tool for anyone accessing the Web with a system that cannot handle the multimedia capabilities of the graphical browsers discussed in Chapter 10, "The One You Keep Hearing About: NCSA Mosaic," and Chapter 11, "Yes Virginia, There Is a Choice: More Graphical Browsers." It has been refined over time to become a thoroughly enjoyable system to use for browsing, and in some cases it can actually be more efficient than other Web clients. If you use the Web for access to documents that do not rely on graphics, or indeed to download documents from FTP sites, you have little need for multimedia. In fact, for that type of access requirement, graphics and other additions can actually be distractions. It is a program well worth considering for specific kinds of access, or simply to find out if the World Wide Web is of use to you in your work.

CERN Line Browser

The CERN Line Mode Browser (sometimes referred to as www), is a character-based World Wide Web browser, developed for use by anyone with a dumb terminal. Currently used mainly as a test tool for the CERN Common Code Library, it was developed by Tim Berners-Lee, one of the original creators of the Web at the European Particle Physics Lab (CERN); Nicola Pellow from Leicester Polytechnic in the UK; and Henrik Frystyk, a student from Aalborg University in Denmark. www is not often used, ironically, as a World

Wide Web browser; rather its usefulness is derived from running it as a background application or from a batch job. It also provides a variety of possibilities for data format conversion and filtering.

The Line Browser currently runs on UNIX, VMS, and VC/VMS. Its current version, 2.12, has been stable at least since June 1994, and is being used as a test tool for the Library of Common Code. To view a demo, telnet to `info.cern.ch`. No user or password is required.

Where to Get the CERN Line Browser

The Line Mode Browser is available via anonymous FTP to `info.cern.ch`.

Starting the Line Mode Browser

The following directions to start the Line Mode Browser assume you are using UNIX.

To access the Line Mode Browser, type

`www`

at your operating system command prompt. With no options, the Line Mode Browser executes with the system default page, `/usr/local/lib/WWW/default.html`, likely set up by your system administrator. You may specify a number of options, a document address, and/or a list of keywords as arguments to your `www` command. Some of these arguments are outlined below. For a complete listing, see the Line Mode Browser online documentation (URL: `http://info.cern.ch/hypertext/WWW/LineMode/Defaults/ QuickGuide.html`).

Options

`-h <hostname>`	Establishes a telnet connection to the remote host specified. This implies a secure mode of execution where all references to the local file system are canceled.
`-n`	Noninteractive mode. This outputs the formatted document to the standard output (already set up), then exits.
`-v`	Verbose mode. Provides a status line in the browser that indicates the program's attempts to read data in various ways. You can also set this from within the browser. See the Commands section.
`-o <filename>`	Redirects output to a specified filename.
`-l <filename>`	Writes a list of visited sites to a specified log filename.

-p <n>	Where <n> is a number, specifies the page length in lines. Default is 24.
-w <n>	Where <n> is a number, specifies the page width in columns. Default is 78, 79, or 80 columns, depending on your system.

Document Address

If you specify a document address, the argument is the hypertext address of the site at which you want to start browsing. If, for example, you wanted to call up the Line Mode Browser with NASA's home page, you could type

```
www http://hypatia/gfsc.nasa.gov/NASA_homepage.html
```

The program would run as shown in Figure 9.4.

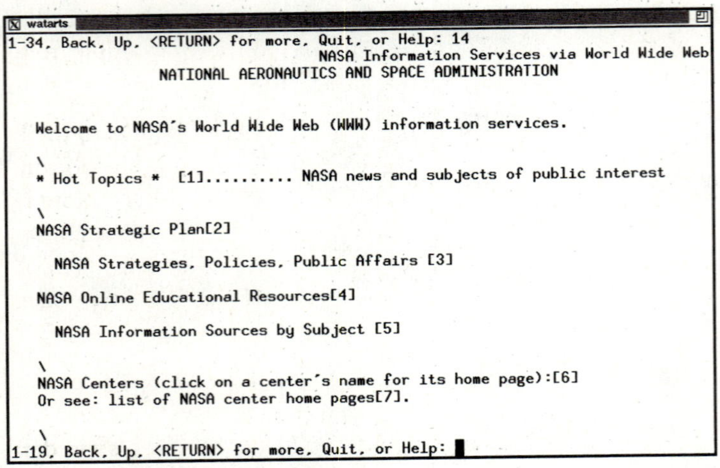

FIGURE 9.4.

The NASA Home Page in the Line Mode Browser.

```
X watarts
1-34. Back, Up, <RETURN> for more, Quit, or Help: 14
                                   NASA Information Services via World Wide Web
             NATIONAL AERONAUTICS AND SPACE ADMINISTRATION


   Welcome to NASA's World Wide Web (WWW) information services.

   \
 * Hot Topics *  [1].......... NASA news and subjects of public interest

   \
 NASA Strategic Plan[2]

    NASA Strategies, Policies, Public Affairs [3]

 NASA Online Educational Resources[4]

    NASA Information Sources by Subject [5]


   \
 NASA Centers (click on a center's name for its home page):[6]
 Or see: list of NASA center home pages[7].

   \
1-19. Back, Up, <RETURN> for more, Quit, or Help: █
```

Keywords

If you referenced an index as your document address, then any words following the document address will be read as keywords and the browser will search the index for those words. Note that this only works on indexed documents.

Leaving the Line Mode Browser

To exit the Line Mode Browser, type **quit** or **q**, **exit**, or **e** from inside the program. All Line Mode Browser commands are case insensitive, so the above may be upper or lower case. You will not be prompted for confirmation.

Navigating in the Line Mode Browser

The CERN Line Mode Browser (www) shows a screen of information and has a command line at the bottom of that screen. From this command line, you may tell the browser to jump to a specific destination, to move forward, to go back, to go home, to get help, to print, and to perform a host of other commands. Each hypertext link has a number next to it in parentheses; to access the site at the end of that link, type the corresponding number at the command line and hit Return or Enter. If one Web page has multiple screens on your display, you may press the Return key to move forward one screen. For many of the text commands (meaning you must type a text string at the command line, followed by a hard return), abbreviations are available. For example, to jump back to the previous site visited, you may type **back**, or **b**.

To move to the top of a Web page, type **top**. To move to the bottom, type **bottom**. The Line Mode Browser is case insensitive, so to execute the bottom command, for example, you may type **BOTTOM**, **bottom**, **bo**, or **BO**, among others. Note that you cannot type **b** for bottom because that abbreviation is reserved for the **back** command. Type **up** to scroll up one screen in a page, and **down** to scroll down (the equivalent of pressing the Return key, as described above). Pretty simple so far. As described, type **back** to jump back to the previous site you visited.

To return to the first document you read, type **home**. To access a specific site, type **go** followed by the URL of that site. If you type go and do not specify any parameters, then the Line Mode Browser will jump to the screen in your system default page, likely stored in /usr/local/lib/WWW/default.html. The command list provides a list of all document titles and corresponding numbers for the hypertext links on the current page. Where no title is available, the document's URL is used. If you type **source list**, you will receive a list of URLs only (and their corresponding numbers). For example, Figure 9.5 shows part of the list of the World Wide Web Virtual Library, without using the source command.

The recall command presents you with a numbered list of the sites you have visited throughout your session. If you wish to revisit one of those sites, type **recall** followed by the list number of that site, and then press the Return or Enter key. A recall list looks something like Figure 9.6.

FIGURE 9.5.

List for the WWW Virtual Library.

```
[N] watarts                                                                    [2]
[54] http://euclid.math.fsu.edu/Science/math.html
[55] http://golgi.harvard.edu/biopages/medicine.html
[56] http://www.met.fu-berlin.de/DataSources/MetIndex.html
[57] http://info.cern.ch/hypertext/DataSources/bySubject/Overview.html#ove12
[58] http://www.comlab.ox.ac.uk/archive/other/museums.html
[59] http://www.oulu.fi/music.html
[60] http://www.mth.uea.ac.uk/ocean/oceanography.html
[61] http://info.cern.ch/hypertext/DataSources/bySubject/Overview.html#ove13
[62] http://info.cern.ch/hypertext/DataSources/bySubject/Overview.html#ove14
[63] http://info.cern.ch/hypertext/DataSources/bySubject/Physics/Overview.html
[64] http://info.cern.ch/hypertext/DataSources/bySubject/politics/Overview.html
[65] http://info.cern.ch/hypertext/DataSources/bySubject/Overview.html#ove15
[66] http://info.cern.ch/hypertext/DataSources/bySubject/Overview.html#ove16
[67] http://www.cis.ufl.edu/~thoth/library/recreation.html
[68] http://info.cern.ch/hypertext/DataSources/bySubject/Overview.html#ove17
[69] http://info.cern.ch/hypertext/DataSources/bySubject/Overview.html#ove18
[70] http://www.pitt.edu/~cjp/rees.html
[71] http://freethought.tamu.edu/
[72] http://coombs.anu.edu.au/WWWVL-SocSci.html
[73] http://www.atm.ch.cam.ac.uk/sports/sports.html
[74] http://www.stat.ufl.edu/vlib/statistics.html
[75] http://www.bgsu.edu/~jzawodn/ufo/
[76] http://info.cern.ch/hypertext/DataSources/bySubject/Virtual_libraries/Overv
iew.html
[77] http://info.cern.ch/hypertext/DataSources/bySubject/coordination.html

1-77, Back, Up, <RETURN> for more, Quit, or Help: █
```

FIGURE 9.6.

Recall Command with the Line Mode Browser.

```
[N] watarts                                                                    [2]
    Women's Studies Programs and Women's Centers[3]

    Women in Academia and Industry[4]

    Gender and Sexuality[5]

    Information Clearinghouses and Resources[6]

    Big Collections of Information[7]

    Unclassified Cool Information[8]



   WOMEN IN COMPUTER SCIENCE AND ENGINEERING
1-42, Back, Up, <RETURN> for more, Quit, or Help: recall

   Documents you have visited:-

R 1)    in UWinfo WEB Home Page
R 2)    in WWW starting points
R 3)    in EINet Galaxy
R 4)    in Business & Commerce
R 5)    in Company, Organization and Consultants (Business & Commerce)
R 6)    in Industries (Company, Organization and Consultants)
R 7)    Women Homepage

1-42, Back, Up, <RETURN> for more, Quit, or Help: █
```

To print the current page, type **print** at the command line. This command will print the document without any numbered references. Output is piped to the command defined by the environment variable WWW_PRINT_COMMAND (lpr by default). You can set your environment variable in UNIX, the syntax depending on whether you are using csh or ksh. For details, see the online documentation for the Line Mode Browser. (URL: `http://info.cern.ch/hypertext/WWW/LineMode/Defaults/QuickGuide.html`).

Help in CERN's Line Mode Browser is available by typing **help** at the command line. The context-sensitive list of commands that appears depends on the version you are using and the hypertext address of the document you are currently reading. The screen you access presents other information besides the commands and their definitions. You can figure out the version number of the Line Mode Browser you are using, and you can view the URL of the current page. A sample help screen is shown in Figure 9.7. Note that not all commands appear in every help screen because of Help's context sensitivity.

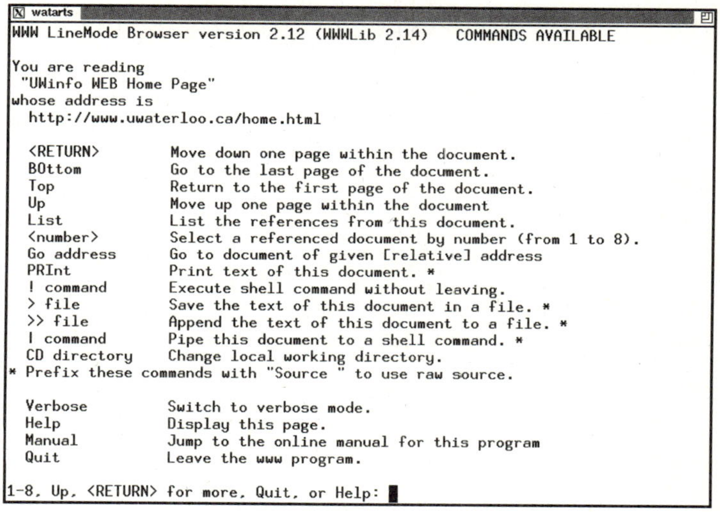

FIGURE 9.7.

*Line Mode Browser
Help Screen.*

```
┌ watarts ───────────────────────────────────────────────────────┐
│WWW LineMode Browser version 2.12 (WWWLib 2.14)   COMMANDS AVAILABLE│
│                                                                  │
│You are reading                                                   │
│ "UWinfo WEB Home Page"                                           │
│whose address is                                                  │
│  http://www.uwaterloo.ca/home.html                               │
│                                                                  │
│   <RETURN>        Move down one page within the document.        │
│   BOttom          Go to the last page of the document.           │
│   Top             Return to the first page of the document.      │
│   Up              Move up one page within the document           │
│   List            List the references from this document.        │
│   <number>        Select a referenced document by number (from 1 to 8).│
│   Go address      Go to document of given [relative] address     │
│   PRInt           Print text of this document. *                 │
│   ! command       Execute shell command without leaving.         │
│   > file          Save the text of this document in a file. *    │
│   >> file         Append the text of this document to a file. *  │
│   | command       Pipe this document to a shell command. *       │
│   CD directory    Change local working directory.                │
│ * Prefix these commands with "Source " to use raw source.        │
│                                                                  │
│   Verbose         Switch to verbose mode.                        │
│   Help            Display this page.                             │
│   Manual          Jump to the online manual for this program     │
│   Quit            Leave the www program.                         │
│                                                                  │
│1-8, Up, <RETURN> for more, Quit, or Help: █                      │
└──────────────────────────────────────────────────────────────────┘
```

List of Line Mode Browser Commands and Other Functions

CERN's Line Mode Browser contains a wide range of commands, many of which are not obvious. Most are shown here.

Line Mode Browser Commands

The following is a somewhat comprehensive list of Line Mode Browser Commands, certainly all you need to navigate. Some of these were described in the "Navigating in the Line Mode Browser" section. It is interesting to note that the Line Mode Browser currently does not allow you to abort a data transfer if it is too slow, as do Mosaic, Cello, and Lynx. This is one of the proposed features for the next version, however.

Command	*Definition*
! *\<command\>*	Executes a shell command from inside www by typing ! followed by the command.
\> *\<filename\>*	Saves the current document to a file specified by *\<filename\>*.
\>\> *\<filename\>*	Appends the current document to a file specified by *\<filename\>*.
Back	Moves back one page.
cd	Changes directory from inside www.
Down	Scrolls down one screen (you can also press the Return key to do this).
Exit, Quit	Leaves www.
Find *\<keyword\>*	Only works on indexed documents, looks for the keyword you specify. Find will be an option listed at your prompt when it is available for use.
Go *\<URL\>*	Jumps to the URL you specify.
Help	Accesses the main help screen, which tells you the version number of the www you are using, the URL of the current page, and a list of all command-line commands.
Home	Returns to the first page you visited.
List	Lists all titles and corresponding link numbers for the links in the current document; where no title exists, lists the URL. Typing **source list** will provide you with a list of URLs and link numbers for the current document.
Manual	Jumps to the main page of the online documentation for www.
Next	Jumps to the site of the next pointer of the menu from which you made your last selection. See below for details.
\<number\>	Jumps to the site corresponding to that number on the screen.
Previous	Same as Next, but for the previous item in the list of pointers.
PRInt	Prints the document. Specify the destination with your WWW_PRINT_COMMAND environment variable.
Quit, Exit	Leaves www without confirmation.
Recall	Produces a numbered list of all the sites you have visited in the current session.
Recall *\<number\>*	Type **recall 5** to revisit site number 5 in your recall list.
Refresh	Refreshes the screen to the way it appeared when you first accessed it. (Note: This command is not very useful.)

Command	*Definition*
Source	Followed by another command, causes raw source to be generated for that command without any MIME headers wrapped around it. You can use this with print, >, >>, and list.
Top	Jumps to the top of the current page.
Up	Moves up one screen.
Verbose	For maintenance purposes, produces messages during data transfer processes.

Using *Next* and *Previous* with the Line Mode Browser

Next and Previous are useful commands when you are browsing through documents with a menu of items from which to choose, and you would like to explore each menu item in full. If, for example, you are reading the list of items in the World Wide Web Virtual Library (URL: http://info.cern.ch/hypertext/DataSources/bySubject/Overview2.html), you will come across the following subset of items:

```
Anthropology [10]
Archaeology [11]
Architecture [12]
```

You may select [11], read about Archaeology, and then decide to move on to [12]. You may do so without first returning to your menu and then selecting [12]; simply type **next** at the command line while in the Archaeology page and you will jump to the Architecture page. Previous works the same way, but for the previous site, so typing **previous** would take you to the Anthropology page.

Performing Keyword Searches with the Line Mode Browser

You may perform a keyword search in the Browser with indexed documents. If a document is indexed, then the command find appears in your prompt as one of your choices. To search for a keyword, type **find** <keyword> followed by **Return**, or **keyword** <keyword> followed by **Return**. If your keyword or keywords does or do not conflict with existing commands, you may omit the word find and the program will automatically interpret your command as keywords to search.

Customizing the Line Mode Browser

You may customize the Line Mode Browser from your shell prompt. Some of the customization features include setting the `WWW_HOME` environment variable, setting the `WWW_PRINT_COMMAND` (UNIX only) environment variable, and creating aliases for some commands. To learn how to set these variables, see the "Customizing www" section of the online manual. (URL: `http://info.cern.ch/hypertext/WWW/LineMode/ Defaults/ QuickGuide.html`). To access the documentation inside www, type **manual** from the command line prompt.

Although it works, and its historical value is undeniable, the Line Browser is a relatively unappealing introduction to the World Wide Web. Not only does it not offer the Web's multimedia features, its navigation system offers none of the ease, or even the attractiveness, of Lynx. By all means, use it as a means of accessing necessary sites, but to experience the Web in anything approaching its full potential you should use the Line Browser as a temporary tool only.

Other Nongraphical Browsers

Lynx and CERN Line Mode are the two most comprehensive nongraphical World Wide Web browsers. Others, of course, have been developed for different platforms, often by hackers wanting to create a new interface for the Web. Many of the nongraphical browsers available never made it past their respective Beta releases. Some are undergoing continued development, some have been scrapped altogether, but they all deserve mention. They are listed in alphabetical order. Figure 9.8 shows a sample "other" nongraphical browser.

FIGURE 9.8.

Sample "other" browser.

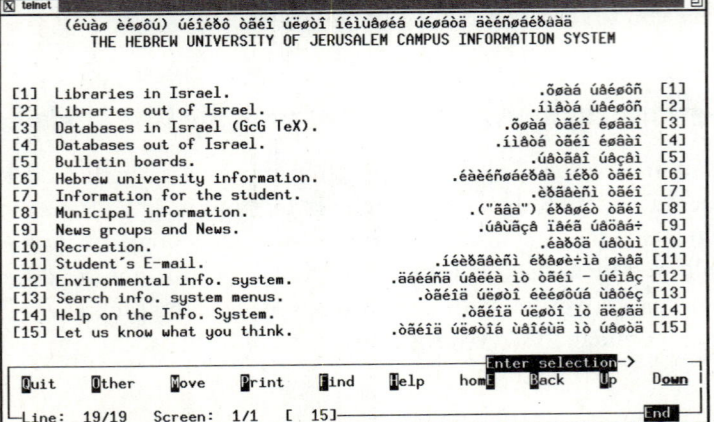

Emacs W3 Mode

Author:	William Perry (`wperry@spry.com`) (`wmperry@indiana.edu`)
Status:	Beta 0.953
Platforms:	UNIX, NeXT, VMS, OS/2, DOS, Windows, Windows NT, Amiga DOS, Macintosh
Availability:	Anonymous FTP from `moose.cs.indiana.edu` `/pub/elisp/w3/w3.tar.Z`

The Emacs World Wide Web Browser enables the user to browse the entire Web, as long as he or she has Emacs or a subset thereof installed. This browser is compatible with Mosaic in that you can share a hotlist file (a file containing URLs of frequently visited sites) between the two applications. You can also share a global history file and a personal annotation directory. It is a highly portable browser, but note that its ability to run on all the platforms listed above depends on the version of Emacs installed on each of the platforms. To make full use of the Web with the Emacs browser, you need the following emacs packages: nntp for news reader, ange-ftp or efs for accessing files over FTP, Gopher (optional), HTML-mode (if you intend to use the group or personal annotation support), and mailcrypt (if you plan to access Web pages that require PGP/PEM encrypted requests).

Rashty VMS Client

Author:	Dudu Rashty (`Rashty%HUJIVMS.bitnet`)
Status:	Alpha
Platform:	VMS
Demo Site:	Telnet to `vms.huji.ac.il` login as `www` select option 2.

Dudu Rashty, from the Hebrew University of Jerusalem, developed a Web client for VMS. The Rashty VMS client is a full-screen browser based on VMS's SMG screen management routines. The browser is bilingual—English and Hebrew—and Hebrew can be replaced with another language if you desire. A good demo of the browser is available via telnet to `vms.huji.ac.il`. Login as `www` and select option 2. You will be presented with the Hebrew University of Jerusalem's Campus Wide Information System, a Rashty Command-Line interface. The browser offers FTP, Gopher, news and telnet connections, as well as access to Web servers.

Tom Fine's Perl WWW

Author:	Tom Fine (`fin@cis.ohio-state.edu`)
Status:	Beta (June 1994)
Platform:	UNIX
Availability:	Anonymous FTP to `archive.cis.ohio-state.edu.` `/pub/w3browser/w3browser-0.1.shar`

Tom Fine's Perl WWW browser is a tty-based browser written in the Perl programming language. This browser was developed for VT 100s and uses full screen with arrow keys and highlighting. (It's similar in appearance to Lynx.) This browser runs on UNIX only. To use this browser, you need to have Perl installed on your system. The browser is available via anonymous FTP to `archive.cis.ohio-state.edu`. The file is located in `/pub/w3browser.w3browser-0.1.shar`. Once you have placed this file in your directory, you need to unpack it with the command `sh w3browser-0.1.shar`. Once this is done, read the README file (that appears when you unpack the `w3browser-0.1.shar file`) for further instructions.

The goal of the Perl browser is to present information on screen as close as possible to the way it would look in a graphical environment. This was done using a program called termcap for all screen manipulations. The browser will unlikely progress past its current Beta version, as Tom Fine himself indicates at the top of his README file. His note nicely sums up the status of the browser:

PERL WWW BROWSER

This software is fairly out-of-date. I only continue to provide it in case someone feels like hacking on it. If you have an interest, though, I also have some code for editing HTML partially implemented, and I can send you that too.

For a better terminal browser, try Lynx—much more up-to-date, fewer bugs, more features, and a somewhat similar interface, although I like mine better :-). Lynx is available for anonymous FTP from `ftp2.cc.ukans.edu`. It may only be vt100, whereas [sic] mine should work on almost any terminal.

It is fairly unlikely that I will ever update this software again, or that I will continue the development of the Perl HTML editor.

Tom
June 8, 1994.

The One You Keep Hearing About: NCSA Mosaic

10

by Neil Randall

Unless you've been hiding under an extremely large rock for the past year, you can't have avoided hearing something about Mosaic. The subject of almost as much media hype as the Internet itself, Mosaic has been called—and with some justification—the Internet's first "killer app." Articles about it have appeared in everything from *The New York Times* through *Wired*, and it's made several appearances on CNN and other TV networks with high-tech interests. And to be quite honest about it, its existence is the reason a book like *The World Wide Web Unleashed* could even be published. What's so special about Mosaic? Before answering that, let's look at what the term "killer app" really means—because in this one instance it really might apply.

Anatomy of a Killer App

A killer app is a computer application, or program, that capitalizes on the strengths of a computer system and applies those strengths to fill a user need, and it does both so well that the user community feels that the application has become essential to their professional or personal lives. If it is a truly killer app, it not only raises these expectations, it fulfills them as well. The result is the lifting of a barrier between user and technology, and inevitably the app becomes identified *with* that technology. The app and the technology become, in many ways, one and the same, and the existence of the app eventually alters the activity it was initially designed to support.

Sounds good, but what does it mean...?

The first killer app for personal computers was Visicalc for the Apple II. Visicalc was the first spreadsheet program, and its design stemmed from what now seems an obvious link between the mathematical power of computers and the mathematical needs of people who work with numbers. When the IBM PC was introduced in the early eighties, Visicalc gave way to Lotus 1-2-3, originally an integrated package (hence its name), but eventually only a spreadsheet program.

Lotus 1-2-3 was one of two killer apps for DOS (we'll get to the other in a minute), and it can be called a killer app because it was so successful at giving PC users the tools they thought they needed that it became the catalyst for change in the kinds of tasks they were being asked to perform. In other words, Lotus 1-2-3 changed the nature of jobs, even careers, and inevitably it changed the way companies did business. Doubt it? Try offering a financial forecasting model to your clients, telling them that because you did it by hand any changes would take a couple days to process. In fact, try putting the financial forecasting model together in the first place without using your spreadsheet.

Visicalc and—much more widely—Lotus 1-2-3 brought personal computers into the business mainstream, changing some of the functions and tasks of business in the process. And they did it so well that people began to believe that there was no other way of accomplishing these functions and tasks. In fact, your spreadsheet program does nothing that you couldn't do by hand, or at the very least with adding machines and sliderules. What it does is make it easier, more easily alterable, and much, much faster.

The other essential killer app of the eighties was WordPerfect. Yes, word processing has been a killer *category* in every PC environment—MacWrite and soon afterwards Word on the Macintosh, for instance—but WordPerfect became as crucially important to business as Lotus 1-2-3, and in fact quite a bit beyond. It extended into the academic world, into governments, and into people's personal lives as well. In fact, people stopped asking, "Do you know word processing?" and started asking, "Do you know WordPerfect?" And because of its capabilities—its formatting, macros, and editing tools—it changed the way documentation (and all other writing) took place. I hate to use the phrase *paradigm shift*, but it probably applies to WordPerfect.

If there was a killer app for the Macintosh, it was Aldus PageMaker. Because the Macintosh from the beginning was hyped as a friendly computer that helped you create attractive publications on-screen and then print them exactly as they appeared (I realize WYSIWYG was never quite *this* smooth), the move to professional page design with PageMaker was a natural transition. The program catapulted the Macintosh into prominence in a previously nonexistent category of computing, desktop publishing, and businesses began to change the way they worked as a result. PageMaker sold Macs the way Visicalc sold Apple IIs and 1-2-3 and WordPerfect sold PCs. The only reason PageMaker is more difficult to consider as a killer app is that serious competition not only quickly developed (as it did with 1-2-3 and WordPerfect) but also quickly managed to gain ground (as was not the case with the others). Still, the idea is the same.

Killer apps fulfill both existing needs and needs that users didn't know they had, but which they develop as a result of using the app. For the Internet, the need was simple: It was wild and chaotic, and it had to be given an interface that the masses could handle. As long as the Net was under the control of the command line vagaries of telnet and FTP, it wasn't going to happen. The first application that came close to killer app status was Gopher, which effectively offered that comfortable interface and became the accepted means of disseminating information across a broad spectrum of platforms and categories. But from the perspective of mass media acceptance Gopher had one significant limitation. In an age where information is in many ways equated with the combination of sound, video, graphics, and text, Gopher's nonmultimedia neverending table of contents (which in many ways it is) didn't quite cut it. Using Gopher is a lot like using a library, and while a library is immensely useful for many things, for better or for worse it doesn't have mass appeal.

Enter Mosaic. Like Lotus 1-2-3 and WordPerfect, it's far from the first in its genre. Lotus had Visicalc before it, WordPerfect had WordStar before it, and Mosaic had the CERN line browser before it and others in the works. What Mosaic did, like the killer apps before it, was to become so popular that people began to associate the program with the genre. Part of the reason was simply that Mosaic began life as a good program and developed well from there, with frequent upgrades and intelligent interface and technology decisions.

A great deal, however, had to do with the fact that it captured its underlying technology—the World Wide Web—almost perfectly. Its by now classic "spinning globe" icon showed people graphically that they were connecting not just to a computer but to the world, and its display had the features that the World Wide Web was designed to have from its inception. The fact that a Macintosh version was available early in the game helped considerably as well, because there was almost no competition whatsoever in this arena. Mosaic came to Microsoft Windows soon after as well. The program became ubiquitous, and—again for better or for worse—became for many users another name for the World Wide Web.

So is Mosaic the Internet's first killer app? To a degree, yes. It has the publicity, it has the brand name status, and it fulfills a considerable portion of the Web's great promise. It has even become a business application, as every killer app inevitably becomes. Users are designing information and sites specifically for it, and all other Web browsers have to strive for compatibility with it. All the signs are there.

But Mosaic hasn't quite reached killer app status, because it can't perform all Internet functions. Its Gopher and FTP capabilities are rudimentary, as are its newsgroup and e-mail functions (which many see as the two major Net applications). Should it do all these things? If it's to become the interface on the Internet, as many of its users think it to be, then yes. But Mosaic might not need them to become a true killer app. As more and more multimedia information is designed for Mosaic specifically, it could well break away from its roots as an Internet meta-tool and take on a life all its own. Maybe (shudder?) as a major application for whatever the infobahn/highway/structure will one day become.

Before We Begin

The three Mosaics covered here are the NCSA versions only. Several software publishers are preparing, or have released, commercial versions of Mosaic, one of which (Spry's AirMosaic) is covered briefly in Chapter 11, "Yes Virginia, There Is a Choice: More Graphical Browsers." A freeware Mosaic for the Amiga computer, Amiga Mosaic or AMosaic, is covered in Chapter 11 because it is not an NCSA release. Interestingly, some members of the original design team for NCSA Mosaic, including the initial developer Marc Andreesen, have left NCSA to form a company called the Mosaic Communications Corporation, but it's not clear as of this writing that the company will be developing Mosaic itself. We'll have to wait and see.

All versions of NCSA Mosaic must be properly configured to work as full multimedia applications. Some details of the configurations are covered in Chapter 12, "Making It

Multimedia: Viewers, Players, and Other Browser Add-ons." For full configuration information, see the respective home pages for the different platforms.

Mosaic for X, Macintosh, and Microsoft Windows: The Common Features

Figures 10.1, 10.2, and 10.3 show the three main Mosaics—X, Mac, and Windows. You may want to refer to these figures as you read this chapter.

FIGURE 10.1.

NCSA Mosaic for X Window.

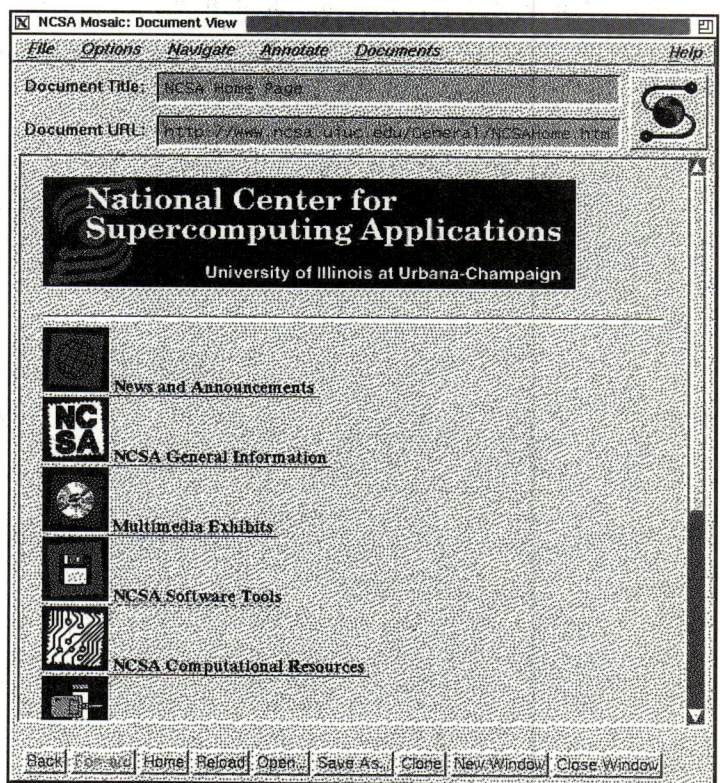

FIGURE 10.2.

NCSA Mosaic for the Macintosh.

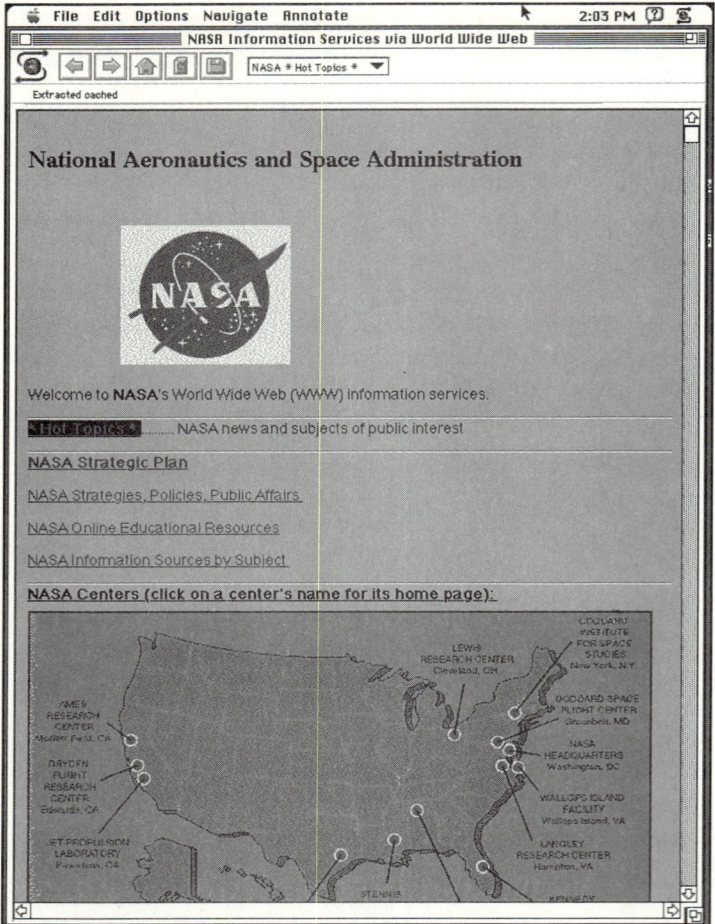

The Document View Window

The most important portion of the Mosaic screen, the document view window, holds the file you're currently viewing. Usually this file is in HTML format, and Mosaic interprets it accordingly, displaying it as a series of headings, lists, graphics, forms, and highlighted links. When Mosaic finds a text file, it displays the file in an unformatted manner. Other types of files it captures in the "temp" directories, although future versions of Mosaic will attempt to show more types of files in the document view window.

FIGURE 10.3.

NCSA Mosaic for Microsoft Windows.

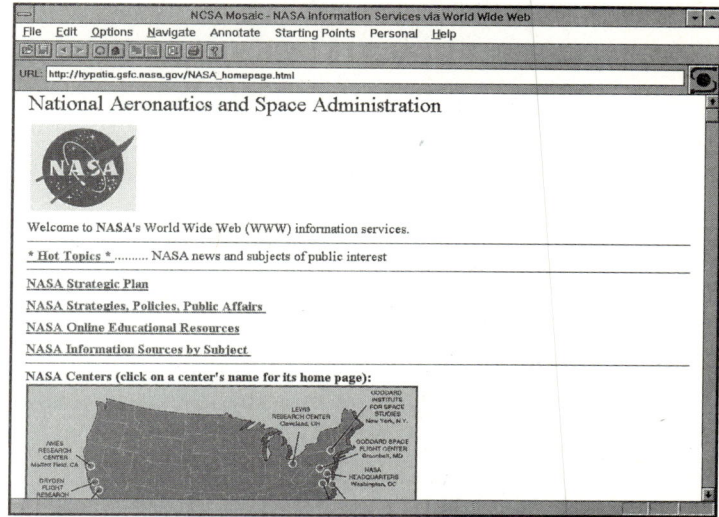

There's little difference in this window across the three computing platforms. And that, as much as anything else, demonstrates why the World Wide Web is so important to computing. Write an HTML document, and any browser on any platform can effortlessly display it. What other programs offer interchangeability of document types across this many platforms? Few at best, and fewer still when the documents become complex. True, this is a Web feature, not a Mosaic feature, but again it's something that the press has attributed to this popular program. (Become popular, it seems, and everything gets credited to you.)

The Spinning Globe

Mosaic's trademark is the spinning globe. Whenever Mosaic attempts to access a URL, the globe spins and lights travel along the arms of the icon. This means absolutely nothing for the program's functionality, but serves a surprisingly important purpose for the user. First, the globe looks sharp; it's an icon that exactly suits the purpose of the program itself, and designs that strong are hard to find even in an icon-laden world. Second, the globe tells the user that something's actually happening that Mosaic is trying to make connections. The more important information in this regard resides on the status bar, but the spinning globe offers reassurance and demonstrates activity. This is oddly significant.

All versions of Mosaic feature the spinning globe; the globes for the three versions are shown in Figure 10.4. On the X and MS Windows versions it lives in the top right corner. For the Macintosh, it's on the left. A few other cosmetic differences exist as well.

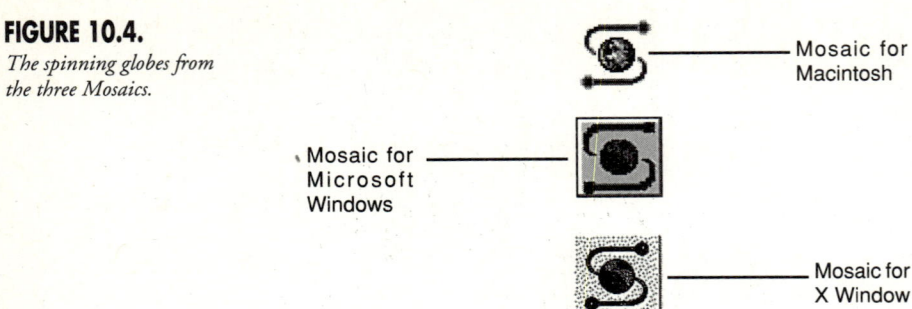

FIGURE 10.4.
The spinning globes from the three Mosaics.

Mosaic for Macintosh

Mosaic for Microsoft Windows

Mosaic for X Window

Actually, the globe serves two other functions. On all versions, clicking on the globe while it's spinning stops—or at least attempts to stop—the current activity. This doesn't always work, especially when Mosaic is engaged in activities such as FTP. And it works less well in general on the MS Windows version than the X version. But for the most part it will do as it's supposed to. The other function exists with the Mac version, in which the globe encloses different icons depending on the function it's performing, whether that function is loading a document, performing an FTP download, or something else. The icon changes each time.

The Status Bar

At the bottom of the document view window is the status bar (called the status *line* in X Mosaic). Like all status bars, its function is to display a status, and in Mosaic's case it displays two important items. When you move the cursor to a hypertext link, the status bar reveals the link's URL address. Then, when you click on the link, the status bar displays the progress of the transaction, a running count of the number of bytes being transferred, and with recent versions of Mosaic, the percentage of the download completed.

Both features are immensely useful. By noting the URL before selecting the link, you can often determine whether or not you want to make the jump. If the link is to a computer on another continent, for example, and you know it's the middle of a business day in that country, you'll know in advance that the connection will probably be slow. As a result, you might not select the link at all. Similarly, as you become experienced with Web access, you'll recognize some URLs on sight, and since you already know what's at the other end you can stop yourself from clicking.

Equally useful is the transaction and download progress indication. This indicator tells you that you're actually making progress (something the spinning globe should relay but often doesn't), and the size of the download guides your decision to keep it going or simply click on the globe and forget about it. Especially with a low-speed connection, having this information can make the difference between information gathering and simply wasting time.

The Vertical Scroll Bar

On the right side of the document view window is the vertical scroll bar. Like the vertical scroll bar in any application, it tells you that the document is larger than the screen in front of you. You use the scroll bar, of course, to access the rest of document.

This seems like a minor feature and an obvious one, but as it turns out it's quite important. Many HTML documents are extremely large, and many contain inline graphics that take up considerable downloading time. While the status bar during download lets you know that information is still loading, the scroll bar becomes the major tool for making use of the entire amount of information being presented. In fact, as you browse the Web, you'll find yourself clicking on the scroll bar every bit as often as on the links themselves.

The scroll bar also points out one design consideration for HTML page designers. There's nothing more frustrating when using Mosaic than seeing progress being made on the status bar for information that the screen doesn't show, and that you'll need to use the scroll bar to access. To an extent it's a good thing, because it shows that the information is extensive, but especially on a slower connection watching a long page or an image-laden page load is excrutiating. It's something to keep in mind, especially for pages that are specifically designed for browsing by home users.

The URL Display

Prominently featured at the top of the document view window is the URL display. This display consists of two parts, the Document Title and the Document URL, except in Mosaic for MS Windows 2.0alpha6, which to save screen space offers the Document URL only. (The size of the spinning globe is also drastically reduced in this version.) Although the URL display can be toggled off, you'll quickly find it to be among the most useful features of the software.

One of the elements of a typical HTML page is the formally designated title. This is what Mosaic displays in the Document Title box. While it's redundant for short HTML documents (the title is normally repeated as the first heading on the page; in fact, some HTML editors do this automatically), the title is extremely useful when viewing long documents. As you scroll down below the first page, the first heading disappears, and you'll often find yourself glancing at the Document Title box to refresh your memory of what document you're actually viewing. The Document Title box offers one other use: This is the title stored when you add the page to the hotlist or, in Windows Mosaic, when you add the page to a specific menu.

The Document URL box reminds you of exactly what document you've transferred to your machine. This is useful for reminder purposes, and once again for hotlisting; this is the URL that goes into the hotlist. But on recent Mosaic releases it's useful for one other thing as well: The Document URL box is editable. If you're viewing one document, and you know that URL of the next one you want to view, you can click in the URL box, type the URL, and hit the Enter key. This is especially useful for documents you're familiar with that have similar URLs to the one you're currently viewing, because rather than search for a link you can simply change the desired section of the URL address and gain access to the next document that way.

The Navigation Buttons

All versions of Mosaic have navigation buttons, although they're in a different place in each version. Mac Mosaic offers navigation arrows on the icon bar at the top of the document view window, Windows Mosaic offers similar arrows on the toolbar (again at the top), and X Mosaic features text buttons, not arrows, and places them at bottom. The function of the buttons in all versions is identical, however. The left arrow (or X's Back button) takes you to the previous page, the right arrow (or X's Forward button) takes you to the next page (that is, where you originally moved to from this page), and the house icon (or X's Home button) loads your specified "home" page.

The home page is yours to decide. At one point, NCSA released Mosaic with the home page specified as one of their own, but recent Mosaic releases have stopped this practice, and for good reason. Because Mosaic was so popular, the NCSA server quickly became severely overloaded. Every time users loaded the Mosaic program, it would launch the NCSA home page, and even though this is alterable, NCSA forgot to consider that many users, especially Windows and Macintosh users, either wouldn't bother to change either home page or wouldn't know how. (In Windows Mosaic's case, changing the default home page meant editing the `mosaic.ini` file, and people tend to be wary of doing this kind of alteration.) Now it's up to you to specify your home page, and whichever one you choose becomes the page the home button takes you to.

The arrow buttons (or X's Back and Forward buttons) seem entirely straightforward, but in fact they can be confusing. When you move from page A to page B, the back arrow returns you to page A and, then, the forward arrow to page B once again. This is fine, but it gets strangely complex, as sometimes it's not exactly clear where the forward button will actually take you. The principle is this: The back button backs you up along the path you've travelled (and it keeps in mind if you've jumped back and forth a few times, so you can easily see the same document keep reappearing), while the forward button returns you to the document that preceded the current document. Because you can jump all over the place, sometimes this system (even though it works) isn't exactly clear. This is especially true of the Windows Mosaic version, which does not cache (that is, keep in memory) documents you've loaded through the History menu; here, a click on the back arrow often lands you in a document you thought you'd discarded long ago, often by reloading it across your connection.

Loading URLs and Local Files

Clicking on hyperlinks is one method of moving from document to document, but there's another. In the File menu of every version are two items, Open URL and Open Local (Open Local File in Windows Mosaic). The first of these lets you type in the URL address of the document you wish to load. The second (see Figures 10.5, 10.6, and 10.7) lets you load a file from a local disk into Mosaic.

FIGURE 10.5.

Loading local files in X Mosaic.

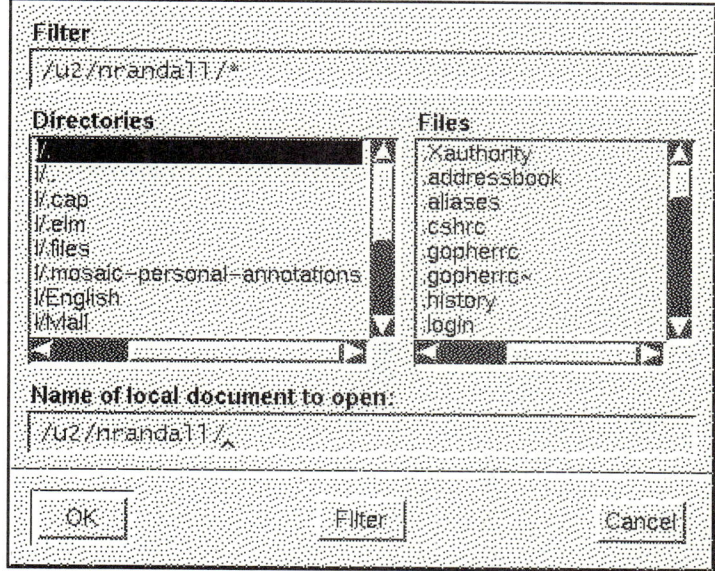

FIGURE 10.6.

Loading local files in Mac Mosaic.

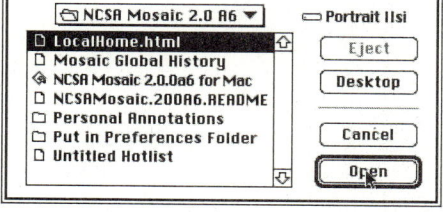

FIGURE 10.7.

Loading local files in Windows Mosaic.

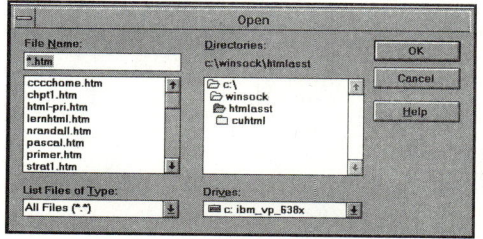

The purpose of Open URL is straightforward. Often, through mailing lists or newsgroups, you'll hear of interesting new Web sites to visit, and you'll be given the URL address in the message. Type that address into the Open URL box, and Mosaic will make the connection and load the document, exactly as if you'd clicked on a hyperlink. For some reason, this box doesn't include a Paste button, which would be extremely useful in such circumstances. Some operating systems include their own universal copy-and-paste mechanisms, but others, such as MS Windows, do not (but the next version of Windows—dubbed, for now, Chicago—will). This means that instead of just pasting the lengthy URL address into the Open URL box, you're forced to type the entire thing, an activity that can try both your patience and your belief.

If you store HTML files on your local drive, you can load them into Mosaic through the Open Local feature. This is a highly useful feature if you're writing HTML code and wish to test the appearance and functionality of a page, or when software authors provide HTML files with their software. This will undoubtedly be a more frequent occurrence as HTML catches on.

Saving Files

In the File menu of every Mosaic version is a Save As ... feature (or, for Windows Mosaic, both Save and Save As features). With this feature, you can save the currently displayed file onto your local disk in one of several formats. The difference in format points to the difference in platforms.

X Mosaic allows you to save in plain text, formatted text, PostScript, or HTML format. Mac Mosaic's options are text and HTML. Windows Mosaic offers saves in text, HTML, or binary format, but as of Windows Mosaic Version 2.0alpha6 this feature had yet to be implemented.

There are several good reasons for saving a file, but the main one is to have the information readily available without having to go out into the Net and find it every time you want to see it. This feature will become increasingly important in the future, as full documents begin to be provided over the Web, but for now the primary interest lies in capturing text files and HTML files to disk. In the case of HTML files, having long files available locally means you can load them into Mosaic instantly (through the Open Local option) without worrying about the destination connections (although the hyperlinks are still dependent on those connections). You can also use them as a basis for your own HTML files.

One warning, however, is that saving HTML documents does not save the corresponding inline graphics (which remain on the remote server). If you load the document from your local machine with inline images toggled on, Mosaic will go onto the Net to find the image files. This can take a great deal of time.

All Mosaics offer another way of saving files to disk: the Option menu's Load to Disk option (or Load to Local Disk in X Mosaic). When Load to Disk is toggled on and you click on a hyperlink, the incoming file is saved on your local disk rather than displayed in the document view window. There are several useful functions for this feature. First, if you know you want to capture a file but you don't actually need to see it, you can turn on Load to Disk and click on the link to transfer the file without losing the file currently displayed. Second, in the case of links to graphic, audio, or video files (or such items as PostScript or other special-format files), Load to Disk lets you store the file and does not activate the viewers of players that would otherwise be necessary. Third, in the case of Windows Mosaic, Load to Disk replaces the more useful Save/Save As function, which as of 2.0alpha6 has yet to be implemented.

The only problem with the Load to Disk feature is that it's a confusing name for novice users. I've spoken with several first-, second-, and even multi-time Mosaic users who have no idea what it means.

Printing

A few months ago, I got into a discussion in a Cello mailing list about Cello's and Mosaic's relative strengths for printing. The point I made at the time was that, given the nature of hypertexts, I couldn't understand why anyone would want to print from one of these programs in the first place. I seemed in the minority, however; in fact, I was shouted down quite energetically. Since I don't even have a printer hooked up to my computer (and almost never use the one on my office network), I figured I must simply be in the minority.

Given the attention by Mosaic's designers to ensuring that the print functions work, I now know this to be true. People want to print out documents page by page as they find interesting ones, and all three Mosaics allow you to do this. In all versions of the program, you can print the document as you like, with each individual version adhering to the standards of that system. Windows Mosaic offers a Page Preview option, for example, while Mac Mosaic includes the standard Mac Page Setup feature. X Mosaic allows you to print in plain text, formatted text, PostScript, or HTML format.

The argument I was given about printing Web pages is that otherwise you can't examine them in a different location or show them to others (at a meeting, for example). This, of course, is very true. But I maintain that, in general, printing a Web page is counterproductive to what that page is trying to accomplish, first because it eliminates the hypertextual concept of the Web environment, and second because it's extremely rare that one or even a series of a dozen pages can convey the flavor of what Web access is truly like.

Printing does make sense for pages that are primarily text, and hence are less likely to be read as you browse past.

I don't expect this argument to diminish, by the way.

For this reason, the designers of Mosaic offer a toggle switch that lets you turn off the loading of inline graphics. X Mosaic stores this switch in its Options menu and calls it Delay Image Loading. Mac Mosaic's version of this command is also in the Options menu and is named Auto-Load Images. Windows Mosaic's, in the same menu as the others, is called Display Inline Images. When Mosaic loads, it has these features on by default; by changing the configuration files you can specify that you want it to load with the toggle off.

This is an extremely useful switch, especially given the tendency of recent HTML documents to use multiple graphics images. Unfortunately, two of the three Mosaics muddy the waters a bit by making the resulting page extremely uninviting. While Mac Mosaic replaces the images with an attractive standard icon, X Mosaic and Windows Mosaic replace them with a gray Mosaic symbol and the tiny word "Image." It's quite ugly, and it should be replaced, even by a camera icon or something similar.

If you enter a page with inline images off, and you wish to display the same page complete with images, you can toggle inline images on and use the Reload command from any of the three versions. (See the next section for details.) Unless you want to see *all* the images, however, this isn't necessary. Often you need to check out only one or two, in which case Mosaic offers a solution. In X Mosaic and Windows Mosaic, moving the cursor over the image symbol and clicking the right mouse button (far left for X systems) commands Mosaic to load that specific image file. Mac Mosaic users accomplish the same thing by moving the cursor over the icon and simply clicking with the mouse's only button. Although this feature isn't immediately apparent when you start using Mosaic, it's a highly useful one to know as you make your way across the Web.

Reloading Documents

All versions of Mosaic offer the possibility of reloading the current document. Called Reload Current in X Mosaic's File menu, Reload in Windows Mosaic's Navigate menu, and Reload in Mac Mosaic's File menu, this feature does the same thing as if you've clicked on a hyperlink featuring your current location. Each version also sports an icon in its toolbar or icon bar that lets you accomplish the same thing.

There are two reasons to reload a document. First, if you've been using Mosaic without automatically loading inline images and you discover you want to see your current document's images, you can toggle the image feature on and then reload the document, thereby revealing the images. Second, if the Mosaic browser has somehow garbled the current document (not surprisingly, this isn't all that uncommon with Windows Mosaic), reloading will restore its appearance. Third, if you're creating your own HTML files, reloading the image lets you see the effects of the changes you're making as you go along. Some HTML editors do this for you, but if you're creating images using a text editor (such as UNIX's vi or Pico, or MS Windows' Notepad), using Reload is obviously much faster than using the Load Local File option all the time.

Loading the Home URL

The home URL is the URL address you specify using Mosaic's configuration tools or by editing the configuration files. Once it's specified, you can move immediately to that URL address by clicking on the Home button in X Mosaic or the Home icon in Mac Mosaic and Windows Mosaic, or by selecting the Home command from the Navigate menu of all three Mosaics. Click once, and you're home (and you thought Dorothy and Toto had it easy).

This command seems almost pointless at first, but in fact it comes in handy quite often. After working your way around the Web for a while, you'll almost certainly find yourself reading pages you had no intention of reading, with no real idea of where you might be (nor do you necessarily care). If your home page is a useful one, and you should make sure that it is, a jumping-off point to a host of other sites, getting back there with one click can save you the time it would take to type the URL address in the Open URL dialog, or even to fire up the History list or Hotlist and find it from there. It's an obvious feature, but a good one.

Configuring Fonts

Although HTML itself controls much of how a document appears when loaded into your browser, Mosaic lets you customize at least one significant feature: fonts. In all versions, you can specify the font that will display for each heading level, and menus, directories, and other document items that Mosaic displays. These items are set in place by the author of the HTML document, but how each is actually displayed is up to you with this customizable Mosaic feature. All versions contain the Fonts feature in their Options menu.

X Mosaic's font configuration system is the least involved of the lot, offering a choice of three varieties of four different fonts. Mac Mosaic's system is the most intricate, with a full dialog box containing several strong options. Windows Mosaic's font system exists entirely through one cascaded menu, each option of which yields a separate font dialog box. The different font configuration systems are covered under their respective versions in the corresponding section later in this chapter.

Being able to configure fonts is as important for Mosaic as it is for any other program, and more important than for many. Much of Mosaic's power—the World Wide Web's power, actually—resides in the usefulness and attactiveness of document appearance, and tailoring this appearance precisely to your liking means that the Web succeeds even more than it was designed to do. For easy reading and browsing, and for showing the Web to other users, font configuration makes a great deal of difference.

The History File

All versions of Mosaic assist you in returning to a document you've previously visited during the current session. Called the History list in Mac Mosaic and Windows Mosaic and Window history in X Mosaic, this feature keeps track of where you've been on your Web travels. By calling it up, you can return to any of these places by clicking on the document you wish to revisit.

Actually, it's not quite as simple as that. Mosaic's history feature works well, and is essential if you do any amount of browsing and returning during your Web sessions, but it's not quite as straightforward as it seems. Each browser has its own logic for which document references it stores, to the degree that switching from version to version (as many people do) can be fairly confusing. This feature isn't even in the same place in all versions: It's in X Mosaic's and Windows Mosaic's Navigate menu, but it's part of the icon/URL area, as a pull-down window, in Mac Mosaic. Furthermore, X Mosaic offers not just one but two forms of document history. The standard one, Window History, displays the URLs visited during the current Mosaic session, but the Global History feature keeps track of all URLs you've ever visited, in all the time you've used Mosaic either currently or in the past.

The history feature is more fully explored in the section below on the individual versions of Mosaic.

The Hotlist

Navigating the Web productively means keeping track of where you've been, so that you can return to the most important (or most desired) documents you've visited. In computer terminology, such a process is known as *bookmarking*, but Mosaic doesn't use this term, even though other browsers (Cello, for instance) and other Internet programs or program types (Gopher, for example) do so very usefully. But Mosaic is nothing if not individualistic, and it refers to its bookmarking item as the hotlist.

When you add a document to Mosaic's hotlist, you're recording that document's URL address and title so that you can easily access it again. Every version of Mosaic treats the hotlist concept entirely differently, and each of the individual sections below will deal with hotlisting in greater detail. Windows Mosaic, for instance, actually has two bookmarking features. One is the hotlist, which is accessible from the Open URL command of the File menu, and another, far more powerful, is this version's exceptional Menu Editor, accessible from the Navigate menu.

It is impossible to overestimate the importance of bookmarking to any Internet browsing tool. Similarly, it is impossible to overstate how much a well-designed bookmarking system adds to the value of a browsing program, and to the use of the Web in general. Mosaic's hotlisting is strong, but with the possible exception of Windows Mosaic's menu editor system, it could be better.

Annotating Documents

Not only is bookmarking important, so is the ability to comment on sites you've visited. For your own browsing, and to help or guide the browsing of others on your network, noting a document's significant content or features saves hours of cumulative time going over the same ground again and again. Wasting unnecessary time this way is one of the Web's very real dangers.

Mosaic solves the problem by letting you annotate any document you're currently visiting. By annotating, you essentially attach a sticky note to the document, so that when you return to the document, or another person on the network visits the site, this sticky note calls out "Read me first." Once again, each version of Mosaic handles the feature differently, and all are dealt with in the individual sections below. To date, in addition, only the X Window and Macintosh versions allow both text and audio annotations (the MS Windows version will surely follow, even though annotation is far weaker in this version than the others so far), and only the X Mosaic version lets you use HTML formatting to make the annotations more noticeable.

An extremely important feature, annotations must become more powerful if they are to realize their full capability, especially across a workgroup.

Caching Documents

Because Web pages are loaded from a remote computer, not your own, they can often take a fairly long time to load. That's because retrieving them depends on so many factors: the speed of your connection, the status of the remote machine and its network (other network activities take priority over you trying to download a page), and if you're working from LAN connection, the status of your own network as well. For modem users, retrieving a Web page is never as fast as you'd like, but even with high-speed connections it can become tedious.

The problem comes when you're working with several Web documents, and you keep returning to one or two of them repeatedly. The last thing you want to have happen every time you want to access a document is for Mosaic to head out into the Net, find the document, make the connection with the remote server, and download the page. Fortunately, the program offers a feature called document caching, designed precisely to avoid this problem. Mosaic keeps the last few documents (you can specify how many, or at least how many bytes) in your local system's memory, reloading them instantly when you request them via the history list, the navigation buttons, or a hyperlink. Essentially, Mosaic checks locally for the existence of a document before sending the HTTP request out to the network.

This feature is not only useful, it's indispensable. In the case of X Mosaic and Mac Mosaic, you can run multiple windows of the program, meaning that you can keep one window with a base document while you browse with the other, but even here the caching system is useful. You don't want separate windows for all frequently accessed documents (things would get extremely cluttered extremely quickly), and caching prevents this from being necessary. Windows Mosaic, as of 2.0alpha6, does not support multiple windows, so caching is simply a necessity if you're going to get anything done at all.

Note that while inline graphics are cached, sound and video files are not, so if you return to a page to access one of these, you'll have to go through the long download all over again.

World Wide Web Starting Points

The Web is a big place, and getting bigger by the hour. As a result, it's impossible for new Web users to figure out where to begin. Mosaic solves this problem by including a collection of useful and popular Web sites (the two aren't necessarily one and the same) that serve as starting points. By the time you've worked your way through even a few of these sites, you'll have both a sense of where you want to be and a hotlist file to take you back to the most interesting spots.

The starting points appear differently in the three versions. In X Mosaic and Mac Mosaic, they're in the Navigate menu, while Windows Mosaic ships with two menus, Starting Points and Personal, both of which feature various sites. The menu items for X Mosaic are Internet Starting Points (a collection of interesting sites) and Internet Resources Meta-Index (a series of Web-based directories and indexes). In Mac Mosaic, these are called Network Starting Points and Internet Resources Meta-Index. Windows Mosaic's much different version of this idea includes two separate top-level menus with all these sites, including important Gopher, FTP, and search sites as well.

It's hard to imagine getting started on the Web without these sites, and some of them you'll use repeatedly no matter how long you've been at it. But it's also hard to imagine users sticking with these and not developing a much more useful hotlist instead.

Help

Mosaic is easy to use. So easy, in fact, that there seems absolutely no reason to have complete documentation for the program. For many users, in fact, the documentation will never be necessary, because everything they need to know is included in one basic instruction: "click on the links." Still, as with just about any program, there's more to Mosaic than just clicking on the links—as this chapter should, by now, have demonstrated. And

Reload Images

When you reload a document (see Reload Current), the inline images are taken from the document cache, not reloaded from source. Sometimes, however, you need to load new versions of the image, in which case select the Reload Images command. This will flush out the cached images and cause a full reload from the server, including all images.

Refresh Current

If something goes wrong with your document's appearance, Refresh Current redisplays it with the original data intact. It doesn't actually reload the document, but rather recaptures the code that resides in memory.

Find in Current...

Particularly in long Web documents, it's handy to be able to search for specific strings of text. This command enables you to do so. This is a perfunctory search mechanism only, with options for a duplicate search but little else. (See Figure 10.9.) In the case of extremely long documents with complex search needs, it's not highly useful.

FIGURE 10.9.

X Mosaic's Find in Current dialog box.

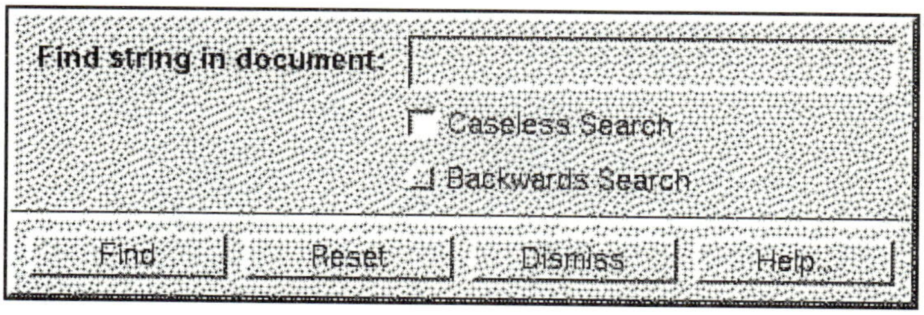

View Source...

This command opens a separate window that displays the source code for the currently displayed file. When you invoke this command, the document you see will contain HTML coding features, letting you see how the document was actually constructed. It's immensely useful if you're developing your own HTML documents, because good ideas can be imitated.

Save As...

When you wish to save the currently displayed document as a file to your local disk, this is the feature to use. You'll be shown an X Window dialog box that lets you select the directory and enter the filename, and you can save the document in one of four formats: HTML, PostScript, or plain or formatted text. This feature is more convenient than Load to Local Disk.

Print...

This command yields the Print Document window (Figure 10.10), with which you can print the displayed file to the printer you choose. As with Save As, you can print in plain text, formatted text, PostScript, or HTML format.

FIGURE 10.10.

X Mosaic's Print dialog box.

| Print Command: | lpr |
| Format for printed document: | Plain Text |

Print   Dismiss   Help

Mail To...

If you find a file you think another user would like to see (or should see whether they'd like to or not), the Mail To command lets you e-mail the file to that user. A rudimentary e-mail window opens (see Figure 10.11), letting you enter the user's e-mail address and, if you wish, a subject line. The file can be sent in one of the four usual formats: PostScript, HTML, formatted or plain text.

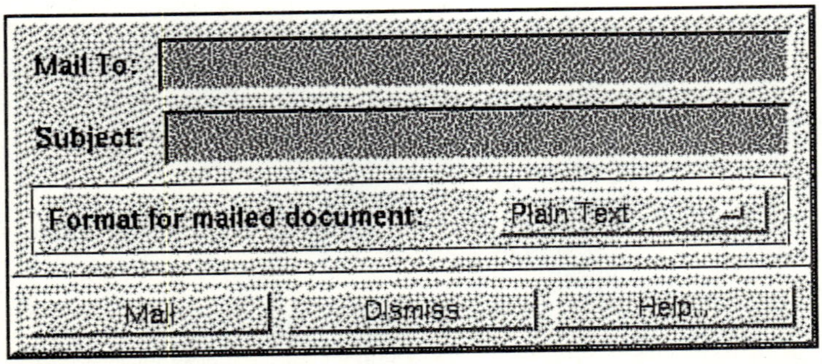

FIGURE 10.11.

X Mosaic's Mail To dialog box.

Mail To:	
Subject:	
Format for mailed document:	Plain Text

Mail   Dismiss   Help

Open DTM Outport...

NCSA Collage is a workgroup-based collaboration program, and this command directly links X Mosaic to XCollage. With the resulting window you specify the necessary port information for sending the document to Collage sessions currently active. Once the port is set, you use the Broadcast Over DTM command to send it to the workgroup.

Broadcast Over DTM

See the Open DTM Outport command, preceding section.

Close Window

With the New Window and Clone Window commands, your X Mosaic session can quickly become next to unwieldy. Close Window lets you get rid of the currently displayed document, leaving the others open. If only one document is loaded when you select Close Window, X Mosaic shuts down without asking your permission; to be used carefully.

Exit Program

After you confirm that you really want to do this, X Mosaic closes all windows and removes itself from memory.

Options Menu

Fancy Selections

X Mosaic lets you cut and paste material from document to document (and to documents in other programs). Fancy selections—surely one of computerdom's more ambiguous and initially meaningless command names—maintains the formatting of the selected text in order to duplicate its appearance as much as possible in the destination document. With this command toggled off, only the text itself is copied.

Load To Local Disk

With this command toggled on, you're presented with a Save Binary File dialog box whenever you click on a hyperlink or access the navigation buttons. This is useful for downloading files such as graphics, sound, and video, which have a separate hyperlink for the FTP function. For capturing the HTML document itself, use Save As instead.

Delay Image Loading

This toggle switch lets you turn off the automatic loading of inline images. It's especially useful for users with modem connections, to avoid long transfer times, but it's also useful if you're looking for information around the Web and don't care about the graphics you might be presented with. A vital feature.

Load Images in Current

Often, when you've turned inline images off, you'll come across a document whose graphics are crucial to its comprehension. If such a document appears, rather than turning on images and reloading the document, select Load Images in Current, which keeps the existing document in memory but accesses the server to transfer all the inline images.

Reload Config Files

This command causes all configuration items to be reloaded, so that X Mosaic is fully aware of all associations and extensions. It's also useful if you alter a file association or other viewer/player information, so you don't have to exit Mosaic and then reload.

Flush Image Cache

Inline images are cached in memory to save retrieval time if you reselect the document in which they originally appeared. They can be large files, however, and you'll quickly accumulate many of them in memory. Flush Image Cache clears this memory for other purposes.

Clear Global History...

X Mosaic maintains a list of all Web documents you've visited, not just in the current session but throughout your entire browsing career. This information is kept in a file called `.mosaic-global-history`, a dot (hidden) file in your home directory. Whenever you retrieve a document, X Mosaic checks this file to see if you've been there before, and from this check it determines whether the links on the retrieved page are shown as previously viewed or still unviewed. Clearing this lets you start over, although bear in mind that it also clears the current session's history as well.

Fonts

This command lets you choose which of three fonts you want to use to view documents (Times, Helvetica, New Century, or Lucida Bright), and the size and style of these fonts as well. Note that these fonts apply to all heading levels.

Anchor Underlines

With this command, you choose the way a hyperlink is underlined. Your choices are default underlines, no underlines, or light, medium, or heavy underlines. With no underlines, the color of the hyperlink is the only way of knowing one exists, so this selection is not recommended for monochrome displays.

Navigate Menu

Back

This command takes you back to the document that appears immediately before the current document in the Window History. Usually it's where you were last, but not always, and especially not when you used the History Window to access the current document.

Forward

Forward takes you to the document that preceded the current one. It differs from Back in that it doesn't use the Window History as its basis, so you can use it to toggle back and forth from one document to another over and over again; confusingly named.

Home Document

This command retrieves the document specified in your configuration file as your "home" document and loads it into Mosaic. Convenient for finding your way out of a hopeless nagivation maze.

Window History...

This important command yields the Window History window, which displays the title of every document you've viewed in your current X Mosaic session. From here you can return instantly to any document in the list, without having to backtrack using the navigation buttons.

Hotlist...

By invoking the Hotlist command, you bring up the Hotlist View window (see Figure 10.12), which shows the documents you've bookmarked to this point. Click on the document you want to retrieve, then on Go To, and Mosaic will connect with the remote server and perform the download. From this window you can also add new documents, or delete documents you no longer want bookmarked.

FIGURE 10.12.

X Mosaic's Hotlist dialog box.

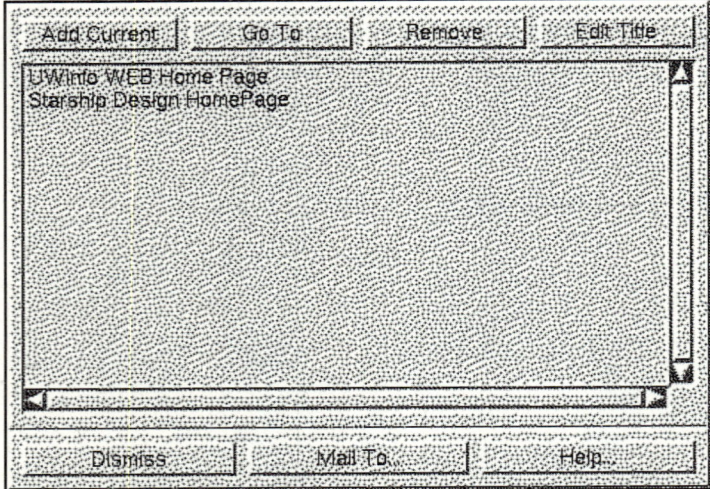

Add Current to Hotlist

When you arrive at a document you wish to bookmark, selecting this command adds the document to your hotlist. From then on, you can access the document using the Hotlist View window.

Internet Starting Points

This command is actually a bookmark; invoking it retrieves an NCSA-prepared document called Internet Starting Points, which offers hyperlinks to a rich variety of information pages throughout the Internet.

Internet Resources Meta-Index

Like Internet Starting Points, this command is a link to a bookmarked page. It retrieves an NCSA-prepared document with hyperlinks to a variety of indexes, directories, and collections of information on the Net.

Annotate Menu

Annotate...

When you want to make comments about a document you've retrieved, for the sake of your future browsing or the browsing of colleagues, the Annotate command lets you do so. (See Figure 10.13.) You enter the comments in the Annotate window that results from selecting this command, and X Mosaic adds a hyperlink on the current page that, when clicked, reveals the comments. You can add as many annotations as you wish. Note that you can type in your annotation and/or include an existing file for yourself or colleagues to read. The Commit button sets the annotation in place.

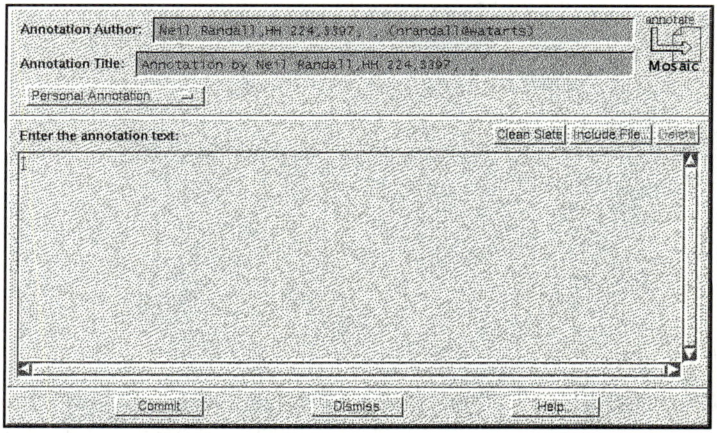

FIGURE 10.13.

X Mosaic's Annotate dialog box.

Edit This Annotation...

When reading an annotation, this command lets you alter the annotation by adding additional text to it or appending a file to it.

Delete This Annotation...

Rather obviously, this command deletes the currently visible annotation.

Help Menu

About...

Here you find standard About material, including version number, resource hyperlinks, developer information, and so forth.

Manual...

This command retrieves the online X Mosaic user manual from the NCSA server.

What's New...

Invoking the What's New command retrieves NCSA's famous What's New With NCSA Mosaic and the WWW page, a regularly (weekly or even daily) updated page showing new resources for Web users. Why it's here and not in the Navigate menu with the other NCSA pages is anyone's guess.

Demo...

This command retrieves the NCSA Mosaic Demo Document, with hyperlinks to a variety of different types of pages, including audio and video demonstrations. As with What's New, it belongs in the Navigate menu, but for some reason isn't.

On Version 2.4...

This tells you which version of X Mosaic you're using (2.4, in this case), and retrieves a file from NCSA that lists changes from previous editions and explains when the next version is scheduled for release.

On Window...

An actual Help screen, On Window gives you information about hotkey commands, menu items, and the parts of X Mosaic's screen.

On FAQ...

This command yields a document offering hyperlinks to Frequently Asked Questions about X Mosaic. If you're having a problem with the program, someone else has probably had it already, and the solution might well be found here.

On HTML...

From here you retrieve a series of Web documents outlining the Hypertext Markup Language (with which Web pages are constructed), with links to tutorials, examples, and other HTML reference documents.

On URLs...

On URLs opens a hyperdocument dealing with Uniform Resource Locators, how they work and what they mean.

Mail Developers

This command opens a rudimentary e-mail window designed exclusively for sending comments, problems, complaints, bribes, and threats to X Mosaic's developers. It automatically includes your e-mail address (as long as you've set it up in the configuration file), and clicking on Send transmits the message. Don't expect a personal response, though; your comments will be logged, but you'll get something along the lines of, "Dear Occupant, we appreciate your ...." How deep the appreciation actually runs is unclear.

NCSA Mosaic for the Apple Macintosh: Features and Menus

FTP Site:	`ftp.ncsa.uiuc.edu`
Directory:	`/Mac/Mosaic`
Filenames:	`NCSAMosaicMac.103.sit.hqx` (Version 1.03)
	`NCSAMosaic200A6.68k.hqx`
	`NCSAMosaic200A6.PPC.hqx` (Power Macintosh)

Mosaic for the Macintosh was released second to X Mosaic, and its developers have spent a great deal of time developing the program to take advantage of the Mac's strengths and idiosyncrasies. Mac Mosaic's unique features include:

- An extensive hotlist editing dialog
- Audio annotations (with X Mosaic)
- The ability to display external graphics as inline graphics
- An easily accessible document history (from the icon bar)
- An extensive and highly usable Preferences configuration box
- An extremely usable (and powerful) Styles dialog box

File Menu

New Window

If you want to keep your current document open as a base, and start browsing from a new Mac Mosaic window, select New Window. Your default home page will be loaded into the new window, and you can go from there. You can open as many new Mosaic windows as you want, although beware of clutter.

Clone Window

This is the same as New Window, except instead of loading your home page, Mosaic creates a new window that contains the same document as the one you were looking at when you selected the option. Very useful for working through a series of linked documents that you need to refer back to.

Open URL...

This command opens a dialog box in which you enter the full URL address of the document or site you want loaded. (See Figure 10.14.) Keep in mind that you must start the URL with the protocol type, which will often be `http://` but might also be `gopher://`, `ftp://`, or any other valid URL address. The important thing is that you enter the *complete* address, or you'll find yourself redoing it until you get it right.

FIGURE 10.14.

Mac Mosaic's Open URL dialog box.

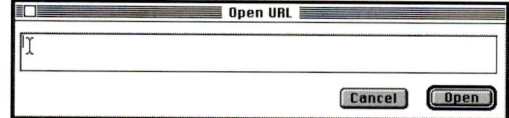

Open Local ...

This command lets you load a file from your local hard disk (or local network disk) into Mosaic. The command presents you with a standard Macintosh dialog box, from which you select the directory and file you wish to load.

Reload Current

Reload Current retrieves the current file from its remote (or local) server, and it's used either to display any changes you've made to the HTML code since you originally loaded it, or to display inline images if you had them toggled off for the original retrieval. One thing to keep in mind is that images, if they were originally loaded, are not loaded again. (They're grabbed from the image cache.)

Close Window

With the New Window and Clone Window commands, your Mac Mosaic session can quickly become unwieldy. Close Window lets you get rid of the currently displayed document, leaving the others open.

Save As...

When you wish to save the currently displayed document as a file to your local disk, use this feature. You'll be shown a Macintosh dialog box that lets you select the directory and enter the filename, and you can save the document in either text or HTML format. (See Figure 10.15.)

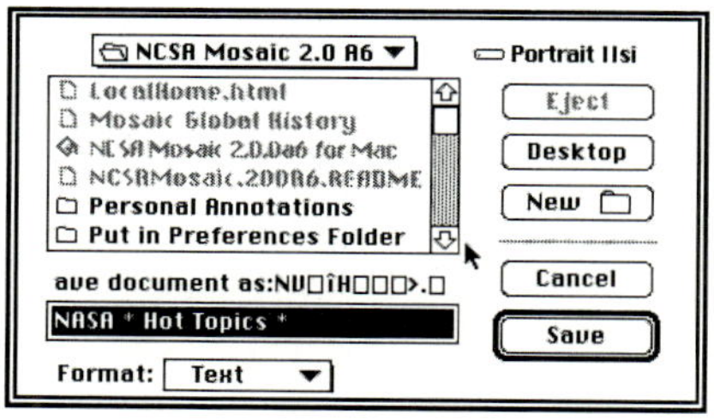

FIGURE 10.15.

Mac Mosaic's Save As dialog box.

Page Setup...

This command brings up the standard Macintosh page setup dialog, from which you can specify the format of the pages as you want them printed.

Print

From this command, you can print the Mac Mosaic document you're currently reading. It will appear on paper as it appears on-screen, tailored by your specifications in the Page Setup command.

Mail Developers

This command opens a rudimentary e-mail window designed exclusively for sending comments, problems, complaints, bribes, and threats to Mac Mosaic's developers. It automatically includes your e-mail address (as long as you've set it up in the configuration file), and clicking on Send transmits the message. Don't expect a personal response, though; your comments will be logged, but you'll get something along the lines of, "Dear Occupant, we appreciate your ...." How deep the appreciation actually runs is unclear.

Quit

Invoke this command to exit Mac Mosaic (okay, so it's obvious).

Edit Menu

Can't Undo/Undo

This is the standard Macintosh command for taking back your last action. If it's dimmed and says Can't Undo, then you can't take the last action back.

Cut

This command lets you cut text from various dialog boxes, such as Annotations. You can't cut text from a Mosaic document itself.

Copy

When you select a block of text with the mouse, you can use this command to copy the text into the Mac's clipboard. Keep in mind, however, that only text is copied. Inlined images are not.

Paste

This is the Mac's standard Paste command, useful in dialog boxes and text fields. You can't paste text into a Mosaic document on-screen.

Clear

This command deletes the text you've currently selected, but it does not modify text in a document in the document view window.

Find...

Choosing the Find command brings up Mac Mosaic's Find window (Figure 10.16), which offers the ability to search for case sensitive text, to search backwards from the current position, and to perform a wraparound search to include the entire Mosaic document.

FIGURE 10.16.

Mac Mosaic's Find dialog box.

Find Again

Once you've initiated a search, Find Again locates the next occurrence of the most recently specified text string.

Show Clipboard

This command, not surprisingly, yields a window that displays the current contents of the Mac's clipboard.

Options Menu

Hide URLs/Show URLs

With this item you can toggle the URL display on and off. The main reason for wanting to do this is to maximize the screen space devoted to the Mosaic document itself, especially important for smaller monitors.

Hide/Show Status Messages

This command toggles the status message area on and off. Again, the main reason is to save display space and processor usage.

Load to Disk

When you find a graphic, sound, or video file within a document (you can tell by the file extension of the file when you move the cursor over it), or when you want to download an HTML, text, or other type of file to your hard disk, toggle on Load to Disk and then click the hyperlink. You'll be presented with a File Save dialog box, at which point you can specify directory and file name. The document will *not* load into Mosaic's main window.

Auto-Load Images

This command toggles automatic loading of inline images on and off. With slow connections (such as modems of any speed), it's a good idea to turn this off by default, toggling it on only when you find a page where the images actually matter.

Use Temp Items

This (somewhat confusingly named) command lets you specify how to store temporary files, which Mac Mosaic uses quite extensively. If Use Temp Items is not toggled on, these files are stored in the system folder (and deleted when Mac Mosaic exits). When checked, the feature stores temporary files in whatever folder you specify.

Remove Temp Items

This command deletes all temporary files, no matter where you've stored them with the Use Temp Items command.

Flush Cache

Mac Mosaic stores document and image information in a memory cache. This command clears out the cache, releasing that memory to the system. During long sessions and with limited RAM, use of this command is highly important.

Preferences...

This is an extremely important command, as it allows you to set the configuration for your Mac Mosaic program. From the resulting dialog box (Figure 10.17) you can specify the default home page, your name, your e-mail address, the colors of the hyperlinks and an underlining style for them, the Temp directory (see Use Temp Items above), and details about the local newsgroup server and a WAIS gateway (used for WAIS searches). From here you also configure the external viewers used by Mac Mosaic to automatically play sound and video files and display documents with specific formats (such as PostScript files). Be sure to spend time learning your way around this dialog.

FIGURE 10.17.

Mac Mosaic's elaborate Preference dialog box.

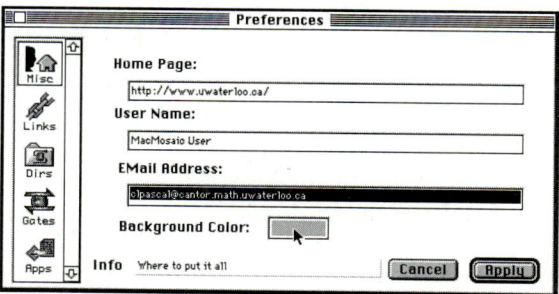

Styles...

This command yields the Styles dialog box, as shown in Figure 10.18. Fairly complex, this box lets you set the appearance of the documents that load into Mac Mosaic's main window, letting you specify a different font and style for each heading and formatting type. You can also control the global appearance of styles from this box. As with Preferences (above), this dialog helps you customize Mac Mosaic to your liking.

FIGURE 10.18.

The Mac Mosaic Styles dialog box.

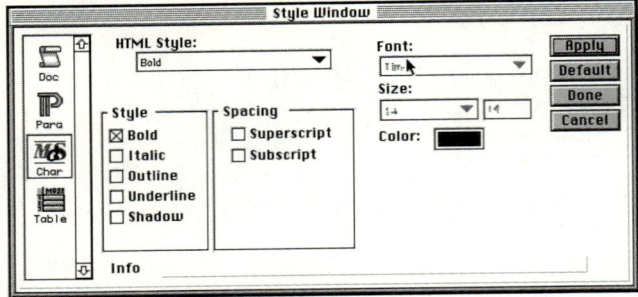

Navigate Menu

Back

Choosing this command takes you back to the previous document. Hardly surprising.

Forward

This command takes you to the next document in the history list.

Home

This command retrieves the document specified in your configuration file as your "home" document and loads it into Mac Mosaic. Convenient for finding your way out of a hopeless navigation maze.

Network Starting Points

This command is actually a bookmark: Invoking it retrieves an NCSA-prepared document called Internet Starting Points, which offers hyperlinks to a rich variety of information pages throughout the Internet.

Internet Resources Meta-Index

Like Internet Starting Points, this command is a link to a bookmarked page. It retrieves an NCSA-prepared document with hyperlinks to a variety of indexes, directories, and collections of information on the Net.

NCSA Demo Page

This command retrieves the NCSA Mosaic Demo Document, with hyperlinks to a variety of different types of pages, including audio and video demonstrations.

NCSA What's New Page

Invoking the What's New command retrieves NCSA's famous What's New With NCSA Mosaic and the WWW page, a regularly (weekly or even daily) updated page showing new resources for Web users.

Mac Mosaic Home Page

This command takes you to NCSA's main page for the Macintosh version of Mosaic.

Mac Mosaic Features

With this command you retrieve an NCSA-prepared page listing the features and known bugs in the current version of Mac Mosaic.

Annotate Menu

Text...

When you want to make comments about a document you've retrieved, for the sake of your future browsing or the browsing of colleagues, the Annotate command lets you do so. You enter the comments in the Annotate window that results from selecting this command, and Mac Mosaic adds a hyperlink on the current page that, when clicked, reveals the comments. You can add as many annotations as you wish. Note that you can type in your annotation and/or include an existing file for yourself or colleagues to read. The Commit button sets the annotation in place.

Audio...

If your machine is equipped with sound recording equipment, you can record an audio annotation using this command. As with Annotate, Mac Mosaic will show the annotation as a hyperlink on the current page. (See Figure 10.19.)

FIGURE 10.19.
*Mac Mosaic's Audio
Annotate dialog box.*

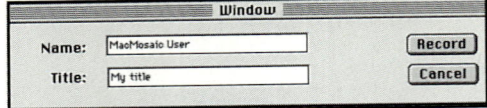

Edit Annotation

When reading an annotation, this command lets you alter the annotation by adding additional text to it or appending a file to it.

Delete Annotation

Rather obviously, this command deletes the currently visible annotation.

Hotlist

Hotlist Interface

Mac Mosaic's Hotlist Interface menu is a hierarchical menu that lets you bookmark documents you want to revisit in the future. From this menu you can create a new hotlist or open an existing one, save the current hotlist, or edit your hotlists. The Edit subcommand brings up the Hotlist dialog box (Figure 10.20), which enables you to delete and rename menu items, or give them new URL addresses.

FIGURE 10.20.
*Mac Mosaic's Hotlist
dialog box.*

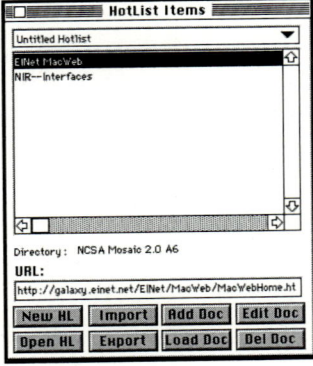

Add This Document

This command adds the currently displayed document title to the hotlist menu itself, making it readily available from that menu.

Balloon Help Menu

About Balloon Help

Here you get typical Macintosh information about Balloon Help.

Show Balloons

Obviously, this command lets you toggle balloon help, but since Mac Mosaic doesn't offer balloon help messages there's not much point.

Mac Mosaic Documentation

This is a hotlist item to NCSA's on-line documentation about Mac Mosaic.

HTML Help

From here you retrieve a series of Web documents outlining the HyperText Markup Language (with which Web pages are constructed), with links to tutorials, examples, and other HTML reference documents.

URL Help

On URLs opens a hyperdocument dealing with Uniform Resource Locators, how they work and what they mean.

FAQ

This command yields a document offering hyperlinks to Frequently Asked Questions about Mac Mosaic. If you're having a problem with the program, someone else has probably had it already, and the solution might well be found here.

NCSA Mosaic for Microsoft Windows

FTP Site:	`ftp.ncsa.uiuc.edu`
Directory:	`/PC/Windows/Mosaic`
Filenames:	`wmos20A6.zip` (most Windows machines)
	`DecMosaic2A6.zip` (Windows NT on the DEC PC)

NOTE

To run versions of Win Mosaic above 2.0alpha2, you must have the Win32 extensions installed (automatic with Windows 95). These are available from the NCSA site as file `Win32.zip`, in the same directory as Mosaic itself. Mosaic for Windows is the most recent of the three releases, but it preceded the Mac Mosaic in releasing a 2.0 version that supported forms. It is an immensely popular program among Windows users with Internet access, which is almost certainly the fastest growing group. Windows Mosaic's unique features include:

- Rich Open URL dialog that offers access to all hotlists

- Full-featured menu editor that lets you create top-level menus for hotlist access

- Print Preview option to see what the document will look like on paper

- Extended FTP Parsing command for fuller FTP directory listings

File Menu

Open URL...

This command opens a dialog box (Figure 10.21) in which you enter the full URL address of the document or site you want loaded. Keep in mind that you must start the URL with the protocol type, which will often be `http://` but might also be `gopher://`, `ftp:/`, or any other valid URL address. The important thing is that you enter the *complete* address, or you'll find yourself redoing it until you get it right. In addition, this dialog box lets you select a URL from any of your hotlists, including the default Quicklist or the menus you've created using the Menu Editor in the Navigate menu. You can select by document title or URL address.

FIGURE 10.21.
*Windows Mosaic's Open
URL dialog box.*

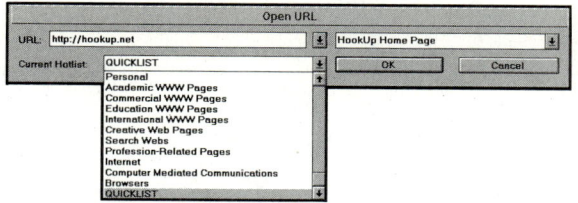

Open Local File...

This command lets you load a file from your local hard disk (or local network disk) into Mosaic. The command presents you with a standard Windows dialog box, from which you select the directory and file you wish to load.

Save

With this command you can save the currently displayed document, but as of 2.0alpha6 it had yet to be implemented.

Save As...

Similar to Save (see preceding), and as of 2.0alph6 not yet implemented.

Save Preferences

This command lets you save the position and size of the Document View window as you currently have it placed, as well as any changes you've made to Windows Mosaic's configuration in the Options menu.

Print...

With this command, you can print the current document. As with all MS Windows programs, however, what you see is not necessarily what you get. To get exactly formatted printouts you'll need to keep your font choices appropriate to your printer and your system's configuration.

Print Preview

This displays a preview of what the printed page will look like.

Print Setup...

This command simply yields the standard Windows print dialog box.

Document Source...

Document Source brings up a separate window showing the source code of the currently displayed document. If the document contains HTML formatting, all HTML codes will be displayed in full. You can save this source file to your hard drive or copy some or all of the file to the clipboard. It's extremely useful for HTML developers, who can study other people's work for inspiration and judicious borrowing.

Exit

This command removes Windows Mosaic from memory (the computer's, not yours).

Edit Menu

Copy

If you've selected text with the mouse, Copy will copy the selection to Windows' clipboard. Unlike the Copy command in X Mosaic and Mac Mosaic, this one does *not* copy text from the displayed document itself, a feature that isn't implemented as of 2.0alpha6. You can copy selections from the Document Title and URL fields (but for some reason there's no corresponding Paste command, which would be endlessly more useful), from the Document Source window, and from any other window in which you enter text manually.

Find...

This command lets you locate specified text strings within a document, and includes a Match Case option for case-sensitive searches and a Find Next command. (See Figure 10.22.) Find does not actually highlight the string in the document when it is found, so it's not quite as useful as it might be.

FIGURE 10.22.
Windows Mosaic's Find dialog box.

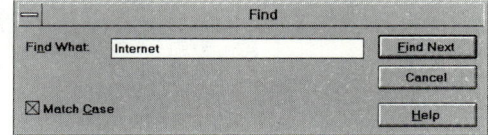

Options Menu

Load to Disk

When you find a graphic, sound, or video file within a document (you can tell by the file extension of the file when you move the cursor over it), or when you want to download an HTML, text, or other type of file to your hard disk, toggle on Load to Disk and then click the hyperlink. You'll be presented with a File Save dialog box, at which point you can specify directory and file name. Note that the document will *not* load into Mosaic's main window, and that filenames will be truncated to match DOS's 8.3 naming standard. You can, however, specify your own filename for each file loaded to disk in this way.

Show Toolbar

This command, when checked, displays Windows Mosaic's toolbar. Uncheck it if you wish to save screen space for the main document.

Show Status Bar

When unchecked, Show Status Bar hides the status bar at the bottom of Windows Mosaic's screen. Unless you're really desperate for screen space, leave it on, because it conveys extremely useful information.

Show Current URL

This command lets you show or hide the URL display. In Windows Mosaic versions preceding 2.0alpha6, this hides the document title as well.

Show Anchor URLs

When you move the cursor over a hyperlink, the destination URL appears on the status bar. This command lets you turn that feature off, presumably for slower processors.

Change Cursor Over Anchors

When you move the cursor over a hyperlink, the cursor changes to a hand with a pointing finger. This disables that feature, again for slower processors.

Extended FTP Directory Parsing

With Extended FTP Directory Parsing, Windows Mosaic displays file sizes and icons in an FTP directory, along with file and directory names. Without it, only the file and directory names are displayed; a very useful feature if you FTP frequently from within Mosaic.

Display Inline Images

This command toggles automatic loading of inline images on and off. With slow connections (such as modems of any speed), it's a good idea to turn this off by default, toggling it on only when you find a page where the images actually matter.

Show Group Annotations

With this command toggled on, Windows Mosaic will display all group annotations with the document when it loads. Otherwise, it will not.

Use 8-bit Sound

This command is necessary for users with 8-bit sound cards, such as the ubiquitous Sound Blaster; 16-bit sound board users need not worry about it.

Choose Font

The Choose Font command lets you tailor the appearance of retrieved documents to your liking. You can specify fonts for all types of headers, menus, directories, and so on. (See Figure 10.23.)

FIGURE 10.23.
Windows Mosaic's Choose Font submenu.

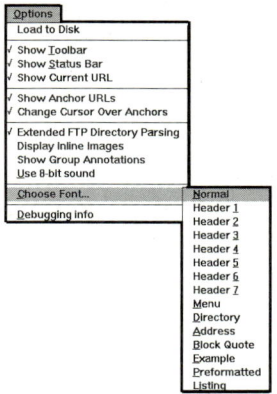

Debugging Info...

Especially useful for developers and systems administrators, Debugging Info can be toggled on to reveal information such as critical warnings, errors, and so forth.

Navigate Menu

Back

This command takes you back to the previous document, unless that document was one you selected from the History window in the Navigate menu, in which case you'll return to the last document you actually retrieved from a server.

Forward

This command moves you forward along the path of documents you originally navigated.

Reload

Windows Mosaic's Reload command reloads the current document into the Document View window. It's useful if the screen becomes garbled (hey, this *is* Windows), or if you have Display Inline Images toggled off and you come across a document whose images you'd like to see.

Home

Selecting this command takes you directly to the Home page specified as such in your `mosaic.ini` file.

History

The History command opens the NCSA Mosaic History window, from which you can jump to a document you visited during that session. Windows Mosaic does *not* maintain a global history file like X Mosaic's.

Add Current to Hotlist

This features adds the title and URL address of the currently displayed document to the current hotlist.

Menu Editor...

One of Windows Mosaic's most useful design features, the Menu Editor (Figure 10.24) lets you not only bookmark items, but place them inside menus and submenus of your choice for future access. With Menu Editor you can add top-level menus (those that appear on the menu bar), and submenus within those menus. You can also edit document titles and change the current hotlist.

FIGURE 10.24.

Windows Mosaic's extremely valuable Menu Editor.

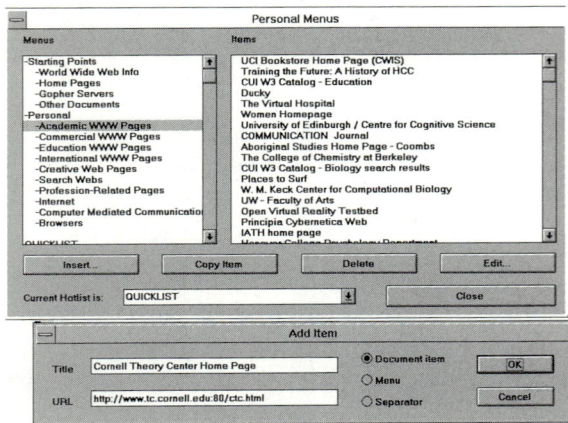

Annotate Menu

Annotate

When you want to comment on a particular document, either for your own reference or that of colleagues, selecting the Annotate command brings up a dialog box (Figure 10.25) that lets you do so. Windows Mosaic will then display the fact that an annotation exists at the bottom of the current page whenever it is accessed in future. This feature is far less useful in Windows Mosaic than in either of the others, however, and Windows Mosaic does not allow audio annotations.

FIGURE 10.25.
*Windows Mosaic's
Annotate dialog box.*

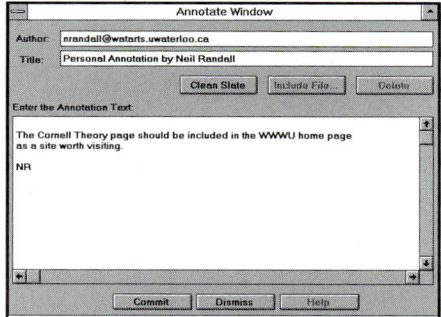

Edit This Annotations

This command yields the Annotate dialog box so you can edit the entry.

Delete This Annotation

This command deletes the selected annotation.

Starting Points Menu

Starting Points Document

This command is actually a bookmark; invoking it retrieves an NCSA-prepared document called Internet Starting Points, which offers hyperlinks to a rich variety of information pages throughout the Internet.

NCSA Mosaic Demo Document

This command retrieves the NCSA Mosaic Demo Document, with hyperlinks to a variety of different types of pages, including audio and video demonstrations.

NCSA Mosaic's What's New Page

Invoking the What's New command retrieves NCSA's famous What's New With NCSA Mosaic and the WWW page, a regularly (weekly or even daily) updated page showing new resources for Web users.

Mosaic for Microsoft Windows Home Page

This command takes you to NCSA's main page for the Windows version of Mosaic.

World Wide Web Info

This submenu contains hotlisted links to pages dealing with the World Wide Web project itself.

Home Pages

Windows Mosaic ships with a wide range of prehotlisted home pages of various institutions. This submenu gives you instant access to any of them.

Gopher Servers

From this submenu, you can access a range of useful Gophers through Windows Mosaic. Several are included.

Finger Gateway, Whois Gateway, X.500 Gateway

These commands access the various gateways specified in your `mosaic.ini` file.

Other Documents

This submenu includes a hotlist of interesting Web documents.

Archie Request Form

From this command you enter a page featuring a page that lets you conduct an Archie search over the Web.

Help Menu

Online Documentation

Selecting this command retrieves the NCSA-prepared documentation for Windows Mosaic.

FAQ Page

This command yields a document offering hyperlinks to Frequently Asked Questions about Windows Mosaic. If you're having a problem with the program, someone else has probably had it already, and the solution might well be found here.

Bug List

This command loads a document dealing with known bugs in the current version of Windows Mosaic. Quite revealing.

Feature Page

Selecting this command gives you a page of new features in the current Windows Mosaic.

Mail to Developers...

This command opens a rudimentary e-mail window designed exclusively for sending comments, problems, complaints, bribes, and threats to X Mosaic's developers. It automatically includes your e-mail address (as long as you've set it up in the configuration file), and clicking on Send transmits the message. Don't expect a personal response, though;

your comments will be logged, but you'll get something along the lines of, "Dear Occupant, we appreciate your ...." How deep the appreciation actually runs is unclear.

Summary

NCSA Mosaic is the most popular Web browser of all, and quite possibly the most popular single piece of Internet software as well. This chapter provides an introduction to Mosaic in its X Window, Apple Macintosh, and Microsoft Windows formats, and compares the strengths and weaknesses of each. Full books on Mosaic are beginning to appear, and if you want to use this software fully, including a full and specific configuration, you're advised to give one of these books a try.

Or maybe not. Mosaic is anything but a difficult program. Like all the graphical browsers, once it's up and running it's next to effortless to work with. You can easily explore the Web, create your hotlists, and download files as you wish, without ever bothering to study a help file. The important points to keep in mind are first, that Mosaic has its share of instabilities, and, second, that when Mosaic doesn't work right it could be the fault of either the program or the Web itself. Mosaic is, in fact, like every other Web browser in this respect.

Yes, Virginia, There Is a Choice: More Graphical Browsers

11

by Neil Randall

IN THIS CHAPTER

Without question, Mosaic is the most famous Web client of all. It has made headlines, it's pictured in mainstream and computer publications alike, and it has come to be something of a synonym, in the public's mind and the minds of many who should know better, for the World Wide Web itself. But equating Mosaic with the Web is more or less analogous to equating your RCA ColorTrak TV with the production and distribution of television programming. The ColorTrak is the gizmo that brings the TV show into your family room, but it has nothing to do with production and distribution. They're two entirely separate technologies, even though both Mosaic and the ColorTrak were developed specifically to display their respective technologies.

Like all analogies, of course, this one breaks down if you think about it for a few minutes. But it's the idea that's important, so let's agree to let it stand.

Mosaic is *not* the World Wide Web. It is nothing more than one of several World Wide Web client programs, better known as browsers. Mosaic simply displays Web documents, just as many other programs do. Chapter 9, "Browsing Without the Glitz: Nongraphical Web Clients," examines the text-based clients such as Lynx and the CERN line mode browser. This chapter presents a selection of graphically based browsers that are entirely independent of Mosaic, the best known of the category.

The fact that I've just spent the past couple of hundred words explaining that the Web and Mosaic shouldn't be confused with each other goes a fair ways toward describing the enormous selling job the designers of any other graphical Web browsers have on their hands.

Making them available is one thing; getting people to actually use them is another. Perhaps the most vocal battle between Mosaic and another graphical browser has been waged over the past year or so by Cello, a graphical browser that offers direct competition for Windows Mosaic, and yet despite its obvious strengths and its seemingly dedicated group of users, it has had difficulty gaining market share (well, freebie share) from the more popular program.

A new Windows entry into the mix, WinWeb (the counterpart to the Mac's earlier MacWeb) seems to be attracting the Cello crowd rather than the Mosaic crowd, and this, too, demonstrates the challenge. There are many users out there who will FTP, install, and use any Web browser that becomes available on the Net, just as there are many word processing users who will happily try any word processing package. But there are just as many of each group who want only the best-known, not even necessarily the strongest-featured, and who won't budge from their initial choice unless forced by some unlikely circumstance. The danger for browser designers is that they'll end up gaining adherents not from the installed base of Mosaic users, but rather from the users of another competing browser.

The point is that competing browsers exist, and each of them has its own specific strengths. It's important for any user of the World Wide Web to be aware of them, because while everyone concedes Mosaic's numerical superiority over all other graphical browsers combined, there's no need whatsoever to concede its technical superiority.

Even in a much smaller program, you might well discover a feature that Mosaic does not offer and that you simply can't traverse the Web without, especially after using that feature even once. Then there's the issue of desiring to avoid the mainstream, something that every critical user of anything eventually wants to do. The hype and the development dollars are all behind the Goliath; let's see what the Davids can do in the background with much less fanfare.

One thing must be said, however, before we look at the alternatives. Essentially, the Mosaics and Cellos and Sambas and Violas and MacWebs and Chimeras all do precisely the same thing: They display HTML documents inside their main viewing window, offering highlighted hyperlinks that, when you select them with your mouse, take you to another document on the Web. That's the purpose of a World Wide Web client program, and that's what these packages all accomplish. The differences among them lie in their individual sets of features. Your choice will be based on appearance, usability, intelligence of design, and incorporation of features that help you use the Web exactly as you wish. The browser you decide upon will be the browser that most closely does what you want it to do.

And one last thing: There's no reason to settle on just one browser. As long as you have room on your hard drive (these programs are relatively small, at least so far), get two or three, and try them all. That way you'll know the differences, and you will probably discover that you'll use one browser for some purposes and another for other purposes. It's simply a matter of firing up the one that will serve the purpose you have in mind at any particular moment.

NOTE

Not all available browsers are discussed in this chapter. Only two X browsers are included, for example, MidasWWW and Viola, while Chimera and tkWWW haven't been given treatment. Similarly, while Amiga Mosaic is dealt with at the end of the chapter, no browser for the NeXT system has a spot. Some of this has to do with my own familiarity with the software in question, some with the fact that not everything can be included, and not everything is in anything approaching widespread use. What are included are the most widely used of the alternative packages.

Browsers for the X Window System

World Wide Web client software for the X Window system has been under development since the inception of the Web project itself. The reason is obvious: The Web was designed as a multimedia information dissemination system for use with GUI systems, X Window was the predominant GUI for UNIX workstations, and UNIX was the essential operating system underlying the Internet itself. It only made sense, therefore, for X Window developers, especially in research institutes, where funding might be made available, and universities, which are typically flooded with UNIX hackers in the guise of both professor and student.

These are indeed the institutions Web clients have come from until very recently. Commercial versions of Mosaic, Cello, and independent browsers are now being released or are at least under development, but before now all the design and development impetus has come from the research labs. Again, this makes sense, given that the Web itself is a product of a university research group as well.

What makes the X clients so appealing is that they run on workstations that typically have large screens and high-speed access. As a result, they show a large amount of information by default, and they do so quickly. What makes them less appealing is the difficulties with installation and configuration that accompany any UNIX and X program running on a local or wide area network, difficulties that put these programs out of the reach of casual users. And, quite simply, most people don't have X stations on their desks at home, which means that the audience for these clients will always be larger organizations.

If you use X Mosaic, you owe it to yourself to check out some of the alternatives. Each has its strengths, each is aware that it must offer something different from the leader, and each tends to be under the development of people who are, if nothing else, easier to get hold of than the Mosaic team. That usually means more immediate support for problems, but it also means that you're dependent on a smaller team's (or even an individual's) sustained commitment to the project. Still, some superb offerings await.

MidasWWW

Publisher:	Stanford Linear Accelerator Center
Latest Version:	2.2
FTP site:	`freehep.scri.fsu.edu`
FTP directory:	`freehep/networking_email_news/midaswww`
FTP filename:	`midaswww-2.1.tar.z` *or* your platform-specific file from `/binaries/`

One of the ways for a program to compete with other programs is to provide enhanced features in specific areas, thereby distinguishing it from the rest. MidasWWW, developed over the past three years at the Stanford Linear Accelerator Center by Tony Johnson, offers precisely those sorts of enhanced features. This is a browser that looks sharp, works well, and demonstrates a strong commitment to user interface considerations.

Figure 11.1 shows a sample Midas screen. There's little to note here, except that all the expected Web components are in place, and especially that the screen's sculpted appearance is extremely strong. It's the kind of screen that instantly attracts, a highly important consideration for any Web browser.

FIGURE 11.1.

Midas screen showing links and inline images.

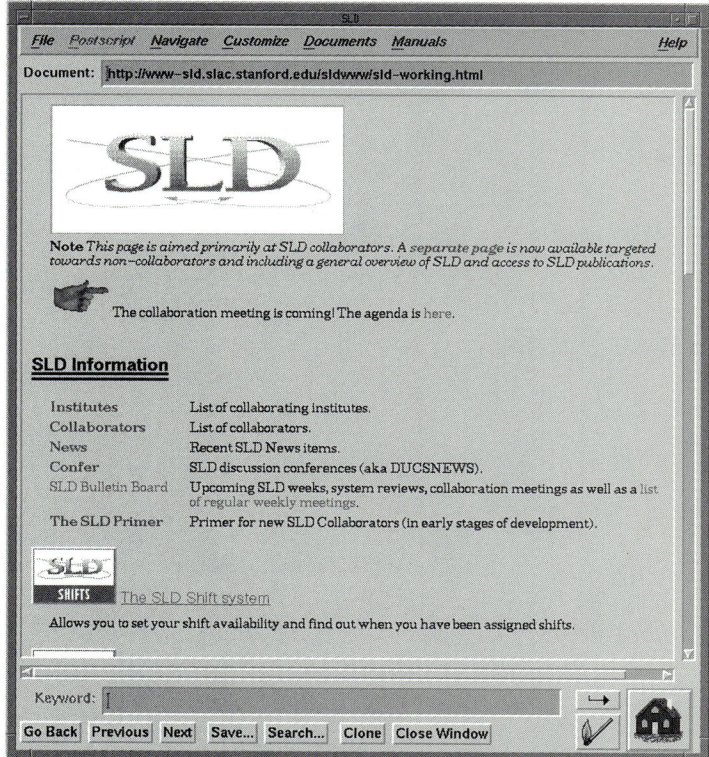

The user interface considerations show up practically everywhere. Figures 11.2 and 11.3 demonstrate Midas's ability to interact with Gopher and FTP servers. Of note in both instances are, first of all, the iconic differentiation among document or function types (notice the easy-to-understand See login messages link at the top of Figure 11.3), and, equally as important, the Open Gopher and Open FTP dialog boxes. In most Web

browsers, you enter an FTP site either as a hyperlink, or by typing in the full URL address in the Open URL dialog. Midas gives you an interface that lets you forget about the URL syntax, and the FTP dialog even includes a space for your username and password (extremely useful to change login types).

FIGURE 11.2.

Midas Gopher screen showing the Open Gopher Document dialog box.

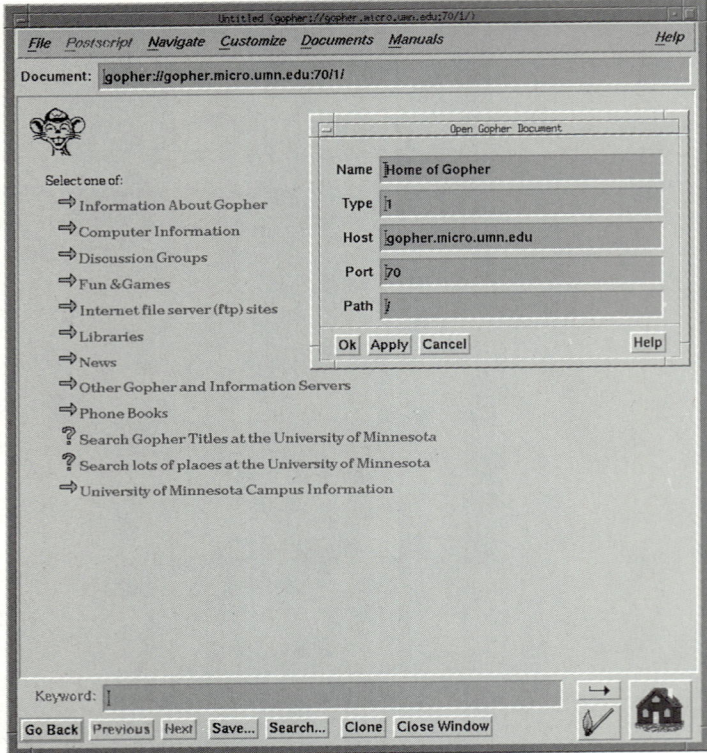

Another important interface consideration appears in Midas's configuration dialogs. Configuring Web browsers isn't fun at the best of times, but in the case of all versions of Mosaic except Mac Mosaic, it's downright painful. Midas offers a series of configuration dialogs (see Figure 11.4) that makes the whole process much simpler, and these include printer setup, default Gopher page setup, and a range of options that are easily changed, either by clicking in the appropriate box or by using the slider controls to customize times and sizes. You can easily enable or disable document caching (shown), font styles and sizes, displays of document title and URL, appearance of hyperlinks, and a range of other options without going through the tedium of editing your configuration files, a process that obviously makes everything easier. Given the importance of customizing your Web client to serve your specific needs, this is a strong feature.

FIGURE 11.3.
Midas FTP screen showing Open FTP Document dialog box.

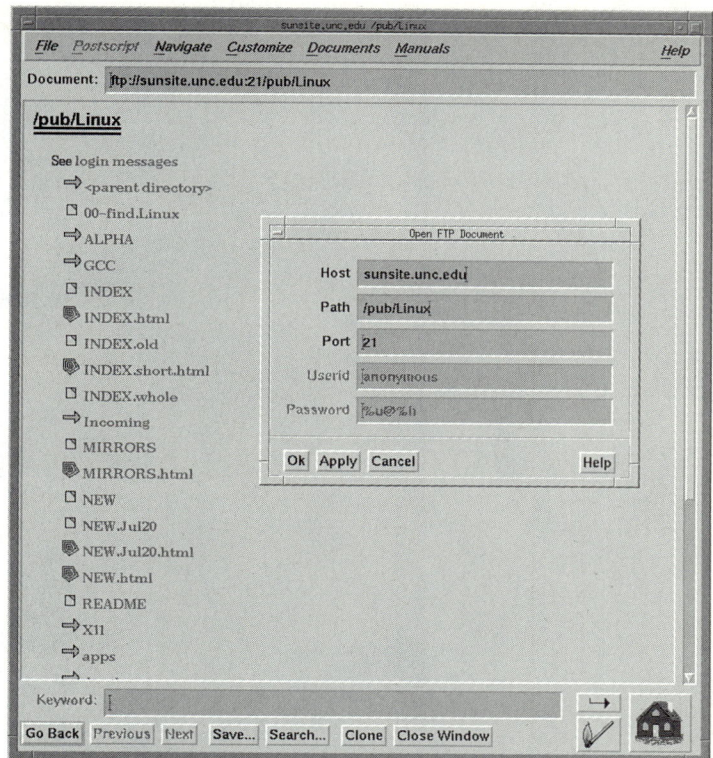

There are even more interface enhancements. Context-sensitive help is available through the On Context command in the Help menu. Clicking on a hyperlink does what you'd expect, but holding down the mouse button on a link brings up a menu that lets you choose between retrieving the document normally, downloading it to your local disk, or opening a new window and displaying it there. Notice that this one feature replaces two clumsy features of X Mosaic and is exactly what's needed. You can even just cancel the process, which is useful if you simply want to ensure that the hyperlink works. This is one of two significant features provided by Midas for HTML page designers; the other, shown in Figure 11.4, is an option that displays illegal HTML tags in documents. The next version of the program (3.0) promises the capability to edit HTML documents as well as view them.

FIGURE 11.4.

Illegal HTML tags option from MidasWWW.

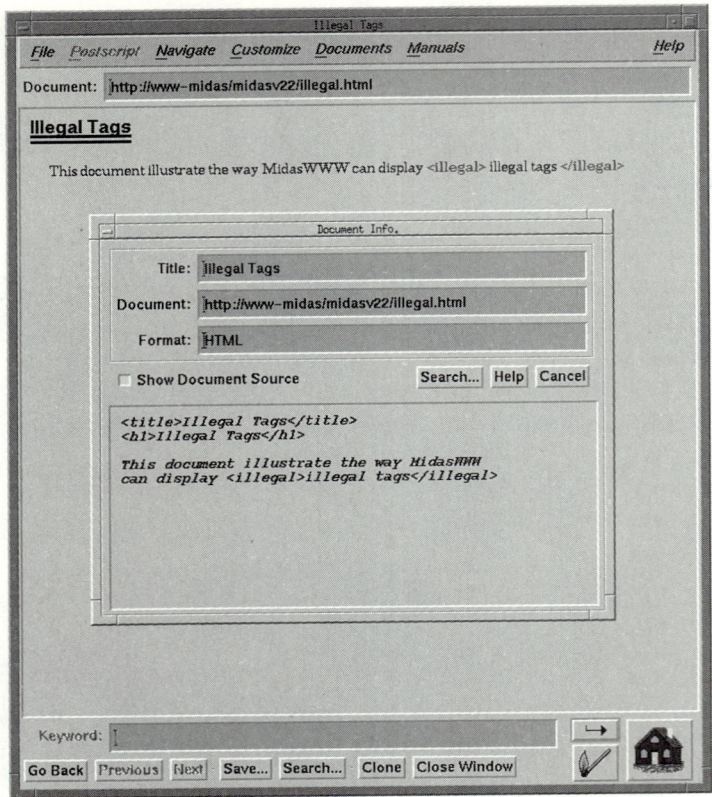

Midas offers a Visited Documents window that in many ways is much stronger than the history feature in any version of Mosaic. As Figure 11.5 shows, this window displays the titles of all the documents you've visited this session, arranging them in hierarchical order. The currently loaded document is indicated by a large yellow dot. The hierarchical view is extremely useful, as it indicates where you can find items, and by clicking on any of the documents you can load it into the main Midas window. But that's not all this window does: From the File menu in the window itself, you can save your current session as an HTML file, at which point you can load it from your local disk. This means that you can capture especially productive sessions and completely re-enact them, a useful design feature for those who navigate the Web frequently and who must do so efficiently.

FIGURE 11.5.

The hierarchical Visited Documents Windows from Midas.

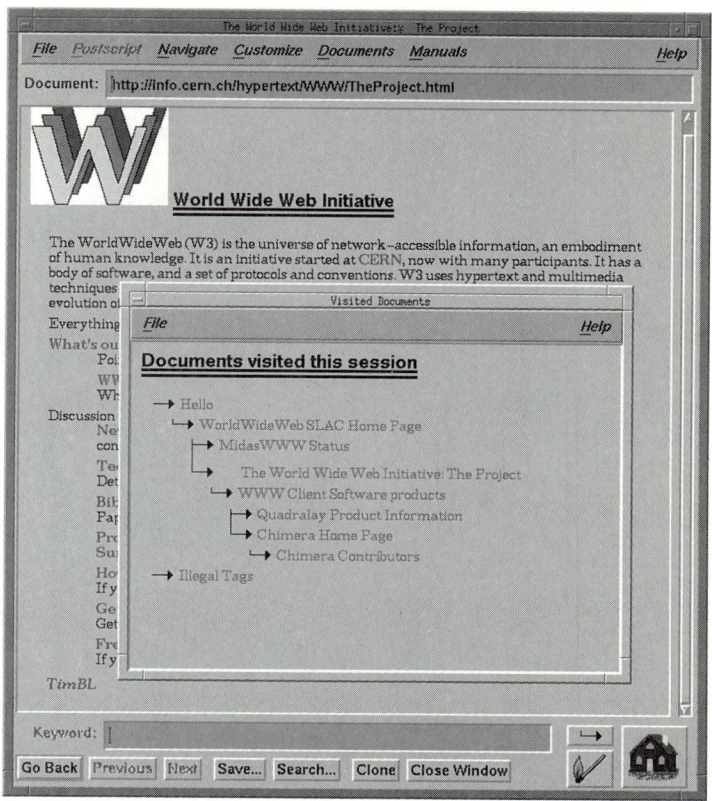

While Mosaic and other browsers require that you install external viewers to view noninlined file types, Midas displays many such files directly in its main window. In other words, the viewers are built-in. Once again, this demonstrates user interface consideration, because setting up external viewers is unnecessarily difficult even in the most easily configured browsers (such as Mac Mosaic). Not all file types are supported, however; to run sound files or video (MPEG) files, you still need an external viewer/player.

Because one of the design team's main reasons for developing Midas was to display scientific papers stored inside publication databases, Midas is especially strong at dealing with PostScript files. Figure 11.6 illustrates Midas's ability to display encapsulated PostScript documents (the tiger is such a document). Figure 11.7 shows how Midas handles multiple page PostScript documents: It opens an HTML document showing the table of contents, from which you can select and view any of the individual pages. One such page, a PostScript document with the kinds of figures and scientific notation PostScript makes possible, is shown in Figure 11.8.

FIGURE 11.6.

*Midas page showing
a PostScript image.*

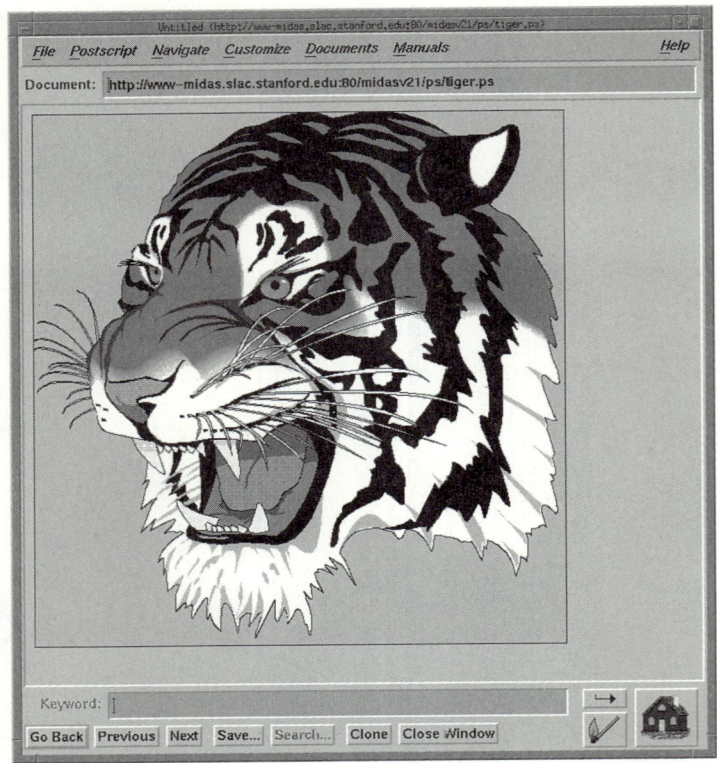

Finally, MidasWWW provides a Next/Previous feature in addition to the Back/Forward
system found on virtually all Web browsers. Effectively, this feature lets you avoid back-
tracking over a whole series of documents you've already viewed by letting you go to the
logical next or previous screen. This is especially useful for such activities as reading
newsgroups, where you need to make your way to a specific point and not meander through
the intermediate areas.

FIGURE 11.7.

HTML Page displayed by Midas showing a Table of Contents for a PostScript document.

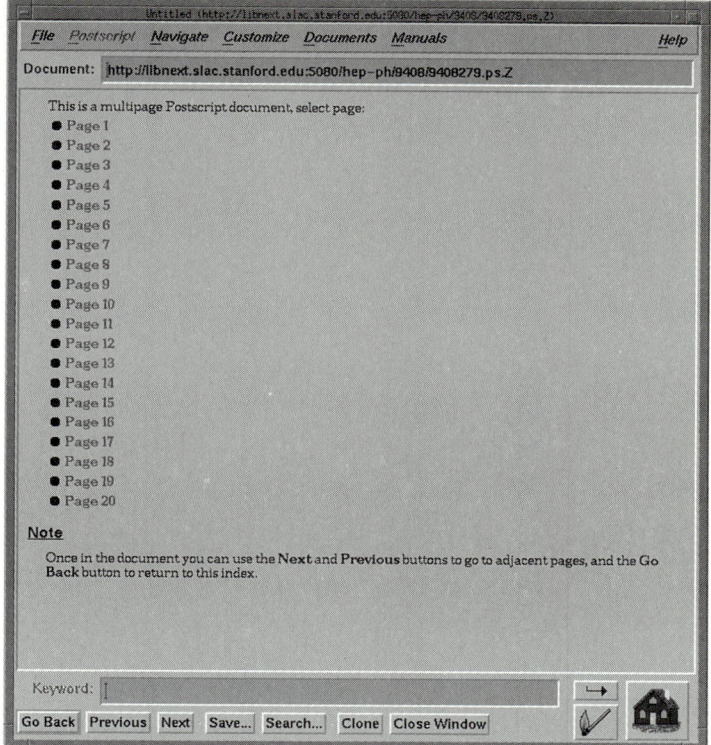

Midas supports forms (and offers a sculpted appearance to forms), and its menu structure contains all the items you'd expect. While it does not support a global history feature, its navigation mechanisms and Visited Documents window make each session productive by helping you avoid the tendency to head off onto an undesired track. For anyone who needs to work extensively with PostScript or other types of files that don't load directly into Mosaic or other browsers, or for anyone who doesn't understand why most browsers require so much additional configuration, MidasWWW is a very strong alternative.

FIGURE 11.8.
Individual PostScript page displayed directly in the Midas view window.

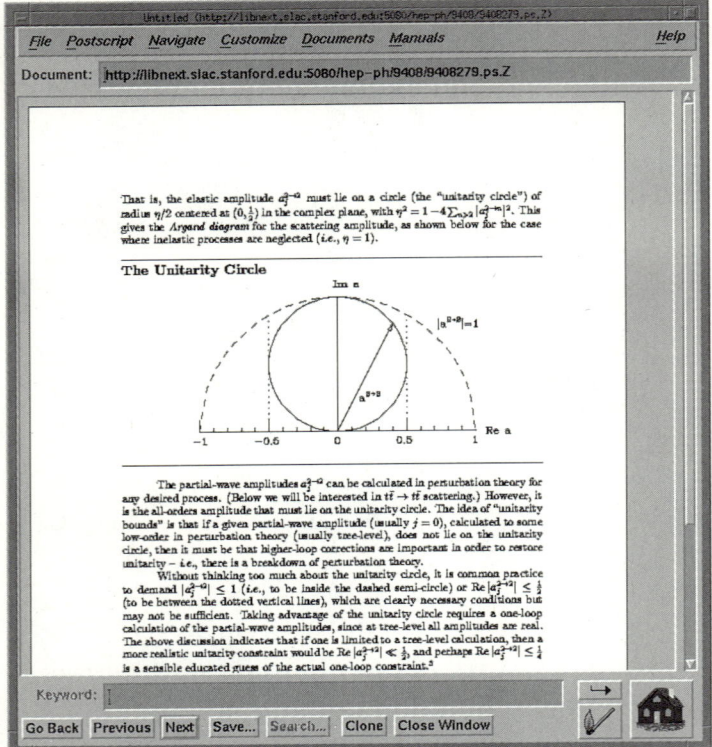

ViolaWWW

Publisher:	O'Reilly & Associates
Latest Version:	3.0
FTP Site:	`ora.com`
FTP Directory:	`/pub/www/viola/`
FTP Filename:	`viola940323.tar` or `viola940323.tar.gz`

ViolaWWW was the first World Wide Web client available for X Window systems. Although it didn't manage to keep up in features or popularity with the later X Mosaic, it appears to be undergoing a rebirth as the designer (Pei Y. Wei) completes his degree and moves himself and his browser from the Experimental Computing Facility at Berkeley (where it began) to the well-known publisher of Internet materials O'Reilly & Associates. Although nothing has been announced to this effect, look for this company (whose most famous Internet site to date is the Global Network Navigator) to possibly start licensing Viola as part of a larger strategy. Maybe not, but it seems logical.

Viola is a full-featured browser, albeit not quite as full-featured, from the standpoint of menu items, as either X Mosaic or MidasWWW. It features a Motif look and feel (sculpted icons, selectable text, all the standard features), it supports HTML fill-in forms, and it is particularly strong at displaying tables and columns, using features of HTML+. A good Viola document, indeed, can look like a published page, as illustrated in Figure 11.9. This document makes use of a specific HTML+ tag <HPANE> to create the columns. In fact, <HPANE> is not an HTML+ standard, but as Figure 11.9 demonstrates, it should be. Because of Viola's history as a language and programming tool rather than just a browser, it is capable of some features that HTML itself does not incorporate.

FIGURE 11.9.

Viola screen featuring document with columns and graphics.

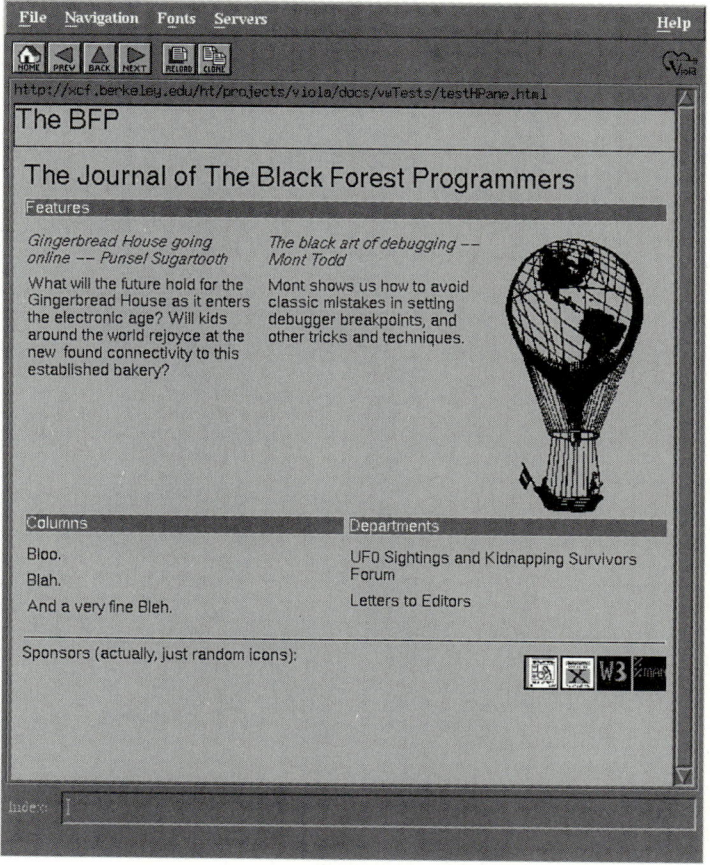

The name Viola is an acronym for Visual Interactive Object-oriented Language and Applications. It is a toolkit that includes several features not found in current versions of HTML, and therefore can display document types and features that X Mosaic and

MidasWWW cannot. If Viola were the standard browser, Web documents would be far richer in both appearance and function, but because it's not, very few people are writing documents that take advantage of all its features. Some of these features are demonstrated in the following pages.

Figure 11.10 shows a sample program built into Viola. This doesn't come as part of the Viola package, but it shows how you can tailor Viola by engaging its programming capabilities. Doodle is a simple drawing program that appears in the main document window.

FIGURE 11.10.

Example of a program appearing in the document window.

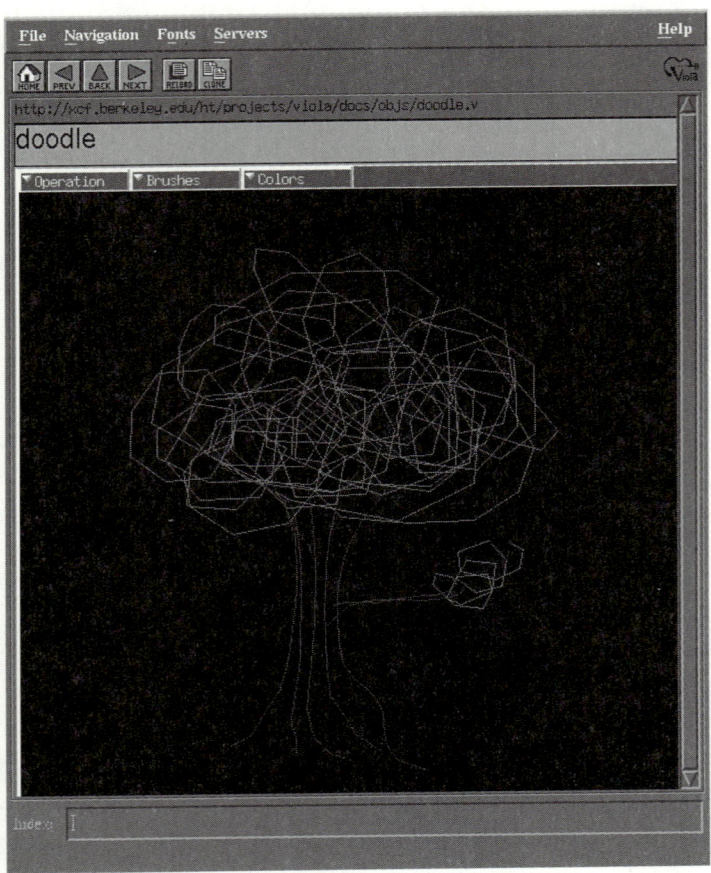

Another example of a Viola document consisting of a Viola-written program is shown in Figure 11.11. In effect, the program becomes embedded into the browser, to the degree that it includes its own interface and capabilities. Again, the secret here is using the Viola toolkit to program both the external program and the browser itself, with the results being an extremely rich environment. Also again, the problem is that this kind of program won't be readily available across the Web, because ViolaWWW is the only client that can take advantage of it, and its use is not widespread enough. For specific customized functions within organizations, however, the possibilities are almost endless.

FIGURE 11.11.

Example of a Viola program embedded in a Viola WWW window.

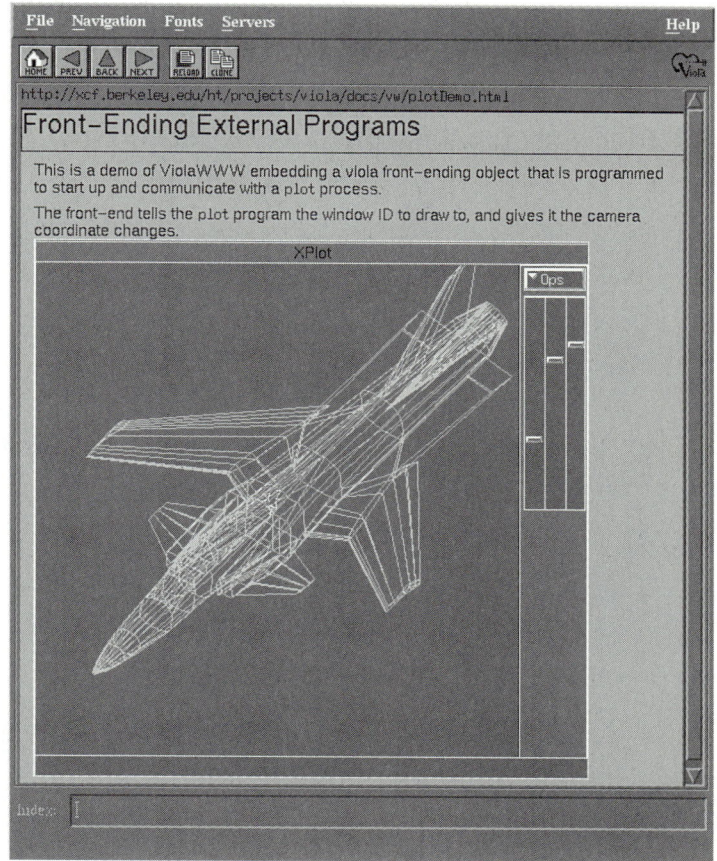

Figure 11.12 shows the main Viola window, with a complex chart drawn into it. As is evident, Viola's is a relatively sparse interface, at least from external appearances. The Home button takes you to your default home page, Back takes you to the previous document and removes the current one from the history list, Previous does the same but leaves the current one available, and Next moves to the next document on the history list. At the bottom is the index line, where searches take place, and it isn't always available.

FIGURE 11.12.

The main Viola window, showing an icon bar at the top.

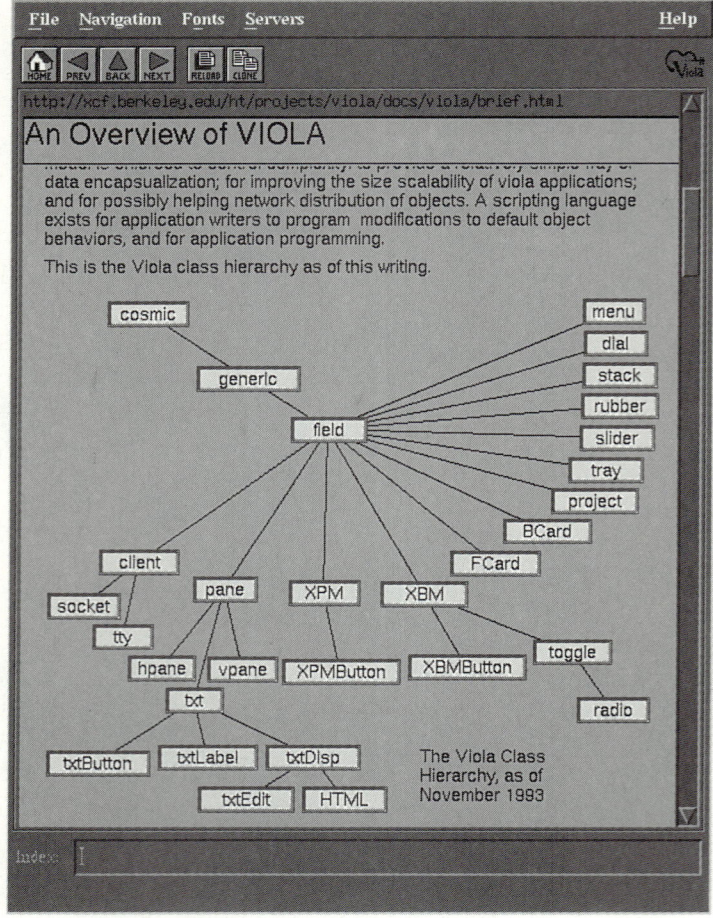

Of particular interest is the Clone icon. This icon opens a new window showing the current document, and this window is called a Navigational Viewer. Its purpose is to act as a launching pad for your Web browsing, and to that purpose it does not change as you use it. When you click on a hyperlink from the Navigational Viewer, the destination document is loaded into the main document window, not the cloned one. The cloned window simply stays in place, waiting for you to select another item from it, which will then take over the main window. This is especially useful when working from long lists of sites (such as the NCSA What's New page or the EINet Galaxy), because you're not forced to return to that site (and hence often reloading the entire document) when you want to make a new selection.

Figure 11.13 shows Viola's support of forms. This example, like Figure 11.9, uses the <HPANE> tag in HTML to offer columns of buttons, and Viola-specific capabilities to offer sliding bars in the item selections and the doodle pad in the Signature box. The appearance of this form is superior to other forms found on the Web because of the browser's inherent capabilities. Again, however, this form will not display on a standard browser.

FIGURE 11.13.

Fill-in form using Viola's programming capabilities.

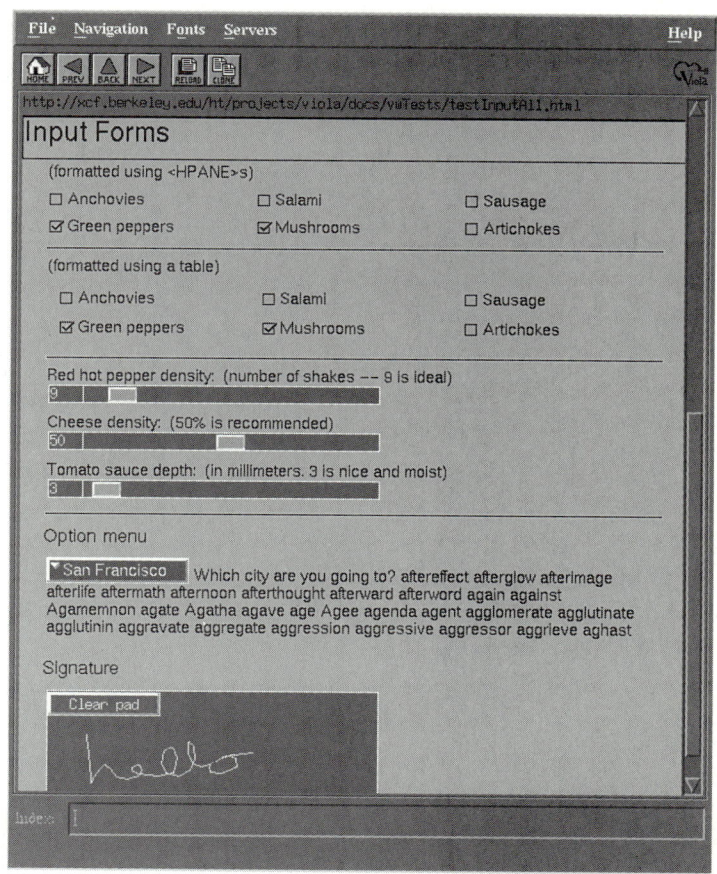

Viola thus offers a rich opportunity for sophisticated document creation. In addition, it features a source code viewer and editor to help you work through HTML authoring. But as a browser for the World Wide Web as it exists today, with the reliance on much less sophisticated HTML documents, it is less useful than either X Mosaic or MidasWWW. In particular, its lack of a hotlisting (bookmarking) feature nearly incapacitates it, since bookmarking has become an absolute must for repeated Web navigation. Once these features are added, as they will be shortly, this browser should see many advanced uses.

Actually, there are two versions of Viola, one that uses the Motif front-end and the older one, which uses the XLib front-end. Users capable of displaying Motif will want that one, since it features the polished and attractive interface sported by the other major X clients, but the versions are generally the same. Some differences are as follows: in the XLib version, you can directly edit the URL display (unavailable in the Motif edition), and, importantly, the XLib version lets you bookmark documents in three menus: Public, Local, and Private. The Motif version of Viola features a history list but not a bookmarking function. According to the designer, however, the two versions will become identical through the course of a few revisions.

Browsers for the Macintosh

Basically, Macintosh users are in the same position as Microsoft Windows users (see the section titled, "Browsers in Commercial Packages for Microsoft Windows," later in this chapter), at least as far as freeware browsers are concerned. They have NCSA Mosaic, and they have two other choices. What differs is the quality of those other choices, although even here there's a strange similarity. Windows users have Cello and WinWeb (both discussed in the Windows section below), while Macintosh users have Samba and MacWeb. Now, there's no way whatsoever that Samba can be reasonably compared with Cello; the latter is so far superior that it's hard to write about them in the same chapter of this book. But WinWeb, in its first incarnation, is distinctly inferior to its Macintosh sister program, MacWeb, so on balance the quality of browsers for the two user bases isn't all that far off. It seems reasonable to give Cello the nod over MacWeb, and WinWeb the definite nod over Samba, so it would seem that Windows users are, indeed, better off.

There are really only two choices for Mac users: Mosaic or MacWeb. Samba is described even by its own creators as "basic," and a quick look at it here will demonstrate the accuracy and the honesty of that assessment. However, there's no need whatsoever for Mac users to feel impoverished. Mac Mosaic is smoother and more stable than its Windows counterpart, and MacWeb is far better than its Windows counterpart as well. The only area in which the Windows versions get the nod is in speed, but not dramatically. None of this will surprise Mac owners in the least.

Samba

Publisher:	CERN
Latest Version:	1.03
FTP Site:	info.cern.ch
FTP Directory:	/pub/www/bin/mac/
FTP Filename:	MacWWW_V1_03.sea

Samba, otherwise known as MacWWW, was the first available Web client for the Macintosh. Developed by the World Wide Web team at CERN, it is worth examining now only for historical interest, because it is underpowered by comparison to all other browsers in this book, arguably even less capable than the CERN line browser itself. There's nothing intrinsically *wrong* with Samba; it works, and it does everything it was apparently designed to do. It's just that it wasn't designed to do very much, and in a year that has given Mac users both Mosaic and MacWeb, Web clients have to do a very great deal indeed. The program is scarcely worth the time it takes to download.

Figure 11.14 gives a good indication of what Samba looks like. As is evident, Samba does not replace the current document with a new document when you access a hyperlink. Instead, it opens a new window. The problem with this approach, obviously, is that the screen becomes extremely cluttered extremely quickly. Again, however, Samba itself isn't really to be blamed for this. As a browser designed to support the Web in its early stages, the design team likely never envisioned the amount of Web activity, and the number of Web sites, now available to even the casual user. Samba is not designed to handle this level of activity, nor was it meant to be.

Still, if you come to this program now, instead of graduating *from* it into something else, its limitations seem difficult to believe, even given its early introduction into the fray. There's no dialog box to allow font changes, for instance, something that's almost a constitutional right among Mac users of Web clients. In addition, you have to double-click on a link rather than single-click, which wouldn't be so bad except that a single click gives you an insertion point wherever you clicked on the link, giving the impression that the text of the link is editable (it's not). Once you double-click, there's no progress indicator telling you how much of the destination document you've transferred, how much remains to be transferred, or even if anything's happening at all. Nor is there any way to stop a transfer once it's begun.

FIGURE 11.14.

Samba with the home page and four additional windows open.

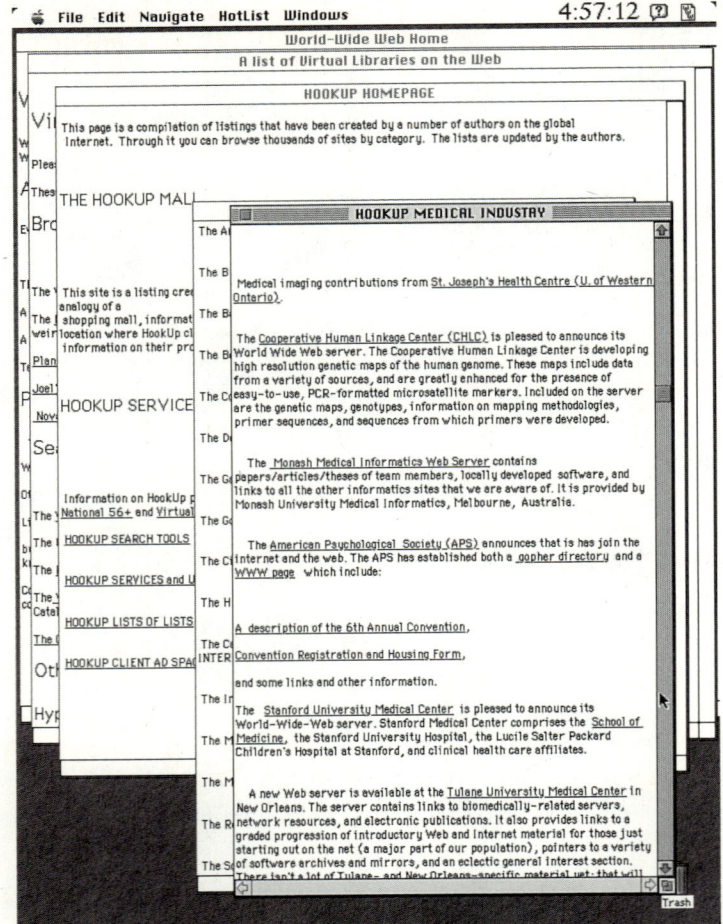

Samba does not display graphics, as shown in Figure 11.15. Nor does it display bullets in lists. In fact, this is a graphical browser only because it is on the Macintosh platform and has its command activated by a mouse, not because it has any connection with graphics per se.

FIGURE 11.15.

A separate window showing a graphical map (nonexistent) in Samba.

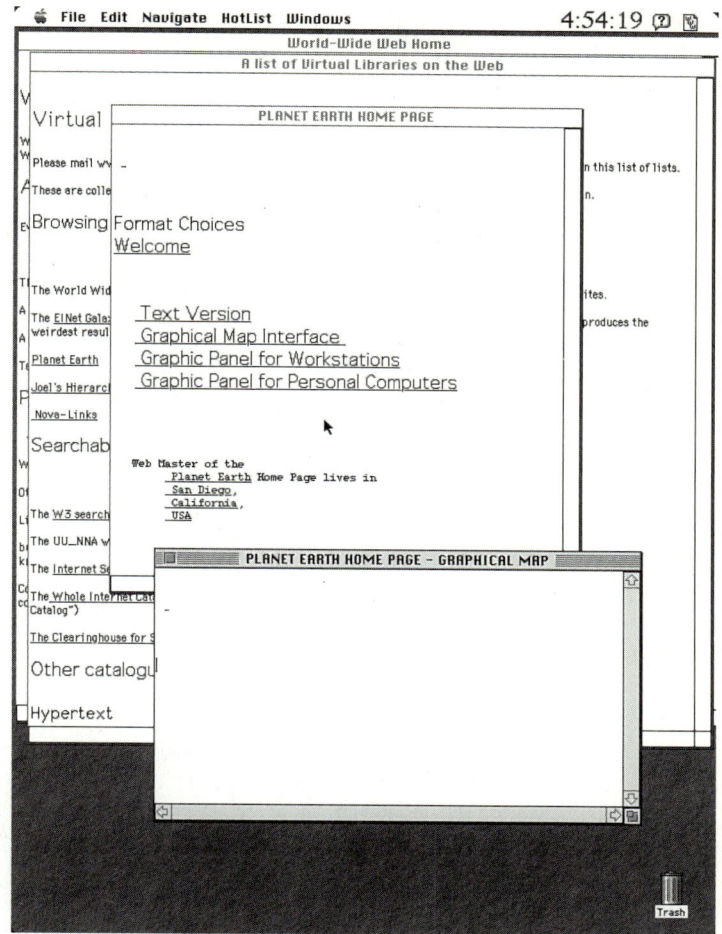

Samba's menus include File, Edit, Navigate, Hotlist, and Windows. Each is rudimentary in function. File contains the standard Mac items, but only Close, Save As (see Figure 11.16), Page Setup, Print, Quit, and Preferences actually do anything. Preferences lets you specify your startup document and whether or not to underline your links (essential with a monochrome Mac), and that's pretty much it. The only possibility with the Edit menu is Copy, which you can do by highlighting text in a document. (Of course, Windows Mosaic can't do this yet ....)

FIGURE 11.16.

The Mac-standard Save As dialog box in Samba.

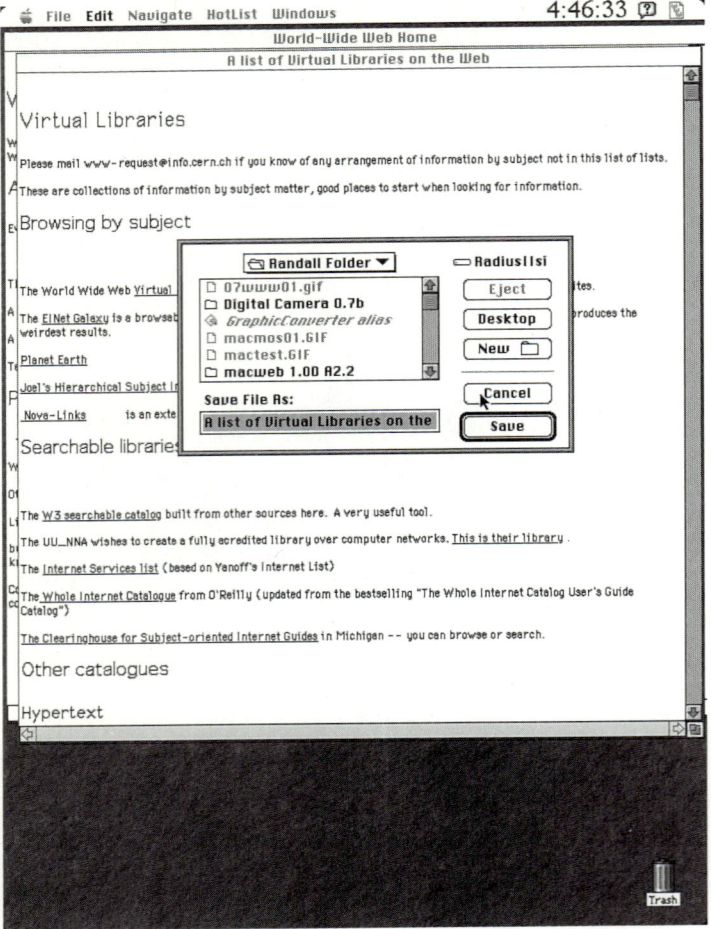

Navigate sports the usual Back and Forward but also includes Previous and Next. Next is a useful but somewhat strange command; if you proceed from Document A to Document B via hyperlink, then click on Next, you'll be taken to the item from Document A that occurs below the link you first chose. Next isn't active at all times. Navigate also lets you open a document by URL, a feature that has become standard in all browsers.

The Hotlist menu offers some built-in documents, and you can add the current document to that list or remove any already on the list. And the Windows menu enables you to move from open window to open window. There's little more to report, except that instead of a permanent URL display, Samba features (from the Windows menu) the Current Document Identifier box shown in Figure 11.17.

FIGURE 11.17.

The Current Document Identifier box in Samba.

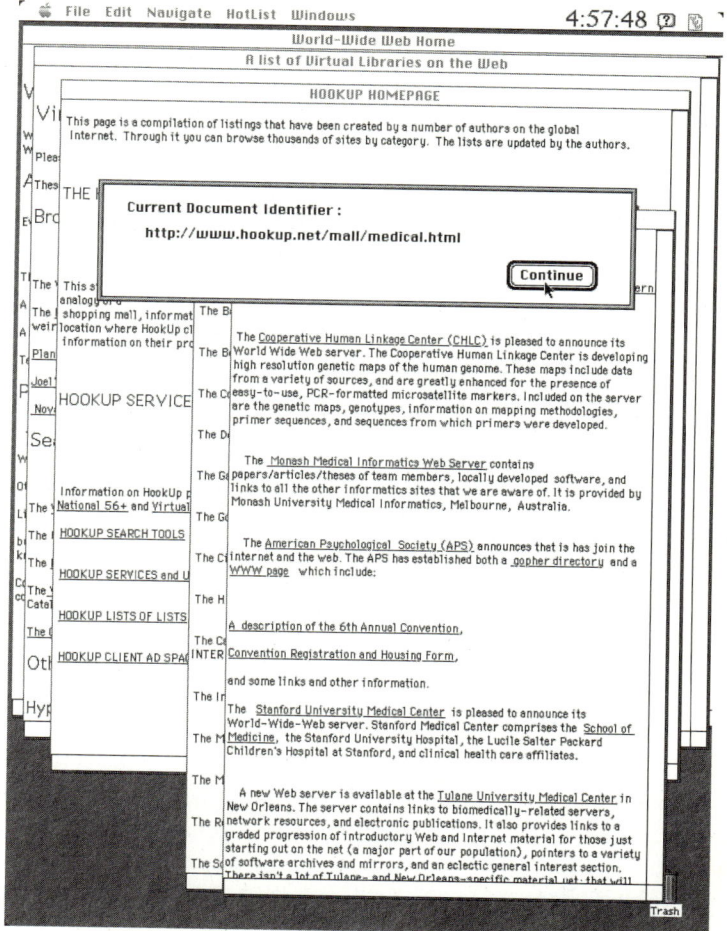

Clearly, this is a browser of limited usefulness, and one that was overtaken so quickly by every other graphical browser that loading it today is almost like stepping back into the dark ages. Interesting, but only as a curiosity.

FIGURE 11.19.

MacWeb page showing support for HTML fill-in forms.

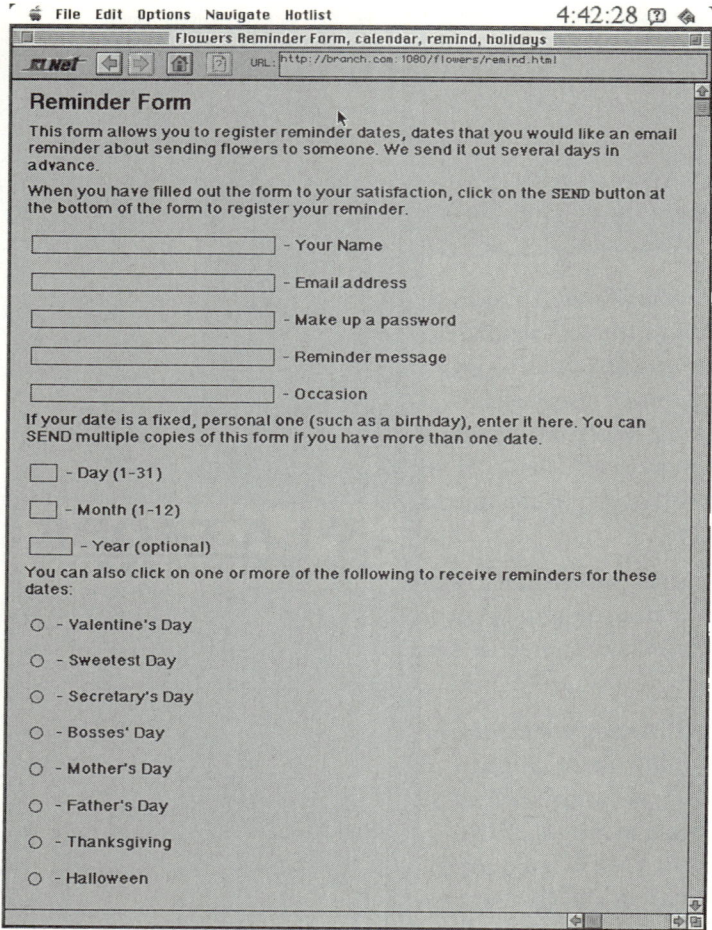

MacWeb can be configured entirely from within. The File menu, for example, features a Preferences item, with which you can specify your default home page, your e-mail address, and the news host you wish to use. Also available here are settings for the hotlist to open at startup and the default folder for temporary files. From the Format section of this dialog (shown in Figure 11.20), you can specify whether or not to automatically load inline images into documents as you retrieve them, whether or not to collapse blank lines (this feature lets you get rid of excess "white space" on documents), what color you want the document window background, and how to handle character translation.

FIGURE 11.20.

The Format dialog box from MacWeb's Preferences menu.

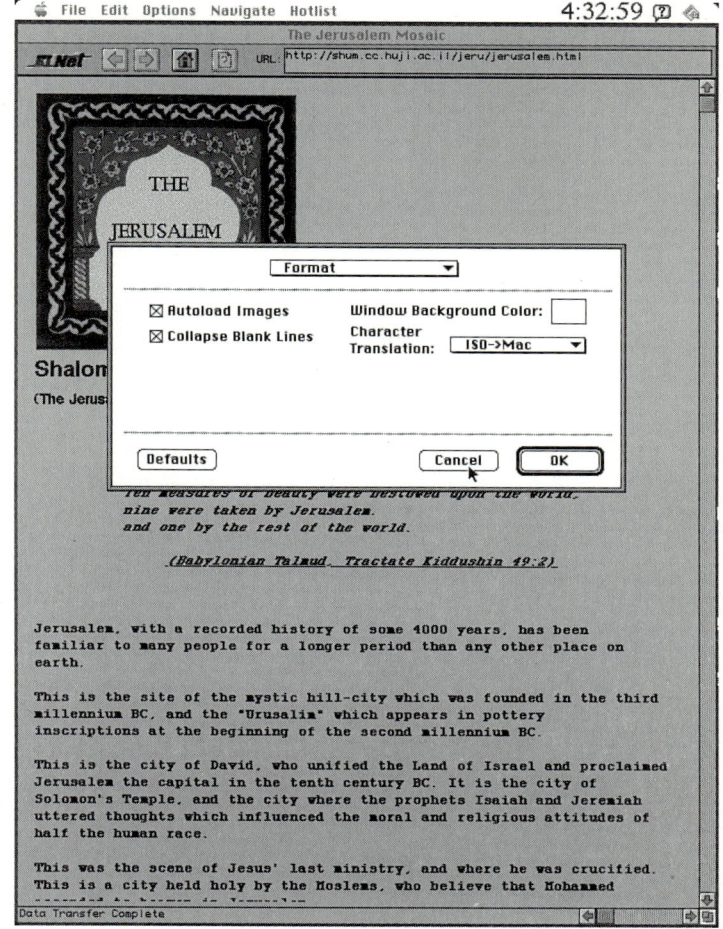

The rest of the configuration possibilities are found in the Edit menu. From here you can access three dialog boxes: Styles, Helpers, and Suffixes. Figure 11.21 shows the main Styles dialog; the pull-down menu at the top of the box lets you set the various elements of the page view. Of note is the Size Is Relative box at the bottom of the box, which enables you to adjust only the root style and have all other styles adjust themselves accordingly. It's similar to the increase or decrease all fonts option found in other browsers.

FIGURE 11.21.

MacWeb's Styles dialog box.

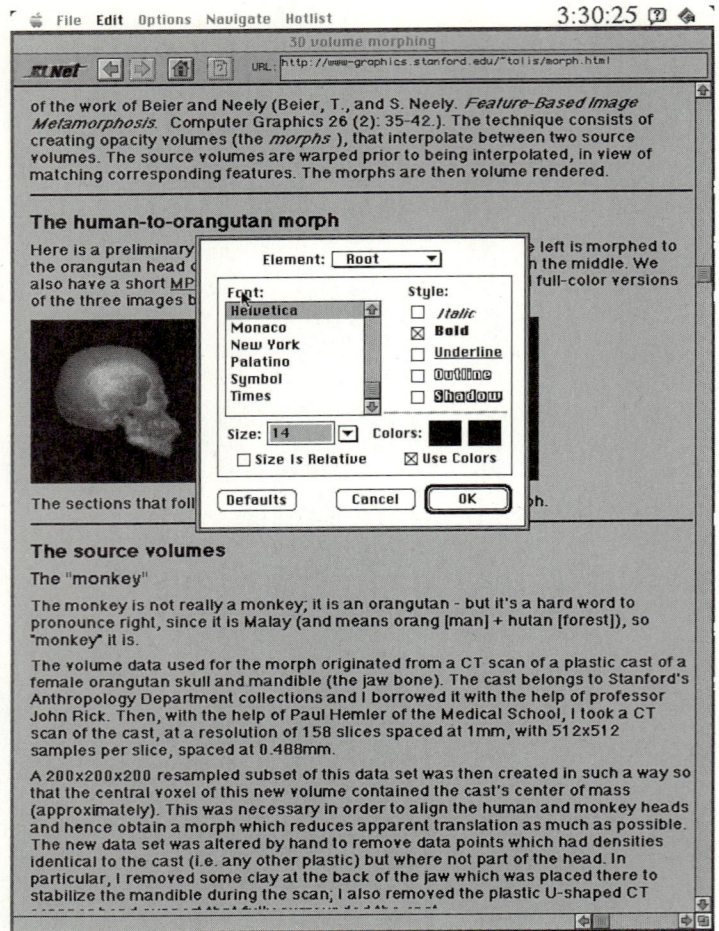

One of the other two configuration menus from the Edit menu is Helpers. As Figure 11.22 shows, this menu enables you to easily determine which tools (viewers or players) will handle which file types. Note that it's possible to set decompression software to handle FTPs of compressed files, an obviously useful feature.

FIGURE 11.22.

The Helpers dialog box from MacWeb.

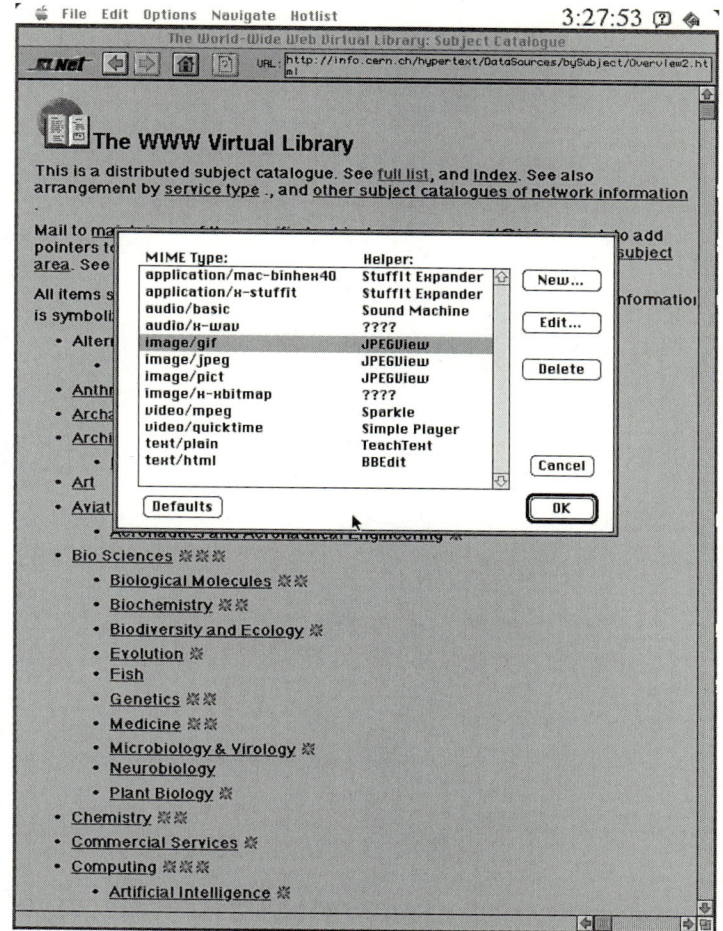

With these helpers in place, you can do all the multimedia things with MacWeb that you can in any other browser. Shown in Figure 11.23 is a QuickTime movie playing through an external player, accessed simply by clicking on the movie link in the document.

FIGURE 11.23.

A QuickTime movie playing on external viewer from MacWeb.

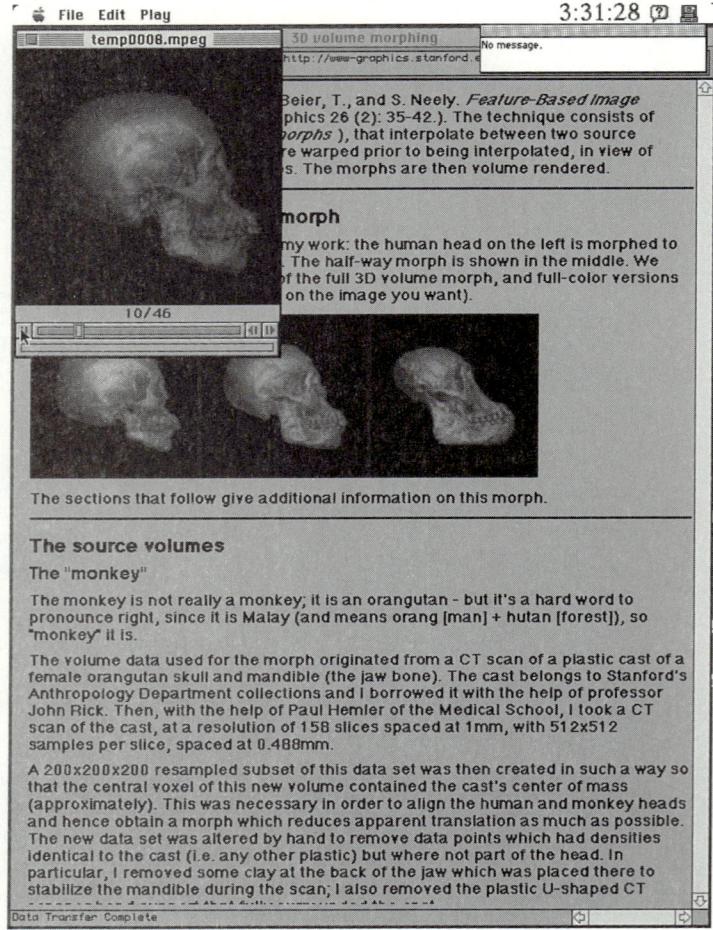

Like the other main Web clients, MacWeb can show you the HTML source code for the current document. As displayed in Figure 11.24, the source code appears in a separate window, from which you can select and copy text, or save to a separate file. The Save As dialog box is displayed in this figure as well.

MacWeb's Navigate menu offers the usual choices, including Forward, Backward, and Home, which also found as icons above the main viewing window. Also here are links to EINet and the EINet Galaxy, although strangely MacWeb doesn't offer the instant search of the Galaxy available in the much less capable WinWeb. There's also a link to the MacWeb home page, as you'd expect.

FIGURE 11.24.

The View Source window and Save As dialog box from MacWeb.

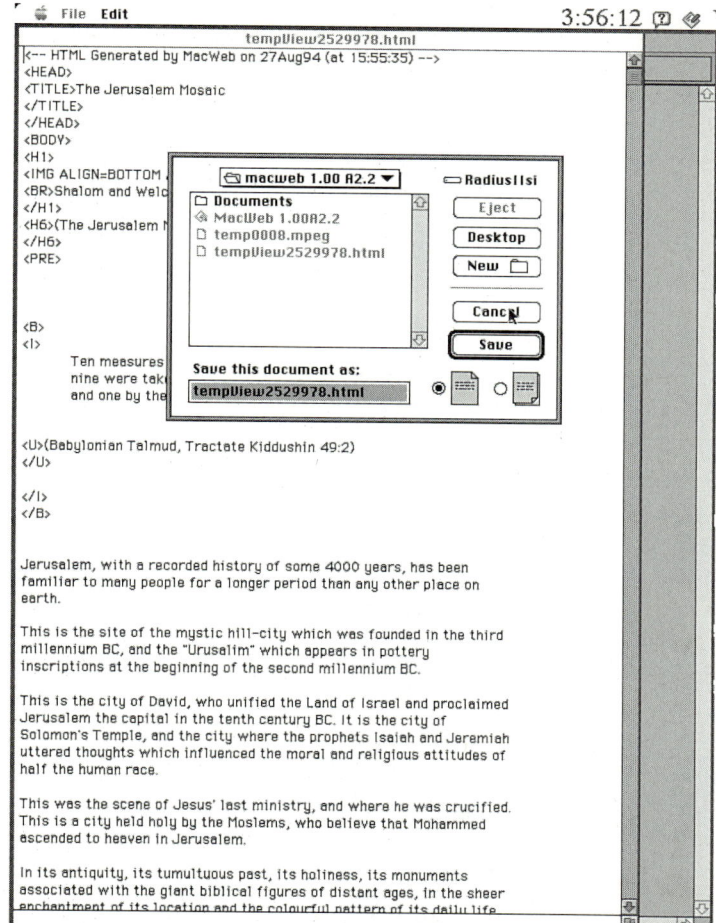

Hotlisting in MacWeb is practically identical to hotlisting in the Mac Mosaic version that preceded the most recent one. A separate Hotlist menu offers two items, Hotlist Interface and Add This Document. With the latter you add the current document to the Hotlist menu itself, while the former offers submenus that enable you to open stored hotlists, begin a new one, edit hotlist entries, and so forth. If you've come over from Mac Mosaic, you'll have no trouble picking up on this feature.

MacWeb's strengths make future versions of this program worth watching for. This is a real competitor to Mac Mosaic, a smaller, more concise program and one perfectly suited to keeping loaded in the background as you work. One or two releases from now, it might well become the preference of many.

Browsers for Microsoft Windows

Microsoft Windows users have several Web browsers from which to choose. Two—Cello and WinWeb—are freely available on the Net. Several others, however, are becoming available commercially, as the Net (and the Web) make their inevitable way towards mainstream popularity. This section examines the two freeware packages in detail, using only a brief amount of space on the commercial offerings. That doesn't mean the commercial browsers aren't worth exploring—indeed, they are—but rather that every other browser in this chapter is available for the price of a download. Besides, within a year there will be several more such packages on the market, and then it will be time to offer a full comparison of the bunch.

There's one other reason for doing things this way. So far, the commercial browsers are either licensed versions of Mosaic (Spry's AirMosaic, for example), licensed versions of Cello (California Software's InterAp), or new creations offered for sale (Netcom's NetCruiser browser and NetManage's Chameleon browser). In none of these cases is the software actually superior to the freeware, not in any truly functional way. The only benefit of these packages is that viewers and players tend to be bundled with them so that you don't have to do so yourself, but until there's a more gripping reason to switch there seems no reason *not* to concentrate on the freeware. Free is free, after all. Soon this may change, but certainly not this year.

Cello

Publisher:	Cornell University's Legal Information Institute
Latest Version:	1.01a
FTP site:	`ftp.law.cornell.edu`
FTP directory:	`/pub/LII/Cello/`
FTP filename:	`cello.zip`

The best known Windows competitor to Mosaic is Cello. Designed by Thomas Bruce of Cornell University's Legal Information Institute, Cello began life as a colorful browser that departed from Mosaic in several ways and in fact was available before Windows Mosaic. From its beginnings, Cello operated without the memory-hogging problems of its competitor, allowing users with SLIP access and slower processors (386-25s, for instance, or even 286s) to make use of a strong World Wide Web client program.

As of this writing, Cello Version 1.0 (with a few minor revisions) remains a good program. This write-up is based on that version. Version 2.0 is just around the corner, according to the designer, and by all accounts it will be a substantially revised package. Included in 2.0 will be support for HTML forms, a crucial feature for all new browsers, and support for multiple documents, meaning that Cello users will be able to have more than one window running (something that X Mosaic and Mac Mosaic offer, but not Windows Mosaic). Other enhancements abound, once again according to the designer, including a new look to the interface and the page itself. But 1.0 is substantial enough to merit a full write-up, which is what this section offers.

Figure 11.25 shows a typical Cello screen, displayed on a 14-inch monitor in 1024×768 resolution. Immediately apparent is the browser's inherent colorfulness. If this book were in color, you'd see the main title of the document, The Virtual Tourist, in a bright red. The image map is similarly colored, and the entire effect of the page—as of all of Cello— is that it appears as a bright, accessible program.

FIGURE 11.25.

Cello showing inline graphics and clean design features.

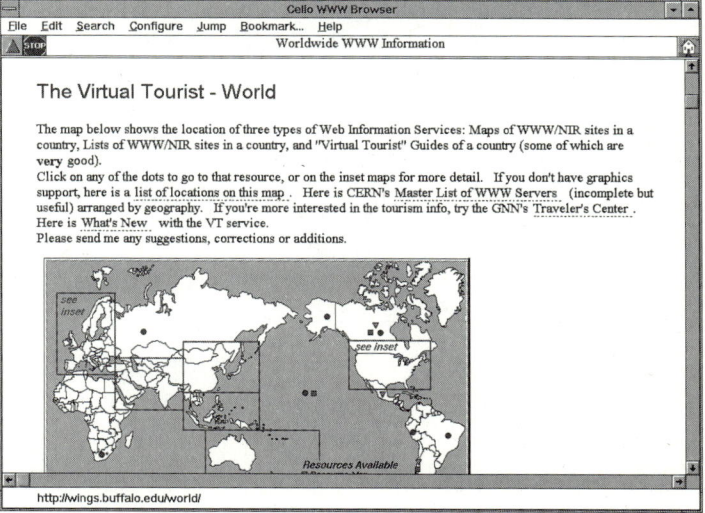

Now, Cello ships this way, with the colors turned on, but you can change all of the fonts with its configuration program, including the colors, so this might seem like unfair praise. Windows Mosaic, by contrast, lets you change fonts but not color of fonts—at least not even remotely easily—so let's let it stand. If you want to truly customize the appearance of your Web documents, Cello makes it possible. You can have every text style in a different color, typeface, and font size if that's what you want, and as long as you don't blind yourself it's fine. Figure 11.26 offers a look at the font configuration dialog, and as you can tell by the bottom left corner, maroon is the color for first-level headings.

FIGURE 11.26.

Font dialog box from Cello, with color choices.

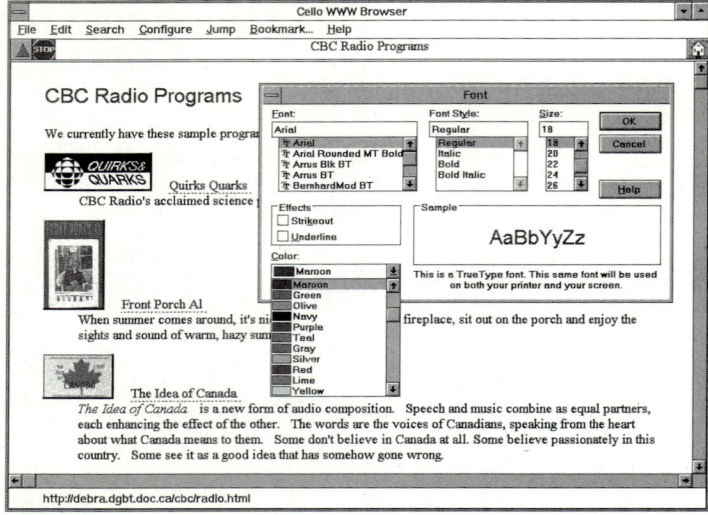

Despite the strengths of this sort of configuration feature, Figure 11.26 also demonstrates one of Cello's less attractive attributes, its underlining appearance. In fact, these dotted underlines alone have caused users to abandon the program for the more attractively highlighted Windows Mosaic, and although this seems a silly reason for switching, that's the nature of working with users of GUIs. It would be nice if Cello offered an underlining choice that meant something, but as the open Configure menu in Figure 11.27 shows, the only options are to have Links Underlined Only either on or off. If they're off, Cello displays hyperlinks with dotted rectangles surrounding the word, also shown in Figure 11.27, and this is truly ugly.

Still, the Configure menu makes it clear how easily configured this program is. The home page, download directory, background color (with full spectrum), e-mail address, mail relay, news server, and WAIS gateway can all be set from this menu, and you can even specify which telnet program you want for those times when hyperlinks open telnet sessions. Such features are similarly available in some browsers, but they aren't available at all through the Options menu of Cello's main Windows competitor. With this kind of interface consideration given to Version 1.0, the new version promises to be even easier to configure.

FIGURE 11.27.

The choices in Cello's Configure menu.

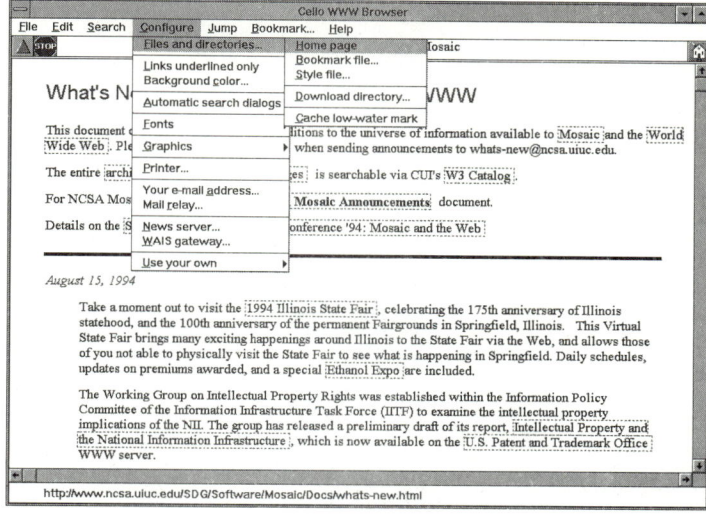

For a beginning Web user, Cello's bookmarking feature is among the easiest of any browsers to understand. For one thing, the feature is actually called Bookmarks, rather than the much less self-explanatory hotlists, and for another it has its own top-level menu name, surprisingly absent from the majority of browsers (surprisingly, because bookmarks on the Web are a constant application). Figure 11.28 shows the Bookmarks dialog box, which lists the bookmarks in alphabetical order and offers a full interface for dealing with them. From here you can dump the entire list to a file to produce an HTML page consisting solely of your bookmarks, you can jump to the bookmarked page, or you can copy the reference to the clipboard. When you find a document you want to bookmark, you use this dialog to do so, clicking on Mark Current Document. This command yields the small dialog shown at the bottom of Figure 11.28, in which you can change the document's title to suit your own purposes.

Unfortunately, Cello's bookmarking system lacks some important features. It doesn't allow categorization, as does Windows Mosaic's Menu Editor. Instead, all bookmarks are lumped together (albeit in alphabetical order), and after a time they're difficult to locate in the list. Furthermore, you can bookmark only 50 entries, after which you have to dump the lot to a file and start over. This will be corrected in Version 2.0 (according to the designer), but for now it presents some very real difficulties.

FIGURE 11.28.

Cello's bookmarking interface and Name Your Bookmark box.

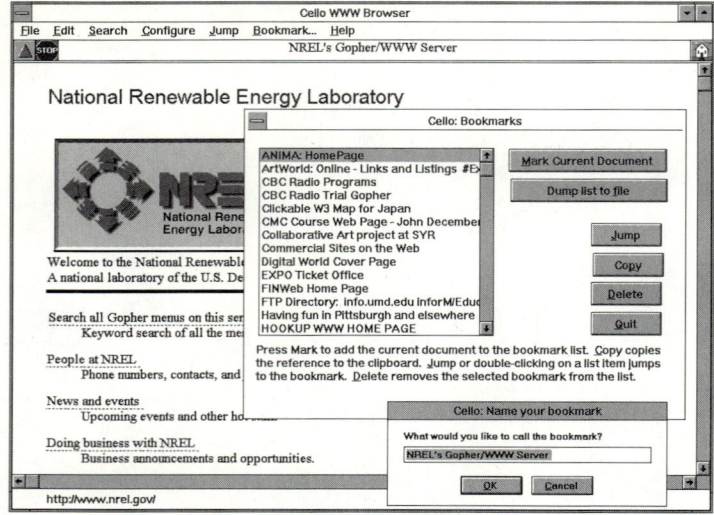

Despite the lack of sophistication of this particular feature, however, Cello sports some ideas that its competition only recently added or indeed hasn't added yet. From before Version 1.0, Cello's Edit menu contained two items, View source and View as clean text. View source offers the same thing as the Document Source option in a variety of browsers, but only very recently in Windows Mosaic: the HTML-coded text version of the file. A very nice feature is View as clean text, which does the same thing but loads the document without the HTML tags. When you see a page you actually want to read (rather than reformat or borrow HTML ideas from), this is an extremely handy feature. An example of the result of using the View as clean text feature appears in Figure 11.29. In fact, the text in the document looks like yhe text in the Cello window.

One area in which Cello shines is its inclusion of local help files. Most browsers don't offer help files, and the various versions of Mosaic have help systems available but only by retrieving files from the Net. Cello's help system ships with the program—the way all MS Windows programs ship—and because it's a hypertext system (again like all MS Windows help systems), getting used to it is effortless. Figure 11.30 shows the help system's content screen. The links from here reveal a host of features that aren't obvious from just looking at Cello's structure, and demonstrate quite nicely why *all* programs, no matter how self-evident they may seem, need a local help system. One such feature is near the bottom of this screen, information for users with low-speed connections. For these users, Cello offers a "peek" mode; if you hold the Control key when clicking on a hyperlink, Cello loads only the first 4096 bytes (4KB) of the resulting file to let you know what's there. Also, since Cello doesn't display the destination URL when you pass the cursor over it, it offers a similar feature: Holding the Shift key while clicking on the link brings up a small box showing the link's address.

FIGURE 11.29.

The result of Cello's View as clean text feature.

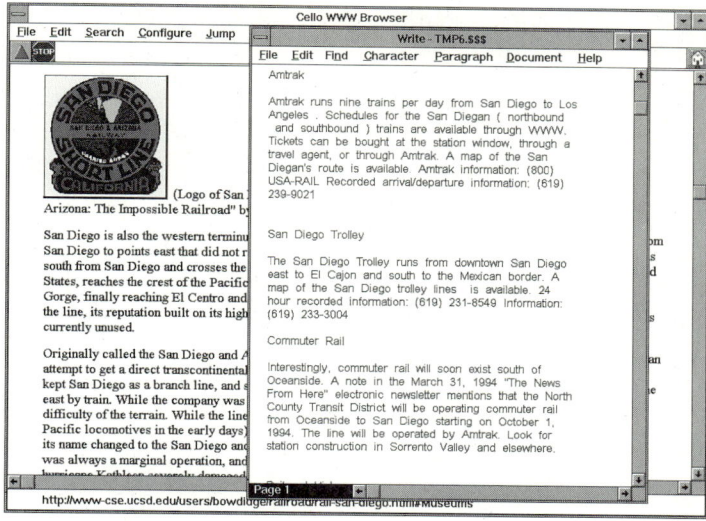

FIGURE 11.30.

The Table of Contents from Cello's help system.

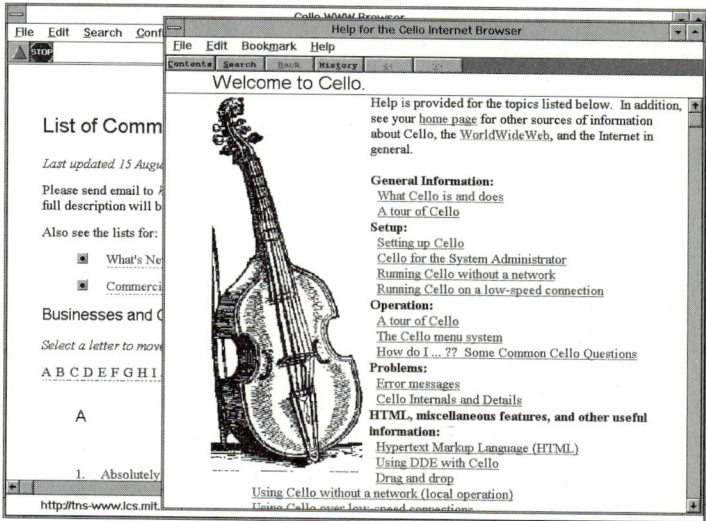

Perhaps the most useful section of the help system deals with writing HTML documents. Included here is the vast majority of HTML codes, their meaning and their usage, to the extent that anyone wishing to start writing HTML pages, or anyone already writing who wants to check out what else is possible through HTML, can do far worse than learn from here. True, there are more comprehensive HTML starter pages out on the Web, but the point is that they're *out* on the Web. Download Cello, and you have an HTML help system available at all times, without the need for actually logging in. As long as Cello is set not to retrieve a file from the Net as soon as it loads, you can use it as a local browser for testing your HTML pages as well.

Figure 11.31 shows one of the HTML pages, this one dealing with the various types of reference codes. Each is explained quite thoroughly, and several examples are available as well. Combine a page like this with Cello's View source command from the Edit menu, and you have a powerful starting kit for HTML authors.

FIGURE 11.31.

The Anchor page from Cello's HTML reference section.

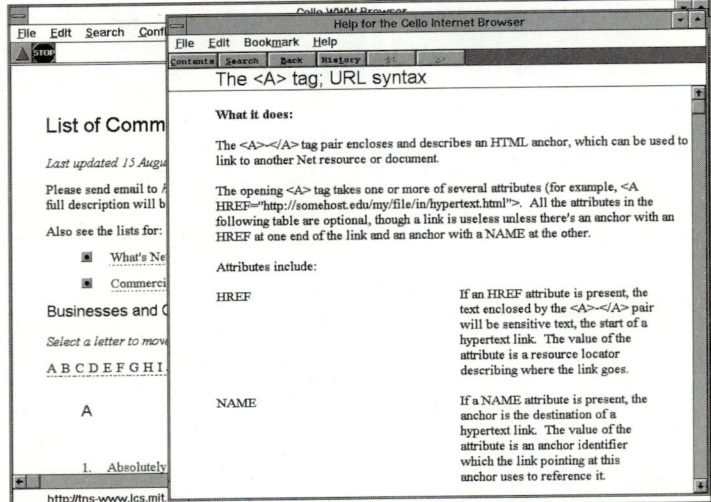

Finally, Cello offers a rudimentary e-mail front end. It appears in two places: in the File menu, where it's designed specifically to mail the current page to anyone on the Net; and in the Jump menu (see Figure 11.32), where it's a simple e-mailer for any purpose (not just to the program's developers, as it is in Windows Mosaic). It's hardly elaborate, and you can't receive e-mail through Cello, but as anyone who's done any evening-long browsing is aware, it's nice not to have to load a separate e-mail package just to send off a quick note.

For Microsoft Windows users, Cello more than rewards the few minutes it takes to download. Version 1.0 is sleeker than Windows Mosaic as far as resource usage is concerned (a huge consideration for Windows systems), and Version 2.0 promises to provide even stronger competition.

FIGURE 11.32.

Cello's built-in e-mail feature, here showing a meaningful exchange between hardworking authors.

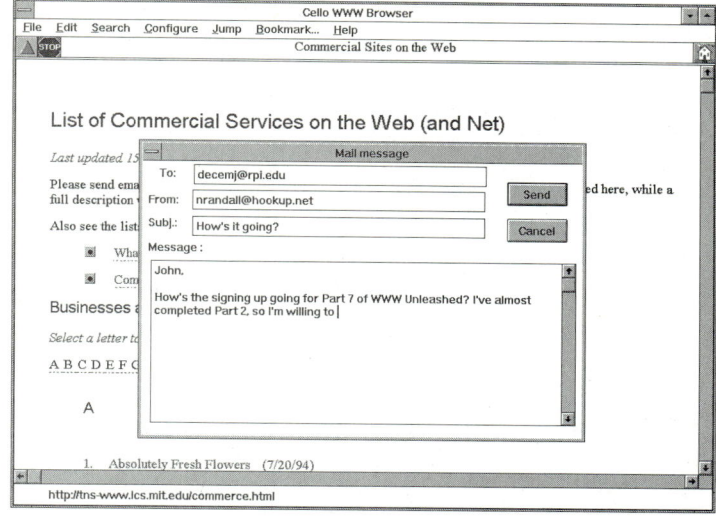

WinWeb

Publisher:	EINet
Latest Version:	1.0alpha2.2
FTP site:	`ftp.einet.net`
FTP directory:	`/einet/pc/winweb/`
FTP filename:	`winweb.zip`

Until very recently, Microsoft Windows users had two WWW clients to choose from: the famous Mosaic and the strong alternative Cello. In mid-1994, another browser became available, MCC's WinWeb 1.0, distributed through EINet, home of the well-known Internet resource site, the EINet Galaxy. If you think there must be a connection between WinWeb and MacWeb, discussed previously in the Mac browser section, you're absolutely right. WinWeb is the Windows version of MacWeb, and many features are similar.

At first sight, WinWeb seems sparse. Its menus are small and few, and it seems to offer none of the user interface dazzle of either Windows Mosaic or Cello. Furthermore, it lacks some of the nicer features of both its competitors, one of which, you'll discover immediately, is the document loading status report on both Cello's and Mosaic's scroll bars. When you click on a hyperlink in MacWeb, you get a box telling you the document is being loaded, and the icon changes to a (sorta cool) connected serial cable, but there's nothing whatever to indicate that something's actually happening. If you've browsed the Web for any length of time, you know how crucial this kind of information is. In fact, neither

Windows Mosaic nor Cello offers *enough* information, and they provide at least some. One of WinWeb's very real strengths in this area, however, is that the progress box features a Cancel button that actually works, at least most of the time. It's more reliable than Cello's Stop button, and it works more frequently than clicking on Windows Mosaic's spinning globe.

Figure 11.33 shows the appearance of a typical WinWeb page. As you can tell, the page looks very much like a kind of stripped-down Windows Mosaic. The current URL address is displayed at the top, as is the URL of the selected link, and the tiny icons appear just beneath the menu bar. (WinWeb and Windows Mosaic, like many Windows programs, are not designed to change icon sizes for different screen resolutions, hence the practically unreadable icons.) The page itself displays quite well, except that selecting nonproportional fonts for the Normal text display often results in an inexact alignment. This is being worked on, according to WinWeb's home pages, for the next version.

FIGURE 11.33.

A typical WinWeb display, displaying inline graphics.

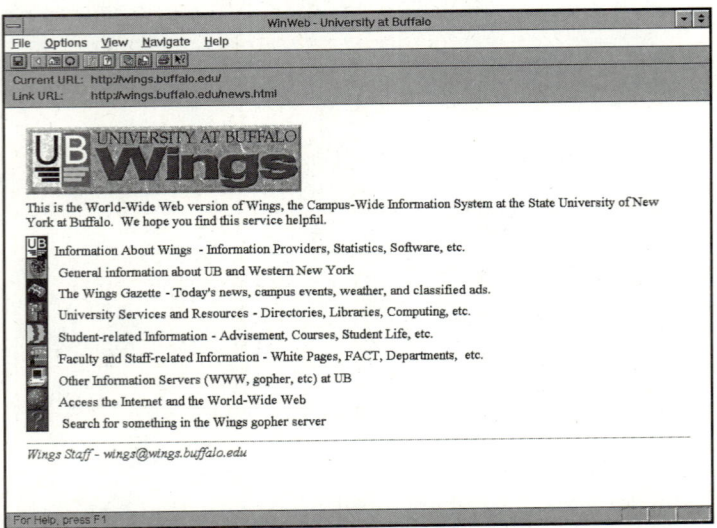

Much of WinWeb's configurability, as with Windows Mosaic, happens in its associated .INI file. However, WinWeb is more customizable that Mosaic directly from within its menus, closer in this regard to Cello. Fonts, home pages, colors, and other attributes can be set from the menus easily and efficiently. Unfortunately, you can't configure nearly as much as you'd like from here, and the result is a browser that appears in its simplicity to be very much a user's choice, but ends up appearing simply lacking in essential features.

Figure 11.34 shows WinWeb's font configuration menu. The program nicely combines its own specific styles menu with a fairly standard Windows font selector, but even here things are missing. Font changes are possible for more HTML headings and text types in both competing programs.

FIGURE 11.34.

WinWeb's font configuration system.

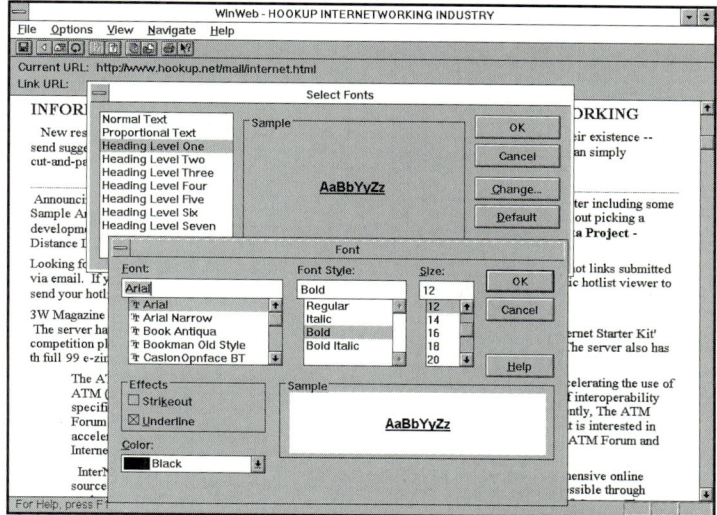

As Figure 11.35 demonstrates, WinWeb handles HTML forms. This might well be the only thing that makes this browser worth more, for the time being at least, than Cello (which won't handle forms until the release of its Version 2.0). The comparison between WinWeb and Cello is inevitable, because both seek to gain market share from Windows Mosaic, and both are extremely kind to MS Windows' precious resources compared with Windows Mosaic. WinWeb will run acceptably on a 2-megabyte Windows machine (inasmuch as *anything* will run acceptably with that little memory these days) and so will Cello. Windows Mosaic 2.0alpha6, by contrast, needs at least 4 megabytes and actually works properly with 6 or 8.

FIGURE 11.35.

An example of an HTML form in WinWeb.

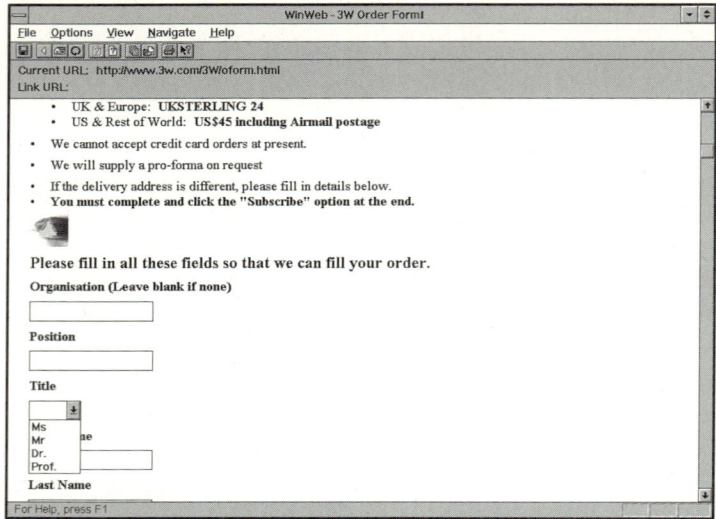

Another WinWeb usability decision appears to need reconsideration. In many Windows products (although neither of the other Web clients), moving the cursor over the icon bar offers text help, often on the status bar, as to what that icon accomplishes. WinWeb gives you that information, but only after you've clicked on the icon. If you want to know what the circular arrow does, for instance, you won't find out until you've activated it. This is a little like pulling a trigger to discover what it does; you'll find out, but you might not like the results. (Incidentally, the circular arrow means Reload Document, a borrowing from Windows Mosaic that would have been much better changed to something more intuitive. Why copy someone else's poor design?)

Two aspects of WinWeb, however, are especially helpful. First, when you select the Load Images command from the Options menu, and you return to a cached document that you originally loaded with*out* images, WinWeb will *not* automatically load the corresponding images. This is a feature that Windows Mosaic and Cello could both profitably copy; in those two browsers, it can be extremely frustrating to avoid image loading on a page you know is graphics-heavy, then toggle graphics on for another page, and then return to the original page and watch the browser go out onto the Net and start transferring the images. WinWeb saves you this agony.

The other strong point is WinWeb's direct tie-in to the EINet Galaxy. Because it's a product of a directly associated team, WinWeb has been built with a dialog box that lets you search the Galaxy without actually entering the Galaxy's HTML page. Effectively, this means that WinWeb offers a built-in Internet search tool, something that's possible in the other two browsers only by accessing a search-specific Web site. Figure 11.36 illustrates the link to the Galaxy.

FIGURE 11.36.

WinWeb's search EINet galaxy dialog box.

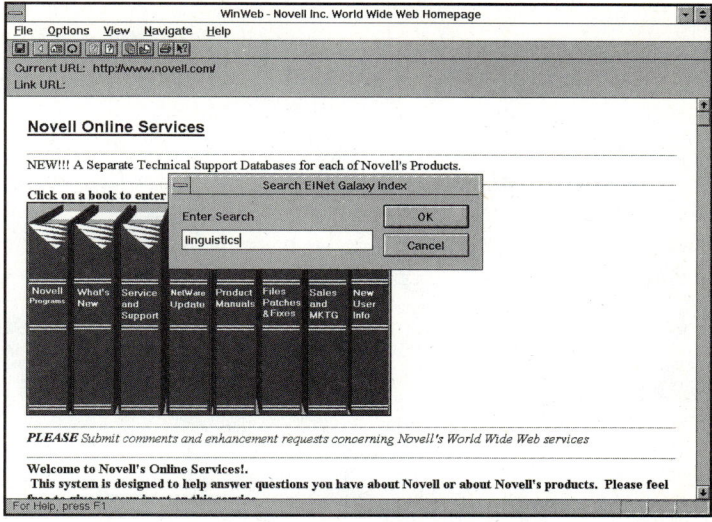

This has been a fairly negative look at WinWeb, and to a degree that's an unfair assessment. The browser in its first general release and its sister product, MacWeb, show a considerably more feature-rich design. Clearly, WinWeb will follow. But if you're looking for a strong Web client for use right now, this one will have to be your last choice.

Browsers in Commercial Packages for Microsoft Windows

While the Internet continues to offer strong Web clients that are also free for the asking, commercially produced and distributed browsers have begun to make their appearance. This is a trend that will unquestionably continue, because the World Wide Web in particular, and the Internet in general, have become extremely hot property over the past six months. Discussed here are two commercially available browsers, AirMosaic from Spry, and the Web browser built into Netcom's NetCruiser software. Both, in fact, are part of a larger collection of Internet tools (although AirMosaic is available separately), and this, too, is a trend that will continue for some time. Packages that feature software for Gopher, telnet, FTP, e-mail, Finger, Archie, WAIS, and the Web will sprout like proverbial mushrooms over the next year or so, all of them trying to capture the market share that the Web's media popularity has created.

AirMosaic

Available either separately or as part of Spry's Internet in a Box package, AirMosaic is the first licensed version of NCSA Mosaic to hit the software shelves, and it's a good one. Windows Mosaic users will recognize immediately that AirMosaic offers essentially the same features as the latest freeware product from NCSA, without the need for downloading and installing the Win32 extensions (as Windows Mosaic 2.0alpha6 demands). Furthermore, AirMosaic offers several other new features that increase usability in some very useful ways, even while sacrificing a bit of Windows Mosaic's richness.

Figure 11.37 shows the Virtual Tourist home page in AirMosaic:

FIGURE 11.37.

The AirMosaic screen featuring the clickable map in The Virtual Tourist's home page.

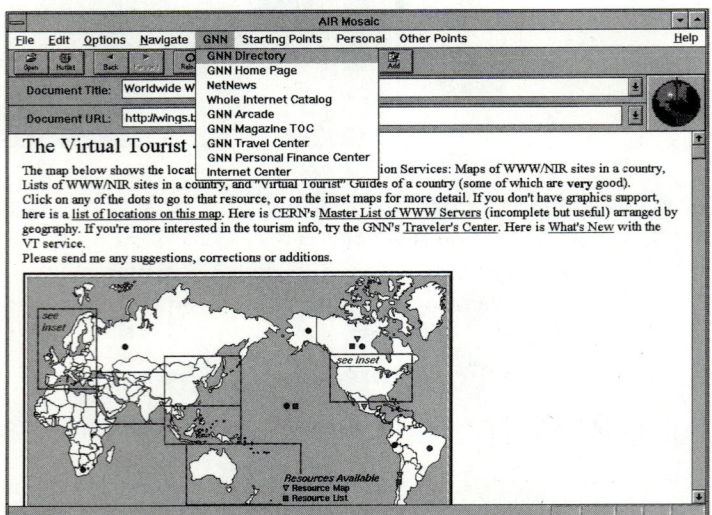

Also shown in Figure 11.37 is AirMosaic's built-in GNN menu, for instant access to the popular magazine and information service. This kind of built-in reference can also be expected, as commercial publishers form links with well-known Internet sites.

Another strong feature of AirMosaic is its configuration menu system. Instead of asking you to edit the `mosaic.ini` file, as the NCSA version does, this browser contains a series of usable menus that let you perform the same functions. Figure 11.38 shows the main configuration menu and one of several adjoining submenus. For obvious reasons, this kind of configuration system is a good idea, especially for a product designed expressly for Internet newcomers.

FIGURE 11.38.

The configuration menus from AirMosaic.

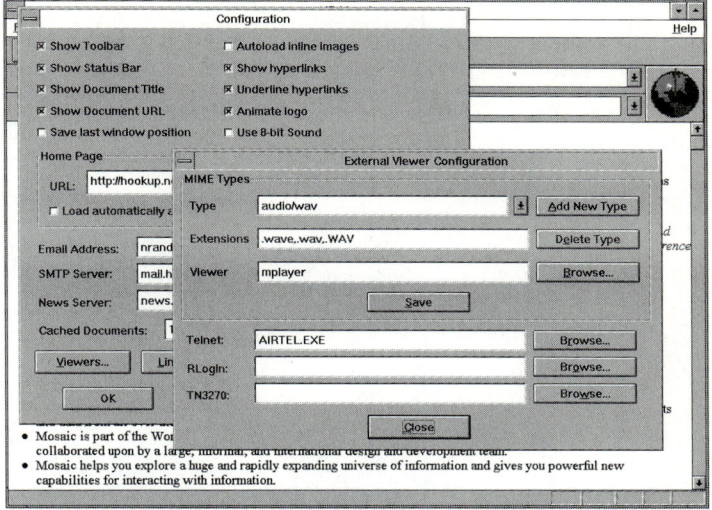

While AirMosaic does not feature Windows Mosaic's excellent menu editor utility, it does let you import your existing hotlist menus directly from your `mosaic.ini` file. The import is quite easy, and the result is a series of menus like those you already have available. Strangely, however, creating new menus isn't included as a feature in AirMosaic as a stand-alone product, which means that non-Windows Mosaic users will have only the rather under-designed hotlist feature AirMosaic offers.

Figure 11.39 shows a final AirMosaic strength, Kiosk mode. Designed expressly for use by libraries or institutions who want to allow Web browsing as a completely contained activity, without the possibility of configuring and toggling of features, Kiosk mode also makes the Windows screen show more of the document. It's useful, although once you're used to the status bar and all the other usual options, Kiosk mode seems a bit flat.

FIGURE 11.39.

NCSA's What's New Page shown in Kiosk mode.

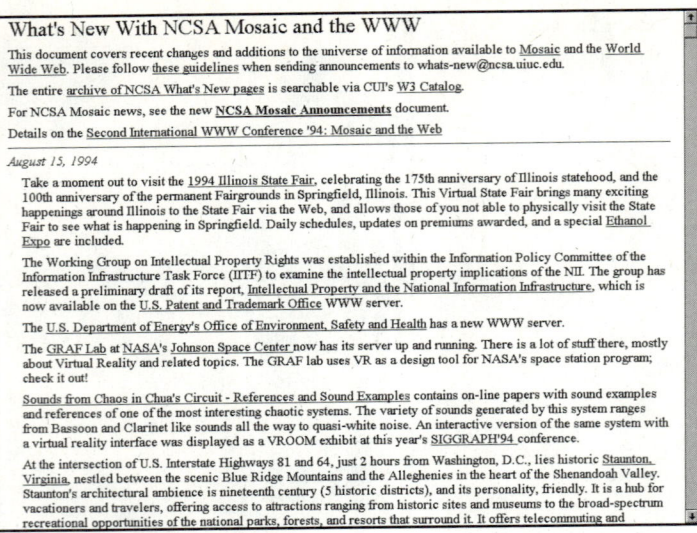

Web Browser from NetCruiser

The WWW browser shown in Figure 11.40 is one of a collection of Net programs that comes with the NetCruiser suite of applications from Netcom. As with Internet in a Box, this suite is designed to save users the trouble of going out onto the Net and downloading and installing the software they'll need. Unlike the Spry product, however, NetCruiser is tied exclusively into a service provider's operation. Without an Internet account with Netcom, you can't use this software.

FIGURE 11.40.

The NASA home page in NetCruiser's built-in Web browser.

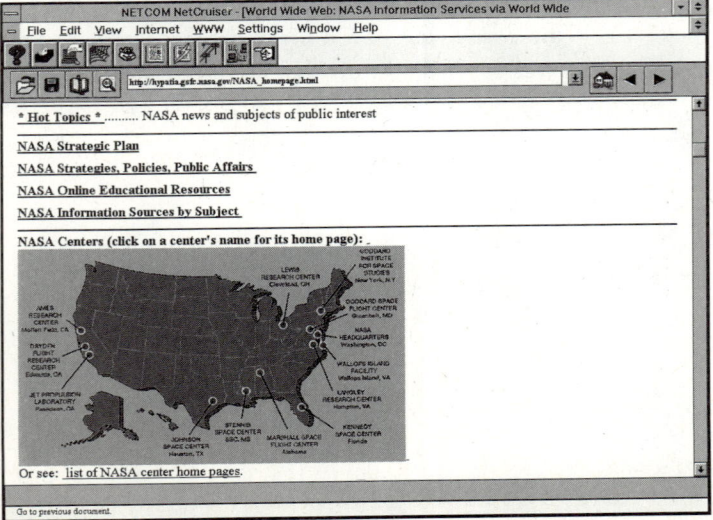

The benefit to an approach like this, of course, is that it's an all-in-one solution for Net denizens who don't want to get involved in the kind of download fever that assaults many of us. In addition, users receive software that is supported (and easily upgraded), and that is tailored for their particular service. It can be an attractive solution for users who want to get on the Net without actually understanding the way it works, and this type of user will increase in number dramatically over the next year or so.

NetCruiser's Web browser is more reminiscent of Cello than Windows Mosaic. In fact, it shares one of Cello's negative attributes, the inability to work with HTML forms (at least as of NetCruiser Version 1.4). In general, though, the browser works well, and it comes with a good base of usable features. During a document load, for example, on the right side of the status bar, the browser displays not only the number of bytes transferred so far, but also the total size of the file, and it does so for each inline image as well. Furthermore, instead of an Open URL dialog, you simply type the desired address into the URL display at the top of the screen. As with Internet in a Box, additionally, users don't have to worry about downloading and installing their own viewers and players; for the most part, they're installed and available right out of the package. The configuration menus, like the Spry product, provide instant access to the most important customization features. The main configuration box appears in Figure 11.41.

FIGURE 11.41.

The configuration dialog box from NetCruiser.

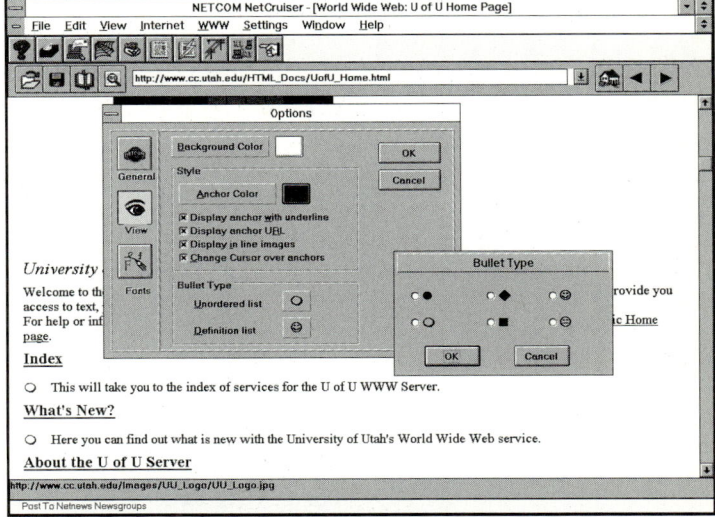

NetCruiser's browser displays cleanly and crisply, and is easy to use. In its obvious nod to simplicity, however, it lacks some of the features found in the more extensive clients. Bookmarking is similar to Cello and just as limiting. The history list works but is rudimentary (but then, so is Windows Mosaic's). But items such as Load to Disk are very good (letting you save the current document to disk, rather than—as in Windows Mosaic and Cello—the next retrieved document), and the whole effort has a feeling of stability to it.

Amiga Mosaic

Publisher:	SUNY Stony Brook
Latest Version:	1.2
FTP site:	`max.physics.sunysb.edu`
FTP directory:	`/pub/amosaic/`
FTP filename:	`Mosaic_1.2._AS225R2.lha`

Web clients exist for other platforms, such as VMS and the NeXT. This chapter makes no attempt at covering every existing browser, however, so here I'll offer only one further example. Commodore's Amiga was one of the first true multimedia computers on the market, and by all rights it should have been a giant hit. But the company's ability to market its products seemed to start and end with the earlier Commodore 64, and the Amiga, despite huge initial hype, never got the audience it deserved. Much of that audience, indeed, opted for the (then) less capable Macintosh instead. Commodore itself folded recently, but rumors have the Amiga itself surviving with another company.

At any rate, Amiga owners have a Web browser to work with, and an interesting one at that. Called Amiga Mosaic, the program looks very much like the Mosaics covered in Chapter 10, "The One You Keep Hearing About: NCSA Mosaic," but this one is *not* distributed or developed by NCSA (which is why it's in this chapter, not the last one). It is the work of a team headed by Michael Fischer, a systems administrator at SUNY in Stony Brook, NY, and it demonstrates the kind of commitment Amiga owners seem to have had since the beginning at creating software for themselves that no one else would make available.

As Figure 11.42 demonstrates, there's little to differentiate Amiga Mosaic from the official Mosaics, at least from an external perspective. Inside, of course, the program is significantly different, primarily because of a reliance (as is common in Amiga packages) on the Rexx programming language, which controls such features as hotlisting. Other small differences are apparent as well, including the omission of the spinning globe, but there's actually less apparent difference between Amiga Mosaic and X Mosaic (for example) than between, say, Mac Mosaic and Windows Mosaic.

FIGURE 11.42.

The Amiga Mosaic main screen.

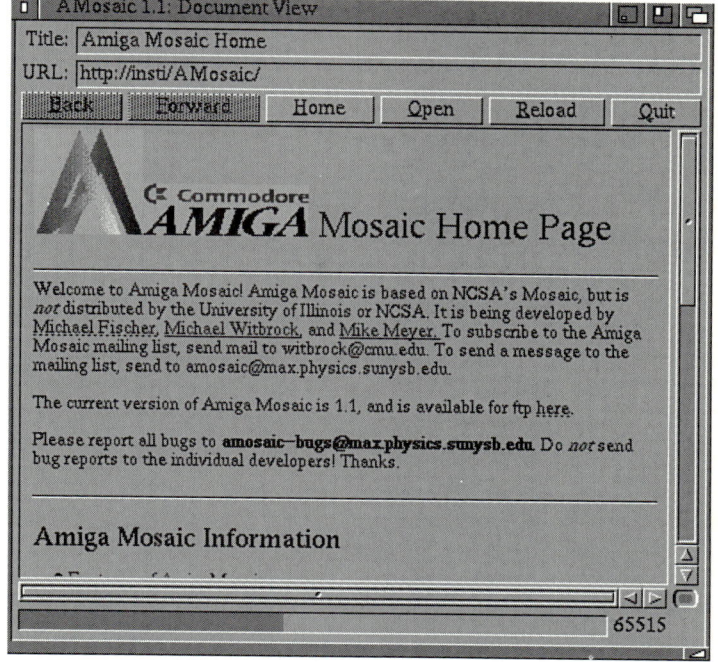

As you'd expect from an Amiga program, the color schemes and other visual elements of Amiga Mosaic are highly configurable. Anyone willing to work with a package like MUI (the MagicUserInterface) can make Amiga Mosaic look exactly as they wish, virtually pixel by pixel. For that matter, anyone willing to work with Arexx can add interface and special functions to the program as well. Good Amiga hackers—and there are tons of these—will take an already strong browser and add whatever they wish.

Making It Multimedia: Viewers, Players, and Other Browser Add-Ons

12

by Neil Randall

Okay. You've found the FTP site for the Web client of your choice, you've downloaded it to your hard drive, you've uncompressed it using the tools on your system, and you've installed it (or in UNIX's case, recompiled after altering the source code) with as little fuss as can be expected. You've fired the browser up, waited patiently for the first HTML page to appear, and, with barely contained excitement, started your exploration of the Web and all its offerings. Inline graphics displayed perfectly, the history list kept you on track, you've played with different fonts and underlining styles, the bookmarks are growing by leaps and bounds, and you've begun to realize how huge the Web has become. All's right with the world.

But suddenly you find yourself face-to-face with an icon that looks like a bit of movie film. And another one, beside it, that appears to be an audio speaker. You click on them, then settle back and watch the status bar for several minutes or maybe even an hour (with modem connections) as the thousands upon thousands of bytes are transferred across the Net. But then, after all that waiting, nothing happens.

So you go on. Everything seems to be working fine, until you come to a display of photographs in an endangered species site. Confidently, you click on the picture of the hippopotamus, then wait as your browser's status bar hits the 300,000 byte mark again. Suddenly, the status line disappears, and you get a message telling you that the program couldn't be found.

What program? Didn't you just FTP and install the thing?

Yes and no. You installed the browser, all right, but your work isn't done yet. You still have to find the viewers and players to go with it.

Browser Add-Ons: Why You Need Them

At this stage in the design of Web clients, they're usually designed to do only a couple things. They display HTML pages, and they display text files. If the HTML page includes a call to a graphic file, the client will display it in the form of an inline image. Some clients are capable of displaying more types of files than others, but for the most part they can handle an extremely limited variety.

To display other kinds of formatted files, or video, sound, and graphic files, you need a variety of external programs. Typically these are called viewers, although players, tools, and add-ons are other names for them. Essentially, the add-ons compensate for the browser's limitations, offering users a means of fully accessing every link they find on the Web.

The four main types of viewers enable you to view or hear the following types of files found on Web pages. Beside each type are some of the typical extensions, although there are certainly others:

- Graphics files: GIF, JPEG (JPG), PCX, TIFF, BMP, MAC, and others
- Sound files: AU, VOC, SND, WAV
- Video files: MPEG (MPG), AVI
- PostScript files: PS

So why don't the browsers do all this themselves? Actually, some do more than others. Look at the write-ups about MidasWWW in Chapter 11, "Yes, Virginia, There Is a Choice: More Graphical Browsers," for example, and you'll see a browser with built-in display capabilities for a range of files. For the others, however, two explanations are possible. The official version is this: By *not* including viewing and playing capabilities, the program is kept smaller, and people can choose their favorite add-ons rather than be forced to use those that are included. The more likely reason is that adding viewers and players would take programming time, effort, and money, and client designers have trouble enough just making the browsers work properly. (The official argument breaks down completely, of course, when you consider that you could be offered the option of overriding the internal viewers in order to specify your own.)

Browser Add-Ons: How to Install Them

Installing add-ons is rightfully the subject of a book all its own, and it is not the purpose of *The World Wide Web Unleashed* to detail the installation procedures. In general, however, the following steps are necessary:

1. Read the browser summary below to see if you have any appropriate add-on programs already.

2. Use your browser—even without any installed add-ons—to navigate to that browser's home page on the Web (see below for URL addresses of home pages), and read any information on that page about add-ons and, importantly, how to install them.

3. Locate and download (FTP) the add-on programs you need.

4. Install the add-ons to your hard disk—this usually requires decompressing them—and make sure they work as standalone programs.

5. Follow the instructions from the home page for installation: This will involve either the configuration tools within the browser itself, or, more commonly, working with the browser's detailed configuration file.

6. Load your browser with the add-ons installed, navigate to an appropriate site (see the listings for your specific browser later in this chapter), and try out your new toys.

The most difficult item in this list is Step 5, by far. Browsers such as MacWeb and Mac Mosaic have built-in configuration dialogs that let you select the appropriate add-on for the appropriate task. So do the new commercial browsers from Microsoft Windows. UNIX browsers, however, and the standard Microsoft Windows browsers (at least for now), all rely on a configuration file that you must edit if you want your add-ons to work with your browser. This task tends to be fairly well-documented, but it's never enjoyable. One note of caution: *before editing a configuration file, save a copy of it for use in case something goes wrong*. If you don't, it will.

To make use of add-ons, you have to instruct the Web client to perform some special duties. That's the role of the configuration files. In essence, you must tell your browser the following:

- Which programs are associated with which file types (suffixes)
- Where the associated programs exist on the hard drive or network

Associating File Types (Suffixes) with Programs

File associations are in no way peculiar to Web clients. Most operating systems can be configured to launch specific programs when files with appropriate suffixes are selected. In Windows, for example, files with a .WRI extension (extensions are also called suffixes) are associated with the small word processor Write, so that if you enter File Manager and then double-click on a file with that extension, you will both launch Write and load that particular file. By default in Windows, for example .DOC files are associated with Word for Windows and .PCX files with Paintbrush, but you can change these if you want by editing the `win.ini` configuration file.

Nor is the principle essentially any different with the Macintosh (where filenames themselves only *appear* to be less significant). The reason you can double-click on the icon for a PageMaker document and have both the program and that document loaded is that the appropriate associations have been established on your system. The difference between Windows and the Mac in this regard is that it's all transparent to you, at least until you want to change anything. For UNIX users, file association is something that must be done through configuration files almost exclusively.

Establishing Program Locations

Not only must you tell your browser which file types to associate with which programs, you must also specify precisely where those programs are located on your hard drive or network.

Once again, the Macintosh browsers are easier than the others in this regard, and typically require only that the program itself be specified in the configuration dialog.

For X Window and Microsoft Windows clients, the appropriate configuration file must be edited to include the full path name to the executable file of the associated program. There is a place to include this information, like the file associations information, in the configuration file of each browser. And keep in mind that if you move these programs to a different location, you'll have to manually edit the configuration files to reflect the change.

Browser Add-Ons: X Window

So much about X Window is dependent upon your particular machine that no discussion of add-ons can possibly be complete. The basic rule of thumb is this: If you have sound capabilities, and a sound player that will play (or at least convert) Sun audio files (that is, those with an .AU extension, the most common form on the Web), then associate the appropriate files with this program.

Similarly, if you're using a graphics package that already displays .GIF and .JPG files well (again, these are the most common types found on the Web), establish it as the external graphics program. Do the same, obviously, for programs that play MPEG video files (or soon Macintosh QuickTime and Microsoft Windows AVI files), and to display PostScript files as well.

Following are the utilities generally considered standard (the nice thing about standards, as one FTP site points out, is that there are so many to choose from). They're also, perhaps not coincidentally, the ones recommended by NCSA in their Mosaic home pages.

Graphics

xv

This is the standard graphics viewer for X Window, although there are others. xv not only views graphics, it makes possible a considerable amount of manipulation and conversion of graphics images as well. And it functions as a good screen capture program as well. It isn't small, though.

> **FTP Site:** `ftp.nsca.uiuc.edu`
>
> **Directory:** `/Web/Mosaic/Unix/viewers/`
>
> **Filename:** `xv-3.00.tar.Z`

Video

Mpeg_Play

This is the standard MPEG player for X Window browsers. It is small and featureless, but it does what you want it to do, which is to show a video file on screen and play it. You can't really control things, or edit the MPEG files, but those features are for more capable programs anyway. If you're using a system that already features strong video capabilities (Silicon Graphics, for example), use its built-in utilities instead.

FTP Site: `ftp.nsca.uiuc.edu`

Directory: `/Web/Mosaic/Unix/viewers/`

Filename: `mpeg_play-2.0.tar.Z`

Sound

The capability to play sound files is determined entirely by your hardware, and if you have sound capabilities then you probably have sound players already. Essentially, however, you need a player that will handle Sun audio files (.AU extension), which is the predominant type of file found on the Web. The standard general player is ShowAudio, which comes as part of a larger package called Metamail (which is also of considerable interest).

FTP Site: `thumper.bellcore.com`

Directory: `/pub/nsb/`

Filename: `mm2.x.tar.Z`

PostScript

Ghostview

Ghostview operates as an interface front-end to the program Ghostscript, and you need both programs to show PostScript documents in your X Mosaic screen. This involves downloading three files, as shown here. Note that Ghostview is a large program, and may take a while to download. Note also that MidasWWW has built-in PostScript viewing capabilities.

FTP Site: `ftp.nsca.uiuc.edu`

Directory: `/Web/Mosaic/Unix/viewers/`

Filename: `ghostscript-2.6.tar.z; ghostscript-fonts-2.6.tar.z;`
`ghostview-1.4.1.tar.z`

Another image format you'll run across is DVI (produced by TeX). The program xdvi displays these files much as Ghostview displays PostScript. Note that you're likely to find fewer DVI than PostScript files, but if you need to view them you'll require a viewer such as this one. Again, however, if you work in DVI format regularly you might already have one.

FTP Site: `ftp.x.org`

Directory: `/contrib/applications/`

Filename: `xdvi.tar.Z`

Sample Configuration File

Following is a sample mailcap file (which I've divided into specific sections), which holds the instructions for sending file types to external viewers in X Mosaic. This example is taken from the NCSA Mosaic Web pages, but on the X Window machine I used it was virtually identical.

Audio

```
# This maps all types of audio data (audio/basic, audio/x-aiff,
# etc.) to the viewer 'showaudio'. Note that '%s' means 'put the
# datafile name here when the viewer is executed'.
audio/*; showaudio %s
```

Graphics

```
# This maps all types of images (image/gif, image/jpeg, etc.)
# to the viewer 'xv'.
image/*; xv %s
```

MPEG Video

```
# This maps MPEG video data to the viewer 'mpeg_play'.
video/mpeg; mpeg_play %s
```

Other Video Types

```
# This maps all types of video *other than MPEG* to the viewer
# 'genericmovie'.
video/*; genericmovie %s
```

PostScript and DVI

```
application/postscript; ghostview %s
application/x-dvi; xdvi %s
```

Browser Add-Ons: The Apple Macintosh

In the area of browser configuration, Macintosh users have it easy. In both MacWeb and Mac Mosaic, file types and add-ons (called "helpers" in true Macintosh style) are configurable from within the program itself. Mac users also have several add-ons from which to choose, from a variety of well-stocked FTP sites. The Mac Mosaic home page from NCSA tells you which ones have been tested with that particular program. Note that not all add-ons will necessarily work with your system; they're listed here simply as a reference.

Graphics

JPEGView

JPEGView is the standard, a viewer capable of displaying JPEG, GIF, and many other file types. You need System 7 to run it, but it's good for many different purposes.

> **FTP Site:** mac.archive.umich.edu
>
> **Directory:** /mac/graphics/graphicsutil/
>
> **Filename:** jpegview3.3.sit.hqx

GIFConverter

Another standard, this program is also capable of displaying a number of document types.

> **FTP Site:** `mac.archive.umich.edu`
>
> **Directory:** `/mac/graphics/graphicsutil/`
>
> **Filename:** `gifconverter2.37.cpt.hqx`

GraphicConverter

An extremely powerful program, this one not only makes it possible for you to view the files, it enables you to convert them to a huge range of formats on several different platforms; includes batch conversion as well.

> **FTP Site:** `mac.archive.umich.edu`
>
> **Directory:** `/mac/graphics/graphicsutil/`
>
> **Filename:** `graphicconverter2.0.sit.hqx`

Video

Sparkle

The standard MPEG video player also converts movies from MPEG to Quicktime format; it's complete with rudimentary VCR-style controls.

> **FTP Site:** `mac.archive.umich.edu`
>
> **Directory:** `/mac/graphics/graphicsutil/`
>
> **Filename:** `sparkle2.12.sit.hqx`

BijouPlay, EasyPlay, PetersPlayer, QuicktimeVCR

These are four of many small Quicktime movie players available for the Mac.

> **FTP Site:** `mac.archive.umich.edu`
>
> **Directory:** `/mac/graphics/graphicsutil/`
>
> **Filenames:** `bijouplay1.33.sit.hqx`, `easyplay2.0.cpt.hqx`,
> `petersplayer1.01.sit.hqx`, `quicktimevcr3.6.sit.hqx`

Sound

SoundMachine

This is the sound player recommended by NCSA for use with Mac Mosaic. It's quite small and works well across a variety of sound formats (including Sun audio files).

> **FTP Site:** `mac.archive.umich.edu`
>
> **Directory:** `/mac/graphics/graphicsutil/`
>
> **Filename:** `soundmachine2.1.cpt.hqx`

SoundApp

An extremely capable utility that lets you play or convert audio files to and from many different formats (including Amiga, Windows, and NeXT).

Browser Add-Ons: Microsoft Windows

Microsoft Windows users, like Macintosh users, have a large variety of utilities to choose from. FTP sites around the Internet, as well as commercial online services, are stocked with audio players, graphics viewers, and video players of all shapes and sizes. Included here are only those easily found in the FTP sites where you can find the browsers as well, but you'll have no trouble finding others if you want them. Check out, for example, the Windows archives at `ftp.sunsite.unc.edu`, among other places.

Graphics

Lview

A good, small, easily installed graphics viewer, Lview handles .GIF, .PCX, and .JPG files with no problem. It converts as well, and it offers other useful graphics tools.

> **FTP Site:** `ftp.law.cornell.edu`
>
> **Directory:** `/pub/LII/Cello/`
>
> **Filename:** `lview31.zip`

Video

This is a very large file (over one megabyte), but it does its job. As with all Windows video, you won't be knocked out by the quality or the size (nor will you be on either of the other platforms, for that matter), but if you need to play an MPEG file, this one is available.

> **FTP Site:** `ftp.nsca.uiuc.edu`
>
> **Directory:** `/Mosaic/Windows/viewers/`
>
> **Filename:** `mpegw32e.zip`

Note that Media Player, which comes with Windows 3.1 and 3.11 (Workgroups), enables you to play Macintosh Quicktime files if you find them. But you also need Quicktime for Windows (available for purchase only, although included with several CD-ROMs) in order to actually view them.

Sound

Despite all the trouble you had getting that sound board to work, you'll now be able to use it to hear audio clips over the Web. Not that there's much worth hearing out there, and not that you'll spend the hours downloading it all, but eventually there will be more. The common file type for sound is Sun audio (.AU extension), but expect to find an increasing number of .WAV files as Windows users become more numerous. Both the sound players below install easily and are unobtrusive, although WPlany doesn't let you stop a file that's currently playing.

Wham

FTP Site: `ftp.law.cornell.edu`

Directory: `/pub/LII/Cello/`

Filename: `wham131.zip`

WPlany

FTP Site: `ftp.cica.indiana.edu`

Directory: `/pub/pc/win3/sounds/`

Filename: `wplny09b.zip`

PostScript

Like MpegPlay, Ghostview is an extremely large program, and if you're using a modem it will take a long time to download. Once in place, however, it's useful for viewing PostScript files from any source, not just the Web; it's well worth having.

Ghostscript/Ghostview

FTP site: `ftp.law.cornell.edu`

Directory: `/pub/LII/Cello/`

Filename: `gs261exe.zip`

Sample Configuration Files

Below are the multimedia portions of sample .INI files from Windows Mosaic, Cello, and WinWeb. Note that the configuration formats are similar as far as external viewers are concerned. Currently, only the commercially available browsers for Windows let you configure these programs without resorting to editing the .INI files.

Windows Mosaic (*mosaic.ini*)

```
[Viewers]
TYPE0="audio/wav"
TYPE1="application/postscript"
TYPE2="image/gif"
TYPE3="image/jpeg"
TYPE4="video/mpeg"
TYPE5="video/quicktime"
TYPE6="video/msvideo"
TYPE7="application/x-rtf"
TYPE8="audio/x-midi"
TYPE9="video/x-avi"
rem TYPE9="audio/basic"
rem There can be any number of TYPEs - just use TYPE10, TYPE11, ...
application/postscript="d:\winsock\gswin\gswin.exe %ls"
image/gif="c:\psp\psp.exe %ls"
image/jpeg="c:\psp\psp.exe %ls"
video/mpeg="c:\winsock\mpeg\mpegplay %ls"
video/x-avi="c:\windows\mplayer %ls"
video/quicktime="C:\QTW\bin\player.exe %ls"
video/msvideo="c:\windows\mplayer %ls"
audio/au="c:\winsock\wham\wham.exe %ls"
audio/wav="c:\winsock\wham\wham.exe %ls"
audio/x-midi="c:\windows\mplayer %ls"
application/x-rtf="c:\windows\write %ls"
rem audio/basic="notepad %ls"
telnet="d:\winsock\winapps\telw.exe"
tn3270=

[Suffixes]
application/postscript=.ps,.eps,.ai,.ps
text/html=
text/plain=
application/x-rtf=.rtf,.wri
audio/wav=.wave,.wav,.WAV
audio/au=.au
audio/x-midi=.mid
image/x-tiff=.tiff,.tif
image/jpeg=.jpeg,.jpe,.jpg
video/mpeg=.mpeg,.mpe,.mpg
video/qtime=.mov
video/msvideo=.avi
```

Cello (*cello.ini*)

```
[Extensions]
gif=e:\psp\psp.exe ^.gif
jpg=e:\psp\psp..exe ^.jpg
au=c:\windows\wplany.exe -u -r 8000 ^.au
snd=c:\wwwproj\viewers\wplany.exe ^.snd
wav=c:\windows\mplayer.exe ^.wav
avi=c:\windows\mplayer.exe ^.avi
mpg=c:\wwwproj\mpeg\mpegplay.exe ^.mpg
```

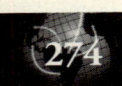
WinWeb (*winweb.ini*)

```
[Launch]
Entry0=image/gif,winvoke wingo.inv lview31
Entry1=text/x-winvoke,winvoke
Entry2=application/x-winexe,winvoke winexe.inv
Entry3=image/jpeg,winvoke wingo.inv wecj1_2
Entry4=video/msvideo,mplayer

Entry5=application/octet-stream,winvoke wingo.inv notepad
[Extensions]
Entry0=.ai,application/postscript,8bit
Entry1=.mime,www/mime,binary
Entry2=.ps,application/postscript,8bit
Entry3=.eps,application/postscript,8bit
Entry4=.execme.csh,applicaton/x-csh,7bit
Entry5=.html,text/html,8bit
Entry6=.c,text/plain,7bit
Entry7=.h,text/plain,7bit
Entry8=.m,text/plain,7bit
Entry9=.f90,text/plain,7bit
Entry10=.txt,text/plain,7bit
Entry11=.rtf,application/x-rtf,8bit
Entry12=.src,application/x-wais-source,7bit
Entry13=.snd,audio/basic,binary
Entry14=.bin,application/octet-stream,binary
Entry15=.z,application/x-compressed,binary
Entry16=.gif,image/gif,binary
Entry17=.tiff,image/x-tiff,binary
Entry18=.jpg,image/jpeg,binary
Entry19=.jpeg,image/jpeg,binary
Entry20=.mpg,video/mpeg,binary
Entry21=.mpeg,video/mpeg,binary
Entry22=.htm,text/html,8bit
Entry23=.exe,application/x-winexe,binary
```

Next Year's Catalog: Web Tools of the Future

13

by Neil Randall

There's a lot to like about the Web. It's informative, it's appealing, it's filled with a sense of adventure. A typical Web session can land you on computers on most of the continents of the world, letting you see the cultural differences in page design and information presentation, all without leaving the comfort of your own mouse. And as long as you have your browser properly configured, you aren't just restricted to the text and graphics on the page itself. At your disposal are full-size graphics, short but fascinating video clips, and sound that can be anything from an announcement to an anthem.

But what the Web does *not* do is every bit as significant as what it *does*. It does not, for example, let you engage in any kind of meaningful e-mail exchange, and surely there's nothing more intrinsic to the Internet itself. Nor does it give you the power to stage live drama or even live videoconferences, and there seems little hope of ever being able to use it as a substitute for television, or for that matter as a substitute for your Sega Genesis. Don't look to the Web even for discussion lists or newsgroups, because any program dedicated to those purposes does a better, more complete, and more feature-filled job. The Web is essentially a program that lets you browse book pages, or at least information documents that resemble book pages in some very real ways.

It's a long, long way from being a truly interactive medium.

True. But the World Wide Web is drawing huge amounts of attention precisely because it's a multimedia dissemination system, one that presents real hypertext and real hypermedia drawn from computers—and hence human minds—from many corners of the world. Because of the Web, the Internet has become suddenly usable, and hence suddenly hot. No, the Web doesn't do everything, and what it does, it does only a fraction as well as it could. But it feels and looks like a true technology of the nineties, and despite its severe limitations it's being looked to as an important source of information and communication in the coming decade.

Part VI of *The World Wide Web Unleashed*, "Whither the Web: Trends and Issues," is devoted to looking at the Web's future. Here, I want to spend a few pages looking at Web-based tools that are already in the works, or rather Internet-based tools that will almost certainly be integrated into the Web. I also want to speculate about what kinds of tools we need to allow the Web to mature into the indispensable technology it currently only hints at becoming. Everything in this chapter is speculation, but it's speculation based on trends and technologies currently underway.

In the last chapter, you saw how to give the Web a rudimentary multimedia look. This chapter examines what it will take to make true hypermedia a reality. It won't happen overnight, but it just might happen one or two steps at a time. Here are some of those steps.

Upgrading What You Have Now

Despite the advances in multimedia computing over the past half-dozen years, the state of multimedia add-ons for Web browsers is, in a word, deplorable. Yes, some excellent graphics browsers are available, but sound players and video players tend to be rudimentary at best.

Worse still, there's no reason for them to be better. Very few worthwhile sound files exist on the Web, and even fewer video files. Any single episode of Nova will provide you with science files of more interest than a week of Web searching would reveal, and any AM-only car radio with only marginal reception outclasses most of the sound offerings out there on the Web. Graphics are better served, but even their quality is highly erratic.

Advances in computer hardware in the past couple years have meant affordable high-quality sound (near CD-quality, in fact) in the form of wavetable synthesis and three-dimensional effects. In the next few years, further advances will mean affordable full-motion, full-screen video, replacing the ridiculously small and unwatchably choppy video we have today.

What this means is that Web information providers can provide truly multimedia documents and files, fulfilling the promise of multimedia only suggested by the Web today.

One problem, and it's a huge one, will remain: The Web is slow. Something seems fundamentally wrong when I can get an instant full-screen, full-motion, live picture from any TV set and from halfway around the world (and have been able to since the 1950s), yet to get even a poor-quality, choppy, prerecorded image from the World Wide Web site a block away from my house I have to sit and wait for it to show up on my machine, and then watch as a few seconds of something too small to be recognizable wiggles around in one corner of my screen. And if I want sound attached to that file—something, once again, that television has done since its earliest days—I have to wait longer, and I'd better not be filled with expectation. Speed matters, and the Web doesn't have it.

Needed, and needed badly, are affordable high-speed access (and I'm not talking about 64kbps here) and much more capable computer hardware and software. Needed, and needed badly, are new and upcoming methods of data compression, compression so tight that a half-hour full-screen video with full sound can appear in seconds, maybe less. It's called "video on demand" in some circles, but whatever it's called, the Web needs it. The multimedia tools of today are not one bit better than the sprite animation and sound reproduction of the Commodore 64 of over a decade ago.

Full Communications

The World Wide Web is proving highly capable as a publishing medium, but extremely disappointing as a force for interpersonal communications. Over the next several months, e-mail and newsgroup capability will improve in Web browsers, as more effort is given to these two fundamental Internet activities. The most likely possibility is initially to incorporate e-mail programs and newsgroup readers into Web clients as add-on tools, then slowly to build them directly into the browser itself. This approach would take the browser further along the path to becoming a full-featured Internet front end, a process that will fulfill its existing promise.

The rationale for this approach is the same as for the development of docucentric (document-centered) software, which is beginning to stumble into existence. In a docucentric environment, users don't load programs, they load documents, and the software tools change depending on the tasks they wish to perform on that document. This is the real basis of the software "suite," the packages containing a word processor, spreadsheet program, database management package, and presentation graphics program. With all these tools available, and all working with essentially the same interface that changes readily depending on the task to be performed, all the software exists to serve the document, not the other way around.

Web clients are already integrated suites. They let you perform FTP and Gopher tasks, and even read newsgroups, send e-mail messages, and telnet to other sites. They tend to do these things halfheartedly (dedicated programs are infinitely better), but they do them. Once fully featured e-mail, newsgroup, FTP, Gopher, telnet, finger, WAIS, Archie, and other Internet tools are built completely into the browsers, the Web can begin to fulfill its role of being all things to all Internetters. When that happens, it can become a technology geared for full communications, not just for the publishing applications which it currently handles so well.

Live Productions

Videoconferencing became an affordable possibility in 1993-94, particularly with the introduction of a new software/hardware genre called desktop conferencing. With this software, and appropriately equipped and configured microcomputers, live video and audio started to make its way from the dedicated videoconferencing rooms (which cost hundreds of thousands of dollars to establish and maintain) and onto the desktop PC or Mac. There are, admittedly, limitations. But with the advent of fiber optic and other technologies, these limitations will be overcome. And prices, as always, will drop.

The World Wide Web must and will begin to support the technologies that make live videoconferencing, and hence live productions, possible. Already in the design and implementation stages on the Internet is a technology set called the MBONE (see `http://www.eit.com/techinfo/mbone/mbone.html` for a full introduction, and `http://www.research.att.com/mbone-faq.html` for an MBONE FAQ), which makes use, partly at least, of a technology called the Real Time Transport protocol (RTP). This protocol

exists for the purpose, as its draft paper tells us, of providing "end to end network transport functions suitable for applications transmitting real time data, such as audio, video, or simulation data over multicast or unicast network services." Furthermore, it is "primarily designed to satisfy the needs of multiparticipant multimedia conferences."

In other words, the technology is already starting to appear that will allow live multicasting over the Internet. As of this writing, either a Sun SPARCstation or Silicon Graphics Indio machine were needed for actually taking part in these multicasts, but ports were underway to the Macintosh as well.

Providers of Web pages should already be looking into providing a World Wide Web interface to real-time MBONE conferencing, because the Web is currently the best Internet interface in existence. Some day in the next year and a half, I want to click on a link to an MBONE videoconference, or maybe even an MBONE talk show, one that I can participate in with people from around the world, in real-time and without the delays and annoyances of Internet Relay Chat, MUDs, or other currently difficult interactions.

But speaking of IRC and MUDs, there's no reason whatsoever that MBONE or MBONE-like technology couldn't be employed to provide the best "face-to-face" international gab sessions or parlor games ever devised.

Tired of the same old pub crowd? How about taking in a pub somewhere across the ocean, not as a passive television-style viewer but as an active participant seen and heard by those physically in the room? Or maybe a virtual pub, with everybody signing in from far away, and a band providing the music from their basement but able to see your reaction anyway. Why not a game of Diplomacy over the Web, with real-time strategy meetings with the leaders of two other players, trying to stop a third from taking over the world?

Farfetched? Sure. But isn't that what interactive technologies are promising? Surely we don't want to settle for occasional interactive input over the set-top superhighway box. Surely we want more, much more. Surely we want a way to shrink the world as never before possible.

Okay, I'm rambling. But the World Wide Web has proven to be a galvanizing force on a global level, and as a familiar and usable front end to real-time global interaction it could be the most fascinating and *important* technology to emerge since, well (dare I say it?), since the printing press. More important than television and radio combined, and maybe more substantive.

I called this mini-section Live Productions. That's because another possibility presents itself over an MBONE-equipped Web: Live, interactive, globally available theater. I'll leave it to the artists to figure out exactly what that entails.

Next Year's Catalog

Of course, the Web was never designed to be anywhere near as extensive as I've suggested it could one day become. It was a hypertext/hypermedia tool, a method of offering easy, graphical access to research documents. Well, it's done that, and although it has a ways to go yet, it's already proven that it can handle its initial role. It's even proven that it can go beyond that role, becoming the center for corporate and financial interest that was very clearly never part of the original plan.

Next year, we'll see the implementation of data security. As a result, we'll see business applications begin to flourish. In all likelihood, we'll start to see tools that will support this kind of activity, although what tools are needed remains amazingly uncertain at this point. There has to be a way to make shopping and ordering easy, because the Web will depend a great deal upon impulse purchasing. And for financial institutions, fast links must be built to live reports and other essential tools, although these will remain expensive and of interest only to those communities.

Obviously, sound and video players will improve as the respective technologies for microcomputers improve. But other technologies remain unintegrated. Will fax boards and scanners gain a use on the Web? Will CD-ROM become fast enough to be considered a worthwhile storage device for files? Maybe, to both questions. What next year's catalog will do, however, is move the Web from its basis in page publishing and into a different mode of information providing. The browsers will be hard put to keep up.

It's possible, of course, that none of these things will happen at all. But with lower costs for cable and/or ISDN access, and the 28.8 kbps modem becoming a standard, the Web will find itself more and more in the mainstream. The tools will follow, as they inevitably do.

PART

III

Web Navigation Tools and Techniques

The Web offers an astounding collection of information and resources. At the same time, many new users remark on the Web's apparent chaos. In my work in training and development, I often hear a user complain, "I can't find what I want." I've also had a student in one of my workshop sessions say he thought the Net was stupid because he had spent much of his class exploration time stuck in the Usenet recipe archive, and he felt recipes were a waste of time. I learned from my experience with that student why users of the Web need to gain skills in navigation tools and techniques to discover the treasure-trove (and weed through the chaos) of information on the Web.

In the chapters in this part, we'll review skills you need to know to effectively gain the Web's wealth of resources. In Part I, "Introduction to the World Wide Web," the Web was introduced from a general point of view. In this part, we'll examine the Web's components in more detail from the point of view of navigation. We'll examine concepts and define vocabulary to describe the Web's structure and spaces as well as specific tools and techniques to find what you want on the Web.

We'll examine the topology of the networks that make up cyberspace and how the Web fits into a global mesh of interconnections. We'll see how the Web's structure links Internet resources and creates information spaces. Through this discussion, you will gain a conceptual map of the Web, with an understanding of how the Web's structures and spaces relate to larger communications networks and Internet tools.

Then you will gain some specific navigation skills, starting with the operation of a popular browser—Mosaic—and look at how you can use its native features for basic navigation. I'll include tips and advice for organizing and conducting your sessions with Mosaic, including ideas for using its options and functions to help you work quickly and efficiently.

In the chapters that follow, we'll look in detail at searching techniques, using a variety of ways to find resources, people, machines, and information on the Web. Building on these techniques, I'll give some advice for methods of "surfing" the Web. By surfing, you can keep current in a resource area and find new and unique resources in some unconventional places. To aid you in searching and navigating, I'll integrate these techniques in a detailed example in the final chapter of this part that illustrates how you can locate specific, subject-oriented, and context information on the Web.

Throughout this part, I'll discuss and summarize key navigation and information resources that you can use to exploit the power of the Web. Appendix C, "Net Directory," contains a summary of these resources and more.

Navigating the Web is an art that requires good grounding in fundamental navigation skills—such as knowing how to use a browser—as well as quite sophisticated searching techniques. Navigating the Web also challenges you to create your own information structure—to select from your experience of the Web a personal "hotlist" of the places and spaces that matter to you most. Throughout this part, you'll gain skills to discover and appreciate the rapidly developing wealth of resources throughout the Web.

Web Structure and Spaces

14

by John December

The first step in learning how to successfully navigate the Web is understanding the Web's structure and information spaces. While Web browsers like Mosaic can enable someone with no knowledge of the topology of cyberspace to use a "point and click" operation to move around, someone knowing how online networks operate together can better understand the workings of the Web navigation tools and the reasons behind navigation techniques discussed later in this part. To tour the structure of the Web, we'll start from cyberspace and then converge on the Web in ever-closer detail.

The Web Within Cyberspace

Cyberspace refers to the mental construct a person generates from experiencing online communication and information retrieval. The science fiction author William Gibson developed this term to describe the visual environments in his novels in which computer users navigate a global network of information resources and services.

The term *cyberspace* is used today to refer to the collection of computer-mediated experiences for visualization, communication, or information retrieval. You can think of cyberspace as the largest context for anything done online or through computers, whether it is a doctor using a virtual reality helmet for visualizing an experimental surgical operation or a student reading a newspaper online.

Within the large context of cyberspace, there is a system for networked communication and information dissemination: the Internet. The Internet is a globally-distributed collection of computer networks that all use the same set of rules (protocols) to exchange information. The Internet is cooperatively-run and constitutes one of the largest systems for human communication ever created. Internet protocols are the basis for exchanging information on the Web, so the Web can be considered to be located within the Internet. Therefore, a Web navigator (someone who uses the Web for information retrieval and communication) needs to know something about the Internet's place in cyberspace.

The Topology of Cyberspace

The topology of cyberspace consists of separate networks and systems that provide for the exchange of information and communication among users. These systems and networks use different protocols, or rules, for exchanging information. The Internet is just one of these online networks in cyberspace.

The Internet uses a special set of protocols to exchange information called TCP/IP or "the Internet protocol suite." The Web utilizes these Internet protocols for communication. Therefore, the Web can be considered to exist within the Internet.

Users of networks other than the Internet have to use gateways (or exchange points) to access resources on the Web. Since not all networks have gateways to the Internet for all the protocols that the Web supports, it is often very difficult for a non-Internet user to make use of the Web.

Commercial online services such as Prodigy, America Online, CompuServe, and others provide users with connections to information. Although some of these commercial services provide graphical interfaces, these interfaces are *not* necessarily views into the Web; there is not yet any direct connection to the Internet's Web from commercial services. Similarly, users of other global networks can't easily access the Web. FidoNet is a network of personal computers worldwide that exchanges information by modems and phone lines, and BITNET and UUCP are other networks used for exchanging information among users. Users of these networks can't directly access the Web (except through electronic mail interfaces).

Figure 14.1 shows the topology of cyberspace, listing major networks in the online world.

FIGURE 14.1.

A topology of cyberspace.

PRIVATE NETS AND SYSTEMS
(e.g., corporate, banking,commerce)

FIDONET

BITNET

UUCP

INTERNET

THE WEB

COMMERCIAL ONLINE SERVICES
(e.g., Prodigy, America Online,CompuServe)

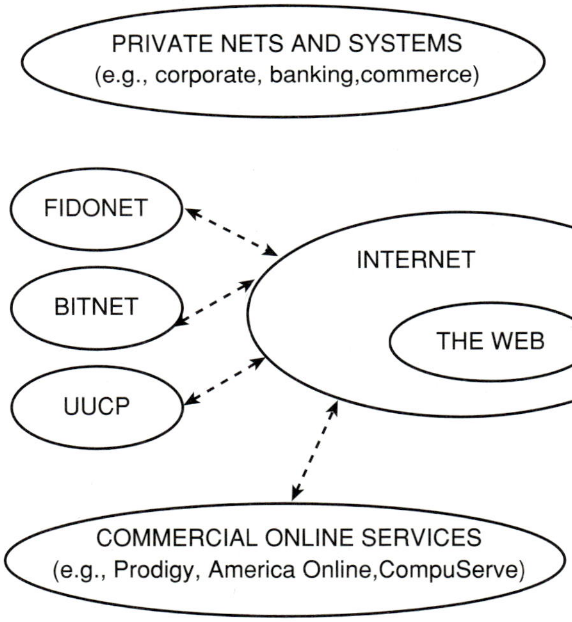

Gateways Among Networks

In many cases, there is no way to exchange information directly among the networks of cyberspace. For example, the world-wide system for exchanging banking transactions is not accessible from the Internet (for obvious security reasons).

In other cases, there is some level of connection among these large networks. For example, BITNET and Internet users can exchange electronic mail through gateways built for that purpose. Similarly, many commercial services provide e-mail gateways from their services to the Internet. Figure 14.1 shows—as dashed lines—some of the electronic mail gateways that exist among the networks of cyberspace.

TERMINOLOGY

When talking about cyberspace, the following brief definitions of its regions may be helpful.

The Matrix—The set of all networks that can exchange electronic mail either directly or through gateways. This includes the Internet, BITNET, FidoNet, and UUCP, commercial services such as America Online, CompuServe, and Delphi, as well as other networks. This term was coined by John S. Quarterman in his book *The Matrix (Digital Press, 1990).*

The Net—An informal term for the Internet or a subset of The Matrix in context. For example, a computerized conference via e-mail may take place on a BITNET host that has an Internet gateway, thus making the conference available to anyone on either of these networks. In this case, the developer might say, "Our conference will be available on the Net."

The Web—Used in its strictest sense, *The Web* refers to all the hypertext on all publicly-accessible Web servers worldwide. In a broader sense, The Web could be used to refer to all publicly-accessible hypertext (on FTP and even Gopher servers). In a still broader sense, The Web could be considered to include all the collected Internet resources that are accessible through a Web browser. This broad meaning, then, would include *FTP space* and *Gopher space* (see below). It would, however, be misleading to say, "We put the documents on the Web" when one has placed them only on an FTP server (as opposed to placing the documents on a Web server). While FTP documents are accessible by Web browsers, the audience for the above statement might be mislead to believe that the documents are on a Web server and perhaps in hypertext. A single Web server with its associated files can be called a web (with a small *w*). For example, you might say, "We're going to have to make a web to describe the new system" (web refers to a single, local web). In contrast: "We'll put the documents on the Web" (Web refers to the global collection of publically-accessible webs, and indicates the speaker's intention to make the local web widely known and publicly available).

The Internet—The Internet is the cooperatively-run, globally-distributed collection of computer networks that exchange information via the TCP/IP protocol suite. The Internet consists of many internetworked networks, called internets (with a small *i*). An internet is a single network that uses the TCP/IP protocol suite, and some internets are not connected to the Internet.

FTP space—The set of all resources accessible through the file transfer protocol. These resources include directories of files and individual files that may be text or binary (executable files, graphics, sound, video) files.

Gopher space—The set of all resources accessible through the Internet Gopher protocol. A Gopher is a system for organizing information in terms of menus. Menu items can be links to other documents or information services.

Usenet—This is not a network at all, but a system for disseminating asynchronous text discussion among cooperating computer hosts. Usenet is not limited to the Internet. Its origins are in UUCP (UNIX-to-UNIX Copy Program) systems, but Usenet is disseminated widely throughout the Matrix and beyond.

As a navigator of the Web, you need to keep Figure 14.1 in mind as a basic operational chart. Remember the following:

- Cyberspace consists of many different networks.
- Because the Web links Internet resources, the Web can be considered to be "located" within the Internet.
- Users of networks can exchange electronic mail or other information through gateways.
- Because most implemented gateways among networks are for electronic mail only, it is easiest to use the Web from the Internet.

When navigating the Web, you may encounter many references to non-Internet activities and other networks in cyberspace. Remember that these activities may not be directly accessible from the Web. Eventually, gateways may be built from these other networks to support the protocols necessary for Web operation.

The Web Within the Internet

Now that we've examined the Web as one part of the Internet portion of cyberspace, let's examine the Web's role with the Internet itself. The power of the Web, as discussed in Part I, "Introduction to the World Wide Web," is that it links Internet resources through a system of hypertext.

From a user's point of view, the Web consists of resources on the Internet that are accessible through a particular Web browser. The Web connects these resources through hypertext written using the Hypertext Markup Language (HTML). Files containing text marked using HTML are located on a Web server and available for Web browsers (clients) to access. The HTML file contains links to other Internet resources. For example,

Figure 14.2 illustrates the connections among an HTML document to other Internet resources.

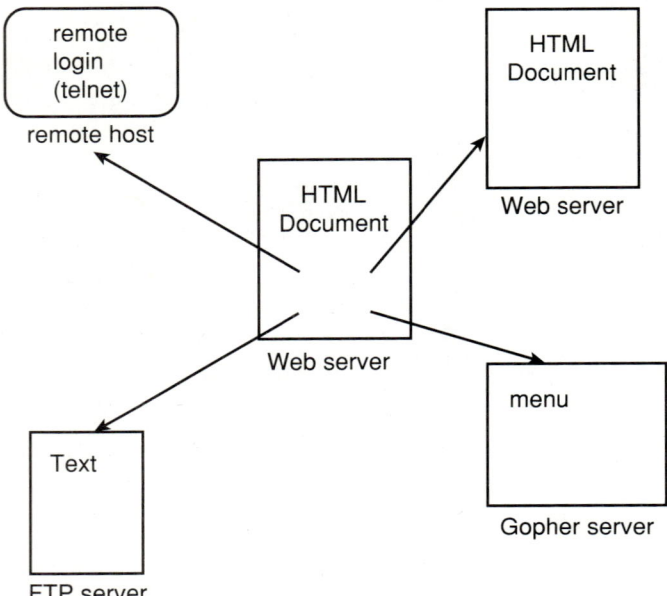

The resources shown in Figure 14.2 include a remote login to a host through the telnet protocol, a link to a text file on a file transport protocol (FTP) server, a link to a menu on a Gopher server, and a link to another HTML document on another Web server. Thus, the Web links disparate resources scattered across the network.

You can think of the "binding together" that the Web does for Internet resources in terms of the protocols that Web browsers can understand. Web browsers use the Hypertext Transfer Protocol (HTTP) as a means to exchange hypertext written in HTML. HTTP is a protocol developed especially for the Web, and was designed to operate quickly for hypertext jumps. Web browsers (discussed in detail in Part II, "Web Browsers and Connections,") can also access information according to other protocols, some of which are shown in Figure 14.2:

■ FTP (File Transfer Protocol)—a protocol used widely for transferring information (text, graphics, video) across the Internet.

■ NNTP (Network News Transfer Protocol)—a protocol used for exchanging Usenet news.

■ Gopher—a protocol for sharing information in the form of menus and documents.

■ telnet—a means to remotely log into a host on the Internet.

Information Spaces In the Web

Now that you've seen the Web's linking relationship with Internet resources, we can examine the structure of the spaces created by the Web's scheme for referring to resources.

Uniform Resource Locators

The basis for identifying the Internet resources the Web links is the Uniform Resource Locator, or URL. A URL consists of a string of characters that uniquely identifies a resource on the Internet. You can think of a URL as a sort of "catalog number" for an Internet resource. When you use a Web browser to open a particular URL, you will gain access to the Internet resource defined by that URL.

The basic format for many URLs is as follows:

```
scheme://host:port/path
```

where

> *scheme* = one of the ways to retrieve or send information via the Internet, such as FTP, NNTP, Gopher, telnet, and others
>
> *host* = the computer host on which the resource resides
>
> *port* = a particular number that identifies the service you are requesting from the computer host; provided if the service is installed on a port different than the standard one for that service
>
> *path* = an identification of the location of a resource on a particular computer host

There are other variations in format that a Web navigator will encounter. All URLs, however, share the same purpose: to identify an Internet resource for linking within HTML hypertext read by Web browsers.

WEB HYPERTEXT TERMINOLOGY

Although the concept of hypertext and its actual use in computer systems has been around a long time, terminology for Web-related hypertext elements is evolving, both in formal definitions and informal usage. The following terms are often used in talking about Web-based hypertext:

Page refers to a single sheet of hypertext (a single file of HTML).

Home page refers to a designated entry-point for access to a local web. Also refers to a page that a person defines as their principal page, often containing personal or professional information.

Hotspot is the region of displayed hypertext that, when selected, links the user to another point in the hypertext or another resource.

For example, here are some URLs (some of which are variations from the pattern shown previously to show different forms a URL can take):

`http://www.eff.org`—This is the home page of the Electronic Frontier Foundation, an organization to advocate the civil liberties of users of online. This home page leads to many other links. This URL actually has no path specified. Only the host name, `www.eff.org` is listed. In this case a default home page is retrieved as a result of accessing this URL.

`ftp://nic.merit.edu/documents/fyi/fyi_20.txt`—This is a text document that answers the question "What is the Internet?" written by E. Krol and E. Hoffman. This URL uses file transfer protocol, and has a host name (`nic.merit.edu`) as well as a path name listed (`documents/fyi/fyi_20.txt`).

`gopher://gopher.cic.net/11/hunt`—This is the URL of a Gopher menu that presents information about a game—the Internet Hunt—that helps players build their skills in locating Internet resources. This URL uses the Gopher protocol. The path name given after the host, `gopher.cic.net` identifies the menu entry for this particular resource.

`telnet://iitf.doc.gov`—This is the URL to the US government's information infrastructure task force's bulletin board. When a Web browser opens this URL, a telnet session will appear (a session in which the user will log onto a remote computer host).

`news:comp.infosystems`—This is the format to access Usenet news delivered according to the network news transfer protocol (nntp).

`http://siva.cshl.org/~boutell/www_faq.html#url`—This is a URL to the World Wide Web Frequently Asked Questions (FAQ) list, the section on URLs. Note that the `#url` part at the end indicates that this URL points to a specific place within the document called an anchor.

`http://www.ncsa.uiuc.edu/SDG/Experimental/demoweb/marc-global-hyp.au`—This is an audio file (`.au` extension) located on a server demonstrating Mosaic's capabilities. This sound file, when accessed by a browser (provided that the user has the appropriate audio player software and hardware installed in the computer), will produce a voice greeting.

`http://uu-gna.mit.edu:8001/uu-gna/index.html`—This is the URL to the home page of the Globewide Network Academy, an organization dedicated to creating a fully accredited online university. Note that this URL has a port number (`8001`), specified by the developers of this page. The standard port number for HTTP access is 80, so that when a port not equal to 80 is set, you should use it in the URL. If you leave off the port number, you will get the following error message:

```
Requested document (URL http://uu-gna.mit.edu/uu-gna/index.html)
could not be accessed.
The information server either is not accessible or is refusing to
serve the document to you.
```

KEY RESOURCES

For finding out more about URLs, see

```
"Uniform Resource Locators."
http://info.cern.ch/hypertext/WWW/Addressing/URL/Overview.html

Andreessen, Marc.
"A Beginner's Guide to URLs."
http://www.ncsa.uiuc.edu/demoweb/url-primer.html


Theise, Eric S. (1994 January 7).
"Curling Up to Universal Resource Locators."
gopher://gopher.well.sf.ca.us/00/matrix/internet/curling.up.02
```

Information Spaces

URLs create information spaces on the Web in terms of the protocol used. For example, you can consider all FTP URLs to be in FTP space, the set of all servers publicly available for anonymous FTP. This space is just one region of the Internet's resources, but represents a vast repository of knowledge to which the Web can connect.

Not only does a URL identify the protocol used for the information, but a URL also often identifies the type of media represented by the resource. For example, the URL shown

above, `http://www.ncsa.uiuc.edu/SDG/Experimental/demoweb/marc-global-hyp.au`, is an audio file. Similarly, there are filename extensions for movies (mpeg) as well as many kinds of graphics (i.e. GIF, JPEG, XBM) and text files (i.e. TXT, PS, TEX). In this way, a URL may identify the *sensory* experience a resource may offer. You can thus consider the information spaces in the Internet to be multimedia spaces. A good source of more information about multimedia is Simon Gibbs' "Index to Multimedia Information Sources," `http://cui_www.unige.ch/OSG/MultimediaInfo/index.html`.

We'll cover techniques for using URLs and writing HTML in more detail in Part V, "Weaving a Web." As a Web navigator, remember that the URL is the basis for some tasks in Web navigation. You will use a URL to call up a specific resource in a browser and use URLs within HTML documents to link resources.

A PEEK AT HTML

In Part V, "Weaving a Web," we'll look in detail how to construct HTML documents. It might be helpful at this point, however, to get a glimpse of what an HTML file looks like. Below is an example. The < and > symbols mark the start and end of tags that are used to identify components of the document.

In this example, I've included several kinds of URLs: HTTP, telnet, electronic mail, Gopher, and Usenet news. Notice how the URLs are enclosed within `<a href="URL">HOTSPOT</a>` markers, where `HOTSPOT` is the part of the displayed text that will be highlighted in the displayed hypertext. Figure 14.3 shows how this HTML file is displayed in the browser. All the items marked labels between < and > are used to interpret the document for display.

```
<HTML>

<HEAD>

<TITLE>

Telecommunications Resources

</TITLE>

</HEAD>

<BODY>

<H1>Selected Telecommunications Resources</H1>

<hr>

<UL>

<LI> <a href="http://gozer.idbsu.edu/business/nethome.html">DELTA</a>
Distributed ELectronic Telecommunications Archive-teaching and learning about
business telecommunications and data communications
```

```
<LI><a href="telnet://ntiabbs.ntia.doc.gov">NTIA</a> National Telecommunications
and Information Administration (USA)

<LI><a href="ftp://ftp.ctr.columbia.edu/CTR-Research">Center for Telecommunications
Research</a> Columbia University, New York, NY

<LI>RITIM-L: Research Institute for Telecommunications and Information Marketing
discussion list: <a href="mailto:listserv@uriacc.uri.edu">Send email to
listserv@uriacc.uri.edu, with the Body: "sub RITIM-L YOUR NAME"</a>

<LI><a href="gopher://info.itu.ch">ITU</a> International Telecommunication Union, a
United Nations agency which coordinates telecommunications

<LI><a href="news:comp.dcom.telecom">The Usenet newsgroup comp.dcom.telecom</a>

</UL>

<hr>

<address> <a href="http://www.rpi.edu/~decemj/index.html">John December</a>
(decemj@rpi.edu) / 24 June 1994 </address>

</BODY>
</HTML>
```

FIGURE 14.3.

Browser display of Selected Telecommunications Resources File.

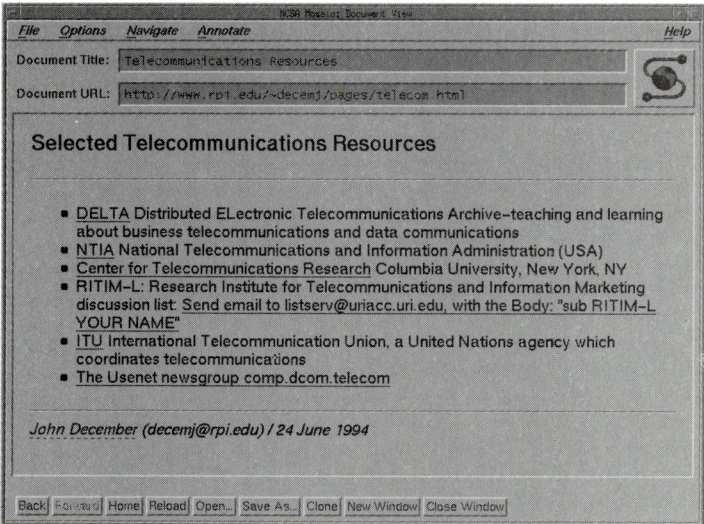

> **TIP**
>
> Since a URL is widely recognized as a standard way to refer to an Internet resource, you might use a URL as a resource descriptor in non-Web settings.
>
> For example, in citing a source in a bibliography, you can list the URL for the source if it has an online equivalent (or only an online version). For example
>
> Polly, Jean Armour. (1993 May 15). "Surfing the Internet: an Introduction." Uniform Resource Locator `ftp://nysernet.org/pub/resources/guides/surfing.2.0.3.txt`.
>
> If you have a Web home page, you might also list its URL on your business card along with other telecommunications identifiers such as this:
>
> Phone: (518)555-1212
> Email: `smith@foo.edu`
> Web: `http://www.foo.edu/~smith/index.html`

Navigator's Check

Your challenge as a Web navigator is to understand the topology of cyberspace and the way the Web links resources. With this knowledge, you can begin to gain skills using a Web browser and learn tools and techniques for navigation. Eventually, you will be able to use the Web to find useful information.

As a Web navigator, you'll need to remember

- The Web is "located" on the Internet, and the Internet is just one of the networks in global cyberspace.
- The Web is a system for linking the vast resources of the Internet together through hypertext.
- The Uniform Resource Locator (URL) is the basis for Web references.

You can envision the Web as a glue that holds together many different kinds of Internet resources. These resources might be information services, multimedia documents, or other Web documents that in turn contain links to other resources. The power of the Web lies in the possibilities its hypertext language, HTML, offers for providing expressive ways to present, organize, and link multimedia information distributed globally.

Browser Operations

15

by John December

Once you have a Web browser installed on your computer (as explained in Part II, "Web Browsers and Connections,") and have an idea of the general layout of cyberspace and the Web (explained in the previous chapter) the next step is learning how to effectively use the functions offered by your browser for navigation. This chapter uses the Mosaic for X browser as an example and describes basic operations as well as tips and techniques for navigation.

Basic Operations

Once you get the Mosaic browser up and running, it presents an interface with a variety of buttons and menu options. In the next chapter, we'll explore how Mosaic supports your navigation through the Web. This discussion focuses on navigation with the native features of the browser itself and assumes you are familiar with basic mouse (point and click) operations and how to use the graphical windowing system on your computer.

Main Panel

The main panel of Mosaic gives you access to the basic operations many browsers offer. The key to effective use of these basic operations is

1. realizing what options are available
2. knowing what these options will do
3. knowing how to use these operations to accomplish useful work

Mosaic's main panel has changed slightly since Mosaic was first introduced, but is basic structure and functionality are about the same. Figure 15.1 shows the main panel.

FIGURE 15.1.

Mosaic main panel.

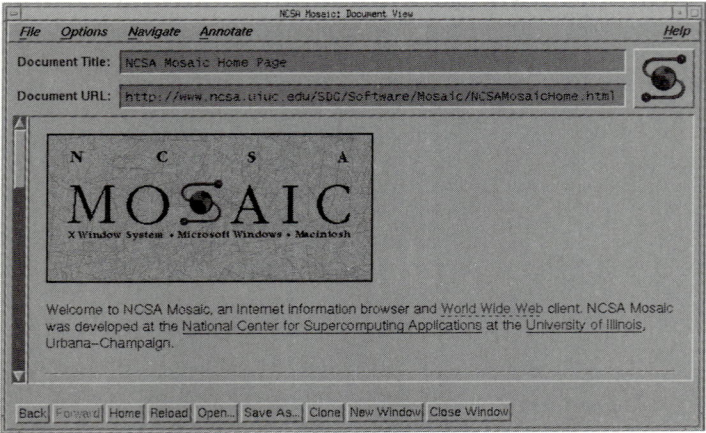

The main panel supports a variety of operations that are divided into functional groups on the display. To access the functions offered, you make use of mouse or keyboard equivalents for commands. Like many graphical user interfaces, Mosaic's features are fairly intuitive. Visual details give you cues for how the interface operates. For example, a series of three dots (...) on the buttons and entries in pull-down menus tell you another pop-up menu will appear as a result of selecting that option.

The operations described here are for the Mosaic for X Window System; your browser may work differently. If you are using an ASCII or line mode browser, the functions described below won't necessarily be grouped in the same way as they are on Mosaic, but similar operations might be available for your browser. The set of operations offered by Mosaic give you the power to navigate the Web very effectively. Therefore, it will help you gain the necessary concepts for browser operations by reading through these sections. Because the actions described are taken out of the context of doing an actual task, the reasons for doing some of them might be unclear to you if you are a new user. On first reading the following sections, though, read them as a way to become aware of possibilities. Later, you'll be able to refer to these in particular situations.

The following sections present the interface (Figure 15.1) starting from the top of the Mosaic main panel and going down.

Title Bar

The title bar is the list across the top of the browser display, and includes

- **File**—A set of options that allow you to operate with files or manipulate the display:

  New Window creates a window that has another Mosaic browser in it, opened to your default home document. You can dismiss this new window by using the File / Close Window function. If you dismiss this new window with File / Exit Program..., you will dismiss both the new window and the original window.

> **NOTE**
>
> You can set what document serves as your home document (see Navigate / Home Document).

  Clone Window is similar to File / New Window, except that this selection brings up the new window with the *same* URL in its display window as the original window (as opposed to bringing up the default home document for your browser).

Open URL... enables you to "open" a particular URL that might point to a resource anywhere on the Internet. This is very useful when you are given a URL to a resource (as opposed to finding a hotspot on a hypertext page linked to a resource). After clicking on this selection, you will be presented with a pop-up menu which allows you to type in the name of the URL to open. This pop-up window will itself have several buttons on it, allowing you to clear the URL name, dismiss the window, and get help.

Open Local... is similar to the File/Open URL... option, but this selection allows you to open a *local* file (in your own home directory, or some other directory that is accessible through your file system). This is a useful option for when you are checking out HTML pages before you place them on a Web server for everyone to obtain.

Reload Current recalls the document you currently have in the viewer from the network, so that any changes that have been made in the document's HTML code (but not changes in images in the document) since you last brought it up are displayed. This is useful when you know that a document has changed since you brought it up. A common situation where this would occur is if you are editing an HTML file and making changes to it. You can edit the source file, use File / Reload Current... and see how your changes have affected the display of the document.

Reload Images does what the File / Reload Current selection does, but also reloads any inline images in the document.

Refresh Current redisplays the X Window that is holding the Mosaic browser. This does *no* network reloading, only redisplaying what is currently in the Mosaic browser. This is useful when, for some reason, the X display of your Mosaic browser was corrupted or damaged (through another overlapping X display or some color mapping problems or errors).

Find in Current... allows you to search for text strings in the document currently displayed in the browser, includes caseless or backwards options.

View Source... displays the HTML source file for the document currently in the browser display. This is particularly useful when you want to see how an HTML feature was written.

Save As... gives you the chance to save the file currently in the display window in your home directory or in a directory accessible on your computer. You can save the displayed file as plain text (with no bullets or underlines), formatted text (with ASCII text representing underlines and bullets), postscript (just as the document appears displayed in the display window), or HTML (the HTML source code for the document).

Print... prints the document to the default printer in either text, formatted text, postscript, or HTML.

Mail to... brings up a pop-up menu that allows you to e-mail the current displayed document to any user.

Close Window closes the given window on which this selection was made. It will close only the window on which the operation is performed, not on any child windows (windows either cloned (created with File / Clone Window) or created new (created with File / New Window) from a parent window.

Exit Program... brings up a pop-up window which asks you to verify that you want to leave the Mosaic program. This command closes all related windows—including children (those cloned (File / Clone Window) or new (File / New Window) from a parent window) or parents (the parent windows of any children).

■ **Options**—This group of menubar selections allow you to control the appearance and interaction with documents displayed in Mosaic.

Fancy selections enables you to preserve the formatting of text within the cut, copy, and paste buffers. For example, if you have a document displayed with a bulleted list, you can use the mouse to copy text from that document and paste it to a text editor in another window. With the (Options / Fancy selections) toggled on, this text will be copied and pasted with as much of the "fancy" things like bullets and underlines as possible.

Load to Local Disk—when toggled on, every time you click on a hotspot in the displayed document, you will get a pop-up window that asks you where you want the given document saved on your local disk. This is commonly used when you are obtaining binary files via Mosaic.

Delay Image Loading, when toggled on, suppresses the display of the inline images in a document. A symbol (Figure 15.2) will appear in the document indicating that an inline image occurs in the document at that spot.

Clicking on this symbol causes the image to be retrieved, loaded, and displayed. This Delay Image Loading option is very useful when you are having a slow network connection or when you are not interested in seeing images and wish to save the time (and network bandwidth) needed to retrieve them. Note that some pages may have hotspots available only through images, requiring you to retrieve the image in order to access the hotspot.

FIGURE 15.2.
Delayed image symbol.

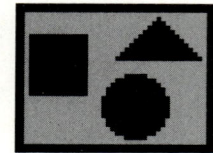

Load Images in Current is used to load (or reload) all inlined images in the current document. This is useful if you have the Options / Delay Image Loading option on and you find that there are many inlined images in the document that you want to see. Selecting Options / Load Images in Current will load all the inlined images at once.

Reload Config Files reloads files that were set up as configuration files when Mosaic was installed on your system (mailcaps and extension maps files). Normally, a user would not need to reload these files.

Flush Image Cache deletes all the inlined images from the "cache" used by Mosaic. All inlined images in the current document will be replaced by the image symbol (Figure 15.2) (see Options / Delay Image Loading).

Clear Global History... removes the complete trace of the URLs that you have accessed using Mosaic or since the last time you cleared the global history. This global history file accumulates in your home directory (filename `.mosaic-global-history`) as you use Mosaic; the first time you visit a URL, it is added to this file. This global history file is very useful if you know you have visited a document but can not remember its URL. This file grows as you use Mosaic, so you should clear your global history occasionally. All the links that are shaded to indicate you visited them will again be highlighted as if you never have visited them. The global history file will accumulate the URLs that you select after clearing the global history, and the global history file will be rewritten after you exit from Mosaic.

Fonts enables you to change the font (the type style and size) in which the documents are displayed. This is particularly useful if you find the default font too hard to read.

Anchor Underlines enables you to change the appearance of the underlines under the hot spots in displayed documents, from heavy underlines to no underlines.

■ **Navigate**—This group of options enable you to move through a document or to open "hotlist" or reference documents quickly.

Back steps back to the previous document you had displayed in the Mosaic window during the current Mosaic session. This option uses the window history file to keep track of this document (see Navigate / Window History...) If you have just begun your Mosaic session, this option will be shaded to indicate that it is not possible to go back. Note that you will go back along the most previous "branch" you have traversed. (For a more detailed discussion, see the *Techniques* section of this chapter).

Forward, if you use the (Navigate / Back) option, will then give you the option to go forward to the document you had gone "back" from. You can continue to select Forward until you've reached the front of your exploration into the Web during this session of Mosaic.

Home Document automatically jumps you to the home document that was established when you started this Mosaic session. You can change the home document by using the -home option when you start mosaic. For example, if you want your home document to be any URL, start Mosaic with the following command:

```
mosaic -home URL
```

where *URL* refers to the document that you want designated as your home document.

Window History... pops up a window that shows you the titles of URLs of documents you have opened during this Mosaic session. You can click on entries in this list to go directly to them. This is particularly useful if you know you have visited something during the current Mosaic session and can't remember what or where it is. Note that this doesn't allow you access to your global history (see Options / Clear Global History...).

Hotlist... pops up a window that enables you to store the title and URLs of any documents (or searches) that you wish. The pop-up window will enable you to add a reference to the current document in the display window to your hotlist (saving the document title and its URL). The hotlist pop-up window will also enable you to go to a selected item in your hotlist, remove an item from your hotlist, edit the title shown for a document, or mail your hotlist to someone. The hotlist is a very useful option. (See more information on effective use of a hotlist in the *Techniques* section of this chapter). Note that the hotlist does not save the given document or resource to your home directory, only a reference to it—its URL—and its title.

Add Current To Hotlist does the same as the Add Current button on the Navigate / Hotlist... pop-up menu. Using this option directly from the Navigate pull-down menu, however, saves you a click of the mouse (but you get no visual feedback that the URL and title were added to your hotlist).

Internet Starting Points brings up a document prepared by the developers of Mosaic to serve as a good set of starting points for exploring the Internet. The document will appear in the Mosaic display window.

Internet Resources Meta-Index is similar to the Navigate / Internet Starting Points option, this option brings up a prepared document in the display window that lists many useful indexes for accessing Internet information.

◼ **Annotate**—This group of functions enable you to create your own notes that will be associated with documents. You can use these annotations to remind you of how to use a resource or other information about it.

Annotate... pops up a window that enable you to enter the text of an annotation.

Audio Annotate... pops up a window that gives you the controls necessary to create a sound file to annotate a document. To use this, you must have the appropriate hardware and software hooked up.

Edit This Annotation... enables you to edit an existing annotation. Start by selecting the annotation, then choose Annotate / Edit This Annotation. You can edit the text in the annotation.

Delete This Annotation...—when you have selected an annotation and it appears in the pop-up window—enables you to delete the annotation.

Document Status Group

The Document status group—a group of two windows—and the globe symbol give you useful feedback about the current resource displayed and Mosaic's retrieval process.

◼ *Document Title* shows the document title of the document currently displayed in the Mosaic window, as defined within the HTML file for the document. A document's title is defined in HTML by the sequence

```
<TITLE> This is the title. </TITLE>
```

If the current document does not have a title as given above, the Document Title window will display

```
Untitled, URL http://foo.bar.com
```

where *http://foo.bar.com* is the URL of the document.

■ *Document URL* is the complete URL for the resource displayed. Sometimes these URLs can be very long. If the URL disappears beyond the right side of this display window, you can either resize the whole Mosaic window or use the cursor and mouse to "push" the edge of this URL:

1. Place the cursor on the right-most letter displayed in the URL window
2. Push down the left mouse button, hold it down, and gently move the mouse to the right slightly

The rest of the URL will scroll by in the window.

You can use the preceding method for capturing the entire URL in the paste buffer. Starting at the first symbol in the URL, hold the left mouse button down and move the cursor to the right until the whole URL is highlighted.

■ *Globe symbol*—if spinning—indicates that Mosaic is retrieving a document from the network. If the globe keeps spinning, it may indicate that the network connection has hung or that the resource is still being retrieved. You can cancel the network retrieval procedure by positioning the cursor on the globe and clicking the left mouse button. This is a very important feature to have, as network connections often do hang, and sometimes you'll find that you are retrieving a resource far larger than you wish.

FUN WITH THE SPINNING GLOBE

Should the globe spin quickly if it is retrieving large amounts of information? Or should it spin quickly when things are not going well ("spinning its wheels")? Or spin slowly to indicate that it is in "high gear" when it is getting data from the network? These were some questions discussed in a debate about Mosaic's globe in an online discussion group.

Resource Display Window

The Resource Display Window is the area below the Document Title, Document URL, and globe symbol. This window displays the resource indicated by the title and URL.

■ *Scrollbar*—If a scrollbar appears, the document is longer than the display window can show. You can use the scrollbar to display the rest of the text (by placing the cursor on the scrollbar box and moving the box down), or jump ahead in the document (by positioning the cursor in the "empty slot" portion of the scrollbar and clicking the left mouse button.

■ *Display* shows the currently selected document. A horizontal scrollbar will appear only when the resources are a fixed width. For most situations, there is no horizontal scrollbar in Mosaic, and the document's text is arranged to fit in the horizontal space available in the Mosaic window (the line breaks will change to accommodate changes in horizontal room for display). You can increase the horizontal space available by enlarging the Mosaic window.

Status Message

Below the Mosaic display window and above the Navigation control buttons is an area where status messages periodically appear. The situations in which status messages appear are as follows:

■ *The URL of a link in the current document*—When you move the cursor over a hotspot in the resource in the display window, the URL associated with that hotspot is displayed as a status message. This is extremely useful as it lets you "look before you leap" into a resource.

■ *During information retrieval*—When you select a link in a document, the status message area will show what information retrieval activities are happening. For example, in response to the selection of the URL `http://www.rpi.edu/~decemj/index.html`, the status messages displayed are

```
Looking up www.rpi.edu
Making HTTP connection to www.rpi.edu
Done sending HTTP request; waiting for response.
Read 1424 of 1424 bytes of data.
```

These messages often are displayed so quickly you won't be able to read them. They are very useful if you are in a situation when Mosaic seems to "lock up." In this case, examine the status message for clues about what might be wrong. If the network seems to be "hung" or you are retrieving far too many bytes of data, you can cancel the network retrieval process by clicking on the spinning globe (see Document Status Group / Globe symbol).

Bottom Buttons

The buttons along the bottom of the Mosaic front panel are commonly used operations. These buttons are mapped to the same functions from the title bar. Their placement as buttons along the bottom make these useful functions quickly accessible.

1. *Back*—equivalent to Navigate / Back
2. *Forward*—equivalent to Navigate / Forward.

3. *Home*—equivalent to Navigate / Home Document.

4. *Reload*—equivalent to File / Reload Current.

5. *Open...*—equivalent to File / Open URL...

6. *Save As...*—equivalent to File / Save As...

7. *Clone*—equivalent to File / Clone Window.

8. *New Window*—equivalent to File / New Window.

9. *Close Window*—equivalent to File / Close Window.

Using Your Browser

Now that we've looked at a list of the operations you can perform from Mosaic's main panel, let's look in detail how you might typically use your browser. Although there is no standard way to use a browser, here are some general guidelines:

- **Keep aware of all indicators**. You want to watch your browser carefully, particularly the globe symbol and the status message line. Watch for these conditions:

  Endlessly spinning globe—this could indicate a network connection has "hung" (is not presently reachable). Look at the status line to see what is happening. If the globe is spinning quickly, this usually indicates a good situation—i.e., Mosaic is quickly retrieving the information you are seeking from the network.

  Huge files—If the globe keeps spinning, and the status message line reports something like this:

  ```
  Read 1024 of 38000999000 bytes of data.
  ```

  you know you are going to be waiting a *long* time for that resource to come up. Consider clicking on the spinning globe.

  Total freeze-up—If the globe is not spinning, there is no message status line and you can't click on anything on the Mosaic main panel, you should wait just a bit longer. For very large files, Mosaic needs some time to load the file in local memory (in which case the globe spinning would have stopped to indicate the end of network data retrieval). If, after a period of time (like 2-5 minutes), Mosaic still seems frozen, you should consider trying to close the Mosaic window or killing the process running Mosaic (you'll need some UNIX skill for this).

- **Expect problems**—The nature of the Internet is that it is cooperative, vast, and complex. As such, not all the computer hosts that hold resources will all be up and operating all the time. Also, machine names, resource names, and other identifiers that make up a URL can change. Therefore, you might run into situations where you have a "stale" URL (one that no longer resolves to a resource). You also might have typed a URL incorrectly.

The URL you click on might not be to an existing resource. You will quickly find this out through an error message in Mosaic's display window, something like

```
404 Not Found
The requested URL /foo.html was not found on this server.
```

You either have a bad URL (recheck your typing if you entered it directly through the Open option) or the URL is no longer valid (it has gone "stale").

The host name in the URL might no longer exist or is temporarily down. You'll see a message like the following:

```
ERROR
Requested document (URL http://foo.bar.com/) could not be accessed.
```

The information server either is not accessible or is refusing to serve the document to you.

The host and document exist, but there is some problem with file permissions or the server itself.

```
ERROR
Requested document (URL http://pass.wayne.edu/foo.html) could not be
accessed.
```

The information server either is not accessible or is refusing to serve the document to you.

To deal with the above problems, the best things to do include

1. Check the URL again to make sure there were no typographical errors if you had entered it yourself.

2. Wait a bit—it may be that network connections or a host is temporarily down. Try again in an hour or a day.

3. Use spider searches (covered in Chapter 19, "Spiders and Indexes: Key word-Oriented Searching") to try to locate resource. Perform searches for portions of the URL or the title of the resource.

4. If you know the maintainer of the information, check to see if they know the status of the resource..

■ **Use the Window History.** As mentioned in the previous list of browser operations, the "Back" and "Forward" buttons take you along the last encountered "path" through the Web during your current Mosaic session. One way to help keep track of where you are in the window history is to use the Navigate / Window History... option to bring up the window history. Position this window on your display so that it doesn't overlap the Mosaic main panel. It will stay up and help you keep track of where you have been. Remember, the window history is dynamic (unlike the global history file which serves as a complete record of your Web visits from session to session). The window history file will lose and gain items as you navigate the Web and contain entries only from your current session. For example, if you are currently in resource A and you follow a link in it to resource B, your history list will read

A
B

Then if you take a link from resource B to resource C, your window history will be

A
B
C

Now, if you go back to resource B (using the Back button) and then, instead of taking the link from resource B to C, you take another link to resource D, your history list will read

A
B
D

Resource C has been "nipped" from your window history list. Resource C will be unreachable via the Back and Forward buttons.

This is not too serious (as you can revisit C from a link in resource B), but keep in mind that this "nipping" can delete a whole branch of your voyage. Let's say that your window history lists reads

E
F
G
H
I
J
K
L
M

and you are presently in M. Let's say that you use your windows history list to quickly go to resource F. You can do this by double clicking on the entry for resource F in the windows history list. (You could have also gone to F from M by clicking Back button seven times.) Now, let's say that at resource F, there's another link, to X, and you take it instead of selecting link G.

Your history list will then read

E

F

X

Everything from G, H, I, J, K, L, and M has been "nipped off." This is no real problem, as you can certainly revisit G, H, I, ..., but you won't be able to use the Forward button to do it from resource F.

- **Act responsibly.** Your access to freely available resources on the Web depends on the thousands of people who invest their time, energy, and money providing information and maintaining machines. Don't abuse this tradition of "shared gifts" by overloading the network—repeatedly obtaining huge graphics or movie files, for example.

  Remember however, that you should feel free to explore. Web browsers work very efficiently. Most work in a "connectionless" fashion—obtaining the resource you request by using the network connections and then "stopping." For example, when you are at a particular site (you have opened a URL referring to a resource at that site), once the resource has been obtained over the network, you are not "using time" on that remote host. Once Mosaic's globe has stopped spinning, you are not using network bandwith to retrieve information, so you can feel free to take your time to examine the information you have obtained. In fact, it is best to carefully look at what you obtain, so that you can best utilize the resources you are accessing without needlessly obtaining something you don't need.

- **You'll encounter other things.** Advances in HTML and Web browsers will bring new kinds of interaction to your screen. Mosaic supports a capability called "Forms" that not all Web browsers support. With Forms, you can enter information into boxes and select controls (like buttons and checkboxes) that are similar to the controls in Mosaic. You'll find that the graphical user interface in Forms is very intuitive.

Techniques and Tips

Once you've become used to the standard operations that you can perform with your browser, the next step in navigating is to put these elements together to navigate well. This section lists specific tips and techniques for using your browser to increase your skills and develop your intuition into how to navigate the Web.

Interpret URLs

The URL given in the window near the top of Mosaic or at the Status Message area on the front panel can tell you many things about the resource to which it refers.

1. The URL can tell you what protocol was used to access the resource across the network. (See discussion of URLs in Chapter 14, "Web Structure and Spaces.")

    An example of when you might want to find URLs using a specific access method: you might want to find *only* Gopher resources about telecommunications. Therefore, you would want to watch out for Gopher resources by looking at the start of the URLs of the resources you encounter.

    Table 15.1 will help you identify the protocol of the URL. We'll talk more about how each of these protocols operates in detail in the next chapter.

Table 15.1. Popular protocols.

Protocols	Name
HTTP	Hypertext transfer protocol—you can expect to find HTML files and possibly other kinds of files at this URL. (Examine file name ending for more clues).
FTP	File transfer protocol—you can expect to find files and directories of files at an FTP site.
news	Usenet newsgroup—this indicates a series of files contributed by people discussing a particular topic.
telnet	Remote login—you can expect a pop-up window to appear which will (possibly) ask you for a login to an information system. Most typically, these information systems consist of menus and choices and are often called bulletin board systems (BBS).
Gopher	Gopher information (menu system)—you can expect a series of menus and choices. You will be able to select menu items to reach other resources.
WAIS	Wide Area Information Server—a system of indexed databases.
mailto	Electronic mail—a link to an application which will allow you to compose a message to be sent to an address via electronic mail.

For example, the URL `http://www.ncsa.uiuc.edu/demoweb/url-primer.html` uses the hypertext transfer protocol, which is the "native" protocol of the Web.

2. The URL can often tell you the format of the resource.

    The URL `http://www.ncsa.uiuc.edu/demoweb/url-primer.html` has an ending of `.html`, which indicates an HTML document. (See Table 15.2 for a list of popular file and URL endings.)

Table 15.2. Popular file and URL endings.

Ending	Name
.html	HTML file (hypertext)
.ps	Postscript, "pretty printed" text with fonts and graphics.
.txt	Text
.tex	TeX or LaTex, typesetting languages using a system of tags
?string	The ? indicates that this URL pointed to a query (a way of finding *string* within a document).
#anchor	This is a URL that points to an anchor (a specific place) within the document.

The file endings in combination with the protocol can give you a clue what to expect at a given URL. However, these are just clues, not necessarily hard and fast rules about what you will find. For example, an HTTP server does not always have just HTML files on it. It is possible to have text and other resources on a HTTP server. Also, you can have HTML documents on an FTP or a Gopher server. The thing to keep in mind is that the protocol name of the URL and the file ending are clues to help you navigate, and can help you develop intuition about Web resources.

3. The document URL can tell you the network host.

   The document URL can tell you from what network host you are retrieving the information. This information is important if

   ■ you are trying to find a specific network host (in which case you are looking for an exact match in the host name)

   ■ if you are looking for a host in a particular geographic region

   ■ you are trying to find the "nearest" network host, in terms of network transfer speed and volume

   In any of these cases, first you can use the name of the host itself as a clue about all these concerns. We can interpret a typical URL: `http://www.uwm.edu/Mirror/inet.services.html`.

   The machine name on which this information resides is

   `www.uwm.edu`

   This name is connected with a particular institution. The last two parts of this name, `uwm.edu`, give a clue about what this institution is. The `edu` part tells me that this is an educational institution. The `uwm` part tells me that the initials of this university are UWM. If that is not enough to clue me into what university this is, I can use the UNIX command `whois` to find out. In a UNIX window, I enter

`whois uwm.edu`

and I find out

```
[No name] (WISC-CSD1-MILW) UWM.EDU 129.89.7.2,129.89.6.2

University of Wisconsin, Milwaukee (UWM-DOM)   UWM.EDU
```

This tells me that the URL shown above is a resource residing on a machine at the University of Wisconsin—Milwaukee.

Table 15.3 lists a brief selection of the kinds of endings for Internet host names in mostly US domains.

For international endings, see the URL `ftp://rtfm.mit.edu/pub/usenet/news.answers/mail/country-codes`.

Table 15.3. Popular Internet domain name endings.

Ending	Description
com	Commercial
edu	Educational
gov	Government
mil	Military
org	Nonprofit organization
net	Network administrative sites (international)

Trying to find the "nearest" network host is a bit more complicated, and beginning or intermediate users might use a geographical rule of thumb for finding a machine that is "closest," in network terms, to their own. This need arises in situations where you are using a resource that may require a large amount of data transfer. To make this transfer easiest on the network and on yourself, you should find the machine that is "closest" to your own in terms of the network.

Naturally, those machines that are geographically close often are the best choice for connections, particularly when your choices are either a machine across the world or one across the street. However, this is not always the case because of the nature of the network topology and connections between your host and your target host.

Moreover, you might want to sometimes use a *distant* host in order to take advantage of off-peak usage of a machine. For example, if you are in New York, and the current time is 11:53am on Saturday, it is 1:52am in the morning on

Sunday in Australia—and probably machines in Australia are experiencing less of a load. So you might want to use an Australian machine rather than one in a busier region, particularly if the resource you are accessing requires a lot of processing by the remote host.

TRICK: FINDING LOCAL TIME

You can find the local time at an Internet domain name by using the UNIX telnet command to port number 13 of that machine.

For example, at the Internet domain uwm.edu (Milwaukee, Wisconsin), the time can be obtained by entering this command at the UNIX window:

```
telnet uwm.edu 13
```

which gives

```
Trying 129.89.7.2 ...

Connected to uwm.edu.

Escape character is '^]'.

Sat Jun 25 10:57:51 CDT 1994

Connection closed by foreign host.
```

At the domain aarnet.edu.au (Australia), `telnet aarnet.edu.au 13`, the time is

```
Trying 139.130.204.16 ...

Connected to aarnet.edu.au.

Escape character is '^]'.

Sun Jun 26 01:57:15 1994

Connection closed by foreign host.
```

The thing to remember is that, as a navigator, there are reasons why you might want to identify the institution sponsoring the machine on which a resource resides. You might need to know the machine's geographic location or local time, or the network route to that machine.

PINGING A REMOTE MACHINE

You might want to use the UNIX `ping` command to do some probing of the network to find a close machine. The routes to which the data is transferred could change all the time, but this "pinging" can give you a clue about how close a host is.

For example, from my machine in Troy, New York, I can ping a host in Milwaukee, Wisconsin by entering this command in a UNIX window:

```
/usr/etc/ping -s uwm.edu
```

I get the output

```
PING uwm.edu: 56 data bytes

64 bytes from 129.89.7.2: icmp_seq=0. time=856. ms

64 bytes from uwm.edu (129.89.7.2): icmp_seq=2. time=1877. ms

64 bytes from uwm.edu (129.89.7.2): icmp_seq=3. time=1751. ms
```

Now if I ping a machine in Ithaca, New York:

```
/usr/etc/ping -s cornell.edu
```

I get the results

```
PING cornell.edu: 56 data bytes

64 bytes from cornell.edu (132.236.56.6): icmp_seq=0. time=92. ms

64 bytes from cornell.edu (132.236.56.6): icmp_seq=1. time=23. ms

64 bytes from cornell.edu (132.236.56.6): icmp_seq=2. time=28. ms
```

This shows me that my test data traveled most quickly back and forth to the Ithaca machine than the Milwaukee machine: 28-92 milliseconds round trip to Ithaca versus 856-1751 milliseconds round trip to Milwaukee.

Use the Hotlist Effectively

The hotlist is one of the most useful features that you will probably use on the Mosaic main panel. It gives you a very basic means to create your own information library, and is one of the major ways that you'll be able to "record" your favorite spots on the Web.

The things to remember about your hotlist are

1. Your hotlist provides you with the fastest and most reliable way to record a Web location—it does not require cutting or pasting from the document URL window (although you could do this if you wanted to record URLs in a separate file) and there is no hand-copying of the URL onto paper (an unreliable way to record a URL, particularly when it is a long URL).

2. Your hotlist gives you rapid access to your favorite Web locations. For example, Figure 15.3 shows the top of a hotlist. In the figure, "Center for Information Technology" is highlighted, so clicking on the "Go To" button takes the user directly to that resource.

FIGURE 15.3.

An example hotlist.

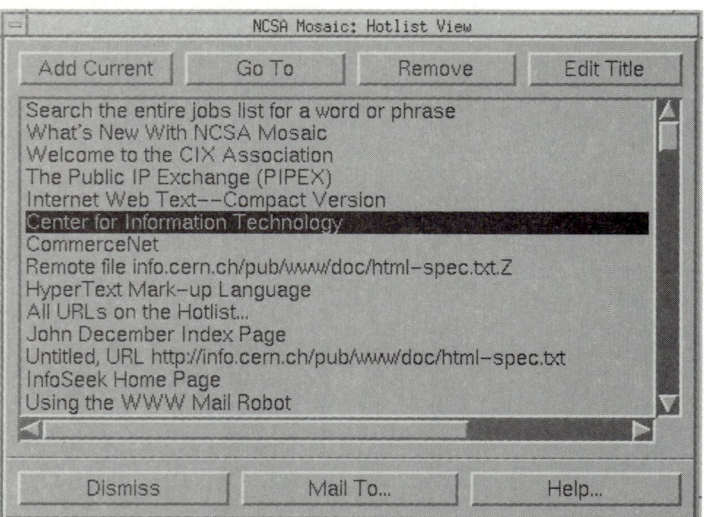

3. Your hotlist accumulates until you change it. Your hotlist is preserved from session to session in a file called `.mosaic-hotlist-default` in your home directory. You can use the hotlist controls to add and remove items from your hotlist or edit the titles of the entries.

When you enter the currently displayed URL into your hotlist, the title added to the hotlist is the same as that shown in the Document Title window. Sometimes this title isn't descriptive, which is why you might want to consider changing it by using the Edit Title button on the hotlist pop-up window.

For example, the entry at the top of the hotlist shown in Figure 15.3 is "Search the entire jobs list for a word or phrase" isn't very descriptive—it doesn't identify the name of the jobs list. To remedy this situation, first double click on the entry to see what it refers to.

In this case, it's the searchable jobs list at the *Chronicle of Higher Education* at URL `gopher://chronicle.merit.edu/77/.ads/.ads-by-search/.all/.waisindex/index`. Then, use the Edit Title button on the hotlist window to change the entry to read "Search the Chronicle of Higher Education's jobs list." Similarly, the entry in the hotlist reading, "Untitled, URL `http://info.cern.ch/pub/www/doc/html-spec.txt`" could stand a revision—it is possible to interpret the URL to get an idea of what this resource is, but a good phrase or set of words would help even more.

Keep Your Hotlist Clean

Since the hotlist is so useful, you should not hesitate to add a beneficial document onto it. However, you will find that your hotlist can get very crowded. Every once in a while, you should go through your hotlist, rename the items to more meaningful names, and remove stale or unimportant links. Eventually, you'll want to use techniques of weaving your own web to create your own pages containing information about your favorite resources (see Part V, "Weaving a Web").

You can keeping your hotlist clean by following these general guidelines:

1. **Keep junk off of it in the first place.** When you find a resource that you know is going to change or you have no interest in it, avoid placing it on your hotlist. This seems obvious, but new users often feel an anxiety about where they "are" within the Web, and the discovery of their hotlist gives them a feeling of being able to "chart" their way through the Web. This often results in very cluttered hotlists. (A cluttered hotlist might be called a warmlist; a totally junked hotlist might be called a coldlist).

2. **Make sure you record "great" finds.** As a converse tip to 1, if you find a resource that seems fantastic, be sure to record it on your hotlist. Sometimes a resource is so amazing, you end up going through it without remembering to put it on your hotlist. You might try to associate any feelings of amazement or excitement with the procedure of Navigate / Add Current To Hotlist. By recording great finds, you'll increase the "temperature" of your hotlist.

3. **Transfer the truly great to another file.** As a matter of routine maintenance, go through your hotlist and record the URLs of critical resources to a separate file. Occasionally, an abnormal exit from Mosaic will corrupt or destroy your hotlist. Because your hotlist should be "hot," make sure that you occasionally back it up so as not to lose critical URLs. At the UNIX prompt, you can do the following:

   ```
   cp .mosaic-hotlist-default hotlist.24jun94
   ```

   or some other scheme to save your hotlist. Or

   ```
   cp .mosaic-hotlist-default hotlist.red
   ```

   and then use a text editor to edit `hotlist.red` to include only your very best finds.

4. **Share your hotlist.** There are ways that you can directly mail your hotlist to another person (by using the Mail To... option on the hotlist pop-up window). There are also utilities to convert your hotlist file into an HTML file which can then be easily browsed by others.

Use Your Global History

As mentioned in the descriptions of the controls on Mosaic's main panel, Mosaic maintains a transcript of your initial visits to Web sites in a global history file. Usually, this file is named

`.mosaic-global-history`

The lines with the file are formatted according to a URL and the date when you first visited the given URL. As an example

```
http://www.rpi.edu/Internet/Guides/decemj/text.html Sat Jun 25 10:46:08 1994
http://www.rpi.edu/~decemj/cmc/people.html Sat Jun 25 10:46:08 1994
http://bingen.cs.csbsju.edu/~jahoffma/letterman/paul.gif Sat Jun 25 10:46:08 1994
http://nistor.paed.uni-muenchen.de/ Sat Jun 25 10:46:08 1994
```

Thus, you can see the URL and the time of your first encounter of it. If you visit a URL again, the new time will not be recorded. The global history list also serves as a database that Mosaic uses to shade hotspots you have already visited. This shading often puzzles new users who wonder how Mosaic remembers where they've been.

Use your global history file as another way to answer the question you may have, "I know I visited a really great site yesterday, but I can't remember the URL and I didn't place it on my hotlist." In this case, use a text editor to read the file `.mosaic-global-history` in your home directory. Examine the dates and names of URLs for clues about your lost, great resource.

The global history file grows larger and larger as you visit more URLs, so you occasionally must purge it (or it will expand to fill your disk space!). Purge your global history by Options / Clear Global History... . You will be given a chance to confirm this, and when you exit from Mosaic, the .mosaic-global-history file will be rewritten.

Have a Backup (Terminal-Based) Browser

Although graphical Web browsers like Mosaic are fantastic, they require a graphical windowing system to use. You may often find yourself in a situation where you don't have the necessary access to the network to run your graphical browser. In such cases, a navigator should be prepared. Find a line mode browser (a good example is Lynx), and either ask your system administrator to install it on your system or install it yourself (see Part II, "Web Browsers and Connections").

A terminal-based browser can work wonders when you are using your dialup account. Indeed, a terminal-based browser can be a quick alternative to Mosaic when you want to look at a file rapidly and you don't care about graphics. For example, the "Selected Tele-communications Resources" file shown in Figure 15.3 looks like this in Lynx:

```
         SELECTED TELECOMMUNICATIONS RESOURCES
    _____

    * DELTA Distributed ELectronic Telecommunications Archive-teaching
    and learning about business telecommunications and data
    communications
    * NTIA National Telecommunications and Information Administration
    (USA)
    * Center for Telecommunications Research Columbia University, New
    York, NY
    * RITIM-L: Research Institute for Telecommunications and Information
    Marketing discussion list: Send email to listserv@uriacc.uri.edu,
    with the Body: "sub RITIM-L YOUR NAME"
    * ITU International Telecommunication Union, a United Nations agency
    which coordinates telecommunications
    * The Usenet newsgroup comp.dcom.telecom

    _____
    John December (decemj@rpi.edu) / 24 June 1994
    Commands: Use arrow keys to move, '?' for help, 'q' to quit, '<-' to go back
    Arrow keys: Up and Down to move. Right to follow a link; Left to go back.
    H)elp O)ptions P)rint G)o M)ain screen Q)uit /=search [delete]=history list
```

While the Lynx display does not have all the graphical features of the Mosaic interface, it is a good alternative. You can go through the online Lynx documentation to discover how to use a Lynx hotlist and other similar options that Mosaic offers.

If you don't have a Web browser available and you need access to a Web resource, you can connect, via telnet, to a Web server. This is generally not a good idea because it drags down the performance of this remote server. However, it may be your only alternative in certain situations. You can find the names of telnet-accessible Web servers in the Web quick reference card for this book.

For example, you can connect with telnet to www.njit.edu and login as www to use the New Jersey Institute of Technology's Web server.

NOTE

Again, do not routinely use this telnet access to the Web. Use it only for demon-stration or limited purposes, as it degrades the performance of the server machine.

Frequently Encountered Navigation Situations and Their Solutions

The list shown at the start of this chapter is a description of the controls on Mosaic's main panel. A new navigator should at least be familiar with what functions are possible and then integrate this understanding with the tips and techniques given previously to solve real-world problems that Web navigators frequently have.

Here are some typical situations that you might encounter as a user of a Web browser. Following each situation is a discussion of how you might deal with it. These situations start out very simple and increase in complexity.

Situation 1: Your best friend tells you that there is a digital confession booth at

```
http://anther.learning.cs.cmu.edu/priest.html
```

Solution: Go to your computer, start up Mosaic, and use the Open..., button. In the space to the right of "URL To Open:," type in the URL and then click the Open button.

Ideally (from the data efficiency standpoint, rather than for interpersonal reasons), your friend would have told you this via electronic mail, in which case you could have used a cut and paste method to put the URL directly in the "URL To Open" box. If the URL is transmitted orally, make sure to write it down correctly, and type it in the "URL To Open" box correctly.

Situation 2: You've just run across a great source and you want to tell your friends about it.

Solution: Send e-mail to your friend giving the URL exactly. Use a copy and paste technique to paste the URL into the letter.

Another solution: Use the File / Mail To... option on the Mosaic's front panel. However, if your friend has a Web browser and the skills to use it, this is a less efficient solution because you are mailing the entire page rather than the reference to it. If your friend does not have a Web browser or the skills to use it, this might be the only alternative to getting the information to him or her.

Advanced solution: put a reference to this resource on your home page (this requires Web weaving skills (see Part V, "Weaving a Web")) and tell your friend to open your home page.

Situation 3: You've just pulled up a great resource, a long list of network terms and their definitions. However, you're not looking up a particular term (in which case you could scroll down the alphabetical listing), but you want to see which entries use the "foo."

Solution: Use File / Find In Current... to search for occurrences of "foo." Use the "caseless" search option to locate occurrences of "FOO" or "Foo."

Situation 4: You've absolutely no clue where you are. You're looking at a resource, but you can't remember how you got there or how to get back to a page you were at an hour ago.

Solution: Bring up your windows history file: Navigate / Windows History. Scroll through this list to see if what you want is there. This method is much faster than hitting the "Back" button repeatedly. Remember, that great page you have in mind might not be on your windows history list because of the "nipping" process described above. It will be, however, on your global history list. To look at your global history list, *exit Mosaic* (in order to rewrite the file), and then use a text editor to examine the clues about time, resource titles, and URLs.

Less Efficient Solution: Click on the Home button, get back to your home page, and try to retrace your steps. This will work only if you can retrace your steps *exactly*. Your first selection off your home page will "nip off" all the remaining sequence in your windows history file.

Navigator's Check

All the preceding information is just the start of your growing expertise in navigating the Web with your browser.

Keep in mind the following:

- Your browser offers an array built-in functions to help you navigate within hypertext, search through resources, and store URL references.
- Interpreting URLs can give you excellent insight into the kinds of resources available through hotlinks displayed in the browser.
- Click on Mosaic's spinning globe to stop network information retrieval.
- Use techniques to manage your hotlist, to keep it clean, and to periodically review its contents.

We'll go on to using resources on the Web for navigation in later chapters. In the next chapter, we'll look at some destinations associated with the protocols associated with URLs. These protocols, as we saw in the previous chapter, represent many different kinds of information spaces.

At the Edge of the Web

16

by John December

IN THIS CHAPTER

A navigator who knows what regions of cyberspace are reachable from a Web browser and knows how to use a browser for navigation can start exploring the Web. In this chapter, we'll begin by navigating the "edges" of the Web—those Internet tools and resources that often are the destinations for the hypertext that makes up the Web, but are not themselves provided through Web servers or made of hypertext.

We'll look at how these tools and resources link with the Web, what they look like when viewed through the Mosaic browser, and the basics of their operation.

What's At the Edge?

As we discussed earlier, the Web consists of hypertext that links Internet resources. These resources can be multimedia information as well as searching tools and interfaces used to find and retrieve information. According to a strict definition of the Web, tools and resources that are not hypertext themselves (i.e., composed of files in HTML) are not actually part of the Web. But as we saw in Figure 14.2, hypertext files written in HTML "point" to many nonhypertext Internet-based resources and tools. These tools and resources can be thought of as being at the "edge" of the Web. Figure 16.1 illustrates these relationships.

FIGURE 16.1.

The edge of the web.

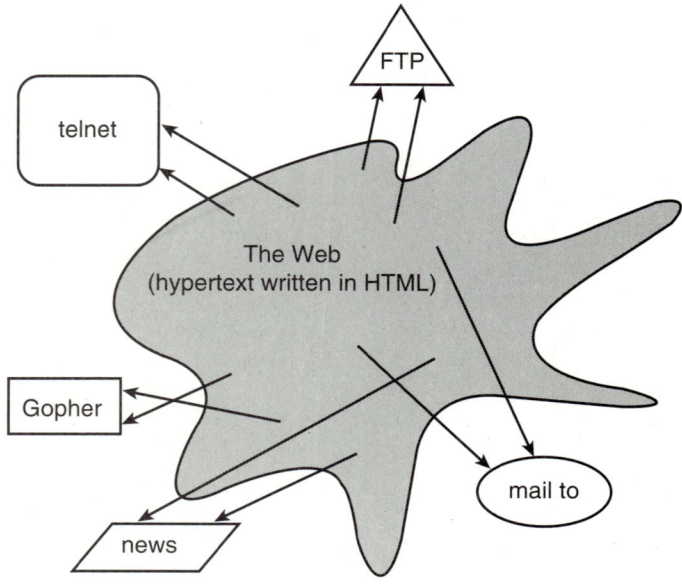

The Web's links reach into the information spaces created by Internet tools and protocols. For example, a link to the FTP resource

`ftp://ftp.ctr.columbia.edu/CTR-Research`

reaches into "FTP space," or the collection of all information on file transfer protocol sites. Similarly,

`gopher://info.itu.ch/`

reaches into "Gopher space," to a particular Gopher offering information about the International Telecommunications Union.

Mail links such as

`mailto:listserv@uriacc.uri.edu`

don't work with Mosaic 2.1, but work in a browser such as Lynx. This link essentially reaches into "mail space," or that portion of cyberspace that can be reached via electronic mail from the Internet (the region known as The Matrix).

All these links into information spaces, then, reach from the Web into other spaces. What happens when you go into these spaces? What does your browser look like? These are the questions we'll investigate in the following sections of this chapter. We'll encounter many "edges" of the Web, illustrating how these information spaces are used, how they look through Mosaic, and techniques and tips for navigating them.

FTP Space

File Transfer Protocol, or FTP, has long been used as a means to share information over the Internet. By using FTP, you can obtain files from remote computers—files of text, executable programs, graphics, movies, sound files—on a wide variety of subjects. Before the invention of Web browsers, the FTP procedure was done by hand, a process in which a user issued commands to a line-mode FTP interface. With a browser such as Mosaic, your entry into FTP space will be seamless and effortless—just a matter of clicking on the hotspot of a hypertext document or menu entry in information systems such as Gopher. Despite this ease of access, however, a navigator needs to pay attention to what happens when entering FTP space. A navigator must learn how to move through an FTP site as viewed through Mosaic, and learn some tips and techniques for dealing with special situations which arise in FTP space. We'll also look at how you can search not just one FTP site, but search thousands of sites with a single tool. We'll begin our journey by going to a sample FTP site and looking around.

An Example FTP site—Center for Telecommunications Research

Let's say that you want to find out something about telecommunications research. A good place to start is an academic center for such research at Columbia University in New York City, the Center for Telecommunications Research. The URL for their site is

`ftp://ftp.ctr.columbia.edu/CTR-Research`

You might have obtained this URL from a friend and typed this link into your browser by hand, using the Open... button on the bottom of the Mosaic browser. Or, you might have used the linking mechanisms of hypertext to follow a hotspot to this URL. Either way, once the Web browser has opened this URL, you will see the display as shown in Figure 16.2.

FIGURE 16.2.

The opening screen for a typical FTP site.

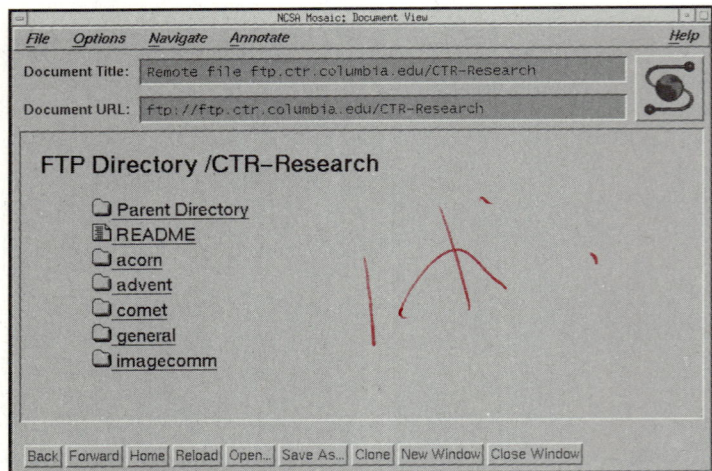

This opening screen for an FTP site is typical. Let's discuss its features.

1. The document doesn't have a descriptive title in the "Document Title" box. This isn't the fault of the developers of this information; rather, it is a limitation of FTP sites as displayed in a Web browser. Unlike the HTML file we looked at in Chapter 14, "Web Structure and Spaces," there is no way to designate a descriptive title from an FTP site for viewing through a Web browser. When FTP sites were invented, there was no consideration about how they would be viewed through a Web browser. (Remember the technique described in Chapter 15, "Browser Operations," for how you can put a descriptive title on this information if you put it in your hotlist.)

2. There is a title across the top of the Mosaic display window: "FTP Directory / CTR-Research." This tells you the location of this information on the host machine (`ftp.ctr.columbia.edu`). The fact that you are in a subdirectory on the host itself (the /CTR-Research part of the URL) lets you know that there are other directories "above" you.

3. There are symbols beside the list items. These give a clue about the file contents. The icon that looks like a folder is a directory of files. The icon that looks like a document is a single file (the README entry). Figure 16.3 shows other icons that you might expect to see at FTP sites (or Gopher in Gopher menus, as will be discussed later).

FIGURE 16.3.

Icons for FTP or Gopher sites.

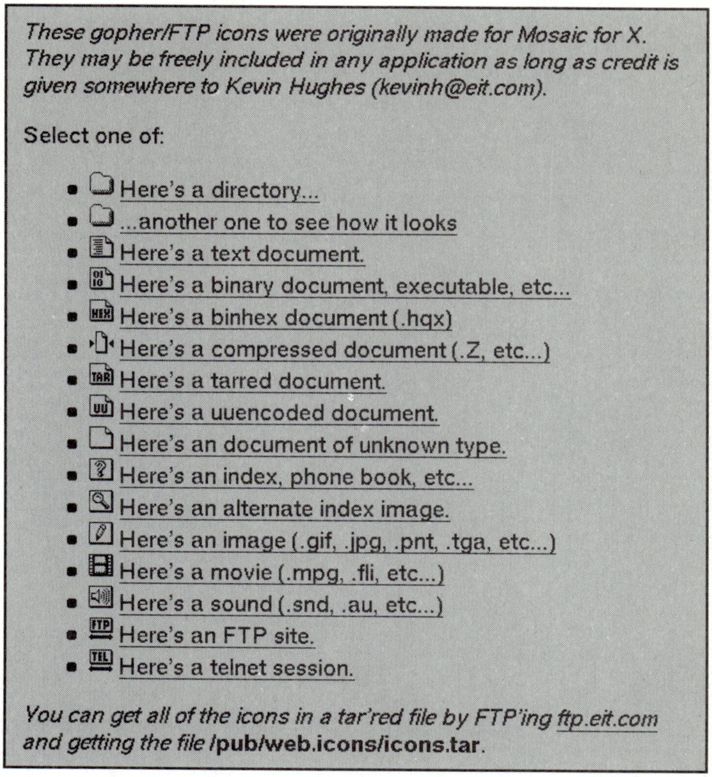

These gopher/FTP icons were originally made for Mosaic for X. They may be freely included in any application as long as credit is given somewhere to Kevin Hughes (kevinh@eit.com).

Select one of:

- Here's a directory...
- ...another one to see how it looks
- Here's a text document.
- Here's a binary document, executable, etc...
- Here's a binhex document (.hqx)
- Here's a compressed document (.Z, etc...)
- Here's a tarred document.
- Here's a uuencoded document.
- Here's an document of unknown type.
- Here's an index, phone book, etc...
- Here's an alternate index image.
- Here's an image (.gif, .jpg, .pnt, .tga, etc...)
- Here's a movie (.mpg, .fli, etc...)
- Here's a sound (.snd, .au, etc...)
- Here's an FTP site.
- Here's a telnet session.

You can get all of the icons in a tar'red file by FTP'ing ftp.eit.com and getting the file **/pub/web.icons/icons.tar**.

4. There are short names (rather than descriptive phrases) describing elements of the list. Because the entries in an FTP menu are the names of files or directories, the names are necessarily short. The entries themselves are all hotspots, underlined and highlighted to indicate that they are links to further information.

Navigating an FTP site

FTP sites, because of the restrictions on information representation (short names, few opportunities for putting phrases or terms on the entries in the lists), you need to recognize several conventions many well-organized FTP sites use. Understanding these conventions is key to navigating an FTP site efficiently.

Because the names in the list at an FTP site are so short, providers of information have recognized the need for more descriptive information and usually offer such a file that explains their site's offerings. The name of this file is often README, such as at the Center for Telecommunications Research FTP site. Often the list of entries will be very, very long. To place the README file in a more prominent position (the entries are usually listed alphabetically by default), a developer will capitalize the README file name or use a name like 00README. There are many variations, but look for a file with a name with variations on README, INDEX, NOTICE, or ABOUT.

Since the README file is probably the best place to start at an unfamiliar FTP site, let's look at the README file from the Center for Telecommunications Research FTP site. By placing the cursor over the README file and clicking the left mouse, the Mosaic browser appears as shown in Figure 16.4.

FIGURE 16.4.

README file for Center for Telecommunications Research site.

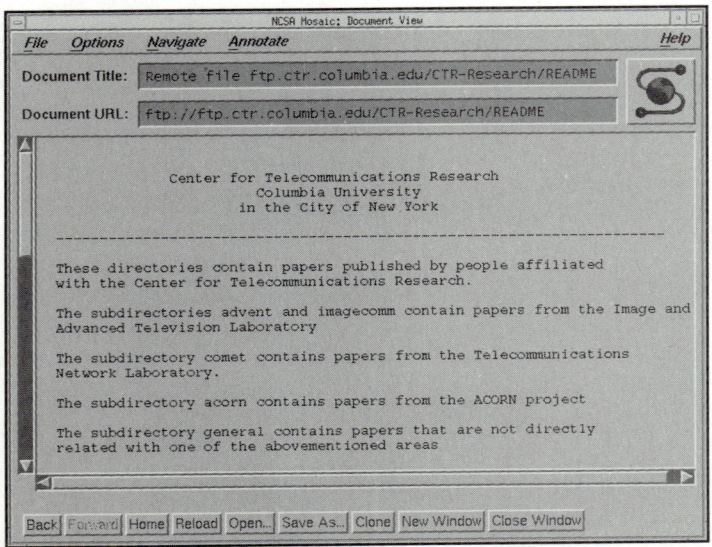

The Mosaic browser shows just the top of the README file's contents. The entire contents of the file are as follows:

```
Center for Telecommunications Research
     Columbia University
     in the City of New York
------------------------------------------------------------------
These directories contain papers published by people affiliated
with the Center for Telecommunications Research.

The subdirectories advent and imagecomm contain papers from the Image and
Advanced Television Laboratory.

The subdirectory comet contains papers from the Telecommunications
Network Laboratory.

The subdirectory acorn contains papers from the ACORN project.
The subdirectory general contains papers that are not directly
related with one of the above-mentioned areas.


------------------------------------------------------------------


Papers with the suffix .ps are in the Postscript format ready to
be sent directly to your postscript compatible printer.
Papers with the suffix .tex are in the TeX format. See the
README file associated with the directory in question for
information on how to format them.

Papers with the suffix .fm are in the Frame Maker format.
Papers with the suffix .mif are in the Frame Maker Interchange Format.


------------------------------------------------------------------


For further information about the Center, you can contact the
center via the following methods:

E-mail:
ctr-info@ctr.columbia.edu

Phone:
(212) 854-2498 (9-5 EST5EDT)

Fax:
(212) 316-9068

Snail-Mail:
CTR Information
Columbia University
Room 801 Schapiro Research Bldg.
530 W. 120th Street
New York, NY 10027-6699


------------------------------------------------------------------


Comments, questions, or problems to archivist@ctr.columbia.edu.
        -Seth Robertson
        seth@ctr.columbia.edu
```

The nice thing about this site's README file is that it gives you an overview of the site, tells you what to expect in each directory, and then gives you information about contacting the administrator of the site. These are all excellent points to have in a README file. Not having this information is often the most difficult part of navigating an FTP site.

Let's go over the Center for Telecommunications Research (CTR) README file, picking out the major points you will need to know for navigation:

1. The sponsoring institution or individual providing the information. You will often encounter FTP sites lacking this information, making it hard to know what institution or individual is providing the information (or even where the information is located) or the date the information was posted. Without this orientation information, it is hard to make a judgement about the information's usefulness or reliability.

   In our CTR example, the sponsoring institution is listed directly at the top of the file and a snail mail (US mail) address is shown at the bottom.

2. The contents of subdirectories. Often, there are many subdirectories at an FTP site, and a good description of each is very difficult to maintain (because of many information contributors at that site or simply a very large number of directories). In any case, look for information in the README file that can give you clues to subdirectory contents. Ideally, the names of the subdirectories themselves will be very descriptive. However, since the information providers are limited in naming directories and files, clues from the README file increase your efficiency in navigating an FTP site. In our CTR example, the contents of the directories are described very well—they clear up the meaning of the directory names like "comet" that might not otherwise yield a clue to their contents. Also, this README file does a very good job of describing the file extensions used in the information within the directories—explaining the file extensions such as .PS, .TEX, .FM, and .MIF. These are particularly important, as a Web browser can't interpret all types of file formats.

3. Further information. You need to have a person to contact in order to direct questions or other information, particularly if you have a problem with the information at that site. From the administrator's point of view, this contact is essential to catch errors and gain some input from users of the information. In our CTR example, a contact e-mail address is given for the person responsible for maintaining the information, so you can contact that person with further comments, suggestions, or questions.

Armed with the information from the README file, our experience of this FTP site can be much more efficient. We might have decided, based on the contents of the README file, that this site doesn't contain the information we want. If so, we can go on to other pursuits, rather than wasting time (and network bandwith) trying to figure out if the information at the site fits our needs or not.

Having viewed the README file, using the Back button on Mosaic's front panel, we'll return to the front screen of this FTP site (refer to Figure 16.2). By using the cursor and mouse, we can enter the subdirectories and encounter more information, each time using the same procedure as when we encountered the first screen: use clues such as README or INDEX files as well as symbols next to list entries to gain clues about the information you are encountering. As you click on entries in the FTP menu, the resources will appear in the Mosaic display window, or, in the case of specially formatted graphics, movies, or postscript files, an external viewer will appear displaying the information. If you have problems with obtaining a file by using FTP, try a "manual method" of using a line mode interface to FTP. You may run into some problems with formats—your Mosaic browser may not be able to display a file, or you encounter a file for which you don't have the appropriate multimedia software to view. See Part II, "Web Browsers and Connections," for more information about browsers and multimedia viewers that go along with them.

Navigating FTP Space

We've looked at one example of an FTP site in detail to see what a typical site looks like and the basics of navigating within it. There are thousands of FTP sites across the world, and, unless the site is focused toward collections of information that you are very interested in, you won't want to browse each one to find something. Navigating FTP space (the collection of all information available at all publicly-accessible FTP sites in the world) is much easier than making a visit to each one. Tools have been developed to find files in FTP space. One such tool available on the Web is called ArchiePlex, a Web-based version of a tool called *Archie* which can search the contents of FTP sites.

A list of ArchiePlex gateways around the world is at URL `http://web.nexor.co.uk/archie.html`. ArchiePlex's interface is in Figure 16.5.

By filling out the ArchiePlexForm and submitting it, you will get back (through the Mosaic interface) a list of all files that match your search string. These files won't necessarily be all the files in the world, only those that are currently in the database on the Archie server you selected in the form. Remember that the string you want to match is a file or directory name at a site, not a descriptive word or phrase. Therefore, you should use short key words.

Archie is a marvelous searching tool for finding things in FTP space based on key words. However, you might want to find an FTP site with a particular name. You could certainly try to guess what that name would be (often it is `ftp.site.domain`), but you might want to examine a list of sites where anonymous FTP access is allowed.

In this case, Archie would not be as useful as such a listing of all FTP sites. Such a listing exists at

`ftp://rtfm.mit.edu/pub/usenet-by-group/news.answers/ftp-list`

By using this list, you'll be able to search for a particular FTP site based on its name. While this monster list is not necessarily comprehensive (because it is maintained by hand), it can serve as a valuable reference while navigating FTP space.

FIGURE 16.5.

ArchiePlexForm.

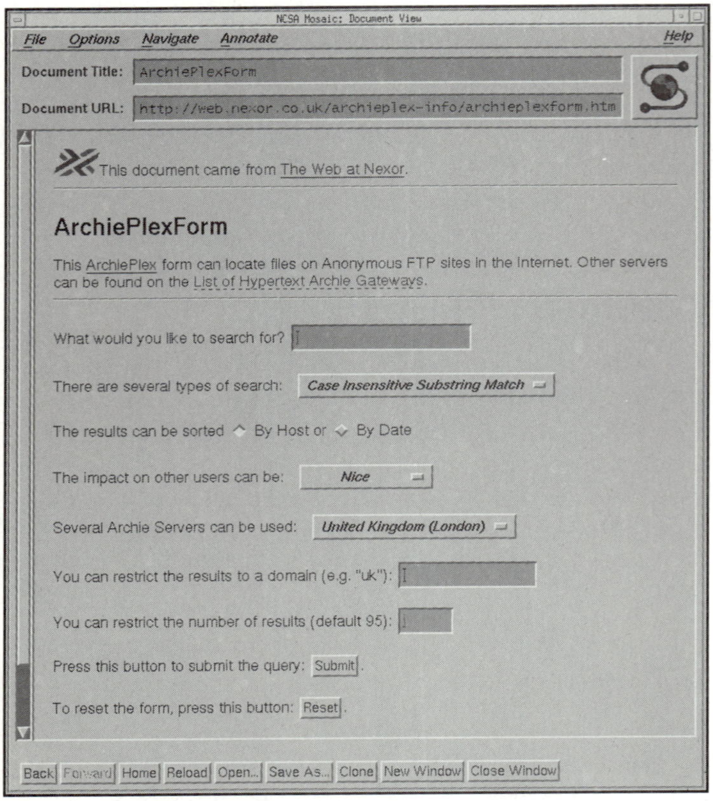

NCSA Mosaic: Document View

| File | Options | Navigate | Annotate | | Help |

Document Title: `ArchiePlexForm`

Document URL: `http://web.nexor.co.uk/archieplex-info/archieplexform.htm`

This document came from The Web at Nexor.

ArchiePlexForm

This ArchiePlex form can locate files on Anonymous FTP sites in the Internet. Other servers can be found on the List of Hypertext Archie Gateways.

What would you like to search for? [   ]

There are several types of search: *Case Insensitive Substring Match*

The results can be sorted ⌃ By Host or ⌄ By Date

The impact on other users can be: *Nice*

Several Archie Servers can be used: *United Kingdom (London)*

You can restrict the results to a domain (e.g. "uk"): [   ]

You can restrict the number of results (default 95): [   ]

Press this button to submit the query: Submit

To reset the form, press this button: Reset

Back | Forward | Home | Reload | Open... | Save As... | Clone | New Window | Close Window

Gopher Space

Like FTP space, Gopher space has long been used as a means to share information over the Internet, and there are thousands of Gopher sites throughout the world. Similar to our earlier discussion of FTP space, we'll first look at an example Gopher site and how to navigate it, then we'll look at how you can search Gopher space itself from the Web.

An Example Gopher Site—Minnesota Gopher

Gopher is an information system designed at the University of Minnesota, and it provides a very efficient way to organize information and provide it for other people to browse on the Internet. The term "Gopher" refers to the University's eponymous mascot, and also hints at the operation of the Internet Gopher itself—to "go for" information.

Just like FTP, there is an off-Web use of Gopher—Gopher clients provide the interface for obtaining information from Gopher servers, just as Mosaic clients (browsers) obtain information from Web server sites. There are even graphical browsers for Gopher, in addition to line-mode Gopher clients. Your Mosaic browser itself acts like a Gopher client when it encounters a Gopher "hole" (a Gopher site in Gopher space).

Let's look at the "mother Gopher," the original Gopher at the University of Minnesota, through Mosaic. The URL

```
gopher://gopher.micro.umn.edu/1
```

refers to this Gopher. Figure 16.6 shows the Mosaic display of the Minnesota Gopher.

FIGURE 16.6.

The Minnesota Gopher.

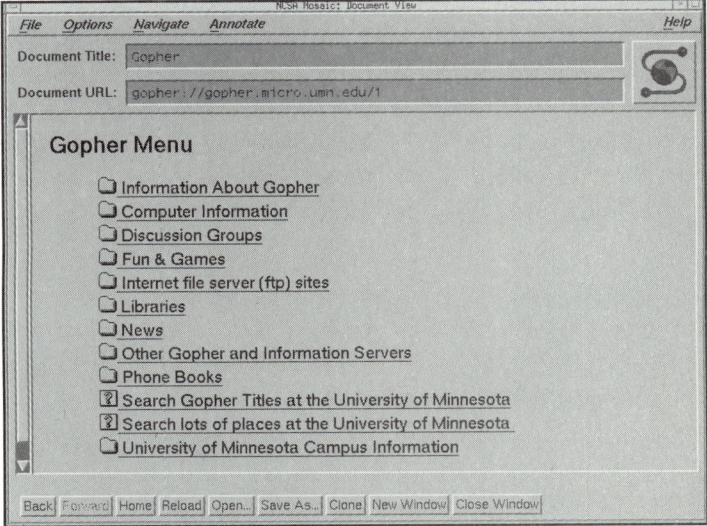

Let's discuss the features of the Minnesota Gopher.

1. Just as in the FTP site in the previous section, the title that shows up in Mosaic's "Document Title" box is just "Gopher." If you save a reference to this Gopher on your hotlist, you can consider using the hotlist's facilities for changing the title that appears on your hotlist.

2. The title in the Mosaic window is "Gopher Menu," and, since it appears in large font in a prominent place in the menu, might be the first clue that you've entered a Gopher hole as you are navigating the Web.

3. The symbols in the Gopher are the same as those at FTP sites on the list shown in Figure 16.3. Just as at the FTP site, you can use these symbols for clues as to what appears beneath the link. In the case of Gophers, a file folder symbol will lead to another menu, and a symbol that looks like a page of text will lead to a document.

4. The Gopher menu has longer names than at the FTP site. This is because the Gopher information system allows for longer, more descriptive names in menu titles.

GOPHER ON MTV!

One of Gopher's claims to fame was that MTV Video Jock (VJ) Adam Curry (now no longer with MTV) wore a Gopher t-shirt on an MTV program. You can view a movie of this appearance as well as still pictures from the "Information About Gopher" menu selection from the front screen of the Minnesota Gopher.

Navigating a Gopher—the Minnesota Gopher

Because Gopher menu entries are more descriptive, you'll often find that you need fewer cues than at FTP sites to navigate them. These longer names mean that a Gopher URL can be a bit more unwieldy, but more descriptive. For example this is a Gopher URL

```
gopher://gopher.tc.umn.edu/11/Information%20About%20Gopher
```

Since the menu entry names are more descriptive, navigating a Gopher requires fewer README file cues. However, you will still want to know

1. the individual or institution providing the information

2. what to expect to find at the Gopher site

3. how to get more information, ask questions, or give feedback

The Minnesota Gopher fulfills these needs very well with its "Information About Gopher" menu entry. By selecting this link, you can browse an extensive directory of information about Gopher itself. A good place to find out more about Gopher itself is from the Frequently Asked Questions (FAQ) list for Gopher. The URL to the Gopher FAQ list is

```
gopher://mudhoney.micro.umn.edu/00/Gopher.FAQ
```

Besides a gold-mine of knowledge about Gophers, the Minnesota Gopher also is a good example of a Gopher-based campus-wide information system for the University of

Minnesota. By selecting "University of Minnesota Campus Information" from the front Gopher menu, you can examine a wide range of information about the university, from Academic Staff to the University of Minnesota Women's Center.

Just as at the FTP site, you'll encounter files and resources in a variety of formats. Unlike an FTP site however, you'll see some unique kinds of resources and connections at a Gopher site:

1. The question mark icon (shown in Figure 16.3 to the left of "Here's an index, phone book, etc.") is a connection to a searching mechanism built into the Gopher itself.

   For example, from the Minnesota Gopher's opening screen, you can select "Search Gopher Titles at the University of Minnesota," your Mosaic display window will show a screen that says

   `Searchable Gopher Index`

   `This is a searchable index. Enter search key words:_`

   In the blank provided, you'll be able to enter a key word or phrase identifying information you want to find at the University of Minnesota. By entering the key words, and pressing Return, you'll generate a list of resources whose titles match the key word or phrase you entered. A Gopher title is the phrase that appears on the Gopher menu. By using this search mechanism, you don't have to browse the complete tree of menus on the Gopher, but have all matching menus, documents or other resources gathered together in a single list as a result of your search request. You can then select items from this list.

2. The telnet icon (shown in Figure 16.3, the bottom of list, to the left of "Here's a telnet session) is a connection to a remote login connection. You can see an example of this on the Minnesota Gopher by, starting from the "front" of the Minnesota Gopher (Figure 16.6), selecting

   `Libraries`

   then

   `Library Catalogs via Telnet`

   You'll see the symbol for a telnet session link next to an entry for "Libraries of the University of Minnesota Integrated Network Access."

   By selecting a telnet session link, you will cause a pop-up window to appear, independent of your Web browser, which brings you into a remote session with a remote computer. (If you are using a nongraphical Web browser such as Lynx, your browser's display will "transform" to the telnet session shown below.)

   By selecting the "Libraries of the University of Minnesota Integrated Network Access," option on the page given by the URL above, a pop-up window will appear like this:

```
UUU  UUU        MMMMM   MMMMM            Welcome to the
UUU  UUU   OF   MM MM MM MM          University of Minnesota
UUU  UUU        MM  MMM  MM     Public Access Information Service
UUUUUUUU        MMMMM   MMMMM

Please Indicate Your Menu Selection Here ===>   and press ENTER
1 - University Libraries/LUMINA      8 - Personnel Information
2 - Computer Facilities              9 - Future
3 - Food Service                    10 - Future
4 - Research News/Deadlines (ORTTA)  11 - Uncle Eddy
5 - Graduate School Information      12 - Gopher
6 - Public Access General Info       13 - Student Access System
7 - Telephone Directories            14 - Future

XQ - 'Exit Quickly' (return to this menu from any screen)
   - or -  (to logoff this menu)
AIS Network Available: Sunday Noon - Sunday at 6:00 A.M.
AIS Network Help:  Monday-Friday, 7:30 A.M. to 4:30 P.M., 624-0555

Message:        Gtway: TN3270GW Term: TCP00413
```

These telnet sessions have their own peculiarities (we'll discuss navigating telnet space in the next section of this chapter). However, the point to remember is that you may find links to telnet space from Gopher space.

We've seen how navigating a Gopher is a bit easier than an FTP site because of the more descriptive names possible in the menu entries and the built-in search mechanisms for finding information at a particular Gopher.

Navigating Gopher Space

While an individual Gopher is easy to navigate, how do you navigate the thousands of Gophers spread throughout the world? Well, as you might suspect, it is far easier than exhaustively burrowing to every Gopher hole in cyberspace. Instead, there is a tool called *Veronica* which does for Gopher space what Archie does for FTP space—search out individual items on servers worldwide.

From the Minnesota Gopher's first menu, you can select "Other Gopher and Information Servers" and look for the menu entry "Search titles in Gopherspace using Veronica." Selecting this entry puts you into a long menu of information as well as query menu entries (entries with a question mark) that allow you to do various kinds of searching in Gopher space. There are many options for this kind of searching, and a good document to consult to help you compose exactly the right Veronica query for you is entitled, "How to Compose Veronica Queries." You can find this document in the "Search titles in Gopherspace using Veronica" on the Minnesota (and many other) Gophers.

You'll obtain a list of entries that match your search specification, and you'll be able to browse the entries, from a single Gopher menu, even though the entries themselves may be scattered across Gopher menus all over the world.

Besides Veronica's power to search Gopher space through key word search patterns, you also can search Gophers by subject area. Subject-related Gophers have sprung up world-wide, growing with the popularity of Gopher itself. Because of the additional expressive-ness offered by Gopher, it is often the preferred information delivery system for many organizations. A very fine collection of subject-related Gophers is called "Gopher Jewels," developed by David Riggins. A Web-based version of Gopher Jewels is at the URL `http://galaxy.einet.net/GJ/index.html`. The opening screen of this Gopher Jewels collection is shown in Figure 16.7.

FIGURE 16.7.

Gopher Jewels Collection.

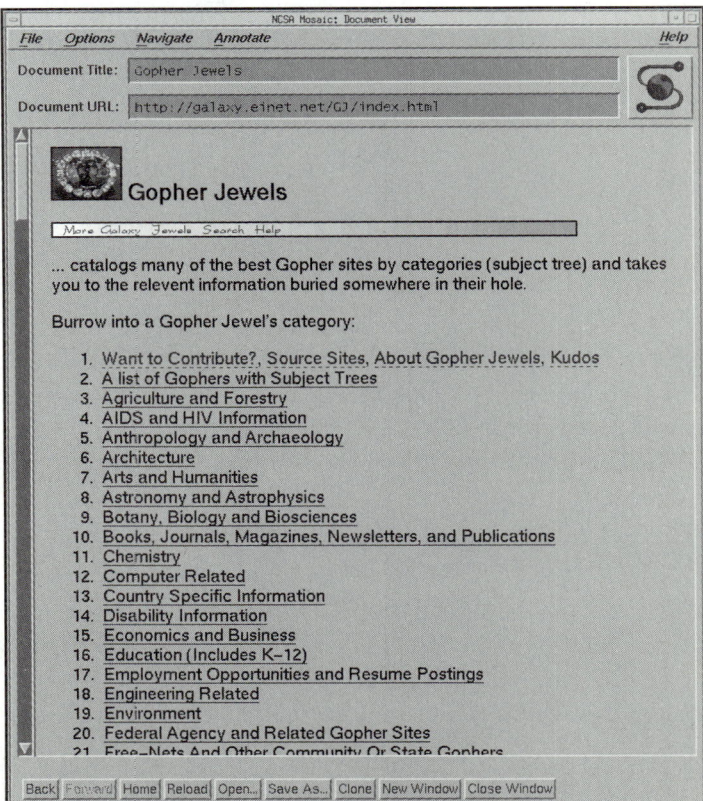

The Gopher Jewels collection gives you a subject-oriented view of Gopherspace. This is particularly useful when you are looking for information related to a particular area of interest, and you don't necessarily know search terms to use (if you did, you could use a Veronica search). In addition, the Gopher Jewels collection also provides a way for you to search the document and directory titles of all Gophers in the collection. This Gopher Jewels search mechanism serves as a Veronica search localized to the Jewels region of Gopher space.

FIGURE 16.8.

Gopher Jewels search screen.

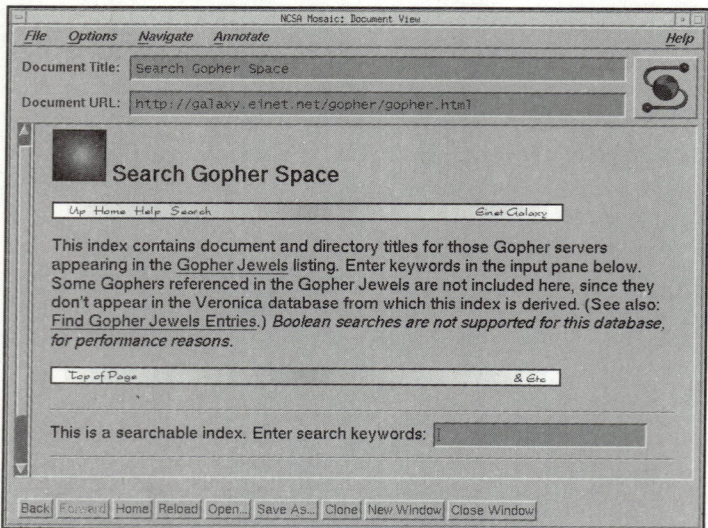

The key word (via Veronica) and subject-oriented (through Gopher Jewels) navigation of Gopher space is useful, but there is still another way to search Gophers—geographically. From the front screen of the Minnesota Gopher, you can select, "Other Gopher and Information Servers" to enter a geographically-based tree of Gophers. In this way, you can attempt to locate a particular Gopher at an organization if you know its geographic location.

Telnet Space

FTP space and Gopher space offered an elaborate, and fairly uniform (as viewed through Mosaic) way of navigating. However, the links to telnet connections from Web documents vary widely in terms of what happens when you enter them. The connection to a telnet session is straightforward—you click on a hotspot, invoking a URL such as

```
telnet://downwind.sprl.umich.edu:3000
```

which causes a pop-up window to appear which allows you to begin the login procedures to the remote computer.

What is different is what happens after you select the hotlink and open the URL. There is no uniform arrangement of how a telnet session on a computer can proceed, and you won't expect to see any of the icons shown in Figure 16.3.

Let's look at a typical session, see how it works, and then talk about general navigating tips for individual sessions and telnet space itself.

An Example Telnet Session—the Weather Underground

The URL

```
telnet://downwind.sprl.umich.edu:3000
```

will take you to the Weather Underground, a public service offered by the College of Engineering at University of Michigan in Ann Arbor. The National Weather Service data in the Weather underground is courtesy of the National Science Foundation-funded UNIDATA Project and the University of Michigan. This service is quite useful for finding out very current weather, earthquake, skiing, and other environmental conditions.

After opening the above URL, a popup window will appear as follows:

```
-----------------------------------------------------------------
*                       University of Michigan                  *
*                       WEATHER UNDERGROUND                     *
-----------------------------------------------------------------
*                                                               *
*           College of Engineering, University of Michigan      *
*           Department of Atmospheric, Oceanic, and Space Sciences *
*           Ann Arbor, Michigan  48109-2143                     *
*           comments: sdm@madlab.sprl.umich.edu                 *
*                                                               *
* With Help from:  The National Science Foundation supported Unidata Project *
*                  University Corporation for Atmospheric Research *
*                  Boulder, Colorado  80307-3000                *
*                                                               *
*        This service is for educational and research purposes only. *
*        Commercial users should contact our data provider, Alden *
*        Electronics, 508-366-8851 to acquire their own data feed. *
*                                                               *
-----------------------------------------------------------------
*   NOTE: — — — —> New users, please select option "H" on the main menu: *
*              H) Help and information for new users            *
-----------------------------------------------------------------
Press Return for menu, or enter 3 letter forecast city code:
```

The service is very descriptive in its opening screen. As a new user, you should pay attention to how you can obtain help in a telnet session. Usually, there is a selection for obtaining help. Look for this to familiarize yourself with the service so you can work most efficiently with it.

Given the information on the opening screen shown above, a user should probably go into the main menu and select the help for new users. By pressing return, the main menu is displayed:

```
WEATHER UNDERGROUND MAIN MENU
*******************************
 1) U.S. forecasts and climate data
 2) Canadian forecasts
 3) Current weather observations
 4) Ski conditions
 5) Long-range forecasts
 6) Latest earthquake reports
 7) Severe weather
 8) Hurricane advisories
 9) National Weather Summary
10) International data
11) Marine forecasts and observations
12) Michigan K12 schools program
 X) Exit program
 C) Change scrolling to screen
 H) Help and information for new users
 ?) Answers to all your questions
Selection:
```

This opening menu shows a common pattern of telnet session—menu selections by numbers or letters. This common arrangement will help you navigate most telnet sessions rather easily. Note on this main menu there are two selections for help—the H selection new users were told to select and the ? selection. It is a good idea to select what you are told to at first—this will give you the introductory information that will help you work well with the interface. Selecting H, we see

```
      INFORMATION FOR NEW USERS OF THE WEATHER UNDERGROUND
      ----------------------------------------------------
Welcome to the Weather Underground! Through our host computer in Ann Arbor,
Michigan, we provide a variety of weather information through this menu-driven,
interactive program. Use of this service is free, as long as the information is
is for personal or educational use. Feel free to access the service as much as
you like, but be aware that during major weather events usage gets quite heavy,
and you may receive the following message:

The Weather Underground is fully loaded. Try again later.

The Weather Underground is limited to 100 simultaneous users, so you will
have to wait until someone else signs off before you can get on. Once you do
get on, please limit the duration of your session so that others may sign on.

BYPASSING THE MAIN MENU
-----------------------
When first entering the Weather Underground, you will get the following
prompt:

Press Return for menu, or enter 3 letter forecast city code:
```

```
At this point, you can either hit <Return> to get the main menu, or
enter a special code that will immediately give you a forecast or observation.
The special codes are explained under the various options available on the main
menu. You may enter any of the following codes at the initial prompt:

1) A 3-letter code for a U.S. city forecast. For example, entering DTW will
give the forecast, plus any warnings or special weather statements for
Detroit.
2) A 2-letter state or province code, to get current observations for the U.S.
or Canada. For example, entering MI will give the current observations for
Michigan.
3) A number between 1 and 20, to get the current forecast for a Canadian
Province. For example, entering 18 will give the forecast for the Yukon.
Note that as a special feature for users who access the Weather Underground
Press Return to continue, M to return to menu, X to exit:
```

This new user information describes typical navigation methods for telnet sessions, including shortcuts for working with the interface. While built-in search mechanisms such as the one for searching titles at the Minnesota Gopher are not always available, the help files and the menu options should provide the user with the clues necessary to navigate a telnet session.

This weather service offers you a wide range of weather information. By using the simple menu interface, you can access current climate, weather, and earthquake reports from all over the world. For example, we can find out about a recent earthquake in Nevada:

```
************************************************************
    Earthquake report for 06/22/94
************************************************************
338
SEXX2 KWBC 220757
THE FOLLOWING IS A RELEASE BY THE UNITED STATES GEOLOGICAL SURVEY,
NATIONAL EARTHQUAKE INFORMATION CENTER: A MINOR EARTHQUAKE OCCURRED
IN NEVADA ABOUT 10 MILES (20 KM) EAST OF CARSON CITY AT 10:10 PM MDT
TODAY, JUN 21, 1994 (9:10 PM PDT IN NEVADA). THE MAGNITUDE WAS
COMPUTED AT 3.5 ON THE RICHTER SCALE. THIS EARTHQUAKE WAS FELT IN
THE CARSON CITY AREA. THERE HAVE BEEN NO REPORTS OF DAMAGE.
```

Navigating a Telnet Session

The Weather Underground is a good example of a telnet session because its menu and help system are typical. Here's some tips for navigating a telnet session:

1. **Read the Screen**—It is a cardinal rule of user interface design that the user will never read a screen :). However, reading the information on the screen and looking through the help files (at least the first time that you enter a telnet

session) can help you in the long term. Look for short cuts to commands if you use a service frequently. Use the help information and the opening screens to get a quick idea of what the service offers.

2. **Hit return**—Sometimes a telnet session screen stops, particularly when you first start it. If this happens, hit the return key on your keyboard.

3. **Set your terminal type**—Sometimes a telnet session will ask you to set the type of terminal you are using. This is so that the session can send graphics or other information to your terminal with the appropriate format. If you are asked a terminal type, unless you know it to be different, you can usually respond with vt100 or xterm safely. If you encounter garbled graphics, logoff the telnet session and try another type.

4. **Quit using a command**—The best way to quit out of telnet session is by using the exit command provided by the session itself. Frequently this command is quit, exit, end, stop, bye, logout, or some other variation.

5. **Be courteous**—When you are using a telnet session, you are actually "on" the remote computer—its processing power is devoted to waiting for your inputs and processing your responses. As such, obtain the information from a telnet session as quickly and efficiently as you can. Sometimes, after a period of time without input from you, a telnet session will terminate on its own. This is very different from a Web browser, in which you are not using the processing power of the remote computer once you've retrieved the resource across the network.

6. **Remember: you're independent**—Once the Mosaic browser spawns the pop-up window of the telnet session, the Mosaic browser itself is free to operate independently. This is a fairly useful feature in situations where you want to use the telnet session's information as part of navigating with Mosaic.

Navigating Telnet Space

Unlike Gopher space and FTP space, there are no tools to cruise through telnet space and find *all* the telnet hosts with particular menu entries. However, there is a wonderful catalog of many telnet-accessible services on the Internet called Hytelnet. Developed by Peter Scott, Hytelnet organizes telnet-accessible services by categories. You can use Hytelnet through telnet itself— by entering the following command at your operating system prompt (assuming you have the telnet program installed on your computer):

```
telnet access.usask.ca
```

and using "hytelnet" as the login name. From a Web browser, you can open the URL telnet://access.usask.ca. However, this telnet session, like the telnet sessions similar to the Weather Underground, creates a drain on the remote computer you are using. You should obtain a client program to most efficiently use Hytelnet. Mosaic acts as a client for you when you use the Web-based version of Hytelnet available at the URL

```
http://www.cc.ukans.edu/hytelnet_html/START.TXT.html
```

The opening screen for this Web-based hytelnet session is shown in Figure 16.9.

FIGURE 16.9.

Web-based Hytelnet.

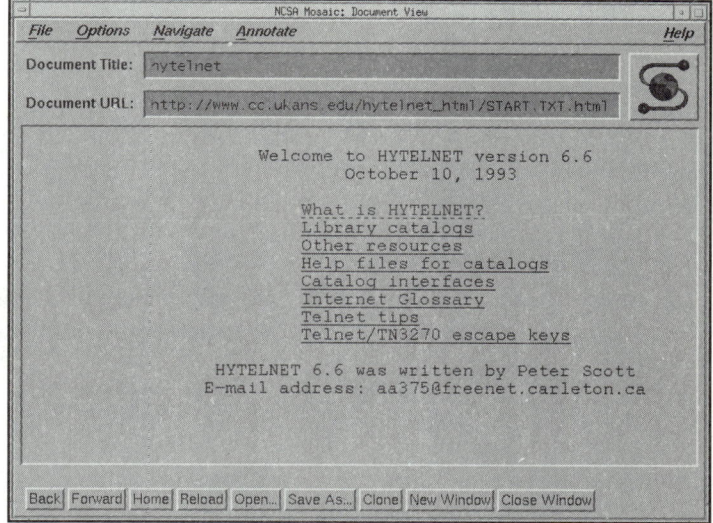

The opening screen of Hytelnet gives you access into a tree of menus that organize telnet-accessible sites and resources into categories. A big category is library catalogs at many universities and public sites. The Web version of Hytelnet will guide you through the process of selecting a telnet session. Eventually, you will reach the point where you will start a telnet session. For example, selecting the Universidade de Sao Paulo from the world-wide libraries list, we see the following in the Mosaic display window:

```
        Universidade de Sao Paulo
 telnet BEE08.CCE.USP.BR or 143.107.70.28
 login: dedalus
 At HELP INICIAL screen, press RETURN
 Select BUSCA
 To exit, hit the telnet escape key
```

In the display above, the word `telnet` is a hotspot. If I put my cursor over the word `telnet`, I see `telnet://bee08.cce.usp.br/` in the status message area of the Mosaic main panel. This tells me that I've reached the edge of the Web-based version of Hytelnet. Clicking on this `telnet` link will cause a window to pop up with a telnet session started at this remote host. From the Hytelnet screen shown in the Mosaic window, I have further information to complete the connection, such as the login name I should use (`dedalus`), and how to get help during the session. (It is possible to search the descriptions of Hytelnet entries for key words or phrases using Galaxy, as we'll see in Chapter 18, "Trees: Subject-Oriented Searching.)"

News Space

While not truly an information system like Gopher, FTP, or telnet, Usenet news is a vast space for communication accessible through Web clients. Usenet includes lively discussion among tens of thousands of people on thousands of topics. Usenet news itself is not confined to the Internet, but flows throughout the Matrix according to a cooperative distribution scheme. Usenet consists of thousands of discussion areas called *newsgroups* that are identified through a hierarchical naming scheme. For example, the newsgroup name `rec.food.restaurants` has three parts to it: `rec` stands for the recreational hierarchy, `food` indicates a subdivision within recreation, and `restaurants` qualifies this newsgroup further. Two other examples of recreational newsgroups are `rec.gambling` and `rec.food.sourdough`.

Tens of thousands of people read Usenet news daily for information or discussion on a wide range of topics. The culture of Usenet and the individual communities of people who participant in the newsgroups is quite complex. If you are a newcomer to Usenet, it is very important that you become aware of the culture, language, practices, and traditions of Usenet itself—it is not just a collection of hardware, software, and network feeds, but a vibrant society, in which individuals contribute their opinions and engage in text-based asynchronous discussions. You can learn more about Usenet in the newsgroup `news.announce.newusers` which is specifically designed to carry information for new users.

Usenet news has its own client programs, or *newsreaders* that give a variety of interfaces for reading and contributing to the thousands of newsgroups. You can use Mosaic as your newsreader, and browse Usenet newsgroups in hypertext fashion. To read a particular Usenet newsgroup (for example `news.announce.newusers`) using Mosaic, you can use the Open... button on Mosaic's main panel and enter the URL `news:news.announce.newusers`

The computer on which you are running Mosaic must have a Usenet server available for it to access, and this server must carry the particular Usenet newsgroup you are attempting to read.

If this is the case, your Mosaic browser will appear as in Figure 16.10.

Navigating Usenet On the Web

Individual entries in a newsgroup are called *articles,* and each article is contributed or posted by someone to that newsgroup. On the Mosaic browser, the article titles are highlighted.

FIGURE 16.10.

A Usenet newsgroup displayed in Mosaic.

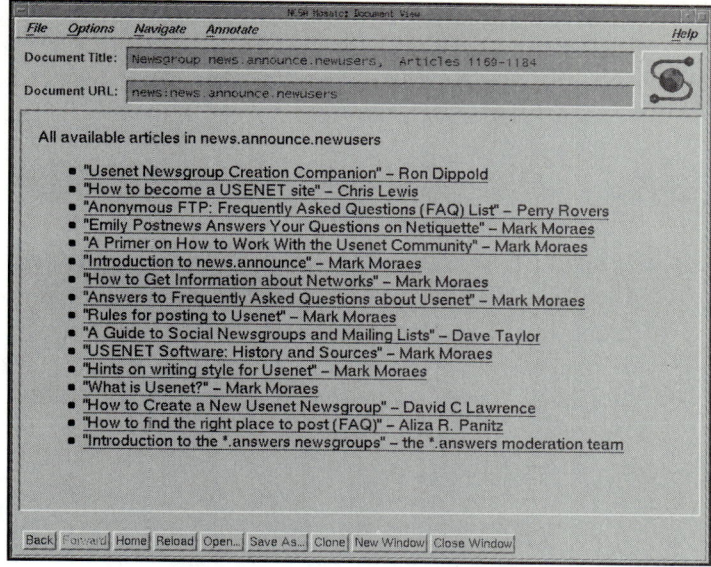

By clicking on an article name, we can see the article's contents.

The article itself will have links in it—to any previous articles to which the given article is a *follow up* (response) and to any other newsgroups where this article has been *crossposted* (contributed simultaneously to several groups). Using Mosaic, you can follow these links to the other articles or the other newsgroups where the article might be crossposted. In this way, the Mosaic interface to Usenet is fairly easy to navigate—following links just as in any other hypertext.

While navigating Usenet, keep these things in mind:

1. Orient yourself to the culture of Usenet. Use the articles in `news.announce.newusers` as a starting point. Then spend time observing the conversation before you consider contributing to any group. (You won't be able to contribute an article to a newsgroup using Mosaic; instead, you'll have to use a special program on your operating system (a Postnews) program).

2. You won't be able to access newsgroups that your local newserver doesn't carry. There are many regional hierarchies for Usenet news that contain newsgroups particular to one region, or specialized hierarchies that aren't necessarily distributed to your site. You'll get an error message `No such group` on your Mosaic display window if you attempt to access one of these newsgroups.

3. You won't be able to access articles that have expired. After a period of time set by your local Usenet administrator, the articles that reach a certain age (have been on

the server for the given period of time) are deleted. It may happen that you find links in articles that refer to an expired article. If you follow such a link, you'll get an error message. Also, if you place a reference to an article on your hotlist, after a few weeks, you might find that the article has expired, and you won't be able to read it again.

4. You won't be able to easily contribute (post) an article to a newsgroup using Mosaic 2.1. Perhaps future versions will include this as a native feature of Mosaic.

5. You won't find many of the news reading navigation features in Mosaic that are offered by other newsreaders. The Mosaic interface, despite its hypertext links among articles and newsgroups, is not very sophisticated as a newsgroup navigator. You'll find that other newsreaders such as `trn`, `nn`, `xrn`, or `rn`, offer many features for rapidly scanning newsgroup contents that Mosaic doesn't provide.

Looking at News Space

If you think of news space as all the unexpired newsgroup articles on all the servers in all the world, you won't be able to search or navigate the entire space. Instead, you are limited to the newsgroups and articles that have propagated to the site where you are reading Usenet news.

A handy list in hypertext, listing many newsgroups and a brief description of each is at

`http://info.cern.ch/hypertext/DataSources/News/Groups/Overview.html`

This list can help you navigate through the hierarchies of groups to find some that might interest you. However, this list, because it was prepared at a Swiss site, won't match the groups that might be available at your site, and it might not contain some new groups that have just developed. With these warnings in mind, a navigator can remember that the anarchy of Usenet is accessible at the edge of the Web, and that Mosaic offers some hypertext features for reading newsgroup articles.

Mail Space: The Matrix

The set of all Internet or gateway-accessible e-mail addresses compromises a rich resource for communication. This space is called *The Matrix*, coined by John Quarterman. Using Mosaic 2.1, however, you will not be able to make use of `mailto` URLs such as

`mailto:listserv@uriacc.uri.edu`

Other Web browsers, such as Lynx, however, recognize these URLs and allow you to enter a session in which you can send e-mail to anyone in the Matrix. Mosaic itself supports electronic mail interaction in some of the options accessible from its main panel (such as File / Mail To...).

While there's no tool analogous to Archie for FTP space and Veronica for Gopher space for The Matrix, you do have some options to find out about e-mail based discussion lists. A searchable index to discussion groups is located at the URL

```
http://alpha.acast.nova.edu/cgi-bin/lists
```

and you can access a WAIS-based index of academic e-mail conferences at the URL

```
wais://munin.ub2.lu.se:210/academic_e-mail_conf
```

Both lists will help you locate an e-mail-based conference or discussion. Neither service will allow you to search through contributed discussions or archives of discussions.

Other Spaces

The previous tour took you through some of the most popular edges of the Web. New kinds of protocols and information systems are being developed all the time which will offer you still other kinds of interfaces. Internet-based activity that is not now directly accessible from the Web such as MU*s (a family of real-time text conferencing systems, often involving social role playing) may develop Web gateways.

ENTERING FINGER SPACE

The `finger` protocol is used to retrieve information about a user with an account on a particular host computer. At the UNIX prompt, you can enter

```
finger decemj@rpi.edu
```

and find out about the person connected with this e-mail account. By including information in a file called `.plan` in your home directory and setting its permissions so that it is readable to everyone, you can create a service based on finger that provides information. A collection of Web-accessible finger-based information services is collected at the URL

```
http://sundae.triumf.ca/fingerinfo.html
```

based on Scott Yanoff's fingerinfo script. The Web-based version of fingerinfo makes use of a way to obtain finger information using a Gopher client. Within Mosaic, you can open the URL

```
gopher://rpi.edu:79/0decemj
```

to see finger information for the user `decemj` on the host `rpi.edu`. By using this Gopher->finger gateway, the Web-based fingerinfo program offers a view into "finger space" at the edge of the Web.

Navigator's Check

Now that we've toured the major spaces at the edges of the Web, we can integrate our knowledge in a single map. The cyber map shown in Figure 16.11 gives you a rough idea of the topology of cyberspace.

FIGURE 16.11.

A cyber map.

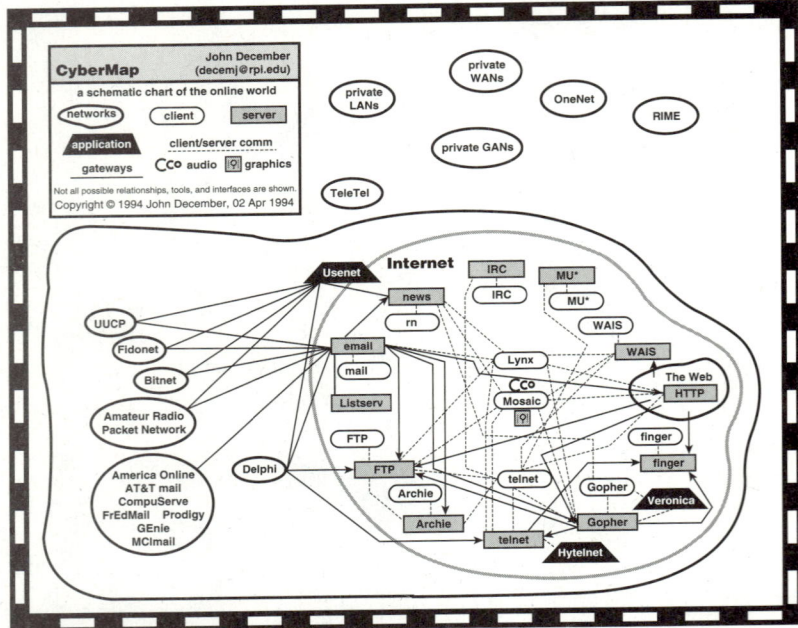

Not all possible relationships are shown on the map—this would be far too complicated! Instead, some illustrative relationships are shown, and the major spaces of cyberspace are charted. You can see how The Matrix encompasses BITNET, UUCP, many commercial services as well as the Internet itself. Gateways make it possible to exchange electronic mail among networks, and other kinds of gateways among tools and protocols allow the flow of information from places like Gopher space to the Web. This map is just a rough approximation of the extent of cyberspace. Like the imperfect charts of the world drawn by early explorers, Figure 16.11 shows only a snapshot of understanding, and will require updating as new tools, information spaces, communication forums, and connections among them are developed.

Notice how the French communication system Teletel (popularly know as Minitel, after the name for the actual hardware terminals used in the system) is approaching the Matrix and the Internet. The critical mass of users offered on the Matrix and Internet lures other networks to build gateways or connect directly to the Internet.

Notice also how the Web is at the heart of the Internet, and how browsers like Mosaic and Lynx access many of the major Internet information protocols and tools.

As a navigator you'll need to create your own map of cyberspace. Figure 16.11 can serve as a general chart, a way of starting. You'll populate your actual experience of cyberspace with the astounding things you'll find and the people you'll meet. The next chapter presents an overview of navigating the Web, and this will be a stepping stone for you to find out still more.

An Introduction to Web Navigating and Searching Techniques

by John December

Navigating the Web requires a variety of skills in dealing with information. Just as we saw techniques in the previous chapter for navigating the edges of the Web, we will look at techniques for navigating the Web itself. And just like FTP and Gopher, the protocol that is native to the web—*HTTP* (hypertext transfer protocol)—creates information spaces that you can navigate in a variety of ways.

This chapter describes concepts and terminology you will need to know in order to make use of techniques covered in the chapters on searching following this one. After exploring an example web, this chapter presents a quick overview of the ways to search the Web. Finally, this chapter discusses some important caveats for using and understanding the limitations of networked information.

An Example Web Page—
Window-to-Russia™

A typical Web page presents a variety of information, possibly using a large variety of multimedia resources. Through Mosaic, a Web page is often very colorful and can have a pleasing layout and design. As such, a Web-based information system can be very appealing to people who want to find information on a particular topic.

We'll look at a particular Web page to illustrate features commonly found. The URL http://www.kiae.su/www/wtr/ points to a Web page called *Window-to-Russia*, and is a project of Relcom corporation to provide worldwide resources to information sources about and from Russia. The top part of the home page is shown in Figure 17.1.

The home page contains elements that you'll find on most Web home pages:

- A descriptive title that appears in the Document Title box on the Mosaic main panel.
- A header which describes the sponsors and originators of the information.
- A short introductory text which tells the purpose of the server itself.
- A warning about special resources that may be required to use this information: (Cyryllic) fonts and the ability to read Russian.
- An appealing arrangement of the link choices, with small icons that help you gain an idea of what the links will retrieve. The icons used in the Russian home page are not standard—unlike the FTP and Gopher symbols (that Mosaic automatically supplies to FTP lists and Gopher menus), there is no standard for icons on Web pages. Developers use whatever they would like. From practice and convention, an arrangement of small icons is often used, rather than many large ones, because many large icons or pictures would require far more time to transfer over the network and slow down the retrieval of the entire page.

■ The bottom of the Russian page (not shown in Figure 17.1) includes contact information for the developers of the page and an address where the developer can be reached.

The preceding list illustrates the kinds of orientation information you should look for on a typical Web server. Although the list of icons and titles on the Russian server are typical, a linear arrangement (reminiscent of a Gopher list or an FTP list shown in the previous chapter) is not necessary. The HTML language allows developers to be very creative in placing hotspots. A traditional arrangement like the Russian server, however, is very effective for quickly summarizing the choices a user has for encountering the information.

FIGURE 17.1.

The Window-to-Russia home page.

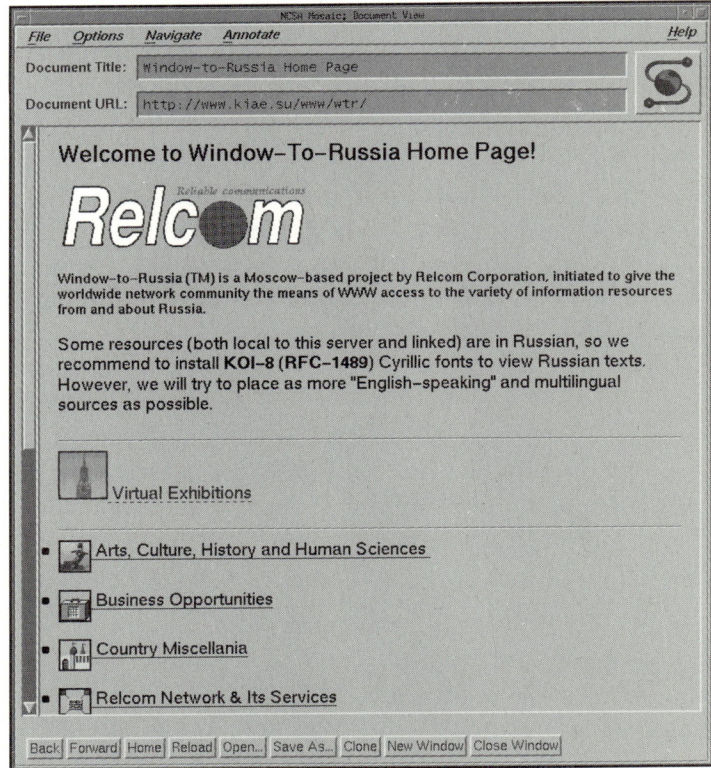

Navigating a Web Page

Now that we've covered the basic elements of a Web page, let's cover some of the basics of navigating the hypertext. Here's some general navigation advice about using Web resources:

■ *Look at all your options*—From any Web page, notice what hotlinks exist and quickly pass your cursor over them, and watch Mosaic's message status area for clues about what kinds of resources these hotlinks are tied to.

Are all the files at the same server? If so, you're looking at a large collection of information, probably developed by the same person or organization. If not, you're probably looking at a page that points to resources not created by the author of that page. This distinction can help you in evaluating the usefulness of the information for your purposes. For example, you might want to get the information directly from a particular source.

What kinds of file extensions at on the URLs? Graphics? Movies? You might be particularly interested in finding multimedia information. Passing the cursor over the hotspots on a web page can help you identify these.

- *Look beneath the surface*—As a follow-up to the above point, you'll need to delve into a web in order to find out what is beneath. The file extension names can give you clues, but only to one level. An `.html` extension on a URL indicates an HTML file connected to the link. This HTML file could be the very treasure-trove you're looking for, or it could be a dead end.

- *Look for orientation marks and guides*—Once you follow a link from one web page to another, what have you found? What cues can you use to go back? On a page "beneath the surface" of another page, look for cues or links back to the home page. Of course, you can always use your windows history or your Back button to return to the home page, but developers of pages often provide a "home icon," repeated throughout the Web pages, that assists you in returning to the start. Moreover, developers will provide other kinds of more complex navigational links, including touch-screen maps, that help you navigate a web.

  For example, on the Russian server, under the "Virtual Exhibitions" link, there is a page with a variety of exhibitions on Russian culture and history. One such link is to the Moscow Kremlin. On the page describing the Moscow Kremlin on-line excursion, is the sentence

  `Begin the excursion.` Alternatively, use `Index` to find a particular place.

  This statement is an excellent guide to choose a way to encounter this information. The first highlighted phrase, `Begin the excursion`, gives a cue that the exhibits will be presented sequentially. The `Index` hotspot offers nonsequential access. By clicking `Index`, the display shown in Figure 17.2 appears.

  The Kremlin tour index is very useful because it gives rapid, random access to the whole exhibit. By looking for such indexes and guides on a Web page, you will be able to navigate them well.

- *Be aware of your window history*—Every time you take a different link from a Web page your window history is renewed from that point on (the "nipping" phenomenon). Thus, a good way to explore a whole web is by following branches in a depth-first manner, going down a branch completely until you reach a page without further links and then backing up. This is not a perfect algorithm for finding every page. The layout of a web is not necessarily a tree in which the links among the pages branch out so that a complete tour of all the pages is easy. Rather a collection of web pages can be arranged in an arbitrary manner (any directed graph).

FIGURE 17.2.

The Window-to-Russia Kremlin tour index.

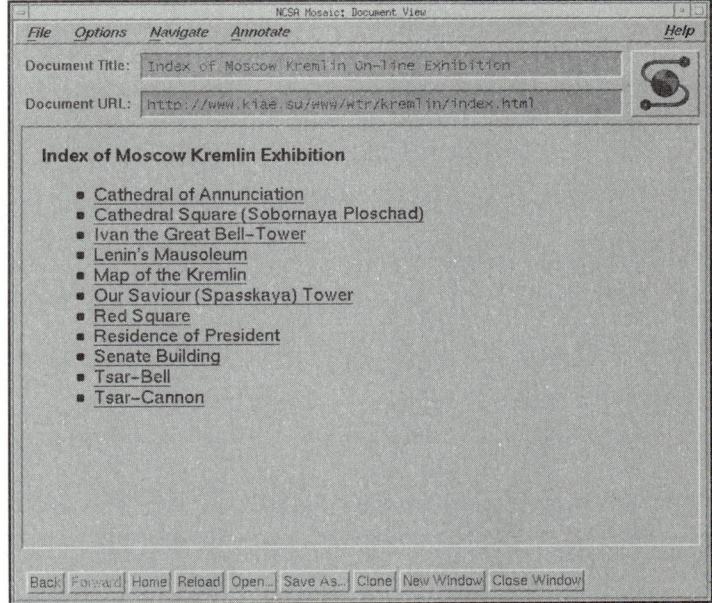

Figure 17.3 shows such an arrangement. Following the link from the Home page to Page A, and then proceeding to D and F will help you tour that one branch. Returning to the home page from F can be as easy as clicking the Back button three times. If you go to page B after this, your windows history file will "lop off" your trip down the A-D-F branch. Your global history file will still retain the time of your visit and the URLs of pages A, D, and F, however, so that the shading of the links on the home page for page A will clue you in to your previous visit.

In Figure 17.3, notice also how page E serves as a kind of index page, actually linking to all the other pages in the web. If, after visiting page B and returning from the home page, you go to page C and then page E, you will find that all the hotspots on page E are all shaded, as you've previously visited all the other pages. Your window history list will include: Home Page, page C, and page E.

As you gain more experience in navigating a web, you'll find that the combination of your windows history used with observing the shading of previously visited links will help you explore a web. Diagrams for hypertext organization like that in Figure 17.3 might help you, although there is no current facility in Mosaic to generate such a diagram. Thus, the burden of providing a good orientation for the reader falls to the web weaver.

■ *Use indexes when available*—It is important to remember that your goal in navigating a web like the Window-to-Russia Home Page is not to exhaustively search the entire web, but to choose the information you would like to see. Often a web will have its entire contents indexed in a searchable database. By entering key words into the input window to the index, you'll get a list of links to pages on the web that match that key word.

■ *Read the text*—Just as many users don't read the text during telnet sessions (because there often is a lot of it), so too do readers often skip over the text on web pages. Instead they focus on the graphics or other features that draw the eye. It is important in navigating to skim through the accompanying text to find important navigation cues. For example, on the Russian page, the statement about Russian Cyryllic fonts could be very helpful when you want to read text later on in this web.

■ *Give constructive feedback*—Many web pages include the name and e-mail address of the administrator (often called *webmaster*). If you find an error—a link that won't work, and you're pretty sure it isn't a temporary problem—send a polite note to the web administrator. Similarly, if you find the organization of the information or links confusing, constructive feedback to the administrator (who may not be the information developer, but might be able to give you the address of the developer) can help improve the usability of the information on the Web.

FIGURE 17.3.

An example web layout.

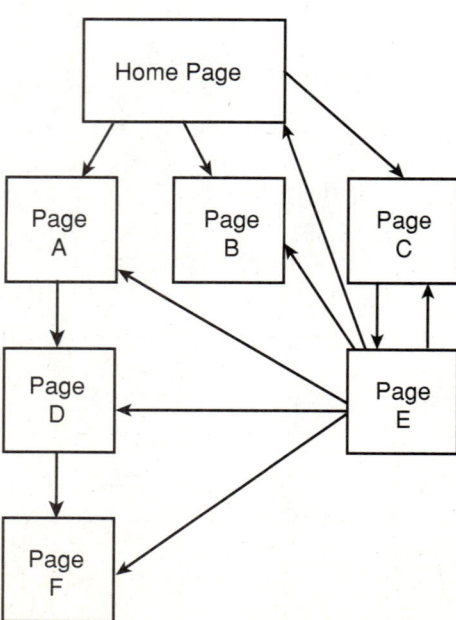

Finding What You Want—Ways of Searching

Now that we've talked about general ways for navigating a single web, let's turn our attention to the whole of the Web itself. Just as FTP space has Archie and Gopher space has Veronica, so does the Web have something analogous—spiders—that help you find things using keyword searches. Moreover, just as there was a mega-list of all FTP sites and a geographical list of all Gophers, so too are there mega-lists and geographical lists of Web sites. The searching mechanisms on the Web, however, are more varied and complex than those for FTP and Gopher, and the variety of searching tools and resources gives you a range of ways to search for a resource that you want.

The next chapters cover ways that you can search the Web.

1. *By subject:* making use of hierarchically-arranged subject catalogs and trees.
2. *By key word:* utilizing spiders (things that crawl on the Web to find resources).
3. *By machine:* using the lists of Web sites.
4. *By surfing:* utilizing techniques, resources, and tools to help you locate new or unusual Web information as well as make serendipitous finds.

Because effectively using the Web to locate information is truly an integrative activity— judiciously combining the above techniques during the course of any one search—this part includes a final chapter which integrates all these techniques in a single example.

Caveats About Networked Information

Although the Web is a treasure-trove, it is important to approach the vast resources it contains with some caution. We cannot bring the same expectations about accuracy and reliability from the print world to the world of the Web. Moreover, we cannot assume print-based standards about authorship or the completeness of a work with regard to Web works.

Origins of Our Expectations About Information and Publishing

We are a culture still relying largely on print to convey information, and our expectations about information accuracy and reliability are based on traditions evolving out of print traditions. The invention of the printing press was revolutionary in human history because it gave people who owned printing presses a way to widely disseminate their ideas. The relatively large expense of owning a press and printing large numbers of copies of a work limited those who would engage in publishing. The scarcity of the printer's resources also caused the printer to make careful judgements about what to publish. This resource scarcity was one factor contributing to the traditions of editorial control over publishing. The development of the scientific method and scholarly traditions of peer review added onto this publishing control an additional layer of requirements for accuracy and completeness. While our culture and institutions have embraced these publishing traditions for centuries, the Web transforms them. The Web allows a person, equipped with the skills this book aims to convey, the power to be a printer as well as an instant, global publisher.

The Web transforms people into information publishers like no other advance in human history. Desktop publishing has enabled the explosive growth of small presses, journals, and publications. However, a person with a desktop publishing system, while arrayed with the tools necessary for high-quality documents in terms of appearance, is limited in terms of reproduction and distribution. If someone writes a book and prints 100 copies of it on a laser printer, who would buy such a book and how would they find out about it? In contrast, a Web-based system of information can include multimedia graphics and interactive elements, and can be available to people with the right equipment (e.g., computers, Internet connections, browser—actually sometimes a *very* steep requirement). This Web-based approach might be far more successful in *distributing* a book or information. However, something has been lost in this process of self-publishing, and that something is the expectation about editorial control and selection that (paper) publishing institutions have.

On the Web, just about anyone can put out almost anything without any checks on its accuracy, completeness, value, or impact on the wider Net community. As a consumer of Web information, then, you will need to develop your skills in evaluating the accuracy, completeness, stability, and value of any information you find. You won't be able to use the attractive appearance of any Web resource as an indicator of quality or accuracy. You'll find most Web resources are offered in good faith with careful attention to detail and concern about accuracy. Moreover, Net-based information can actually can go through a very active peer review process in which users correspond with the information provider and offer comments and corrections. Not everything on the Web is junk, nor is everything accurate.

Things To Remember When Accessing and Using Web Resources

There's no simple way to evaluate the value of Web information. You can use your own experience and judgement, rely on people you trust, or consult others who use the same information.

Here is a checklist of some things to keep in mind when using Web resources:

- *They are not always accurate.* Just because you "read it on the Web" doesn't mean that something is true, just as seeing something on TV or reading it in the newspaper doesn't make it true. The appealing graphical display Mosaic gives to the Web, with fonts and well-formatted displays, may mislead a user to "feel" that the information is accurate. While there is certainly not any Web-wide conspiracy about spreading false information :), inaccuracies can have a way of propagating on the Net in particularly virulent ways (see URL `news:alt.folklore.urban` for some discussions about how people can think something is true when it simply isn't.)

  The key points to keep in mind about accuracy are:

  1. *Can you trust its source?* Is the provider of the information an expert in the field? The importance of this question depends on the kind of information you are looking for.

     For example, if you run across of list of "smileys" (symbolic shorthand for facial expressions) on the Web, you can consider if the author consulted other comprehensive and authoritative listings in the field. In the field of smiley's, David W. Sanderson is the "Noah Webster of Smiley's" (: *The Wall Street Journal* :) and has published a (paper) book as well as created a smiley server program containing a large amount of known smileys. On the other hand, you can probably judge a good smiley yourself. The determiner for your trust is your purpose—are you looking for a comprehensive list or just one good smiley?

  2. *Are there others who point to the same information or resource as a reliable source?* Is the source you found a very odd occurrence in an obscure corner of the Web? If so, the information might have great value, or it might be just ramblings. In any case, you might ask peers or practitioners in the field. If the source is often cited, you still should be critical—how valuable to you is the source of information for your purpose?

  3. *Is the information accurate?* For example, is the Frequently Asked Questions (FAQ) list for the Usenet newsgroup `alt.war.civil.usa` accurate? Does someone you know who is knowledgeable in the field consider it an accurate (although not necessarily complete) source of information? In general, Usenet newsgroup FAQs encounter a great deal of scrutiny by newsgroup participants, all of whom are interested in the field and many of whom practice professionally in the area of expertise. However, there will be errors and misinformation—the key is to check out how authoritative the source is considered for that field.

4. *What is the original source of the information?* For example, the Weather Underground gets its information from U.S. National Weather Service data and forecasts. This attests to a reliable, "official" source. In other cases, the source of the information might be a laboratory or a professionally-run server. However, you can't always expect "official" sources for Web-based information.

A Web server is often set up by an administrator or technician as an experiment, with content provided haphazardly. One should not expect the Web server at `www.foo.edu` to always be the "official" voice of Foo University. Check for claims made on the Web page itself. Just because the Web page might include a graphic of the official University logo (which can be easily scanned in), the information it contains is not necessarily official. Generally, official servers have names like `www.foo.edu`, rather than `mickey.unix5.cs.foo.edu` (although it is not all that difficult to manipulate the name that appears on a server). Keep in mind that an official server will normally have a Web administrator assigned, with phone contact as well as e-mail contact information. And of course, the tone and organization of the information itself on the server will give you many clues about the "officialness" of the server and its information.

- *They might even be illegal.* There are law firms that specialize in communications law that routinely cruise the Nets looking for licensed commercial software available at FTP sites illegally, or illegally-provided information and copyright infringements. Information that has high monetary value is not often placed on the Net for free. Therefore, be suspicious of sites that claim to have commercial software available for free, and be suspicious of information providers who give out copyrighted works without permission of the copyright owners. Many publishers of books, however, create support sites for samples of a copyrighted work as part of a marketing strategy—look for notices of copyright and ownership. As a consumer of information, respect these copyrights, as the traditions of intellectual property and copyright law encourage individuals to create more valuable works.

- *They are not always complete.* Information you find on the Web is not all that there is. For example, we'll see in the next chapters how you can find multiple collections of information on a particular subject in many different places on the Web and at the edges of the Web, yet still come up short for certain topics. Moreover, the Web itself isn't even close (yet) to containing the sum of all human knowledge! The holdings of even a modest university library far outstrip the Web in terms of completeness of coverage in many subjects.

- *They are not always peer-reviewed.* Information on the Web is often created by a sole author, without a formal process of peer-review. Peer-review processes have long been used in scientific communication to make sure information is accurate and complete, and that there are no errors of logic or presentation that devalue the work. Some Net-based information (for example, in peer-reviewed electronic journals) has gone through review processes as rigorous as for print-based publications. However, a great deal of Net-based information has not. Often, the review process is informal, such as in the case of Usenet newsgroups or a frequently-accessed information resource. You might contact the provider of the information and ask about any review done on the information or resource. It may be that they have more background information as well as an opinion on its value.

■ *They are not a substitute for libraries (and librarians).* Some people, finding the Net and the Web a treasure-trove of information, easily accessible through clicks of a mouse button, might ignore other means of gathering information. The Net is not a substitute for a library or a good reference librarian. (In fact, you'll find many good reference librarians are Net-savvy themselves.) The key to remember is to not assume that just because you've used all the methods described in this book for finding all the Web-accessible information on a subject, your research is complete. Your library may hold even more information.

Navigator's Check

We've seen the basic layout of a typical Web site and how to navigate it. While going through the Web, keep these points in mind:

■ A Web page usually offers many informational cues and navigation aids to help you use the information presented efficiently.

■ Your windows history can be a useful navigational aid; keep in mind the "nip-ping" phenomena.

■ The chapters that follow will cover how you can search the Web by subject, key word, machine, and through surfing.

■ Be critical and cautious of network information; it isn't always true.

Trees: Subject-Oriented Searching

by John December

18

There may be many situations where you want to learn about a subject without necessarily having a precise idea of the specific topics you would like to study. You wouldn't necessarily want to use the keyword searching mechanisms we saw in previous chapters, Archie and Veronica, to search FTP space and Gopher space, because you would not have a specific set of filenames or keywords to look for. Rather, you'd want to locate collections that present broad categories of information organized according to subjects. We've already seen an example of a subject-oriented compilation in Gopher space (the Gopher Jewels collection). There are similar, Web-based collections of subject-oriented resources.

When you want to find collections of information or individual resources related to a particular subject, you'll need to seek out the many subject-oriented collections on the Web. There is no single source for subject-oriented information on the Web, although there are some very complete collections, and a few key places on the Web provide excellent jumping-off points.

This chapter outlines resources, tools, techniques, and tips that you can use to find subject-oriented information on the Web. Using subject-oriented searching methods alone probably won't help you find all the information you might need. Instead, consider subject-oriented searching as just one technique that you can use to search the Web.

This chapter uses the metaphor of the tree as a way of providing a useful analogy for what you will explore during subject-oriented searching.

> **NOTE**
>
> The correct, mathematical term for many Web information structures described here is *graph*. A graph is a structure of *nodes* (documents) and *edges* (links). A *tree*, in the mathematical sense, is a special kind of graph that branches similar to the way a real-life tree's branches grow—upwards, without reaching back towards the ground. The structure of most subject-oriented collections, however, is not always in the form of a mathematical tree. A Web-based collection can include arbitrary branching (not always just "growing" in one direction). However, in this chapter, we'll use the term tree in its more informal sense, and understand that the Web-based trees can allow for branching in any direction.

The Web is full of trees—lists and directories of resources, many arranged hierarchically so that you can go down a series of selections to find what you want. Like the yellow pages of a phone book, the labels on the branches of these trees include subjects, topics, and subtopics.

As we look at techniques for searching these trees, remember that there is no single tree that organizes all subject-based information for the entire Web or Internet. You'll have to use a variety of techniques to seek out appropriate subject-oriented trees and use surfing techniques (covered in Chapter 21, "Surfing: Finding the New and Unusual") to keep abreast of other useful subject trees that pop up all the time.

The sections that follow introduce many of the most popular subject trees on the Web and at the edge of the Web. To help you follow this survey and to compare the trees, this chapter uses the environment as an example subject for searching.

Resources for Subject-Oriented Searching

We've already discussed one very valuable subject-oriented tree, the Gopher Jewels Collection in Chapter 16, "At the Edge of the Web." The Gopher Jewels collection, based on Gophers, is at the edge of the Web (accessible through a Web browser, but not in hypertext itself). Because good subject-oriented trees attempt to collect information from the whole Internet, you'll find that there are few trees totally contained within the Web. Instead, most trees extend to the edges of the Web (and thus contain links to nonhypertext documents).

CERN's Virtual Library

CERN is a center for high-energy physics research in Switzerland and is the birthplace of the Web itself. Therefore, CERN's subject tree, an early outgrowth of the initial Web development, is a comprehensive source of subject-oriented information.

The URL of the CERN Virtual Library is `http://info.cern.ch/hypertext/DataSources/bySubject/Overview.html`

CERN's tree is mostly Web-based, that is, its branches and individual items reach into the Web fairly deep, although eventually individual pages within the tree reach the edges of the Web.

Figure 18.1 shows the front page of the Virtual Library, showing the top-level organization. You'll notice that the subject breakdown is not necessarily along standard lines (such as a Library of Congress Subject division); rather, new subjects are added as individuals with interests have resources to link into the existing Virtual Library.

FIGURE 18.1.

CERN's Virtual Subject Library.

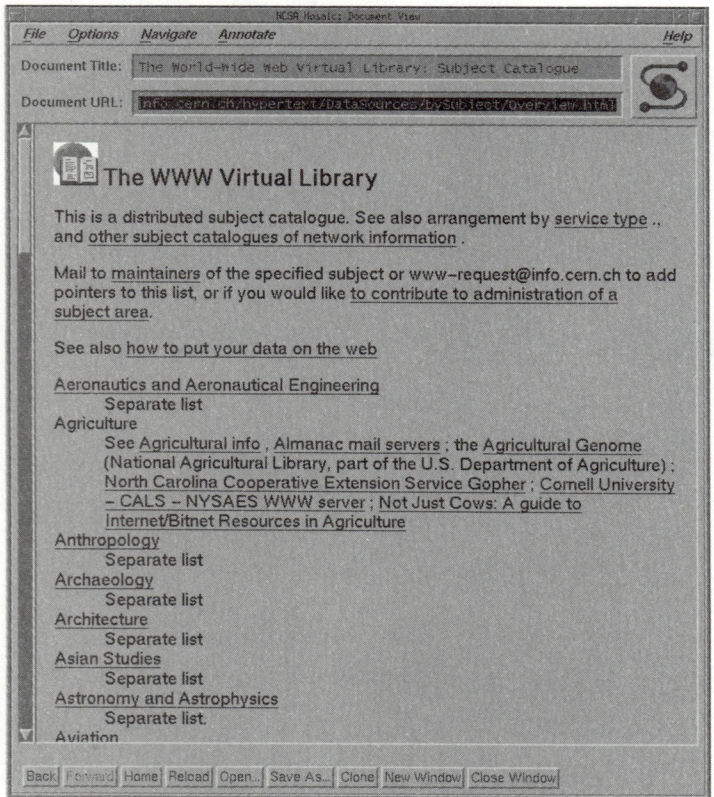

Navigating the Virtual Library is quite simple. You can get more specific in your search by following the tree's branches. You'll encounter more pages with lists of more specialized subjects and topics. This multiple page approach, in which the tree is very tall (contains many levels of hierarchy) is common in Web-based trees. The entire tree itself is not hosted entirely on CERN's machine (`info.cern.ch`), but you'll encounter pages on many different hosts as you go deep enough into the tree. In this way, the Virtual Library represents a massive, collaborative effort to gather and present information on a wide range of subjects.

Let's use our example of seeking environmental information as a means to illustrate individual tree-offerings and to compare trees. The front page of CERN's Virtual Library has an entry for "Environment." Selecting this link, we obtain the page shown in Figure 18.2. Because the list is so long, the bottom portion is shown in Figure 18.3.

FIGURE 18.2.

CERN's Virtual Subject Library entry for Environment 1.

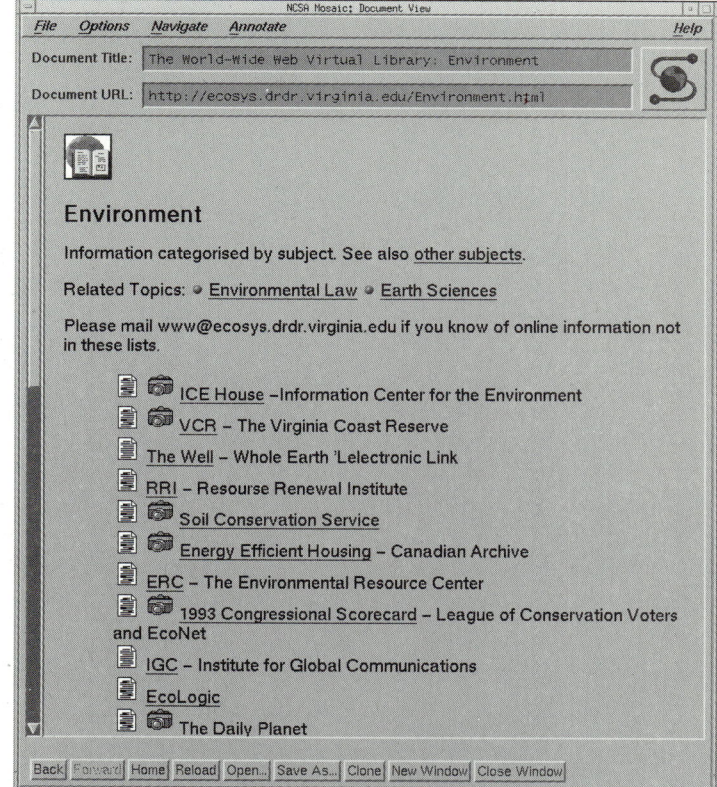

FIGURE 18.3.

*CERN's Virtual Subject
Library entry for
Environment 2.*

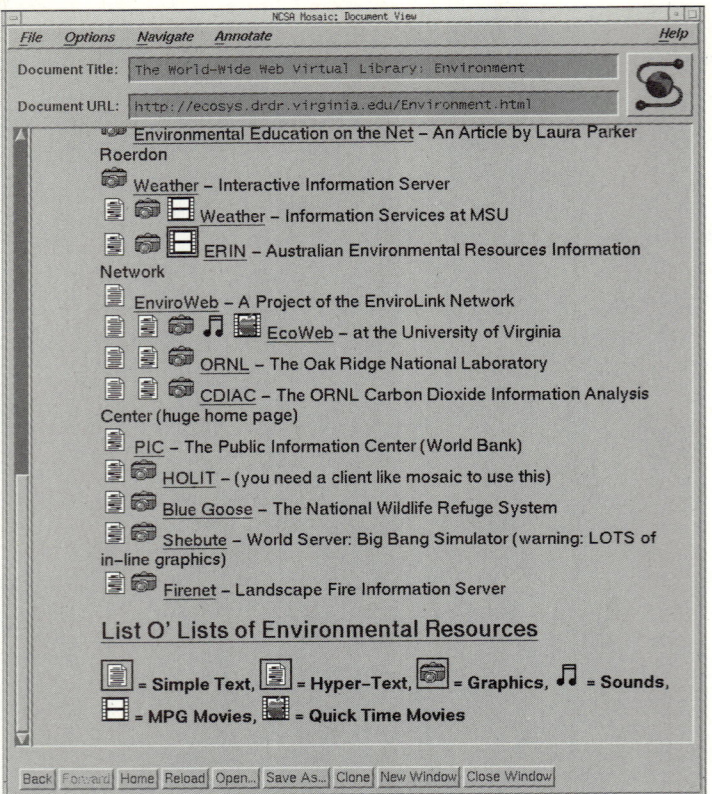

The Virtual Subject Library page for the environment is impressive. The multimedia guide at the bottom of the page defines the media formats you will find in the pages. Notice that the host for this page, ecosys.drdr.virginia.edu, is also the host for EcoWeb, a collection of resources devoted to local recycling and environmental concerns (Figure 18.4).

This environment page is typical of Virtual Library pages—containing a rich set of links for topics and subtopics. We'll see how other trees offer similar collections, but their contents are different, as they grew independently.

FIGURE 18.4.

EcoWeb.

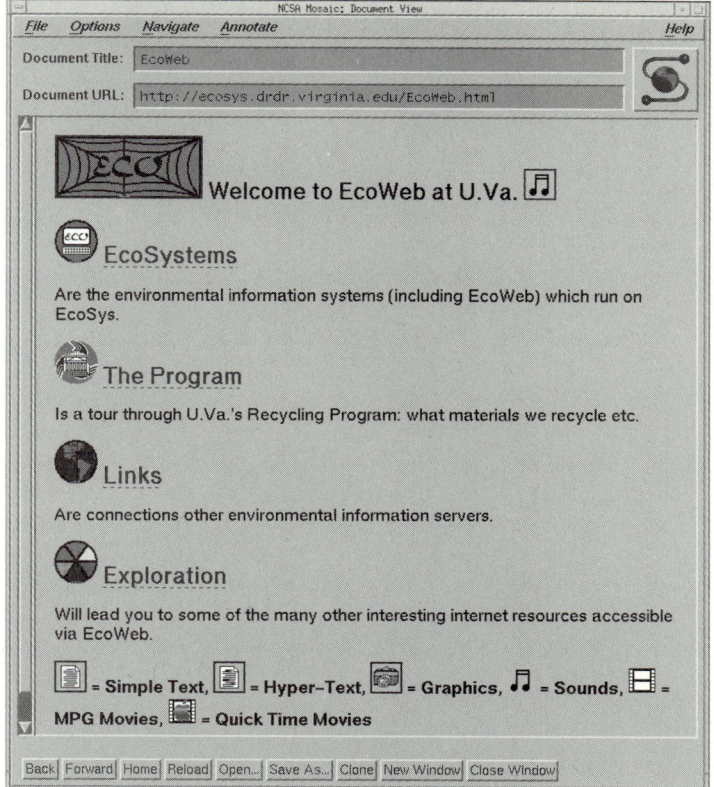

Galaxy from EINet

While the Virtual Subject Library at CERN contains a great deal of links into the Web, the important thing to remember in searching trees is that you shouldn't rely on only one as a sole source for subject-oriented information.

Let's examine another subject tree, called Galaxy, developed by EINet, a commercial provider of network communication and services. While CERN's Virtual Library was essentially a noncommercial, cooperative venture, EINet's Galaxy is offered to the Web for free, courtesy of a commercial company. Galaxy enhances EINet's reputation as a provider of network information and communication services while at the same time contributing a valuable public service to the Web community. Galaxy's URL is `http://www.einet.net/ galaxy.html` and its front page is shown in Figure 18.5.

FIGURE 18.5.
EINet's Galaxy.

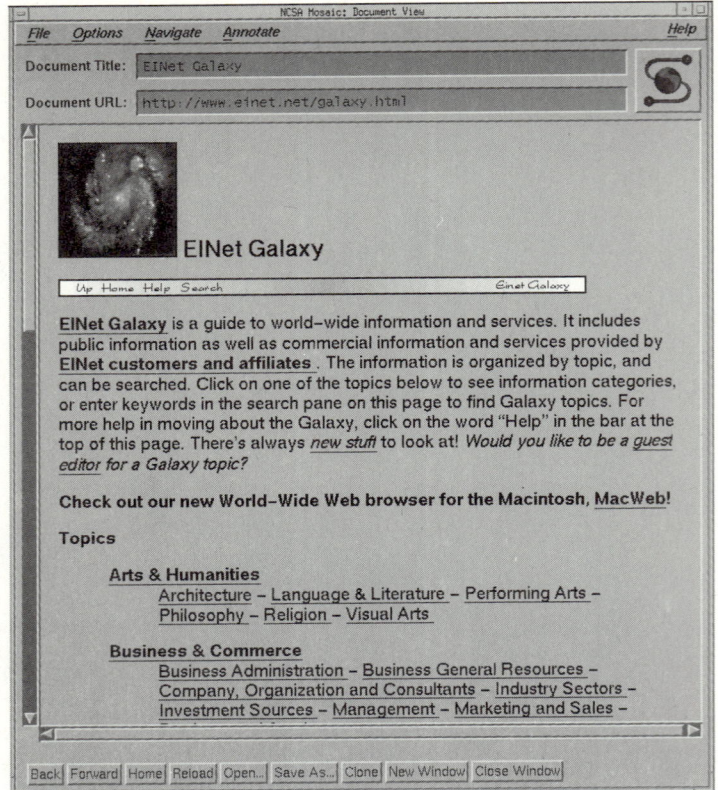

Like CERN's Virtual Library, Galaxy's front page shows a hierarchical organization of subjects, arranged in broad subject categories listed alphabetically, with links from the front page to other pages containing further information. Unlike the Virtual Library, however, Galaxy provides a search mechanism for finding entries in the Galaxy web.

This search mechanism, located at the bottom of the front page (Figure 18.6) gives you a quick way to find information which may be buried deep within the Galaxy tree. For example, a user might not be sure from the front page which subject classification to follow for environmental information. A quick search using the search mechanism yields a link to a page for the environment located in the Community subdivision on the home page (which a user might not have seen on first coming into Galaxy). The top of the environmental page is shown in Figure 18.7.

FIGURE 18.6.

EINet's Galaxy search mechanism.

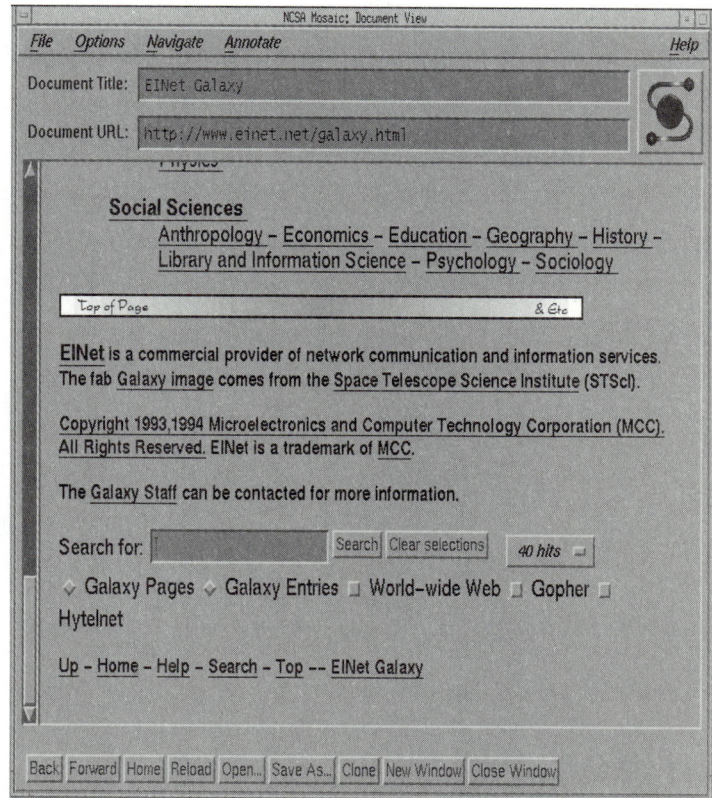

This environmental page contains a similar organization to the CERN's environmental page, with links to pages that further refine the subject area of the environment to specific topics (agriculture, air & water quality, ecosystems, and so on), as well as links to specific documents, directories, and collections.

FIGURE 18.7.

*EINet's Galaxy environ-
mental page.*

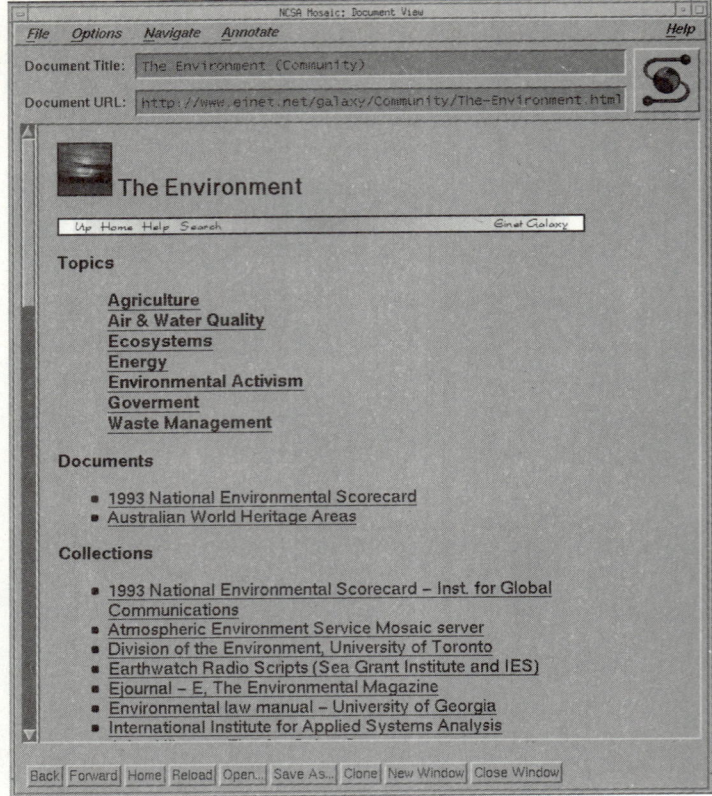

What sets Galaxy apart from the CERN's page are its facilities for growing (for allowing users to fill out a Form to add information to the page) as well as built-in searching mechanisms for gaining maximum reach into the Web space, Gopher space, Hytelnet entries, and WAIS indexes for terms related to the environment.

Figure 18.8 shows the "Search Results for Keywords" section of the page, with links to search results from the Web, Hytelnet menu entries, Gopher space, and WAIS indices related to the key word "environment." We'll discuss key word searching in the next chapter in detail.

FIGURE 18.8.

EINet's Galaxy adding and search facility.

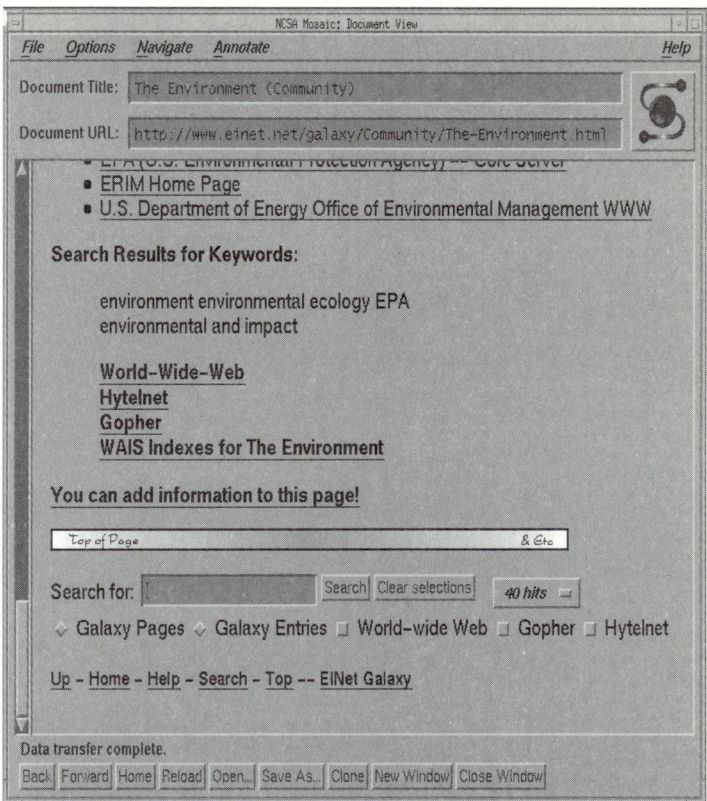

Galaxy's links to these search results are useful because they organize the results using *WAIS* (Wide Area Information System) technology. WAIS technology retrieves documents based on a request from a user according to a system of indices, and returns a list of documents to the user along with a "score" for each "hit" in the database, with a higher score indicating a greater relevance to the user's search request. This searching and scoring takes into account the user's search string (which might contain Boolean expressions or wild cards) as well as word frequency, density, frequency, and other characteristics of the texts in the database.

The "You can add information to this page!" link is also a valuable addition. It allows the user to enter a Form (Figure 18.9) to add additional information to Galaxy's database.

FIGURE 18.9.

EINet's Galaxy annotation form.

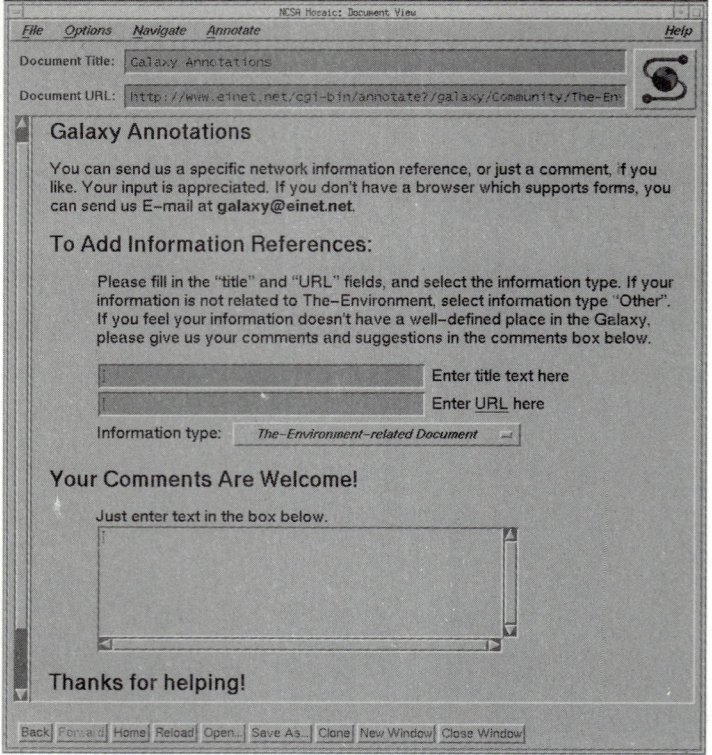

While subject trees such as CERN's Virtual Library welcome submissions via e-mail, Galaxy's Forms-based facility makes it easy for someone to add information, and it helps the user supply all the necessary information for an entry into the subject tree.

The Whole Internet Catalog from O'Reilly

O'Reilly & Associates is an information publisher that has established a strong presence on the Internet through its Global Network Navigator (GNN) information system. The Whole Internet Catalog (WIC) portion of GNN is an extension of the resource section in Ed Krol's *The Whole Internet User's Guide and Catalog*, a paper-based book O'Reilly first published in 1992. Like Galaxy, the O'Reilly's WIC is a public service to the Web community supported by a commercial firm, extending O'Reilly's reputation as an information provider both on the Net and in its (paper-based) book publishing business.

Like CERN's Virtual Subject Library, GNN's Whole Internet Catalog (WIC), provides a tree structure showing various subjects on its front page (Figure 18.10).

FIGURE 18.10.

O'Reilly's Whole Internet Catalog.

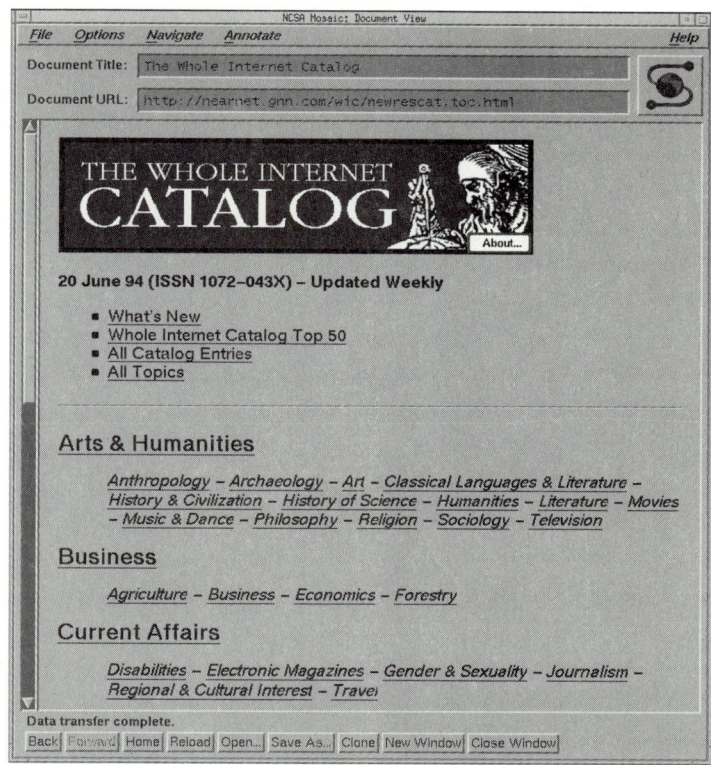

Continuing our illustrative search for environmental information, we can select the "Science" link on the WIC front page, and obtain a page listing many subjects within the field of science, including a link to "Environmental Studies," shown in Figure 18.11.

The WIC's entries contain descriptive text underneath the links. For example, under the link for the "1993 National Environmental Scorecard," you can find text, written by people at GNN, describing what this resource offers before you select it. The pages of the WIC also offer an index into this descriptive text and titles for all GNN entries, including related GNN information including GNN's Travel, Internet, and Finance MetaCenters. The box for this index search is shown at the bottom of Figure 18.11. In this way, WIC's catalog helps the user hone in quickly on the sources required.

FIGURE 18.11.

*O'Reilly's Whole Internet
Catalog Environment
Page.*

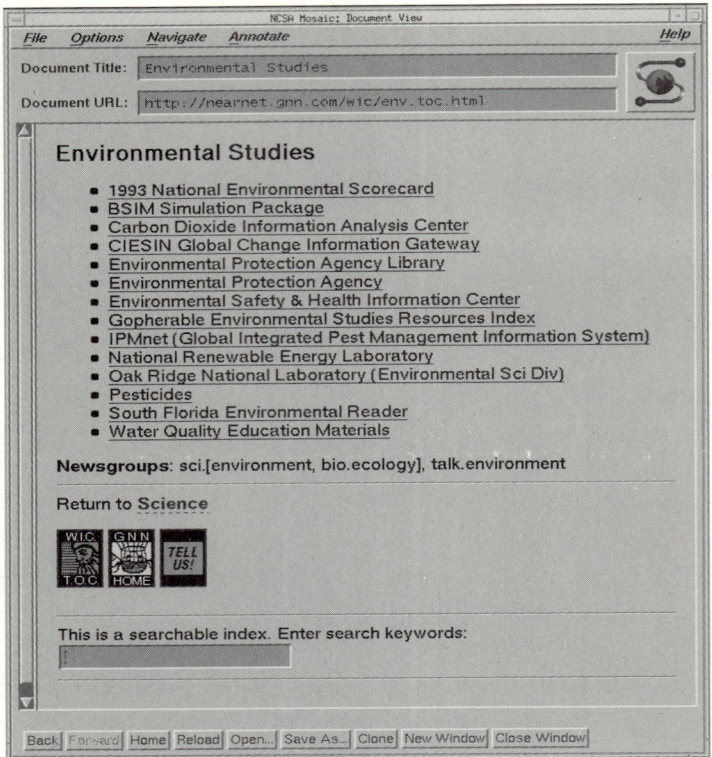

Usenet FAQ Archives

The global asynchronous text conferencing system known as Usenet has grown very quickly over the years since its inception in 1979, a project of two graduate students at Duke University, Jim Ellis and Tom Truscott. Today, Usenet newsgroups number in the thousands, covering a very wide range of topics on just about every human pursuit or subject imaginable. Participants in Usenet newsgroups contribute articles to ongoing discussions. These articles propagate through the Matrix (not just the Internet) for others to read and respond to. This process of discussion is ongoing, with some newsgroups experiencing hundreds of new articles per day. Since articles eventually expire (are deleted from the local systems on which they are stored), information within the individual articles can eventually be lost. Longtime participants in the newsgroup can often face the same questions and discussions from new users over and over again. It is from this need to transmit accumulated knowledge that the tradition of Frequently Asked Questions (FAQ) lists arose.

FAQ lists evolve out of newsgroup discussion. Sometimes one person decides to record the results of a discussion about a particular question, then post this question again with

its answer periodically in the newsgroup. In this way, longer lists of such questions and answers develop and are often reposted to the newsgroup for further comment as well as an informational service to new readers. While periodically posted to the newsgroups, these FAQs could often get lost in the hundreds of other articles or don't appear at the right time for new users to see. Therefore, a more static form of housing these FAQs developed at an FTP site on a machine at MIT. The machine, `rtfm.edu`, holds these FAQs for newsgroups, making them available via anonymous FTP. The resulting list of FAQs covers a wide variety of subjects. The entire collection of Usenet FAQs can be found at the URL `ftp://rtfm.mit.edu/pub/usenet/`. A Web-version of access to FAQs posted to the newsgroup `news.answers` is maintained by Tom Fine at

`http://www.cis.ohio-state.edu/hypertext/faq/usenet/FAQ-List.html`

and is shown in Figure 18.12.

FIGURE 18.12.

Usenet FAQs.

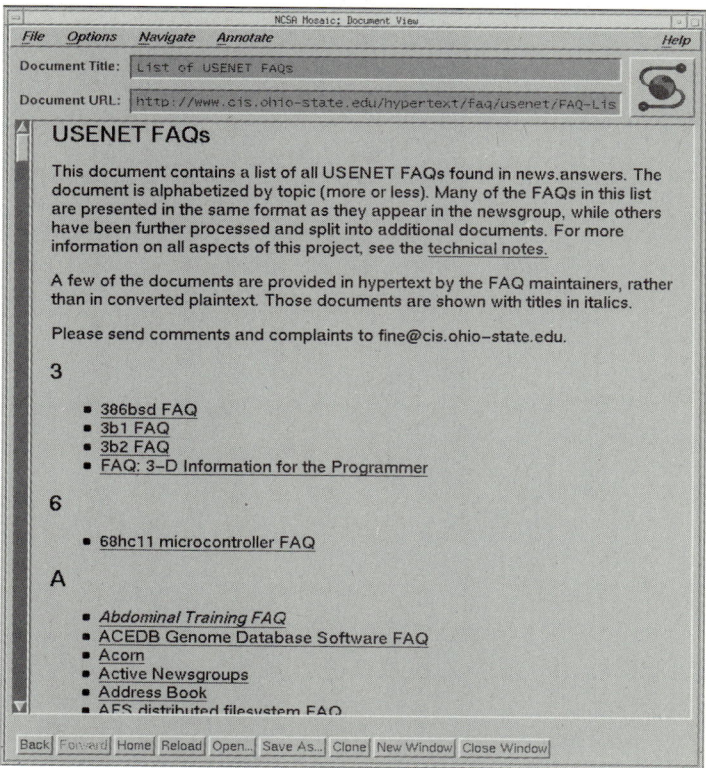

Usenet FAQs are generally in text form, although the collection shown in Figure 18.12 includes many that are in HTML. The information in the FAQs can often include very rich discussion of the field of study, as well as descriptions of other information and online resources. Usenet FAQs, because the newsgroup names are so specialized, are often very particular (and peculiar). For example, you can see a very specialized FAQ listed in Figure 18.12 called *Abdominal Training FAQ*. Usenet FAQs are therefore very useful for finding very specific information on a particular topic.

Continuing our search for environmental information, we can scroll down the list of Usenet FAQs and find no entry for environmental information. Using the File / Find In Current... also yields no results. Going to FTP space, we can try the collection of all Usenet FAQs at `ftp://rtfm.mit.edu/pub/usenet`. Looking in the Usenet by newsgroup directory, we find a promising newsgroup, `sci.environment`, and find that it contains several FAQs: "Ozone Depletion FAQ" (in four parts), and an "FAQ on Sea Level, Ice, and Greenhouses." These FAQs are very specialized, and contain a great deal of information, including references to published, peer-reviewed articles on the subject. As mentioned previously, this specificity in FAQ coverage is typical of Usenet—very complete on specific subjects, but not necessarily offering a comprehensive selection of subjects and topics.

The Clearinghouse for Subject-Oriented Internet Guides

While the Usenet FAQs provide a great deal of information on a variety of subjects related to newsgroups, another subject-oriented collection at the University of Michigan provides a collection of guides in some areas outside of newgroup subject divisions. Like the Usenet FAQs, the Michigan collection consists of subject-oriented guides. However, the Michigan collection's intent is to gather guides which help people discover further *Internet* resources, and thus is very useful for obtaining guides which help you locate further information on the Internet.

The home page for the Clearinghouse is `http://www.lib.umich.edu/chhome.html` and is also available through Gopher and FTP (URLs are given on the home page). Although most of the guides are in text, some have HTML analogues, and others have no plain text equivalent. In the Clearinghouse, there is a wide variety of subjects represented in the humanities, social sciences, sciences, and multiple subjects.

The Michigan Clearinghouse does have two guides about the Environment, one by A. Phelps, and one by T. Murphy and C. Briggs-Erickson. The Phelps Guide includes a caveat that it is not intended to be a comprehensive guide but to represent sources of information on the Internet. As such, this guide can be a useful introduction to finding other sources. The Murphy and Briggs-Erickson guide on the environment, mentioned in the Phelps Guide, gives a more comprehensive view of Net-based information, including listings of major environmental organizations and networks, resources for specific topics in the environment, regulations and standards, regional concerns, online library catalogs, and

a further bibliography. Thus, the Michigan guides can be very useful in locating more resources on the Net.

Gopher Trees

Just as CERN's virtual library broke Web space into a subject-oriented tree structure, so too do various Gopher trees. We've already talked about the Gopher Jewels collection (URL `http://galaxy.einet.net/GJ/index.html`) in a previous chapter. There are other Gopher space subject trees available that aid in finding subject-oriented resources. The subject tree at URL `gopher://burrow.cl.msu.edu/11/internet/subject` provides a large variety of subject trees from many institutions, as well as Gopher links to the Michigan collection and Gopher Jewels.

To find a particular subject on the Gopher trees, you could investigate each Gopher tree separately. You could also use a Veronica search to find information about the environment. A good place to start if you want to use the tree-like method for searching is Gopher Jewels. There is an entry for "Environment" on the list at `http://galaxy.einet.net/GJ/index.html`, shown in Figure 18.13.

FIGURE 18.13.

Usenet Gopher Jewels environment page.

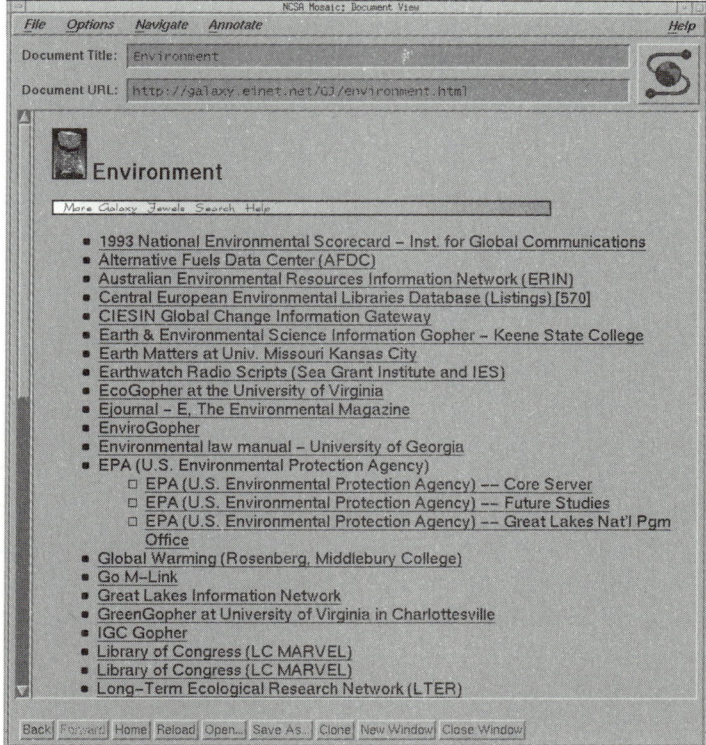

You can see that the Gopher Jewels page for the environment contains links to many Gophers, and some of the names should be familiar to you from our previous searches for environmental information.

Other Trees

On the Web, there are many other subject-oriented classifications of Net resources. In fact the proliferation of subject-oriented trees has been so virulent, probably a tree of subject trees will soon develop :). Here are some of the other Web-based trees that provide a way to search for subject-oriented information.

- **DA-CLOD**—(Distributedly Administered Categorical List Of Documents) URL `http://schiller.wustl.edu/DACLOD/daclod`. This is an effort to create a categorized database of links to subject-oriented information on the Internet. Like Galaxy and O'Reilly's WIC, the DA-CLOD project attempts to organize and gather subject-oriented information. Like Galaxy, it employs a method by which users add items to its database through a forms interface.

- **Mother-of-all BBS**—URL `http://www.cs.colorado.edu/homes/mcbryan/public_html/bb/summary.html`. This is an interactive system for collecting subject-oriented information developed by Oliver McBryan. Users of this BBS can add items or create new directories on the bulletin board. The information— even the organization—of this bulletin board is contributed and determined by users themselves.

- **Planet Earth Home Page**—URL `http://white.nosc.mil/info.html` Richard P. Bocker created this web that collects a wide variety of links on starting points ranging over many Net resources. Unlike other hierarchies, this one does not allow *automatic* additions to the menus and entries, although the developer accepts suggestions.

- **Joel's**—URL `http://www.cen.uiuc.edu/~jj9544/index.html` Joel's Hierarchical Subject Index (JHSI), is a project created by Joel Jones which collects and organizes information on the Internet based on a hierarchical division of knowledge. Although the contents of some of the tree's branches are sparse, the coverage of the structure itself is fairly complete.

- **Yahoo**—(Yet Another Hierarchically Odoriferous Oracle) URL `http://akebono.stanford.edu/yahoo/`. This is a very rapidly growing collection of subjects, including entertainment and many "nonacademic" subjects. It is possible for users to add to the hotlist at any point in the hierarchy, but these additions are moderated by the Yahoo developers. Thus, Yahoo, like many of the trees we've looked at, grows as users contribute more information.

FIGURE 18.14.

Yahoo Home page.

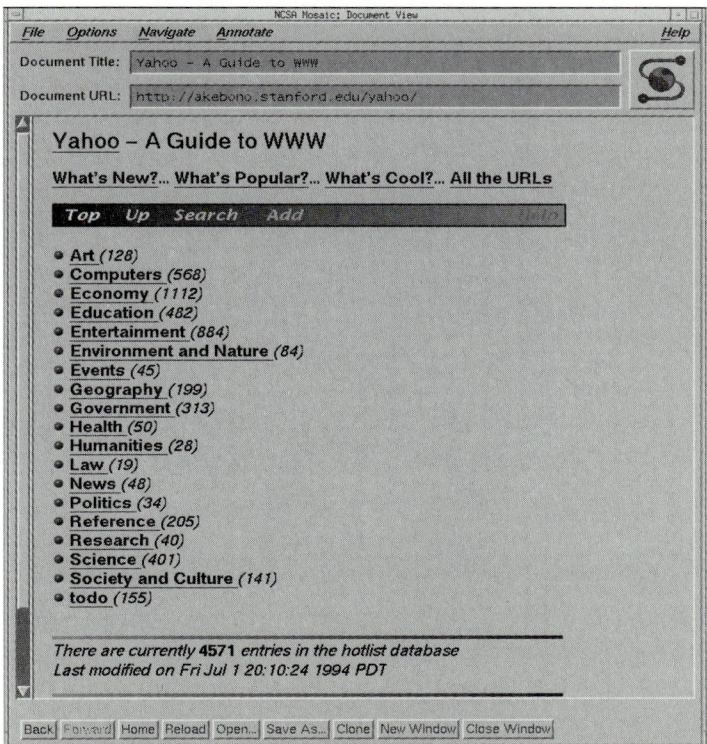

- **CyberNet**—URL `http://cybersight.com/cgi-bin/cs/s?main.gmml`. CyberNet is a commercial venture for providing "alternative" information, provided by Internet Marketing, Inc. The goal of these developers is to provide information that will attract viewers which will then attract advertisers.

Indices

Besides Web sites that offer a series of pages to access information on the Web, there are some subject-oriented indices that can give you jumping-off points to information on the Internet.

The **Meta-Index** from UICU (The University of Illinois, Champaign-Urbana (home of Mosaic) maintains a Meta Index at `http://www.ncsa.uiuc.edu/SDG/Software/Mosaic/MetaIndex.html`. This is the same list that you can obtain from the Navigate / Internet Resources Meta-Index through the Mosaic control panel. It gives you access into a list of indices of Web resources.

Scott **Yanoff's List** of special Internet collections is one of the most cited guides to subject-specific guides on the Internet. Begun as a list of just six items in 1991, this list has continued its popularity. The hypertext version at `http://www.uwm.edu/Mirror/inet.services.html` and can give you jumping-off points to subject-oriented information on a range of subjects. The list summarizes a wide variety of information and resources that are very useful for showing "what's out there" on the Net.

A list of **Information Sources** for the Internet and Computer-Mediated communication at `http://www.rpi.edu/Internet/Guides/decemj/internet-cmc.html` is useful for finding sources of information about the Internet itself. Included in this guide are links to many subject-oriented collections and indices, as well as resources discussed in this book.

Hand-crafted indices like the ones shown above have some value in guiding you to subject-oriented and other information, particularly if the index is well-organized and the author is well versed in what is available on the Net. These indices might give you a start in finding specialized subject-oriented trees.

Organizations and Individuals

While guides that are organized around subject classifications and lists are very useful, don't overlook other sources of subject-oriented information. Look for home pages of organizations and individuals who are experts in a particular area. Often, their pages will contain links to major sources of information for a particular area of study.

META CENTERS

The idea of gathering links to scattered Net resources into one Web page or a set of pages is behind an information structure called a meta center. A meta center is something much more than just another subject-oriented page. Rather, it gathers all commonly used information for a particular subject as well as background information, links to discussion groups on Usenet, and pointers to individuals and organizations with further expertise in an area. The best meta centers are collaboratively built, with contributions coming from experts in the field from all over the Net.

A meta center

- is pan-organizational. It doesn't represent just one organization's viewpoint of a topic, but contains links and contributions from many major organizations and individuals that have capabilities in that area

- is pan-protocol. It is not restricted to gathering just Web or Gopher links, for example, but includes links to resources regardless of where they are, including references to e-mail-only, or off-Net connections such as phone numbers and bibliographies of print materials

- develops original, authoritative resources. Its cooperating participants develop material which provides information to its participants and the Net community as a whole. Usenet newsgroups have been doing this a long time with the development of FAQs.

- supports multiple activities. It contains not just resource listings on a topic, but also white pages of individuals with expertise in that area, as well as lists of activities, connections to real-time and e-mail-based conferences and other forums for participants to interact in detail about that activity. It may have online conferences, based on e-mail or the interactive Forms capability of HTML.

- are collaboratively developed. Not just the work of one individual or even a group of individuals in one organization, a meta center draws the attention of experts in the field, fosters their contributions to knowledge, and provides for a community "memory," either through an online newsletter, magazine, or journal.

The last two qualities—activities involving discussion and collaboration—are what set aside a meta center from just a resource collection or a reference web page. After all, the power of the Web lies in the connections it fosters among people and the diverse activities and resources these people take part in creating.

Finding specific organizations and individuals with expertise in certain areas is part of key word searching, covered in the next chapter. Often the links within resources you locate through the subject trees will contain links to organizations and people, and these links may reveal more relevant information.

Techniques and Tips for Subject-Oriented Searching

In wading through the vast amount of information available within subject trees on the Web, it is helpful to know some basic techniques for managing the information and finding what you want. As the illustrative discussion about environmental issues has shown, we can find a variety of pages dealing with a subject in several different subject-oriented trees. Glance back over the figures showing the results from the major trees: CERN's virtual subject library, EINet's Galaxy, and GNN's WIC. Notice how there is variation in what is presented as well as some overlap. Also keep in mind that the composition of these pages *changes frequently,* so the figures shown in this book are more of a historical reflection than what is probably out on the Web right now.

As you navigate the Web's trees to find what you want, keep these techniques in mind:

1. **Search broadly at first.** If you don't have the URL of what is considered to be an authoritative or standard source in a particular area, check the main subject trees listed previously (Virtual Library, Galaxy, Whole Internet Catalog, USENET FAQs, Michigan's Clearinghouse, Gopher Jewels, and perhaps several of the other trees mentioned). Go down the tree until you find the page that contains your subject area. Save a reference to this page on your hotlist and then go to the next tree. In this way, you can gather the pages within the trees referring to your area before you evaluate which page to look at in detail. In this way, you'll gain a broad view of the major collections in many spaces in the Web and at its edge. References to sources that appear in many tree collections often are the ones to look at first.

2. **Look for authoritative sources.** The "authoritative" source for information varies by the subject matter. For example, if you're looking for space travel-related information, seek out NASA or other space-agency Web pages. You might use the subject-trees to find the general collections and background information, but then draw most heavily for your work from the most authoritative sources. The level of "authoritativeness" might not always include academic or scientific authority—you may be looking, for example, for an entertainment-oriented or nontraditional source. In this case, consider the more informal/alternative trees, such as CyberNet, that tend to be more open to new links such as Mother-of-All-BBS, or trees that have developed reputations for a broad range of informal resources, such as Yahoo.

3. **Travel lightly at first.** Save references (URLs on your hotlist) to promising documents before you download their entire contents to your local directory. Although the first source you find may seem like the most comprehensive, it might be that you later find you want just a particularly well-done, focused collection of information, perhaps just the contents of one link from one of your previous findings.

4. **Use tools.** Use the indices offered by any of the trees—for example, the Galaxy's search mechanism. You'll employ key word searching techniques also in looking for subjects. (See the next chapter for more information on key word searching.)

5. **Look for major collections.** Look for a page that brings together as much of the subject information you seek in a coherent form, rather than saving URLs pointing to this same information scattered in bits and pieces across the Net. For example, you'll find many references and links to resources connected to the

United State's High Performance Computing and Communications (HPCC) initiative. Rather than save links to this program that are scattered in many places, save a single link to the Web server to the entire HPCC project, `http://www.hpcc.gov`. Not all subjects will have a similar, unifying server for official information, but seek out major collections.

6. **Collaborate.** Don't underestimate the power of asking others who have looked for information in the subject area of your interest for help in finding Net resources. If a newsgroup that relates to the subject you are interested in doesn't have any information in its FAQ, ask in the newsgroup itself or ask one of the frequent contributors to the newsgroup.

7. **Start your own collection.** If your subject area is so specialized that you don't find a collection of URLs on it elsewhere, start your own page on this subject (see the Part V, "Weaving a Web").

8. **Follow clues.** Use your Web navigation skills and techniques to following links on pages to lead you to more information. For example, look for major indices and listings and links to search engines. Often page developers include these kinds of links as an afterthought and they are not readily apparent. Look at the home page of the page developer. Often that person is an expert in the field.

9. **Keep cool.** Be patient in examining the Web—severs go down temporarily, or you'll feel endlessly lost in information. Take a break from Net cruising, remembering to save URLs of places that seem key to your search.

10. **Be wary.** Be cautious about information and judge it critically. If you are doing a serious report or research, be very careful about using a Net resource as a reference. Apply the same level of critical perspective you would take toward printed sources and ask yourself if there is a more authoritative, paper-based source. If so, seek it out and use it.

11. **Be flexible.** Don't get stuck in any one server or web for too long, particularly if it doesn't seem to yield results. Try another information space (such as Gopher, or Hytelnet, or discussion lists). If the subject-oriented approaches given previously don't work, try the key word-oriented approaches discussed in the next chapter.

Navigator's Check

There are many subject-oriented trees on the Web and at the edge of the Web. A few major ones have established themselves as large collections of resources.

These major trees are

- CERN's Virtual Library `http://info.cern.ch/hypertext/DataSources/bySubject/Overview.html`
- EINet's Galaxy URL `http://www.einet.net/galaxy.html`
- O'Reilly's Whole Internet Catalog URL `http://www.ora.com` (use this URL as a front door to choosing the O'Reilly server closest to you)
- USENET FAQs URL `http://www.cis.ohio-state.edu/hypertext/faq/usenet/FAQ-List.html`
- Michigan's Clearinghouse for Subject-Oriented Guides to the Internet URL `http://www.lib.umich.edu/chhome.html`
- Gopher Jewels URL `http://galaxy.einet.net/GJ/index.html`
- Gopher Trees URL `gopher://burrow.cl.msu.edu/11/internet/subject`

Other subject trees vary in their coverage, tone, completeness and organization:

- DA-CLOD (Distributedly Administered Categorical List Of Documents) URL `http://schiller.wustl.edu/DACLOD/daclod`
- Mother-of-all BBS URL `http://www.cs.colorado.edu/homes/mcbryan/public_html/bb/summary.html`
- Planet Earth Home Page URL `http://white.nosc.mil/info.html`
- Joel's Index URL `http://www.cen.uiuc.edu/~jj9544/index.html`
- Yahoo (Yet Another Hierarchically Odoriferous Oracle) URL `http://akebono.stanford.edu/yahoo/`
- CyberNet URL `http://cybersight.com/cgi-bin/cs/s?main.gmml`

Some handcrafted lists might help you with jumping-off points to find other resources:

- Mosaic Meta-Index Navigate/Internet Resources Meta-Index or URL `http://www.ncsa.uiuc.edu/SDG/Software/Mosaic/MetaIndex.html`
- Yanoff's List URL `http://www.uwm.edu/Mirror/inet.services.html`
- Information Sources URL `http://www.rpi.edu/Internet/Guides/decemj/internet-cmc.html`

Whether collaboratively built or built under the guidance of commercial organizations employing knowledge workers, the subject-oriented trees available for finding information won't lead you to all the information on a subject that you want. You'll find much information that seems worthless to you along with the nuggets that seem extremely valuable. The development, maintenance, and even the veracity and value of Web information can easily be called to question. You will find, however, that the explosive growth in Web-based and Net-based information will continue, along with (hopefully) advances in information quality.

Spiders and Indexes: Keyword-Oriented Searching

by John December

19

If your goal is to find a specific piece of information, and you are not necessarily interested in finding contextual or related information through a subject-oriented search of trees, your best bet is to use a spider. A spider is a term for a class of software programs that wander through the Web and collect information about what is found there. (Another term is "robots" or "wanderers," but the term "spider" will be used throughout this chapter.) Some spiders crawl the Web and record URLs, creating a large database that can be searched. Other spiders look through HTML documents for URLs and keywords in title fields or other parts of the document. The nice thing about spiders is that they are *automated*—after initial setup, and with proper care and feeding, they can industriously scour the Web, recording the patterns of the links and keywords in documents, creating a valuable database for users to query.

In this chapter, we'll look at what spiders do and how you can use them to find specific information on the Web, based on searching for specific words or phrases in documents. There is no "super spider" that is omniscient in terms of knowing everything that is on the Web or understanding what you want. But you will find that many of the spiders that exist now can give you a very big start on locating resources on the Web.

Introduction to Spiders

One of the challenges in making sense of any large body of information is how to find something in it. Books have indexes. If you have a file in your word processor you can usually use the "find" command to search for a specific occurrence of a string. But the Web itself, before the development of searching mechanisms, was a tangle of links, branching and forking, an inscrutable mesh. To find resources, users of the Web had to use handcrafted lists and indexes—which are not always reliable, current, or complete. The situation was ripe for the development of automated mechanisms to index the Web's information spaces. Historically, there were precedents for automated programs to search information spaces—Archie and Veronica helped users make sense of the vast repositories of FTP space and trees of Gopher space long before the first spiders crawled out onto the Web. It was no surprise, then, that Web developers created spiders and Web users make use of spiders often.

Spider-Like Programs

We've already talked about some tools that behave in a similar way to spiders in other information spaces. Archie catalogs FTP space so that it can easily be searched. The product of Archie's searches is a database that can yield a list of file names and directories that match a key word search pattern. Similarly, Veronica traverses Gopher space, finding menu titles or documents that conform to a user's wishes. But Archie and Veronica do not crawl on the Web—at least in their original forms—so they do not search Web servers for documents and keywords. But their action is analogous to that of spiders. Table 19.1 summarizes tools used to search spaces by key word patterns.

Table 19.1. Keyword searching tools.

Space	Tool	URL to Web-based page
FTP	Archie	`http://web.nexor.co.uk/archie.html`
Gopher	Veronica	`gopher://gopher.tc.umn.edu/11/` `Other%20Gopher%20and%20Information%20Servers/` `Veronica`
telnet	Galaxy	`http://www.einet.net/galaxy.html`
WAIS	WAISgate	`http://www.wais.com/directory-of-` `servers.html`
Web	spiders	`http://web.nexor.co.uk/mak/doc/robots/` `robots.html`

Basic Spider Use

Spiders take advantage of the structure of the Web by automatically traversing its links to gather information. Spiders can "crawl" across links in one HMTL document to another through a URL reference. Once at the next document, the spider can use the tagging structure of HTML to obtain key information about a document and its links. This *semantic-*carrying content of HTML is key to the success of powerful spiders. Veronica and Archie have nothing like it currently in FTP space and Gopher space. The combination of structure and language gives spiders an edge in being able to successfully index the Web.

Here's the basic procedure for using a spider:

1. Open the URL of its home page.
2. Enter a query string in an input area. This query is usually implemented through a forms interface. The form of the query itself could be just a set of key words, or the search facility could allow for search patterns or Boolean expressions. Other options in the query could allow for searching references, titles, or text within documents.
3. Submit the query. According to the size of the database, this query is usually processed interactively (right away), rather than "batched" to run at a later time. This search for information is done against the database—the spider is not dispatched to walk the web for each request.

4. Access the results. These results are usually in the form of a Web page, dynamically created by the query interface. When the results are given interactively, the Web page will usually appear in your Mosaic display window.

5. Interpret the results. The list of results returned might or might not contain what you are looking for. The usual form of the results is a list of page of hypertext containing links. You can look the names of the URLs for clues about what they refer to, or open the URL itself.

Things To Look for In Spiders

While the procedure of using a spider is fairly straightforward, the complex question about spider results is this: "Is this all there is on the Web about X?" The answer should not necessarily be a resounding "yes," because you cannot be assured about the meaning of the actual results until you know more about the spider—its feeding and care—as well as how it handles search expressions.

Here are some things to look for when you're using a spider:

1. *How is the spider fed?* What is the process for a spider encountering new information? New resources at new URLs are developed all the time. While there are commonly accessed lists that contain such URLs, how does the spider find out about them—what is the spider's diet? Is it fed a selected set of the same "root" URLs, or is it given an amalgam of "fresh" URLs often? How does the spider find out fresh URLs (URLs that are not yet referenced in any existing Web document)?

2. *How often does the spider walk?* Since the Web and its documents change continuously, how often does the spider revisit sites and documents? Given its diet (determined by question set 1 above), how often does it execute its foray into the Web?

3. *Is the spider caged?* Is the spider limited to a fixed set of Web servers or URLs and not allowed to wander off these? Are there file types or special structures which the spider ignores?

4. *Can the spider leave the Web?* Most spiders in existence now stay strictly on the Web (only traverse Web servers and HTML documents). Some spiders can touch the edges of the Web (look through documents at FTP sites, for example).

5. *Does the spider behave?* Is the spider responsible in its behavior (not overloading a single server, not dragging down the Web's performance, and identifying itself)? A well-behaved spider should not enter restricted areas or go onto a server if it is specifically forbidden. A spider should also walk slowly, with sleeps in between its

accesses, so that it doesn't overload a single server. A spider should also ideally walk on a server during its nonpeak usage, so that it doesn't disturb users.

6. *What does the spider know?* When the spider traverses the Web, what is the information it records? Is it just URLs? Text in HTML hotspots? All the text in a document?

7. *How can you communicate with the spider?* What type of searching patterns can you use to query its database?

Because of their automated nature, poorly-behaved spiders can cause problems on the Web. If you want to create your own spider, get in contact with experienced spider developers to share technical and ethical information.

While the above questions can help you understand how a spider works, not all of these questions are easy to answer. Technical details involved in spider operation are developing and evolving rapidly. You might not be able to get all the answers to the above questions, even from the spider developers. The key is that you'll have to be flexible in trying alternative spiders and interpreting the results of what you find. The spiders we'll examine in the following subsections are currently being used widely on the Web to locate information. There will certainly be new ones developed, so you'll need to build your skills to understand the features and limitations of existing spiders and discover new ones.

A Gallery of Spiders

Unlike Archie and Veronica, which seemed to have exclusive domain over their respective information spaces, spiders are a mixed lot. This section outlines some of the most popular current spiders. Certainly, more will develop and the spiders here will evolve. Look for features that give you flexibility in searching in these spiders. Then you can find out how newer spiders implement these same or similar capabilities.

The World Wide Web Worm

The World Wide Web Worm was developed by Oliver McBryan to help make sense of the myriad of references on the Web. As such, it has been one of the most successful searching tools on the Web, winning a "Best of the Web '94" award for a navigational aid. The Worm (as it is affectionately known) searches the Web for URLs, title strings, and reference links. The home page of the Worm is at the URL `http://www.cs.colorado.edu/home/mcbryan/WWW.html`. Figure 19.1 shows a portion of the Worm's home page, showing the Worm's two main forms of searching mechanisms.

> **NOTE**
>
> Don't confuse the World Wide Web Worm with a computer security-related term for a software program (virus) intended to cause a computer system to crash. The World Wide Web Worm is benign.

FIGURE 19.1.

World Wide Web Worm search form.

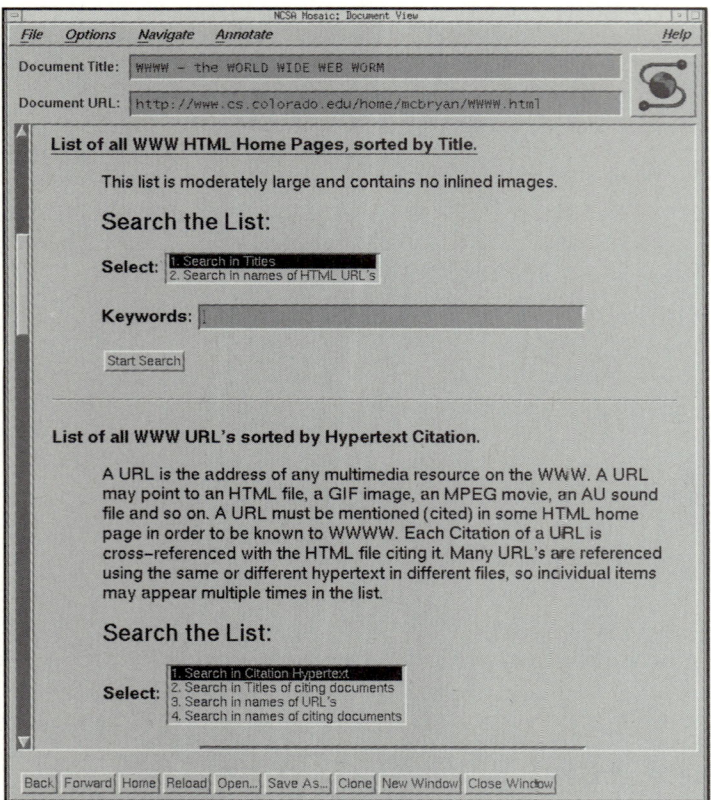

In all searches using the Worm, the key word pattern must be exact (no wildcards currently implemented) and in the order of occurrence. The pattern is case-insensitive (will return a match for the string regardless if the letters are in upper- or lowercase).

Here are the options for searching:

1. Searching a list of all known HTML pages. This list includes the URL of the page and the title of the page, as given within the tags used in HTML to designate a title (`<TITLE>...</TITLE>`). You can search this database by looking for key words or strings within the URLs or within the title names.

2. Searching the database of HTML pages and links within them. The Worm keeps track of what documents cite other documents on the Web, so that you can search a database for these patterns. The arrangement of the database information is two-tiered: there are citing documents that contain references to cited documents. Your options for searching this database are as follows:

- Search in Citation Hypertext—The citation hypertext is the text in the "hotspot" of an HTML file, the clickable portion that links to another resource.

  With this selection, you'll find the URLs in the database that match your search criteria, and you'll be given links to the documents that cite (refer to) these URLs. In this way, you can use this searching mode to find patterns of citation in the Web.

- Search in Titles of citing documents—This option will give you a list of "hits" on the strings within the titles of the citing documents.

- Search in names of URLs—With this option, you'll obtain all the URLs in the database which contain your search string and links to the documents that cite these URLs.

- Search in names of citing documents—This option refers to the names of the URLs (filename directory name, host name, or other identifiers in the URL) of the citing documents.

The home page of the Worm contains examples of search possibilities. Here are some examples that illustrate the power of the Worm:

1. Find all the HTML pages at the Electronic Frontier Foundation's Server (www.eff.org).

   Solution: Search the List of all WWW HTML pages. Select 2. Search in names of HTML URLs. Enter key words www.eff.org.

   Results (the text is shown below with boldface indicating hotspots, the actual page returned had active links):

   www.eff.org

   ```
   Return to Searching
   -------------------


   1. Computers and Academic Freedom
      -------------------------------
   2. Electronic Frontier Foundation
      -------------------------------
   3. Welcome to the Big Dummy's Guide to the Internet
      -------------------------------------------------
   ```

```
If you received an empty return list, but expected a non-empty one, please read
here.
....


Return to Searching
..................


WWW is being developed by Oliver McBryan
```

2. Find all the HTML pages that have the word "Fun" in their title.

   Solution: Search the List of all WWW HTML pages. Select 1. `Search in Titles.` Enter keyword

   fun

```
Return to Searching
..................


1. A General Purpose Function Network Workbench and Simulator - DigiPlumb
   ..................................................................


2. A Tool for Construction of Functional Models of Distributed Applications and
Protocols - STRAPPS
   ...........................................................................
..................


3. Analysis and Simulation Branch Functional Statement
   ...............................................

4. Andy's Fun Page
   .............

5. COMMA Fun and Games (Cardiff)
   ..........................

6. COMMA Fun and Games (Cardiff)
   ..........................

7. Doctor Fun
   ..........

8. Doctor Fun
   ..........
```

(list continues)

Notice that the above list included matches such as function in the search. The list continued to 83 items.

3. Find all the HTML pages that refer to resources on any Los Alamos National Lab machine.

   Solution: Search "List of all WWW URLs sorted by Hypertext Citation."

   Select 3. Search in names of URL's. Enter keywords.

   Results:

```
lanl.gov


Return to Searching
-----------------


1. Uniform Resource Identifiers
   ---------------------------
      o cited in:
                  http://www.gatech.edu/projects.html
      ----------------------------------
2. [IMAGE]
      o cited in:
                  http://esther.la.asu.edu/asu_tes/TES_Editor/dsn_solarsyst.html
      ------------------------------------------------------------
3. CNLS
   ----
      o cited in:
                  http://info.cern.ch/hypertext/DataSources/WWW/Geographical.html
      ------------------------------------------------------------
4. CNLS
   ----
      o cited in:
                  http://info.cern.ch/hypertext/DataSources/WWW/Servers.html
      ------------------------------------------------------------
 5. Gen. Relativity and Quantum Cosmology o cited in:
http://cui_www.unige.ch/OSG/Catalog/changes.html 6. Gen. Relativity and
Quantum Cosmology
      ------------------------------------
      o cited in:
http://info.desy.de/pub/userWWW/projects/Lattice/Misc.html 7//cui_www.unige.ch/
OSG/Catalog/changes.html
      ------------------------------------------
```

```
6. Gen. Relativity and Quantum Cosmology
   ------------------------------------
     o cited in:
http://info.desy.de/pub/userWWW/projects/Lattice/Misc.html
                 ------------------------------------------------


7. Gen. Relativity and Quantum Cosmology
   ------------------------------------
     o cited in:
http://info.desy.de/pub/www/projects/Lattice/Misc.html
             ------------------------------------------------
```

(list continues)

The flexibility of the Worm to sort through hypertext citations makes it possible to find the pages that cite a page—a valuable capability for information seekers as well as page maintainers.

WebCrawler

Like the Worm, the WebCrawler finds references to URLs on the Web and makes the resulting database that it builds available for searching. Unlike the Worm, however, the WebCrawler makes indexes of the *contents* of documents it finds, in addition to URLs, hotspot text, and titles like the Worm.

The WebCrawler was developed by Brian Pinkerton, its home page is at URL `http://www.biotech.washington.edu/WebCrawler/WebCrawler.html`, and it is shown in Figure 19.2.

The WebCrawler, like the Worm, returns a set of links that match a given key word search. However, the WebCrawler has some important differences:

- It records not only URLs starting with `http`, but other protocols, including Gopher, FTP, and others.

- Its search pattern is for words, not strings. This means your search for `electronic frontier` will turn up matches for those two words anywhere on a page. You can control this search string by using the switch to toggle on and off the "and" function for the words (if the button is pushed in, all the words in your search string must be on the the page for a successful hit).

- Its output is arranged by a "score" in which resources judged (through the indexing algorithm of the crawler) best are listed first.

Since the WebCrawler indexes the contents of documents, in addition to the information that the Worm collects, the Crawler is a powerful search tool. The flip side of it is that the Crawler must work very, very hard in order to perform this total text search of all documents in the Web and at the Web's edge (in Gopher space, FTP space, or other protocols accessed from some HTML file). The Worm, collecting less information, travels lighter than the Crawler, but knows less about the URLs it finds. The Crawler, since it collects more information from each document, knows more, but probably can visit fewer URLs in the same amount of time as the Worm.

FIGURE 19.2.

WebCrawler search form.

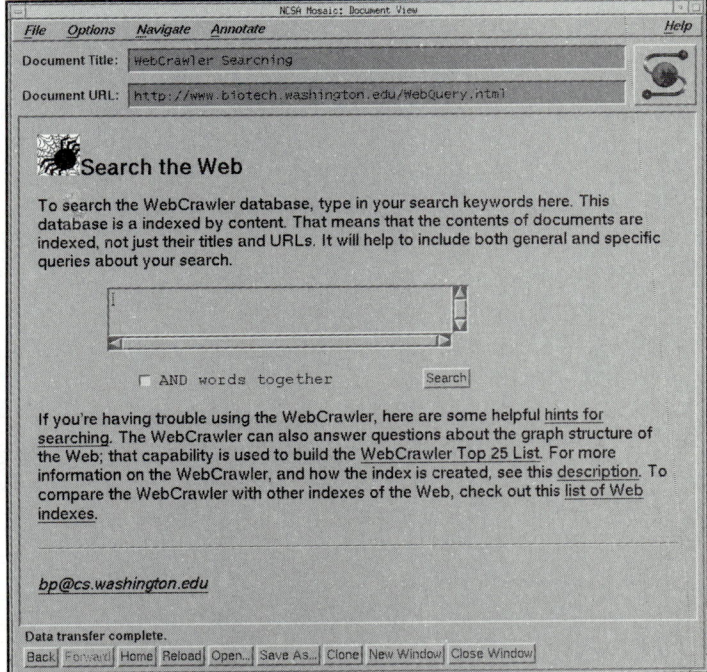

JumpStation

The JumpStation, developed by Jonathon Fletcher, references information on the Web by document title or header, although extensions of this are in the works for the JumpStation. The JumpStation's home page is at `http://www.stir.ac.uk/jsbin/js`, and its search form is shown in Figure 19.3.

The beta version of the JumpStation will count the occurrences of words in the document, remove references to common words like "and," "a," and "the," and use this index of words and occurrences in the document as a way of determining the subject of the document. The JumpStation also will make use of the `<header>` and `<title>` tags in HTML documents. In this way, the JumpStation, like the Crawler and the Worm, attempts to cull out important keywords from documents to perform a search. The next version of JumpStation is also expected to have a "server scanner" service, which will allow you to search the URL database by a partial name of the server you are interested in.

FIGURE 19.3.

JumpStation search form.

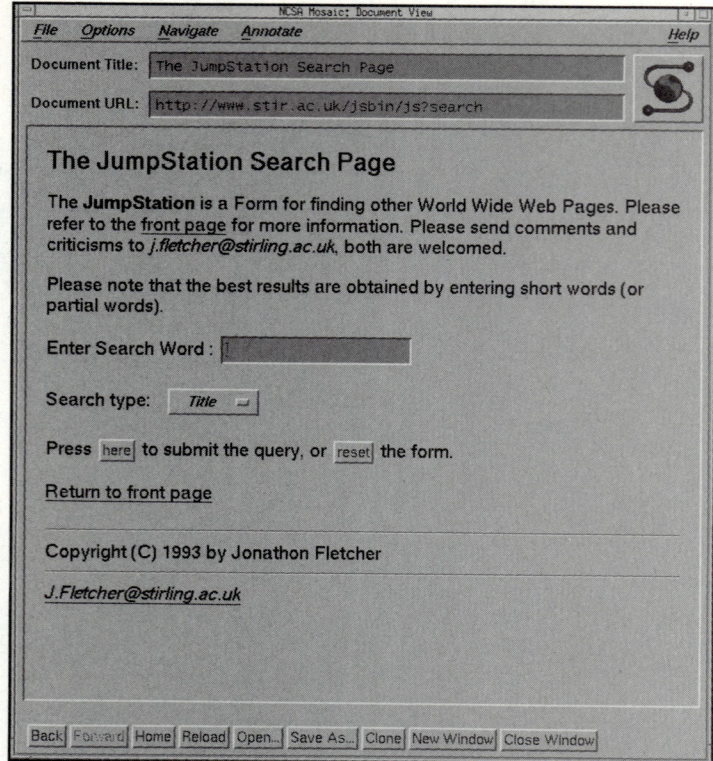

The RBSE Spider

The RBSE (Repository Based Software Engineering Program) Spider, developed by David Eichmann, works like many of the spiders described above, roaming the Web collecting URLs. The search form for the RBSE spider is at URL `http://rbse.jsc.nasa.gov/eichmann/urlsearch.html`, and its front page is shown in Figure 19.4. Its unique features are

- It indexes the full text of HTML documents.
- It traverses links that have patterns of `.html` and `http:/` in them.
- It uses an Oracle database for storing references.
- It uses a version of WAIS technology to present the results to the reader.

The RBSE Spider accepts as input a set of search key words that are part of a URL or a word in a HTML document. It will return pages that fit this search pattern, arranged in descending relevance—the higher the score, the more relevant the document.

FIGURE 19.4.

RBSE Spider search form.

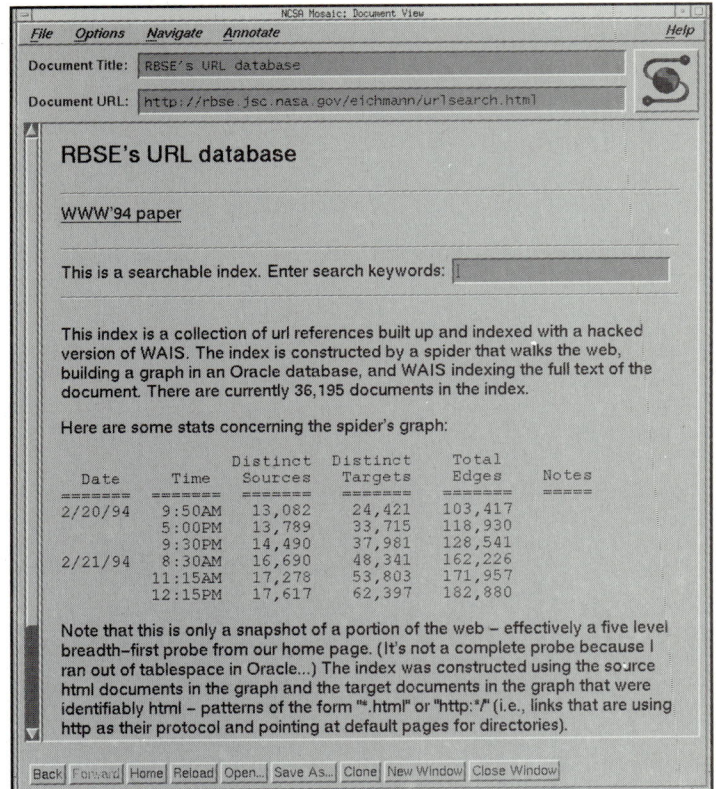

Web Nomad

The Web Nomad organizes information into large pools of URLs organized by topic. Its URL is `http://www.rns.com/www_index/intro.html`, and its front screen is shown in Figure 19.5.

To use the Nomad, you type in a topic name. Nomad retrieves items from the database that match the topic name. If there are no matches, a search will be done against the URLs in the database for matches to that topic name. James Aviani, Web Nomad developer, says that this scheme is useful because it takes very little space to run. Keywords in the actual text of the resources are *not* indexed, like in the WebCrawler. Rather, the Web Nomad is useful for finding starting points, not necessarily for full Web searches. Because the Nomad travels light, it travels often and can cover a lot of the Web.

FIGURE 19.5.

Web Nomad search form.

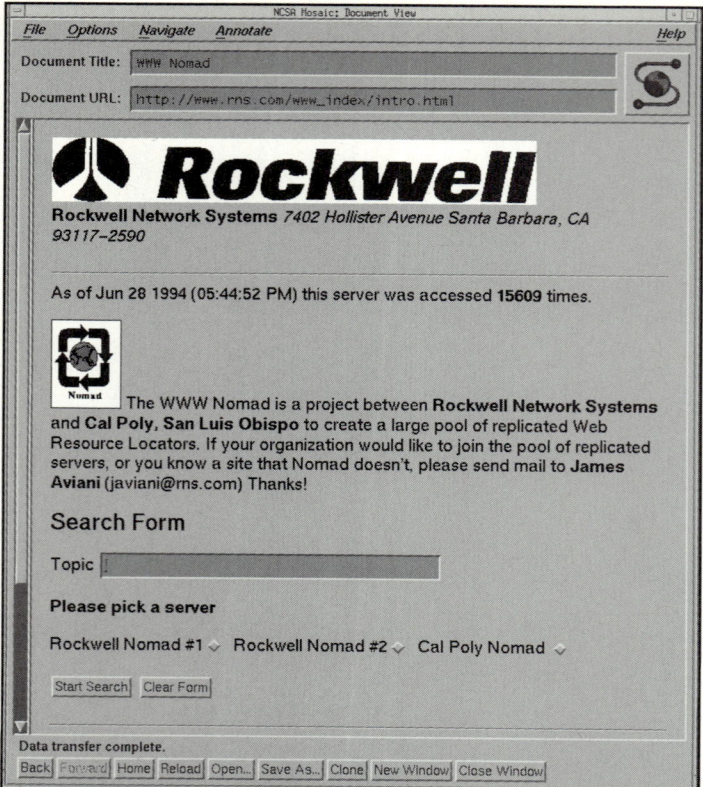

More Spiders!

Spiders are extremely useful in finding information in the Web. So useful, in fact, that many new ones are in development. Check out the list of active spiders at the URL `http://web.nexor.co.uk/mak/doc/robots/active.html`.

LATE-BREAKING SPIDER NEWS

The numbers in brackets in this text refer to the URLs given at the end of this article.

Computer-Mediated Communication Magazine[1] /

Volume 1, Number 5 / September 1, 1994 / Page 3

NEW SPIDERS ROAM THE WEB

by John December[2] (`decemj@rpi.edu`)

THE WEB (August 28) Two newer, smarter tools for finding and indexing resources on the Web have been released this summer. The Carnegie Mellon University[3]'s Center for Machine Translation[4] announced the public availability of its Lycos _ WWW search engine[5] on August 12th, and the Internet Research Task Force Research Group on Resource Discovery[6]'s Harvest System[7] has been presented in several papers during the summer.

Both systems are now in place for public use. The Lycos and Harvest systems attack a problem that has plagued many information spaces before the Web—how can a user find resources related to a topic or locate a specific resource? In FTP space[8], there's Archie[9]; in Gopher space[10], there's Veronica[11]. For the Web, there is a variety of robots, wanderers, and spiders that have been crawling through the Web and collecting information about what they find.

Oliver McBryan's Web World-Wide Web Worm[12], released in March, was a very early ancestor to the newer species of spiders on the Web today. The Worm collected a database of over 100,000 resources and still provides the user with a search interface to its database (current to March 7, 1994). Both Lycos and Harvest build on the Worm's techniques, provide more current databases, and collect them in a more efficient manner.

Lycos

In an e-mail interview, Dr. Michael L. Mauldin[13], a developer of Lycos, described the spider's unique features. Lycos' software ancestry is from a program called "Longlegs" written by John Leavitt[14] and Eric Nyberg[15], and the term "Lycos" comes from the arachnid family Lycosidae, which are large ground spiders that are very speedy and active at night, catching their prey by pursuit rather than in a web. Lycos lives up to its name—rather than catching its "prey" (URLs on a server) in massive single-server sweeps, Lycos uses an innovative, probabilistic scheme to skip from server to server in Webspace.

The secret of Lycos' search technique lies in random choices tempered by preferences. Lycos starts with a given URL and collects information from the resource, including

■ Title

■ Headings and Subheadings

■ The 100 most "weighty" words (using an algorithm which considers word placement and frequencies, among other factors)

■ First 20 lines

■ Size in bytes

■ Number of words

Lycos then adds the URL references in the resource to its queue. To choose the next document to explore, Lycos makes a random choice (among the HTTP, Gopher, and Ftp references) with built-in "preferences" for documents that have multiple links into them (popular documents) and a slight preference for shorter URLs (to keep the database oriented to the Web's "top").

While many early Web spiders infested a particular server with a large number of rapid, sequential accesses, Lycos behaves. First, Lycos' random-search behavior avoids the "multiple-hit" problem. Second, Lycos complies with the standard for robot exclusion[16] to keep unwanted robots off WWW servers, and identifies itself as 'Lycos' when crawling, so that webmasters can know when Lycos has hit their server.

With more than 634,000 references in its database as of the end of August, Lycos offers a huge database to locate documents matching a given query. The search interface[17] provides a way for users to find documents that contain references to a keyword, and to examine a document outline, key word list and an excerpt. In this way, Lycos enables the user to determine if a document might be valuable without having to retrieve it.

According to Dr. Mauldin, plans are in the works for allowing users to register pages and for other kinds of searching schemes. Another related project underway is WebAnts[18] aimed at creating cooperating explorers, so that an individual spider doesn't have to do all the work of finding things on the Web or duplicate other spiders' efforts.

The Harvest Project

The Harvest Information Discovery and Access System[19] reaches beyond being merely a spider, but involves a series of subsystems to create an efficient, flexible, and scalable way to locate information. Harvest is an ambitious project to provide a way to create indexes and provide for efficient use of servers. Work on its development has been supported primarily by Advanced Research Projects Agency[20], with other support from the Air Force Office of Scientific Research (AFOSR)[21], Hughes, National Science Foundation[22], and Sun[23]. Harvest is being designed and built by the Internet Research Task Force Research Group on Resource Discovery[24].

The philosophy behind the Harvest system is that it gathers information about Internet resources and customizes views into what is "harvested." According to developer Mike Schwartz,[25] "Harvest is much more than just a 'spider.' It's intended to be a scalable form of infrastructure for building and distributing content, indexing information, as well as for accessing Web information." The complete capabilities of Harvest are beyond the scope of this news article; for further information, the reader is directed to The Harvest Information Discovery and Access System web page[26].

Harvest consists of several subsystems. A Gatherer collects indexing information and a Broker[27] provides a flexible interface to this information. A user can access a variety of collections of documents. The Harvest WWW Broker[28], for example, includes content summaries of more than 7,000 Web pages. This database has a very flexible interface, providing search queries based on author, keyword, title, or URL-reference. While the Harvest database (the WWW pages) isn't yet as extensive as other spiders', its potential for efficiently collecting a large amount is great.

Other subsystems further refine Harvest's capabilities. Subsystems for indexing/searching provide ways for for a variety of search engines to be used. For example, Glimpse[29] supports very rapid space-efficient searches with interactive queries while Nebula[30] provides fast searches for more complex queries. Another Harvest subsystem, a Replicator, provides a way to mirror information the Brokers have and an Object Cache meets the demand for managing networked information by providing the capability to locate the fastest-responding server to a query.

While spiders like the Worm could successfully crawl through Webspace in first part of 1994, the rapid increase in the amount of information on the Web since then make this same crawl difficult for the older spiders. Harvest's systems and subsystems are extensive and provide for efficient, flexible operation, and its design addresses the very important issue of scalability. Similarly, the Web Ants[31] project addresses this scalability issue through its vision of cooperating spiders crawling through the Web. The promise for the future is that systems like Harvest and Lycos will provide users with increasingly efficient ways to locate information on the Nets.

References in this document

[1] http://www.rpi.edu/~decemj/cmc/mag/current/toc.html

[2] http://www.rpi.edu/~decemj/index.html

[3] http://www.cmu.edu/

[4] http://www.mt.cs.cmu.edu/cmt/CMT-home.html

[5] http://lycos.cs.cmu.edu/

[6] http://rd.cs.colorado.edu/~schwartz/IRTF.html

[7] http://rd.cs.colorado.edu/harvest/Home.html

[8] http://hoohoo.ncsa.uiuc.edu/ftp-interface.html

[9] http://web.nexor.co.uk/archie.html

[10] gopher://gopher.micro.umn.edu/1

[11] gopher://gopher.unr.edu/11/veronica

[12] http://web.nexor.co.uk/mak/doc/robots/robots.html>

[13] http://fuzine.mt.cs.cmu.edu/mlm/home.html

[14] http://thule.mt.cs.cmu.edu:8001/jrrl-space/home-page.html

[15] http://www.mt.cs.cmu.edu/ehn/release/

[16] http://web.nexor.co.uk/mak/doc/robots/norobots.html

[17] http://lycos.cs.cmu.edu/cgi-bin/pursuit/

[18] http://thule.mt.cs.cmu.edu:8001/jrrl-space/webants.html

[19] http://rd.cs.colorado.edu/harvest/

[20] http://ftp.arpa.mil/

[21] http://web.fie.com/web/fed/afr/

[22] gopher://stis.nsf.gov/11

[23] http://www.sun.com/

[24] http://rd.cs.colorado.edu/~schwartz/IRTF.html

[25] http://rd.cs.colorado.edu/~schwartz/Home.html

[26] http://bruno.cs.colorado.edu/harvest/

```
[27] http://rd.cs.colorado.edu/brokers/

[28] http://rd.cs.colorado.edu/brokers/www-home-pages/query.html

[29] http://glimpse.cs.arizona.edu:1994/

[30] http://canopus.cse.psu.edu/NEBFS/nebula.html

[31] http://thule.mt.cs.cmu.edu:8001/jrrl-space/webants.html
```

Indexes

While all the above spiders have the same characteristic of being *automated* Web searching facilities that look through the Web, there are other resources that can help you locate resources on the Web based on keyword patterns. The following sections outline some tools and resources that are used to pull out information from collections of URLs and unify many searching mechanisms into Forms-based interfaces. These are not true spiders, but interfaces to URL collections that behave similarly to the interfaces to the databases of URLs generated by spiders. Their purpose, just like the spiders, is to help users find specific resources in the Web.

CUI W3 Catalog

The CUI W3 catalog is a collection of URL references built from a number of hand-crafted HTML lists (Figure 19.6). The CUI W3 Catalog (URL `http://cui_www.unige.ch/cgi-bin/w3catalog`) periodically scans these lists and produces a database of the URLs and hotspot text in them. The CUI W3 forms interface allows a user to query this database for key word patterns.

The limitation of the CUI W3 Catalog is that it depends on human-made documents for information about resources. However, it still is very useful as these lists, although potentially limited in coverage and accuracy, can help in very focused searches. Thus, the searches for information related to the content covered by the lists shown in Figure 19.6 can be very helpful.

ALIWEB

The name ALIWEB stands for "Archie-like indexing for the Web," and it attempts to do for the Web what Archie intended to do for FTP space. Archie, along with its ability to collect the names of directories and files at FTP sites, has a facility associated with it that allows for maintainers of files to describe those files. Done by hand, this feature never

worked out to be as successful as the automated activity of Archie. ALIWEB seeks to accomplish this for the Web and seems to be more successful, with its more appealing Forms-based interface to collect information from developers. ALIWEB should not be confused with Web-based interfaces with Archie—ALIWEB is an index to Web resources, while the Web-based Archie interface ArchiePlex indexes FTP space.

FIGURE 19.6.

The CUI W3 Catalog document set.

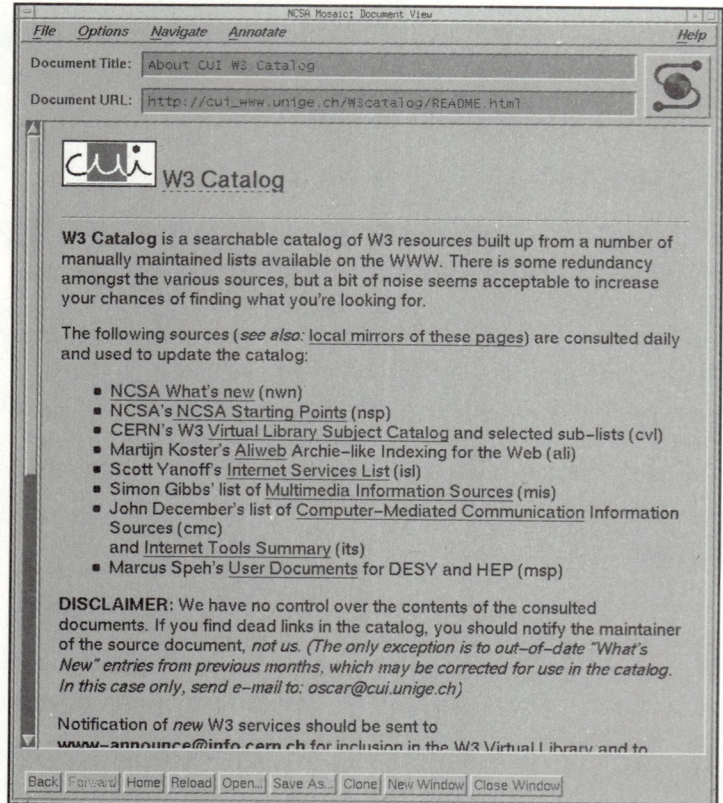

ALIWEB's home page is at URL `http://web.nexor.co.uk/aliweb/doc/aliweb.html`. The way ALIWEB works is that people write index files in a specific format and store these files on their server. They inform ALIWEB about these files, and ALIWEB regularly retrieves these files and creates a database from them. The result is a fairly up-to-date database of available resources.

Unified Search Engines

We've talked about a bewildering amount of spiders and catalogs that index resources on the Web. Is there some place where you can easily access a list of them? The answer is yes.

These collections of keyword-based search tools, sometimes called "unified search engines" exist in several places:

- Oscar Nierstrasz's Meta index (Figure 19.7) at URL `http://cui_www.unige.ch/meta-index.html`

- Martijn Koster's SUSI, at URL `http://web.nexor.co.uk/susi/susi.html`

- Twente University's External Info at URL `http://www_is.cs.utwente.nl:8080/cgi-bin/local/nph-susi1.pl`

FIGURE 19.7.

Meta Index search form.

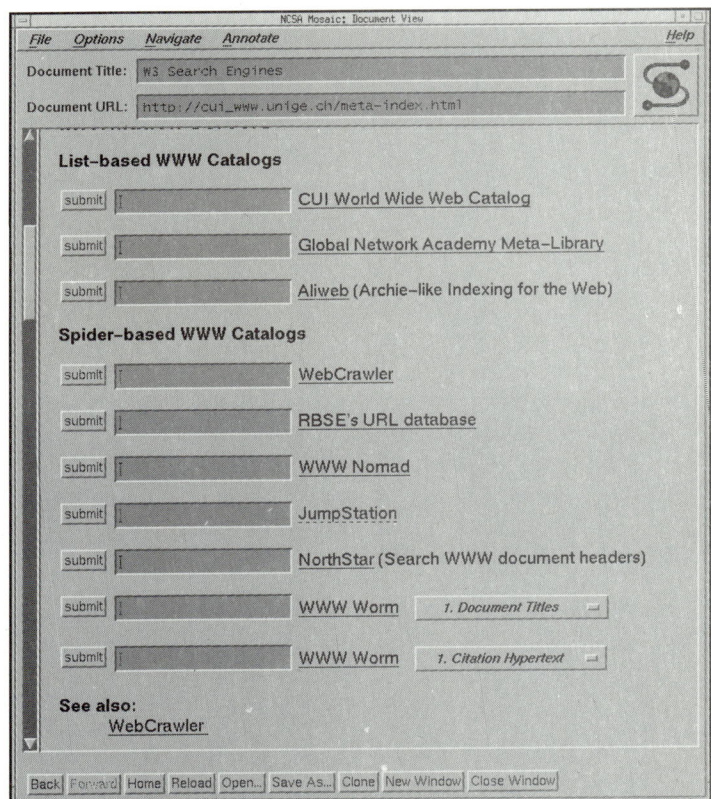

The Meta Index, shown in Figure 19.7, is a typical example of a collected search engine.

The Meta Index serves as an interface to many different indexes through a Forms interface. These collected search engines are useful, both because they give a one-stop approach for key word-oriented searching, but also because they help users build an awareness of the kinds of tools on the Web for such searching, including links to the home pages of the tools themselves. Thus, the user can choose which index would be best as a place to search.

Tips and Techniques for Using Spiders

We've talked about spiders and indexes that are useful for finding information based on key word searches on the Web. All these tools have their strengths and limitations, and are perhaps some of the most useful tools on the web for finding specific information. Using these tools takes some getting used to, though. Here are some tips and techniques for making the best use of them.

1. Know the limitations of the spider or index that you are using. The above survey briefly covers the strengths and weaknesses of current spiders. There will be more spiders, and spiders evolve over time, so you'll need to keep abreast of developments.

   If one spider yields poor results, try another. Some spiders, due to the area they often walk on the Web or because of their diet, might seem to have more resources in your areas of interest than others. (Perhaps specialized spiders could develop, known for their ability to walk known subject-oriented areas of the Web.)

2. Be respectful and patient of the spider developers and databases. Spiders, if not properly behaved, can run rampant on the Web, possibly causing many administrators to ban spiders from their hosts, taking away from the spiders' original intent as a helpful searching tools for the Web. Therefore, be patient with a spider administrator—don't pressure him or her to walk a spider. Assure yourself that the spider's developer and administrator follows "Guidelines for Robot Writers," URL `http://web.nexor.co.uk/mak/doc/robots/guidelines.html`, written by Martin Koster, Jonathon Fletcher, and Lee McLoughlin.

3. If you get extensive search results from a spider search and they are important to your work, save the search results to an HTML file on your local directory (in HTML). This is necessary because, in most cases, you will not be able to save the search results as a URL reference in your hotlist.

4) Be flexible in your search strategies. Sometimes a subject-oriented approach can yield results, as well as surfing methods (discussed in Chapter 21, "Surfing: Finding the New and Unusual") or machine-oriented methods we'll talk about in the next chapter.

Navigator's Check

Finding a specific resource in the enormous information space of the Web is a difficult task. Spiders can help in this task, but the conflict between searching broadly (finding out something about a lot of things) and searching deep (finding a lot about a few things) is always in balance. Some spiders, like the Worm, collect specific text set apart by the tags in HTML documents. Others, like the WebCrawler, search more deeply and make indexes of the entire contents of documents. Other indexes search through URL collections for patterns of key words. These indexes, sometimes relying on hand-crafted lists or manual maintenance of information, also have their limitations.

The key to using spiders and indexes effectively is

- Understand that finding information on the Web is a complex task and no spider has infallible knowledge of the Web.

- Be aware of major spiders and spider collections. Use a variety of spiders in performing searches.

- For the spiders that seem most helpful to you, learn the details of their searching pattern options and how they work. Attempt to answer these questions (abbreviated from list earlier in this chapter):

  1. How is the spider fed?

  2. How often does the spider walk?

  3. Is the spider caged?

  4. Can the spider leave the Web or touch its edges?

  5. Does the spider behave?

  6. What does the spider know?

  7. How can you communicate with it?

Machines: Space-Oriented Searching

by John December

IN THIS CHAPTER

While the subject-and keyword-oriented searching methods from the previous two chapters might locate what you want for particular subjects, another searching problem is to find resources based on geographic location. In this space-oriented searching method, you search lists that present a geographic breakdown of information (often using protocol-specific lists of servers, such as lists of all Web servers by geography, and lists of Gopher servers by geography), looking for a particular machine in a region or at a certain institution.

Besides using a list of Web servers for space-oriented searching, you can search lists of machines in other information spaces. We've already seen the FTP site list in Chapter 16, "At the Edge of the Web." While all the lists don't have a pleasing graphical interface, they provide a way for you to find institutions, resources, and organizations based on geographic location.

The Virtual Tourist

What if you are interested in the country of Turkey, and you want to get an idea of what Web sites are in the country? A Web spider search (see previous chapter) might turn up references to Turkey, but not necessarily to just information related to the country of Turkey. Further, let's say you don't really want to look at just a text-based list or find isolated instances, but you'd rather see the "lay of the land" of Turkey in cyberspace.

There is a tool for exactly this purpose, called the Virtual Tourist, developed by Brandon Plewe. The URL of the Virtual Tourist is `http://wings.buffalo.edu/world`, and its front page is shown in Figure 20.1.

The Virtual Tourist accomplishes several things. First, it serves as a visual interface into the geographic distribution of World Wide Web servers. Second, it gathers geographical, tourism, and cultural information about many geographic regions. Third, it does all this through a cooperative system of hypertext documents that is voluntarily developed. Fourth, it effectively employs the graphical information maps feature available through Mosaic. By clicking on a symbol or boxed region, the user obtains more information about that region. In this way, the Virtual Tourist accomplishes very much.

FIGURE 20.1.

Virtual Tourist front page.

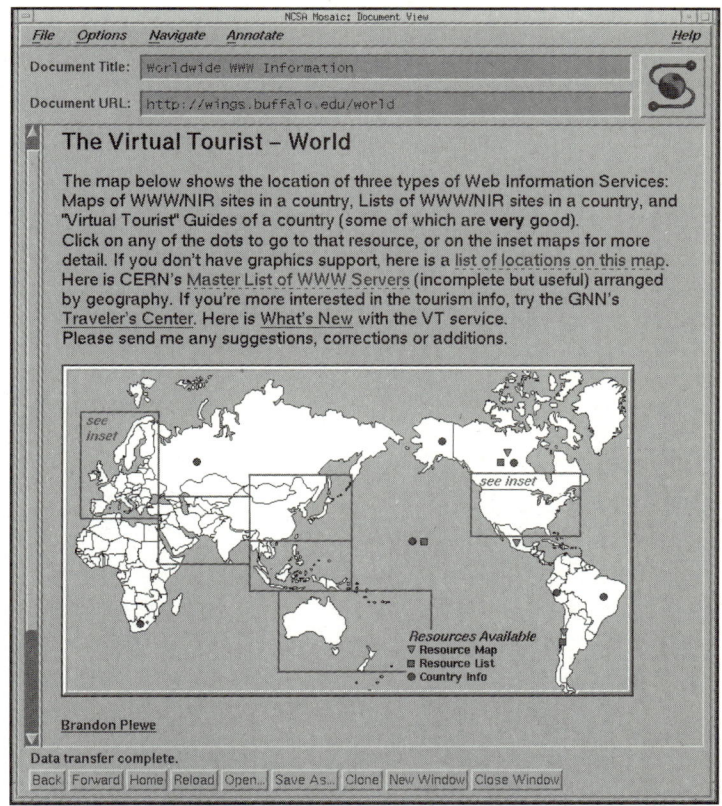

Let's continue our example of curiosity about Turkey. By clicking on the box over southwest Asia on the world map (Figure 20.1), we obtain the Southwest Asia map (Figure 20.2).

Note that in Figure 20.2 there are several choices for Turkey: the resource map, a resource list, or country information. The resource map gives a visual perspective of the layout of cyberspace in Turkey. The results are shown in Figure 20.3.

FIGURE 20.2.

Southwest Asia map.

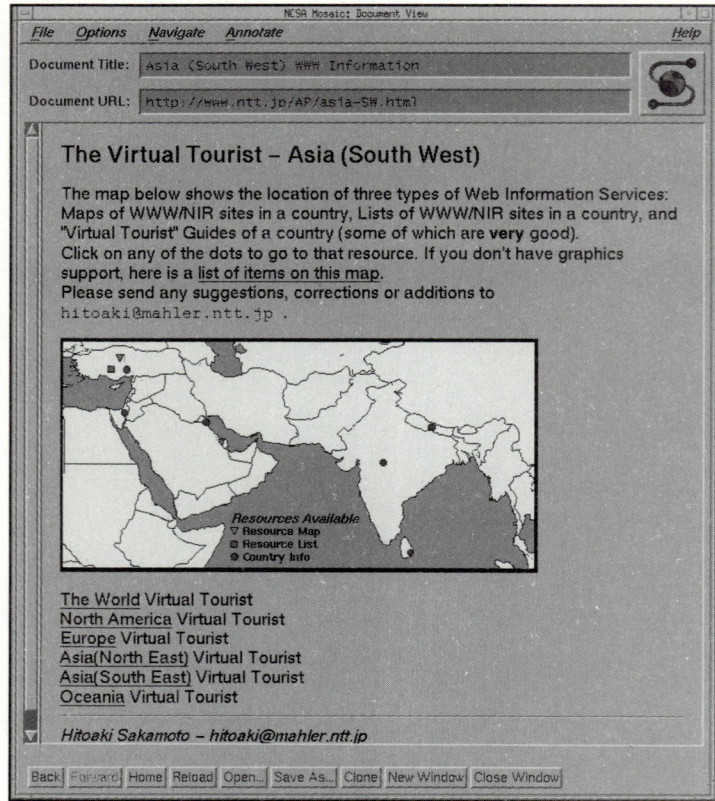

Notice how the Turkey map differs slightly in style from the Southwest Asia map, a difference that allows for expressive variation in how administrators at individual sites want to represent their region, while still retaining the functionality and intent of the Virtual Tourist itself. The Turkey map shows the locations of Web sites that have registered with the developer of the map shown. It quickly gives an idea of locations in the region where you might find Web servers. Let's examine the link labeled METU on the Turkey map. Clicking on the square next to the label "METU," we obtain Figure 20.4.

FIGURE 20.3.

Turkey map.

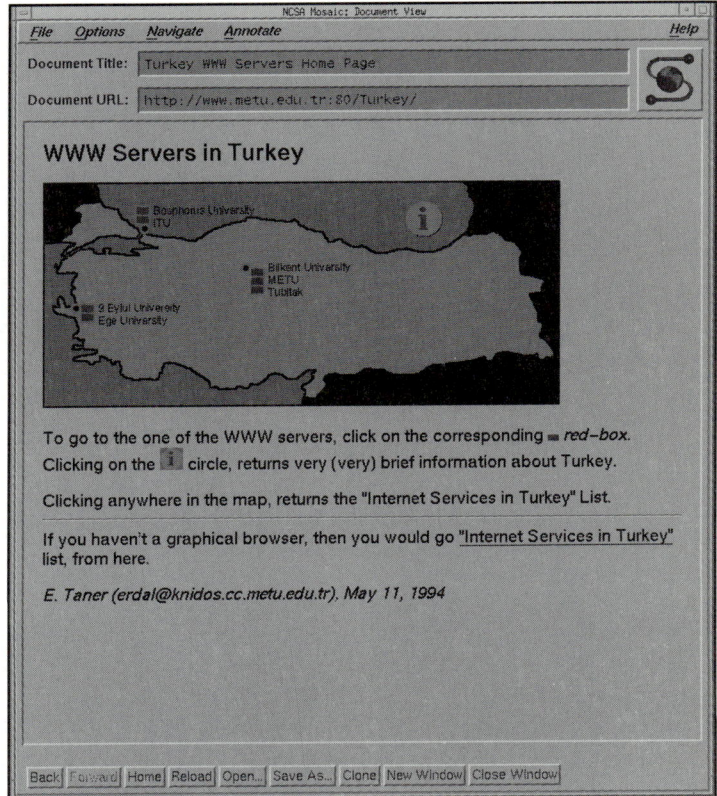

This page gives us a launching point for more information about Middle East Technical University. Although we might have found this same home page with a Web spider (as well as hits for each word in the name of METU), we might not have been able to locate other contextual information so easily, such as the Turkey country information as well as neighboring universities. Moreover, the graphical map interface is fun to use.

If you want to browse a hypertext (nongraphical) list of Web servers, you can open URL `http://info.cern.ch/hypertext/DataSources/WWW/Servers.html`. This list gives you links to many of the country maps shown throughout the Virtual Tourist as well as a means to scan keywords or phrases easily (using Mosaic's File / Find In Current...).

FIGURE 20.4.

Middle East Technical University home page.

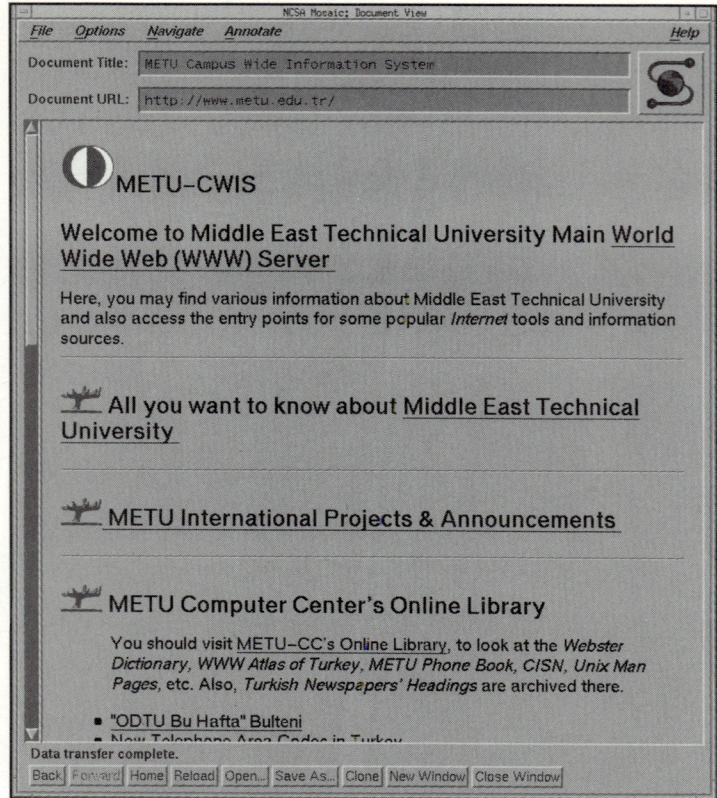

Directory Servers

Another kind of space searching involves trying to track down individuals using Directory Services. There are a a variety of "white pages" electronic directory services based on various schemes with names such as whois and X.500.

The page at http://honor.uc.wlu.edu/directories.html is an entry point into a collection of directory servers. Part of the breakdown of directory servers by geography is shown in Figure 20.5.

FIGURE 20.5.

Directory servers by geography.

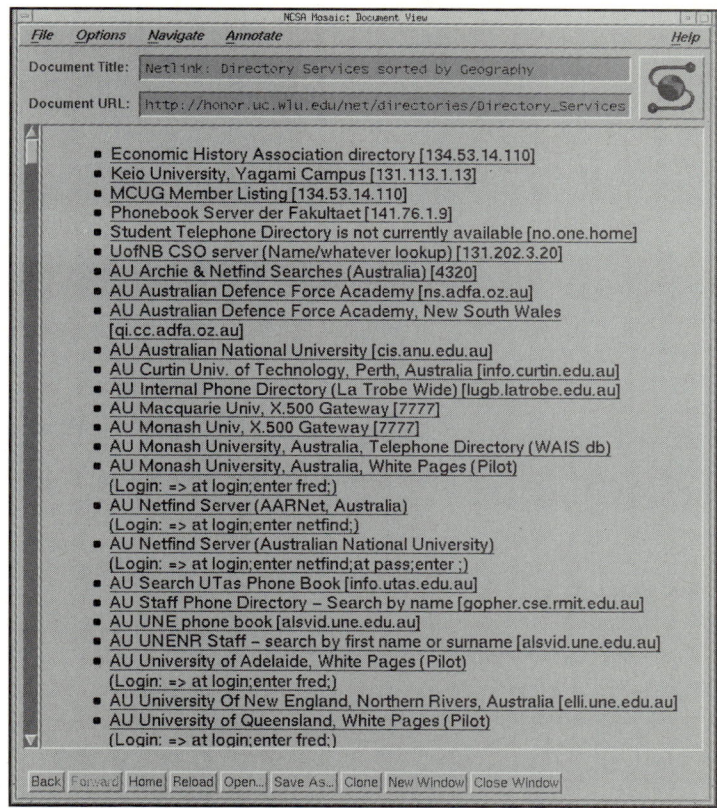

There is no simple solution to finding a person on the Net using the Net itself; often you'd be better off to contact the person directly by telephone! However, directory services are improving. As an experiment, you might try to locate yourself in the directory service. You might be surprised that doing so can be more difficult than you might think.

Telnet Space: Hytelnet

We've already talked about Hytelnet in Chapter 16, "At the Edge of the Web." Hytelnet also organizes telnet-accessible resources by geography. Hytelnet is particularly useful for services that adopted online technology early—libraries and community-based Free-net systems—since telnet is a widely available interface for dial-up modem users. Hytelnet's offerings for "Other Telnet-accessible resources," at URL `http://www.cc.ukans.edu/hytelnet_html/SITES2.html`, shown in Figure 20.6, give you a flavor of what to expect.

FIGURE 20.6.

Other telnet-accessible resources.

```
                    Other Telnet-accessible resources
<ARC000> Archie: Archive Server Listing Service
<CWI000> Campus-wide Information systems
<FUL000> Databases and bibliographies

<DIS000> Distributed File Servers (Gopher/WAIS/WWW)
<BOOKS>  Electronic books
<FEE000> Fee-Based Services

<FRE000> FREE-NETs & Community Computing Systems
<BBS000> General Bulletin Boards
<HYT000> HYTELNET On-line versions

<NAS000> NASA databases
<NET000> Network Information Services
<DIR000> Whois/White Pages/Directory Services

<OTH000> Miscellaneous resources
```

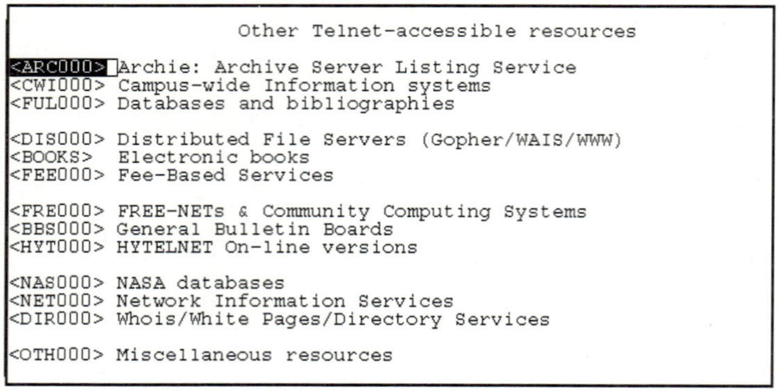

Gopher Space and Notes on Space Migration

We've already talked about Gopher in Chapter 16, "At the Edge of the Web." You can browse for Gophers by geographic region. Many campus-wide information systems have been implemented as Gophers, as these institutions quickly adopted Gopher as "the next generation" of information delivery tools, after many libraries adopted telnet. Certainly, there are more libraries now using Gopher, and many universities and libraries are migrating to the Web.

You can use this "space migration" phenomenon to judge where in cyberspace you'd be most likely to find a particular institution. Many new, commercial ventures are going directly to the Web, and most new systems built after 1994 seem destined for the Web. This might change, and the integration Gopher offers with the Web (through information servers such as GN) may encourage many developers to remain in Gopherspace. However, if spiders never learn to leave the Web, you may see more information providers leave Gopherspace because their information won't be indexed by important forms of searching tools available on the Web.

Navigator's Check

We've covered a variety of ways that you can search for institutions, resources, and people using a geographic space or information space as a criterion. Table 20.1 summarizes major lists for each.

Table 20.1. Summary of space-oriented searching for machines.

Space	*URL of List*
FTP	`http://hoohoo.ncsa.uiuc.edu/ftp-interface.html`
Gopher	`gopher://gopher.tc.umn.edu/11/`
	`Other%20Gopher%20and%20Information%20Servers`
Web	`http://wings.buffalo.edu/world`
telnet	`http://www.cc.ukans.edu/hytelnet_html/START.TXT.html`
Directory	`http://honor.uc.wlu.edu/directories.html`

Surfing: Finding the New and Unusual

21

by John December

We've covered some major ways to find information on the Web and at its edges: navigating through trees for subject-oriented information, using spiders to find keyword information and lists of machines to find institutions, people, and resources in space-oriented (geographical as well as information space) lists. All these are valuable searching and navigating methods and may truly yield what you want. However, the Web isn't always so neat and tidy. As you've seen, spiders are imperfect, and every hand-crafted resource index is imperfect. Until the development of advanced artificial intelligence software (smart spiders) that can efficiently and intelligently scour the Web and the Net for resources, you'll have to use the most powerful intelligence agent possible—*you.*

In this chapter, I ask you to drop your spiders, subject trees, and machine lists and learn how to surf. Or, if discovering the new and the quirky is something you want to do anyway, surfing might be your thing. The term *surfing* used here refers to the experience of encountering information and communication in cyberspace in nonlinear (and sometimes nonlogical) ways.

There are some practical reasons for learning how to surf:

- To keep up with new and developing tools that will help you use the Net more effectively
- To build your awareness of resources and activities in your field of study or area of interest
- To experience serendipity—a rare moment when you find something very useful among the large volume of information on the Net
- To stay current in your awareness of what is out there as well as possible on the Net
- To develop your awareness of the state of Net information quality in your area of interest

Surfing is an active, wide-ranging navigation activity that requires you to not rely on any single software tool or list, but to employ a set of skills drawing on insight for the *feel* of the Net. You can't surf by just clicking down lists of resources, although that activity is a part of surfing. You can't surf by just using spiders, trees, or space maps of the Net, although you will use all of those searching techniques and skills in combination to surf. Surfing means crawling and running along the links of the Web and beyond its edge into the trees of Gopher space, the archives of FTP space, and the scores and lists of WAIS responses. While other means of searching rely on your analytic, logical skills to find resources, surfing involves using your intuition, a feeling that can only develop over time in a holistic experience of a network's resources and the people behind it. The philosophy of surfing draws on the principle that you might not know what you want on the Web, but you'll know it when you see it.

Introduction to Surfing

The key to surfing is to remember that you *integrate* all searching methods with your own developed *intuition and subjective judgement* drawing on *a set of specialized and advanced navigation techniques* driven and tempered by your own *personal style and tastes.* Surfing involves working subjectively from a logically acquired set of information using skills that are both analytical and physical. Surfing involves the feeling you have when you are encountering networked information and communication. If you do not have all senses or body movements possible, you can develop what you have to experience the Net. To surf involves transferring many network-access techniques acquired through language, logic, and analytic reasoning, to intuitive responses and muscular reactions, much the way a tennis player practices a serve over and over both to perfect it and to make it automatic and available in the dynamic flow of a competition.

This may sound like I'm advocating a very strange approach to finding and experiencing network information. You don't have to change your life or abandon all reasoning, but only be open to a different way of looking at how you interact with the people and resources on a network. Moreover, in this view of my "guide to surfing," you can pick and choose from among the techniques described here. Choose what works best and seems right for you.

Initial Considerations

When surfing, you'll find that you will be physically, emotionally, and mentally taxed—you'll encounter large amounts of information rapidly and make quick judgements about where your attention and concentration should go next. Carpal tunnel syndrome and other physical ailments are realistic concerns, particularly if you use repeated physical actions to perform a task. You should consult a physician if you experience any pain or discomfort using a keyboard, mouse, or computer monitor.

You'll also need to keep track of the time of day you surf and the amount of time you spend. If you share resources, don't tie up a computer. Surfing is not necessarily a waste of time, but you will be using time and finding many, many resources you don't want; therefore, use good judgement about the resources you tie up. Moreover, you might find that you lose track of time when you are accessing large amounts of information—you might even consider setting an alarm so that you don't overdo it! Late nights and weekends are usually off-peak usage hours for Web access at your local site (but these same times may be peak hours somewhere else on the Web). Surfing during your local off-peak times will usually help minimize the drain on the network while giving you better responses.

Coping with Information

Many people find the large amount of information they encounter on the network daunting. If you are a new user, you'll need to develop skills to skim hypertext. You should read in detail only those resources and pages that are the most valuable to you. Without skills to cope with large amounts of information, you'll suffer information overload and flounder in less valuable information. Your goal is not to read everything, but to discover what's out there and become current in Net resources related to your area of interest. Here are some tips to avoid information overload:

1. **Pace yourself.** Only you know how much computer interaction you can take. If you know that an hour's worth is going to give you a headache or frustrate you, it's probably best not to push yourself beyond that. You will become more adept at surfing as you are rewarded with valuable information from the Net, not as a result of pushing your tolerance limits.

2. **Don't read everything.** While you'll need to use the navigation skills we talked about in Chapter 15, "Browser Operations," and pay attention to the indicators on your browser while going through the Web, don't feel compelled to read all the text on a screen. In my own classes, I've seen many students start at the top of a screen and read down. This is not necessarily the best strategy. We'll talk about specifics in the next section, but be aware that surfing does not necessarily mean reading word-for-word all the text on a screen.

3. **Pay attention to the information's space, texture, and cues.** While encountering networked information, ask yourself the following:

   ■ What *information space* is this? (Gopher, FTP, WAIS, HTTP?) The answer to this question helps you perform the basic navigation skills we talked about in Chapter 15.

   ■ What is the *information's texture*? By texture I mean the media composition and organizational structure of the information. Hypertext in HTML is one identification of a media texture. Another example of a media texture is a Gopher or FTP menu that has many multimedia icons (for sound, binary files, graphics, movies). Besides medium, another aspect of texture is information structure: Do you see many symbols for directories or directories and files? Still another aspect of information texture is interconnections: Are you at the home page of a much larger set of connected documents? Or are you at a document buried deep in a web? This texture information gives you immediate clues about the site's organization as well as what kind of material you'll find there. If you've just come into a site and the texture of what you see is varied (many different icons for directories, text files, graphics files all mixed together), you may have stumbled into the "back closet" where you'll expect to see very little orientation or explanatory information. In contrast, you might reach the "front door" of a site, with "About this server" or "README" links immediately apparent.

■ What navigation *cues* can you see immediately? For example, in hypertext, can you see links back to a "front" or home page? If at an FTP site, do you see a file folder for "Parent directory"? If on a Gopher, can you see any menu entries for orientation information? What navigation cues (links back to home, links to parent directories, links to README files or orientation information) can you see? Are you at the home page for a group of documents?

■ What information *cues* can you see immediately? What text appears in the "Document Title" window on the front panel of the Mosaic browser? What does this title mean to you? What does the URL tell you about the host and resource type? What does the heading information in the document tell you? Is there a clearly stated purpose for the resource you are looking at?

4. **Travel light.** Avoid saving information or files until you are sure you want them. If you consider a resource potentially valuable, put a reference to it on your hotlist. I've seen students often want to print a page they find interesting. This perhaps comes from being attuned to print and wanting to "feel" information in a familiar medium, rather than on the computer, which, to a new user, may seem a capricious barrier been themselves and the information. At first, you may feel a need to print screens and save files to your home disk. There may be good reasons to do so (resources *can* disappear or their network connections become lost). However, as you gain experience, you'll feel more confident that you will be able to track down a resource again, perhaps by using a spider. By traveling light, you'll save disk space, time, resources, and attention, and you'll also free yourself up to move on to new resources.

5. **Move on.** Surfing involves the discovery phase of encountering information. You should certainly spend some time while surfing contemplating the value and meaning of what you find, but you shouldn't get bogged down in any one particular site. Avoid the tendency some new users have to consider the first site they find on a particular subject to be the definitive one. The composition of sites and quality of "definitiveness" changes dynamically. In a manner of hours or minutes, a developer at one sight might add valuable resources another site doesn't have. In fact, you can't consider any information on the Web to be static.

The point of the preceding advice on coping with information is to increase your ability to sift through large volumes of information and communication. This will increase the probability that you'll find valuable resources with the quantity and quantity you desire.

Equipment

Not everyone has high-speed connections to the Internet offering rapid access to resources, particularly graphics. If you have a slow Internet connection, you should consider turning graphics off (Options / Delay Image Loading) on the Mosaic main panel. Also, you'll have to access the network during off-peak hours. A slow Internet connection also means that you'll pay closer attention to the texture of information you find—you might need to avoid graphics and movie files, or be more selective in the ones you access.

Outlook

Unlike the previous chapters in which I've discussed searching in terms of an "indexing mode" (by subject, by keyword, by space), the goal for surfing is not necessarily to find information according to an indexing mode, but to encounter information *for its own sake*. You might possibly encounter information just for the purpose of building awareness, or with the intent of grabbing URLs and references within hypertext so that you can later navigate more carefully using other techniques.

Skills

In order to encounter large amounts of information using a Web browser, you'll need to have good basic navigation skills (see Chapter 15, "Browser Operations") as well as good file management skills. You should know how to save and manage files in directories, as well as know the basics of navigating in your computer's operating system.

Surfing

Prepared with an awareness of how to cope with information overload, special considerations for the equipment you have, and an understanding of an outlook, let's look in detail at some techniques. I'll describe some general considerations that you can use in any situation and also provide examples to illustrate specific techniques.

We'll start by looking at preparations you can take and then some ideas for coming up with starting points for surfing. Then, we'll look at how you can use these starting points to encounter more information.

Preparations

Find a comfortable place to work with the computer. Often it is helpful to have an environment in which you won't be distracted and you can concentrate fully. You might consider turning off any incoming message icons (like a mailbox icon) that may be on your screen, and image loading (Options / Delay Image Loading) on the Mosaic browser.

You'll also want to have an e-mail communications program available and links to your favorite spiders, trees, or machine lists in your hotlist.

Starting Points

Your first goal is to get started in a process of encountering information. Although you don't need to have a specific mode of information discovery in mind when you start, you need to have some link that will take you to entry points.

Here are some techniques to generate starting points:

1. **What's new pages.** When Mosaic was developed, its creators started an HTML page entitled, "What's New with NCSA Mosaic." Begun as a simple service to help the Web community, it grew in popularity to become one of the most accessed documents on the Web and won the "Most Important Service Concept" in the "Best of the Web '94" contest. Because of this award and the popularity of Mosaic's "What's New," many more information providers have created "What's New" pages of their own. These pages serve as some of the most valuable entry points for encountering new networked information. Through tradition, and because it is closely tied to the rapid growth of the Web associated with the development of Mosaic, the "What's New with NCSA Mosaic" page is perhaps one of the best single starting points on the Web, serving the need for a central forum for information about the Web, not necessarily just to Mosaic-related resources.

   The Mosaic "What's New" page's URL is `http://www.ncsa.uiuc.edu/SDG/Software/Mosaic/Docs/whats-new.html` and its appearance is shown in Figure 21.1.

FIGURE 21.1.

What's New With NCSA Mosaic.

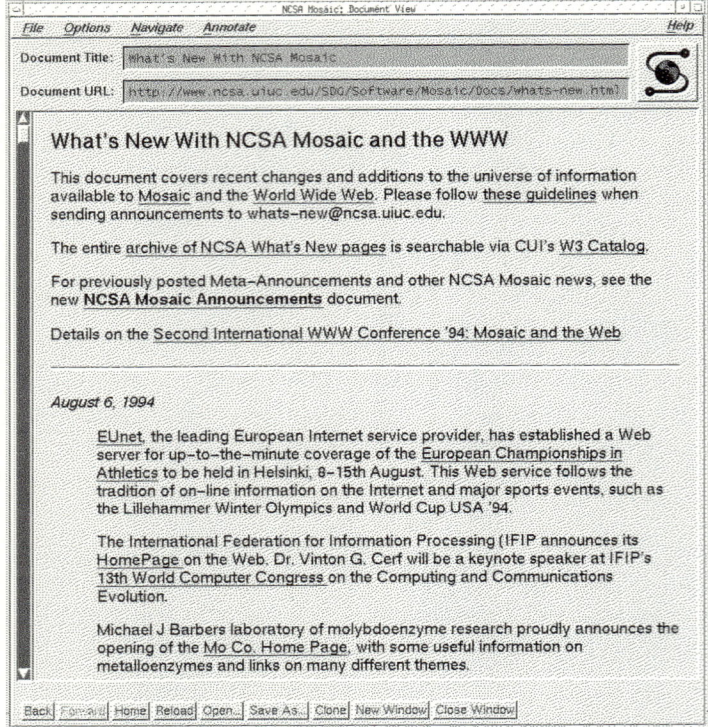

The Mosaic "What's New" page serves a Web-wide interest audience. If you're interested in new resources in this context, this page is a good starting point.

There are specialized "what's new" pages, particular to specific servers, that can benefit you. A technique to find these pages is to use a Web spider to locate the phrase "What's New." If you know you want to surf in a particular subject area, examine the list for a "What's New" page on servers that you know will give you the best coverage for that subject. How do you know which servers will give you the best coverage? You can examine the results of a Web Crawler search for key words in your area of interest.

2. **Personal Home Pages.** The plethora of links on the Web makes individual perception valuable, and the personal home pages of people that share your interest often contain links to new resources and information, sifted by their tastes and judgement. These personal home pages may give you excellent jumping off points into the Web. There is no central "white pages" for the Web, although there are several initiatives being developed to collect home pages. (See `http://www.rpi.edu/Internet/Guides/decemj/icmc/culture-people.html`).

A WebCrawler search for the keywords "personal home page" (and perhaps further words in your area of speciality) will yield both personal home pages of individuals as well as collections of home pages. Finding such a Web community devoted to your area of interest may be a goldmine for interesting personal home pages.

3. **Institutions.** As you explore the Web, you'll find that the Web servers of institutions (academic, commercial, nonprofit) contain just the links you want to have for exploring the Web. However, the caveat here is that institutional Web servers vary in information maintenance and development activities. You'll have to explore these institutional pages (obtained through any of the search techniques we've talked about so far) to find out which ones develop links to *new* resources most consistently. If you find institutional links with good new Web information coverage in your area of interest, these may be good surfing starting points.

4. **Language strategies.** To find sites with a with a particular (cultural, scientific, or information) orientation, use your knowledge of language conventions of that community to locate resources. For example, if you are looking for information about youth activities on the Web (actually a very well represented topic with the large proportion of younger people using the Web), use spider searches for title terms like "cool sites" or "fun sites." Use search terms for specialized vocabulary of that community or culture. Search for keywords that serve as language markers (words or phrases that uniquely identify members of a community) or terms that distinguish one community from another.

5. **Guessing.** This is a technique that perhaps is least likely to succeed but its payoff could be great. Let's say that you want to find out about a new company called XYZ Corporation. You suspect they probably have a Web server. You could do a spider search, but if no spider has yet visited the XYZ corporation's server, its page will not show up in any database. A scan of the What's New Mosaic Page (through the CUI Catalog mentioned in Chapter 19, "Spiders and Indexes: Keyword-Oriented Searching") might also yield a match, or a search of a geographical listing of Web servers. Let say these don't yield a match. What do you do?

   Try opening the URL `http://www.xyz.com`. You'll get an error message if the server does not exist or if the server's public access to files is turned off. If you are lucky, you'll find the home page for XYZ company neatly appear in the browser display window.

6. **Random.** This is perhaps the riskiest and least likely way to yield good information but can be used as a creative way to build your awareness of the kind of resource you might be looking for and possibilities for Web communication and expression.

> **NOTE**
>
> Yuval Fisher has created a page with "not exactly a thousand" points that connect to URLs all over (see Figure 21.2). This is perhaps the most random you can get.

FIGURE 21.2.

A Thousand Points of Sites.

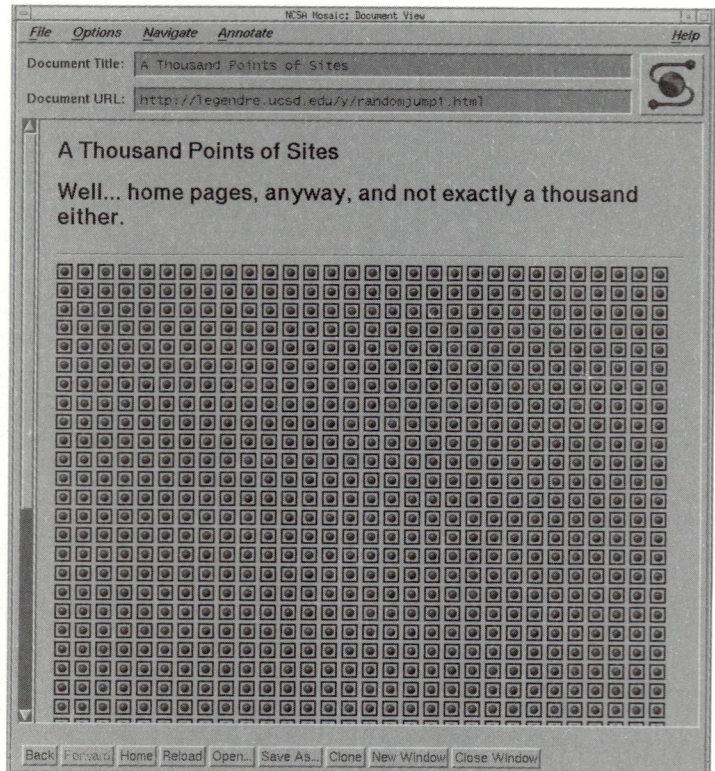

Other (nearly) random ways to enter the Web:

- Comprehensive lists of Web servers, generated from spiders. Find these lists by doing a spider search on "web sites."
- Try a Worm title search (so that the order of the words matter) on "web sites" in addition to a WebCrawler search.
- Use the Virtual Tourist or CERN's Web server list as starting points.

Another way to get (nearly) random sites to explore is to look for "free-for-all" pages. These pages developed out of early applications of the HTML Forms facility for allowing people to add links to a page. The resulting free-for-all pages grow very rapidly, as they are a shared, public space for announcing new resources. You'll find several free-for-all pages, and their contents will often be oriented to a particular outlook or area of interest. These lists serve as a kind of public wall on which hypergraffiti in the form of links are placed. Because these are often unmoderated (unlike the NCSA "What's New" postings), the tone of the entries is far from "official."

The preceding techniques are specific ways to generate starting points. Like other activities in surfing, there is no single technique that can yield the results you want, nor is there a comprehensive list of logical procedures to find the best starting points. You'll develop your own techniques, but remember: Generating starting points for surfing is not the same as simply applying search strategies; rather, it involves integrating and extending your current awareness of what the Web does and could potentially offer.

Into the Web

Using one of the techniques for starting points given previously, and armed with the advice given earlier for coping with information, you're ready to start surfing. Because all sessions are different, therefore, I'll use an example to illustrate, and then I'll cover more general techniques and tips.

Here's the example: I'm interested in cyberspace—what people are doing, why, and what artifacts, communication, and information exist there. This is a huge subject area, but it is an area of study in which I need to keep current, particularly with regard to new Web resources. I'll go through a step-by-step session in which I add to my current knowledge of what is out there.

■ Starting point. I know the Mosaic "What's New" list contains a gold mine of new *applications* of cyberspace tools like the Web, and these are interesting in themselves as objects of study, but I'd like to scan the Web for new developments or thought in the study of cyberspace. There's no single institution that studies cyberspace in all its details; therefore, I won't select an institutional Web sever as a jumping-off point. Rather, I'll use the WebCrawler to generate a list of possible resources. Using WebCrawler, I use the keyword cyberspace. I use this word because I know it is a marker in the community of people who study online communication. I get the results shown in Figure 21.3.

FIGURE 21.3.

Web Crawler search results for cyberspace.

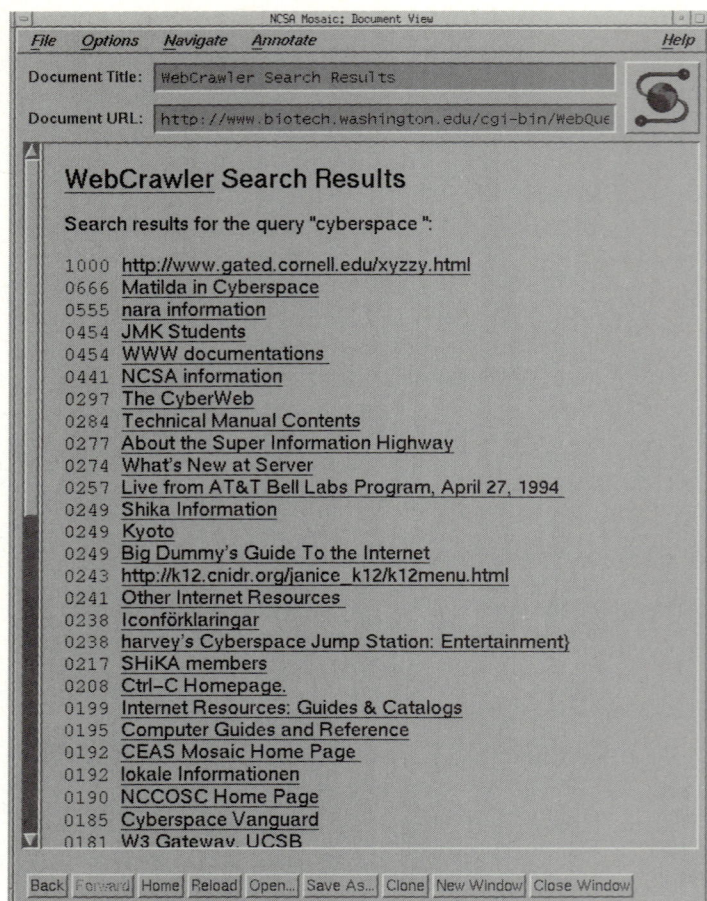

■ I immediately look over the list that I've generated.

1. I quickly judge the size of the search results by glancing at the scrollbar on the left of the Mosaic panel. It shows about half of the list exposed. This size feels about right. If I had generated far too large of a list (or received no hits at all), I would have revised the WebCrawler search.

2. Because the Crawler uses an indexing system to assign "scores" to retrieved resources, I know that the documents that are likely to be my best matches are at the top. I quickly note the value of the second document display— 0666. I know the first document is always 1000 and the scores go down from there. I look down the list of scores and see that they drop by roughly 100 for each entry, level off in the 200s, and go down to the 180s. This

slope in the score tells me that the 200–180 range documents will be roughly the same in their treatment of the word cyberspace. I make a mental note that I seem to have a high hit group (the first six items) and a moderate hit group in the 200s to upper 100s.

3. I look over the titles in the list. I notice the prefix Cyber occurring in some titles, a language hint of a resource that could be very relevant. I also see references to Internet and Web documentation. I'm not necessarily trying to build my awareness of that area of cyberspace now, so I mentally "shade out" those titles on the list.

4. I look for any odd items—items that are unusual in terms of what I've seen before or in the title displayed.

   The very first resource, http://www.gated.cornell.edu/xyzzy.html, is untitled. This tells me that the author probably did not use appropriate <TITLE> tags in the document to give it a title. This cue tells me that this source might be a personal page or a very unofficial document. The name of the document xyzzy.html puzzles me a bit; it seems like the name of a test file. This may be a work in progress.

   The very last resource (not shown in the figure) has the title "Chalmers University of Technology." This raises my interest. I place the cursor over this title to see the URL to which it points. The URL is http://www.chalmers.se/Home-E.html. The document has a low score, but maybe this university now has a Department of Cyberspace! 8-).

   None of the other titles in the list particularly piques my interest, but all the titles with cyber or related words catch my attention.

3. Based on my scan of the Crawler list, I decide it will serve as my surfing "base" for a while. I can't put the results of this search as a reference in my hotlist, so I'll make sure I don't click on the "Back" button while in this screen and take a different path from that document until I'm through with this list as my base. (If I did, my Crawler search results in the windows history would be "nipped off.")

4. I'm so curious about the "Chalmers University of Technology" that I choose that link first. (Logic might have said to choose the document with the 1000 score first, rather than the very last!) In the Chalmers document (Figure 21.4), I immediately note *space, texture,* and *cues.*

FIGURE 21.4.

*Welcome to Chalmers
University of Technology.*

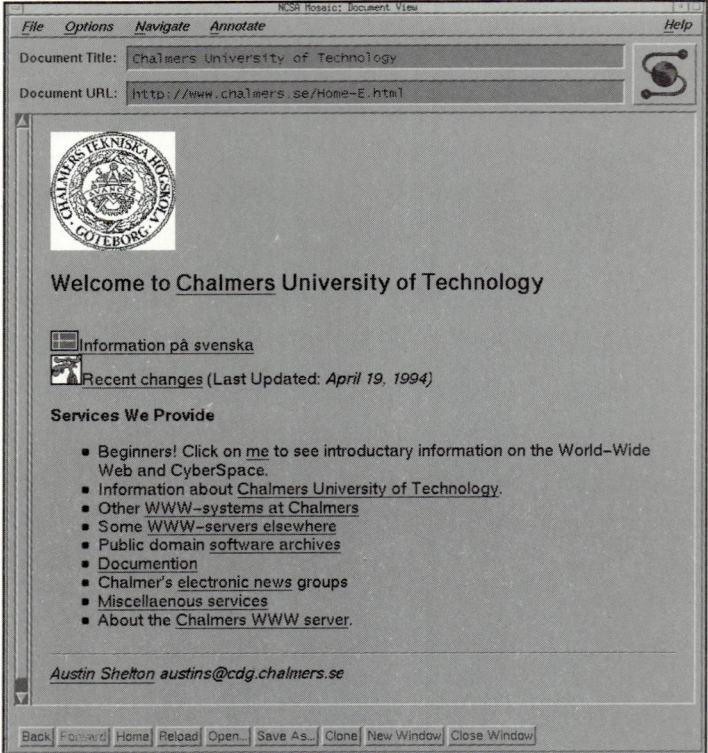

I can see by first glance that I'm in a standard campus wide information system welcome screen. I knew before I even entered this screen that it would probably be in hypertext (the `.html` ending of the URL). The images shown in Figure 21.4 originally were delayed; I retrieved them by clicking on them once.

The appearance looks "official." It looks like a university-sponsored page rather than in informal page by a student, particularly since the URL doesn't have an extremely long name. I note that there is a link on the name "Chalmers" itself, possibly leading to more explanation.

I note the Swedish flag and the Swedish phrase next to it. The cartoon icon next to the "Recent changes" link gives me a more informal feel about the page. I know the "recent changes" link leads to the "What's New" service for this server.

Other cues I note are that the page developer's name, link, and e-mail address are at the bottom.

Based on all this information about space, texture, and cues, I feel more assured that I'm in a very common form of a university Web page.

Now I'm curious about why this page matched `cyberspace`. At first, I don't see the word at all (it is not in any of the hotspots). So I use the File / Find In Current... option from the Mosaic main panel to find the word `cyberspace`. It appears in the first bulleted item, in the phrase "information on the World-Wide Web and CyberSpace." I realize that this is the kind of new information I don't want to surf right now, so I make a mental note that the WebCrawler's scoring was a pretty good indicator in this case and click on the "Back" button.

5. Since my worst-scoring document was not what I wanted, I try the best-scoring one. After clicking, I see the single phrase,

```
This section of cyberspace is temporarily inaccessible.
```

This is not a standard error message (generated as a response from a Web server), but rather text that someone wrote in this file as a holder until he or she could complete the project. The sentence itself doesn't convey anything about the project and does not imply that the project deals with cyberspace itself. This document probably received a high score because the word "cyberspace," proportionate to the total number of words, is higher than in the other documents. I make a mental note that the WebCrawler's scoring can do this. I click on the "Back" button.

6. Now, I decide to tackle the "high-scoring group." Of these, the second item, "Matilda in Cyberspace" seems most promising as possibly an account (or even fiction) dealing with cyberspace. I click on the link, and get a message in the Mosaic window:

```
Matilda in Cyberspace has moved to snazzy.anu.edu.au.
The URL is http://snazzy.anu.edu.au/Matilda/start.html.
Select to connect.
```

I click on the "Select to connect" link and see Figure 21.5.

I quickly see that this is a kind of "What's New" for Australia. I don't necessarily want this kind of information, and I'm about to leave when my eye catches the link under the page developer's name. The label is "Centre for Networked Access to Scholarly Information."

This is a serendipitous discovery—or is it? A person developing online information may perhaps be more likely to use the term cyberspace. In turn, that individual's work may revolve around the area in which I'm interested, including issues such as networked scholarly information.

FIGURE 21.5.

Matilda in Cyberspace.

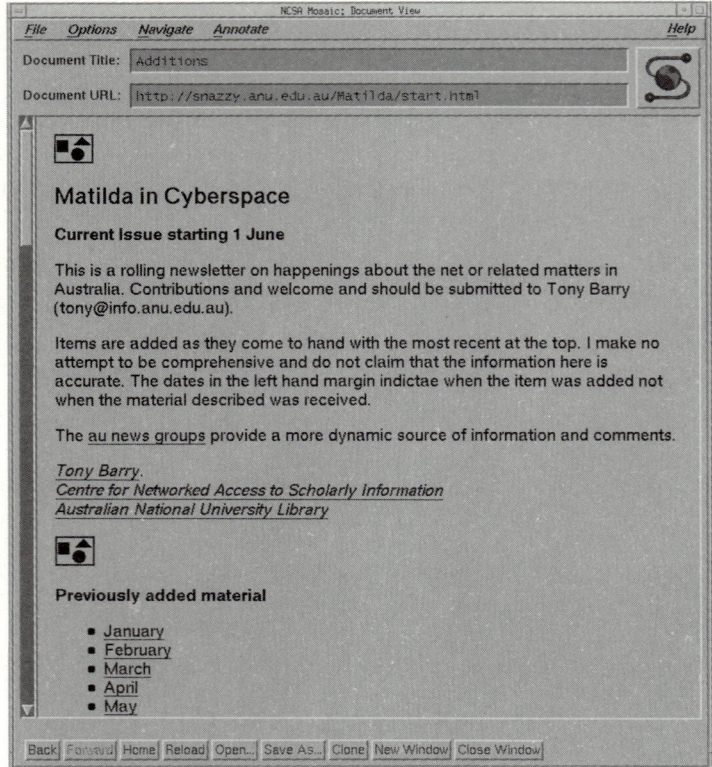

I click the link to "Centre for Networked Access to Scholarly Information," and get the message:

```
404 Not Found
The requested URL /Default.html was not found on this server.
```

Hmm. I know that a Web server can be set up to serve a default document (that is, when `http://host` is the URL, given without a filename path).

Therefore, I'll open the URL to the server, without giving a pathname to a specific file. I copy the `http://info.anu.edu.au` portion of the URL, using the mouse and cursor into the copy buffer. I click the "Open.." button and paste the URL in the URL to open box. Then I click the "Back" button on Mosaic's main panel. Why didn't I click the "Open" right away? Because it has been my experience that trying to bring up a new URL on the same host that caused the error message currently displayed in the Mosaic for X Window never seems to work. (This is an example of a tools-experience sense that comes with use.) After clicking on the "Back" button, I open the URL `http://info.anu.edu.au`. I get the screen shown in Figure 21.6.

FIGURE 21.6.

Electronic Library Information Service at ANU.

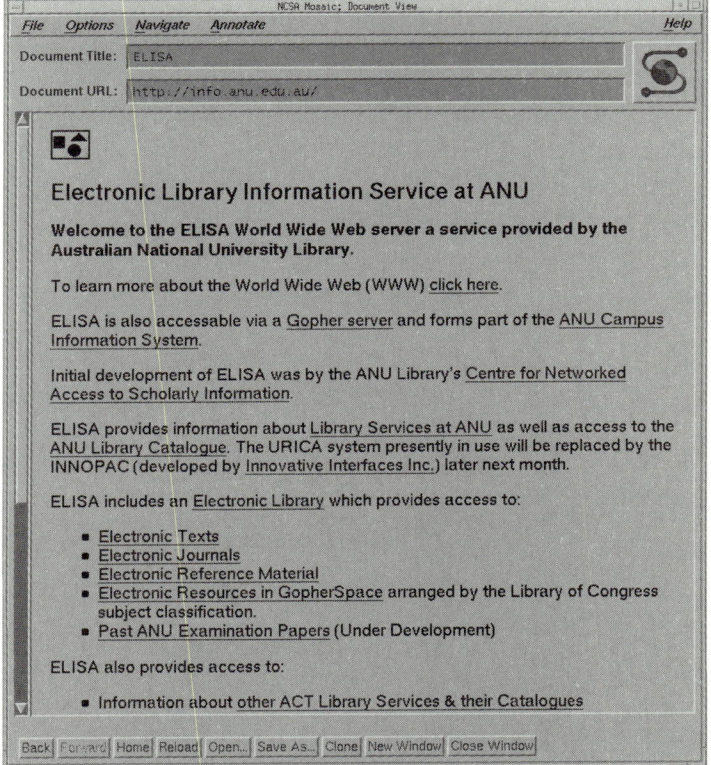

I see that this particular screen is oriented to the service at the Australian National University Library. However, the existence of the "Centre for Networked Access to Scholarly Information" there should provide a further place for exploring later on. I add the URL to my hotlist.

7. I click the "Back" button enough times so that I'm back to my WebCrawler search results. I see another promising entry, "Cyberspace Vanguard." Placing the cursor over it, though, I see that its URL, `http://thule.mt.cs.cmu.edu:8001/sf-clearing-house.html/zines/cyberspace-vanguard.html` indicates this is probably a science fiction magazine.

8. I look through my WebCrawler list and don't see any other entries that stand out. Having experience browsing cyberspace-related links, I recognize many entries from previous sessions. At this point, I think about making a new base for exploration. I don't return to Figure 21.5, "Matilda in Cyberspace," because I already have that entry on my hotlist for a later, more detailed perusal. My original search term "cyberspace" was very broad, and it brought me hits that were not—once seen in context—a good match. I return to the WebCrawler and

use the search terms `study network communication community`. Again, I generate a list. My approach to scanning this list is to use a similar methodology as illustrated in steps 1–7 shown previously. However, if I'm truly trying to build my awareness, I should be cautious about using the same spider, as its database is limited by where it has crawled.

9. I decide to do a subject-based search. I bring up Galaxy's (Figure 18.5) page, and look through its top-level menu. Under the main heading for "Community," I find the link "Networking and Communication." This is a subject list I often peruse to maintain my knowledge of community-based networking and communication resources.

10. I quickly scan the "Networking and Communication" list. Since this list is hand-crafted (that is, individual developers add information to it as opposed to being a spider-generated list), I know that its criteria for inclusion is different from that for a WebCrawler search. The individual entries may be more relevant (I know from experience that Galaxy's entries usually are quite good). Scanning quickly through the entries in the list, I try several, evaluating the information space, texture, and cues, as well as the question "do I want this to be a new base?" for surfing. I want to find a good selection (one to two Mosaic screens-full) of links from which to explore and use as a base. I continue, looking for serendipitous discoveries to put on my hotlist, and keeping an eye out for new forms of information presentation.

The preceding list is actually a fairly brief portion of my surfing session, about five minutes' worth. Since I hadn't spent much time in Galaxy recently, I revisit some of the subject trees dealing with my areas of interest: Engineering & Technology/Computer Technology, Reference & Interdisciplinary Information/Internet & Networking. This checking-over of a topic tree that I like builds my awareness of new resources.

You can see from the above account that

- I move as efficiently as possible, making use of cues about space (what information space is it), texture (media form, structure, and organization), and others, such as navigational and information/cues.

- I employ a *base*—a single Web page, list, or results of a spider search to return to several times after delving down its branches. If I find another base while searching, I may abandon the original one (although I often end a surfing session by clicking the Back button many times), and re-encounter bases further up the windows history list.

- I use my hotlist to store promising entries, not passing final judgement as to the value of the resource, but gathering links that I will later go through as part of a regular hotlist and web-weaving maintenance session. In the hotlist maintenance session, the hotlist itself serves as a base.

■ I let my interests and intuition, not always logic, guide me in my search (A good example is my check of the *lowest* scoring document first from the WebCrawler search). Through experience, I know right away when I see a novel way of presenting information on the Web or a novel *kind* of information on the Web. This catches my eye to look further. By making mistakes and also finding valuable things, I build my awareness.

Tips

The previous section described a sample session of using a variety of methods to search for information. There's no typical surfing session—and the actual technique relies on previous awareness and accumulated understanding. Here's some specific tips that may help you build this awareness:

1. Have a set of regular pages that you check, possibly including the following:
   - ■ "What's New" pages
   - ■ Your favorite spider search
   - ■ Your favorite subject tree links
   - ■ Home pages of people who have similar interests

2. Collaborate with others on locating, identifying, and reviewing network resources. You may work out a shared resource database among a group of people with similar interests as yours. You can use this as a regular way to collaborate.

3. Regularly surf. Set aside a time period in which you regularly sweep through your starting points. Remember, allow for new and unique resources to come to your attention through "What's New" pages. Find out how often your favorite spider walks and recheck its database for matches against phrases you've used before.

4. Build your own mental model of the Web and its resources. You might try to sketch it graphically or create a verbal or hypertext map of resources important to you. Try not to *duplicate* existing collections of resources, but to point to them through your own links.

Navigator's Check

We've seen how surfing integrates our other searching methods—trees, spiders, and machines—into a process of seeking and trying out links. Surfing relies heavily on your awareness of the structure of the Web, finely tuned navigation skills for using your browser, and the use of searching techniques. Surfing might be the least likely form of searching to yield useful results; but, without surfing as a technique within your repertoire, you won't be able to easily find new resources, make new connections, or see what can be possible.

As a general guide to surfing, remember the following:

- Have a set of starting points that you regularly check, including "What's New" pages, as well as subject trees in your area, and the home pages of institutions and individuals.

- Based on your starting points, arrive at (possibly generating through a spider search) a page with the "right" number of links on it. Use this page as a base for exploring the links leading off it.

- Abandon the base page for a new base as soon as you find a page that exceeds the first base in terms of your judgement of the link's value.

- Work this pattern recursively; save all promising links in your hotlist.

- At a later time, go through your hotlist and examine the links more carefully for relevance and value; share the valuable links with people who have common interests as yours.

Elephants: Putting It All Together and More

22

by John December

No, *elephants* are not still another kind of creature that roams the Web. I'll use elephants (the real-world kind) as an example topic for an information search of the Web and Net in this chapter. This example will put to use the navigation techniques we've covered so far. This example also will show some of the flexibility of technique and critical skills used during information gathering and retrieval.

Searching for Elephants

We've already talked about how the Web and the Net are not necessarily a good source for peer-reviewed academic, research, or other kinds of official information. This more rigorously reviewed information can best be found in a (paper-based) library (although, gradually, more of this kind of material is making its way to the Web). What the Net might be able to do is to help you gain awareness of collections, people, and institutions that may point you to other useful resources on the Net or off of it. In fact, this associative, context-generating nature of Net information, particularly typical of the Web, may be the ultimate power of the Net—to bring you into contact with the people and resources directly involved in the detailed study of a subject.

All the search strategies we've talked about in this part won't help you discover everything there is to know about elephants. Only a small fraction of information and resources about the detailed, scientific study of elephants is on the Net, and it would be a mistake to lead you to believe that the Net can tell you everything. Indeed, we've seen how the Net tools for even finding what's on the Net are imperfect. Moreover, the Net itself isn't a "black box" where questions go in and answers come out, but a collection of resources behind which are *people*—imperfect or passionate, knowledgeable or naive, helpful or cynical. Don't look upon our search through the Net as simply a process of encountering data—people made all of it, and the human side of the resources may be the most valuable connection you might make.

Having said this, let's use our elephants example to illustrate both the value as well as the pitfalls of finding Net information about a topic. Let's say your situation is as follows: You are gathering information about elephants for an audience of high school sophomores. You're not exactly sure what kind of resources you want—there are no set information requirements you must fill, but you know you generally want to find the following:

- Context information—everything from geographic and climate data about where elephants live to political and social issues involved with elephants' interaction with people

- Specific information—material about elephants themselves, what they eat, their life cycles, status of species endangerment, social groups, etc.

- The role of elephants in human activities—circus elephants and, for example, elephants as workers

■ Perhaps even artistic or literary works that involve elephants

You know you want more information than just this, but you're not sure what that might be (you'll know it when you see it). Let's assume also that you have good library skills, you're on good terms with your reference librarian, and that you'll be able to (and will) locate authoritative sources of information to verify Net resources, whenever the nature of the information and how you use it requires a close check for accuracy. Situations requiring close checks could be when the Net information you find is used in research, in formal academic contexts, or any other situation where the accuracy of the information is paramount or when you have a "gut feel" that such a check is necessary. You'll find that some kinds of information don't need such a thorough check in certain contexts. For example, if you find a photograph of an elephant, you'll have to decide whether you can judge whether it is an elephant or not (and verify the kind of elephant represented in the image if that is important).

Starting Points

I've mentioned how the Net is a powerful way for you to make connections with people of specific interests and expertise. Don't mistake this close connection to experts as an excuse not to do the Web-work of making a good-faith effort to find out information on your own, particularly basic fact information. You might "listen in" on an electronic mail discussion group devoted to a particular speciality, but the transient nature of mail is such that the participants are not usually involved in discussing basic or orientation information about their specialty.

STARTING AT THE WRONG PLACE

Don't use close connections with groups of experts as an excuse for not doing your homework. The following electronic mail message originally occurred in a discussion group called `comp.risks`, which is devoted to discussing risks to the public from computers and users of them. The discussion group, `BIOSPH-L@UBVM.BITNET`, mentioned in the post, is an electronic discussion list, distributed through electronic mail, devoted to discussing issues related to the biosphere.

```
Getting information from discussion groups
by
Dan Yurman (dyurman@igc.apc.org)

Perhaps one disturbing trend as more people use Internet is the practice
by college students of using subject matter listservs as sources of first
resort for information they should be looking up in their university library.
Every year BIOSPH-L@UBVM.BITNET, a list dealing with environmental issues, is
```

flooded with ill-expressed questions that should not be addressed to the list. These include questions such as "what is hazardous waste," etc. Another which came up today was a question which could be answered by using the Statistical Abstract of the US or any World Almanac, etc.

Last year a hot debate erupted when a graduate teaching assistant at a major, dare I say, top 10, Eastern university, assigned a class of undergraduates to use Internet to seek information on research paper topics. The TA did not instruct the students to use the library first and then pose well formulated questions to the net. BIOSPH-L was flooded with questions on basic environmental science.

Both the TA and the students were outraged by the complaints they received from list readers who objected to being asked fundamental questions that ought to be dealt with by the students themselves. The root cause appears to be neither the TA nor the students had any idea who was at the other end of the line. All they saw was a computer that should be giving them answers.

What was said to them repeatedly is this. The courtesy issue is that traffic on BIOSPH-L is voluntary. If you want people to take the time to answer your questions, indicate you have done some legwork on your own and have a genuine problem looking for additional information. Otherwise, you are soaking up volunteer resources which could be better used to meet needs not answered elsewhere.

Also, neither the students nor the TA took kindly to suggestions that if they absolutely insisted on using computer terminals instead of (gasp) books, that there are online services which for a fee will gladly give them the information they want.

If going directly to experts is not the best place to start, what is? I suppose our ideal find would be an "Elephant Home Page" or the "Elephant MetaCenter" on the Web—an integrated presentation of resources and discussion on the many aspects of elephants, put together and maintained collaboratively by experts in the field. How might we find this?

1. A subject search might not be the quickest way. Elephants are more of a topic within larger areas of knowledge such as environmental or biological fields. Since we want to find out more about elephants than just their biology and environment, a subject-based approach may throw us into too many different subject-oriented searches.

2. A keyword oriented search sounds like a good start. The word *elephant* can't be used in too many other contexts, so the number of "false hits" we could get might be low.

3. A space-oriented search might not be a bad idea, either. Where do elephants live? Are there institutions in that geographic area with collections of information about elephants? A thing to keep in mind here is that the knowledge center for elephants might not be based in the same geographic region where elephants live.

4. Surfing probably isn't the way to start at all. We are trying to improve our awareness of Net resources about elephants, but we've no base to start from. We don't yet know of any starting points for surfing (What's New pages, free-for-all pages) that are specialized enough to yield us good results. Surfing for elephants is out for now.

Based on our options, it looks like a keyword search would be a good start. We've a selection of spiders to choose from (see Chapter 19, "Spiders and Indexes: Keyword-Oriented Searching"). Do we know of a specialized spider, perhaps an environmental or biological one? Our ideal would be an elephant spider, a spider that crawls on webs where elephant-related information is usually found. As of now, we really don't know of one. Among the spiders we do have:

1. Spiders that collect information from titles in HTML documents. *Pro:* This spider travels lighter, perhaps covers more ground. *Con:* The term *elephant* has to be somewhere in the title of the document.

2. Spiders that contain full text indices of Web pages. *Pro:* Any occurrence of the word *elephant* in the document will be a hit. *Con:* Any occurrence of the word *elephant* in the document will be a hit; and spiders that do this kind of searching can't travel as far.

Although a full-text spider search may represent a smaller part of the Web, it sounds more likely to lead us to relevant resources. A title search might yield something only if the word *elephant* is in the title field of the HTML document. A great page to find might have a title "All About Elephant Resources on the Web."

A WebCrawler Search for Elephants

Let's use the WebCrawler to do a full-text search of Web documents in its database. After entering the keyword `elephant` in the input box of the WebCrawler, we get the results shown in Figure 22.1.

FIGURE 22.1.

WebCrawler search results for elephant.

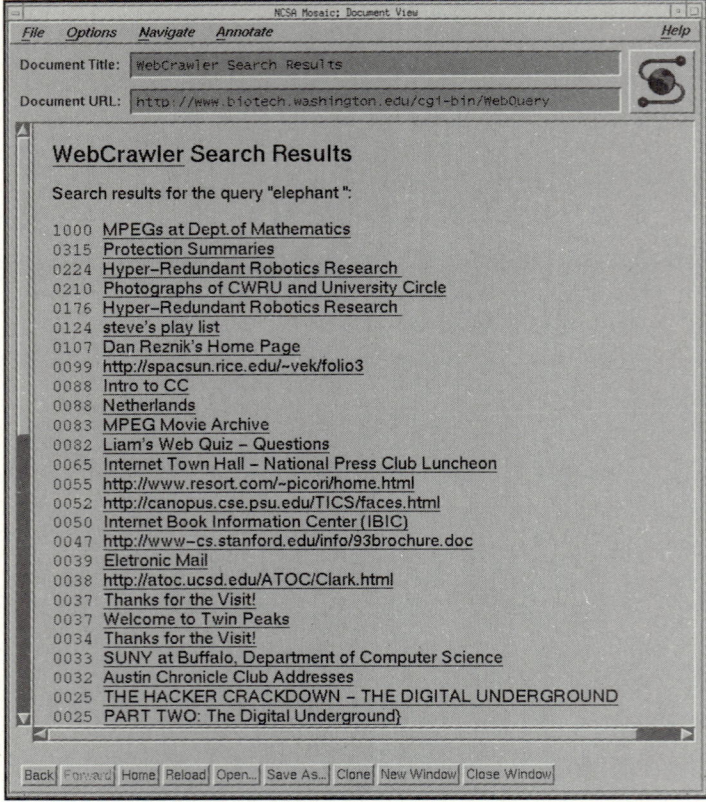

Some entries in the list look more promising than others. Remember, the word *elephant* appears in these resources, and the ones at the top have a higher score, so are judged (by the indexing system the WebCrawler uses) to be more relevant. This list is essentially a base from which we can use surfing techniques to examine other areas that seem interesting or relevant.

A quick scan of the list shows the following titles:

- "MPEGs at Dept. of Mathematics"   This is the very first entry. It is also refers to *MPEGs* which are a kind of movie format. The "Dept. of Mathematics" worries me, though. It clues me into suspecting that the use of the word *elephant* there is incidental, although the thought of an elephant movie (perhaps the Math department has one as a demonstration of MPEG movies) sounds enticing as a resource to get the attention of the audience.

- "Protection Summaries"   This sounds promising. Placing my cursor over the hotspot, I see that the URL is http://ash.lab.r1.fws.gov/cargo/protect.html. The gov in the host name indicates it is a U.S. Government Source. I'm not sure to what domain `fws.gov` refers. My guess is "Fish and Wildlife Service." If so, this could be a very authoritative source.

■ "Hyper-Redundant Robotics Research"   Robotic elephants would probably really catch the attention of the audience. But again, my suspicion is that the word *elephant* is used only incidentally.

Scanning down the rest of the list, I see a few other entries that I might check out further. The biggest lead so far, though, is the "Protection Law Summaries." I click on its hotspot and get what is shown in Figure 22.2.

FIGURE 22.2.

Protection Law Summaries.

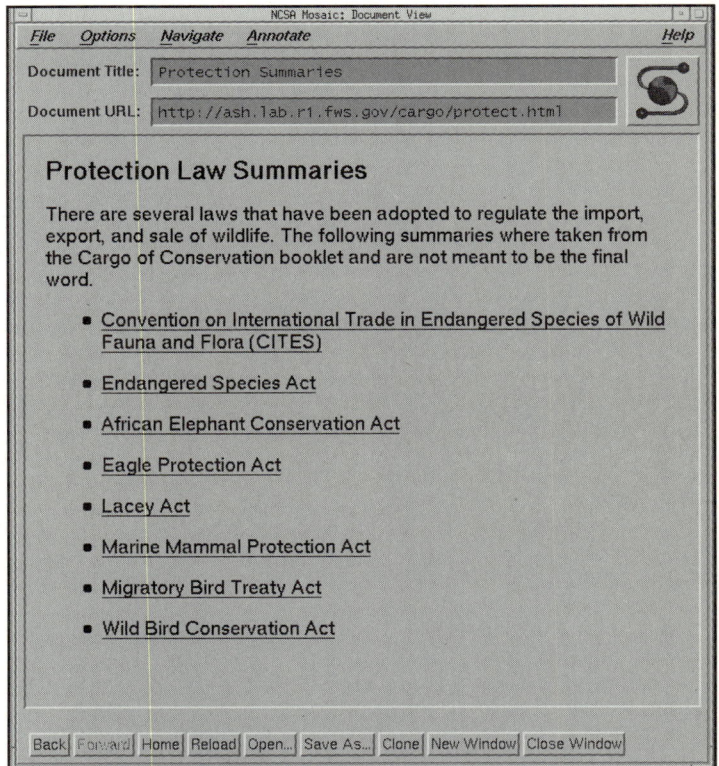

This looks like a good information source. I place a reference to this on my hotlist. The page refers to the "Cargo of Conservation booklet," which might be a lead on a government document to find.

Moreover, the "African Elephant Conservation Act" looks like a great specific source. I click on this link to find a narrative describing the act itself (a summary, not the actual legislation). This summary is written for the level of my audience. I save the reference to

it on my hotlist and quickly scan the document for any other links. There are none. I click the Back button. On the "Protection Law Summaries" page, the "Convention on International Trade in Endangered Species of Wild Fauna and Flora (CITES)" looks like good information, but I don't want to stray too far from information specifically about elephants. I've saved a link to this "Protection Law Summaries" page in my hotlist for detailed examination later.

On the "Protection Law Summaries" page, I begin to wonder if there are higher-level pages on the same Web server. There are no navigation links to them, but I see from the URL that I'm in a subdirectory called "cargo." I wonder what is at the top level for this host. I open the URL `http://ash.lab.r1.fws.gov` and find I'm at Figure 22.3.

FIGURE 22.3.

Forensic Science Web Server.

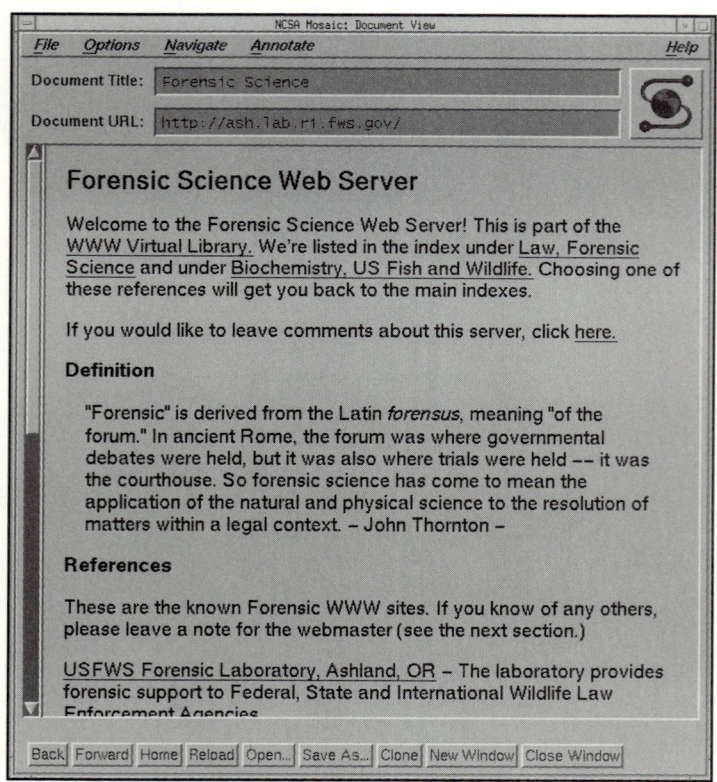

The title throws me off a bit: *forensic science?* But the narrative at the top of the page helps me realize that I'm now in CERN's Virtual Library subject tree. This particular page, as the narrative states, is part of "Law, Forensic Science" and "Biochemistry, US Fish and Wildlife." I don't understand the connection—although I suppose biochemistry has a great deal to do with forensic science. The link to "Biochemistry, US Fish and Wildlife" is promising as more background information. I click on it and see that I'm in the "Biosciences" page for CERN's Virtual Library subject tree, Figure 22.4.

FIGURE 22.4.

The World-Wide Web Virtual Library: Biosciences.

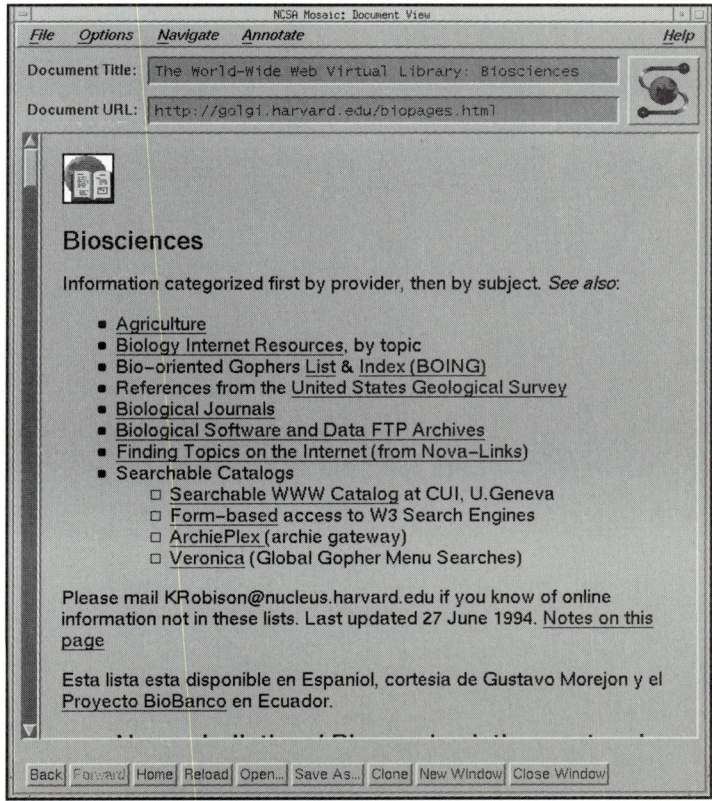

Again, I feel I'm straying from my specific interest in elephants, although I'm finding good background information. In fact, this Biosciences page looks like it could be a good source to keep for surfing after I exhaust some other possibilities back on the WebCrawler results page. After scanning down the Biosciences list quickly to see if anything like "All about elephants" jumps out at me, I save a reference to the page on my hotlist and hit the Back button until I'm back at the WebCrawler search results page (Figure 22.1).

At this point, I feel that I've obtained some good links to general biological information that I can search through later to find references to elephants. But I really want to get more specific. I look at the WebCrawler search results with the idea of finding something very particular to elephants. I try the following:

■ **"MPEGs at Dept. of Mathematics"** The MPEG movie listed is "Moglie and the little elephant," apparently a movie kept by this department as a demonstration of

MPEG capabilities. I click on the selection, which takes a while to come up (an entry in the list tells me the movie is 285KB). The movie takes so long to come up, I decide right away I would not use a direct link to it for the presentation or as a resource. I watch the movie—it is a cartoon not appropriate for our audience.

■ I find similar incidental or nonsignificant uses in several other links. However, I do find something serendipitous. On "Dan Reznik's Home Page" home page, he identifies himself as a graduate student in Computer Sciences/Robotics at the University of Wisconsin—Madison. I wonder why he had the word *elephant* on his page. I look down the page and see Figure 22.5.

FIGURE 22.5.

A robotic elephant trunk.

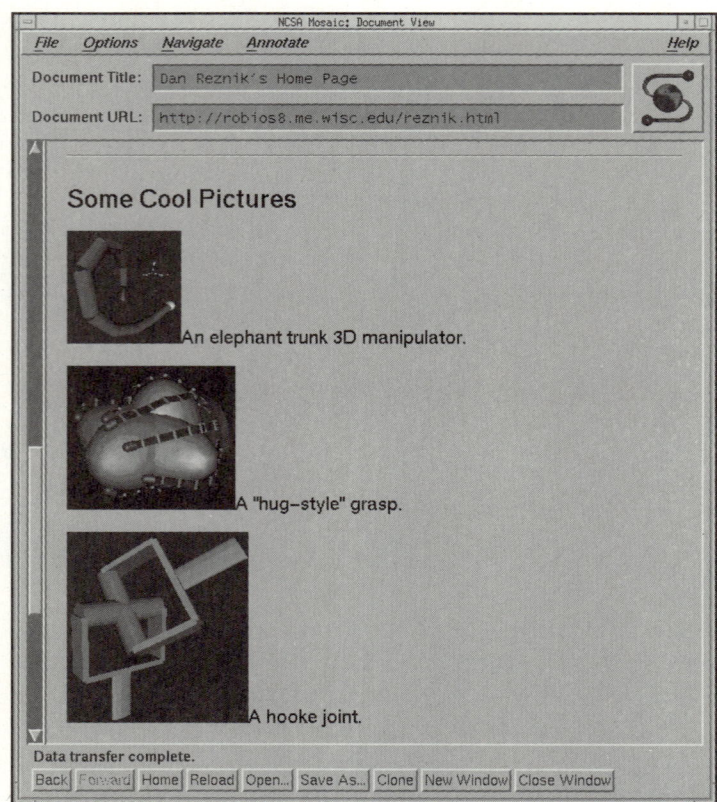

Ah, an "elephant trunk 3D manipulator." Wouldn't it be interesting to show my audience a robotic model of an elephant trunk? I save a reference to Dan Reznik's home page for later investigation. After checking some more links on other sources, I'll probably e-mail him and ask specific questions about the robotic elephant trunk.

■ Enthused by the idea of including a discussion of an elephant trunk's operation as modeled by a robot, I check out the link "Hyper-Redundant Robotics Research." It takes me to `http://robby.caltech.edu/~jwb/locomotion.html`, and I search for the term *elephant,* finding the following quote:

```
"Hyper-redundant" robots have a very large degree of kinematic redundancy, and
are analogous in morphology and operation to snakes, elephant trunks, and tentacles.
```

This seems to tell me that the phrase *elephant trunk* is used as an analogy for certain kinds of robots. I locate the writer of this page, through the link, `http://robby.caltech.edu/~jwb`, Joel Burdick, Associate Professor, Department of Mechanical Engineering, California Institute of Technology. This department and the one in Wisconsin, could be information sources for modeling elephant trunks with robotics.

I'm still not satisfied that I've found specific information about elephants themselves. Naturally, any good library would have an encyclopedia entry for *elephant* that would give me all the basic facts, but I'm looking for something more specialized. I could continue to collect related information which already could form a good deal of resources for our audience by continuing to surf the WebCrawler results page. However, I'll take a different approach and try to get where the elephants live.

A Space-Oriented Search for Elephants

After searching through the Web's links for subject and keyword information, I've decided to try to find elephants using the Virtual Tourist maps of geographically organized Web resources. I open the URL for the Virtual tourist (shown in Figure 20.1 in Chapter 20). Now my problem is knowing where elephants live in the world. At this point, it might be helpful to consult a basic encyclopedia article to identify geographic regions where elephants live. Working from the Virtual Tourist, I try the sector of the map including India. This is the southwest Asia map shown in Figure 20.2. I click on the dot on the country of India and obtain Figure 22.6.

This looks like a good lead. By focusing on one country where elephants live, I may get an idea of their interaction with people. I save the link to this page on my hotlist. I also take a quick look at the web developer's home page by opening the URL `http://enuxsa.eas.asu.edu/~sridhar`. He is Sridhar Venkataraman. I use the India information page as a base for surfing. The page contains a good selection of links. In the "India Travel Guide" link, I find the "Rec.travel Guide to India (1993 June, version 1.0)," part of the Usenet newsgroup hierarchy, `rec.travel`, FAQ archive. Kaye Stott is the editor of this document at URL `ftp://ftp.cc.umanitoba.ca/rec-travel/asia/india/india-guide`, and I use the File / Find In Current... operation to locate a reference to elephants:

Urban traffic in India is a miasma of vehicular and non-vehicular traffic, including such diverse things as cars, semis, motor-rickshaws (three-wheeled taxis), bicycle-rickshaws, motor scooters, elephants, goats, dogs, children, chickens, bearers, push-carts, camels, buses, etc.

FIGURE 22.6.

Information about India.

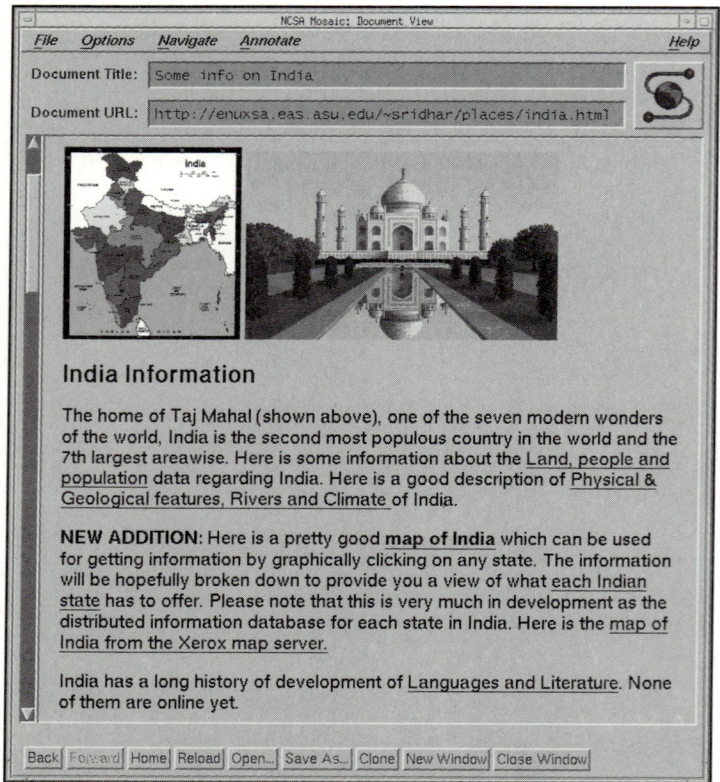

This is a vivid description of how elephants interact with people in India, another lead. I save the URL in my hotlist.

I can continue to use the methods shown above to find information about elephants. Although I've not found the "Elephant Home Page," I have found some links that I could use to perhaps start putting one together.

Other Searches: Background and Experts On Elephants

The other side of a subject search involves getting background material for any particular topic. Knowing what background material is available for a topic is an awareness skill that you can develop using the techniques in this part to locate specific subject-oriented collections. Your body of knowledge about what kind of reference and background material is available will grow as you know the Net more. I know that I could get weather and climate information, political information, and perhaps some more specific statistics about elephants. I could locate picture archives that probably contain pictures of elephants. I could also locate discussion lists that may cover some of the detailed environmental issues related to elephants. So far, in the small segment I've completed above, I've found the following:

- A description of specific legislation related to elephant protection
- A lead on a possible use of a robotic model of an elephant's trunk
- A rich source of information about India, a country where elephants are found

Navigator's Check

You can see from this example that searching the Net cannot substitute for a library or the skills of a good reference librarian. On the Net, certain topics that may seem at first glance to be fairly basic lead one on a chase throughout network links to try to locate information that might easily be found in a general reference work. The above example, however, did show us that we can locate some specific background information. Applying more of the techniques we've covered in this part, you'd be able to put together even more links. In this process of discovery, keep the following techniques and tips in mind:

1. Use background information that you can obtain from "traditional" general sources, such as encyclopedia articles and books, to guide you to a list of keywords, subjects, and world locations to search for information.

2. Use this background information to generate a series of keyword, subject-oriented, and space-oriented searches on the Web. Use techniques of surfing to quickly go through large amounts of information to find the "nuggets" you want.

3. Keep track of these nuggets of valuable URLs on your hotlist. During the course of your search, you may run across people who are interested in the same topic; contact them and collaborate on building a web page or a meta center around your topic. For skills in creating HTML documents and webs, see Part V, "Weaving a Web."

PART

IV

Exploring the Web

While our search for information on the Web for a particular topic might not yield a wealth of information (such as in the "Elephants" example in the Chapter 22), looking at the completed webs of some organizations can yield information at an astounding depth and richness. In the chapters in this part, we'll explore how the Web can be used in areas ranging from entertainment, commerce, education, science, technology, communication, government, and communities. We'll show how the Web provides organizations and individuals with many ways to deliver timely and authoritative information to audiences worldwide.

While not every organization offers the same degree of information depth, we'll explore some webs that are exceptionally strong in particular areas. The Web itself is a new medium, and during the research for this part, many webs were still under construction (you'll even see some construction sign imagery in some of the illustrations). Therefore, if you explore these same webs with your browser today, you'll find that they very well may have improved on their offerings as shown here. Also, you can use Appendix C, "Net Directory," as a source for more entry points to explore the Web.

The goals of these Web exploration chapters are

- To raise your awareness of what kind of communication can be possible on the Web
- To give you a glimpse of "what's out there" in selected application areas
- To showcase several award-winning webs (some of the winners of the "Best of the Web" contest are shown here)
- To illustrate several design and communication techniques

You'll find that the depth and maturity of some of these webs may surprise you. For example, the European Space Agency's Information System in Chapter 26, "Science and Technology," can lead researchers to a vast range of astronomical and space science data. The OncoLink Web in that same chapter illustrates a depth of oncology-related information that is maintained by experts and carefully presented and updated.

These examples illustrate the potential of the Web for presenting detailed, quality information. By exploring the Web, you may find that the way you think about and use information changes. In subject and topic areas such as the European Space Agency's Information System and OncoLink, authoritative, current, comprehensive, and carefully maintained information is on the Web now. Soon, your first stop for obtaining information on a range of other topics may become the Web.

Business and Commerce

23

by Neil Randall

To look at the World Wide Web now, I find it hard to believe that, not very long ago, business activity on the Internet was strictly forbidden. The Web is still dominated by the presence of academic and research activities, but the presence of business and commerce is growing at a very brisk pace. Not everyone would suggest that this is a good thing; but whether we like it or not, the Web, like the Internet itself, is an entity increasingly populated by commercial interests.

Commercially *populated* is one thing, but whether or not the Web ever becomes a commercially *driven* entity is the question foremost in many Net-watchers' minds. So far, it hasn't been. The Web was initiated as a communications medium for the exchange of scientific research, and it remains a vital community nurturing a range of scholarly endeavors. Its development has been driven by the needs of the academic community, in both its traditional and experimental facets. In meeting these needs, the Web has emerged as both a database service and a multimedia communications tool, because these are the two foremost requirements for scientific and research organizations.

Enter business. Already on the Internet for a variety of reasons, including research and development capacities, business became interested in the Web almost as soon as it appeared. A hypermedia environment available to the entire world offered all sorts of commercial potential because it enabled appealing, interactive access.

When Mosaic for X appeared and turned some of those promises into reality, the race was on. Businesses started to make their appearances on the Web for reasons such as marketing, customer service, product information, and ordering. Today, commercial activity on the Web has increased to the point that new companies are adding accessible Web pages practically daily, and a What's New page for commercial sites (`http://tns-www.lcs.mit.edu/commerce.html`) is being updated almost as often as NCSA's famous What's New page for the entire Web. Put simply, it's exploding.

If the Web becomes commercially *driven*, as it well might, given the current efforts to make it fully secure for data transmission (meaning that classified data or credit card numbers, and so on, can be safely communicated through the Web), then there's every chance that the Web as we know it, including the scope and speed of its development, will change significantly. Nobody knows what that means, except that in the world of business and commerce, shared research and development is rarely *allowed*, let alone encouraged. Nor, in fact, is sharing of anything else. This is not to label business as the bad guys; it's simply to recognize that the priorities of business and academe are entirely different from one another.

Obviously, we'll just have to wait and see.

> **NOTE**
>
> This chapter introduces you to the variety of business and commerce entries on the Web. No attempt whatsoever is made at comprehensiveness. Instead, I have focused on a small sampling of the commerce-related Web sites currently in existence, trying to point out the typical, the detailed, and the creative. From it, you'll get a good indication of the range of activity in this important area.

Finding Business and Commerce Sites on the Web

With all the commercial activity appearing on the Web, what's needed is a Web page that provides the links necessary to access all the main players. There are other ways of finding Web information, of course (see Part III, "Web Navigation Tools and Techniques"), but using the Web's search tools shouldn't be necessary for something this obvious. And besides, it's often more useful to browse than to search, especially if you don't know exactly what you're looking for.

Fortunately, a few pages have appeared to help you find the business information you need. Others also exist, but the two shown here are easily accessible and reasonably well-organized. Take your pick, or try both.

List of Commercial Services on the Web (and Net)

The major list of business and business-related sites on the Web, the Commercial Services site (`http://tns-www.lcs.mit.edu/commerce.html`) serves an extremely useful function. Here, on one fairly long HTML page, appear dozens of links to businesses, business services, nonprofit organizations, and sites that collect several businesses together. For a business user looking to find out how other companies are currently using the Net, this is an invaluable page from which to start.

As is obvious from Figure 23.1, the page's design centers around the alphabetical list. You can scroll through the A, B, etc. sections manually, or you can click on the letter you want from the alphabet line in the middle of the figure. This line, actually, is one of the questionable design aspects of the page, because it appears to contain only one link (that is, its one underlined element) when in fact it consists of 27 anchor links. Still, as soon as you use it once its function is clear, so this is only a moderate issue.

FIGURE 23.1.

Commercial Services on the Web (and Net) main page.

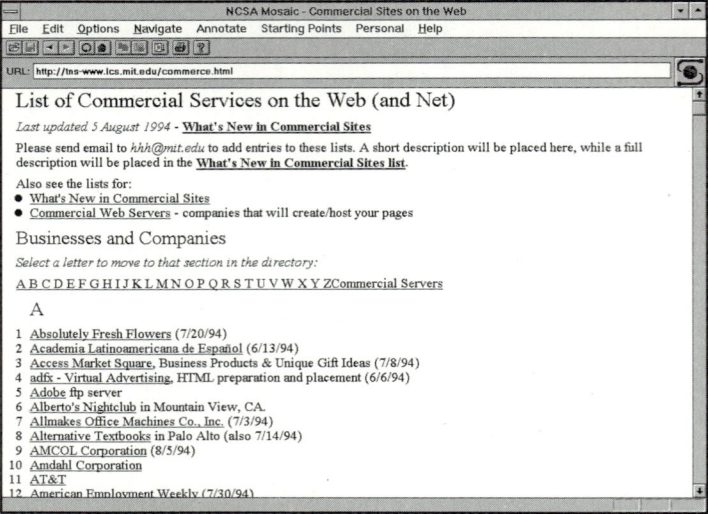

There's one other confusing design issue. The main page (Figure 23.1) does not contain all the business links available. Some businesses can be found only on the List of Commercial Web Servers page, whose link is found at the end of the alphabet line and further down the page. As an example of how this causes potential confusion, when I was trying to locate a florist's page I knew about, Grant's Florist and Greenhouse, pressing G on the main page didn't get me there. I happened to know the company is part of a larger server, so I clicked on the Commercial Servers link, browsed through to Branch Information Services, and found it there. Clearly, this system needs some work.

The main page offers links not only to the List of Commercial Servers page, but also to the equally useful What's New in Commercial Services on the Web page (Figure 23.2). Updated frequently, this page offers a look at recent entries onto the page, organized (like NCSA's extremely popular What's New page) by date. It's well worth turning to on a regular basis.

SPRY NetAccess

Another page directing Web users to business sites is SPRY, Inc.'s NetAccess (`http://www.spry.com/netacc.html`). Concentrating in its initial stages on links to players in the computer industry, NetAccess subdivides participating firms into the categories Computer Software, Computer Hardware, Internet Service Providers, Internet Services, Hardware/Software Publications, and Business Internet Organizations. Clearly the site has to expand its offerings if it is to succeed as a full business and commerce reference, but even in its initial stages the categorization model works well.

FIGURE 23.2.

What's New in Commercial Services on the Web (and Net) page.

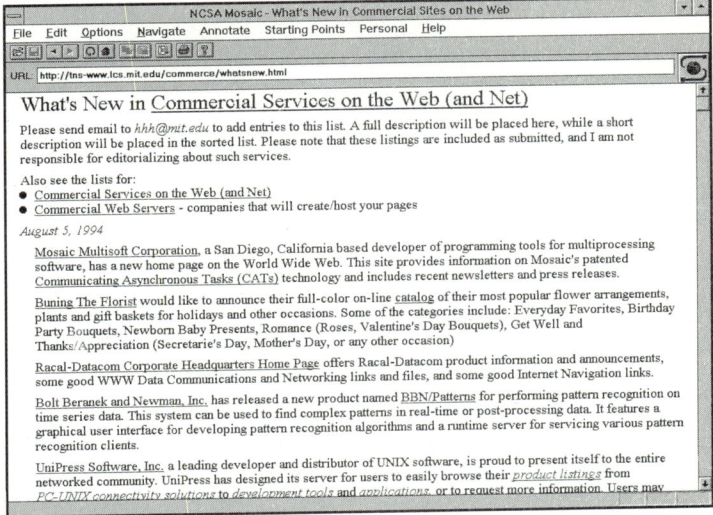

More useful, of course, would be a blurb of information about each company, appearing beside or under their links. (This is true of the Commercial Services site above as well.) While such detail would add to the heft of the page—and if NetAccess expands as it plans to, such heft could be a problem—the computer industry offers a wide range of products and it's not easy to know what company produces the products you might be looking for.

Actually, this leads to another design suggestion for the future, the possibility of providing a product index as well as a name index. For any site that seeks to provide useful information about one particular industry, in fact, such product and service indexes are almost necessary. Sometimes, certainly, users look for a specific firm, but just as often (perhaps more so) users are searching for companies who produce certain kinds of products. In the case of NetAccess's home page, and as you can see in Figure 23.3, Santa Cruz Operations, Silicon Graphics, and Sun Microsystems could all be included under a product index item called UNIX. Of course, many companies have multiple index listings.

Figure 23.4 shows a link from SPRY's home page to their Hot Home Pages section. From here another business directory exists, which is updated according to what the designers think is currently interesting.

FIGURE 23.3.

NetAccess main page offering categorizations according to business type.

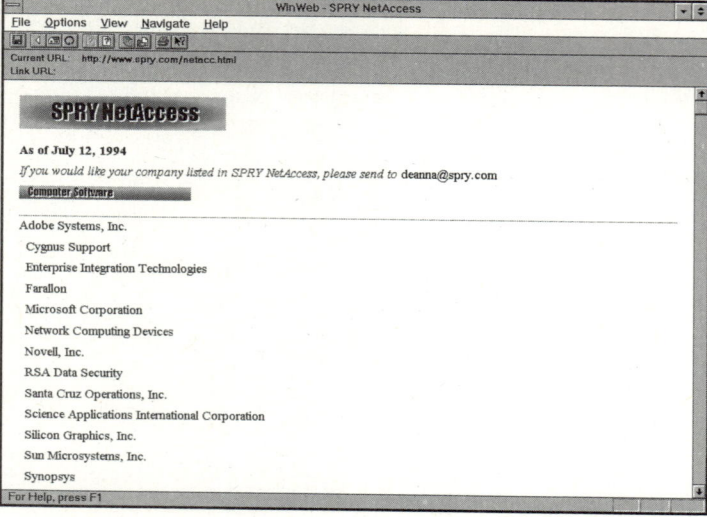

FIGURE 23.4.

Business section of Hot Home Pages directory through SPRY home page.

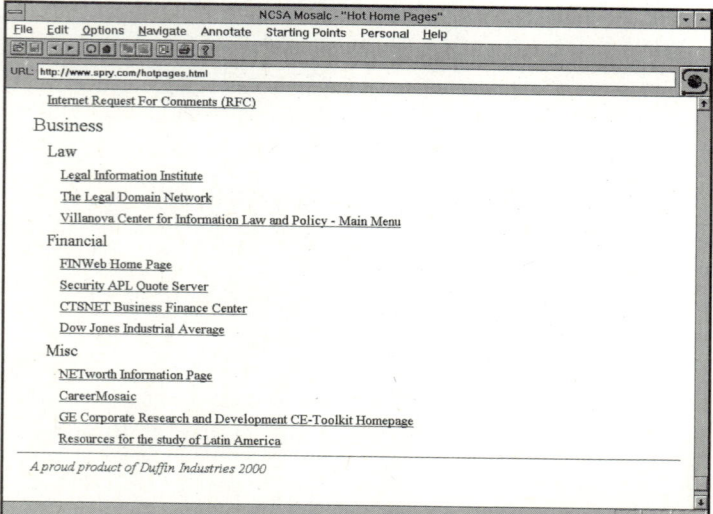

Special Interest Business Sites

Essentially focusing on small business sites, this section looks at a very few of the growing number of fascinating Web pages aimed at highly specific markets. The importance of these sites is obvious: Here we see the World Wide Web being used as an inexpensive means for businesses to make their products known to more potential buyers than would likely be possible in any other way short of full-scale and highly expensive mass media advertising. And even in the mass media publications or broadcasts, there's no guarantee that anyone will actually pay attention.

So are these companies using the Net for advertising, an activity once frowned upon by the Internet community at large? Yes, blatantly. But while these pages demonstrate the possibility—and play into the fear—that one day the Net will be saturated with the electronic version of direct mail advertising, there is no pressure for anyone to access these sites, nor do they appear unless you want them to. If you wish, you can avoid them completely, but if even one of them solves a hobby or gift-buying need, you'll be glad you have access to them.

AutoPages of Internet

Cars and computers must mix, right? After all, car owners are just as critical about other people's machines as computer owners are, and both groups want nothing less than the best, the fastest, the most technologically advanced. They also want the machine that will give them the most prestige. Of course, there's one fundamental difference; Computer owners don't routinely polish up their old Altairs and Apple IIs and parade them around an antique computer show to the oohs and ahs of admiring onlookers (and now, in the tape-drive only class, we have this apartment-beige Vic-20 ...).

The Automobile Sellers HomePage (`http://www.clark.net/pub/networx/autopage/autopage.html`) offers a place on the Web for people to advertise their classic or exotic cars and motorcycles for sale. As shown in Figure 23.5, the page has links to Exotic Cars and Classic Cars, and links further down provide access to car dealers and manufacturers, articles and reviews of interest, and pages explaining how to advertise on the AutoPages Web site and even how to earn a commission by soliciting advertising. As a business, this is the equivalent of a specialty buy-and-sell paper, and the fact that it's so focused in scope is precisely what makes it interesting. Hobbyists and collectors will find themselves accessing the page regularly.

Figure 23.5 shows the top of the Exotic Cars page. Each of the links provides information about the cars, including contact names and prices. As of this writing, these pages were only in their beginning stages of construction, so not as much was included as will be in the future. It's easy to foresee a page about each car that would offer interior and exterior views, a look under the hood, and perhaps even an audio file so the potential buyer can listen to the purring of the engine.

FIGURE 23.5.

Automobile Sellers home page.

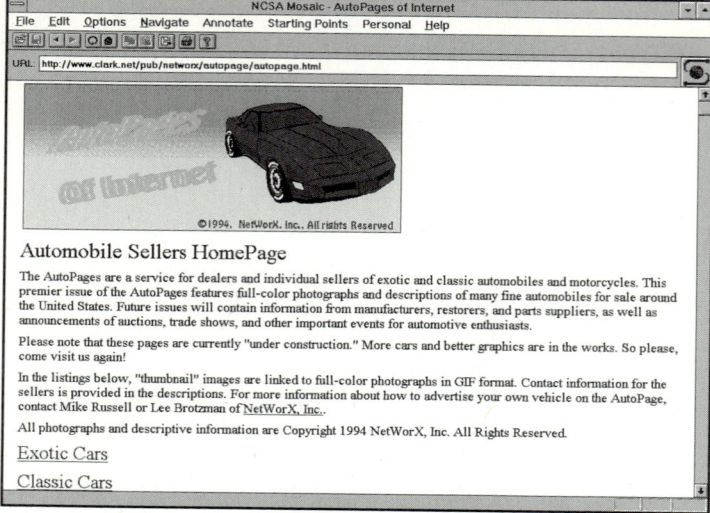

FIGURE 23.6.

AutoPages Exotic Cars page, with links to information about specific cars.

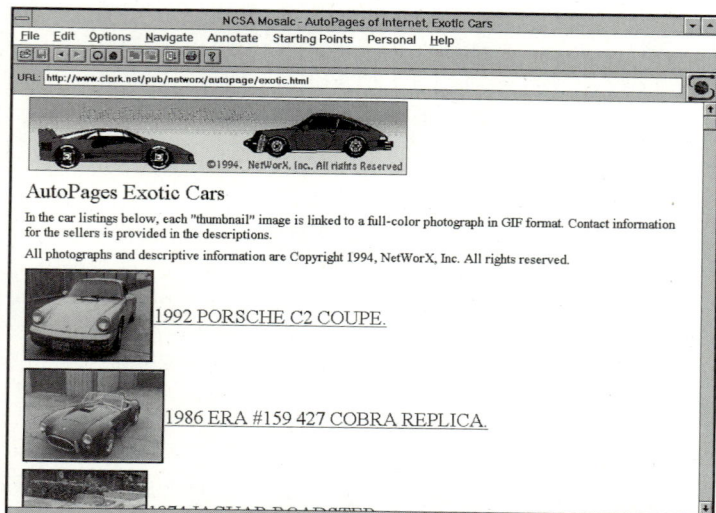

The Vermont Teddy Bear Company

As Figure 23.7 points out, the Vermont Teddy Bear Company was the entrepreneurial result when someone tried to buy a particular product and couldn't find it anywhere. Most people just walk away and complain; the true business mind assesses the situation, realizes a need, and summons up the energy and the money to fill the newly discovered void. In the case of American-made, high-quality, special occasion teddy bears, why not use the

Internet for getting the word out about your product? The demographics seem to point to the kind of income-generating parental type this entrepreneur is after.

FIGURE 23.7.

Vermont Teddy Bear Company home page.

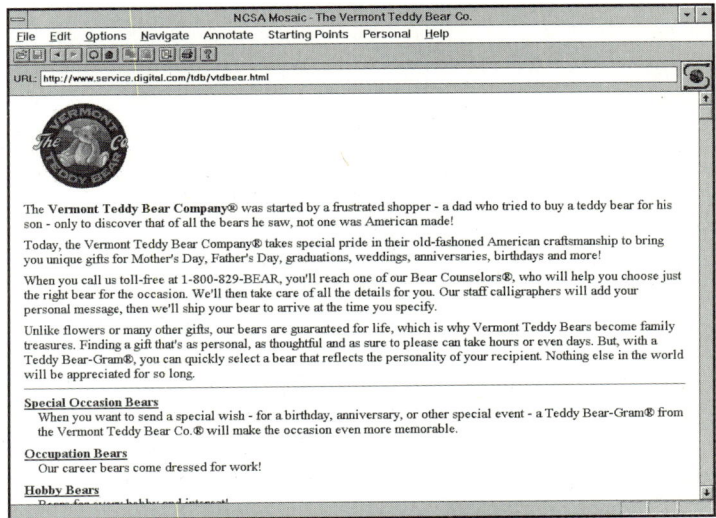

The home page (`http://www.service.digital.com/tdb/vtdbear.html`) offers a well-written explanation of why the company exists and the kinds of services available to you. A company that makes available a "Bear Counselor" at a toll-free 800 number understands its potential market and wants to make that level of service—and the commensurate level of price—extremely clear to prospective customers. The links throughout the rest of the page are to the specialty bears available for order, everything from occupation bears through sports bears, and wisely include a short blurb about what you'll find when you click.

Figure 23.8 displays the result of one of the links, the Artist Bear. Here we see a picture of the bear and the prices of the two sizes available, as well as a link to ordering information. We also find a problem with this site: The graphics are far too large for easy accessibility, especially by modem. Considering that the majority of this company's customers will likely come from the growing hordes accessing the Web through modems, the page shown in Figure 23.8 practically guarantees one-time only access. It takes forever to download at 14.4 kbps, and at the very least should be split into separate pages for each bear. In addition, each bear should appear as a much smaller graphic, with the option to download a larger graphic via FTP (that is, clicking on the option link).

I make this point for the Vermont Teddy Bear Company but not, say, the Bank of America because of the importance to this company—and not BOA—of the dial-up modem customer.

FIGURE 23.8.

Sample offering from Vermont Teddy Bear Company.

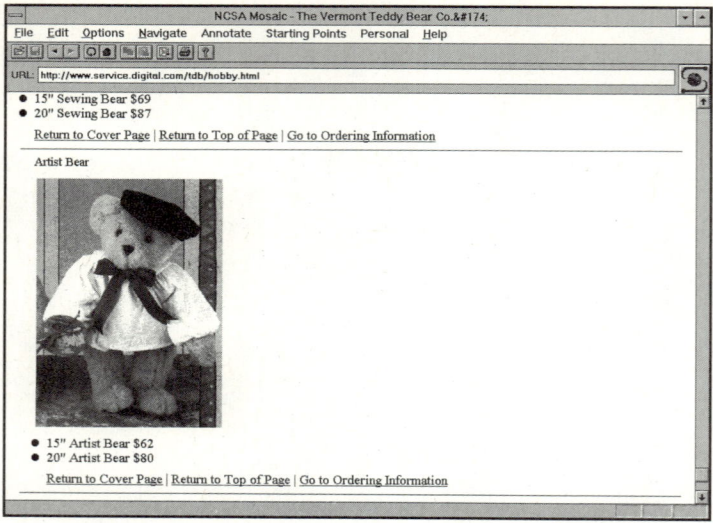

Solar Panel Power

The Solar Panel Power site (`http://www.wilder.com/solar.html`) demonstrates a trend that is only beginning among specialty business sites on the Net, the online product brochure. More than the Virginia Teddy Bear Company, which was more a catalog of available products, this site offers a look at a specific product and information about how to order it. The only difference between this brochure and one you receive in the mail is that this one is aimed at a different class of consumer. Potentially the site will have a fill-in form for ordering, but even that won't be much different (except in speed) from the traditional brochure.

The strength of the design of the home page (Figure 23.9) lies in its simplicity, clarity, and use of color and special (but unostentatious) bullets. The logo is especially well-rendered (it's in sun-like reds and yellows with black lettering), and the bullets play on the logo theme (they're little suns, too). The writing itself is perfectly acceptable for its purpose, although eliminating an exclamation point or two wouldn't hurt, and the separate paragraph nicely answers the one question we all have about this product.

This clarity and graphical strength carries over to the explanation page, How Solar Panel Power Works (Figure 23.10). Here we see exactly the kind of graphic we would expect in a well-executed product brochure, and it's fairly clear that only the limitations of HTML prevent it from being even better. From the standpoint of the modem customer, these graphics are too large for acceptable downloading, but if users really *want* to see the full explanation they can reload the page with the inline graphics option turned on. Note that my criticism of the size of the graphics on this page is different from that on the Virginia

Teddy Bear page, because there the size of the graphic was much less important. Here they add significantly to the explanation of the device.

There is, unfortunately, no order form on the site.

FIGURE 23.9.

Home page advertisement for Solar Panel Power device.

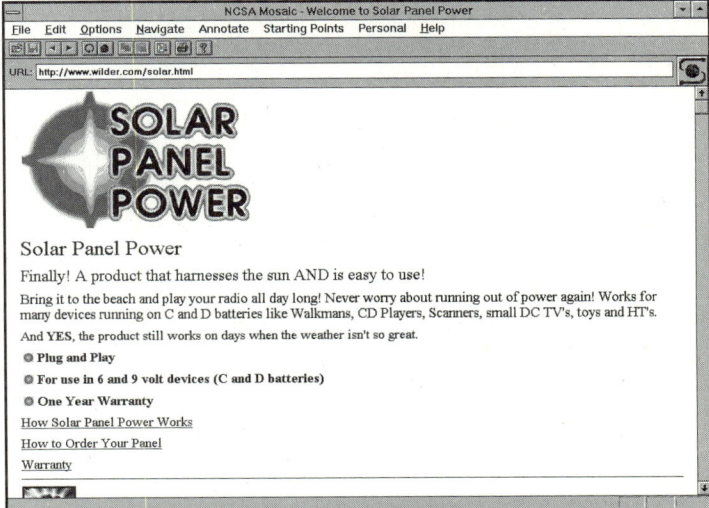

FIGURE 23.10.

Brochure-like hyperdocument showing information about Solar Panel Power.

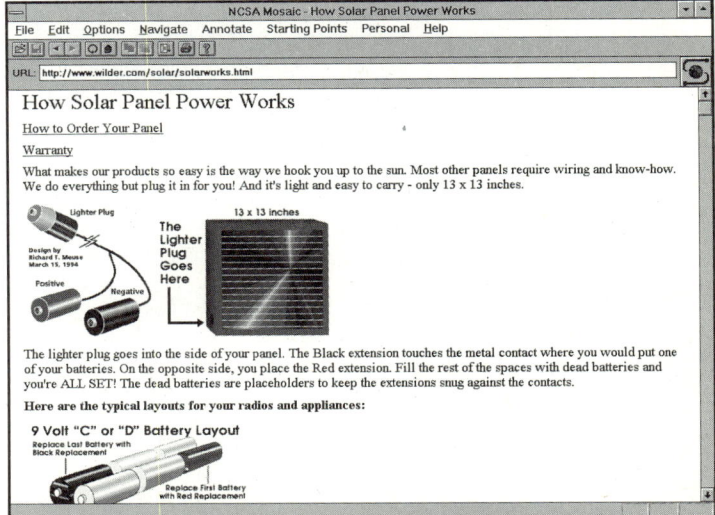

Colorburst Studios

If the Colorburst Studios online catalog gives you a sense that we're moving into Home Shopping Network territory, you're right. The difference, of course, is that with these pages you don't have to sit through endless ads about things you have no interest in. If you want a piece of Niobium Jewelry, this is where you can find it—and you don't need to see the fake Norman Rockwell paintings and obsolete computers along with it.

The designers of the catalog (`http://www.teleport.com/~paultec/catalog.html`) obviously have the Web user in mind, as shown in Figure 23.11 by the explanation of graphic sizes in the first paragraph. Interestingly, they suggest that you write for a printed catalog for more complete information, a curious suggestion given the fact that they already include so much information online. This point demonstrates that we're still a long way from having all the available products from even Web-savvy proprietors on the Net, and that it will be a while before direct mail marketing is seriously challenged.

FIGURE 23.11.

Colorburst Studios home page with product information and order form link.

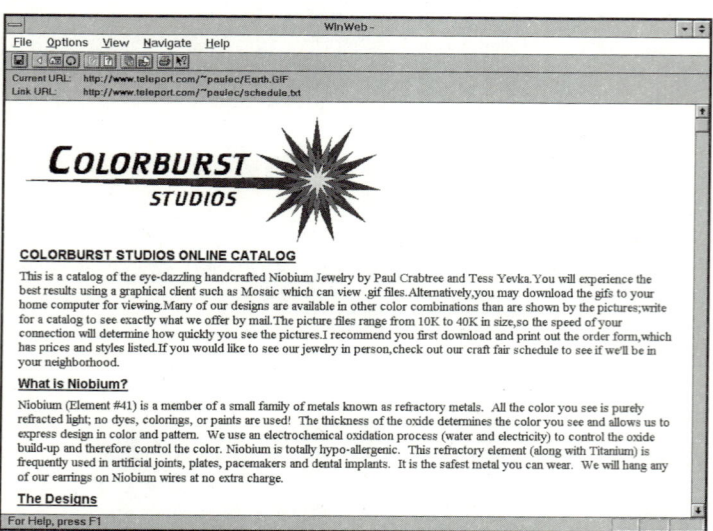

The two links in the first paragraph show one of the drawbacks of embedding links inside paragraphs. Using WinWeb (as shown here), which doesn't underline the links, and a monochrome monitor, nicely simulated in this book, the links are almost invisible. But on a color monitor and with underscoring they're fine, and more effective in some ways than separately listed links. The link to the craft fair schedule is instantly attention-getting.

Figure 23.12 shows a list of the actual products offered by Colorburst. Each of the links is to a downloadable `.gif` file rather than another page, and while this is definitely better than loading individual inline images for each product, it means that the customer must make a decision—perhaps based on modem speed—whether or not to actually see the product. A sample design or two as an inline graphic might be a better idea.

FIGURE 23.12.

Product section from Colorburst Studios home page with links to downloadable graphics.

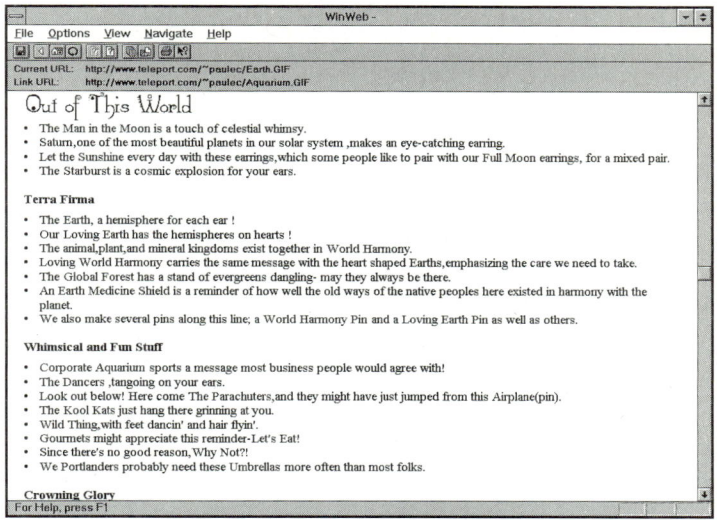

Arctic Adventours

Given the fact that the tour industry caters to people who are interested in travel, and often travel to exotic places around the globe, the Internet seems an inevitable choice of venues for placing marketing and information materials. So far a few tour operators have jumped on the bandwagon, including Norway's Arctic Adventours shown (`http://www.oslonett.no/data/adv/AA/AA.html`) in Figures 23.13 and 23.14.

There's not a huge amount of information on these sites, but then again there isn't much in most tour catalogs. Links point to separate pages about specific tours, where you can find, at the very least, the details you need to determine if you're even interested. A nice touch is the link to the yacht Arctic Explorer, and another good link is to the GIF images from various parts of the world. Because of the GIFs, the site loses little of the color it would have on a glossy printed version, although the GIFs take much longer to download than they would to glance at in print.

Figure 23.14 follows a specific tour link from the home page. This is fairly standard tour brochure information, necessary for the customer to make decisions about possible tours of interest. The polar bear graphic reinforces the fact that these are Arctic tours you're looking at, not Caribbean or Mediterranean tours, and therefore helps eliminate anyone seeking sun and sand. There are few links inside the text itself, but these could and should be developed further. The point of a Web site, after all, is to hyperlink elsewhere, not just to contain exactly the same information found in a printed brochure.

FIGURE 23.13.

Arctic Adventours' main page offering glimpses of their offerings.

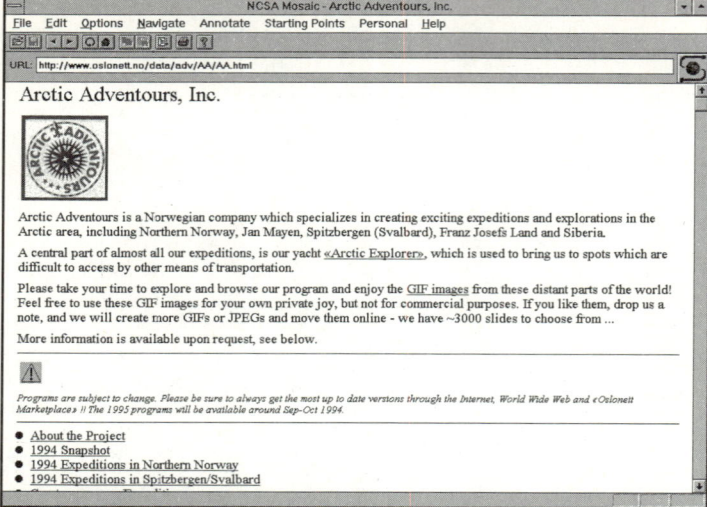

FIGURE 23.14.

Details about one of Arctic Adventours' programs.

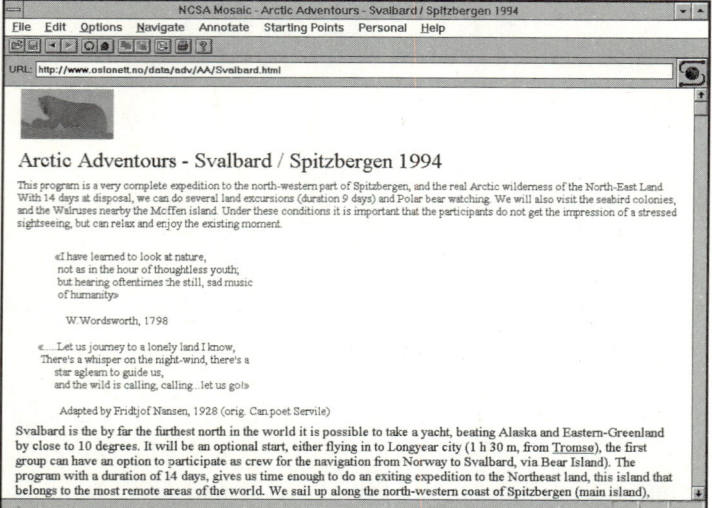

Large Corporations on the Web

The possibilities of Web use by large corporations is a topic of considerable interest as we approach the mid-nineties. Always on the watch for new ways of attracting, serving, and maintaining customers and clients, large businesses see the Net as a very real possibility for all of these important activities. Predictably, however, they're approaching Net presence very cautiously, partly because of security issues and partly because no concrete figures exist to suggest how many people are reachable this way. Because of both concerns,

the tendency is to direct funding elsewhere, and in corporations an unfunded project is a nonexistent project.

Which is not to suggest that Web activity hasn't begun. A quick scan of the Commercial Services site demonstrates that large corporations are beginning to assert an Internet presence, and while many of these are (understandably) computer companies, others are out there and still others on the way. For some companies, the Web has become a site under very real development, with firms like Digital and Hewlett Packard already sporting numerous pages devoted to product support and information. Others are joining in and will inevitably continue to do so.

The other interesting point about large corporate presence on the Net is that it signified a change to the Internet as it has existed in the past. If Net presence is deemed a good thing by corporate America (and by good I mean profit-generating, either directly or indirectly), then expect the Web to experience nothing less than an explosion of big-business activity, to the extent that the balance of functions the Internet seems to be capably dealing with will almost certainly be swung in business's favor. That won't necessarily have negative ramifications, but it's something the Internet community is extremely wary of.

CommerceNet

From the standpoint of large business presence, CommerceNet is one of the most significant new sites on the World Wide Web. Page through its directories and you'll find the planned participation of some Fortune 500 giants, and although the site isn't anywhere near ready for prime time, it simply can't be ignored as a harbinger of things to come.

CommerceNet (`http://www.commerce.net/`) is a consortium, a project jointly sponsored by a number of corporations to take advantage of the Internet's vast promise. From the home page (Figure 23.15) through the individual pages, even in their under-construction state, it's clear that these sites will bear little resemblance to the product information pages we saw among the small companies above. The promise here is for fully developed, fully operational sites, using the World Wide Web (and Mosaic in particular) not only as a means of generating awareness, but also as a means of transacting real business in real-time.

Clearly, it will take months, perhaps a year or more, for important things to happen. The biggest stumbling block, as you might imagine, is security. Given a chance to do banking over the Net today, nobody in his right mind would do so. It's just too risky. For that matter, resist the impulse to send your credit card number over the Net as well. While the likelihood is that nothing will happen, there's very little in place to prevent it. One of the CommerceNet consortium's stated goals is to develop Web security to the extent that such transactions are as safe as they are over, say, automatic telling machines, which means as secure and cracker-proof as they're likely to get.

FIGURE 23.15.

CommerceNet home page, with full graphics interface.

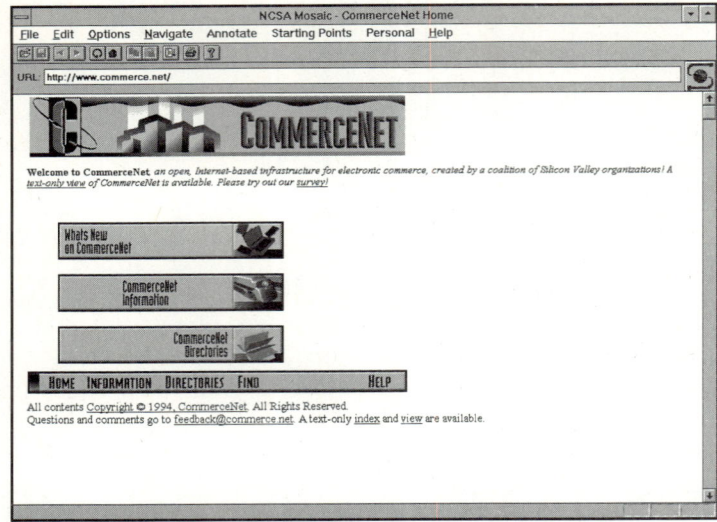

The home page shows the graphic-based design of CommerceNet, although it's clear from the subhead that a text view is available. The design works as a series of push buttons, and it works well. Figure 23.16 shows a similar interface from a subsequent page, with more buttons but demonstrating the potential for detail. Unfortunately, nothing is particularly well organized or complete as yet, so it's hard to get a good read on what the site will finally look like.

FIGURE 23.16.

CommerceNet's directories, with links to participants and partners.

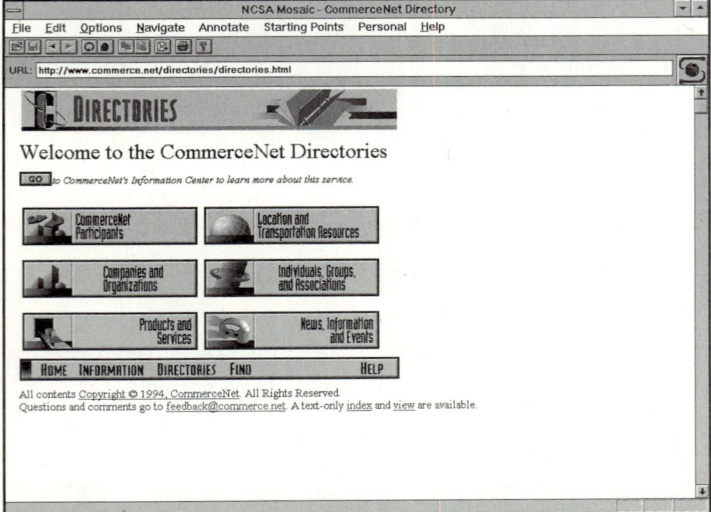

Canadian Airlines International

The Canadian Airlines International site on the Web (`http://www.CdnAir.CA/`) demonstrates more of the Web's promise, but ironically it shows how far the Net has to go in some important business regards. Here we have access to a good range of useful information about the airline, including flight and departure details. Eventually, in fact, we'll be able to use this site to order airline tickets and make hotel and automobile reservations as well—the complete package, including tours.

The problem is, you can already do all this on the commercial online services. So while this site is ahead of many in its efforts to provide reservation and ordering services, it's still way behind the less hyped services. In fact, it's years behind in a number of ways. Of course, this is true of just about all Web-based ordering activities; we've been able to shop in CompuServe's or America Online's malls for a long time, and nobody's been going ga-ga over those.

So let's not go ga-ga. But let's keep in mind the Web's size, its growth rate, and its stupendous problems with security and interactivity. (This isn't just a couple of computers joined together, remember.) With those things firmly in mind, we can see the potential of the Canadian Airlines site, and even without it we can remark on the clean design and the orderly interfaces. Figure 23.17 makes this abundantly clear.

FIGURE 23.17.

Home page for Canadian Airlines International with link to flight information.

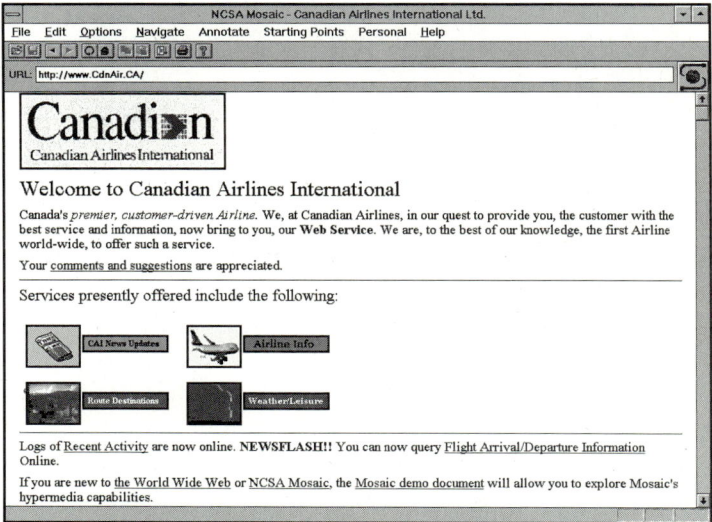

Figure 23.18 shows one way the Web can help make information extremely accessible. You can click on any continent on the gorgeously rendered map and be given a closer view of that continent, with information about the destinations. Start merging this with reservation information and you have something very real to go on.

FIGURE 23.18.

Page with clickable map to details on Canadian Airlines destinations.

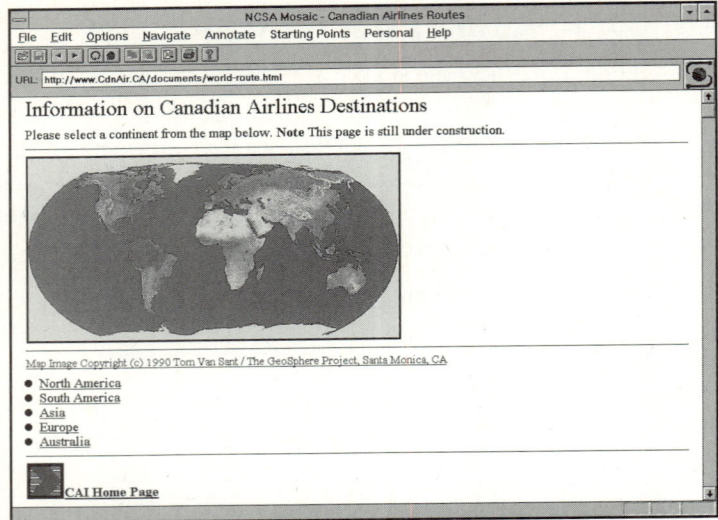

Lockheed Missiles and Space Company

As the home page displayed in Figure 23.19 shows, the Lockheed Missiles & Space Company (`http://www.lmsc.lockheed.com/`) specializes in developing space systems, missiles, and other high-tech products. It's pretty obvious the company earns its keep primarily through defense department contracts (the civilian space missile market is extremely limited these days, although watch out for those James Bond villains), and that probably has a great deal to do with why the home page offers an immediate link to the Public Information Office and transcriptions of recent press releases. You have to think that Lockheed spends a fair amount of energy on public and press relations, and the Web very clearly helps this process along.

The site doesn't offer a great deal of information beyond public information and some technical details, but it represents an example of a government-related corporation using the Web to demonstrate a commitment to public education about its role. Of course, there's no indication here of how much information is given and how much is classified (we can assume that we'll never see most of this company's technical data on the Web); nevertheless, this is an important example of one corporate use of the Net. If you've ever wondered about the companies that land the lucrative (or at least once-lucrative) defense contracts, give this page a look.

FIGURE 23.19.

Lockheed home page, with press releases and company info.

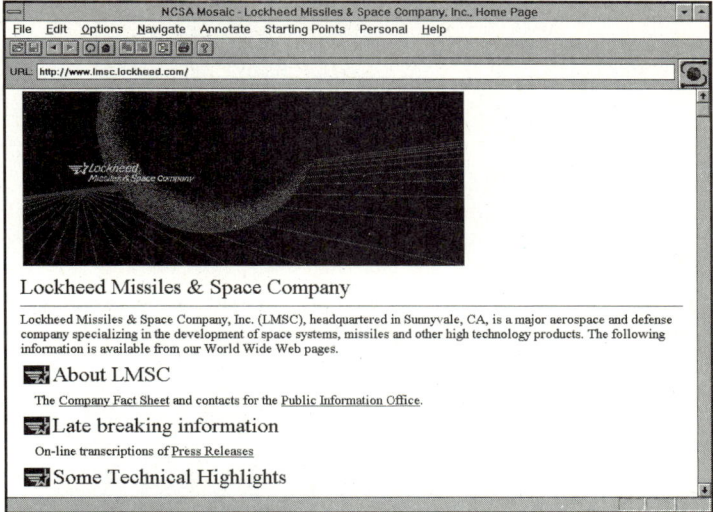

The design of the home page is straightforward, with appropriately iconic custom bullets and easy to understand links. Clearly, the page is meant for viewing through high-speed connections, however (the graphics take forever to download across a modem), and this seems a bit strange given the *public* focus of the information. (In other words, don't forget the little guys, folks.) Figure 23.20 shows the accessible Lockheed press releases page, and although not notably designed, it's quite functional.

FIGURE 23.20.

Lockheed page for access to company press releases.

Bank of America

Part of the CommerceNet initiative, Bank of America has hit the Web with a series of pages that show nothing less than truly significant potential. The home page (`http://www.commerce.net/directories/participants/bofa/bofa.home.html`)consists of one huge clickable map in the form of a large, colorful logo (see Figure 23.21). It offers no concession to text-only users but clearly demonstrates the four financial activities that will be possible from this site in the near future.

FIGURE 23.21.

Bank of America home page, completely and exclusively graphic.

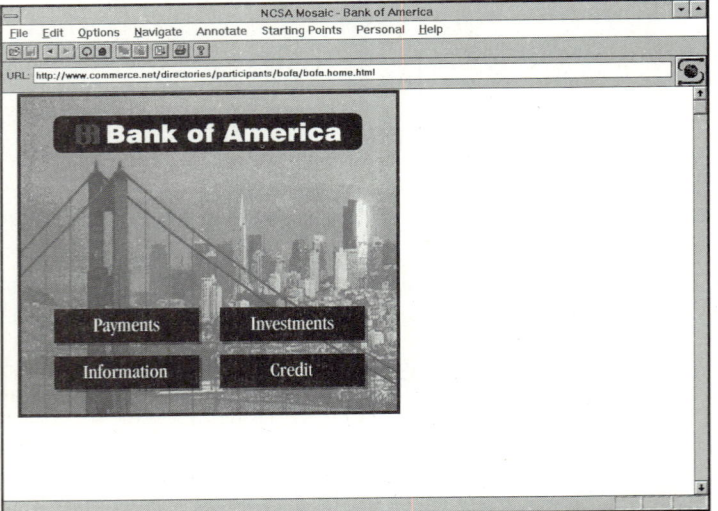

Figure 23.22 shows the results of clicking on the Payments icon (as of this writing, actually, it's the result of clicking on any icon). The purpose is obvious. Somewhere along the line, Bank of America customers will be able to make payments of a variety of types over the Web, first by filling in the check-like blanks and then clicking on the Paper Check, ACH Payment, or Wire Transfer buttons. Here we see a solid use of the HTML fill-in form, with the arrows signifying selection menus. It takes little imagination to see how we might turn to this or a similar page in the future and make the transactions from our computers.

The stumbling block, once again, is security. At this stage in the Web's existence, services such as those proposed here by the Bank of America simply can't happen. But let the Web security gurus get their act fully together (and a lot of money is being spent by CommerceNet and others to make this happen), and you might find yourself Web-Banking before too long. While making payments this way might not seem too exciting, checking and making investments certainly is.

FIGURE 23.22.

Proposed payments form for the Bank of America site.

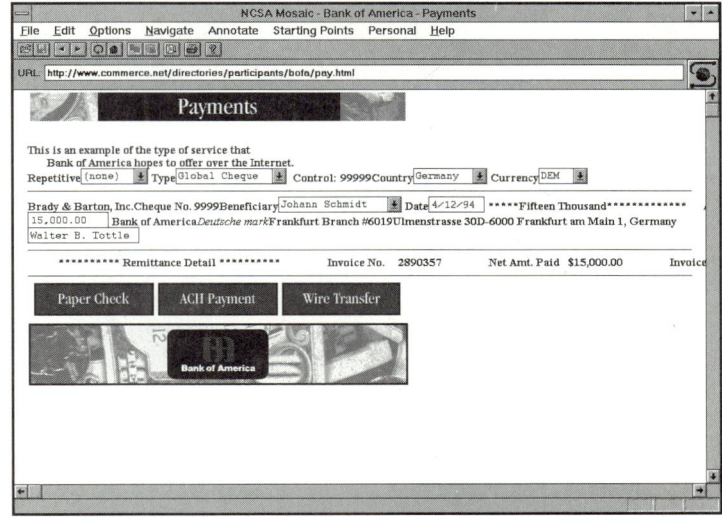

Hewlett Packard

As shown in the guided tour of the Web in Chapter 6, Hewlett Packard has one of the best developed corporate sites on the Web at this time. Shown in Figure 23.23 is the Services and Support home page (`http://www.hp.com/Services.html`), which loads with the large (overlarge for modem use) imagemap graphic that contains the buttons you need to traverse the site. Apart from the sheer size of this map, it is clearly and colorfully designed and extremely easy to understand, and in fact fits with the theme of the HP access pages throughout the site. For modem users, four of the items are accessible from the links at the bottom of the page.

Figure 23.24 illustrates the extent of HP's offering. Here is a well-organized FTP site, fully accessible from the Web, that demonstrates the extent to which corporation can, even now, be using the customer and technical services potential of the Net. It's not hard to imagine HP's customers, especially MIS staffers, coming to rely on this page from the time they install new HP products until the day they exchange them for others.

Nor is this anywhere near the full extent of the material available from this site. Press releases, question and answer sessions, educational items (see Figure 23.25), and other support details are here as well, and the HP customer is advised to check it out frequently. This is one of the most impressive business sites available.

FIGURE 23.23.

Hewlett Packard home page showing graphic with clickable buttons.

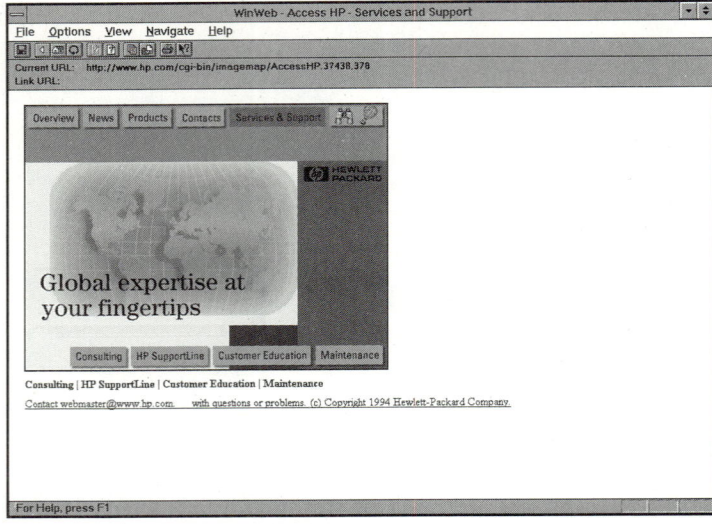

FIGURE 23.24.

HP Peripheral Anonymous FTP Site page with links to technical information.

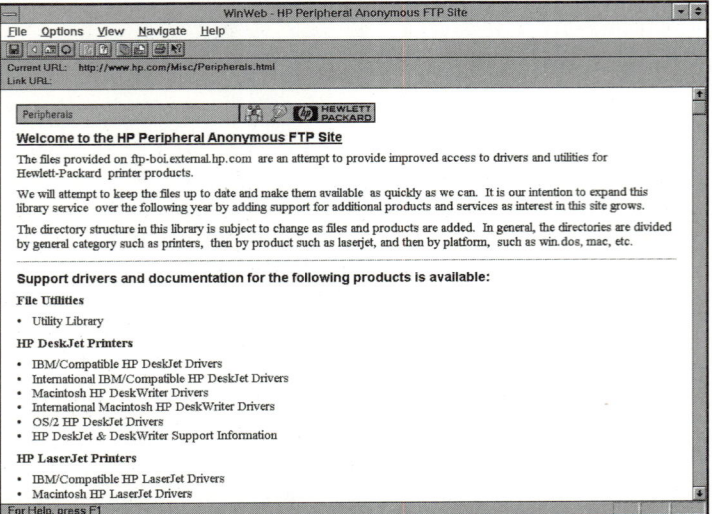

Digital Equipment

Very similar in completeness to Hewlett Packard's site is Digital Equipment's extensive and highly useful area (http://www.service.digital.com/home-g.html). Like HP, Digital leads off on its home page with a clickable imagemap (the "DigitalCity Map" towards the bottom of Figure 23.26), but Digital's main graphic representation, the science-fictionish window view at the top of the page, is far different in tone and function from HP's. It also takes a great deal of time to load, but once again the assumption is that Digital customers will likely have the connections needed for high-speed access.

FIGURE 23.25.

One of HP's customer education pages with information about product-oriented course.

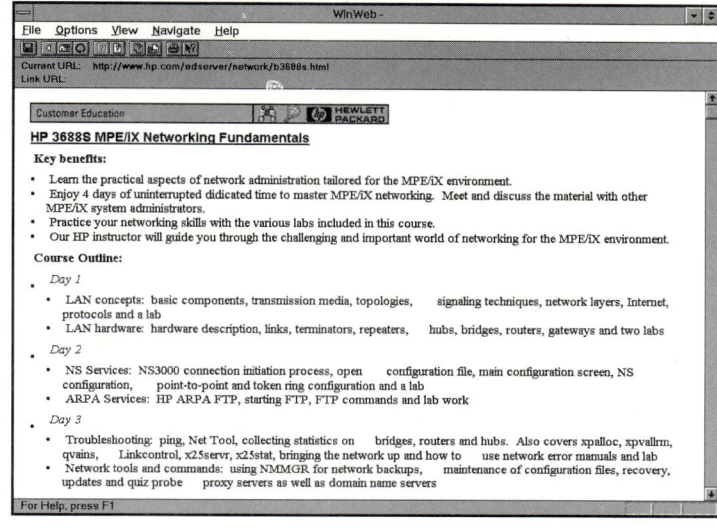

FIGURE 23.26.

Digital Equipment's main page with large graphic and clickable display.

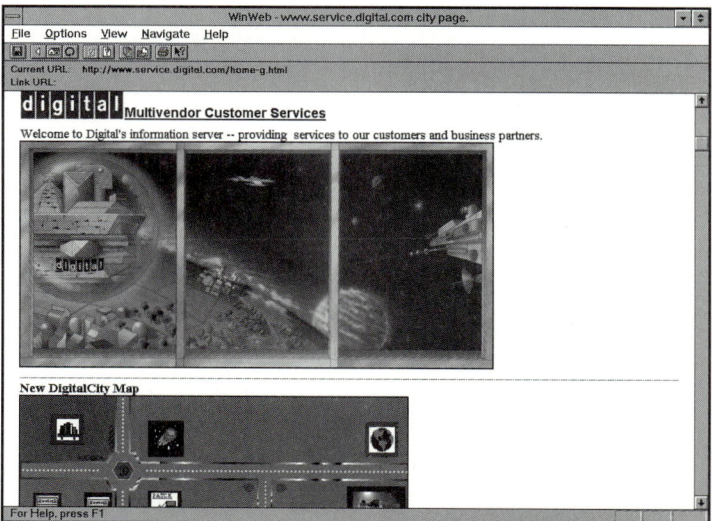

The DigitalCity Map is a good idea, but it's confusing. The map's key (not shown here) doesn't really help you understand what each of the icons means, and few are obvious enough to stand on their own. One that is, however, is the "Patch" icon, which leads to the page displayed in Figure 23.27. As with HP's FTP site, the Patch page offers Digital's customers downloadable files that contain software patches (corrections), an immensely useful feature for anyone in charge of installing and maintaining Digital equipment. Digital offers a huge amount of technical information on these pages, including technical reports

and documentation along with educational items. From a customer and technical service perspective, this is another impressive Web business site.

FIGURE 23.27.

Digital patch information page with searchable database.

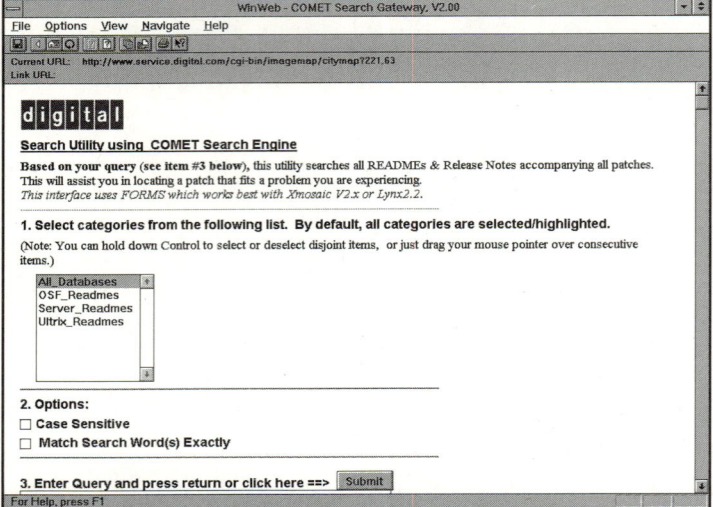

Dun & Bradstreet

Dun & Bradstreet has an old and venerable presence in the financial and information community, and the fact that they have established pages on the Web suggests that they're aware of the Net's potential for finance-based organizations. As is evident from Figure 23.28, the company's home page (`http://www.corp.dnb.com/`), this site includes links to several important financial, research, and service firms, and there's every reason to believe that this clickable image will eventually include others as well.

So far, however, the available material is almost solely basic information about the services each firm offers. The AC Neilsen page from this site, for instance (Figure 23.29), is primarily a page of textual details functioning as little more than a window in a brochure. Still, the links to Neilsen offices around the world and its new products show a commitment to providing much more material as the site develops, placing the D&B site in a situation very similar to that of many large business offerings to date.

FIGURE 23.28.

Clickable diagram from Dun & Bradstreet's information page.

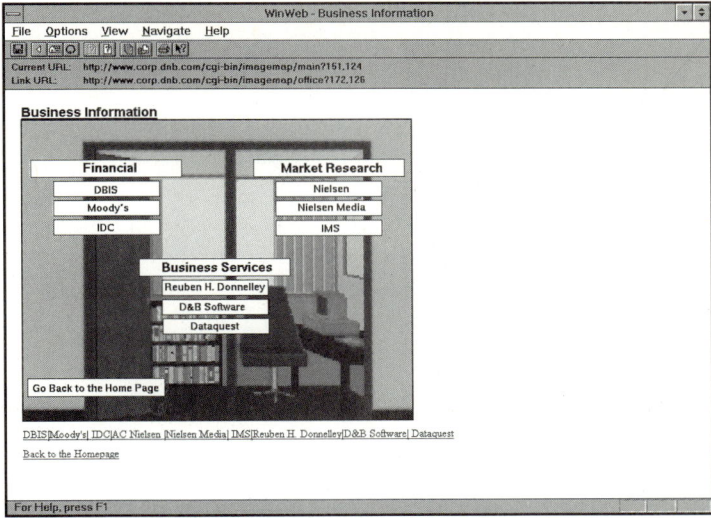

FIGURE 23.29.

AC Neilsen information page from Dun & Bradstreet site.

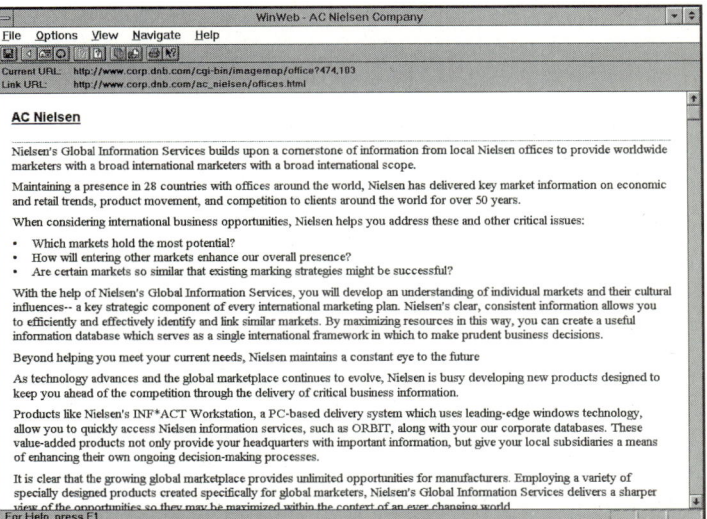

The importance of the D&B area is that it tells us what the future of the Web holds. This company and its associated companies will establish a joint presence on the Web, and the range of services offered is potentially unlimited. Expect more of this kind of site in the future.

Industrial Malls

Large companies can afford to establish their own Internet connections. Small companies, for the most part, cannot. For that reason, we're seeing an increasing number of "industrial malls" coming into operation on the World Wide Web. Like a real industrial mall, the principle behind these e-malls is that one company owns and maintains the structure, collecting rent from and thereby giving a business presence to its tenants. Rather than a building, of course, the e-mall landlord owns and maintains a full Internet connection, renting disk space and bandwidth to the tenants for a setup fee, a monthly fee, and, in some cases, a page design fee as well. The possibilities are varied, depending on the site.

The advantage for the tenants is that they obtain an Internet presence without the significant cost in both equipment and labor of installing their own connection. They don't have to worry about system upgrades, hard disk failures, UNIX trivia, or anything else. They just assert their presence, pay for the amount of e-space they take up, and open their name to 20 million Internet users. The disadvantages are that they don't have the freedom to develop full Internet integration into their company's daily activities, and that they don't have unique URL addresses (although this isn't always true). But since most Web users point and click their way into a site rather than type in the actual URL, this latter point probably doesn't matter anyway.

Expect industrial malls to increase continually, in both number and quality. This is an obvious entry point onto the Web for a great many businesses, and not just small ones.

Downtown Anywhere

As its home page (Figure 23.30) says, Downtown Anywhere (`http://www.awa.com`) is "conveniently located in central cyberspace." It's structured very evidently according to the town metaphor, with a main street, a library and newsstand, and just about everything else you'd find in, well, downtown anywhere. The idea behind the site is to collect a wide variety of businesses and services in one spot, creating not just an industrial mall but a virtual town, and the early development is strong enough to lend some credibility to the possibility of future success.

FIGURE 23.30.

Downtown Anywhere's home page with links to commercial pages.

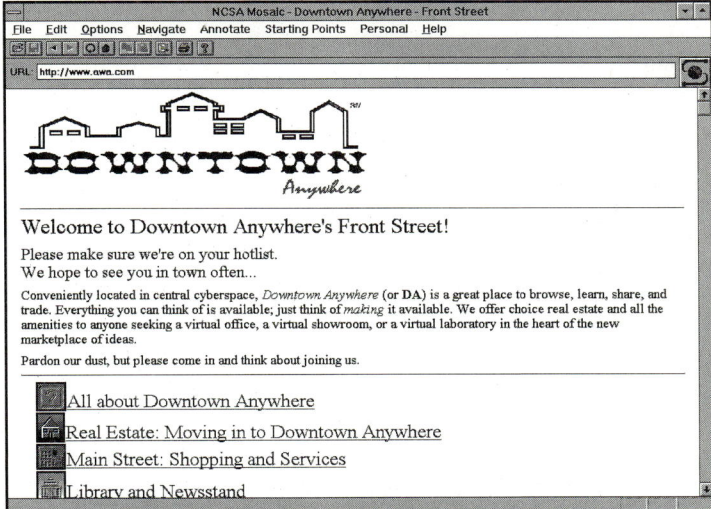

This is an exciting site. Browse it for a while, and you start to feel a sense of "town-ness" building up. Of course, it helps to experience the "static-ness" of some other mall sites to feel this, but it really does seem to happen. Inevitably, the strength of the town itself is only as strong as its inhabitants, but that's true of real towns as well. Not everything in Downtown Anywhere is going to attract your immediate attention, but the concept certainly should.

After a truly enticing home page, the interior pages seem comparatively drab, however. Main Street, shown in Figure 23.31, looks no different from any other hastily developed collection page on the Web, and clicking on several of the links reveals that the site is in its very early stages. Considering what the site's designers did with the home page, Main Street—which should be the one central fully developed attraction—just doesn't cut it from the standpoint of esthetics. It's functional, but it should be much more. Still, it's a site well worth watching.

FIGURE 23.31.

Main Street from the Downtown Anywhere site.

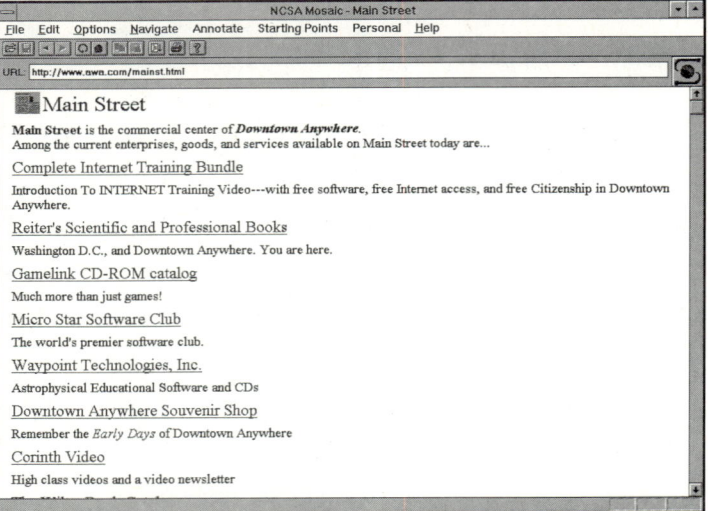

BizNet Technologies

Unlike Downtown Anywhere, BizNet Technologies (`http://128.173.241.138/shopping.html`) has organized its tenants around the metaphor of the shopping mall. The concepts are similar, but when the metaphors are fully developed the two sites will end up with very different atmospheres. So far, however, the sites appear alike, but this is hardly surprising; interface designers have always been much better at coming up with metaphors than developing them fully. Still, the shopping mall is a metaphor you'll run into frequently on your Web travels, so it's worth exploring here.

The home page (Figure 23.32) is clear and attractive. It's brief (this will change as more stores are added), and the logo is clever and appealing (it omits Antarctica, but that's probably acceptable). One of the interesting points about this site is that it's not just a collection of shops. Instead, it mixes a flower shop with an apartment site and two other not completely obvious tenants (Durability, Inc. and Home Technologies, Inc.), a combination that makes you want to start browsing to see the differences. Apartment blocks in particular are very rare on the Web.

Inside, the pages are of varying degrees of interest, but in at least one case they prove more complete than many such pages. The Busch Entertainment site (Figure 23.33) not only explains the nature of the company's theme parks, but offers links to several of them, and following these links takes you on a mini-adventure of its own. This is different from many e-malls, where clicking on most tenant's names yields one or maybe two isolated pages; the Busch site makes use of the Web as it was designed, as a full hypertext environment.

FIGURE 23.32.

BizNet's home page, including links to a variety of businesses.

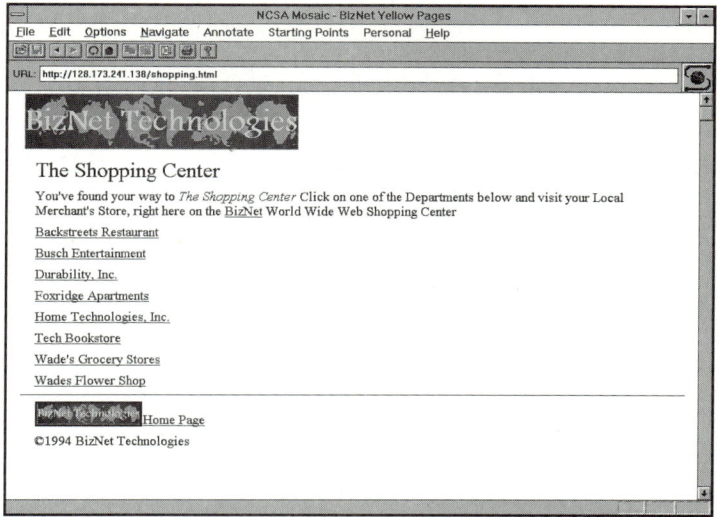

FIGURE 23.33.

Busch Entertainment page from BizNet collection.

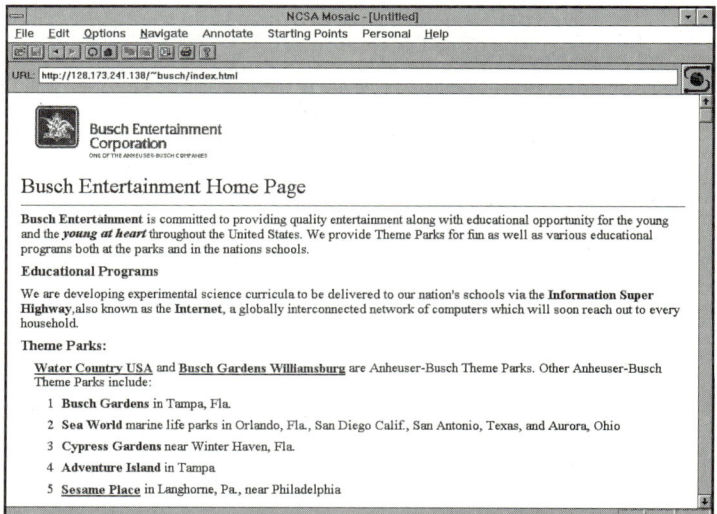

NetMarket

Among industrial malls on the Web, NetMarket (`http://www.netmarket.com`) is unique. Not only is it designed to house a variety of businesses (which isn't unique at all), it is also structured so that you open an account that covers all the offerings in the mall itself. Establish the account, and you can go shopping inside any of NetMarket's stores (which were few at the time of writing). This is an extremely interesting idea because it encourages e-shoppers to stay in that particular mall for all their shopping needs. Rather than

establish accounts with each individual store, you need only one to get your shopping going. This is also potentially dangerous from a personal finances standpoint, of course, but such is the nature of credit card shopping.

Figure 23.34 shows the HTML form in the account creation page. Note that you can create your account fully over the Net, or you can call or write NetMarket to arrange the account otherwise. Note also that your account is active as soon as you send the form. That means you can impulse shop until you drop. At this stage, it's probably not a good idea to send credit card information through the Web, but if you're interested in doing so, why not contact NetMarket and see what they have to say?

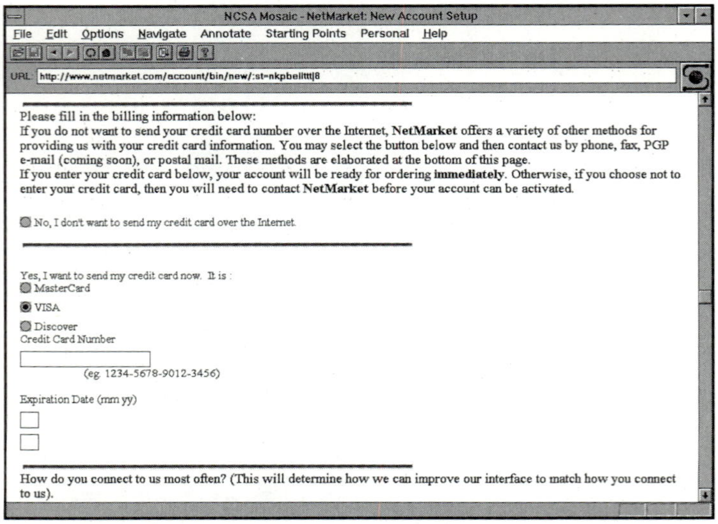

FIGURE 23.34.

NetMarket account setup form with fill-in radio buttons.

Inside NetMarket, the most fully developed site (as of this writing) is Noteworthy Music Compact Discs. Their home page (Figure 23.35) displays the colorful push-button interface common throughout NetMarket, and its options are intriguing. Cleverly, the store offers either a browsing or a searching choice, including complex searches. You have the option of a multimedia display as well, an extremely promising idea for CD buyers.

Figure 23.36 shows the extent of Noteworthy Music's site. Below the Page button you can see that this is the first of 775 pages! Surely this is a CD-buyer's dream, a fact that is confirmed by the running purchase total displayed immediately below the top menu. The idea here is to browse or search for what you want, clicking on the button beside the item to select it, then watching your dollar total increase until you're satisfied you have the items you want and have spent the money you can afford. Then you can finish the transaction. Noteworthy's interface takes some getting used to (practice a few times before actually launching an order), but it's powerful.

A very interesting site, and probably a harbinger of the future.

FIGURE 23.35.

Noteworthy Music's main menu with links to order forms.

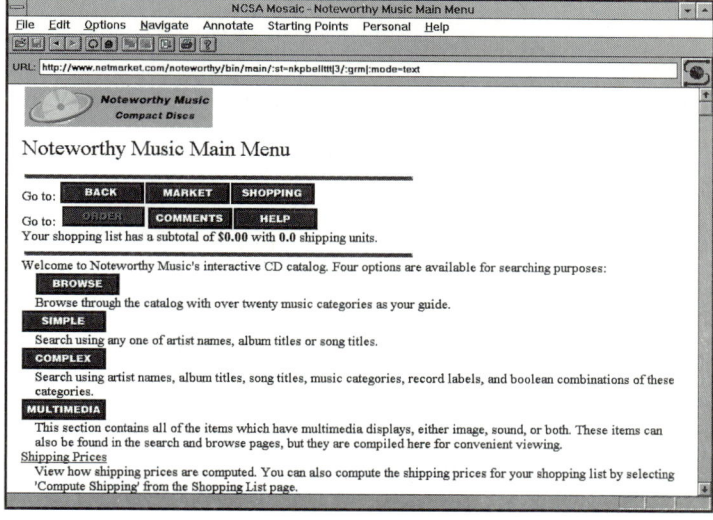

FIGURE 23.36.

Noteworthy Music's browsable and searchable catalog of CDs.

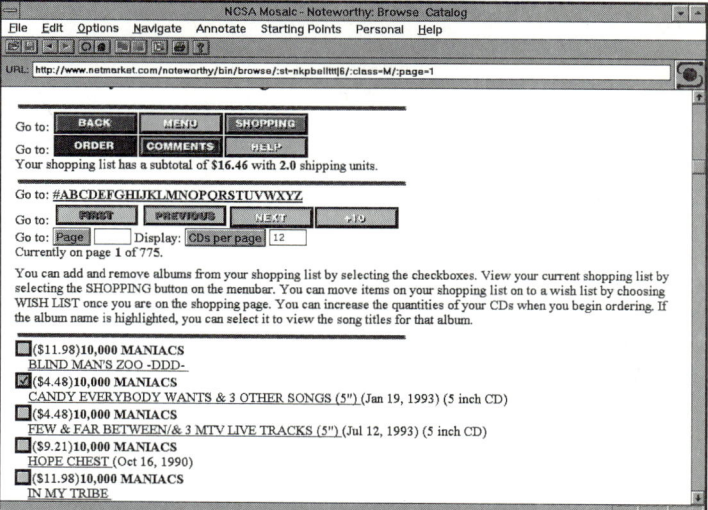

Business Services on the Web

Even as businesses develop Web presence, so do the corresponding business services. One of the most prevalent services, as you might expect, are the Internet site providers, but I've foregone those in favor of two less obvious examples. These two sites demonstrate that the nature of Web-based business services is yet to be determined, but we can expect the same range of services over the Net, eventually, that we have in the non-Net world.

There's one problem: The Net as it now exists is extremely public, and many business service companies cast an image that suggests they deal with a very elite (that is, very large business) clientele. How this translates onto the Web remains to be seen.

Corporate Agents, Inc.

An interesting site, Corporate Agents (`http://www.corporate.com/`) is an example of a business service designed to appeal to small businesses or individuals wishing to start or expand a business. Its purpose as a company is to help its clients incorporate. Incorporating is a good idea for many businesses for a variety of reasons, yet it's a process that, for the uninitiated, seems awash in legalities and lawyers. What makes Corporate Agents' site an especially clever one is that it uses the democratizing basis of the Internet as a means of making its point that incorporating is neither all that difficult nor necessarily all that expensive. In other words, it's a service that seems especially suited to the Net itself, which has thousands of small-business or would-be small-business users.

The home page (Figure 23.37) is sparse but easy to follow, although the logo should probably be redone for Web purposes. The crucial links for many are "Why Incorporate" and "Incorporation Fees," and these are nicely stressed right up front.

FIGURE 23.37.

Corporate Agents home page, with links to explanations.

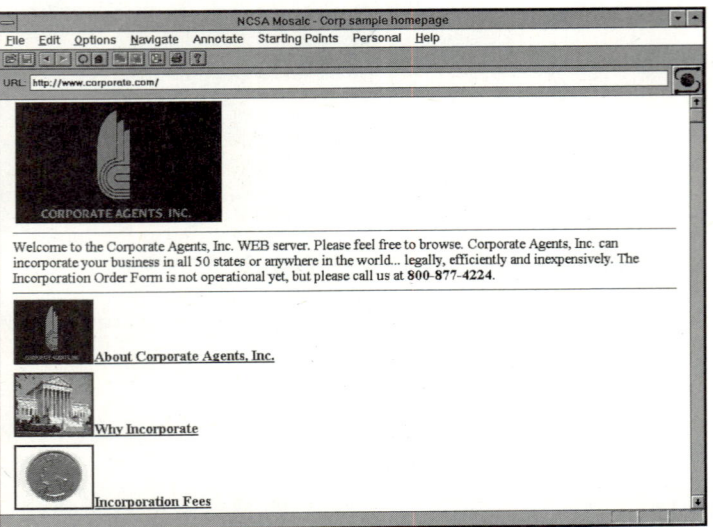

Figure 23.38 offers a look at the company's actual products, "corporate kits" that you can order from them, although not over the Web itself. This shot is taken from the middle of the page, and it shows a picture of the kit and a bulleted list of what's in the kit. It would be a good idea if some of the items themselves were given a fuller explanation (or perhaps a link to a separate information page), but what you need is right here.

FIGURE 23.38.

Information about corporate kits from Corporate Agents.

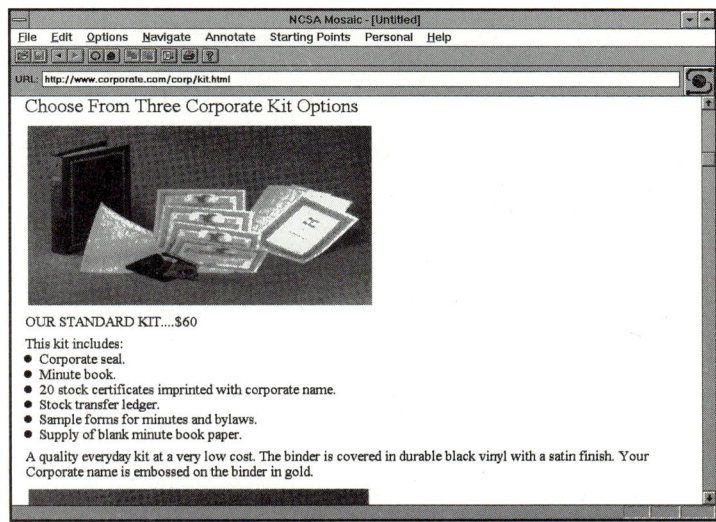

Graphics Visualization and Usability Center

Although sparsely developed at this stage, we can expect more from the Graphics Visualization and Usability Center (`http://www.gatech.edu/pitkow/survey/survey-1-1994/graphs/results-general.html`) in the future. We can also expect similar sites to pop up across the Net. What business continually needs is detailed demographic information so that it can track and target potential customers, and because of its chaotic nature the Internet does not easily provide such information. This lab's home page (Figure 23.39) offers a very brief look at who's using the Net, and although it's only very generally useful, it provides some insights all on its own. (The relatively small percentage of users in the 36-50 range strikes me as extremely odd.)

Clearly, this is interesting material. Just as clearly, business needs much, much more of it, and in much finer detail and across a much larger range of sampling categories and types. While not construed as a business service per se, this center's Web offerings demonstrate the need for such sites. It's also an intelligent site from the standpoint that, from this graph alone, the center is likely to receive consulting requests from major clients, and that's something many centers and labs are looking for. In other words, this page might act as a teaser for business users to contact the center and contract for more information.

FIGURE 23.39.

Graphics Visualization and Usability home page showing demographic chart.

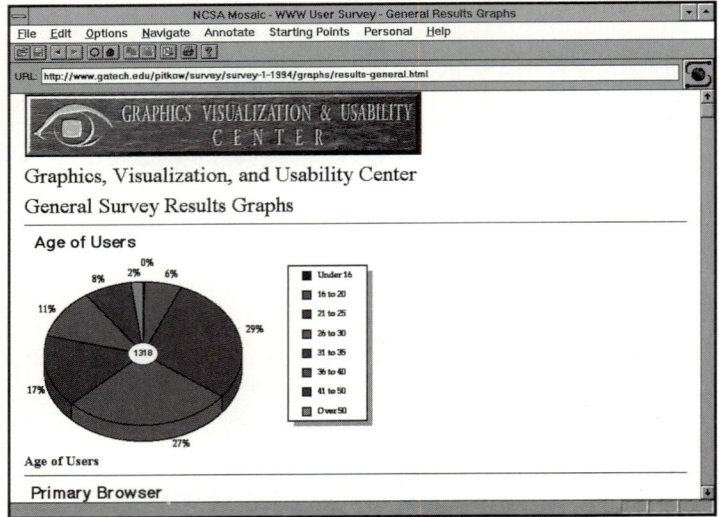

Municipality-Based Business Pages

We've seen a virtual downtown on the Web, so why not a real one? One subcategory of the industrial mall is the municipality-based collection of business sites, of which several are now appearing on the Web. While it's true that shopping on the Web itself doesn't require users to know where they are geographically (that's one of its pluses), the idea behind presenting information about businesses in real communities is that the real business dollar is still very much geographically based. In some cases, these municipality-based sites offer travelers a look at what they can expect when they visit that location. In others, and perhaps more importantly, the site shows businesses who their corporate neighbors will be if they move there.

Keep in mind that one of the most significant municipal tasks is to attract new business. As more and more businesses develop an Internet presence, it makes good sense for municipalities to attract these businesses by demonstrating that the municipality itself has a strong business presence. That might be a factor in a firm's decision to move to one location rather than another. And that could be the most significant thing about these pages.

Businesses in Utah

Utah doesn't spring into the mind when thinking of major business states, so the Businesses in Utah site (`http://www.utw.com/UtahBusi.html`) makes a great deal of sense. From the home page (Figure 23.40) you can see that the state's businesses are aware of the Net and have developed at least some Web presence, although some of the explanations could be expanded for more immediate interest. Still, one of the links is to the world-famous WordPerfect Corporation, and this is an obvious place to start.

FIGURE 23.40.

Home page for Businesses in Utah showing links to partipating firms.

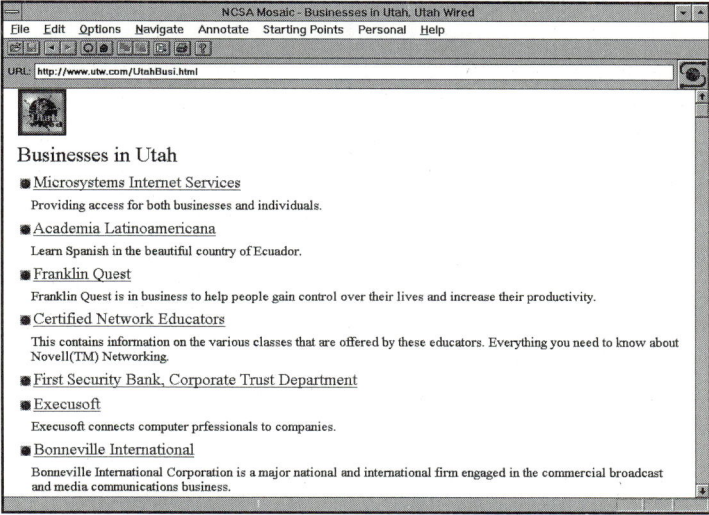

Figure 23.41 shows one of many WordPerfect pages available. This is an information page for WordPerfect for UNIX users, one of the strong design touches being the 3-D buttons at the top of the page. In fact, this page is nothing more than a product information document—there are no patches or bug-fixes available—but it's useful from the standpoint of demonstrating what other information WordPerfect provides. Expect this site to improve dramatically in the near future.

Figure 23.42 demonstrates how a company can gain presence by being associated on the Web with a large company. Appearing with WordPerfect on the Utah business home page is a local Orem company, Computer Recyclers. Although the logo could be better scanned, it's attractive, and the large links are clear and unambiguous. The fact that a browser on the Utah page can switch from large corporation to small local business makes Web presence a particularly attractive possibility for the latter.

Quadralay Corporation, Austin, Texas

Some states have taken a far stronger initiative than others in getting the information superhighway up and running, and Texas is one of them. Among the most prominent Net sites in the state is that of the capital, Austin (`http://www.quadralay.com/www/Austin/Austin.html`), developed by Quadralay Corporation and sporting some of the most interesting business-related information on the Net.

FIGURE 23.41.

WordPerfect for UNIX information page from Utah Businesses.

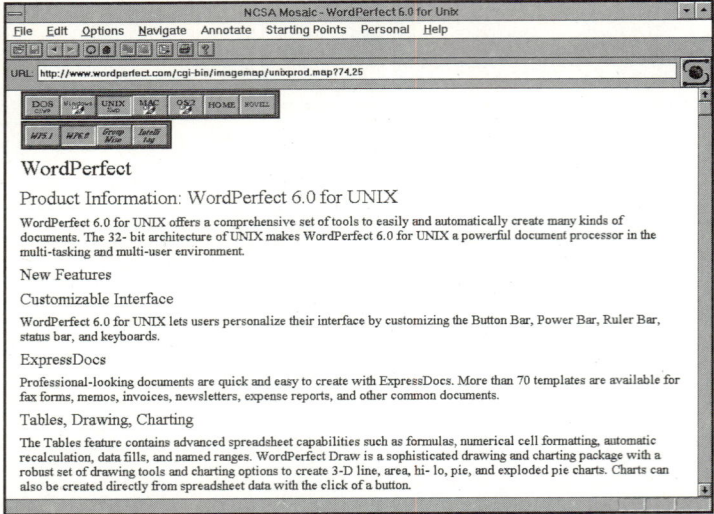

FIGURE 23.42.

Computer Recyclers page from Utah business page.

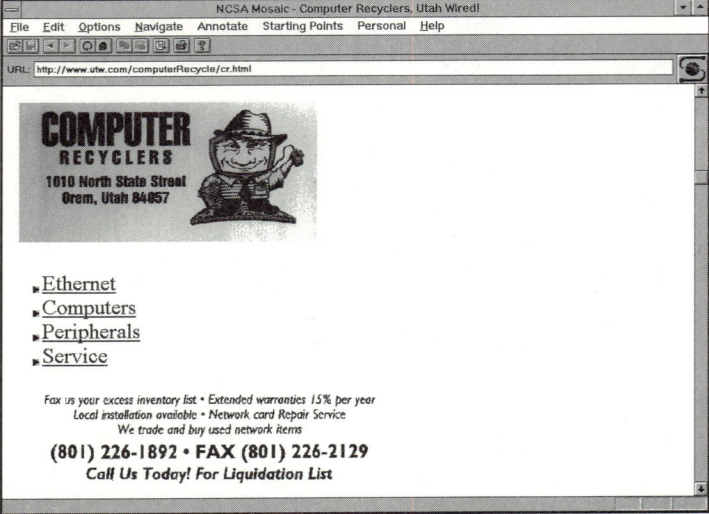

Figure 23.43 shows the Austin home page, with links to information about universities, the county, and the state capital, and with a well-structured set of links to a wide variety of businesses, organizations, and interests further down the page.

FIGURE 23.43.

Quadralay's Austin home page, offering links to a wide range of Austin sites.

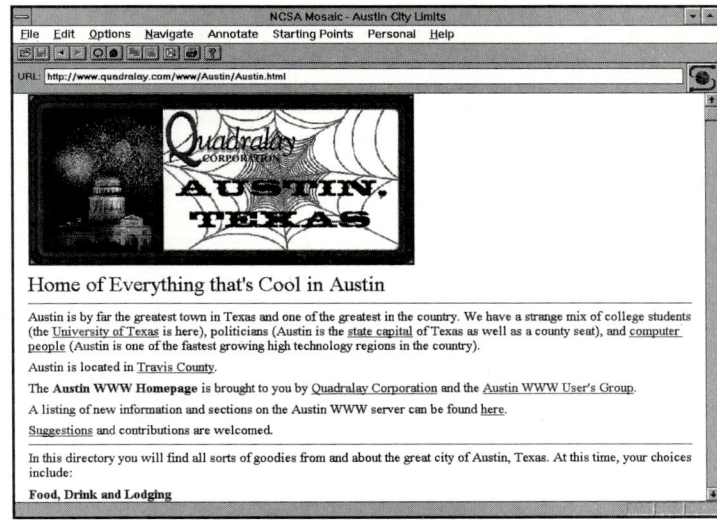

One of the links leads to the Austin Business page (Figure 23.44), and even here you'll find more than the usual assortment of information. Central, of course, are the companies that have developed an Internet presence, but this page features organizations "dedicated to helping Austin-based businesses" as well, an important consideration for any firm browsing the Web and thinking of making a move.

FIGURE 23.44.

Austin Business main page with both companies and business-oriented organizations.

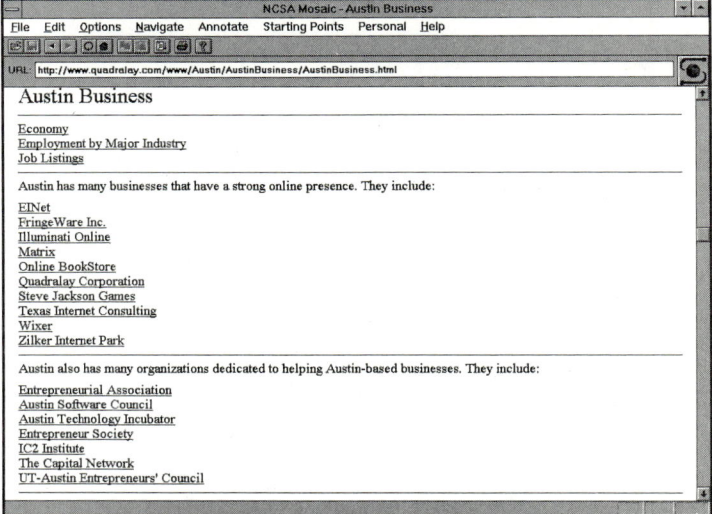

Also available here are details about Austin's economy and employment possibilities. One other link offers information about the Texas Capital Network (Figure 23.45), whose goal is a very clear indication of how actively Austin is seeking to attract new businesses into the area. This is a very well-developed site, and one that is frequently updated. It's probably the best example on the Web so far of a municipality's support of its business community.

FIGURE 23.45.

Texas Capital Network main page, with links to detailed information.

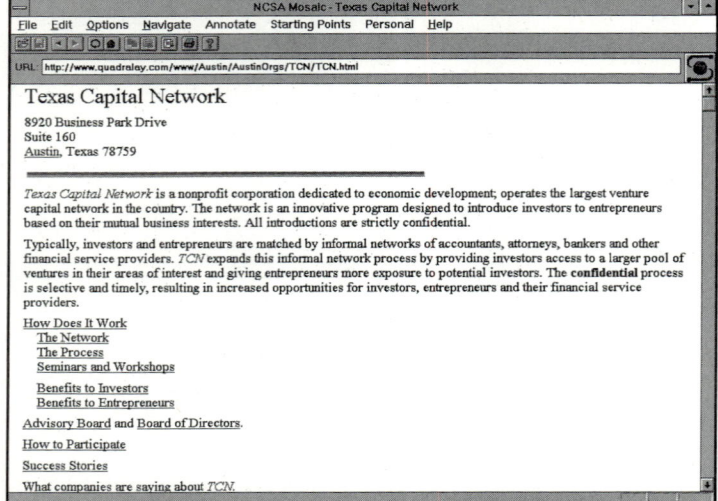

Explorer's Check

Chapter 23 provides a look at a few of the business and commerce sites currently accessible on the World Wide Web. Even from this small sampling it's easy to see the potential of the Web-based commerce, whether from the standpoint of customer service or full-scale product browsing and ordering.

The next year will see an explosion of commercial activity on the Web, as businesses in greater and greater numbers come to realize the Web's potential for advertising, public relations, and, very simply, public awareness.

Niche products and services, international business ventures, and fully developed support sites will spring up continually in 1995 and beyond, to the extent that we might easily find ourselves doing business on the Web in ways that we can only begin to envision now.

The Web isn't likely to replace any existing business venues, but it will certainly add to the possible means of conducting global and local commerce. It's simply too large and too inexpensive for the business sector to ignore.

Entertainment and the Arts

24

by Neil Randall

This chapter, if truly unleashed, would be huge, unruly, and guilty of some of the sheer frivolity and silliness that characterizes some of the entertainment and arts activity on the Web itself. Presented in the next few pages is a glimpse, *and only a glimpse*, of the sheer variety of fascinating sites accessible through even casual browsing, a variety that is increasing with each passing week. Strangely enough, though, and despite the enthusiastic contributions to the Web by artists and entertainers alike, these categories of activity are among the most disappointing material out there. Somehow, it just shouldn't be that way.

The Web has the technological power to foster new kinds of entertainment and new approaches to the arts. Both groups, indeed, have been active since the Web's inception, especially since the graphical browsers began to appear.

But so far very little—if anything—is available on the World Wide Web that isn't available on other media, and in better formats. Collections of great art dot the Web, but nothing available so far even begins to approach the pleasure of visiting a museum, paging through a well-designed art book, or experiencing similar collections on CD-ROM. The Web should be a place for artists to congregate and display their works in progress, but even this has barely begun to occur (at times for obvious reasons of financial exigency, but not always). And where, it might be asked, is the Net's great promise of collaboration, something we might expect to be rampant? It's out there, as this chapter will show, but in very small doses.

And so with entertainment. While the Web allows the kind of interesting "on the site" activity that occurred during the Woodstock '94 festival, and will presumably feature that kind of activity in the future, few entertainment designers have shown much creativity in what they have to present. Some interesting archives exist, and many things on the Web are entertaining without necessarily meaning to be so, but in very few places are we seeing the kind of around-the-world join-in-the-fun type of activity that seems so natural for a global network. Where are the games? Where are the creative and inventive games? Where are the contests, the trivia diversions, the collaborative ventures, the coffee shop chats, the next-to-live bands? Where are the plays we might visit, the books we might interact with, the ... well, you get the idea.

What's a bit mystifying about all of this is that artists and entertainers have always been among the first to bend technology precisely to their needs and wants. The arts often venerate the past, but artists fully realize that new technologies allow them to make their statements, construct their worldviews, offer their insight, or simply display their talents, in a host of new ways. The entertainment industry has historically taken any promising technology and similarly co-opted it for the sake of mass interest, a tendency of which television is only the most obvious example. (It was originally supposed to be of primary interest to educators, let's remember.)

I'm not saying there isn't a significant commitment to entertainment and the arts on the Web today; I'm saying, instead, that the efforts so far have been surprisingly conservative, backwards-glancing, and tentative. If you're an entertainer or an artist and you're reading this right now, consider this a plea to use the Net to its fullest. You have a point to make, and there's now a new way of making that point. And many of us around the world are glued to the set waiting.

The Arts: Projects

Any number of ways present themselves for detailing information on the Web about the arts. We could start with a guided tour of the museums and the archives, or we could launch immediately into a display of some of the Web's more interesting "weirdness." Instead, we'll head somewhere in between, opting for a good beginning collection of activity and moving outwards.

ANIMA

One of the best sites for opening an Internet arts expedition is found in ANIMA, an acronym for the Arts Network for Integrated Media Applications. Part of the often creative `wimsey.com` series of pages out of Vancouver, ANIMA offers not only resources of its own, but a solid basis for further exploration. Figure 24.1 shows part of the ANIMA home page (`http://wimsey.com/anima/ANIMAhome.html`), with colorful links to a range of fascinating (and not so fascinating) material.

FIGURE 24.1.

The ANIMA home page, leading to a number of different artistic sites.

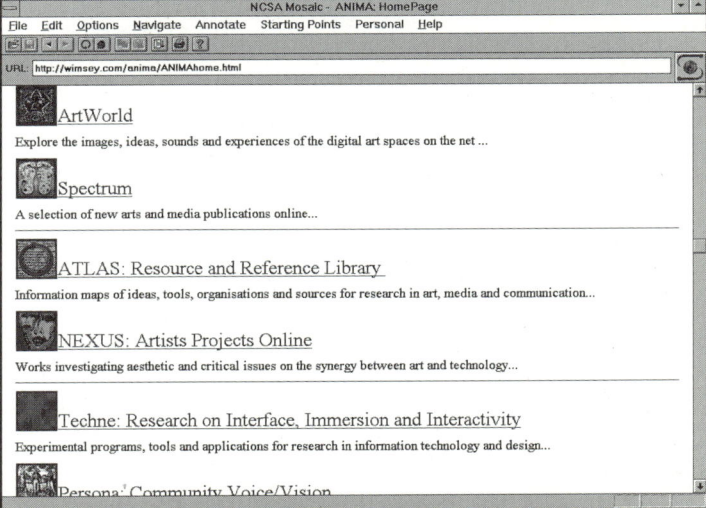

The links, in fact, are ANIMA's real strength. All links are to other pages on `wimsey.com`, and demonstrate how committed this site is (or at least has been) to scouring the Web in search of items of artistic and artistic/theoretical interest. The first significant link is to ArtWorld, a highly personalized page—and in many ways clumsily and even unattractively designed—that provides a huge range of options for the artistic traveler. One such page of links is shown in Figure 24.2, a few of which we'll visit later. While this page has little to recommend it from the standpoint of sheer design (perhaps ironically given its origins), it demands recognition through its function as gateway to the Web's artistic wonders and blunders.

FIGURE 24.2.

A series of artistic links from the pages of ArtWorld.

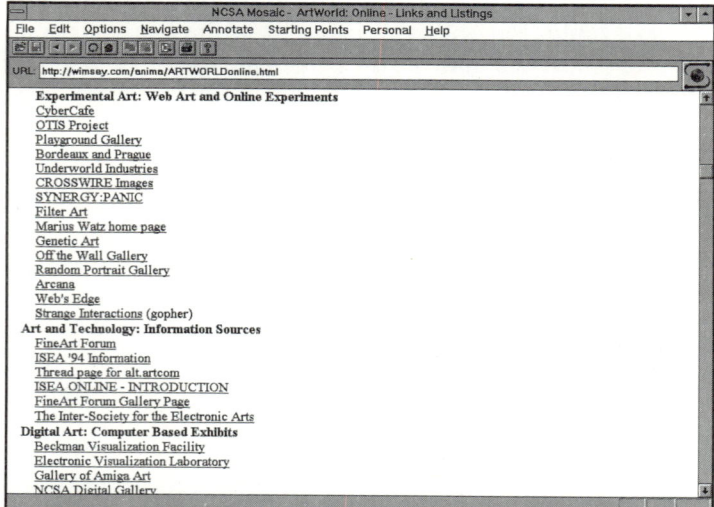

Yet another ANIMA subpage is ATLAS, the Arts and Technology Resource and Reference. The issues raised here deal with the importance of technology to the arts, and also, of course, the problems associated with the association. From links to sites and essays dealing with the electronic media, electronic literature, computer interfaces, and technology and social issues, this site can commandeer hours of your reading time. Figure 24.3 shows links to some of these issues. A somewhat similar page, and just as interesting, is the link to Techne: Interface, Immersion and Interactivity Research.

Finally in ANIMA, we have NEXUS: Network Projects by Artists. While this page (Figure 24.4) isn't anywhere near as full of exciting and inspiring art projects as you'd hope, what appears at this site is precisely the kind of activity the Web needs much more of from the artistic community. Here we see artists at work, displaying what they've done and what they've found themselves capable of using the technology for. They comment on the technology, demonstrate collaborative approaches, and so on, and here again you could spend

a good deal of time. Not all of this is well-designed, but that's not exactly the point. It's ideas we're after here, and ideas we get—even if some of them are off a bit into left field.

FIGURE 24.3.

Part of the ATLAS home page.

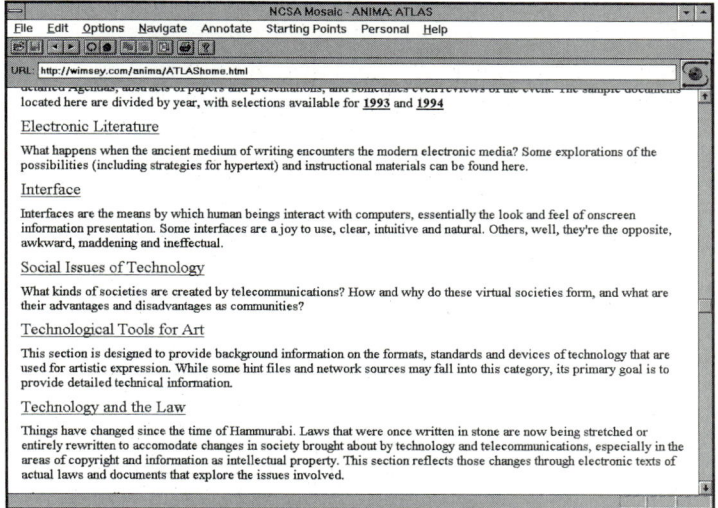

FIGURE 24.4.

Some of the projects in the NEXUS home page.

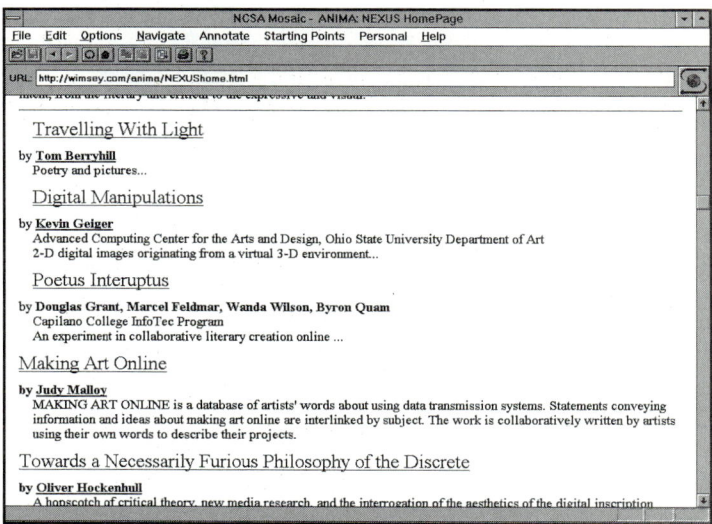

The real criticism of ANIMA is that it doesn't change often enough. Something of this promise should have new offerings constantly, but that simply isn't happening. In fact, not a huge amount has been added since the site opened. Even so, from here you can see the arts on the rest of the Web, so at the very least it's an excellent place to begin.

The OTIS Project

Coming to us from the well-known `sunsite.unc.edu` site is the OTIS Project, an online gallery and collaboration project (`http://sunsite.unc.edu/otis/otis.html`). OTIS stands for Operative Term Is Stimulate, and for the most part that's exactly what it does. Some of the material isn't worth a repeat visit, but that applies to all galleries, digital or physical. What's important is that the project is going on, and that it seems to be thriving quite well. OTIS's home page (Figure 24.5) shows the obvious artistic bent of its contributors (each of the bars represents a separate page or series of pages). For those with slower connections, the OTIS directory is available without inline images at `http://sunsite.unc.edu/otis/schmotis.html`.

FIGURE 24.5.

The OTIS Project home page.

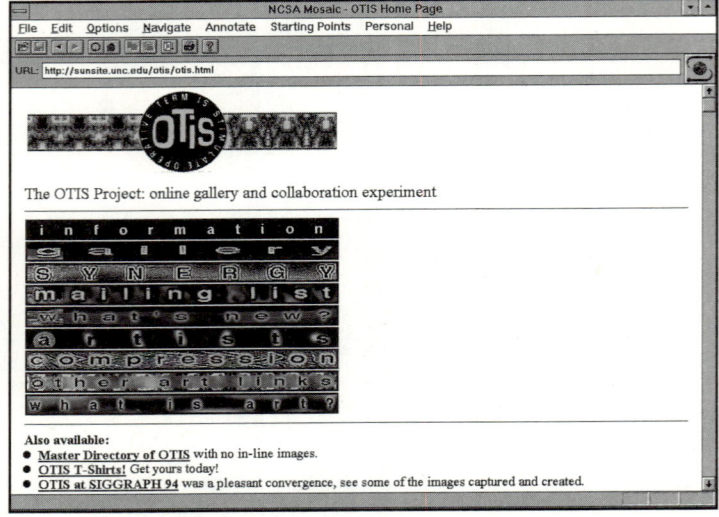

The first link from the home page takes us to the OTIS Gallery. Here we see nothing but a long list of links to further pages (Figure 24.6), but what a list! Pick a medium, any medium, and see what the gallery has to offer. For me, Morphs, Jewelry, Math-art, and Collaborations were must-sees; I only wish this page offered a better indication of what lies behind each link. In the case of jewelry, for instance, no artwork existed at all, and the same held true for morphs; there was, however, an invitation to submit your own art for the category, which is, after all, the point. And the etchings link, like the paintings link and others, takes you to a collection of JPEG and GIF files available for downloading, but nowhere is there a guide to the size of these files. Trust me; they're not small. Still, a few hours spent downloading some selected items will give you a very strong collection, and this is only one site on the Net.

FIGURE 24.6.

The various mediums (media?) from the OTIS Gallery

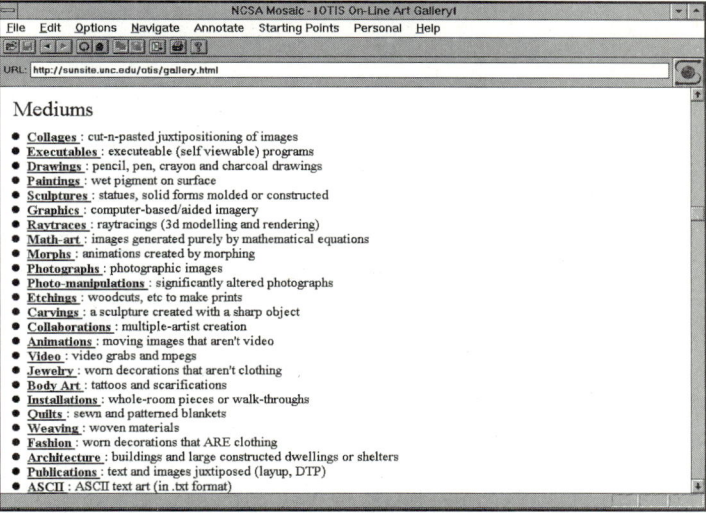

Perhaps the most interesting area of the OTIS site is the collection of collaborative art projects called Synergy. The purpose behind the project is, as its home page points out (Figure 24.7), exactly what the Net should be good for. One person starts a picture/drawing/construction, usually by offering an overall concept with very little detail, and anyone from the Net is free to add to the overall idea or contribute details or even offshoots. Eventually the picture is completed, at which time another picture on the same theme is begun, or the artists start another Synergy project entirely. So far, the results have ranged—predictably—from the bizarre through the terrible and the intriguing, but the idea itself remains continually appealing.

FIGURE 24.7.

The Synergy home page, with links to details about the collaborations.

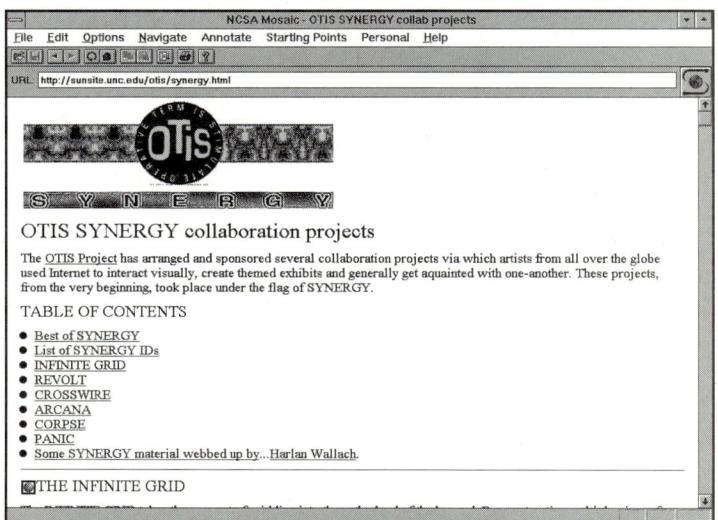

Using sheer morbidity as a guideline, let's look at one of the Synergy collaborations in a bit more detail. This one is called CORPSE, the idea being to assemble an entire corpse from body parts contributed by other artists. Figure 24.8 offers links to rules of contribution, thumbnail sketches, and (below the figure) to various attempts at corpse assembly. The results, which I've decided not to display in this chapter, are extremely mixed but always at least interesting.

FIGURE 24.8.

The CORPSE project from OTIS Synergy.

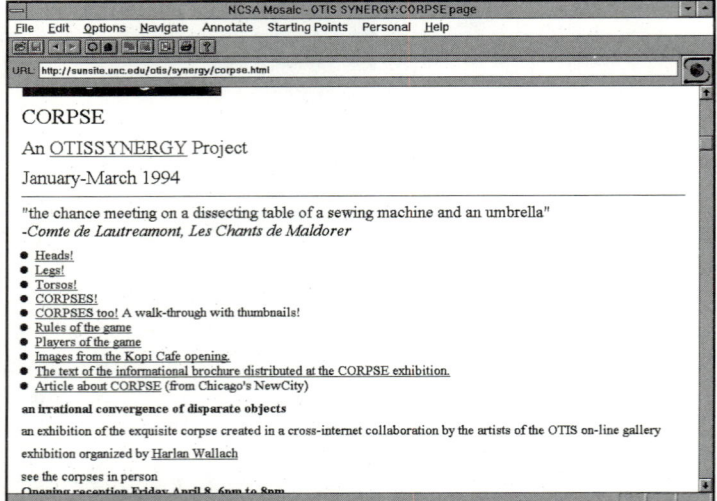

Kaleidoscope

Another project site for artists is Kaleidoscope (`http://kspace.com/`), whose home page (Figure 24.9) is subtitled "Where Independent Artists Sell their Work to the World." In fact, a stroll through this site reveals that there are indeed pictures of works of art offered for sale, and although no forms accompany the site instructions exist for ordering. The most interesting design approach for the site lies with its home page, however. A colorful, unusual clickable "map" takes you to whichever section of the wheel you choose, and as you can see the artistic possibilities are endless. As of this writing, however, some of the categories were underdeveloped.

Cyberkind

Another opportunity for collaborative art, or at least the unusual presentation of art, exists in the literary world. Figure 24.10 shows the home page for Cyberkind, subheaded "prosaics and poetics for a wired world." Here, as you might expect, are literary works of a variety of types, and one of the more attractive logos on the Web. The page is clear and well-designed, and if you have literary material of the kind this site is after, you should consider contacting the editor about submissions.

FIGURE 24.9.

The Kaleidoscope home page, with the clickable wheel.

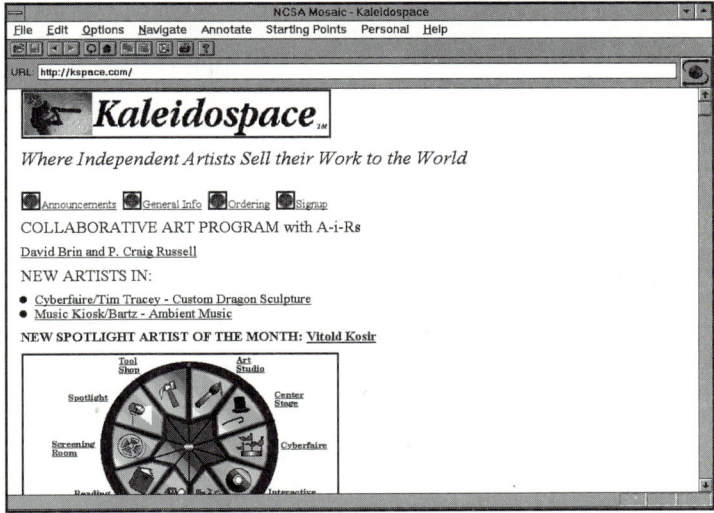

FIGURE 24.10.

Cyberkind's home page, with guidelines for aspiring writers.

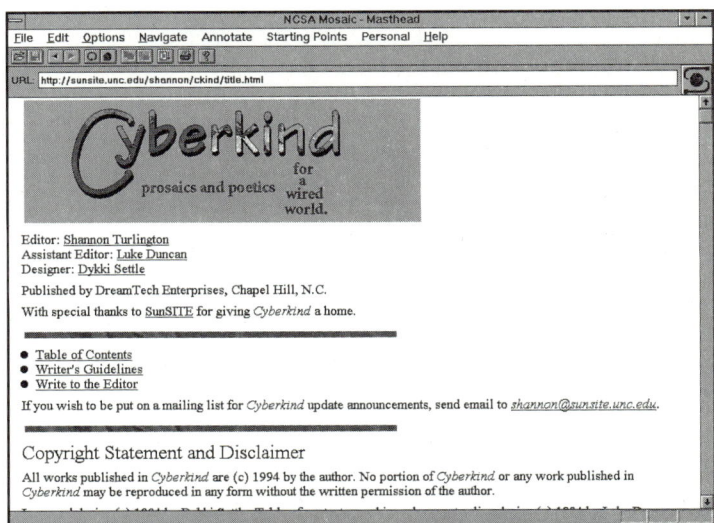

All sites of this kind offer extremely mixed reading (and viewing), but Figure 24.11 demonstrates the type of activity well-suited for Internet-based literary demonstration. "The Complex, Adaptive, Dynamic, Autocatalytic, Multicultural Hypertext Poem" is a title you won't easily find in your local bookstore, especially since the hypertextuality is important to this particular concept. For poets, in fact, the Web offers an opportunity to reach thousands more people than would normally buy a book of poetry anyway. Given the high price of printed books today, and the fact that almost nobody makes a living writing poetry, it wouldn't be surprising to see more poets start publishing on the Web. If the idea is experimentation, or simply expanded audience, why not?

FIGURE 24.11.

One literary venture from the Cyberkind site.

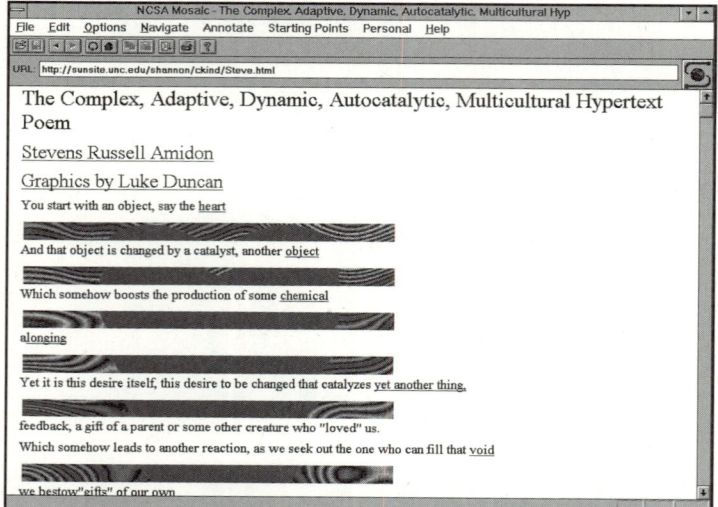

The Arts: Museums and Galleries

Of course, what would an arts medium be without galleries? Traditionally, galleries have benefited the arts community in one major way: They provide a place for works of art to be on permanent or temporary display to the public. Their assumption is that people will actually want to look at works of art, an assumption that appears to be correct, if the fact that many are still open is any indication. Galleries also provide a place (sometimes) for artists to present new works of art, and consequently a place where the public can watch for new artistic developments. The arts community has raging debates about the role of galleries, quite naturally, but those outside that community who are interested in art for any reason rarely question the galleries' usefulness, perhaps even necessity.

Each of the preceding project sites is also a gallery. Here, however, we'll look at the more traditional style of gallery, the art museum. In these galleries, which have a real-world counterpart (that is, an actual building) outside the Net, works are displayed not as a means to find additional contributors, but rather because either the artists are dead or, if still alive, their work is deemed of public interest (by the gallery, society, whatever). The function of the World Wide Web in this context is to provide a means for users around the world to visit these galleries, albeit in a limited way. In fact, the online versions of the some of these galleries operate essentially as an advertisement for the galleries, a means of building awareness. In the first gallery of this section, however, this isn't the case.

art gallery

Names don't get much less pretentious than this one, and in fact it nicely blends the contributors' gallery of the OTIS type with the traditional gallery of the Louvre type. See the upcoming section, "The Louvre." Maintained entirely by one person, as many Web galleries are, the art gallery (`http://heiwww.unige.ch/art/`) features a limited selection of works along with commentary, and the inevitable links to other art sites on the Web, as shown in Figure 24.12.

FIGURE 24.12.

The art gallery home page, with links to a variety of displays.

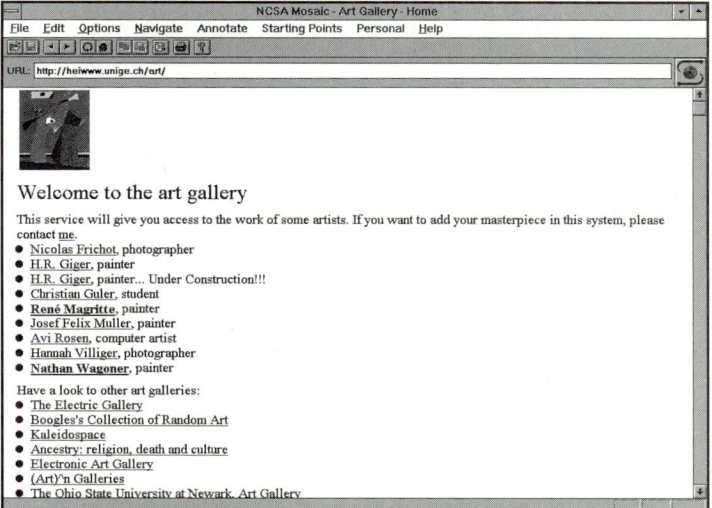

One of the links is to an exhibit of works by Rene Magritte, and here we see the impressive collection of holdings of this gallery. All of the links shown in Figure 24.13 (and this is only a portion of the full page) are to further pages that display the work of art and offer commentaries about it. Whereas the OTIS gallery offered downloadable graphics files, these are viewable on the Web itself, a solution that is instantly more attractive. The problem with downloads is that they demand external viewers (in most instances) and often hard disk space (even when they're not permanently stored), and they simply don't fit with the spirit of navigating and viewing that the Web offers. This is a good site.

FIGURE 24.13.

Links to the specific art works of Rene Magritte.

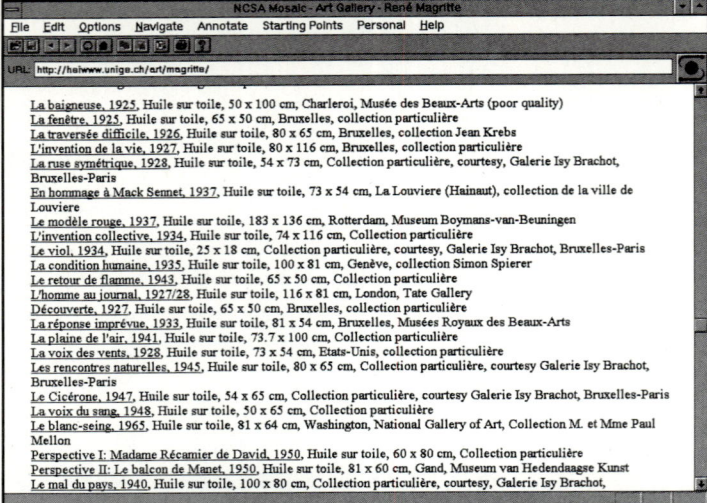

Krannert Art Museum

Our first real-world gallery is the Krannert Art Museum, physically located at the University of Illinois at Urbana-Champaign (which, perhaps not incidentally, is also the home of NCSA), and electronically available at

```
http://www.ncsa.uiuc.edu/General/UIUC/KrannertArtMuseum/KrannertArtHome.html
```

As Figure 24.14, the home page, makes clear, the function of the Krannert Web site is to introduce long-distance viewers to the museum and to offer a sampling of some of the treasures contained in the real building. A very sharp map of the museum is available, as well as an extremely useful list of educational resources.

Figure 24.15 shows a typical exhibit from the Krannert site. Here, three samples of the museum's collection of 20th century art are given (relatively) small representations, and clicking on the links downloads a larger version. Like the rest of the Krannert Museum, this is a well-designed page: clear, colorful, and highly accessible. The limited amount of information is actually a plus, because of the tendency of Web pages to cram rather than present. Still, having only three works on display is a bit disappointing, and might have the negative effect of suggesting that the museum itself is poorly stocked.

FIGURE 24.14.

The Krannert Art Museum home page.

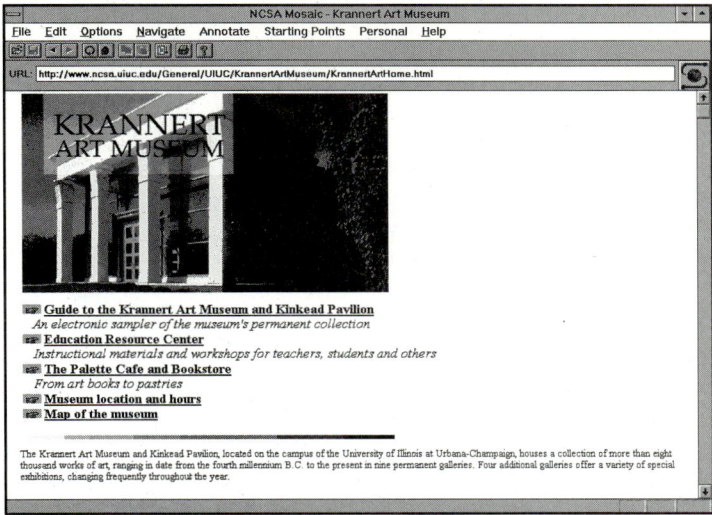

FIGURE 24.15.

The Twentieth-Century Art page from the Krannert Museum.

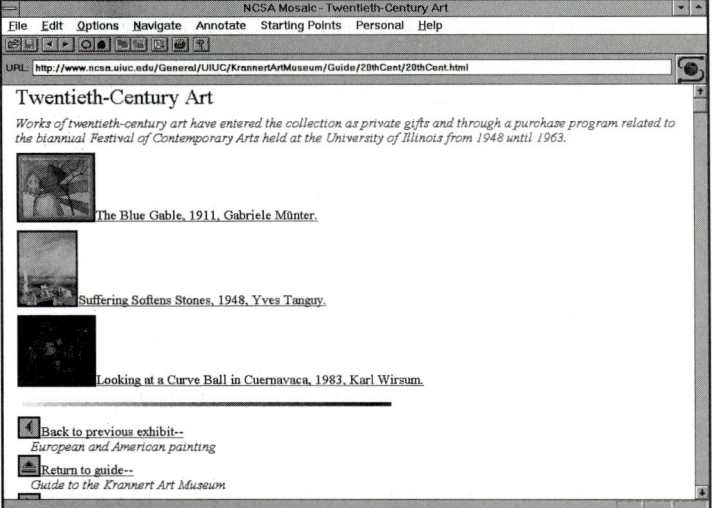

The Louvre

No art museum in the Western world has the prestige of the Louvre, and it's nice to see its presence on the Web (`http://mistral.enst.fr/~pioch/louvre/`). It's even nicer to see that the site is well-designed and maintained, because it would be wrong to expect anything less of an institution like this one. Of course, the nicest thing of all would be to be

able to sit back and tour every item in every exhibit in every room of the real museum, something that wouldn't likely even make a dent in the potential attendance at the place. In fact, it might even entice visitors who wouldn't otherwise come to see it.

What we have in this site is a fractional sampling of the material available in the museum itself. Figure 24.16 is the home page, which clearly states that three exhibits are currently being offered. Of these, strangely enough, the tour of Paris might well be the most complete, but the two internal exhibits are at least worth seeing.

FIGURE 24.16.

The Louvre home page, with links to a tour of Paris.

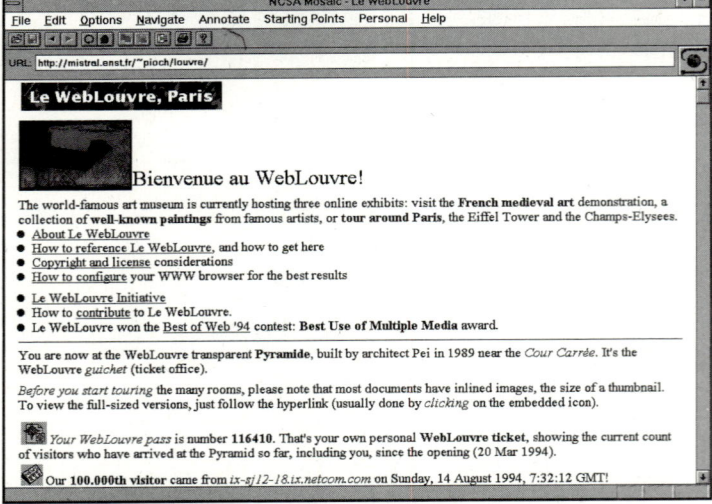

Figure 24.17 offers an introduction to the Famous Paintings exhibition. Again a well-developed page with attractive and small inline graphics leads us in an uncluttered fashion through the offerings. This page demonstrates the importance of a clear and uncomplicated entrance to a Web site, and it's almost as if the Louvre knew something about building accessibility. At any rate, all items are appealing, but keep in mind that they're definitely limited in what they display thereafter.

A click on the Impressionism category leads to a small but worthwhile list of artists, including the Dutch painter/printmaker Johan Barthold Jongkind. Here is an example of the use of the Web to spur interest in an item that physically exists. One look at Jongkind's "The Church of Overschie," even at this size, makes you realize first, that you have to see it in order to appreciate it fully; and second, that you want to see it to grasp what appears to be superb effects of color and texture. The text of the page—especially the French text—makes the real site all that much more appealing.

FIGURE 24.17.

The entry to the Famous Paintings exhibition at the Louvre.

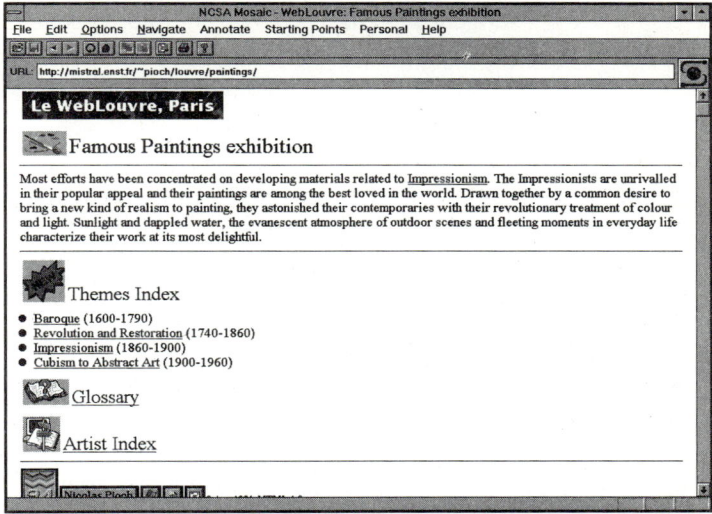

FIGURE 24.18.

A sample work of art from the Jongkind display at the Louvre.

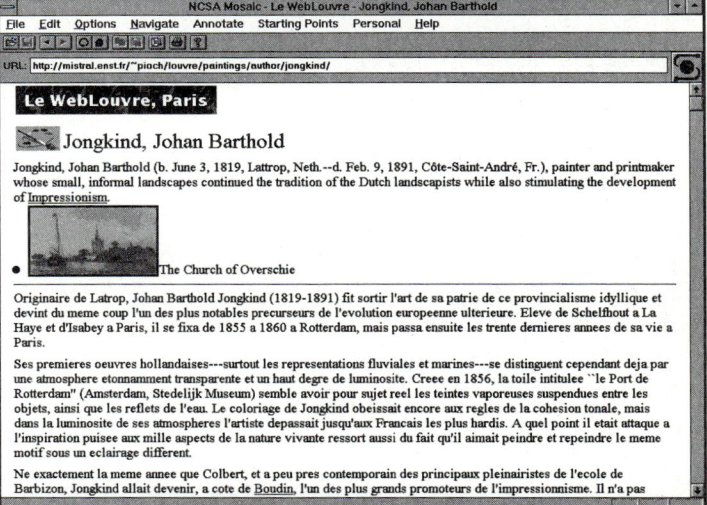

The Arts: Publications and Collections

There are so many arts-oriented sites on the Web worth visiting that it would require an entire book, rather than one single chapter, to capture them all, even at this early stage of the Web's career. Here we'll look at a sampling of other efforts, which I've lumped under the category Publications and Collections. These are indicative of the kind of material available for the diligent searcher, but I've not chosen them because they're necessarily representative. Right now, there's really no such thing as a representative collection of sites, since designers are putting forth a considerable effort to be creative and remain individualistic. Still, they demonstrate some important trends.

RUNE

RUNE (`http://www.ai.mit.edu/~spraxlo/rune/RUNE.html`) is one of many arts-oriented publications finding its way onto the Web. It's not necessarily the best, the most complete, or even the most provocative, but it offers a glimpse at some of the potential for authors and publishers in this regard. In many ways, the Web is a perfect vehicle for this kind of publication because there's rarely sufficient funding available to offer these journals in print. In addition, the Web offers a potentially larger audience, even given the fact that many visitors will simply take a look and click elsewhere. Journals such as *RUNE* have a nearly impossible time finding shelf space in even the better periodical outlets, whereas on the Web they are always available, and they can be advertised in newsgroups, mailing lists, and on the Web itself.

Figure 24.19 shows the home page for *RUNE*, with an enticing set of links for anyone of a literary bent.

FIGURE 24.19.
RUNE home page.

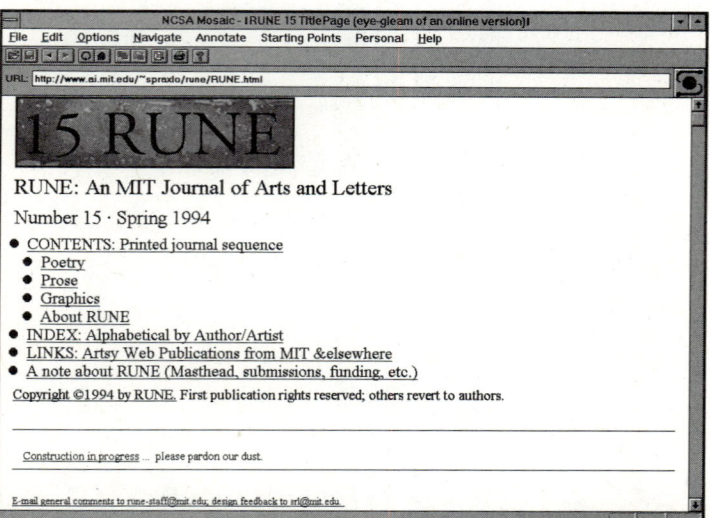

CBC Radio

The Canadian Broadcasting Corporation has a reputation for being anything but "with-it," but you wouldn't know it by looking at their Web site (`http://debra.dgbt.doc.ca/`

cbc/cbc.html). Here we have not only information about the nationwide (in Canada) radio network, but also lists of products available for ordering and a link to a fascinating area called Illustrated Audio (a necessity if the Web is to fulfill its communicative potential). Figure 24.20 displays the CBC Radio's home page, with links to specific tools that allow you to play audio files on your machine.

FIGURE 24.20.

The CBC Radio trial home page.

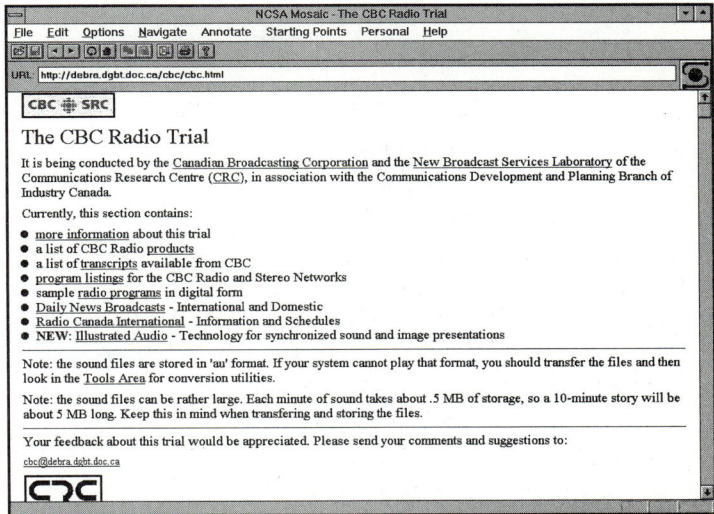

From the sample radio programs link on the CBC home page, you arrive at Figure 24.21, which offers links to several representative CBC programs. While several of these are of interest to many people (although admittedly The Idea of Canada might have limited appeal), the best known of the bunch is unquestionably Quirks and Quarks, a science explanation program. Clicking on any of these links takes you to a page that offers downloadable audio files, each containing a sample of a particular show. Some are several minutes long (and thus extremely long to download), but others are shorter and more instantly accessible.

J.R.R. Tolkien

The next two sites demonstrate how one solitary fan of a given artist can simultaneously fuel a passion for that artist's works and make a huge amount of valuable information available to a world-wide community at the same time. Figure 24.22 (http://herald.usask.ca/~friesend/tolkien/rootpage.html) is a truly impressive page featuring links to just about anything you could possibly want to know about the author of *The Lord of the Rings* and a host of other material, and it clearly represents hundreds of hours of searching, compiling, and presenting. Figure 24.23 (http://www.cs.indiana.edu/

hyplan/awooldri/Xanth.html) shows a similar site dealing with the Xanth novels of Piers Anthony, somewhat less complete but equally impressive in its display of sheer labor. In both cases, however, that labor is a labor of love.

FIGURE 24.21.

A sampling of available CBC programs.

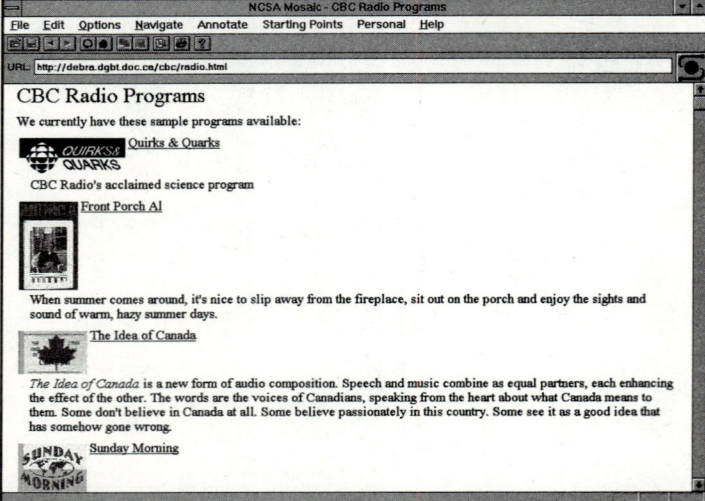

FIGURE 24.22.

The J.R.R. Tolkien home page, with links to newsgroups and many other sites.

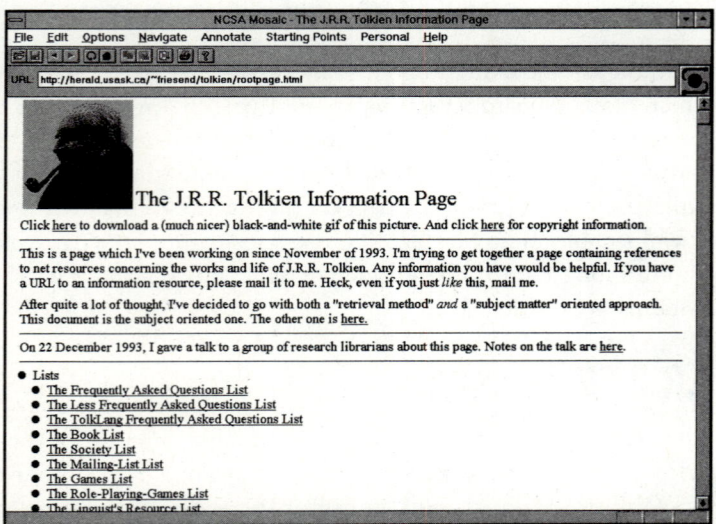

FIGURE 24.23.

Xanth home page, with newsgroup and text file links, among others.

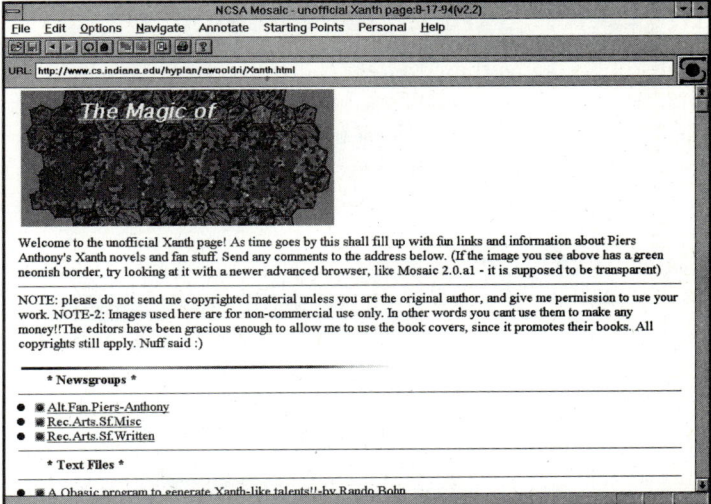

Entertainment: Television

Well, why not? Television and the World Wide Web are linked, of course, especially as the multimedia nature of the Web begins to kick in. Given enough bandwidth, and high enough speeds, the Web has the potential to become part of the promised interactive television technology that's been bandied about for the past several months, and I suspect it won't be an extremely long time before Web sites are used as supplemental activities for TV programs. Is there any doubt that right now, in 1994, a Web site that featured outtakes, fill-in episodes, trivia contests, and interviews with the cast members of "Beverly Hills 90210" or "Melrose Place" would be an immediate success? The age group is right, the familiarity with computers is right, and the Web is almost as hyped as the shows. Newsgroups about these and other shows—everything from "The Simpsons" through "Star Trek" (all incarnations) and just about everything else— are already hugely popular, and they offer nothing but text and opinions.

Whether or not we'll see television-style programming over the Web, the way we're seeing magazine-style publishing, remains to be seen. Just don't be surprised, given the possibility of such ventures as the Internet Multicasting project, to find Web "stations" listed beside the real stations in the *TV Guide*. Not this year, certainly, but who knows what the latter half of this century might bring? And who knows, additionally, whether the possibilities are exciting or terrifying?

The Lurker's Guide to "Babylon V"

"Babylon V" has garnered a loyal following partly because of its similarities to and important departures from "Star Trek." As far as entertainment archive information is concerned, the Lurker's Guide to Babylon V (`http://www.hyperion.com/lurk/lurker.html`) is probably the most impressive on the Web. The home page (Figure 24.24) is clear and free of (often) unattractive lists, and it leaves no question of what's available on the site.

FIGURE 24.24.

Babylon V home page.

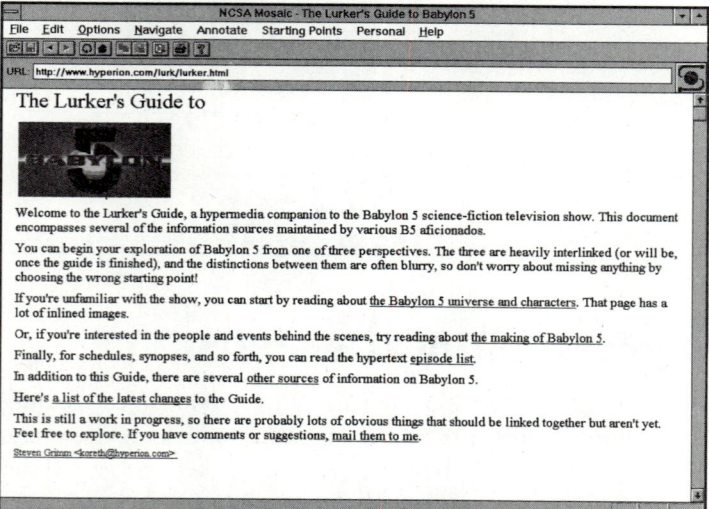

What the home page doesn't do is demonstrate the richness of what's behind the links, as here any viewer (except the absolutely most knowledgeable) will find information they might not have known they wanted. Figure 24.25 displays a series of links that begin to show the amount of material available, and this, while enticing, isn't anywhere near the most attractive of the lot. Other pages offer pictures and information about the actors and their careers, and still other pages offer still other details about other aspects of the show— well worth examining if you're thinking of putting together a worthwhile archive. If nothing else, this site shows how much sheer work is involved.

"Star Trek: The Next Generation"

And, of course, where would any self-respecting global network be without its requisite share of Star Trek material? Beginning with a (perhaps inevitable) picture of the Enterprise, the home page for "Star Trek: The Next Generation" (`http://www.ee.surrey.ac.uk:80/Personal/STTNG/`), shown in Figure 24.26, offers a clear structure and equally clear links. If you're a fan of the now-completed but forever-to-be-rerun series, or even if you're just a casual viewer or someone trying to construct a similar site, this one is worth visiting. One of the problems, however, is that there's surprisingly little good material on the Net about any of the Star Treks, other than copious text files about aliens and starships and endless discussions about the possibilities of Warp factor travel and the like, and this site suffers in that way. But that's hardly its own fault.

FIGURE 24.25.

The Making of Babylon V page.

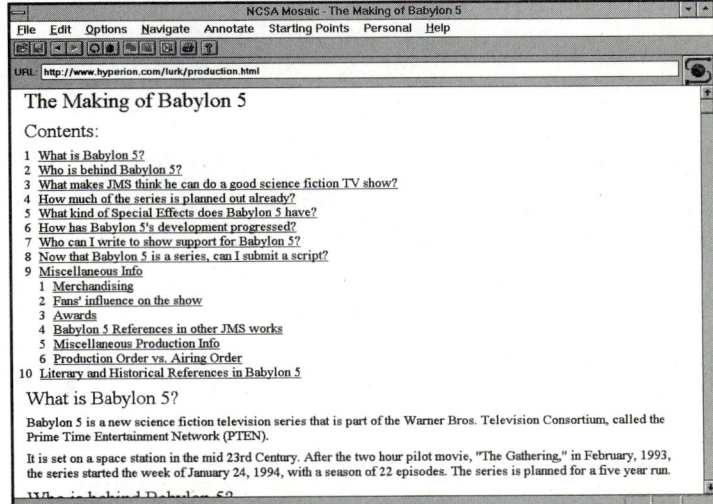

FIGURE 24.26.

Star Trek: The Next Generation home page.

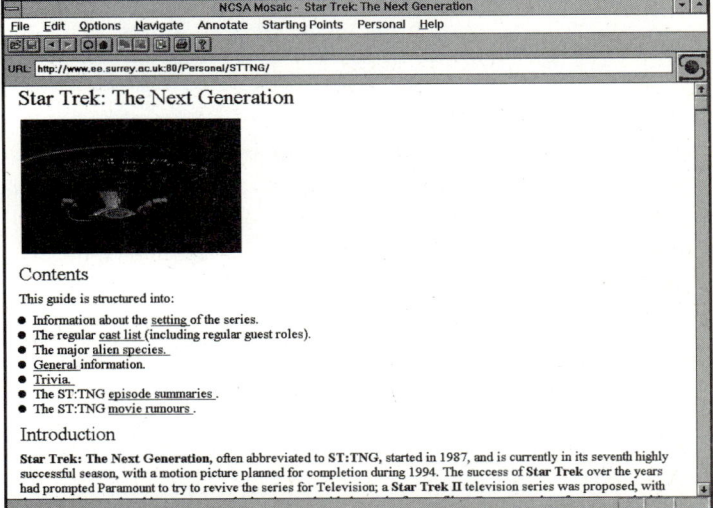

Lunar Institute of Technology

Since we're on the science fiction theme, let's take a look at how we might actually bring the Babylon Vs and the Star Treks into existence. At first glance, and without actually reading the title or anything else (a common possibility while surfing the Web), the Lunar Institute of Technology home page (`http://128.194.15.32/~dml601a/ssd/sdhp.html`) looks like all kinds of other university or research institute home pages on the Web. All it needs is a logo with a coat of arms, and links to a course calendar or two, and it's all there. Figure 24.27 shows the home page, compete with attractive iconic links to the, uh, faculties.

FIGURE 24.27.

The Lunar Institute home page.

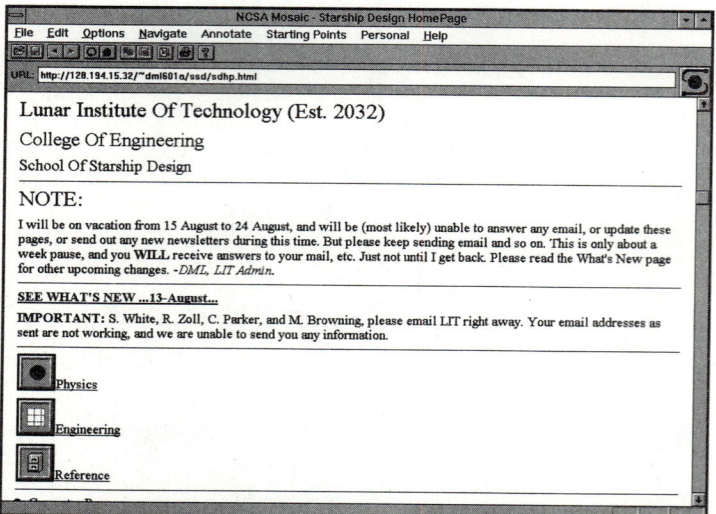

And what's being researched at the Lunar Institute? Lots, actually. As Figure 24.28 demonstrates, serious research is being undertaken about items like the Starwisp, a technology that would allow a craft to reach Alpha Centauri in a mere 21 years. By that time, "Full House" should have finished its rerun schedule and Windows 95 will be on the market, so you won't have actually missed much. In fact, the Lunar Institute itself might be in operation.

A fun site, and highly creative.

FIGURE 24.28.

The Starwisp research page from the Lunar Institute.

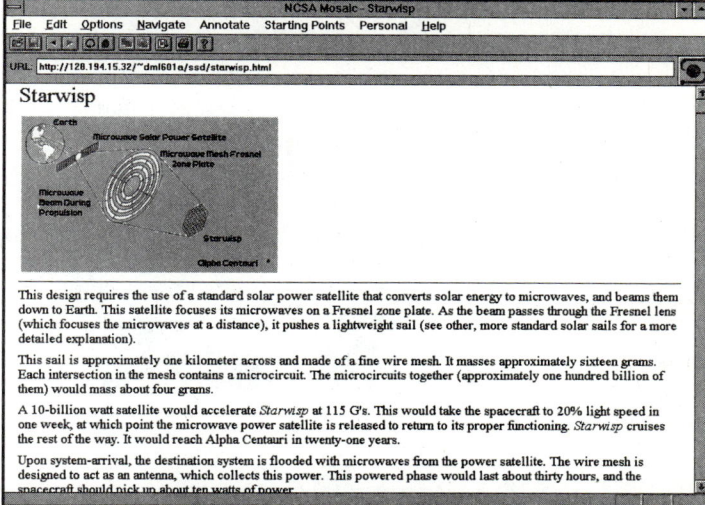

FOX Broadcasting

Well, I mentioned "Beverly Hills" and "Melrose Place," didn't I? And here we have it: a FOX Broadcasting site (`http://www.clark.net/pub/aaron/my-html/fox.html`). It's not an "official site" (one developed by FOX), but at this point few sites are. Like most, this one's constructed by a fan, and like most it represents hours of devoted work. If you're a fan of FOX programming in general, you'll spend more time than you can afford seeing what's here. The home page, shown in Figure 24.28, offers links to several FOX programs.

FIGURE 24.29.

The FOX Broadcasting home page.

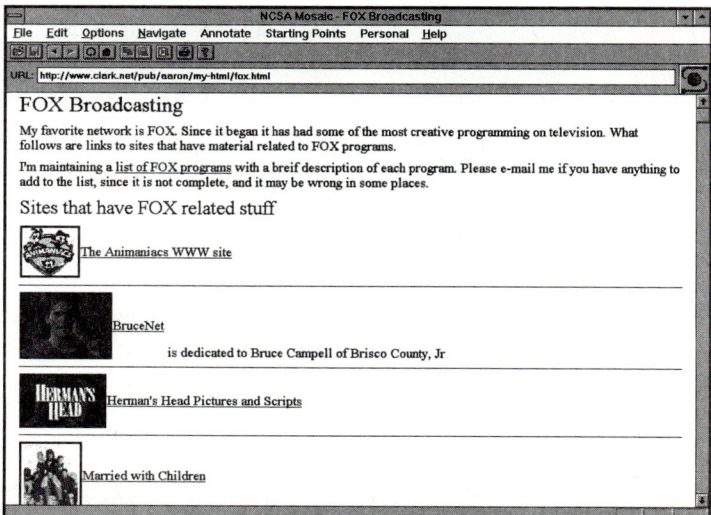

Who knows which FOX program is the most popular among these, but the X-Files page (Figure 24.30) is as richly detailed as any being offered. In addition to a sound icon that lets you hear the program's theme music, there's an episode guide, a FAQ, two FTP sites, a collection of related art and fiction, a survey, and fan club information. The page is indicative of many fan pages in demonstrating that you're likely to meet people with common interests all over the Net, and any X-Files fan will find at least some happiness here.

FIGURE 24.30.

The X Files page from the FOX site.

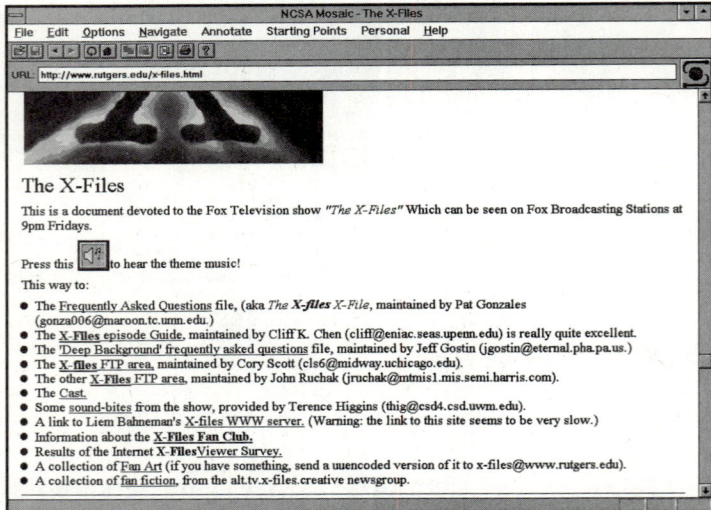

Entertainment: Sports

Not surprisingly, several Web sites offer sports-related pages. During the 1994 World Cup, an official site offered advance information such as schedules and ticket availability, and during the course of the tournament, updates were available as well. This was also the case during the 1994 Winter Olympics in Lillehammer, Norway, with an official Norwegian site featuring medal results, medal standings, graphics, and news material about the games. Look for a huge amount of detailed Web-based information about the 1996 Summer Games in Atlanta, and this is only natural for tournaments such as these: They all appeal to the world, and that's what the Internet attracts.

But there's room on the Web for more than just world-wide interests. The New York Rangers have a home page, as do several other sports clubs, and the Canadian Football League (which has now expanded into U.S. cities) also has an official site. There's no reason for minor leagues and minor teams not to have sites as well, since the cost of renting Web space is extremely small considering the benefits that a well-maintained site can offer in public relations and fan information. Statewide or interstate competitions could benefit as well; the name of the game is getting the word out, and offering interested people continual updates on what's transpiring. In the case of major sports events, such as the World Cup, the European Cup, the Super Bowl, the Stanley Cup playoffs, or the World Series, Web sites can help maintain fan enthusiasm and satisfy fan obsession.

World Wide Web of Sports

The World Wide Web of Sports (`http://tns-www.lcs.mit.edu/cgi-gin/sports`) offers links to a variety of professional and amateur sports. As the home page (Figure 24.31) shows, the format is brief but clear, and the information provided useful but hardly mesmerizing. Being able to get video highlights from yesterday's baseball games requires two things—a high-speed Internet connection and the actual playing of baseball games (as I write this, there's a bit of a strike going on)—and it would be nice to have full box scores and revised rosters.

FIGURE 24.31.

The Major League Baseball section of the World Wide Web of Sports page.

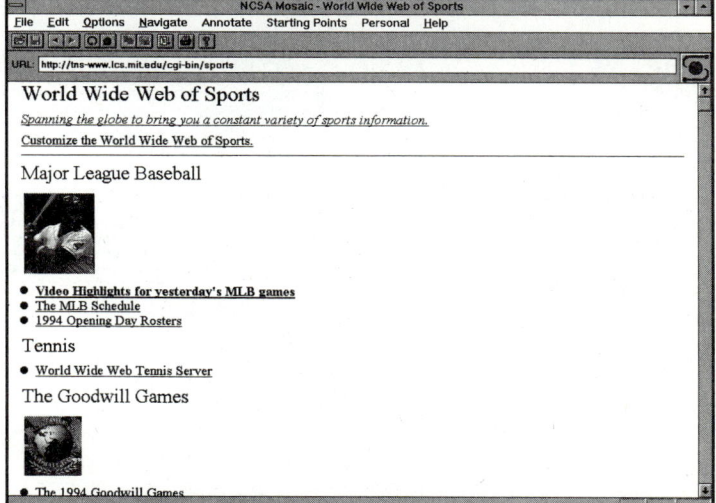

Figure 24.32 shows the result of clicking on the Video Highlights link. The top link shows the CNN screen showing the final results of the game, and clicking on any link takes you further to the highlight. You're far better off watching CNN itself for real highlights, but this page points nicely to the possibilities of the future. Highlights on demand, anyone?

One of the more interesting features in this site is shown in Figure 24.33. Here, you can create your own HTML page that bypasses links to sports you're simply not interested in. This is interactive webbing at its height, allowing you not just to bookmark the pages you want to visit but in fact to change the ones you find. Expect more of this from similar sites in the future.

FIGURE 24.32.

The Major League Baseball highlights page.

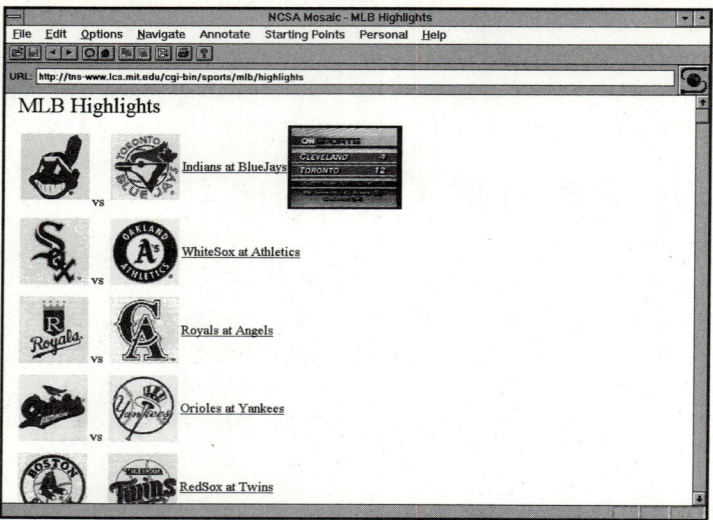

FIGURE 24.33.

The Create Your Own Sports Page site.

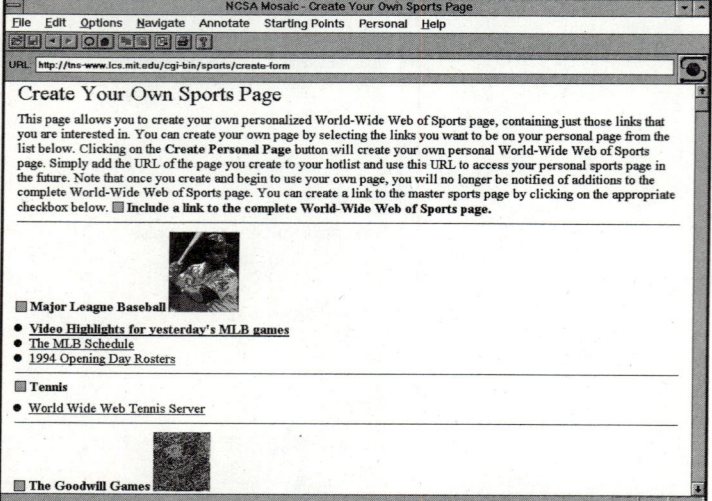

Entertainment: Games and Interactivity

If there's one area where the Internet has been surprisingly weak, that area is the games department. Yes, MUDs (Multi-User Dialogs, text adventure games available through telnet) are a fact of Internet life, but while some people find them addicting and some designers are using them for very worthwhile purposes, they hold utterly no appeal for a wide range of users. One reason is that they're text-only (with a few very limited exceptions), and in a world of colorful, highly graphical computer games this is less than acceptable. Anyone who's spent even twenty hours a year for the past three years trying out even one hot new game each time knows that text games aren't even available any more. Graphics, sound, full multimedia are the hot ticket items, and gamers will settle for nothing less.

Obviously, the Web is too young and too slow to offer anything approaching even the most rudimentary graphic games. It's not too young or too slow to offer interactive gaming, but there's virtually nothing available. This is surely a resource (both creative and financial) just waiting to be mined.

In the meantime, the Web has proven adept at offering support for players of existing games, and at least a couple of examples of interactive fiction. A few examples are explored here.

Advanced Dungeons and Dragons and Other RPGs

Take a look at this page while you can. TSR, the publishers of Advanced Dungeons and Dragons, has recently taken a hard stance against any use of its name or its trademarks on the online services, so this extremely attractive gaming page (`http://www.acm.uiuc.edu/ duff/index.html`) might well have a short lifespan. As the home page demonstrates (Figure 24.34), the site offers pointers to items of interest to players of AD&D and other role-playing games, including information and archives about mailing lists and newsgroups. The Boris Vallejo painting is a perfect attention-getter from this crowd—Vallejo is the artist against whom all other fantasy artists are judged—and the clear contents and purpose of the page make it highly accessible. Unfortunately, there are no links to any individual games, and the undesired impression is that there's not all that much here.

FIGURE 24.34.

The Advanced Dungeons and Dragons and RPGs home page.

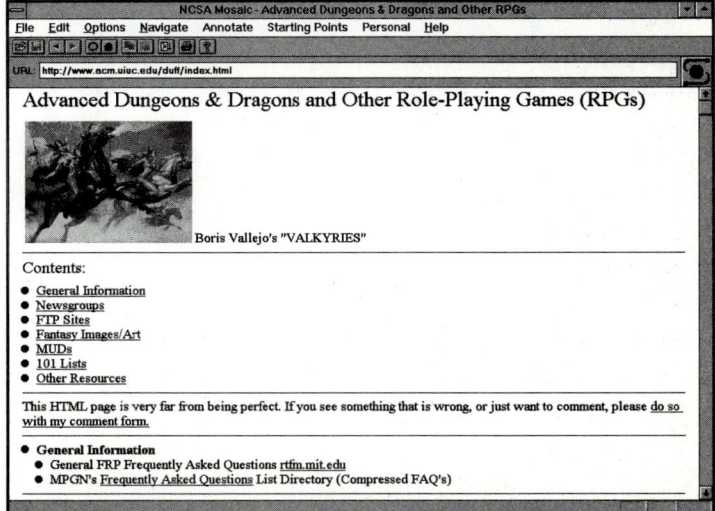

Of particular interest to those collecting the work of Vallejo and his colleagues is the Fantasy Art link. Figure 24.35 offers a very attractive group of sample graphics files that can be downloaded from one specific archive, with a pointer to a second. Also of interest to HTML designers is the designers' candid comments about the tribulations of trying to construct a useful page. Not only do the comments add to the personal element (important in hobby pages), they also encourage interaction.

FIGURE 24.35.

Fantasy Art page from the RPG site.

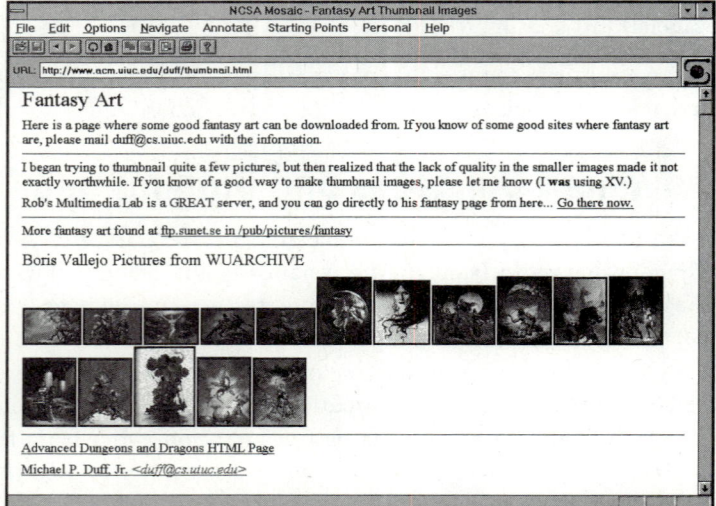

Myst and ShadowRun

Figures 24.36 and 24.37 show a recent trend on the Web that has the potential to be extremely useful to gamers. These pages offer support and guidance for players of two particular computer games, of the same nature found in the forums of online services such as GEnie or America Online. The Myst page, in fact, (`ftp://ftp.netcom.com/pub/carasso/www/myst.html`) operates as a mini-hint guide, and it's easy to see how a page like this could prove invaluable for those stuck at a particular point (in most adventure games, this happens at least two or three times). There's no money in it for the author, but there isn't for those who post hints and tips to the commercial online forums, either. That's not the point.

The Myst home page makes use of large font sizes for its main questions. While the size is perhaps too large for good aesthetics, it more than accomplishes its goal of drawing attention to the purpose of the page and simultaneously avoiding the problem of too much white space on pages with limited content. The ShadowRun home page, shown in Figure 24.37, builds its appeal around the idea of comprehensiveness; anyone interested in the ShadowRun game (`http://www.ip.net/shadowrun`) will find this page a starting point to a variety of Internet activities.

FIGURE 24.36.

Home page for the popular Myst adventure game.

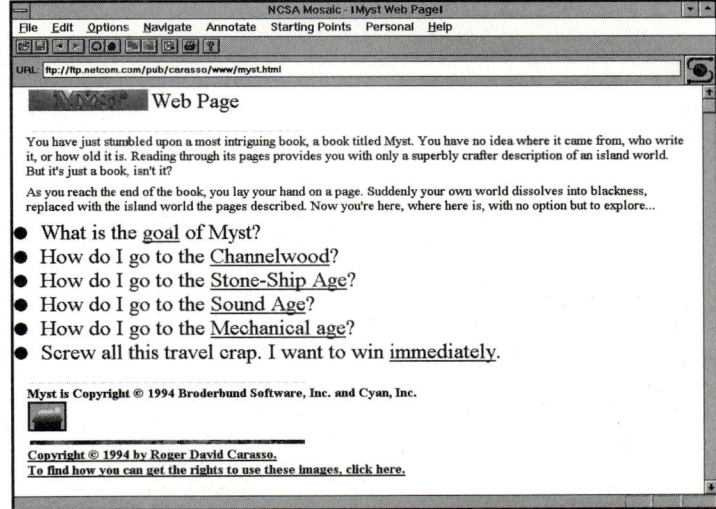

The value of pages like this is that they promote community among game players. Computer gaming by its nature (for now, at least) is a solitary activity, and there are so many games available that it's often difficult to find anyone nearby who plays the same game you do. But there's certain to be a group of people somewhere on the Net who share your interest, and these pages help you find them.

FIGURE 24.37.

Home page for resources about the ShadowRun game.

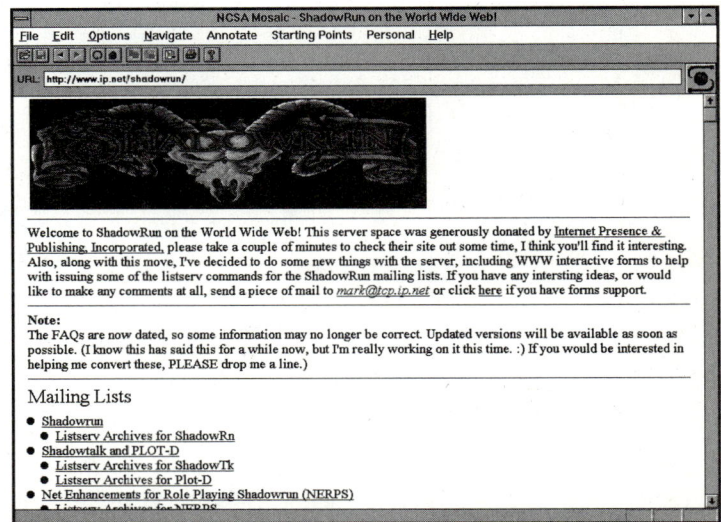

The Doomsday Brunette

Somewhere in our youth, most of us encountered the reading phenomenon known most popularly as "choose your own adventure." The idea was to read a page, then make a decision about what the character should do next. Instructions at the bottom of the page then told you what page to turn to, based on your decision, and the story proceeded from there. All in all, you'd make a few dozen decisions by the time the story ended, and if you ended up with an unsatisfying ending you just started over and decided differently.

Multiple-path novels found a new home with the Macintosh after the introduction of Hypercard. In fact, they proliferated. *The Doomsday Brunette* (`http://zeb.nysaes.cornell.edu/CGA/ddb/demo.cgi`) is the same kind of novel, a hypertext-based multiple-path story found on the World Wide Web. Actually, as its author makes clear on the home page (Figure 24.38), the full version of the story is available for download as an MS Windows hypertext program, one that allows you to read through the first three chapters before asking for a few bucks to go on. (The beginning of Chapter 1 is shown in Figure 24.39.) Publishing this shortened version on the Web does two things: first, it gets readers hooked; second, it lets non-Windows users give it a try as well (and, presumably, they can ask that it be released for their own platform).

FIGURE 24.38.

The Doomsday Brunette home page.

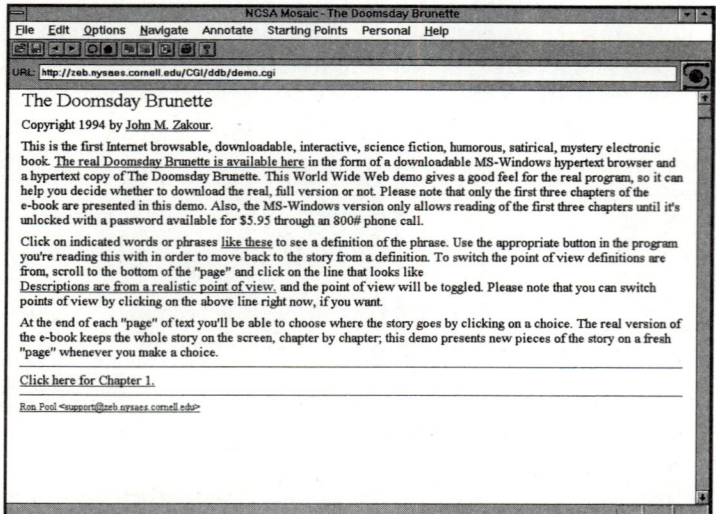

The importance of this endeavor is that it represents the kind of fiction that the Web makes entirely possible. Second, it represents a way for new authors to get published, without the huge barrier of going through a print publisher, who don't usually offer first-time authors anything approaching real money anyway. There's no reason why such a publishing venture couldn't be profitable, and it's a superb way of trying out experimental fiction.

FIGURE 24.39.

Chapter 1 from The Doomsday Brunette.

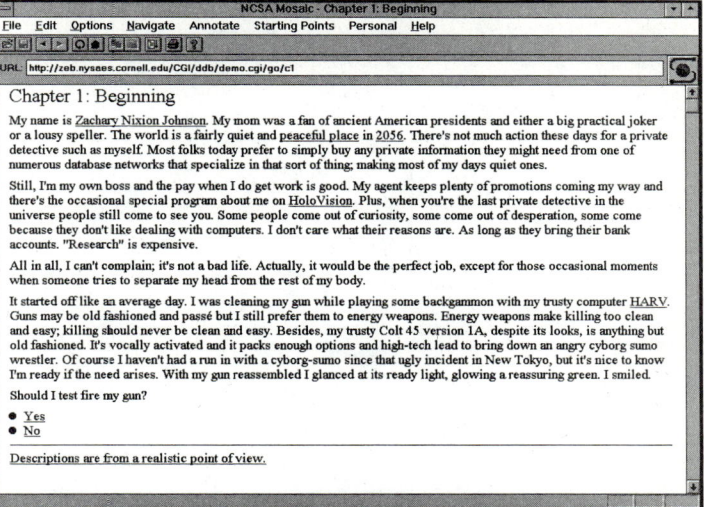

Entertainment: Divinity

I couldn't resist.

Actually, it's an interesting site (`http://128.194.15.32/~ahb2188/elvishom.html`). Not only do we have details about the King (Figure 24.40), we also have a guided picture tour of the only house that Paul Simon ever named a song after. In fact, this is the kind of picture tour (Figure 24.41) that public relations and marketing people could use very advantageously, especially for the purposes of enticing people to visit the real thing.

FIGURE 24.40.

The Elvis Presley home page, with the guy's middle name actually spelled right.

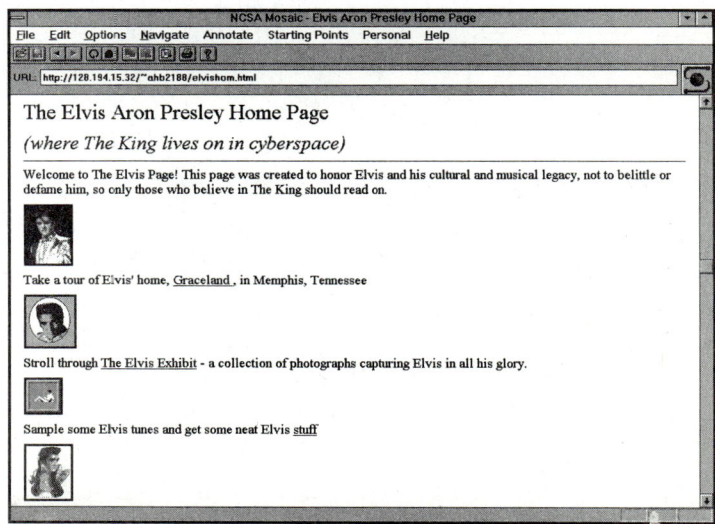

FIGURE 24.41.

The Graceland Tour, complete with musical prelude.

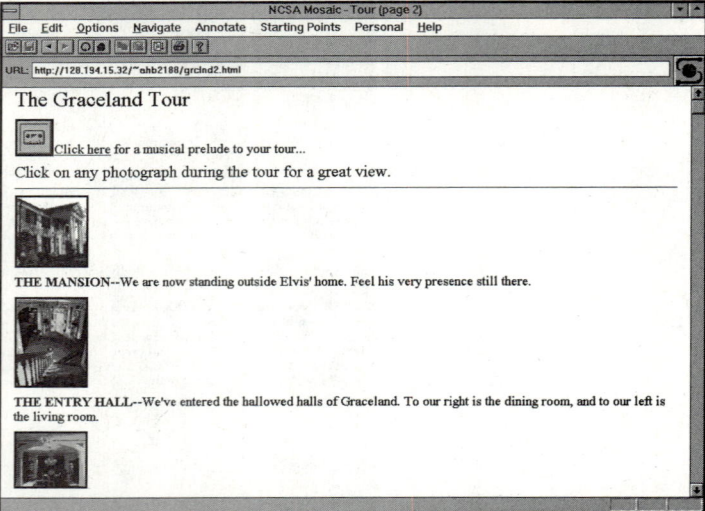

Explorer's Check

This has been a brief tour through a portion of the growing number of entertainment-related pages on the World Wide Web. The pages are indicative of the kind of entertainment activity occurring on the Web, and while you will be able to add several references of your own within hours after starting to browse the Web, the basic idea remains that entertainment on the Web is largely an underdeveloped area.

There are plenty of sites available, and plenty of variety as well, but only in a few cases are the sites as useful as a good entertainment book or CD-ROM. On the other hand, they're cheaper (unless you pay by the hour, perhaps), so for that reason alone they're worth visiting. For highly specific entertainment information, however, the Web is not the best choice of media.

Education, Scholarship, and Research

25

by John December

Historically, one of the strengths of computer networks has been their capacity for bringing people together. Educators such as those at the Open University in the United Kingdom, the New School for Social Research in the United States, as well as at other institutions, have long recognized this and have used computer networks for education. While scholars still examine the value of and the best processes for online learning, the Web creates information spaces and communication opportunities that represent a wide range of activities.

This chapter presents some examples of how the Web can be used for education and for specific applications that awaken students' minds to the excitement of learning. Other examples show how educators have created webs to reflect their activities, projects, and resources.

Next, this chapter surveys how scholars can use the Web to share ideas, collaborate on research, and develop materials for their students. Like many information systems before it, the Web has its limitations and weaknesses. A primary weakness is that there is still relatively little educational material available through the Web. However, the examples shown here demonstrate a remarkable richness in innovation and creativity. By exploring these, you can gain a sense of enthusiasm for learning beyond the physical walls of the classroom.

Exciting Students to Learn

While a traditional classroom relies on a single teacher to provide students with a view into knowledge, the Web can offer direct connections from knowledge producers to students. The example presented below describes the JASON project, an effort to involve students in exploration. It is just one illustration of how many educators can collaborate to create an online learning environment that extends from the classroom to the world.

In 1985, Dr. Robert D. Ballard (now Director of the Woods Hole Oceanographic Institution's Center for Marine Exploration) and a research team discovered the wreck of the *R. M. S. Titanic* on the floor of the North Atlantic Ocean. In order to photograph the vessel's interior, the team designed a submersible robot called Jason. In 1989, due to the success of the Jason and the curiosity of school children who wanted to know how his team discovered the *Titanic*, Dr. Ballard founded the JASON project. In 1990, the JASON Foundation for Education was formed "to excite and engage students in science and technology and to motivate and train their teachers." (See Figure 25.1.)

In the JASON Web (URL `http://seawifs.gsfc.nasa.gov/scripts/JASON.html`), Dr. Robert Ballard talks about the project's purpose: "to excite young people in the fields of science and engineering by involving them in the excitement that we as scientists and engineers enjoy... [to] involve them in moments of discovery... [to] take young people to interesting research sites and let them participate in live exploration" (URL `http://seawifs.gsfc.nasa.gov/JASON/JASON6/ballard_purpose.au`). One feature of the JASON project is *telepresence*, in which scientists, using remote sensing devices, involve others in the process of discovery.

The JASON Project home page (Figure 25.1) serves as a clearinghouse for information about the project, as well as tutorials and information for participants.

FIGURE 25.1.

The JASON Project home page.

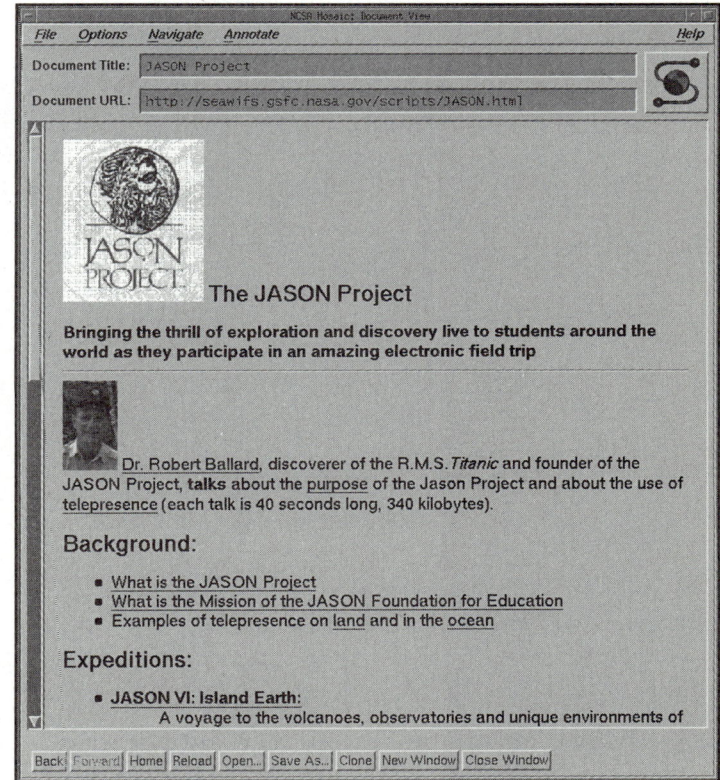

Designed for students in grades four through twelve, the JASON Project material offered through the Web page provides an overview of past and future expeditions. These expeditions involve the use of telepresence, the technology of the JASON submersible robots, as well as in-class activities and observations at many sites throughout the world. Figure 25.2 shows the page providing an overview of the 1995 expedition to "Island Earth," the environment of Hawaii.

FIGURE 25.2.

The JASON Project's "Island Earth" overview.

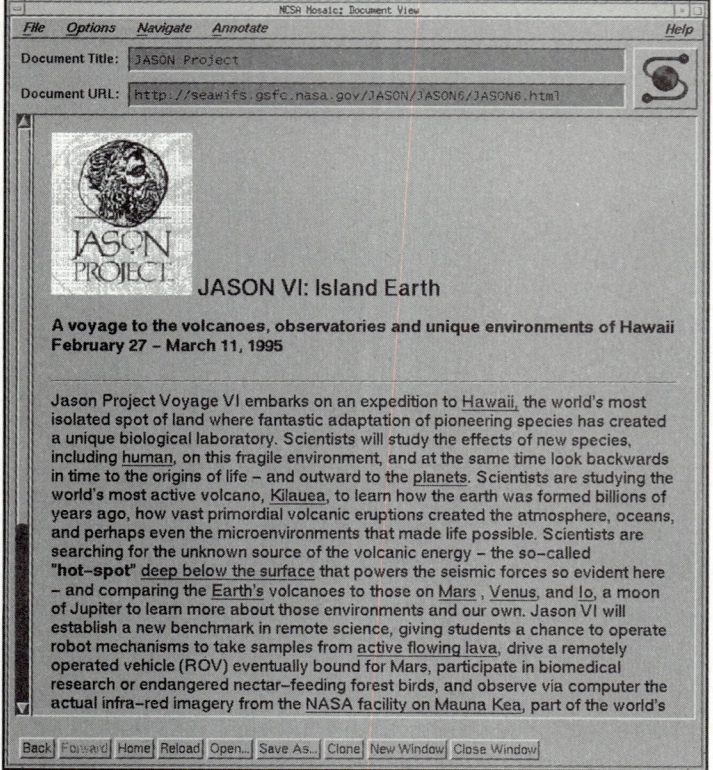

The Web materials on this overview page place the voyage in context—linking it to information on the Web related to Hawaii's natural features such as background material about the origins of planets, volcanoes, and other natural features. The home page for the voyage, shown in Figure 25.3, links to additional material.

This additional material provides specific information about Hawaii, demonstrating the strength of the Web to contextualize a project by bringing together diverse information sources. In this way, the JASON Project Web creates an excellent set of preparatory materials that teachers can use to familiarize themselves and their students with what they will experience during the telepresence phase of the expedition. While the JASON Project Web is not the focus of the expeditions, the background material, information, and specific guides the JASON Web offers support the entire project—making it visible and accessible to still more students worldwide.

FIGURE 25.3.

The JASON Project "Island Earth" home page, showing links to additional material.

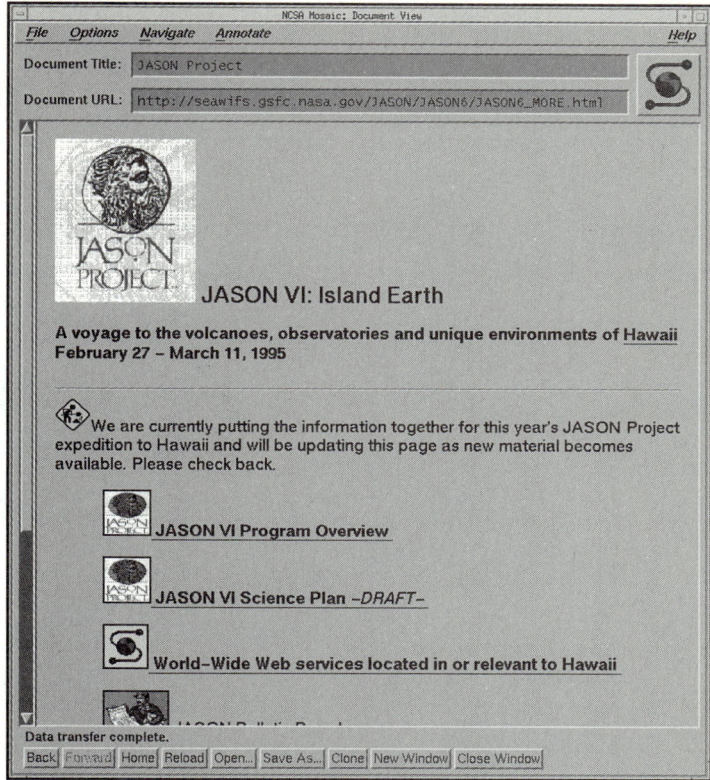

Schools on the Web

While specific projects like JASON demonstrate how the Web can be used to support educational projects, other applications of the Web show how schools can build webs to provide information to their own students and teachers, as well as to connect their site to the larger world of the Web.

While electronic mail, real-time text conferencing, and online tutorials have been used in the education community for several years, the Web brings a unique aspect to these online efforts by helping educators create information spaces that present the "face" of a school to anyone on the Web who ventures in for a visit. This section describes several school webs and surveys the kinds of information that have been created.

Hillside Elementary School

Hillside Elementary School is located in Cottage Grove, Minnesota, in the southeast section of Minneapolis-St. Paul. In March 1994, sixth-grade students at the school began work on their own web, as part of a joint project between the University of Minnesota's College of Education and Hillside. The Hillside home page is shown in Figure 25.4.

FIGURE 25.4.

The Hillside Elementary School home page.

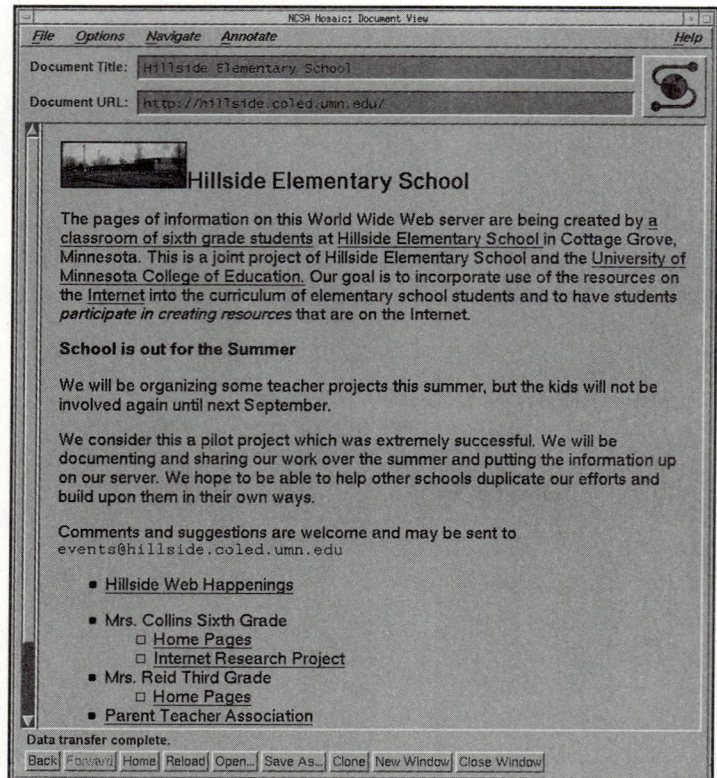

The goal of the Hillside web is to foster the use of the Internet in the curriculum by helping students access the Web for information as well as create their own information. As part of this work, a teacher at the school, Chris Collins, created an Internet Research Project Assignment, in which the students had to locate and use references to Web resources for a research paper (URL `http://hillside.coled.umn.edu/research/assignment1/assignment1.html`). Mrs. Collins also provided the students with a "JumpPage" listing various Web documents for references to HTML, Web searching tools, and resource lists.

The sixth-graders produced a variety of reports on subjects ranging from Antarctica to weather, each incorporating links to Web resources. In addition, each student created his or her own home page, as well as helped Mrs. Reid's third-grade students create their own home pages. Announced on the "Mosaic What's New" page (URL `http://www.ncsa.uiuc.edu/SDG/Software/Mosaic/Docs/whats-new.html`), their project attracted a great deal of attention in the spring of 1994, logging 500-1000 connections per day during the week after it was first announced.

The longer-term goals of the teachers at Hillside are to document their work and to share their experience through their Web server so that others might build on their efforts. Hillside provides a directory to other elementary schools on the Web at URL `http://hillside.coled.umn.edu/others.html`.

The Virginia L. Murray Elementary School

Like at Hillside, the teachers at Virginia L. Murray Elementary school in Ivy, Virginia, worked with a nearby college of education to develop a Web server. Working with the Curry School of Education at the University of Virginia, along with a grant from Albemarle County, the Parent-Teacher Organization, and money from the school's budget, the school established an Internet connection in February 1994. The top of Murray Elementary's home page is shown in Figure 25.5.

The home page contains links to class pages and the library, as well as local resources such as a Mosaic tutorial written by graduate students in the Curry School of Education and a tutorial written by Theresa McMurdo and Jason Mitchell for fourth- and fifth-grade students called, "How Light Works." By providing links to local sources, the Murray school can share resources that other schools may find valuable. By linking to resources on the Web itself, the Murray school creates relationships beyond its own walls.

FIGURE 25.5.

Virginia L. Murray Elementary School home page.

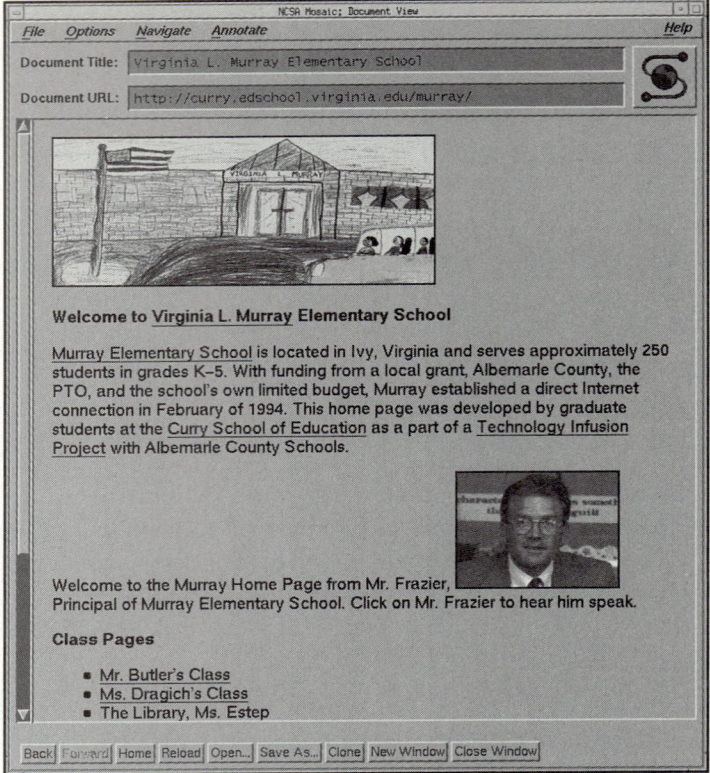

Thomas Jefferson High School for Science and Technology

Thomas Jefferson High School for Science and Technology in Alexandria, Virginia, was founded in 1984 as a special *magnet* school (a school that receives a special designation within a school district for excellence in a range of subjects). Although students at Thomas Jefferson excel at the school's offerings in science and technology, they share a wide variety of interests, and these interests are reflected in their web (URL `http://boom.tjhsst.edu`). (See Figure 25.6.)

The Jefferson Web was originally run by a student administrator, Nathan J. Williams, who trained his teacher, Donald W. Hyatt, in the summer of 1994, then left to start school at MIT. The Jefferson web presents a wide variety of information about the school, including reference information for students, and records happenings (News Items) accessible from links on the home page.

FIGURE 25.6.

Thomas Jefferson High School for Science and Technology home page.

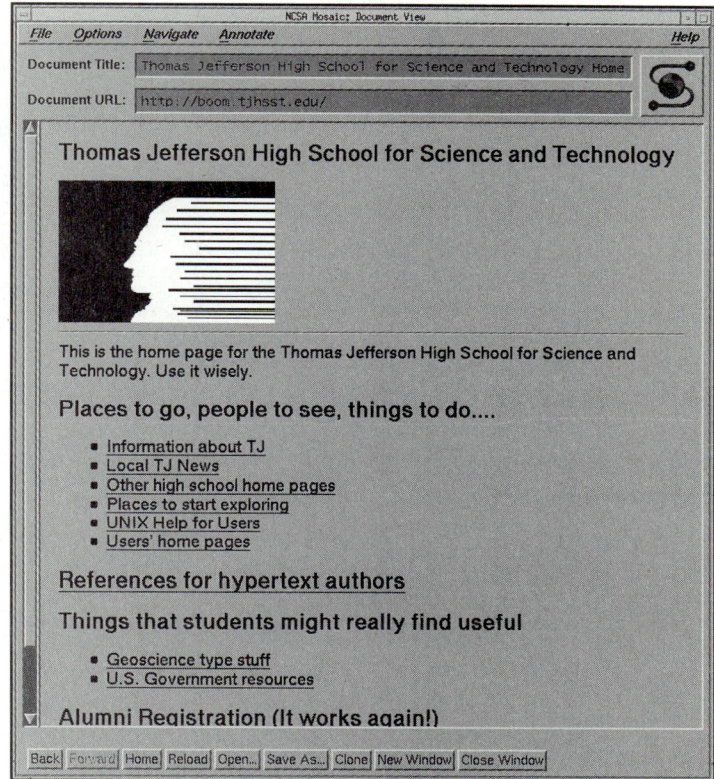

The Thomas Jefferson Web includes extensive information about its technology labs, particularly its Computer Systems Laboratory, including detailed descriptions of its educational focus on Artificial Intelligence, Computer Architecture, Supercomputer Applications, Computational Physics, and Computer Systems Research.

Links within several of these categories provide detailed course descriptions, including statements of objectives and assignments. For example, the page for the Artificial Intelligence course is shown in Figure 25.7.

FIGURE 25.7.

General Description page for the Artificial Intelligence course at Thomas Jefferson High School for Science and Technology.

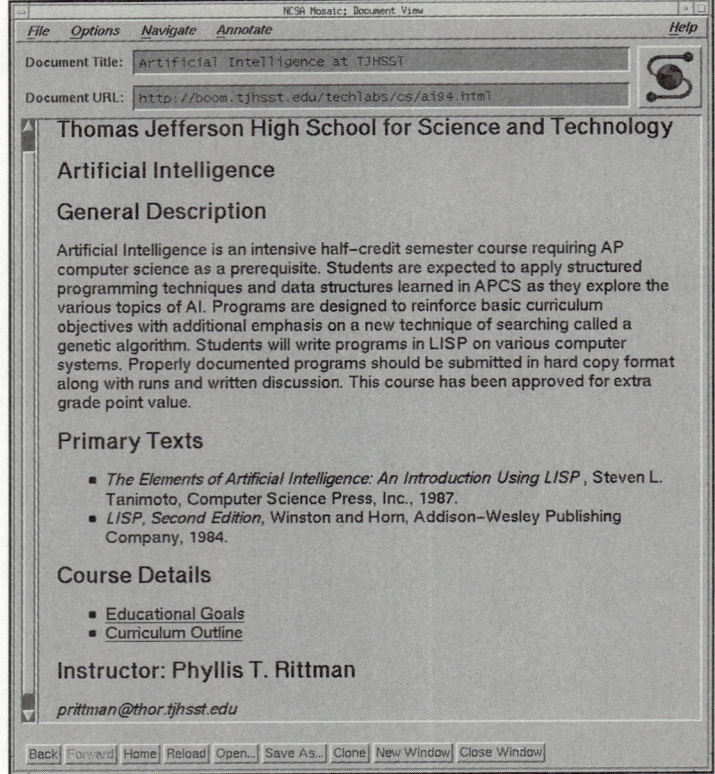

As shown in Figure 25.6, Thomas Jefferson's front page contains links to information about its Geoscience department as well as to home pages of people at the school. The front page also contains a link to a database that keeps track of alumni of the school by class year. In this way, the Thomas Jefferson Web page functions not only as an information space for its current students, but as a gathering-point on the Web for its alumni—relationships that may yield additional connections and ideas to increase the information and knowledge that the Thomas Jefferson web can offer.

Claremont High School

Claremont High School in Claremont, California, is another high school with a web. Its home page is shown in Figure 25.8.

The Claremont Web page contains links to information and resources at Claremont High School, such as links to resources related to its academic departments, information resources about the Internet, and reports about the web server. Like the Thomas Jefferson web, the

Claremont web provides a mix of resources and links that help students at the local school make sense of the Internet as well as locate information to support their education at the school.

FIGURE 25.8.

Claremont High School WWW home page.

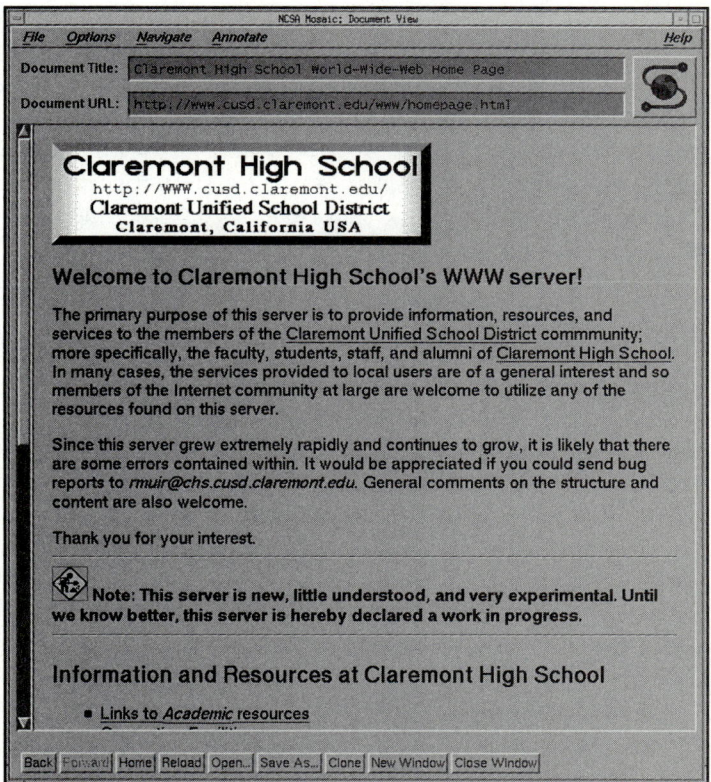

Community Colleges

While the elementary and high school webs described in the preceding sections provide information for students and educators located at a single campus, other academic institutions serve a more dispersed and diverse student population. One such example is the Maricopa Community College District in Arizona, the second-largest multi-college community college system in the United States. Established in 1962, Maricopa serves the needs of a varied student population with an average age of 30, of whom 80 percent are employed, 50 percent with full-time jobs. Maricopa schools offered more than 180,000 credit hours during the 1993-94 academic year. This student population requires high-quality, relevant education that can flexibly help them succeed academically while maintaining busy lifestyles.

Maricopa Center for Learning and Instruction (MCLI) operates a web that provides a set of links, bringing together information to support its active academic community and linking together the Gophers and other information servers that individual institutions within the Maricopa Community College District operate. The Maricopa web links offices, departments, and campuses within the district and has been recognized as a model for "motivating, infusing, and promoting innovation and change in the community college environment" (URL `http://hakatai.mcli.dist.maricopa.edu/`). CAUSE, the association for managing and using information technology in higher education, and Novell, Inc. presented Maricopa with the 1993 CAUSE Award for Excellence in Campus Networking, citing Maricopa's "exemplary campus-wide network planning, management, and accessibility" (URL `gopher://cause-gopher.colorado.edu/00/awards/networking/1993-net-award-winners.txt`).

The top of MCLI's home page (URL `http://hakatai.mcli.dist.maricopa.edu/`) is shown in Figure 25.9.

FIGURE 25.9.

The home page for Maricopa Center for Learning and Instruction.

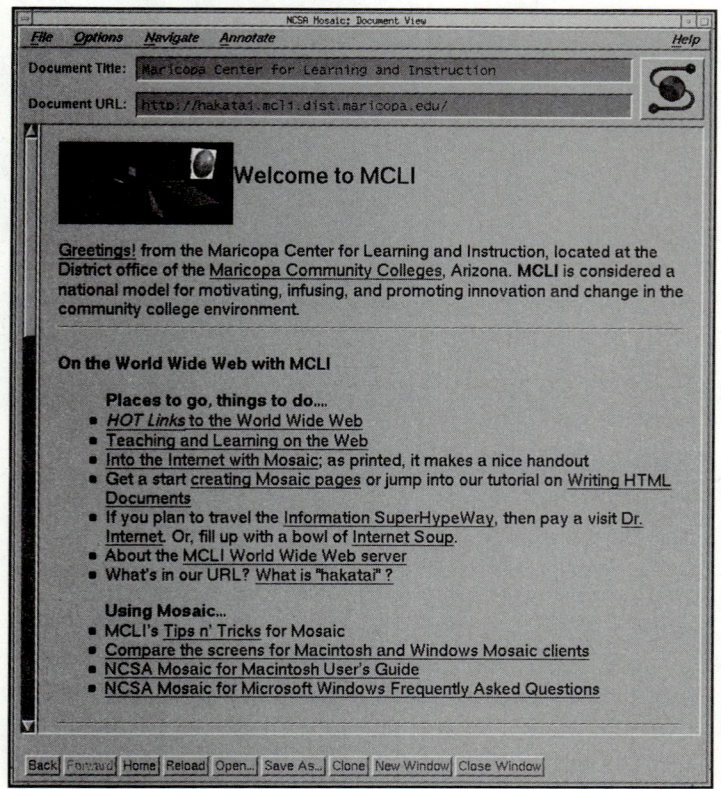

The front page provides links to a wide variety of Web and Internet orientation information as well as more information about Maricopa's publications, projects, library, and campuses. These links furnish a wealth of information about Maricopa's educational offerings. MCLI's publications offered through links on the home page include the *Labyrinth*, focusing on instructional technology, and the *Forum*, covering teaching and learning methodologies. A project called Ocotillo, deriving its name from a plant indigenous to Arizona that branches reach up and out, is a "think tank" that reports on issues such as emerging technologies, information literacy, intellectual rights, and technology-based training. These reports, available in the Maricopa web, provide valuable resources that relate how Maricopa deals with these issues while utilizing technology for education.

The MCLI page also contains links to information about the Library and special projects like Learning English Electronically, and links to Gophers, such as MariMUSE, a Gopher of the Learning Collaboratory located at Phoenix College supporting education through access to resources, faculty directories, and links to individual colleges and centers. (See Figure 25.10.)

FIGURE 25.10.

Links within the Maricopa Center home page.

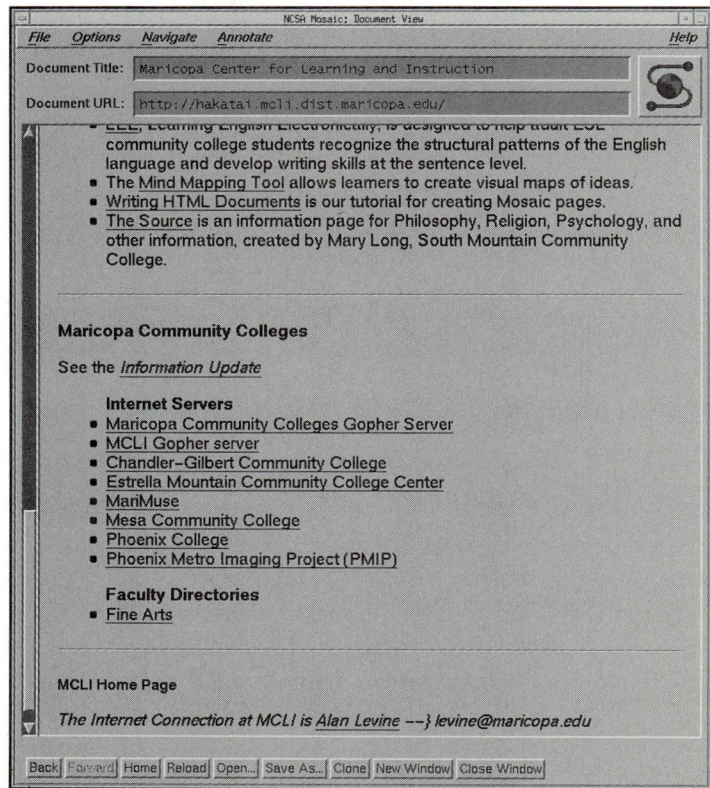

The Maricopa Web demonstrates how a diverse collection of many campuses can combine to create an information space to support education as well as explore the uses of educational technology.

Colleges and Universities

The number of colleges and universities with home pages is large and growing very quickly. As of August 1994, Mike Conlon's page of American Universities at URL `http://www.clas.ufl.edu/CLAS/american-universities.html` has more than 400 entries, and Christina DeMello's page of American and International colleges at URL `http://www.mit.edu:8001/people/cdemello/univ.html` lists hundreds of college-level webs worldwide. In Chapter 27, "Communication, Publishing, and Information," campus-wide information systems are discussed as an example of organizational communication. This section focuses on selected college course material created for the Web.

Online Course Information

The University of Texas at Austin maintains a collection of pointers to course material (much of it college-level) used for instruction (URL `http://www.utexas.edu/world/instruction/index.html`). The offerings include material in the following subjects: Anatomy, Archaeology, Architecture, Art and Art History, Astronomy, Biochemistry, Biology and Botany, Chemical Engineering, Chemistry, Communication, Computer Science, Finance, History, Language Lab, Management Information Systems, Mathematics, Medicine, Nuclear Engineering and Engineering Physics, Physics, Psychology, and Religious Studies.

The material present in this collection varies in depth and coverage. Most of the web pages offering course information simply point to ASCII or other notes files used in the course, and no course listed was delivered *solely* through the Web without face-to-face teacher-student interaction.

One course web (URL `http://www.rpi.edu/Internet/Guides/decemj/course/cmc.html`) is shown in Figure 25.11.

The graduate-level course, Computer-Mediated Communication (CMC), was taught at Rensselaer Polytechnic Institute by Dr. Teresa Harrison. Participants investigated the nature of CMC's impact on interpersonal, work, and societal contexts. The students also were exposed to some technologies and skills necessary to take part in CMC on the Internet and visited an IBM groupware facility.

FIGURE 25.11.

Computer-Mediated Communication course web.

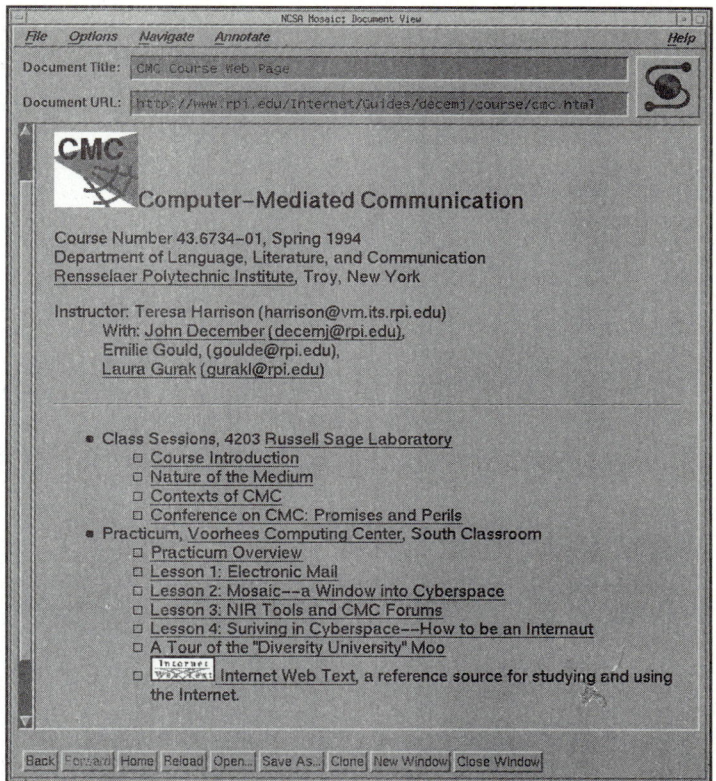

The CMC course web's front page provides the information found on many college syllabi: instructor name, course number and location, and an outline of the course contents. Links on the page allow the student to browse a hypertext version of the syllabus. In cases where required readings were available online, links were made from the syllabus directly to these readings. The front page also links to the lessons used in the practicum portion of the course, in which the students use workstations to access various Internet resources. The text for this online portion of the course, *Internet Web Text*, URL `http://www.rpi.edu/Internet/Guides/decemj/text.html`, shown in Figure 25.12, links the student to Internet resources, including orientation material, guides, reference information, browsing and exploring tools, subject and word-oriented searching tools, and information about connecting with people.

By providing both course and study information, the CMC course web shows how a web can be used both as an information system and a learning tool.

FIGURE 25.12.

Internet Web Text.

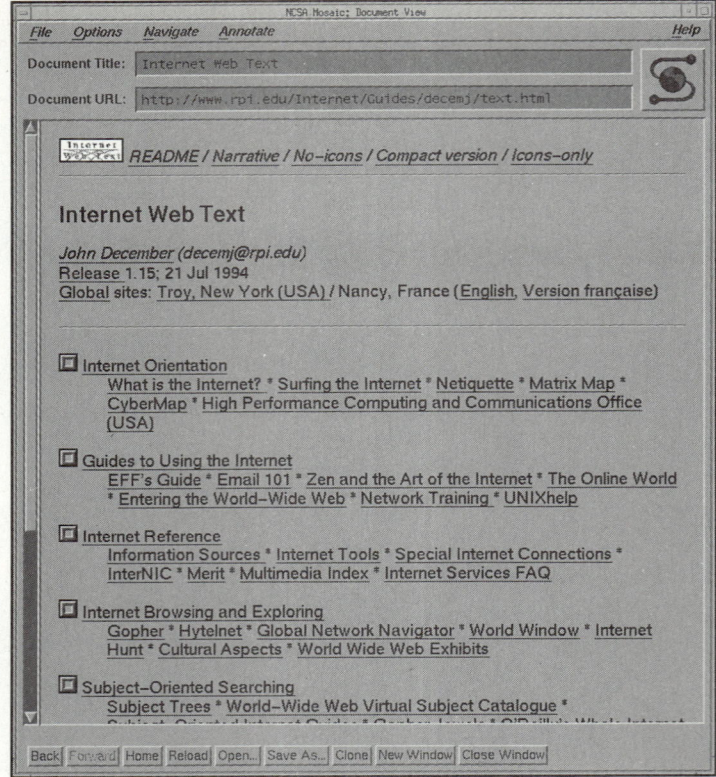

Another example of a course web is Brian Butler's undergraduate Management Information Systems course taught in the summer of 1994 at Carnegie Mellon University. Figure 25.13 shows the online information page for the course (URL `http://www.gsia.cmu.edu/bb26/70-451/`).

This page links the student to a variety of information, not just the course outline itself and the syllabus and schedule, but to final exam study hints, lecture notes, and course readings when they were online. The instructor also provided links to assignment questions, with the answers provided after the students turn in the assignment. The exam, study questions, and assignment solutions also contain links to the relevant lecture notes. For example, Figure 25.14 shows exam answers, with links to the relevant lectures.

FIGURE 25.13.

Online Information page for a Management Information Systems course at Carnegie Mellon University.

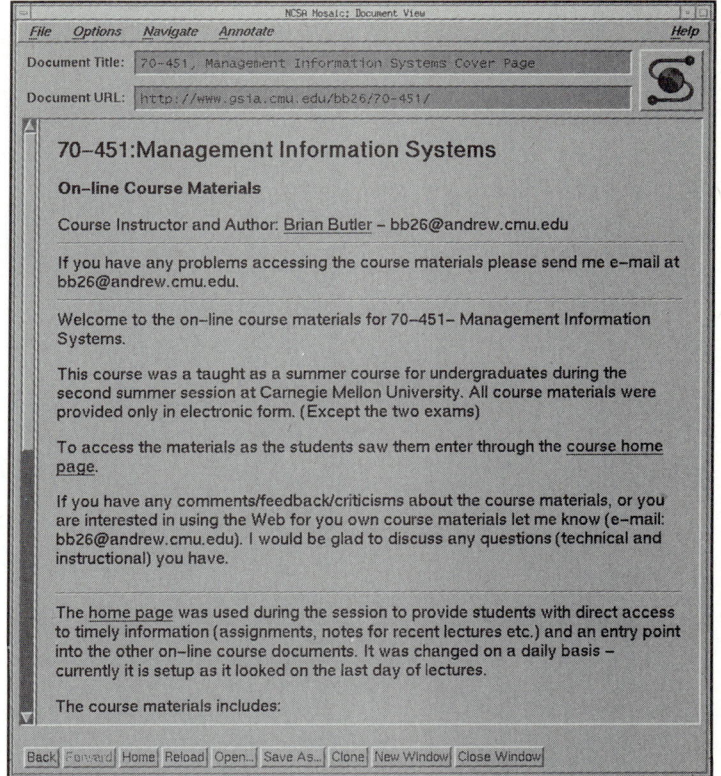

According to the instructor and author of this course material, Brian Butler, this web provides students with access to course materials and also prompted him to ask the questions shown at the bottom of Figure 25.15.

The MIS course web is a good example of how course materials can be provided through a web. Direct student-teacher interaction plays a part in learning, but a web such as that shown for the MIS course, as well as the others shown in this section, may help a busy student access current course materials. Placing these materials on the Web, the instructors help expand and extend the context of the information they present—the classroom ceases to be provided only in a particular physical space at a particular time, and the sources of information and instruction materials are not supplied only by the instructor.

FIGURE 25.14.

MIS exam answers with links to relevant lectures.

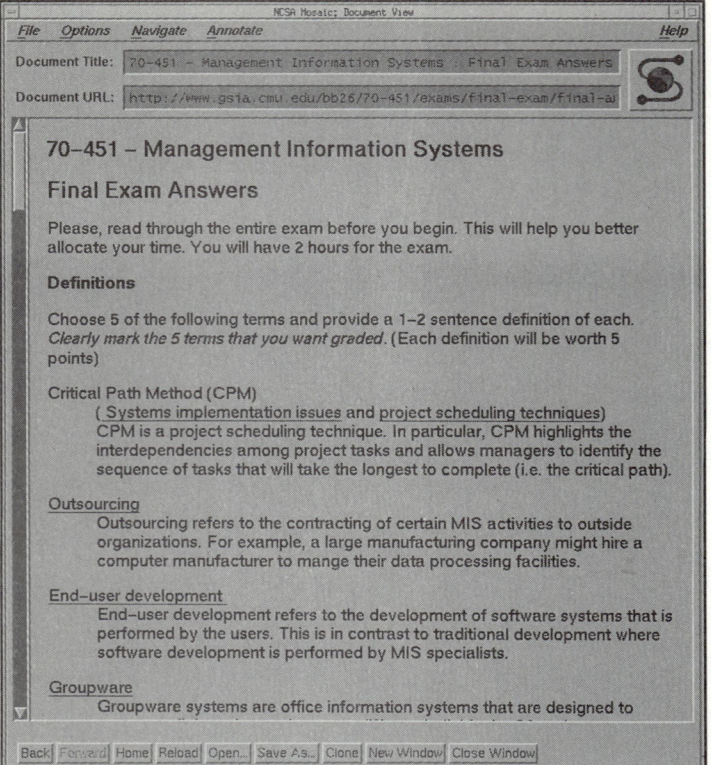

Tutorial Modules

In addition to information that supports an educational institution or a particular course, there are many webs that contain detailed tutorial and materials for learning. These webs delve into very specific topics to help students grasp a concept or learn information. Unlike the course webs described above, these tutorial modules are examples of the Web being used to teach students particular content.

FIGURE 25.15.
MIS course materials questions.

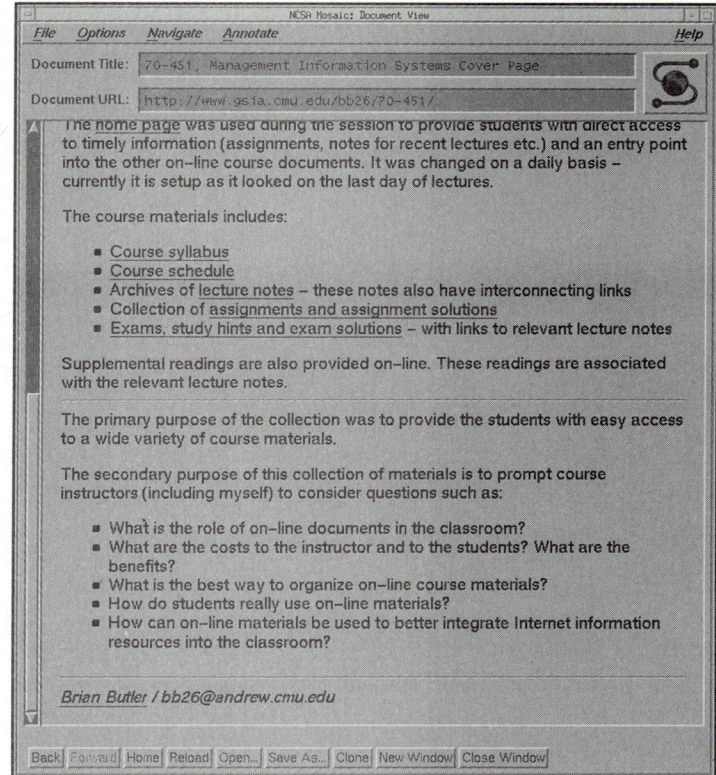

A Tutorial Module—the Knee

Michael L. Richardson at the University of Washington has prepared Anatomy Teaching Modules (URL `http://www.rad.washington.edu/AnatomyModuleList.html`), which guide the user through normal knee anatomy and normal distal thigh anatomy. (See Figure 25.16.)

The first module, Normal Knee Anatomy 1, takes the reader through a discussion of knee anatomy (Figure 25.17).

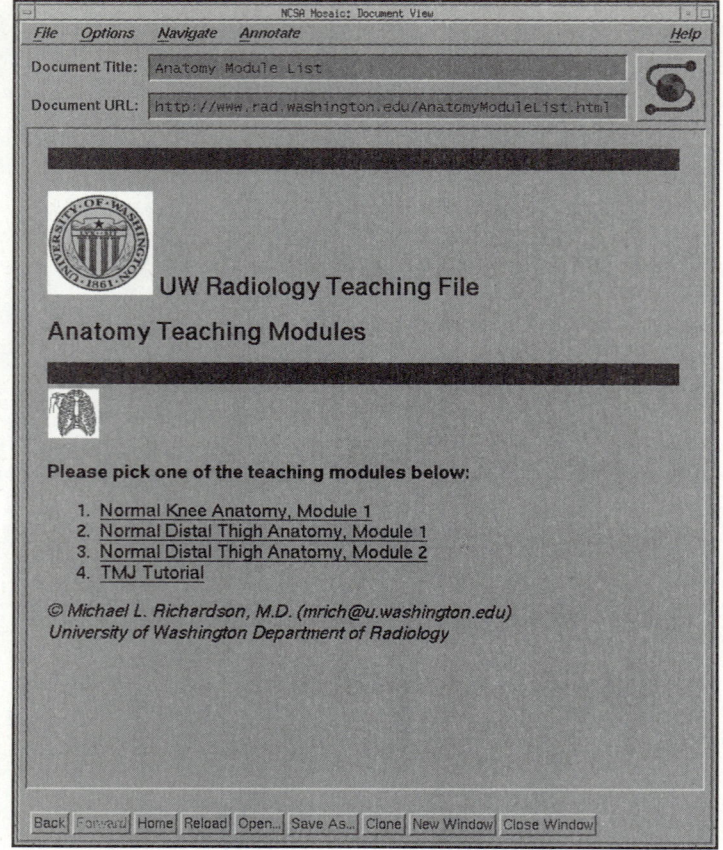

The Normal Distal Thigh Anatomy 1 includes images as well as a movie showing the operation of the distal thigh. These modules use a combination of graphics and text to help students learn. While similar materials (without the movie) could be presented in a book, the Web version can be customized and immediately updated by the instructor and is accessible worldwide, available to anyone who would like to learn.

FIGURE 25.17.

Normal Knee Anatomy 1.
(Copyright Michael L.
Richardson, M.D.
Reprinted by permission.)

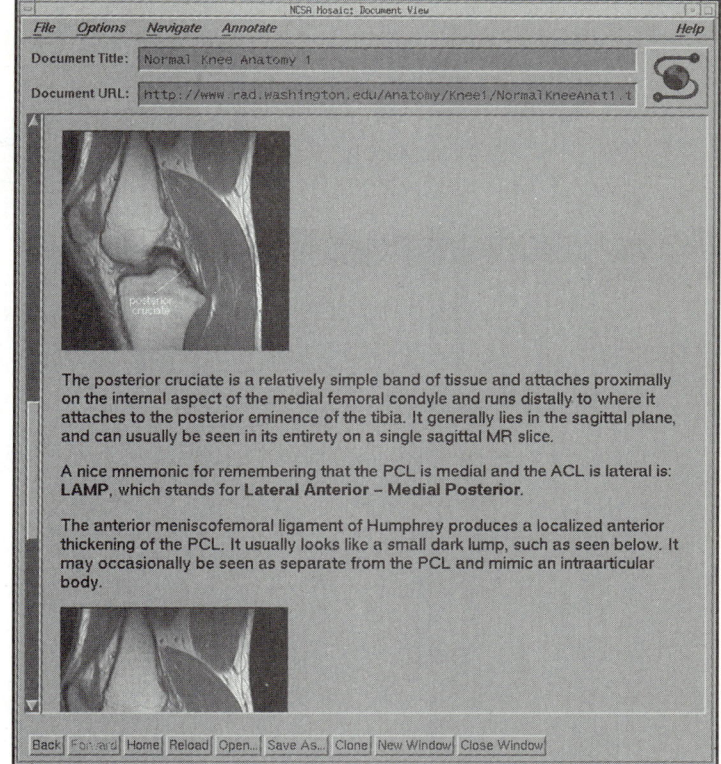

An Interactive Training Module—A Frog Dissection Kit

The Lawrence Berkeley Laboratory in California, in work sponsored by John Cavallini of the U. S. Dept. of Energy's Energy Research Division, Office of Scientific Computing, has created a virtual frog that can be dissected online. This online "frog" was created as part of the Whole Frog Project, an effort with the purpose of providing high school biology students with a tool for exploring a frog's anatomy using high-resolution MRI imaging and 3-D surface and volume rendering software. As a result of this work, the project has created not only a useful tool but also has demonstrated the value of computer-based 3-D visualization and whole-body, 3-D imaging as a curriculum tool.

The Whole Frog Project home page, at URL `http://george.lbl.gov/ITG.hm.pg.docs/Whole.Frog/Whole.Frog.html`, links into a preview of the Frog Dissection Kit as well as tutorials. Figure 25.18 shows the interactive program with the frog's skin still on. (This is the Mosaic version using the graphical information map feature as well as HTML Forms; a version which can be used in Mosaic for Windows is also available.)

FIGURE 25.18.

Frog Dissection Kit. (Copyright 1994 by Lawrence Berkeley Laboratory. Reprinted by permission.)

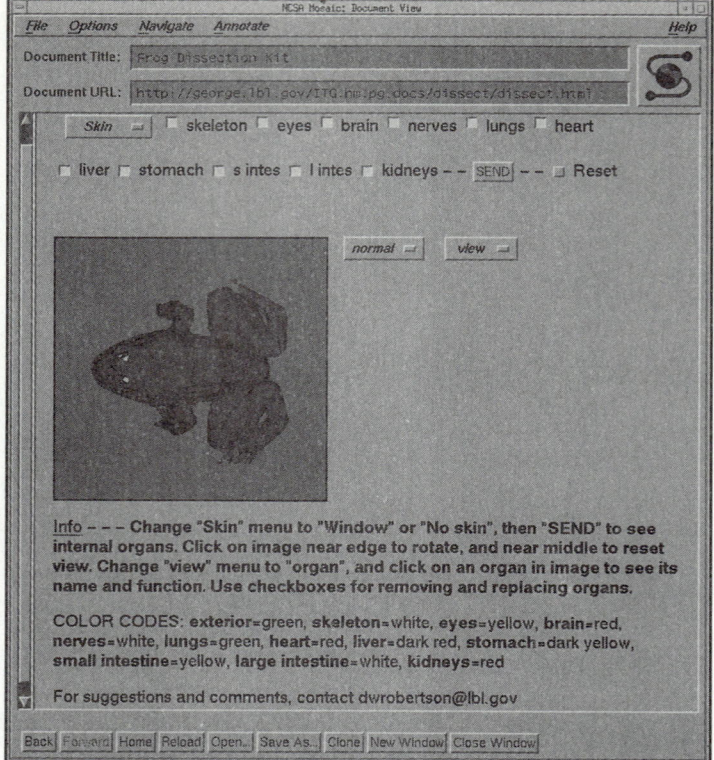

By clicking on the image of the frog near an edge, the student can alter the position of the frog—changing the view to a side or bottom view, for example. By using the selector bar (currently set to "Skin" in the above figure), the student can "open up" the view of the frog to see inside the skin through a "window" or remove the skin entirely. (Figure 25.19 shows the frog with no skin.)

The kit offers the students a variety of ways to focus on particular organs and systems. By selecting the checkboxes at the top of the menu, a student can "remove" selected organs. For example, Figure 25.20 shows the frog with the skeleton, nerves, and intestines removed.

FIGURE 25.19.

Frog with no skin. (Copyright 1994 by Lawrence Berkeley Laboratory. Reprinted by permission.)

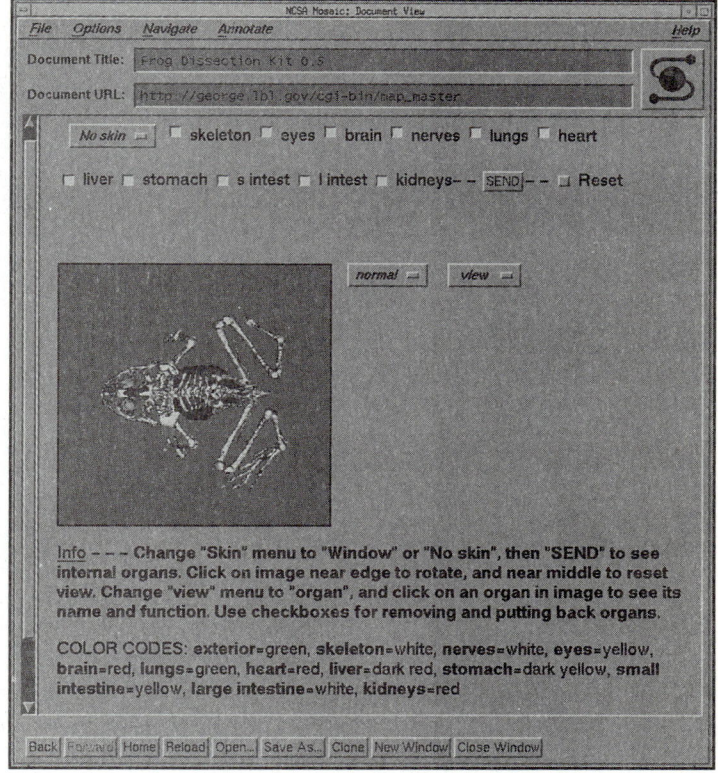

The online virtual frog is valuable both as an educational resource—giving students an interactive program for learning—and as a model for using graphics for this kind for education.

FIGURE 25.20.
Frog with selected items removed. (Copyright 1994 by Lawrence Berkeley Laboratory. Reprinted by permission.)

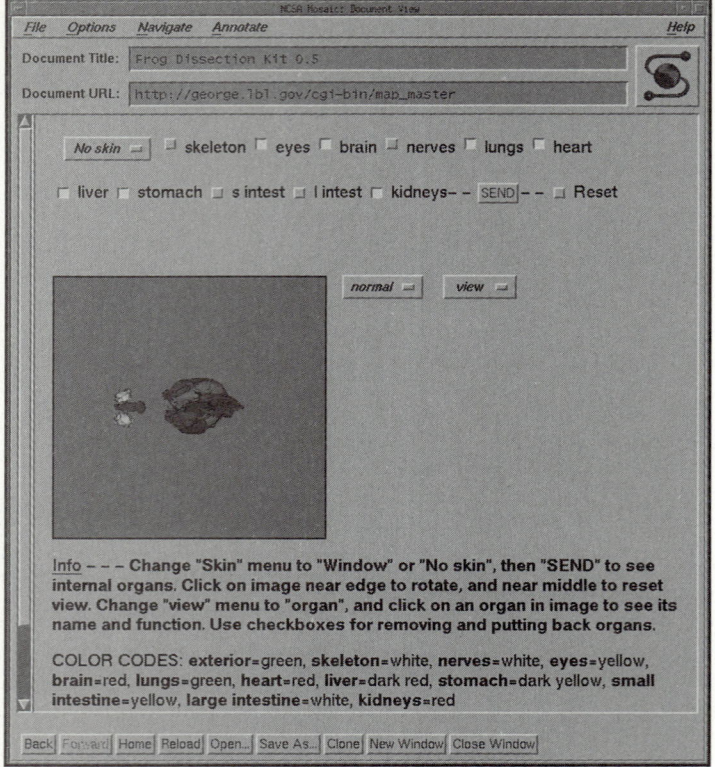

Educational Resources

In addition to webs that support information for and about education offered at schools, a wide variety of online resources is available to support educators. In this section, you'll explore some major collections.

AskERIC: K-12 information

AskERIC is a service providing information for K-12 educators. Part of the ERIC (Educational Resources Information Center) Clearinghouse on Information and Technology, AskERIC is a project funded by the United States Department of Education.

Based at Syracuse University and sponsored by the Schools of Information Studies and Education, AskERIC's Virtual Library connects teachers to resources through a variety of online means (e-mail, FTP, and Gopher, as well as the Web). AskERIC also provides connections to Network Information Specialists (NIS) who can answer questions from

K-12 staff related to education. The overview portion of AskERIC Virtual Library's home page, URL `http://eryx.syr.edu/Main.html`, is shown in Figure 25.21.

FIGURE 25.21.

The overview portion of the AskERIC Virtual Library home page.

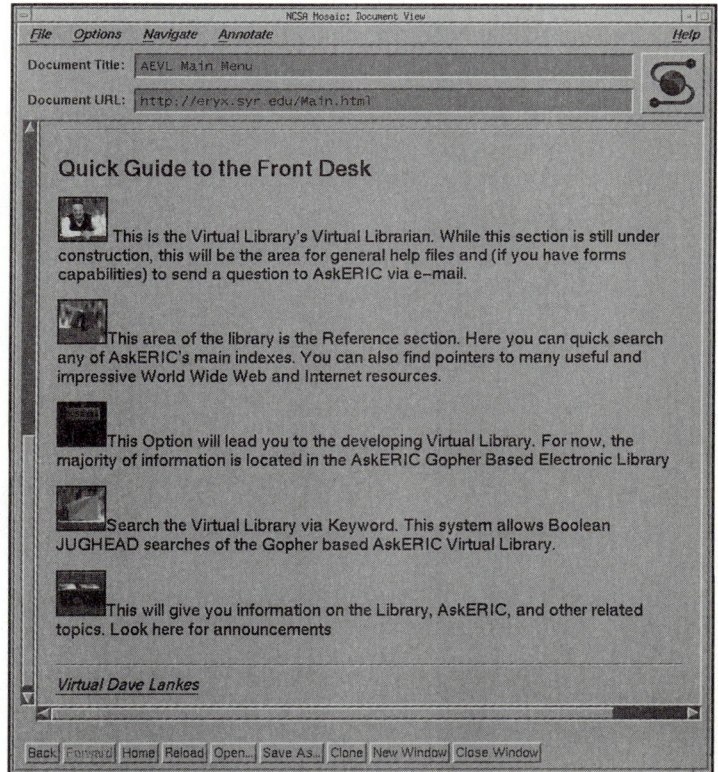

The AskERIC Virtual Library (AEVL) gives K-12 educators automated access to more than 700 lesson plans, archives of Listserv discussion, and pointers to Internet services. The Reference desk (Figure 25.22) includes indexes, remote reference sources, and related Web sites.

The AskERIC web also links to specific lesson plans. For example, Figure 25.23 shows the front page for the NASA SIR-C Education Program.

SIR-C stands for Spaceborne Imaging Radar-C, a type of imaging radar produced by the Jet Propulsion Laboratory for the National Aeronautics and Space Administration (NASA). SIR-C will be onboard Space Shuttle flights, and the SIR-C educational (SIR-CED) program's goal is to involve middle school and high school students in an experience of discovery and learning, with the benefit of helping students improve math, science, and geography skills. The teacher's guide for the program includes a special unit on spaceborne imaging radar, and computer and in-class activities (Figure 25.24).

FIGURE 25.22.

The AEVL Reference page.

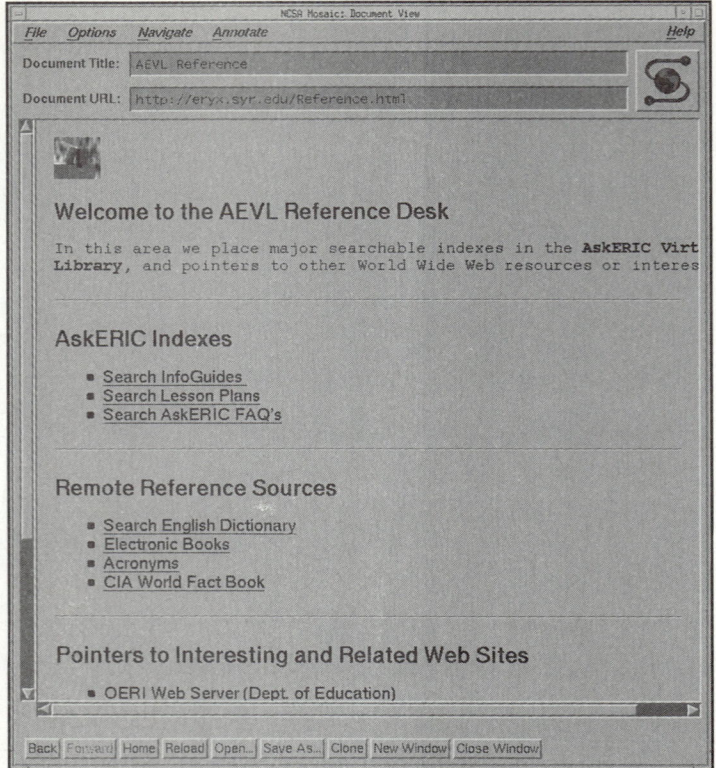

Written exercises in the lesson plan involve students in exploring data collection aboard the space shuttle's Earth Observing System as part of lessons on concepts in remote sensing. Part of the goal of these lessons is also to spark students' interest about the environment. Put together by people at the Jet Propulsion Laboratory (Anthony Freeman, JoBea Way, and Ellen O'Leary) as well as teachers in the Los Angeles Unified School District (Kathleen Crandall, David Gunderson, and Robert Veas), the program combines excellent teaching with exciting content.

AskERIC itself is in development—don't be surprised if AskERIC's web looks different than pictured here—in a research and development effort to support the Virtual Library and the NIS services. Efforts are underway to create new resources as well as a new virtual interface. The ultimate goal is to have a seamless, intuitive, "point and click" interface that will help guide educators to the resources and answers they need.

FIGURE 25.23.

The front page for the NASA SIR-C Education Program.

The AskERIC system thus combines a source of help for teachers in K-12 through a virtual library with Network Information Specialists available for answers and a research and development program aimed at improving the contents and interface of AskERIC's offerings.

The DeweyWeb

Like AskERIC, the DeweyWeb at the University of Michigan is a project to both provide information and facilitate communication. DeweyWeb accomplishes this by providing links to resources as well as a computer-mediated communication activity called Interactive Communications & Simulations (ICS) World Forum.

Figure 25.25 shows the top of the DeweyWeb's home page, URL `http://ics.soe.umich.edu/`. The work on the DeweyWeb extends work done with the World School for Adventure Learning, Indiana University, ICS at the University of Michigan, and the International Arctic Project.

FIGURE 25.24.

The table of contents page for the SIR-CED Teacher's Guide.

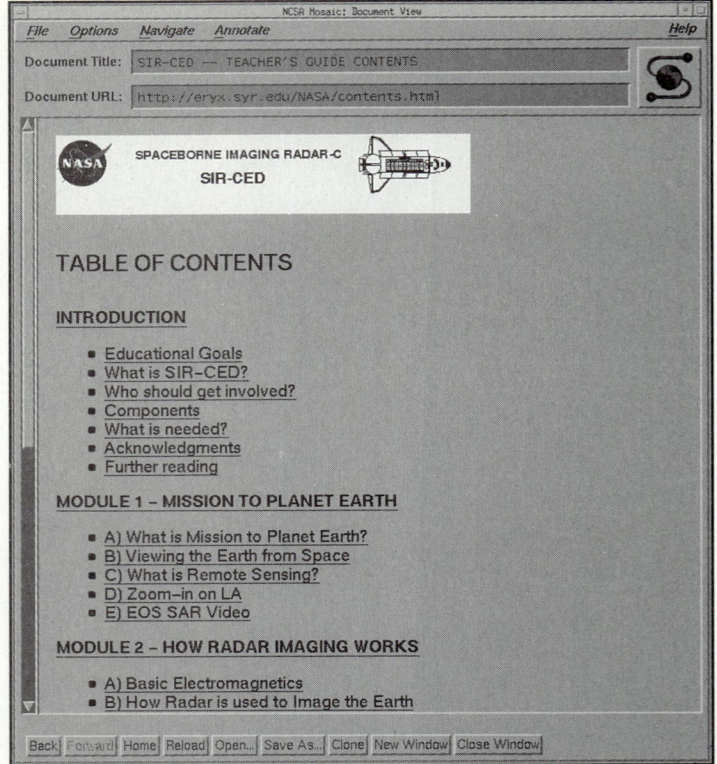

One ICS Forum involves schoolchildren around the world in tracing the training activities of the International Arctic Project in preparation for a trip across the Arctic. This project is called "Journey North." Figure 25.26 shows the home page for this project.

The Journey North helps students learn more about the Arctic, including the environment, wildlife, and culture. The Web links to "Arctic Bites," a collection of writings relating to the Arctic, information and news about the 1994 International Arctic Project team, and a "Wild Adventurers" section where students can report their own observations of wildlife (Figure 25.27).

Thus the DeweyWeb, like JASON and many of the other projects described here, illustrates how both information and involvement can excite students to learn.

FIGURE 25.25.
DeweyWeb home page.

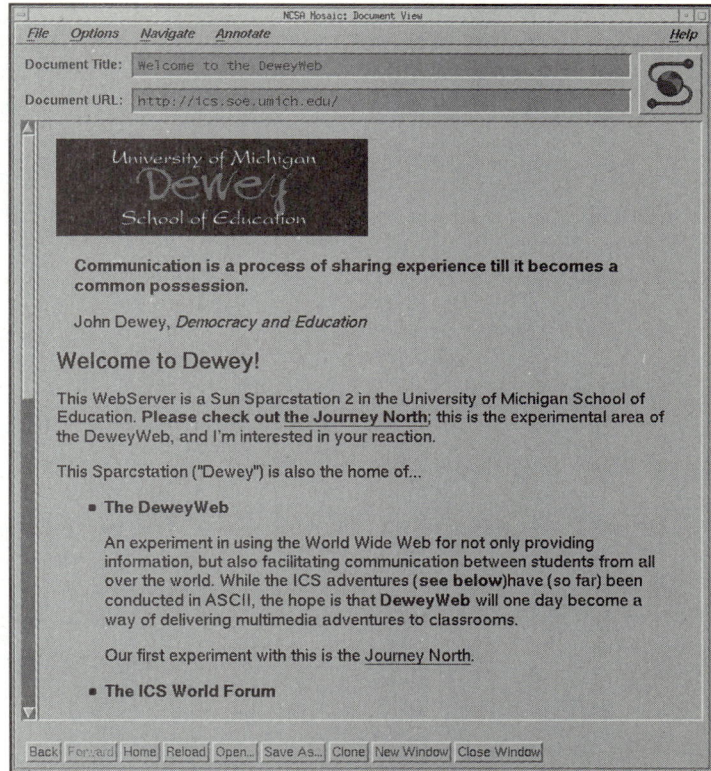

Educational Online Sources: Help and Pointers for Information

With the philosophy of creating a "central meeting" place for information about education, Educational Online Sources (EOS) has grown a vast web of information for educators. The goal of EOS, according to Joel Parker Henderson, is to help teachers grasp concepts and skills necessary for primary and secondary educators, to consolidate resources and information, and provide basic information about how to use the Internet. These goals address the need for providing annotated citations of educational sources in FTP, Gopher, mailing lists, and webs (Figure 25.28).

EOS includes collections of webs, a Gopher, a file list, educational Gophers, Usenet newsgroups, Internet guides, and subject-oriented resources. The long-term goal is to continue development (including a newer URL than shown here); if you can't find the EOS Web at the URL (http://eos.org) or through a Web spider search (Chapter 19, "Spiders and Indexes: Keyword-Oriented Searching"), you can contact EOS at 1-800-ASK-EOS-1.

FIGURE 25.26.

The Journey North home page.

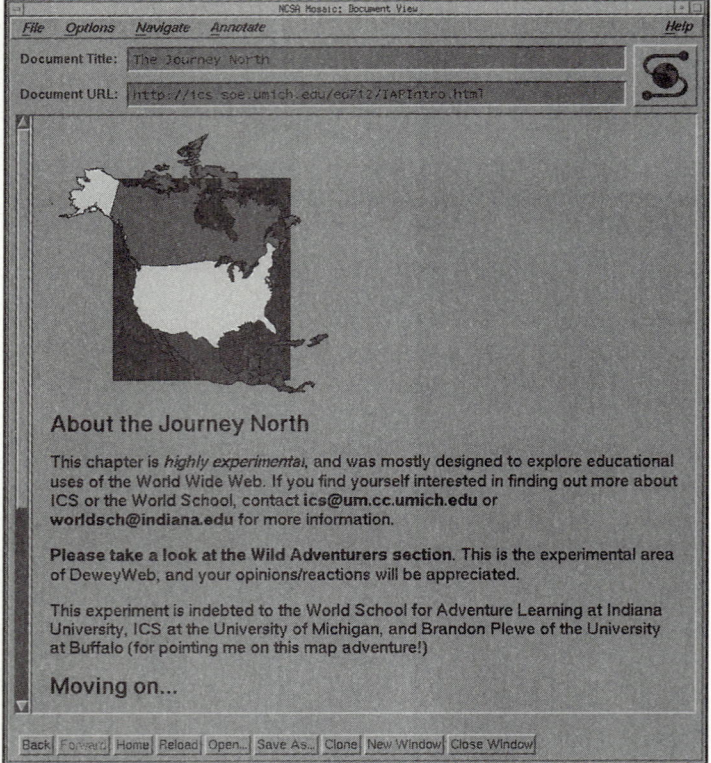

Scholarship and Research

Human knowledge has accumulated over centuries through the careful work of scholars who create, critique, and disseminate information and research. These scholars, working through a continuous process of interchange with peers, experts, and students, require communication in order to generate and evaluate new knowledge. While traditional forums for scholarship such as paper-based journals and in-person conferences and gatherings have been used for centuries, scholars today have adopted the power of the Net to fulfill many of their needs.

Net-based scholarship is a routine part of the lives of many scholars today. This has come about through the widespread use of computer networks for electronic mail as well as the demonstrated propensity of networked communication to foster communities of people interested in specialized knowledge. The plethora of Usenet newsgroups, electronic-mail-based discussion, and the wide number of subject-specific Net and Web resources are testaments to this phenomenon. Part of this power to create communities of interest lies in the ability of the Web and Net to draw people together who are geographically dispersed, yet share the same passion for an area of study.

FIGURE 25.27.

Tracking the Journey North page from the Wild Adventurers section.

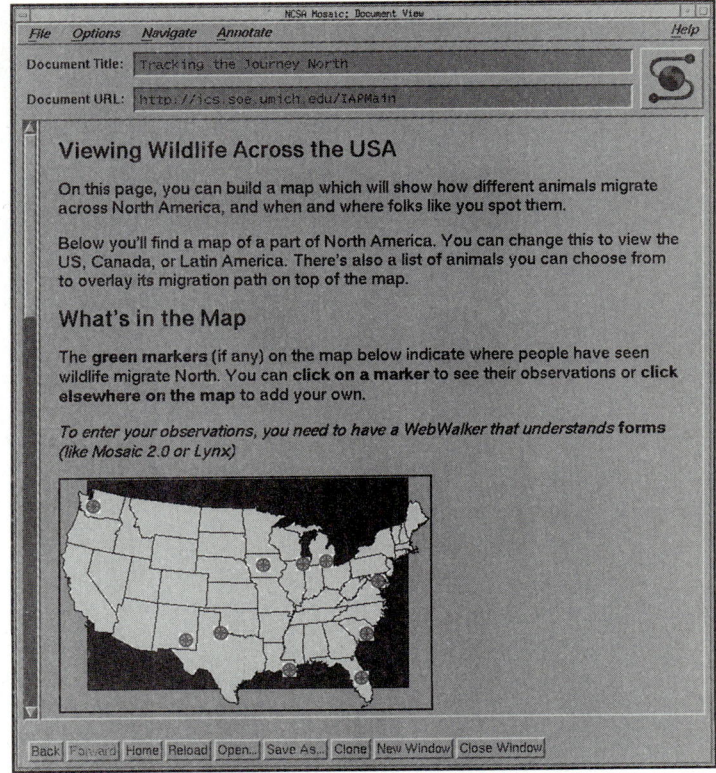

Tools like the Web provide the means to create shared resources in a different way than electronic mail or other Net-based means for communicating and sharing information. While electronic mail discussions or archives of files often require compartmentalized development, Web structures can expressively present and evoke ideas and foster cooperation and collaboration. The hypermedia links that the Web makes possible facilitate interchange and shared development in a way that other networked information delivery systems, such as electronic mail, file transport protocol, or Gophers, do not. The Web opens doors to hypermedia as well as networked communication that can be shaped to meet the needs of an audience through text layout, design, and rhetorical devices. (See Part V, "Weaving a Web.") Moreover, by integrating the views of Internet resources (Chapter 16, "At the Edge of the Web"), the Web also provides a platform for gathering information from a diverse set of Internet protocols. This integrative and collaborative nature of Web communication holds great promise for future scholarship on the Web.

This section explores some example resources and organizations devoted to enhancing online scholarship. These examples range from the Jeffersonian idea of an "Academical" Village to organizations that foster information-sharing, research, and learning online.

FIGURE 25.28.

*Educational Online
Sources Web list.*

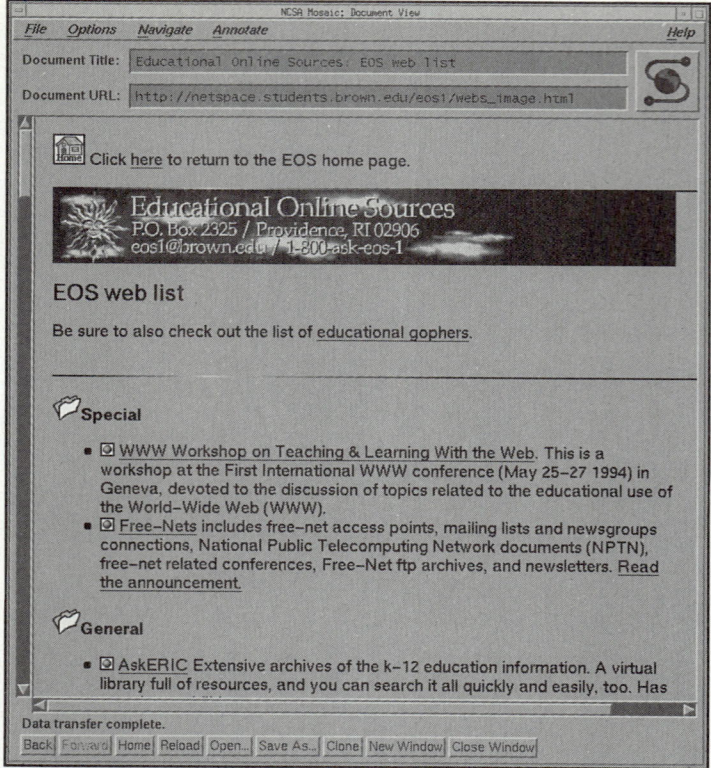

These organizations and resources attempt to fulfill a challenging mission: to help scholars search for information, communicate and collaborate with colleagues, analyze information, disseminate findings, and prepare curriculum and instruction. With increasing opportunities on the Web to pursue these activities, scholars can exchange ideas at many different levels of formality—ranging from chance and serendipitous connections struck on an electronic mail discussion list or on a Web-based communication forum (see Chapter 27) to the more formal exchanges in peer-reviewed electronic journals. By assisting in this scholarly communication, the Web itself may help bring about Thomas Jefferson's dream of a community of scholars exchanging ideas and working together, as you'll see in the first example.

Jefferson Village Virginia, An Electronic Academical Village

Thomas Jefferson's idea for a society in which people work and learn in an integrated environment, sharing interdisciplinary ideas and growing in understanding, may be happening on the Web. The University of Virginia in Charlottesville has created an "Academical Village." The home page for this village (URL `http://jefferson.village.virginia.edu/home.html`) is shown in Figure 25.29.

Unlike Jefferson's village based on geography, the Institute for Advanced Technology in the Humanities (IATH) at the University of Virginia in Charlottesville uses technology to support humanities-related scholarship. Founded in 1992 with a grant from IBM as well as support from the University, IATH's Web now supports a range of holdings, including publications, research reports, a magazine (*Postmodern Culture*), and technical reports to support humanities scholarship.

FIGURE 25.29.

The home page for the Institute for Advanced Technology in the Humanities at the University of Virginia.

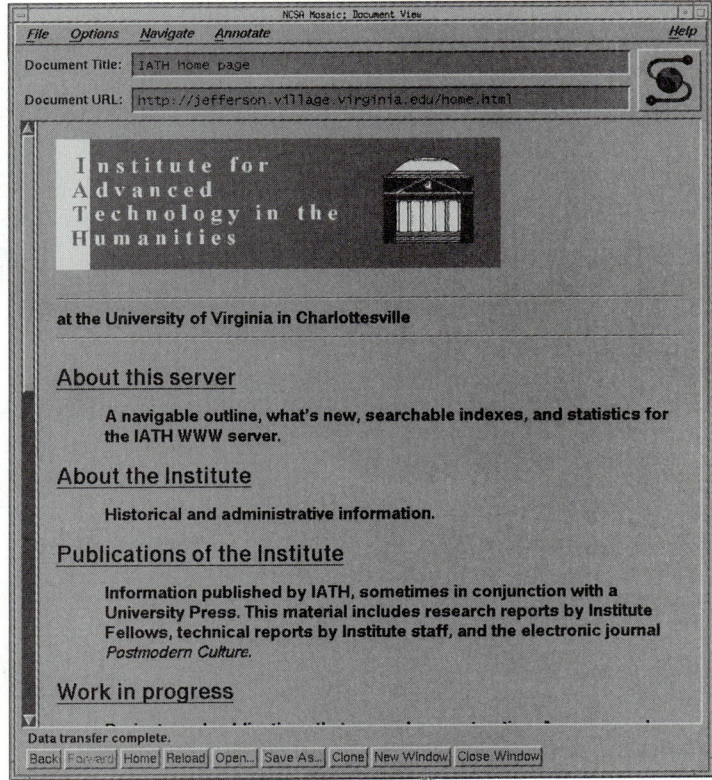

The research report holdings range from hypertext reports such as Mike Gorman's report on "Bell's Path to the Telephone," to "Noun Classification in Swahili," by Ellen Contini-Morava. The Rossetti Archive (Figure 25.30) contains many writings and pictures of Dante Gabriel Rossetti (its goal is to eventually contain Rossetti's complete works) in a hypermedia web, URL `http://jefferson.village.virginia.edu/rossetti/fullarch.html`.

The Rossetti Archive illustrates the depth of coverage that a Web-based hypermedia archive can offer; it includes images of paintings, drawings, and designs, texts of poems and fragments, commentary, prose works and fragments, manuscripts, and translations.

The Institute for Advanced Technology in the Humanities, through institutional support and the commitment of scholars, has developed a web with the potential to enrich all who venture into it. Because the Web "breaks walls" of geography, politics, and culture, people worldwide can make use of the collection of knowledge in Jefferson Village.

FIGURE 25.30.

The D.G. Rossetti Hypermedia Archive.

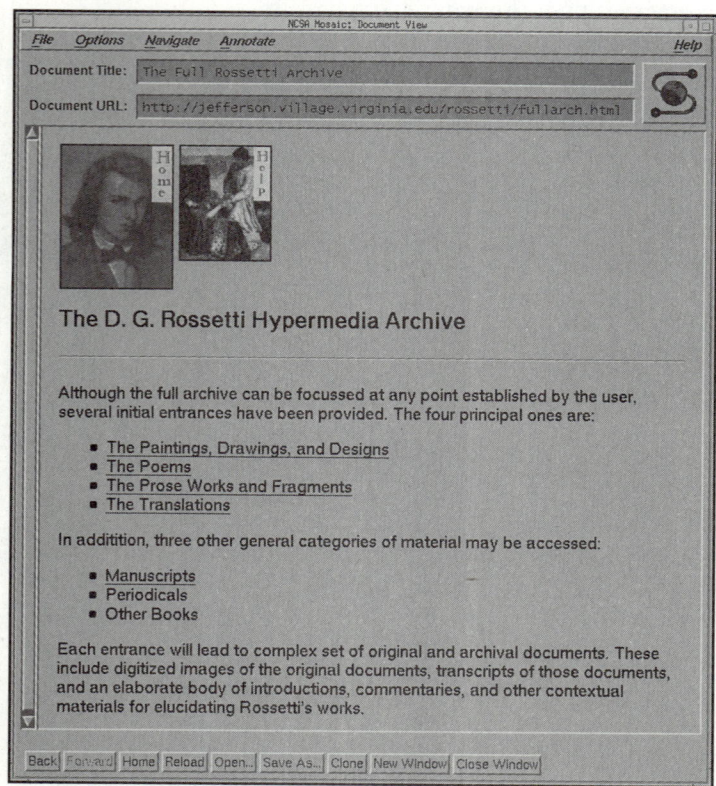

Coalition for Networked Information

While the University of Virginia's Jefferson City Web focuses on a specific area, humanities scholarship, the Coalition for Networked Information (CNI) focuses on promoting the creation and dissemination of networked information in all scholarly disciplines. CNI's home page located at URL `http://www.cni.org/CNI.homepage.html`, is shown in Figure 25.31.

FIGURE 25.31.

The home page for the Coalition for Networked Information.

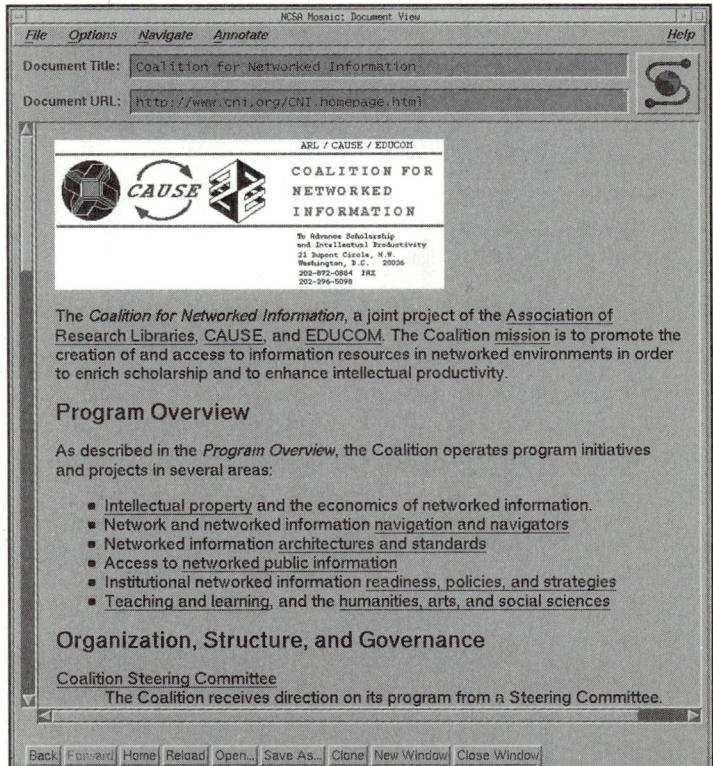

CNI itself is a collaborative project—often a hallmark of valuable Web collections—among a group of information-related organizations: Association of Research Libraries, CAUSE (the association for the management of information technology in higher education), and EDUCOM (a consortium of higher education institutions to facilitate information resources for teaching, learning, and scholarship). CNI's home page contains links to information about

- ■ Intellectual property
- ■ Projects dealing with networked navigation and navigators

■ Architectures and standards for networked information

■ Networked information policies for institutions

■ Teaching and learning

■ Links to other services provided by participating organizations: Coalition for Networked Information, Association of Research Libraries, CAUSE, and EDUCOM

CNI's work includes initiatives to explore important issues for making networked information available and useful to all scholars.

The Scholarly Communications Project

As CNI works to foster the use of networked information, the Scholarly Communications Project at the Virginia Polytechnic Institute and State University works to provide scholarly materials through electronic communication. The Home page of the Scholarly Communications Project, shown in Figure 25.32, is located at URL `http:// borg.lib.vt.edu/`.

Begun in 1989 as an effort to pioneer the electronic dissemination of scholarly materials, the Scholarly Communications project today includes publishing the following:

■ Electronic journals, including: *Journal of the International Academy of Hospitality Research, Community Services Catalyst,* and *Journal of Technology Education*

■ Abstracts of the print quarterly *International Journal of Analytical and Experimental Modal Analysis*

■ Research data of *Journal of Fluids Engineering*

The project develops electronic editing skills and provides participants with a means to experiment in various display formats on the Internet. The project offers texts through ASCII at an FTP site, through Gopher and WAIS, and through the Web.

Fostering Specialized Scholarly Connections

In-person meetings, conferences, and symposia have long been forums for scholars to meet and exchange ideas. These meetings, however, have required scholars to physically relocate to be in touch with other scholars. These in-person connections are invaluable because of the way interpersonal dynamics and the shared experience of a conference bring participants together. In fact, many participants might consider the "connections" made at a scholarly conference as important as or even more important than the information transmitted. Fostering similar kinds of "connections" in online environments is an important part of scholarly activity on the Web. This section examines some organizations and resource collections that bring scholars together.

FIGURE 25.32.

The home page for the Scholarly Communications Project of Virginia Polytechnic Institute and State University.

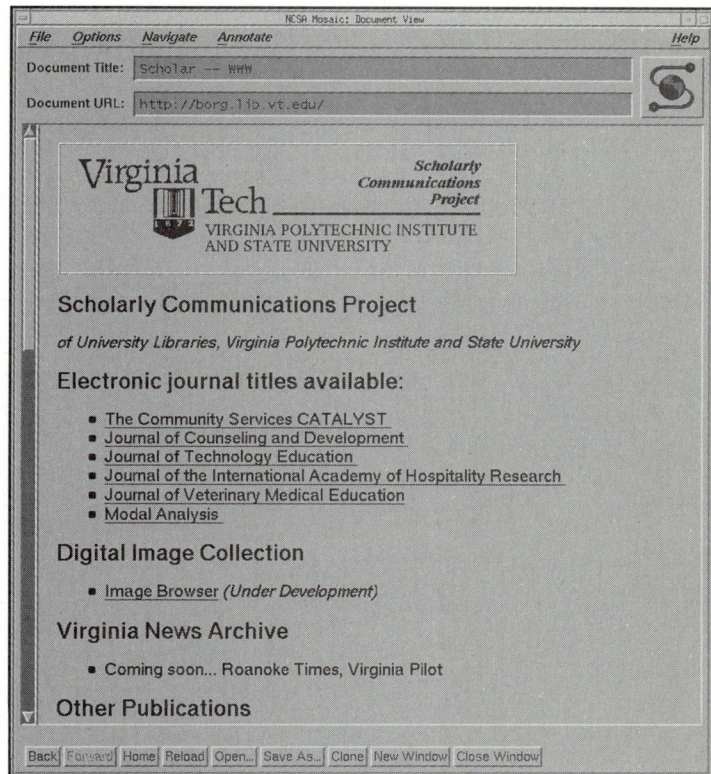

University of Waterloo Scholarly Societies Collection

Many scholarly societies have recognized the value of networked information and communication for their membership and have created online forums. However, how does a scholar find an organization of interest? One way could be to use keyword or subject-oriented searching methods (Chapter 18, "Trees: Subject-Oriented Searching," and Chapter 19, "Spiders and Indexes: Keyword-Oriented Searching"). However, a comprehensive, professionally maintained collection can serve the needs of a scholar or interested student much more efficiently.

The University of Waterloo Library has created such a collection of pointers to scholarly societies. The Waterloo collection facilitates access to electronic resources maintained by scholarly organizations, as defined on the Waterloo Web page at URL `http://www.lib.uwaterloo.ca/~society/overview.html` as "organizations in which membership is determined by scholarly credentials, not by the existence of a contract of employment or of visitation rights, as in the case of a research centre."

The Waterloo collection lists almost one hundred organizations that have Web pages, Gophers, or FTP archives providing information for members or the public. Figure 25.33 shows the holdings of the Web pages collection of scholarly societies.

The University of Waterloo's collection serves a valuable service because it acts as a central branching-off point for scholars seeking to find organizations in a particular field of interest. It also provides an excellent means to locate authoritative information for a particular subject area, as many societies also maintain resource collections in their members' area of expertise.

FIGURE 25.33.

Web pages of Scholarly Societies with subject area listing.

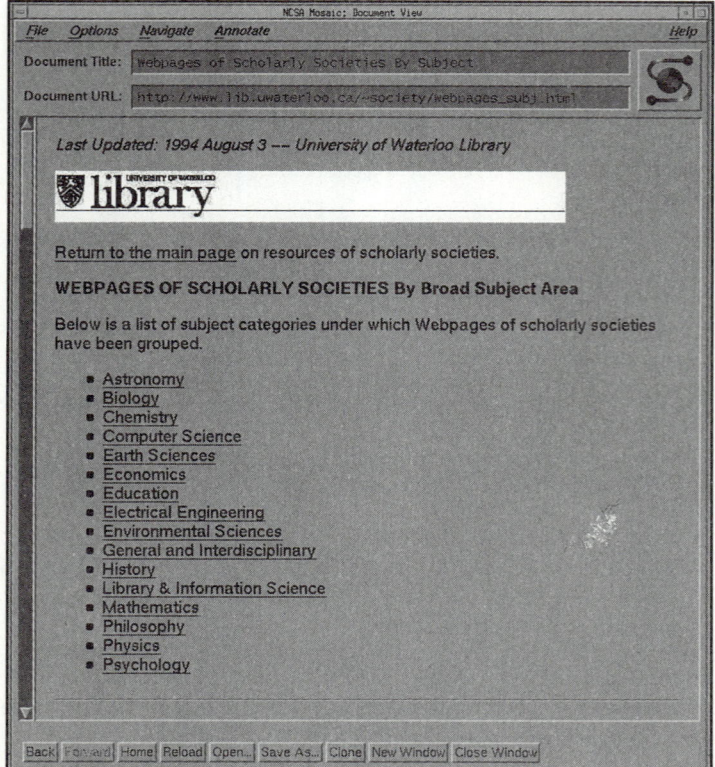

The Communication Institute for Online Scholarship

The Communication Institute for Online Scholarship (CIOS) is a nonprofit organization co-directed by Timothy Stephen and Teresa Harrison, both associate professors of communication at Rensselaer Polytechnic Institute in Troy, New York. The goal of CIOS is to facilitate communication-related scholarship through the use of computer and information technologies.

CIOS operates Comserve, an online service for scholars interested in human communication research. Begun from an idea by Timothy Stephen and Teresa Harrison for scholarly electronic communication in 1985, Comserve today serves a community of thousands of users at more than 50,000 e-mail addresses in 80 countries. Comserve functions as a resource library, a news service, an electronic "white pages," a computer conferencing system, a database of journal indexes, and a distributor of electronic announcements and surveys. The philosophy guiding Comserve is to provide high-quality services for communications scholars with as much distributed responsibility as possible. The emphasis for Comserve's growth and development is to continue to improve the quality of the scholarly discussion taking place as well as to increase the value of the materials stored in Comserve's resource library.

Comserve provides both a model for scholarly online communication and a forum for studying online scholarly interaction. Since Comserve provides a full range of services to meet scholarly needs for communication and resource sharing, it can give other scholarly organizations some direction in designing Net- or Web-based forums for interaction. Comserve also facilitates the study of online communication itself, through its hotline discussions focused on the study of Computer-Mediated Communication as well as through its resource library holdings, communication journal indexes, and online journal related to the study of communication.

The full range of Comserve's services is available through electronic mail. For more information send the message "Send Comserve HelpFile" to `Comserve@Vm.Its.Rpi.Edu`. The CIOS Gopher is at URL `gopher://cios.llc.rpi.edu/`.

The Centre for Networked Access to Scholarly Information

While efforts to increase scholarly interaction worldwide often have great impact, local efforts can also show success in helping scholars make use of networked information and communication. The Centre for Networked Access to Scholarly Information (CNASI) at the Australian National University Library aims to deliver online information to the University's academic community (Figure 25.34).

The efforts of CNASI (URL `http://snazzy.anu.edu.au/`) include

- A Campus-Wide Information System (CWIS)
- An Electronic Library Information System at Australian National University (ELISA)
- Daily Reuters Newsbriefs
- Developing electronic resources in the area of Asian Information, through the cooperation of the National Library and the Research School of Social Sciences
- Establishing a national network of centers for teaching resource materials
- Establishing a central gateway to access all Australian Gophers
- Creating a directory of Australian electronic mailing lists
- Providing access to course materials to students
- Developing links to network information materials, government information, and electronic journals

FIGURE 25.34.

The home page for the CNASI Web server.

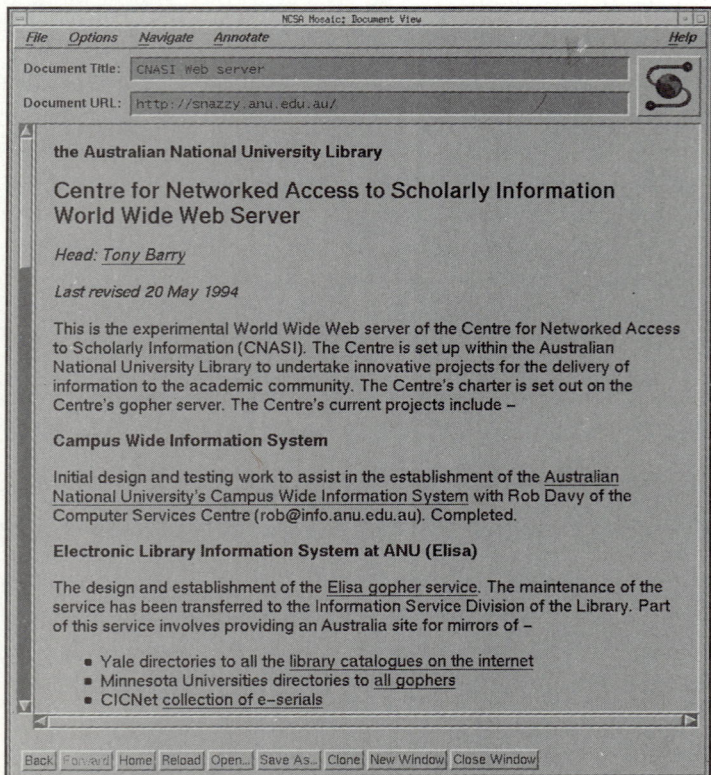

Although the CNASI Web, as well as related Gophers, is still under development, its current state demonstrates the potential scope of how university-wide access to networked resources can be developed.

Brown University's Institute for Information Research and Scholarship

The Institute for Information Research and Scholarship (IRIS) was established in 1983 at Brown University to explore the ways computing technology can be used for research and teaching. Now absorbed into Brown's Computing and Information Services department, IRIS provides hypertext materials in a variety of specialized areas.

One example is the "The Religion in England" Web, (URL `http://www.iris.brown.edu/iris/RIE/Religion_OV.html`), developed as part of an IRIS project to provide contextual information for a course in English literature. Developed by a team of authors—David Cody, George P. Landow, Anthony S. Wohl, Robert Aurellano, and David B. Stevenson— the web offers a very rich set of background information on all aspects of religion in England (Figure 25.35). David B. Stevenson converted its Storyspace (a Macintosh-based hypertext system) version to the Web.

FIGURE 25.35.

The Religion in England Web.

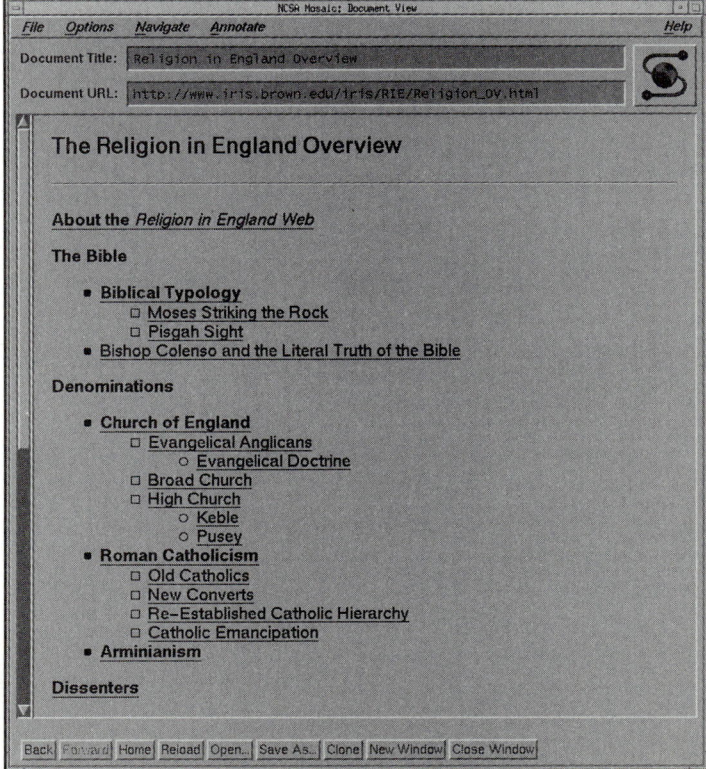

The depth and richness of the contextual information offered by the Religion in England web is an example of what can be done for a specialized use. The value of the Web-based version of this hypertext is that this web can be freely used by students and scholars worldwide to gain an understanding of religion in England.

Explorer's Check

The Web can serve as a tool for scholars and educators to not only express their ideas, but also share their knowledge within a community of scholars and students. Elementary and secondary schools as well as community colleges and universities have all joined the Web with information and instructional material.

Organizations such as the Coalition for Networked Information foster the use of networked information in education and research through innovative and authoritative collections of information and guidelines on important issues and topics.

Specialized forums such as Jefferson Village Virginia, the Scholarly Communications Project, and the Communication Institute for Online Scholarship foster scholarship in broad areas of interest by creating forums and structures to disseminate, create, and critique knowledge.

At the local level, scholars can develop webs to support specific needs. Australian National University's Centre for Networked Access to Scholarly Information and Brown University's Institute for Information Research and Scholarship demonstrate webs that support a local need and at the same time serve to inform and educate all students on the Web.

Through the pioneering efforts of these online organizations, scholars can continue to build structures that fully explore the potential of the Web for communicating, sharing information, and creating scholarly communities.

Science and Technology

26

by John December

IN THIS CHAPTER

Since the Web itself was invented by CERN, an organization that is part of an active scientific community (see Part I, "Introduction to the World Wide Web"), it is no surprise that science and technology subjects are well-represented on the Web. This chapter describes webs that present science and technology information for public and professional education as well as directly for use in research. The ability of the Web to expressively convey multimedia information through a graphical browser such as Mosaic is well-represented among these examples, with many webs using hypermedia to inform and educate the user.

These webs also illustrate the value of having domain experts (people with expertise in the knowledge domain represented by the web) involved in developing web information. Systems of peer-review and quality checks are essential to providing reliable web information, and many of these webs show exceptional involvement by domain experts. Moreover, these webs also illustrate the way specialized science webs can serve the public good through the collective efforts of several organizations.

The first section explains how OncoLink, a service for disseminating information about cancer, provides not only an excellent service for practitioners in the field, but also serves the public by providing accurate information to learn about this important topic. Many organizations already strive to educate the public through materials and courses—often provided for free. The Web facilitates the dissemination of detailed, current, educational materials that utilize the expressive power of hypertext and multimedia on a global scale.

Most of the webs described in this chapter were still in their infancy (under a year old) when they appeared as shown here. Their developers will have increased the offerings on these webs since. Also, in my narrative of each web, I'll stress various aspects of the information contained in the web itself. Therefore, my description is not a complete guide to the total offerings in each web, but highlights significant aspects and special needs that each web meets.

OncoLink: Quality Information for Specialists and Patients

Oncology is the study of cancer, and comprehensive and up-to-date educational information is critical for the treatment of patients, education of health care professionals, and the development of the field of oncology itself. The University of Pennsylvania's Cancer Center meets this need through OncoLink, a multimedia, Web-accessible Oncology resource. Supported by the Radiation Oncology Department and founded by E. Loren Buhle, Jr., Ph.D and Joel Goldwein, M.D., OncoLink was the first multimedia cancer resource collection established on the Internet. For its excellence, OncoLink earned the International Best of the Web Award for Best Professional Service in 1994. Its home page (URL `http://cancer.med.upenn.edu/`) is shown in Figure 26.1.

FIGURE 26.1.

OncoLink home page.

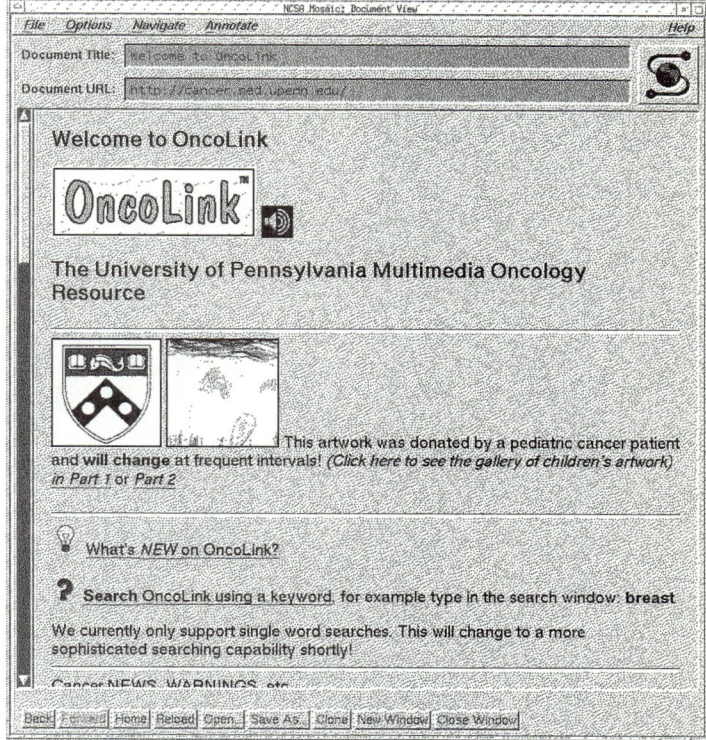

OncoLink supports a wide variety of information for

- The rapid collection and dissemination of information related to oncology
- Education for health care personnel
- Education for patients, families, and the general public

While many information webs provide a variety of links to outside resources, OncoLink's stress is on developing high-quality, well-organized, peer-reviewed information pertinent to the field of oncology and its specialties.

OncoLink offers information in several general categories:

- Specific Diseases such as Breast Cancer, Ovarian Cancer, Cervical Cancer, Gestational Trophoblastic Disease

■ Specialities within Oncology such as Pediatric (Figure 26.2), Gynecologic, and Radiation (Figure 26.3)

■ Patient support and information; for example, psychosocial support (Figure 26.4), Cancer FAQ, and topical information on subjects like smoking, pain, and prevention

■ News such as meeting and conference announcements

■ Pointers to cancer-related Internet information

■ Administrative information

Within each category, accessible from the home page, other web pages offer a variety of information. Figure 26.2 shows the top of the Pediatric Oncology page and Figure 26.3 shows the top of the Radiation Oncology page.

FIGURE 26.2.

The Pediatric Oncology page (top).

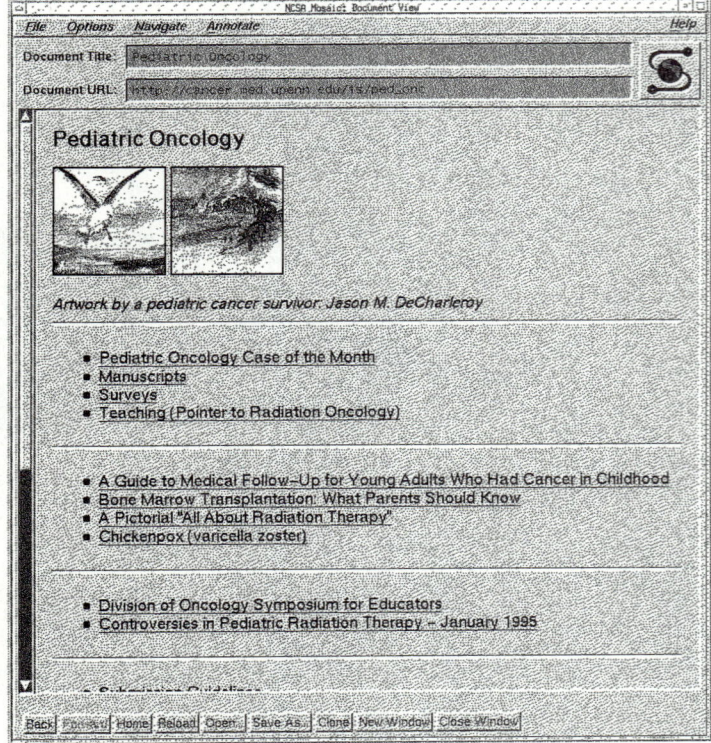

FIGURE 26.3.

The Radiation Oncology page (top).

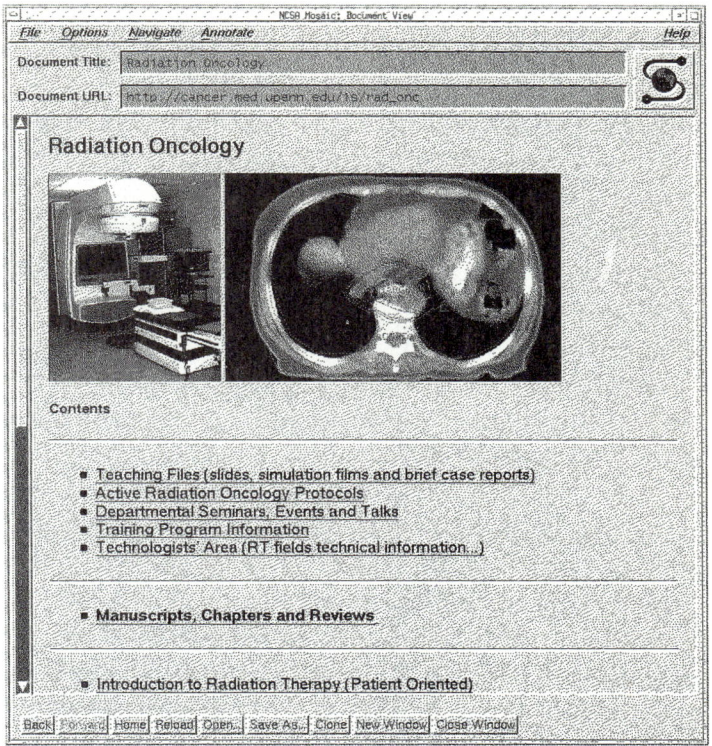

The individual page designs make good use of techniques to package information into distinct conceptual categories. The pages also illustrate how graphics can be used to add information as well as visual appeal to a page without being obtrusive. Since OncoLink's information is also accessible via Gopher, the images may not be available to all users (and those with nongraphical Web browsers). OncoLink's design takes this into account by not providing important information solely through graphics. For example, on the Psychosocial Support page, shown in Figure 26.4, images add an element of beauty to a page that may help ease a patient into information that otherwise may look cold and impersonal on a computer screen.

OncoLink's users are worldwide, and a group of seven cooperating editorial advisors reviews the information provided. The audience for OncoLink includes physicians, health care workers, patients, and the public. As a provider of important information to this audience, OncoLink developers very responsibly include disclaimers acknowledging the limitations of Web information—stating that the information is for informational purposes, that it does not imply University of Pennsylvania Cancer Center endorsement, and

that the information is not a rendering or substitute for medical services and care. This disclaimer is important, because it reveals the necessary limitations of Web-based information itself: It does not replace appropriate medical care, but rather provides better information in order for patients and providers to obtain and experience quality care.

FIGURE 26.4.

The Psychosocial Support page.

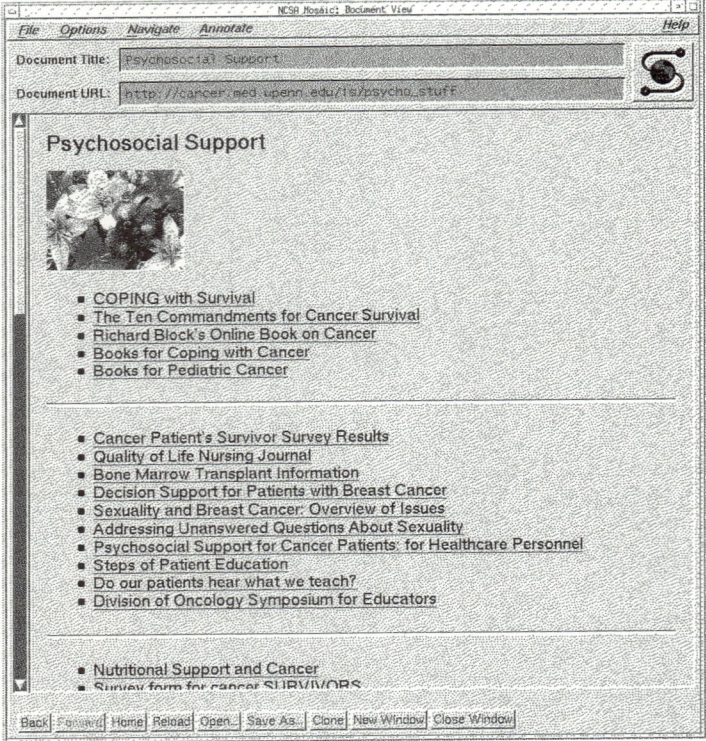

OncoLink has experienced great popularity, and the statistics offered about its use demonstrate extensive access. OncoLink was announced via Usenet on March 7, 1994. Between its official announcement and July 31, 1994, users accessed OncoLink an approximate average of 3,000 times per weekday and 1,000 times per day on the weekend. Moreover, accesses were from more than forty-five countries (see Figure 26.5), although the majority, 52 percent, were from the United States.

The global reach of OncoLink shows how it not only meets a unique need, but also brings connections to the developers—establishing relationships that may grow over time with international researchers. These relationships may, through feedback and involvement, improve the quality of information on the OncoLink web.

FIGURE 26.5.

OncoLink use.

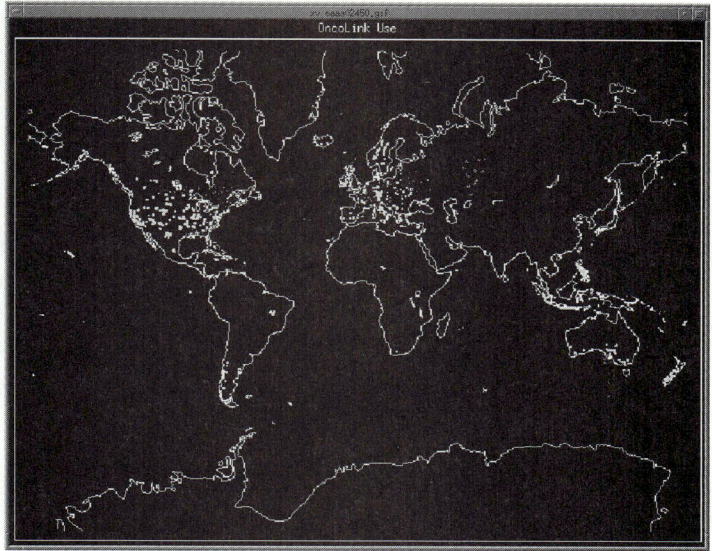

OncoLink's authoritative, comprehensive collection of oncology information, combined with a peer review process to ensure the highest quality information, packaged in a good web design with careful analysis of web use, makes OncoLink an excellent example of how the Web can be used for advancing and explaining science.

The European Space Information System: Multinational Scientific Information

There are many challenges that arise when presenting scientific information from a variety of sources to a variety of audiences dispersed worldwide. The European Space Information System web demonstrates that a high-quality information system to support researchers and developers can be created and maintained.

The European Space Agency (ESA) consists of 14 member states: Austria, Belgium, Denmark, Federal Republic of Germany, Finland (January 1, 1995), France, Ireland, Italy, the Netherlands, Norway, Spain, Sweden, Switzerland, the United Kingdom, and Canada (as a participating member). The diversity of languages and cultures, as well as the complexity of the science involved in space research, challenges information providers to present timely, accurate information to support scientists and researchers. Figure 26.6 shows the ESA's home page (URL http://www.esrin.esa.it/htdocs/esa/esa.html).

FIGURE 26.6.

European Space Agency home page.

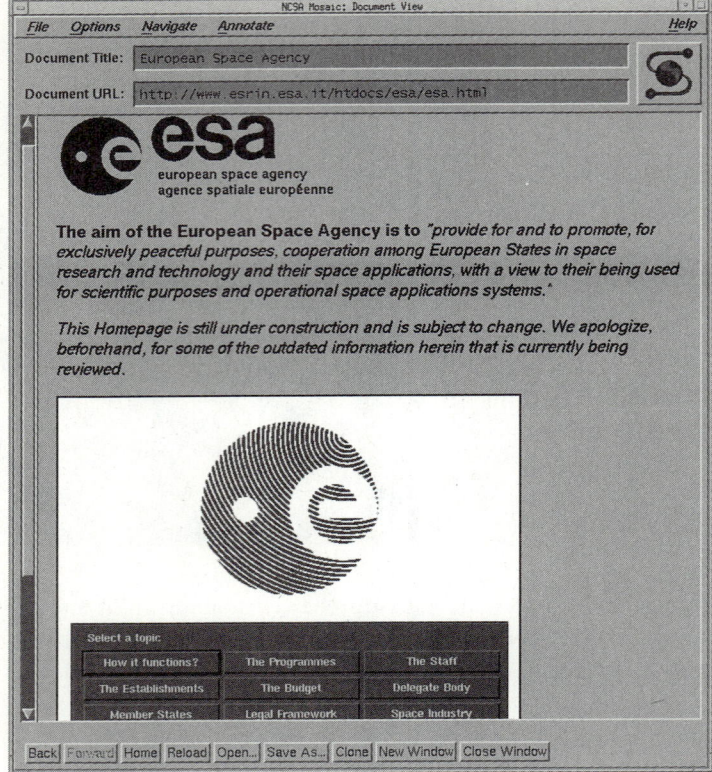

As part of the complex task of keeping members informed as well as providing the space science community access to scientific data, images, and resources, the ESA provides information through the European Space Information System (ESIS) web shown in Figure 26.7 (URL `http://www.esrin.esa.it/htdocs/esa/esa.html`).

The ESIS web provides extensive links to astronomical databases and catalogs, a space science bibliography (including a forms interface), space physics catalog and datasets, and a space physics bibliographical service.

FIGURE 26.7.

European Space Information System home page.

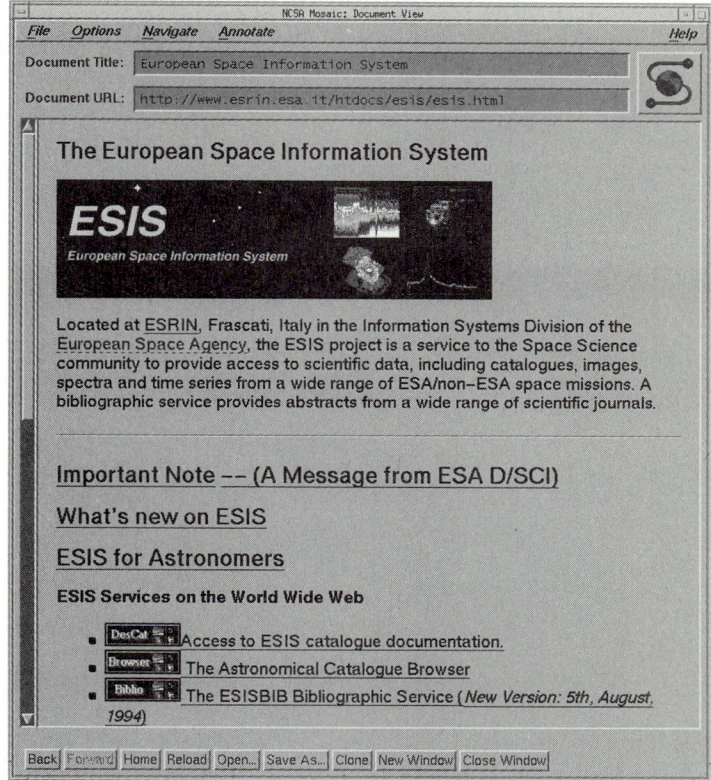

Only a *partial* listing of the astronomical databases illustrates the wide variety of and locations for information:

- SIMBAD: information on individual astronomical objects, at the Centre de Donnees Astronomique de Strasbourg, France
- STARCAT: European Coordinating Facility for European use of the Hubble Space Telescope and the European Southern Observatory and Space Telescope, in Garching bei Muenchen, Germany
- Canadian Archive Data Centre in Victoria, B.C., Canada
- Villafranca Satellite Tracking Station data, near Madrid, Spain

The ESIS web utilizes several kinds of graphical interfaces to guide the user through this data. For example, Figure 26.8 shows the view of the interface available for the system itself. Figure 26.9 shows the ESIS Imaging Application interface.

FIGURE 26.8.

Overview of ESIS.

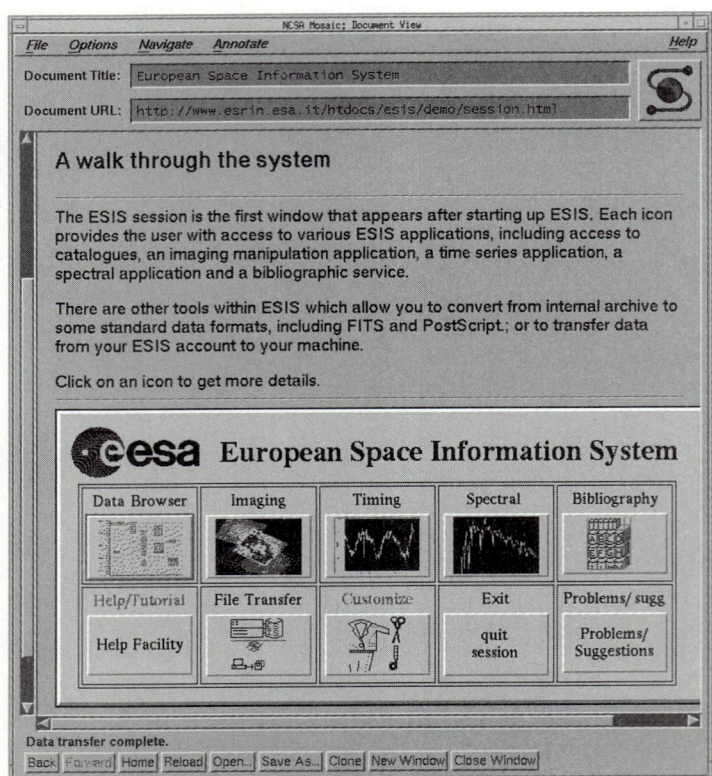

FIGURE 26.9.

*ESIS Imaging
Application.*

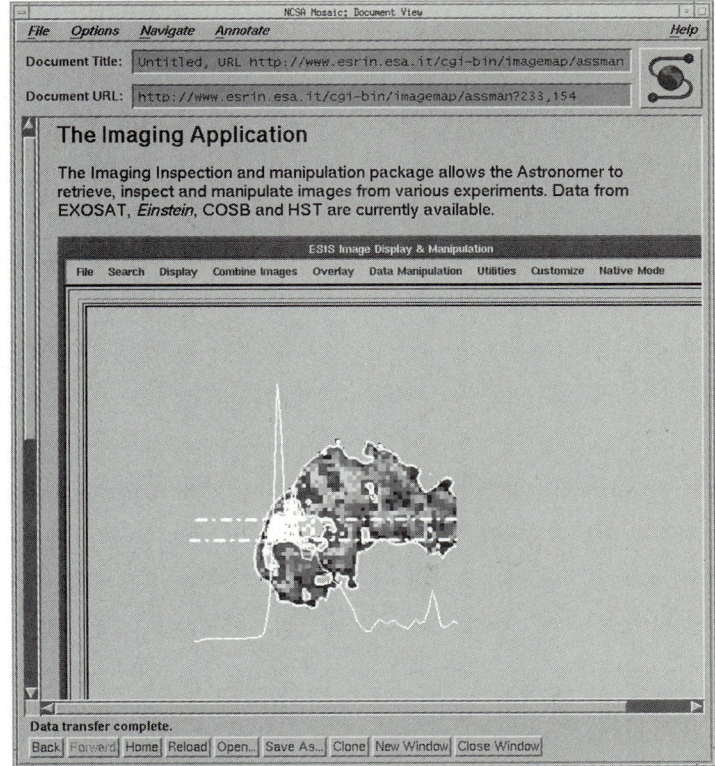

The ESIS web provides further links to services for space physicists (the ESISBIB biblio-graphical service shown in Figure 26.10), as well as links on the Web to space research sites and other space agencies.

FIGURE 26.10.
*The ESISBIB Biblio-
graphical Service.*

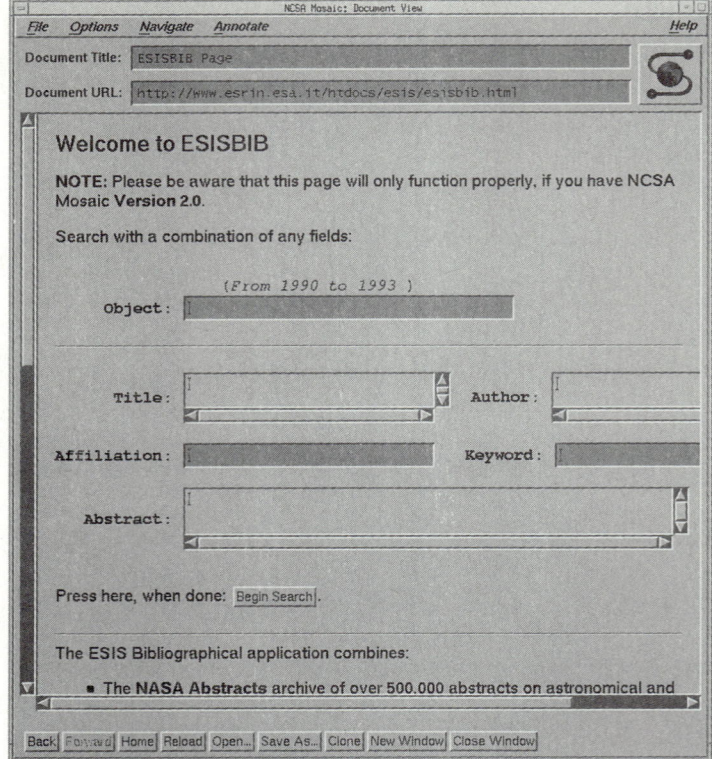

The ESIS also offers reprints of publications, a newsletter, and a user's guide.

The ESIS is a good example of how a community of scientists from diverse organizations can cooperate to share valuable scientific information, not only for their own benefit, but for the benefit of the wider scientific community as well. In this way, the ESIS web itself serves as a focal point for sharing space science information, fostering connections and associations that can enrich the progress of science itself.

Institute for Telecommunication Sciences: Science in Service to People and Government

While the mission of ESIS is multinational and draws on many kinds of databases from multiple sources, other scientific webs provide information from more localized sources. The Institute for Telecommunication Sciences is a U.S. government research and engineering organization. As such, it has special requirements to serve its employers (the U.S. taxpayers) as well as the government agencies it serves through the work it performs.

The ITS is part of the National Telecommunications & Information Administration (NTIA) (URL `http://www.ntia.doc.gov/`) which in turn is part of the U.S. Department of Commerce (URL `http://www.doc.gov/`). The goal of the Department of Commerce is to promote U.S. business and trade, and as part of this work, the Department of Commerce calls on the NTIA to advise the President on telecommunications and information policy matters and to present these policies before Congress. In cooperating with other federal government agencies, NTIA also contributes to the United States' initiative to develop the Information Infrastructure Task Force (IITF), chaired by the Secretary of Commerce. Within the context of these government relationships, the Institute for Telecommunication Sciences (ITS) serves NTIA with research and engineering to promote advanced telecommunications and information infrastructure. The ITS also serves as a focal point for helping federal agencies, state and local governments, and corporations and organizations solve telecommunications problems.

The ITS home page (URL `http://www.its.bldrdoc.gov/its.html`) is shown in Figure 26.11.

In its mission to serve as a research and engineering arm of the NTIA, ITS works in areas such as:

- Radio spectrum use analysis
- Telecommunication standards development
- Telecommunications systems performance and planning
- Applied research (for example, radio wave modeling)

The goal of ITS is to benefit the public and private sectors through its products (engineering tools, standards, research results) and services (training for industry and government users). Reflecting this purpose, the ITS web offers organizational information (a breakdown of the divisions and groups is shown in Figure 26.12) and access to files and programs; for example, computer models of high-frequency propagation.

FIGURE 26.11.

Institute for Telecommunication Sciences home page.

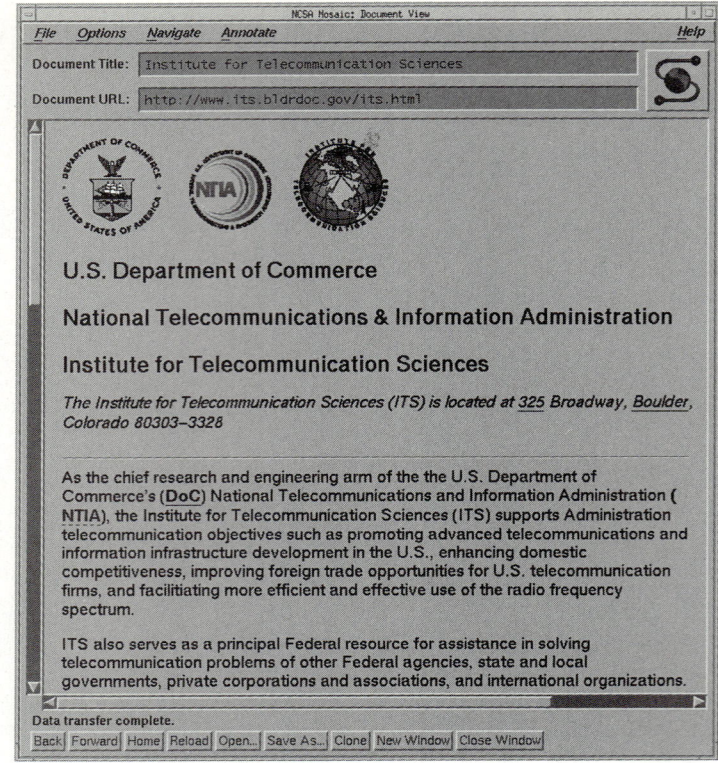

FIGURE 26.12.

Institute for Telecommunication Sciences divisions.

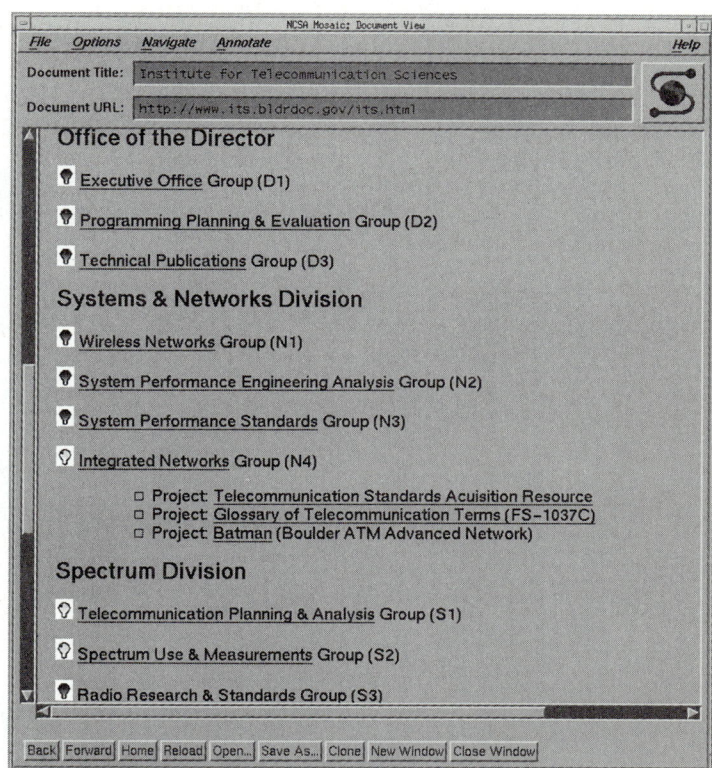

Figure 26.13 shows Integrated Networks Group's group-level web offering links to projects on which the people in the group are working and to home pages of people in the group.

FIGURE 26.13.

ITS Integrated Networks Group.

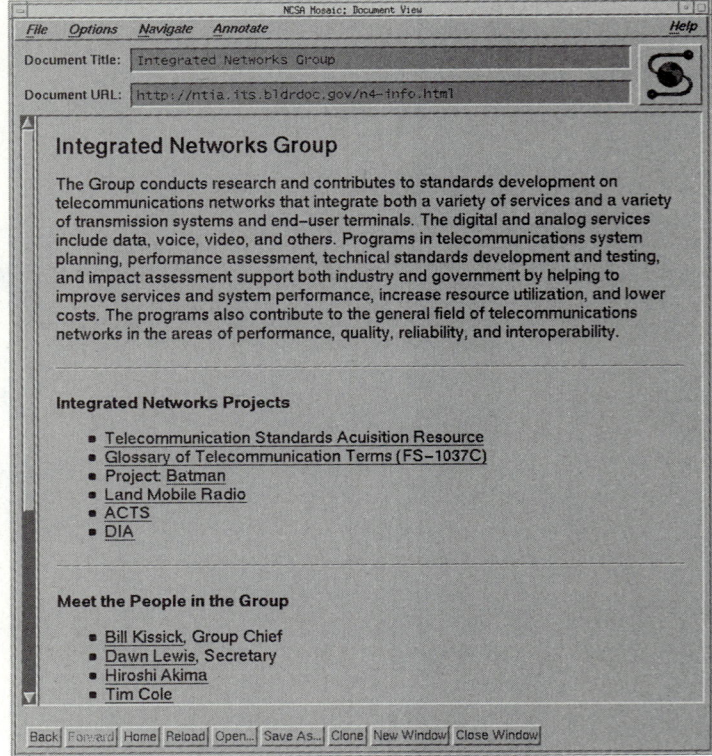

Moving one step down again, following the link to the BATMAN project, we see another detailed web summarizing this project.

The BATMAN (The Boulder Asynchronous Transfer Mode Advanced Network) project is a technology trial of Asynchronous Transfer Mode [ATM], a type of computer communication in which units of data called cells are exchanged independently from source to receiver. The value of this page is that it serves as a focal point for the project as well as the cooperating organizations and participants. The page provides general information for the public.

FIGURE 26.14.

ITS BATMAN home page.

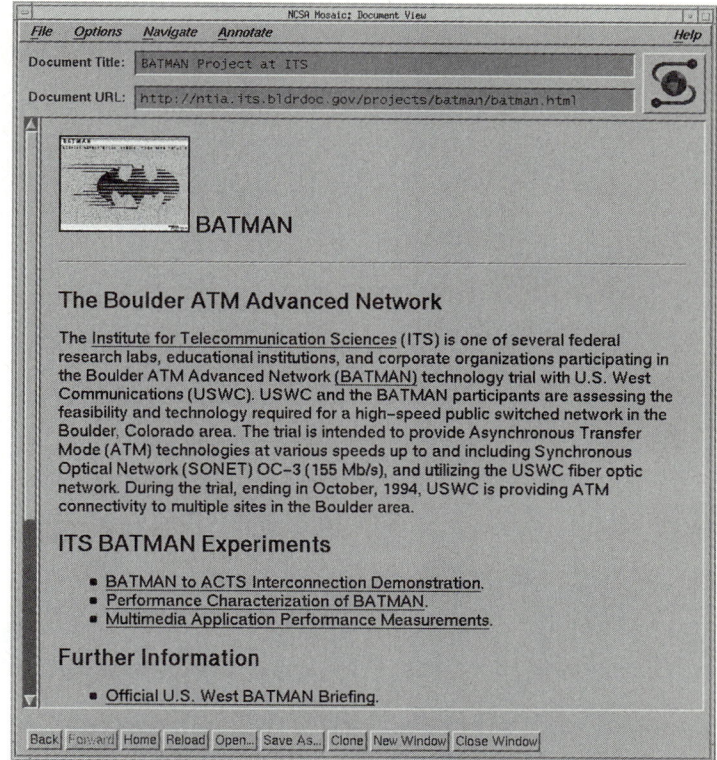

The ITS BATMAN page points to a BATMAN page at the University of Colorado, one of the participating institutions. From the ITS BATMAN page, you can obtain specific technical information such as a diagram showing an overview of the BATMAN network topology (Figure 26.15).

By combining selected technical information such as that shown above, with a good set of administrative and contact information, the ITS web serves both the public and private sectors as an information source for government engineering and research in advanced telecommunications. In this way, the ITS web shows a particular attention to organizational information needs—an important aspect in complex government, university, and corporate interaction.

FIGURE 26.15.
*BATMAN network
topology.*

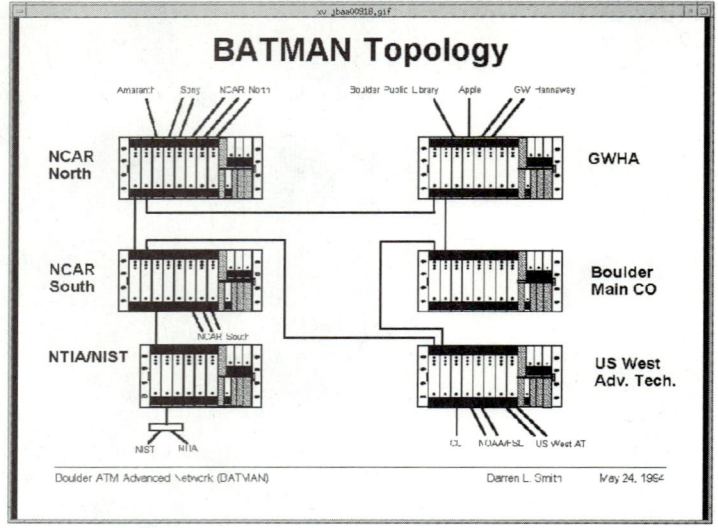

Artificial Life Online: Breaking New Ground in an Emerging Discipline

The webs examined so far deal with scientific subjects that have a long history and body of research, but the Web can be especially helpful to disseminate information about an emerging field and discipline. A web in a (relatively) new field of scholarly inquiry can broaden the range of information people can access and serve as a gathering point for scholars interested in the discipline.

Artificial Life Online, developed by Chris Langton and Scott D. Yelich, is a forum for people interested in the study an emerging area for research and study. The Artificial Life web text itself states that artificial life is "[recreated] biological phenomena [made] from scratch within computers and other 'artificial' media" (URL http://alife.santafe.edu/ 0/System/bbs/lib/html/alife-def.html). The study of artificial life thus attempts to *synthesize* systems that act like living things, as opposed to the traditional biological approach of analysis (taking apart or examining living organisms to analyze how they work). While artificial life study aims to create advances in the understanding of biology, it also can be applied to complex systems that have many interacting parts—such as computer networks, nanotechnology, and industrial assembly. Figure 26.16 shows the home page of the Artificial Life web.

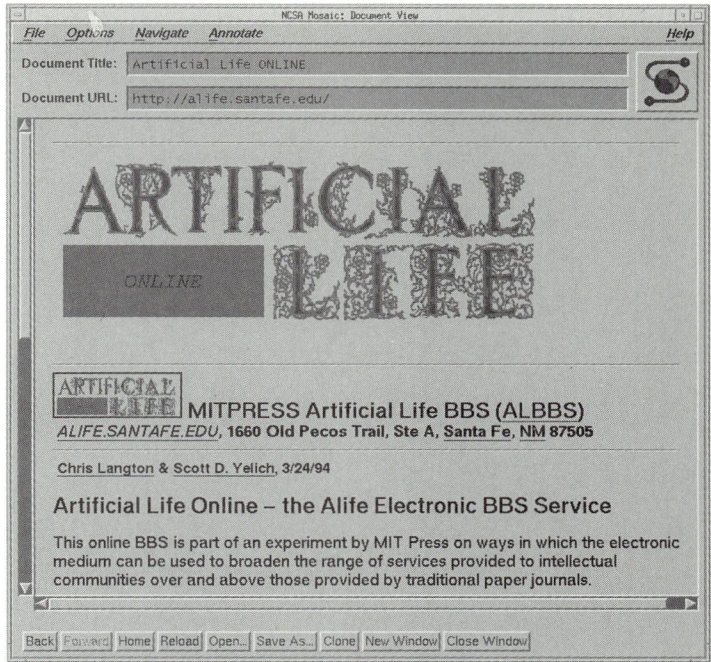

FIGURE 26.16.
Artificial Life Online home page.

The developers of the Artificial Life web have created many features to support scholarly communication:

■ Information about *Artificial Life*, a quarterly journal from MIT Press (text not online)

■ Links to Usenet discussion groups that discuss related issues (including links to local information at the Santa Fe Institute)

■ Software available via FTP, including "Cellsim," a cellular automation simulator; "Polyworld," an artificial world for studying evolution; "Echo," an ecological simulation

■ A bibliographic database, including entries from the First Alife Workshop

■ Curricula materials, such as suggestions for Artificial Life courses and syllabi contributed by educators in the field

■ An archive of papers by authors who wish to gather comments

■ A list of upcoming conferences, seminars, and other events of interest to the Artificial Life community

■ Links to WWW resources related to Artificial Life

This extensive offering of activities supports a variety of ways scholars can contribute and discuss ideas. Besides the Web-accessible offerings, Artificial Life Online also sponsors discussion lists and the Usenet newsgroups mentioned above. The offerings on the Artificial Life Online web support a range of communication, from formal publication (the *Artificial Life* quarterly) to informal discussions (mailing list and Usenet newsgroups) to review processes (paper review area). The Artificial life BBS thus gathers a community of scholars around an emerging discipline, educates interested others, and provides a focal point for further research and discovery.

The International Society for Optical Engineering: Supporting Professional Development

The International Society for Optical Engineering (SPIE) is a nonprofit association of professionals working in the optical sciences. The goals of SPIE are to advance research, education, and applications. The SPIE web "brings the latest technological breakthroughs to the doorstep of individuals and organizations all over the world" (URL `http://www.spie.org/web/member_guide/about_spie.html`). The SPIE web's home page is shown in Figures 26.17 and 26.18.

The SPIE web offers a variety of information to support its membership in a rapidly changing field. The Membership Guide for SPIE points out, "Keeping abreast of the latest developments in optics, electro-optics, and optoelectronic engineering has always been a challenge. Today, rapid changes throughout the industry make this challenge even more imperative" (URL `http://www.spie.org/web/member_guide/individual_member.html`).

With more than 11,500 members in 64 countries, SPIE's membership is truly worldwide and multidisciplinary, with organizations supporting SPIE in education, industry, medicine, and government. Each year SPIE sponsors more than 200 technical conferences and meetings and offers more than 400 courses in conjunction with technical meetings, some broadcast live over the National Technological University satellite network. SPIE also publishes more than 200 conference proceedings a year, 30 books, a refereed technical journal *(Optical Engineering)*, and *OE Reports*, an industry newspaper.

FIGURE 26.17.

SPIE home page (top).

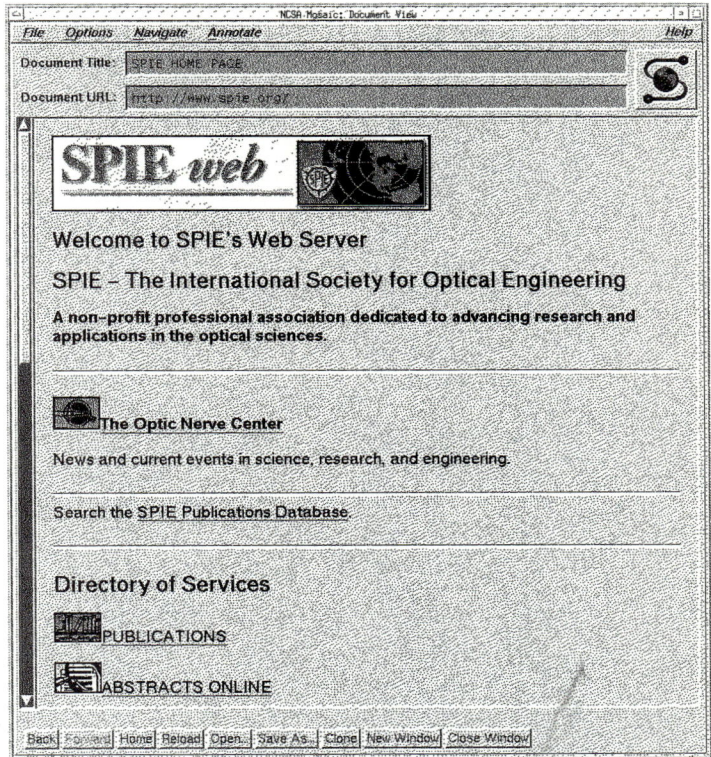

With this range of activities, a web supporting its members must have the breadth to cover the concerns of a diverse, geographically dispersed community while at the same time covering each topic with enough depth to justify the work of creating and maintaining the web itself. SPIE's membership includes industry and academic researchers, educators as well as students. By making their web server publicly accessible, SPIE's web audience also includes the general Web public who may be seeking expert information in the field of optical engineering.

What makes the SPIE web a good example of a professional society web is the variety, depth, and breadth of information it provides. For example, Figure 26.19 shows a collection of standards information offered.

FIGURE 26.18.

SPIE home page (bottom).

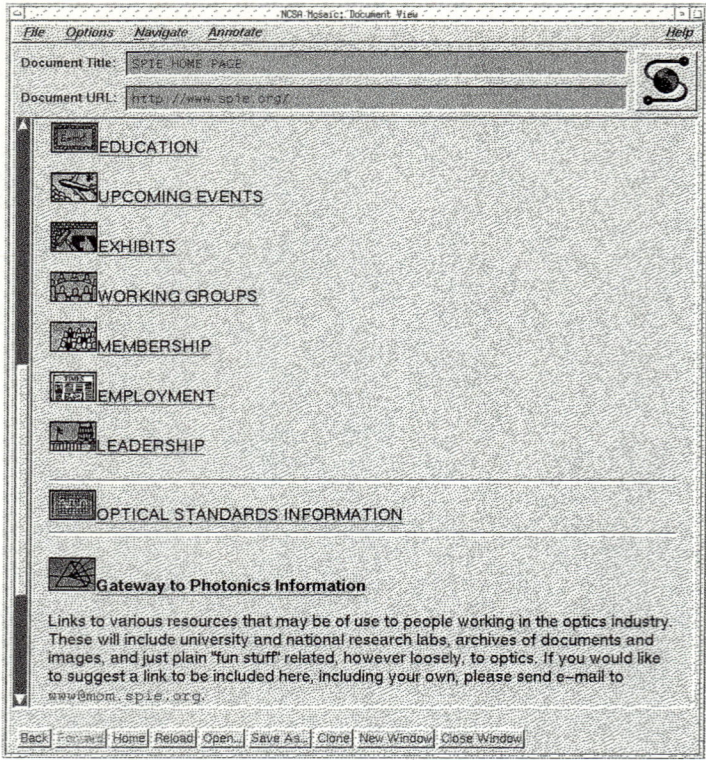

By maintaining this collection of online standards, the SPIE web simplifies the information retrieval process for researchers while presenting an excellent overview for students.

Another example of the SPIE web's depth and breadth is the contact information it offers. The SPIE web provides an *Optics Education* directory online. This directly lists more than 200 college and university programs in North America and the world, published with assistance from Lawrence Livermore National Laboratory and Control Optics Corporation. This guide is comprehensive, and its presentation on the SPIE web serves as an invaluable contact resource for students. The SPIE web also includes a complete listing of corporate members as a bridge from SPIE to industry.

FIGURE 26.19.

SPIE Optical Standards collection.

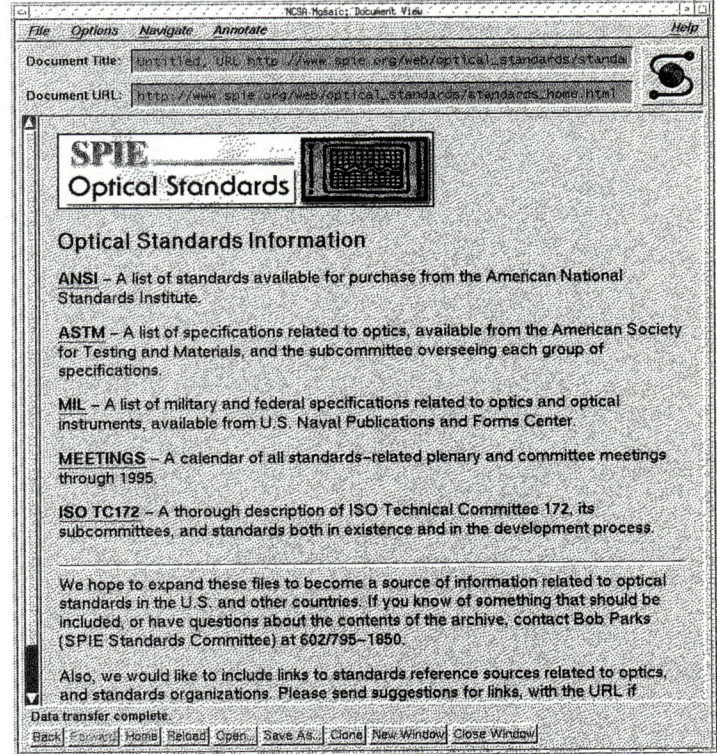

The SPIE web also offers a gateway to information resources on the Net related to the optics industry, as well as a database of more than 20,000 abstracts available for searching by scholars and researchers for noncommercial purposes.

By providing a range of services, the SPIE web demonstrates how a scholarly society web can support scientific research for a diverse and dispersed community. Indeed the SPIE web itself serves as an important focal point for the organization, serving as SPIE's "front door" on the Web.

Knowledge Wealth from Laboratories

Besides efforts such as the preceding examples that involve multinational efforts to bring scientific and research communities together, there are webs that highlight the accomplishments of a single laboratory or research center. Through their webs, these labs offer a wealth of knowledge to interested researchers, potential participants, and the general public. From the examples in this section, you'll see how these webs are a rich source of unique information on the Web.

QUEST Protein Database Center

QUEST (QUantitative Electrophoresis STandardized) Protein Database Center is a U.S. National Institutes of Health biomedical research technology resource. Located in Cold Spring Harbor (New York) Laboratory (CSHL), which provides services in addition to core research, the QUEST web's goal is to support the "construction and analysis of Protein Databases" (URL `http://siva.cshl.org/index.html`).

The home page for the QUEST web (URL `http://siva.cshl.org/`) is shown in Figure 26.20.

FIGURE 26.20.

QUEST home page.

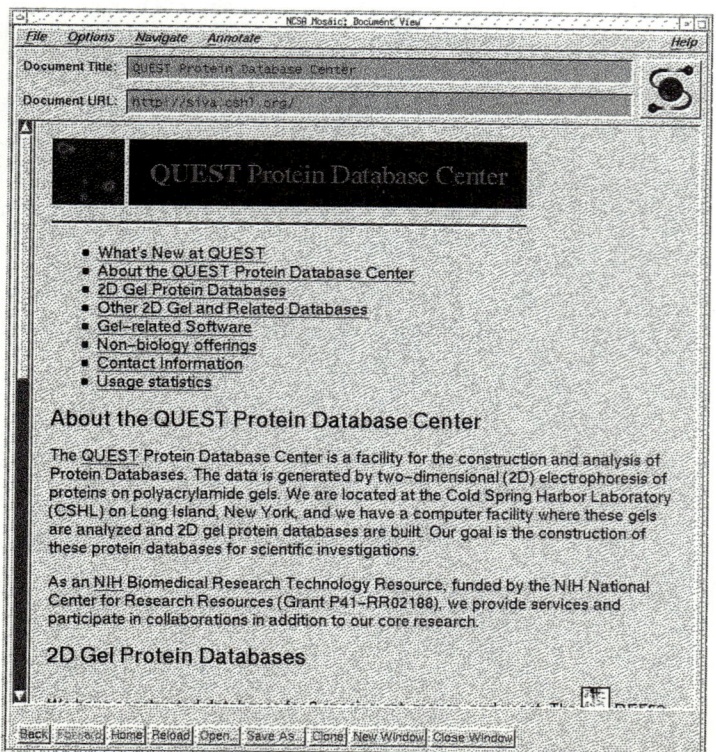

The QUEST web provides a detailed glimpse into protein research. For example, Figure 26.21 illustrates the image representation of a 2-D Gel Protein Database for a rat protein.

FIGURE 26.21.

Rat Protein Database.

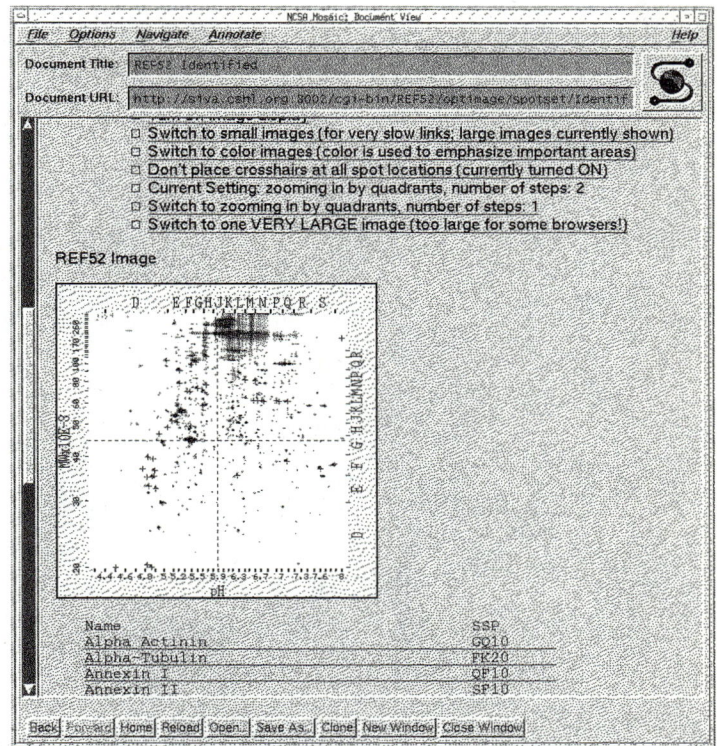

The QUEST web also provides:

- Links to software for analysis and comparison of protein patterns
- Links to other related databases in Switzerland and at the Laboratory of Mathematical Biology, National Cancer Institute

The QUEST web is a good example of a single lab providing access to an extensive database of information through a graphical interface on a specific subject.

Ergonomics in Telerobotics and Control Laboratory: Multimedia Presentations

The Ergonomics in Telerobotics and Control (ETC) lab is part of the Human Factors Laboratories in the University of Toronto's Department of Industrial Engineering.

The researchers of ETC lab (home page, URL `http://vered.rose.utoronto.ca/`, shown in Figure 26.22) work in a variety of areas including telerobotics, virtual reality, and other perception- and display-related projects.

FIGURE 26.22.

Ergonomics in Telerobotics and Control Lab home page.

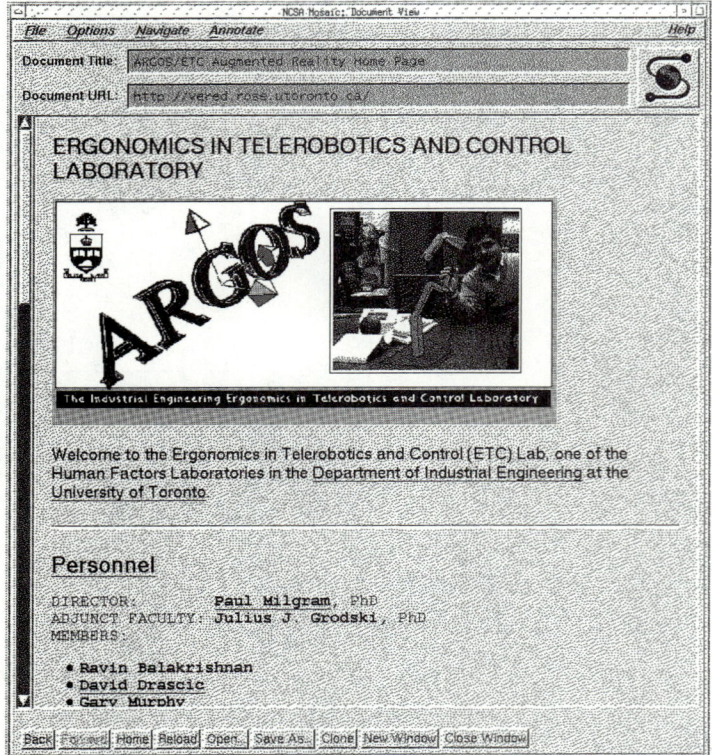

One project of the ETC lab is "Input/Manipulation in 3D Environment." This project has a page containing important reference information for the project itself (Figure 26.23).

FIGURE 26.23.

*Input Manipulation in
3D Environment.*

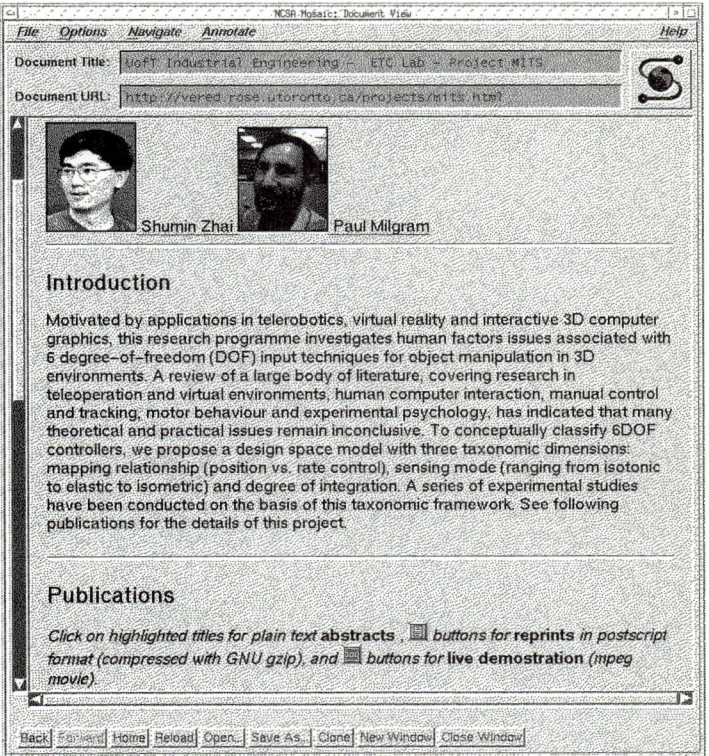

The developers of the ETC web use multimedia to illustrate the projects of the lab. The "Input/Manipulation in 3D Environment" page links to the home pages of the scientists working on the project as well as to information about the project itself—in the form of PostScript papers and mpeg movies of project demonstrations. A frame from the movie *Virtual Robotic Control* is shown in Figure 26.24. By viewing these movies, a user can get an idea of how the projects operate in a way that he could not with a textbook.

The ETC lab, like the Cold Spring Harbor Lab already mentioned, explains scientific work to the public and interested researchers, using innovative techniques for graphics and multimedia. The web pages for the labs are like an "open" lab tour always available to those who are interested, expanding public knowledge, drawing the attention of researchers, and creating relationships with researchers in these fields worldwide.

FIGURE 26.24.
Frame from movie,
Virtual Robotic Control.

Infrared Processing & Analysis Center

Another scientific laboratory with a web is the Infrared Processing & Analysis Center (IPAC), operated by the California Institute of Technology, Jet Propulsion Laboratory under contract to the National Aeronautics and Space Administration (NASA). IPAC's home page, URL `http://www.ipac.caltech.edu/`, is shown in Figure 26.25.

The goal of IPAC is to perform the intensive processing NASA requires for infrared astronomy investigations as well as contribute scientific expertise on infrared imaging projects to the astronomical community. In pursuit of these goals, IPAC offers a variety of information through its web.

Online User Services include resources and tools for observation planning, astronomical catalog scanning, sky atlas retrieval, and data processing services by e-mail. Also available are an archive for the Infrared Astronomical Satellite and Infrared Space Observatory tools. Project information is available for the 2 Micron All Sky Survey (to complete a map of the entire sky in near-infrared wavelengths), the Infrared Astronomical Satellite, the NASA/IPAC Extragalactic Database, the Astrophysics Data System, and the Midcourse Space Experiment (MSX). Another area contains links to news and information from the staff, bulletins, and the IPAC Newsletter. These services provide a unique collection of detailed information about infrared imagery.

FIGURE 26.25.

Infrared Processing & Analysis Center home page.

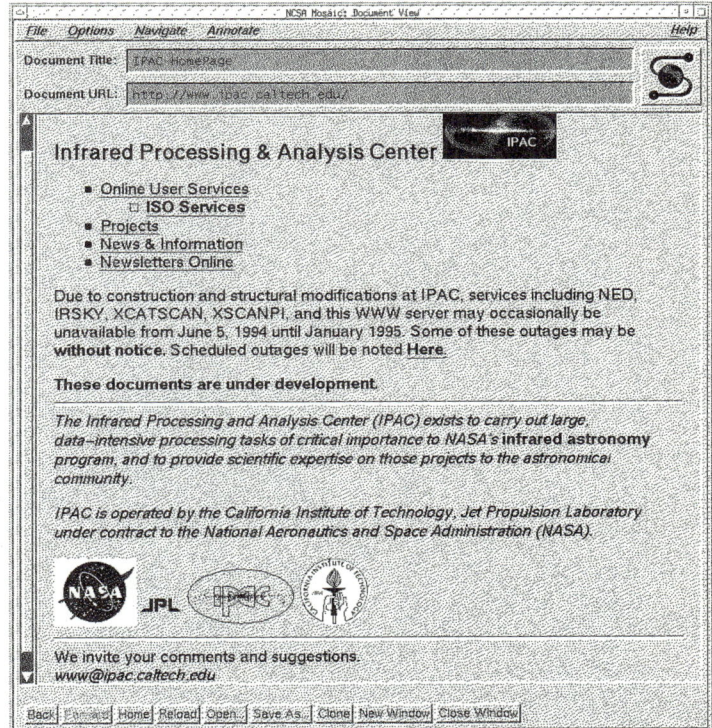

The Bulletins area of the web contains links to ongoing or special astronomical events. For example, the Supernova 1992bu in NGC 3690 was discovered in 1992 at NASA's Infrared Telescope Facility on Mauna Kea, Hawaii. The team of researchers from IPAC, CalTech, and the University of Hawaii provide a discussion of images of the supernova (Figure 26.26).

Another example of IPAC's offerings is the Infrared Sky Survey Atlas (ISSA) Postage Stamp Server, a tool to retrieve two-degree areas of the sky from the Infrared Sky Survey Atlas. Figure 26.27 shows the web page for the interface to the server.

FIGURE 26.26.

Supernova 1992bu in NGC 3690 images.

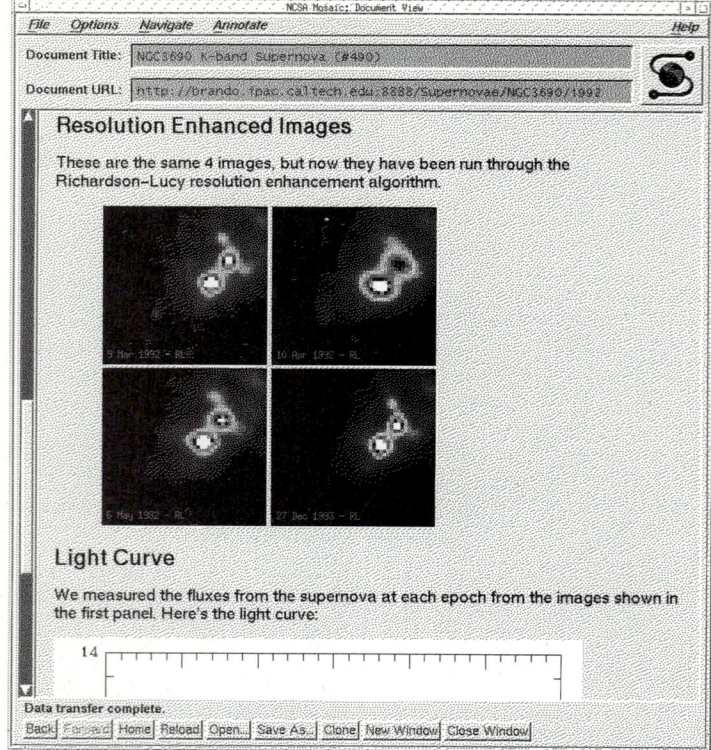

By entering the name of an object or a position, the user can retrieve an infrared image of the sky.

This service, along with IPAC's extensive information on infrared astronomy, makes its collection a valuable part of the rich resources about astronomy online.

FIGURE 26.27.

ISSA Postage-Stamp Server.

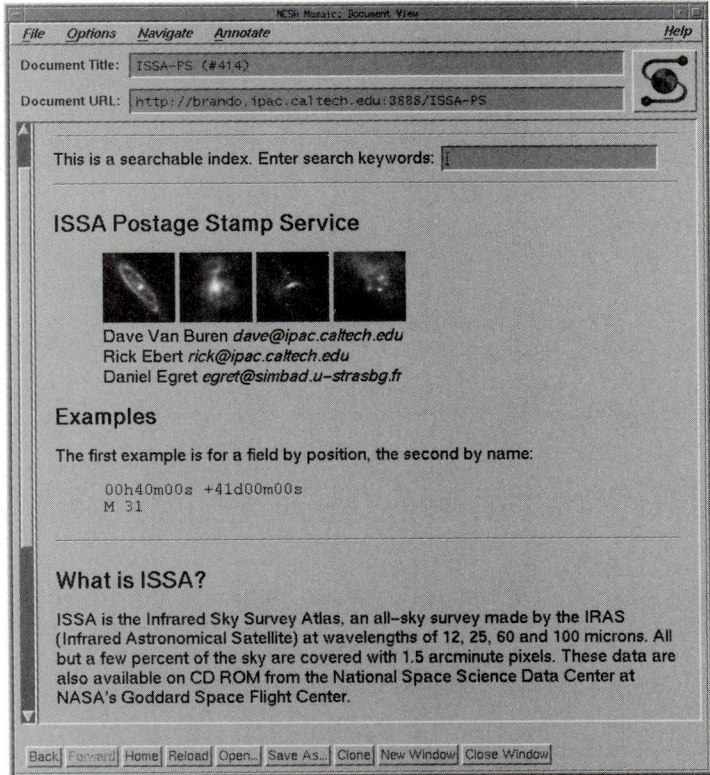

The MEMS Information ClearingHouse WWW HomePage

The Information Sciences Institute at the University of Southern California is a research facility of the School of Engineering focusing on information processing research and advanced communication systems (URL `http://www.isi.edu/`). As part of the ISI's projects, the Microelectromechanical Systems (MEMS) Information ClearingHouse was established by the U.S. Advanced Research Projects Agency's Electronic Systems Technology Office (ESTO). The goals of the MEMS Information ClearingHouse are to create information systems and perform basic research in technology products and processes (URL `http://esto.sysplan.com/ESTO/`). The MEMS home page (URL `http://mems.isi.edu/mems`) is shown in Figure 26.28.

FIGURE 26.28.

The MEMS Information ClearingHouse WWW HomePage.

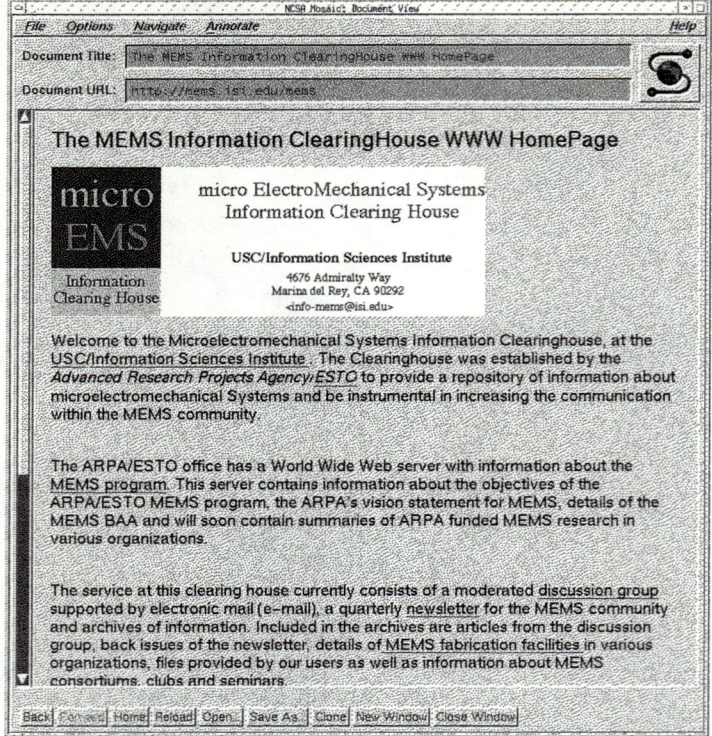

Microelectromechanical systems include micro-devices (such as sensors and actuators) that are arranged into large collections to form an overall microdynamic system (URL `http://esto.sysplan.com/ESTO/MEMS/`). The clearinghouse offers information and interaction about MEMS in a variety of formats, including a discussion group (e-mail), a quarterly newsletter, and information archives (Figure 26.29). These archives offer a detailed set of information for research relevant to MEMS.

FIGURE 26.29.

MEMS Information ClearingHouse Information Archives.

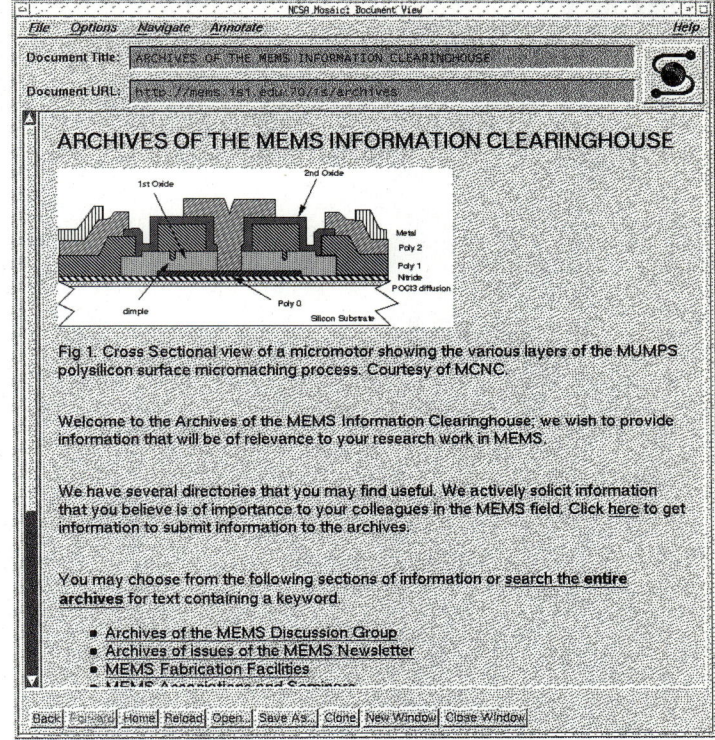

Gateway to Antarctica: Ongoing Explorations and Knowledge

In 1992, the International Centre for Antarctic Information and research (ICAIR) was established to serve as a central location for the collection and use of scientific and environmental information on Antarctica and the Southern Ocean. ICAIR is an independent organization within the Royal Society of New Zealand and is a joint initiative between New Zealand, the United States, and Italy. As part of its mission, the ICAIR collects and presents a variety of databases, geographic information systems, and remotely sensed imagery. The ICAIR web, called "Gateway to Antarctica," (URL `http://icair.iac.org.nz/`), is shown in Figure 26.30.

FIGURE 26.30.

Gateway to Antarctica.

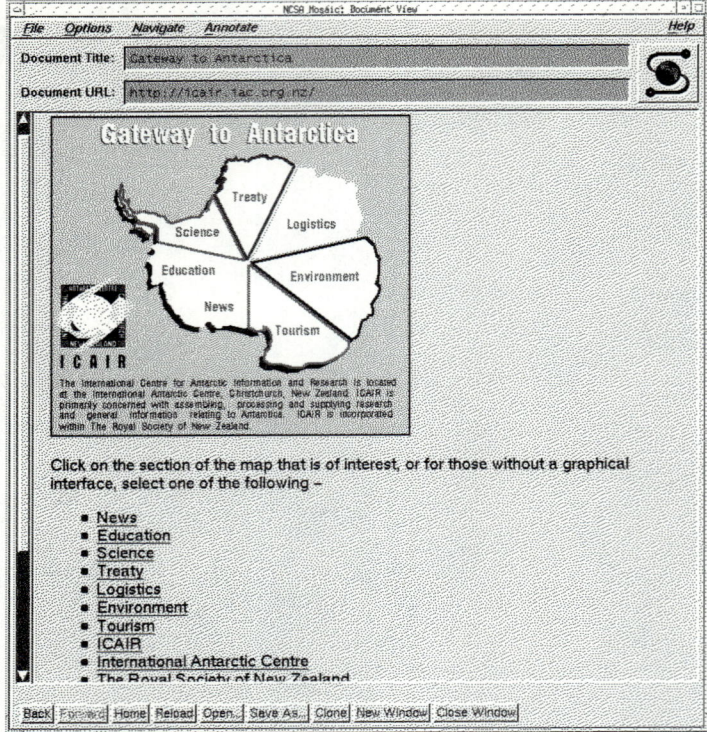

The ICAIR web offers a variety of links (shown in the figure) to major information sources about Antarctica. For example, the science page links the user to information sources such as the contents pages from issues of *Antarctic Science*, the Antarctic Address Book (listing contacts of people who are interested in Antarctica), and a variety of reports and map catalogs. (For an example, see Figure 26.31.)

FIGURE 26.31.

Catalog of Ross Sea area coverage.

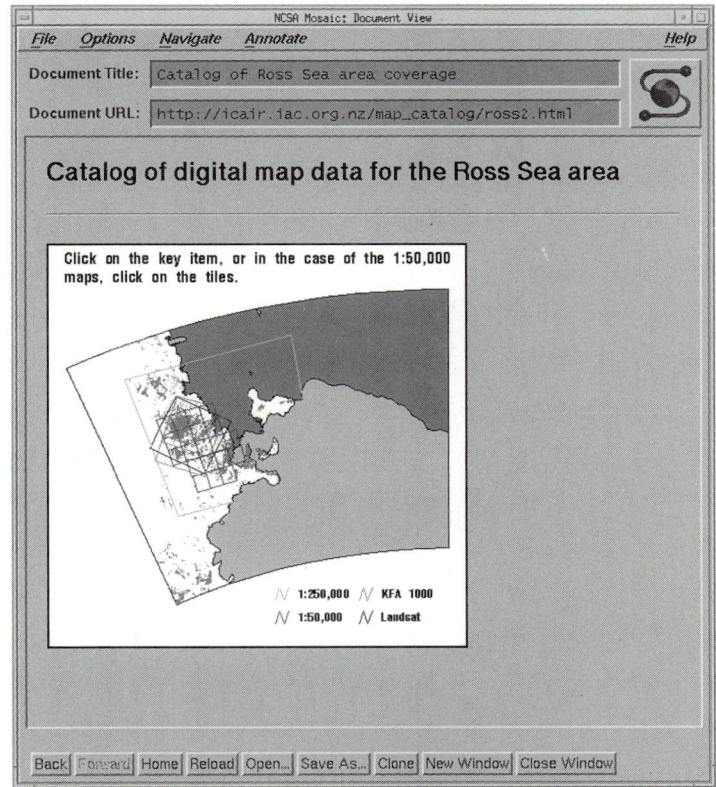

In addition to scientific information, the ICAIR web provides information to place the entire region in context—international treaty information, logistic information for expeditions, and even tourism information such as a visitor's introduction to Antarctica and its environment. By showing leadership in collecting, reviewing, and presenting comprehensive information about the Antarctic, the ICAIR web demonstrates how an international organization can cooperate to provide accurate, up-to-date information about its area of speciality that can benefit the larger Web community.

WebElements: A Science Information Server

While many of the preceding webs provide detailed views of very complex, team-produced science and technology, there are many opportunities for the individual researcher to contribute to science information on the Web. Dr Mark J. Winter of the Department of Chemistry at The University, Sheffield in England has prepared a web called "WebElements" (URL `http://www2.shef.ac.uk/chemistry/web-elements/periodic-table.html`), shown in Figure 26.32.

FIGURE 26.32.

WebElements.

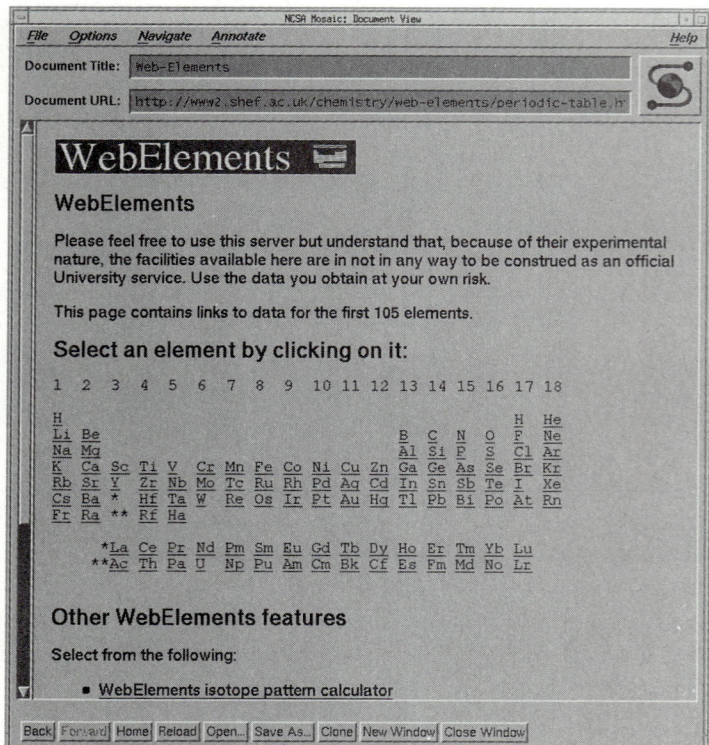

While not an official service of the university itself and still under development (as the web page states), the WebElements page demonstrates how a single individual can provide a useful interface to scientific information on the Web. By clicking on a symbol shown in the figure, the user can get a page containing information about the element. Small, focused efforts like WebElements can add to the scientific offerings on the Web. With appropriate peer review and fact-checking, such services have the potential to enable other developers to draw upon them for advancing science itself.

Explorer's Check

Because many scientific organizations were early adopters of World Wide Web technology, the offerings on the Web in the fields of science and technology are unusually abundant. Ranging from multinational efforts to coordinate access to information from a wide variety of databases such as the European Space Information System to the focused collection of peer-reviewed information about a field of knowledge like OncoLink, scientific information on the Web, in fields and specialities for which it exists, is often deep and rich.

Programs like The International Society for Optical Engineering draw professionals together to increase knowledge in a field. Other organizations such as the Institute for Telecommunication Sciences create webs serving the public interest for research and engineering.

Laboratories share their wealth of knowledge through webs that allow other scientific researchers to access databases and information sources. Webs such as Artificial Life Online create a forum for scientists to participate in developing new areas of knowledge. While the work of scientific organizations is extensive and impressive, there are many opportunities for individuals to create focused webs to disseminate scientific information.

Communication, Publishing, and Information

by John December

27

IN THIS CHAPTER

The Web is essentially a communications medium, making it possible for organizations, individuals, and groups to connect in a variety of ways. The applications discussed in the other chapters in this part reflect this; they all show examples of the Web as a communications tool. This chapter, however, focuses on Web communication in more detail, presenting applications in various contexts—individual, group, organizational, mass publishing, and specialized areas such as surveillance and information. These examples illustrate the flexibility of the Web as well as the ingenuity of people who mold and use it to fit their needs.

The communication categories individual, group, and mass, while useful guidelines to the scope of the communication contexts discussed here, are not necessarily clear-cut on the Web. While traditional notions such as what distinguishes a "mass" publication from an "individual" can shape our expectations about Web information, the Web itself can blur or break these expectations: an individual's home page might attract a larger audience than a "mass" publication such as an online newspaper. Similarly, the boundaries of organizations can blur. While organizations can provide very specialized information spaces, people often collaborate in dynamic communities on and at the edge of the Web.

Individual Communication

The tradition of having a personal "home page" is just that—a tradition. While there's no technical reason why a person must have a page describing himself or herself, the practice of having one has evolved with the development of the Web. The origins of providing personal information over the network include the .PLAN files offered through the finger command (see page 608); however, the personal home page allows a far more expressive and flexible format than a .PLAN file.

A person creates a home page in the same way any other HTML page is written. (This is explained in Part V, "Weaving a Web.") The user makes a home page publicly available through a means that may vary from server to server, based on technical issues as well as administrative policy.

The information found on a home pages varies widely, and reflects the diversity and personalities on the Web. There are no set formats, no one style or substance to include. In this section, four examples illustrate a variety of approaches to providing a web page that expresses one's personality.

Jane Patterson's Home Page

The first home page example is Jane Patterson's, shown in Figure 27.1.

FIGURE 27.1.

Jane Patterson's home page.

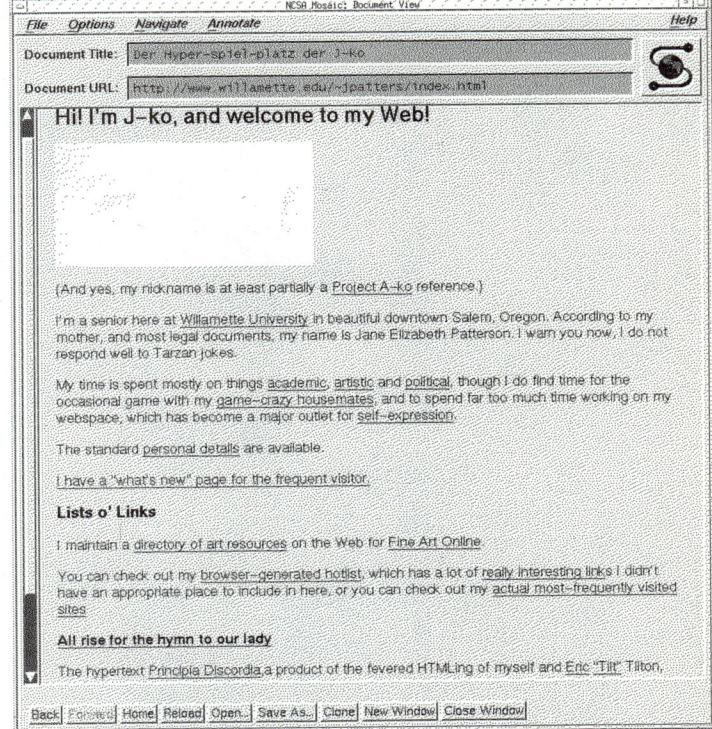

Jane has created links to express her identity within the context of her work at her university (links to Willamette) as well as other pages that outline her academic, artistic, and political interests. This extensive collection of links is a more thorough presentation than a typical home page, and it indicates the richness possible. Through personal home pages, people can *network* (a practice by which people grow a set of relationships in order to share information, resources, experiences, and advice) in a new way.

For example, Jane's page contains a link to "My REAL Hotlist," the places she often visits. This helps people who share some of Jane's interests get connected with even more resources that may interest them. Also, "network friendship circles" can become expressed through links on home pages; for example, Jane's link to Eric "Tilt" Tilton, a person with whom she works on a hypertext *Principia Discordia* project.

Ellen Spertus' Home Page

Ellen Spertus' home page is another example. Through links to the projects, individuals, and organizations connected to her work, she has created an intricate and very detailed personal information space. Part of her home page is shown in Figure 27.2.

FIGURE 27.2.

Ellen Spertus' home page.

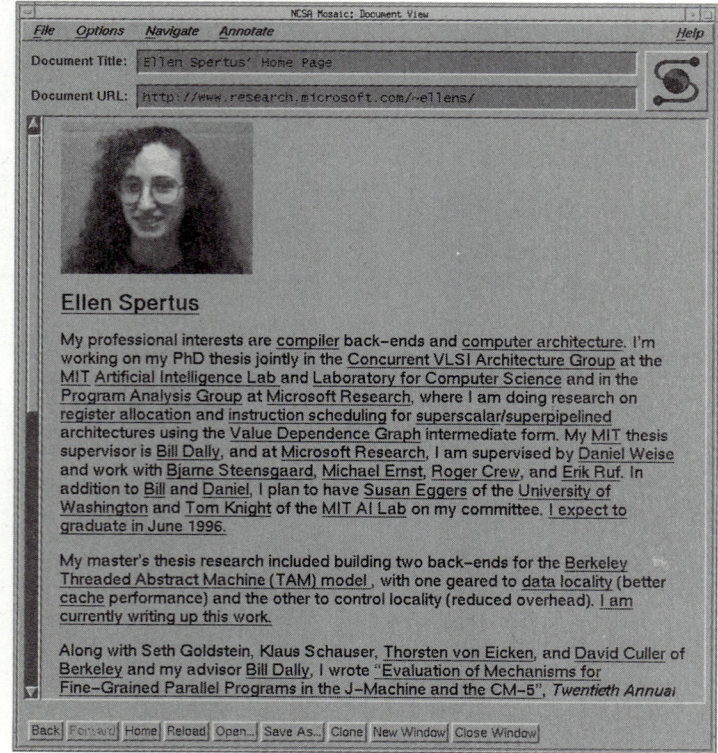

Ellen's home page illustrates how a personal web page is frequently a treasure-trove of material related to an area of expertise or study (Chapter 18, "Trees: Subject-Oriented Searching"). Ellen's page illustrates how her contributions to knowledge in her fields of expertise augment the Web itself. For example, a link on her home page from the term "superscalar" to the free online dictionary of computing (URL `http://wombat.doc.ic.ac.uk/`) includes a definition that she contributed (URL `http://wombat.doc.ic.ac.uk/?superscalar`).

Michael Witbrock's Home Page

Michael Witbrock's home page conveys his personality, identity, and creativity through a balanced design and creative use of graphics. Figure 27.3 shows his "Fabulous Sepia Home Page."

FIGURE 27.3.

Michael Witbrock's Fabulous Sepia Home Page.

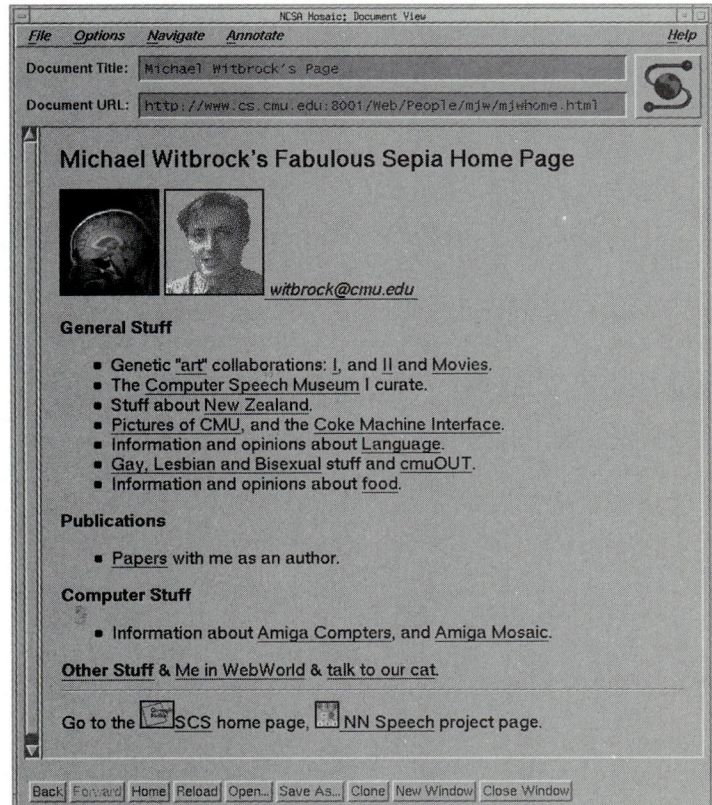

Michael's page contains references—both personal and professional—that convey his interests. This set of links creates an information and also a social space that expresses humor ("talk to our cat"), professional accomplishments ("Publications"), and the context in which he works ("SCS [Carnegie Mellon's School of Computer Science] home page"). Thus, Michael's page, like Ellen's and Jane's, shows personal "places of interest" as well as specific knowledge, information, and works that the author has created.

FINGER: AN EARLIER "PERSONAL BROADCAST" SERVICE

Just like the personal information available on a home page on the Web, users of UNIX systems have made use of the features of the "finger" command to provide a personal set of information for retrieval by any user on demand. A user can make finger information available by creating a text file called .PLAN in his or her home directory and making this file readable and executable to anyone. When someone uses the command:

```
finger user@host.dom
```

where "user@host.dom" is the electronic mail address of the "fingeree," the contents of the .PLAN file will displayed to the "fingerer."

It's a good idea to carefully consider what personal information you want to give out through finger (or your Web home page)—remember, it is available *globally*.

bianca's Shack

While many home pages express a fairly conservative view of life, others can adopt a very expressive, artistic view, and thus provide a gathering point for a culture or subculture. Figure 27.4 illustrates bianca's Shack, a collection of musings and art about a wide range of subjects. The figure shows the graphical information map (Chapter 34, "Advanced HTML Features") interface.

According to Chris Miller, a participant in bianca's Shack, the page exists as a jumping off point on the Web for "artists, hackers, poets, and minstrels dedicated to making the Internet a happy and open place, where everyone may always be at play in the streams."

As these four examples illustrate, the individual communication expressed through the home page varies in style and content. The Web has an enormous potential to give people a means for creativity and self-expression. Home pages can open up the genius of individuals to everyone on the Web.

FIGURE 27.4.

bianca's Shack.

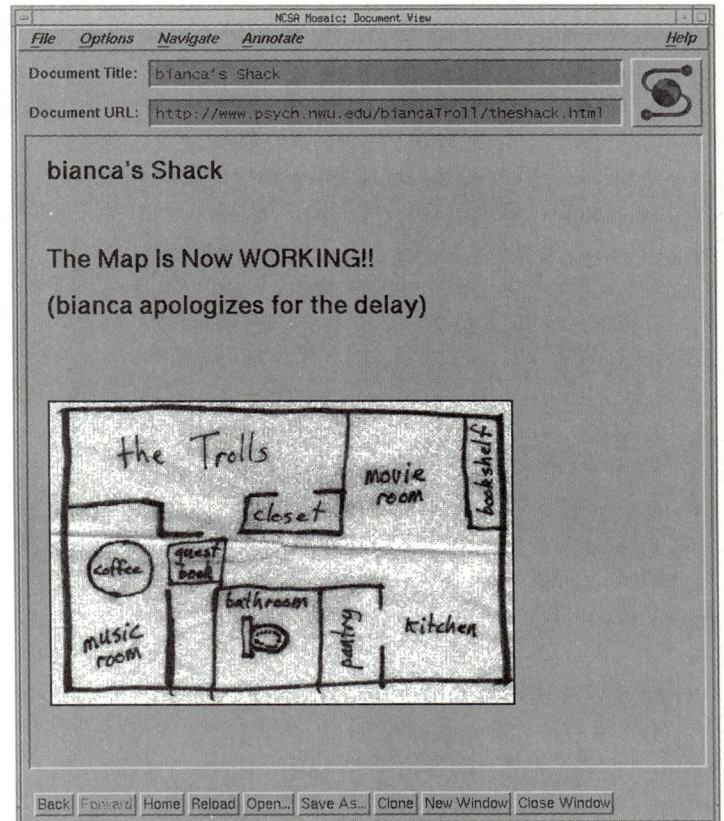

Group Communication

While personal home pages represent the life and view of individuals, there are many other webs that create forums for groups of people to communicate and form group identities. Many of the pages make use of the interactive forms (see Chapter 34)—a process of "interactive webbing" by which people can contribute to a common space for network distributed hypermedia writing.

"Hypergraffiti Walls": "Free for Alls"

Perhaps the forerunner of applications of interactive webbing was a page called "Free For All," offered originally on the NCSA (National Center for Supercomputing Applications) web. "Free for All" was an HTML page allowing users to add any URL and a brief explanation for it. The contributors of these URLs had the ability to remain "anonymous" while posting (so that readers of the page would not necessarily know who posted what to the link) and the tone of the page quickly became "graffiti-like" with a wide range of entries. The page also grew very large, so that as of summer 1994, it was not available on its original server. Since then, other "Free for Alls" began operating; you can locate them through a spider search (Chapter 19, "Spiders and Indexes: Keyword-Oriented Searching"). Use keywords "free for all" or "graffiti wall."

Web Interactive Talk

While hypergraffiti can create group communication on one level (in which each participant contributes just a link in a sequence of links), other systems for adopting to the Web for group communication have been developed.

One is Web Interactive Talk (WIT), URL `http://info.cern.ch/hypertext/WWW/WIT/User/Overview.html`. WIT was originally developed by Ari Luotonen and Tim Berners-Lee following the 1994 World Wide Web conference in Switzerland.

In WIT, a user can contribute a new proposal for discussion or respond to an existing proposal within the context of a list of topics in a discussion area. Although similar to other discussion systems such as Usenet or mailing lists, WIT differs in at least one important aspect: The contributions do not "evaporate" after the user submits them because they are not distributed through a propagation scheme. Rather, the postings are stored on the computer hosting the discussion area(s). Using this feature, the goal is to create a permanent "knowledge base" in which the same topic is not introduced time and time again. This important difference between WIT and both Usenet and mailing lists could possibly change the kind of communication taking place. For more discussion on this topic see Chapter 41, "Conferencing on the Web."

A Virtual Web Community: WebWorld

While applications to create discussion areas foster connections and the exchange of ideas, a subtle shift in interactive webbing to include a graphics display creates a different kind of environment—a WebWorld. Figure 27.5 shows the front entrance to WebWorld, an application developed by Ron Britvich to use interactive webbing and graphics to create a virtual world open to anyone for building.

FIGURE 27.5.

WebWorld.

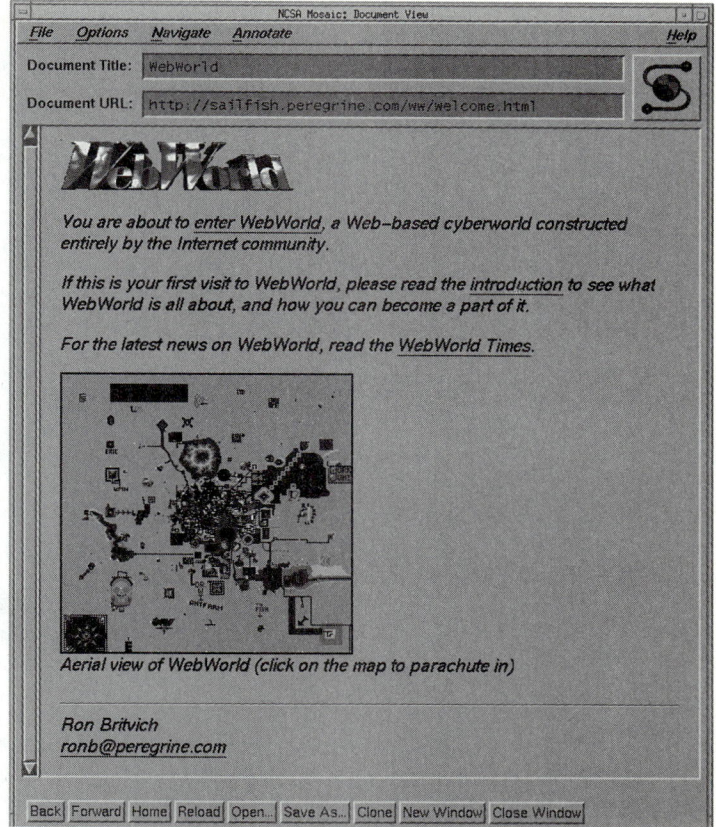

Figure 27.5 includes links to introductory information about WebWorld: the *WebWorld Times* newspaper, introductory information, and an aerial map of the WebWorld itself. WebWorld consists of "neighborhoods" into which the user can "parachute" by clicking on the aerial map of WebWorld. An example neighborhood is shown in Figure 27.6, which shows a 3-D view of a WebWorld neighborhood. The picture shows a variety of structures (pyramids and boxes), that are URL links to resources on the Web or pointers to another place in WebWorld itself. You can see the landscape (trees) as well as water and undeveloped land (grey).

FIGURE 27.6.

A WebWorld neighbor-hood, Mainland.

People can build various objects in the neighborhood using several links and symbols. The user can create containers that can then contain whole "WebWorlds" inside as well as links to any arbitrary URL. Figure 27.7 shows the same view of WebWorld as Figure 26.6, except in two dimensions to enable a user to build a new structure.

The shapes shown in Figure 27.7 correspond to the structures that a user can build on undeveloped land or on land that they have already used for development. A user cannot "destroy" a structure that someone else has built. A builder creating a container, however, can choose an option that will allow others to build structures within that container. In this way, WebWorld is essentially a multidimensional version of a "Free for All" hypergraffiti wall.

FIGURE 27.7.

Building in a Webworld neighborhood.

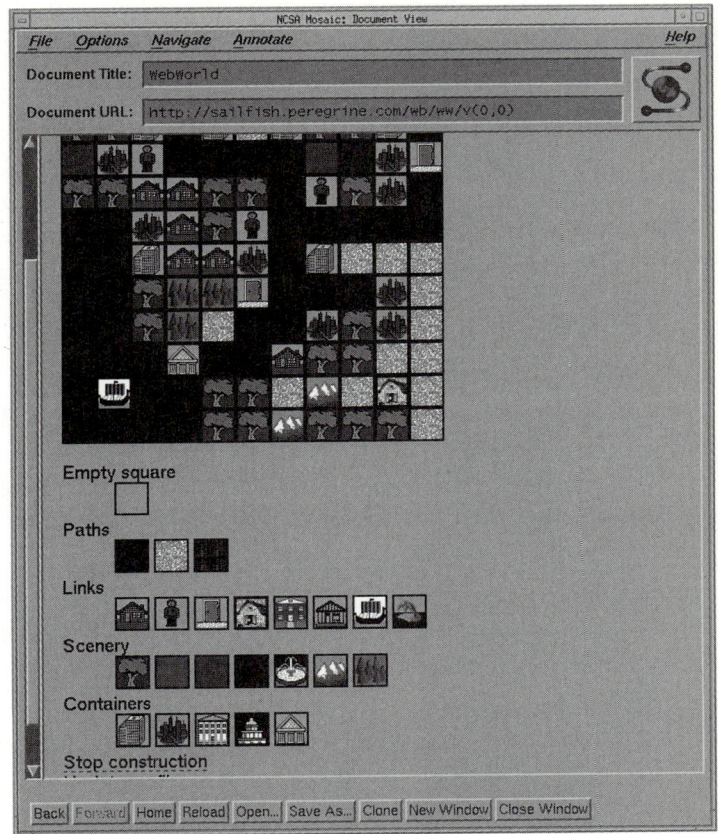

However, WebWorld's suggestive shapes, reminiscent of a real-world cultural landscape, evoke a sense of neighborhood (and also commonality and continuity of links; that is, people see that others are building the same "kind" of links rather than the heterogeneous entries on a hypergraffiti wall). The real-life need for WebWorld developers to "get along" with their neighbors as well as the serendipitous "meetings" that can occur give WebWorld many characteristics of a community.

Jay's House: Melding a MOO with the Web

While WebWorld presents a very lively visual display and a carnival-like atmosphere with its intricate links, the streets of WebWorld are very quiet. Aside from the occasional pedestrian (represented in WebWorld by an "eye" icon), there's no way for the inhabitants to communicate except through structures and links (and of course, off-Web communication such as e-mail).

In contrast, a much older group communication system called a MOO provides for lively talk and interchange. The term "MOO" stands for MUD—Object Oriented. The term "MUD" stands for "Multiple User Dimension/Dialogue/Dungeon" and is a term for a class of computer programs that allow users to traverse and build a text-based virtual world.

A MOO is a variant of a MUD that borrows ideas about its structure and operation from a computer software engineering technique known as "Object-Oriented" programming, in which software components are considered to be "objects" consisting of encapsulated data (nouns) and operations that can be performed on that data (verbs). In a MOO, everything is an object—even the inhabitants—and object-oriented concepts such as inheritance provide builders in a MOO with ways to create still more objects.

So while the streets of WebWorld are colorful and quiet, the corridors and links of a MOO are lively with conversations and objects, in a world made of text. Instead of WebWorld's colorful graphics, builders in a MOO must rely on their skills with words to create imagery. While most MOOs are not connected to the Web (most are available for use through special client software or through telnet access), there's a MOO called Jay's House that has nestled some of its functions into the Web.

The Web entrance for Jay's House MOO (JHM) is at URL `http://jh.ccs.neu.edu:7043/`. This entrance provides links to helpful information about JHM and some views of the goings-on of the JHM itself.

For example, from the Web entrance for JHM, you can

- Look at the objects in JHM "The Big Book of Objects"
- View the help system
- See who's currently logged into JHM
- View background materials, including papers and other information about JHM

While the Web entrance for JHM allows you to see many features of JHM, the true interactivity is still available only through a MOO client or a telnet session. However, JHM demonstrates a truly intriguing possibility—the first steps toward integrating the lively real-time interactions possible in a MOO with the Web.

Organizational Communication

While applications using interactive webbing lead to intriguing structures, an organization that needs to communicate information to its members requires less interactivity and more information and usability. An organization needs to inform its members to support their activities, to create a sense of belonging in the group, and to communicate to others what that group is all about. The next section covers some Web applications that organizations use to reach their members.

Campus-Wide Information Systems

Colleges have the mission to provide for the educational development of students and to support staff, faculty, and all others involved in the life of the college. A college community is a whole world unto itself, with a great variety of information needs ranging from building locations, library hours, course offerings, departments, and other information about the academic and support community.

A type of system for delivering information for a university or college called a Campus-Wide Information System (CWIS) has developed out of this need. Telnet and Gophers were the systems of choice for many initial CWIS's , and today Gophers still meet many needs for information. However, the development of the Web has brought many CWIS developers to Web-space. Polly-Alida Farrington maintains a list of CWIS's at URL `http://www.rpi.edu/Internet/cwis.html`, including links to Gopher, telnet, and Web-based CWIS's.

One example of CWIS is St. Olaf College's Web Server, URL `http://www.stolaf.edu`, shown in Figure 27.8.

FIGURE 27.8.

St. Olaf College home page.

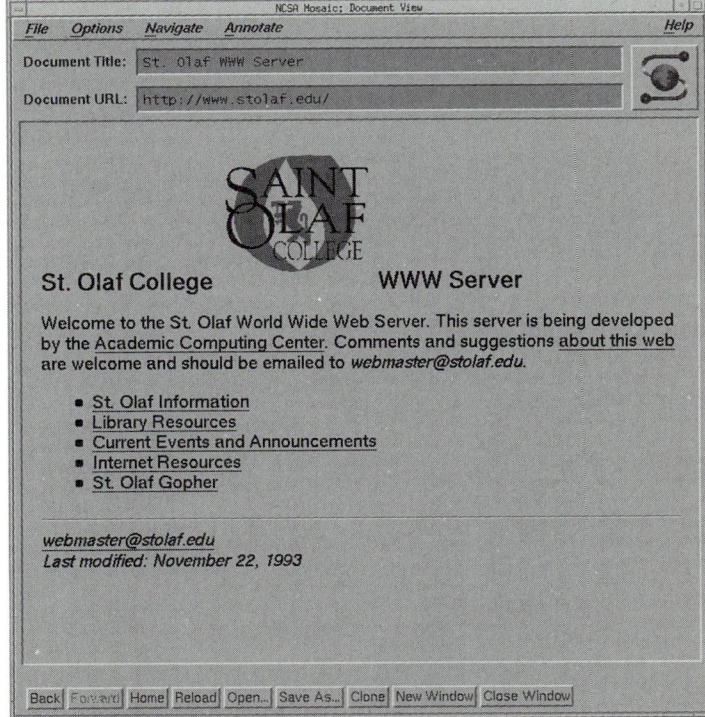

St. Olaf's CWIS offers a rich set of information to support its campus community. From links on the front page, you can reach the services shown in Figure 27.8—information about St. Olaf, the library, current events, resources, as well as St. Olaf's Gopher-based CWIS. St Olaf's CWIS also offers the following:

■ An interactive campus map (Figure 27.10), URL `http://www.stolaf.edu/stolaf/stolaf/map/top.html`, showing the buildings on campus and offering text, audio, or picture information to describe the building.

FIGURE 27.9.

St. Olaf's campus map.

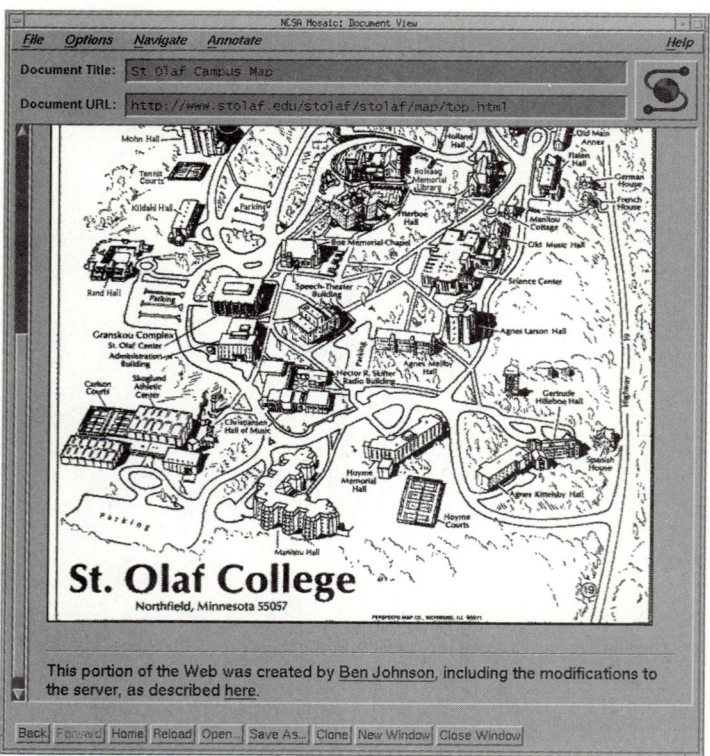

■ A *complete* course catalog, URL `http://www.stolaf.edu/stolaf/courses/top.html`, with hypertext links to current class and lab schedules.

■ A special collection of U.S. State Department Travel Advisories and Consular Information Sheets, URL `http://www.stolaf.edu/network/travel-advisories.html`. St. Olaf is the designated Internet and BITNET distribution point for this information, so it is among St. Olaf's unique offerings.

■ A hypertext interface to its library catalog interface, URL `http://www.stolaf.edu/library/unofficial_pals.html`.

■ A complete presentation, including the full audio, of the St. Olaf Choir's signature piece, "Beautiful Savior," URL `http://www.stolaf.edu/stolaf/depts/music/stolaf_choir/top.html`.

FIGURE 27.10.

St. Olaf's Choir.

Through a collection of unique resources and "standards" (customary information that many colleges offer), St. Olaf's CWIS supports the current campus community, potential staff and students, and even alumni who want to find out what's "going on" at the campus.

A Commercial Organization—MathWorks, Inc.

A commercial organization shares many of the interests an academic organization has to provide information and support connections among people. In the case of a commercial organization, however, these connections include those among customers, employees, and the general public. A commercial organization's web often provides many of the same functions as an academic CWIS, but with some differences—most notably a focus on product support and domain (the subject area in which the commerce is conducted) information to a geographically dispersed audience.

MathWorks, Inc. produces MATLAB, a scientific and engineering software tool. As shown in Figure 27.11, MathWorks home page offers links to

- What's New notices
- Product information
- MATLAB forum—a collection of resources useful to customers
- Contact information

FIGURE 27.11.

MathWorks, Inc. home page.

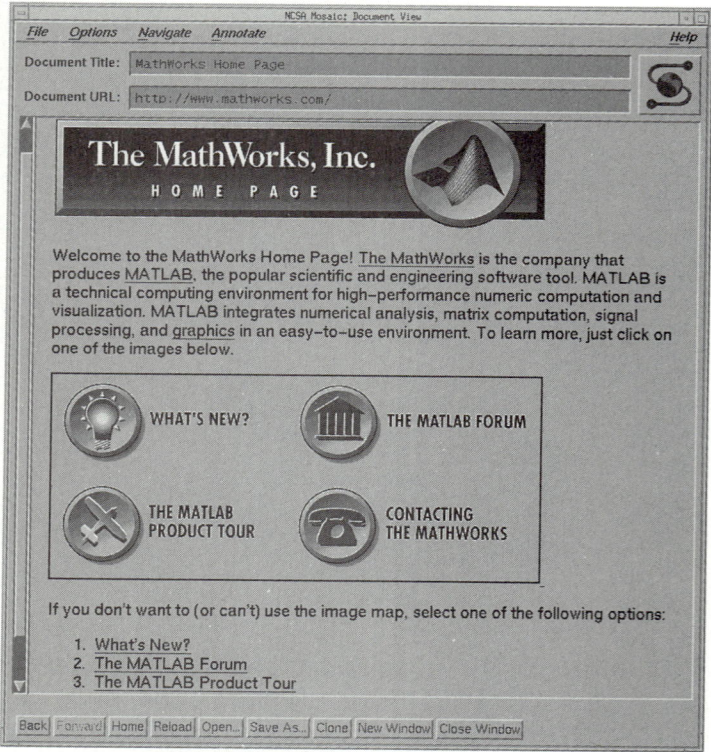

Like the St. Olaf CWIS, the MathWorks web provides an extensive set of links and pages. Unlike the St. Olaf web, however, which addresses the concerns of people located within a geographic region, the MathWorks web seeks to address a worldwide audience of customers, potential customers, and employees.

To accomplish this, MathWorks provides a graphical interface that serves throughout its web to guide the user to information about the company as well as its products and services. Since MATLAB is a scientific visualization tool, the MathWorks web also hosts a MATLAB Gallery that contains exemplary applications of MATLAB.

FIGURE 27.12.
MATLAB Gallery.

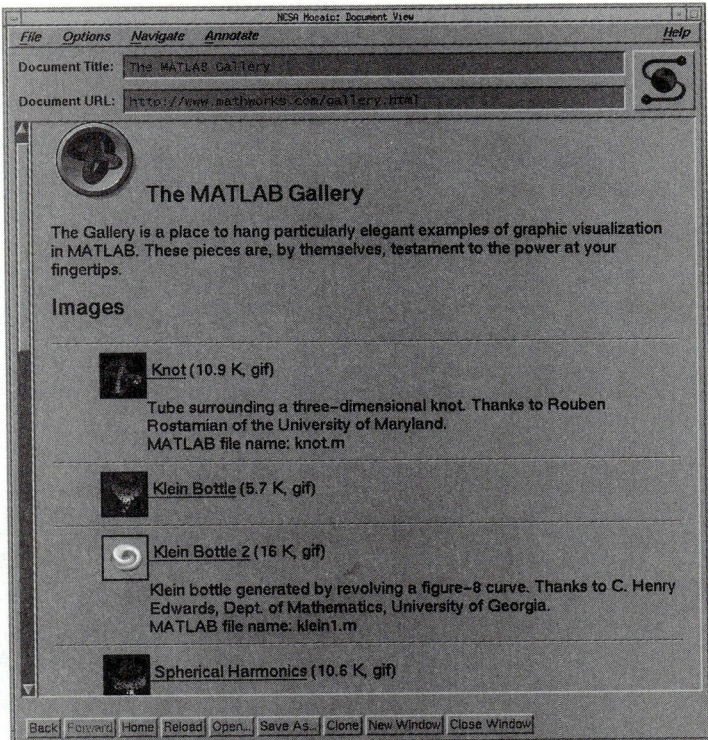

Since MATLAB runs on workstations that also often support Web browsers for X such as Mosaic, customers using MATLAB can use a session of Mosaic to learn more about the product and its applications online.

A Nonprofit Organization—The Computer Professionals for Social Responsibility (CPSR)

The Computer Professionals for Social Responsibility (CPSR) is an alliance of information technology professionals who are concerned about public policy issues dealing with information technology. Unlike a campus CWIS or a commercial Web, CPSR's membership is not co-located geographically. Therefore, the CPSR web functions as a critical tool to provide information for its members who are spread throughout the world.

FIGURE 27.13.

The Computer Profession-als for Social Responsibility home page.

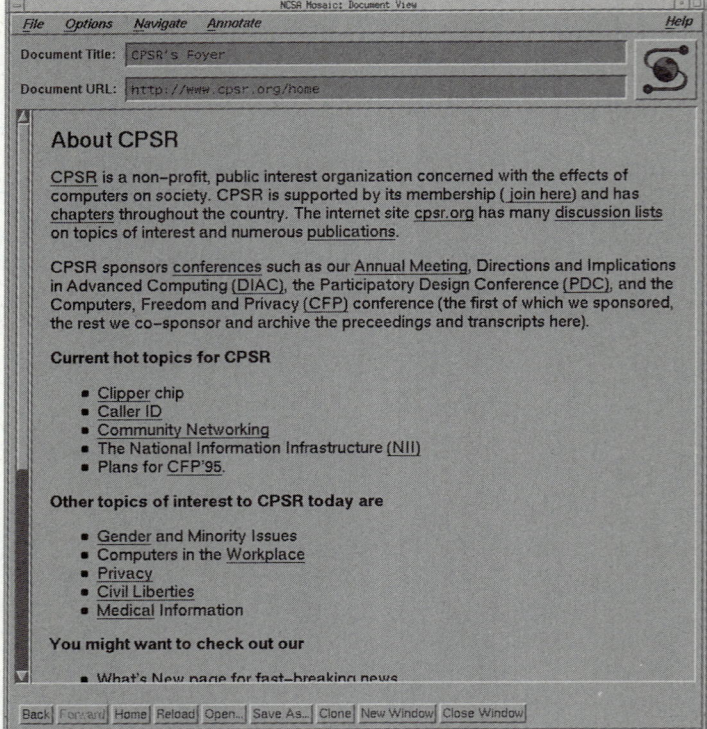

CPSR's web, therefore, delves deeply into both organizational information about CPSR and issues of interest to CPSR members or potential members. Moreover, since CPSR's web also functions to serve part of its mission to provide public information on critical issues, its holdings in many areas are quite extensive. For example, its Gender and Minority Issues directory contains extensive links to online resources. (See Figure 27.14.)

The CPSR web, like the MATLAB web, thus reaches its geographically dispersed constituents with relevant domain information. While a campus CWIS can draw on cultural artifacts and activities from the physical world its members inhabit, the dispersed organization must create an entirely virtual world and thus create an information space that, for the users, *becomes* the organization.

FIGURE 27.14.

The Computer Professionals for Social Responsibility Gender information.

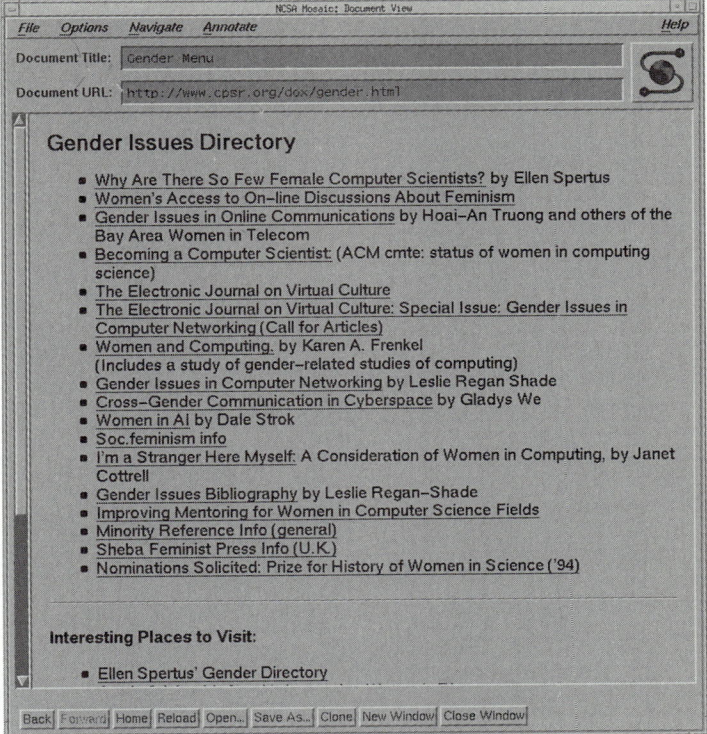

Publishing

While the operation of the Web blurs the distinction among communication contexts—individual, group, and mass—the intent of many Web offerings is to reach a large audience. Although mass communication through the Web is still an emerging practice, publishers of paper-based information have crossed over to the Web. In many cases, the result of this crossover is an online publication that continues some print traditions and conventions. Another aspect of mass communication involves supporting off-Web activities such as radio broadcasting and product sales. This section explores examples of several of these forms of Web-based publishing.

A Newspaper—the *Palo Alto Weekly*

The *Palo Alto Weekly* is a twice-weekly, free newspaper distributed in the Palo Alto, California area. Covering events of local interest such as land use, community policing, government and education, as well as features such as health and fitness sports, and arts and entertainment, the paper serves its communities with a variety of information. The home page of the Web version of The *Palo Alto Weekly* is shown in Figure 27.15.

FIGURE 27.15.

The Palo Alto Weekly home page. (Copyright 1994 Embarcadero Publishing Company. All rights reserved. The Palo Alto Weekly and the Weekly logo are registered trademarks of Embarcadero Publishing Company. Other trademarks or registered trademarks are the property of their respective owners. Reprinted by permission.)

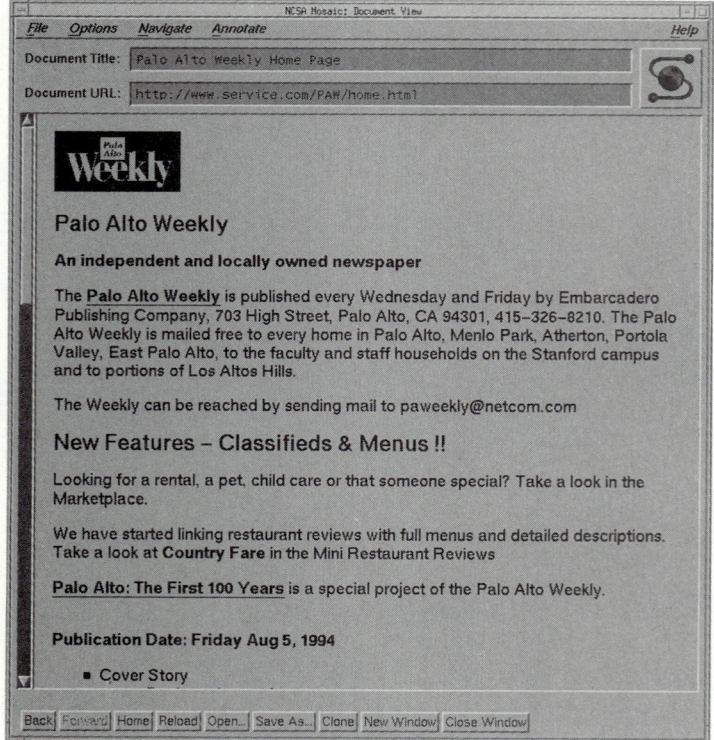

Internet Distribution Services, Inc. provides the Web services for the paper, and the offerings through the Web include an index and links to back issues as well as the full text of the current issue. Aside from distributing the text through the Web, the paper itself contains no unusual Net-references or interaction (no hypertext links in the Web-version text, for example). In this way, The *Palo Alto Weekly* demonstrates simultaneous publication on paper and on the Web.

A Zine—Cyberkind

Unlike The *Palo Alto Weekly*, there are many publications intended for mass, public use that exist solely on the Web with no paper equivalent. John Labowitz maintains a list of online magazines (or *zines*—a term used to describe a small or self-published periodical, particularly network-based ones, although the term now encompasses many periodicals, some of which involve extensive professional and commercial involvement) available on the net at URL `http://www.ora.com:8080/johnl/e-zine-list/`. The origins of zines go far back before the start of the Web, growing out of the early use of bulletin board systems and electronic mail. People realized that they could be publishers by creating content that has an appeal to a wide audience and distributing that content through informal and formal channels, including electronic mail and/or computer bulletin board systems.

While early zines consisted of ASCII text, Web-based versions have sprung up, exploiting the possibilities offered by hypertext in both the design of the magazine itself and in the articles. While The *Palo Alto Weekly* used many hypertext features in its Web presentation, it uses none within the text of its articles. In contrast, one example of an online magazine, *Cyberkind*, shown in Figure 27.16, uses hyperlinks in both its design and content.

FIGURE 27.16.

Cyberkind home page. (Logo and design Copyright 1994 by Dykki Settle. Table of contents graphic and separator line design Copyright 1994 by Luke Duncan. Reprinted by permission.)

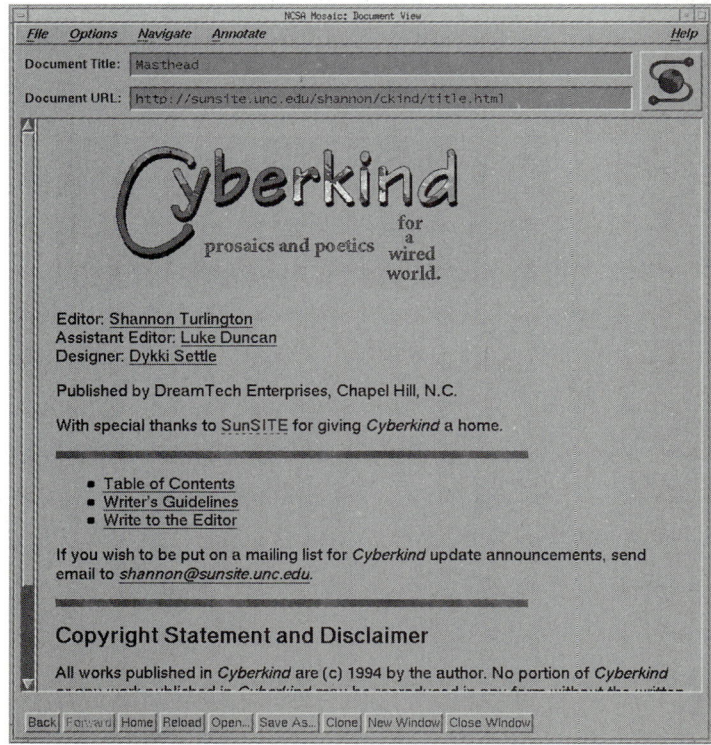

Edited by Shannon Turlington, *Cyberkind* offers a mix of nonfiction, poetry, and fiction that has some relation to cyberspace or online discourse. The result is a publication with a unique appeal, available Web-wide to anyone would like to read or contribute.

Online Publishing—Electric Press

While paper-based publications and zines can reach a mass audience with news, opinion, features, and other traditional journalism content, other Web services work to present services and products to build "presence" on the Web and support widespread attention to a particular customer's content as the focus of a web. For example, the Electric Press (home page shown in Figure 27.17) offers a range of products and services to create business opportunities on the Web.

FIGURE 27.17.

Electric Press home page.

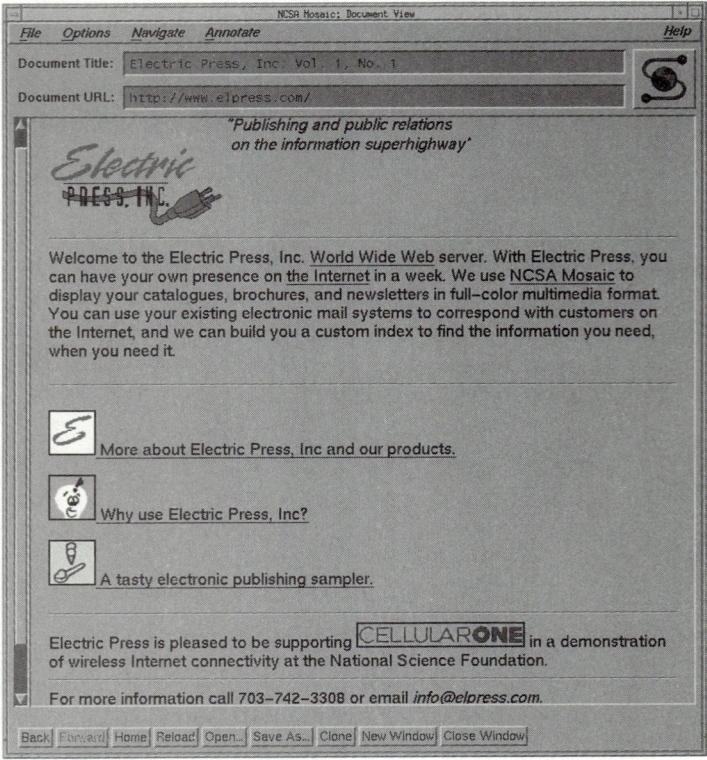

Distribution of mass information has long been supported by advertisers—in the case of free community (and most other) magazines, advertising is the main source of revenue. Operating within the context of the Web, developers have recognized the widespread "free" nature of Web information and use a model of providing customers directly to advertisers through attractive information and interaction. The Electric Press is an example of an organization that provides specific products and services to (potentially) bypass the journalism content and directly link an advertiser to customers to offer information "advertisements" through a Web server or other network communication. This same model of direct advertiser-customer connection can be seen in many commercial Web applications. (See Chapter 24, "Entertainment and the Arts.")

Supporting Mass Communication—Canadian Broadcasting Corporation (CBC) Radio

While the content offered by The *Palo Alto Weekly* as cast in paper and on the Web both involve reader interaction at times they choose (asynchronous communication), other traditional mass-media outlets support their Web-based communication in different ways. The Canadian Broadcasting Corporation's Radio services, working with the New Broadcast Services Laboratory of the Communications Research Centre (CRC) (URL `http://clark.dgim.doc.ca/about-crc.html`) in Canada have created a Web page (Figure 27.18) containing links to supporting information as well as the full sound recordings about CBC broadcasts.

CBC's Radio Trial is the first presence of a national broadcaster on the Internet, and its offerings at its Web site are extensive. The collection includes popular, general-interest programs such as "Quirks and Quarks" (a science program), "Basic Black" (featuring people with unusual activities), and "Sunday Morning" (CBC's flagship current affairs program). The CBC's web links users to audio files of segments of each program, program schedules, and information about how to order supporting products such as transcripts and recordings.

A new product offered on CBC's web is Illustrated Audio, a synchronization of text and image—giving images a sound track and defining a new file format (.Ia, illustrated audio). Thus, the CBC has innovatively moved beyond just sound to merging pictures and images and making these available to a global audience on a demand basis—a different model than just broadcast radio. CBC's whole effort demonstrates the power of the world's first broadcast mass-medium to move into the world's newest.

FIGURE 27.18.

CBC Radio home page.

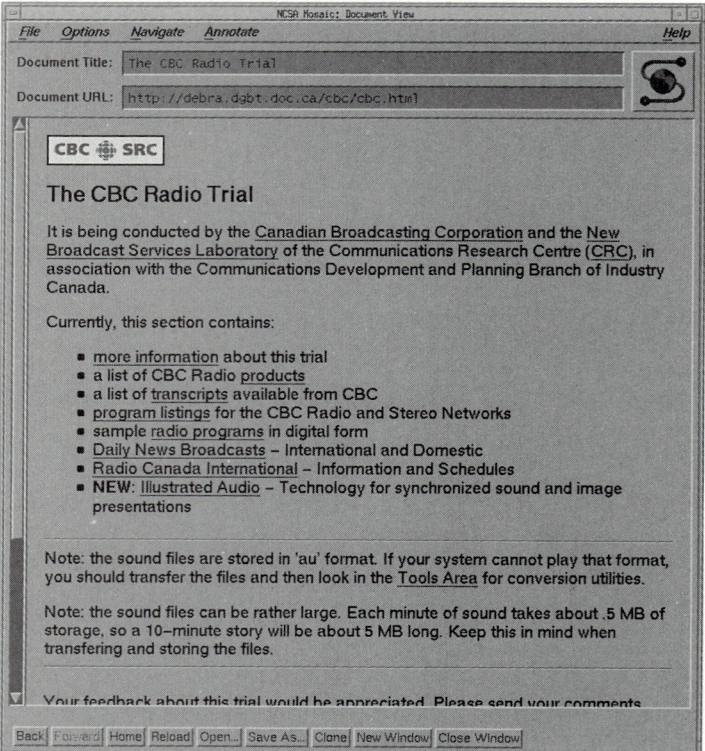

Supporting Offline Sales— O'Reilly & Associates

O'Reilly & Associates is an information publisher specializing in Internet, UNIX, and X Window System information. In October, 1993, O'Reilly launched Global Network Navigator (URL http://gnn.com), an online information service to the Internet community that presents a variety of news and information about Internet activities (a news service), the Whole Internet Catalog (a resource listing), an Arcade area for entertainment, and several "meta-centers" providing information about Travel and the Internet.

As part of GNN, O'Reilly offers links to a variety of "market resource centers"—webs containing information from commercial developers. A good example of these resource centers is O'Reilly's Resource Center, a page supporting offline sales of O'Reilly's paper and other material products. Figure 27.19 shows the front page of the O'Reilly center.

FIGURE 27.19.

O'Reilly & Associates Resource Center home page. (Copyright 1994 O'Reilly & Associates, Inc. Reprinted by permission.)

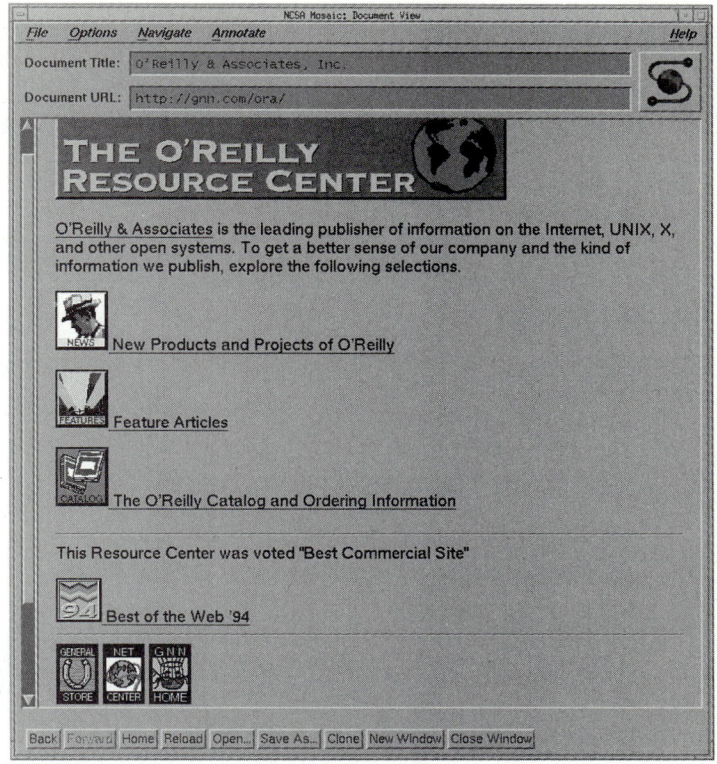

The O'Reilly Resource Center won a "Best of the Web '94" award for commercial webs in 1994. By combining the O'Reilly Resource Center with the other free offerings on its web, O'Reilly provides support for offline sales of products. The web contains links to new O'Reilly products, such as tradeshows, t-shirts, and software. Also linked to the front page is a catalog containing detailed descriptions of O'Reilly products (books and audiotapes). By making this complete product information available through the Web, within the context of popular content that people can browse (within GNN itself), O'Reilly has pioneered Web-based publishing.

Surveillance

While the above applications for communication deal in varying degrees with the size of the audience intended for the communication, this section deals with a specialized kind of communication—surveillance—and how it can be used for remote sight and temperature sensing.

Sight—Spy on Dennis Gannon, Research Director of the Center for Innovative Computer Applications

Dennis Gannon is director of CICA (The Center for Innovative Computer Applications at Indiana University) (URL `http://www.cica.indiana.edu/`). In the spring of 1994, he had a new workstation installed in his office equipped with a small camera on the top of it. One of the graphics programmers at CICA, without telling Dennis, hooked up the camera to a screen-capture program and added it to the "What's New" page for CICA, without going into Dennis Gannon's office. The result, shown in Figure 27.20, allows anyone with a Mosaic browser to "spy" on Dennis Gannon.

FIGURE 27.20.

Spy on Dennis Gannon.

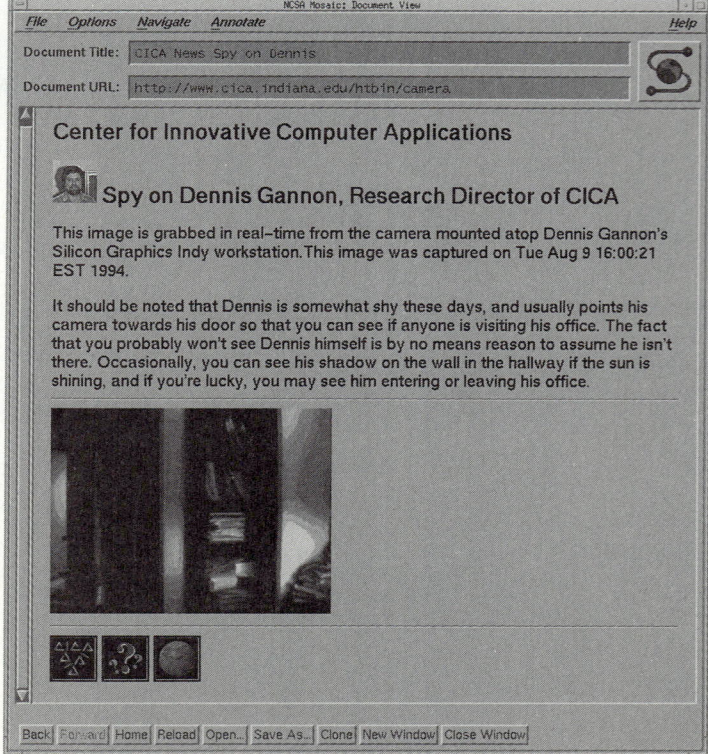

Subsequently, the graphics programmer let Dennis in on the joke—and the page remained on the CICA web. This application provides a demonstration of an innovative application: remote sensing via the Web. Normally, Web users expect to encounter text and graphics and perhaps animations, movies, or sound files, but the Web itself can be used to extend the human senses. There are other applications similar to the CICA camera that "spy" on areas of a campus, the world's best surfing beaches (SurfNet, URL `http://sailfish.peregrine.com/surf/surf.html`), or a coffee pot. (See the next section, "Beverage Surveillance.")

Temperature—The Roof of the Engineering Center at the University of Colorado

The Web can also extend your sense of temperature—at least through a temperature scale. Oliver McBryan created an application (Figure 27.21) that connects a remote sensing device to a Web page.

FIGURE 27.21.

University of Colorado Engineering Center roof temperature.

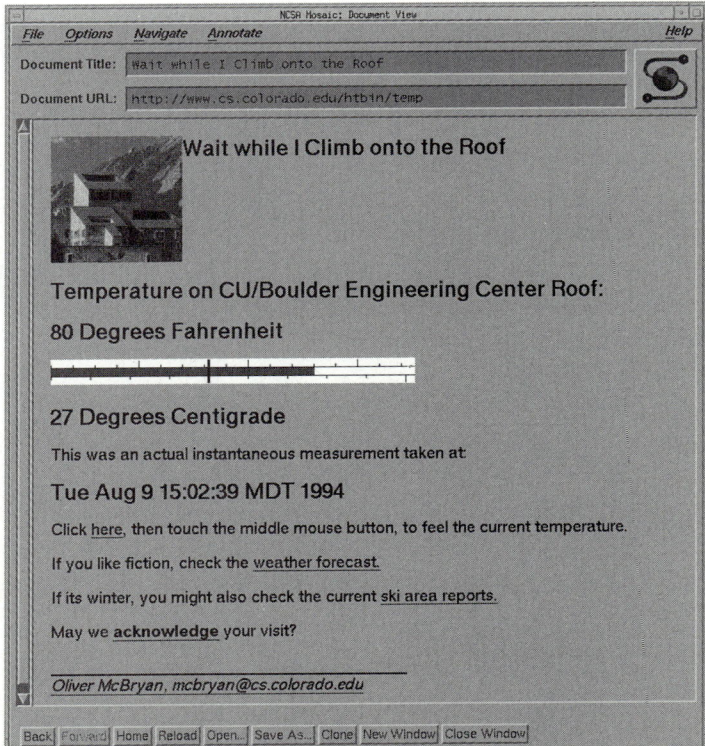

While the statement "Click here, then touch the middle mouse button, to feel the current temperature" is a humorous addition—or perhaps a challenge along the lines of the finger-vending machine interface in the specification for the finger protocol (see next section, "Beverage Surveillance"—the temperature sensor, along with similar applications on the Web, extends the bounds of what can be communicated across networks.

Beverage Surveillance

Just as Web home pages have some origins in the .PLAN files offered by the finger command, so do applications for Web surveillance. A connection for an interaction between the finger command and vending machines was specified in the Network Working Group's RFC (Request For Comments), a document that specified an Internet Activity Board standard for a protocol for the Internet community. RFC 1288, "The Finger User Information Protocol" by D. Zimmerman, includes this statement on page 7:

> Vending machines SHOULD respond to a {C} request with a list of all items currently available for purchase and possible consumption. Vending machines SHOULD respond to a {U} {C} request with a detailed count or list of the particular product or product slot. Vending machines should NEVER NEVER EVER eat money.

Obviously, this specification was provided in jest, a humorous turn to an otherwise (to casual readers at least) dry technical specification. But graduate students and computer scientists (some of whom can be quite literal-minded) have implemented the finger command to operate as specified. There are a variety of Internet-accessible vending machines on the net. For example, checking on the machine at the University of California at Berkeley, `finger coke@xcf.berkeley.edu` (equivalent to URL `gopher://xcf.berkeley.edu:79/0coke`), we can see the state of the machine:

```
Login name: coke                 In real life: Coke is it!
Directory: /usr/users/coke       Shell: /usr/users/coke/bin/coke
Last login Sat Jul 23 15:03 on ttyp2 from nyx10.cs.du.edu
Plan:
Stock Value: $311.23  Total Balance: $116.32 Loss Percentage:  0.00%
Outstanding real debts:        stas 14.99    mlee 10.76      scott 4.06
blojo 1.78      genie 1.61      grady 0.10    dougo 0.08
Current Stock List:
    ? DRINKS                 0                    5 Oreo Cookies
   34 Coke                   3 Box of Ammo 40    31 Death Chip Cookies
   21 Pepsi                  0                     2 Crackers
    5 Dr Pepper              0                    20 Cup Cakes
   30 Dads Root Beer         0                     ? Danish
   20 Sprite                 0 FOOD               14 PowerBar
   24 Hansens               13 Cheese Roll        41 DarkMilkyWay
   37 Clearly Canadian       0 Death Muffins       3 Good Beef Jerky
   62 Snapple               12 Rugala Pack        12 reeses
   61 Gatorade              22 Death Cookies       4 fritos
   59 Martinelli            30 1 mark of Sausage   6 Twix
```

```
    48 Fruit Bowl        23 Nutrageous       2 Nabisco
    12 Koala             27 Skor Bars        2 HoHos


Hail our Coke Warriors:
Total           Daily Total     Coke         Power Bar    Gatorade
645 cgd         2 blojo         72 cgd       70 bernt     55 bernt
595 bernt       1 marco         66 marco     53 stas      44 scott
583 marco       0 empty         25 seidl     4 hh         32 cgd
431 blojo       0 empty         24 genie     3 wei        7 marco

Not logged on.
```

Extended to the Web, this idea can lead to another kind of beverage surveillance: coffee. The Trojan Room Coffee Machine at URL `http://www.cl.cam.ac.uk/coffee/coffee.html` (see Figure 27.22) provides the user with a way to get a real-time view of the amount of coffee in the pot. While obviously only useful to members of the research lab, its operation extends the interaction between the Web and machines, providing a view of how the Web itself can extend one's senses.

FIGURE 27.22.

The Trojan Room coffee machine.

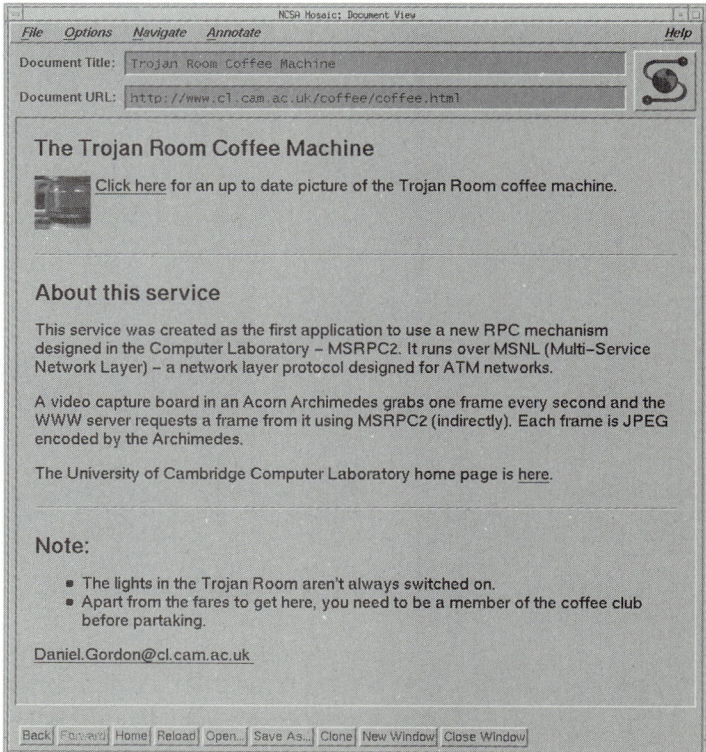

Weather

While surveillance for pictures of beverage levels and other "spy" cameras make for interesting exercises in linking the Web to the larger world, other applications of remote sensing are particularly useful. For example, real-time weather forecasts and reports have long been made available over the Internet, mostly through text interfaces. With the widespread development of graphical browsers, current weather imagery—satellite cloud cover images, forecast maps, and digital radar summaries—have been made available over the Net.

Charles Henrich at Michigan State University has developed an Interactive Weather Browser, weaving together many existing weather data sources into an easy-to-use Web interface. Figure 27.23 shows the front page.

FIGURE 27.23.

Interactive Weather Browser.

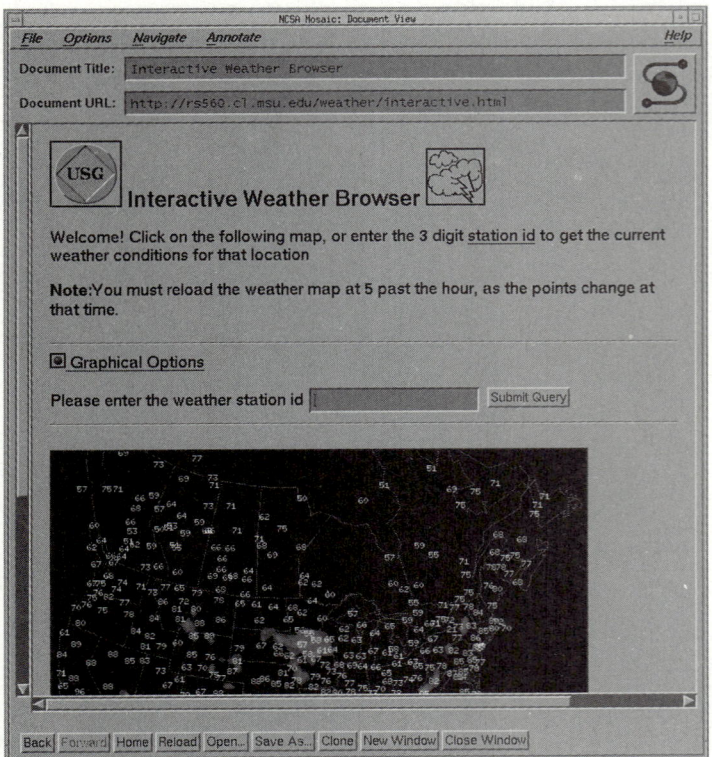

The Interactive Weather Browser enables a user to view the current conditions map as well as obtain a National Weather service forecast for a weather station by entering the station's name or by clicking on the current conditions map. Although these weather services are offered in different forms in other areas of the Net and Web, Charles Henrich's Weather Browser brings these together in an easy-to-use forms interface. The result is that the user can access the remote sensing devices available to the National Weather Service through the Web.

Information

Communication being at the heart of the purpose of all webs, the dissemination of information is part of any web. There are webs and organizations, however, that focus specifically on information itself (for example, the Coalition for Networked Information mentioned in Chapter 25, "Education, Scholarship, and Research").

Networked Information Discovery and Retrieval

The Clearinghouse for Networked Information Discovery and Retrieval (CNIDR) was created in 1992 by a three-year grant from the National Science Foundation (NSF) for the purpose of fostering the coordination of networked information tools so that they are compatible and consistent. CNIDR also educates and supports NSF investigators in the use of networked information retrieval tools and participates in standards development with the Internet Engineering Task Force and the Coalition for Networked Information.

The CNIDR home page, URL `http://cnidr.org/welcome.html`, is shown in Figure 27.24.

Within the CNIDIR web, more information is available about CNDIR projects. These efforts are to make information more available, easier to retrieve and more organized on several information systems:

- The Web
- Wide Area Information Server (WAIS) and freeWAIS
- Gopher
- Archie

Thus, CNIDR is an example of an organization that is organized around the study of information itself, and its web is a natural outgrowth of its work.

FIGURE 27.24.

Clearinghouse for Networked Information Discovery and Retrieval.

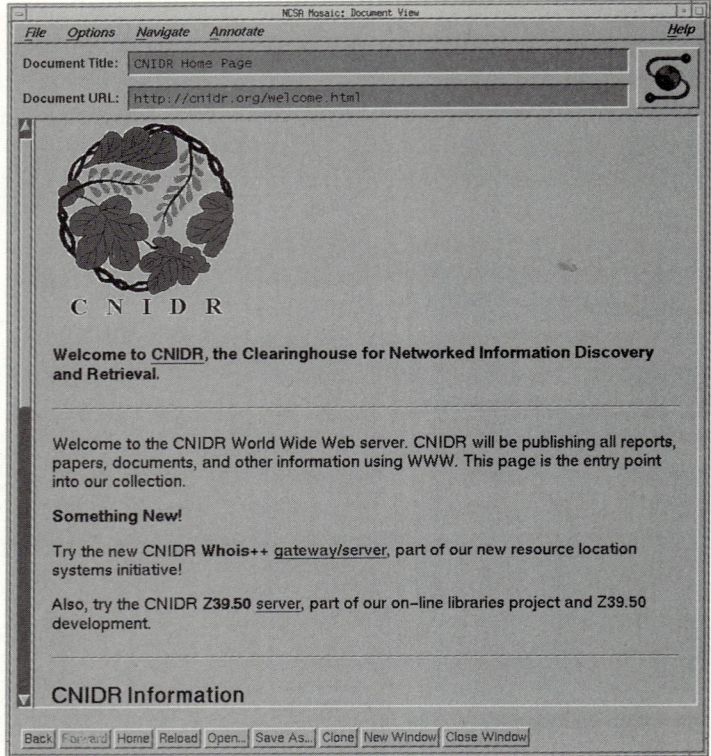

The U.S. Library of Congress Web

Libraries are information treasure-troves, and many libraries now offer some Web-based services. The United States Library of Congress has a web that contains links to not only the online information catalog of the library, but also to online exhibits and collections (Figure 27.25).

The links shown in Figure 27.25 provide the user with the ability to view exhibits that otherwise may have required a trip to Washington, DC to see. These multimedia exhibits include popular Web destinations including "Scrolls From the Dead Sea" and "The Vatican Library." In this way, the Library of Congress web demonstrates how libraries contain not only written texts, but cultural expressions in multimedia forms.

FIGURE 27.25.

U.S. Library of Congress home page.

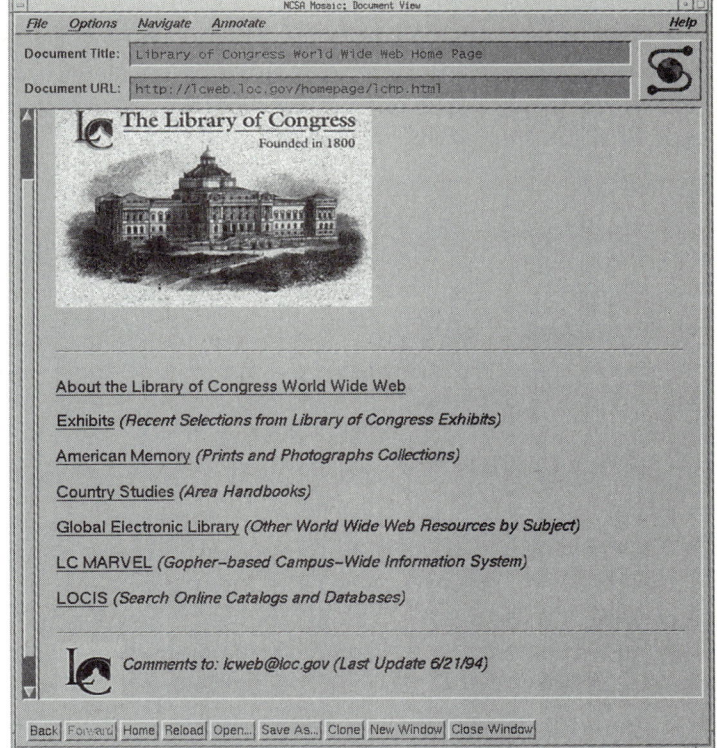

Explorer's Check

Since communication is one of the oldest activities of humans, it is no surprise that people continuously adapt and shape technology to achieve communication with each other. In fact, many observers of networked communication note that people taking part in online communities and groups is one of the recurrent aspects of online activity—and that the pull of people toward each other is often far stronger than interest in information and data. Moreover, many would argue that the impact of online human communication on shaping our culture is far more profound than the technical details of the tools and conduits themselves.

In this chapter, you've seen how individuals can create their own online "personas" in the form of hypertext home pages, linking their personal work with other works and thus creating elaborate information and social spaces that establish points of departure for others who may share similar interests. The interactive forms feature opens up new possibilities for people to contact each other, to create online hypergraffiti, to create virtual communities such as WebWorld, or to provide interfaces with communication systems such as MOOs.

Organizations have a special need to communicate information and at the same time create a sense of community through shared information. Campus-Wide Information Systems provide these links in academic settings. Commercial and nonprofit organizations also solve their problems in keeping their geographically dispersed memberships informed and motivated through their webs.

On the Web, new possibilities open for mass communication. Publishing can take the form of a direct translation of a print publication to a web. Another option is to provide asynchronous access to synchronous mass media, such as the online archives of CBC's radio programs. Online zines can create a whole medium that has no offline equivalent by making full use of the Web's features in both design and content.

People can create "sensory doorways" glimpsing real-time conditions or scenes in places all over the world. These applications range from demonstration exercises such as the Trojan Room coffee machine and other remote sensing exercises to valuable applications such as Charles Henrich's Weather Browser.

Like communication, information itself is at the heart of all webs. Organizations such as the Clearinghouse for Networked Information Discovery and Retrieval work to increase the interoperability and use of tools to discover and retrieve information in online systems. As such, their web provides a wealth of information about supporting information itself. Other information organizations—libraries—also exploit the power of the Web to disseminate information widely. The U.S. Library of Congress, continuing its role as an information storehouse, uses the Web to make its exhibits available to still wider audiences.

These examples show how the Web can be applied to communication in varying contexts. Still in its infancy, Web communication is potentially a very rich future activity, mainly as a result of the genius of individuals working out ways to contact each other and to extend what they can know through the Web.

Government and Communities

28

by John December

National governments have recognized information and telecommunications technologies as sources of wealth in their economies. Initiatives to develop computer and communications networks, such as the networking project by the United States Defense Advanced Research Projects Agency in the 1970s, eventually can lead to global communication networks (for example, the Internet). At the community level, people are also developing information and communications systems, such as Free-Nets, to link people and valuable community information together. The result of these government and community networking initiatives is an increasingly dense mesh of networks at all levels—community, state, region, nation, and world.

This chapter surveys webs that support national information infrastructure plans as well as government and community information. While these webs are not necessarily the information infrastructure called for in national plans, the webs themselves demonstrate possibilities for and government commitment to advanced forms of information delivery. This chapter presents examples of the range of government information available on the Web, including pages from international organizations, government agencies, and a U.S. Senator. Finally, some community-based information systems demonstrate how people are creating ties with each other and the world.

National Government Initiatives

Many nations and economic regions are taking active steps to create national information infrastructures, including the European Community, Japan, Singapore, Canada, and the United States. In this section, we'll look at some web sites that governments have established to disseminate information about their national infrastructure initiatives.

Canada

The Canadian government has developed plans to develop an Information Highway—a national infrastructure that builds on Canada's existing strength in information technologies. In a video conference speech to the "Powering up North America Conference" in February 1994, the Minister of Industry, John Manley, described a vision for a Canadian information infrastructure that would improve communications in the country as well as spark economic growth (URL `http://debra.dgbt.doc.ca/isc/ Canadian.Information.Highway/manley.speech.feb.2.1994`). Canada's goal is to create an infrastructure that will "give all Canadians access to the employment, educational, investment, entertainment, health care and wealth-creating opportunities of the Information Age" (URL `http://debra.dgbt.doc.ca/isc/Canadian.Information.Highway/ Building.Canada's.Info.Infrastructure.April94.txt`). This ambitious plan will bring together the academic, government, cultural, and community wealth of Canada through networked communication and information access.

Figure 28.1 shows the home page for the Electronic Document Distribution of Industry Canada (URL `http://debra.dgbt.doc.ca/isc/isc.english.html`), which makes information about Canada's plans available over the Web.

FIGURE 28.1.

Industry Canada.

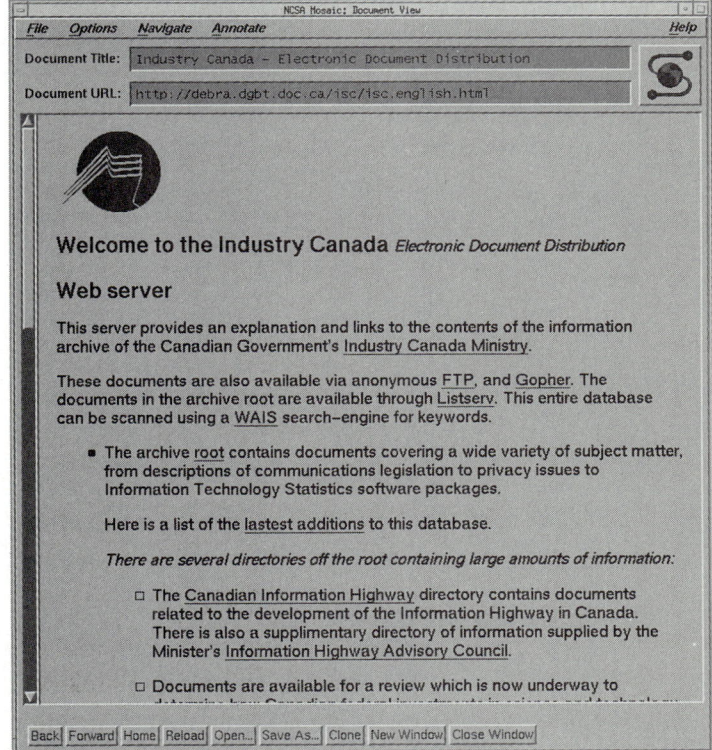

The Industry Canada web also offers many detailed documents describing Canada's infrastructure plans, including links to

- Technology Networking Guide, a directory guiding Canadian companies to develop information technology
- An archive of news releases related to the infrastructure efforts
- Gazette notices listing information about telecommunications regulations and legislation from the Communications sector of Industry Canada

By gathering information about their information infrastructure initiative and delivering it over the Web, the Canadian government helps all citizens of Canada access these plans in a manner that is very much in keeping with the ultimate goals of the Canadian Information Highway initiative itself.

Japan

GLOCOM (URL `http://www.glocom.ac.jp`) is the Center for Global Communications at the International University of Japan in Tokyo. A research center focusing on the impact of computer-based communication, GLOCOM examines a wide range of issues, including Japanese government information policy. GLOCOM's web contains a report on Japan's plans for information infrastructure, shown in Figure 28.2 (URL `http://www.glocom.ac.jp/NEWS/MITI-doc.html`).

FIGURE 28.2.

Japan Program for Advanced Information Infrastructure.

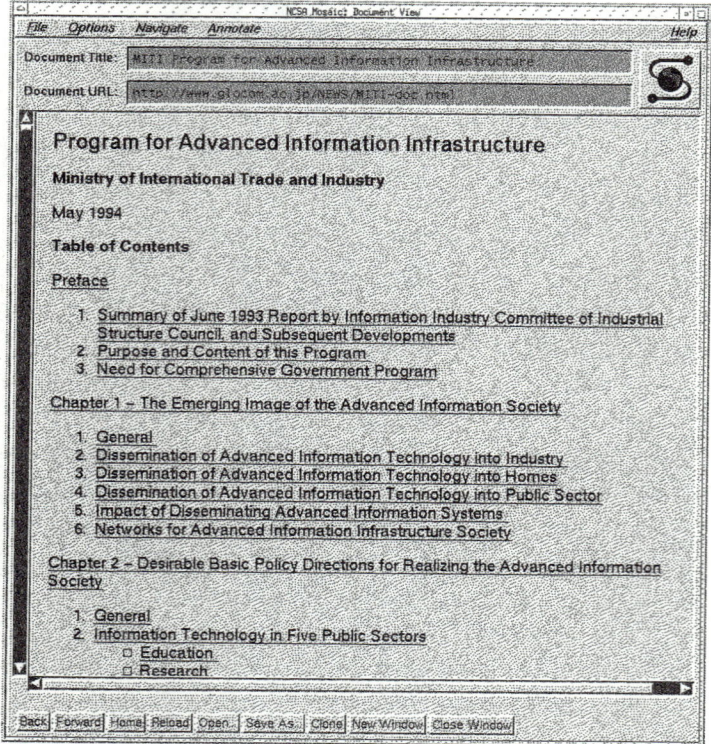

Japan's plan for information infrastructure, like the plans of other nations, acknowledges a shift in economic activity from manufacturing to intellectual activity and articulates a vision of a comprehensive government program to promote information technology. The May 1994 report (Figure 28.2) on the GLOCOM web offers a detailed statement of the program. Japan's plan pays particular attention to a future "Advanced Information Infrastructure Society." According to the plan, people in this information society will "ultimately be able to obtain and process information from anywhere in the world no matter where they are located, through a variety of media, and to easily transmit their own information to any point in the world."

Other key webs related to Japan's initiative include:

- Communications Research Laboratory, Koganei, Tokyo, URL `http://www.crl.go.jp/`

- Nippon Telegraph and Telephone Corporation, URL `http://www.ntt.jp/index.html`

- Internet Initiative Japan Inc., URL `http://www.iij.ad.jp/`

Singapore

The National Computing Board (NCB) of Singapore has a vision for an "intelligent island"—an intensive, country-wide information technology (IT) infrastructure intended to improve the quality of life and create competitive business advantages for Singapore. Figure 28.3 shows an information page about this plan called "IT 2000."

FIGURE 28.3.

Singapore Information Technology 2000.

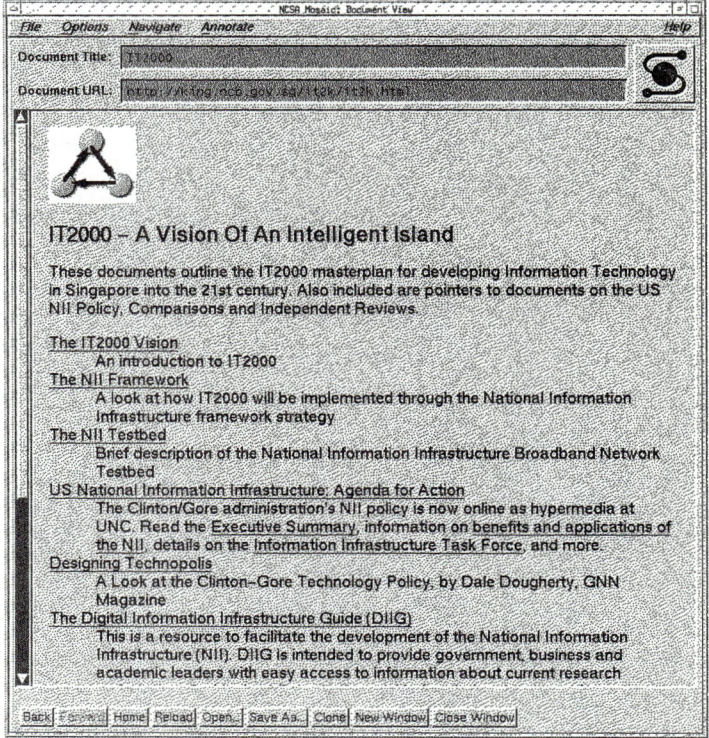

The IT2000 plan is comprehensive, aimed at interconnecting "computers in virtually every home, office, school, and factory" (URL `http://king.ncb.gov.sg/it2k/it2kv.html`). The framework for the development includes integrating legal and technical policy and standards with infrastructure (networks and services) to support applications (Figure 28.4).

FIGURE 28.4.

Singapore NII framework.

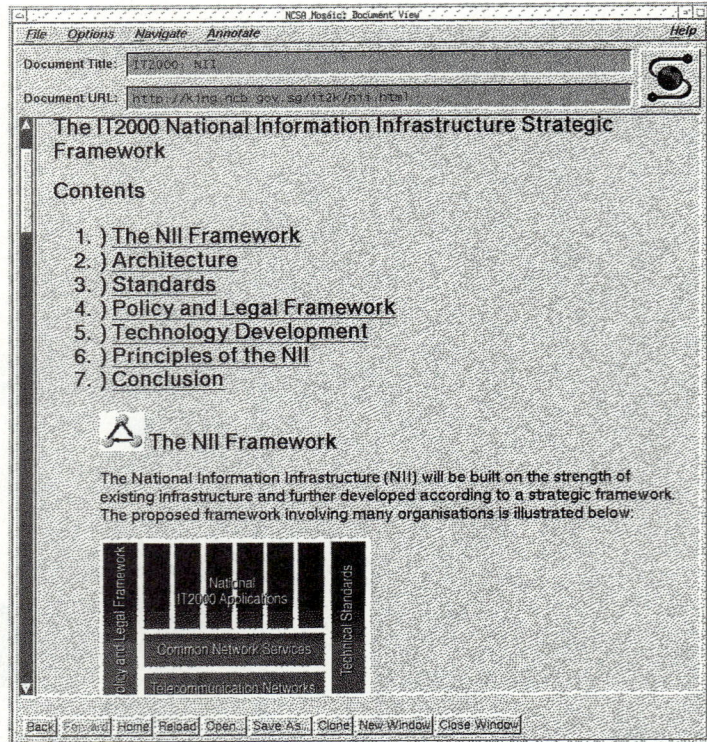

Singapore's framework is more comprehensive and requires greater government involvement and top-down planning than many other national plans. While the United States' plan (below) focuses on a few key areas such health care, education, libraries, and government information, the Singapore plan targets a larger range of *economic* sectors (URL `http://king.ncb.gov.sg/it2k/it2kv.html#study`):

- Construction and Real Estate
- Education and Training
- Financial Services
- Government
- Healthcare

- IT Industry
- Manufacturing
- Media, Publishing, and Information Services
- Retail, Wholesale, and Distribution
- Tourist and Leisure Services
- Transportation

Thus, the Singapore plan reaches farther into all the sectors of the national economy than many other national plans. Sandy Sandfort, writing in *Wired* (1.4), speculates on the outcome of Singapore's ambitious plan: "Perhaps a cosmopolitan, more robust Singapore will emerge, or maybe it will be consumed. What does seem clear is that the information technology bell cannot be unrung."

The United States

The United States has taken an aggressive approach to developing a National Information Infrastructure (NII). President Clinton, in his 1994 State of the Union message, stated the goal of working "with the private sector to connect every classroom, every clinic, every library, and every hospital in America to a national information superhighway by the year 2000" (URL `http://ntiaunix1.ntia.doc.gov:70/0/papers/documents/state_of_union.txt`).

While efforts for national communications networks were underway decades before—with the development of the forerunners to the Internet, ARPAnet, as well as growth and development of communication technologies, the Clinton Administration has made networked communication a national goal. Through the leadership of Al Gore, first as a Senator, then as the Vice President, a National Information Infrastructure Agenda has been developed that seeks to create "a seamless web of communications networks, computers, databases, and consumer electronics that will put vast amounts of information at users' fingertips" (URL `http://ntiaunix1.ntia.doc.gov:70/0/papers/documents/nii_agenda_for_action.txt`).

The National Information Infrastructure Act (H.R. 1757) was passed in July 1993 and is an extension and acceleration of the High Performance Computing Act (P.L. 102-94) of 1991. To support this effort online, the Information Infrastructure Task Force (IITF) has developed a web server (URL `http://iitf.doc.gov/`), shown in Figure 28.5.

FIGURE 28.5.
*US Information
Infrastructure Task Force.*

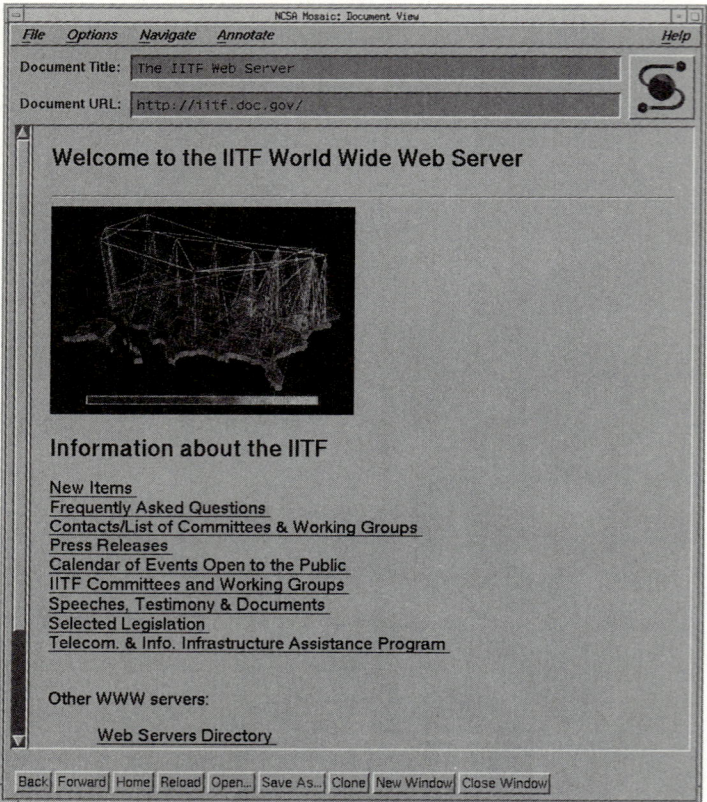

The IITF web contains links to a variety of supporting information, as shown in the figure above. Since it is a government-oriented server, it contains a large selection of documents, testimony, speeches, and reports revolving around the legislative efforts to create a national information infrastructure. For example, a portion of the executive summary of a report called "Framework for NII SERVICES" is provided that outlines some issues about how NII services will be provided. Figure 28.6 shows a view of how relationships and roles might emerge in a US NII.

Other information in the IETF web includes summaries and transcripts of hearings that have been held to debate and discuss how a national infrastructure might develop. The IETF web is part of other major webs related to the US NII project, including the following:

■ The National Coordination Office for High Performance Computing and Communications, URL `http://www.hpcc.gov/`

- U.S. Department Of Commerce, URL `http://www.doc.gov/`
- The Digital Information Infrastructure Guide, "a collection of information about projects and organizations working on the development of the NII," `http://farnsworth.mit.edu/diig.html`
- National Information Infrastructure Testbed, `http://www.esi.com/niit_top.html`

FIGURE 28.6.

National Information Infrastructure relationships.

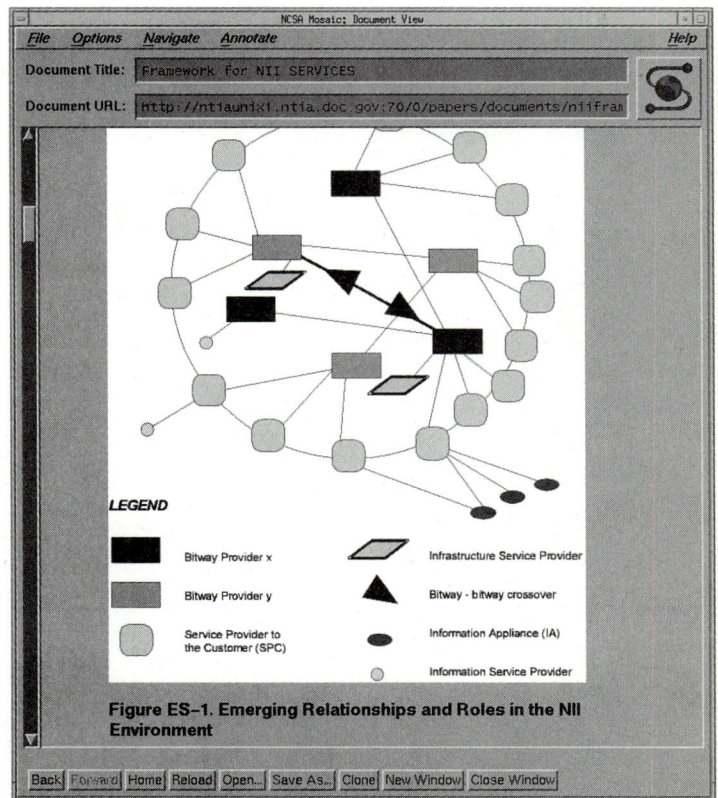

Figure ES–1. Emerging Relationships and Roles in the NII Environment

While the US NII project is not specifically focusing on the Web as a basis for an NII, the use of the Web illustrates how timely and valuable information about information infrastructure can be delivered online.

International

Besides national governments, a range of international organizations use the Web to deliver information to the general public as well as members. These webs are particularly valuable when current, detailed information is needed from an organization that may be distributed across the globe.

The World Health Organization

The goal of the World Health Organization (WHO) is "the attainment by all peoples of the highest possible level of health" (URL `http://www.who.ch/WHOis.html`). As part of this broad mission, WHO directs and coordinates international health work, promotes technical cooperation, and assists in emergencies. WHO advances disease-prevention work, the improvement of living and working conditions, health services, and education. Headquartered in Geneva, Switzerland, WHO also proposes and makes recommendations about health policy and promotes international standards for food and other substances. The WHO web is shown in Figure 28.7 (URL `http://www.who.ch/`).

FIGURE 28.7.

World Health Organization home page.

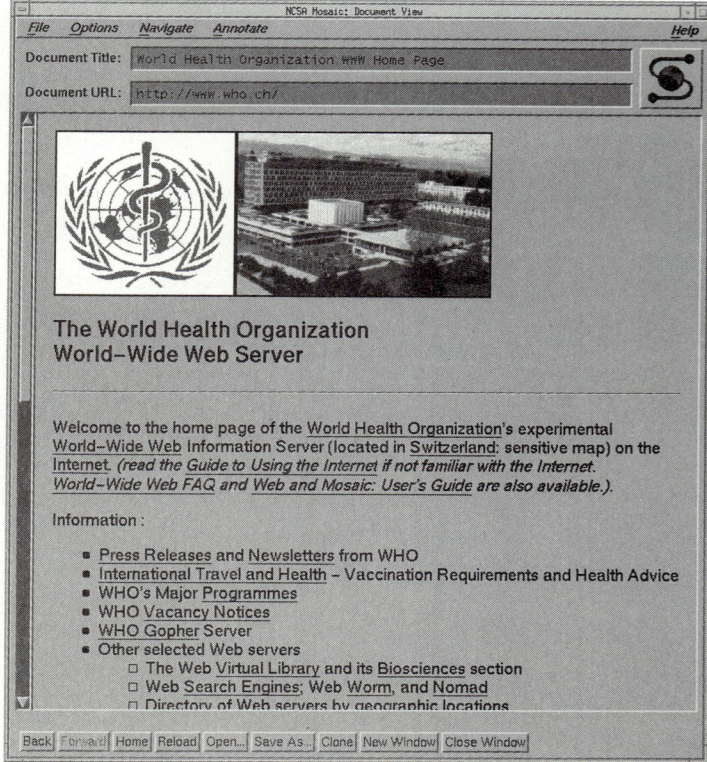

The WHO web offers a wide variety of information, general web links, and a link to the WHO Gopher and related organizations (for example, the World Bank). The WHO web offers access to a variety of informational publications online, including the following:

- Press releases (for example, An Update on the Cholera Strain in Rwandaa 25 Jul 1994)
- Several newsletters
- Environmental health
- Influenza
- AIDS
- WHO library Digest for Africa

Figure 28.8 shows a page linking to descriptions of WHO's major programs.

FIGURE 28.8.

World Health Organization Major Programs.

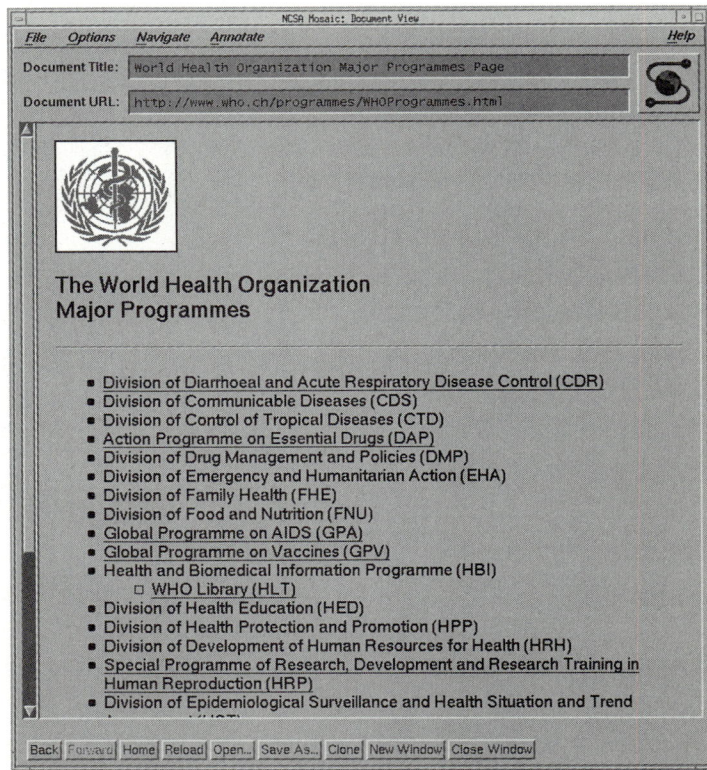

The information on the WHO web is very specific—including not only background information, for example on Acute Respiratory Infections and Diarrheal Disease Control, but detailed bibliographies and ordering information for WHO publications on these subjects.

The WHO web demonstrates how an international organization with a complex mission can create an information system to disseminate useful information to the public and to serve as an information and education system for any user.

The World Bank

The World Bank is an international agency that lends money to poor countries for development, finances private sector projects, advises governments and businesses on investment, and promotes foreign investment ("The World Bank Home Page," URL `http://www.worldbank.org/`). The home page is shown in Figure 28.9.

FIGURE 28.9.

World Bank home page. (Copyright the World Bank. Reprinted by permission.)

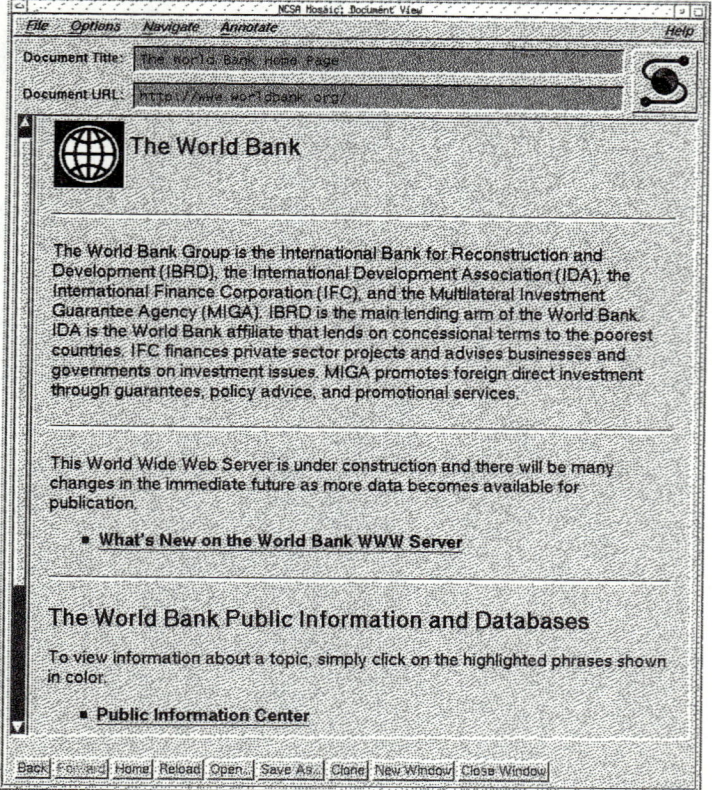

The World Bank's web provides an offering of public information as well as descriptions of World Bank publications that are for sale. The public information center on the World Bank web is one aspect of a new policy of the bank, approved in August 1993, which makes operational information available to the public that had previously been restricted to official users. This public information includes items such as:

- Economic reports
- Environmental information
- Assessments and analysis
- Data sheets
- Global environmental facility document
- Environmental documents
- National environmental action plans
- Project information, policy papers, and reports

These links include searchable indexes as well as many detailed information sheets; environmental datasheets, for example, include more than 500 documents. By creating a single web source for their documents, the World Bank's web can truly serve all interested people worldwide by providing access to detailed and current information.

Government Information

National government plans for information infrastructure are just one part of the government information offered through the Web. In the United States, for example, many federal agencies and offices have web servers. Figure 28.10 shows a partial list of agency webs from the Federal Information Exchange, Inc., a private company operating several multi-agency information services.

This section uses two example webs to illustrate federal information on the Web—a government agency and a legislator.

FIGURE 28.10.

U.S. Federal webs.

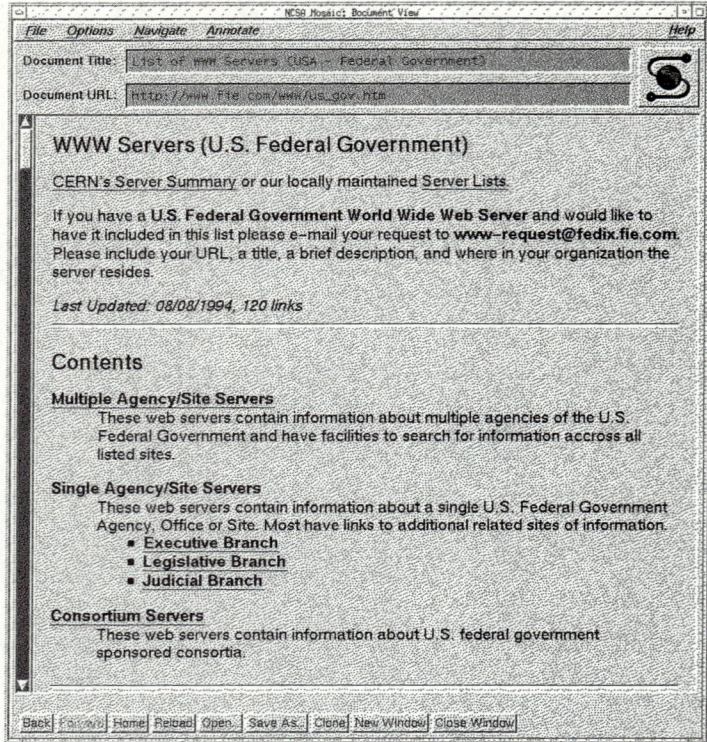

U.S. Department of Transportation

As shown in the list in Figure 25.9, there is a wide variety of U.S. government agencies with web servers. As an example, the U.S. Department of Transportation (DOT) offers a web, URL `http://www.dot.gov/`, as shown in Figure 28.11.

The U.S. DOT web contains a wide variety of material about the agency, including:

- A link to the DOT Gopher
- A list of operating agencies
- Text of National Public Radio coverage of the process of "reinventing" DOT
- Recently published information and tips on locating information about DOT online
- Acquisition, procurement, and grant management information
- The U.S. Dept. of Transportation Telephone Directory

FIGURE 28.11.

U.S. Department of Transportation web.

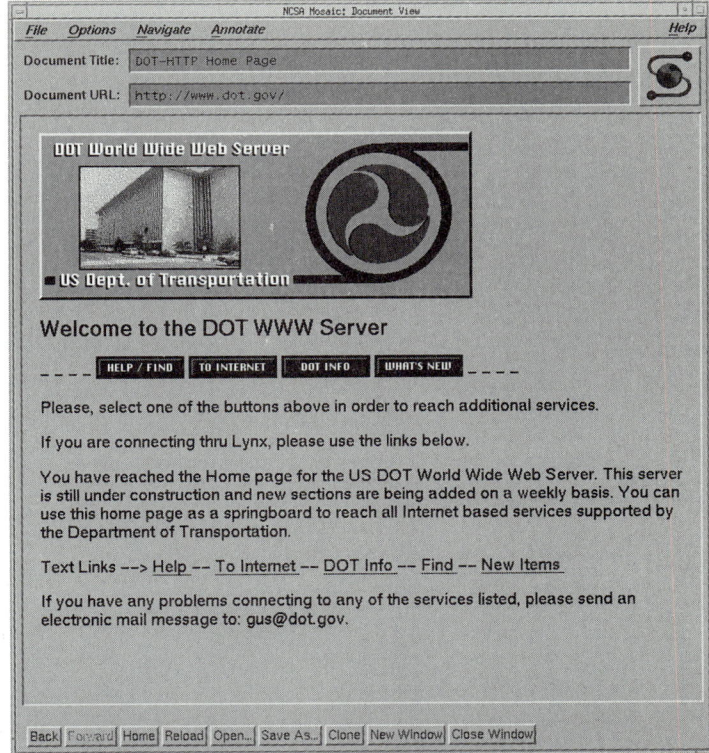

The DOT thus can serve both its employees (the many people working in DOT's operating agencies) and its employers (the American taxpayers) by providing links to agency and government information. Moreover, the DOT web is just one part of DOT's overall strategy to use information technology throughout its operations. The DOT web, still under development when shown in the preceding image, will eventually contain more links about the agency and easier access to information so that citizens anywhere can use it.

U.S. Senator Edward Kennedy

Senator Edward Kennedy (D-Mass) was the first United States Senator with a web page. Eric Loeb and John C. Mallery at the Artificial Intelligence Laboratory of Massachusetts Institute of Technology developed the page as part of the Intelligent Information Infrastructure Project. The top of Sen. Kennedy's page is shown in Figure 28.12 and another section illustrating more information available about legislation and the commonwealth

itself is in Figure 28.13. (Note that in Figure 28.12, a notice posted indicates that the U.S. Senate rules place a freeze on Network information distribution in the sixty days before an election, when this image was taken.)

FIGURE 28.12.

Senator Edward Kennedy home page (top).

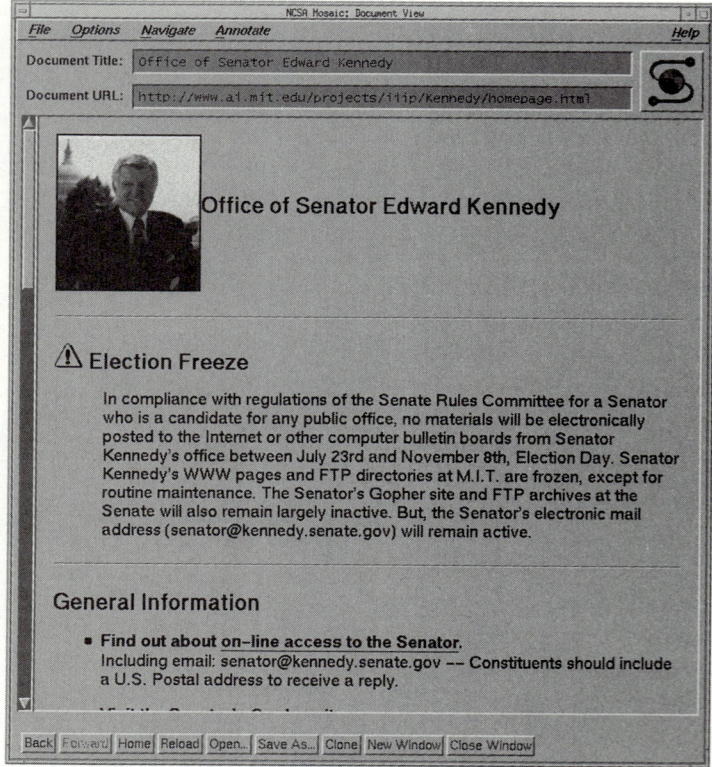

Senator Kennedy's web contains an excellent collection of information for his constituents and other people who might be interested in the U.S. political process. The United States Senate itself has a Gopher, and the web gives a pointer to the Senator's Gopher menus. Besides legislative and budget information and press releases, the web links to important information for the citizens of Massachusetts:

■ A collection of press releases from the Senator's office that highlight important developments and issues about Massachusetts and New England

■ A Web resource map of Massachusetts, (created by the UMass Astronomy Department) showing graphical information maps to Internet resources in the commonwealth (as part of the Virtual Tourist, discussed in Chapter 20, "Machines: Space-Oriented Searching")

■ A variety of World Wide Web links to other links of interest to Massachusetts citizens, and other U.S. infrastructure and government information

FIGURE 28.13.

Senator Edward Kennedy home page (middle).

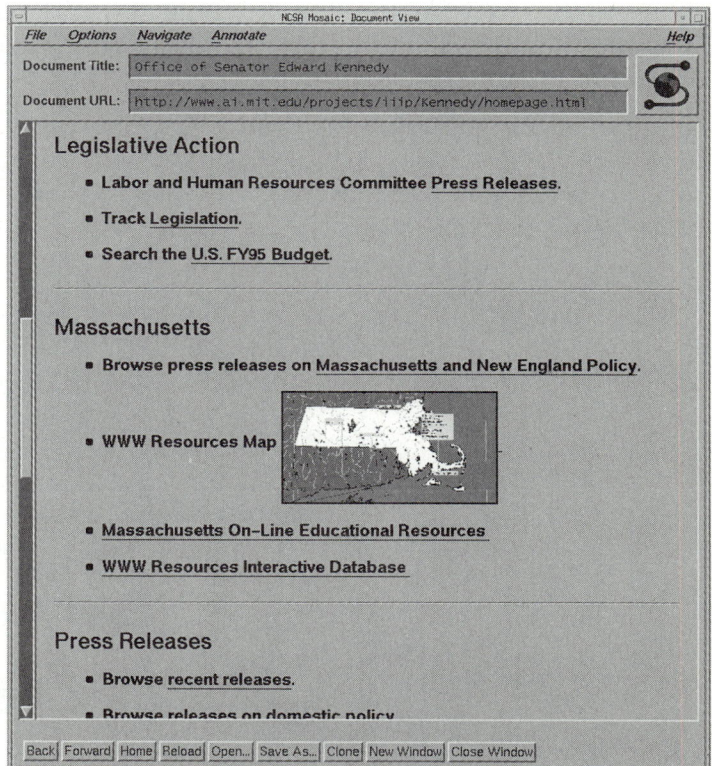

By combining links specific to the Senator's record and activities with information sources relevant to citizens, the Kennedy web offers constituents a way to keep track of government activities that is far more flexible and detailed than any noninteractive news source.

Community Networking

Like national governments and international organizations, regional and metropolitan communities need to provide information structures for their citizens. People have been developing community-based networking for more than a decade—the first community network was Dr. Tom Grundner's public health information bulletin board "St. Silicon's Hospital and Information Dispensary," in Cleveland, Ohio in 1984. This service eventually developed into the Cleveland Free-Net. In 1989, the National Public Telecomputing Network (NPTN) was formed to help other communities form similar networks (URL `ftp://nptn.org/pub/nptn/nptn.info/basic.guide.txt`).

Today, community networks extend across the world, with many offering connections through telnet, Gopher, and the Web. Peter Scott (the creator of HYTELNET) maintains a Free-Nets home page (Figure 28.14) that offers a variety of links to Free-Nets as well as background information on them.

FIGURE 28.14.

The Free-Nets home page.

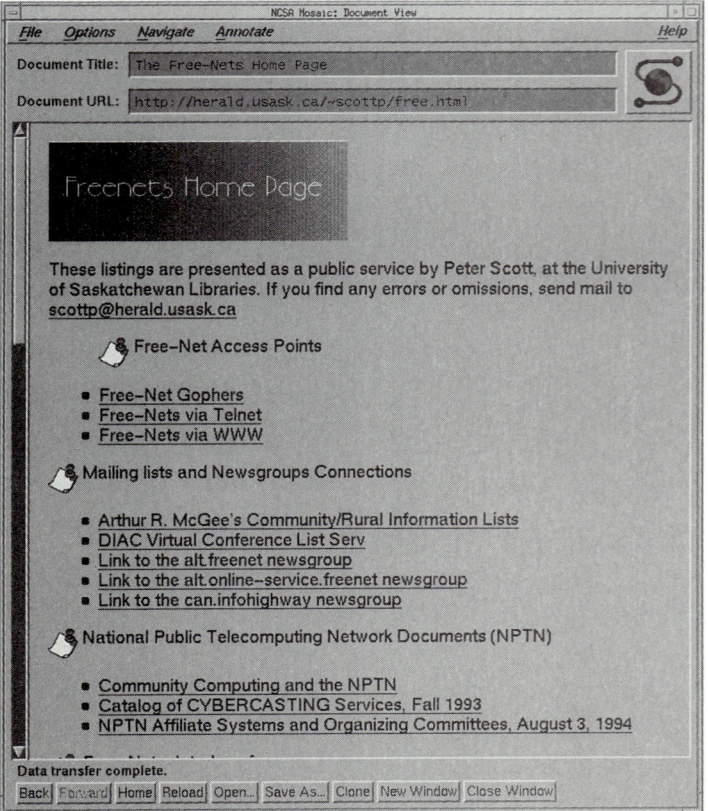

The rest of this section highlights some networks that support communities.

The Silicon Prairie

As part of a collaboration between the National Center for Supercomputing Applications (NCSA) and the Champaign (Illinois) County Chamber of Commerce, Alaina Kanfer and Gordon M. Taylor of NCSA created a web to demonstrate how information about a community can be presented. Figure 28.15 shows the front page of "The Silicon Prairie," Champaign County, Illnois, URL `http://www.prairienet.org/SiliconPrairie/ccnet.html`.

FIGURE 28.15.

Champaign County web page.

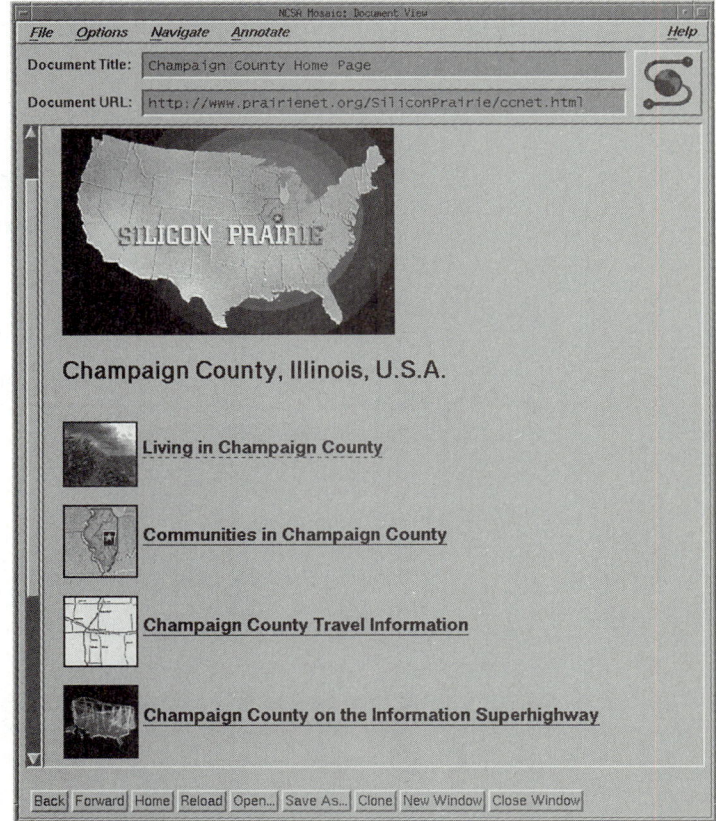

The Champaign County web offers information about its natural and cultural attractions as well as community information. For example, links on the "Living in Champaign County" page connect a user to the University of Illinois at Urbana-Champaign as well as a brief history of the county. The web also offers community profiles, travel information, and detailed information about the county. The Champaign web describes plans for Prairienet (Champaign County's Free-Net) to link all county citizens to information. Another development, the Champaign County Network (CCNet), will offer webs related to organizations and individuals.

St. Petersburg, Russia

The 1994 Goodwill Games brought a great deal of attention and activity to the city of St. Petersburg, Russia. The home page of St. Petersburg's web shows this emphasis (Figure 28.16).

FIGURE 28.16.

St. Petersburg, Russia home page.

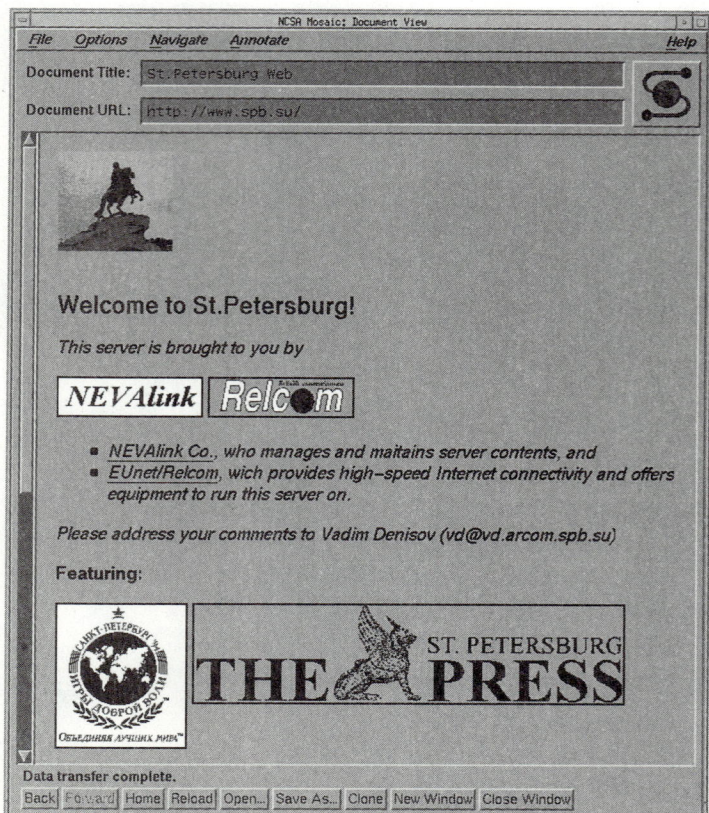

The St. Petersburg web offered detailed information about the progress of the Goodwill Games while they were being held there in 1994. Other information includes the full text of *The St. Petersburg Press,* the city's English-language daily newspaper covering news as well as the culture and lifestyle of St. Petersburg's restaurants, shops, transportation, and other tourist attractions. The web also contains "St. Petersburg Pictures Gallery" (Figure 28.17), which shows a variety of scenes.

FIGURE 28.17.

St. Petersburg picture gallery.

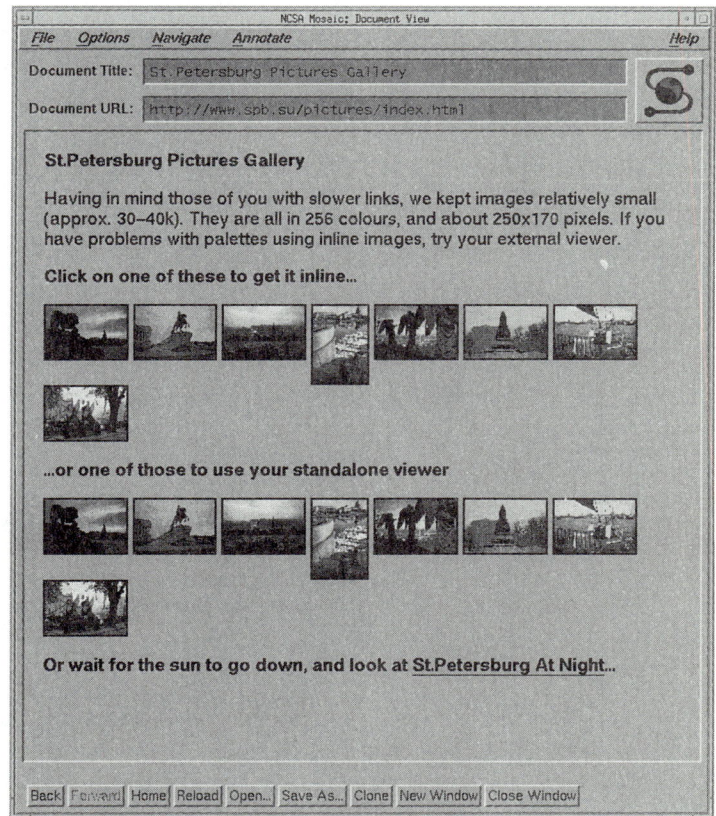

By using St. Petersburg's web, particularly the picture gallery and the detailed cultural guide offered by *The St. Petersburg Press*, you can get a unique glimpse into a city with a long history. While the St. Petersburg web does not offer all the connections that older Free-Nets might offer (it doesn't have online conferencing and discussion areas), it nevertheless demonstrates how a city can increase its connections to the world, leveraging the attention of a popular event held there into more publicity for the city itself.

San Carlos, California

The city of San Carlos is located in the San Francisco Bay Area of California. As part of the Association of Bay Area Governments (ABAG), San Carlos has developed the web shown in Figure 28.18 (URL `http://www.abag.ca.gov/abag/local_gov/city/san_carlos/schome.html`).

FIGURE 28.18.

San Carlos, California home page. (Copyright 1994, The City of San Carlos. The City of San Carlos Seal, the City motto "The City of Good Living" and "San Carlos On Line" are trademarks of the City of San Carlos. All rights reserved. Reprinted by permission.)

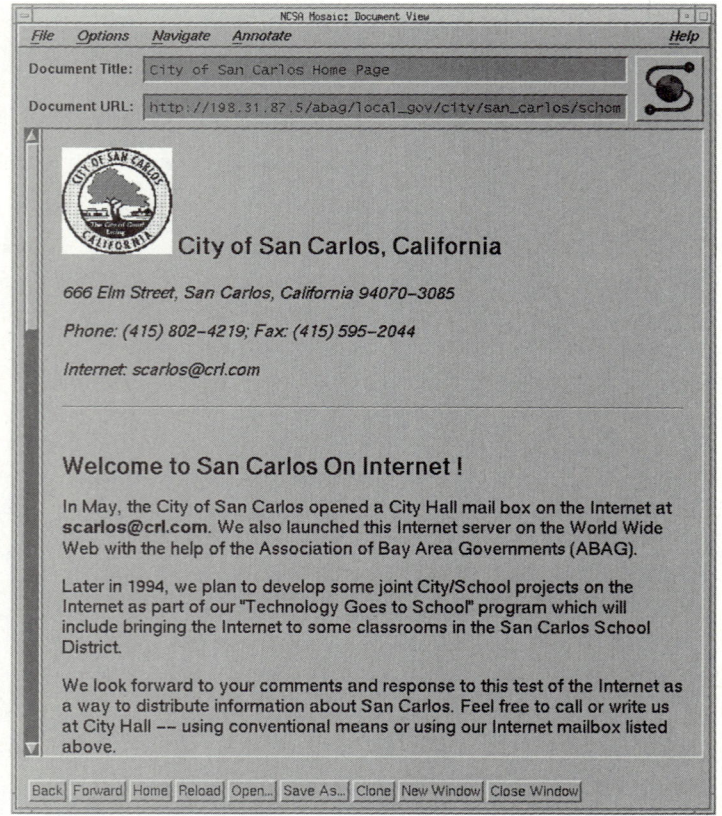

The San Carlos web links citizens to information about

- What's New on the San Carlos web
- City Hall
- City regulations
- Fire Department
- Parks & Recreation
- Transportation
- Business
- Schools

Begun in May 1994 and still under rapid development, the San Carlos web is an example of what a city can do to connect its citizens to information. The links under development on the home page show the potential for even more detailed information. For example, a link in the Business links area is to a company called Bay Area Model Mugging (BAMM), a company offering a range of classes in self-defense techniques. By providing information at this level of detail, a citizen can rely on the community web for up-to-date and detailed information, and a remote user can gain a good idea of the community itself.

Boulder Community Network

The Boulder Community Network (BCN) web was launched in July, 1994, as a project involving many of Boulder, Colorado's educational, civil, and corporate organizations, including Apple Computer and the University of Colorado at Boulder. BCN offers a variety of links relating to "Information Centers" relating to many aspects of city life (see Figure 28.19), URL `http://bcn.boulder.co.us/`.

The goal of BCN is to gather together community information important to citizens and at the same time ensure that all citizens have access to this information.

According to Ken Klingenstein, Director, University of Colorado Computing & Network Services, the web is a work in progress. The process of BCN's growth will include not only increasing the information offered, but also adding a research agenda in cooperation with the Schools of Journalism and Mass Communication, Computer Science, and Sociology. Scholars in these departments will investigate the impact of computer-mediated communication and delivery of information on the community. As the vision statement for BCN points out, Boulder offers a combination of advanced technology institutions that can serve as a testbed for a community of the future (URL `http://bcn.boulder.co.us/bcn/vision.html`). By providing links to information about these plans on the Web and tying the web to the research process of local academics, the Boulder Community Network is poised to both invent and understand the future.

FIGURE 28.19.
Boulder Community Network home page.

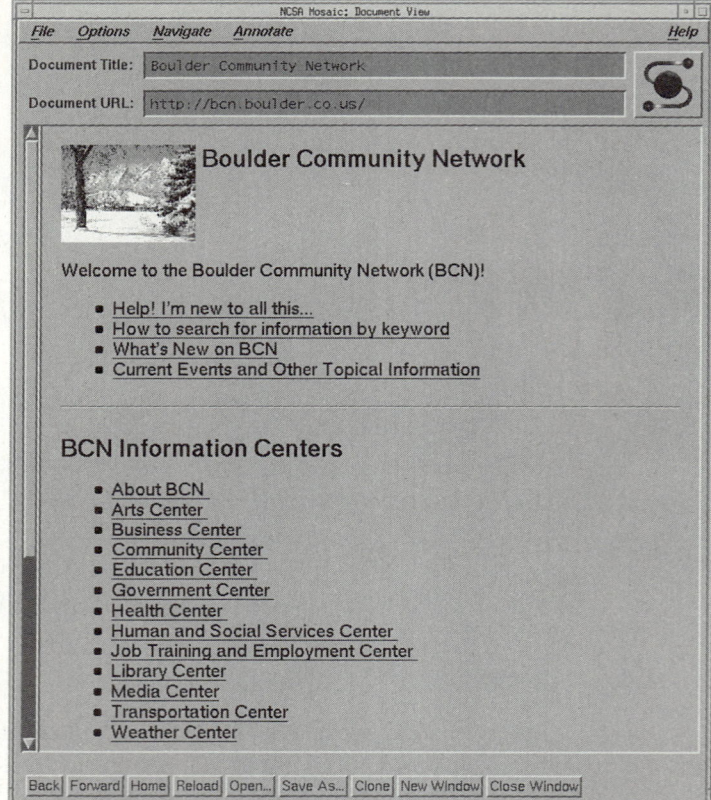

South Dakota

South Dakota has developed a web that meets the need for a state-level information system. The front page of the graphical version of the South Dakota web, located at URL `http://www.state.sd.us`, is shown in Figure 28.20.

FIGURE 28.20.

State of South Dakota web page.

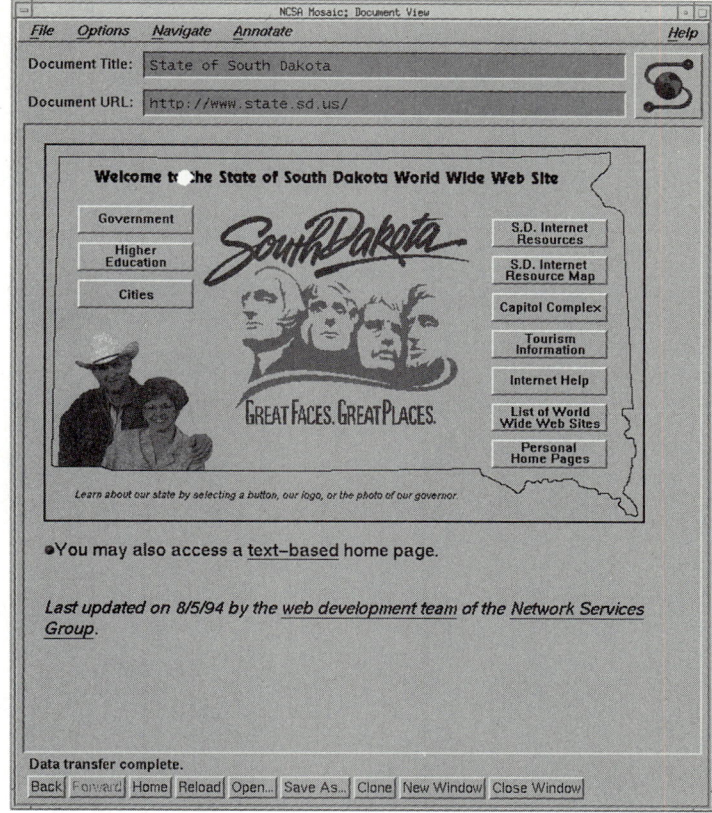

The South Dakota server offers a good collection of government information, with a graphical interface to information about branches and offices. (For example, Figure 28.21 shows the breakdown of the Executive Branch.)

FIGURE 28.21.

State of South Dakota Executive Branch.

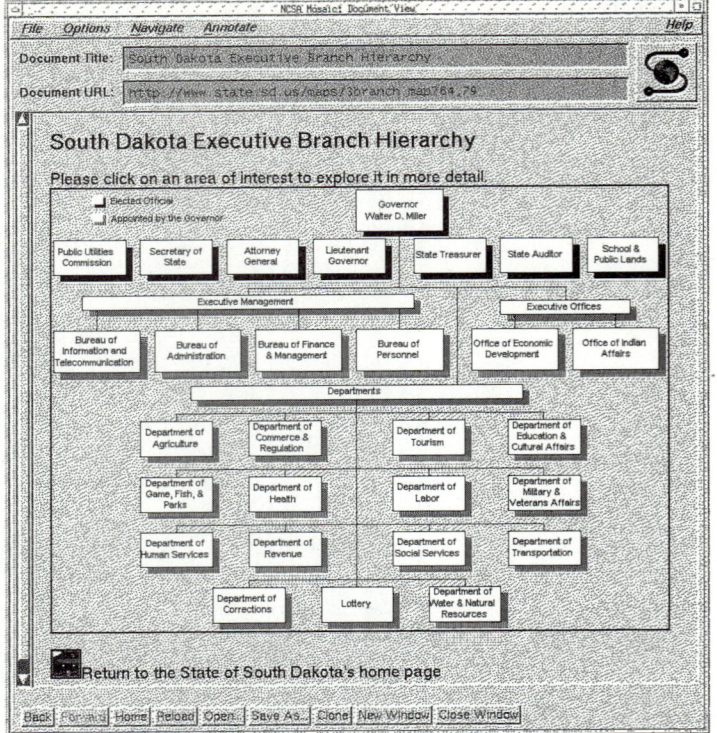

By clicking on a box within the diagram, the user can obtain a description of the office or department. Similar diagrams show the Judicial and Legislative branches of the South Dakota government.

The web also has a tour of the Capitol Complex in Pierre, complete with a map and pictures of the buildings and features. There's also a collection of information about the state's attractions, such as one of its most famous, Mount Rushmore National Monument (Figure 28.22).

FIGURE 28.22.

Mount Rushmore National Monument.

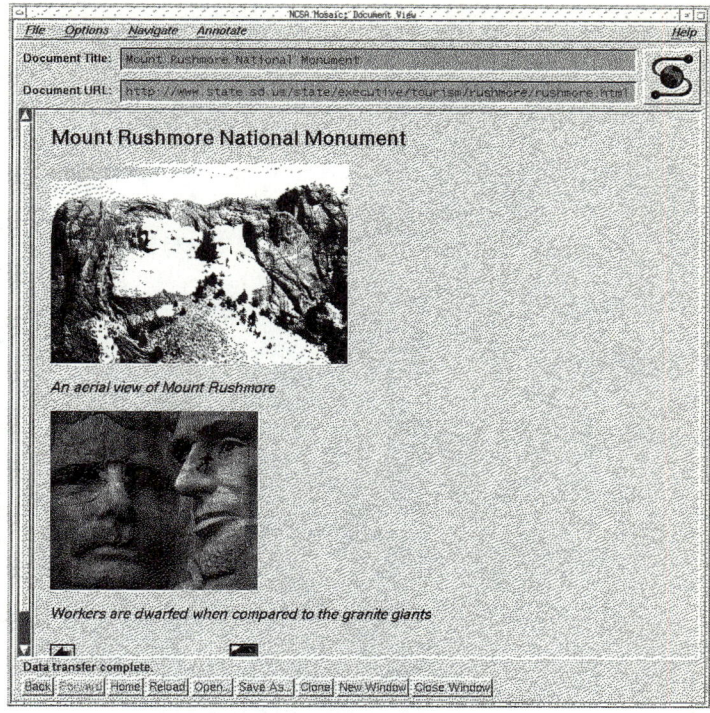

Other tourism information includes the Crazy Horse Memorial, Oahe Dam, and natural features and activities in the state. By combining extensive government, education, and tourism information, the South Dakota web accomplishes on a state-wide level what many community-based networks are striving to accomplish—an information system that helps residents by providing important information for their lives as citizens and as life-long learners, and which presents a best "face" to the larger world on the Web.

Blacksburg Electronic Village

Blacksburg Electronic Village (BEV) in Virginia is a cooperative effort to create a comprehensive information infrastructure to support an entire community. Using the strength and talents of the partners in the program—Virginia Tech, Bell Atlantic, and the Town of Blacksburg, Virginia—the project attempts to create a "critical mass" of users so that people can and will use electronic means to interact and gather information. Figure 28.23 shows the home page of BEV (URL `http://www.bev.net/BEVhome.html`).

FIGURE 28.23.

Blacksburg Electronic Village home page.

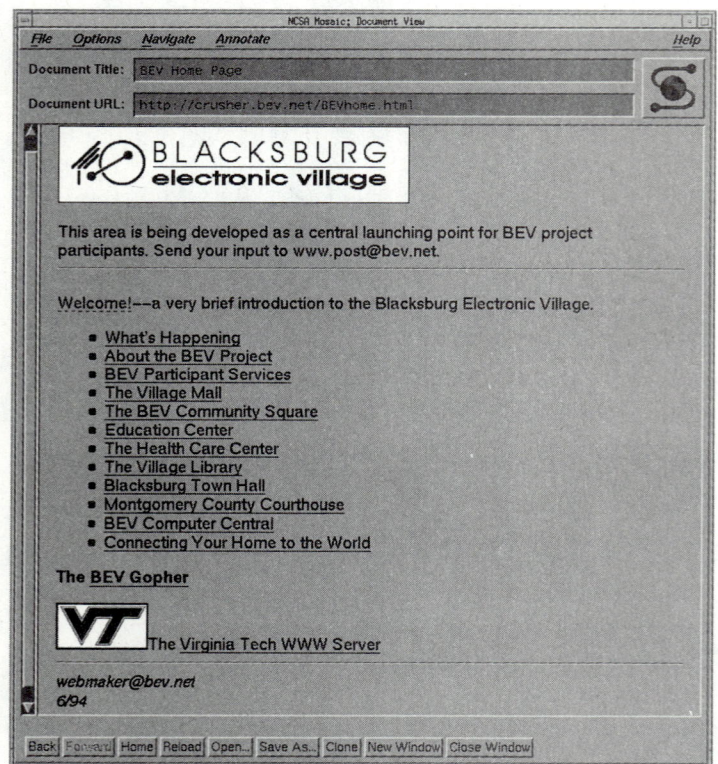

As an electronic village that reflects the activities of a real community, the offerings on the BEV web include features that you would expect to find in a community—such as links covering aspects of education, health, government, and cultural activities, as well as support information for using the BEV web. The "Community Square," for example, provides links to local attractions and activities, such as a restaurant guide, local organizations, and general interest information. In the "Village Mall" area, you can find out the weekly specials and look at the menu of restaurants such as Backstreets (Figure 28.24), and even obtain a coupon for specials on pizza and calzone from the Backstreets home page.

FIGURE 28.24.

Backstreets Restaurant home page.

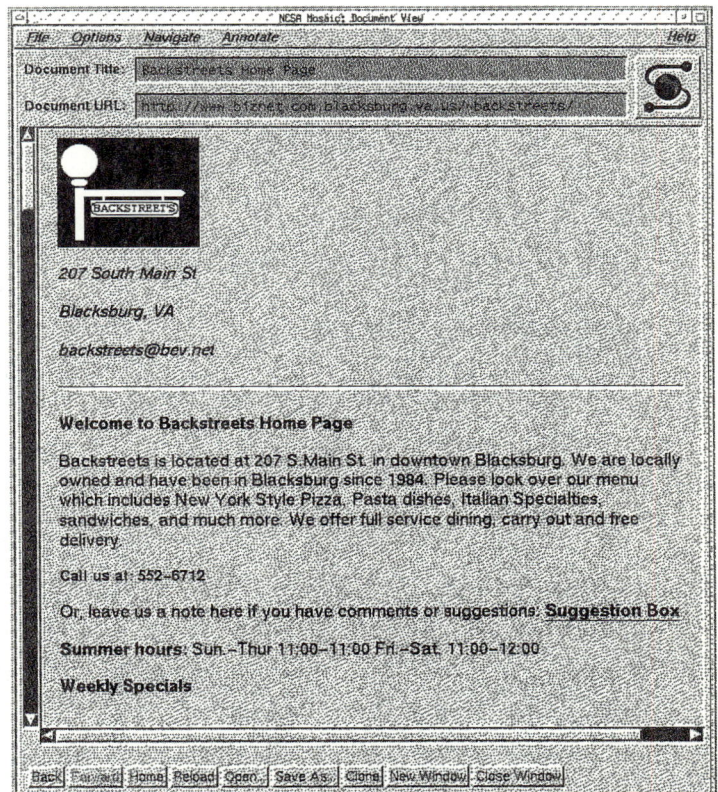

The BEV web's goal is to provide an information infrastructure that can support many information needs a citizen might have. For example, in addition to the links mentioned above, the BEV web includes information about the following:

- Movie schedules at local cinemas
- Bus schedules
- Recycling drop-off points
- Supermarket specials

The Blacksburg plan takes community networking to a very detailed level. The goal of the developers is to develop a "community of the future" in which the routine use of networked information and communication will increase the quality of life, expand educational and business uses of the Web, and create an online system for citizens to participate more effectively in civic activities.

Explorer's Check

Just as people throughout history have collaborated to create governments at the local, regional, and national levels, governments and communities today create webs to support the needs and interests of citizens.

National governments have recognized information as a valuable resource not only for economic wealth but also as a way to supply information to citizens about a variety of topics. Many countries now are developing initiatives for national infrastructures to increase the use of information technology by citizens. Using a variety of approaches, Canada, Japan, Singapore, and the United States supply webs of information that support these plans.

International organizations have recognized the Web's power to supply detailed information for a worldwide constituency on demand. Both the World Bank's and the World Health Organization's webs illustrate the value of Web-delivered information.

At the federal, state, and local levels, governments and communities have created webs to enrich and inform their citizens. South Dakota's web shows how a web can provide extensive information for a state's citizens and at the same time inform and attract others to the state. At the community level, a range of activities has been occurring for more than a decade—Free-Nets to support community information at a variety of levels of detail, including the ambitious plan of Blacksburg Electronic Village to provide a complete information infrastructure for its citizens.

PART

V

Weaving a Web

The personal computer revolution of the 1980s fueled the desktop publishing revolution of the 1980s and 1990s. Today, another revolution is taking place—the network publishing revolution—and the World Wide Web and browsers like Mosaic are a big part of it. What started as a simple means for exchanging electronic messages over computer networks in the 1970s has developed into a range of sophisticated systems for computer-mediated communication. Network information systems like the Web open up new opportunities for communication that have never been possible before.

This new revolution in publishing is taking place not just on desktop computers, but through global computer networks. While desktop publishing tools provide users with sophisticated ways to control how information is presented, network publishing processes emphasize user involvement and choice. Tools for creating hypertext webs involve not just shaping the information content but involving the information user interactively.

Instead of the static, goals-oriented products that paper-oriented desktop publishing often produces, network products are frequently dynamic, involve interactivity, place more control in the hands of the user, and are based on a different model for distribution. This model is demand-broadcast, in which the content is served (broadcast) globally upon a demand from a user, who selectively encounters content according to interest.

> **NOTE**
>
> Throughout this part, I use the convention of using the term *web* (lowercase) to denote a local collection of hypertext pages, to distinguish it from the term *Web*, representing the global collection of all publicly accessible webs.

Creating a web to inform, persuade, entertain, or affect a user is not a simple task. But in this part, we'll explore some ways you can be a network publisher by using existing tools and delivery mechanisms for the Web.

You'll find that some of the procedures for developing information are different from print-based communication design and composition methodologies, while other guidelines and principles for effective communication can still apply to the Web.

You'll see that the web development process I describe here borrows many principles from such academic disciplines as composition, technical communication, and rhetoric, as well as ideas from software and user-interface design methodologies. The very act of weaving a web involves your ability to manage a *process* of information development, drawing on your ability to

- Plan, analyze, design, implement, and develop information using an iterative, cyclic process of refinement
- Develop information and communication structures using network-distributed hypermedia and computer-mediated communication
- Use techniques of visual communication, language, and layout design to package, sequence, and cue information for a user
- Produce elements of a web such as audience information, purpose and objective statements, domain information, web specification, and web presentation
- Understand the domain of expertise you are conveying in your web and continually adjust and update your knowledge and the information served out on your web

We'll start this part by looking at how Web browsers like Mosaic have changed the process of developing and delivering information and thus have altered our conception of information itself. Then we'll examine a way you can employ an iterative process of planning, analysis, design, implementation, and development to weave webs. We'll look at the details of using HTML as well as specific techniques for design and implementation.

You'll discover that the Web offers opportunities for publishing that are unique in human history, and that developing a literacy in composing webs is key to successful Web publishing. Since a web weaver must be a good web navigator as well as familiar with what kinds of applications are possible, this part assumes that you are familiar with the material in Part III, "Web Navigation Tools and Techniques," and Part IV, "Exploring the Web."

Communication Processes on the Web

29

by John December

The Web is a very new medium for communicating with other people. However, this novelty doesn't mean that you have to re-invent the art of creating a message and structuring its content to reach a particular audience through the Web. Instead, you can draw on a large body of knowledge about crafting information from the ancient art of discovering the means of persuasion (rhetoric) and the relatively modern field of technical communication. These fields, rooted in static or noninteractive media such as paper, film, or recorded sound, can enrich the process of weaving a web.

> **NOTE**
>
> The term *web* with a lowercase *w* will be used here to refer to the local hypertext you create, in order to distinguish from the *Web,* the collection of all hypertext publicly available on servers worldwide.

Borrowing some ideas from disciplines such as computer software engineering and user interface design, this chapter outlines a web-weaving methodology that addresses the dynamic nature of Web communication.

This chapter covers some of the implications of the Web's transformation of the information development process. It reviews how the Web changes communication processes involving *mediated* communication (that is, communication that employs an object—such as paper, a graphic, a screen display, a user interface, a computer network—to convey a message). It explores some of the characteristics of Web communication that set it apart from traditional forms.

This chapter begins with a review of how Web communication is different from other forms of mediated communication. It then gives an overview of what these changes hold for a new process of information development and communication on the Web.

How Is the Web Different from Other Communication?

Communicating on the Web is different from communicating through paper-based means such as brochures, reports, letters, memos, and other documents because it involves a different kind of *encoding* process (that is, how you create it using hypertext) as well as a different kind of *decoding* process (that is, how users perceive it through network-distributed browsers and servers). While it is beyond the scope of this chapter to enumerate all of these differences, those related to web-weaving will be described.

NOTE

The preceding paragraph doesn't use the term *reader* because the Web includes multimedia as well as hypertext, and the experience styles of the users of the Web (as you saw in Part III, "Web Navigation Tools and Techniques") aren't necessarily best described by the term *reading* as well as by the term *using* information.

No longer constrained to a single physical object such as a piece of paper, Web communication becomes independent of time and space constraints, and is limited only by the interface (for example, a browser such as Mosaic) working in conjunction with the distribution mechanism (for example, a computer network). The user is also less constrained because he or she has more choices for interaction with the universe of information available on the Web than with a paper-based form of communication.

Web communication differs from communication in traditional media in the following ways:

1. Web communication involves different *space and time constraints,* taking on a different *form,* and employing a different *delivery* mechanism than traditional media.

   For example, when you receive a paper memo in your in-basket, you might first pile it with all the other things you must deal with: reports, electronic mail, meetings, voice mail, postal mail, express mail, and so on. All of these kinds of communication compete for your attention in terms of the space and time they occupy. The memo on your desk is more likely to get your attention than the one in the bottom drawer of your filing cabinet or the one that arrived last week. In addition, these forms of communication compete in terms of what form and delivery mechanism they employ. A brightly-packaged express mail letter (a special form of communication) usually commands more attention than a plain manila envelope, particularly when you must sign for the express mail (a special form of delivery).

   On the Web, however, the user chooses the time and space for communication. The form of the communication's display (how the hypertext file will be shown, in terms of font and appearance) is set by the user's browser, and the delivery mechanism is the same for all information—along the hypertext links of the Web itself. While access to information on the Web is constrained by awareness of it and the skills necessary to retrieve it, all information is potentially equally accessible. For example, is the 1948 company report in a storage room equally accessible to you as the memo sitting on your desk today? If delivered over the Web, that 1948 company report becomes not only more accessible to you but to any number of other users at the same time.

The form of the web itself—hypertext—is different from the linear flow of print on paper. Whereas memos and other communications offer themselves as separate objects, branches off a hypertext document can link to and thus relate one document or piece of a document to another, resulting in contextual relations among documents. Links from Web documents can be to hypermedia resources, interactive documents, or information delivery systems.

2. Web communication takes place within a context much larger than a single site or organization, involving social and cultural structures shaped by traditions, shared meanings, language, and practices developed over time.

The Web, like many other forums for computer-mediated communication on networks, has rapidly created specialized information and communication spaces. On computer networks, social and information spaces exist that are, by tradition, set aside for particular purposes. Behavior in these spaces is governed by collective agreement and interaction, as opposed to a single organization's rules of operation.

Community norms developed on networks inhibit advertising in noncommercial spaces. Just as going to a public place and shouting "Buy my widgets!" could be done, this a method of advertising that may bring derision, particularly if it disturbs the decorum (or other chaos :)) the people in that public space had been previously enjoying. Although there may be no "Net cops" monitoring what is said and done, inappropriate communication risks invoking the wrath of a community. In contrast, the same widget seller in the market bazaar (or the Web-equivalent virtual mall) would be welcomed, because the users going into that marketplace know that they will see ads. The enthusiastic widget seller may be eagerly approached by those looking for very good widgets.

Examples illustrating appropriate and inappropriate advertising demonstrate the developed sense of community responsibility and tradition that has evolved over time in networked communities. Web traffic occurs in the context of these traditions. In contrast, the inter-office memo and the internal report exist within a closed environment—closed not just by proprietary considerations, but by the space and time limits inherent in the paper memo as a communications medium. This is not to say that there are no private, proprietary spaces on the Web. Indeed, an organization or individual would not even have to link the hypertext to the Web, and servers can support restricted access via passwords and machine names. However, a local community can still evolve on private, internal webs, and display all the cultural and psychological effects that have been occurring in computer-mediated communication systems for decades—community building, socioemotional interactions, evolving social practices, and conflicts.

Since communication on the Web exists within a larger community, the information provider must cope with the relationships arising from these connections. Web communities evolve over time, and relationships may cross national, cultural, language, and space and time borders. The challenge for this larger Web community is to negotiate the norms for individual interactions appropriately.

3. Web communication is dynamic. Traditional information development practices have long recognized the iterative nature of the process of creating and delivering information. Web communication, however, involves not only iterative development, but offers a delivered artifact that is conceptually and physically very different than that in traditional media. Web communication need not be fixed in its delivered form and exists within an information flux.

   When you write a report, you often go through the process of copyediting, revision, review, user testing, and revision again. Eventually, the deadline clock ticks, and there is a final form that the information takes. Although changes can be made—and there are very possibly second, third, and more editions of the work created—the sense by all parties involved is that the work is "completed" when it is etched into a medium, such as paper, a CD-ROM, a computer disk, or video tape.

   On the Web, hypertext links, the multiple interactions with and among users, and the changing Web information universe all mark the Web as a medium attuned to flux rather than to stasis. Although you can create a web and deliver it to the world through a Web server, your job as an information developer is not done—in fact, it is just starting. You must not only manage the technical operation of your server, but also feedback from users and your web's place in the constant flow of new information introduced on the Web. In managing this change—since keeping track of document versions is not built into Web servers—you may also need to develop archiving procedures if you want to keep track of incremental changes.

Although the implications for how the Web changes communication go beyond even considerations of space, time, form, delivery methods, context, and information dynamism, these issues are enough to raise your awareness of how the Web medium differs from traditional media. The full implications of this change for our society and culture as a whole are still being worked out; we are still living through these changes as well as creating more of them.

A Traditional Information Development Process

The characteristics of Web communication described above—changes in space, time, and form relationships, as well as a shift in expectations about information context and change—necessitate a change in the processes people use to develop information for the Web.

Perhaps in high school you learned a process for composing an essay using a three-part model—an introduction, a body, and a conclusion. Such a model, evolving through thousands of years of human experience with written texts, serves as an information development method that can still be effective today in many situations. While the relationship between web information and its user is different from that between printed text and its reader, composing webs can involve many of the principles gleaned from centuries of experience in shaping communication.

One field on which you can draw for ideas about web composition and design is the field of technical communication. Practices and methods of technical communication developed in the twentieth century as a result of increased industrialization and knowledge specialization. Today, the need for computer documentation, descriptions of technological innovations, and legal and environmental documentation fuel the need for many forms of technical communication.

One way you can view technical communication is as a set of processes involving information development. These processes occur within a problem domain and yield specific products, such as a finished report or document.

Figure 29.1 shows the processes, products, and techniques of a technical communication model.

FIGURE 29.1.

The technical communication process.

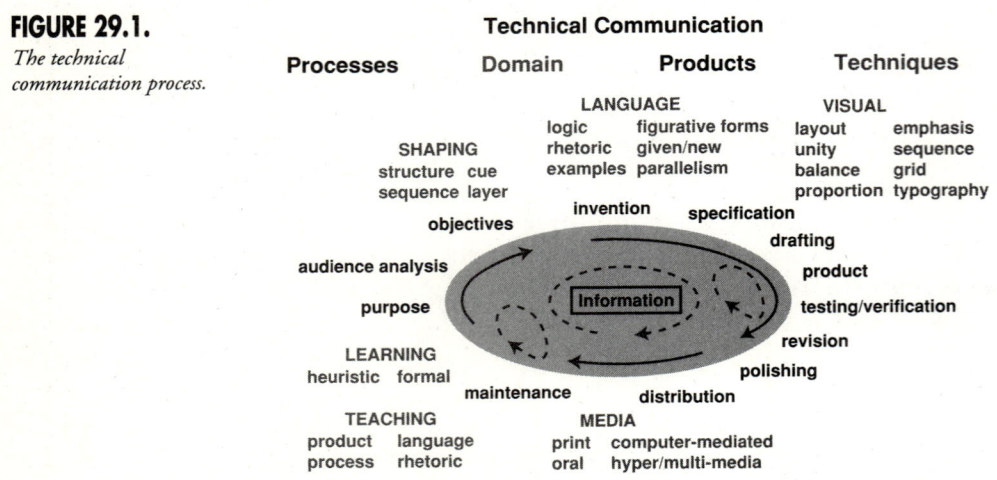

These processes operate within an information domain. For example, your information domain might be from the field of banking, or, more specifically, the information needed to operate an automated teller machine. In such a case, your challenge might be to accomplish a specific purpose, such as instructing customers how to use the machine to make a deposit, withdraw money, or check on an account balance. Based on this purpose, you can state information objectives such as the following:

- To inform the customers how to identify themselves and their account
- To present the deposit, withdrawal, and balance options, including variations and combinations such as savings, checking, and loan accounts
- To accept the customer's choices for interaction
- To give the customer feedback concerning the transaction process
- To conclude the transaction with the appropriate result—whether it is cash in the drawer, a balance slip printed, or some error condition

Based on the objectives for the automated teller machine information, you can then create a specification for how this information should take shape: Should you display the information on the screens of the machine? Should you provide a poster next to the machine with the information on it? Will you write a brochure explaining the machine that you will send to all customers? This specification answers these questions about the form and the medium of the information. This specification can get very detailed about the form of the information, including exact sizes, type fonts, and other details.

Continuing the automated teller machine example, consider how you might develop the information that will be displayed on the video screen of the machine. You need to develop a detailed statement of exactly what you want your information to accomplish. Once you get this exact statement, you'll move on to the phase of designing the information product (an individual screen display) itself. In this design process, you can weigh all your options for how the screens should look, and how the user will interact with them. These options include the screens' sequence, contents, wording, and appearance. Developing this information, you can draw on design principles such as layout, typography, and other considerations.

In the automated teller machine example, you eventually must create all the *products* of the information development process—the purpose statement, objectives, specification, and design. In creating these products, you'll employ a variety of processes. First, the purpose and objectives themselves were influenced by a thorough understanding of audience (the users of the machine). What do people care about when using an automated teller machine? Do they want to know the bank's reputation? the total cash on hand in its vaults? Common sense and knowledge of the audience help answer these questions. The act of coming up with a purpose statement requires some idea of audience and an understanding of what that audience wants to and needs to know.

The transition from having objectives defined and making specifications for information to achieve these objectives involves a process of invention, of coming up with creative ideas to accomplish a goal and solve a problem. For example, how can you let a user know that he or she has inserted the bank card into the machine backwards? How should you handle the user's request for how much money he or she wants from the account? These kinds of questions, derived from the objective statements, determine the information specifications. For example, your objective to accept the customer's choices for interaction (whether to make a deposit, a withdrawal, or to check on the account balance) might take on an additional specification, such as "to take the user's choice for interaction through a numeric keypad on the automated teller machine."

With the processes and products leading up to the specification of the automated teller machine information, you can now draft a final product. Since this example involves using a machine—rather than a brochure or paper report—your actual design must involve experts in the mechanics and operation of that machine. You must know how to encode the commands to achieve a particular effect or screen display and how to decode inputs from the user—the buttons the user pushes on the machine—into information the system can accept and use.

When your initial design is complete, obviously you want to test it—first, with some tests in your own lab, and then with tests by real customers in mock situations (some customers might wince at risking their own bank balances in an untested new system). Based on this testing, as well as verification that all your objectives have been met, you can polish the result, or even restart the process of audience analysis, invention, drafting, and design. When you have a final form for the automated teller machine that meets your objectives, you can distribute and then maintain the system.

How the Web Transforms the Information Development Process

The automated teller machine example in the preceding section has many characteristics similar to a development and design process that can be used to weave a web. The example emphasizes user interactivity, user interface design, and human-computer interaction issues. Is this same model of information development appropriate for weaving a web? Yes and no. The traditional technical communication process matches web weaving in the following ways:

■ A traditional information development process often recognizes the importance of understanding the user's needs, perceptions, abilities, and ways of interacting with the information.

- A traditional information development process employs an iterative, even cyclical, approach in which specific products are created by processes, employing techniques to shape information.

The traditional technical communication process does not match web weaving for the following reasons:

- The Web offers unique space and time possibilities.
- Web messages have a form and delivery largely determined by the user's equipment and options not under the total control of the information developer.
- Web information is often extremely dynamic and exists within a larger information and social context.

An Information Development Process for the Web

How can you create a development process for the Web, drawing from techniques of information development processes based largely on static mediated communication? This is not an easy question to answer. However, you can develop information for the Web by using an information development process that relies on your knowledge of the Web's unique characteristics while at the same time using a basic design and development process similar to that used by many technical communicators, writers, designers, and software developers.

This section previews a web-weaving methodology that serves as the basis for the next chapters in this part. These chapters cover the planning, analysis, design, implementation, and development processes for weaving a web. Although these processes might seem like an encumbering amount of work to go through, a well-designed web has a far greater value than one that is hastily put together, particularly if your web is for business or professional communication. For casual web developers, the methodology can still help, to illuminate possibilities for structuring information and techniques to improve the overall effectiveness of a web.

An Overview of a Web-Weaving Methodology

Figure 29.2 illustrates a methodology that can be used to develop webs. At first glance it seems similar to Figure 29.1 (which is a more traditional technical communication methodology). The web-weaving method contains many of the same elements, but web-weaving processes are more open-ended because the final product (an operating web) is often not as permanently fixed as traditional media.

FIGURE 29.2.
A web-weaving methodology.

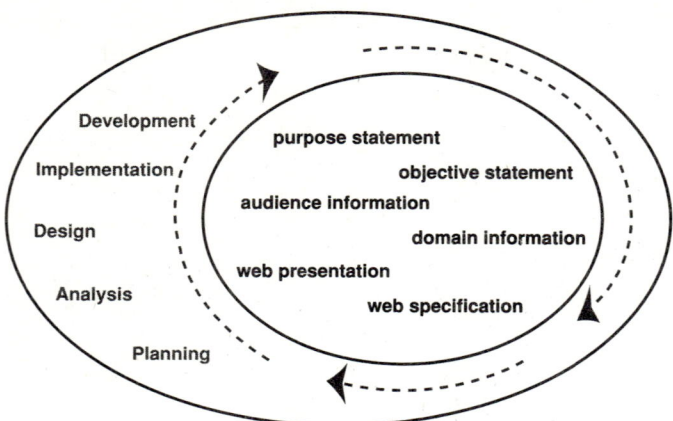

In the example, automatic teller machines were installed and occasional checks were made to make sure they were working correctly, but a web is often never completed (many webs offering a static set of information can often have large sections that remain stable, however). The traditional technical communication approach, although recognizing the need for review, revision, maintenance, and re-release of information products, eventually stops because of the encoded nature of the medium—etched in paper or even in the workings of an automated machine, the information becomes "set" and there is no further development. Web information exists in the constant flux of the global Web, is used by new users with new kinds of browsers, and often involves much user-developer interaction. Therefore, web weaving often requires that the processes performed on information elements are continuously done.

Moreover, web elements themselves are subtly changed from elements in a traditional communication process. While the traditional approach to technical communication saw audience analysis as a crucial part of shaping information, the web-weaving methodology recognizes audience information as an intrinsic element of the web itself. Information about an audience must be gathered, planned for, analyzed, designed, and implemented in the information presentation itself. In a web, audience information plays a crucial role in publicity and user feedback. Thus, all processes in web weaving depend on audience information.

These web elements and processes are interconnected, and decisions web weavers make rely on these interconnections. As such, there is redundancy in the methodology. If any one element or process is weak, another stronger element or process may be able to compensate. For example, a good implementation can sometimes make up for a bad design. A good objective statement can make up for a poor purpose statement. The goal is not to have these weaknesses, but to counter the inevitable problems that result.

The following chapters in this part go into the details of this web-weaving methodology. The following are the elements:

- **Audience information**—a store of knowledge about the target audience for the web as well as the actual audience who uses the information. This information includes the audience's background, interests, proclivities, and all detail helpful to shaping the information to suit the users' needs. All this information may not be complete at any time during the web-weaving process; only a store of information will develop over time. The audience information may be very useful and accurate at one time; it may then pass out of currency as different users start accessing the web.

- **Purpose statement**—an articulation of the reason for and scope of the web's existence. At all times during web development, a web weaver should have a succinct purpose statement for the web. This statement might be in general terms, such as "to create a presence for our company in cyberspace" or it may be very specific, such as "to provide information about our company's new line of modems." This purpose statement itself is dynamic—over time, an organization that started a web to "establish presence in cyberspace" may want to make that web serve another, more specific, purpose. A succinct statement of this purpose, at whatever level of generality, serves as a guidepost for the web-weaving processes.

- **Objective statement**—flows from the purpose statement and defines what specific goals the web should accomplish. For example, an objective statement based on the purpose used in the preceding paragraph—"to provide information about our company's new line of modems"—might include a statement of the modems the company offers and what kind of information should be given (pictures, prices, schematics, and so on). Like the audience information and purpose statements, the objective statement is dynamic, and it may become apparent later in web weaving to define still others. Therefore, the objective statement will change as the purpose of the web changes, but also as the information about the audience changes. For example, it may be that the audience looking at the modems might be suddenly very concerned about display buttons on the devices themselves. In that case, an objective might be created to include pictures of modems in the web itself.

- **Domain information**—a collection of knowledge about the subject domain the web covers, both in terms of information provided to users of the web and information the web weavers need. For example, a web offering modems for sale might also necessarily draw on a variety of information about the use, mechanics, principles, and specifications for modems. While not all this information would necessarily be made available to the users of the web, this domain knowledge may be essential for the web developers to have. Often, this domain knowledge makes a good complement to the information the web already offers. For example, a modem manufacturer with a good collection of modem facts might find that interested buyers visit that web for technical information about modems and, in the course of this visit, be informed of a company's products.

■ **Web specification**—as in the automated teller machine example, the specification statement describes, in detail, the elements that will go into a design. The specification statement lists what pieces of information will be presented as well as any limitations on the presentation. For example, one part of a specification might state that the picture of the modem must be placed on the same hypertext page as a link to an order form. The specification, as with all the other elements of the web, may be in constant flux.

■ **Web presentation**—the means by which the information is delivered to the user. The presentation is the result of design and implementation processes that build on the web specification. In these processes, creative choices are made among design and presentation techniques to achieve the web specification as well as considerations for efficiency, aesthetics, and known web usage patterns.

From this list of the elements involved in the web weaving methodology, you can see that there are many interactions and relationships among them. In fact, all of the elements depend on the best information being available about the other elements in order to be successful. For example, a web weaver needs to know if the objective is to sell modems or educate people about modems if he or she is designing a particular piece of a web. Similarly, the elements interact with the *processes* of the methodology.

The processes of the methodology are the following:

■ **Planning.** This is the process of choosing among competing opportunities for communication so that overall goals for the web can be set. These goals include anticipating and deciding on targets for the audience, purpose, and objectives for the information. Planning is also done for domain information through a process of defining and specifying the supporting information that must be collected, how it will be collected, and how the information will be updated. A web planner anticipates the skills called for by the web specification as well as the skills needed for constructing particular parts of a web. For example, if a specification for a design calls for using a forms (a feature supported by HTML) interface, the web planner needs to identify the need for web implementors to have these skills. The web planner also anticipates other resources needed to support the operation and development of the web. For example, if user access statistics will be gathered, the plan for the web must account for the need to procure and install a web statistics program.

- **Analysis.** This is a process of gathering and comparing information about the web and its operation in order to improve the web's overall quality. An important operation is one in which a web analyst examines information gathered about the audience for its relevance to some other elements or processes in web weaving. For example, information about the audience's level of technical interest can have a great deal of impact on what information should be provided to a user about a particular product or topic. Similarly, analyzing the web's purpose in light of other new developments, such as the contents of a competitor's web, must be an ongoing process. An analyst weighs alternatives and gathers information to help with a decision in the other processes of planning, design, implementation, or development.

- **Design.** In this process, a web designer builds on the web's specification and makes decisions about how a web's actual components should be constructed. This process involves taking into account the web's purpose, audience, objective, domain information, and specifications. A good designer knows how to achieve the effects called for by the specification in the most flexible, efficient, and elegant way. However, because it relies so heavily on the other processes and elements in web weaving, the design process is not more "important" than any of the others, but it requires a thorough grounding in implementation possibilities as well as knowledge about how particular web structures affect an audience.

- **Implementation.** This is the process of actually building the web itself, using hypertext markup language (HTML) (or improvements on it). The implementation process is perhaps most like software development because it involves using a specific syntax for encoding web structures using a formal language in computer files. Although there are automated tools to help with the construction of HTML documents, a thorough grounding in HTML as well as an awareness of how designs can best be implemented in HTML enriches the web implementor's expertise. (See Chapter 35, "HTML Editors and Filters," for more information.)

- **Development.** This is the process of making sure that the other processes continue and that the web itself is being presented well to the World Wide Web. The web development process involves directing the analysis of audience information, usability, and use patterns; publicizing the web's availability and purpose; monitoring usage; and making sure that the planning and design processes continue for new conditions and information.

While this methodology for weaving a web won't work flawlessly in all situations, it can serve as a basis for looking at the issues of web weaving. You may find that the actual processes and elements you use are some variation on these. Being aware of what elements and processes are involved in web development is key: Once you are aware of what you might face, you can most flexibly grow a successful web.

Weaver's Check

When you weave a web, you are making paths through the tangle of links that make up the Web. Unlike the linear paths that paper books present to readers, hypertext paths in a web give the user a different experience of space and time constraints, form and delivery methods, context, and information flux, than do traditional forms of mediated communication. The key in weaving a web is to meet the user's needs.

A web-weaving methodology, like traditional communication or composition methodologies, employs a set of elements and processes for creating and shaping information. Web weaving involves processes of planning, analysis, design, implementation, and development, as well as elements including audience information, purpose and objective statements, domain information, web specification, and web presentation. A web-weaving methodology uncouples the processes from the communication elements more than in a traditional process. The Web-weaving methodology described here results in a final product—an operating web—that can be considered to have a life cycle with periods of change and growth rather than a final static form.

The next chapters explore each of the processes of web weaving described in this chapter.

Planning a Web

30

by John December

Frequently great things can be done without a plan. Sometimes, well-planned things meet with dismal failure. Often, well-planned projects are successful. Although planning a web is not required, a well-planned web can help web weavers meet their goals and improve the quality of the information they provide.

The previous chapter described the differences between Web information and traditional forms. These differences make planning an important part of web weaving.

This chapter first looks at what you can and cannot plan for when weaving a web. Then it looks in detail at how to plan for the six key elements of web weaving: audience information, purpose statement, objective statement, domain information, web specification, and web presentation. As you will see in this chapter, this process of planning a web is incremental (moves in small steps) and is cyclical (moves in cycles).

What You Cannot Control

In weaving a web and making it available to the public to freely browse, there are a range of factors over which you have no control. The first step of the planning process is to recognize these factors and consider how they will affect your particular web. The factors over which you have no control include user behavior, browser display, links into your web, and what's behind the links out of your web.

User Behavior

You cannot control how the user is going to access and use your information. You might assume that the user will enter your web at its "front" or "top" page, but it is possible to link into your web at any arbitrary point given its URL. While your intent may be to guide your user down a series of pages in your web, as shown in the left picture of Figure 30.1 (the wine bottle model), users can actually enter your web at any arbitrary link (the pin cushion model in the right side of Figure 30.1).

FIGURE 30.1.

A user can enter your web at an arbitrary point.

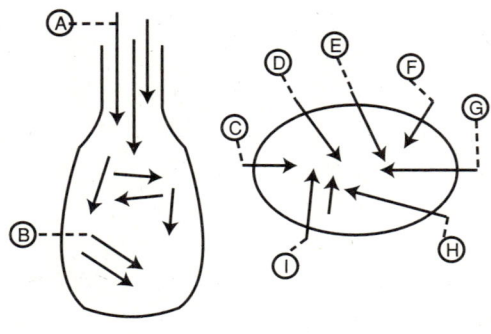

Wine Bottle   Pin Cushion

This means that you must take this arbitrary linking to your web into account during planning as well as in the other processes of weaving: analysis, design, implementation, and development (as described in detail in later chapters). During the planning stage, it is possible to *intend* to build a web with a different entry pattern than the pin cushion model. In fact, it is often possible to shape general user behavior toward a wine bottle model by using the right navigational cues, web publicity (publicity is the process by which you make your web and its features known), and other design features. At the planning stage, it is important to identify what model of user behavior you are aiming for and state it explicitly. While you can't control user behavior, an explicit statement of how you would like a user to access your web serves as a guide in later processes and elements in web weaving.

Just as you can't control a user's entry point into your web, you cannot shape the user's path through it. While navigational cues and the links you make available will guide the user on a likely path through your web, the planning process of web weaving cannot make explicit assumptions about what this entry point is or how the user will traverse the information.

It is important to note that not being able to control a user's entry point or path through your web is not necessarily an undesirable feature. In fact, many would say that this is precisely the power and benefit of hypertext—the user can follow links based on his or her interest or thought process.

The User's Browser and Display

As described in Part II, "Web Browsers and Connections," there are a wide variety of browsers available to view the Web. In planning a web, you must recognize that you might not know what kind of browsers your users will have. Moreover, new browsers are in development, and future browsers are certain to provide more and different features than the ones presently available.

Therefore, different users, based on their browser's operation, will experience your web differently—from an ASCII display of your web (in Chapter 14, "Web Structure and Spaces") to a hypermedia experience with Mosaic (Figure 14.3). Therefore, in planning for your web, you need to think about what kinds of information will be essential. For example, if you place important or essential information in a graphics file, not all browsers will support that display, and the information will be lost to some users.

Just as you might not know what browser the users of your web will have, you can't control exactly how information is displayed in a browser. This is a very big change from traditional desktop publishing, in which every aspect of font style and size, alignment, and other layout features can be carefully controlled. In fact, such control and fine-tuning has been a big part of a desktop publisher's job for a long time.

However, the hypertext markup language (HTML) works on a completely different philosophy for presenting information. HTML is a *markup* language, which means that the *structure* of a document is marked with tags. For example, an ordered list starts with the tag <OL>; each item in the list is preceded by <LI>, and the list ends with </OL>. Thus, the *meaning* of the text is marked within the HTML document, rather than the appearance.

Some say that this separation of content from display frees up the writer to concentrate more on producing good content than worrying about how it looks (HTML is thus said to be a presentation-independent language). This same feature disappoints others, however, who are fond of presentation-dependent tools such as WYSIWYG (what you see is what you get) word processors.

HTML in covered in more detail in Chapter 33, "Implementing a Web: Basic Hypertext Markup Language (HTML)," and Chapter 34, "Advanced HTML Features." For the planning process, you must recognize that the tags in an HTML document define the structures of a document but do not define how these structures are displayed. For example, in some browsers, the ordered list is normally displayed with Arabic numerals, starting from 1, in a vertical list slightly indented from the previous list. However, a browser could be designed that reads the same HTML file and displays the same ordered list with Roman numerals and the list items arranged in a block paragraph form.

In fact, there is no reason why future browsers may not have preferences whereby the user can control how ordered lists are displayed. Moreover, font style and size, while controlled to some degree by HTML tags that suggest different levels of headings, are ultimately under control of the browser. In the Mosaic browser (Chapter 15, "Browser Operations"), the user can alter the appearance of text by choosing from four different fonts in three different sizes each. In other browsers, such choices are not possible.

Links Into and Out of Your Web

In the course of weaving a web, you may make many links to other resources on the network that you don't control. In so doing, realize that resources often move, making the link no longer valid (the link is then said to be *stale*). A user following a stale link from your document will encounter an error message and not get the information you had originally intended for him or her to access, thus degrading the experience of the user in your web.

Realize that you can't control this. Even if a link isn't stale, an error message might result when a remote computer host is down temporarily. Users should realize that this is an unavoidable aspect of web navigation (Part III, "Web Navigation Tools and Techniques"). While you may have relied for a long time on a particularly beneficial resource to be available to your web's users, that resource may eventually go away, leaving a stale link and information missing from your web.

Not only can a link you create from your web to an outside resource go stale, but it can also change in unexpected ways. This can be particularly troubling when you are linking to resources created by people for very informal reasons (for example, a school project or a hobbyist's project).

For example, you may have linked to a very nice photograph of a train at a remote site, a photograph key to your web's information content. The hobbyist who made that photograph available, unless by an agreement with you, is under no obligation to forever offer a picture of a train through that link. It may be that the hobbyist changes the image at that link every month. Next month, your users retrieve a photograph of a tree. This example helps you see how link maintenance and coordination is an important part of web weaving, and that the planning process involves recognizing that remote resources might not always be stable or readily accessible.

Just as you can't control what resources exist at the links out of your web, you cannot control the links into your web. When publicly available, any link in your web—any URL that resolves to an HTML page that you provide—can be used in any other work on the Web. (You can make a statement explicitly forbidding these links, but this kind of restriction is rarely done on the Web and itself may be considered a breach of "community tradition.")

Someone linking to your web could misrepresent its purpose or content, perhaps unintentionally. For example, while your web might be "The XYZ Company's Modem Products," someone at a remote site might identify your link as a "instructions for hooking up to a computer bulletin board." You can track down references to your web by using a Web spider (Chapter 19, "Spiders and Indexes: Keyword-Oriented Searching"), and you will often be able to correspond with anyone who may have misinterpreted the meaning or purpose of your web; you can't, however, control all links into your web.

While this benign case of a misunderstanding of your web's purpose may be something you can easily fix, it is not clear if you will be able to suppress or stop malicious references or links to your web. The legal issues involved are not worked out.

For example, you might run across someone who describes your modem products web as "the lamest modems made" or even maliciously spreads your web's URL among large groups of people, with instructions to "click on this link until the server crashes." The latter case is a bit more clear-cut—there are explicit rules of conduct that most users, at least at institutional sites, must follow, and these often include rules against intentionally damaging any equipment. Moreover, the commonly held set of traditions on the Net itself would definitely prohibit maliciously crashing a server.

However, another view is that the user who makes the comment "the lamest modems made" about your web may be simply exercising his or her freedom of speech, and there might be nothing you can do about it. In actual practice, you'll find that links into your web will be made in good faith, and you will be able to clear up any misinterpretations of your web's purpose.

What You Can Control: Planning

Now that you've surveyed some of the major factors that you cannot control in web weaving, it's time to look in more detail at the specific elements that your plan should cover.

The purpose of planning is to choose among competing opportunities, options, and choices. Specifically, you need to plan particular aspects of each of the web-weaving elements: audience information, purpose statement, objective statement, domain information, web specification, and web presentation. This chapter goes into detail about how planning works for each of these elements.

Audience Information

Part IV, "Exploring the Web," presents a large number of ways the Web can be used in many contexts. The applications in Part IV along with navigation skills in Part III can help you consider what you want to do in your web. Creating effective communication, particularly mediated communication, requires that you plan what you want to communicate to whom. Information about the target audience for your information is crucial for creating successful communication. In fact, many would consider information about your audience to be your most precious resource.

Knowing your audience is important because it, like the purpose statement, helps shape the whole information content of your web as well as its "look and feel." If you do not have a specific audience in mind for your web, a specific audience will use your web, and their experience of it may be positive or negative as a direct result of the choices you make about the way you present your web. A web influenced by accurate information about its intended and actual audience should have a higher probability of successfully communicating its intended message and information.

Excellent planning for audience information involves two steps: defining your audience and then defining the information that it is important to know about that audience:

1. Define your target audience. In a simple statement, describe the audience you want to reach with the information in your web. For example, you may want to reach "scholars who are interested in geology." Although this statement is simple, it serves as a valuable guide for developing many of the other elements in web weaving. A plan to reach the audience "everyone interested in science" is a very broad one. Although a web might be successfully created which reaches this audience, it may be an unrealistic audience planned for a new web.

One technique for helping you define your audience is to generate a cluster diagram. Draw a diagram such as the one shown in Figure 30.2, in which you show overlapping circles representing different audiences that you might target, as well as their relationships. For example, you might be interested in reaching just professors at universities who are geologists, or any scholar (someone seriously pursuing the academic study of a subject at a high level).

FIGURE 30.2.

A cluster diagram of an audience.

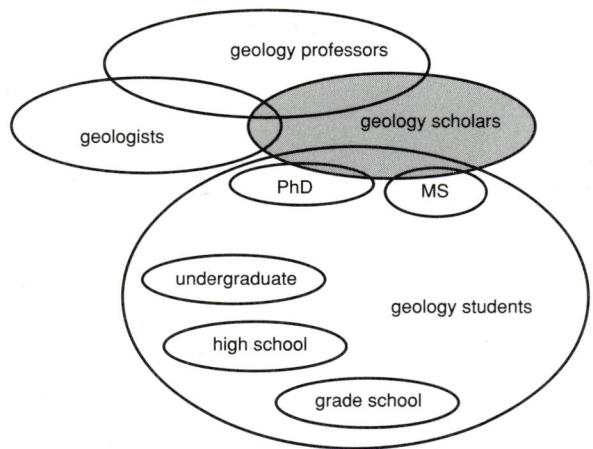

Draw ovals to represent the audiences and their relationships (such as overlapping or inclusion). Also show related audiences—even if you might not want to reach them—as a way of explicitly defining who you might *not* want to reach. For example, Figure 30.2 shows a large oval for students. You might not plan to reach grade school and high school students, but you might include them in your diagram in order to show their relationship to members of your target audience. For example, many scholars may teach younger students. As such, some of your target audience (geology scholars) may have in interest in gathering and developing material for younger audiences or issues involved in teaching.

Continue this clustering process until you've zeroed in on what you can say is the specific audience you want. Maybe you'll decide after looking at this diagram that you want to target only professional geologists who are also geology professors. Thus, the cluster diagram helps you more carefully define your target audience. Note that you can target multiple and overlapping audiences, not just a single group.

2. Define information you will need to know about the audience. Based on your audience description, what information about them would be useful? For example, if you plan to reach scientists interested in geology, what characteristics of these scientists are important to you? Educational level? Area of specialization?

Personal characteristics such as age, height, and weight? For some purposes and some audiences, different information will be important. For example, weight and height information might be important if you are trying to sell the scientists clothing or equipment for their research that depends on their body characteristics. Otherwise, such information might be totally irrelevant. The key is to identify the *relevant* information about your audience in the planning stage. In later stages, you'll use this list as a basis for gathering information and analysis.

Since the planning process itself is incremental and continuous, you might find that you don't know exactly what information about your audience will be important later on. You can use the cluster diagram you made to generate characteristics of that audience. With your target audience shaded to help you focus on it, generate lists of your audience's characteristics, concerns, and activities. (Figure 30.2 shades the geology scholars audience.) Write down this list as quickly as you can, including entries without judgment about the relevance of that entry.

Here's an example:

Geology scholars—characteristics:

> *highly educated*
> *interested in earth processes*
> *skilled in critical thinking*
>
> *…*

Geology scholars—concerns:

> *funding for projects*
> *publishing findings*
> *getting the right equipment*
> *teaching*
> *valid research methodologies*
> *locating related publications*
>
> *…*

Geology scholars—activities:

> *attending conventions*
> *conducting research*
> *communicating with the public*
> *teaching*
> *gathering samples*
> *serving in industry roles*
>
> *…*

Continue these lists until you've included just about everything you can think of that relates to your audience's characteristics, concerns, and activities. Some items may naturally fall into several categories; notice that "teaching" showed up both as a concern and an activity.

The next section shows how planning for your purpose helps you select the audience information you intend to gather and maintain. After defining your purpose, you can return to these lists and choose which of these items is relevant or important for the purpose you've defined. The set of characteristics you select as important will serve as the database of audience information you are concerned about collecting and maintaining.

Purpose

The statement of purpose serves as the driving force throughout web weaving. The purpose helps you choose what information about your audience you must gather and maintain, and it influences the form of your web's presentation. Not having a succinct purpose statement for why the web is operating in the first place makes it very hard for web designers to choose among techniques to present information. Without a statement of purpose, web analysts have no basis for evaluating if the web is operating effectively. Moreover, a web without a clear purpose often carries a cloudy message to the user—upon entering, the user will wonder What is this for? and have no clue as to an answer.

To define your purpose, you need to make a statement about what you want your web to do, which identifies the following elements:

- The subject area. What area of knowledge serves as the context for what your web conveys? This area of knowledge does not have to be a traditional Library of Congress subject classification (such as geology or biology). It might be "information about the odd-bearing division of XYZ Industries."

- The audience. Your purpose statement contains the audience identification within it. This audience identification is a part of the purpose statement because so much of the "What are we doing?" question about your web revolves around the specific audience you are trying to reach.

- The level of detail at which information is presented. Your purpose might be, for example, "to provide a comprehensive overview of geology for geology scholars" or it might be more specific, such as "to present basic reference material about geology for geology scholars." This level of detail influences how much domain information you will need to gather and maintain.

- The user's expected benefit or response. What will users of your web gain from it? The purpose statement might include the phrase "in order to keep current in the field of geology" or "in order to keep up with current developments" or some combination of these kinds of statements.

As you can see from this list, planning the purpose statement forces you to make many decisions about the message you want your web to convey. A well-formed purpose statement serves as a touchstone for all the other web-weaving processes and elements. Indeed, the purpose statement itself may play a very important role as one of the first pieces of information about your web that is presented to users.

Here are some actual purpose statements that contain many of the points in the previous list. Notice that the more complete the statement of purpose is, the easier it is for a user to answer the question "What is this for?"

- ■ "This information server (`ftp.arpa.mil`) provides selected information about the activities and programs of the Advanced Research Projects Agency (ARPA). It initially contains information provided by the Computing Systems Technology Office (CSTO) and associated information about the High Performance Computing and Communications Program. Additional capabilities will be added incrementally to provide additional information."

  —from the *ARPA home page,* URL `http://ftp.arpa.mil/`

- ■ "The purpose of this center is to serve the needs of researchers, students, teachers, and practitioners interested in computer-mediated communication (CMC). This center helps people share resources, make contacts, collaborate, and learn about developments and events."

  —from the *Computer-Mediated Communication Studies Center,*
  URL `http://www.rpi.edu/[126]decemj/cmc/center.html`

- ■ "This project is intended as a demonstration vehicle to show how information useful for teaching and learning about business telecommunications and data communications may be effectively shared over the Internet."

  —from the *Distributed ELectronic Telecommunications Archive (DELTA)*
  home page, URL `http://gozer.idbsu.edu/business/nethome.html`

- ■ "The purpose of this server is to provide access to a wide range of information from and about Japan, with the goal of creating deeper understanding about Japanese society, politics, industry, and, most importantly, the Japanese people."

  —from the *Center for Global Communications home page,*
  URL `http://www.glocom.ac.jp/index.html`

Objective Statement

Once you have planned for the purpose of the web, who the audience is, and what you need to know about the audience, you need to combine all this information to arrive at a specific statement of web objectives. As such, an objective statement is much more specific

and lengthy than a purpose statement. An objective statement makes clear the specific outcomes and information that will implement the stated purpose of the web. Thus, the objective statement expands on the general descriptions given in the purpose statement. However, an important difference exists: While the purpose statement stays the same, the objective statement may change as new information about the domain or audience becomes available.

A phrase in the purpose statement such as "to provide access to a wide range of information from and about Japan" (Center for Global Communications home page, URL `http://www.glocom.ac.jp/index.html`) could be implemented with a variety of specific objectives. The objectives could include showing Japanese cultural information, geographical and climate information, and selections of online Japanese publications. While the purpose statement says "here is what we are going to do," the objective statement says "here is the information that will do it."

Unlike the purpose statement, the objective statement need not necessarily be written on the web's home page. Instead, an objective statement is "behind the scenes" information that guides the development of other elements in web weaving.

For example, from the statement of purpose given for the Computer-Mediated Communication (CMC) Studies Center, the statement "help people share resources" can be used to generate a set of specific objectives as follows:

> *Purpose:* help people share resources
>
> *Objective:* provide a list of resources with links to the following:
> > major online collections of CMC-related material
> > bibliographies
> > academic and research centers related to CMC
> > online journals

Over time, this objective statement may change by expanding to include links to other kinds of forums for subjects related to CMC. Also, changes in the objective statement may require that features are removed from the web.

Planning the objective statements gives you a head-start on another web-weaving element: domain information.

Domain Information

Domain information refers to information and knowledge about the subject area of the web, including both online and offline sources of information. Domain information includes not only information that will be presented to users of the web, but it includes all information and knowledge the weavers of the web need to know in order to do a good job.

Therefore, the collection of domain information serves as an "information store" from which both the developers and users of the web will draw. It may be that the purpose of the web itself is to provide an interface to this information store; or it might be that this information store is only incidental to the purpose of the web and plays only a supporting role as background information for the developers. In either case, planning for domain information is essential. These are steps for planning for domain information:

1. Define what domain information is necessary for the weavers to know and what information will be provided to users. Are there specialized databases to which you must gain access? Is there an existing store of online material that will serve as a basis for user information? What kind of background in the discipline do weavers of the web have to appreciate and understand in order to effectively make choices about information content and organization? What other material might be needed, either by the users of the web or by the developers?

2. Plan for the acquisition of domain information. Once the information store is defined, how can it be obtained? For example, is there a large collection of information files easily accessible? Or is there a paper-based information source that the web developers should read or a course they should take before trying to build the web? For example, developers working in creating a web about geology should have some appreciation for the topics and subdivisions of the field in order to make judgments about how information should be presented.

3. Plan for updating and maintaining the information. It is not enough to define and acquire a database. If it is time-dependent information, when will it lose its usefulness? How will it be updated? Who will update the information? What will be the costs of this updating and maintenance?

The degree of attention paid to domain information acquisition and maintenance varies a great deal according to the purpose of the web itself. For example, a web that purports to be an interface to current satellite imagery of the earth's clouds must necessarily have constantly updated domain information. In contrast, a web for information about British literature might require updates as new knowledge is formed, but not on an hourly or minute-by-minute basis.

Web Specification

The web specification is a refinement of the objective statement in more specific terms, adding a layer of constraints or other requirements. These requirements may restrict or further describe in detail what the web will offer and how it will be presented.

The web specification, for example, takes the objective statement "to provide links to bibliographies in the field" and makes it specific—with a list of the URLs that will be provided. The specification statement can also characterize limitations on the information and its presentation, such as "no more than 10 bibliographies will be listed on the resources page; if more are required, a separate bibliographies page will be made."

The specification, however, doesn't dictate how the web should look (this is the goal of the web design process). Rather, the specification acts as a guidebook for the designers and implementors who will create the actual files of the web itself. The specification should completely identify all resources (for example, links; web components such as forms or graphical image maps; other resources such as sound, image, movie, or text files) that should (or can) be used in the web.

Similar to how the objective statement can change while accomplishing the same purpose, the specification statement can change while accomplishing the same objective. (For example, the URL to a resource required by an objective statement might change.)

The major issue in planning for the specification is to make sure that the people developing the web have the tools, training, and time necessary to weave the web according to specifications. For example, one part of the specification could state that a customer can order a product by using the Forms feature of HTML. In such a case, the planning process must identify the ability to build these forms as a skill web implementors must have.

The web specification can also *exclude* specific items. For example, the specification may state that the Forms feature of HTML is *not* to be used (because many browsers do not support Forms) or that no graphics are to be used. Thus, the specification acts as a list of "building blocks" and "tolerance limits" that can satisfy the objective statement for the web.

Web Presentation

Although the audience definition, purpose and objective statements, and domain information are most closely associated with the planning process of weaving a web, the development of a web's presentation must also be planned.

The web's presentation is the whole "look and feel" of the web, along with its actual implementation. Web designers planning for the web's presentation rely heavily on the web specification statement as a basis for making choices.

Planning for web presentation involves verifying that resources are and will be available to support the files on the server that comprise the Web. Therefore, the person planning for the web's presentation must work closely with the web server administrator (sometimes called the *webmaster*) whose duties include allocating space or setting any special file or directory permissions so that the web presentation can be implemented.

Web planners also anticipate needs for the web's presentation by doing the following:

- Generating a set of possibilities for web presentation based on current or possible specifications. These possibilities might include sample HTML pages or, if the specifications allow, graphical image maps or forms to help the user interact with the information

- Planning the work schedule necessary to implement the web according to specifications, including how much time it will take to implement and test web pages, verify links, and implement changes based on new specifications

- Creating and maintaining a pool of generic web components (for example, common web page layouts or Forms to serve as templates for web implementation)

- Creating a mockup of the web based on an initial specification. This mockup could be quickly created from generic web components and offer a rapid prototype to be used in the other web weaving processes

While the web implementors working on the web's presentation are the ones to actually write HTML files, the implementors aren't the "author" of the web itself. As you can see from this chapter and Chapter 29, there are many processes involved in weaving a web. Whether it is one individual involved or a whole team, all weavers take part in creating an effective web.

Weaver's Check

It may seem like a lot of work, and you might rather just dive into writing HTML before planning, but taking the time to plan a web can raise the probability of a web's success. Thinking about and anticipating issues of audience, purpose, objective, domain information, specification, and presentation can lead to the creation of a web that best conveys an intended message and may save time and energy in the long run.

A web weaver cannot control many factors of a web: user behavior, the user's browser and display, and links into or out of the web. A web weaver can make efforts to ensure that web-weaving processes work together continuously and involve each of the six elements of a web (audience information, purpose statement, objective statement, domain information, web specification, and web presentation). During the planning process, a web planner must pay attention to the following:

- Defining the web's intended audience and important characteristics about the audience

- Formulating a purpose statement that identifies the web's subject area, intended audience, level of detail, and expected user benefits or response

■ Making an objective statement that specifically tells *how* the web's purpose will be accomplished by enumerating the resources and information

■ Defining the web's specification—a complete enumeration of the specific resources that will accomplish the objectives and any restrictions or special circumstances, including identification of special skills, tools, or resources needed by the web developers

■ Identifying the domain information necessary to support the information the web serves to the users as well as to support developers, including planning for acquiring and updating this information

■ Planning for the web's presentation by verifying that a Web server is available that has enough space for the expected web size, planning the time table for implementation and the resources needed, anticipating needs by developing or acquiring a generic set of web components, and making a mockup of the web based on the specification

■ The planning process may never stop. The intended audience for the web, its stated purpose, objective, domain information, specification, and presentation could change, thus requiring a revisit to all of the web's elements affected by the planning process.

A well-done planning process can keep a web fine-tuned and always ready for growth, change, and improvement. The next chapters look at the roles of other processes involved in web weaving and how they build on the work done in planning to continuously improve the web.

Plan Worksheet

TARGET AUDIENCE

1. Definition

    One-sentence statement:

    More complex description:

    Cluster diagram:

2. Information about audience

    Characteristics:

    Concerns:

    Key concerns based on purpose definition (below):

PURPOSE

1. Subject area:
2. Audience (defined previously):
3. Level of detail:
4. User's expected benefit/response:
5. Succinct purpose statement:

OBJECTIVE STATEMENT

1. Specific goals to accomplish the purpose:
2. Restrictions:

DOMAIN INFORMATION

1. Information necessary:
   a. Web team:
   b. Information served:
2. Acquiring information:
3. Updates and maintenance:

SPECIFICATION

1. Limitations on information:
2. Limitations on media:
3. Resources (for example URLs; web components such as forms or graphical image maps; other resources such as sound, image, movie, or text files) that should and can be used in the web's design:

PRESENTATION

1. Look and feel possibilities:
2. Work schedule:
3. Skills required:
4. Components:
5. Mockup web:

Analyzing a Web

31

by John December

Whether your web is already operating or you have just planned it, you might ask your-self: "Is the web accomplishing (or will it accomplish) the planned objectives?" You can answer this question through a process of analysis, in which you gather information about your web's elements (audience information, purpose and objective statements, domain information, web specification, and web presentation) and compare it with information about how users have used or will use your web. The analysis process also involves gathering information about other webs that may be accomplishing a similar purpose or reaching a similar audience. When done in conjunction with the other people involved in the other web weaving process, analysis serves as a check of the web's overall quality and effectiveness. Web analysis seeks to uncover the answers to the following questions:

Is the web accomplishing its stated purpose and meeting its planned objectives?

Is the web operating efficiently?

Are the intended benefits/outcomes being produced?

While a definitive answer to these questions might be impossible to obtain at all times, web analysis can serve as a check on the other weaving processes. This chapter looks at how you can go through web analysis at any time during your web's development. This analysis process involves gathering information and comparing it to feedback from users, server statistics, and information about your web's elements.

Analyze the Web's Elements

Figure 31.1 shows an overview of information useful in analysis. In the figure, the web's elements are in rectangles, and supporting or derived information is in ovals. Key checkpoints for analysis are shown in dashed circles, labeled A through E. At each checkpoint, the web analyst compares information about the elements or information derived from the web elements to see if the web is working or will work effectively.

The information about the web elements and derived information will vary in completeness depending on how far you are into actually implementing the web. You can obtain information about the web elements from the results of the planning, design, implementation, or development processes. If you've just started the planning process, you can analyze the checkpoints for which you have information. You can obtain the derived information through examining web statistics. Ideally, you'll be able to observe representatives from your intended audience as they use your web. If you don't have a working web ready, these audience representatives may give feedback on a mockup of your web, its purpose statement, or a diagram of its preliminary design.

The key to the analysis process is that it is meant to check the overall integrity of your web. Results from the analysis process are used in other processes to improve the web's performance. For example, if analysis of the web's domain information shows that it is often out of date, the planning process would need to be changed to decrease the time between updating the domain information. The analysis process on the web's elements helps all processes of web weaving work correctly and efficiently. The following sections go through each of the analysis checkpoints shown in Figure 31.1.

FIGURE 31.1.

The Web's elements must work together to meet objectives.

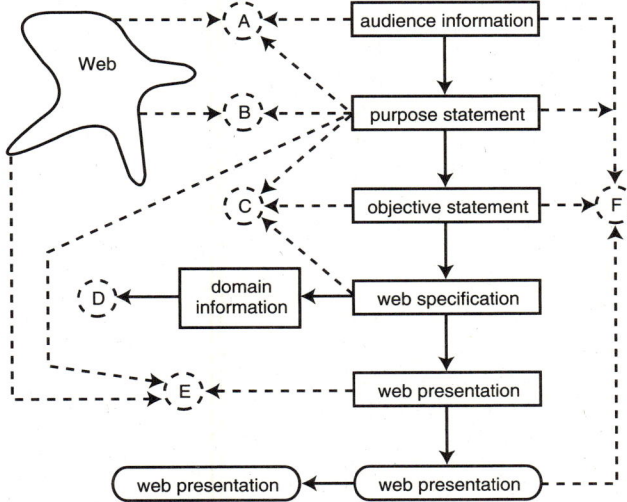

Does the Audience Exist on the Web for the Given Purpose? (Checkpoint A)

Before spending too much time in the planning process defining and describing a target audience, you should check first to see that this audience could make use of your web at all. While the interests of all the people who use the World Wide Web is growing increasingly diverse, a routine check of the Web's demographics or contents may tell you something about the size of the audience you want to reach.

Up-to-date, accurate demographics of Web users are difficult to obtain (mainly because getting this information is a complicated task). Moreover, even an up-to-date demographic profile of *current* users may not say anything about the massive number of people who are beginning to use the Web. Therefore, comparing a description of your target audience with any demographic statistics should be done with caution, and only gives you a "rough feel" about whether the audience you seek is out there. The Graphics, Visualization, and Usability Center at Georgia Tech (URL `http://www.gatech.edu/pitkow/survey/`) has compiled a good collection of demographic statistics.

Without demographic statistics, the other way to see if your audience is on the Web (or the Net) is to check for subject-oriented information resources and forums that are interest items of your audience. (Chapter 18, "Trees: Subject-Oriented Searching," details how to locate subject-oriented resources.) For example, if your target audience is geologists, what online information already exists that shows geologists as active on the Web and the Net? You can do the following to find out:

- Search subject-oriented trees for resource collections related to geology.
- Locate institutions—academic, commercial, or research—that are involved with geology.
- Check Usenet newsgroups and FAQ archives to see what geologists are active on the Net.
- Check to see if there is an online mailing list devoted to geology.
- Check to see if professional societies or publications in the field of geology offer an online forum or information service.

You can interpret the results of your check of demographic statistics or Net resources related to your subject in two ways. First, if you find nothing, it might mean that your audience has made no forays into the Net—no newsgroups, no mailing lists, no online collections of resources at major institutions. Based on this, you could decide that your web would therefore fill a great need for this audience. In contrast, you might conclude that this particular audience is not interested in online communication at all. To decide which of these two alternatives is more accurate, you should consult representative audience members. Check with people you know in the field, and ask them, "What if you had an online system for information and communication?" Because online electronic mail discussion lists have been around longer than many network communication forums, an online mailing list that your target audience uses can be a good source of information about that audience's interests.

Another aspect of this analysis of audience information is to make sure that the purpose for your web is one that meets the audience's patterns of communication, or at least patterns that they are willing to engage in.

For example, you may find that certain audiences are not willing to have a publicly available forum for discussion and information because of the nature of their subject matter. For example, computer security systems administrators might not want to make detailed knowledge of their security techniques or discussions publicly available on a web server.

Certainly, private businesses or people involved in proprietary information may not want to support a web server to share everything they know. However, it may be that these same people would be interested in sharing information for other purposes. For example, computer security administrators might want to support a site that gives users advice about how to increase data security on computer systems. Thus, the web's purpose statement must match the audience's (or information providers) preferred restrictions on the information. Current technology can support password protection or restricted access to Web information, so that specific needs for access can be met.

Through a check of the audience, purpose, and communication patterns for that audience, you can quickly detect logical problems that might make a web's success impossible.

For example, if your web's purpose is to teach new users about the Web, you might have a problem if your audience definition includes only new users. How can new users access your web in the first place? In this case, it may be that you should redefine your audience to include web trainers as well as the new users they are helping. This more accurate audience statement reflects the dual purpose of such a training web—getting the attention, approval, understanding, and cooperation of trainers as well as meeting the needs of the new users. By having an accurate audience statement, all the other processes in web weaving, such as design and development, can work more efficiently because they take the right audience into account.

Is the Purpose Already Accomplished Elsewhere on the Web? (Checkpoint B)

Just as you don't want to reach an audience that doesn't exist, or target an audience for a purpose they don't want to achieve, you don't want to duplicate what is being done successfully by another web. Checkpoint B is the "web literature search" part of the analysis: "Is some other web doing the same thing as what you want to do?" "What webs out there are doing close to the same thing?" These questions should be asked at the start of web development as well as continuously during the web's use. New webs and information will be developed all the time, and someone else may develop a web to accomplish the same purpose for the same audience as yours.

To find out if someone has built a web for a specific audience and purpose, use the subject and keyword-oriented searching methods of Chapter 19, "Spiders and Indexes: Keyword-Oriented Searching." You might also try "surfing" for a web like yours or for information related to your audience and purpose. (See Chapter 21, "Surfing: Finding the New and Unusual.") During this process, save these links; if they are relevant to your audience and purpose, they become part of the domain information on which your own web's developers and users can draw.

The other benefit of this web literature search is that you can find webs that may be accomplishing the same purpose for a different audience. These webs may give you ideas about the kinds of information you want to provide for your audience. Also, you may find webs that reach the same audience but for a different purpose. These webs can give you useful background or cognate information that you could include as links in your own web. If you find a web that reaches the same audience for the same purpose you are considering, you can consider collaborating with the developers and further improve the information.

Do the Purpose, Objective, and Specification Work Together? (Checkpoint C)

One of the most important elements for the integrity of your web is the purpose, objective, and specification triad. These three elements spell out why your web exists and what it offers. The purpose statement, as you saw in the last chapter, serves as the major piece of information that your potential audience will read to determine if they should use your web. If the purpose statement is inaccurate, the audience might not use your web when they could have benefited from it, or they might try to use your web for a goal they will not be able to accomplish.

The check of the purpose-objective-specification triad is to make sure that something wasn't lost in the translation from the purpose (an overall statement of *why* the web exists) to the objective statement (a more specific statement of *what* the web will do) to the web specification (a *detailed enumeration* of the information in the web and constraints on its presentation).

It may be that during the development of the specifications, a piece of information was added that has no relation to the stated purpose. Or it might be that some aspects of the stated purpose are not reflected in the specification at all.

One way to do this check is to make a diagram that traces the links from the purpose statement to the objective statement to the specifications, both top-down and bottom-up. For example, Figure 31.2 shows how a purpose can be matched to specific objectives. Each objective gives rise to specifications for the web. From the bottom up, every specification should be traced to an objective and each objective to some aspect of the purpose.

The diagram shown in Figure 31.2 is incomplete in that the specifications would include a list of *all* URLs used in the web as well as a more complete specification of the database. Figure 31.2 shows just the categories for this specification information. When filled out completely, however, every URL and component of the specification should be traced back to an objective and each objective traced back to the purpose statement. If there is a mismatch, more planning must be done to re-state the purpose, objectives, or specification so that they all match.

FIGURE 31.2.

The Web's purpose, objectives, and specification must work together to accomplish the same aim.

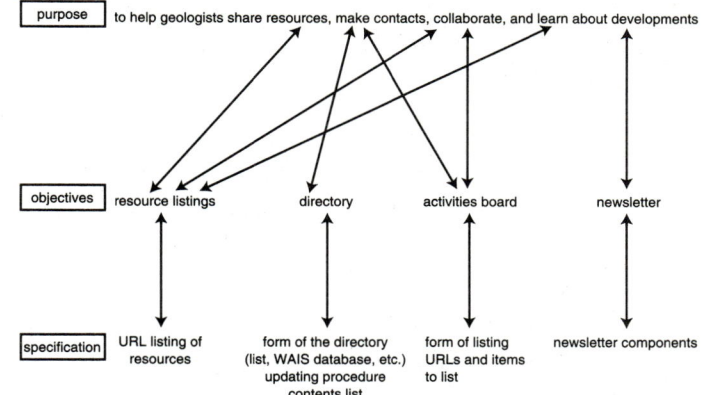

Is the Domain Information Accurate? (Checkpoint D)

The quality of the domain information you serve from your web and use in the web's development affects the users' perceptions of your web's overall quality. Inaccurate or incomplete information will hinder web developers as well as lead to dissatisfaction by your web's users. The domain information must be checked to make sure that it is accurate, updated, and complete. Periodic checks can be made according to the nature of the domain.

Recall from the definition given in Chapter 29 that there are two kinds of domain information: the information your web developers need to understand enough to plan, analyze, design, implement, and develop the web; and the domain information that your web provides to its users. Remember also that domain information of the first type need not be located on the Net at all—it may include textbooks or courses that the web developers use as a means of getting up to speed in the area of knowledge the web covers. This kind of domain information can also serve as reference information throughout the course of web weaving.

Verifying the accuracy, currency, and completeness of the domain information is a difficult task because you must have adequate knowledge of the subject matter to make a judgment about the veracity of all domain information. While the verification of off-Net resources such as books and courses can be evaluated according to the judgment the domain information analyst uses for similar offline materials, the Net information included in the first type of domain information and all the second type of domain information can be checked through a process of Net-access and retrieval.

The following is the process for checking Net-accessible domain information. For domain information provided to developers but not users of the web (the first type of domain information, which is Net-accessible), check the web page provided to developers in the same manner as described in the following list:

1. **Verify the freshness of links.**

   If the web is operational, use the links provided in the web itself to ensure that the links are not stale or the resource has not moved.

2. **Check the accuracy of the information.**

   If the web purports to respond with the correct solution to a problem given a set of inputs (for example, a physics problem answer through a Forms interface), have a set of conditions that lead to a known result. Test the web to verify that it yields the same answer, and vary the test cases you use.

   Use reliable and authoritative sources, where available, to verify the new information added in the web since the last analysis. If necessary, contact the developer of that information and discuss his or her opinions of the information's accuracy.

   In the case of databases, make sure that they are as current as they possibly can be. This is crucial, for example, if your web serves out time-dependent data such as earthquake reports. If you are not getting a direct feed from an information provider who supplies the most current information, check to make sure that the most current reports or data have been downloaded to the database that you use in your web.

3. **Check the completeness of the information.**

   Compare all specifications to items in the database. Are there any specifications calling for information that is currently missing?

   Check locations on the Net (using methods of navigation described in Part III) to locate more current or reliable domain information.

   Check locations on the Net to find other domain information that might be helpful as background to developers. Also look for information that could be part of the objective statement of the web.

4. **Check the appropriateness of the information.**

   Is the information at the right level of detail? Are the web weavers getting the right level of information for their work? Are the web's users given the right amount of information, or is there an "information overkill" or an oversimplicity in what is offered?

   Is any of the information not appropriate for serving or providing to your users or to the Web community at large? Is any of the information unethical, illegal, obscene, or otherwise inappropriate? Check links to outside information to verify that users will not encounter inappropriate material. Clearly, for outside sources of information, you will be limited in your ability to control inappropriate information. Include this check in your analysis process to make decisions about what outside links you want to use.

Is the Web Presentation Yielding Results Consistent with the Web's Design and Purpose? (Checkpoint E)

In this checkpoint, your goal is to determine if your web, based on server statistics or feedback from users, is being accessed consistently with how you want it to be used. One part of this consistency is to find out if the web server's access statistics show any unusual patterns. Your web server administrator should be able to provide you with a listing of your web's files and how many times they have been accessed over a given period of time. While this file access count is a simple measure of usage of your web, using it may reveal some interesting access patterns.

For example, a check of your web's files might show the following access pattern over the past 30 days:

File	Number of Accesses
top.html	10
about.html	9
overview.html	1000
resources.html	800
people.html	20
newsletter.html	8

This shows a fairly uneven distribution of accesses in which a single file is accessed many times (the 1000 shown here for overview.html). Compared to the small number of accesses to a "front door" (top.html) of your web, this pattern shows a problem unless this imbalance was intended. Also, the statistics show the newsletter isn't getting read very much, while the resources are being accessed quite a bit.

In order to interpret your web's access statistics, ask yourself these questions:

■ Does the overall pattern of accesses reflect the purpose of the web?

■ Does the pattern of access indicate a "balanced" presentation, or are some pages getting disproportionate access? Does this indicate design problems? (See the next chapter.)

■ If the web's "front door" page isn't getting very many accesses, this could indicate problems with the publicity about your web.

Another aspect of verifying your web's consistency of design and purpose is to see that it is listed and used in appropriate subject indexes related to the subject of your web. Do you find links to your web on home pages of people working in your field? Is the general reputation for your web good? You can find answers to these questions by doing web spider searches to find what pages on the web reference your pages. Check major subject trees to see if your web is represented in the appropriate categories. Much of this analysis of your web's "reputation" is useful in the development process. (See Chapter 37, "Developing a Web.")

Another aspect of your web's design efficiency is access time. Go through the pages on your web and time how long the retrieval takes. Pay particular attention to pages that are large or pages that contain many in-line figures. Consider how long it would take users at remote sites or with slow connections to download these pages. Your local access time may often be much shorter than for your audience, so that a long local access time required to download a page may indicate a still longer access time for the remote audience. Report this information to the designers and implementors.

Also, check your web using several different browsers. If your web has been viewed with Mosaic, try Lynx and see how it appears. You may discover that some HTML features have to be adjusted for use in an ASCII browser such as Lynx. Report problems with the display of the web in various browsers to the designers and implementors so that they can adjust the HTML used in the web.

Do the Audience Needs, Objective, and Results of Web Use Correspond to Each Other? (Checkpoint F)

It is very important that you determine whether your audience's needs are being met by your web. To do this, you must compare the audience information (your audience's needs and interests) with the objective statement and the intended and actual benefits and results from your web. Information about the actual benefits and results of your web's use will be the most difficult to come by. There are several methods, however, that may help you get a view of the effects of your web:

■ *Ask users.* Design and distribute a survey. This could be done using the Forms feature of HTML if you are willing to use features not found on all web browsers. You could distribute the survey by e-mail to a random sample of users (if such a sample can be constructed from either a listing of "registered" users or derived from web access logs). Include in this survey questions about user satisfaction. Are the users satisfied that the web meets their needs? What else would the users like to see in the web? How much do users feel they need each of the features your web offers?

■ *Survey the field.* Is your web used as a standard reference resource in your field of study? This is similar to the analysis performed at Checkpoint E, but rather than just focusing on the occurrence of links in indexes and other web pages, you need to analyze your web's reputation in the field of study or business as a whole. Do practitioners generally recommend your web as a good source of information?

■ *Are you accomplishing your purpose?* Are there outcomes occurring that you specifically stated in your purpose? For example, if one phrase of your purpose is to "foster research in the field," is there any evidence to support this? Is there research published that was sparked by the interactions your web fostered? If you have a commercial web, how many sales can you say the web generated? Determine some measure of your purpose's success and apply it during the analysis process.

Another way to look at Checkpoint F is to ask the broader question: Is the web doing some good? Even though your web may be under development and its objectives have still not truly been met, is there at least some redeeming value of your web? What benefits is it offering to your specific audience or even to the general public? For example, a commercial site that also provides some valuable domain information is performing a public service by providing education about that topic.

Another approach is to conduct research using theory and methods from the fields such as Computer-Mediated Communication, Computer-Supported Cooperative Work, Human-Computer Interaction or other disciplines that can shed light onto the dynamics of networked communication. These fields may yield theory that you can use to form testable hypotheses about how your web is working to meet users' needs, foster communication, or effectively convey information.

The key to Checkpoint F is to make sure that the other checkpoints—A through E—are working together to produce the desired results. You'll notice that Checkpoints A through E in Figure 31.1 each touch on groups of the web's elements. Only Checkpoint F spans the "big picture" questions: Are the *people who use your web* (audience information) getting *what they need* (purpose, objective, benefits/results) from it?

Weaver's Check

You can analyze your web to determine its communication effectiveness. This process of analysis involves gathering information about your web's elements and supporting information to make sure that your web does the following:

■ Attempts to reach an audience that has and will use Web access (Checkpoint A)

■ Contributes new information (accomplishes goals that haven't already been done) (Checkpoint B)

■ Is self-consistent (its purpose matches its objectives and specifications) (Checkpoint C)

■ Is correct (the domain information it presents is accurate, up-to-date, and complete) (Checkpoint D)

■ Is accessed in a balanced manner, both in terms of its own files and in terms of outside links into it (Checkpoint E)

■ Is accomplishing objectives that meet the needs of its intended audience (Checkpoint F)

Designing a Web

32

by John December

As a Web navigator, you've probably used webs that seemed to have *the right stuff*—information was at the right level of detail and the arrangement of pages and links guided you quickly to what you needed. While a positive web experience depends a great deal on your subjective preferences, a web designer can create a web look and feel that can increase the probability that most users will have a positive experience in a web. Because all users are different in their abilities and tastes, it is impossible to design a web that meets all user needs. Using the web weaving processes and elements, combined with an understanding of users' web experiences, a web weaver can create an effective design for a specific audience and purpose.

A web's design includes its "look and feel" and takes into account all the elements of web weaving—audience information, purpose and objective statements, domain information, and web specification—and combines these to produce a description of how the web can be implemented. Web implementors then use this design and the web specifications to create a working web.

A web designer makes many choices about how to best achieve the effects called for by the web specification. The web designer also draws on a repertoire of techniques for packaging, linking, and cueing information utilizing one or more design methodologies. Throughout this process, the web designer is sensitive to a user's experience of the web's information space, texture, and cues. There are very practical issues involved in designing—such as considerations for inline images and graphics, how much to put on a single page, and what should be linked and what should not. Over time, a web designer gains a sense of judgement and experience on which he or she draws—ultimately making web designing an art in itself.

The design process, however, is just one process in the interlocking web-weaving processes. A successful web requires that all process and all elements work together. Thus, we'll see in this chapter how designing a web draws on the elements that the other web-weaving processes have helped develop.

Figure 32.1 illustrates how the web design process takes information from all elements of web weaving and combines them to produce a "look and feel" design that is then used by the implementation process to create a working web. By separating the design from implementation process, information about the web's structure and operation can be cast in a hypertext language-independent form. That is, while the design process is influenced by knowledge of what is possible in the target design language, its product can be implemented in any language that can capture the features used in the design. In this way, this design process can be used with successors or alternatives to the widely used hypertext markup language (HTML).

FIGURE 32.1.
The web design process combines web elements.

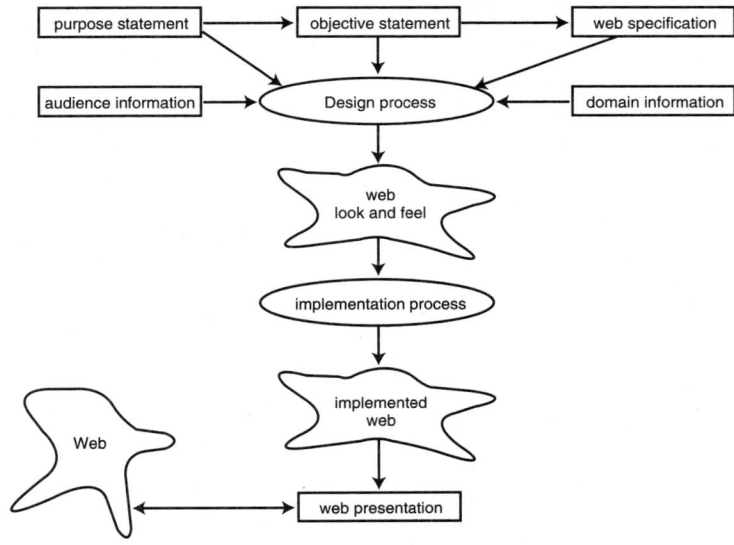

This chapter first reviews the experience of a web user, emphasizing many of the aspects of user experience described in Part III, "Web Navigation Tools and Techniques," but from a design perspective. This review is meant to highlight how this design process is essentially *user-centered*—that is, it draws on audience information and the designer's understanding of how people navigate in webs.

Following the review of user experiences of a web, some basic design methodologies are described—top/down, bottom/up, and incremental/in-time. These terms should be familiar to people who develop software, as they take their inspiration from software engineering. In web designing, there is not necessarily one methodology that should be followed throughout the web design or implementation process, particularly as the design process—like all the other processes of web weaving—can continue even after the web is deployed and used. Instead, the designer should be aware of the different design methodologies and be prepared to flexibly use any one of them at various times during the process of web design.

Aside from having a set of design methodologies to flexibly draw upon, the designer should also have a set of techniques for packaging, linking, and cueing information. The nature of hypermedia demands a strong attention to the user's experience of space, texture, and cues. The best way to manipulate the user's experience is by judiciously packaging the information in the right amounts on pages and in sections of pages, linking these pages to support the user's needs, and cueing the user to information and navigation aids.

Throughout this chapter, you'll see how the design process itself works with each of the elements of web weaving to produce a look and feel for the web. Because this chapter is more of a survey of design issues than a case study, we'll see this design process in a more sequential form in the hypothetical case study in Chapter 38, "Putting It All Together: A Case Study."

Principles and Goals

Throughout the design process, try to keep the following principles in mind:

1. Meet the user's needs. The web is not built for the personal taste of the designers, the convenience of the implementors, or the whims of the planners. Rather, the web serves the audience for which it is designed. Meeting the needs of the users is the first priority for the web.

2. Efficiently use resources. In designing and implementing a web, select features that meet the users needs with the least amount of space, access time, graphics, and long-term maintenance requirements. That is, aim for web features that are efficient to operate, elegant to use, and easy to maintain.

3. Create a consistent, pleasing, and efficient look and feel. The design of the web should aim to give the user an impression on all its pages that reflect a common organization and consistent visual cues. Each page of the web should cue the user to the web's identity and page purpose. The web's overall appearance should help the user accomplish their objectives through interfaces which strike a balance between simplicity and completeness, and aim for an aesthetically-pleasing appearance.

We'll now look more closely at specific issues a designer needs to consider in order to weave a web consistent with these principles.

User Experience

The idea of developing any product in a *user-centered* manner—that is, one in which the needs, interests, characteristics, abilities, knowledge, skills, and whims of the user are central in the whole process—may not seem like a radical idea. After all, a web is meant for users to find information and accomplish specific objectives. Not all web designers, however, are sensitive to the role of the user. In fact, because user information is often difficult to plan for and analyze (see Chapter 30, "Planning a Web," and Chapter 31, "Analyzing a Web"), it is often overlooked. Moreover, the idea of the user is not as simple as it may seem. Who is the user of your web? Your web planning process should have produced a good set of audience information—a definition of the audience and an enumeration of audience characteristics.

In moving to the design process, however, it helps a designer to be aware of the needs of any general web user. In Chapters 17 through 21, we saw how in navigation, a user needs to look at specific things when encountering a display in his or her browser window. The user asks, "What is this? What is it made of? What is it for? What can I do with it? How do I get what I want?" The user is not concerned with the fine points of web's design. Instead, the user is concerned with getting his or her job done correctly and efficiently. Therefore, this review of a user's general experience helps the designer become more aware of the perceptive qualities of web information—what I call information space, texture, and cues.

Information Space

The eager Web navigator clicks quickly on a link, looks over the display in the browser, and asks, "What is this?" One of the fundamental pieces of information that a Web navigator needs to know when encountering a new display on his or her browser is: What information space is this; have I entered a Gopher? An FTP site? A WAIS session? A Web server?

While this information is not necessarily crucial to the *semantic* or meaning of the web, the kind of information space you present to the navigator immediately establishes *user expectations* about how to navigate and even what kind of information might be found at that site. For example, a Gopher information space presents menus of information, each entry of which may be another menu, a link to a document, a link to a search, or a link to a telnet session. This information structure sets up user expectations about *navigation*. At the same time, through traditions and practices (that do change over time), a user gains expectations about what *kinds* of information Gophers often present. A user of a Gopher might expect to encounter tree-like information: subject catalogs and organizational or campus-wide information systems (although not exclusively, but these are very common applications of a Gopher).

Therefore, the web designer must make choices—within the web specifications—about what information spaces will be presented to the users and how these information spaces should be presented. Often, the web specifications require that an existing information system be used in the web, such as an FTP site that already contains most of the files of information to be presented to the user. It may even be that the web specifications call for integrating other spaces into the web, such as a Gopher server. The key for the designer is to contemplate the user's experience of these spaces individually and how they can be used in combination. Specifically, a web designer should consider the following:

1. **Difference in space interface**

   As shown in Chapter 16, "At the Edge of the Web," the appearance of the information spaces at the edge of the Web differ. The user who encounters an FTP site through a Web browser such as Mosaic has a different experience than seeing that same information through a web or a Gopher. As such, this difference can have a big impact on the look and feel of your web. A designer should examine the web specification and enumerate the different spaces it requires. It may be that none are specified, in which case the designer could make the choice to serve all information through the web. The designer should also, however, consider the needs of the users: Will someone need to access this same information through an FTP session? The answer to this question requires input from the planning and analysis processes, and, if FTP access is required, it should be stated in the web specification. A good designer, however, is aware of issues raised by the information spaces used in the web.

2. **Space overload**

   If web developers decide to include different types of information spaces in the web, such as several FTP sites and several Gophers, the designer needs to consider how this variety might be best integrated to create a consistent look and feel. The web designer might object if such a variety would lead to space overload or to too many information systems with disparate styles of interfaces in the web. The benefit of a browser like Mosaic is that, although the information spaces at the edge of the web are different, Mosaic provides consistent functionality in each (point and click mechanism, similar graphical representation). Combined with the uniformity the browser itself brings (displays all spaces in same typeface, uses same symbols where possible), a designer may judge that a number of different spaces in the web will still meet the users' needs. In other words, the final decision comes down to the characteristics of the users: Are they concerned with a uniform appearance? Do they have experience using an existing information space for the same purpose? For example, do they already use a Gopher or FTP space, or will a variety of information spaces detract from their experience of the web?

3. **Space transitions**

   If multiple information spaces are to be used in the web, consider how transitions between them are designed. A transition to an FTP space, if the users are not familiar with using one, might be a bit daunting. In an FTP space observed through a Web browser, the textual cues may be dramatically reduced. Consider what level of transition would be right for your users, ranging from none to a transition page that explains the use of the FTP, Gopher, or other information space.

4. **Web layers over spaces**

   As a designer, you may decide to put a web layer over an information space by preparing a web page that contains links into the information space. This allows greater flexibility for describing the information. The drawback is that implementation and maintenance of these web layers can be expensive. If there are only a few links, this may be a good way to link to the information space while retaining the expressive possibilities of the web.

Figure 32.2 illustrates how a web layer can be designed on top of an FTP space.

FIGURE 32.2.

A web layer over an FTP space.

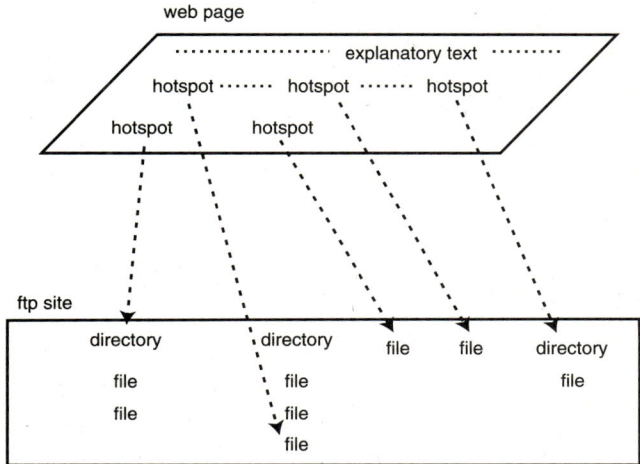

The figure shows how the links from the web page's hotspots can be made into the directories or specific files at the FTP site. The benefit of this layering is that you can include explanatory text, placing the meaning of the files at the FTP site within the context of the meaning of the information presented on the web page. Notice, though, how this linking requires a coordination of the web page with the structure of the FTP site, requiring more links than if just one link were made to the FTP site. This requires an increase in implementation time as well as maintenance.

Information Texture

Just as web users gain a great deal of cues from the kind of information space they are in, they must pay attention to the information's *texture*. In this section, I'll first define three aspects of information texture and then discuss specific strategies the designer can consider with regard to them.

Information texture refers to the medium in which the information is encoded, the structure of the information, and the connections to and from the information. Just as the user of a web looks quickly to find cues about the information space he or she is in, so too does the user look for cues about information texture. By examining cues of media type, information structure, and connections, the user quickly gets a handle on how to extract information.

Media type is one aspect of information texture. A user entering an FTP site, for example, might encounter a long list of files which display a variety of media types—graphics, a movie, text files, and directories, for example. This variety (or uniformity, in the case of all the same kinds of media presented to the user) is the media type, which is one aspect of the information's texture. A quick look at the possible graphical symbols at an FTP site or a Gopher, for example (see Figure 16.3) quickly sets up a set of user expectations about *what* will be found there and the *interface* required to sense that information. A user entering a long list of sound files, for example, knowing that his or her sound player is not hooked up to their web browser, knows immediately that the site contains information that he or she cannot use.

Another aspect of information texture is information structure. Structure is the overall organization of the information within the display of the browser. The structure could be characteristic of an information space, such as the list of files at an FTP site, a menu from a Gopher, or it might be a ordered or unordered list within an HTML file. Structure is the pattern by which the information is presented. Simple structures, like lists or menus, are immediately recognized by the user.

Other structures, such as the complex interspersing of paragraphs, ordered and unordered lists, figures, and forms using HTML may be more difficult at first for the user to perceive. In either case, the structure of the information sets up expectations in the user about how to deal with the information. If the list shown on the browser display is numbered, and it continues down the page, a user quickly forms the expectation that the rest of the list will be available by using the scrollbar. In more complicated structures that are possible in webs, the structure of the information, although more expressive, might include paragraphs and lists, and the user might not know what to expect on the rest of a page or on other pages.

Just as media type and structure contribute to the information's texture, so do the connections that are either explicit or implied. The media type and structure contribute to information about connections. An FTP site listing, for example, often includes a folder at the top of the list with the label "parent directory" next to it. This folder is a connection, and it sets up in the user's mind a knowledge of the information he or she is presently encountering is possibly connected to some other information (hierarchically "up" in the case of FTP sites). In the case of a web, these connections might be to pages that are either more general or more specific in information content than the page the user is presently viewing. Moreover, the user wonders, "Where in the hierarchy (in the case of FTP sites or Gopher menus) am I?" or "Where in the mesh (in the case of webs) am I?" The connections to this other information, revealed by cues (see next section), can have a great impact on setting up a user's expectations about how to deal with the information shown.

Based on the previous discussion of information texture, the designer can appreciate some factors of the user experience while encountering information. The information texture sets up user expectations about *what* has been found and *how* to deal with it. As a designer, the following specific strategies might help in dealing with the way a user perceives information texture:

1. **Media type**

   What matters to the user most, the media type of the information or the content conveyed? Some users might want to locate all sound files on a web. Other users only want relevant information presented as it relates to meaning, with media type flagged (a symbol shown to alert the user of the media type for a link in the web). As a designer, your user's needs will dictate how you choose to arrange resources according to media type.

2. **Information structure**

   What degree of guidance do your users require to make use of the information? A list of items conveys less context information than a narrative paragraph, but is more to the point, particularly if the user knows exactly what the list is for and what each item on the list means. As a designer, in creating web pages, you'll constantly need to balance expressiveness with terseness.

3. **Connections**

   When does the user need the information? In the case of introductory or help information, how can you place it so that it is easily available at the major web entry points as well as at other appropriate places? How can you place a web page at exactly the right spots in a web so that its meaning is enhanced by connections to other pages? These are the main issues dealing with connections you face as a designer. The answer, of course, lies in the users needs:

   - How often would the user need to see this information?
   - When would the user need to see this information?
   - Why would the user need to see this information?

   These questions can help you determine the placement of pages within a web.

Cues

While information texture is often the first thing a user might notice on entering a web, cues are the next part of a user's experience. While information space and information texture have set up expectations in the user about "Where am I?" "What is this?," cues are the features in a web that say to a user "Here is what this is" (information cues) and "Here is how you get there from here" (navigation cues).

Information cues are the features of the text or graphics on a web page that help the user know the page's purpose, intended audience, contents, and objective. In other words, information cues help the user know what the page is for and what it contains. Notice that in our discussion of the user's experience, we've not yet talked about the user encountering the substance of the information's content yet. We're still at the stage of helping the user get oriented. A careful presentation of information cues can get the user oriented quickly, and thus enable the user to more efficiently use the information.

Some examples of information cues are

The title of the document (both as it appears in the "Document Title" window on the Mosaic browser and the words that appear most prominently at the top of the page). The user expects some sort of meaningful title in document—a holdover perhaps from encountering print. A meaningful title that conveys the purpose, audience, and objectives for that web page serves well to orient the user. For example, a title such as "Business Divisions of XYZ Industries, Listed by Region" immediately helps the user know what to expect on that page.

The sponsoring organization. Who created this web? Is it an official web server for an organization or a web put out by an individual?

A statement of purpose. This can flow directly from the purpose and objective statements. During design, however, you will need to customize the level of detail and the wording of the statement to be appropriate to your audience's needs on each page. I'll cover this more in the later section in this chapter about applying the design process to the purpose and objective statement elements.

A statement of objective. Similar to the statement of purpose described above, the objective statement can flow directly from the prepared objective statement, customized for the level of detail and audience needs.

A hint at the contents. Sometimes this can take the form of a list (even a hypertext list) of what the page contains. It is not necessary, however, (nor desirable all the time) to do this. A well-worded paragraph that gives a narrative of the web's contents might be best.

Headings. The use of well-worded, prominently placed headings can enable a user to quickly scan a page to get an idea of the contents. These headings should carry specific meaning, such as "An Overview of XYZ Products" as opposed to "Section One."

In writing headings, seek parallelism in phrasing. For example, your top-level headings might read as follows:

Opening the URL

Printing the Document

Exiting the program

Notice how each of the headings starts with the same "*-ing*" verb form. Compare this to

URL opening

Printing the Document

How to exit from the program

This mismatch in phrasing lacks the consistency of the previous set of headings.

The maintainer of the document. Users will find errors, have questions, or want to otherwise give feedback about the content of a document. The maintainers address often appears at the bottom of the page with at least an e-mail address given and possibly a link to his or her home page. The maintainer might also provide comment boxes or other features to explicitly seek feedback.

While information cues help a user make sense of a page's purpose and contents, navigation cues help the user do the following:

■ Understand where the page fits into the larger web

■ Learn how to leave the page or web quickly

■ Find out how to obtain further information

There are a variety of navigation cues that can help a user move through a web. All cues need not be present on each page of a web, but these cues should be easily available to the user:

■ Links to home pages—links to the top or home page of your web. These help the user who is lost to get back to the beginning to start over. The presence of these links helps users who have entered your web by some other method than the top (see Figure 30.1) to reach the front page. When used in a consistent title bar or foot bar on the page (see the upcoming Design Techniques section), the presence of your home page link acts as a marker to help identify each page as a part of your web.

■ Links to related pages in your web. One of the benefits of hypertext is that you can offer choices to your user about what to encounter next. A well-chosen selection of links to information in your web (or outside of your web) that relates to the information on a given page adds this "associative dimension" to the page's topic.

■ Links to help/indexes/README pages. In many places throughout your web, it is helpful to create links to indexes, help pages, or README pages that help a user understand where they are in your web and what other information they can get. A link to a help or index page can play a part in a consistent title bar or foot bar on all the pages of your web (see the upcoming "Design Techniques" section).

■ Expert links. These are "fast track" links that help a user who is familiar to your web to quickly go to featured resources, bypassing introductory or explanatory pages.

Design Methodologies

While there is no one way to weave a web, you can choose among a variety of approaches. No one way will necessarily work best all the time; therefore, you might even consider varying the approaches while developing the same web.

Top Down

If you have a good idea about what your whole web should contain, a top-down method of design might be best. In the top-down methodology, you start with a front or top page (often called the "home" page) for your web and work branching off from there. You might even create prototype "holder" pages that contain only minimal information but hold a place for later development in the web.

The benefit of the top-down approach is that you can develop your pages according to one central theme or idea. That is, you have a good chance to affect the look and feel of the whole web very powerfully because all pages are designed according to the top page look and feel. A good way to do this is to design a set of templates for types of pages in your web and use these during the implementation process.

Bottom Up

If you don't have a good idea of what the final web will look like (or even exactly what it will do), but you know how specific pages will look and work, it might be that working from these specific pages to the top page is the way to proceed. This is particularly true if you already have existing pages as a result of the development of some other web or service.

If you have no pages from which to start, you can begin by designing *leaves*—pages that accomplish specific objectives—and then linking them together through intermediate pages to the top page. The benefit of this design is that you are not constrained by the style of a top page in the leaf pages. Instead, you design the leaf pages in exactly the right style based on their function. Later, you adjust the pages to create a common look and feel for the whole web.

Incremental/In-time

Similar in ways to both the top-down and bottom-up approaches, the incremental/in-time approach develops pages "just in time" when they are needed. It may be the case that an initial top page is needed and specific leaf pages that implement particular objectives. These are created and linked together with the understanding that later, intermediate pages may be added. This works well if you want to very quickly have a working web that will grow incrementally, rather than being deployed all at once.

Design Techniques

Designing a web and dealing with the issues raised above about user experiences and design methodologies requires a designer to employ a variety of techniques to achieve particular effects. These techniques have to do with shaping information for user's needs and abilities and expressing a consistent look and feel for the whole web. Like many aspects of web weaving, design techniques are an art in themselves, and having a good repertoire of them increases your value as a web designer.

Package Information in the Right-Sized Chunks

Humans can process only so much information at a time. Helping your users process information is your overall challenge as a web designer and a specific task in your design is to package or "chunk" information in pieces that do not overwhelm your users. As a general guideline, the number of pieces of information to have in the user's attention at any one time is five, plus or minus two. While you'll have to judge what constitutes an information "piece" and decide exactly what constitutes the field of "a user's attention," the key idea is to chunk information as follows:

- So that the amount of information on any one page doesn't overwhelm the user.
- So that you can create reusable pages, that is, if each page you create accomplishes one specific purpose, it can be a useful link throughout the entire web for that purpose. In this way, you can flexibly include a page of information in as many places as appropriate to the user's needs, but only create that information once.
- So that you can focus the user's attention. The chunks of information, when created around ideas, concepts, and ways of thinking familiar to your users, will help a user focus on one topic at a time and build their knowledge incrementally.

How can a designer do this chunking? There are several techniques. As a first step for all of these techniques, the designer must gather the documents that represent the information to be presented in the web. This information should be listed in detail in the web

specifications (created by the planning process) and reflected in the objective statement. Information to be served to users and useful to designers should be in the store of domain information.

Here is a clustering technique to arrive at packages of information for a web:

1. Start with a copy of the objective statement for the web. Circle the nouns in the objective statement.

2. Using a simple graphics drawing program, type in the circled nouns and move them until related ones are close together. Define this *relatedness* in terms of the user's perspective. Ideally, you would know how the user thinks about the information your web will provide. Does a user think in terms of subjects or topics (the subject categorization of the nouns) or in terms of processes (what you do with the nouns)? Try both arrangements and show each version to a representative user, asking "Which clustering of words is most useful to your work (the work that the web intends to support)?" The benefit of hypertext is that you may be able to implement both views of the same information.

3. In the word cluster diagram, draw more nested circles around the words that relate. In the case of a topic-oriented clustering, this can proceed along a hierarchical breakdown of the topic. In a process-oriented clustering of words, this can be done by grouping nouns that the same processes act upon. After all words are in at least one loop (even if there is just one phrase in each loop), group loops together by drawing lines around related groups. For example, Figure 32.3 shows how the nouns given in the (partial) objective statement in Chapter 30, "Planning a Web."

   Computer-Mediated Communication (CMC) Studies Center

   purpose: to help people share resources

   objective: to provide a list of resources with links to major online collections of CMC-related material, bibliographies, academic and research centers related to CMC, online journals, and other resources

   Note in the figure that the "online journals, online resources, and online bibliographies" group is also grouped with "research center home pages." This reflects, at the level of clustering shown, a separation of what the web offers into *people, activities,* and *resources.* A different clustering could have been done—the list of people grouped with the online resources and the research center home pages grouped with the list of activities. This would have reflected a research/activities and resources slant to this information (with people looked upon as resources, possibly in supporting or informational roles).

4. Continue clustering until you draw a final loop around all the clusters. This final loop acts to show that the clustering diagram is "finished" and no other clustering can be done.

FIGURE 32.3.

Information cluster diagram.

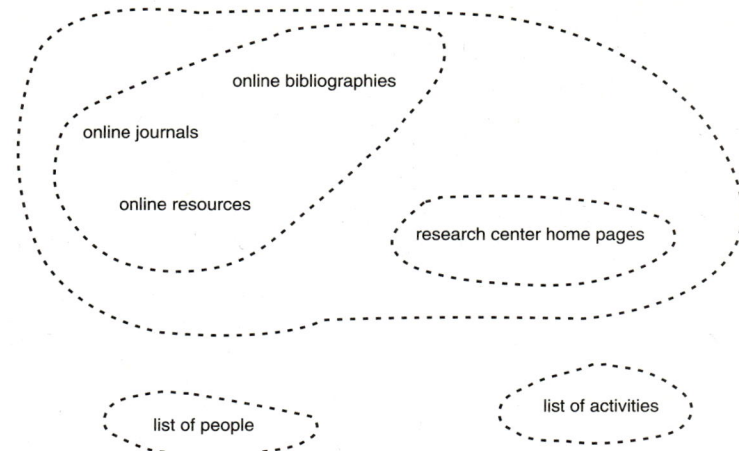

Your clustering diagram now can serve as a map to breaking down your web into packages. A *package* is a web page or group of web pages that are closely related, as defined by the above clustering process. Eventually, each package must be defined as a web page or set of web pages. One simple transformation from a cluster diagram to packages is to make each loop a package. In other words, if we had a loop around the three outer loops shown in Figure 32.3, we would have the following packages:

1. A package with links to a list of people, activities, and resources
2. A package containing a list of people
3. A package containing a list of activities
4. A package ("list of resources" from 1) containing links to online resources, online journals, and online bibliographies
5. A package containing online resources (from 4)
6. A package containing online journals (from 4)
7. A package containing online bibliographies (from 4)

You can see how this cluster method works even with a simple example to give you a quick way to create a preliminary set of packages of information. The next step is to transform packages to pages:

1. A simple transformation is to make each package a page, paying close attention not to overload any given page. Based on Figure 32.2, you would obtain seven pages, described in the list previously.

   To assure that no page gets overloaded, for each page, estimate the total number of *kinds* of links and how much of each. For example, the list of people page might contain just one kind of link—to a personal home page. Let's say there's

50 people on the list. That would mean that this page contains 50 links to personal pages plus other navigation or information links (say there are five of these). This yields 50 instances of one kind of link and five instances of navigation links. This is not necessarily an unmanageable combination for a single web page. However, if there were 500 people in the directory, it might be a problem to put the whole directory on one page. The main issue is scalability. The directory could grow to a page that size will cause performance problems. The design decision at this point might be to include the preliminary listing, but then to investigate using a database or other lookup scheme for the lists of people.

2. A better transformation might be to create a page for every noun in the cluster diagram and a page for every package that has more than one noun phrase in it. Using this method for Figure 32.2, a total of nine pages would be made—six pages would be created for each noun phrase and three pages would be created to handle links to the following:

>   A page linking to the online bibliographies, journals, and resources pages

>   The page linking to the page described in 1, above (online pages), and the research center home pages page

>   A page linking to the page described in 2, a list of people page, and a list of activities page

Link Pages Together

Once you have a set of pages, you need to design how they will link together. The cluster diagram showing packages and pages is a good start toward seeing how these links might be made. The following methods will yield an initial linking of pages that can be built upon using some other linking techniques (see index, title bar, and foot bar methods). To get an initial link diagram, do the following:

1. Link pages in a hierarchy determined by the nesting of packages shown in the cluster diagram. Link pages within the same package together. For example, using this method, we can link the nine pages generated by the second method shown above for package->page breakdown. Figure 32.4 shows the initial link diagram using this method. The benefit of this scheme is that the hierarchy of pages helps guide a user through the information. The downside is that the user must follow a particular path to reach a page—a path that might be several links long from the home page.

FIGURE 32.4.
*Link by package
hierarchy.*

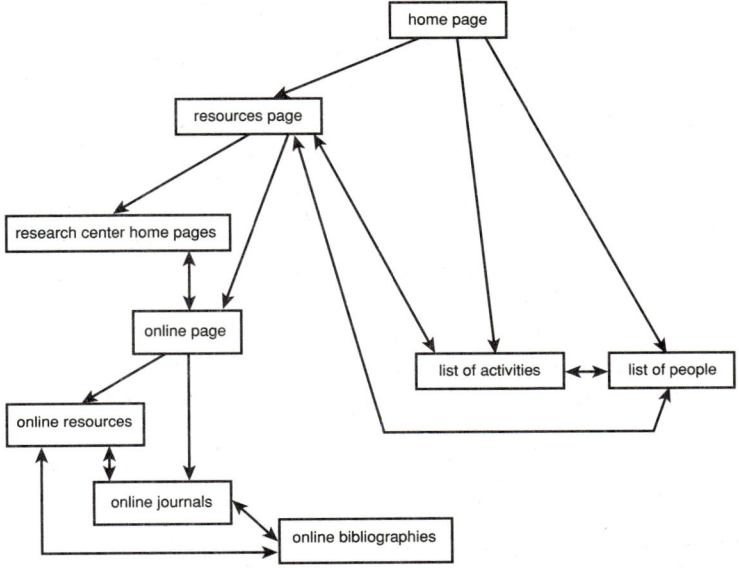

2. Create pages for only the *leaves* of the package hierarchy shown in Figure 32.3
    (that is, only pages generated from the noun phrases in the objective statement)
    and link every one of them to each other. This creates a nonhierarchy web, in
    which all the pages of information called for by the objective statement are
    available to every other page. For webs with a small number of total pages, this
    might work well; for large webs, the number of links required will grow large very
    rapidly as the number of pages increases. Figure 32.5 shows a nonhierarchy link
    of all the leaf pages of Figure 32.3. The benefit of this structure is that all pages
    are just one link away from any other page. The downside is that there is no
    information hierarchy to help the user cope with the link choices from any given
    page, and that this technique is not scalable (requiring many links for large webs).

There are obviously many more variations of these linking schemes, but the two directions above—linking for hierarchy and total (nonhierarchical) linking—have their advantages and disadvantages. Other methods for linking include the following:

1. *By need*—In a test situation, give representative users a problem (a set of ques-
    tions or an "information hunt" type of exercise) that they solve by using the
    information given in the web pages. Observe the order in which the users access
    the pages in search of information to solve the problem. Based on these observa-
    tions of user access, link the pages together based on minimizing the number of
    links a user must typically traverse to solve the problem.

FIGURE 32.5.
Completely link all leaf pages.

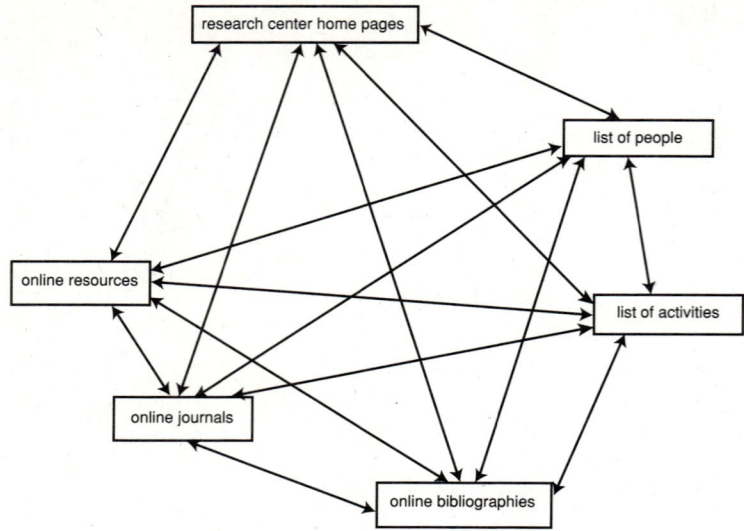

2. *By association*—Have representative users rank how closely each of the pages relate to each other (for example, on a scale of 1 to 5 with 5 being a strong association). Provide double links between pages with association scores over the average for all links (or use some other criterion that generates something short of a complete, double linking of all pages).

Specify Overall Look and Feel with a Universal Grid

Besides the package, page, and link diagrams, the web designer can make several other products to help express the look and feel for the web. One of these diagrams is a universal grid for the entire web, a diagram that sets out the function and arrangement for text, cues, and links on any given page.

For example, a universal grid is shown in Figure 32.6.

The purpose of the universal grid is to create a template to give all pages of the web a uniform look. This uniform look helps the user of the web know what cues to expect where on each page. Notice how the universal grid shown in Figure 32.6 doesn't specify exactly what has to go into the footer and header for each page; this could vary according the purpose for each page or type of page.

FIGURE 32.6.

Example universal grid.

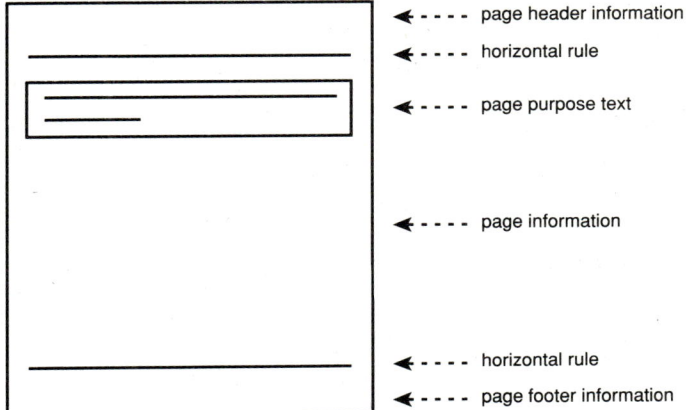

- ◀ - - - - page header information
- ◀ - - - - horizontal rule
- ◀ - - - - page purpose text
- ◀ - - - - page information
- ◀ - - - - horizontal rule
- ◀ - - - - page footer information

Use Repeated Icons

Another technique for creating a unified look and feel for the web is to use repeated icons to represent classes of information or an icon representing the web itself. These repeated icons could be specified in the universal grid. For example, Figure 32.7 shows the universal grid from Figure 32.6 with repeated web icon (an icon that represents the whole web) and a repeated topic icon (an icon that represents the particular topic this page addresses) in the header information.

FIGURE 32.7.

Example universal grid with repeated icons.

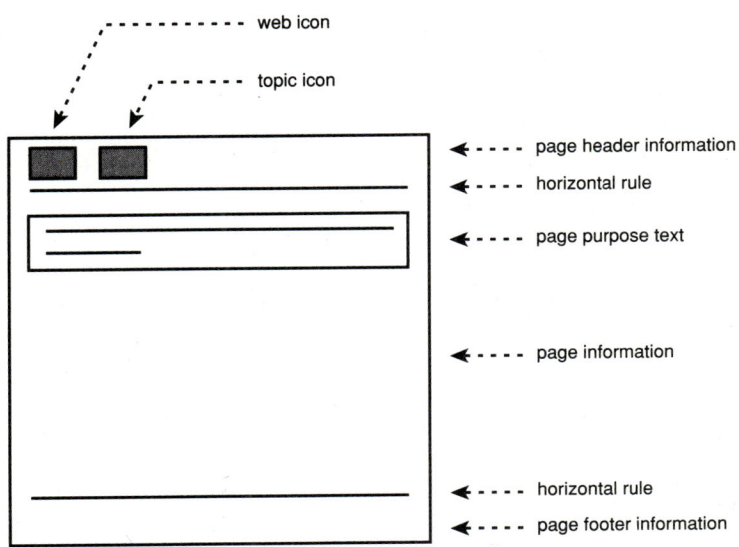

- web icon
- topic icon
- ◀ - - - - page header information
- ◀ - - - - horizontal rule
- ◀ - - - - page purpose text
- ◀ - - - - page information
- ◀ - - - - horizontal rule
- ◀ - - - - page footer information

These repeated icons help the user gain a sense of consistency in all the pages from this web. The topic icon helps cue the user to the purpose of the page. Because these icons are repeated, the user benefits because the browser loads a given icon only once, and then can use it (without reloading) on any other page in the web. In this way, repeated icons can give the web a strong sense identity for each page. This is particularly important when a pin-cushion access pattern (Figure 30.1 in Chapter 30) is expected for the web—the repeated icons help let the user know where they are.

Create and Use Web-Wide Navigation Links

Just as repeated icons provide the user with information cues on each page, navigation cues and links can help the user move through an entire web.

One technique for creating a web-wide navigation link is to make an index page which links to every page of the entire web. For webs with a large number of pages, this can clearly create problems, but the concept is to provide a central point for the user to locate a page that he or she knows is in the web somewhere but can't remember how to get to it. An index page is particularly important for webs linked using a hierarchical technique (see Figure 32.4). For example, the index page for the web in Figure 32.4 is shown in Figure 32.8.

FIGURE 32.8.

Index page for hierarchically linked web.

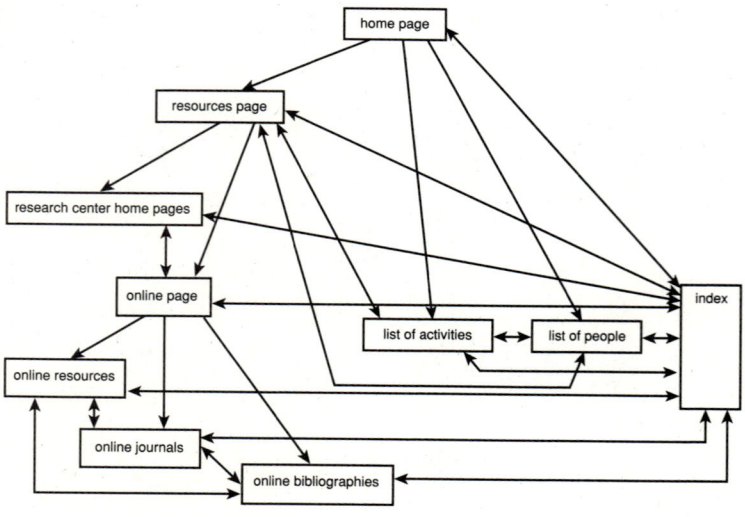

Given that an index page is created, the index itself then can become part of the universal grid, either in the title bar or in a foot bar. Local or specialized indexes of pages within the same package could also be created and placed on pages within the same package.

Another web-wide navigation link might be to the top or home page for the entire web. Often, the web icon itself can serve as this link. Placing this link on the universal grid, the home page for the web can be just one link away from any page in the web. Just like the other elements of the universal grid, these repeated navigation links can help a user make sense of an arbitrary web page, particularly in pin-cushion access patterns.

Use Web Elements for Information Cues

Within each page of your web, look for opportunities to use the audience information or purpose and objective statements for explanatory or information cues. For example, you've carefully planned which audience you are targeting for your web in the planning process. Why hide this information from the user? An explicit statement of the target audience, written with the appropriate wording for a particular web page, can help the user immediately see if he or she is right for the information on that page.

The purpose statement is perhaps the web element you'll draw on the most in providing information cues to your user. Purpose statements can serve as a powerful "mission statement" for communicating the web's intent with users. Since every page of the web reflects its purpose, you'll find that every page can contain a variation of the purpose statement that is specific to the function the given page is serving.

Similarly, the objective statement can be put to use on pages worded for the right level of detail and serve as an important information cue for the user. For example, one objective statement might be

> "To list online bibliographies in the field of geology."

This can translate directly to introductory text at the top of the page that meets this objective:

> "This page lists online bibliographies in the field of geology."

While not all translations between web elements and information cues used in the web design will be as easy or mechanical, the web designer should take full advantage of the store of wording and language in these elements.

Design Problems

While the above techniques can help you create a consistent look and feel for your web, there are specific problems that can detract from a web's design. These include problems with a lack of navigation and information cues ("the page from outer space"), a page with large access time required or with an over-complex information texture and structure ("the monster page" and "multimedia overkill"), a page with an uneven information structure ("the uneven page") and problems with linking ("meaningless links") in pages. All these

design problems *may* lead to problems—there are exceptions where many of these same effects I critique here may play an integral role in effectively accomplishing a purpose. The key is that these design problems are issues that web designers should be aware of, not as iron-clad rules or formulas. Moreover, every designer may create one of these problems at one time or another, such as a page evolving over time, accumulating links until it gradually becomes a "monster." Rather, these are issues to consider when designing (or analyzing) a web.

The Page from Outer Space

One of the most frustrating things you may find as a web navigator is a page like the one in Figure 32.9.

FIGURE 32.9.

The page from outer space.

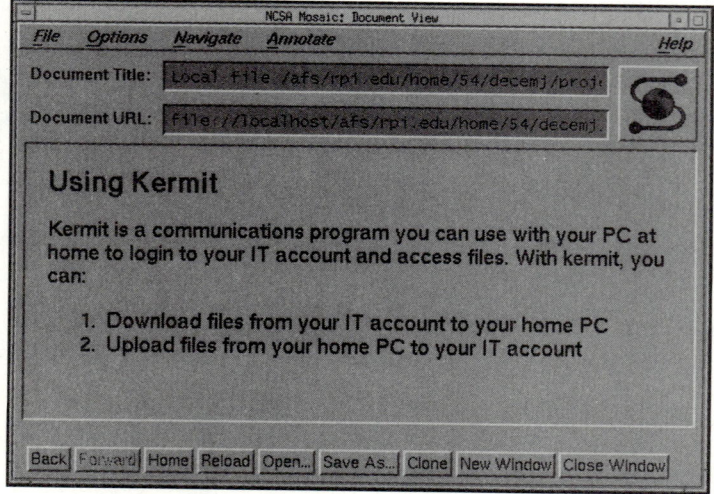

The page is well-written: it has a descriptive heading, it includes a narrative that guides you through its main points about using kermit. However, a navigator who enters this page would have many questions: Who wrote this page? Why? What web is it a part of? What is does "IT" stand for?

The page shown in Figure 32.9 has no information cues, not even a <TITLE>, to cue the user to the purpose of the page. Since there are no links on the page, we can't easily locate the home page for this web (a navigator would have to use the technique of opening a URL consisting of just the beginning part of the URL for this page). The information on this page—apparently instructions about what kermit can do—is contextless, and therefore of little use. Moreover, a navigator coming into this page has *no easy way* to find out the answers to the above questions; the page has no links, no context, no cues. Hence the phrase "the page from outer space."

Avoid creating pages that have no cues. You generally cannot assume the user will encounter your web according to the wine bottle model of access (Figure 30.1 in Chapter 30). Moreover, you're not taking advantage of the power of the Web itself if you treat the information on each page as just a "slab" of text with no links to other context, information, or navigation cues. Most importantly, you're closing off user interaction and feedback. A user encountering the page in Figure 32.9 would have no contact point for even asking the above questions. On the other hand, there's no need to provide links to every conceivable scrap of information related to the topic of the page. The key is to balance the number of cues versus completeness of information. As a rule of thumb, ask yourself what a user would do to get more information from a given page. There should be at least one cue or link on that page to help them at some level, even if it is a link to the home page.

Variations on the "page from outerspace" include home pages that give information that has little meaning in a global context. For example, you might see the following as a title for a page:

> "Department of Physics home page"

What university? What country? What continent? Although the skilled navigator can (usually) obtain the answers to the questions by looking for clues in the URL, the designers of this page apparently did not realize that their page reaches a global audience.

Although it's usually not necessary to qualify a geographic location as: "Department of Physics, Delta University, Delta, Mississippi, USA, North America, Earth," as a designer, you should have some sense of how many cues to give in order to help a user place your information in the global context of the Web. Don't assume that your organization, city, or state name is recognized worldwide. Often, qualification to the country level is enough.

The Monster Page

Just as the "page from outer space" had too few cues to help the user effectively place the information in context, so too can a page get too cluttered with links, graphics, lists, and other effects. There are two major problems with cluttered pages:

1. *Access time*—If there are many inline images, or there is a great of text on the page, the access time for that page can be enormous. (Read about my own monster page and my redesign of it in Chapter 39, "Challenges for Web Information Providers.")

2. *Information overload*—If you put too much information on a single page, the user simply will not be able to cope with it. The physical limits of the browser display will by default chunk the information on the page into screenfuls of information accessible by the scrollbar or other system in the browser. Rather than having the browser chunk the information the designer should determine these chunks.

There are situations, though, where a long list of similar items is best browsed in one long list and any breakup of the information would be arbitrary.

The strength of hypertext is that information can be chunked into pages, so that these pages can then be encountered by users according to their need. The "monster" page, with its overabundance of links and cues, creates too much noise for the user to pick out the essential information.

Multimedia Overkill

New designers using the facilities of a browser such as Mosaic often include many inlined images as well as links to graphics, sounds, movies, or other multimedia files. When not needed, this multimedia overkill can lead to the same problems associated with the "monster page" discussed previously. The multimedia used in a web must play a key role in accomplishing an objective that directly meets a user's need. Chunking links to these resources, just like chunking links among pages, can be done using the cluster diagram and packaging techniques outlined above.

Another issue related to multimedia overkill is using the same graphics in several different places in a web without using a link to the same graphics file, which requires that the Web browser must reload the image every time it is used. If you use a repeated image in a web, link to the same file (same URL) every time you include it on a page. By doing this, the Web browser can load the file just once and display it on many other pages in the web.

The Uneven Page

An uneven page is one that contains information at vastly different or incongruous levels of detail. For example, Figure 32.10 shows the home page of the ABC University's Information Technology Department. The design and context information is adequate—a link to the university's home page is given, a link to an index is shown, and the page is signed by the webmaster.

The items in the list given on the page, however, are very incongruous—"Faculty Directory" seems on the same level of importance as "Research Programs" and "IT Department's Mission." But the next two links—"How to Use Kermit" and "CS 101 Final Grades"— seem to be at some other level of detail.

A page often becomes uneven through a process of iterative accumulation of links. The webmaster in the case of the ABC IT Department probably added links as they were developed. This unevenness, however, weakens the coherence of the page—the user begins to wonder what this page is supposed to accomplish. Naturally, a page reflecting a deliberate "grab bag" or collection of links would display this unevenness. Usually, unevenness can be a problem on major home pages or pages that have a specific, often high-visibility purpose in the web. Every time you add a link to a page, ask if it fulfills the purpose of that page or in some other way helps the user with that information.

FIGURE 32.10.

An uneven page.

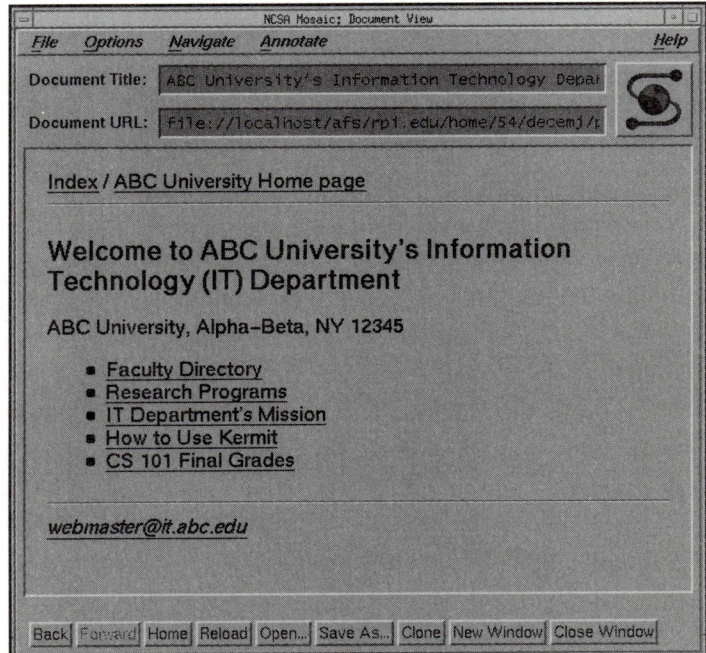

Meaningless Links

Just as links can be uneven, they can also fail to add any meaning to the information presented. Of course, any stale link fulfills this criterion, but stale links shouldn't be intentionally designed into a web.

One manifestation of a meaningless link is a "vacuous" link that takes the user to a resource or document with no apparent connection to the meaning conveyed on the original page. Every link should somehow extend the meaning of a page. The link in the following sentence

```
Welcome to <a href="abc.html">ABC</A> University's Home Page</A>
```

from the term ABC to the file abc.html should contain some background or historic information about the University's name (because the link was made to "ABC" as opposed to "ABC University's Home Page"). If this link is to a special project by the page designer or some other unrelated or unpredictable subject, the link is vacuous.

Another form of vacuous link is a sentence such as

```
For more information, click <a href="info.html">here</A>.
```

The hotspot, here, has no meaning within the sentence. A better choice might be

```
You can get <a href="info.html">more information</A>.
```

Another kind of meaningless link is the trivial link, in which a link is made to some re-source or document that relates to the original page, but only trivially in the given con-text. For example, you might find this sentence on the home page of ABC University:

```
Welcome to ABC University's Home <a href="page.html">Page</A>
```

If the link from Page to the file page.html is to a dictionary definition of the word *page,* it is a trivial link because the information isn't essential in the context of a university's home page. In the context of a narrative about Web vocabulary and terms, this same link (from "page" to a definition of the term) might be essential.

Another kind of meaningless linking occurs when a designer creates a web with very small chunks and excessively links these chunks together. This creates a mesh of pages, and each page carries very little context and content. This requires the user to traverse a great num-ber of pages in order to accumulate meaning or context. This is the opposite of the "mon-ster page" effect and represents hypertext taken to an extreme. In some cases, however, this effect is highly desired, such as in hyper-art, hyper-fiction, or hyper-poetry, where the medium of hypertext may be stretched to its limit. As a general rule, though, each page should accomplish a specific, self-contained purpose, so that the user has a feeling of at-taining a goal rather being left with a need to follow still more links.

Weaver's Check

Designing a web involves considering the user's experience and meeting the user's needs by shaping information. In doing this, a designer strives to follow the principles and goals of a user-centered web design process to weave a web that works efficiently and is consis-tent and aesthetically pleasing.

The web designer understands a user's experience of information space, texture, and cues, and uses design techniques to package and link information in a way that best meets a user's abilities and needs. The designer can approach the overall process of web design in a top-down, bottom-up, or in-time/incremental methodology. The web designer uses a variety of techniques to specify the look and feel of the web—though a cluster diagram showing web packages and pages, through a link diagram, or a universal grid for an over-all pattern for page development.

There are many problems a weaver may unintentionally create in the process of web design: a page with no accessible context ("the page from outer space"), a page with an overabundance of information texture or information ("the monster page"), a page with too many multimedia effects, particularly inline graphics ("multimedia overkill"), an uneven page with items at inconsistent levels of detail, and meaningless links that distract from the user's ability to gain useful information.

The overall process of web design involves both acquired skills in information design and also acquired experience in design problems and their solutions. No web design is flawless, but the task of the web designer should be to always strive to improve a web's design to better meet the needs of users.

Implementing a Web: Basic HyperText Markup Language (HTML)

by John December

33

All Web browsers must recognize a version of HyperText Markup Language (HTML) that is called Level 1 (sometimes called basic HTML). Level 2 HTML, which is still being refined, includes features such as Forms that only certain Web browsers understand. Level 3 HTML, sometimes called HTML+, includes tables, figures, and mathematical equations and is still being defined.

Once you've developed a design for a web, the next step is to implement the design. This chapter covers Level 1 HyperText markup language (HTML), the language used to express ideas and information for a hypertext browser to read. In the next chapter, "Advanced HTML Features," we'll look at some features of Level 2 HTML; Chapter 35, "HTML Editors and Filters," covers tools that can help you create HTML files; and in Chapter 36, "Implementing a Web Design," we'll explore how to implement a specific web design in HTML. You'll find that the tasks involved in writing basic HTML documents are really not overly-complex. In practice however, the coherent design and operation of a web is far more complex than just writing in HTML—just as typing skills are just one part of being able to write a good document.

HTML, similar to a computer programming language, requires you to express your thoughts in a specific structure in order for the "computer" (in this case, the hypertext browser) to understand. While HTML is not as complicated as some computer programming languages, writing HTML requires that you follow specific rules to "tag" or "mark" the parts of your document. This marking sets HTML apart from free-form prose or text created in a word processor. In fact, the whole idea of marking up a text to express its structure comes from a very different approach than the What-you-see-is-what-you-get (WYSIWYG) word processors that you might have used. In a WYSIWYG word process, you concentrate on a document's *appearance*. Using HTML, you concentrate on the document's *structure*.

There are tools that help you create HTML documents in a WYSIWYG manner (covered in Chapter 35, "HTML Editors and Filters"). It will be important for you, however, particularly if you will work extensively on developing HTML files, to be familiar with HTML itself. Also, a close look at HTML helps you see how information within these files is shaped and what is possible.

This chapter presents a detailed tour of basic HTML. First, some background is given describing the purpose behind HTML and why a browser-independent (also called presentation independent) markup language helps developers. Then, the details of HTML are covered, demonstrating how different features of HTML express the structure of a document.

■ Making sure that the < and > all match up when composing an anchor. For example:

```
The <A HREF="http://info.cern.ch/hypertext/WWW/MarkUp/Tags.html">Elements of
HTML</A>
```

are head, body, and graphics.

Notice how the anchor starts with <A and ends with </A> and what's in between are the HREF label, the URL of the resource, the hotspot for the hypertext. Missing just one of the ", >, <, or / will cause an error.

■ Verifying that many browsers will read the HTML file without problems. In developing HTML, you'll find that some browsers are forgiving in that they let you get away with small errors in your HTML code. Another browser might not be, so it is a good idea to check your HTML code in at least one other browser than the one you're using for development.

■ Linking to other documents using relative links. When you write an HTML document, you can refer to other HTML files that are located on your server by using relative links within your HTML. For example, if you are writing the top HTML document (top.html), and you are referring to the index document (myindex.html) that is located in the same directory, you can link from top.html to myindex.html as follows:

```
<A HREF="myindex.html">Index</A>
```

Anyone who links to your top document, perhaps from a distant host, will use the link

```
<A HREF="http://your.host.com/Project/top.html>Top Document</A>
```

When this user clicks on the Index hotspot, the reference to myindex.html will be resolved to be the URL

```
http://your.host.com/Project/myindex.html
```

even though you had only used myindex.html in your HTML document. This is called *relative naming (or relative addressing or linking)*.

Getting Started—Basics

Because there are certain tags that you will have in all HTML documents, it is a good idea to make a template for yourself (create a file called template.html) that contains all the basics:

```
<HTML>
<HEAD>
<TITLE>title</TITLE>
</HEAD>
```

```
<BODY>

<ADDRESS>your name (your email address)</ADDRESS>

</BODY>
</HTML>
```

Now let's put some information onto this template and step through some of the most commonly used HTML structures.

1. *The title.*

   Think up a good one. As we saw in looking at spiders in Chapter 19, "Spiders and Indexes: Keyword-Oriented Searching," the title is often used as an identifier of your HTML document on the Web. Therefore, your title should be meaningful outside of the context of your document's contents (but not be overloaded with every conceivable buzzword to grab a spider's attention). For example, your document might be the overview for your company's products. Using the title "Overview," however, won't have any meaning to anyone else who might come across this title. The title "Overview of XYZ Industry Product Line," instead, will have more meaning to anyone seeing your document's title in a spider list.

   Put the title between the <TITLE> and </TITLE> brackets in the HEAD of the document.

   ```
   <TITLE>Overview of XYZ Industries Product Line</TITLE>
   ```

   Remember, this title does not show up in the document's representation in a browser. You'll have to repeat the document's title, if desired, in the text itself (as a heading possibly).

2. *Headings.*

   The six levels of headings give the opportunity to create an information hierarchy within your document. As such, the heading elements are used to indicate *semantic* hierarchy, not necessarily to take advantage of the varying sizes of type that the headings might offer in some browsers. Therefore, you should attempt to use these headings in sequence, starting with level 1 <H1>, and continuing to <H6> in stepsizes of 1 (that is, not jumping from using heading 1 to heading 6). If you find you are tempted to violate this rule (that you want to use a high-numbered heading to take advantage of the type display change in browsers like Mosaic), remember that not all browsers will support a type size change—so that while your Mosaic users see small type with <H6>, your Lynx users are seeing the same-sized type as with heading <H1>.

   Similar to the title, the headings too should be as descriptive as possible, particularly because there are some spiders that use heading information as a means to index your document's content.

The very first heading you put in a document could reflect the purpose of the document itself. For example, continuing with our XYZ Industries example, the first heading in our document might be XYZ Industries Product Line. We put this as a major heading as follows:

```
<H1>The XYZ Industries Product Line</H1>
```

Since this entire page is devoted to the XYZ Industries Product Line, we wouldn't normally put another <H1> header on the page. We might include <H2> and <H3> headers for information one or two "levels down" from the product line description. You'll find, however, that the nature of hypertext gives you the opportunity to avoid this nesting of parts within the same HTML page. Therefore, you'll find it uncommon to have many layers of headings on a page. If you find yourself nesting information to many levels of headings, you should consider breaking up the document into several HTML pages.

3. *Paragraphs.*

The text that you type into an HTML file outside of any of the elements marked off by the < and > tags will be placed into paragraphs. Only the <P> tag marks the end of a paragraph, no matter how many blank lines or intervening spaces there are. Moreover, most browsers "chew up" any extraneous white space between words, so that you won't be able to "format" your text using spacing (use preformatted text, <PRE> for this).

So after your heading, you can explain a little bit about XYZ Industries product line:

```
Founded in July 1994, XYZ Industries has
rapidly become a world leader in
HyperWidget and Odd-Bearing Machine (OBM) technologies.
<P>
XYZ's product line includes industry standards
such as the HyperWidget 2000 and OBM 411, as well as such
innovations as the
Alpha-class HyperWidget line that allows hyper-window mapping
on
VR (Virtual Reality) helmets or displays.  With XYZ's
products,
you can be assured of
the highest quality and state-of-the art design. <P>
```

Notice in the above example, I used only a <P> to break the paragraphs. For readability in my HTML source file, I might have placed a blank line between the paragraphs, but it would not have been required. Note also, that the line breaks in the HTML source file don't matter. The browser will break lines and wrap lines of text based on how wide the display area for the text is, not based on the HTML source (unless a `<BR>` were used).

4. *A List.* Lists provide a very useful way to focus a user's attention on a series of items. As described above, you have a variety of choices for lists. Generally, you'll use a sequential list for steps or directions that must be done in a particular order, or for a list of counted items.

   Since we want to impress the potential customers about the wide range of products that XYZ Industries offers, we'll use a numbered list to emphasize the quantity of items shown.

   ```
   The XYZ products currently available for sale and delivery are:
   <OL>
   <LI>OBM 411, 412, 413, and 440
   <LI>HyperWidget 2000, 2000A, 2000A-XL, and 2000A-XL-G
   <LI>Alpha, beta, gamma, and delta class HyperWidgets for VR
   applications
   </OL>
   ```

   You can quickly change a list that is ordered to an unordered list by changing the starting tag from `<OL>` to `<UL>` and the ending tag from `</OL>` to `</UL>`.

5. *A Link.* Looking over what you've written about XYZ Industries' products, you might notice that you've used many highly technical terms and jargon that may be company or industry-specific. For example, the term "VR" was defined (Virtual Reality) but not explained. As we saw in the previous two chapters, what you need to explain largely depends on your audience's knowledge and interests. Assuming that an educated customer would be reading about XYZ's product lines, you wouldn't necessarily have to go into great detail about every term. However, if you do want to provide a way to help a user who wants to find out more about a topic, a link is a very useful way to connect information—in fact, this is the heart of writing hypertext.

   To help the user who is interested in finding out more about Virtual Reality, let's make a link from the phrase "Virtual Reality" in our document to a page that presents a large selection of resources for virtual reality at the URL `http://guinan.gsfc.nasa.gov/W3/VR.html`. Note that, as discussed in the previous chapters about planning and analyzing a Web, we need to take special care when we link to resources outside of our web—paying attention to link freshness and appropriateness.

To make the link in our text, we have to modify a few lines:

```
Alpha-class HyperWidget line that allows hyper-window mapping
on
VR (<A HREF="http://guinan.gsfc.nasa.gov/W3/VR.html">Virtual
Reality</A>)
```

Notice that the basic form of making a link is

```
<A HREF="URL">Hotspot</A>
```

Where URL is the Uniform Resource Locator for the document, and Hotspot is the explanatory text for the link that is usually highlighted (or underlined) in the browser.

Getting Started—Some Flairs and Details

In the previous section, we've done the most common things you'll do in an HTML document—we've set up the heading and body tags, given the document a title, put in a heading, written some paragraphs, created a list, and put in a link. There are a few other flairs that you can put in your document to add visual cues—things to draw and focus the user's attention. These include small images and horizontal lines, as well as details like a link to your home page in the address of a document, a revision link in the head of the document, and comment lines in the HTML source code.

1. *A logo.* Our page for XYZ industries, while providing an overview of products, seems a little dry. One flair you can add is a small logo or inline image in the document. First, you need to create the logo itself with tools on your computer and create a file in a graphics format that can be recognized by the browsers you expect your users to have. A common type of graphics file that works is a GIF (Graphics Interchange Format) file. Also, keep in mind, of course, that browsers that cannot display inline graphics won't show the logo, and that (currently) GIF, XPM, and XBM are the only supported inline image types.

   Once you've got the XYZ industries logo created (in file xyz-logo.gif in the same directory as your HTML page), add the following line just below the <BODY> element:

   ```
   <IMG SRC="xyz-logo.gif" ALT="XYZ Logo"> XYZ Industries
   ```

   The inline image element <IMG > will bring the image in the file given directly into the text of the document. We've also added text to the right of the logo to identify the full name of the company. Note also that we've used the ALT=" " option to include a descriptive title that will be displayed in browsers which do not support graphics. This is important because otherwise, the users of these browsers will just see the word IMAGE and might wonder what they're missing.

2. *Horizontal lines.* Just as the fine lines going horizontally across the top of a page in a magazine serve to bracket the text visually for a pleasing appearance, so too can you create horizontal lines in your HTML pages to help bracket text. The key is not to over-use these lines, but use them selectively to help guide the reader's attention in your document. If you find yourself making too many horizontal lines, you should consider making separate pages out of the regions on the page you're marking off with the horizontal lines.

Let's add horizontal lines just after the logo:

```
<IMG SRC="xyz-logo.gif" ALT="XYZ Logo"> XYZ Industries

<HR>
```

and just after the end of our product list:

```
The XYZ products currently available for sale and delivery are:

<OL>

<LI>OBM 411, 412, 413, and 440

<LI>HyperWidget 2000, 2000A, 2000A-XL, and 2000A-XL-G

<LI>Alpha, beta, gamma, and delta class HyperWidgets for VR

applications

</OL>

<HR>
```

The two horizontal lines created by <HR> serve to bracket the body of text that contains the page's main information, with the header being the logo and the signature being the address at the bottom of the page. In this way, this organization corresponds closely with a letter style, in which a company logo starts off the letter, a signature ends it, and the content of the letter is bracketed in between.

3. *Your address.* An address for the developer of the page is important to have; what if there were an error in the page or if a customer actually wanted to buy a OBM 411? Without a contact address at the bottom, it would be hard for a customer to make contact. Note that a contact address is *not* required in an HTML document, and it could come at the top or bottom (or anywhere) in a page.

The contents of the address can be the name of the developer for the page or an organizational unit's name and email address. There also can be a link to a home page for that person or organizational unit.

```
<ADDRESS><A HREF=="http://www.xyz.com/units/cc.html">Corporate

Communications</A>

(cc@xyz.com)</ADDRESS>
```

Note that a link was made in this address to the home page for corporate communications at the URL http://www.xyz.com/units/cc.html.

4. *Revision link.* Similar to the tradition of signing a page so that users can contact the developers, so too is including a revision link in the header of the document a valuable (but not necessary) detail. The revision link is made as follows:

```
<HEAD>
        <TITLE>Overview of XYZ Industries Product Line</TITLE>
        <LINK REV="made" HREF="mailto:cc@xyz.com">
</HEAD>
This will direct anyone who wishes to find out
more about the revision of this document to
contact cc@xyz.com.  While this same information
is included in the ADDRESS element, its inclusion
in the HEAD element (which is not actually displayed)
makes it accessible to browsers that recognize
the special function of the LINK REV element.
```

5. *Comments in the HTML code.* Just as the ADDRESS and LINK REV elements added important contact information as well as documentation to your HTML file, so too can you add comments to your source code itself. While comments are not required (as well as not displayed) in the browser, they can add significant value to your work by providing background and administrative information, labeling the information so that developers know who wrote it, why, and any special considerations for it. You bracket each comment within <!— and —>. For example:

```
<!— Author:    M.U. Langdon (mul@xyz.com) —>
<!— Dept:      Corporate Communications —>
<!— Date:      10 Jul 94 —>
<!— Purpose:   overview of XYZ products—>
<!— Comments:  check with Sales to get the latest enumeration
of model numbers. —>
```

The XYZ Industries Product Line Page

Now that we've gradually added HTML code to the XYZ Industries product page, let's look at the whole page with our changes:

```
<HTML>
<!— Author: M.U. Langdon (mul@xyz.com) —>
<!— Dept: Corporate Communications —>
<!— Date:   10 Jul 94 —>
<!— Purpose:   overview of XYZ products—>
<!— Comments:  check with Sales to get the latest enumeration of model numbers.
—>
```

```
<HEAD>
<TITLE>Overview of XYZ Industries Product Line</TITLE>
<LINK REV="made" HREF="mailto:cc@xyz.com">
</HEAD>

<BODY>
<IMG SRC="xyz-logo.gif" ALT="XYZ Logo"> XYZ Industries
<HR>

<H1>The XYZ Industries Product Line</H1>

Founded in July 1994, XYZ Industries has
rapidly become a world leader in
HyperWidget and Odd-Bearing Machine (OBM) technologies.
<P>
XYZ's product line includes industry standards
such as the HyperWidget 2000 and OBM 411, as well as such innovations as the
Alpha-class HyperWidget line that allows hyper-window mapping on
VR (<A HREF="http://guinan.gsfc.nasa.gov/W3/VR.html">Virtual Reality</A>)
helmets or displays.   With XYZ's products,
you can be assured of
the highest quality and state-of-the art design. <P>

The XYZ products currently available for sale and delivery are:
<OL>
<LI>OBM 411, 412, 413, and 440
<LI>HyperWidget 2000, 2000A, 2000A-XL, and 2000A-XL-G
<LI>Alpha, beta, gamma, and delta class HyperWidgets for VR applications
</OL>
<HR>

<ADDRESS> <A HREF="http://www.xyz.com/units/cc.html">Corporate Communications</A>
(cc@xyz.com)</ADDRESS>

</BODY>
</HTML>
```

Figure 33.1 shows the page displayed in Mosaic, and Figure 33.2 shows it displayed in Lynx. Note how the displays differ, yet the same logical structure is expressed.

FIGURE 33.1.

XYZ Industries Product Line page (Mosaic).

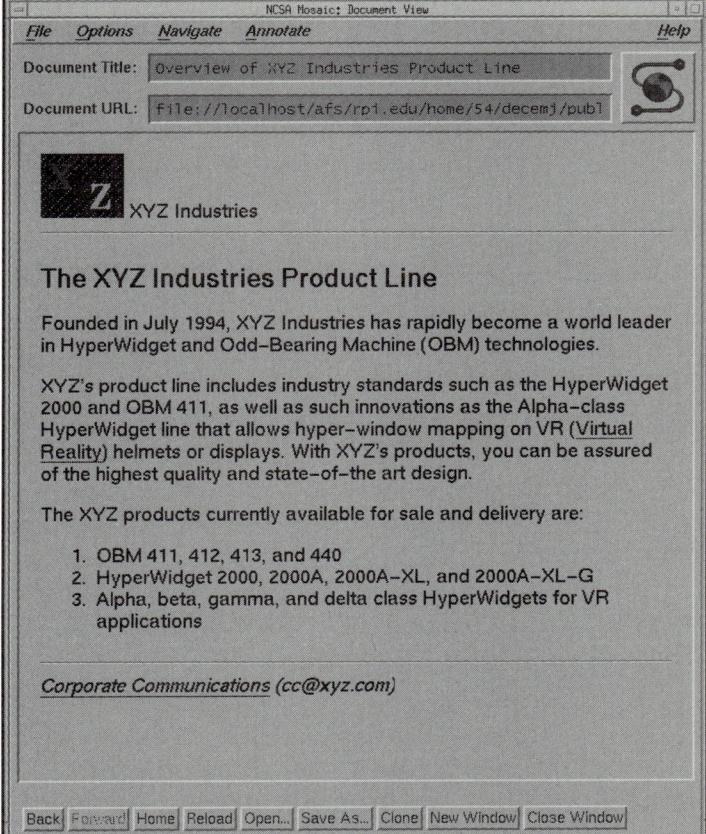

FIGURE 33.2.

XYZ Industries Product Line page (Lynx).

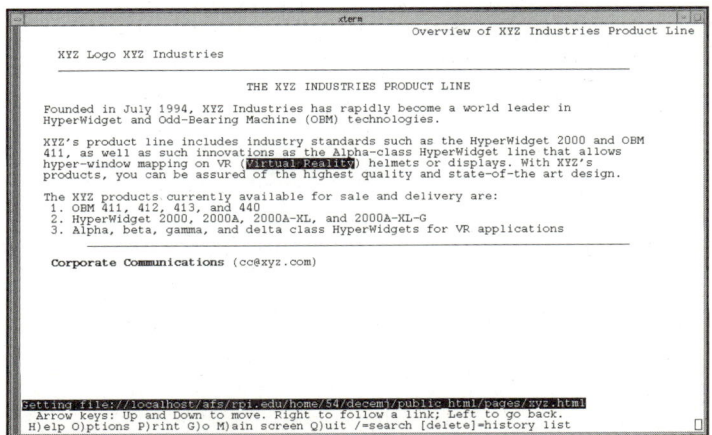

More HTML Features

While our XYZ Industries product page illustrates many common features of HTML, there are a some features that deserve a closer look because of their complexity and their special uses.

Anchors

We've already seen one kind of anchor that links a "hotspot" in your text to another document somewhere out on the Net:

```
Alpha-class HyperWidget line that allows hyper-window mapping on
VR (<A HREF="http://guinan.gsfc.nasa.gov/W3/VR.html">Virtual Reality</A>)
```

Another kind of anchor links a hotspot in your document to another place in your document (for example, if you want to allow the reader to jump quickly to another section). At the hotspot, make your link as follows:

```
You can find more about this same topic
at the <A HREF="#JUMP-TO-NAME">Jump Spot</A> later in this
document.
```

Notice that instead of a URL after `HREF="`, I included a `#` and a string of characters `"JUMP-TO-NAME."` At the point in your document that is the destination for this jump, make an anchor like this:

```
<A NAME="JUMP-TO-NAME"></a>
```

This will allow users of your document to jump from your hotspot to the portion of the text marked by the destination anchor.

A variation on this anchoring is when the document is at a remote place. In your own document, you can jump to this specific place in the remote document like this:

```
You can find more information about
of
<A HREF="http://www.zippy.com/products.html#JUMP-TO-NAME">Zippy Products</A>.
```

Notice that I've included the full URL of the document and then I used `#JUMP-TO-NAME` to mark the anchor point in that document where I want the user to jump.

It is ok to put an anchor in an HTML element, such as

```
<H1>The <A HREF="http://www.xyz.com">XYZ Industries</A> Product Line</H1>
```

But *do not* put an HTML element in an anchor, such as

```
<A HREF="http://www.xyz.com"><H1>The XYZ Industries Product Line</H1></A>
```

The reason for this is that the HTML specifications prohibit an HTML element placed in an anchor; semantically it doesn't make sense (because an anchor should be a "hotspot," not a list, heading, or other element).

Nesting

You can nest lists, for example

```
Regions of the USA and representative states and cities
<UL>
<LI>East
        <OL>
        <LI>New York
                <MENU>
                <LI>White Plains
                <LI>Latham
                </MENU>
        <LI>Delaware
        </OL>
<LI>Great Lakes
        <OL>
        <LI>Michigan
                <MENU>
                <LI>Troy
                <LI>Escanaba
                </MENU>
        <LI>Wisconsin
        </OL>
<LI>Midwest
<LI>Plains
<LI>West
</UL>
```

But don't try to nest physical or logical character highlights:

```
<B><I>The House of Seven Gables<I><B> is a great book.
```

The above *won't* give you bold italics.

Logical Versus Physical Tags

The tags used for character highlights (bold, italics) are either *physical,* that is, they define the *appearance* of the characters:

```
<B>Bold</B>
<I>Italics</I>
<U>Underline</U>
<TT>Fixed-width</TT>
```

or *logical,* that is, they define the *meaning* of the characters highlighted:

```
<STRONG>Strong emphasis, often same as bold</STRONG>
<VAR>A variable name</VAR>
<CITE>A citation</CITE>
```

You'll notice that the physical tags go against the HTML and SGML philosophies of marking the meaning and structure rather than the appearance. However, the existence of the physical tags is an acknowledgment that bold, italics, and other forms of character highlights *are meaningful* in certain contexts. The logical tags provide an alternative means to mark the semantic meaning of the character highlights. For example, the logical tag style uses a `<STRONG>...</STRONG>` to indicate emphasis rather than `<B>...</B>`. These logical alternatives help you achieve an appearance-independent HTML file. However, one problem with logical tags is that a tag's appearance might not correspond to the context in which it is used. For example, a `<CITE>Citation</CITE>` tag is typically rendered in italics. This may be fine for many contexts. However, it may be that citations within your discipline or field of study should always be marked by quotation marks around the cite (short stories or poem titles, for example). Therefore, the logical tags in many cases provide a useful alternative to the physical tags and should be used where possible. But in situations where the rendering of the characters is important—such as where a particular physical style is required—you'll have to use a physical tag.

Nicks and Cuts

Whenever you develop an HTML page, spend some time examining it in several different browsers. Often, particularly when working with links to graphics displayed by Mosaic, you'll find marks and irregularities in the display. One example is a "nick" that can occur when making a logo a hotspot. For example, you may make a logo a hotspot as follows:

```
<A HREF="xyz.html"><IMG SRC="xyz-logo.gif"> </A> XYZ Industries
```

However, Mosaic's interpretation of the space between the `<IMG SRC="xyz-logo.gif">` and the end of the anchor, `</A>` causes a nick to appear in the Mosaic display as shown in Figure 33.3. The nick is a small line between the logo and the label `XYZ Industries`. Taking out the space will remove the nick.

FIGURE 33.3.

A nick in an icon hotspot (magnified).

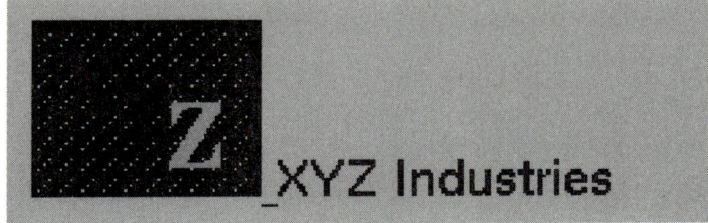

Similarly "cuts" can appear under other conditions in specific browsers. For example, if you include a physical tag such as <I> within a hotspot, such as

```
You can find more about this same topic
at the <A HREF="#JUMP-TO-NAME">Jump <I>Spot</I></A> later in this document.
```

You'll find that some browsers display a cut or discontinuity in the display of the anchor line in Jump Spot. While curing all nicks and cuts is not crucial to a successful HTML document (and it actually goes against the philosophy of HTML itself to not worry about a browser display), sometimes fine-tuning your HTML can help make its appearance more pleasing in your target browser. If you find an unusual display in your browser, it might even be an indication that you are misusing some aspect of HTML, and the browser can't determine a satisfactory way to resolve your error.

Weaver's Check

HyperText markup language (HTML) is a way to express information and ideas in hypertext. Based on a philosophy of marking up the meaning of a text rather than its appearance, HTML gives you a great deal of flexibility in defining semantic structures in your document but discourages attempts to manipulate the appearance of your text in any particular browser.

HTML itself is written in ASCII text files following a specific format for elements and entities. Head elements identify information *about a* document such as its title that are not displayed directly in a browser. Body elements such as headings, lists, blockquotes, preformatted text, and physical and logical character highlights mark the structure of a document. Graphics elements allow you to imbed inline images in a document. Entities are special characters that you can have displayed in most browsers.

To create HTML files, it's a good idea to make a template to hold the basic tags to mark the head, body, and address parts of a document. Based on this template, you can add headings, paragraphs, lists, and links. You can improve the appearance of an HTML file with horizontal rules and inline images. You can help document an HTML file through comments, the address element, or a revision link in the head of the file.

There are fine points of making anchors, nesting elements, and physical and logical tags that can help you be prepared for special situations or when you're struggling with the structure of your document. Finally, a careful examination of a document in a variety of browsers may show up a variety of anomalous displays—nicks and cuts— that can be cured by removing spaces or fixing errors in the HTML itself.

We've seen how writing HTML, although conceptually fairly straightforward, involves a great deal of syntax and fine points that might make it cumbersome to routinely produce. There are tools to assist you in preparing HTML code (see Chapter 35, "HTML Editors and Filters"). Also, you'll find that the basic HTML covered in this chapter doesn't do everything you want. The next chapter provides an overview of features of HTML Level 2, an extension of HTML that all browsers do not necessarily understand.

KEY HTML RESOURCES

HTML Information from CERN, URL `http://info.cern.ch/hypertext/WWW/MarkUp/MarkUp.html`

WWW & HTML Developer's JumpStation, by Barry Raveendran Greene, URL `http://oneworld.wa.com/htmldev/devpage/dev-page.html`

Advanced HTML Features

34

by John December

The basic HTML covered in Chapter 33, "Implementing a Web: Basic HyperText Markup Language (HTML)," constitutes a language set that every Web browser should recognize. The development of the browsers like Mosaic has brought new features to the HTML language that extend hypertext in a profound way: by adding features which provide more ways to *interact* with the user. These features include Forms and graphical information maps, both supported by Mosaic 2.0, but not necessarily recognized by other Web browsers. Both Forms and information maps are useful in eliciting information from users, as well as implementing new methods of interactive Web-based communication.

This chapter presents a very brief overview of these advanced HTML features to raise your awareness of what is possible. Techniques, practices, and tools for developing Forms and graphical information maps are still under development. For more information, consult tutorials given in the resources listed at the end of this chapter. Information for the discussion about Forms and graphical image maps in this chapter comes from the documents in the following sidebar:

INFORMATION MAP TUTORIAL

"Graphical Information Map Tutorial," URL `http://wintermute.ncsa.uiuc.edu:8080/map-tutorial/image maps.html` (originally written by Marc Andreesen).

"Mosaic for X Fill-Out Form Support," URL `http://www.ncsa.uiuc.edu/SDG/Software/Mosaic/Docs/fill-out-forms/ overview.html`.

Forms

Forms are features to elicit responses from the user through a graphical user interface consisting of fill-in blanks, buttons, checkboxes, and other features to get input from the user. After the user fills in Form values, the entries can be used by an arbitrary script (a list of commands for a computer to perform) or a separate computer program created by the implementor. In this way, a form can interface with any other program the implementor designates—another database, an accounting program, or a program to handle a user's order for a product.

This section focuses on the HTML aspects of forms, rather than on the implementation of scripts or programs to handle the output (these scripts and programs vary widely based on the application and the script or program language).

The Form Tag

A Form tag is used in an HTML document just like an element. A Form tag looks like this:

```
<FORM ACTION="URL" METHOD="POST">Form contents</FORM>
```

where URL is the query program or server to which the contents of the fill-in fields of the Form will be sent. METHOD identifies the way in which the contents of the form are sent to the query program. Mosaic documentation suggests always using the form POST because it allows for the form contents to be sent to the query program in a data structure as opposed to being appended to the URL. The form itself is defined in the area

```
Form contents, and tags possible are described below.
```

Tags in a Form

There are a variety of tags that can be used within a form to provide interfaces for user response.

1. The INPUT tag.

    The INPUT tag is the basic way to get input from the user in a variety of situations. These situations include asking for a user's name (when an exhaustive list of possibilities is not desirable) and also when a strict enumeration of user choices is possible (for example, a user's gender). Here's an example input tag that queries the user for a name (using text):

    ```
    <INPUT TYPE="TEXT" SIZE=40 NAME="NAME">
    ```

    An input tag can have various values for TYPE, including the following:

    TEXT (shown previously) is used for any alphanumeric string entry.

    NUMBER causes the input to be read as a number.

    PASSWORD causes the text to be read as an alphanumeric string, but with the characters displayed as stars when entered.

    CHECKBOX enables the user to toggle a single button on or off.

    RADIO enables the user to choose to toggle on exactly one button out of a set of buttons.

    SUBMIT is a pushbutton that causes the current form to be submitted to the query program.

    RESET clears all values that a user might have entered in the form and sets them to their default settings (a way for the user to start over).

    The SIZE portion of the INPUT tag determines how wide a box or input area is displayed.

The NAME portion of the INPUT tag designates the variable name that will be used in the data structure sent to the query program. This name is then used to pull the value of the user's response from the data structure.

The VALUE field is used to specify default values. For example

```
<INPUT TYPE="NUMBER" NAME="quantity1" VALUE="12" SIZE=5><BR>
```

will set the default value for this entry to be 12. That is, the user might change this value, but upon entry to the form and after a RESET, the form's value will be set at 12 (and a 12 will be displayed in the input area).

2. The SELECT tag. Like the INPUT tag, the SELECT tag is for querying the user for values. The basic structure of a SELECT tag is as follows:

```
<SELECT NAME="select-menu" SIZE=2 MULTIPLE=2>
<OPTION> View the product.
<OPTION> Call for help.
<OPTION> Request a catalog.
<OPTION> Exit this form.
</SELECT>
```

In the SELECT tag

NAME designates the symbolic name for use in the data string submitted to the query program.

SIZE, if missing or set to 1, will make the SELECT tag an option menu (displayed with all the options shown). If SIZE is 2 or more, the number of options indicated by SIZE will be shown in a scrollable list.

MULTIPLE sets the number of options that can be chosen from the list.

3. The TEXTAREA tag. This tag is used to allow the user to enter several lines of text.

An example TEXTAREA tag is

```
<TEXTAREA NAME="comments" ROWS=4 COLS=30></TEXTAREA>
```

The attributes of the TEXTAREA tag are the following:

NAME is used to identify the text in the data structure sent to the query (or other) program.

ROWS are the number of vertical rows displayed for user entry.

COLS are the number of horizontal columns displayed for user entry.

An Example Form

Let's put all this together and construct an example form. Here's the HTML code:

```
<HTML>
<HEAD>
<TITLE>Example Order Form</TITLE>
</HEAD>

<BODY>

<H1>Order Form</H1>

Please fill out the following form.
<P>

<FORM METHOD="POST" ACTION="http://hoohoo.ncsa.uiuc.edu/cgi-bin/post-query">
Your Name:        <INPUT TYPE="TEXT"   size=32 NAME="NAME"><BR>
Customer Number: <INPUT TYPE="NUMBER" size=10 name="CUSTOMER-NUMBER"><BR>
<P>

Size?
<INPUT TYPE="radio" name="SIZE"   value="S">S
<INPUT TYPE="radio" name="SIZE"   value="M">M
<INPUT TYPE="radio" name="SIZE"   value="L">L
<INPUT TYPE="radio" name="SIZE"   value="XL">XL<BR>
<P>

<SELECT NAME="select-menu" SIZE=2 MULTIPLE=2>
<OPTION> View the product.
<OPTION> Call for help.
<OPTION> Request a catalog.
<OPTION> Exit this form.
</SELECT>
<P>

<TEXTAREA NAME="comments" ROWS=4 COLS=30></TEXTAREA>
<P>

<INPUT TYPE=submit value="Order Product">
<P>

<INPUT TYPE=reset  value="Cancel Order">
</FORM>
<P>

</BODY>
</HTML>
```

Figure 34.1 shows the appearance of this form.

FIGURE 34.1.

A Mosaic Form.

```
┌─────────────────────────────────────────────────────────────┐
│                    NCSA Mosaic: Document View          ▫ □   │
│  File   Options   Navigate   Annotate              Help      │
│ Document Title:  Example Order Form                    ╭──╮  │
│                                                        │ ◉│  │
│ Document URL:  file://localhost/afs/rpi.edu/home/54/decemj/p │
│ ┌─────────────────────────────────────────────────────────┐ │
│ │ Order Form                                              │ │
│ │ Please fill out the following form.                     │ │
│ │                                                         │ │
│ │ Your Name: [                                        ]   │ │
│ │ Customer Number: [            ]                          │ │
│ │                                                         │ │
│ │ Size?  ◇ S  ◇ M  ◇ L  ◇ XL                              │ │
│ │                                                         │ │
│ │ ┌───────────────────────┐▲                              │ │
│ │ │View the product.      │▼                              │ │
│ │ │Call for help.         │                               │ │
│ │ ┌───────────────────────────────────────┐▲             │ │
│ │ │ I                                      │▼             │ │
│ │ │                                        │              │ │
│ │ │◄                                      ►│              │ │
│ │ └───────────────────────────────────────┘              │ │
│ │ ┌───────────────┐                                      │ │
│ │ │ Order Product │                                      │ │
│ │ └───────────────┘                                      │ │
│ │ ┌───────────────┐                                      │ │
│ │ │ Cancel Order  │                                      │ │
│ │ └───────────────┘                                      │ │
│ └─────────────────────────────────────────────────────────┘ │
│ Back Forward Home Reload Open... Save As... Clone New Window Close Window │
└─────────────────────────────────────────────────────────────┘
```

When the form is filled in by the user, as shown in Figure 34.2, and the SUBMIT button is pressed ("Order Product"), the results are sent to the demonstration query program (at URL `http://hoohoo.ncsa.uiuc.edu/cgi-bin/post-query`) and the results are shown in Figure 34.3. This test server is provided by NCSA developers to echo the data structure submitted by a POST query. The implementor could develop his or her own program which would have used the Form values in some other way.

Graphical Information Maps

Just as HTML Forms are a way to elicit input from the user, so too are Graphical Information Maps. While Forms provide a template for information that the user fills in, the graphical information map is a way for a user to respond through graphics. Essentially, a graphical information map provides a way for any part of an arbitrary image (in a graphics file) to be linked to a particular URL. A common application is in point-and-click maps (Figure 34.4) that enable you to find out information about a particular area or building.

FIGURE 34.2.

A filled-in HTML Form.

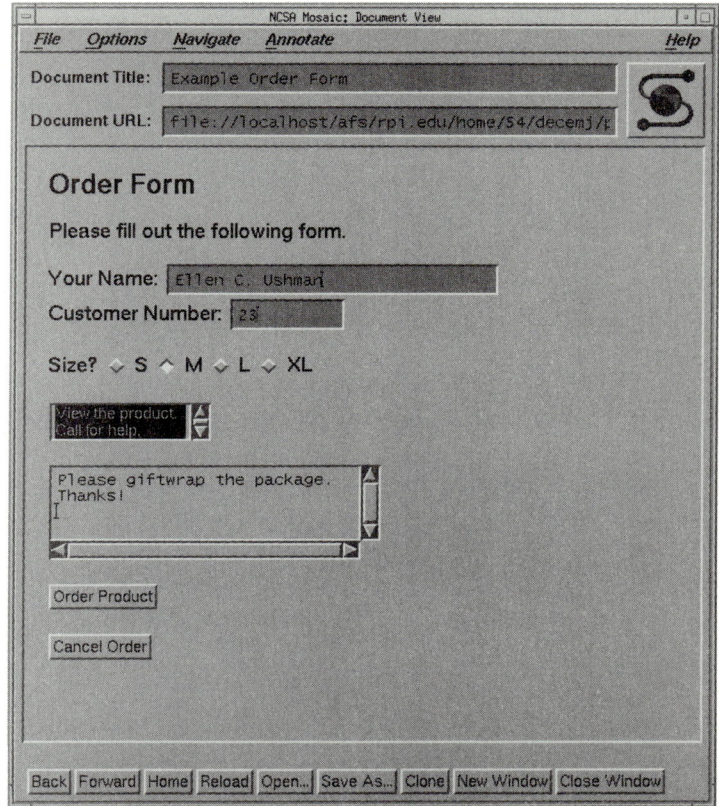

Map Specification

To use a graphical information map, you must have several things in place, which may require skills from setting up the Web server itself. You must

1. Have a HTTPD server installed and operating.

2. Have write privileges to the conf/imagemap.conf file (the server administrator would have to give you these permissions if you aren't the server administrator yourself).

3. Have the "imagemap" program compiled in the cgi-bin directory of the server. (See URL http://hoohoo.ncsa.uiuc.edu/docs/Overview.html.)

FIGURE 34.3.

An HTML Form results.

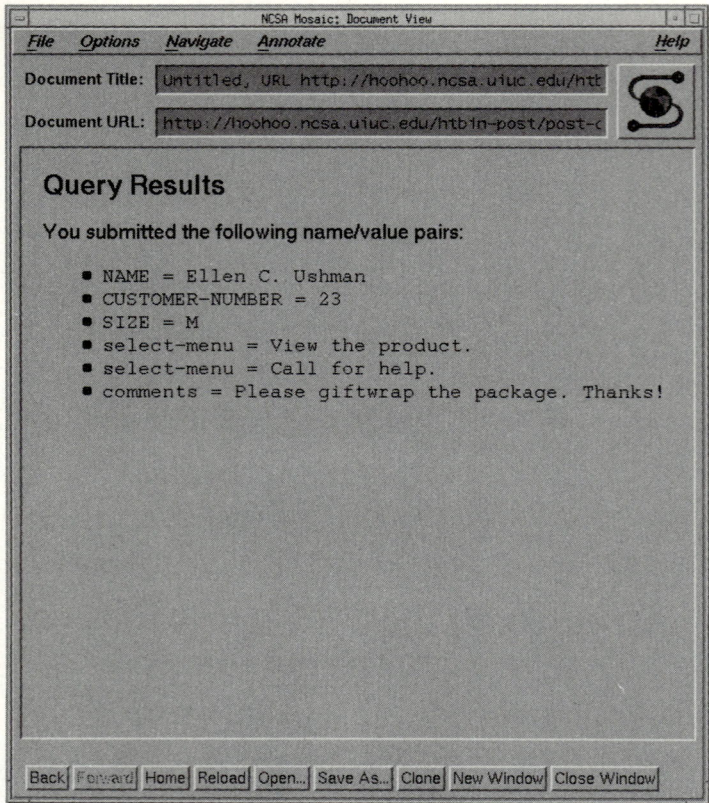

Once these are in place, the next steps are

1. Create an image. There are a variety of drawing and painting and drawing tools available. A typical file ending for the image file is Graphical Interchange Format (GIF). Other inlined-image formats include xbm and xpm. For example, your image file might be `info.gif`.

2. Create an image map file. This file specifies what URL will be opened as a result of a user clicking on a region of your image.

    The general format of this image map file is as follows:

    ```
                default default-URL
        rect URL      UL-corner  LR-corner
        rect URL      UL-corner  LR-corner
        rect URL      UL-corner  LR-corner
    ...
    ...
    ...
    ```

where `default-URL` is the resource that is opened if the user clicks on any region not designated in one of the other lines of the file.

The `rect` identifies each line as a rectangle. The URL after `rect` is the resource that will be opened if the user clicks on the image in the rectangle bounded by the upper-left corner (`UL-corner`) coordinates (given in x, y pairs in pixels) and the lower-right (`LR-corner`) coordinates.

FIGURE 34.4.

A touch-sensitive campus map.

3. Put a line in the `conf/imagemap.conf` file:

```
infomap:/yourhome/yourdirectory/info.map
```

`Infomap` is the symbolic name recognized by the server as the name of your map. After this name, the full pathname of your image map file (relative to the `conf/imagemap.conf` file) is given.

4. Add a reference to your map in an HTML file:

```
For more information, click on part of the image below:
<A HREF="http://yourhost.domain/htbin/imagemap/infomap">
<IMG SRC="info.gif" ALT="IMAGE MAP" ISMAP></A>
```

A Glance Ahead: Extensions to HTML

Extensions to HTML are still in development as of this printing. These extensions are expected to allow for

- Figures with captions
- Tables
- Mathematical equations
- Fill-out forms
- Segmentation of large documents into nodes
- Style sheets

and many other features that will make it a much more expressive and powerful language than basic HTML.

These extensions are expected to be a compatible *superset* of HTML, so you should expect that most of what you write now in HTML will be recognized by browsers designed for HTML extensions. There will be differences, however. For example, an HTML paragraph is expected to have both a start and an end tag as follows:

```
<P>
For example, an HTML+ paragraph is expected
to have both a start and an end tag.
</P>
```

However, HTML code written without the </P> tag will still work as long as the browser can recognize the end of the paragraph (implied by another <P> tag, for example).

Weaver's Check

Some features that the Mosaic browser can access are not available to other Web browsers, but provide very useful ways to interact with users. The Forms interface allows the implementor to create a form, complete with checkboxes, fill-in slots, scrollable text entry, and other features. Once the user completes this form and clicks on the Form feature designated as the SUBMIT button, the values in the form are sent to a query (or other) program created by the implementor.

Graphical information maps are another way to get information from a user. Instead of the static template a Forms interface presents, a graphical information map allows the implementor to map any geometric region of an inline image to a particular URL. In this way, graphical information maps help developers create very user-friendly, point-and-click interfaces.

KEY RESOURCES

"WWW & HTML Developer's JumpStation," by Barry Raveendran Greene, URL `http://oneworld.wa.com/htmldev/devpage/dev-page.html`

WWW Weavers, a collection of links to assist web weavers, by Chris Beaumont, URL `http://www.nas.nasa.gov/RNR/Education/weavers.html`

Cyberweb, a resource collection for Web information providers and users, from Charm Net, URL `http://www.charm.net/~web/Web.html`

"MapMarker (a tool for clickable image maps) Home Page," by Peter Murray-Rust, URL `http://www.dl.ac.uk/CBMT/mapmarker/HOME.html`

NCSA Mosaic Tutorials, URL `http://www.ncsa.uiuc.edu/SDG/Software/Mosaic/Docs/mosaic-docs.html`

HTML Editors and Filters

35

by Thomas Boutell and Laura Lemay

Faced with the task of creating HTML (Hypertext Markup Language) documents, it is natural to wish for an easy, friendly way of creating them. If you have a large number of existing documents, you probably want a straightforward way to convert them to HTML without rewriting them; this is the purpose of HTML filters. Fortunately, HTML filters, which are discussed later in this chapter, are fairly numerous.

When creating new documents, it is natural to expect a WYSIWYG (What You See Is What You Get) environment, in which you can immediately see the final appearance of your work. After all, word processors have provided such features for years.

But now the reality: Although there are plenty of HTML editors that claim to make your task easier, few of them succeed. Some editors attempt to provide a WYSIWYG environment and a few attempt to help you write correct HTML documents, but only a few products make a credible showing in all three categories: ease-of-use, WYSIWYG environment, and the creation of correct documents that look good on many different browsers. There is also a much smaller group of editors that attempt to be even remotely WYSIWYG. And an even smaller group actually attempt to help you write correct HTML documents. Fortunately, there are a few products that make a credible showing in all three categories.

As has been discussed in earlier chapters, HTML documents consist of a collection of tags in angle brackets, such as <EM> for emphasis and </EM> to close it. Learning to follow these tags is relatively easy, since their names are fairly intuitive, but memorizing all of them and keeping the order straight is more work than you may want to do by hand.

All HTML editors provide convenient tag-insertion menus and button bars, but editors *should* be able to insert closing tags for you and make sure that your document follows the HTML standard. Unfortunately, though, most of the presently available editors are essentially text editors with pretty buttons provided to insert tags. They do nothing to help structure your document, and in most cases their only WYSIWYG feature is the ability to invoke Mosaic or another browser as a WYSIWYG previewer.

You may point out that you can create such a collection of macros yourself using your favorite word processor, and you're right. Some of the best editors are macro packages for Microsoft Word and WordPerfect (under the Microsoft Windows and Macintosh environments), and for the Emacs editor (under UNIX).

BEFORE YOU FETCH THESE PACKAGES...

Anonymous FTP sites and URLs are provided for each package described in this chapter, but remember that Internet sites are subject to rapid change. Also remember that sites are often overloaded by too many attempts to retrieve the same package. Before obtaining one of these packages from the URL provided, make an effort to locate it at a site near your own by using the Archie program that is available from nearly all Internet sites (such as any UNIX shell account provider you may use).

Non-WYSIWYG Editors

Most standalone HTML editors for Microsoft Windows or for the Macintosh have no WYSIWYG features. They do, however, attempt to provide other benefits. The following section describes several such editors for a variety of platforms.

HTML Assistant

One of the most popular editors for Microsoft Windows is HTML Assistant, available by anonymous FTP from `ftp.cuhk.hk` in the directory `pub/www/windows/util/htmlasst.zip`. HTML Assistant is essentially a text editor, dressed up with buttons which can insert the more commonly used tags of HTML (see Figure 35.1).

FIGURE 35.1.

HTML Assistant.

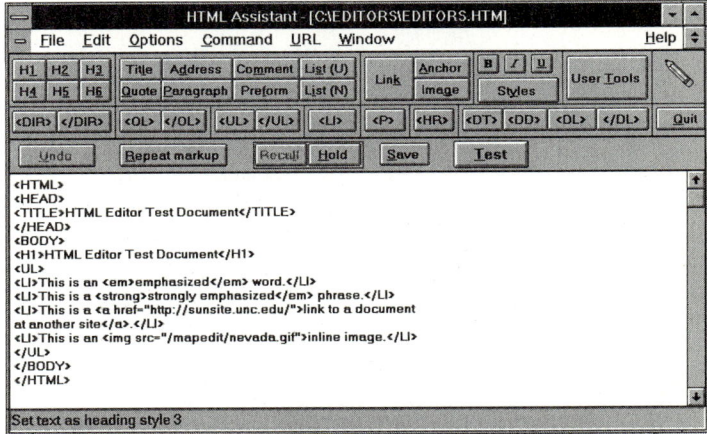

Perhaps its best feature is the ability to automatically instruct your World Wide Web browser to load or reload the document, providing a preview capability. HTML Assistant also has good online help.

In addition, HTML Assistant helps the user construct URLs, providing a history of frequently linked-to URLs and also providing a menu of the usual access methods (`http:`, `ftp:` and the like) to construct links more quickly.

An important disadvantage: HTML Assistant cannot open files larger than 32K in size. This restriction makes it impossible to open large HTML files, such as the WWW Frequently Asked Questions (FAQ) list, which was used as a test document.

HTMLed

HTMLed for Microsoft Windows is a newer package, available by anonymous FTP from `ftp.cuhk.hk` in the directory `pub/www/windows/util/htmled10.zip`. Much like HTML Assistant, HTMLed is a gussied-up text editor with convenient buttons for the insertion of HTML tags (see Figure 35.2). However, HTMLed lacks many of the features of the latest versions of HTML Assistant. HTMLed has no capability to assist in building anchors (except for a history capability), and no online help.

FIGURE 35.2.

HTMLed.

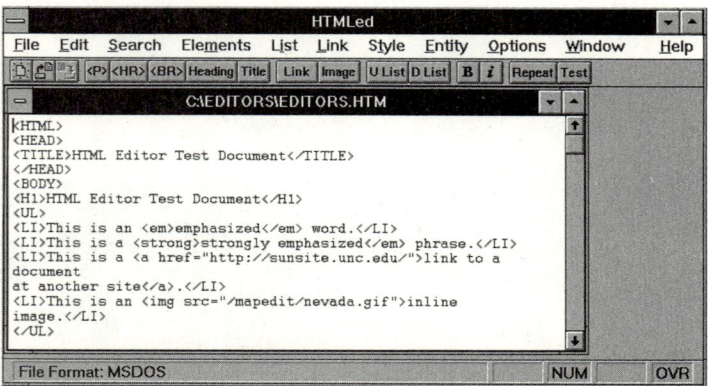

The strongest feature of HTMLed may be a conversion facility provided for *intelligently* inserting tags at the beginnings and ends of lines in a particular portion of the document (see Figure 35.3). This makes it easy to convert a plain ASCII text document into a reasonable HTML document.

HTMLed does attempt, in a very limited way, to encourage good HTML style by inserting both opening and closing tags when elements are inserted from its tool bars. It has other interesting macros such as a macro to create the following commonly-seen structure:

```
<TITLE>The title text</TITLE>
<H1>The title text</H1>
```

Unfortunately, this is not correct HTML. The title tag should be within the `<HEAD>` tag at the beginning of the document, and the `H1` tag should follow later within the `<BODY>` tag.

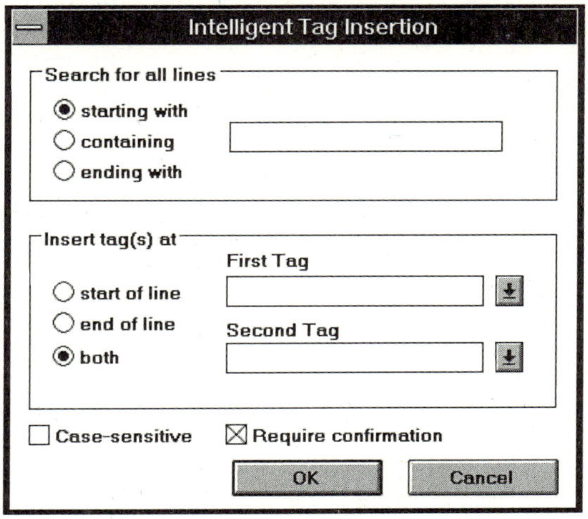

FIGURE 35.3.
HTMLed Intelligent Tag Insertion.

In addition, HTMLed has the same problem as HTML Assistant: it cannot open large files. Worse, it does not produce a clear error message when failing to do so.

Products such as HTML Assistant and HTMLed are essentially stopgaps. What they truly reveal is the need for editors that actually understand HTML to a significant degree, helping the user to create correct documents. The more the editor knows about HTML, the more it will be able to help you.

HTML.edit

HTML.edit is a freeware HTML editor for the Macintosh. HTML.edit is available by anonymous FTP at most common Macintosh archives such as sumex or its various mirrors (try the Gopher archive at `gopher://catfish.lcs.mit.edu`, for example). HTML.edit is written in HyperCard, and behaves much like a HyperCard stack, but does not require the HyperCard program in order to run.

HTML.edit is quite complete, allowing you to insert most HTML tags (including `<HTML>`, `<HEAD>` and `<BODY>`) into a simple text file. Inserting links is particularly easy; HTML.edit allows you to easily create both links to other documents and create anchors within this document.

Besides the standard HTML tags, HTML.edit also contains an automatic indexing feature (for easily creating linked Table of Contents listings), a command for inserting paragraph (`<P>`) tags at the end of every paragraph in the selected text (which makes converting plain text files particularly easy), and a window of special characters (diacriticals and other "entities") where when you click on a character, the appropriate HTML code for that character is inserted.

The biggest problem with HTML.edit is its interface. HTML.edit opens with an index page (card) that lists several files, and includes buttons for saving, deleting and editing files (see Figure 35.4).

FIGURE 35.4.

HTML.edit Index Card.

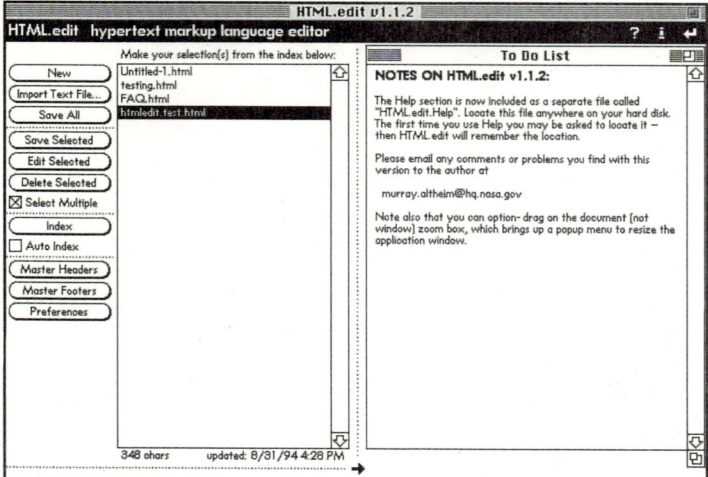

The relationship between the files in the list and the HTML files on the disk was somewhat confusing. The lists were entirely different. A quick read through the online help file cleared up the confusion: the index card allows you to create a system of HTML files (sort of like a project in Think C, or a Book file in FrameMaker), and easily create links between them (the files in the index appear in a menu for inserting links). To have a file listed in the index page, you must import it into HTML.edit first.

The cards for actually editing HTML files are slightly more straightforward, but are littered with extra buttons and menus whose effects are mysterious and confusing (see Figure 35.5). The window itself is divided into three parts: a header, a body, and a footer. The header and the footer are one line wide, and it was difficult to figure out how to resize them without reading the help. There are also buttons and menus everywhere: a tool bar with pull-down menus, a set of navigation buttons along the button edge, and several other clickable items whose effects were not immediately apparent. Once again, after reading the online help, things were much clearer.

The help for HTML.edit implies that when you import an HTML file into HTML.edit, the HTML tags in that file are parsed, and errors are pointed out. Several intentional grievous errors to the sample file were made (closing a <STRONG> tag with </em>, leaving off a closing tag for an anchor </a>, and creating a mythical tag <ruff>). HTML.edit imported the file with not a single complaint. It did, however, recognize and correct a <TITLE> tag in the <BODY> section, and moved it to the <HEAD> section.

FIGURE 35.5.

HTML.edit editing windows.

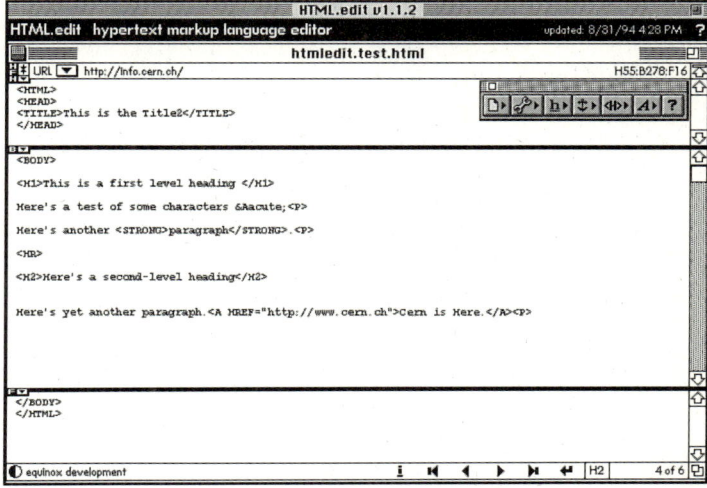

Like HTML assistant and HTMLed, HTML.edit has a limit as to the size of imported files (30K), imposed by the HyperCard engine. The online help does provide a "cheat" for getting around the limit by putting parts of the file in the header and footer windows.

Simple HTML Editor

Simple HTML Editor (SHE), for the Macintosh, is freeware, and is available by anonymous FTP from `ericmorgan.lib.ncsu.edu`, in `/Public/simple-http-editor.hqx`. SHE is a HyperCard stack and requires the HyperCard program to run (see Figure 35.6).

The interface is simple; an HTML menu allows the insertion of many popular HTML tags including titles, heading tags, paragraphs, comments, rule lines, links and character formatting (it does not provide document tags such as `<HTML>`, `<HEAD>`, or `<BODY>`).

There is also a small tools palette that allows you to insert tags by selecting icons. Most of the menu items (and palette icons) require some amount of text to be selected before SHE imports the tags.

You can import files into SHE by using the Open... menu item. Be forewarned, however, that SHE has a size limit on imported files that it does not tell you about. Worse, when you try to import larger files (such as the Frequently Answered Questions file), SHE silently cuts off any portion of the file that exceeds the limit. No error or warning message is ever produced; you just find out when you get to the end of the scrolling window that the end of your file is missing.

SHE is acceptable for small, simple files, but the functionality is limited. HTML.edit is more general and comprehensive for editing HTML files on the Macintosh.

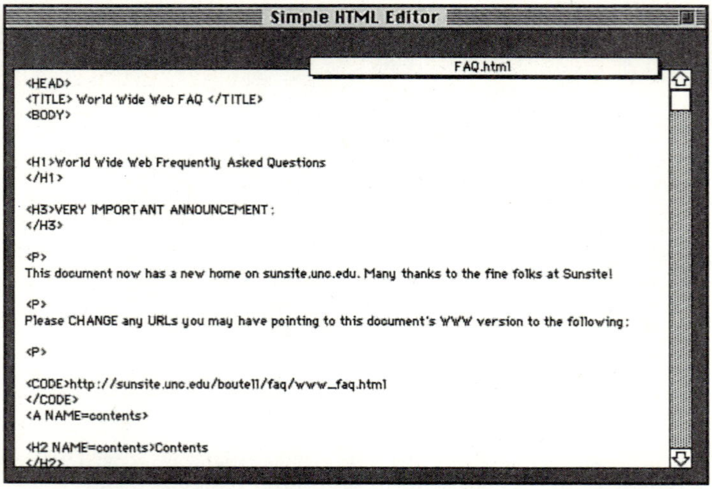

FIGURE 35.6.

SHE.

```
                                          Simple HTML Editor
                                    ┌──────────────────────────────────────┐
                                    │                FAQ.html                │
<HEAD>
<TITLE> World Wide Web FAQ </TITLE>
<BODY>

<H1>World Wide Web Frequently Asked Questions
</H1>

<H3>VERY IMPORTANT ANNOUNCEMENT:
</H3>

<P>
This document now has a new home on sunsite.unc.edu. Many thanks to the fine folks at Sunsite!

<P>
Please CHANGE any URLs you may have pointing to this document's WWW version to the following:

<P>

<CODE>http://sunsite.unc.edu/boutell/faq/www_faq.html
</CODE>
<A NAME=contents>

<H2 NAME=contents>Contents
</H2>
```

Extensions for Alpha and BBEdit

Alpha and BBEdit are two popular text editors for the Macintosh, and both have extensions available that allow insertion of HTML tags into the file you're editing, allowing you to use the powerful capabilities of a general text editor as well as insert HTML tags. Alpha is a shareware programmer's text editor; BBEdit's interface is friendlier, but is a commercial application (there is a freeware "lite" version with fewer capabilities).

The BBEdit HTML extensions (and the freeware version of BBEdit as well) are available by anonymous FTP at most common Macintosh archives such as sumex or its various mirrors (try the Gopher archive at gopher://catfish.lcs.mit.edu, for example). See Figure 35.7 for an example of the HTML menu in BBEdit after the extensions have been loaded.

The Alpha HTML extensions (and the Alpha editor) are available by anonymous FTP at cs.rice.edu. As of Alpha version 5.92b, the HTML extensions have been incorporated into the main Alpha release. For earlier versions of Alpha, get the file html.0.14.sit.bin from the Alpha/contrib directory on cs.rice.edu (ftp://cs.rice.edu/public/Alpha/contrib/html.0.14.sit.bin).

See Figure 35.8 for an example of the HTML menu in Alpha after the extensions have been loaded.

FIGURE 35.7.

BBEdit.

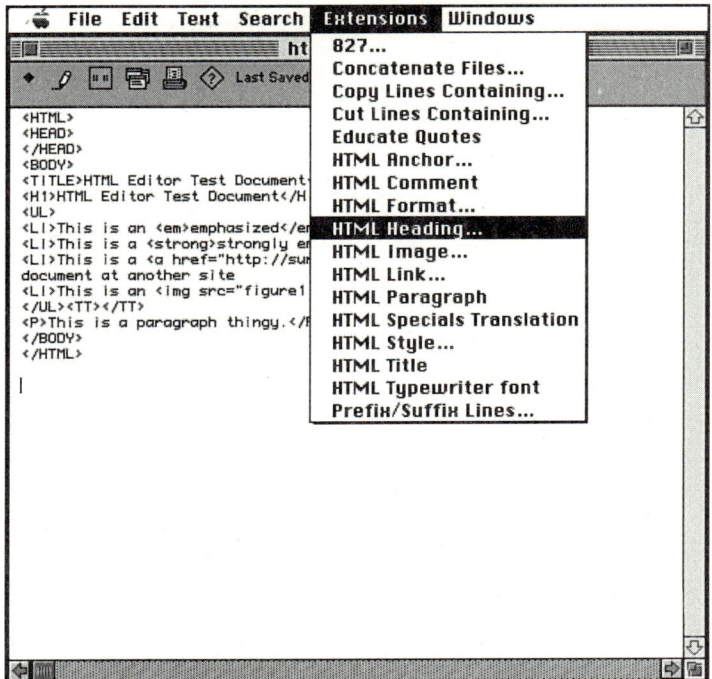

FIGURE 35.8.

Alpha.

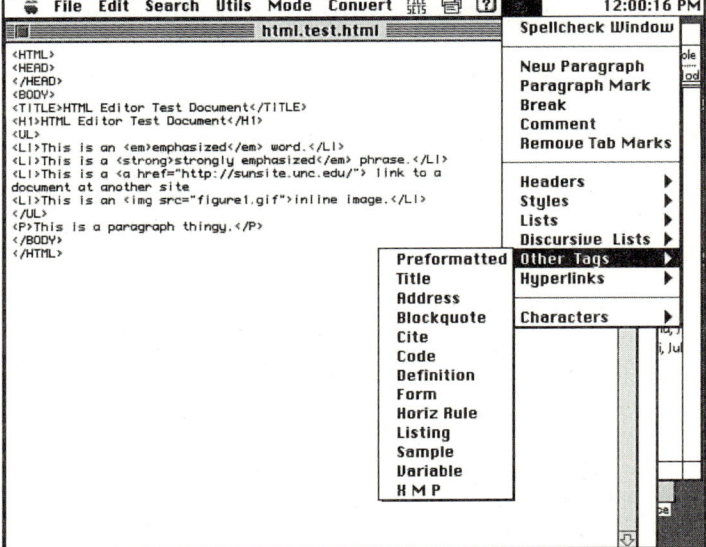

Near-WYSIWYG Editors

A truly WYSIWYG HTML editor is impossible. The reason is that there are many different browser packages, including the Windows, Macintosh and UNIX flavors of Mosaic and many others such as Chimera (for X11), Cello (for Windows) and Lynx (for text environments such as DOS and UNIX shell accounts). Each browser has its own idea of how to display HTML text, and its own formatting conventions.

What's more, even if all of your readers were to use the same browser, they still wouldn't see the same thing. Many users change the font settings, the window size, and other attributes of their browser to suit their personal taste.

Many of the worst documents on the web try to assume that text will wrap at a particular point on the line, or that every user will have a particular font size, or that a convenient bug found in one browser will also exist in every other browser. When using near-WYSIWYG editors, be sure to remember that if your document depends on the exact window width, font size or other idiosyncrasies of your browser, it will probably look terrible on another user's display.

Near-WYSIWYG features are a great help, because they allow you to see at a glance whether you have turned on <em> (emphasis, *italic* on most browsers), <strong> (strong emphasis, **bold** on most browsers), <H1> (header one, very large on most browsers) and the like. They also allow you to see at a glance how deeply you have nested list elements such as <UL> (unnumbered list, displayed with "bullets" for each item on most browsers). But it is just as well that they do not match browser displays exactly, since it would be a mistake to assume that the display of every user's browser will precisely match that of your editor.

CU_HTML

CU_HTML is a template package for Microsoft Word for Windows that provides an impressive near-WYSIWYG environment for creating HTML documents. (Both Word 2.0 and Word 6.0 are supported. At the time of this writing the Macintosh version of Word is not supported.) CU_HTML can be obtained by anonymous FTP from `ftp.cuhk.hk` in the directory `pub/www/windows/util/cu_html.zip` (see Figure 35.9).

CU_HTML is quite useful for creating new HTML documents and immediately seeing the results. Since it is a template package, it works within Microsoft Word, which ensures a full-featured editing environment; but since it provides several DLLs of its own, it is capable of things that even most stand-alone editors can't handle, including inline image display, which few other editors can do effectively at this time. (The inline images do have to reside on your file system, but this is quite often the case. Inline links to outside images cannot be easily created, however.)

FIGURE 35.9.

CU_HTML.

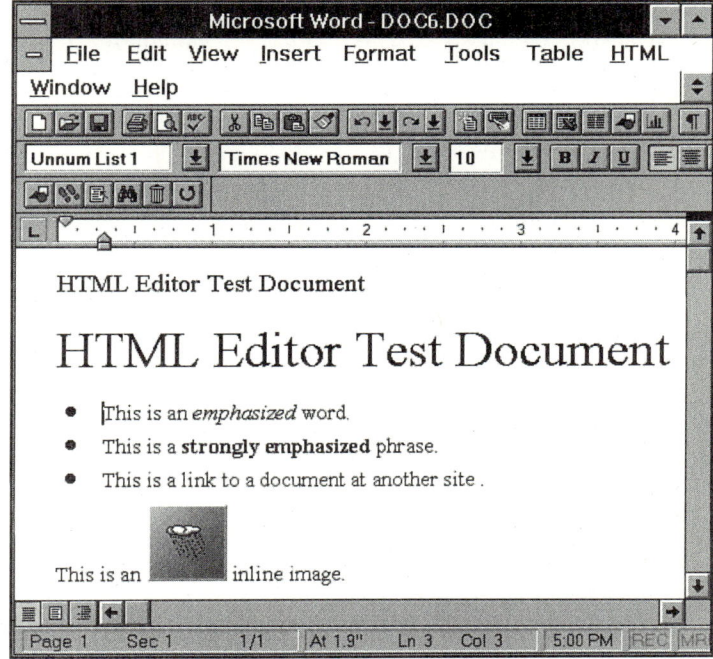

FIGURE 35.9.

CU_HTML.

CU_HTML provides a collection of styles that allow header levels 1 through 6, emphasis, strong emphasis, addresses and the like. CU_HTML also provides a small toolbar of frequently used operations, such as the creation of links.

Link creation with CU_HTML is most elegant when the document you are linking to exists on the same system. In that case, you can take advantage of the file dialog box provided to seek out the file you want to link to. In the case of links to documents located on other servers, CU_HTML is actually less elegant than HTML Assistant, since it does not provide the convenience of a history of frequently used URLs.

CU_HTML and Existing Documents

The greatest weakness of CU_HTML is that it cannot be used to edit existing HTML documents. CU_HTML documents continue to exist in the Word for Windows DOC format, side by side with HTML versions which are exported, one-way, from the system. As with the other editors, it was not possible to effectively edit a large existing HTML document, the WWW FAQ List. Recreating every tag in an existing document is not an acceptable price to pay for a WYSIWYG environment.

If you will be creating new documents or converting ASCII documents, and already have access to Word for Windows, CU_HTML is worth careful consideration. If you have a large collection of existing HTML documents, or expect to inherit one, you will probably want to look elsewhere.

ANT_HTML

ANT_HTML is also a template package for Microsoft Word for Windows. Much like CU_HTML, ANT_HTML provides a near-WYSIWYG authoring environment. ANT_HTML, however, differs in several respects. ANT_HTML can be obtained by anonymous FTP from ftp.einet.net in the directory EINet/pc (see Figure 35.10).

ANT_HTML has most of the same advantages and disadvantages as CU_HTML; it cannot edit existing HTML documents, but has strong capabilities for the creation of new ones. Like CU_HTML, it can handle inline GIF images, but ANT_HTML does not provide DLLs for this, instead requiring that you acquire appropriate filters for the images you want to insert.

ANT_HTML has stronger documentation and a more comprehensive tool bar, providing buttons for most of its operations instead of just a few. Also, it makes a point of inserting both opening and closing tags when an element is inserted.

FIGURE 35.10.

ANT_HTML.

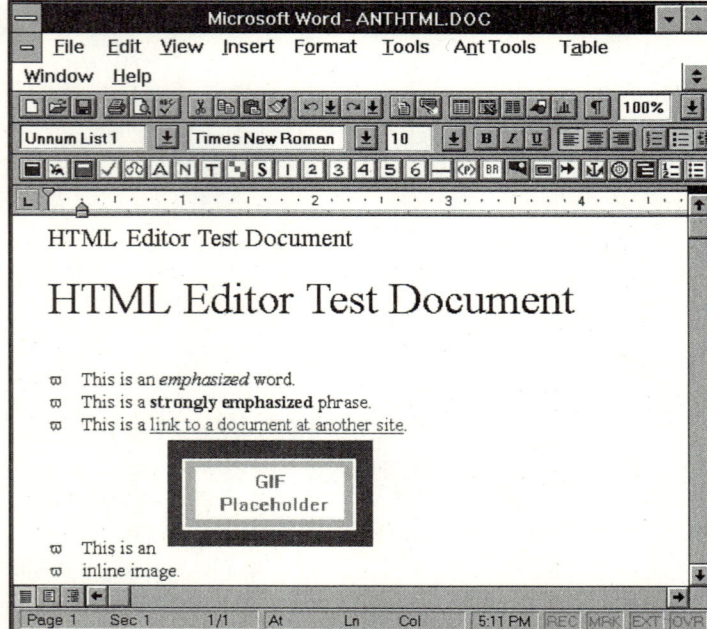

ANT_HTML and Existing Documents

Like CU_HTML, ANT_HTML cannot be used to edit existing HTML documents in a WYSIWYG fashion. Unfortunately, this is not easily understood from the documentation, and considerable time was lost trying to convert the Frequently Asked Questions document to take advantage of the styles ANT_HTML provides.

As with CU_HTML, if you will be creating new documents or converting ASCII documents, and already have access to Word for Windows, ANT_HTML is worth careful consideration. While ANT_HTML puts more functionality on the button bar and does a better job with nested lists, CU_HTML is preferred because of its superior display. Neither package, though, is suitable for editing existing HTML documents.

Softquad HoTMetaL: Above the Crowd

The strongest editor as of this writing is Softquad HoTMetaL, which is available for both Microsoft Windows and Sun SPARC (UNIX) systems. (It is likely that it will be available for other UNIX platforms by the time you read this.) HoTMetaL is a commercial product, but the entry-level version is freely available by FTP; the commercial version, HoTMetaL Pro, has more features and should be available for purchase in the immediate future. HoTMetaL is available for anonymous FTP from `ftp.ncsa.uiuc.edu` in the directory `/Web/html/hotmetal/Windows`.

Unlike CU_HTML, HoTMetaL is a stand-alone program and does not require a word processor. Softquad is truly remarkable in that it provides both a reasonably-close-to-WYSIWYG display and a good sense of the structure of your HTML document. What's more, it actively encourages good HTML style, by only allowing you to insert tags where they are legal. For instance, your entire document must be enclosed in an `<HTML>` tag, and the `<TITLE>` element must be enclosed in a `<HEAD>` tag.

These requirements may seem like nit-picking, but in actuality they are very worthwhile because they make it possible for future clients to request only certain portions of your document in much less time, and also because they allow your documents to be examined by SGML-supporting programs. (HTML is a particular case of SGML, a more general language for describing markup languages like HTML. Most HTML documents don't comply with the SGML DTD, or rule set, that formally defines HTML.)

NOTE

In Figure 35.11, display of tags is turned on. They can be toggled on and off freely and need not be displayed all the time.

FIGURE 35.11.
Softquad HoTMetaL.

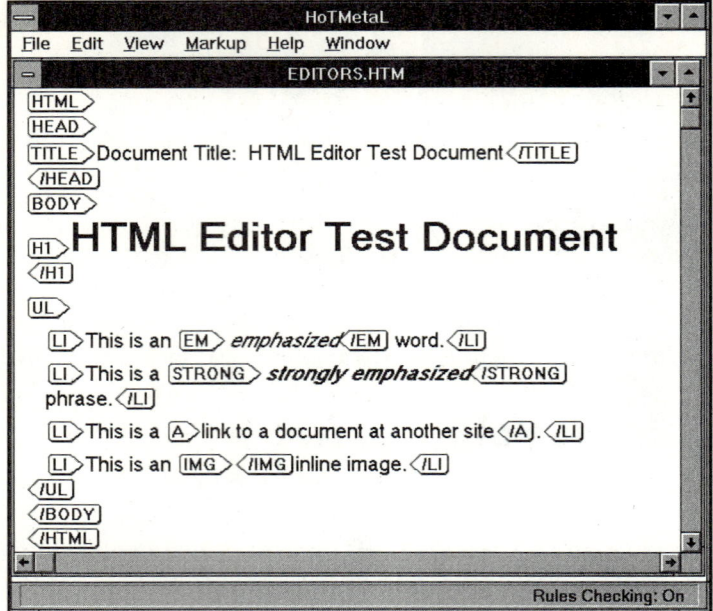

The Word for Windows-based packages do have some advantages over HoTMetaL; note that the GIF image in the above document is not visible. But HoTMetaL's ability to ensure that you insert only the tags that make sense at a particular point outweighs the disadvantages.

Existing Documents and HoTMetaL

The greatest disadvantage of HoTMetaL at this time is its inability to load many older documents that do not conform closely to the official rules of HTML. In practical terms, this means that most documents cannot be loaded, or they can only be loaded with a "relaxed rules file" which HoTMetaL automatically tries when the strict rules fail.

When you attempt to load an older document into HoTMetaL using the strict rule set, you will probably receive a message saying that your document is not fully compliant, and specifying a line number (which in my experience is not always correct) where the first violation of HTML takes place.

By way of example, it was hoped that HoTMetaL would be suitable to edit the World Wide Web FAQ (Frequently Asked Questions list). Unfortunately, it was impossible to open it with the strict rule set *o r* the relaxed rule set. It is certainly true that it would be possible to load the document if it were completely compliant with the rules, but bringing it into compliance is one of the things that one would like to be able to do with the editor!

As an example, see Figure 35.12, which contains the error message that HoTMetaL produced for the first version of the `editors.htm` file shown in Figure 35.11. In the first version of the file, I had attempted to close a `<STRONG>` tag with an `</EM>` closing tag (the correct tag is `</STRONG>`).

FIGURE 35.12.

HoTMetaL error message (refusal to load file).

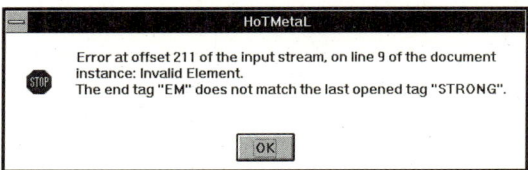

"So why can't it load the document anyway, show me where the errors are and let me fix them?" It should be possible, but as of this writing HoTMetaL can't do it. The HoTMetaL authors have stated that this feature will be available in HoTMetaL Pro (at least in the commercial version). HoTMetaL Pro will also include a cleanup program that will attempt to fix problems with old HTML files before they are imported. Nonetheless, for the creation of new documents, HoTMetaL is tough to beat.

HTML Editor

HTML Editor for the Macintosh is an interesting combination of a non-WYSIWYG text editor that simply inserts tags, and a WYSIWYG editor that allows you to see what your text might look like in its final form. HTML Editor is available by anonymous FTP at `cs.dal.ca` in the file `/giles/HTML_Editor_1.0.sit.hqx`. The documentation is available as a separate file at `ftp://http://dragon.acadiau.ca:1667/~giles/HTML_Editor/Documentation.html` (see Figure 35.13).

HTML Editor is shareware, and at $25 is a bargain, given its capabilities.

HTML Editor allows you to insert tags into text using menus, buttons, and command keys. It includes a rather complete set of HTML tags, and any missing tags can be specified in a "User Tags" window. When you insert a tag, the tag text itself appears in a light grey color (if you have a monochrome monitor, there is no color difference) and when you type, the text you enter is in an appropriate format for that tag. For example, Headings (`<H1>`, `<H2>`, and so on) are in a larger font and boldface (see Figure 35.13). The default formatting appears to be Mosaic-like, but HTML Editor allows you to change the styles for each tag and then reapply those new styles across the document.

You can preview the text you have written, both within HTML Editor using the "hide tags" button, or by selecting the Mosaic button, which loads the browser of your choice (Mosaic by default; it can be customized through the Preferences... dialog box). Or at least, that was the theory; it didn't seem to work reliably.

FIGURE 35.13.
HTML Editor.

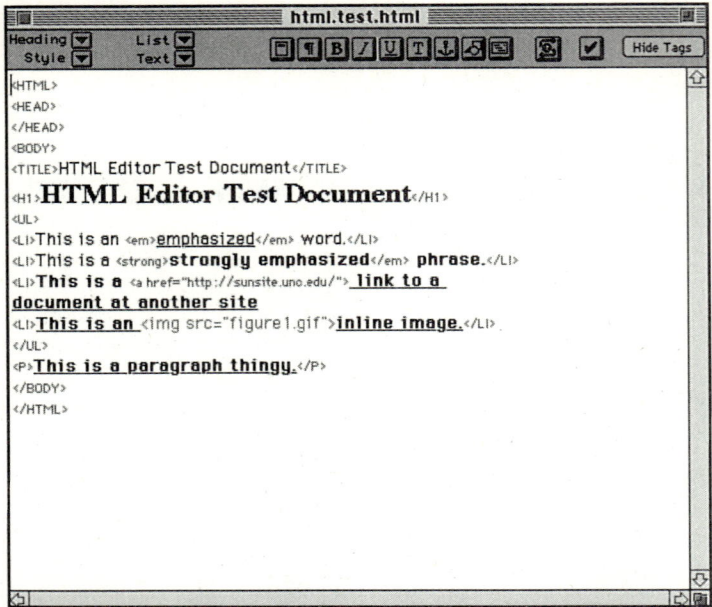

Opening existing HTML documents is straightforward, and there are no file size limits as far as was discernible. You have a choice in the preferences dialog box of whether to "auto-style" the text you are importing; with auto-style turned on, the HTML tags are turned on and the text is formatted in appropriate ways. Turning auto-style off imports files much faster, but they appear in all the same font.

It was possible to import the Frequently Asked Questions file with auto-style turned on, and although the translation took many minutes, the result was accurate and impressive.

Like HoTMetaL, HTML Editor did not understand how to handle the file with errors in it. However, it did do HoTMetaL one better: it loaded the file, and simply skipped over the erroneous tag that closed a . Or rather, the style skipped over the tag; the tag was still included, which made for quick debugging of the text.

The only quibbles with HTML Editor are that it doesn't have document tags such as <HTML>, <HEAD>, <BODY> (although you can easily specify those in the User Tags window), and it doesn't allow printing (but printing is promised in a later version).

tkWWW

tkWWW is a combined World Wide Web browser and editor based on the Tk/Tcl toolkit. As such, it currently runs only on UNIX systems with the X Window System, but ports of the Tk/Tcl toolkit to Microsoft Windows and the Macintosh are well on the way (see Figure 35.14).

The Tk and Tcl packages can be obtained by anonymous FTP from `ftp.cs.berkeley.edu` in the directory `/ucb/tcl`; tkWWW itself can be obtained by anonymous FTP from `harbor.ecn.purdue.edu` in the directory `/pub/tcl/extensions` as the file `tkWWW-*.tar.Z` where `*` will be the latest version number. Version 0.12 was evaluated (note that this is still a beta version).

FIGURE 35.14.

tkWWW.

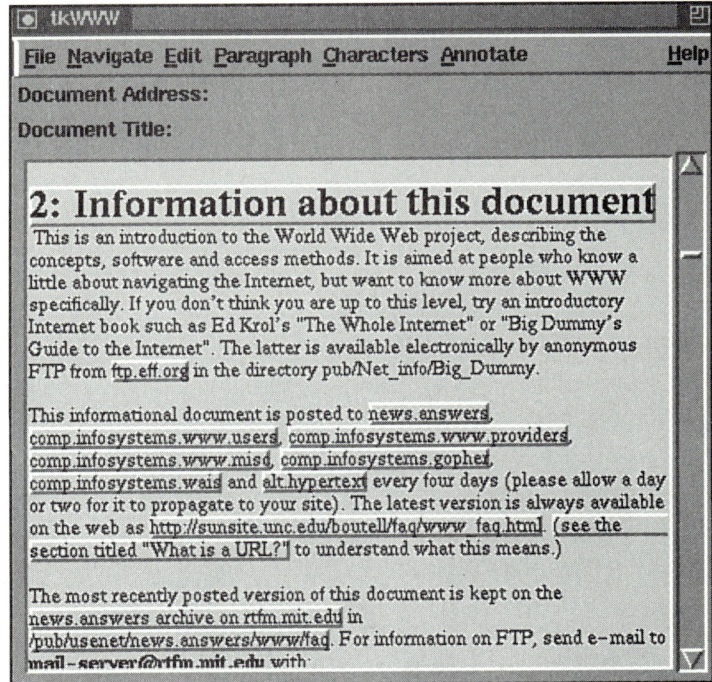

tkWWW is another near-WYSIWYG editor, and since it is also a browser, it can lay claim to a certain degree of true WYSIWYG. If you create a page with tkWWW as an editor and then view it with tkWWW as a browser with the same font settings and window size, you will indeed see exactly the same thing. (However, tkWWW is not a terribly impressive browser from a visual standpoint. It's unlikely many will abandon Mosaic in favor of tkWWW for general web-surfing purposes.)

tkWWW stacks up well, feature for feature, when compared to other HTML editors. Unlike HoTMetaL, tkWWW does not allow you to see the structure of your document directly. Instead, tkWWW insulates you completely from the HTML, a valid approach in its own right.

In HoTMetaL, you create an HTML document and HoTMetaL ensures that you do so by the rules; you remain aware of the tags throughout the process. In tkWWW, you create a document by selecting list items, text styles and the like from menus and observing the visible results, and tkWWW outputs correct HTML when you save the document. The HoTMetaL approach ensures that you have full control over your document, but requires more knowledge; the tkWWW approach is very user-friendly but can lead to surprises if you attempt to simply make the document look right on the screen rather than use meaningful styles.

Unlike most editors discussed so far in this chapter, tkWWW could load the Frequently Asked Questions document. Unfortunately, it could not save that document. Instead, it produced a blank error message and offered a stack trace of its code.

To be fair, tkWWW is still in beta test. It did load, save and edit a smaller test document.

htmltext

htmltext is an HTML editor based on the Andrew Toolkit. As such, it runs on UNIX systems with the X Window System. Ports to Microsoft Windows and the Macintosh are not expected in the near future (see Figure 35.15).

htmltext is available by anonymous FTP from `ftp.cs.city.ac.uk` in the subdirectory `pub/ htmltext`. If you do not have a system for which a binary is provided (at the time of writing a binary for SunOS 4.1.X was available), you will need to obtain the Andrew Toolkit as well; Andrew is available as part of the "contrib" tape of the X11 distribution (which is available by anonymous FTP from many sites). Use Archie to locate a site near you.

htmltext is quite similar to tkWWW in its capabilities. Both are near-WYSIWYG, and both take the approach of insulating the user from the actual HTML tags.

If you define *WYSIWYG* as *looks like it will look in Mosaic,* htmltext is decidedly the closest thing to WYSIWYG available at this time. The htmltext display looks very much like that of the X Window System version of Mosaic. (Note that since there are many other browsers, and even many possible font settings for Mosaic, it is not generally a good idea to depend on this resemblance.)

Like tkWWW, htmltext places the features of HTML in a set of menus and allows you to work with the document in a word processor-like manner. Unlike tkWWW, htmltext has the full power of the Andrew Toolkit behind it, which means that many traditional word processing features are available, including spell checking. Also unlike tkWWW, htmltext can display inline images if they are located on the same system.

This is both a blessing and a curse, because the Andrew Toolkit, fully installed, requires between 70 and 100 megabytes of disk space to build. There is a binary standalone version of htmltext available for SunOS 4.1.X which requires only a few megabytes, but some features are disabled due to the absence of the rest of Andrew. (This binary version was used in the evaluation, however, and no significant frustrations were encountered.)

FIGURE 35.15.

htmltext.

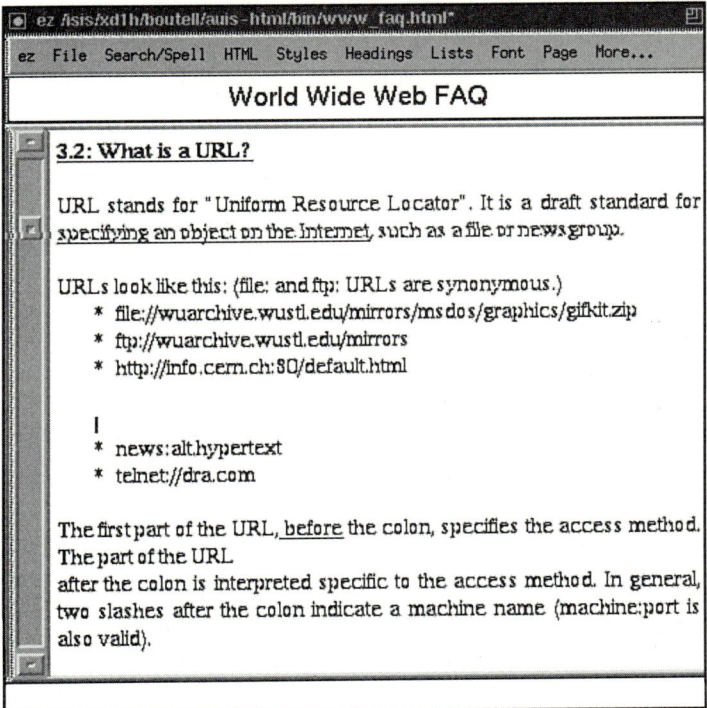

Like tkWWW, htmltext can load the Frequently Asked Questions document. Unlike tkWWW it can also save it.

Unfortunately, however, htmltext does not appear to understand nested lists fully. Nested lists were used to create an outline at the beginning of the Frequently Asked Questions document. But when the document is saved with htmltext, the resulting HTML is incorrect; in areas where lists are nested, seemingly random portions of the text are missing. It is difficult to be certain what htmltext is objecting to in the document.

Also, the highest level of list is not properly opened and closed. This is probably done to exploit the coincidence that some versions of Mosaic will display a flush-left list when the list is not actually opened, but it is not correct HTML and it definitely shouldn't happen to a document that dealt correctly with lists when it was loaded.

htmltext is an impressive editor, one very suitable for simple tasks. Until its list-handling features improve, however, it will not be suitable for large documents such as the Frequently Asked Questions document. Nonetheless, htmltext came closer than most editors evaluated to being able to handle that task.

Converting Your Documents: HTML Filters

While HTML editors have a long way to go, HTML filters are quite well-developed. A sizable number of filters have been created to convert from existing formats such as WordPerfect, nroff/troff, RTF (Rich Text Format) and TeX to HTML.

In some cases, you may find that conversion is an ideal solution, and you may not wish to create HTML documents directly. Given the state of HTML editors, this is a possibility worth considering.

Converting from WordPerfect

WPTOHTML is a collection of WordPerfect macros which convert from WordPerfect versions 5.1 and 6.0 for DOS to HTML. It is available by anonymous FTP from `oak.oakland.edu` in the directory `SimTel/msdos/wordperf`, as the files `wpt51d10.zip` and `wpt60d10.zip`.

At the time of this writing, a conversion package from WordPerfect 5.2 for Windows is not available.

Note, however, that WordPerfect can read and write RTF (Rich Text Format), which can also be converted to HTML (see the next section).

Converting from Microsoft Word

See CU_HTML and ANT_HTML, described above in the WYSIWYG editors section, for two good ways of transforming Word for Windows documents into HTML documents.

For a more automatic form of conversion, see the section on Rich Text Format, immediately following. (Microsoft Word can load and save RTF as well as the normal DOC format.)

Converting from RTF (Rich Text Format)

RTFTOHTML is a utility that converts files in RTF to HTML, preserving styles as well as links to other documents. RTFTOHTML binaries are available for Macintosh and Sun SPARC platforms, and source code is also available in order to build it for your own system if you have access to a compiler. RTFTOHTML is available by anonymous FTP from `ftp.cray.com` in the directory `src/WWWstuff/RTF`.

The Macintosh version of RTFTOHTML also includes a sample template file for Microsoft Word that contains a set of styles that match the HTML tags (see Figure 35.16). Like

CU_HTML and ANT_HTML's templates, this provides an excellent way to write HTML documents on the Macintosh and allows them to be easily converted.

FIGURE 35.16.

RTFTOHTML style sheet for Microsoft Word.

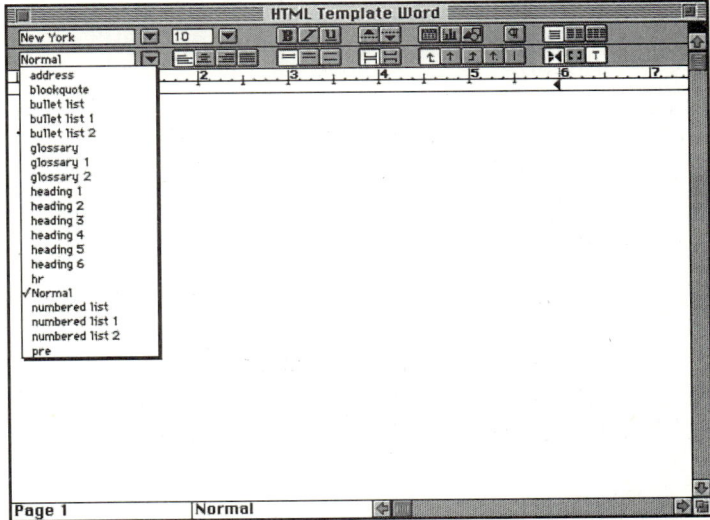

Converting from FrameMaker

fm2html is a set of scripts for UNIX systems, written mostly in Perl, that convert files written in FrameMaker to HTML. The fm2html package was written by Jon Stephenson von Tetzchner at Norwegian Telecom Research and is available by anonymous FTP at `bang.nta.no:/pub/fm2html.tar.v.0.n.m.Z.`.

The conversion from Frame document to HTML is quite sophisticated, and includes mechanisms for converting hypertext links into HTML links, tables into preformatted text, and even translates imported images into GIF files (with the GhostScript and PBM filter programs installed). A 30-page FrameMaker file was translated with 10 imported PostScript graphics, tables, and several internal links using this filter, and the results were excellent.

Although fm2html is only available for UNIX, versions of FrameMaker exist for many different systems (including the Macintosh and Windows), and the files are binary-compatible across platforms. If you have access to a UNIX system with which to do the final translation, you could easily write your documents on any platform for which you had FrameMaker.

Converting from TeX and LaTeX

LaTeX (a variant of TeX) is a common format on UNIX systems, and is much more expressive than HTML in many ways. Converting it to HTML is a tough job. There is, however, an excellent package for this which succeeds amazingly (some would say to the point of overkill).

LATEXTOHTML does a very thorough job of converting LaTeX to HTML, even to the point of creating inline images for LaTeX equations. You can obtain LATEXTOHTML by anonymous FTP from `ftp.tex.ac.uk` in the directory `pub/archive/support/latex2html`, but the authors specifically request that you attempt to locate a copy closer to your site using the Archie file-finding program (installed at virtually all Internet sites). LATEXTOHTML requires that your system have an up-to-date version of the Perl script language installed.

VULCANIZE is a simpler program, also in Perl, which takes care of most nonmathematical LaTeX documents in a more straightforward manner. You can obtain VULCANIZE via the Web (URL is `http://www.cis.upenn.edu/~mjd/vulcanize.html`). Complex mathematical LaTeX documents cannot be converted without a more sophisticated package such as LATEXTOHTML, but most documents simply don't fall into that category. In the words of the author, Mark-Jason Dominus, "for a program that doesn't work, it is remarkably successful."

ADDITIONAL SOURCES OF INFORMATION

For additional information about HTML editors and filters, consult CERN's collection of tools for generating HTML (URL is `http://info.cern.ch/WWW/Tools/Overview.html`).

You can also consult NCSA's list of filters and editors (URL is `http://www.ncsa.uiuc.edu/SDG/Software/Mosaic/Docs/faq-software.html`).

Conclusion

For those hoping to create World Wide Web documents dynamically in an elegant WYSIWYG environment, the future has not quite arrived. On Windows PCs and UNIX systems, Softquad HoTMetaL comes very close to the goal, but is still too frustrating for those who want to edit existing documents. On the Macintosh, HTML Editor does an excellent job. The other editors are even more disappointing, though still useful in their present form. On the Macintosh, however, the exceptional HTML Editor comes very close to the mark, failing only in the area of document tags such as `<HTML>`, `<HEAD>` and `<BODY>`.

HTML filters, on the other hand, are in good shape, although they do tend to require UNIX systems or at least software with a UNIX background that PC users may be unfamiliar with. In the future, as more and more Web servers are installed on PCs, we will probably see one-piece conversion programs for Microsoft Windows and the Macintosh.

With the growing acceptance of HTML and the World Wide Web technology, however, there is little doubt that the capability to read and write HTML will soon make an appearance in mainstream word processors themselves. IntelliTag, an SGML editing package, is already available for WordPerfect; it won't be long before WordPerfect and Word both come with HTML capability as standard equipment.

In the meantime, the authors of HoTMetaL for Windows and UNIX, HTML Editor for the Macintosh and other products like them have an opportunity to create superior solutions tailor-made to the needs of World Wide Web information providers.

Implementing a
Web Design

36

by John December

If all the processes of web weaving operate well together, and you've mastered the skills to write HTML, you're ready to implement a web design. To do this, you'll need the products of the design process—the look and feel diagrams; the package, page, and link chart; the web specification—as well as information from the other processes of web weaving, including audience information, the purpose and objective statements, and domain information.

As an implementor, your challenge is to turn the design into working web. To do this, you'll need to be fairly organized and have excellent knowledge of HTML and the computer system on which your web will be developed and deployed. You'll also need excellent writing skills, talent for layout and design, and a sense of how the audience uses and thinks about the information you're presenting.

In this chapter, we'll go over a sample web implementation. First, we'll start off with some general considerations for setting up the web. Then, we'll go through a step-by-step process of creating a prototype web. Throughout this chapter, we'll use the "ElectricMarket," an imaginary Web department store as an example.

A SEMINAL HYPERTEXT ARTICLE

Vannevar Bush's article, "As We May Think," which appeared in July 1945 issue of *The Atlantic Monthly* has inspired generations of hypertext designers and implementors.

Denys Duchier has created a hypertext version of this article, reproduced with the permission of *The Atlantic Monthly,* which is available at URL http://www.csi.uottawa.ca/~dduchier/misc/vbush/as-we-may-think.html

General Considerations

In implementing a web design, you'll not only create files of HTML, but you will work with people—web planners, analysts, designers, developers, and users. You'll also have to be on good terms with your webmaster (the person who is responsible for the deployment and maintenance of your web server itself).

You'll need to recognize that your work, like the work of the other processes in web weaving, may never end as long as the web is deployed. Therefore, you'll need to develop your own system to deal with the multitude of changes in design that inevitably occur in a good web. You'll have to be aware of the latest methods for maintaining directories and files on your computer system as well as be responsible for backups and coordinating with the webmaster for your web's security.

You'll need to compose text to explain features of your web. Often, you'll be able to use wording from the audience information, purpose and objective statements, or other web-weaving products generated from the planning and design processes. You'll often need to customize this prose to guide the user through the specific situations occurring in the pages you'll implement.

Working with People

Although much of your time as web implementor will be spent constructing HTML files, you'll also work with other people. Even if you are the sole weaver of your web—the planner, analyst, designer, implementor, and developer—you'll still need to work with representatives from a very important group: the users of your web. Without a representative user, or at least a close analysis of their characteristics and a good understanding of them, a web can get off base and miss meeting their needs. The analysis process of web weaving (Chapter 31, "Analyzing a Web") is means to check that the audience needs are being met on the "big picture" level. As implementor, you'll be intimately concerned with minute decisions about the construction of hypertext—the placement of hotspots, links, and composing specialized features such as Forms or graphical information maps. While a good web designer should have created a look and feel for the web, and the web specification should be able to be implemented without any problems, there will still be decisions you will have to make. It is impossible to fully specify every last detail of a web. In fact, the only record of this set of minute decisions is the web itself.

Therefore, it is important that you keep lines of communication open and operating with the following individuals:

- Web planners

  What do you know about the audience that might help the planners identify or meet their needs better?

  Are there parts of the design that you know are not meeting the needs of the audience or are extraneous to the purpose or objective of the web?

  What are the planners considering for the future? This information may help you anticipate future directory or file requirements or other future requirements that you might begin to implement as prototypes.

  Do you feel that some parts of the purpose or objective of the web have not been expressed in the web specification or design?

  What skills do you need to implement the web itself? Are there specialized skills or resources that you don't have?

- Web analysts

  What performance problems are you aware of in the web's design (many images on one page, huge pages, problems with interfaces to databases)? You can inform the web analysts to pay particular attention to these areas of the web for timing and user feedback.

What are the patterns for web use? Consider how you can help the analysts interpret the file use statistics. Do you know of a particular page that seems to be either under- or over-used considering its purpose?

What overall performance concerns do the web analysts have? For example, if the purpose of the web is to get orders for products, is the number of orders low? Do you know this may be because the order form, for example, is implemented in a manner that makes it difficult to use? What other aspects of the implementation might be causing problems or dissatisfaction in users?

■ Web designers

What aspects of the web design are impossible or awkward to implement?

What design decisions haven't been considered or specified with sufficient detail for you to implement?

What issues of look and feel or linking in the web design do you think need to be changed or modified?

What overall concerns do you have about how the web design is meeting the purpose and objective of the web?

■ Web developers (web development is covered in next chapter)

What suggestions do you have for publicity and timing of web announcements and public releases?

What features of the web do you feel need to be brought more to the attention of users?

What problems do you see with the current way web development (publicity, inputs to the planning analysis and design processes) is being done?

■ Audience representatives

Do you have access to a pool of representative audience members for testing your web's implementation? The analysis processes should involve a detailed study of the results of your web's use. Direct feedback from users in how you've implemented a web feature can also be very valuable.

Could you use the Forms capability of HTML to include response-forms or comment boxes for eliciting user feedback?

As implementor, you'll often be the one to get e-mail from users (because of a stale link or a problem with your web). What sense do you get about the users overall satisfaction with the web based on this feedback? What suggestions or comments might you pass on to planners, designers, and developers?

Overall, you'll find that the people-processes in implementing a web can be as complex—if not more so—than developing the HTML itself. This should not be a great surprise. After all, the web you weave is created and used by people, and people are notoriously inexact and changing. In all these interactions, keep your patience and listen: your inter-personal communications skills in eliciting constructive criticism will be a major factor to help you implement the web in the best way possible.

Planning Your File and Directory Structure

Essentially, you weave a web from files of HTML. There may be just one file, or there may be hundreds. In either case, you should be sensitive to issues of file naming and source code control. After all, if the users can't find or access the files, the web isn't useful.

1. Have a consistent, stable server name. Work with the webmaster to create a publicly known name for your server that can remain constant, even though the actual machine that supports the server may change. For example, a name like

   ```
   www.company.com
   ```

   is a good one, since it uses a common convention: the string www in front of the company's network domain name (company.com). A poor choice would be something like

   ```
   unix5.its.itd.td.company.com
   ```

   Not only is the name long and not descriptive (maybe too descriptive since it reflects the company hierarchy all the way down to the web server machine). What if the web server is moved from the unix5 machine to the unix6 machine? You don't want to have to tell all your users to change their hotlists or web pages to accommodate the name change. Instead, choose a name for you web server that is descriptive and can remain constant.

2. Organize your files in a way that is consistent but allows for growth. Just as you don't want your users to have to change their URL references to your web because of a server name change, don't force them to change their URLs because of changes in directory structure.

   Plan your directory structure so that it can remain stable, even as other projects are added to your server. For example, don't put all the files for the very first web project you have in the top-level directory of your web server. This will cause a crunch later on when you add other projects.

   So, for example, instead of the first project (for example, the "star" project) having the home page

   ```
   http://www.company.com/star.html
   ```

consider

```
http://www.company.com/star/home.html
```

where the directory name you use (in this case, star) is a short, descriptive name of the project itself. At the project level, you can use the structure of the web design (the package, page, and link diagram) as the basis for a directory structure. Above the project level, if you know that your server will contain a great deal of information besides projects, consider

```
http://www.company.com/projects/star/home.html
```

which will leave room for

```
http://www.company.com/projects/delta/home.html
```

```
http://www.company.com/documents/catalog/home.html
```

```
http://www.company.com/services/orders/home.html
```

and other development. Although it's not impossible to change naming schemes, it's best to design an extendible naming scheme at the start. Naturally, you don't want to go to the other extreme and have an labyrinthine directory structure such as

```
http://www.company.com/projects/new/info-tech/startups/tuesday/morning/star-
project/home-directory/home.html
```

3. Consider using a source code control system, such as SCCS (Source Code Control System) on UNIX platforms to maintain configuration control over files, particularly if your web is large or there are many web weavers. Source code control systems have facilities for maintaining information to regenerate previous versions of files. So if you have to go back to a previous version of your web, you're prepared. Systems of source code control can also keep track of who makes changes to files and when. The whole process of web design, implementation, and management may be amenable to such tools. Use them where it makes sense. For small projects, these tools may create far too much overhead for them to be beneficial. For large projects, they may be essential to keep track of the many changes made in the web files.

Composing Text and Page Layout

You'll need some writing ability to implement a web. Not only will you need to know how your audience uses language, but you'll need to know how they think about the information you're presenting. In many cases, you'll be able to "steal" wording and text right from the purpose and objective statements, audience information, and domain information. With just a bit of change, this text can serve different purposes in the web implementation.

For example, each web page should have enough text to cue the user to the purpose of the page and how it's used. This text should be aimed at the needs of the user for that particular page—a customized statement of purpose, a concise overview of what information is on that page, and instructions for using the information. The designer might not have specified this language down to the wording level, but this language is important. Use a spell checker and proofread the text for grammar and syntax errors.

While the look and feel diagrams from the design process should set goals for the overall appearance of each page, the implementor still will make many decisions about the details of each page layout. The implementor should make use of the following guidelines in creating a page:

1. Keeping in mind that you can't control how any particular browser may display your HTML file, work with the features of HTML to create, as much as possible, a grid pattern to suggest an information hierarchy. To reveal the grid pattern for a page design, draw vertical lines on the left side of the start of every element on the page. Figure 36.1 shows the grid pattern for a sample look and feel design.

FIGURE 36.1.

Gridline pattern on a page.

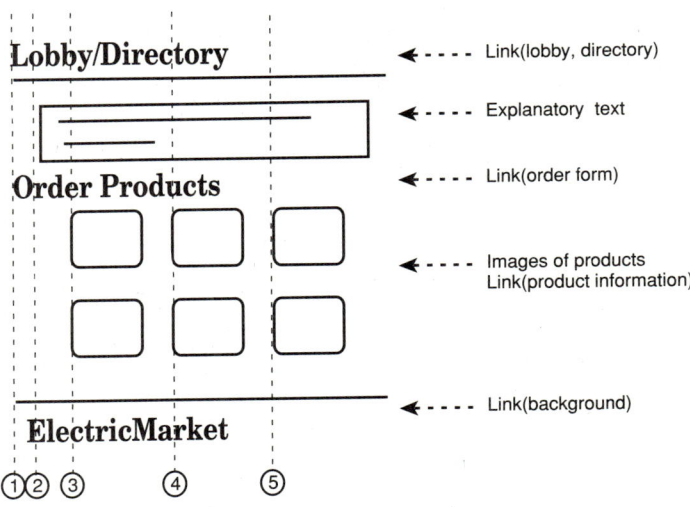

Note in this sample that there are five gridlines. The gridlines identify where the user sees vertical alignment, and this alignment implies equal functionality and purpose. Do the five gridlines on the page show an equal level of purpose?

Gridline 1 seems to indicate the headers at the first level of information—the "Lobby/Directory" and "Order Products" are cues to the reader about major functions.

Gridline 2 seems extraneous. Why slightly indent the label for "Electric Market?" Moving this label over to align with gridline 1 will reduce the number of gridlines by one and thus simplify the information hierarchy of the page. The explanatory text can be moved to the left, to gridline 1. Because it is set off from the "Lobby/Directory" labels by a horizontal line and the "Order Products" label by a change in font size, the indentation to gridline 2 is an extraneous emphasis of the functional difference.

Gridlines 3, 4, and 5 function only to separate the images of products. However, the placement of the products implies an information hierarchy. What products are listed first? Are the products on the same row similar? Are the products on the same gridline similar? The implementor might suggest to the designer that, if the present arrangement of products has no meaning (that is, the gridlines aren't conveying different categories of products), that the products could be arranged in a vertical list or on separate pages. The downside of using a vertical list is that the list of products consumes a great deal of page real-estate, so the user might not be able to see all the items on the same screen. The answer to what to do about these gridlines lies in the users. How do the users want to see the products? By category? In one big list? Does the arrangement on the gridlines confuse them?

Gridlines thus reveal the information hierarchy implied in the arrangement of the elements on the page. Most browsers do an excellent job of interpreting HTML and aligning text along gridlines. You should check how several browsers handle a page. Each browser may make different alignments, but by choosing appropriate (reflecting semantic structure) HTML features consistently (lists, horizontal lines, paragraphs, line breaks), you can influence an information hierarchy.

2. Use typographic changes to focus a user's attention. On a page, photographs, drawings or icons, and particularly color, will very quickly grab the user's eye. Next, bold headings, large letters, and page features with empty space around them will catch the reader's attention. On a page, where do you want the user's attention to go? The diagram in Figure 36.1 shows the guide links to the "Lobby/Directory" as very dominant on the page. Are the "Lobby/Directory" links central to the purpose of the page, or are they just navigation links?

   Browsers display letters and fonts differently. Be aware of how the major browsers —your users—are most likely to use display your pages. Look at the pages through different browsers. Locate the areas of the page where the dark/light contrasts caused by the typography or the color in images draw the user's eye. Are these the areas of the page that best reflect its purpose? If not, adjust the page elements by toning them down: make the font smaller, eliminate a diagram or a photograph or make the text smaller. Use the high-contrast elements to guide the reader's attention to the most important parts of the page.

3. Use a given/new information chain to compose text and present information on a page. While hypertext allows nonlinear reading of a web, each web page (at the surface level) still presents a linear set of information for the user. To deal with

the information on a page, the user might apply the convention: start at the top and left, read to the right and down. (Many Western cultures use these conventions, but people from other cultures may have a different reading pattern. Also, surfers might not read a page like this; see Chapter 21, "Surfing: Finding the New and Unusual").

At the prose level, take advantage of reading sequence by using an *information chain*—taking the reader from a point they know to new information. For example, if someone on the street asks me where the library is, I might say the following:

Starting from this corner, go east until you reach Second Street.

Turn north along Second Street until Congress Street.

Just north of Congress, you'll find the library.

In each sentence of these directions, I link a place the listener knows to a new place, and I repeat this new place as the known place in the next sentence.

Used with expressive variation, the information chain technique, used at the sentence as well as paragraph and page level, can help guide your user through information.

4. Use parallelism in phrasing and information wherever possible. Just as you used the gridlines to match up information at the same level of importance or functionality, use parallel phrasing to match information in lists and headings. In lists, use entries in all the same grammatical form. For example,

Products include:

- apples
- oranges
- bananas

rather than

Products include:

- four bags of apples
- some oranges
- banana

5. Use a consistent voice when addressing the user. If you've made a decision to use direct address, be consistent. For example, the instructions at the top of a page for resources might be

"This page contains links to well-known resources in the field of Astronomy. You can access these resources by following the highlighted links in the list. If you have suggestions for more links, or have questions, please contact the page developer at the address given at the bottom of this page."

Rather than

"This page contains links to well-known resources in the field of Astronomy. *The user* can access these resources by following the highlighted links in the list. If *y o u* have suggestions for more links, or have questions, the page developer at the address given at the bottom of this page *can be contacted....*"

This second example shows some inconsistency. At one point the user is referred to in third person ("the user can access") and then addressed directly ("If you have any suggestions..."). Finally, the writer uses passive voice ("the page developer....can be contacted") in which the agent of the action implied in the sentence (the person doing the contacting) is not explicitly mentioned.

6. Adopt an appropriate tone for your prose and other features. If your web is meant for professional use, avoid "cute" diagrams or colloquialisms. Every part of your web conveys something about its purpose and its developers. While helping the user feel relaxed and even entertained can help the effectiveness of the web, too many "fun" additions can make the users take your web less seriously than you might have intended. On the other hand, the lack of graphics or human elements can make a web seem very dry and not the expression of a vibrant, active information community. A good way to adopt an appropriate tone is to notice how the audience members themselves talk about the information covered by the web. Also note the tone of supporting or background literature (part of the domain information).

Implementing a Design

Now that we've reviewed some general considerations about naming files and directories and shaping information and prose, let's delve into implementing an example web design.

For our example, we'll assume that we've been given design information about ElectricMarket, an innovative Web-based department store. So far, only a portion of the ElectricMarket web has been designed, but you're told to implement a prototype.

Gathering Information

The first step in implementing a web design is to gather the following information:

1. Design information—look and feel and package, page, and link diagram

   Look and feel diagrams. You are given one for a generic page (Figure 36.2), one for a department page (Figure 36.3), and one for a product information page (Figure 36.4).

   Package, Page, and Link diagram. (Figure 36.5)

FIGURE 36.2.

ElectricMarket generic look and feel diagram.

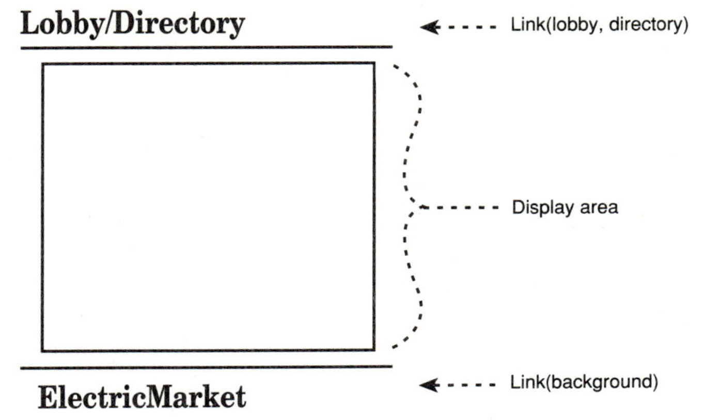

Lobby/Directory ◄ - - - - Link(lobby, directory)

- - - - - Display area

ElectricMarket ◄ - - - - Link(background)

FIGURE 36.3.

ElectricMarket Department look and feel diagram.

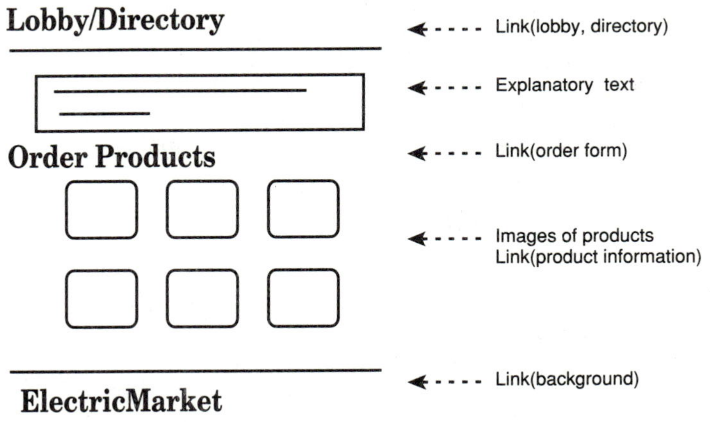

Lobby/Directory ◄ - - - - Link(lobby, directory)

◄ - - - - Explanatory text

Order Products ◄ - - - - Link(order form)

◄ - - - - Images of products
Link(product information)

ElectricMarket ◄ - - - - Link(background)

FIGURE 36.4.

ElectricMarket product information look and feel diagram.

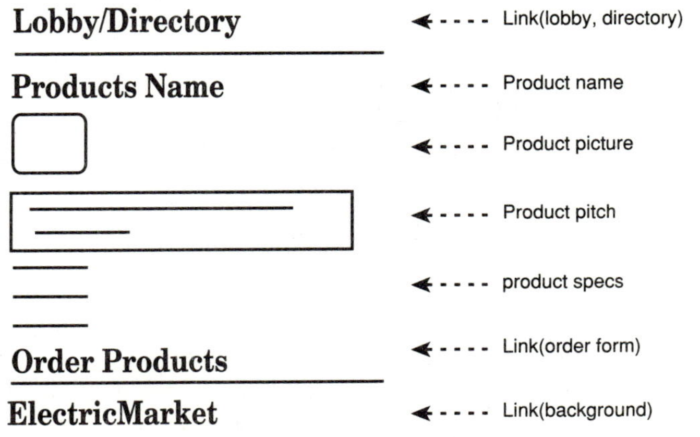

Lobby/Directory ◄ - - - - Link(lobby, directory)

Products Name ◄ - - - - Product name

◄ - - - - Product picture

◄ - - - - Product pitch

◄ - - - - product specs

Order Products ◄ - - - - Link(order form)

ElectricMarket ◄ - - - - Link(background)

FIGURE 36.5.
ElectricMarket package,
page, and link diagram.

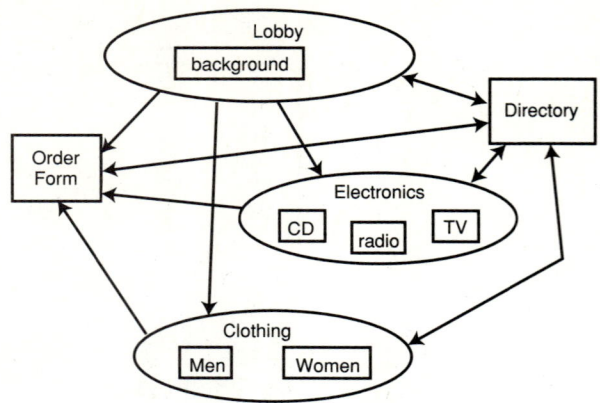

2. Audience information

   Target audience: younger net surfer with disposable income; old enough to have a credit card

   Important aspects about audience: interested in new gadgets, personal electronics, new clothing styles; willing to buy products over the Net

3. Statement of purpose

   "The purpose of the ElectricMarket is to attract buyers interested in electronics and clothing products and solicit sales of these products."

4. Objective

   ■ To attract the attention of potential buyers to the ElectricMarket web

   ■ To inform users of the products available

   ■ To reach a sales volume that justifies the cost of web deployment and development

   ■ To achieve customer satisfaction and get feedback on what we should offer in our product line

5. Domain information. You are given a variety of collections:

   Product information—all specs on products

   Buyer profiles—information from past studies and profiles of target audience members

   Company background—mission statement, history, and product lines

   Materials from competitor's catalogs and webs

6. Web specification

You are given these limitations on web information:

Company background. Wording can come from current paper brochure "About ElectricMarket, Inc." condense to 100-300 words, no current stock or profits information.

Department offerings. List the products from different departments on separate page.

Product presentation. Pictures should be no smaller than 2cm × 2cm, no larger than 4cm × 4cm.

Product information available at ftp://ftp.em.com/products/, data that should be displayed: size, color, price, catalog number.

Designing a Directory and File Structure Tree

Once you've gathered the previous information, you're ready to start planning the web. The first step is to plan how you will organize the files and directories to hold the ElectricMarket project. Based on the package, page, and link diagram, you can create a structure as shown in Figure 36.6.

FIGURE 36.6.

ElectricMarket directory structure.

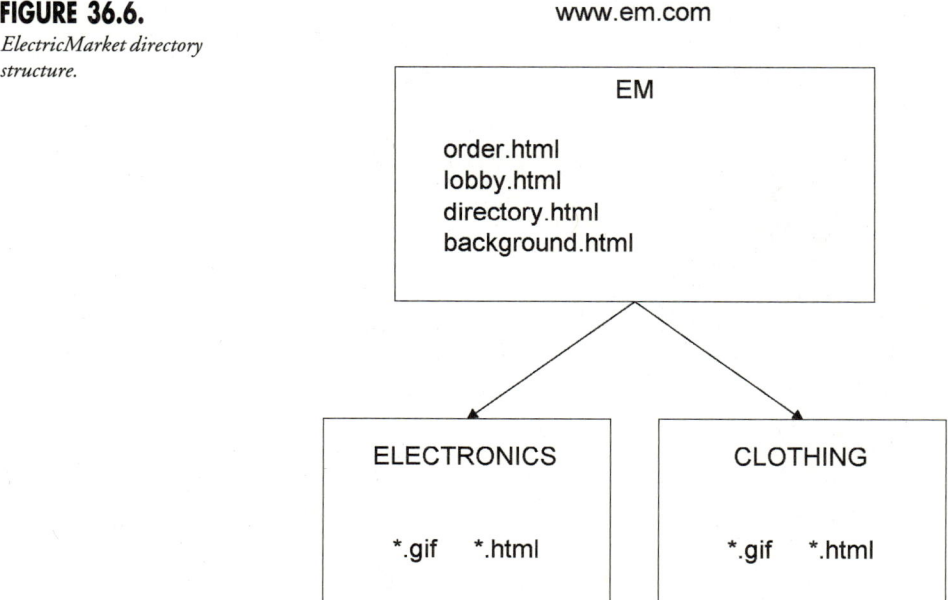

Making Templates

Based on the look and feel diagram shown in Figure 36.2, 36.3, and 36.4, you can construct a template that will help start the implementation of each page of the web.

First, a template like the following can serve as a basis for the whole look and feel of all the other pages:

```
<HTML>
<!— Author: K.C. Deemark (kcd@em.com) —>
<!— Dept: Web Weaving —>
<!— Date:   11 Jul 94 —>
<!— Purpose:   overall look and feel template for ElectricMarket —>
<!— Comments:  bring to next meeting for approval. —>

<HEAD>
<TITLE>ElectricMarket—Page Title</TITLE>
<LINK REV="made" HREF="mailto:kcd@em.com">
</HEAD>

<BODY>
<A HREF="../lobby.html">Lobby</A> / <A HREF="../directory.html"> Directory</A>

<HR>

<H1>Page Title</H1>
page explanation / overview / salespitch
<P>

page information
page information
page information
page information
page information
page information
page information
page information

<HR>

<ADDRESS> <A HREF="../background.html">ElectricMarket</A></ADDRESS>

</BODY>
</HTML>
```

This universal template appears through the Mosaic for X browser as shown in Figure 36.7. Notice how the features as displayed in Mosaic differ from the "look and feel" sketch in Figure 36.1.

```
<HR>

<ADDRESS> <A HREF="background.html">ElectricMarket</A></ADDRESS>

</BODY>
</HTML>
```

Making a Prototype

Link the templates you've generated according to the package, page, and link diagram (Figure 36.5). You'll create a web as shown in Figures 36.8 through 36.12.

FIGURE 36.8.

Prototype lobby.

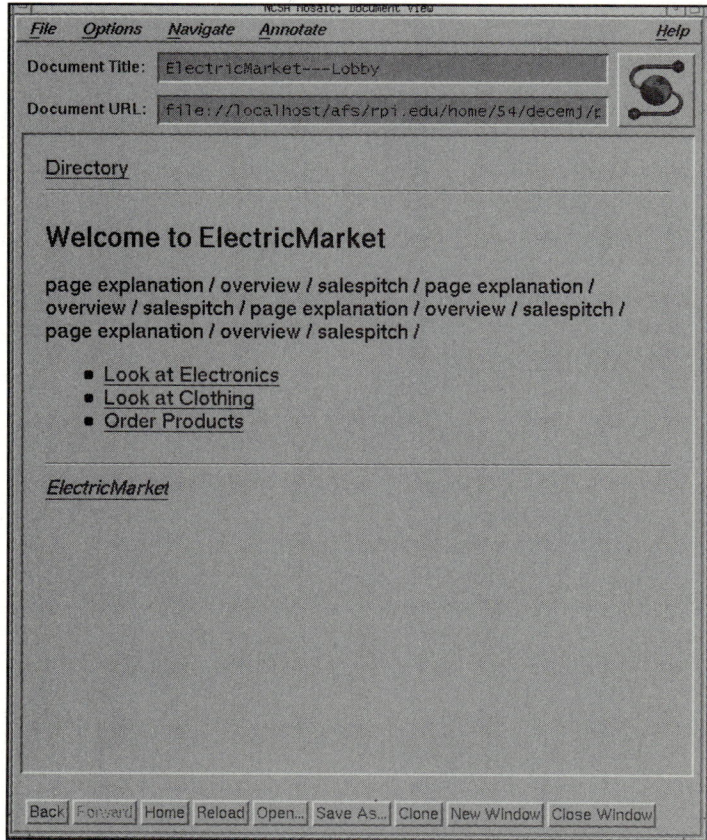

FIGURE 36.9.

Prototype directory.

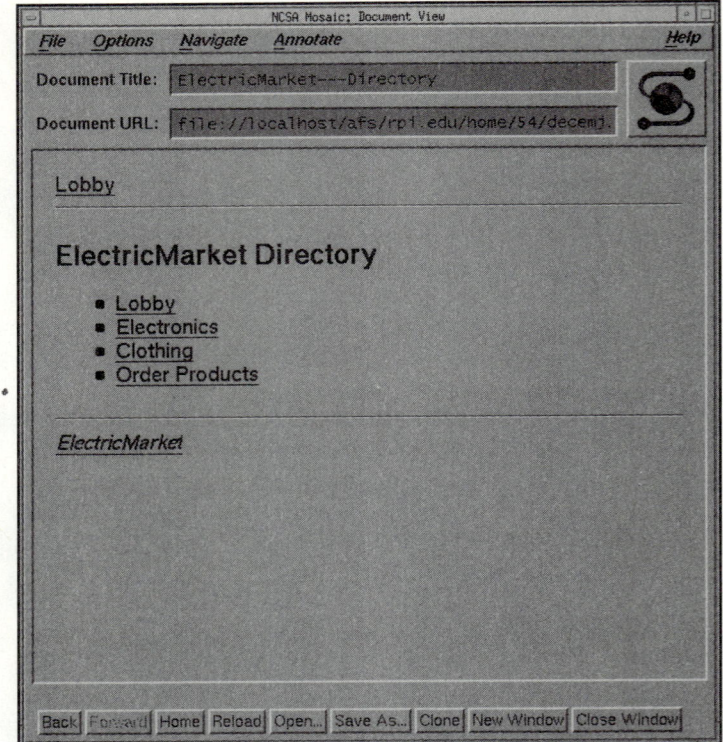

Testing Your Prototype

Ideally, once you've generated the prototype, you'll test it on the following individuals:

1. On yourself—Click through the web and see how things work. Try a simple task that you know users would probably do (find the page for a certain product, for example). The look and feel diagram and the package, page, and link diagrams never really capture the experience of an actual working web. Ask yourself the following:

   How does this work together?

   Is there any page that seems unneeded?

   Do you feel that the web conveys the sense of a consistent, coherent design?

   Take your concerns to the designer and change problems associated with your implementation.

2. On designers—Have the designer who created the look and feel and other design products go through the prototype with you. What opinions do they have about how the web looks, and how the major pages fit together?

3. On other weavers—Check with the planners, analyst, and developers of the web. What suggestions do they have based on seeing the prototype?

4. On representative audience members—If possible, have a member of the target audience go through the prototype web. Elicit any comments you can from them. It may be that the prototype is too rough for the audience member to be able to say exactly how they feel about it, but observe how the audience member navigates through the prototype. Identify the problems they have. These comments can help you quickly identify areas where you might have to provide additional guidance and information.

FIGURE 36.10.

Prototype order form.

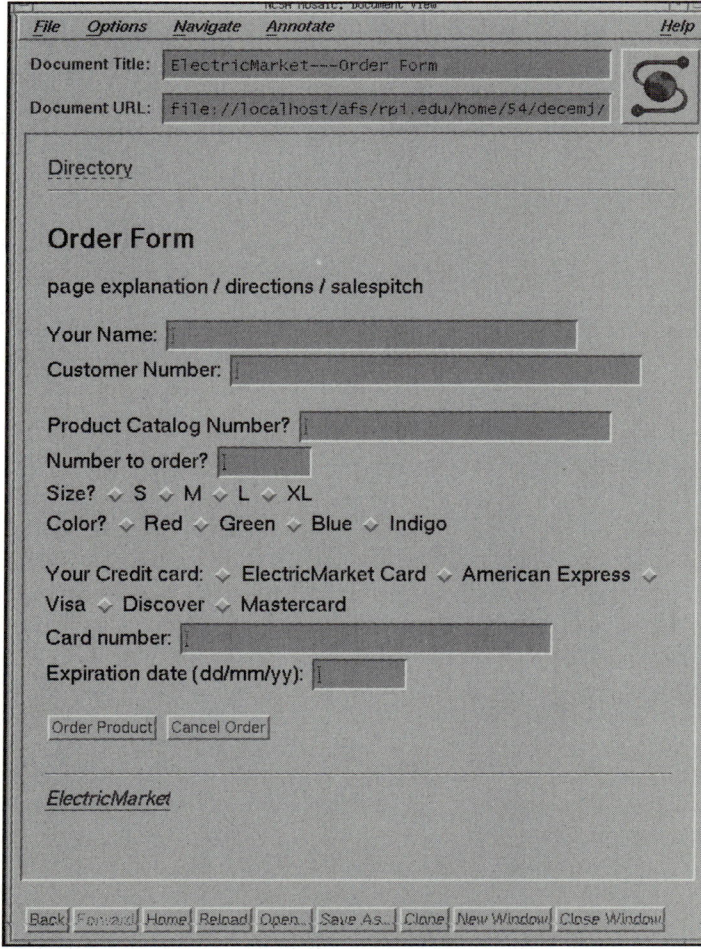

FIGURE 36.11.

Prototype department page.

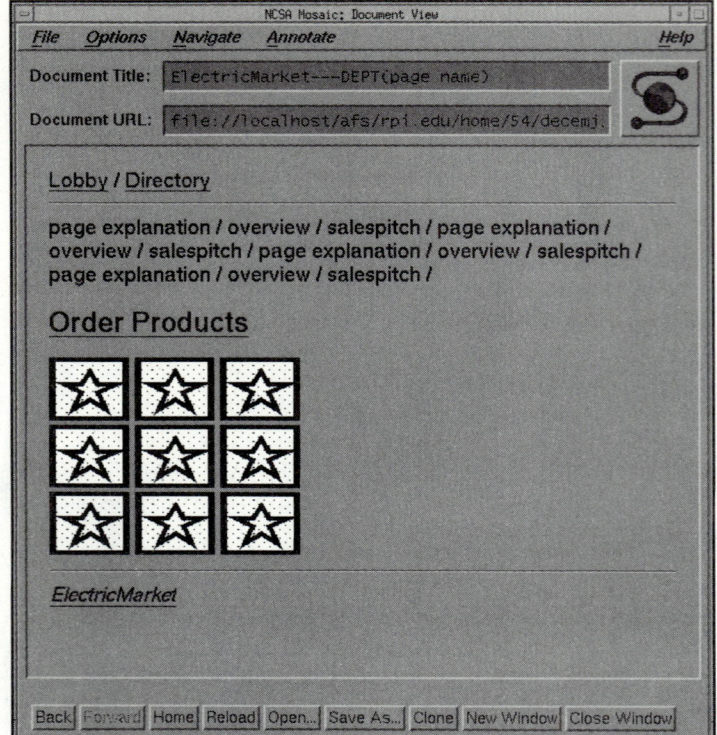

Continuous Implementation

Once you've built and demonstrated a prototype and gained some comments from other web weavers and audience members, you can continue implementation based on these results. It may be that the comments from the prototype may even lead to a redesign. More likely, some parts will be redesigned while the implementation of other parts of the web can go forward. Remember, the redesign of the web will probably be more or less continuous over the deployed life of the web. As an implementor, you'll need to adjust to a process of change and growth in the web.

Continue to implement areas of the web, always seeking feedback as described above for the prototype. In a way, the web itself is always an "evolving prototype." As implementor, the key is to continue to craft HTML files and keep track of changes to design (particularly when it affects all files such as changes in the look and feel of the universal template).

In the long-term, you'll have to be concerned with web maintenance, both the maintenance of the HTML features as well as the information (wording) in the files themselves:

1. Work closely with the web analyst to detect stale links. If possible, use automated programs to do this.

2. Routinely check the web pages for any updates you need to make in the wording and presentation of the information. This can be particularly crucial if web planners make a major change in the target audience or purpose of the web.

3. Routinely check the web's access statistics. (The webmaster should be able to set up a program to collect these.) Look for links that show up in the error logs for the server—they may be stale or malformed links.

4. If you must change the name of a file, provide a link in the old file's name for a period of time with a "link moved" notice, and provide users with a link to the new file. Using a carefully-designed directory and file naming plan, you should be able to avoid as many of these "link moved" notices as possible.

5. Continue to build your store of knowledge about HTML (and its extensions) and identify new ways to more efficiently implement the web's design.

FIGURE 36.12.

Prototype product information page.

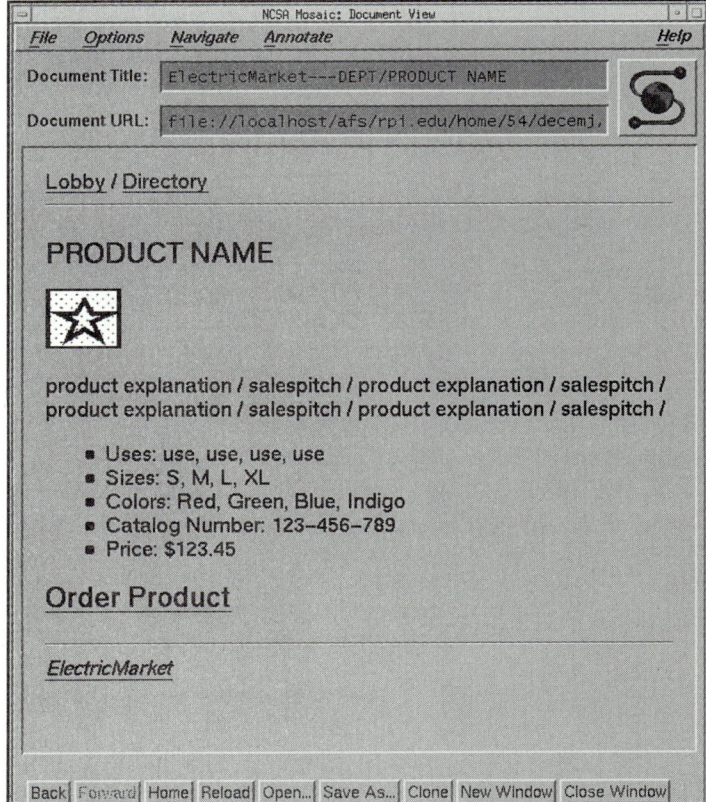

Weaver's Check

Implementing a web is a demanding part of web weaving. As implementor, you must work closely with others—the web planners, analysts, designers, and developers.

Working with HTML files and directories is also part of a web implementor's job. Plan a stable, extensible structure for the Web server's name, directories, and files. Use configuration control systems, when appropriate, to keep track of changes and alterations in the web's files and templates.

In creating individual web pages, consider general principles for presenting information: grid; typography; given/new information chain; and consistent, appropriate voice and tone.

If you're just starting a web, first gather all the information you can from the other processes and web elements: look and feel diagrams; package, page, and link diagrams; audience information, purpose and objective statements; domain information; and web specification.

Building a web prototype is the next step in implementing a new web. Create templates based on the look and feel diagrams for the whole web and as well as templates for pages that serve other functions. Link these pages based on the package, page, and link diagram to create a web prototype.

Test the prototype yourself, and then seek comments from web designers, planners, analysts, and developers. If possible, have a representative audience member look over the prototype web and comment on it.

In the long term, you'll continuously implement the web; change and growth are characteristic of good webs. Develop a process of implementation and testing and open communication with other web weavers and representative audience members. Fine tune the web so that it best expresses its design and accomplishes its overall objectives.

Implementing a web is very challenging—it draws on your technical abilities to create and manage a complex system of HTML files, your expressive capabilities with language and design elements, and your communication skills in asking for and receiving feedback to continuously improve the web.

Developing a Web

37

by John December

If you weave a web, will they come? Will your web server statistics rise long after your grand opening? Will users' hotlists include your URL? Will your target audience find increasing levels of satisfaction with your web? The answers to these questions lie in how you promote, improve, and grow your web. The constantly changing needs of your users make keeping a web current, accurate, and relevant an enormous challenge.

As a web developer, your work will involve keeping the general Web public and your web's users informed about the purpose and offerings of your web. You'll need skills in public relations, interpersonal communication, mass communication, and listening. The need for continuous web development arises from the dynamic environment in which web information exists. New resources, new information, and new forums for communication come into existence all the time. These changes alter the context in which your users experience your web. If you don't grow your web and continue its development, your web will inevitably lose value to your audience.

This chapter presents some strategies for developing a web, including techniques for publicity, attention to quality, and continuous development.

Publicity

The users and potential users of your Web experience information overload. Every moment, new services and information become available on the Web, some of which grabs your audience's attention. Making your web known to the Web public at large is a difficult task. There's no central "What's New Page" to announce a new web to the world (although NCSA's What's New page serves this purpose to a large degree). Moreover, there are few subject-related "What's New Pages," so someone interested in what you have to offer might not easily come across your Web.

There are, however, strategies you can take to publicize your web. This publicity has several goals:

1. To inform the general Web public as a whole of the existence of your web and what it has to offer

2. To attract the interest of your target audience members and let them know about how your web meets their needs

3. To educate your current web users of new developments on your web

The work you've done in composing purpose and objective statements and gathering audience information will be key to the success of web development. You'll draw on the wording of your purpose and objective statements to create publicity statements for the Web (Web releases), and you'll draw on your audience information to know where to place these Web releases. In the sections to follow, I'll describe strategies for reaching a variety of Web audiences. I'll start out with the most general audience and then describe how to focus on the narrower audience you are trying to reach with your web. Finally, I'll review how you can keep publicity and information flowing to your current web users. Before we look at how you can create Web releases, however, we need to review their timing.

Publicity Timing

No one likes to go into a brand-new shopping mall that still has sawdust and equipment spread all over. Similarly, your audience won't have a good experience if you announce your web's "grand opening" too soon. As a web developer, you'll need to work closely with other web weavers, particularly the web implementors and planners, to decide when your web is ready to "go public." Before this time, the web implementor and web master must make sure that the general public cannot access the files that comprise your web on the server. (The web server itself will often have to go public for testing before your web's public release.)

One of the most intense times for your web will be just after Web-wide announcements of its availability. This initial wave of interest will bring Net surfers, the curious, indexers, resource aficionados, and a variety of others to your web for a first look. Don't announce your web publicly until you're ready to make a good first impression. When your web is "ready" is a subjective judgement. Remember your web is never "done," so you'll have to decide on what web objectives must be met before public release, and have the web in place and well-tested before this public release.

In the following sections, we'll look at how to create and disseminate general (Web-wide) and targeted (focused to a specific Web audience) publicity. Your goal is to implement a series of periodic announcements that catch the attention of Web-wide and targeted audiences. The basic techniques for doing this include writing announcements at varying levels of detail and releasing these to appropriate forums.

Timing and content issues are a part of this dissemination process. You don't want to release so much periodic publicity that you saturate the audience's attention for your web. This may happen if the audience sees a release from your web every time some minimal change occurs. Use more frequent publicity for more specific audiences. For general audiences, announce only the "big stuff." Another technique is to use a resource on your web that has proven to be a popular item as "teaser information" that can help draw attention to your web's publicity.

General Web Releases

Reaching a Web-wide audience to announce your new web, or updates to it, is not easy. Despite the enormous demand for such a service, there are few services on the Web to

offer up-to-date, widely-recognized, "What's New" announcements for a Web-wide audience.

There are several reasons for reaching a Web-wide audience. First, you want to announce your web as part of the whole Web itself, to allow the whole Web community to benefit from or use the information you provide. Second, reaching a general audience for your announcement might be a key way to reach your target audience, or to spark an interest in your subject by a member of the general Web audience. Third, the general announcement serves as a public announcement of your Web's availability so that indexers and other Web-information gatherers can then evaluate your Web and place it within their web indexes and resource lists.

There are several considerations in creating a general web release:

1. **Audience.** The ultimate audience for your web, of course, is the audience you've defined and analyzed in the web weaving processes covered in the previous chapters. However, in creating a general web release, step back from this audience just a bit and focus on explaining your web's purpose and offerings from a general point of view—from a context outside of your web.

   For example, in the previous chapter we looked at an example design for ElectricMarket, an imaginary web-based department store. The audience for ElectricMarket are those that are interested in buying the products offered: electronics or clothing. We'll talk about how to target this specific audience in the next section on focused web releases, but for a general web release, you need to focus not just on your target audience, but on any Web user.

2. **Commercial or noncommercial.** Just as we discussed in Part III, "Web Navigation Tools and Techniques," the Web is a community of people, not a neutral collection of machines and software. As part of Web community traditions, there are places set aside for commercial activity and acceptable ways to advertise. These usually involve the following:

   Designated marketplaces—virtual malls and directories that are clearly labeled or intended to be commercial

   Commercial "What's New" lists and sponsored advertising in other webs

   Commercial asynchronous text discussion or information lists, such as commercial newsgroups or company-sponsored mailing lists

   The key is to *not* place a commercial advertisement where the standards of the Web community don't allow it. Many places on the Web welcome commercial announcements (such as NCSA's "What's New" page). Observe the information outlet for a while to see if commercial announcements are placed there or ask a moderator or frequent participant in the forum what would be appropriate.

3. **Appropriate forum.** Just as commercial advertisements are not acceptable—by Web community standards—where they don't belong, so too are nonrelated announcements in a subject-specific information or communication forum. For example, there are a variety of subject-specific web indexes (see Chapter 18, "Trees: Subject-Oriented Searching") as well as subject-specific newsgroups and mailing lists. Choose only the most appropriate forums for announcements. You'll be using subject-specific forums for focused web releases (next section). For general web releases, make sure that the forum you choose is intended for general Web audiences.

4. **Purpose.** Describe your purpose in terms that appeal to a general person on the Web. For the ElectricMarket example from the previous chapter, a general announcement could describe the web as a new, innovative shopping web and as a place to find out more about new products in electronics and the latest fashion trends.

5. **Tone, depth, length, and content.** General web releases should be very brief. In large forums like NCSA's "What's New" page (described later), the guidelines call for a concise paragraph and stipulate the format of the entry. Follow the guidelines of the forum closely.

   Adopt a tone and choice for details that will attract the attention of a general audience, as opposed to an exhaustive list of what your web has to offer. Choose only the major links of your web to include in your announcement, rather than including links to many pages. These extra links clutter the announcement, and you may unintentionally place users too deep in your web, bypassing the introductory pages you've carefully designed and built.

   For example, the ElectricMarket's general announcement might read as follows (this example is hypothetical; the URL won't access a web):

   The `<A HREF="http://www.em.com/EM/lobby.html">ElectricMarket</A>`,
   a new, innovative shopping web, is now open. The ElectricMarket
   offers a wide variety of the latest electronics and fashion
   for the discriminating shopper, complete with product images
   and detailed specifications.

   This general announcement doesn't go into too much detail of exactly what electronics are offered or what other features the store has. Rather, it mentions keywords to catch the attention of a Web user who is interested in shopping or electronics or clothing products. A spider reading your announcement will catch the important key words: market, shopping, electronics, and fashion.

Once you've developed a well-worded general web release that appeals to a general Web audience, you need to choose some forums that will disseminate this release.

Some Web-based outlets include the following:

1. Moderated Web forums.

    NCSA's "What's New," URL `http://www.ncsa.uiuc.edu/SDG/Software/Mosaic/Docs/whats-new.html`

    The InterNIC's "Scout Report" URL `http://www.internic.net/scout-report/`

2. Unmoderated Web forums. "Free for All's" (locate these by a Web spider search for "free for all").

    These are lists of hypertext, in which you can add items at will (usually through Forms). Because they are essentially unmoderated and often run by individuals on a very informal basis, the tone of these lists can vary from serious to scatological. Obviously, you'll need to decide if the tone of this list is appropriate for your web's announcement. Frequently, you'll only be able to add a short title and a short description.

Let's look in detail at one of the major outlets for general web releases—the "What's New" page at the National Center for Supercomputing Applications (NCSA), URL `http://www.ncsa.uiuc.edu/SDG/Software/Mosaic/Docs/whats-new.html`. This page won a 1994 "Best of Web" award for Most Important Service Concept. Brandon Plewe, who coordinated the contest, wrote about the NCSA What's New page: "Probably the single most accessed page on the Web, this service has helped unknown thousands keep up with this fast-moving virtual world." The NCSA page quickly rocketed to popularity because it met a need; people want to know "what's going on" and learn about new developments and resources.

NCSA's page has also grown in popularity because it is located at a centrally-known place (for Mosaic users) and is moderated. Although originally meant just to carry information about Mosaic, the service quickly included announcements for a Web-wide audience, and now serves as a gathering point and common-experience base for Web users (just like watching major network newscasts. ("Did you see that on the CBS News last night?" "Did you see the latest in 'What's New'?")

Located at the home of Mosaic, the page has at least a cachet of being "official," although no claims are made about the announcements or links contained on the page. It is moderated through a process of electronic mail: you send an announcement to the address shown on the top of the page, following a suggested set of guidelines (URL `http://www.ncsa.uiuc.edu/SDG/Software/Mosaic/Docs/submit-to-whats-new.html`). These guidelines include a request for a one paragraph, concise announcement in the third person, with no headers, inlined images, or bold text.

There are other forums that are often appropriate for general web releases:

1. Net-happenings mailing list. To subscribe, send e-mail to `listserv@is.internic` `.net` with the body, `subscribe net-happenings` *YOUR NAME*. You'll receive e-mail about the list and how to submit items to it.

2. NewNIR-L—announcements of new Network Information Retrieval and Online Public Access Catalogue Services. To subscribe, send e-mail to `listserv@itocsivm.csi.it` with the body: `subscribe NEWNIR-L` *YOUR NAME*. Archive: `http://www-chem.ucdavis.edu/nir/nirwww.html`.

3. Usenet `Comp.infosystems.announce`—announcements of new WWW sites or information services.

4. New Commerce—"What's New in Commercial Services on the Web (and Net)," URL `http://tns-www.lcs.mit.edu/commerce/whatsnew.html`.

5. "Meta-List of What's New pages"—`http://www.seas.upenn.edu/~mengwong/` `whatsnew.list.html`, by Meng Weng Wong.

6. Infobank's collection of "What's New" lists—`http://www.clark.net/pub/` `global/new.html`.

Focused Web Releases

As part of the publicity for your web, general announcements are great for spreading the word about the existence of your web and possibly catching the attention of the audience you are targeting. However, focused web releases also should be part of your overall strategy to seek out your specific audience.

Instead of wording your announcement for a general audience as for a general web release, instead, write a focused web release with your audience's greater knowledge of the subject in mind.

For example, our ElectricMarket announcement would read as follows:

```
The <A HREF="http://www.em.com/EM/lobby.html">ElectricMarket</A>
a new, innovative shopping web, is now open. The ElectricMarket
offers a wide variety of the latest electronics—including
watch tvs, CD-ROM viewers, personal digital assistants, and
a full range of personal area network (PAN) supplies.
You can also check out the latest fashion trends, from the
Webs of Europe to the far-East.
You'll find detailed product specifications, including
images, sounds, and motion videos. While shopping, you
can get helpful advice on our in-store
<A HREF="telnet://moo.em.com/">MOO</A>, and
access a <A HREF="wais://wais.em.com/">WAIS database of
fashion reviews</A>.
```

This announcement provides specific keywords to grab the readers attention. Its increased detail would be too much for a general audience, but would engage the attention of an audience interested in electronics, particularly the ElectricMarket's strength in personal electronics.

There are many ways to find outlets for focused web releases:

> Subject-specific indexes (see Chapter 18, "Trees: Subject-Specific Searching")
>
> Subject-specific Usenet newsgroups and mailing lists
>
> Professional organizations and societies
>
> Individuals involved in indexing network resources

Current Web Releases

Not only do you have to keep the general public and your potential audience informed, you'll also need to provide information about what is new on your web to your web's users.

The best way to do this is to create your own "What's New" page and keep a link to it prominently displayed on your web's home page or in its index.

You can craft the wording of these current web releases to be more specific than either the general or focused web releases. You can assume that your readers have some familiarity with your web and also very strong interest in the details of a new service or feature of the web. Naturally, you'll post current web releases more frequently than general or even focused web releases. A current web release, for example, might be placed on your web's "What's New" page to announce even a minor change in a resource, or the addition of a set of new links. You shouldn't send minor changes to Web-wide "What's New" services like NCSA's "What's New." Minor changes are usually only appropriate for your web's own "What's New" page.

Quality

The user's experience of your web is the indicator of your web's health. If the user gets the information he or she needs, you're doing your job. Maintaining a web at a high level of service, however, is not easy. You'll need to make an effort to keep your web relevant to your audience's needs, accurate, and complete.

To develop the quality of your web, use results from the analysis process. Examine the contents of your web's access statistics files, and look for patterns. Are the files that are currently getting high access appropriate to your web's purpose? You also can contact users directly and find out how they are using your web—either through a survey form (or comment box) on your web or through a voluntary e-mail list.

A successful web can build on its success. The key to making a web successful is recognizing the dynamic nature of the Web as a communications medium, and carefully attending to the intricacies of the web-weaving processes.

Here's some specific things you can do:

1. Usability testing

   Laboratory. Invite a sample of audience members as subjects to use your web to accomplish a specific objective. For example, your web might provide a list of resources related to your web's field of specialization. Devise a series of test questions that draw on your web's information. Use these items as test questions for the subjects and observe how they use your web to attempt to find these resources.

   Field. Observe audience members in their own settings as they use your web. This is may be difficult, particularly if your users are geographically dispersed. This may be more feasible for studies of "company" webs, in which there are groups of co-located users.

2. Feedback

   If a voluntary registry of users is available, send a survey to a random sample of users and ask about their overall levels of satisfaction and use of your web. Note: when your users voluntarily register, inform them that they might receive such a survey.

   Provide a Forms interface to elicit user feedback. (Note how this is a self-selected means of getting feedback versus a direct questionnaire sent to a sample of users as suggested previously.)

3. Iterative analysis

   The analysis checkpoints for your web defined in Chapter 31, "Analyzing a Web," serve as a way to examine the overall integrity of your web. As web developer, work closely with the web analyst (you might even be the same person!) to improve on these checkpoints and possibly add more. Devise other checks and tests, particularly for issues that are giving you trouble, such as a large database, or low use of a resource that is identified as critical in your web.

Continuous Development

Because the information space in which your web operates constantly changes, as does as the domain information that you present in your web, you'll need to recognize that deploying and operating a web involves continuous development. You usually can't just set a web up and then let it run. The amount your web changes will depend on your users' needs, the nature of the domain information, and other factors such as the growth of competitive webs.

Here's some specific strategies for continuous development:

Keep all web weaving processes going. Make sure that the people working on the planning, analysis, design, and implementation processes are communicating, working together, and continuously striving to improve the web for the greater good of the user.

Keep abreast of publicity outlets. New outlets to explain or announce your web will develop all the time. Keep track of new developments in "What's New" pages as well as subject-oriented resources related to your web.

Keep informed of similar or competitor's webs. New webs will come into existence that may share your web's purpose and audience. Examine how these webs work; if appropriate, you might consider collaborating with another web, so that you each might focus on a specialization and share the results.

Keep abreast of your audience's professional societies, trade shows, conventions, periodicals, related Web resources, and changing interests. You may have to do this through off-Web channels (on the Net) or print magazines, journals and newsletters. Know what your audience is involved with and how their interests and pursuits are changing.

Build your web's reputation for quality, comprehensiveness, and user service. Do this through a continuous process of defining what these issues mean in terms of your web's goals. For example, what does your web's objective statement define as "comprehensive"? Consider how you can integrate these issues into the planning and analysis processes.

Aggressively meet your defined audience's needs and purpose. Explore ways to offer new services using innovative delivery methods before other webs do, rather than merely follow the norm.

Weaver's Check

A web developer's concerns are for both public relations as well the overall excellence of the web. A developer should release web publicity at appropriate times and in appropriate forums, worded for the level of interest of the audience. General web releases reach a Web-wide audience and are usually placed in "What's New" pages or submitted to mailing lists. Focused web releases try to reach the specific audience that the web addresses, through specialized or topic-related forums. Current web releases inform the web's current users, and can be offered through a "What's New" page specific to the web.

Besides publicity, a web developer is concerned with the web's quality and continuous improvement. Keeping the other web weaving processes (planning, analysis, design, and implementation) operating and the people involved in these processes communicating is a big part of web development. A web developer also looks for opportunities to expand the web's service offerings or to suggest improvements for design or implementation. Working closely with the web analyst, a web developer can identify areas of the web that may lack publicity and educate the users about these features.

A web developer works with the whole web-weaving team to help insure that the web continuously improves in quality and value and is represented well to the whole Web.

Putting It All Together: A Case Study

by John December

38

For the first time in human history, individuals and organizations can be global publishers instantly through the Web. With this opportunity, vast quantities of information will be disseminated on top of the flood of information and communication already flowing on the Net and in other media.

Web information will add to this information flood both in terms of quantity and in terms of the *kind* of information disseminated. Web communication takes place in an environment where all information is potentially equally accessible. The Web's information space is in flux because of a continuous stream of new information, and existing information constantly changes in its relationships with other information. Thus, developing information and communication on the Web challenges web weavers to adopt new skills and new methodologies to take advantage of the exciting possibilities.

Because of the Web's information dynamism, the web weaving methodology outlined in the previous chapters occurs in a much more complex way in the real world than was described in the chapters. In my own work, I switch very quickly from web analysis and planning to implementation and design—not necessarily in a neat order or with clean breaks between work on processes and web elements.

Developing complex information structures with networked hypermedia requires a methodology that has flexibility and change built into it, and I attempt to evoke these qualities in this hypothetical case study.

This chapter presents the case of the Kappa Company (an imaginary organization), describing how a team of its information developers weaves a web, starting from an inspiration from the company's president.

How you weave your web for your organization or your personal use will vary widely based on what you want to accomplish. However, the case of Kappa is typical: an enthusiastic beginning followed by a process of fits, starts, and surprises.

The Kappa Company Web

The example for this chapter is an imaginary company that offers—according to one of its brochures—*integrated solutions for today's business problems*. In other words, Kappa does whatever is necessary with products and services to meet customers' needs. Kappa develops and sells business software and training courses, and analyzes customer needs for information and online services. They're a natural candidate for adopting Web communication.

Kappa—in business for five years—has 100 employees, and although it has experience in analyzing online communications services for its customers, it does not have expertise with the Web. The president of Kappa, Anne Smith, is interested in moving onto the Web, and recently attended an international conference on Mosaic and the Web. Returning to Kappa headquarters with enthusiasm, President Smith calls Lynn Jones, a key information developer in the company. Lynn is the sole person in the company dedicated to developing information *about* Kappa—information for company reports, publicity, company brochures, and proposals. In the short time since the company started, Lynn has created or overseen the design of all the information about Kappa presented to prospective clients.

President Smith's corner office is on the 33rd floor of Kappa headquarters, overlooking a compact but rapidly growing downtown in a sunny, midwestern city. Lynn has no idea why the president called her in, and is concerned about possible cutbacks or "rightsizing." But as soon as Anne and Lynn sit down at the window alcove, Lynn knows that its not bad news—the lore of Kappa is that Smith never delivers bad news at the alcove.

President Smith tells Lynn, "This information highway thing, we need to get on it."

Lynn appears puzzled. Knowing the president had gone to the Web conference, Lynn suspects that this has something to do with that.

President Smith shrugs her shoulders as if surrendering to some inevitable point and says, "We need to build a Mosaic server."

To Lynn, it makes sense now. Mosaic's alluring view into the Web—probably prevalent at the conference—easily seduces. Lynn understands the president's error in the term *Mosaic server,* but also recognizes the genuine interest the president has. Lynn nods her head to show she understands. President Smith continues.

"We need the global reach—the flexible way we can provide information about ourselves to attract clients, inform people about what we do, and understand the medium itself so that we might be able to advise our clients on how to use it. We need to have a presence on the Web."

Lynn says, "I'd be glad to do it."

"Great, You have all the budget you need." President Smith stands up and says, "I have a meeting."

Lynn knows this is her cue to get moving.

Putting a Team Together

Now all Lynn needs to do is obtain the equipment and software and the Internet connections, and make a server. Right?

Well, not exactly. Since Lynn is an information developer, she knows that the actual content of what will be on the Web server will be crucial to accomplishing the goals of establishing a Web presence.

The skills of the talented people who obtain the hardware and install the software and network connections to get a Web server operational is crucial. Without them, there would be no Web server. Similarly, without excellent content, there would be no reason why anyone would use a web from the Kappa Company.

Lynn pulls a team together—a mix of software, hardware, and Kappa product experts—people who know how to work with hardware and software, along with people involved directly with the potential audience of the web, including a sales representative, an account manager, and a customer service person.

Setting Goals

In their first meeting, the team brainstorms what the web server could possibly do—what "a presence on the Web" could mean. Writing down as many ideas as possible on the whiteboard in the conference room, the team generates and then synthesizes ideas. They arrive at the following list:

Goals for Web Server

Information for prospective customers

Information supporting current customers

Kappa services and products catalog

Background information about Kappa

These goals imply reaching an audience that members of the team know: potential and existing customers. The team knows information about Kappa that they can use to reach these customers now: information about products, services, company background, and even the sales pitches to potential customers.

Lynn has a collection of brochures, company reports, and full access to all company information. The sales representative, Karen, explains that she sees a trend in Net-literate customers showing increasing interest in the Web and knows some customers who are developing their own webs, either directly in their business or as part of their own interests and hobbies.

The customer service representative, Mark, has a great deal of stories about what people want to know—the continued questions that prospective customers always seem to ask on the 800 phone number they use for sales and support.

The people with technical knowledge of the hardware and software necessary to bring the web server into operation know all the issues about networks and security.

After the first meeting, the web server developers (the webmasters) want work on their own to create an operational server. Still keeping the lines of communication open, Lynn sets the web masters free, allowing them to dedicate their time to getting the necessary hardware and software up and running.

With the rest of the team, Lynn needs to get an idea of what content could be possible. Lynn, several other information developers, and a graphic designer at Kappa will acquire skills in Web navigation (see Part III, "Web Navigation Tools and Techniques") and learn HTML by reading some books (see the previous chapters of this part). They'll install and use Web browsers (see Part II, "Web Browsers and Connections") to experiment on their own. They'll also spend time getting familiar with Web applications (see Part IV, "Exploring the Web").

Learning

After a few weeks, the initial enthusiasm seems drowned in a sea of new terms and concepts—URLs, spiders, Gopher, Mosaic, Lynx, HTML. The team members have spent time searching for subjects and keywords, surfing, and researching their competitors' webs.

President Smith, however, seems a bit confused. She's spent tens of thousands of dollars on the project, but when she visits the cubicles of the team members, she sees only the bright graphics of web pages like the Late Night with David Letterman home page (URL `http://bingen.cs.csbsju.edu/letterman.html`) or the *Star Trek* Page (URL `http://www.cosy.sbg.ac.at/rec/startrek/index.html`). Once in a while, she sees small, jerky MPEG movies of people on bicycles or scientific visualizations of gas jets on a team member's computer monitor.

The developers seem entranced—surfing through colorful pages on webs covering every conceivable subject, and making their own home pages with photographs and lists of their hobbies. The Kappa web server isn't public yet, so these pages aren't being provided to anyone worldwide, but President Smith begins to wonder if the Web is a very expensive waste of time.

President Smith asks Lynn for a written plan for how the "Mosaic server" (no one has corrected President Smith yet) is going to benefit the customers of the company. Moreover, she asks Lynn how they could possibly make money on information that they will be *giving away for free* on a public web. And not only giving it away for free to potential customers, but to all their competitors as well. President Smith warns, "Our competitors will be able to see, in intimate detail, exactly how we are serving our customers, enabling them to steal our market share even faster."

The Planning Process

Lynn calls a meeting of the web team and brainstorms more specific goals. The team members' immersion in what the Web has to offer has raised their awareness of many kinds of webs. They've honed their skills in navigating the Web (Part III, "Web Navigation Tools and Techniques") and in writing and designing with basic HTML (Chapter 32, "Designing a Web" and Chapter 33, "Implementing a Web"). They're actually very anxious to get started with a public web. One of the team developers has already created a "Kappa Home Page," and wants to make it available for public use right away.

Lynn senses that it's time to start planning exactly what their web should do before the force of the team's enthusiasm pushes them into deploying a web too soon. They also need to address President Smith's very serious concerns about making money from something (information) that they will give away for free.

Lynn calls the team together and again brainstorms all aspects of their web—what should go in it, and what should not.

Gradually, they see a pattern emerging. They recognize that just because the Web offers a wide range of possible ways to communicate: hypermedia, movies, graphics, interactive Forms, and graphical information maps, they're not obligated to implement a particular feature just to display the technology. Moreover, just because they *could* present all kinds of information about the company and its inner workings, they don't have to. It seems obvious to Lynn that they, as a team, can carefully plan what information goes public and what does not—a balancing of choice that Lynn has always been familiar with in the many reports and presentations she's designed.

President Smith, seeing the vast amounts of information on demonstration webs, might have assumed a web would, somehow by its own volition, "suck up and serve out" all the information a company might have to offer. Lynn knows they have choices, and that, given the President's mood and the team's enthusiasm, it is time to start making those choices now.

Lynn opens the meeting by asking, "Why are we building this web?" Through a process of discussion, the team comes up with some answers:

- To help customers make better use of our products
- To reach customers who might be interested in our company
- To attract customers to buy our services and products
- To inform our own employees about our products and services
- To have a Web "presence"

Although this list seems to be getting at why they are building the web, Lynn still wonders what all this *means,* particularly that last point. What is a "Web presence?" Pressing on this point, Lynn helps the team elaborate on the meaning of "Web presence":

> To tell potential customers what products we have, just as we do now in the paper catalogs and brochures that we distribute. The advantage the Web can give us is global reach, and no marginal cost increases for each electronic catalog distributed via the Web.

> To let customers know our company, so that someday they may have us in mind when they need us, just as we are doing now in our print ads and television commercials. The advantage of the Web is that its information is customer-driven: through the Web's hypertext, the customer selects the information and level of detail they want.

> To help current customers see what other products we offer and to provide them with specific information they can use on demand. We're doing this to some degree with our sales calls, but the Web offers a more flexible way for customers to find this out. Satisfied with our initial products and services, they can link to our home page and find out more about what we have to offer.

> To use the Web as a locus for doing business, much as the downtowns of cities formed because of the ease of communication with other businesses and proximity to business services, support information, and supplies. The Web is evolving as a place where business needs can be met. A presence on the Web also means that our customers can include a link on their own web pages with a hotspot that says, "Here is where we bought our business software for project X." These links foster and continue relationships. Without a Web presence, we do not even show up within the larger context of Web information—in the indexes, lists, and directories on the Web, or in any Web spider search. Our Web presence is just one more form of communication. No company today would question having a phone (although the Web may change this) or a Fax machine (they might change this, too). The Web and the Internet are part of an infrastructure for communicating and doing business, for providing the customer the means to acquire the information they want when they want it, rather than relying on face-to-face or voice communication at mutually agreeable times and places.

Lynn is now satisfied with how the team has defined the reasons for going onto the Web in more detail. They've mentioned specific benefits in terms of how things have been done (such as business contacts through sales calls and advertisements and customer information through 800 numbers) and in terms of what new things are possible (most notably, the idea of the Web presence leading to new kinds of relationships through hypertext links).

Now Lynn pushes the team to explore what content they could possibly create to address these issues. What kind of information could we provide? To whom? Why? The team arrives at several points:

> We can provide on the Web all the information we are presently giving away— promotional brochures, annual reports, product catalogs, and all other supporting company material. We can do this on the Web for the same reason we are now in print: to inform our customers about what we can offer. Our competitors have access, in one way or another, to this information already. Online, we can have an opportunity to help a potential customer see our total company, rather than the limited view a sales catalog might bring. They can see our products and services as a total plan to help them meet their needs.

> Our web will serve not just as a marketplace where we know our customers will often visit, but a communication and information space. We'll include a contact e-mail address and ways for our customers to give us direct feedback. Also, we'll provide valuable information to the Web as a whole. We could do this by providing information in our area of expertise. For example, we can provide techniques and tips for using our products in specific business applications or information about other resources on the Net that our customers might often need.

> Our web can serve as a visible focal point that conveys important information about our company in a way that no paper source can. Current and prospective employees can find out about our products, company background, and current activities in one central location. Paper sources quickly go out of date or become unavailable, while our web's information can be updated instantly.

Lynn is happier with the results of this meeting, but is still concerned. It seems as if there's a great deal of talk, but not enough specifics. Highbrow philosophies of new frontiers in communication sound great, but the reality is that they must decide what is going to go in the HTML files served out on their web, and that those files must be able to demonstrate *cost recovery* (in other words, pay their way) in terms of increased sales. At the next meeting, Lynn intends to bring a plan worksheet and prompt the team to become more specific about the purpose and objective for the web server. Meanwhile, Lynn realizes she needs to placate President Smith before the web project itself is canceled.

An Answer for President Smith

Lynn visits President Smith the afternoon after the planning meeting. On the overhead projector in the president's office, Lynn puts up her first chart:

- Information fosters relationships
- Relationships bring us customers

Smith's brow furrows, and she says, "I've been president of this company for five years and now you tell me we're in the business of *relationships*? I should read fewer books by Tom Peters and more by Leo Buscaglia?"

Lynn looks again at the chart. "No," she says. "We want to build a web that can help us keep in contact with current and potential customers in many of the ways we're doing already, only our web could bring us a global audience. The information we provide about Kappa's products can be the most current and comprehensive available."

"OK," President Smith says. "I can see that—our catalog all over the world at the speed of light. But where's the value in the information we serve out on our web? Are we going to charge the customers to access it because it's a more convenient way to order?"

Lynn knows that the discussion could quickly devolve into an endless debate over charging policies on networks—pay-per-view versus flat rates versus free access. Lynn looks directly at President Smith and quickly says. "The information we give away in our web has no value to us or anyone until it leads to a relationship."

"There's the word *relationship* again," Smith says, "I'm not going to pay for ten color workstations and two hundred person hours a week for relationships."

"But you will pay for a team of five salespeople on the road…" Lynn says.

"Well," Smith says, "that's how we get our orders. That's where the money comes from."

"…and $10,000 a year for print ads and $500,000 a year for internal documentation and reports and thousands a month for phone service and FAX numbers and office rent.…"

"You're giving me the *it's a part of doing business* line—I don't buy it. You can't tell me that providing color workstations for everyone is just a way of doing business."

Lynn began to wonder if the project might be canceled. Not only didn't they have a clue about what would be served out on the web, but the president herself was losing faith in the project. All the collaboratively-brainstormed points on the white board in the conference room seemed to fade, seemed less important than this direct challenge—the president of the company wondering why tens of thousands of dollars had already been spent for something that hadn't shown any results.

"Where are our customers?" Lynn asks.

Anne Smith leans forward, straining her eyes to see Lynn. She hesitates, then says, "Out there…," and gestures toward the large picture window overlooking the boxy towers of downtown, with its late-80s slick-tech architecture that the city residents regarded with considerable pride. It *looked* like a serious downtown, a place where business people on their lunch hour could wander on the street among hotdog vendors and the swirl of brief-cased salespeople—a flow that didn't change very much over the years, but still seemed the highlight of many workers' days.

"How are they going to find us?" Lynn's voice was lower, almost a whisper.

Anne lowered her voice, matching Lynn's in a mock-whisper, "Our address is printed on all our sales literature: 21 North Water Street."

"That's not our address anymore," Lynn said.

"Did I miss something, Lynn?" the president asked.

"Our address is `kappa.com`."

"Lynn," Anne said, straightening up in her chair, "I've always respected your work. You develop all the print, radio, and television materials that explain our company to the public and customers; you direct the product catalog and the sales brochures. You've even scripted the presentations that sales representatives give to customers. You know how we communicate in every medium we use. You know this isn't a starship—we're not talking about some journey into cyberspace."

"Our customers are using online communication."

"I know," Anne said. "I developed the procedures for analyzing our customer's needs for online news, information, and stock quotes. I know online services. That Mosaic server you want to build is very different."

Lynn brightened. "The server is very different. It can give our customers—both current and potential—a way to gain updated and comprehensive information about us on their own terms any time they want to."

Lynn paused. President Smith seemed weary with the whole subject.

Lynn continued, "We've always met our customers on their terms and become part of their way of doing business. We don't question the need for phones, advertisements, or Fax machines because our customers have them. The Web server can be a part of this same information and communication infrastructure. It's not going to work miracles. It would be unfair to judge it in any other way than as a medium for communication, and its success will depend on how we use it, not on any of its inherent properties."

President Smith looked at Lynn and back at the chart still beaming onto the screen from the overhead projector.

Lynn continued, "We want spiders to find us and intelligent agents to know us. We want to be able to be distinguished in a new medium that breaks from the one-way media like print or TV and involves the user in shaping information. We want our company to be a part of the relationships our customers will choose to have. Our customers are using the Web in increasing numbers. Our potential customers are out there, increasing traffic on the Web by hundreds of thousands of percent in a year."

Lynn paused, sensing that nothing she had said was convincing President Smith.

"OK," Smith said, "go ahead with the server for now. Once you get an initial operational web, I'll take a look at it. I'll invite a group of customers to give it a try, and I'll watch them. Then we'll go from there."

A Plan Worksheet

Lynn and her team, after going over the details of possibilities and brainstorming what they want to do on the web, carefully write down a plan by filling in a web planning worksheet.

PLAN WORKSHEET

Kappa Web Team

Plan A

TARGET AUDIENCE

Discussion: While our ideal audience will be customers ready to buy our products and services, we recognize that Web surfers and the curious may use our web, and we won't discourage this. Moreover, our long-term goal will be to include support for an increasingly wider audience: employees (current, prospective, and past), investors, business partners, and other people with key relationships to our company. However, our initial plan will be to reach a specific, targeted audience whose needs our sales team and customer service representatives know well: potential clients interested in the business applications we develop and sell.

1. Definition

   One sentence statement: Potential customers identified by our sales team as likely prospects for buying our products and services

   More complex description: These customers are:

   ■ In a business with little or no in-house software development or consulting support (they have a need for our products/services)

   ■ Willing to take part in advanced forms of technology and interfaces (have an existing set of equipment, people, and skills involved in modern communication, such as computers, networks, and some computer-mediated communication)

   ■ Either already have and use an Internet connection and one or more Web browsers, or are willing to have our sales staff assist in installing and providing some training in their use

Cluster diagram. Figure 38.1 (shown at the end of this worksheet) illustrates the overlapping possible audiences for the web. We'll target the shaded portion—those who are web literate or willing to try, and who are identified by our sales staff as likely customers or past customers. We'll also target Web indexers, including spiders, agents, or people concerned with gathering or cataloging information on the Web.

2. Information about audience

   Characteristics

   - Technology adopters
   - Results-oriented
   - Need rapid communication for products and services
   - Need updated, comprehensive product support information
   - Want current and comprehensive sales and promotional literature

   Concerns

   - Value and quality in products and services
   - Meeting their own business needs/customer needs
   - Reliable, trustworthy partners

   Key concerns based on purpose definition (to follow)

   - Product information is current, complete, and correct
   - Customer support will be continuing and reliable
   - Security and privacy will be ensured and respected

PURPOSE

1. Subject area: Kappa company current software products and services

2. Audience (defined previously)

3. Level of detail: Equivalent to sales literature we already provide to customers, giving full details of what we sell, can develop, or services we provide. This does not, of course, include customized services or products, or proprietary products (products developed for a company and sold exclusively to them).

4. User's expected benefit/response: Ideally, sales. But just as we recognize that developing customers means spending time to inform them about what we

can do, we understand that what we serve on our web may help keep our name in the customer's mind for the next time they need our products or services.

5. Succinct purpose statement:

To provide potential customers a comprehensive collection of information about Kappa products and services.

OBJECTIVE STATEMENT

1. Specific goals to accomplish the purpose:

Provide a comprehensive and current product catalog

- All current software products, including demos when available, detailed reviews and documentation
- Software development team capabilities

Present a services list

- Business areas in which we have strength and have succeeded in the past
- Willing customers can provide case studies

Provide free domain information

- A well-checked, authoritative guide to technologies in which we excel
- Background information in our areas of expertise

2. Restrictions:

No proprietary information about our own customers or Kappa itself (President Smith will clear all information).

Tone of web should be low-key—not heavily "sales," but more informative/helpful to potential customers, even providing a good collection of useful information for free.

DOMAIN INFORMATION

1. Information necessary:

Web team: All members know Kappa's operations, products, and services well. Sales and customer service representatives will do a series of presentations on customer needs and concerns. Existing background, sales, and other information—on paper and online will be gathered and placed in a central library.

Information served: Existing electronic version of product and services catalog will be translated to HTML. A database of company background information and domain information to be given away (see objective statement) will be gathered.

2. Acquiring information:

Kappa employees who are directly involved in creating domain information used will be trained in HTML. The most authoritative and complete version of all information for this project will be the one on the web.

3. Updates and maintenance:

As part of regular duties, people supplying domain information will keep it continuously updated with the most current available information.

SPECIFICATION

1. Limitations on information:

Proprietary (see objective) restrictions

Competitive—President Smith will meet with sales representatives and other web team members regularly to evaluate any information that may be too valuable to serve out on the web.

Appropriate legal and ethical considerations—Information will be presented according to all copyright and other laws, and will represent the best interests of the company in fostering good customer relations by following Web customs and practices, including considerations for multicultural communication.

2. Limitations on media:

Initial web will provide text and graphics; multimedia will be incorporated according to customers' needs.

Forms support will not be used until such time when security measures are in place; our current 24-hour 800 telephone number will be offered to customers to place orders.

3. Resources:

List of in-house URLs: sales, company background, product, service, and domain information directories will be established on the server.

Outside links will be evaluated for background domain information.

PRESENTATION

1. Look and feel possibilities:

   A fairly conservative overall look, focusing most on providing useful content that meets customer needs, with graphics playing a role to enhance information and navigation.

2. Work schedule:

   We'd like to deploy an in-house prototype for invited customers to evaluate with President Smith in three to five weeks; we'd like to hook up our web to the Web in three months.

3. Skills required:

   Web planning, analysis, design, implementation (basic HTML), and development

4. Components:

   Web designers and implementors have already developed some candidate components

5. Mockup web:

   A mockup web which demonstrates functionality and "look and feel" will be operational for a review by the President in three weeks.

FIGURE 38.1.

Kappa audience cluster diagram.

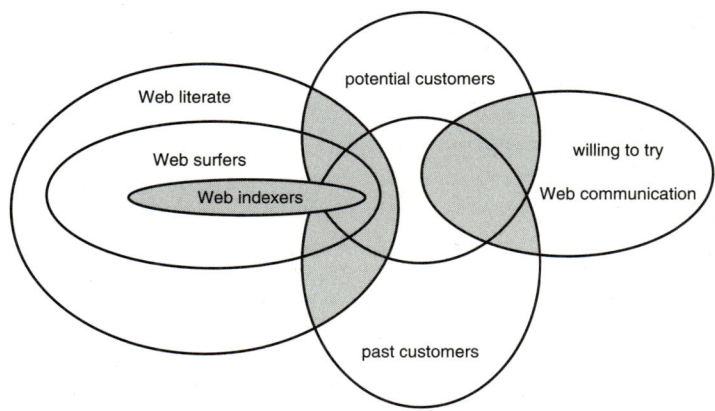

Preliminary Analysis

After the initial confusion, now it all seems too easy to Lynn and her team. They've created a written plan, and President Smith seems placated, at least for three more weeks until they have a mockup web operational. But is the plan sound? Will this web be successful? Because there is no operational web, only a limited amount of analysis can be done (see Figure 31.1 in Chapter 31). Lynn and her team identify the analysis that can be done based on the web plan so far:

- Is the web attempting to reach an audience that has and will use Web access (Checkpoint A)?
- Is the web contributing new information (accomplishing goals that haven't already been done) (Checkpoint B)?
- Is the web self-consistent (that is, its purpose matches its objectives and specification) (Checkpoint C)?

Lynn assigns Jack, a member of the web team who had seemed particularly adept at finding Web resources and surfing the web, to be web analyst. Jack's first tasks are to analyze checkpoints A, B, and C for their proposed web. Jack will find out more about where their target audience "hangs out" on the Web and the Net and locate any existing webs that may be supplying similar information. He'll continually work with the web planners, designers, and implementors to make sure that the web's purpose, objectives, and specifications match. He'll coordinate with the web developer to identify problem areas in the web or opportunities for other publicity outlets. Jack spends time surfing the Web to find out about current Web offerings and similar Web audiences. At the same time, he gathers useful background domain information.

A Preliminary Design

Jose, the graphic designer on the web team, doesn't know HTML. But he knows the layout and design of the existing product catalog well—he developed it for Lynn. Lynn assigns him the task of web designer, and Jose spends time at his personal computer using a drawing program to create sketches that can be used as a basis for the appearance of web pages. Jose's knowledge of layout and design principles helps him articulate a professional look for the pages. Although his sketches can't be implemented directly (he still struggles to adjust to the non-WYSIWYG nature of HTML and web browsers), the sketches give all the web team members a sense of having something concrete to look at and critique.

Jose also spends a great deal of time navigating and exploring the Web itself (Part III, "Web Navigation Tools and Techniques" and Part IV, "Exploring the Web"), and he gains a sense of what kinds of structures and layouts are possible, while at the same time retaining his own aesthetic vision for the Kappa web—that is, not being swayed by some of the poor web designs he finds. He even interacts with some webmasters, making constructive suggestions for improving their web's appearance, and they appreciate his insights.

Jose's concept for the universal grid for the Kappa web is in Figure 38.2, and he spends time with Karen, Mark, Lynn, and other team members asking about comments as well as how this universal grid can be used to generate grids for other types of information: the product catalog, the domain information page, and so on.

FIGURE 38.2.

Kappa universal grid.

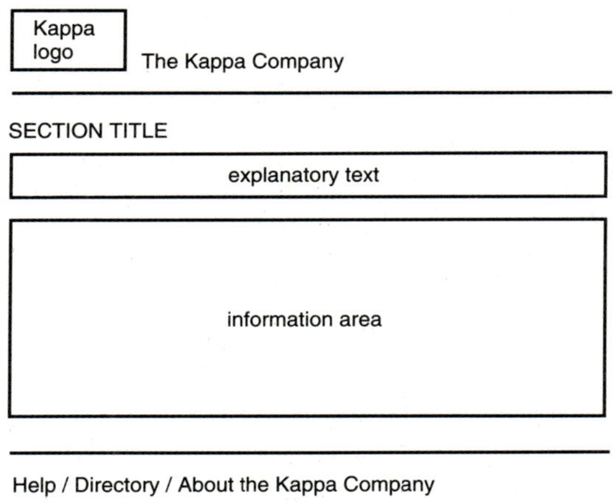

Jose also works from the written plan and drafts an introductory statement for the Kappa home page:

"This is the home page for Kappa, a diversified company offering products and services for networked business information systems worldwide. From links on this page, you can find out more about our company, products, and the field of business communications."

More Tasks for Team Members

Lynn is pleased that team members now can independently produce information for the web. She assigns Jack, the web analyst, to also develop the store of domain information by identifying scholars and other people on the Web who maintain business information related to Kappa's products. Jack asks each if they would be willing to allow the Kappa web to link to their pages.

Lynn assigns Holly and Bill to be web implementors. Both have shown a keen ability to compose in HTML. Holly had already made a preliminary home page for Kappa, and her personal home page is extensive, with links to where she had gone to school and worked before, as well as links to Web resources she likes. Bill has been a software developer with Kappa for three years, and his ability to manage collections of files and directories is well-known among the Kappa software team.

In addition, she assigns Karen to work with Jose in the web design. Karen has an M.S. in technical communication, and she has developed her own web on her MacIntosh at home. She knows many customers who have developed their own webs as a hobby. Both Karen and Jose will work closely with Holly and Bill to work out ideas for what could be possible and what can be done.

Lynn spends some time surfing the Web herself—finding potential outlets for Web-wide and focused web releases—as well as getting a feel for the culture and customs she encounters. She notices that President Smith's visits to the cubicles of the web-weaving team are becoming more frequent. Lynn looks up one morning to see Smith standing quietly behind her, looking at the Tango Server (URL `ttp://imtsun3.epfl.ch:8000/tango/`) in Lynn's Mosaic browser. Lynn senses it will be best to have a prototype completed soon.

Moving Toward a Prototype

The team members increase the specificity of their plans to include the actual URLs that Jack, Bill, and Holly have designated as repositories for domain information. Jose and Karen have a large set of story boards showing screen designs for the Kappa web. They show these to President Smith, and she says she likes seeing something concrete, but seems impatient, as if the story boards where somehow a small consolation for the talent, time, and money she's spending on the web. In the course of explaining to Smith why they can't precisely control the appearance of their web in the many different browsers that their audience might have, Jose very diplomatically explains that they're creating a "Web server," not a "Mosaic server." Smith squints a bit and seems disappointed that they're not going to be able to guarantee that each customer will look at their web through Mosaic. Smith vividly remembers the colorful displays at the conference and wonders if they will be able to appeal to the customers through the dull text in nongraphical browsers.

After another meeting of the whole web team, in which they look through all the story boards defining the look and feel of the web, including Karen's package, page, and link diagram (Figure 38.3), they decide to start implementing a prototype.

Holly and Bill design a directory structure and make templates that implement the look and feel designs. The web team members seem more excited one afternoon when they all gather in Holly's cubicle to see the working prototype, with all links working to prototype pages (the home page is shown in Figure 38.4).

Bill works out a translation scheme to turn their current products catalog to an HTML-like format that can easily be converted to correct HTML. This enables the team to quickly offer a great deal of content on their web: descriptions of their entire line of software products.

FIGURE 38.3.

Kappa package and link diagram.

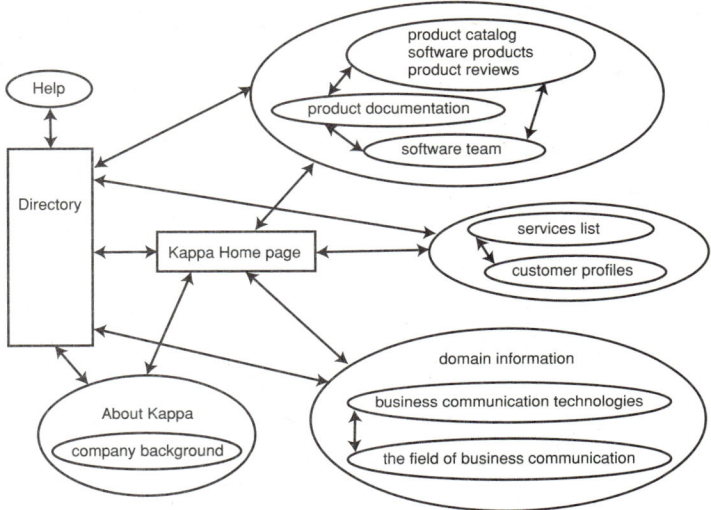

FIGURE 38.4.

Kappa home page.

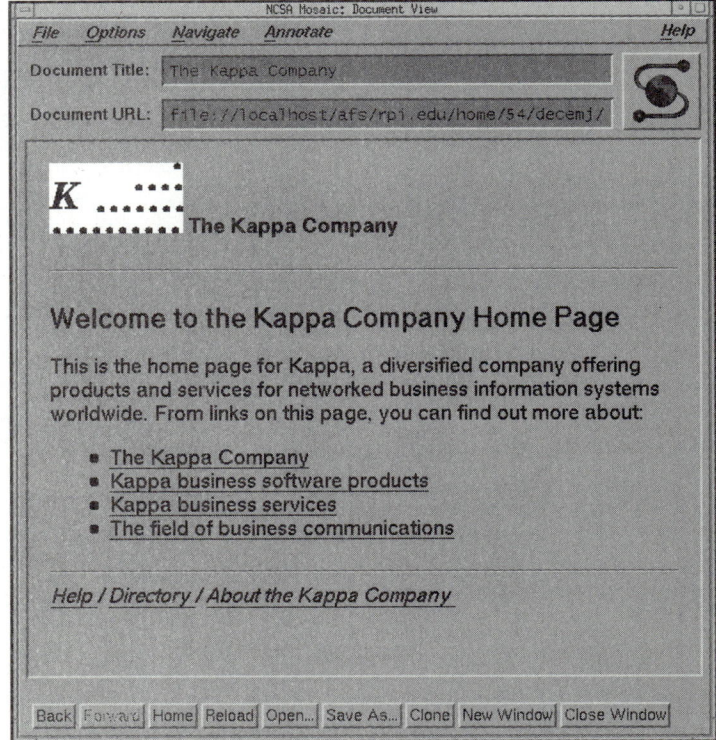

After several weeks of moving through the processes of planning, design, analysis, and implementation, Lynn finds that they have a prototype web with at least as much content as their existing sales brochures. They've more branches to add in the background domain information section, but they have completed all the product pages. The services list is the same as they offer customers now, but more current than the paper copies in circulation.

A Prototype

In a meeting with President Smith at Holly's cubicle, the web team members watch while President Smith uses the Kappa web. She's impressed by how much information is available—a complete catalog of the company's business software products, as well as all the information that they normally provide to customers through sales brochures.

"I'm impressed," President Smith says, "Do you think the customers are going to use this?"

"I think so," Lynn says. "It's already the most current and comprehensive source for information about our products."

"What do you mean?" President Smith asks.

Lynn explains, "We've included pages about our two newest software products—PANMate (Personal Area Networks interface to local area networks) [Figure 38.5] and Cygnus14 (spreadsheet)."

Lynn continues, saying, "These two products won't show up in our paper catalog until the next quarterly printing, and those catalogs probably won't be widely circulated for six months."

President Smith squints and clicks again on the screen for PANMate (Figure 38.5). She knew that this should be one of their hottest selling items; no one else has ever marketed PAN-LAN interface software. Their sales force is out there now, she thought, spreading the word at the speed of airplanes and rental cars, while the web she's looking at could deliver current information to customers immediately.

"Let's get on the Web with this now," says President Smith.

Development

Lynn knows that the web team will have to work carefully on their web before deploying it, despite the pressure to release it right away. Already, salespeople want to know when Kappa's home page will be ready so that customers can link to it. Lynn holds more planning sessions with the web team, and meets with Jack about his continued analysis of the web's integrity. Lynn talks more with Karen and Jose about design ideas, and with Holly and Bill to check that they have the skills and equipment to do the implementation correctly.

FIGURE 38.5.

Kappa's PANMate product page.

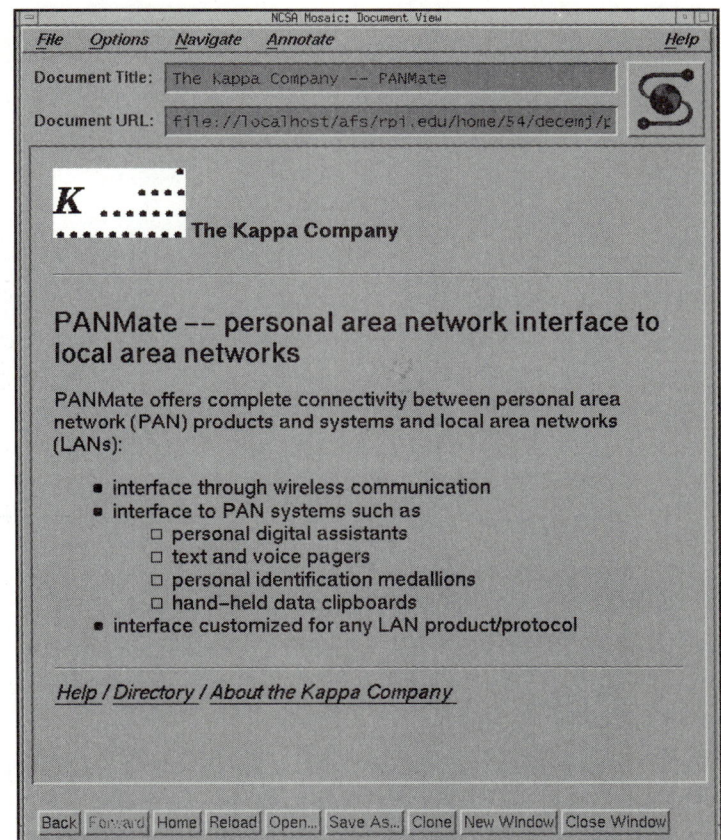

President Smith invites a focus group of customers to Kappa headquarters to use and view the prototype web. One long-time customer in the group, actually a good friend of President Smith's, tells her, "I didn't realize your company offered so many products and services." Later, Smith tells Lynn to connect the Kappa web to the Web, and to announce it to the world.

Lynn had already crafted general and focused web releases. She'd tracked down some outlets for Web-wide releases as well as some places she could place announcements to reach their target audience. Lynn places a full-page print ad in a well-known business communications trade journal (Figure 38.6).

Lynn hopes the ad will catch the attention of the Web-literate and perhaps catch the attention of those who might be interested in knowing what Kappa is doing. Lynn smiles to herself, knowing the ad will perhaps rankle their competition just a little bit.

FIGURE 38.6.
Kappa's print ad.

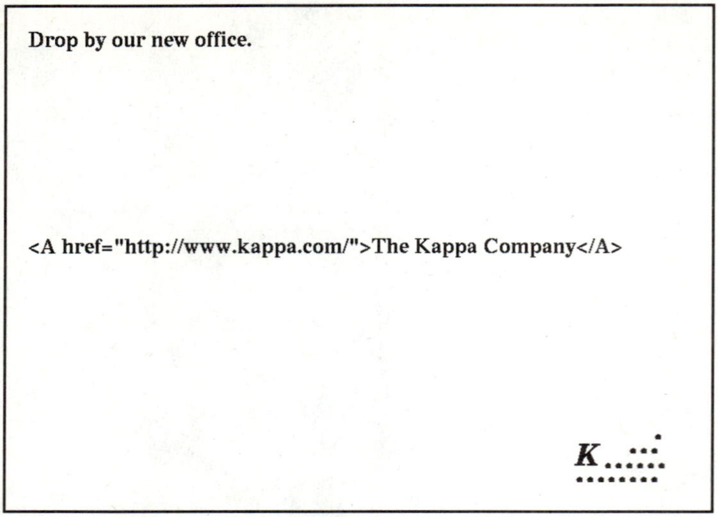

Drop by our new office.

<A href="http://www.kappa.com/">The Kappa Company</A>

K ......::

Weaver's Check

Weaving a web is not a simple exercise. Although you can quickly get a HTML page up and running on a server, a carefully crafted web, one designed to accomplish a set of objectives for affecting a specific audience, is a complex task.

Web weaving requires people skills as well as technical skills in communication and shaping information. A group of people—or even a single individual—can employ an iterative, incremental process of creating audience information, objective and purpose statements, a web specification, and a web presentation through processes of planning, analysis, design, implementation, and development.

The imaginary narrative describing the Kappa Company's experience might not be typical to your situation, but you'll probably face many of the same issues. These issues include identifying and understanding the people you want to reach with your web, more precisely stating why you want to reach them, and defining your web's content. You'll be under pressure from whomever is funding your work (or yourself if your doing your own web) to justify spending time and talent on creating something that's essentially just ephemeral electric transmissions throughout a patchwork of world-wide networks. A well-done web, however, can extend the range of your communication. With the increasing number of individuals, businesses, schools, and universities using the Web, you'll be able to communicate with more people, more flexibly, and with greater impact.

VI

PART

Whither the Web: Trends and Issues

The Web as a technological innovation is still evolving. Initiatives by the World Wide Web Organization (W3O) (URL `http://info.cern.ch/hypertext/WWW/Organization/Consortium/W3OSignature.html`) will guide the evolution of the Web so that it will continue to support a wide variety of applications. The W3O will promote activities such as the collection and dissemination of standards for the Web's infrastructure, clients, and servers; the examination of advanced Web concepts and data models; protocol design and support; and other work to encourage the Web's stable evolution and operation. These initiatives, under the guidance of an international organization, will undoubtably bring new perspectives and help foster the Web's continued success.

Beyond the technical level, the Web is a vibrant, social space, bringing with it still more issues to examine. Today, people use the Web to create information and communication in ways that rival our physical and cultural landscapes in terms of complexity and potential. This intensive use reflects the Web's role as a tool and foreshadows the way tool-using humans will continue to employ the Web in unexpected and chaotic ways, not necessarily following any one set plan or prediction.

So while the evolving Web may be guided in its technical development, and perhaps shaped by tradition and practices in its expressive and social dimensions, other challenges will arise that are, as yet, unenvisioned. Therefore, the chapters in this part attempt to complete this book by raising questions and identifying issues related to the future of the Web. While the state of the Web, covered in the previous chapters, reveals a growing, complex communication infrastructure, that description doesn't fully evoke what the future may hold.

Part VI examines issues and raises questions related to specific aspects of the potential and possibilities of the Web. Ranging from the details of information collection and management (Chapter 39, "Challenges for Web Information Providers") to speculations about the Web's ultimate value as a technology (Chapter 42, "The Web: Essential Technology or Trivial Pursuit?"), these chapters delve into topics that will have some impact on the Web's future use and development. Chapter 40, "The Future of Web Commerce," examines issues important to commercial use of the Web, surveying the current state of Web commerce and identifying important future considerations. Chapter 41, "Conferencing on the Web," looks at how Web-based communication can support human communication, critiquing current systems and offering perspectives for the future development of Web-based conferencing. Chapter 43, "Challenges for a Webbed Society," raises some issues our society may face as Web-based communication changes relationships and expectations about information and communication, and its effect on human experience. Finally, Chapter 44, "Who's in Charge? Tomorrow's Toolmakers," surveys how future standards and tools may yet evolve.

While these chapters clearly don't exhaust the issues related to the future, they touch on aspects that will grow in importance as we continue to unleash the promise of the Web.

Challenges for Web Information Providers

39

by John December

Developers are producing information on the Web, and users are accessing it at a break-neck rate. Web traffic on the National Science Foundation (NSFNET) Backbone (just one conduit for exchanging Internet packets) increased from a monthly transfer total of 78 megabytes in December 1992 to 1,056,081 megabytes (over 1 *terabyte*) in July 1994. It would be cliché to call this an "information explosion." However, this rapid growth in Web use begs the question—what is the meaning of all this "information" transmitted so feverishly? What are the considerations for making sense of it and improving information quality? So while there certainly has been an explosion of activity, traffic, servers, and data or "stuff" presented on the Web, an explosion of information leading to knowledge and wisdom—to significance—is still in its nascent stages.

Without tools and methodologies for gathering, evaluating, managing, and presenting information, the Web's potential as a universe of knowledge could be lost. In an increasingly thin soup of redundant, poor quality, or incorrect information, even the smartest Web spiders won't be very effective. A flood of information unfiltered by the critical and noise-reducing influences of collaboration and peer review can overwhelm users and obscure the value of the Web itself. The Web certainly needs solutions in information discovery and retrieval—indeed, developing intelligent spiders, worms, robots, and ants is crucial to making sense of the Web. The Web will also need new protocols, tools, browsers, hypermedia interfaces, and software. But along with these tools for information discovery and delivery, we must develop information-shaping capabilities—skills to select and present information on the Web. These information-shaping abilities cannot be based on machine intelligence alone. Human wisdom, judgment, and aesthetics must play a part in improving the quality of Web information.

In this chapter, I first explore the growth in Web activity in terms of increased Web servers, traffic, and information. I then survey some indicators of a growing diversity and expanding extent of Web communication. These growth indicators dramatize the need to increase information quality. Next, I describe lessons learned through my experiences in gathering, managing, and presenting Internet information. Finally, I discuss information quality in terms of issues Web information providers face.

Web Growth

An extensive user community has developed on the Web since its public introduction in 1991. In the early 1990s, the developers at CERN spread word of the Web's capabilities to scientific audiences worldwide. By September 1993, the share of Web traffic traversing the NSFNET (National Science Foundation Network) Internet backbone reached 1 percent. On December 8, 1993, John Markoff reported on Mosaic on the front page of the business section of *The New York Times*. At the same time, Mecklermedia's Internet World '93 conference and exposition in New York City featured colorful views of the Web through

NCSA's Mosaic, released (Version 1.0) just a few months before. By January 1994, the Web comprised 2.6 percent of NSFNET backbone traffic. Web growth, however, includes not just traffic increases. Web growth can also be seen in terms of the number of servers, amount of traffic, and increasingly various kinds of information offered.

Growth in the Number of Web Servers

Matthew Gray, writing in his web page "Growth of the World Wide Web" (URL `http:/ /www.mit.edu:8001/afs/sipb/user/mkgray/ht/web-growth.html`), reports a dramatic increase in the number of servers. Using his "World Wide Web Wanderer" (W4) program, Gray found the results shown in Table 39.1.

Table 39.1. Increase in Web servers.

Date	Number of identified Web servers
Jun 1993	130
Sept 1993	204
Oct 1993	228
Nov 1993	272
Dec 1993	623
Mar 1994	1,265
Jun 1994	3,184

Gray notes that this W4 survey does have limitations, and these figures should be looked on as representative of what W4 could find. However, these figures give a good snapshot of the rapid growth in the number of Web servers—one part of the "information explosion" on the Web. Each server represents the work of one or more administrators (webmasters) as well as people who provide information in large or small local webs on each server. Each of these servers, then, is potentially a large source of even more information, analogous to television stations ready to broadcast to the masses—and the June 1994 figure is like a world with more than 3,000 channels. Moreover, by August 1994, SG-Scout (`http:// www-swiss.ai.mit.edu/~ptbb/SG-Scout.html`) robot had located over 7,000 Web servers.

Growth in Web Traffic

Along with an increasing number of Web servers, there have been dramatic increases in Web traffic. According to NSFNET backbone statistics (URL `ftp://nic.merit.edu/ nsfnet/statistics`), during the first several months of 1994, the Web's share of NSFNET backbone traffic increased from 2.6 percent in January to 6.1 percent in June, surpassing

Gopher in terms of bytes transferred in March. Note, however, that this is a limited measurement of traffic only over the NSFNET backbone. (Other estimates place the Web still behind Gopher in terms of traffic; see http://www.cc.gatech.edu/gvu/stats/NSF/merit.html.) This is significant because Gopher, just a year before, was ahead of the Web—in January 1993, Gopher's share of the backbone was 0.8 percent (the Web's was 0.002 percent), and by June 1993, Gopher was at 1.61 percent (Web 0.515 percent). The Web thus has overtaken Gopher—an information system that had reached wide popularity and had a large base of deployed information in place previous to the Web's widespread use. This "byte ratings" race on the NSFNET backbone, shown in Table 39.2, dramatizes the pull the Web has for information and traffic.

Table 39.2. WWW traffic over NSFNET backbone—in megabytes/month.

Month/Year	WWW Traffic	Gopher Traffic
Dec 92	78	34,247
Jan 93	122	43,238
Feb 93	512	60,897
Mar 93	3,613	79,024
Apr 93	8,116	89,074
May 93	17,298	103,870
Jun 93	35,701	111,881
Jul 93	48,728	139,006
Aug 93	50,779	148,795
Sep 93	75,401	198,096
Oct 93	122,174	250,785
Nov 93	172,340	291,133
Dec 93	225,443	309,691
Jan 94	269,129	374,681
Feb 94	347,503	396,066
Mar 94	518,084	480,690
Apr 94	671,950	517,625
May 94	799,163	555,708
Jun 94	946,539	567,479
Jul 94	1,056,081	555,089

The preceding statistics show a dramatic increase in Web traffic. The *daily average* number of Web bytes exchanged in July 1994 (34,067 megabytes) exceeds the *monthly* total for May 1993. Also, notice that there was a slight *decrease* in the number of gopher bytes transferred from June to July 1994.

Growth in Web Information Variety

While there's no quantifiable way to characterize the variety and extent of Web information available, it is possible to gain a qualitative sense by examining the "What's New With NCSA Mosaic and the WWW" page at URL http://www.ncsa.uiuc.edu/SDG/Software/Mosaic/Docs/whats-new.html.

The NCSA "What's New" page is a good indicator of the growth of the variety, quantity, and extent of information provided through the Web, particularly resulting from the popularity of the Web as a result of Mosaic development and use. The "What's New" page's archives go back to June 1993. The June 1993 page had 26 entries (11,426 bytes). A typical entry from that month is

```
June 25, 1993

    A Web server has been installed at the Centre Universitaire
    d'Informatique of the University of Geneva. Information
    about various research groups at the CUI is available, as
    well as a number of other experimental services.
```

Six months later, the December 1993 page had 124 entries (40,750 bytes), including not only institutional offerings such as:

```
December 10, 1993

    A new Web server is online at the Nippon Telegraph and
    Telephone Corporation, in Tokyo, Japan, serving
    Japanese information. This server contains documents in
    Japanese, as well as notes on Japanese encoding
    methods and WWW browsers that can display Japanese.
```

but also more informal information:

```
December 10, 1993

    The first ice hockey team on the Web!


December 26, 1993

    A J.R.R. Tolkien information page is now online at
    University of Waterloo.
```

By June 1994, the "What's New" page included 297 entries (146,684 bytes), and included more specialized webs such as:

```
June 29, 1994

   The protein H-Bond analysis software, HBPLUS, now has a WWW page.

June 27, 1994

   For lovers of plastic arts a page on stone sculpture from
   Zimbabwe has been placed on the Web. See these pages on
   Shona Sculpture! There also is a list of exhibitions on the
   subject. These pages are regularly expanded as new
   information becomes available.
```

These entries illustrate the trend during the spring and summer of 1994 for increasingly specialized webs to appear. These webs, in many cases, exist on institutional and organizational web servers, which had been previously announced or just developed.

Also, during the early part of 1994, subject trees continued to flourish. Established subject-oriented webs such as CERN's Virtual Library (URL http://info.cern.ch/hypertext/DataSources/bySubject/Overview.html) continued to grow, while newcomers like Yahoo (URL http://akebono.stanford.edu/yahoo/) grew at an astounding rate. According to Yahoo developer Jerry Chih-Yuan Yang, Yahoo started late March 1994 with about 100 links. It then grew as shown in Table 39.3.

Table 39.3. Yahoo database growth.

1994 date	Number of URL Links
Mar	100
May 9	1666
Jun 1	2823
Jun 15	3607
Jul 11	5479
Jul 23	6121
Aug 5	7337
Aug 11	8265
Aug 17	8566

Therefore, along with an explosion in the number of Web servers and traffic, there has been an expansion in content—both in terms of amount and diversity—with many institutional "official" webs as well as informal, entertainment, and individual webs growing in the numbers of the links they contain. Older subject trees such as CERN's Virtual Library operate according to a more conservative model involving distributed moderators (people who oversee development of an individual topic page within the virtual library) and have grown steadily during this same period. However, some informal, single-site trees (exemplified by Yahoo) have grown very rapidly.

Challenges from Growth for Information Providers

With all this growth—in Web servers, traffic, and information—what issues face the providers of Web information? Because an information provider's first concern should be the information user's needs, information discovery and retrieval tops the list of concerns. Web spiders (Chapter 19, "Spiders and Indexes: Keyword-Oriented Searching"), particularly newer spiders such as Lycos (URL `http://lycos.cs.cmu.edu`) and systems such as Harvest Brokers (URL `http://www.town.hall.org/brokers/www-home-pages/query.html`) help solve parts of the information discovery and retrieval problem. Subject-oriented webs (Chapter 18, "Trees: Subject-Oriented Searching") also assist users who want to browse information according to subject.

But another aspect of the user's needs happens *after* the user discovers and retrieves information—issues of content and presentation become very important. With rapid Web growth, the user can no longer easily browse alternate or multiple sources for the same or related information—the Web information space becomes "saturated"—that is, there is so much information that a human being can't adequately compare the value of available information sources on a particular subject or topic. Along with saturation, growth in the Web's information space leads to "pollution"—redundant, erroneous, or poorly maintained information that can obscure other information.

This is not to say that Web growth has created no valuable information nor that there can be a universal standard for information quality. Parts III and IV of this book highlight many valuable webs. Information saturation and pollution are an offshoot of diverse, distributed, creative, and chaotic development—much like the "noise" in Usenet. The goal of information providers is not to eliminate this "noise" on a global scope or crush creative expression—this would lead to unacceptable levels of control, censorship, loss of diversity, and undue dominance of one taste for information over another. Information space saturation often leads to competition among information sources, and this competition can drive web weavers to implement information quality increases in order to garner attention and use.

So while saturation and pollution are issues that information providers should consider, the goal is not to seek out or eliminate offending webs or excoriate web weavers. Diversity of web information and views is *not* pollution or saturation. Rather, pollution and saturation occur when individual information providers don't meet their user's needs or interests. The challenge is for information providers to best define—according to the needs of their users—the content and presentation methods that define quality information. This may include eliminating web structures and information that other webs already offer (reducing redundancy) or correcting erroneous or poorly presented information. In Part V, "Weaving a Web," I propose a methodology web weavers might use to achieve this process of meeting user needs and continuously improving a web.

While information spaces such as traditional media (TV, radio, newspapers) exhibit both saturation and pollution, these aspects are not as salient because of editorial and institutional control. For example, there's a great deal of news during a single day, and I don't have time to sort it all out and decide what is important (saturation) or correct (pollution). Therefore, I choose various media—such as a network evening news broadcast or a weekly news magazine—to select and filter that information for me. So while I won't attend to wire reports or C-SPAN during the day, I can depend on Dan Rather or Bernard Shaw to provide a daily selection of what happened that is important. I choose information sources based on my previously developed trust of their work.

On the Web, however, there's no Dan Rather. Web information providers must become aware of the nature of their medium:

- **Surface cues are gone on the Web**. All Web information is presented equivalently through a browser. Cues that might indicate quality or value (production values in a television broadcast, paper and print quality in a magazine) are gone. Individual Web browsers transform HTML files using a specified mechanism—so the surface cues about quality don't come from the interface. Instead, as covered in Part V and as discussed later in this chapter, the design of webs and arrangement of information in the HTML file are the main contributors to perceptions of quality differences. It is as if everyone had the same television production team, but they could only change the content and arrangement of the information to differentiate their show from others.

- **Web information providers don't face scarcities in presentation media**. While scarcities of resources and time in print and broadcast media lead to traditions of editorial selection and control, Web publishers don't often face similar time or resource constraints for dissemination (unless, of course, due to disk size or other constraints). The 22 minutes Dan Rather fills each night forces a selectivity (and a corresponding simplification) of content. On the Web, without constraints, information providers are not necessarily compelled to be selective about providing information. Like cheap, suburban land, Webspace can thus fill with banalities.

- **Web information encounters different patterns of peer review.** Voices of experience are not always heard on the Web. Unlike the peer review processes formal scholarly work often undergoes, the traditions for Web information review are not mature. Often, Web information can encounter a maelstrom of comment and critique similar to what a Usenet FAQ list faces. In other cases, collaborators or experts in a field or topic assist in reviewing and correcting Web information. In still other cases, "peer review" has little meaning: personal information (home pages), artistic expressions, and other information on informal webs (opinion, descriptions, product information, etc.) doesn't necessarily require close critique aside from accuracy checks to be valuable. Moreover, measures of value and "correctness" gained from traditional media can't be applied to a medium that is highly dynamic and, by its nature, is *always* incomplete.

The challenge for information providers is to be aware of these issues arising from Web growth and the dynamic nature of Web information. Providers can consider how their information can

1. Meet user needs.
2. Cue the user about the level of quality and completeness.
3. Face some noise-reducing filtering or selectivity, as the result of review or critique where appropriate.

I see a tendency for an institutional imprimatur to be increasingly useful as a rule of thumb for ensuring some of these aspects of quality (borrowing the "trusted information source" described earlier for encountering news). For example, I might seek out the Web page of a university or government research center for information related to a particular topic. This information is valuable, ultimately, because specialists and experts maintain it.

Still other challenges for information providers go beyond these considerations for information space saturation and pollution resulting from Web growth. These challenges involve the details of implementing specific information structures and developing *processes* for gathering, selecting, and presenting online information. To illustrate these issues, in the next section I discuss some lessons I've learned from my experience in providing information.

A Case Study: Tracking Internet Information Sources

Through my work providing information about the Internet and Computer-Mediated Communication (CMC), I've gained insights into issues facing information providers. My experience includes developing a list of information about information. In this list

(URL `http://www.rpi.edu/Internet/Guides/decemj/icmc/top.html`), I attempt to organize and present information sources describing the Internet and computer-mediated communication technologies, applications, culture, discussion forums, and bibliographies. In this section, I describe my experience and discuss lessons I've learned.

Background

In May 1992, I began an independent study project (as part of doctoral work at Rensselaer Polytechnic Institute) investigating the Internet and how it can be used for communication. As part of this project, I located information sources about the Internet. I listed these resources and posted the result to `alt.bbs.internet` (the only Usenet newsgroup at that time with the word "internet" in it). I received some comments and feedback, and I added items to the list as a result of suggestions and further searches of the network. I tried to organize the list so that it would be easy to read, listing Internet descriptions, information services, electronic publications, societies and organizations, newsgroups, and a bibliography. After further revision, I placed the list on my university's FTP site, and posted an announcement of its availability and updates to `alt.internet.services` (a newsgroup formed after `alt.bbs.internet` people grew tired of having non-Internet BBS-related items posted to their group). Over the next year, I continued to gather information, drawing on items to include from mailing lists and my own use of Archie, FTP, Gopher/Veronica, WAIS, and the Web.

The reason for my approach in developing a list of information about information was that I found many useful documents describing the Net that were available over the Net. Rather than duplicating these efforts, my goal was to develop a list summarizing where I could obtain further information sources. I could then use my list to obtain information to help people become familiar with the Internet, or as a tool to define areas to examine in the field of CMC. The process I used to develop this information has evolved over the years, and has contributed to my skills and ideas about information discovery and selection, presentation formats, usability and design issues, information value and quality, and the context in which I should present my list to others. My development process has included gathering information, presenting it in a variety of formats, improving usability and content, and presenting it in a context where it would elicit more reactions and involvement with others specialized in my field of study.

Gathering Information: Discovery and Selection

I've noticed a similar pattern for information space development throughout my work with Internet information. File transfer protocol, telnet, Gopher, and the Web all created new information spaces, and the ways these spaces became populated with information were similar:

1. Developers introduced an information presentation protocol or system.
2. Users contributed information to the resulting information space, leading to
   a. Information space saturation—a plethora of information servers and an abundance of content. This abundance grows to such a degree that the space can't be encountered without information layering or filtering through handcrafted indexes or other guides to the spaces.
   b. Information space pollution—redundant, erroneous, or poorly maintained information becomes replicated throughout the space, obscuring other information.
3. Developers created tools to automatically traverse the space and glean information about resources. The result of this automated gleaning is a database which can be queried through a keyword or other indexing scheme.
4. With greater visibility of the available resources, redundancy decreased and specialization increased. Specialized information servers, often under the guidance of experts in the subject area of the information, created new levels and standards for quality. Often, lists or indexes of information servers also contribute greatly to this process. (For example, the well-known Gopher Jewels showcases specialized gophers, discouraging duplication and encouraging specialization.)

The preceding pattern occurred with FTP (Archie as the automated indexer), Gopher (Veronica), and the Web (Spiders).

By observing and making use of this information space life cycle, I have tried to locate the updated and authoritative source for all the information I present. For example, during the summer and fall of 1992, I made use of Archie to locate directories describing the Internet. So while, in release 1.0 of my list (23 May 92), I had three entries for descriptions of the Internet:

```
o INTERNET DESCRIPTIONS ANONYMOUS FTP HOST   FILE OR DIRECTORY/
---------------------- --------------------  --------------------------
Zen & Art of Internet   ftp.cs.widener.edu   pub/zen/
NWNet Internet Guide    ftphost.nwnet.net    nic/nwnet/user-guide/
Hitchhikers Guide       ftp.nisc.sri.com     rfc/rfc1118.txt
```

I later was able to add more (from release 1.50, 01 Aug 92):

```
o INTERNET DESCRIPTIONS ANONYMOUS FTP HOST   FILE OR DIRECTORY/
---------------------- --------------------  --------------------------
New User's Questions    ftp.nisc.sri.com     fyi/fyi4.txt
Hitchhikers Guide       ftp.nisc.sri.com     rfc/rfc1118.txt
Gold in Networks!       ftp.nisc.sri.com     rfc/rfc1290.txt
Zen & Art of Internet   ftp.cs.widener.edu   pub/zen/
Zen ASCII version       csn.org             pub/net/zen/
```

```
Guide Internet/Bitnet    hydra.uwo.ca        libsoft/guide1.txt
NSF Resource Guide       nnsc.nsf.net        resource-guide/
NWNet Internet Guide     ftphost.nwnet.net   nic/nwnet/user-guide/
SURANet Internet Guide   ftp.sura.net        pub/nic/infoguide.*.txt
NYSERNet Internet Guide  nysernet.org        pub/guides/Guide.*.text
CERFNet Guide            nic.cerf.net        cerfnet/cerfnet_guide/
DDN New User Guide       nic.ddn.mil         netinfo/nug.doc
AARNet Guide             aarnet.edu.au       pub/resource-guide/
```

Using Archie, coupled with a growing awareness of the duplication of resources in FTP space, I searched for the "definitive" editions and versions of each document. I eventually identified major FTP repositories for Internet information which offered well-maintained collections. As these sites changed and evolved, I added additional pointers to my list. Gradually, I began to see more redundancy at FTP sites—many administrators would copy an entire set of documents to their site. As these documents evolved into later additions, many outdated copies would remain online. By monitoring newsgroups, I gained information about new information as well as updates to existing documents. Where possible, I focused on collecting links to well-maintained FTP sites, such as those maintained by people with an interest in having a good collection, such as at Network Information Centers (NICs).

After discovering a resource, I evaluated it for possible inclusion in my list. Before the development of information space-searching tools like Veronica and Web Spiders, I had to rely on newsgroups and mailing lists to discover information sources. After the development of space-searching tools, I could be more selective about which sources to include because I knew the space searching tool itself was available for users to find sources in the space. I used Veronica to glean gopherspace, and spiders to search the Web. (The World Wide Web Worm, the first widely used spider, was available in March 1994.)

After searching tools were introduced for each space, I knew a user should be able to locate sources based on any given keyword. This fact led me to redefine the purpose of my list. For example, one section in my list included electronic journals, services and publications:

```
o JOURNAL/SERVICE   Subscribe with email to       Body of letter
~~~~~~~~~~~~~~~~~~   ~~~~~~~~~~~~~~~~~~~~~~~~~~~~~   ~~~~~~~~~~~~~~~~~~~~~~
Comserve            comserve@vm.ecs.rpi.edu        Send Comserve Helpfile
EJC/REC             comserve@vm.ecs.rpi.edu        Directory EJCREC
EJournal            listserv@albnyvm1.bitnet       subscribe ejrnl YourName
Netweaver           comserve@vm.ecs.rpi.edu        Send Netweave Winter91
RFCs                rfc-info@isi.edu               help: ways_to_get_rfcs
```

A user could create such a list by keyword searches of a database of mailing lists—but how would the user know which keywords to use? Moreover, the process itself of locating these addresses and resources, if repeated, would be laborious. Thus, I began to realize that another aspect of my list's value was collecting semantically related specialist information that could not be easily generated by using an information space-searching tool.

The information space life cycle also caused me to reevaluate the value of my list in other ways. Early in an information space's life cycle, when just a few servers exist, a handcrafted index into the information in the space isn't necessary, as users could, in a relatively short period of time, become familiar with resources. Later, as the space fills with information, a list becomes more valuable—as a reminder of where the major or definitive information sources are. When the information space fills to the point where space-searching tools are developed and used widely, indexing instances of resources and documents in that space becomes less necessary.

However, as the information space matures, space saturation and pollution start to set in. The space tool searches turn up many duplicate or out-of-date entries, so that a handcrafted index that carefully lists the most authoritative collections or updated editions becomes more important. Finding these accurate collections became my goal as each information space matured.

Table 39.4 shows the changing contents of my list at representative release dates. (There were incremental releases between the ones shown here.)

Table 39.4. Number of entries in Information Sources List.

	FTP	*EMAIL*	*USENET*	*TELNET*	*GOPHER*	*HTTP*	*PAPER*
Release 1.00, 23 May 92	20	5	7	0	0	0	
Release 1.50, 01 Aug 92	75	12	17	0	0	0	14
Release 2.00, 19 Jan 93	120	21	27	0	0	0	21
Release 2.50, 10 May 93	188	41	31	0	0	0	25
Release 3.00, 03 Nov 93	303	85	36	20	41	13	44
Release 3.14, 01 Dec 93	317	107	36	23	47	40	48
Release 3.20, 22 Jan 94	340	148	37	38	60	101	49
Release 3.25, 11 Feb 94	319	156	37	32	180	649	64
Release 3.62, 21 Aug 94	363	209	37	42	191	764	67

Release 3.00 was the first in HTML (and other) formats, and the release in which I first listed resources in Gopher, telnet, and HTTP. Release 3.62 marked the start of a major shift in my efforts toward consolidating references in my list. Note the slowed expansion of FTP, e-mail, and Gopher entries in the later releases.

I see a strong trend now toward specialized, Web-based collections of information that are collaboratively maintained by experts in the field. The Web offers more expressive possibilities than Gopher, a more uniform interface than telnet sessions, and the capability to integrate information from a variety of protocols (Gopher, telnet, FTP, and so on). Most importantly, the Web, because it is based on hypertext, encourages linking to specialized information rather than reinventing or duplicating it. Thus, my goal now is to locate higher-level, well-maintained collections in my area of interest. At the same time, I try to keep aware that many of the users of my list don't use the Web for information retrieval and try to list non-Web sources of information as well. However, I see the best resources gradually moving to the Web, and the best collections which integrate many resources in multiple protocols on the Web. Therefore, I see an inevitable shift toward a greater proportion of Web-based information sources in my list.

Presenting Information: Formats, Usability, and Design

With the growth of my list, I've made changes in its format and design. My early list included a short name for the resource, then its location at an FTP site or e-mail address. I distributed my list as an ASCII file, using a scheme for formatting the information into three columns, with dividers to help the user distinguish between sections, subsections, and divisions of the information:

```
 _ _ _ _ _ _ _ _ _ _ _ _ _ _ _ _ _ _ _ _ _ _ _ _ _ _ _ _ _
 Section -1- THE INTERNET AND SERVICES
 ===================================================================
 This section lists information about the Internet, services available
 on it, and topics related to computer networking.

 o INTERNET DESCRIPTIONS ANONYMOUS FTP HOST FILE OR DIRECTORY/
 ~~~~~~~~~~~~~~~~~~~~~~~  ~~~~~~~~~~~~~~~~~~  ~~~~~~~~~~~~~~~~~~~~~~~~~~~
 New User's Questions    ftp.nisc.sri.com    fyi/fyi4.txt
 Hitchhikers Guide       ftp.nisc.sri.com    rfc/rfc1118.txt
 Gold in Networks!       ftp.nisc.sri.com    rfc/rfc1290.txt
```

In the fall of 1993, several people asked if I had an HTML version of my list. Kevin Hughes (at that time at Honolulu Community College) created a version of my list in HTML that he had generated using a C program. Although I had not planned for it, my list's fairly consistent format made it possible for him to write software to scan and translate my list into HTML. However, I realized that my list could be improved by making my format more consistent to accomplish this (and other) translations.

Based on the idea that I wanted to create a *database* for my list's information from which I could then generate a variety of formats, I devised a simple markup system for the "raw" data. Using this system, I marked the entries in my list by semantics. For example:

```
#SECTION INTERNET

#SUB-SECTION Introduction

#SUB-SUB-SECTION Motivation

#FTP "Gold in Networks!:a description of gold nuggets in the network, by J.
Martin"
    %HOST nic.merit.edu  %FILE documents/fyi/fyi_10.txt %CHECKED 02-Oct-93

#HTTP "Internet: a column about the Internet from the Magazine of Fantasy and
    Science Fiction, Feb 1993, by Bruce Sterling" %HOST www.lysator.liu.se
    %PORT 7500 %FILE etexts/the_internet.html  %CHECKED 25-Mar-94

#SUB-SUB-SECTION Overviews

#FTP "Hitchikers Guide: describes the Internet (circa September 1989), by Ed Krol"
    %HOST nic.merit.edu  %FILE documents/rfc/rfc1118.txt %CHECKED 11-Oct-93

#FTP "Surfing the Internet: a narrative of what the Internet has to offer, by
    Jean Armour Polly" %HOST nysernet.org
    %FILE pub/resources/guides/surfing.2.0.3.txt %CHECKED 11-Oct-93

#FTP "What is the Internet?: by Krol and Hoffman" %HOST nic.merit.edu
    %FILE documents/fyi/fyi_20.txt %CHECKED 11-Oct-93
```

I wrote a Pascal program to use this marked-up version of my list as data and then generated HTML, LaTeX (typesetting language), and text versions of my list. Figure 39.1 illustrates this multiformat generation process.

FIGURE 39.1.

Information Sources List generation.

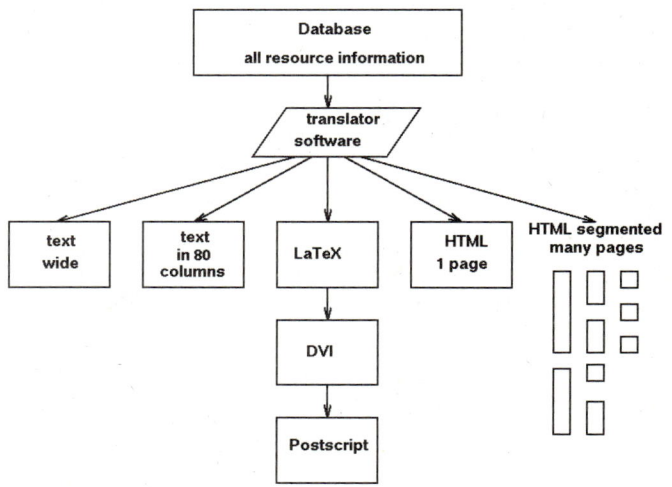

Using my translation program, I could easily generate an ASCII list in a format similar to what I had previously been offering my users:

```
|_____
* Section -2- INTERNET
|===================================================================
o Introduction
- Motivation
Gold in Networks!:      ftp  nic.merit.edu      documents/fyi/fyi_10.txt
Internet:               http www.lysator.liu.se :7500/etexts/the_internet.html
- Overviews
Hitchikers Guide:       ftp  nic.merit.edu      documents/rfc/rfc1118.txt
Surfing the Internet:   ftp  nysernet.org       pub/resources/guides/
                                                surfing.2.0.3.txt
What is the Internet?:  ftp  nic.merit.edu      documents/fyi/fyi_20.txt
```

The HTML version of the list proved to be very useful, as it not only listed the resources, but gave the user the links to retrieve the resources through hotspots in the document.

As my list grew, however, a serious usability problem arose. The size of the list, particularly in its HTML form (one very large page) caused problems with some Web browsers (crashing them). Therefore, during the summer of 1994, I modified my translation program to also create a "segmented" hypertext version (Figure 39.2).

FIGURE 39.2.

Segmented Hypertext version.

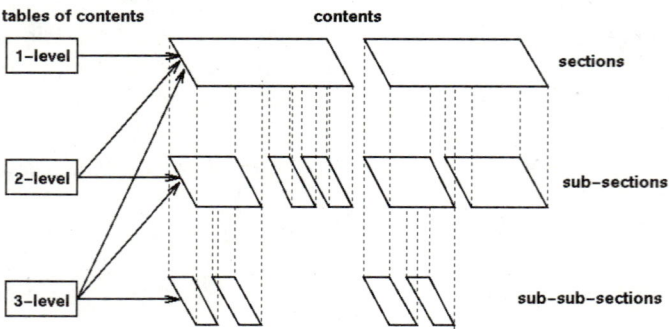

This segmented version divides the file into various-sized "chunks": sections, subsections, and sub-subsections (which had already been marked in the database file). Using automatically generated tables of contents at one, two, or three levels, users can retrieve just the part of the document they need. This dramatically reduces the amount of download time for a user. Moreover, the separation of the list into files of varying sizes allows the user to select the amount of information they want to encounter. This change was essential for the continued usability of the document itself. The list's size before segmentation was over 150K, requiring large amounts of time to download as well as frustrating the user with information overload.

Improving Content

In the course of improving my processes for information retrieval, selection, and presentation, I've also developed processes for improving various aspects of my list's content. The content aspects include:

Accuracy of sources. In the early days of widespread use of the Net, any information about how to use it or understand it was welcome. Today, the variety of information sources requires me to seek out only those sources that are most accurate and usable for my list. The dynamic nature of the Net and the plethora of alternate operating systems, tool versions, and user customization make it impossible to check each source for accuracy. However, I've kept informal track of which sources have proven, in the opinion of others and through my own checking, to be reliable. In some cases, particularly with very new and emerging tools and resources, there may be only a single source of information in existence. Later, as other information is developed, I try to point to resources that are accurate, high-level, and appeal to a variety of audiences (beginners, advanced users, administrators).

Link freshness. Since Net resources constantly change, keeping links updated in my list is a constant task. Ultimately, I would like to have tools or methods to automatically verify the existence/location of a resource at a given URL. Through an interface to such a tool, I could verify or correct links in my database automatically. Without such a tool, I rely on user reports as well as periodic sweeps by hand through my list to verify links. I've also developed a sense of which links will be more stable than others. (Older institutional and organizational links are often more stable as opposed to those developed by individuals or those that are relatively new.)

Reducing redundancy. I seek to link to highest-level, stable, comprehensive information sources for the topics I cover. A positive trend in this direction is the development of topic-specific collections of information. For example, I now don't have to offer a wide selection of links to information about developing HTML files. Instead, I can link to a few good collections, including WWW & HTML Developer's JumpStation (URL `http://oneworld.wa.com/htmldev/devpage/dev-page.html`), maintained by Barry Raveendran Greene of the Johns Hopkins University Applied Physics Lab, and WebWeavers, (URL `http://www.nas.nasa.gov/RNR/Education/weavers.html`), a collection of links to assist web weavers, maintained by Chris Beaumont. Some redundancy in my list helps users see alternate views of the same information. However, once an information source appears to have surpassed other similar sources for accuracy, completeness, and usability, I'll tend to list just that resource, particularly when it collects and organizes links to other instances of information that I can eliminate from my list.

Improving annotations. My database format allows for a short name for a resource and an optional longer description. This longer description gives me the chance to add value to the information by providing a good description of the resource. Oscar Nierstrasz (when he was at the Centre Universitaire d'Informatique (CUI), l'Université de Geneve) included my list as a source in the CUI Web Catalog (URL `http://cui_www.unige.ch/w3catalog`), so I am aware of how these descriptions play a role in making this catalog more valuable.

Providing alternate views. I've created other hypertext guides to provide higher-level and alternate views into my list. By developing the Internet Web Text (URL `http://www.rpi.edu/Internet/Guides/decemj/text.html`), I've tried to layer the abundance of information so that newer users can encounter it in a variety of ways and in smaller "chunks." By providing narrative, list-oriented and graphical views, I hope to provide users with a variety of ways to learn about the Internet.

Expanding the Context and Activity

I've recognized that my list of information sources is just one part of developing my understanding in my area of study. Therefore, I've started another stage that I've seen can be important in developing online information—gathering a community of people interested in the information itself. The tradition of Usenet FAQs is very rich because participants share and build elaborate information artifacts in the context of a group identity (for example, there often seems to be a strong sense of community and group ownership of a FAQ). On the Web, subject-specific information doesn't necessarily rise directly out of such group forums.

With this need to gather a group of peers, I've created a Web-based forum for sharing information and connecting with other people interested in computer-mediated communication (URL `http://www.rpi.edu/~decemj/cmc/center.html`). The Computer-Mediated Communication Studies Center (Figure 39.3) includes a resource collection, a directory of people interested in CMC, a list of activities, and a publication, *Computer-Mediated Communication Magazine.*

By expanding the context in which I develop my list, and by gathering domain experts interested in the same field, I'm starting to make the important transition from information to knowledge.

Lessons Learned

In developing my CMC Information Sources list, I've learned lessons which may be useful to information providers:

1. It is possible to develop and maintain a handcrafted index to Internet resources where:

a. The list adds value over what could otherwise be easily obtained (either through another list or index or through space-searching tools).

b. The list is continuously updated and improved in terms of selectivity, usability, design, and content.

c. The list is offered in a variety of formats.

FIGURE 39.3.

The Computer-Mediated Communication Studies Center.

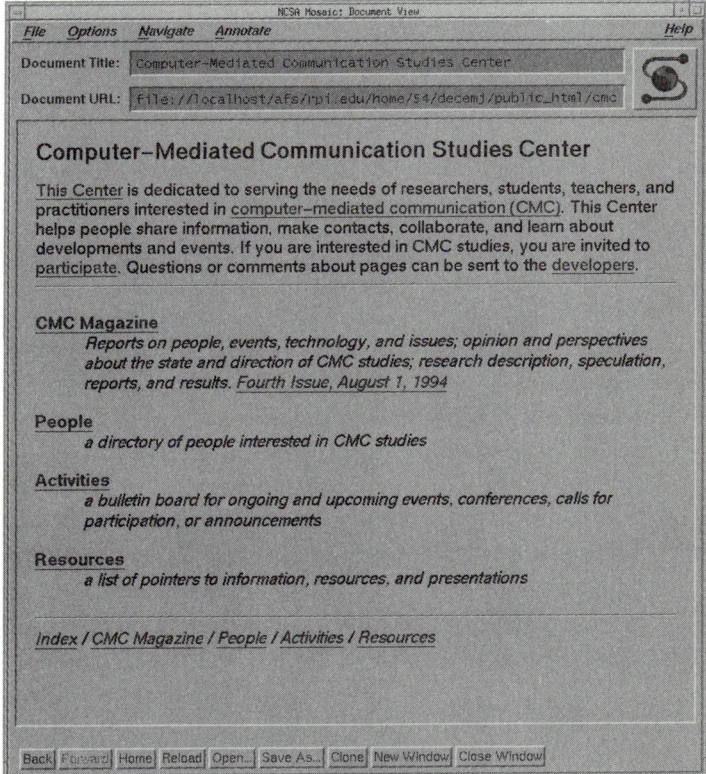

2. A single database combined with a translator program is essential to providing multiple formats of a list. It would be far too difficult for me to create and maintain the individual files required for the segmented hypertext version. I would not even attempt to make a single LaTeX version of the file by hand.

3. In order to develop a successful list, the list maintainer should

a. Keep aware of current developments in Internet resources.

b. Become knowledgeable in the domain area represented by the field of study of the list. The maintainer should also rely on domain experts to help advise on the significance and value of information sources.

    c. Be available and accessible for comments from users and domain experts and timely maintenance of the list based on these comments.

    d. Provide leadership/vision toward making the list serve the interests of the users by seeking out opinions and testing the information frequently.

    e. Ask for and acknowledge the assistance and collaboration of others in shaping the information in the list.

    f. Actively seek and install new resources, links, or information presentation methods in the list.

    g. Provide periodic publicity and announcements about the list to appropriate online discussion forums and indexes.

    h. Seek a replacement when no longer able to develop the information in the list or when absent for an extended period.

4. A resource list exists within a larger context in which its value as information can be used to create or develop knowledge (and hopefully, eventually wisdom). In order to accomplish this, a resource list should be presented and used within a community of people interested in the information, in order to provide the critical review as well as suggestions to improve it.

5. A resource list's ultimate value lies in the judgment and care of the list maintainer. Annotation becomes very important; and, as the information spaces which the list points into become saturated and polluted, the judgment about what to leave out becomes even more important. Eventually, the list maintainer relies on others who create more focused and specialized collections of information to provide excellent destinations as links.

6. It is important to recognize the limitations of Web-based information. In most academic disciplines, important journals, books, and other scholarly materials are still on paper. Net-based information should recognize this, and point the user to appropriate paper-based resources.

Toward Web Information Quality

Based on the preceding discussions, this section presents an approach toward defining Web information quality.

Toward a Notion of Web Information Quality

Quality is a difficult term to define for a particular domain or product. Total Quality Management, derived from W. Edwards Deming's principles, includes ideas such as continuous improvement and multidisciplinary responsibility for improving a product.

Information quality has much in common with product quality. Like a physical product, information should meet users' needs (satisfy the customer). Implementing this principle in specific information development practices and web design features, however, is not so straightforward, as the needs a user has vary greatly from application to application. However, this is a preliminary statement for web information quality:

> Quality as a goal for Web information involves a continuous process of planning, analysis, design, implementation, and development to ensure that the information meets user needs in terms of both content and interface.

Thus, quality is more a process of continuous improvement rather than a set of the characteristics of a finished object (a web). Due to the dynamic nature of Web information and the context in which it exists, any outward sign of a web's quality can change over time even if the web itself doesn't change. In Part V of this book, I describe a methodology for weaving a web using a user-centered, continuous process emphasis, with the goal of building up information so that it can lead to knowledge. An information developer can view quality as emerging from processes. However, more specific characteristics for the quality of products resulting from these processes can be stated. Quality Web information is

- **Correct:** Within its stated scope, purpose, and the context of its presentation, Web information should give the user cues as to its purpose, scope, and status. Developers should ensure that the information presented in the web stays consistent with these stated characteristics. For example, OncoLink (see Chapter 26, "Science and Technology") is peer-reviewed, and functions in a specific role within the medical community (not as a substitute for professional medical care). In other words, Web information must not only be factually correct , but also include cues that help the user know the web's particular definition and scope of "correctness" as well as appropriate use.

- **Accessible:** While information presented with a web, when viewed with multimedia equipment, can present a rich experience for the user, web developers must ensure that these "bells and whistles" don't make important information inaccessible to some users. Web developers should know their audience's requirements, but need not abandon the use of graphics or sound to conform to the least capable browser. However, if significant segments of the target audience do not have multimedia capabilities (or want such features), the web should be designed so that important information is not masked behind features the users can't or won't access.

- **Usable:** From the functional perspective, the web should deliver the information users need with a minimum amount of clutter, in a design that captures the information taking full advantage of hypertext. This means that text is not in one monstrous file (as my CMC information sources file was in its state before I "segmented" it). Rather, the pages in the web should aim to capture a single unit of user attention—not with so little information that the user has to "thrash" through multiple links in the web to find meaning, but not with so much information that the user is overwhelmed by a single page.

■ **Understandable:** The web should contain cues and employ composition principles that build and shape meaning. Web developers can use techniques from writing methodologies used in paper and other media—audience analysis, rhetorical devices (for example, parallelism, analogies), and technical communication techniques (for example, chunking information, cueing the reader, ordering information). Hypertext is not constrained to be linear—however, in local doses and at surface layers, hypertext is linear prose. Hypertext can be thought of as text that is not constrained in a single expressive object (such as a web) or to a single perspective for meaning. Web-based hypertext is *unbounded* text that derives meaning from its links that branch into Webspace. Making meaning at a local level within hypertext, however, still involves crafting prose (or using visual or aural elements) to create meaning. To do this, a developer needs to use effective composition principles as opposed to forcing a user to "construct" meaning by decoding unorganized pieces of information.

■ **Meaningful:** Within its stated scope and context of presentation, a quality web should somehow reach for a significance beyond itself, a meaning that can help a user form new relationships among information. From these new relationships, new knowledge or insights may form. For example, Le WebLouvre (URL `http://mistral.enst.fr/~pioch/louvre/louvre.html`) is an online art gallery, containing online exhibits and a tour of Paris. While the "information" presented by art is not as obviously "useful" as scientific information in webs, it nonetheless functions as art does in our culture—evoking a feeling of human identification such as emotion or association. Thus, "meaning" is not purely a transfer of information content, but emerges as a result of encountering that information. A web should not merely present information, but assist users in analyzing and interpreting that information within a larger context. In fact, this contextualizing aspect of meaning is one of the strengths of the Web itself.

What Information Providers Need to Increase Quality

The Web has the potential to help people articulate and arrange information more expressively than any other information delivery system in history. In order to tap into this potential, and to ensure and develop notions of quality such as those outlined earlier in this chapter, the following methodologies and tools for information providers might be developed:

■ Tools to assist in web design and implementation.

- Automated tools for maintaining HTML files or to create and enforce web "look and feel" design decisions.

- Automated tools for web maintenance (to verify link freshness) and assist in other tasks of web development.

- Higher-level languages that articulate web constructs and structures above the HTML level, capturing notions of inheritance (from object-oriented design methodologies), packaging (module concept from procedural programming languages), and information-shaping (from rhetoric, composition, and technical communication techniques).

  These higher-level languages might include a logical level over Uniform Resource Locators (or Identifiers), that captures abstraction in naming. For example, a link to a national Network Information Center (NIC) could be expressed as a generic term within an anchor that is instantiated in a web-generation scheme to an appropriate URL specific to a given parameter (for example, yielding a a specific link for a web for Europe, another link for a web for Australia).

- Automated tools to help a designer evaluate a web's performance—accesses by page, perhaps graphically represented, to alert web designers to how the web's information is actually being used. (See WebViz's approach to this at `http://www.gatech.edu/pitkow/WebViz/WebViz-html/WebViz.html`.)

- Methodologies to support web planning, analysis, design, and development.

- Techniques for web usability testing.

- Methods for web audience analysis.

- Techniques for information presentation that help a diverse audience of users find different "ways into" or views of a body of information.

While some of the preceding tools and methods might involve computer-assistance or automation (for example, link freshness checks), the key element in successful webs is human intelligence and judgment. A management system for information providers should thus include automated procedures along with ways for information providers to contribute judgment and knowledge. For example, in information discovery, hand-crafted indexes are costly in terms of time, but can lead to valuable results for specialized uses. While automated methods (WAIS, Veronica, Archie, WWW Search engines) can scan a large amount of information, the raw search results can bewilder an inexperienced user. Combining human judgment with the strength of automated tools may ultimately lead to more powerful ways to gather and shape information.

Finally, web information providers need an information-literate audience. Information literacy includes the ability to access, evaluate, and use networked information in the pursuit of a goal. Helping a user gain this literacy and progress from using information to gaining knowledge involves presenting the right information at the right time in the right context. Often, web developers can do this by providing a variety of ways to access, view, and understand the continually changing resources on the Internet.

What Information Providers Can Do to Increase Quality

The growth of Web information challenges information providers to increase quality in these areas:

Content

1. Draw on domain experts to judge and critique information, and to suggest content development and improvements.
2. Tirelessly work for authoritative sources and fresh links to them.
3. Recognize the value of and encourage collaboration in developing content.

Presentation

1. Use techniques to cue users about the purpose, offerings, status, and usability of web information.
2. Use HTML design techniques that exploit the power of hypertext. "Chunk" information into manageable pieces. Use links to refer to concepts and information rather than reproducing it.
3. Keep graphics, multimedia and other features serving the best interests of the users. This includes minimizing them when necessary, and including them when appropriate.

Discovery

1. Keep aware of subject-oriented collections as well as indexes on the Web. Publicize the web's information so that it is included in appropriate indices and subject trees.
2. Be aware of schemes for spider indexing. Design document hotspots, titles, and other features to provide the best information for spiders.
3. Provide your web's information within the context and communities of its intended audience so that your users (and potential users) know your web's offerings and new developments.

Innovation

1. Unceasingly work for innovative techniques for your web's presentation and content so that it meets your users' changing needs.
2. Creatively experiment in nontraditional expression to exploit new hypermedia features and techniques that meet your users' needs.
3. Adjust your web development processes to allow for new ideas, approaches, and techniques, so that creativity can flourish.

Summary

If there were only a few Web resources, users could easily find and compare them to identify the most useful ones for their needs. However, with an increasingly large and diverse universe of Web servers, traffic, documents, and audiences, even smart Web spiders can't identify the resources that are correct, complete, or most useful for a given purpose.

The Web itself is a means of *expression*, not just a conduit for delivering information. The challenge for Web information providers is to increase the quality of information they deliver—both in terms of its content and methods of presentation. Therefore, Web information providers must examine the processes by which they gather, present, and improve their web's information.

By refining skills and techniques for gathering and presenting information and tapping into the wisdom of experts for critical review, web information providers can engage in a continuous process of quality improvement. Methods for presenting Web information can draw from fields such as technical communication, rhetoric, and composition to shape information. Web information providers can also draw on concepts and practices from software engineering to inform design and implementation techniques. Automated tools and higher-level hypertext languages can provide more abstract levels above HTML, so that larger units of thought and web structure can be articulated. Ultimately, the challenge for a Web information provider is to acknowledge the dynamic nature of Web information and recognize that information quality is not just a set of outward characteristics or design decisions, but a part of a continuous process in which content and presentation are adjusted to meet user needs. Webs that more completely articulate information so that it can become knowledge may be the key to the Web's continued growth.

The Future of Web Commerce

40

by Andrew Dinsdale

Can any of us predict how the World Wide Web will look and be used in five years time? At current growth rates, the Web will become a popular medium for entertainment, information, education, and business, but how far away are we? Laying the cables to allow millions of users to connect to the Web as well as the research and development needed to make the Web an effective medium will cost millions of dollars, yen, pounds, and deutsche marks. Thus, the future of the Web will depend on commercial involvement and acceptance.

Science fiction authors, such as William Gibson (*The Neuromancer*) and Neal Stephenson (*Snow Crash*), have described a so-called "Cyberspace" or "Virtual World." The Web is the first tangible incarnation of the global communities depicted in these fiction works. We can use e-mail to communicate with friends and colleagues all over the world, partake in synchronous discussions in MUDs (Multi-User Domains, text-based meeting places), and connect to server computers without the need for high-level computer science studies. The possibilities appear endless, and these new virtual worlds will certainly include a virtual marketplace.

The function of the marketplace is to bring together buyer and seller. There must be methods of bringing goods to market and encouraging buyers to attend, a place to meet, and a transaction system. Organizations are complex; not only do they depend upon interactions between departments but with other players in the world. Players include the government, other businesses, workers, consumers, and the media, to name a few. Web technology, the interconnection created by servers, personal computers, modems, and phone lines, merely enables a new system of interaction and the latest marketplace.

Over the last year, more companies started using the Internet to communicate internally and with the public. The electronic press release, e-mail–based customer support, and more recently, "Net-Presence," have become popular. The Web is a new medium for companies to bring information to those who need it; further, it allows for meetings and transactions to be performed. The Web contains consumer fillable forms with the function of the 1-800-ORDER-NOW phone number; ordering takes place within the medium that brought the message. The Web is the promotional tool, the ordering device, the organizational communication method, and the "place." Soon the virtual world will allow computer-mediated education, doctor's visits, entertainment, shopping, and banking; in fact, many events from real-life (RL) will take place in this Virtual Reality (VR).

Or so we are led to believe. Currently, the idea of a "Global Virtual Marketplace" is perhaps vaporware. *Vaporware* is the term applied to not-yet-developed software and hardware. The real marketplace potential of the Web is far from reality. In a few years we will look back at the current attempts at net-marketing and think of them as "alpha tests." Yes, there is a place to meet; those with browsers can be encouraged to attend (if they know the URL); and with a Web form you can order from electronic storefronts. Business associates can collaborate and work via e-mail, and multimedia files can be moved around the network with great ease. There are many potential pitfalls and problems that need to be solved before the Web becomes a true marketplace, however.

This chapter introduces the depth of these problems and demonstrates how they will impact the development of a commercial Web. Some potential solutions are offered, but the aim is to act as a "think-tank" discussion and promote cognizance of the problems.

Mosaic for the Masses?

A hard fact is that Mosaic is not sitting in every personal computer. Those connected to the Internet via subscriptions to the major "Online" companies do not have real access to the Web. Also, the TCP/IP pipes needed are not, as yet, commonplace. The lowest common denominator of Internet access is an e-mail address and, even though Web traffic (measured in "packets") is increasing at an alarming rate, e-mail will remain the de facto standard for a number of years to come. A problem facing those at the forefront of Web commerce is the complexity inherent in accessing the Web. Not only does the potential customer need a PPP or SLIP connection (unless they have a dedicated access at work or school), they also have to understand how to install software without a handy setup disk, know FTP to get a copy of a Web browser, decompress it, and learn the fundamentals of "Packet Drivers" and modems to get on ramp.

The Net is a hard phenomenon to understand, and computerphobes are scared enough of even the simplest applications. Fortunately, most Web browsers appear intuitive once installed; a key issue is getting them that far. Mosaic, the most popular browser, has been licensed to some software companies, so a possible solution will be a package that is easy to install and use. The user's education level is crucial; the generation raised on Nintendo and with computers in the classroom may have a better chance.

Another recent development is TIA—The Internet Adaptor—a software solution that allows those with standard UNIX shell accounts to access the Web via a "pseudo-SLIP" connection. This will allow thousands of users to run graphical interfaces such as Mosaic and Cello without a privileged and expensive TCP/IP account. (For further information write to SoftAware@marketplace.com or see http://marketplace.com.)

Caution: Construction Ahead—Expect Delays

A major consideration is insufficient bandwidth. As Web use increases, the current network "back-bone" or infrastructure will not be sufficient for the likely demand. When NASA offered .GIF files of Jupiter's encounter with the comet Shoemaker-Levy 9, "traffic" on the Internet was brought to a standstill, showing the metaphor of the Info-Highway as too true—but only with respect to traffic jams, not speed. The current Web is not amiable to the movement of even simple files. When the average home user dials in to access the Net, it is at 9,600 or 14,400 bps—a speed too slow for downloading pictures, let alone multimedia presentations. But who is going to build the Internet to a sufficient state to support a true and virtual marketplace, and further, who is going to pay for it?

The momentum to build the infrastructure necessary for a virtual world has been building for a number of years. These moves are akin to the building of the telegraph and railroads of the nineteenth century. The creation of a true I-way will undoubtedly be through the marriage of private companies with public agencies with utilities. The global nature of the Web will make the construction even more complex. In the United States, the Clinton-Gore administration has certainly committed a lot of energy and time to the development of a National Information Infrastructure plan. As planned, the Net will allow for information and entertainment delivery; it will be a medium that allows online shopping, game playing, libraries, news, banking, telecommuting, and education. One sure thing we can predict is that whatever is planned and no matter how many "lanes" are created, eventually the traffic on the I-way, as with RL highways, will be congested.

This will certainly be the case if the I-way backbone and the Web model form the basis of the video-on-demand projects currently under development by IBM, the Baby-Bells, and Silicon Graphics. The speed of lines needed and improvements in data compression techniques necessary to move a movie through the Internet, from the server to the client, lay in the future. The current compression standard that shrinks bite-sized movies and small sound files is not sufficient for proposed uses of the I-way—truly interactive entertainment may be far away.

Control of the Web

Another consideration is who governs such an international network, sets the rules, and discusses policies. Future development and funding of the Web may depend upon answers to this important issue.

The Web is primarily a communication tool; other communication media such as television, telephone, and postal mail have fair use and censorship rules laid down by statute and cultural expectations. In the United States, where freedom of speech and of the press is protected, there are workable limitations imposed on "hate" speech and pornography. Could domestic censorship laws cover the International Web? The Net is already portrayed as having a cultural standard akin to anarchy. Already, X-rated discussion groups exist, and servers could easily be established to promote racist or discriminatory rhetoric and criminal activity. How can this be controlled? Could a governing body rate or even monitor all sites?

The issue of Net control could fill books, and those vocal in the debate consider the Net to be a place worth protecting. Organizations such as the Electronic Frontier Foundation have recognized that the legal provisions of the real world do not transfer well into the digital one. The ongoing Clipper chip debate over an attempt to place a tappable encryption device in all telecommunications is being fought by civil liberty activists as an intrusion on privacy. In a virtual world, all transactions could be monitored remotely, allowing many potential abuses of power.

Without answers to the control issue, questions regarding copyright and protecting published information in the electronic form will be harder to solve. Digitized materials will be "tangible" products on the Web. What will prevent these from being illegally reposted and copied? Even though it might become easy and profitable for content to be transferred, publishers and "application" producers will put off selling digitized products if this threat is too great.

On a micro or company level, "control" of Net usage could become a big factor. With all the potential information flying around, customers and workers are going to learn to deal with information overload. E-mail brings a new level of internal and external communication, combining business and personal uses. Employees subscribing to only a few e-mail lists may receive 100 or more messages per day, meaning an awful lot of unproductive time. Add to this lost business hours due to addicted employees Web-surfing, playing in MUDs, and reading alternative newsgroups, and it's clear companies will need to monitor the Net's effects on employee productivity. There are ways to limit or "filter" mail, but some companies already have to take greater measures and close down internal mail systems so RL work gets done.

Transaction and Network Security

One of the most important issues facing the development of commerce on the Web is the transaction system. Customers and sellers are aware of the risks of RL credit card fraud; carbon copies of transactions, unscrupulous shop assistants, and even someone looking over one's shoulder can lead to your credit card number being used by a criminal. Even giving out credit information when ordering by mail and telephone is a scary thought to many. Transactions on the Web offer their own series of risks, basically because transferring data via e-mail or WWW forms is not, with a few exceptions, thought to be secure.

Placing sensitive and personal information online and transferring it to a server is probably as safe as any method of credit transaction—but the perception is otherwise. Electronic information is readily movable and relatively easy to access; movies such as *War Games* have shown the havoc a wily "cracker" can create. Data cracking and telecommunication technology go hand-in-hand, and many understand that if anyone could commit credit card fraud, it is a determined hacker.

Cryptography (or crypto) means little to the majority of the population; such mathematical methods of encoding and decoding messages are the realm of spies and the secret services. Crypto, however, and a brand of this known as "Public Key Encryption," seems to offer a solution. A problem in itself is educating consumers about how public key encryption works. The scope of this chapter only allows a brief outline, and the next few sentences further emphasize the complexity.

In the 1970s Whitfield Diffie, a computer scientist, developed a crypto system for which a secure channel was not a necessity. In the Diffie system everyone has two keys: a "public" key that can be widely disseminated and stored, and a private, "secret" key. The sender uses the recipient's public key to produce an encrypted text; the recipient turns this text back into plain text using the private secret key. The sender's "digital signature" can also be checked. This would have been encrypted using the sender's secret key, and the recipient would use the sender's public key to decrypt the signature. Three researchers used this system to construct the Rivest-Shamir-Adleman (RSA) system that allowed for the safe passage of keys and messages in a method more robust than any previous method.

A current example of secure transactions using crypto can be seen in the CommerceNet pages. CommerceNet is demonstrating a system developed by RSA, NCSA, and Enterprise Integration Technologies. New WWW forms will allow the contents to be encrypted using various methods, including public key, providing a secure communication mechanism between client and server. (At the time of writing this demo was available at http:/ /www.commerce.net/information/examples/demo/cl.secure/cl.info.html.) The CommerceNet home page is shown in Figure 40.1.

The deployment and acceptance of such encryption in the United States is currently subject to a federal embargo. The export of U.S.-made crypto is restricted due to a "munitions" classification. This restriction is certainly detrimental to the creation of electronic commerce in the United States and suggests that answers to the "secure channel" problem will come from elsewhere; the United States will be left behind. Governments should be working with the financial institutions to develop regulations and "printing" net-cash certificates, not formulating policies to paralyze the virtual marketplace. This embargo, and the apparent complexity of crypto, may hinder its acceptance so that other short-term solutions will be necessary.

Downtown Anywhere (http://www.awa.com), a virtual city and Net developer known for its novel approaches for providing companies with Net presence (charging either a rent for server space or a commission on what is sold online), has an easy answer to the security problem. Their solution has been to create a "virtual" economy based on software, common sense, and understanding that the problem is more about perception of risk than actual risk. The customer can give Downtown Anywhere a credit card number via a toll-free phone number or by mail (modes of communication protected by existing laws). In return the customer receives a personal payment password that can be used when ordering with Web forms. When a transaction is completed, the "owner" of the password is sent an e-mail receipt and his or her credit card is charged. Another payment option allows the customer to build credit in a virtual bank—Downtown Anywhere debits the customer's credit card account by however much is transferred into the virtual bank and the customer is free to spend her virtual money with less risk by using a personal password. In their system, all credit information is stored and transactions are handled offline. (See Figure 40.2.)

FIGURE 40.1.

The CommerceNet home page.

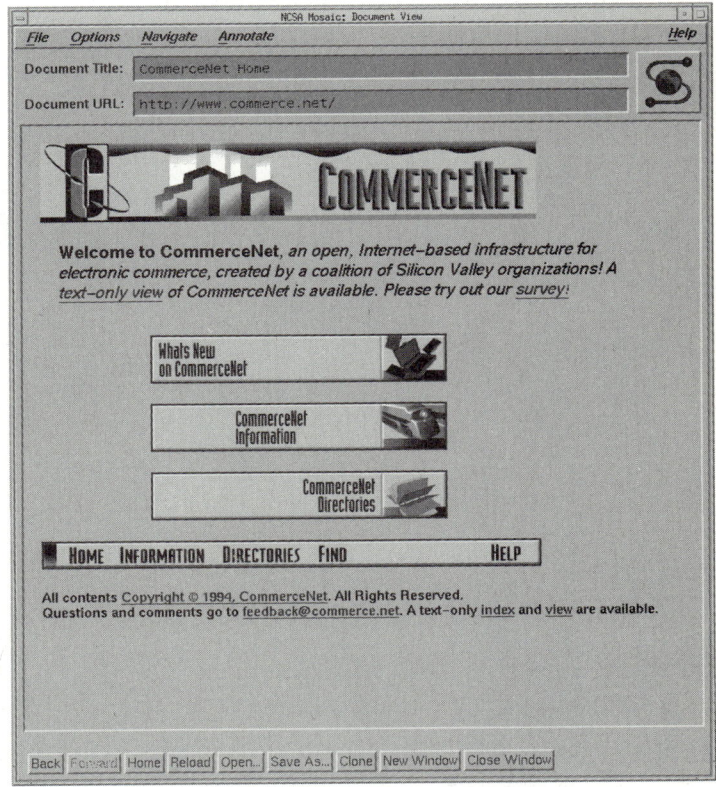

Just considering crypto and various net/digi cash initiatives as the solution to this problem is not enough. Educating—or should that be *convincing*—Web customers that tools such as "Secure Mosaic" really are secure will be a public relations job. Developing robust crypto is important, but most of our trust in such systems will come from the reputation of the companies concerned. The Bank of America and major credit card companies are working on such systems, and in the next few years an accepted method should be in place. The answer could be as simple as recognizing the perceived problem and, like Downtown Anywhere, finding a solution.

FIGURE 40.2.

*Downtown Anywhere's
Front Street.*

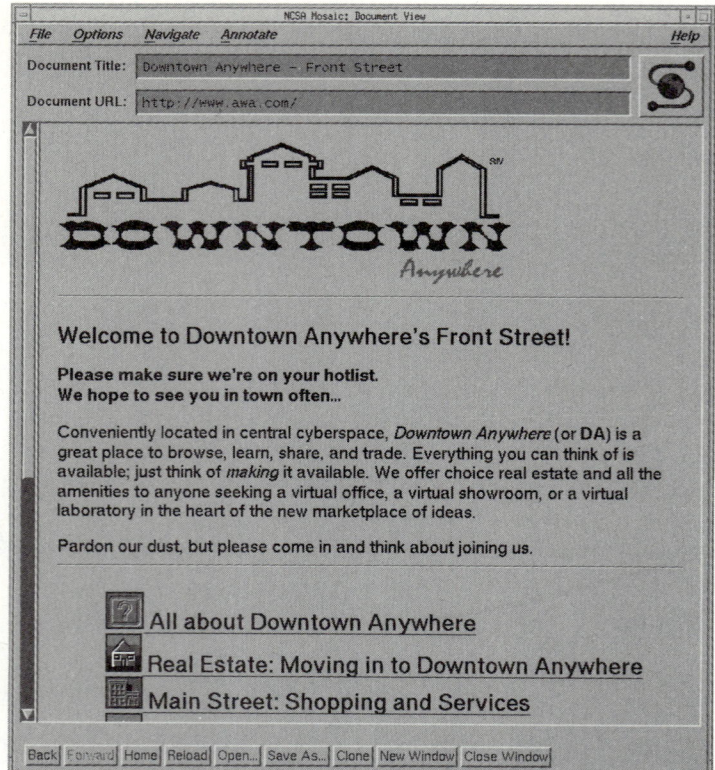

Discussion of this issue is hot in a number of online forums, and many people have concluded that the Web offers an opportunity for a new form of transaction based on strong and unbreakable encryption—in a particular transaction the communication could be three-way and instantaneous between the buyer, seller, and credit company/cyberbank. A related issue, concerning confidentiality and secrecy, is that with information in the electronic form it will become easier to move vast databases of sensitive information around—making industrial espionage, intrusions of privacy by clever hackers, and risks of employees selling secrets even greater. If the future of Web commerce is to be a serious proposition, unbreakable and easy-to-use crypto is a necessity.

Commercial Interests in Communication Technology

A question in many boardrooms and on all of our lips is quite simply, "Who is going to pay for all this?" One method often mentioned is Pay-Per-View/Use (PPV)—stressing further the need for a safe transaction system. The multimedia ability of the Web allows, in theory, text, graphics, sound, and motion to be downloaded. The Web will one day allow the movement of "virtual products," so you will read your daily newspaper on-line, buy and transfer digitized music to disk, get copies of computer games and programs, and transfer other information to your client for personal use. Customers might simply pay for what they get or subscribe to the on-line *New York Times*, the online Columbia Digitized Music Club, or the Nintendo Games Server.

Taking a simple look at changes in communication technology highlights a strange consistency in the interaction between what may be termed "commercial interests" and the actual medium developed. The invention of the printing press allowed development of newspapers; soon advertising space was being sold that helped build revenue for the publishers, helped improve coverage and print processes, and helped reduce the cover price. These improvements combined to boost readership. The circle continued—greater circulations led to increased revenues, better newspapers, and more advertising revenue. The story of radio is similar, and the early advertisers, in fact, enabled the creation of programming that became part of the American culture. Even before radio show sponsorship, the manufacturers of crystal sets had applied for, and been granted, licenses to broadcast. Selling the "hardware," even then, depended on the presence of "software." The story of television is even more vivid in our memories, and the union between commercialization and media content clearer still.

To sell the medium, manufacturers needed killer applications: shows, special effects, sports, and events such as Superbowls, World Cup finals, and NASA moon landings. These applications are intertwined with commercial interests—ads, messages, and sponsorship—but the "virtual marketplace" of the traditional broadcast media is one-way. Even the home shopping channels with their telephone ordering systems are part of the traditional broadcast model. The consumers have no say in what products they can learn about, and can only learn as much as is broadcast to them. The potential of the World Wide Web is to make a marketplace where communication is two-way and users have total free choice on where they web to and how deep they learn.

The broadcast model is not congenial to corporate communications. The cost and lack of editorial control are prohibitive in the use of the traditional media to carry public relation style messages. The broadcast model does not allow organizations to stay fully in contact with their "publics": the government, share holders, the media, suppliers, customers (past, present, and potential), and the same groups in other countries. To accomplish such contact, companies use the telephone, mass mailings, and personal visits—but to produce feedback or communication back from these "publics" requires even more effort and expense: information-gathering such as customer surveys with low response rates, following up on suppliers, and paying for toll-free customer lines. The potential of the Web is to cure some of these communication problems.

Commercial interests, then, should be driving the Web and building the infrastructure, tools, and policies to aid in its development. The Web, if built to its true potential, will become a place where power is not tied to the presence and ownership of raw materials or geographic location, but to ideas and knowledge. It is in the best interests of companies to get involved, not simply because it is trendy or out of fear of missing the boat, but because the Web offers some real solutions and possibilities. Those companies that take advantage of the Web will reap the benefits, especially as more of the so-called publics are using the Web themselves.

Becoming part of the Virtual Marketplace is relatively easy—many organizations already have a computing guru somewhere in their ranks, so setting up a dedicated server may be a possibility. An alternative route is to set up a presence in one of the Virtual Mall, Web city or Net-Presence services. (Any organization with an eye on the Web should peruse the Interesting Business Sites on the Web page located at URL `http://www.rpi.edu/~okeefe/business.html.`)

All other media developments were funded and created with advertising dollars and commercial interests in mind. The mass media is a creation of the advertising industry. The Net, so far, is the exception and has developed very well without commercialization. In fact, the Internet culture is aghast at obvious sales pitches, including the notorious attempts of certain Green Card lawyers to sell their services by mailing to thousands of Net users.

As the Web model stands today, there is no real room for mass advertising. Only the so-called "Net presence" is accepted, and that will not sell 400 million cans of cola. So far, the American advertising industry has not become involved seriously with the development of the National Information Infrastructure or in collaborations with the computer, telephone, and cable companies involved in hard-wiring the Web and developing the applications. The advertising and promotions industry could offer input at this early stage, input that might influence a commercial direction on the I-way. Certainly commercial involvement could reduce the cost to the consumer and subsidize a PPV system; further, advertising billings could pay for development of the backbone. In fact, it is in the best interests of the advertising, public relations, and communication industries to get involved—their futures might depend on it.

Companies need to consider the Web as a viable part of a promotional strategy. A marketing lead is needed—it is not surprising to learn that many Net presences have been established by computing departments with no input from marketers. The Web proves to be part public relations, part selling tool, and part advertisement. Documentation present in Web pages needs to be consistent with the content, messages, and images portrayed in other promotions. The Web should become part of, and converge with, the rest of the promotional mix. It will soon be the norm to include e-mail addresses and even URLs in press advertisements, literature, and on business cards. If only the advertising industry would take a more aggressive stance, the future of an exciting and profitable new medium of business might be secured.

Encouraging Participation

The future of Web commerce lies in educating decision makers about inherent advantages of the system. PC sales are set to remain high, placing computers in many homes, and over the next few years almost all computer owners will be accessing the Net. In 1993 the media hyped up the promise of 500 channel interactive television. The popular press was abounding with stories of mergers between cable, computer, and telephone companies. Although some experiments have taken place, and set box/server technology will one day put such entertainment in our homes, the topic has fallen into disfavor with the media, and the hype has turned into a backlash.

Media coverage of the Internet, especially relating to business on the Net, has again promised the world and raised expectations, in the short term a little too high. It now appears that companies are waiting for the Internet to deliver. The role of the media is often to help the diffusion of new ideas and new technologies, but in the case of the Net it appears that the blind are leading the blind as few reporters really know what's going on, and those who do are writing for special interest publications. Within the popular media, we see little or no mention of how to get connected or how to use the Net. (See URL http://pass.wayne.edu/business.html for a thorough introduction to getting started in Net-based business.)

Media portrayals suggest that doing business on the Net will allow companies to reach 20 million literate, wealthy, educated professionals via an e-mail message. Unfortunately, for the marketers at least, that is far from the truth. Expectations on the future of the Net have been running too high, and a media backlash might result if it fails to live up to anticipations. One thing that might be missed in the backlash is that the Net, unlike interactive TV, is already a tried and tested medium of communication. Eventually, with current growth rates, a virtual marketplace on the Web will have a healthy customer base.

Toward Virtual Reality

The convergence of telecommunications and microprocessing has brought us the World Wide Web. Two different technological revolutions started by Charles Babbage (the analytical engine, the precursor to the computer) and Guglielomo Marconi (the father of radio) have merged to create a new industry—and new complex possibilities with even more complex problems. Computer-mediated business is now functionally possible, and a virtual world is within our grasp. In fact, Gibson's cyberspace is perhaps closer than we realize as virtual meeting places become accepted in business and social life.

The current view given by Web GUI's and MUDs is 2-D and text reliant, but software such as Meeting Place will soon give a graphical front-end to these worlds. Further, Virtual Reality (VR) researchers are working on a VR Markup Language (VRML is based on the principles of SGML, HTML and VR) that will produce a 3-D view of the Web. The same technology used by the Web will be transformed into a 3-D networked cyberspace that VRML-browsers can attach to. According to Chris Hand, VR researcher at De Montfort University, England, "There can be no doubt that in five years time, a proportion of international business transactions will take place in 3-D virtual worlds on the Net. When that happens, [Neal Stephenson's] *Snow Crash* will follow in the footsteps of Musashi's *Book of Five Rings* as the latest Wall Street strategy guide." (For more about graphical meeting places see URL `http://www.cms.dmu.ac.uk/~cph/Publications/MS/article.html`.)

Before this potential can be realized, and virtual worlds of the Web become a reality, many obstacles need to be overcome. There needs to be a solid, high bandwidth infrastructure, secure transmission and online storage of information, and an acceptance and understanding of this new media by consumers and the business community. Solutions to some of the problems will come from the computer engineering field and perhaps from dedicated management consultants. Many answers will be found by experimental organizations learning from their bruises. It is possible that companies are holding back because they do not understand the terminology and the technology or because they are watching the brave souls "out there" and learning from others' mistakes.

Testing this new medium appears risky, but when decision makers are educated enough, high-profile companies will go online. The "chicken and the egg" theory is perhaps making many companies unwilling to commit venture dollars to the relatively unconstructed and uninhabited virtual world. Pioneers such as Sears managed to reach new markets far from stores via the new media of mail order more than 100 years ago. When something as accepted as the Sears catalog used to be goes online, it will set a new benchmark for the Web and prove the existence and future of a Virtual Marketplace. This author is excited to be around and involved in what is the most important marketing revolution of all time. Remember though, the Web is not a thing, resource, or marketing tool, but a creation of whomever gets caught up in it. Future technology will enable its creation; however, its future depends on participation, understanding, and foresight.

Conferencing on the Web

41

by David R. Woolley

Bianca's Smut Shack is definitely one of the most happening spots on the Web. Alongside music reviews and tips about fun things to do in Chicago is a "room" where you can converse with the surly troll that lives atop Bianca's dresser. The troll likes to ask prying personal questions and responds mostly with insults. You can also sign the guest book, leaving your name, e-mail address, and favorite recipe. Or if you're feeling more scatological, you can step into Bianca's bathroom and read the graffiti left by other visitors. If you wish to add your own anonymous pearls of wisdom, just choose a wall and let loose. Since HTML is available, you can spice up your message with large type or italics, or even include active links to other Web pages.

Although graffiti boards like Bianca's are fun, they're not of much practical use. But they do offer a key feature that lies at the heart of all online conferencing systems: the ability to post a message in a public place for others to read. Conferencing has been available on the Internet for years in the form of Usenet newsgroups. When support for forms input was added to HTML, it opened the door to conferencing on the Web.

What do I mean by "conferencing?" It's an overworked term, but it will have to do until something better becomes generally accepted. For my purposes, conferencing is a form of group discussion that uses text messages stored on a computer as a medium for communication. Usenet newsgroups, CompuServe forums, message boards on America Online, and Lotus Notes discussion databases are all examples. I'm *not* referring to real-time video or audio conferencing, nor to facilities like CompuServe's CB Simulator or America Online's chat rooms, which instantly relay typed messages between participants who are online at the same time.

Graffiti boards offer little structure for the posted messages. Each new message is simply tacked on to the top (or bottom) of the page. In this sense, these Web pages resemble the early electronic bulletin board systems that began to pop up in the late seventies and early eighties. It is possible to write a message responding to an earlier posting, but since it is just tossed into a big pot along with unrelated messages, with no connection between the original message and the reply, it's difficult to carry on an extended conversation.

For true conferencing, some structure is essential. In particular, the system must support "threading," the ability to sequentially read the messages that make up one discussion. You need to be able to read all the way through the conversation about where to get the best sushi in Boise without having celebrity gossip and announcements about used stereo equipment for sale mixed in. A few conferencing systems now evolving on the Web offer such threading. But how much structure do you need?

WIT: The Perils of Too Much Structure

W3 Interactive Talk makes for a nice acronym, but it's something of a misnomer. It sounds like a chat system akin to CompuServe's CB Simulator. In reality, WIT is a highly structured conferencing system designed for group decision making.

WIT was a quick hack by Ari Luotonen of CERN, who put it together in a few days immediately following the WWW '94 Conference. Participants of the conference desired a way to carry on prolonged group discussions about technical issues related to Web development.

The weaknesses of Usenet and mailing lists for such a purpose are well known. Mailing list discussions have no inherent structure at all, making it difficult to maintain more than one or two threads of conversation. In a Usenet newsgroup, a message can be posted specifically as a response to another message, but the overall structure tends to be rather chaotic. Also, Usenet messages typically disappear within a week or two, leaving no permanent record of what points have been raised and what issues have been settled.

By contrast, a WIT discussion takes the form of a permanent, continuously expanding hierarchical tree. The tree can branch out indefinitely, but the top three levels of the hierarchy have specific purposes and are labeled accordingly:

- **Topic**—an issue to be resolved
- **Proposal**—a statement up for discussion, related to a topic
- **Argument**—an argument for or against a proposal

Arguments are also called "articles"; the two terms are used interchangeably. There can be arguments to arguments, and arguments to arguments to arguments, and so on. Any participant can start topics and write proposals or arguments.

When you enter WIT, you see a welcoming message describing the purpose of the discussion area, followed by a list of topics. Selecting a topic takes you to the page for that topic. Topic, proposal, and argument pages all have a few things in common: a title, date, author's name, and text. They differ in what appears below the text, though. A topic page lists only the proposals associated with the topic. But a proposal page shows the entire tree of arguments branching off of the proposal. An icon next to each argument indicates its type: a white checkmark for an agreement, a red X for a disagreement. (See Figure 41.1.) An argument page is similar to a proposal page, except that only the portion of the tree branching off of that particular argument is displayed.

FIGURE 41.1.
A WIT proposal.

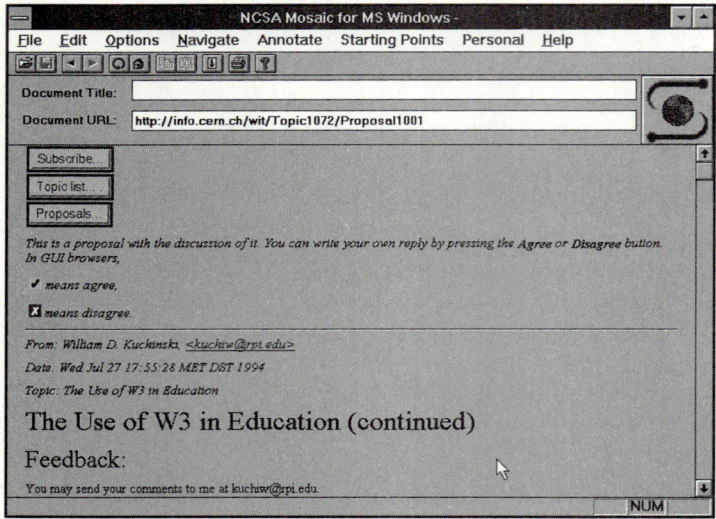

The list of checkmarks and Xs can give you a quick sense of how a proposal is being received without requiring you to read all of the arguments. Looks can be deceiving, though: an agreement to a disagreement (are you still with me?) shows up as a white checkmark, although it argues *against* the proposal!

Of course, as soon as WIT was released, the structure of WIT itself became the most popular subject of discussion. One problem noted by many participants is that each article is forced to either "agree" or "disagree." What if you want to add a pertinent comment that does neither? What if you agree with some points of a proposal and not with others? Some people suggested adding a third button next to Agree and Disagree, labeled "other" or "idea."

Another problem is that every branch off of a topic is labeled a "proposal." But some topics need to branch into subtopics rather than proposals. One participant suggested that, in addition to proposals and arguments, there might be questions, answers, merits, demerits, summaries, categories, qualifies, and reframes. Another suggested that proposals be broken down into subproposals called "points." Yet another asked for a way to rank arguments on various scales, such as serious to humorous, or friendly to flaming.

The limitations imposed by WIT's structure become immediately apparent when you start to use it for a discussion. Most of the suggestions for improving it center on extending the structure to accommodate a wider variety of comments. Yet the more classifications that are added, the more confusing and hard to use the system becomes. Deciding exactly where to place a response and how to categorize it becomes a major chore. And inevitably, arguments develop over such choices ("That's not a summary, that's a new proposal!") Eventually, either the system will collapse under its own weight, or the participants will begin to ignore the structure and use it however they please.

Since WIT was implemented so quickly, a lot of obviously needed features were left out. For example, navigation between messages is rudimentary, and there is no good way to find messages written since your last visit. But even with improvements in these areas, WIT's structure will make it awkward for general-purpose conferencing.

HyperNews: The Next Usenet?

HyperNews is probably the closest thing to a general-purpose conferencing system on the Web so far. Like WIT, HyperNews uses a hierarchical tree structure, but it's a simpler structure with only two types of messages: base articles and responses.

The creator of HyperNews, Daniel LaLiberte, hopes that it will evolve into a next-generation replacement for Usenet. One of Usenet's biggest problems is its redundancy: Each widely distributed newsgroup is replicated on countless news servers around the world, consuming huge amounts of disk space. Consequently, messages must be thrown away quickly to make room for new ones. This, in turn, leads to another kind of redundancy, as people repeatedly ask the same questions and hash out the same issues. Rather than building a repository of knowledge, Usenet is forever locked into a cycle of destroying and re-creating the same knowledge time and time again.

Figure 41.2 shows a Hypernews discussion (`http://union.ncsa.uiuc.edu/hypernews/2.shtml`).

FIGURE 41.2.

A HyperNews discussion.

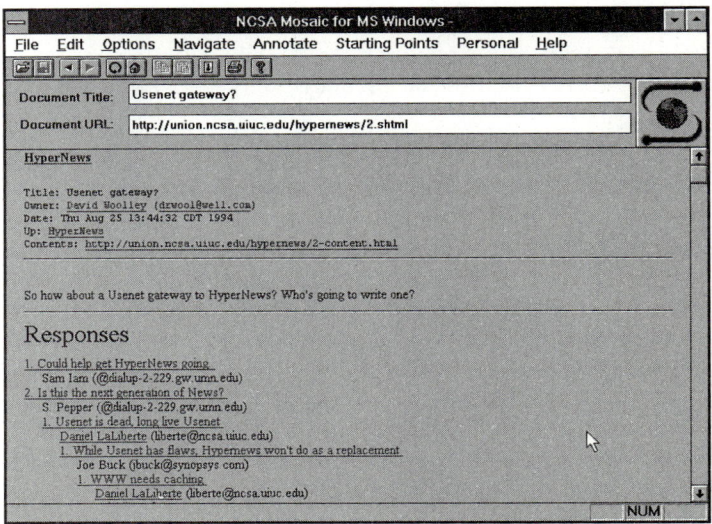

A HyperNews discussion does not rely on such massive replication. It can exist on a single server, yet still be available worldwide through the Web. Since each HyperNews server only needs to host a few discussions, it should be possible to keep messages for a much longer time, perhaps forever.

LaLiberte's vision extends beyond conferencing. HyperNews, or something like it, could be used as a structure for organizing vast amounts of information. For the purposes of finding a particular piece of information, HyperNews would appear as a hierarchical tree with general subject areas near the top and finer divisions of knowledge further down. But since lateral connections between documents are also possible, the true structure would be a constantly evolving web. Some areas of the web would be mostly discussion, while others would be mostly static information, but responses would be possible anywhere. LaLiberte has some innovative, yet-to-be-implemented ideas regarding discussions, such as allowing a message to be linked as a response to multiple articles, and the ability to snip off a subtree of responses and attach it somewhere else in the web.

This is an ambitious concept, to say the least, and LaLiberte does not claim to have solved the myriad thorny issues it raises. I am less convinced than he of the value of keeping everything forever. Do we really need to save every byte posted to `alt.mcdonalds.ketchup` for the benefit of our children's' children?

In any case, while HyperNews holds interesting possibilities, the current implementation is a bare-bones system at about the same early stage of development as WIT; that is, not ready for prime time.

LaLiberte has recently joined NCSA, where he is applying many of his ideas to an annotation system that will let readers leave comments for the owners of Web documents. Flexible access controls will allow an owner to accept annotations either from the general public or from a specified group of people only, and determine whether annotations are visible to others. If visitors are able to read and respond to annotations by other people, annotation begins to blur into conferencing.

What Makes a Good Conferencing System?

Ask 100 experienced conferencers what makes a good conferencing system, and you'll get 100 different answers. As with any kind of software, people tend to like whatever they are used to. For instance, some swear by GUIs, others swear at them. But almost anyone who conferences regularly will readily point out flaws in their own favorite system.

There is no one perfect solution for all people and all purposes. But having used a variety of systems over the past 20 years, I think I can make a few generalizations about what seems to work well.

Separate conferences for broad subject areas. This is a nearly universal feature. Whether the discussion areas are called conferences, forums, newsgroups, or notesfiles, they provide a basic level of organization. Besides focusing on different subjects, different conferences often have very different atmospheres and social conventions. People become "regulars" only in the conferences that most interest them.

Threaded discussions within conferences. This sometimes takes the form of a tree structure, in which each topic is the starting point for a branching tree of responses. But while a hierarchical tree is a good way to organize static information, it does not work as well for conversation. It is easy to get lost in the tree, and often hard to figure out where to attach a response. Discussions tend to fragment and dissipate. I prefer a star structure, in which each topic has a simple chain of consecutive responses attached to it. This form is easily understood by most people because it closely resembles "real life" conversation.

Informative topic list. A reader should be able to easily see a list of the topics in a conference. At minimum, it should show each topic's title and some indication of the amount of activity in the topic: the number of responses, date of the last response, or both. The topics should be sortable both by topic start dates and by last response dates.

Respect for the integrity of topics. A reader should always be able to go back to the beginning of a topic and follow it all the way through to the most recent responses. Of course, it is necessary to clear out obsolete material to avoid clutter (and because nobody has infinite disk capacity) but pruning should be done by deleting entire topics after they have fallen into disuse. Some systems (notably Usenet and CompuServe) throw away older messages even if they are part of an active discussion.

Support for both frequent readers and casual browsers. A browser wants to choose a conference manually and scroll through the list of topics, dipping in here and there, moving backward or forward sequentially through topics, returning repeatedly to the topic list. A frequent reader wants to cycle automatically through a customized list of conferences, skipping topic lists entirely and getting immediately to the new unread messages. Most conferencing systems are biased toward one type of reader or the other; few support both well.

Search and filter tools for readers. A reader should be able to search messages by date, author, or keyword. Word searches on both topic titles and message texts should be possible. Frequent readers should also have tools for controlling what they see; for example, a way to "forget" topics so that any subsequent responses are skipped automatically.

Access control. Both public and private conferences are useful in different situations. A conference host or moderator should have flexible control over who can access the conference and what level of access each participant has. For example, it should be possible to give some participants read and write permission, others read only, and others no access. This, of course, runs counter to a widespread anarchist sentiment on the Net. Anarchy is marvelous—the Web might never have evolved without it—but being unable to have private discussions among chosen friends or colleagues is just a different form of tyranny.

Host tools. The host of a conference should have good tools for managing topics; for example, weeding out obsolete topics, archiving those that are worth saving but no longer active, and moving a divergent thread of a topic to a new topic of its own.

Speed. Frequently used functions like advancing to the next message should require only one key press or pointer click and should happen instantly when selected. If the system is slow or cumbersome, people simply won't use it much.

What I have laid out here is an ideal. No conferencing software that I know of excels at everything. The systems that have been successful are those that do some of these things well enough that they capture a critical mass of enthusiastic users, who then provide the content and culture that attracts others.

Why Conference on the Web?

The capabilities that the Web has to offer are enough to make a veteran conferencer salivate.

For years we have been shackled to plain ASCII text. People have responded creatively to ASCII's limitations, inventing customs like smileys ;-) to express emotions and *stars* for emphasis, and even creating gigabytes of ASCII art (imagine a full-page picture of Snoopy cursing the Red Baron here). Some will bemoan the passing of this era, but the expressive capabilities of HTML text far surpass those of plain ASCII. Many sizes of type! Real italics! Bold text! And so on.

The Web's multimedia capabilities will add another dimension to conferencing. Many of us have long dreamed of including pictures and sound in our messages, and the Web will finally make this possible. Some of the uses will be trivial: ASCII smileys will give way to full-color smiley cartoons. Some uses will be annoying (imagine every instance of "LOL"— net shorthand for "laughing out loud"—being replaced with a recorded laugh track). But there are many situations where a picture really is worth a thousand words.

Hypertext links embedded in messages offer endless possibilities. One obvious application is to make the author line of every message an active link to the author's home page. This would eliminate the need for the long signatures often attached to Usenet articles, which add clutter and disrupt the flow of conversation. Links can reduce the need for quoting earlier messages, as well. Instead of copying the text of the message, just include a link to it.

Links could also be used to post a message in two or more conferences in which it is relevant. For Usenet readers, this probably brings up hateful images of "spamming"—the posting of identical messages to every newsgroup in the world. But if a message is *linked* to multiple conferences rather than replicated, then you will only see it once. If it appears again in another conference, the software will recognize that you have already seen it and skip over it.

There are practical reasons to use the Web for conferencing, also. There is an expanding plethora of Web client and server software to choose from, supporting a wide variety of hardware. Much of it is free. No proprietary system is likely to match the Web in terms of universality of service.

One of the Web's great strengths is that it provides a common user interface for Internet utilities like FTP, Gopher, and WAIS. It is natural to extend this to conferencing, as well. People should be able to reach everything the Internet has to offer without leaving the familiar environment of their Web browser.

Finally, a conferencing system on the Web would scale well. Since the data can be distributed across any number of servers, there are no inherent limits to growth.

What About Usenet?

You might be wondering, why not just make Usenet available through Web browsers?

Mosaic does provide a way to read newsgroups, but it is very primitive: There is no threading, it doesn't keep track of what you have read, and worst of all, you can't post messages. There is no reason that it has to remain this way; full-featured newsreaders certainly could be integrated into Web browsers like Mosaic.

Yet it might not be done. Web browsers are already large and complex programs, as are good newsreaders. Combining the two is not a trivial task. Will the benefits justify the costs?

It will not be possible to make the best use of the Web's capabilities through Usenet. For instance, a Usenet message could contain HTML formatting and hypertext links, but it would be readable by other Web users only. To anyone using a standard newsreader, the HTML codes would look like garbage.

Furthermore, Usenet suffers from some fundamental problems, particularly the massive replication of data discussed earlier. Usenet is probably not the right model to carry forward into the future.

Issues and Challenges

There are a number of problems to be solved before any of today's Web-based conferencing systems will be ready for heavy use. Following are a few of the most interesting ones.

What's new? Regular readers of a conference want to see only the new messages added since their last visit, so the system must keep track of what each reader has seen. Either the client or the server could do this, and it's not clear which is the better choice. Web servers are designed to be "stateless"; that is, they simply respond to each request as it arrives and do not keep track of what clients are doing. Requiring the server to remember what messages have been sent to each client violates the spirit of the Web's design. On the other hand, client software is not "aware" of the distinction between a conferencing system and any other Web document.

Dynamic document creation. Conferencing requires that displays be customized for each user in various ways. For example, you might want to see a list of topics that contain the word "kangaroo," or use a "bozo filter" to screen out messages written by certain individuals. Hence, the server cannot simply ship existing HTML documents, but must create customized documents on the fly according to the specifications of each client.

Uploading. Users need to be able to upload existing files into the conferencing system, rather than always having to type messages into a Web form.

Images in messages. While the ability to include images and sound into messages is one of the most exciting features Web-based conferencing has to offer, it might also be one of the most difficult to implement. A message containing an HTML reference to an existing image is no problem, as long as the image is already available on some Web server. But how can a user get a *new* image to the server? Ideally, the user should be able to draw a picture with her favorite "paint" program, drag it into a document editor with the mouse, type a message, and click the Send button. But this will require much more sophisticated HTML document editors than exist today, as well as coordination between the Web server, the Web client, and the document editor.

Speed. This is crucial not just for conferencing, but for any highly interactive application. For users without a high bandwidth connection, the Web can be agonizingly slow when moving from one page to another. Using the Web at 14400 BPS feels about the same as using an ordinary dial-up BBS at 2400 BPS. Some of the sluggishness is built in—the Web was designed for shipping files around the world, not for quick response to keys. But client software could do a lot to alleviate the problem:

- ■ Display each page *as it is being received*, rather than waiting for the entire document.
- ■ Abort the transmission immediately if the user selects any link.

I can't emphasize enough how important this is! Conferencing involves skimming over a lot of stuff to find the most interesting nuggets, so you need to be able to move around quickly.

Where To from Here?

Although Usenet has its problems, there will likely be efforts to integrate it into the Web. The trend has been for the Web to incorporate more and more of the Internet, and Usenet is one of the last pieces of unconquered territory. Newsreading capabilities of Web browsers probably will improve, although they might never match the features of traditional newsreaders.

A more promising approach might be to create a gateway between Usenet and a native Web conferencing system such as HyperNews; that is, a mechanism that automatically copies all messages from a newsgroup into a Web-based system and vice versa. This could give the Web system a running start, but would not tie it permanently to the problematic Usenet architecture.

Meanwhile, work is moving forward on Web systems for voting, annotation, and other types of collaborative projects, which have the potential to evolve toward conferencing. There are also efforts underway to set up Web gateways to existing conferencing software such as Lotus Notes and EIES.

How will it all turn out? It's too early to know. The Web continues to evolve rapidly, chaotically, and unpredictably. But it's safe to say there *will* be conferencing on the Web. The promise it holds is too great to ignore.

Resources of Interest to Readers

Bianca's Smut Shack

`http://bianca.com/btp/`

WIT

`http: //info.cern.ch/hypertext/WWW/Discussion`

HyperNews

`http://union.ncsa.uiuc.edu/hypernews.shtml`

List of collaborative Web projects

`http://union.ncsa.uiuc.edu:80/hypernews/related.shtml`

Computer-Mediated Communication Studies Center (index of people, activities, and resources related to CMC)

`http://www.rpi.edu/~decemj/cmc/center.html`

The Web: Essential Technology or Trivial Pursuit?

by Neil Randall

42

The World Wide Web, like the Internet itself, was conceived and designed as a technology for serious applications. The Net's purpose, as documented in any number of books and articles, was to keep open the communications channels necessary for the defense of a nation. The Web was designed to provide a means by which members of a scientific community could access the findings of their colleagues easily and thoroughly, a function different from the Net's in degree but not in kind. Whether or not either design team foresaw the trivial use to which their projects would eventually be turned is unknown, but it is highly unlikely. When one is thinking of the survival of a nation or the dissemination of scientific knowledge, newsgroups about Barney and Web pages displaying traffic citations rarely come to mind.

In many ways, the Web retains its serious origins. By "serious" I don't mean solemn (although they're obviously not mutually exclusive), I simply mean something closer to "worthwhile." Inevitably the question arises, *Worthwhile to whom?*, but it's one I will leave unanswered. I'll merely take it on faith that we all recognize worth when we see it, and that we know the difference between the serious and the trivial. The point is that an increasing amount of activity on the Web has crossed precisely into the realm of the trivial, and the real question becomes: *How far in this direction can it afford to go?*

North American culture—Western culture, in fact—has a rich and relentless history of turning technologies to trivial purposes. This tendency has been examined in detail by philosophers, sociologists, and social critics alike, most of them taking the stance that this is ultimately a negative process. One of the most vocal recent critics of our love affair with high technology is Neil Postman, whose *Amusing Ourselves to Death* raised a considerable stir in the late eighties, and which remains today a book very much worth reading. (Postman himself has become practically a parody of himself in recent writings and appearances, but that doesn't diminish the thought-provoking arguments of that book.) The fundamental thesis of *Amusing Ourselves to Death* is that we have openly accepted and readily embraced a technological lifestyle that ultimately allows only the trivial and the ephemeral, and that the influence of this lifestyle is so strong that there seems no way of reversing the process.

Much as it's tempting to answer Postman with a smirk and a knowing "Lighten up, Neil," a few minutes of contemplation render his arguments difficult to ignore. The single most ubiquitous multimedia technology in our lives is television, and while it has its moments of brilliance and wonder, such moments are very few and very far between. One July night in 1969, it's true, we all sat glued to the set as a human being stepped onto the surface of a world that was not our own, but on another summer night, this time twenty-five years later, what kept us at the set was a white van being escorted down a freeway by an unbelievably large contingent of police. In between, for every Watergate trial there were a thousand "Full House" and "Saved by the Bell" episodes, for every Berlin Wall destruction there were fifty thousand "Wheels of Fortune." Trivia reigns, and pointlessness is rampant.

Entertainment has come to mean *mindless* entertainment, and the result has been the almost inevitable phenomenon known as channel surfing. If nothing matters, everything is as important as everything else.

In many ways, I disagree with Postman. He allows no place for the significance of global communication that the Internet makes possible, a significance that exists no matter how many unnecessary responses we might receive to a one-liner posted on a mailing list. After the publication of my previous book, *Teach Yourself the Internet: Around the World in 21 Days*, I was contacted by readers in Norway, England, Malaysia, Singapore, Australia, and New Zealand, all within the span of two weeks; and this is significant communication, nontrivial communication, if only because it happened at all. Recently I was deluged with e-mail from various parts of the globe on another Internet matter, and that, too, was significant. And that's just e-mail. If I consider the Web, and the resources now available to me that I could not get in any other way, or at least I *would* not get in any other way, I have no choice but to conclude that this is communication of an extremely important kind. Potentially, at least, the Net—and through it, the Web—is a technology that does not trivialize.

But there are signs that the Web is following the path of television, from once-promising communications and education medium to a medium that encourages and applauds the dissemination of ephemera and inconsequentia. There are signs, in other words, that the Web has lost control of its future, and that it will become, increasingly, little more than a trivial pursuit. It might be less passive than television, and it might be more difficult to master, but those things alone don't make it worthwhile. In the rest of this chapter, I examine this trend and its implications.

Early in its history, accessing the Web was somewhat like accessing a well-stocked research library. What was available were studies, discussion papers, proposals, and screen after screen of information about research institutes, universities, and the Internet itself. Today, a Web session is less like browsing a research library than poring through the shelves of an extremely well-stocked magazine store. In such a store (which are distressingly few), you'll find magazines on every topic imaginable, and the styles will range from the scholarly to the effectively nonliterate, from the profound to the puffy, from the consequential to the trivial. Stores like this are exciting for anyone who craves information, and the Web today offers a similar range of material. The research reports and technical discussion papers are still there, but so are the details about university programs, the galleries of experimental art, the tours of cities and tourist attractions, the articles about social injustice, and the archives of "M*A*S*H" and "Married With Children." And, just like in the bookstore, you can hop from one to the other with impunity and without guilt. That's what it's there for.

The question that faces the Web of the future is: When does it stop being a well-stocked anything? When does it turn its back on its origins in research, and even on the fascinatingly eclectic entity it has become? When does the seriousness—the consequentiality—disappear,

and when will it all be given over to the trivial? When, in other words, will the Web be an entertainment medium only?

Impossible? Hardly. Throughout the twentieth century, almost all major technologies have begun with a focus on significance but have become, in varying degrees, purveyors of entertainment. And not just entertainment, but *mindless* entertainment, primarily. Television in its infancy was seen as a tool for education and other serious information; its early history is punctuated with predictions that it would remain relatively undeveloped, that it had no real chance of capturing radio's audience, that it would find its chief use in the schools but not the homes. These predictions, obviously and dramatically, were wrong. The microcomputer in its infancy was seen as a smaller version of the data processing machines that were changing the face of research and business, but were doing little for the average person, and until the introduction of the Commodore VIC-20 (and later the Atari 400), there was little to change that initial perception. Earlier, radio itself changed from an information source to an entertainment medium, until by the end of the 1950s there was little on the radio but popular music and popular talk.

Whatever these technologies had once been, for any number of reasons they were changed into entertainment technologies. The microcomputer is the least changed of the three because it has also become a leading force in business, industry, and even government, but there's no question that the growth of multimedia has once again raised the possibility of a whole-scale entertainment revolution. And telephony, which has always blended the twin possibilities of consequentia and trivia, has allied itself with the computer in the development not only of online services, but of the thing known today as the information superhighway. The superhighway is touted as being the most important communications development in the past several decades, perhaps in history, but even the early perceptions suggest that it might be little more than a conduit for the ordering of entertainment and other unnecessary products. It will be overtaken, say the pundits, by the inevitability of mass entertainment.

Which brings us back to the World Wide Web. As perhaps the first real indication of what the superhighway might be like, the Web represents an opportunity to get it right. Coexisting right now are research, business, artistic, community, and entertainment interests alike, in much the same way as they coexist in information technologies such as libraries. But libraries are far different from bookstores, another information technology; very few bookstores offer anything approaching a balanced selection, because the emphasis in book popularity is increasingly on entertainment, whether it takes the guise of the mediocre best-seller or the ubiquitous self-improvement genre. Much as we like to encourage people to read, the fact is that there's no real qualitative difference between reading most best-sellers and watching most dramatic or comedic programs on television. They're all part of Theodore Sturgeon's "95 percent of *anything* is junk," and there's nothing intrinsically wrong with them. The problem is that they squeeze out the rest of the stuff because people become unaware that anything else exists. Or, once aware, they have no idea how to approach it.

The year 1994 will go down in Internet history as, among a few other things, the year the Web hit the big time. But the explosion of interest has not necessarily been kind to the Web's actual "product." At this stage, it exists primarily *not* as a medium for depth of knowledge, but rather as a platform for breadth of information. And information, as we well know, has little to do with knowledge itself. We have information from the universities about graduate programs and research activities, but rarely do we have access to anything more than a cursory glance at the substance of the institution's activities in these areas. We have superbly designed pages from government institutions like NASA, but what we're presented with is often the stuff of coffee-table books, excellent for acquiring broad overviews but useless as a research base for anyone even halfway through secondary school. Yes, we have hordes of details about government bills and proceedings, but that's information we could quite easily get anyway (albeit not as conveniently). And, more importantly, we're seeing business using the Net for superficial marketing, and jes' folks using the Net as a personal medium for publicly showing their hobby horses.

The keyword in many of these activities is "superficial." To be sure, there's plenty of room for the superficial, but one of the great dangers of our time is that *everything* is given a superficial treatment. Except for the truly dedicated, nobody bothers with in-depth analysis, because in-depth analysis is never required of us. Human resources people rely on canned psychological tests for their hiring of personnel, rarely bothering to question whether the specialists with a deep understanding of these tests would consider them valid. Science is presented to us in popular formats in an attempt to make it accessible to everyone, when in truth many scientific concepts can be comprehended only with years of specialist training. Newspapers like *USA Today* demonstrate that in-depth reporting is simply pointless, and so on and so on and so on. The problem is not that the superficial is bad—it's not, and it can at least create awareness—but rather that, after a time, the superficial is regarded as the only knowledge needed. The board game *Trivial Pursuit* demonstrated quite clearly that we respect a person's knowledge of inconsequentia much more than a specialist's depth of understanding, and *Trivial Pursuit* was a game precisely for its time.

So am I being Neil Postman here, decrying all this for the sake of a return to the old days? To a degree, sure, except that the old days hold neither appeal nor interest for me. They weren't any better, no matter what Postman and others suggest. People have always sought the trivial; they just didn't have as much of it as we have today. Our explosion of visual media has ensured that trivia proliferates, and we've reached the stage where it is both unavoidable and treasured. It's only natural, of course, that trivia will overtake the World Wide Web as well.

What I want to reiterate, however, is that trivia itself isn't the problem. When recognized for what it is, trivia is harmless or even helpful. It does, I repeat, create awareness. The problem lies, once again, in our tendency to equate trivia with knowledge, and thus to value the overview, the summary—in short, the superficial. Most Web sites today have very little actual substance. A glossy home page offers links to one or two other pages within the site, and these quite typically offer a brief amount of information. The home page also offers links to other sites on the Web, and thus acts as a launching pad for further exploration of the topic, whether or not the remote sites are related to the content of the home page in any meaningful way. A few hours of following these links rarely yields anything that will sustain interest. Imagine a book offering nothing but tables of contents and abstracts, along with some graphics, and you have a pretty good idea of what the Web tends to be like.

But the Web hasn't gone completely over the top yet. Not by a long shot. Through a well-designed Web site you can gain access to FTP archives, where you can often find sustained analyses or studies of the topics in question, usually in the form of a PostScript, TeX, or other word processing or spreadsheet file type. Download it, and you have substance. Some Web sites offer page after detailed page of information, so much that reading everything will build an awareness of the topic (or the company or the program) that takes you far beyond the superficial. Even some entertainment sites offer in-depth looks at the subject matter, and thus become endlessly visitable if that's your area of interest. The good sites are out there, and they're well worth exploring.

But much of what appears on the NCSA What's New Page is of interest only to the person who mounted the site in the first place. Next time you access this site, or the Scout Report or the Commercial Sites list or any other page that collects a wide range of new sites, spend a couple hours exploring as many links as you can. Take note of which links initially grabbed your attention, and then, after accessing them, how many were ultimately disappointing. I'm willing to bet that at least 80 percent of everything you visited was less than it could have been, and that even if the page said "Under Construction," you're not likely to head back there again. Too many Web pages seemed designed as one-time appearances rather than continually developing presences, and too many are simply experiments to see if anyone will bother navigating to them.

The danger in all of this is that the growth of trivia on the Web will mean that its initial purpose will be lost. That purpose, you'll recall, was to provide a means for people to acquire knowledge and improve expertise in a manner and at a speed never before possible. By its very hypertext/hypermedia nature, the Web offers the opportunity to present information in a way that users can glean what they need from one site and then effortlessly find additional information from other sites. At its best, the Web already does this, acting like an almost endless book on the topic in question, one in which you don't have to return to the library to follow the footnotes and learn even more. Or, to use a different analogy, it's a means of moving from one televised feature about a topic to twenty others on the same topic, all without moving from your chair. Even entertainment sites can make use of this idea by stocking their sites with rich collections of material and pointing clearly and usefully to other repositories of relevant information. Many such sites are currently "under construction," but many are just as clearly not. The fear of Web-watchers everywhere is that the first group will never get constructed, while the second will go forth and multiply simply because construction isn't an issue.

If the Web becomes as trivial as television—and there is nothing in history that has sustained that level of inconsequentia for so long and with such success—then it will be abandoned by the people who could make the best use of it. In all likelihood, the abandonment has already begun. The signs are clear that the next eighteen months or so will see an explosion of purposeless home pages leading nowhere, or informational "teasers" that exist only to pique interest in something that is explored no deeper. If the Web were not an active medium, one that requires an actual decision to move from one site to the next, this explosion of trivia would not matter. But to ask people to choose a site, only to insult them when they arrive, is not just stupid, it's a crime against the promise of the Web itself. Perhaps we'll see the next generation of browsers include the kinds of filters that will warn of these sites in advance, but it's far more reasonable to assume that we'll be spending hours of our own precious time sifting through them ourselves. The greatest danger of all is that sifting through the trivia will become the central, and the accepted, World Wide Web activity.

Challenges for a Webbed Society

43

by John December

There are subtle, complex changes taking place in human communication, thought, and relationships within online communication and information communities. The Web is part of these changes, enabling new forms of communication and information delivery, and fostering new associations among people. One challenge for our society is to grapple with the questions raised by these changes. How might our culture, society, and communication patterns change as a result of widespread Web use?

In this chapter, I approach these questions by focusing on specific ways the Web alters communication, thought, and society, and on what issues arise from such changes. For people involved in the task of installing Web servers and for users trying to make sense of browsers and HTML, the Web may seem to consist only of a set of technical details, protocols, and network connections. However, communication on the Web, like human communication over computer networks for the past several decades, displays characteristically human qualities, including emotional, chaotic, surprising, and at times passionate or mundane exchanges. The Web illustrates how the inevitable pull of human beings toward each other in any communication system alters relationships, the way people think, and what they expect from communication.

The Scope and Extent of Web Transformations

Although the Web has changed the face of networked information dissemination dramatically over the past years, it is a much larger question whether the Web has or will ever change our society and culture significantly. The use of any communication technology evolves in the context of broader societal change, in ways so subtle that we may never be able to detect them.

Predictions

Many inventions in human history were thought to be the ultimate catalysts for sweeping social change: The telegraph would eliminate wars, the telephone and television would bring democracy and education to the people, and computer-mediated communication would transform society as Hiltz and Turoff envisioned in *The Network Nation: Human Communication via Computer* (Reading, MA: Addison-Wesley, 1978).

So the idea that the Web is *the* technology that will transform our culture must be tempered by noting the hollow predictions about earlier technologies. Humans often utilize technology in far too complex and quirky ways for neat predictions to come true.

While not always far-reaching in their effects on society, technologies have gradually and subtly changed communication patterns, relationships, and expectations. With 24-hour cable news, we expect to see a dramatic or important event as it happens. With global telecommunications, we expect to reach nearly anyone worldwide by telephone. Participants in global computer-mediated communication forums like Usenet expect to communicate with other people interested in very specialized discussion topics. Like Marshall McLuhan's vision of a global village, the electronic landscape today binds us together with connectivity we expect to access instantly.

So while the Web may fail to live up to any prediction that it will radically alter our lives immediately, its qualities as a communication technology may have some effect on future expectations and communication patterns. Also, the Web already offers unique features—interactivity and one-to-many broadcasting capabilities—that set it apart from previous communication media. The Web fulfills several "niches" within the communications landscape like few technologies before it and offers a new set of expectations about information that break the traditions of linear print.

The Web Fulfills a Dream and a "Gap"

Vannevar Bush, in a landmark article called "As We May Think" in the July 1945 issue of *The Atlantic Monthly*, described his vision of a device for helping the human mind cope with information. Bush observed that previous inventions expanded human abilities to deal with the physical world, but not floods of information and knowledge. Observing that the human mind works by association through "some intricate web of trails carried by the cells of the brain," Bush proposed a device he called a "memex" which could augment the human mind through "associative indexing." Bush's vision was for a system of information which could link documents in "trails" that could be saved and shared with others.

The Web fulfills Bush's dream of a memex in many respects. While a "universe" of knowledge is still evolving on the Web, the hypertext "trails" on Web pages are associative indexes that people save and share. The Web can link information in useful ways, giving rise to new insights—a transformation of information to knowledge that Bush described in terms of applications in law, medicine, chemistry, and history. An HTML version of Bush's article, developed by Denys Duchier, at URL `http://www.csi.uottawa.ca/~dduchier/misc/vbush/as-we-may-think.html`, contains links to several applications that fulfill Bush's predictions.

The Web offers other correspondences to many features of Bush's memex. There are "trails" within the subject trees of information on the Web that connect extremely useful documents and resources. Web browser hotlists serve as "trails," where people record their stops of interest along paths through the Web. As Bush predicted for his memex, there are many people on the Web today "who find delight in the task of establishing useful trails through the enormous mass of the common record." The Web's basic structure rests on

Bush's principle of associative indexing, and the flourishing of information on the Web in the last few years demonstrates its potential as a "universe of documents."

In addition to fulfilling many needs identified by Bush for human intellectual activity, the Web also fills a "media gap" identified by Tetsuro Tomita. In his essay, "The New Electronic Media and Their Place in the Information Market of the Future," (in *Newspapers and Democracy: International Essays on a Changing Medium*, A. Smith, editor. Cambridge, MA: MIT Press, 1980), Tomita observed a pattern in the way traditional communications methods were used to reach audiences. Methods such as letters, telegrams, and conversation reach a very small audience in amounts of time ranging from immediate (telephone) to several days (a letter). Mass media such as radio and television, newspapers, books and movies reach very large audiences in times ranging from immediate (radio, television) to weeks (magazines) to months (books). But the middle range—audiences of 10 to 10,000 people reached within times ranging from immediate to a day—is a gap filled by few traditional media. This is too small an audience for mass media and too large an audience for personally controlled (traditional) media. Yet this is the audience and time delay gap that many forms of computer-mediated communication fill, including the Web.

The Web offers immediate delivery of information to specialized audiences. There are many examples of webs that draw audiences in the range of Tomita's media gap—in fact, these audiences are what the Net seems to support in abundance. Specialized groups in Usenet and specialized webs do not necessarily appeal to massive audiences (in the 100,000 to millions range), but to quirky, specialized groups of hundreds or several thousand people. Before the invention of computer networks, an individual could not easily seek out several hundred others interested in a specialized hobby or area of interest, when those people were spread worldwide. No traditional media offered a personally available means to accomplish this, but the Web does, and filling this "media gap" is certainly a contributor to its popularity and growth.

Changes in Communication Characteristics

As part of fulfilling the needs identified by Bush for a system of associative thought and by Tomita for reaching specialized audiences in the media gap, the Web alters many characteristics of communication:

1. **Time and space constraints.** Like many forms of computer-mediated communication (CMC), the Web provides a way for users to create communication artifacts that can be accessed by anyone at any time. The benefits of this asynchronous communication are
   - People don't need to be co-present in order to exchange a message.
   - People can communicate with and associate online with others based on interest rather than geography.

2. **Power and communication control.** The power of the press lies with those who own a press. On the Web, everyone with the necessary skills owns a press.

   Dissemination of ideas on a mass and medium scale is no longer filtered through organizations and institutions but can come directly from individuals. Net and Web-based magazines (zines) (URL `http://www.ora.com:8080/john1/e-zine-list/`) can flourish rapidly or die quickly based on the ambition or interest of their publishers.

   Even without the label "zine," all web pages serve as "publications" that anyone can access. On the surface, this is a dramatic shift from institutions as holders of the publishing key. However, the cacophony of voices on the Net generates "noise," causing users to seek guidance according to signposts—institutionally sponsored or established commercial publishers, or web pages that have grown reputations for various purposes.

   The Web can shatter institutional control over knowledge (which relies on geographic proximity of members, and boundaries on knowledge dissemination) and give control to individuals and ad hoc, online groups.

3. **Expressive possibilities.** The Web offers expressive possibilities that no other information space has provided before. The Web's text is unbounded—not constrained to a single artifact or work—but can include links deep into other works by other authors. Web text thus can be neverending, finding continuing associations into the texts it links into and from texts that link to it.

4. **Relationships among people and information.** Paper texts reference each other—in fact, this is the basis for scholarly works and the "great conversation" of literature. However, the association on paper is referential (in the form of a citation, excerpt, or summary of the other work) rather than associative (a live "link" directly to the other work). Moreover, a paper reference is bounded (cast in the medium and space of the referring text) rather than unbounded (changing the user's focus of attention entirely into the space of the referred text via a hypertext link).

   Associative linking fosters relationships among people in addition to relationships among information. Experts in a particular field create pools of knowledge on their home page. When other people link into these pages, cliques of experts form. These cliques might be based on information or on hobbies, interests, culture, or political leanings. The result is that "electronic tribes" can form that meld cooperatively, linking people in associations that could not be possible any other way. For example, related information from a subject page in CERN's Virtual Library (URL `http://info.cern.ch/hypertext/DataSources/bySubject/Overview.html`) reveals collections of experts, institutions, and organizations all interested in a particular subject or topic. This linking creates visibility and associations among participants.

Through links, the Web reveals relationships among information and people. Unlike the linearism of text that integrates ideas in a single form, the Web relies on creating linked relationships among disparate pieces of information to build meaning. Unlike the ephemeral, synchronous communication spaces of Internet Relay Chat and MU*s, where text-based conversation flows and is usually never recorded, Web linking reveals relationships—and these links form a record of information relationships.

Issues and Challenges

As the Web alters communication and information patterns, the resulting change raises issues our society must face for individual, group, and societal responsibility. Moral and legal issues will arise in the areas of individual behavior, societal responsibility for issues of access and information literacy, and the new relationships, communication, and thought patterns the Web fosters.

Individual Behavior: Packet Ethics

The current Internet/Web relies on an open-access model: Anyone can follow a public link in a web page and call up a resource, whether it is a 300-byte HTML file or a 1.8 Megabyte MPEG movie. While the relatively limited number of Web users today and adequate network bandwidth make this model feasible, its future is threatened if there are far more Web users without a proportional increase in bandwidth. Essentially, the problem relates to the "tragedy of the commons" situation: A commonly held resource (network bandwidth), when made freely available to all, sometimes results in users abusing the resource.

This issue is not yet a serious problem on the Web for several reasons. First, unlike a grazing commons for livestock, network bandwith is not consumed permanently, but only temporarily occupied. Second, advances in network technology have made more bandwidth available, and the bandwidth that exists is not needed all the time. Although popular Web servers are noted for their degraded performance during busy times, it is unlikely that all potential Web users will try access at the same time. In fact, the telephone system depends on this same principle: If everyone with a phone tried to make a call simultaneously, there would be "phone jams."

So while the aggregate behavior of users dispersed across a network often might not cause serious bandwidth problems today, widespread patterns of bandwidth-intensive individual behavior, in extreme cases, can. What about the user who heavily accesses graphics or movies on the Web? While there may be no laws to stop this user, an agreement between the user and the Internet service provider might restrict such activity. If the user violated this agreement, he or she could lose the account. However, on a much larger scale, enforcement and the definition of what is "overuse" is harder to pin down. Our society and sense of "etiquette" has only begun to address this and other issues about behavior in a public network space.

While Arlene H. Rinaldi's excellent Net Etiquette guide (URL `ftp://ftp.lib.berkeley.edu/pub/net.training/FAU/`) touches on many practical issues of personal behavior, larger questions remain that are not easily resolved or codified. For example, what about individuals who provide information that may be

- Illegal in some jurisdictions where it could be downloaded (for example, non-exportable encryption programs or information that is banned in a particular country or state)
- Offensive to others beyond mere "disagreements," but violating cultural and community standards for offensiveness
- In violation of copyright laws or counter to Net traditions for information dissemination and intellectual property protection
- Intended to undermine or overthrow a government

Court cases may test these issues and prompt legislation. However, our laws and customs today aren't prepared to answer the issues these situations raise.

Societal Responsibility: Access Issues

If the Web becomes a major form of communication for government, commerce, and education, how can we assure that everyone has access to it? Access is more than just physical—it means not only having the ability to use the hardware and software to access the Web, but having the knowledge (information literacy) to make use of the content. Today, we struggle to teach print literacy to people. What will the world be like when information literacy skills are needed in addition? Experts in communication today would be hard-pressed to even define Web information literacy, much less be prepared to create curriculum for a variety of educational contexts. At the same time, Web communication is here, and those who are skilled can take advantage of it.

Moreover, many initiatives for providing skills in networked communication focus only on physical access to networks and tools. Skilled people to set up the equipment and train people in Web-based communication is another, perhaps scarcer, resource. Networked communication today requires a fairly specialized set of skills. While the Web masks the details of some communication activities (like FTP commands or the details of a telnet connection), it raises still more issues (for example, the fine points of HTML page design or how to create a working Mosaic form).

How will our society deal with a form of communication that requires such specialized knowledge on relatively expensive equipment? The U.S. Library of Congress has a Web server (URL `http://lcweb.loc.gov/homepage/lchp.html`), but whom does it serve? Can a society justify creating an elite information infrastructure, one that enriches only the privileged with the resources, skills, and knowledge to use it?

Human Relationships: Balancing Online and Offline

If modern civilization obliterates safe public spaces for people to meet and freely interchange ideas, how will our society deal with such spaces formed only online? Will psychological dependence on networked communication create imbalances in offline relationships? Research in computer-mediated communication has not answered these questions with regard to Web-based communication, and answers won't necessarily come soon or easily. (For example, the debate about television's impact on our society continues.)

If network activity becomes a major form of human communication, people may associate more freely online because they are not slowed by geographical or temporal limits. How will our institutions (government, education, religious) change to accommodate these new associations? Institutions often act as a force to help people achieve a group identity, but if people can create their own group identity in the form of network-based alliances, how will this change offline institutions? What will happen to those institutions whose power and influence are usurped by groups performing the same function online?

Ultimately, the communication possibilities offered by the Web can't help but change human relationships. People no longer might identify with a physical neighborhood for companionship or advice; they can turn to a cyberspace neighborhood, based on mutual interests and association, as a source for support and information. (This has already happened for many people in many online communities.) Will this continue to erode physical public space? In the long term, the relationships the Web fosters will certainly continue to raise more questions as well as open up new ways for people to associate.

Summary

Like failed urban planning and architecture schemes, technology developed to transform society often falls flat. The Web, a technological invention that has spread through voluntary use, perhaps has an advantage over such inventions. Despite the rapid growth of Web traffic and activity, however, the significance of the impact of the Web on our society remains unknown.

There are several characteristics of the Web that may indicate its power to change our lives. The Web very closely fits Vannevar Bush's description of a tool essential for extending human thought. Similarly, the Web fits very well into Tetsuro Tomita's "media gap" of audiences and time constraints that traditional media do not reach. As a means of communication, the Web transcends time and space constraints; alters power and control; makes possible new, expressive styles; and creates new relationships among people and information.

Our society is just beginning to face issues that may have more serious impacts if Web use becomes more widespread. Individual and societal responsibilities for Web use, access, and training have not been defined, and the way Web-based communication alters human relationships has not yet been examined in detail. In the long term, human interaction online can't be planned or predicated any more than the growth of vibrant, exciting cities. Our society is only beginning to identify the changes the Web may have already brought to communication.

Who's in Charge? Tomorrow's Toolmakers

44

by Neil Randall

By now, you've read enough of *The World Wide Web Unleashed* to know that the Web is in a constant state of change. This is typical of all computer software and systems, of course, but such is the Web's popularity that it seems to be inviting more than its share of updates, off-shoots, and innovations. The purpose of this chapter is to direct you to information about those changes—all of it available, as you'd expect, on the Web itself.

Note that these changes aren't pie-in-the-sky announcements about multimedia and its glitzy future. Instead, these are ventures now in the works, or in some cases nothing more than the sort of evolutionary upgrading seen throughout the computer industry. For many users, none of these projects will directly matter; the Web tools they'll use are whatever they get, and what's in development now simply isn't of much interest. For most readers of this book, however, this is precisely the stuff that makes for excitement, concern, and maybe even participation.

And speaking of participation, there's still time to get involved in the Web's development. While it's no longer as easy as it might have once been, if you're committed to the future of the World Wide Web, and you have the skills to lend to the project, you might consider contacting any of the locations and teams listed here.

This is especially true if you have the qualifications and you're willing to work for nothing, as some of the work is going ahead with minimal funding. If you're really good at what you do, however, there are jobs to be had in hacking the Web, and while definitely not plentiful, these jobs are almost certain to be exciting—and just a bit exasperating as well, which is no surprise.

If you think you're capable of helping out, fire up your browser and check out the following URL: `http://info.cern.ch/hypertext/WWW/Bugs.html`. Here you'll find details about work needed for the following topics (as of this writing):

- Posting to newsgroups
- Better reading of newsgroups
- Stronger mail sending
- Full mail reading
- Virtual Reality on the Web
- Linking into various document types
- Advanced search engines
- Printing text from hypertext pages
- Slide shows
- Gopher+ protocol
- Increased variety of gateways

- Stronger WAIS integration
- Relational database gateways
- Transport level gateways
- Full semantic linking
- Graphic overview of Web structure
- Advanced phone-line protocol
- MOO and IRC integration
- Tutorials
- Demos

And so on ...

Lots to do, huh?

HTTP: The Protocol of the Web

The Internet Engineering Task Force (IETF), in conjunction with CERN, continues to work on HTTP, the Web's standard protocol (and the one you keep typing over and over again in the Open URL box). For full information about the protocol and its future, see `http://info.cern.ch/hypertext/WWW/Protocols/HTTP/HTTP2.html`. Here you'll find explanations of the protocol's features and additional notes about features and problems that are not part of the official IETF draft specification.

HTML+: The Language of the Web

The URL `http://info.cern.ch/hypertext/WWW/MarkUp/MarkUp.html` offers a thorough look at the IETF specifications for HTML and HTML+ (the upgrade to HTML), the language in which Web pages are written. (See Part V, "Weaving a Web.") Included on this page is a link to a well-written HTML style guide (several others are available on the Web), a guide to such fancy items as clickable maps and indexes, and a full HTML specification in hypertext form. Also here are minutes of IETF meetings, which are less dull than the minutes of many meetings you've attended in your career.

Access Authorization

Access authorization has to do with the highly contentious and important area of concentration known as Web security, although this certainly isn't all of that issue. From the URL `http://info.cern.ch/hypertext/WWW/AccessAuthorization/Overview.html` you can get a thorough look at what's been accomplished in this ongoing project (again part of CERN's Web project), and some of the issues yet to be resolved. Included are several user manuals and a testing page as well.

Common Gateway Interface

The Common Gateway Interface (CGI) promises to be crucial to the Web's future, especially since it is the interface that handles the kind of programming seen in the handling of data generated by Web fill-in forms. Part of the NCSA initiative (with CERN), CGI continues to develop in myriad ways. Included at `http://hoohoo.ncsa.uiuc.edu/cgi/` are links to sample CGI programs, guides to creating and handling forms data, and the full interface specification.

The CERN/MIT Initiative

In July of 1994, CERN and MIT announced a joint initiative designed to extend the Web project significantly. The entire press release is available at `http://www.lcs.mit.edu/lcs/consortium.html` in all its press-release-like glory, and while it necessarily contains the kind of hype you'd expect from such an announcement, inside you can find important statements about the future of the Web itself. This is the most direct statement yet of the tie-in between the World Wide Web and the Global Information Infrastructure, the concept that has (sensibly) replaced Al Gore's National Information Infrastructure to become the information superhighway.

The important points in the announcement come from Michael L. Dertouzos, director of MIT's Laboratory for Computer Science. He is absolutely correct in claiming in the press release, "Right now, it takes a great deal of time and patience to browse through the Internet.... The key to tomorrow's information market is to make it possible for machines to talk to each other and relieve us of the painstaking details of doing the work ourselves. We aspire to enhance the Web by developing the 'bulldozers and backhoes' of the information age, that will work *for* us—not the other way around." If the consortium can remove from the Web the sense that we're serving its needs rather than it serving ours, it will be a long-term project worthy of both support and praise. But the reality remains to be seen.

Of perhaps the greatest importance here is the notion of a global infrastructure for information. But it's a concept that will require a huge amount of cooperation, and inevitably—and perhaps fatally—political concerns will rise to prominence.

Enhanced (Secure) Mosaic

In one of the most inevitable events in computing history, several companies have decided to license and improve NCSA Mosaic. Chapter 11, "Yes, Virginia, There is a Choice: More Graphical Browsers," dealt briefly with the commercialization of Mosaic, but much more is happening in the area than was covered there. Of particular note are the efforts to make Mosaic a more stable, more usable, and more *secure* package; the last of these improvements is an absolute requirement for the convergence of the business and the Web, and we can expect a great deal of money and effort being placed behind these projects.

In an August 24, 1994 press release Spyglass, Inc. announced that the University of Illinois at Urbana-Champaign had "announced a master license agreement assigning to Spyglass all future commercial licensing rights for the University's NCSA Mosaic graphical Internet browser." In the same press release, the company announced its first four licensing partners and the uses they will make of the popular Web client.

According to the release, which can be found at http://www.spyglass.com/mos_home.htm, enhanced Mosaic will feature a wealth of improvements over the version available free from NCSA. Among these are the following:

- Reliability. (Admittedly, we could use this.)
- Feature-matched versions across all three desktop platforms (which will eliminate the need for a large part of Chapter 10 of this book).
- Dramatically faster performance. (This will be nice.)
- User-interface improvements, to conform with industry standards (in other words, boring but at least predictable).
- Reduced memory requirements, by as much as two-thirds. (Fewer stack overflow errors in the Windows version would be good as well.)
- Easy installation (replacing the FTP and guess method).
- Support for multiple windows (available in some versions now).
- An online Help system. (It would be nice not to rely on the NCSA server being available.)

Nothing beyond the obvious here, and it's not until the promised release 2.0 of enhanced Mosaic that truly interesting things will start to happen. Here we begin to see the security and authentication issues that are hindering development today, including full payment-processing capabilities necessary for online purchasing. Also starting to appear at this time will be significantly enhanced multimedia capabilities, and this, too, will prove to be important.

Another interesting and related development is the founding, in April 1994, of the Mosaic Communications Corporation (see http://mcom.com). Of significance here are the founders' names. The first is Dr. James H. Clark, who was the founder of Silicon Graphics, Inc., and who oversaw SGI's success in what was already a crowded and seemingly limited market. The second is Marc Andreesen, who designed and developed X Mosaic in the first place.

Mosaic Communication Corporation was formed not only to offer enhanced versions of Mosaic, but also to create and market other, similarly usable, Internet and superhighway tools. The company's home pages do not make clear the particular projects being worked on at this time (although the Resolution Controller looks like an essential component that will compensate for varying network speeds), but what's clear is that this is yet another high-profile reworking of what is now a free piece of software.

The importance of all of this is that Mosaic—and hence the Web—will become a commercial product with commercial support, a commercial future, and (less excitingly) a commercial price tag. It's inevitable, it's probably necessary, but anyone reading this book will soon look back on the NCSA days as wild, carefree, and nostalgic.

Other Web Clients

Here we go again, dumping everything that isn't Mosaic into a category labeled "other." It's inevitable, and it remains to be seen whether anything will change that. Possibly, the commercialization of Mosaic will remove it from general circulation in its freeware form, or at least stop it at a certain stage in its development, thereby opening the door for other browsers to step in and become the leader in this still-important category.

The fact is that not everyone wants or needs a commercially supported Web client, especially since many of the enhancements promised by Spyglass, the Mosaic Communications Corporation, and other companies will be available perhaps even earlier on the noncommercial versions. There's simply no way the UNIX community is going to abandon the notion of freely distributed software available through FTP sites, and it's a notion rapidly coming into the Macintosh and Windows environments as well. As a result, we can expect to see continual work on MacWeb and WinWeb, on Cello and Viola, and on all the other smaller Web browsers that will appear as well. Some of these browsers might never support the kind of secure payment systems promised by the commercial Mosaics, but other methods of payment will inevitably be developed.

Appendixes

Internet Access Providers

A

IN THIS APPENDIX

This appendix lists companies and organizations that provide dial-up access to Internet services for individuals. For more information on different types of Internet access and what to look for in an access provider—especially in relation to accessing the World Wide Web—see Chapter 8, "Getting Connected: Accessing the Web."

Geographical and Area Code Summary— US and Canadian Providers

Following is a listing of North American Internet provider names arranged by the state or province that the provider services, and then by area code. Details and contact information for each provider follow in the next section.

Alabama

205

Nuance Network Service

Alberta

403

Alberta SuperNet Inc.
CCI Networks

Arizona

602

CRL
Data Basix
Evergreen Internet

British Columbia

604

Cyberstore Systems Inc.
DataFlux Systems Limited
Wimsey Information Services

California

213

CRL

310

CERFnet
CRL
Netcom

408

a2i Communications
Netcom
Portal

415

CERFnet
CRL
Institute for Global
Communications (IGC)
Netcom
The WELL

510

> C - Cnet Communications
> CERFnet
> CRL
> HoloNet
> Netcom

619

> CERFnet
> CTS Network Services
> Netcom

707

> CRL

714

> CERFnet
> Digital Express Group (Digex)
> Netcom

818

> CERFnet
> Netcom

909

> Digital Express Group (Digex)

916

> Netcom

Colorado

303

> CNS
> Colorado SuperNet
> Netcom

719

> CNS
> Colorado SuperNet

District of Columbia

202

> CAPCON Library Network
> Clarknet

Florida

305

> CyberGate
> Gateway to the World
> IDS World Network

407

> IDS World Network

Georgia

404

> CRL
> Netcom

Illinois

312

> CICNet
> InterAccess Co.
> Netcom

708

> CICNet
> InterAccess Co.
> XNet Information Systems

815

> InterAccess Co.

Louisiana

504

Neosoft

Manitoba

204

MBnet

Maryland

301

CAPCON Library Network
ClarkNet
Digital Express Group (Digex)

410

CAPCON Library Network
ClarkNet
Digital Express Group (Digex)

Massachusetts

508

The World

617

Delphi
Netcom
North Shore Access
The World

Michigan

313

Msen

810

Msen

Missouri

314

Neosoft

Nevada

702

Evergreen Internet

New Hampshire

603

MV Communications, Inc.

New Jersey

609

Digital Express Group (Digex)
Global Enterprise Services, Inc.

908

Digital Express Group (Digex)

New York

212

Echo
Maestro Information Service
Mindvox
Netcom
Panix
Pipeline

516

    Panix

718

    Echo
    Mindvox

North Carolina

704

    Interpath
    Northcoast Internet
    Internet Access, Inc.

910

    Interpath

919

    Interpath

Ohio

513

    Freelance Systems Programming

614

    OARNet

Ontario

416

    Internet Online Inc.
    UUNorth Incorporated

519

    Data Tech Canada
    Hookup Communication
    Corporation

Oregon

503

    Agora
    Netcom
    Teleport

Pennsylvania

412

    Telerama

Rhode Island

401

    IDS World Network

Quebec

514

    Communications Accessibles
    Montreal, Inc.

Texas

214

    Netcom
    Texas Metronet

512

    Netcom

713

    Neosoft

817

    Texas Metronet

Utah

801

Evergreen Internet

Virginia

703

CAPCON Library Network
ClarkNet
Digital Express Group (Digex)
Meta Network
Netcom

Washington

206

Eskimo North
Netcom
Olympus
Teleport

Packet Network/Toll-Free Access

CompuServe Packet Network

IDS World Network
The WELL
The World

PSINet

HoloNet

SprintNet

Delphi
Meta Network
Neosoft
Portal

Tollfree/800 Access

CERFnet
CICNet
CNS
CRL
Global Enterprise Services, Inc.
Msen
Neosoft

Tymnet

Delphi
Holonet

Providers in United States and Canada

a2i Communications

Area code(s)	408
Voice phone	408-293-8078
E-mail address	info@rahul.net
Dial-up number	408-293-9010, login as guest
Services provided	Shell, Usenet, e-mail, Internet access, including telnet and FTP

Agora

Area code(s)	503
E-mail address	info@agora.rain.com
Dial-up number	503-293-1772
Services provided	Shell, Usenet, FTP, telnet, Gopher, Lynx, IRC, mail, SLIP/PPP coming

Alberta SuperNet, Inc.

Area code(s)	403
Voice phone	403-441-3663
E-mail address	info@supernet.ab.ca
Services provided	Shell, e-mail, Usenet, FTP, telnet, Gopher, SLIP/PPP

CAPCON Library Network

Area code(s)	202, 301, 410, 703
Voice phone	202-331-5771
E-mail address	capcon@capcon.net
Services provided	Menu, FTP, Archie, e-mail, FTP, Gopher, telnet, WAIS, Whois, training

CCI Networks

Area code(s)	403
Voice phone	403-450-6787
E-mail address	info@ccinet.ab.ca
Services provided	Shell, e-mail, Usenet, FTP, telnet, Gopher, WAIS, WWW, IRC, Hytelnet, SLIP/PPP

CCnet Communications

Area code(s)	510
Voice phone	510-988-0680
E-mail address	info@ccnet.com
Dial-up number	510-988-7140, login as guest
Services provided	Shell, SLIP/PPP, telnet, e-mail, FTP, Usenet, IRC, WWW

CERFnet

Area code(s)	619, 510, 415, 818, 714, 310, 800
Voice phone	800-876-2373
E-mail address	sales@cerf.net
Services provided	Full range of Internet services

CICNet

Area code(s)	312, 708, 800
Voice phone	800-947-4754 or 313-998-6703
E-mail address	info@cic.net
Services provided	SLIP, FTP, telnet, Gopher, e-mail, Usenet

ClarkNet (Clark Internet Services, Inc.)

Area code(s)	410, 301, 202, 703
Voice phone	800-735-2258, ask for extension 410-730-9764
E-mail address	info@clark.net
Dial-up number	301-596-1626, login as guest, no password
Services provided	Shell/optional menu, FTP, Gopher, telnet, IRC, news, Mosaic, Lynx. MUD, SLIP/PPP/CSLIP, and much more

CNS

Area code(s)	303, 719, 800
Voice phone	800-748-1200
E-mail address	service@cscns.com
Dial-up number	719-520-1700, 303-758-2656
Services provided	Shell/menu, e-mail, FTP, telnet, all newsgroups, IRC, 4m, Gopher, WAIS, SLIP, and more

Colorado SuperNet

Area code(s)	303, 719
Voice phone	303-273-3471
E-mail address	info@csn.org or help@csn.org
Services provided	Shell, e-mail, Usenet news, telnet, FTP, SLIP/PPP, and other Internet tools

Communications Accessibles Montreal, Inc.

Area code(s)	514
Voice phone	514-931-0749
E-mail address	info@cam.org
Dial-up number	514-596-2255
Services provided	Shell, FTP, telnet, Gopher, WAIS, WWW, IRC, Hytelnet, SLIP/CSLIP/PPP, news

CRL

Area code(s)	213, 310, 404, 415, 510, 602, 707, 800
Voice phone	415-837-5300
E-mail address	support@crl.com
Dial-up number	415-705-6060, login as newuser, no password
Services provided	Shell, e-mail, Usenet, UUCP, FTP, telnet, SLIP/PPP, and more

CTS Network Services (CTSNet)

Area code(s)	619
Voice phone	619-637-3737
E-mail address	support@cts.com
Dial-up number	619-637-3660
Services provided	Shell, e-mail, Usenet, FTP, telnet, Gopher, IRC, MUD, SLIP/PPP, and more

CyberGate

Area code(s)	305
Voice phone	305-428-4283
E-mail address	sales@gate.net
Services provided	Shell, e-mail, Usenet, FTP, telnet, Gopher, Lynx, IRC, SLIP/PPP

Cyberstore Systems Inc.

Area code(s)	604
Voice phone	604-526-3373
E-mail address	info@cyberstore.ca
Dial-up number	604-526-3676, login as guest
Services provided	E-mail, Usenet, FTP, telnet, Gopher, WAIS, WWW, IRC, SLIP/PPP

DataFlux Systems Limited

Area code(s)	604
Voice phone	604-744-4553
E-mail address	info@dataflux.bc.ca
Services provided	Shell, e-mail, Usenet, FTP, telnet, Gopher, WAIS, WWW, IRC, SLIP/PPP

Data Basix

Area code(s)	602
Voice phone	602-721-1988
E-mail address	info@data.basix.com
Services provided	Shell, Usenet, FTP, telnet

Data Tech Canada

Area code(s)	519
Voice phone	519-473-5694
E-mail address	info@dt-can.com
Dial-up number	519-473-7685
Services provided	Shell, e-mail, Usenet, FTP, telnet, Gopher, WAIS, WWW

Delphi

Area code(s)	617, SprintNet, Tymnet
Voice phone	617-491-3393
E-mail address	info@delphi.com
Dial-up number	617-492-9600
Services provided	Gopher, FTP, e-mail, Usenet, telnet

Digital Express Group (Digex)

Area code(s)	301, 410, 609, 703, 714, 908, 909
Voice phone	800-969-9090
E-mail address	`info@digex.net`
Dial-up number	301-220-0258, 410-605-2700, 609-348-6203, 703-281-7997, 714-261-5201, 908-937-9481, 909-222-2204, login as `new`
Services provided	Shell, SLIP/PPP, e-mail, newsgroups, telnet, FTP, IRC, Gopher, WAIS, and more

Echo

Area code(s)	212, 718
Voice phone	212-255-3839
E-mail address	`info@echonyc.com`
Dial-up number	212-989-3382
Services provided	Conferencing, e-mail, shell, complete Internet access including telnet, FTP, SLIP/PPP

Eskimo North

Area code(s)	206
E-mail address	`nanook@eskimo.com`
Dial-up number	206-367-3837
Services provided	Shell, telnet, FTP, IRC, Archie, Gopher, Hytelnet, WWW, Lynx, etc.

Evergreen Internet

Area code(s)	602, 702, 801
Voice phone	602-230-9339
E-mail address	`evergreen@libre.com`
Services provided	Shell, FTP, telnet, SLIP/PPP, others

Freelance Systems Programming

Area code(s)	513
Voice phone	513-254-7246
E-mail address	fsp@dayton.fsp.com
Dial-up number	513-258-7745
Services provided	telnet, FTP, FSP, Lynx, WWW, Archie, Gopher, Usenet, e-mail, etc.

Gateway to the World

Area code(s)	305
Voice phone	305-670-2930
E-mail address	m.jansen@gate.com
Dial-up number	305-670-2929
Services provided	Dial-up Internet access

Global Enterprise Services, Inc.

Area code(s)	609, 800
Voice phone	800-358-4437
E-mail address	market@jvnc.net
Services provided	Dial-in Internet access

HoloNet

Area code(s)	510, PSINet, Tymnet
Voice phone	510-704-0160
E-mail address	support@holonet.net
Dial-up number	510-704-1058
Services provided	Complete Internet access

Hookup Communication Corporation

Area code(s)	519, Canada-wide
Voice phone	800-363-0400
E-mail address	info@hookup.net
Services provided	Shell, e-mail, Usenet, FTP, telnet, Gopher, WAIS, WWW, IRC, Hytelnet, Archie, SLIP/PPP

IDS World Network

Area code(s)	401, 305, 407, CompuServe Network
Voice phone	401-885-6855
E-mail address	info@ids.net
Dial-up number	401-884-9002
Services provided	Shell, FTP, Gopher, telnet, Talk, Usenet news, SLIP

Institute for Global Communications (IGC)

Area code(s)	415
Voice phone	415-442-0220
E-mail address	support@igc.apc.org
Dial-up number	415-322-0284
Services provided	E-mail, telnet, FTP, Gopher, Archie, Veronica, WAIS, SLIP/PPP

InterAccess Co.

Area code(s)	312, 708, 815
Voice phone	800-967-1580
E-mail address	info@interaccess.com
Dial-up number	708-671-0237
Services provided	Shell, FTP, telnet, SLIP/PPP, etc.

Internet Online, Inc.

Area code(s)	416
Voice phone	416-363-8676
E-mail address	vid@io.org
Dial-up number	416-363-3783, login as new
Services provided	Shell, e-mail, Usenet, FTP, telnet, Gopher, IRC, Archie, Hytelnet

Interpath

Area code(s)	919, 910, 704
Voice phone	800-849-6305
E-mail address	info@infopath.net
Services provided	Full shell for UNIX, and SLIP/PPP

Maestro Information Service

Area code(s)	212
Voice phone	212-240-9600
E-mail address	info@maestro.com
Dial-up number	212-240-9700, login as newuser
Services provided	Shell, e-mail, Usenet, telnet, FTP, Archie, IRC

MBnet

Area code(s)	204
Voice phone	204-474-9590
E-mail address	info@mbnet.mb.ca
Dial-up number	204-275-6132, login as mbnet with password guest
Services provided	Shell, e-mail, Usenet, FTP, telnet, Gopher, WAIS, WWW, IRC, Archie, Hytelnet, SLIP/PPP

Meta Network

Area code(s)	703, SprintNet
Voice phone	703-243-6622
E-mail address	info@tmn.com
Services provided	Shell, e-mail, FTP, telnet, conferencing

Mindvox

Area code(s)	212, 718
Voice phone	212-989-2418
E-mail address	info@phantom.com
Dial-up number	212-989-1550
Services provided	Shell, e-mail, Usenet, FTP, telnet, Gopher, Archie, IRC, conferencing

Msen

Area code(s)	313, 810, 800
Voice phone	313-998-4562
E-mail address	info-request@msen.com
Services provided	Shell, e-mail, telnet, FTP, Usenet, Gopher, IRC, WAIS, SLIP/PPP

MV Communications, Inc.

Area code(s)	603
Voice phone	603-429-2223
E-mail address	info@mv.mv.com
Dial-up number	603-424-7428
Services provided	Shell, Usenet, FTP, telnet, Gopher, WAIS, SLIP/PPP

Neosoft

Area code(s)	713, 504, 314, 800, SprintNet
Voice phone	713-684-5969
E-mail address	info@neosoft.com
Services provided	Shell, Usenet, FTP, telnet, Gopher, SLIP/PPP, etc.

Netcom On-Line Communications Services

Area code(s)	206, 212, 214, 303, 310, 312, 404, 408, 415, 503, 510, 512, 617, 619, 703, 714, 818, 916
Voice phone	800-501-8649
E-mail address	info@netcom.com
Dial-up number	206-547-5992, 212-354-3870, 214-753-0045, 303-758-0101, 310-842-8835, 312-380-0340, 404-303-9765, 408-261-4700, 408-459-9851, 415-328-9940, 415-985-5650, 503-626-6833, 510-274-2900, 510-426-6610, 510-865-9004, 512-206-4950, 617-237-8600, 619-234-0524, 703-255-5951, 714-708-3800, 818-585-3400, 916-965-1371; login as guest
Services provided	Shell, e-mail, Usenet, FTP, telnet, Gopher, IRC, WAIS, SLIP/PPP

North Shore Access

Area code(s)	617
Voice phone	617-593-3110
E-mail address	info@shore.net
Dial-up number	617-593-4557, login as new
Services provided	Shell, FTP, telnet, Gopher, Archie, SLIP/PPP

Northcoast Internet

Area code(s)	707
Voice phone	707-444-1913
Services provided	Shell, FTP, telnet, Gopher, SLIP/PPP

Nuance Network Services

Area code(s)	205
Voice phone	205-533-4296
E-mail address	info@nuance.com
Services provided	Shell, Usenet, FTP, telnet, Gopher, SLIP/PPP

OARNet

Area code(s)	614
Voice phone	800-627-8101
E-mail address	info@oar.net
Services provided	Shell, SLIP/PPP

Olympus

Area code(s)	206
Voice phone	206-385-0464
E-mail address	ifo@olympus.net
Services provided	Shell, FTP, telnet, Gopher

Panix Public Access UNIX and Internet

Area code(s)	212, 516
Voice phone	212-787-6160
E-mail address	info@panix.com
Dial-up number	212-787-3100, 516-626-7863, login as newuser
Services provided	Shell, Usenet, FTP, telnet, Gopher, Archie, WWW, WAIS, SLIP/PPP

Pipeline

Area code(s)	212
Voice phone	212-267-3636
E-mail address	infobot@pipeline.com
Dial-up number	212-267-6432, login as guest
Services provided	Pipeline for Windows software, e-mail, Usenet, Gopher, telnet, Archie, FTP, WAIS

Portal Communications Company

Area code(s)	408, SprintNet
Voice phone	408-973-9111
E-mail address	info@portal.com
Services provided	Shell, e-mail, Usenet, FTP, telnet, Gopher, IRC, SLIP/PPP

PSI

Area code(s)	North America, Europe and Pacific Basin; send e-mail to numbers-info@psi.com for list
Voice phone	703-709-0300
E-mail address	all-info@psi.com
Services provided	Complete Internet services

Teleport

Area code(s)	503, 206
Voice phone	503-223-4245
E-mail address	info@teleport.com
Dial-up number	503-220-1016
Services provided	Shell, e-mail, Usenet, FTP, telnet, Gopher, SLIP/PPP

Telerama

Area code(s)	412
Voice phone	412-481-3505
E-mail address	sysop@telerama.lm.com
Dial-up number	412-481-4644
Services provided	Shell, e-mail, Usenet, FTP, telnet, Gopher, IRC, SLIP/PPP

Texas Metronet

Area code(s)	214, 817
Voice phone	214-705-2900
E-mail address	`info@metronet.com`
Dial-up number	214-705-2901, 817-261-1127; login as `info`, with password `info`
Services provided	Shell, e-mail, Usenet, FTP, telnet, Gopher, IRC, SLIP/PPP

UUNorth Incorporated

Area code(s)	416
Voice phone	416-225-8649
E-mail address	`uunorth@north.net`
Dial-up number	416-221-0200, login as `new`
Services provided	E-mail, Usenet, FTP, telnet, Gopher, WAIS, WWW, IRC, Archie, SLIP/PPP

VNet Internet Access, Inc.

Area code(s)	704, public data network
Voice phone	800-377-3282
E-mail address	`info@vnet.net`
Dial-up number	704-347-8839, login as `new`
Services provided	Shell, e-mail, Usenet, FTP, telnet, Gopher, IRC, SLIP/PPP, UUCP

The WELL

Area code(s)	415, CompuServe Packet Network
Voice phone	415-332-4335
E-mail address	`info@well.sf.ca.us`
Dial-up number	415-332-6106, login as `newuser`
Services provided	Shell, e-mail, Usenet, FTP, telnet, conferencing

Wimsey Information Services

Area code(s)	604
Voice phone	604-936-8649
E-mail address	`admin@wimsey.com`
Services provided	Shell, e-mail, Usenet, FTP, telnet, Gopher, WAIS, WWW, IRC, Archie, SLIP/PPP

The World

Area code(s)	508, 617, CompuServe Packet Network
Voice phone	617-739-0202
E-mail address	office@world.std.com
Dial-up number	617-739-9753, login as new
Services provided	Shell, e-mail, Usenet, FTP, telnet, Gopher, WAIS, WWW, IRC

XNet Information Systems

Area code(s)	708
Voice phone	708-983-6064
E-mail address	info@xnet.com
Dial-up number	708-983-6435, 708-882-1101
Services provided	Shell, e-mail, Usenet, FTP, telnet, Gopher, Archie, IRC, SLIP/PPP, UUCP

Australia

Aarnet

Voice phone	+61 6-249-3385
E-mail address	aarnet@aarnet.edu.au

Connect.com.au P/L

Areas serviced	Major Australian capital cities (2, 3, 6, 7, 8, 9)
Voice phone	1 800 818 262 or +61 3 528 2239
E-mail address	connect@connect.com.au
Services provided	Shell, SLIP/PPP, UUCP

Germany

Contributed Software

Voice phone	+49 30-694-69-07
E-mail address	info@contrib.de
Dial-up number	+49 30-694-60-55, login as guest or gast

Individual Network e.V.

Area serviced	All of Germany
Voice phone	+49 0441 9808556
E-mail address	in-info@individual.net
Dial-up number	02238 15071, login as info
Services provided	UUCP throughout Germany; FTP, SLIP, telnet and other services in some major cities

Inter Networking System (INS)

Voice phone	+49 2305 356505
E-mail address	info@ins.net

Netherlands

Knoware

E-mail address	info@knoware.nl
Dial-up number	030 896775

NetLand

Voice phone	020 6943664
E-mail address	Info@netland.nl
Dial-up number	020 6940350, login as new or info

Simplex

E-mail address	simplex@simplex.nl
Dial-up number	020 6653388, login as new or info

New Zealand

Actrix

Voice phone	(04) 389-6316
E-mail address	john@actrix.gen.nz

Switzerland

SWITCH—Swiss Academic and Research Network

Voice phone	+41 1 268 1515
E-mail address	`postmaster@switch.ch`

United Kingdom

Almac

Voice phone	+44 0324-665371
E-mail address	`alastair.mcintyre@almac.co.uk`

Cix

Voice phone	+44 49 2641 961
E-mail address	`cixadmin@cix.compulink.co.uk`

Demon Internet Limited

Voice phone	081-349-0063 (London)
	031-552-0344 (Edinburgh)
E-mail address	`internet@demon.net`
Services provided	SLIP/PPP accounts

The Direct Connection (UK)

Voice phone	+44 (0)81 317 0100
E-mail address	`helpdesk@dircon.cu.uk`
Dial-up number	+44 (0)81 317 2222

> **NOTE**
>
> **Note to Providers:** If you would like to be included in future versions of this list, for use in subsequent editions of this book as well as other Sams Internet books, send an e-mail message to Mark Taber <`mtaber@netcom.com`>.

Web Reference

B

This appendix lists some key online resources for finding out and using the Web.

Introduction

Overviews

- WWW overview/CERN: overview of the Web, from Conseil Europeen pour la Recherche Nucleaire (CERN) European Laboratory for Particle Physics, Geneva, Switzerland (birthplace of WWW) (`http://info.cern.ch/default.html`).

- WWW info/EARN: What is World-Wide Web, a narrative introducing and explaining the Web, from European Academic Research Network Association (EARN) (`http://www.earn.net/gnrt/www.html`).

- WWW Guide/Hughes: Entering the World-Wide Web, A Guide to Cyberspace, by Kevin Hughes (`http://www.eit.com/web/www.guide/guide.toc.html`).

FAQs—Frequently Asked Questions Lists and Answers

- WWW FAQ/Boutell: Frequently Asked Questions Lists and Answers about the Web—covers user, provider, and general information, maintained by Thomas Boutell (`http://sunsite.unc.edu/boutell/faq/www_faq.html`).

- WWW FAQ/CERN: Frequently Asked Questions on W3, by Tim Berners-Lee at CERN (`http://info.cern.ch/hypertext/WWW/FAQ/List.html`).

Access and Information

- WWW via telnet: an example of using WWW via telnet (to CERN) (`telnet://info.cern.ch`).

- WWW via email: obtain a web file (e.g., HTTP) via e-mail; URL = Uniform resource locator; send message body www URL, note—use sparingly, from CERN (`mailto:listproc@www0.cern.ch Body: help`).

- WWW bootstrap: how to get some starter information for accessing the Web, by Tim Berners-Lee at CERN (`http://info.cern.ch/hypertext/WWW/FAQ/Bootstrap.html`).

- WWW Clients: a list of programs (Web browsers) that allow you to access the WWW, from CERN (`http://info.cern.ch/hypertext/WWW/Clients.html`).

- WWW ftp info: some information files about the Web, includes papers, guides, and draft specifications, from CERN (`ftp://info.cern.ch/pub/www/doc/`).

Net Directory

by John December

There are many online information sources that can help you learn more about the Net. The following listings contain descriptions of sources of information about the Internet, applications of the Net, Internet technology, and online culture. Each section will help you find more information about the Internet or connect you directly to examples of how the Internet or Web can be used.

Each entry is of the following form:

■ *Name: Description* (URL)

Where

Name is a short name or title for the resource

Description is a longer annotation describing the resource

URL is the Uniform Resource Locator of the resource

This list is a selection of annotated links from my list, "Information Sources: the Internet and Computer-Mediated Communication," (URL `http://www.rpi.edu/Internet/Guides/decemj/icmc/top.html`)

Internet

The Internet is a vast collection of resources, encompassing tens of thousands of cooperating organizations and tens of millions of users. This section provides you with information to find out more about the Internet on many different levels:

■ Introductory information to orient you to what the Internet is and what is possible on it

■ Collections of official Internet standards and technical documentation

■ Training resources, collections, and courses

■ Information about navigating the Internet, including guides and special collections

■ Navigators and tools that help you find people or resources on the Internet based on a search by subject, keyword, information space, or list

Introduction

Motivation

Gold in Networks!: a description of gold nuggets in the network, by J. Martin (`ftp://nic.merit.edu/documents/fyi/fyi_10.txt`)

Internet: a column about the Internet from the Magazine of Fantasy and Science Fiction, Feb 1993, by Bruce Sterling (`http://www.lysator.liu.se:7500/etexts/the_internet.html`)

Overviews

- Hitchikers Guide: describes the Internet (circa September 1989), by Ed Krol (`ftp://nic.merit.edu/documents/rfc/rfc1118.txt`)
- Surfing the Internet: a narrative of what the Internet has to offer, by Jean Armour Polly (`ftp://nysernet.org/pub/resources/guides/surfing.2.0.3.txt`)
- What is the Internet?: by Krol and Hoffman (`ftp://nic.merit.edu/documents/fyi/fyi_20.txt`)
- Xerox Video: An Overview of the Internet and World-Wide Web, by Xerox Palo Alto Research Center (`http://pubweb.parc.xerox.com/hypertext/wwwvideo/wwwvideo.html`)

Facts

- Internet Index: A list of interesting facts about the Internet (Inspired by "Harper's Index"), by Win Treese (`http://www.openmarket.com/info/internet-index/current.html`)
- New User's Questions: answers questions commonly asked by new users, by Malkin and Marine (`ftp://nic.merit.edu/documents/fyi/fyi_04.txt`)

History

- Internet History/ISOC: Internet Society's collection of Internet history (`gopher://gopher.isoc.org/11/internet/history`)
- Internet History: Master's Thesis, Henry Edward Hardy (`ftp://umcc.umich.edu/pub/users/seraphim/doc/nethist8.txt`)
- Internet Timeline: events in the history of the Internet by Robert H'obbes' Zakon (`http://tig.com/IBC/Timeline.html`)
- Netizen Anthology: the Netizens and the Wonderful World of the Net-an anthology, Ronda Hauben, Michael Hauben (`ftp://wuarchive.wustl.edu/doc/misc/acn/netbook/`)

Collections

NICs (Network Information Centers)

- ■ InterNIC web: information, directory, and registration services (`http://www.internic.net`)
- ■ InterNIC DS Web: Directory and Database Services Home Page (`http://ds.internic.net`)
- ■ Merit: network information center (`ftp://nic.merit.edu`)

Series

- ■ EIN Web: Internet Engineering Notes (`http://www.cis.ohio-state.edu/hypertext/information/ien.html`)
- ■ Internet Docs: Internet Documentation (RFCs, FYIs, etc.) from InterNIC (`http://ds.internic.net/ds/dspg0intdoc.html`)
- ■ Internet Handbook: a list of RFCs by subject and category (`ftp://sri.com/netinfo/internet-technology-handbook-contents`)
- ■ STD: Internet Standards, sub-series of notes within the RFC series which document Internet standards (`ftp://nic.merit.edu/documents/std/`)
- ■ RFC Index: an interactive RFC index, searches an index and builds a list of URL's to all matches, by Brandon Gillespie (`http://www.usu.edu/~brandon/RFC/`)
- ■ RFC repositories: repositories where RFCs are located (`ftp://isi.edu/in-notes/rfc-retrieval.txt`)
- ■ RFC Web: Internet Request For Comments (RFC) in HTML (`http://www.cis.ohio-state.edu/hypertext/information/rfc.html`)

Training

Collections

- ■ CBL: Computer-Based Learning Unit, The University of Leeds, United Kingdom (`http://cbl.leeds.ac.uk`)
- ■ DELTA: Distributed ELectronic Telecommunications Archive-teaching and learning about business telecommunications and data communications (`http://gozer.idbsu.edu/business/nethome.html`)

■ Introducing the Internet: Merit's Directory of miscellaneous introductory Internet information (`ftp://nic.merit.edu/introducing.the.internet/`)

■ ITTI: Information Technology Training Initiative, a United Kingdom-wide initiative to provide training materials about or using Information Technology (`http://info.mcc.ac.uk/CGU/ITTI/ITTI.html`)

■ NETTRAIN archive: NETTRAIN (networking training) discussion list archives (`ftp://ubvm.cc.buffalo.edu/nettrain/`)

■ NOCALL: Northern California Association of Law Libraries (NOCALL) and the Southern California Association of Law Libraries (SCALL) to encourage use of the Internet and provide training assistance to our members (`ftp://ftp.netcom.com/pub/loftus/buddies/home.html`)

■ Schneider Bib: a bibliography of Internet Training Materials, by Karen Schneider (`ftp://alexia.lis.uiuc.edu/pub/training.bib`)

■ Start Web: Where to Start for New Internet Users (in HTML), by James Milles (`http://www.law.cornell.edu/test/newusers.html`)

■ Trainmat: Training Materials Gopher (`gopher://trainmat.ncl.ac.uk`)

■ Web Training: University of Toronto Instructional and Research Computing Group (UTIRC) World Wide Web home page, information about HTTP, HTML, and networked multimedia training and technology (`http://www.utirc.utoronto.ca/home.html`)

■ Wheeler: Internet Training handouts, by Bill Wheeler (`ftp://s850.mwc.edu/nettrain/`)

■ Yale: YaleInfo Internet Help (`gopher://yaleinfo.yale.edu`)

Resources

■ About Internet: a collection from the InterNIC (`http://www.internic.net/infoguide/gopher/about-internet.html`)

■ New users list: New Internet User's Top 10 Reading List (`http://www.sips.state.nc.us/docs/top-10.html`)

■ Start: Where to Start for New Internet Users, by James Milles (`ftp://sluaxa.slu.edu/pub/millesjg/newusers.faq`)

Exploring

■ Beginners/Suarez: The Beginner's Guide to the Internet for DOS and Windows, by Patrick J. Suarez (`ftp://oak.oakland.edu/pub/msdos/info/bgi13a.zip`)

- DOS Internet Kit Web: public domain programs that enable Ethernet or serially connected PCs to access Internet services, packaged as a kit, by Dean Pentcheff (`http://tbone.biol.scarolina.edu/~dean2/kit/kit.html`)

- Internet Hunt Gopher: a game for learning about the Internet; Hunt Questions, Results, and Comments (`gopher://gopher.cic.net/11/hunt`)

- Internet Navigating: Navigating the Internet Workshop List, by Richard J. Smith (`ftp://ubvm.cc.buffalo.edu/navigate/`)

Courses

- CMC: a graduate course in computer-mediated communication (CMC) with some network training components (`http://www.rpi.edu/Internet/Guides/decemj/course/cmc.html`)

- Compass in Cyberspace: Internet Training from John S. Makulowich (`http://www.clark.net/pub/journalism/brochure.html`)

- Gopherin: a course for cyberspace, by Jim Gerland and Rich Smith (via FTP) (`ftp://ubvm.cc.buffalo.edu/gophern/`)

- Intro/Internet: one of several prototype classes and texts sponsored through the Globewide Network Academy (`http://uu-gna.mit.edu:8001/uu-gna/text/internet/index.html`)

- ISS 101: Internet survival skills, a course from Dr. Kenneth Hensarling (`http://kawika.hcc.hawaii.edu/iss101/101mods.html`)

- Gopherin course: Jim Gerland and Rich Smith's course about Gopher (via Gopher) (`gopher://wealaka.okgeosurvey1.gov/11/K12/GOPHERN`)

- LeJeune Course: course materials and files, by Urban A. LeJeune (`ftp://pilot.njin.net/pub/Internet-course/`)

- Navigating: Navigating the Internet, workshop for teaching the Internet via email, by Richard J. Smith (`gopher://jake.esu.edu/11/Help/net_stuff/training`)

- Surfing: a course given at Florida State in Internet use (`http://www.cs.fsu.edu/surfing.html`)

- Syracuse: courses offered by the Syracuse University, School of Information Studies (`http://eryx.syr.edu/bmis/bmis.html`)

Tutorials for Specific Applications

- Ackermann tutorial: Internet Services and Resources for Computer Scientists, by Ernest Ackermann, Department of Computer Science, Mary Washington College, Fredericksburg, VA (`ftp://s850.mwc.edu/pub/tutorial`)

- Competencies: Competencies for Electronic Information Services, by John Corbin (`mailto:listserv@uhupvm1.uh.edu Body: GET CORBIN PRV4N6`)

- Discussion help: the art of getting help-guidelines for seeking help in discussion groups (`mailto:rre-request@weber.ucsd.edu Subject: archive send courtesy`)

- HTML Assistant: an MS Windows text editor with extensions to assist in the creation of HTML hypertext documents to be viewed by World Wide Web browsers like Cello and Mosaic, by Howard Harawitz (`ftp://ftp.cs.dal.ca/htmlasst/htmlafaq.html`)

- HTML Developer's: WWW + HTML Developer's JumpStation, by Barry Raveendran Greene (`http://oneworld.wa.com/htmldev/devpage/dev-page.html`)

- HTML Guide/NCSA: A Beginner's Guide to HTML from National Center for Supercomputing Applications (`http://www.ncsa.uiuc.edu/demoweb/html-primer.html`)

- HTML info/CERN: HyperText Markup Language (HTML), Working and Background Materials, from CERN (`http://info.cern.ch/hypertext/WWW/MarkUp/MarkUp.html`)

- Mosaic Web Index: An index to the National Center for Supercomputing Applications (NCSA) Mosaic online documentation and tutorials on the NCSA Web server (`http://www.ncsa.uiuc.edu %FILE SDG/Software/Mosaic/Docs/web-index.html`)

- NIR/CMC Tools/December: a list summarizing Internet tools and computer-mediated communication forums; includes pointers to guides or information about each tool, by John December (`http://www.rpi.edu/Internet/Guides/decemj/itools/top.html`)

- Tutorial gateway: a filter for a CGI-compliant HTTP server that makes it slightly easier to develop tutorial style questions for Web users (`http://www.civeng.carleton.ca/~nholtz/tut/doc/doc.html`)

- UNIX Help: Novalinks's Unixhelp for users (`http://alpha.acast.nova.edu/UNIXhelp/TOP_.html`)

- UNIX Man Pages: HyperText interface to UNIX manpages, by Michael Fisk (`http://nmt.edu/bin/man`)

- UNIX tutorials: a collection of UNIX and computer information, from East Stroudsburg University (`gopher://jake.esu.edu/11/Help/Tutorials`)

- URL: Curling Up to Universal Resource Locators, by Eric S. Theise (`gopher://gopher.well.sf.ca.us/00/matrix/internet/curling.up.02`)
- URL guide/NCSA: A Beginner's Guide to URLs, by Marc Andreessen (`http://www.ncsa.uiuc.edu/demoweb/url-primer.html`)
- Usenet and trn: An Introduction to Usenet News and the trn Newsreader, by Jon Bell (`ftp://cs1.presby.edu/pub/trn-intro/`)
- WWW Developers (CyberWeb): a resource center for WWW developers (`http://www.charm.net/~web/Web.html`)
- WWW Weavers: a collection of resources related to developing information on the World Wide Web, by Chris Beaumont (`http://www.nas.nasa.gov/RNR/Education/weavers.html`)
- WWW talk/Wallach: The World Wide Web, Everything you've always wanted to know, but were afraid to ask, by Dan Wallach (`http://www.cs.princeton.edu/grad/Dan_Wallach/www-talk/talk0.html`)
- WWW talk/Berners-Lee: WWW Seminar, Transparency track, by Tim Berners-Lee , Robert Cailliau, CERN (`http://info.cern.ch/hypertext/WWW/Talks/General/Transparencies.html`)

Navigating

Access

- Access + Providers: listings of Internet service providers for dial-up, direct lines, and international connections, by Global Network Navigator (`http://nearnet.gnn.com/gnn/meta/internet/res/access/index.html`)
- NIXPUB: Public/Open Access UNIX, by Bux Technical Services (`ftp://rtfm.mit.edu/pub/usenet/alt.bbs/Nixpub_Posting_(Long)`)
- Service Providers: Network Service Provider WWW Servers (`http://www.eit.com/web/www.servers/networkservice.html`)

Tools

- GNN's Tools: a list of tools and supporting documents, from Global Network Navigator (`http://nearnet.gnn.com/gnn/meta/internet/res/tools/index.html`)
- Internet Browsers: Sources for Internet Browsers and Client Software (`http://life.anu.edu.au/links/syslib.html`)

- Internet Tools/EARN HTML: European Academic Research Network Association Guide to Network Resources Tools in HTML (`http://www.huji.ac.il/www_help/earn.html`)

- Internet Tools NIR: a status report on networked information retrieval tools and groups, by Joint IETF/RARE/CNI Networked Information Retrieval Working Group (`ftp://mailbase.ac.uk/pub/lists/nir/files/nir.status.report`)

- Internet Tools/December HTML: HTML (segmented) version of a list summarizing Internet tools and computer-mediated communication forums, by John December (`http://www.rpi.edu/Internet/Guides/decemj/itools/top.html`)

- Internet Systems UNITE: a list of Internet tools and systems, by User Network Interface To Everything (`ftp://mailbase.ac.uk/pub/lists/unite/files/systems-list.txt`)

Guides

- De Presno Guide Gopher: full text of the Online World book by Odd de Presno (`gopher://wuecon.wustl.edu:10672/11/online`)

- EFF's Guide: (formerly Big Dummy's Guide) a guide from the Electronic Frontier Foundation (EFF) to the Internet in HTML (`http://www.eff.org/papers/bdgtti/bdgtti.html`)

- EFF's Guide Search: search the EFF's Guide to the Internet (`http://alpha.acast.nova.edu/cgi-bin/srch.cgi/search/bigdummy/mylist`)

- Email 101: describes how to use email as well as other Internet features, by John Goodwin (`ftp://mrcnext.cso.uiuc.edu/etext/etext93/email025.txt`)

- Entering/WWW: Kevin Hughes's guide to the web (`http://www.eit.com/web/www.guide/`)

- HWGUIDE: a hypertext version of Noonan's Guide to Internet/Bitnet (`ftp://sunsite.unc.edu/pub/docs/about-the-net/libsoft/hwguide.txt`)

- InfoPop: a WINHELP (hypertext) guide to the Internet, CompuServe, BBS systems, and more, by Wally Grotophorst (`ftp://ftp.gmu.edu/library/`)

- Internet Companion (parts): A Beginner's Guide to Global Networking by Tracey LaQuey (`ftp://ftp.std.com/OBS/The.Internet.Companion/`)

- Internet Guide: A guide to Internet/Bitnet, by Dana Noonan (`ftp://sunsite.unc.edu/pub/docs/about-the-net/libsoft/guide1.txt`)

- Internet Tour: A Short, Semi-Guided Tour of the Internet, from Kapor Enterprises (`http://www.kei.com/internet-tour.html`)

- Internet Web Text: an index to the Internet's resources; links to orientation, guides, reference materials, browsing and exploring tools, subject and word-oriented searching tools, and information about connecting with people, by John December (`http://www.rpi.edu/Internet/Guides/decemj/text.html`)

- La toile d'araignee: French translation with European-oriented resources, by Francois Charoy, of John December's Internet Web Text (`http://www.loria.fr/~charoy/ToileInternet/text.html`)

- Library of Congress: a directory of Internet User Guides (`ftp://ftp.loc.gov/pub/iug/`)

- Meng's: Holistic Guide to the Internet, by Meng Weng Wong (`http://ccat.sas.upenn.edu/mengwong/guide.html`)

- Neophyte: Network Knowledge for the Neophyte, Stuff You Need to Know in Order to Navigate the Electronic Village, by Martin Raish (`ftp://hydra.uwo.ca/pub/libsoft/network_knowledge_for_the_neophyte.txt`)

- NWNet Internet Guide: NorthWestNet's User Service Internet Resource Guide (`ftp://ftphost.nwnet.net/user-docs/nusirg/README.nusirg`)

- NYSERNet Internet Guide: New York State Education and Research Network Guide to the Internet (`ftp://nysernet.org/pub/guides/Guide.V.2.2.text`)

- SLAC: Introduction to the Internet, a narrative about the Internet from SLAC (Stanford Linear Accelerator Center), by Joan Winters (`http://slacvm.slac.stanford.edu/FIND/internet.html`)

- SURANet Internet Guide: updated as infoguide.MM-YR.txt (`ftp://ftp.sura.net/pub/nic/`)

- SURFnet Guide: SURFnet is the Dutch academic network (`ftp://ftp.nic.surfnet.nl/surfnet/user-support/docs/training/`)

- WWW/Mosaic: User's Guide, by Craig I. Schlenoff (`http://elib.cme.nist.gov/fasd/pubs/schlenoff94.html`)

- Zen Web: Zen and the Art of the Internet (1st edition), by Brendan Kehoe, in HTML (`http://sundance.cso.uiuc.edu/Publications/Other/Zen/zen-1.0_toc.html`)

Collections

- GNN's Internet Center: Global Network Navigator's (O'Reilly) Internet Information Center (`http://nearnet.gnn.com/gnn/meta/internet/index.html`)

- Hypermedia/Internet: Hypermedia and the Internet, by David Green (`http://life.anu.edu.au/education/hypermedia.html`)

- Info Deli: a collection of Net information, by Peter Kaminski (`ftp://ftp.netcom.com/pub/info-deli/bookmark.html`)
- NetCruiser: NETCOM On-Line Communications Services, Inc.'s online guide (`http://www.netcom.com/glee/cruiser.html`)
- NMIS: Networked Multimedia Information Services (NMIS), conduct research and develop new multiprogramming and services for delivery on the internet (`http://nmis03.mit.edu:8001`)
- NOSC Page: list of Internet-related sources, by Richard Bocker (`http://white.nosc.mil/internet.html`)
- Naval Research Lab: NRL Network Research Navigator, strong on technical aspects of networking (`http://netlab.itd.nrl.navy.mil`)
- Stanford: Stanford Medical School Internet Page (`http://med-www.stanford.edu/hypertext/net/Net.html`)
- The Net: descriptions of how to access information through Mosaic/Web, by Robert Thau (`http://www.ai.mit.edu/the-net/overview.html`)
- Stanford WWW Links: a variety of resource links, by Don Geddis (`http://www.stanford.edu/otherLinks.html`)
- Tractatus CyberNauticus: information about the Internet and the Web, by Denys Duchier (`http://kam1.csi.uottawa.ca:3000/tractatus.html`)
- Yale: General Overview of Worldwide Internet Resources (`http://www.cs.yale.edu/HTML/WorldWideWebTop.html`)
- U of TX: Internet Information Resources, from the University of Texas (`http://fiat.gslis.utexas.edu/internet/internet.html`)
- Yahoo's Internet: pointers to the subject classification Computers-Internet (`http://akebono.stanford.edu/yahoo/Computers/Internet/`)

Specialized Guides of General Interest

- Dern's Info: Daniel Dern's Internet Info, News and Views (`gopher://gopher.internet.com:2200/11/`)
- Agricultural Guide: Not Just Cows, by Wilfred Drew (`gopher://snymorva.cs.snymor.edu/hhGOPHER_ROOT1:[LIBRARY-DOCS.HTML]`)

Navigators

- GNN: Global Network Navigator from O'Reilly (`http://gnn.com`)

- Hytelnet: assists users in reaching Internet libraries, Free-nets, CWISs, BBSs, and other information sites by telnet, by Peter Scott (`http://www.cc.ukans.edu/hytelnet_html/START.TXT.html`)
- NetLink: connects you with a wide variety of services (`http://netlink.wlu.edu:1020`)
- Nova Links: Nova Southeastern University, in Ft. Lauderdale Florida (`http://alpha.acast.nova.edu/start.html`)
- WorldWindow: a service of the Washington University Libraries (`telnet://library.wustl.edu`)

Searching

New or Noteworthy

- Best of Web: a gallery of best of Web Award Winners (`http://wings.buffalo.edu/contest`)
- Best of GNN: Global Network Navigator's Best of honorees (`http://nearnet.gnn.com/gnn/meta/internet/feat/best.html`)
- Best of/PC Week: a collection of sites from PC Week Labs (`http://www.ziff.com/~pcweek/pcwbests.html`)
- Commerce New: what is new in commercial services on the Web (`http://tns-www.lcs.mit.edu/commerce/whatsnew.html`)
- CUI W3 Catalog: changes to the various W3 Catalog sources for the past week (`http://cui_www.unige.ch/W3catalog/changes.html`)
- Fishnet: a weekly list of odds and ends of postings and information from the Internet (`http://www.cs.washington.edu/homes/pauld/fishnet/`)
- InfoBank: InfoBank's collection of new lists (`http://www.clark.net/pub/global/new.html`)
- Infobot: hotlist database (`ftp://ftp.netcom.com/pub/ksedgwic/hotlist/hotlist.html`)
- Net-Happenings: archives of a moderated mailing list that announces conferences, publications, newsletters, network tools updates, and network resources (`http://www-iub.indiana.edu/cgi-bin/nethaps/`)
- New NIR: new network information resources from the NEWNIR-L mailing list (`http://www-chem.ucdavis.edu/nir/nirwww.html`)
- NovaLinks New: What's New on the Internet collection (`http://alpha.acast.nova.edu/misc/netnews.html`)

■ Scout Report: a weekly publication offered by InterNIC Information Services to the Internet community as a fast, convenient way to stay informed on network activities (`http://www.internic.net/scout-report/`)

■ Useful/cool things: daily showcase of one pointer to something useful on the Internet, and one pointer to something cool (`http://www.teleport.com/~lynsared/useful.html`)

■ webNews search: a database of recent articles from Usenet news about the Web (`gopher://twinbrook.cis.uab.edu/7GO/webNews.70`)

■ What's New/Meta: a list of what's new pages, by Meng Weng Wong (`http://www.seas.upenn.edu/~mengwong/whatsnew.list.html`)

■ What's New/Web: What's New With NCSA Mosaic; actually shows Web-wide new resources (`http://www.ncsa.uiuc.edu/SDG/Software/Mosaic/Docs/whats-new.html`)

■ Yahoo new: What's New on Yahoo Hierarchical Hotlist (`http://akebono.stanford.edu/yahoo/new.html`)

Resource Lists

■ ALICE: Annotated Listings for Internet and Cyberspace Explorers (`http://www.umanitoba.ca/ALICE/index.html`)

■ Awesome List: a list of useful resources, by John Makulowich (`http://www.clark.net/pub/journalism/awesome.html`)

■ CMC resources: resources related to the study of Computer-Mediated Communication, from the CMC Studies Center (`http://www.rpi.edu/~decemj/cmc/resources.html`)

■ December List: information describing the Internet and computer-mediated communication technologies, applications, culture, discussion forums, and bibliographies, by John December (`http://www.rpi.edu/Internet/Guides/decemj/icmc/top.html`)

■ Drakos List: Subjective Electronic Information Repository, by Nikos Drakos (`http://cbl.leeds.ac.uk/nikos/doc/repository.html`)

■ Email Services: a list of services available via email, by David DeSimone (`ftp://sunsite.unc.edu/pub/docs/about-the-net/libsoft/email_services.txt`)

■ GNN's Internet Page: Internet information, from Global Network Navigator (`http://nearnet.gnn.com/wic/internet.toc.html`)

■ Hot/Cool List: What's Hot and Cool on the Web, art/music/interesting emphasis (`http://kzsu.stanford.edu/uwi/reviews.html`)

- InfoBank: Information Bank's collection of Internet resources links (`http://www.clark.net/pub/global/front.html`)

- Internet/Disk: reference information about the Internet (`http://www.eff.org/pub/Publications/CuD/Internet_on_a_Disk`)

- Internet-EIT: Enterprise Integration Technologies Web Resources (`http://www.eit.com/web/web.html`)

- Internet FAQ: Internet Services Frequently Asked Questions (FAQ) list for `alt.internet.services` Usenet newsgroup (`ftp://rtfm.mit.edu/pub/usenet/news.answers/internet-services/faq`)

- Internet Meta-Index: Internet Resources Meta-Index, from the National Center for Supercomputing Applications (NCSA) (`http://www.ncsa.uiuc.edu/SDG/Software/Mosaic/MetaIndex.html`)

- MaasInfo Indexes: The index of indexes of Internet online files, by Robert Elton Maas (`ftp://NCTUCCCA.edu.tw/documents/Internet/MaasInfo/`)

- May List: lists telnet sites/services, by CC May (`ftp://aug3.augsburg.edu/files/bbs_lists/nal008.txt`)

- Planet Earth: Planet Earth home page, a list of things on the Internet, by Richard Bocker (`http://white.nosc.mil/info.html`)

- Power Index: from Web Communications, lists a variety of resources in many categories (`http://www.webcom.com/power/index.html`)

- Smith's BigFun List: telnet, FTP, and other sites, by Jeremy Smith (`ftp://owl.nstn.ns.ca/pub/netinfo/bigfun.txt`)

- ThesisNet FAQ: a summary of academic resources pertaining to cyberspace (`http://www.seas.upenn.edu/~mengwong/thesisfaq.html#ftp`)

- Thousand/Sites: A Thousand Points of Sites, a random way (!) to encounter web sites (`http://legendre.ucsd.edu/Research/Fisher/Home/randomjump.html`)

- Tong's Collection: Links to other sites, a miscellaneous collection of information and entertainment, by Andrew Tong (`http://www.ugcs.caltech.edu/~werdna/info.html`)

- Yale Overview: General Overview of Worldwide Internet Resources (`http://www.cs.yale.edu/HTML/WorldWideWebTop.html`)

- Yanoff List HTML: hyptertext markup language version of Scott Yanoff's Special Internet Connections listing of resources by subject (`http://www.uwm.edu/Mirror/inet.services.html`)

- Websurf: includes a variety of links to web information, personal pages (`http://pubweb.ucdavis.edu/Documents/Quotations/web/websurf.html`)

■ WWW/Internet: a collection of links to manuals and demos (`http://tecfa.unige.ch/info-www.html`)

Subjects

■ CERN's Virtual Library: a large hypertext collection of information organized by subject (`http://info.cern.ch/hypertext/DataSources/bySubject/Overview.html`)

■ CSOIRG Home Page: The Clearinghouse for Subject-Oriented Internet Resource Guides at the University of Michigan chool of Information and Library Studies (`http://www.lib.umich.edu/chhome.html`)

■ CyberNet: unique subjects on the net (`http://venus.mcs.com/~flowers/html/gcybernet.html`)

■ DA-CLOD: a categorized database of links to subject-oriented information on the Internet (`http://schiller.wustl.edu/DACLOD/daclod`)

■ Galaxy: a service of EINet, a collection of information, searchable via index or by topic trees (`http://www.einet.net/galaxy.html`)

■ GNN WIC: Global Network Navigator's Whole Internet Catalog, from O'Reilly and Associates (`http://nearnet.gnn.com/wic/newrescat.toc.html`)

■ Gopher Jewels web: a collection of subject-specific gophers (`http://galaxy.einet.net/GJ/index.html`)

■ Internet at Large: subject-oriented listing (`http://www.sdsc.edu/1/SDSC/Geninfo/Internet`)

■ IWT Narrative: Internet Web Text's narrative about subject-oriented searching (`http://www.rpi.edu/Internet/Guides/decemj/nar-subject.html`)

■ Joel's List: Joel's Hierarchical Subject Index (`http://www.cen.uiuc.edu/~jj9544/index.html`)

■ Lib/Congress: US Library of Congress code for classifying resources on the Net (`gopher://info.anu.edu.au/11/elibrary/lc`)

■ Mother/BBS: Mother of all BBSs, a project to allow users to add information to a subject tree, developed by Oliver McBryan (`http://www.cs.colorado.edu/homes/mcbryan/public_html/bb/summary.html`)

■ Planet Earth: Richard P. Bocker created this web to collect a wide variety of Internet resources (`http://white.nosc.mil/info.html`)

■ Subject Lists: Resources Classified by Subject (LC Classification) (`gopher://info.anu.edu.au:70/11/elibrary/lc`)

- UMBC Web: University of Maryland-Baltimore County, exceptional Internet based resources by subject category (`http://umbc7.umbc.edu/~jack/subject-list.html`)
- USENET FAQ Index: forms-based gateway to usenet FAQs, by INTAC (`http://www.intac.com/FAQ.html`)
- USENET news.answers: a hypertext presentation of the answer lists posted in the news.answers newsgroup (`http://www.cis.ohio-state.edu/hypertext/faq/usenet/FAQ_List.html`)
- Waterloo Web: lists the academic departments at the University of Waterloo and useful net resources for each (`http://www.lib.uwaterloo.ca/~nrc/template.html`)
- WAIS Servers: directory of wide area information servers (`wais:/cnidr.org:210/directory-of-servers?`).
- WAIS sources: a collection of WAIS sources (`gopher://liberty.uc.wlu.edu/11/internet/indexsearches/inetsearches`)
- WSPS: Web Self-Publishing System, a publicly updatable database of resources (URL's) on the internet organized using a hierarchy of groups, facility for adding (`http://sparc57.cs.uiuc.edu:8000`)
- Yahoo: Yet Another Hierarchically Odiferous Oracle, an extendible collection of subjects (`http://akebono.stanford.edu/yahoo/`)
- Yanoff List HTML: hyptertext markup language version of Scott Yanoff's Special Internet Connections listing of resources by subject (`http://www.uwm.edu/Mirror/inet.services.html`)

Keyword

- Academic lists: searchable index of academic email conferences (`wais://munin.ub2.lu.se:210/academic_email_conf`)
- ALIWEB: Archie-Like Indexing for the Web, by Martijn Koster (`http://web.nexor.co.uk/aliweb/doc/aliweb.html`)
- Archieplex: Archie via Web-Access Archie servers (search FTP sites) via the web (`http://web.nexor.co.uk/archie.html`)
- CUSI: SUSI, by Martijn Kosterrch interface; a forms-based interface into many indices, engines, and Web Spider databases (`http://web.nexor.co.uk/susi/cusi.html`)
- Discussion groups: search a list of discussion groups, Bitnet and Internet interest groups (Dartmouth list) (`http://alpha.acast.nova.edu/cgi-bin/lists`)

■ External info: collects some of the most useful search engines available on the WWW (`http://www_is.cs.utwente.nl:8080/cgi-bin/local/nph-susi1.pl`)

■ Gopher Jewels Search: Search the Gopher Jewels (a collection of subject-oriented gophers) (`http://galaxy.einet.net/gopher/gopher.html`)

■ GNA Meta-Library: search the Globalwide Networking Academy (GNA) library of resources and information (`http://uu-nna.mit.edu:8001/uu-nna/meta-library/index.html`)

■ Hytelnet Web search: search all Hytelnet resource entries, via a web form, from Galaxy (`http://galaxy.einet.net/hytelnet/HYTELNET.html`)

■ JumpStation: referencing the information available on the World Wide Web (`http://www.stir.ac.uk/jsbin/js`)

■ SIMON: Searchable Index (`http://web.elec.qmw.ac.uk:12121/server/search.html`)

■ WAISGATE: WAIS to WWW gateway, search WAIS databases through search terms (`http://server.wais.com/directory-of-servers.html`)

■ Web Catalog/CUI: is a collection of URL references built from a number of hand-crafted HTML lists, from Centre Universitaire d'Informatique, l'Universite de Geneve (`http://cui_www.unige.ch/cgi-bin/w3catalogcui_www.unige.ch/cgi-bin/w3catalog`)

■ Web Search Engines: a meta-index of search engines on the Web, with a forms interface, from Centre Universitaire d'Informatique, l'Universite de Geneve (`http://cui_www.unige.ch/meta-index.html`)

■ Web Spiders info: search the web for information about resources, collecting information into a database which can be queried; e.g., Web Crawler, Web Nomad, Web Worm, RBSE database, Lycos (Araneida, Lycosidae, Lycosa), Harvest Brokers; entry from Internet Tools Summary (`http://www.rpi.edu/Internet/Guides/decemj/itools/nir-tools-spiders.html`)

■ Web Spiders web: Wanderers, Spiders, and Robots; includes list of known robots/spiders, guidelines, standard for robot exclusion, by Martijn Koster (`http://web.nexor.co.uk/mak/doc/robots/robots.html`)

Spaces

■ FTP sites Web: the "monster" list of FTP sites (`http://hoohoo.ncsa.uiuc.edu/ftp-interface.html`)

■ Gopher sites: list of all Gophers (long) (`ftp://liberty.uc.wlu.edu/pub/lawlib/all.gophers.links`)

- telnet-hytelnet: (`telnet://hytelnet@access.usask.ca`)
- list of lists: interest groups (`ftp://sri.com/netinfo/interest-groups`)
- list of lists/email: interests groups (`mailto:MAIL-SERVER@SRI.COM Body: send interest-groups.txt`)
- MUDS: mudlis* files list MUDs (`ftp://caisr2.caisr.cwru.edu/pub/mud/`)
- WAIS servers: Wide Area Information Server to Web gateway (`http://www.wais.com/directory-of-servers.html`)
- Web Servers: a long list of registered WWW servers listed alphabetically by continent and country (`http://info.cern.ch/hypertext/DataSources/WWW/Servers.html`)
- Web Sites (Virtual Tourist): a geographic map to aid in locationg Web sites and other resources (`http://wings.buffalo.edu/world`)
- Web sites index: index to WWW sites, by John Doyle (`http://herald.usask.ca/~scottp/home.html`)

People

- Directory services: a collection of white pages servers to look up people (`gopher://gopher.nd.edu/11/Non-Notre%20Dame%20Information%20Sources/Phone%20Books-Other%20Institutions`)
- Finding people: a collection of resources to help you locate a specific person on the Net (`gopher://yaleinfo.yale.edu/11/Internet/People`)
- Home Pages: a collection of personal home pages lists (`http://www.rpi.edu/Internet/Guides/decemj/icmc/culture-people-lists.html`)
- Knowbot: provides a uniform user interface to heterogeneous remote information services (Internic Point of contacts, MCImail, x500 databases, finger, nwhois, etc.) (`telnet://info.cnri.reston.va.us:185`)
- Netfind: a simple Internet "white pages" user directory (`http://www.rpi.edu/Internet/Guides/decemj/itools/nir-utilities-netfind.html`)
- Searching for People: e-mail addresses, phone books, from Washington and Lee (`gopher://liberty.uc.wlu.edu/11/internet/personsearches`). 1.6 Directories
- American Universities: (`http://www.clas.ufl.edu/CLAS/american-universities.html`)
- CS Depts: (`http://www.cs.cmu.edu:8001/Web/People/anwar/CS-departments.html`)
- CWIS Web: a listing of Campus-Wide information systems, by Polly-Alida Farrington (`http://www.rpi.edu/Internet/cwis.html`)

■ Commercial List: List of Commercial Services on the Web (`http://tns-www.lcs.mit.edu/commerce.html`)

■ Dartmouth Merged SIGL: Special Interest Group Lists (`ftp://dartcms1.dartmouth.edu/siglists/`)

■ Electronic Conferences: browse or search the Directory of Scholarly Electronic Conferences, by Diane K. Kovacs (`http://www.austin.unimelb.edu.au:800/1s/acad`)

■ Electronic Conferences: gopher presentation of the Directory of Scholarly Electronic Conferences, by Diane K. Kovacs (`gopher://info.monash.edu.au/11/Other/lists`)

■ Electronic Zines/Jrl: An Index to Electronic Journals and Zines (`http://www.acns.nwu.edu/ezines`)

■ Electronic Journals/ARL: Association of Research Libraries Directory of Electronic Journals and Newsletters (`gopher://arl.cni.org:70/11/scomm/edir`)

■ Electronic Journals/Strangelove: Directory of Electronic Journals and Newsletters, by Michael Strangelove (`ftp://ftp.cni.org/pub/net-guides/strangelove/`)

■ Electronic Magazines/archive: an archive of various electronic magazines (`ftp://etext.archive.umich.edu/pub/Zines/`)

■ Electronic Resources: lists resources (CWIS, texts, guides, WWW, WAIS, etc.) by University of Waterloo Library (`gopher://watserv2.uwaterloo.ca/11/servers`)

■ EZines List: summary of electronically-accessible zines, by John Labovitz (`ftp://etext.archive.umich.edu/pub/Zines/e-zine-list`)

■ EZines Web: summary of electronic zines by John Labovitz (`http://www.ora.com:8080/johnl/e-zine-list/`)

■ Finding Lists: how to find LISTSERV lists (`mailto:listserv@vm1.nodak.edu` `Body: get NEW-LIST wouters`)

■ Free-Nets Home Page: Free-net information, presented as a public service by Peter Scott, at the University of Saskatchewan Libraries (`http://herald.usask.ca/~scottp/free.html`)

■ Free Databases: a catalog databases that are available without payment (`ftp://idiom.berkeley.ca.us/pub/free-databases`)

■ Internet Computer Index: lists of PC, Macintosh, and UNIX-related resources (`http://ici.proper.com`)

■ Interest Groups List: The Lists of Lists, a listing of special interest group mailing lists available on the Internet (`ftp://sri.com/netinfo/interest-groups.txt`)

- Japanese: key information sources on Japan currently available over the Internet (`http://fuji.stanford.edu/japan_information/japan_information_guide.html`)

- Net Orgs: Outposts on the Electronic Frontier, International, Groups Supporting the Online Community (`ftp://rtfm.mit.edu/pub/usenet/news.answers/net-community/orgs-list`)

- Nonprofits: Nonprofit Organizations on the Internet, by Ellen Spertus (`http://www.ai.mit.edu/people/ellens/non.html`)

- Online books: On-line books (`http://www.cs.cmu.edu:8001/Web/books.html`)

- Online bibs: On-line Bibliographies and Journal Contents (`http://www.cs.cmu.edu:8001/Web/bibliographies.html`)

- Online journals: On-line Journals (`http://www.cs.cmu.edu:8001/Web/journals.html`)

- Online libraries: (`http://www.cs.cmu.edu:8001/Web/e-libraries.html`)

- PAML: Publicly Available Mailing Lists, by Stephanie da Silva (`http://www.ii.uib.no/~magnus/paml.html`)

- Publisher's Catalogs: (`http://jester.usask.ca/~scottp/publish.html`)

- Reference: Reference Resources via the World Wide Web (`http://vm.cfsan.fda.gov/referenc.html`)

- Software downloads: publicly available sites for software (`http://alpha.acast.nova.edu/downloads.html`)

- Technical Reports: technical reports archive (`ftp://daneel.rdt.monash.edu.au/pub/techreports/`)

- Virtual Tourist: geographical directory of WWW Information Services (`http://wings.buffalo.edu/world`)

- WAIS sources: a brief description of the content of many WAIS sources on the Internet, grouped into relevant categories (`ftp://kirk.bond.edu.au/pub/Bond_Uni/doc/wais/readme`)

- WAIS Directory of Servers: (wais://cnidr.org:210/directory-of-servers?)

- WAIS Databases: a hypertext list (`http://kaml1.csi.uottawa.ca:3000/wais.html`)

- WWW Catalogues: A collection of WWW Home pages in many areas, by Oliver McBryan (`http://www.cs.colorado.edu/homes/mcbryan/public_html/bb/summary.html`)

- WWW Sites: comprehensive list-a long list of WWW sites gathered through an automated program, Webwanderer, by Matthew Gray (`http://www.mit.edu:8001/afs/sipb/user/mkgray/ht/compre3.html`)

APPLICATIONS

People use the Internet and Web for many purposes and applications. Part IV of this book contains detailed discussions of some of these applications. The listing here includes examples of applications as well as pointers to information about Internet and Web-based applications in the following areas:

- Commerce: information about commerce on the Internet and Web as well as resource lists to locate additional marketplaces.
- Communication: information about applications for individual, group, organizational, mass, societal, surveillance, and scientific communication.
- Education: resource lists and information about schools on the Net.
- Entertainment: some example lists of fun resources.
- Government: information about intiatives for national information infrastructures, and pointers to information supplied by governments.
- Information: dissemination and retrieval and library applications.
- Scholarship: information and pointers to organizations concerned with online scholarship.

Commerce

Information

- Business/Corporations: lists of business and corporations on the Net (http://akebono.stanford.edu/yahoo/Economy/Business/Corporations/)
- Business sites: Interesting Business Sites on the Web, by Bob O'Keefe at the School of Management, Rensselaer Polytechnic Institute (http://www.rpi.edu/~okeefe/business.html)
- Business uses: Commercial Use (of the net) Strategies Home Page, by Andrew P. Dinsdale (http://pass.wayne.edu/business.html)
- Career Tech: high-tech companies offering career information (http://www.service.com:80/cm/)
- Commercial List: a longer list of many Commercial Services on the Web (http://tns-www.lcs.mit.edu/commerce.html)
- Commercial Services: from The World (gopher://gopher.std.com:70/11/Commercial)

- Computer+Communications: Computer and Communication Company Sites on the Web, by James E. (Jed) Donnelley (`http://www-atp.llnl.gov/companies.html`)
- Daily business news: daily sources of business and economic news (`http://www.helsinki.fi/~lsaarine/news.html`)
- Entrepeneurs: useful business information and services for entrepreneurs (`http://sashimi.wwa.com/~notime/eotw/EOTW.html`)
- FITC: Fairfax Information Technology Center; Continous Acquisition Lifecycle Support (CALS); enterprise integration, electronic commerce and business processing, re-engineering (`http://axil1.csrc.gmu.edu`)
- IBC: Internet Business Center is a World-Wide Web server for information specifically related to business use of the Internet (`http://www.tig.com/IBC/`)
- IBD: Internet Business Directory, product/service information (`http://ibd.ar.com`)
- Stock Quotes: QuoteCom, a service dedicated to providing financial market data to Internet users (`http://www.quote.com`)
- Thomas Ho: favorite Economic Commerce WWW resources (`http://biomed.nus.sg/people/commmenu.html`)
- Virtual Inc: lists of companies on the Net (`http://www.peregrine.com/web/virtual/welcome.html`)
- What's New/Commerce: what is new in commercial services on the Web (`http://tns-www.lcs.mit.edu/commerce/whatsnew.html`)

Marketplaces

Lists of Marketplaces

Yahoo Marketplaces list: (`http://akebono.stanford.edu/yahoo/Economy/Business/Corporations/markets/`)

Some Instances of Marketplaces

- CommerceNet: Internet-based infrastructure for electronic commerce, created and operated by a consortium of major Silicon Valley users, providers and developers under Smart Valley, Inc. (`http://logic.stanford.edu/cit/commercenet.html`)
- Digital's Emall: Digital Equipment Corporation's Electronic Shopping Mall (`http://www.service.digital.com/html/emall.html`)

- GNN Marketplace: Global Network Navigator (GNN) Marketplace (`http://nearnet.gnn.com/gnn/mkt/mkt.intro.html`)
- Global City: books, hardware, software, and a variety of services (`http://kaleidoscope.bga.com/km/KM_top.html`)
- Internet Mall: Shopping on the Information Highway A monthly list of commercial services available via the Internet (`ftp://netcom.com/pub/Guides/`)
- Internet Plaza: Internet services for companies that would like to sell products online or provide information about products online (`http://xor.com/plaza/index.html`)
- Internet Shopping Network: products from hundres of vendors, along with query interface (`http://shop.internet.net`)
- MecklerWeb: a communication and marketing system (`http://www.mecklerweb.com/demo.html`)

Communication

Individual

- CMC-Interpersonal: list of interpersonal tools for CMC (mail, talk) (`http://www.rpi.edu/Internet/Guides/decemj/itools/cmc-interpersonal.html`)
- Home Pages: a collection of personal home pages lists (`http://www.rpi.edu/Internet/Guides/decemj/icmc/culture-people-lists.html`)

Group

- CCCC: Computerized Conferencing and Communications Center at New Jersey Institute of Technology (NJIT) (`http://it.njit.edu/njIT/Department/CCCC/default.html`)
- Collaborative Comm: Collaborative Networked Communication-MUDs as Systems Tools, by Remy Evard (`http://www.ccs.neu.edu/USER/remy/documents/cncmast.html`)
- CRTR-U of CO: Collaboration Technology Research Group (group user interfaces, distributed editors, workflow systems, cooperativee grown information systems), University of Colorado (`http://www.cs.colorado.edu/homes/carlosm/public_html/ctrg.html`)
- CoMMedia: Cooperation, Communication and Multimedia program, Norway (`http://www.ludvigsen.dhhalden.no/webdoc/this_server.html#commedia`)

- Communication Archive Web: Sunsite Communication archive-papers, logs, information, including April Fools Page, maintained by David Barberi (`http://sunsite.unc.edu/dbarberi/communications.html`)
- HyperNews: readers respond to any articles they read in the HyperNews web (`http://ginko.cecer.army.mil:8000/hypernews/hypernews.html`)
- Internet Citizen's Band: Internet group teleconfrencing program (`http://www.echo.com/~kzin/icb.html`)
- Internet Relay Chat(IRC): real-time, many-many text discussion divided into channels (`ftp://cs.bu.edu/irc/support/`)
- IRC FAQ: Internet Relay Chat Frequently Asked Questions and Answers (`http://www.kei.com/irc.html`)
- MOO Papers: Pavel Curtis' collection of MU* papers (`ftp://ftp.parc.xerox.com/pub/MOO/papers/`)
- MUD resources: Generic MUD Resource Page, MUDs with WWW pages; MUD pages, archives, gophers, services (`http://bunda.gb.nrao.edu/muds/muds.html`)
- NCW: National Center for the Workplace (NCW) Gopher (`gopher://uclink.berkeley.edu:3030/1`)
- Project H: an ongoing computer-mediated collaboration, on a Comserve-sponsored hotline, of more than a hundred international researchers (`http://www.arch.su.edu.au/PROJECTH/index.html`)
- SHARE: A Methodology and Environment for Collaborative Product Development (`http://www.eit.com/projects/share/share/share-home.html`)
- Tools: a list of Internet tools for group communication (`http://www.rpi.edu/Internet/Guides/decemj/itools/cmc-group.html`)

Organizational

- CORPS: Computing, Organizations, Policy, and Society, study of computerization in organizations, Information and Computer Science, University of California, Irvine (`http://www.ics.uci.edu/CORPS/`)
- CWIS Web: a listing of Campus-Wide information systems, by Polly-Alida Farrington (`http://www.rpi.edu/Internet/cwis.html`)

Mass

Lists

- Campus Newspapers: Campus Newspapers on the Internet, by Jonathan Bell (`http://ednews2.asa.utk.edu/papers.html`)
- Internet news: Internet accessible news, Newspapers, tv, radio, press services, and publications, by C. Sam Sternberg (`ftp://ftp.shell.portal.com/pub/jshunter/news.html`)
- Commercial News/Web: a list of commercial news services on the WWW, by Gary Ritzenthaler (`http://www.jou.ufl.edu/commres/webjou.htm`)
- Communication Resources: Communications and Mass Media Resources, links, reviews, and resources for scholars and those interested in Journalism, Mass Media, and Communications Research, by Steve Brown (`http://www.jou.ufl.edu/commres/commhome.htm`)
- CyberNews: student-run media connectivity, newsire on the Internet (`http://www.hmc.edu/www/people/teverett/cybernews/Home.html`)
- Daily business: daily sources of business and economic news (`http://www.helsinki.fi/~lsaarine/news.html`)
- GSN: Global Student Newswire, a collaboration of student journalists, by Gary Ritzenthaler (`http://www.jou.ufl.edu/forums/gsn/`)
- Journalism: Journalism List of Internet Resources, by John S. Makulowich (`ftp://rtfm.mit.edu/pub/usenet/news.answers/journalism-net-resources`)
- Media List FTP: e-mail addresses of media outlets, by Adam Gaffin (`ftp://ftp.std.com/customers/periodicals/Middlesex-News/medialist`)
- Movies and TV: Nova Link's Movies and TV information (`http://alpha.acast.nova.edu/movies.html`)
- Periodicals: electronic periodicals and journals (`gopher://gopher.cic.net/11/e-serials`)
- SPJ: Society of Professional Journalists (`ftp://netcom5.netcom.com/pub/spj/html/spj.html`)
- TV Schedules: the schedules of some television channels/shows (`http://white.nosc.mil/television.html`)
- Tools: a list of Internet tools for mass communication (`http://www.rpi.edu/Internet/Guides/decemj/itools/cmc-mass.html`)

Application Areas

- ■ Amateur Radio: (http://www.mcc.ac.uk/OtherPages/AmateurRadio.html)
- ■ Ham Radio: (http://www.acs.ncsu.edu:80/HamRadio)
- ■ Live TV: demonstration consists of live video and audio using the vsdemo VuSystem application that uses a live television source on the VuNet (http://tns-www.lcs.mit.edu/cgi-bin/vs/vsdemo)
- ■ Satellite: The Satellite TV Page (http://itre.uncecs.edu/misc/sat.html)

Outlets

- ■ BBC Networking Club: (http://www.bbcnc.org.uk)
- ■ C-SPAN: Cable-Satellite Public Affairs Network (gopher://c-span.org)
- ■ CBC Home Page: Canadian Broadcasting Corporation (http://debra.dgbt.doc.ca/cbc/cbc.html)
- ■ ITR: Internet Talk Radio (http://www.ncsa.uiuc.edu/radio/radio.html)
- ■ Cyberspace Report: a public affairs radio show aired on KUCI, 88.9 FM in Irvine, California (http://www.ics.uci.edu/~ejw/csr/cyber.html)
- ■ PBS: United States Public Broadcasting Service (gopher://gopher.pbs.org)
- ■ Palo Alto Weekly: (http://www.service.com/PAW/home.html)
- ■ USA Today: news summaries (http://alpha.acast.nova.edu/usatoday.html)
- ■ VOA gopher: Voice of America (USA) (gopher://gopher.voa.gov)

Societal

- ■ Cyberpunk: texts for understanding technology and culture, from the English Server (http://english-server.hss.cmu.edu/Cyber.html)
- ■ Friends + Partners: USA and Russia information and communication (http://solar.rtd.utk.edu/friends/home.html)
- ■ Net Revisited: The Network Nation Revisited, a bachelor's thesis examining Hiltz and Turoff's predictions for CMC on societal change, by David Belson (http://www.stevens-tech.edu/~dbelson/thesis/thesis.html)

Surveillance

- ■ bsy's List: Internet Accessible (non-Coke) Machines, connections to many surveillance and remote sensing examples (http://www.cs.cmu.edu:8001/afs/cs.cmu.edu/user/bsy/www/iam.html)

■ Camera in office: Spy on Dennis Gannon, Research Director of Center for Innovative Computer Applications (`http://www.cica.indiana.edu/htbin/camera`)

■ SurfNet: a window to the world's beaches (`gopher://sailfish.peregrine.com/surf/surf.html`)

■ Temperature: Temperature on CU/Boulder Engineering Center Roof (`http://www.cs.colorado.edu/htbin/temp`)

Scientific

■ CS Tech Reports: Computer Science Technical Reports Archive Sites (`http://www.rdt.monash.edu.au/tr/siteslist.html`)

■ EnviroWeb: environmental information source on the Internet (`http://envirolink.org`)

■ NAS web: National Academy of Sciences (`http://www.nas.edu`)

■ SPIE Web: services from The International Society for Optical Engineering (SPIE) (`http://www.spie.org`)

■ WATERS: Wide Area Technical Report Service (`http://www.cs.odu.edu/WATERS/WATERS-GS.html`)

Education

■ AskERIC Web: Educational Resources Information Center, Clearinghouse on Information and Technology, federally-funded collection of education-related resources (`http://eryx.syr.edu/Main.html`)

■ Center/Excellence: Center for Excellence in Education, to help our best students and teachers keep the United States competitive in science and technology, and to nuture international understanding among potential leaders of many countries (`http://rsi.cee.org`)

■ CERN Education: virtual library entry for education (`http://info.cern.ch/hypertext/DataSources/bySubject/Education/Overview.html`)

■ Chronicle web: ACADEME THIS WEEK, offers guide to contents of The Chronicle of Higher Education and all Positions Available ads, calendar of events, deadlines for grants, papers, fellowships, put out every Tuesday at noon EST (`http://chronicle.merit.edu`)

■ Cisco: education archive (`http://sunsite.unc.edu/cisco/edu-arch.html`)

- CITD: Centre for Instructional Technology Development, Bladen Library at Scarborough Campus, University of Toronto (`http://library-www.scar.utoronto.ca/CITD/CITD.html`)

- COL: Commonwealth of Learning, distance education techniques and associated communications technologies (`http://www.col.org`)

- CoVis: Learning Through Collaborative Visualization, Northwestern University (`http://www.covis.nwu.edu`)

- DeweyWeb: facilitating communication between students from all over the world (`http://ics.soe.umich.edu`)

- Dr. E's Compendium: Dr. E's Eclectic Compendium of Electronic Resources for Adult/Distance Education, by J. H. Ellsworth (`ftp://ftp.std.com/pub/je/dre-list.txt`)

- NDLC: National (USA) Distance Learning Center (`telnet://ndlc@ndlc.occ.uky.edu`)

- Distance Ed DB: contains full text of *Mindweave*, edited by Mason and Kaye (`telnet://icdl@acsvax.open.ac.uk`)

- Diversity U Web: a web-page front-end to Diversity University, an experiment in interactive learning through internet, Web page by Andrew Dinsdale (`http://pass.wayne.edu/DU.html`)

- EOS web: Educational Online Sources, pointers for education, from Brown University (`http://netspace.students.brown.edu/eos1/`)

- Educational Technology: The World-Wide Web Virtual Library-Educational Technology (`http://tecfa.unige.ch/info-edu-comp.html`)

- Education Technology Initiatives: Higher Education Funding Councils for England, Wales, Scotland and Northern Ireland now support three major initiatives in the UK which are aimed at improving universities' awareness and use of technological innovations in teaching and learning (`gopher://gopher.csv.warwick.ac.uk/11/remote/other-remote/edu-tech`)

- Empire Schoolhouse: Empire Internet Schoolhouse, a selection of K-12 resources, projects and discussion groups (`gopher://nysernet.org:3000/11/`)

- EnviroWeb: a project of the EnviroLink Network, sponsors many online environmental education initiatives (`http://envirolink.org`)

- ETB/NLM: Educational Technology Branch (ETB), part of the Lister Hill National Center for Biomedical Communications (LHNCBC) at the National Library of Medicine (NLM) (`http://wwwetb.nlm.nih.gov`)

- Exploratorium: a collage of 650 interactive exhibits in the areas of science, art, and human perception (`http://www.exploratorium.edu`)

- Galaxy education: collection of resources about education from EINet Galaxy (`http://galaxy.einet.net/galaxy/Social-Sciences/Education.html`)

- GENII: Group Exploring the National Information Infrastructure (`http://www.deakin.edu.au/edu/MSEE/GENII/GENII-Home-Page.html`)

- GNA: Globewide Network Academy, a non-profit corporation, affiliated with Usenet University; goal is to create an fully accredited online university (`http://uu-nna.mit.edu:8001/uu-gna/index.html`)

- HUB: mathematics and science education (`http://hub.terc.edu`)

- iCDL: International Centre for Distance Learning, in the United Kingdom on the campus of the Open University, disseminating distance education information worldwide (`http://acs-info.open.ac.uk/info/other/ICDL/ICDL-Facts.html`)

- IKE Web: IBM Kiosk for Education (`http://ike.engr.washington.edu/ike.html`)

- ILT: Institute for Learning Technologies as part of the Columbia University Virtual Information Initiative (`http://www.ilt.tc.columbia.edu`)

- ILC-Southampton: Interactive Learning Centre, University of Southampton, United Kingdom (`http://ilc.ecs.soton.ac.uk/welcome.html`)

- JASON Project web: A journey to the rain forest, caverns, Mayan ruins and coral reef of Belize (`http://seawifs.gsfc.nasa.gov/JASON/JASON.html`)

- KidLink: gopher aimed at 10-15 year olds (`gopher://kids.ccit.duq.edu`)

- K-12/Armadillo: annotated directory of K-12 resources from Rice University (`http://chico.rice.edu/armadillo/Rice/K12resources.html`)

- K-12 Info/CNIDR: includes global schoolhouse project and Janice's K12 Cyberspace Outpost (`http://k12.cnidr.org`)

- K-12 Briarwood: collection of K-12 resources of the Internet, including a Curriculum Database (`gopher://gopher.briarwood.com`)

- K-12 NASA/Langley: NASA Langley Research Center's HPCC K-12 Program (`http://k12mac.larc.nasa.gov/hpcck12home.html`)

- K-12 NASA/NAS: pointers to online Educational Resources, by Chris Beaumont (`http://www.nas.nasa.gov/HPCC/K12/edures.html`)

- K-12 Schools on Internet: pointers to information service for school or school district (`http://big-bird.pomona.claremont.edu/schools.html`)

- LRDC: Learning Research and Development Center at the University of Pittsburgh-thinking, knowing, and understanding in and beyond school (`http://www.lrdc.pitt.edu`)

- NCSA education: National Center for Supercomputing Applications Education Program Home Page (`http://www.ncsa.uiuc.edu/Edu/EduHome.html`)
- Maricopa: Center for Learning and Instruction, Maricopa Community Colleges, Arizona (`http://hakatai.mcli.dist.maricopa.edu`)
- NCET: National Council for Educational Technology Information Service (UK) (`http://datasun.ncet.org.uk`)
- OISE Gopher: Ontario Institute for Studies in Education (`gopher://porpoise.oise.on.ca:70`)
- Online LC: Mount Allison University's Online Learning Centre-tele-education (`gopher://pringle.mta.ca`)
- Primary/Sec: Answers to Commonly Asked Primary and Secondary School Internet User Questions (`ftp://nic.merit.edu/documents/fyi/fyi_22.txt`)
- Teacher Education: Society for Technology and Teacher Education (STATE), the University of Virginia, and the University of Houston have collaborated to establish a Teacher Education Server on the Internet (`http://curry.edschool.virginia.edu/teis/`)
- TECFA: an academic team active in the field of educational technology at the School of Education and Psychology of the University of Geneva (`http://tecfa.unige.ch/tecfa-overview.html`)
- US Dept of Ed Web: United States Department of Education (`http://www.ed.gov`)
- USENET University: an online a society of people interested in learning, teaching or tutoring (`ftp://nic.funet.fi/pub/doc/uu/FAQ`)
- Web teaching: WWW for instructional use, a collection of course materials, from the University of Texas at Austin (`http://www.utexas.edu/world/instruction/index.html`)

Entertainment

- Coke Machines: bsy's List of Internet Accessible Coke Machines (`http://www.cs.cmu.edu:8001/afs/cs.cmu.edu/user/bsy/www/coke.html`)
- Games: Games FAQS and other entertainment resources (`http://wcl-rs.bham.ac.uk/GamesDomain`)
- Interactive games: Zarf's List of Interactive Games on the Web (`http://www.cs.cmu.edu:8001/afs/cs.cmu.edu/user/zarf/www/games.html`)
- WWW/Sports: World Wide Web of Sports, Spanning the globe to bring you a constant variety of sports information (`http://tns-www.lcs.mit.edu/cgi-bin/sports`)

■ Yohoo's: Entertainment section from Yohoo (`http://akebono.stanford.edu/yahoo/Entertainment/`)

Government

Initiatives for Information Infrastructures

These government-sponsored initiatives and organizations to implement or support national or state information infrastructures.

■ Canada: Industry Canada Ministry, Canadian Information Highway directory (`http://debra.dgbt.doc.ca/isc/isc.english.html`)

■ Europe: European Council report on specific measures to be taken by the European Community and the Members States for information infrastructures (`http://www.earn.net/EC/bangemann.html`)

■ France: Reseau National de Telecommunications pour la Technologie, l'Enseignement et la Recherche (`http://web.urec.fr/docs/renater/renater.html`)

■ Japan-IIJ: Internet Initiative Japan Inc. (`http://www.iij.ad.jp`)

■ Japan-MITI: Japan's Ministry of International Trade and Industry, program for advanced information infrastructure (`http://www.glocom.ac.jp/NEWS/MITI-doc.html`)

■ Singapore-IT200 Web: (`http://king.ncb.gov.sg/it2k/it2k.html`)

■ Singapore-ITI: Information Technology Institute (ITI), the applied R and D arm of the National Computer Board (NCB) of Singapore (`http://www.iti.gov.sg`)

■ USA-HPCC Web: the National Coordination Office (NCO) for High Performance Computing and Communications (`http://www.hpcc.gov`)

■ USA-Info highway: pointers to information about efforts to create information networks at government and private levels (`http://ai.iit.nrc.ca/superhighway.html`)

■ USA-NII DIIG: The Digital Information Infrastructure Guide (DIIG) is a resource to facilitate the development of the National Information Infrastructure (NII) (`http://farnsworth.mit.edu/diig.html`)

■ USA-NII Testbed: National Information Infrastructure Testbed (`http://www.esi.com/niit_top.html`)

■ USA-NII Web: The White House Information Infrastructure Task Force Web (`http://iitf.doc.gov`)

- USA-NII Related: Related Efforts in the National Information Infrastructure (`http://www.acl.lanl.gov/sunrise/RelatedInfo/OtherProjects.html`)
- USA-North Carolina: North Carolina Information Highway (NCIH) home page (`http://encore.concert.net/welcome.html`)

Information Supplied by Governments

Government-sponsored or government-related information, particularly dealing with CMC issues.

- Fedix: Federal Information Exchange, Inc., access to a wide variety of governemnt data (`http://www.fie.com`)
- Galaxy's Government info: page from EINet's Galaxy showing a large collection of government information (`http://www.einet.net/galaxy/Government.html`)
- GILS: Government Information Locator Service (`ftp://ftp.cni.org/pub/gils/`)
- Govt/Citizenship: information about federal agencies, guides, policy, and other government information (`gopher://eryx.syr.edu`)
- Govt Information: Internet Sources of Government Information by Blake Gumprecht (`ftp://ftp.nwnet.net/user-docs/government/gumprecht-guide.txt`)
- US Govt Gophers: a collection of government gophers (`gopher://peg.cwis.uci.edu:7000/11/gopher.welcome/peg/GOPHERS/gov`)
- US Govt Webs: List of WWW Servers (USA - Federal Government), from Federal Information Exchange (`http://www.fie.com/www/us_gov.htm`)
- US Patents and Trademarks: includes Intellectual Property and the National Information Infrastructure issues (`http://www.uspto.gov`)
- US House of Representatives: (`gopher://gopher.house.gov:70`)
- US Senate: (`gopher://gopher.senate.gov:70`)

Policy

These pointers relate to public policy issues or government-citizen interaction, or legal issues.

- ACE: Americans Communicating Electronically (`gopher://cyfer.esusda.gov/11/ace`)
- Communications law: Pepper and Corazzini, L.L.P. specializes in communications law (`http://www.iis.com/p-and-c`)

- Intellectual Property: Working Group on Intellectual Property Rights, a sub-group of the Information Infrastructure Task Force (`http://www.uspto.gov/niiip.html`)

- Internet Economics Collection: a collection of documents that have to do with the economics of the Internet, information goods, and related issues, by Hal Varian (`http://gopher.econ.lsa.umich.edu/EconInternet.html`)

- MIT-RPCP: MIT's Research Program on Communications Policy (`http://farnsworth.mit.edu`)

- Politics: a collection of etexts on miscellaneous political topics (`gopher://fir.cic.net/11/Politics`)

- Tap Info: reports on activities relating to federal information policy (`ftp://ftp.cpsr.org/taxpayer_assets`)

- Telecom legislation: (`ftp://ftp.govt.washington.edu/legislation.telecom/`)

- Voters Telecom Watch: monitoring important bills and alerting the public at crucial times in the life of a bill (`gopher://gopher.panix.com/11/vtw/vtwinfo`)

- Warren Gopher: a collection of electronic newsletters distributed by Jim Warren on the subjects of political action and government access through the use of computer communications (`gopher://gopher.path.net:8102/1`)

Information

Dissemination and Retrieval

- ACM/SIGIR: Association of Computing Machinery (ACM) Special Interest Group on Information Retrieval (`http://info.sigir.acm.org/sigir/`)

- Addressing: Uniform Resource Identifiers/Locators/Names (URI, URL, URN) (`http://info.cern.ch/hypertext/WWW/Addressing/Addressing.html`)

- Advertising: Coalition for Networked Information, Electronic Billboards on the Digital Superhighway, A Report of the Working Group on Internet Advertising (`ftp://ftp.cni.org/CNI/wg.docs/modernization/adpaper-draft.txt`)

- CARL/Uncover: tables of contents and article level access to over 16,000 unique multidisciplinary journals, reflecting the collections of selected CARL System and other libraries (`telnet://database.carl.org`)

- CATRIONA: CATaloguing and Retrieval of Information Over Networks Applications (`http://www.bubl.bath.ac.uk/BUBL/catriona.html`)

- CGI: Common Gateway Interface, a standard for external gateway programs to interface with information servers such as HTTP servers (`http://hoohoo.ncsa.uiuc.edu/cgi/overview.html`)

- CHAT: Conversational Hypertext Access Technology, natural-language interface (`ftp://debra.dgbt.doc.ca/pub/chat/`)

- CIT: Center for Information Technology, a laboratory operated by Stanford University, the encoding, storage, communication, manipulation, and use of information in digital form (`http://logic.stanford.edu/cit/cit.html`)

- CIIR-UMass: Center for Intelligent Information Retrieval, University of Massachusetts, Amherst (`http://ciir.cs.umass.edu`)

- CNI Web: Coalition for Networked Information, promotes creation of and access to information resources in networked environments (`http://www.cni.org/CNI.homepage.html`)

- CWI: Centrum voor Wiskunde en Informatica, Centre for Mathematics and Computer Science, Amsterdam, Netherlands (`http://www.cwi.nl/default.html`)

- CNIDR Web Page: Coalition for Networked Information Discovery and Retrieval Home Page (`http://cnidr.org/welcome.html`)

- Cyberweb: useful information for information providers (`http://www.charm.net`)

- Doc Center: Document Center, a hard copy document delivery service for government and industry specifications and standards (`http://doccenter.com/doccenter/home.html`)

- DIMUND: Document Understanding Information and Resources (`gopher://dimund.umd.edu`)

- Info Provider: discussion of WWW and other servers from an information provider standpoint (`http://info.cern.ch/hypertext/WWW/Provider/Overview.html`)

- Integrated Information: A Vision of an Integrated Internet Information Service, by Weider and Deutsch (`ftp://venera.isi.edu/internet-drafts/draft-ietf-iiir-vision-01.txt`)

- Interpedia: mission is to be a primary source of information for Internet users, and a guide to many of the online resources available (`http://www.hmc.edu/www/interpedia/index.html`)

- IRLP: Internet Resource Location Project (`http://www.cs.colorado.edu/home/gc/cs/genbbb_wwww.html`)

- IRTF: Internet Research Task Force Research Group on Resource Discovery (IRTF-RD) (`http://rd.cs.colorado.edu/~schwartz/IRTF.html`)

- ISI-USC: University of Southern California (USC) Information Sciences Institute (ISI) (`http://www.isi.edu`)

- ISRI-UNLV: Information Science Research Institute, University of Nevada, Las Vegas (`http://www.isri.unlv.edu`)

- Lycos: a research program in providing information retrieval and discovery in the WWW, using a finite memory model of the web to guide intelligent, directed searches for specific information needs (`http://fuzine.mt.cs.cmu.edu/mlm/lycos-home.html`)

- NIR Gopher: Networked Information Retrieval Gopher (`gopher://mailbase.ac.uk`)

- OCLC Research: Toward Providing Library Services for CMC (`ftp://ftp.rsch.oclc.org/pub/internet_resources_project/report/`)

- PCP: Principia Cybernetica Project (PCP)-the computer-supported collaborative development of an evolutionary-systemic philosophy (`http://pespmc1.vub.ac.be/RELATED.html`)

- Riddle: Rapid Information Display and Dissemination in a Library Environment (`ftp://ftp.cwi.nl/pub/RIDDLE/`)

- SGML Review: a biased review of SGML, by Tim Berners-Lee (`http://info.cern.ch/hypertext/WWW/MarkUp/SGML.html`)

- SIGNIDR: Special Interest Group on Networked Information Discovery and Retrieval (`http://www.wais.com/SIGNIDR/`)

- UNITE Archive: User Network Interface To Everything (`ftp://mailbase.ac.uk/pub/lists/unite/`)

- UWI: UnderWorld Industries, nodes that wish to share information with other UWI nodes (`http://zapruder.pds.med.umich.edu/uwi/uwi-info.html`)

- WISE: World Wide Information System for Support of Research and Development Efforts (`http://zgdv.igd.fhg.de/zgdv/Dept.uig/research.html#WISE`)

- Z39.50: Network Information Dissemination Standards (`http://www.research.att.com/~wald/z3950.html`)

Library

- Access: catalogs and databases (`ftp://ftp.unt.edu/library/libraries.txt`)

- ALA: American Library Association (`gopher://gopher.uic.edu/11/library/ala/`)

- ALIX: Automated Library Information Xchange; Advice, opinion, and software by and for librarians; a service of the Federal Library and Information Center Committee, Federal Library Network (`telnet://alix.loc.gov:3001`)

- ARL Web: Association of Research Libraries Web server (`http://arl.cni.org`)

- BUBL Web: The Bulletin Board for Libraries Web server (`http://bubl.bath.ac.uk/BUBLHOME.html`)

- Galaxy LIS: Library and Information Science listing from Galaxy (`http://www.einet.net/galaxy/Social-Sciences/Library-and-Information-Science.html`)
- Library Resources: Library Resources on the Internet-Strategies for Selection and use, Ed. Laine Farley (`ftp://dla.ucop.edu/pub/internet/libcat-guide`)
- Lib resources/Northwestern: Library resources on the Internet, from Northwestern University (`http://www.library.nwu.edu/DOCS/LibResources.html`)
- Lib webs: Library Information Servers via WWW, by Thomas Dowling (`http://www.lib.washington.edu/~tdowling/libweb.html`)
- RLG: Research Libraries Group, Inc., a not-for-profit membership corporation of universities, archives, historical societies, museums, and other institutions devoted to improving access to information that supports research and learning; includes access to Eureka (search system), RLIN (library support system), and Zephyr (Z39.50 services), database, citation files, Ariel document delivery (`http://www-rlg.stanford.edu/welcome.html`)
- US LOC web: United States Library of Congress web (`http://lcweb.loc.gov/homepage/lchp.html`)

Multiple

- FARNET stories: Federation of American Research Networks (FARNet) descriptions of 51 Reasons for a National Information Infrastructure (NII) (`gopher://gopher.cni.org/11/cniftp/miscdocs/farnet`)

Scholarship

- CIOS: Communication Institute for Online Scholarship, a nonprofit organization for online communication scholarship; gopher server (`gopher://cios.llc.rpi.edu`)
- CNI: Coalition for Networked Information, a project of the Association of Research Libraries, CAUSE, and EDUCOM to promote the creation of and access to information resources in networked environments in order to enrich scholarship and to enhance intellectual productivity (`http://www.cni.org/CNI.homepage.html`)
- IATH: Institute for Advanced Technology in the Humanities at the University of Virginia in Charlottesville, an effort to bring Jefferson's educational ideas of exchange across disciplines and integrated living and learning (`http://jefferson.village.virginia.edu`)

- IRIS-Brown: Brown University's Institute for Information Research and Scholarship, explores ways technology can be used for research, teaching, and learning (`http://www.iris.brown.edu/iris`)

- Scholarly Communications Project: of University Libraries, Virginia Polytechnic Institute and State University, a project to pioneer electronic communication of scholarly materials (`http://borg.lib.vt.edu/z-borg/www/scholar.html`)

- Scholarly Communication Reports: Quarterly Technical Reports (`ftp://borg.lib.vt.edu/pub/vpiej-l/reports`)

- Scholarly Societies web: University of Waterloo Library maintains links to gophers and other servers of scholarly societies (`http://www.lib.uwaterloo.ca/~society/overview.html`)

- Scholarly Communication study: University Libraries and Scholarly Communication, A Study Prepared for The Andrew W. Mellon Foundation, by Anthony M. Cummings, Marcia L. Witte, William G. Bowen, Laura O. Lazarus, and Richard H. Ekman, November 1992 (`http://www.lib.virginia.edu/mellon/mellon.html`)

- Scholarly Publishing: Centre for Networked Access to Scholarly Information at Australian National University Library (`http://info.anu.edu.au`)

Technology

The technology of the Net involves a wide spectrum of telecommunications and computing equipment and software. This technology supports the infrastructure of the Net itself as well as the applications that run on it. This section provides pointers to information about computing, multimedia, virtual, network, and telecommunications technologies and resources.

Computing

- ACM Gopher: Association for Computing Machinery's gopher information server (`gopher://acm.org`)

- ACM Web: Association for Computing Machinery (`http://info.acm.org`)

- CACS-U of S LA: Center for Advanced Computer Studies, University of Southwestern Louisiana (`http://www.cacs.usl.edu/Departments/CACS/`)

- CPU Info Center: central processing unit (CPU) information, includes press announcements, papers, machine information, by Tom Burd (`http://www.ncsa.uiuc.edu/General/MetaCenter/MetaCenterHome.html`)

- HPC Archive: London and South East Centre for High Performance Computing, archive on high performance computing, includes articles and facility to add articles (`http://www.lpac.qmw.ac.uk/SEL-HPC/Articles/index.html`)
- NCHPC-USA: National Consortium for High Performance Computing, U.S. research institutions to advance massively parallel processing systems (`http://info.lcs.mit.edu`)
- NCSA-USA: National (USA) Center for Supercomputing Applications (`http://www.ncsa.uiuc.edu/General/NCSAHome.html`)

Developing

- NIMT: National Institute for Management Technology, Ireland (`http://www.nimt.rtc-cork.ie/nimt.htm`)
- NIST-USA Web: National Institute of Standards and Technology WWW Home Page (`http://www.nist.gov/welcome.html`)
- NSF-USA Gopher: National Science Foundation (USA) Gopher (`gopher://stis.nsf.gov:70/11`)
- NTTC-USA: National Technology Transfer Center (`http://iridium.nttc.edu/nttc.html`)

Human Interaction

- ACM/SIGCHI: Association of Computing Machinery (ACM) Special Interest Group on Computers and Human Interaction (`gopher://gopher.acm.org/11[the_files.sig_forums.sigchi]`)
- HCI Index/deGraaff: Human-Computer Interaction Index web (`http://www.twi.tudelft.nl/Local/HCI/HCI-Index.html`)
- HCI Launching Pad: Human-Computer Interaction resources and pointers, by Keith Instone (`http://www.cs.bgsu.edu/HCI/`)
- HCS: Center for Human-Computer studies, at Uppsala University, Sweden (`http://www.cmd.uu.se`)

Multimedia

Audio

- CERL: The CERL Sound Group (U of IL) (`http://datura.cerl.uiuc.edu`)

- Clips: Sites with audio clips (`http://www.eecs.nwu.edu/~jmyers/other-sounds.html`)
- Internet Multicasting WWW: Home page for the Internet Multicasting Service (`http://www.cmf.nrl.navy.mil/radio/radio.html`)
- MIDI: Musical Instrument Digital Interface (`http://www.eeb.ele.tue.nl/midi/index.html`)
- Mbone FAQ Web: Frequently Asked Questions (FAQ) on the Multicast Backbone (MBONE) (`http://www.research.att.com/mbone-faq.html`)
- Music Resources: (`http://www.music.indiana.edu/misc/music_resources.html`)
- Say: Text to Audio (translate text to sound) (`http://utis179.cs.utwente.nl:8001/say/form/`)
- IUMA: Internet Underground Music Archive (`http://sunsite.unc.edu/ianc/index.html`)

Graphics

- ACM/SIGGRAPH: Association of Computing Machinery (ACM) Special Interest Group on Graphics (`gopher://siggraph.org`)
- AIG-Manchester: Advanced Interfaces Group (AIG) at the Computer Science Department at the University of Manchester (`http://www.cs.man.ac.uk/aig/aig.html`)
- CVC-MS State: the Center for Visual Creation, a Silicon Graphics National Training Center (`http://WWW.ERC.MsState.Edu:80/CVC/`)
- CVU-GA Tech: Georgia Institute of Technology's Graphics, Visualization, + Usability Center (`http://www.gatech.edu/gvu/gvutop.html`)
- Images: short descriptions and links to servers on the web which serve computer generated animations, visualizations, movies and interactive images, by Thant Nyo (`http://midget.towson.edu:8000/home.html`)
- Scientific Visualization: Annotated Scientific Visualization URL Bibliography (`http://www.nas.nasa.gov/RNR/Visualization/annotatedURLs.html`)
- Thant's: animation index (`http://mambo.ucsc.edu/psl/thant/thant.html`)
- Video: demonstration of vsbrowser, a video file browser (`http://tns-www.lcs.mit.edu/cgi-bin/vs/vsbrowser`)
- ZGDV: Zentrum f_r Graphische Datenverarbeitung e.V., Computer Graphics Center (`http://zgdv.igd.fhg.de`)

Multi

- Media Lab: MIT Media Lab Home Page (`http://debussy.media.mit.edu`)
- MICE: Multimedia Integrated Conferencing for European Researchers (`http://www.cs.ucl.ac.uk/mice/mice.html`)
- Multimedia Index: Multimedia Information Sources, by Simon Gibbs (`http://cui_www.unige.ch/OSG/MultimediaInfo`)
- Multimedia Lab BU: Multimedia Laboratory at Boston University (`http://spiderman.bu.edu`)
- NYU-Digital: New York University Center for Digital Multimedia (`http://found.cs.nyu.edu`)
- Rob's Multimedia Lab: (`http://www.acm.uiuc.edu:80/rml`)
- Sunsite Multimedia: multimedia presentations based on SunSITE (`http://sunsite.unc.edu/exhibits/exex.html`)
- TNS Tech demo: Technology Demonstrations-multimedia (`http://tns-www.lcs.mit.edu/vs/demos.html`). 3.4.4 Hypermedia
- ACM/SIGLINK: Association of Computing Machinery (ACM) Special Interest Group on Hypertext/Hypermedia (`gopher://gopher.acm.org/11[the_files.sig_forums.siglink]`)
- Bush, Vannevar: As We May Think, article from July 1945 issue of The Atlantic Monthly about hypertext (`http://www.csi.uottawa.ca/~dduchier/misc/vbush/as-we-may-think.html`)
- H Hyperbook: a simple hypertext markup language (`http://siva.cshl.org/h/h.body.html`)
- Hypermedia Lab-TAMU: Texas A and M Hypermedia Research Lab (`ftp://bush.cs.tamu.edu/pub/home.html`)
- Hypertext resources: lists of articles, systems, organizations and resources, by Volker Zink (`http://www.uni-konstanz.de/FuF/Inf-Wiss/IW/hypertext_e.html`)
- Hypertext systems: An Overview of Hypertext and IR systems and applications (`http://info.cern.ch/hypertext/Products/Overview.html`)
- HTML Web: a collection of top-level information, from CERN, about hypertext markup language (`http://info.cern.ch/hypertext/WWW/MarkUp/MarkUp.html`)
- Hypertext terms: glossary of terms from the WWW project, from CERN (`http://info.cern.ch/hypertext/WWW/Terms.html`)
- MapMarker: a tool for creating clickable maps for HTML (`http://www.dl.ac.uk/CBMT/mapmarker/HOME.html`)

Virtual

- DIS: Distributed Interactive Simulation (`ftp://ftp.netcom.com/pub/frankc/dis.html`)
- Meme: virtual world development system (`http://remarque.berkeley.edu/~marc/home.html`)
- Meta VE: Meta Virtual Environments (`http://www.gatech.edu/gvu/people/Masters/Rob.Kooper/Meta.VR.html`)
- MIT Media Lab: access to Massachusetts Institute of Technology's Media Lab (`ftp://media-lab.media.mit.edu/access/`)
- MIT TNS: MIT's Telemedia, Networks, and Systems Group (`http://tns-www.lcs.mit.edu/tns-www-home.html`)
- OVRT: Open Virtual Reality Testbed Home Page, to facilitate the development of standard interfaces and testing methodologies to the many novel types of human interface devices which when integrated form a Virtual Reality system (`http://emo.ncsl.nist.gov/~sressler/OVRThome.html`)
- VRML: Virtual Reality Markup Language (`http://www.wired.com/vrml/`)
- VR collection/Texas: (`gopher://ftp.cc.utexas.edu:3003/11/pub/output/vr`)
- VR Page/Cardiff: (`http://www.cm.cf.ac.uk/User/Andrew.Wilson/VR/`)
- VR Page/Chris Hand: Research, Papers, Archives, Events, User Groups and so on (`http://www.cms.dmu.ac.uk:9999/People/cph/vrstuff.html`)
- VR Page/Luke Sheneman: (`http://www.cs.uidaho.edu/lal/cyberspace/VR/VR.html`)
- VR Web: Virtual Reality Web Page (`http://guinan.gsfc.nasa.gov/W3/VR.html`)
- VR Archive: Sunsite Virtual Reality archive-papers, information, maintained by David Barberi (`http://sunsite.unc.edu/dbarberi/vr.html`)
- VR Testbed: Open Virtual Reality Testbed Home Page (`http://nemo.ncsl.nist.gov/~sressler/OVRThome.html`)
- VSR: Virtual Shared Reality Project (`http://nfhsg3.rus.uni-stuttgart.de/virtual/index.html`)

Networks

Access

These documents help with gaining or finding out about access to networks.

- Connecting to Internet: What Connecting Institutions Should Anticipate (`ftp://nic.merit.edu/documents/fyi/fyi_16.txt`)
- DLIST: a list of dedicated line Internet providers, by Susan Estrada (`mailto:dlist@ora.com Body: Please send DLIST`)
- Internet Access Guide: Access Guide to introducing.the.internet, by Ellen Hoffman (`ftp://nic.merit.edu/introducing.the.internet/access.guide`)
- NII: National Information Infrastructure (`http://sunsite.unc.edu/nii`)
- NIXPUB: Public/Open Access UNIX, by Bux Technical Services (`ftp://rtfm.mit.edu/pub/usenet/alt.bbs/Nixpub_Posting_(Long)`)
- PDIAL: The Public Dialup Internet Access List, by Peter Kaminski (`ftp://rtfm.mit.edu/pub/usenet/news.answers/pdial`)
- PDIAL search: directory provides information on service providers in Northern California, Southern California, and the United States. It was compiled from the Internet pdial listing (`http://www.commerce.net/directories/news/inet.prov.dir.html`)
- PSGnet/RAINet: networking in the developing world, low-cost networking tools, computer networking in general (`gopher://gopher.psg.com`)
- Rural Datafication Web: bring the power of the Internet to rural and otherwise underserved communities (`http://www.cic.net/rd-home.html`)

Administration

- Domain Name Survey: an attempt to discover every host on the Internet by doing a complete search of the Domain Name System (`http://www.nw.com/zone/WWW/top.html`)
- Internet Servers: Building Internet Servers, a collection of information and links from Charm Net (`http://www.charm.net/~cyber/`)
- SNMP: simple network management protocol project group, at the University of Twente, the Netherlands (`http://snmp.cs.utwente.nl`)

Networking

- ATM forum: worldwide organization, aimed at promoting ATM within the industry and the end user community (`http://www.atmforum.com`)
- ATM Research: Asynchronous Transfer Mode (ATM) Research at Naval Research Lab (`http://netlab.itd.nrl.navy.mil/ATM.html`)

■ Bitnet info: a large collection of documentation about Bitnet and EARN (`ftp://lilac.berkeley.edu/netinfo/bitnet/`)

■ Cell Relay: cell-relay or broadband technologies (ATM/DQDB/SONET, etc.) including research papers, standards, product information, mailing list archives, and events (`gopher://cell-relay.indiana.edu/1`)

■ Ethernet page: resources related to the Ethernet (IEEE 802.3) local area network system, by Charles Spurgeon (`http://wwwhost.ots.utexas.edu/ethernet/ethernet-home.html`)

■ FredMail Network: Free Educational Mail, an informal set of nodes to exchange information (`http://www.cerf.net/~noc/HTML/fredmail.html`)

■ IBM's collection: networking information, protocols, standards (`ftp://networking.raleigh.ibm.com/pub`)

■ International Connect: International Connectivity Table, by Larry Landweber (`ftp://ftp.cs.wisc.edu/connectivity_table/`)

■ Internet Country Codes: FAQ about country codes (`ftp://rtfm.mit.edu/pub/usenet/news.answers/mail/country-codes`)

■ Internet Domain Names: Relationship of Telex Answerback Codes to Internet Domains (`ftp://nic.merit.edu/documents/rfc/rfc1394.txt`)

■ Internet/Networking EINet: list of resources related to Internet and Networking from EINet's Galaxy (`http://galaxy.einet.net/Reference-and-Interdisciplinary- Information/Internet-and-Networking.html`)

■ Internet Protocols: listings of working groups and information about protocols—applications, internet, next generation, network management, operational requirements, routing, security, and much more (`http://netlab.itd.nrl.navy.mil/Internet.html`)

■ ISDN info: collection of Integrated Services Digital Network (ISDN)information, from Bellcore (`ftp://info.bellcore.com/pub/ISDN/`)

■ Network Research sites: a list of network researching sites (`http://netlab.itd.nrl.navy.mil/onr.html`)

■ Networking Overview: Overview of information available (`http://web.doc.ic.ac.uk:80/bySubject/Networking.html`)

■ PSGnet/RAINet info: networking in developing world, low-cost tools, networking in general (`gopher://rain.psg.com`)

■ NREN Information: Merit's directory of National Research and Education Network information (`ftp://nic.merit.edu/nren/INDEX.nren`)

■ Personal IP: PPP, MS-Windows and other information and links about connecting with Internet protocols, from Charm Net (`http://www.charm.net/ppp.html`)

- PCLT: PC Lube and Tune; informative introductory material on PC hardware, networks, and newer operating systems (`http://pclt.cis.yale.edu/pclt/default.htm`)
- RSA info: information on many cryptographic related topics (`ftp://rsa.com`)

Security

- CERT FTP: Computer Emergency Response Team at Carnegie Mellon Univ. (`ftp://cert.org/pub/`)
- Cryptorebel/Cypherpunk: Vince Cate's Cryptorebel and Cypherpunk page (`ftp://furmint.nectar.cs.cmu.edu/security/README.html`)
- CSC: Computer Systems Consulting, system security issues information (`http://www.spy.org`)
- First: Forum of Incident Response and Security Teams (`http://first.org`)
- Hack/phreak: resources, happenings, connections, from Randy King (`http://www.phantom.com/~king/`)
- SAIC: Science Applications International Corp, computer security (`http://mls.saic.com/mls.security.text.html`)
- Security index: Computer and Network Security Reference Index, by Rodney Campbell (`http://www.tansu.com.au/Info/security.html`)
- SHEN: A Security Scheme for the World Wide Web (`http://info.cern.ch/hypertext/WWW/Shen/ref/shen.html`)
- Site Security: Site Security Handbook, FYI 8, guidance on how to deal with security issues in the Internet, eds. Holbrook, Reynolds (`ftp://nic.merit.edu/documents/fyi/fyi_08.txt`)

Statistics

- IBC Stats: Internet Business Center's collection of Net statistics-shows lists of Net cities, states, Net Presence by industry, from The Internet Group (`http://tig.com/IBC/Statistics.html`)
- Internet Charts/ISOC: charts of traffic, connectivity, hosts, etc., from the Internet Society (`ftp://ftp.isoc.org/isoc/charts/`)
- Internet Growth: charts showing the Internet's past and projected growth, by Texas Internet Consulting (`ftp://tic.com/matrix/growth/internet/`)

■ NSFnet stats/GVU Center: Georgia Tech's Graphics, Visualization, and Usability Center NSFNET Backbone Statistics Page, includes graphs of statistics (`http://www.cc.gatech.edu/gvu/stats/NSF/merit.html`)

Maps

■ ARPAnet Map: an index of Interface Message Processors on the ARPAnet (circa 1986) (`http://web.kaleida.com/u/hopkins/arpanet/arpanet.html`)

■ Internet Maps (Europe): (`ftp://eunet.fi/nic/pub/netinfo/maps/`)

■ Internet Maps (Many): (`ftp://ftp.uu.net/inet/maps/`)

■ Internet Maps (NSFNET): (`ftp://nic.merit.edu/maps/`)

■ Internet Maps (SuraNet): (`ftp://ftp.sura.net/pub/maps/`)

■ Internet/Matrix: maps from MIDS (Matrix Information and Directory Services) (`gopher://gopher.tic.com/11/matrix/maps/matrix`)

■ USENET Maps: Maps of Usenet news feeds/backbones (`ftp://gatekeeper.dec.com/pub/maps/`)

■ UUCP Maps: Unix-Unix Copy Protocol Map Data (`gopher://agate.berkeley.edu:4324/1uumaps`)

■ WWW Resource Maps: The Virtual Tourist, a collection of maps from all over the world to help you locate Internet sites and resources (`http://wings.buffalo.edu/world`)

Telecommunications

■ ATP-LLNL: Advanced Telecommunications Program at Lawrence Livermore National Laboratory (`http://www-atp.llnl.gov/atp/`)

■ CTR-Columbia U Web: Columbia University Center for Telecommunications Research (CTR) (`http://www.ctr.columbia.edu/CUCTR_Home.html`)

■ Data Comm/Networking: Data Communications and Networking Links, by Don Joslyn (`http://www.racal.com/networking.html`)

■ INT-France: Institut National des Telecommunications, France (`http://arctique.int-evry.fr`)

■ Tele/Communications: Information Sources about Communications and Tele-communications (`http://www.tansu.com.au/Info/communications.html`)

■ Telecomm Archives: files about telecommunications, from the Usenet group comp.dcom.telecom (`ftp://lcs.mit.edu/telecom-archives/`)

- TelecomInfo: from New York State Department of Education gopher (`gopher://unix5.nysed.gov/11/TelecommInfo`)
- TIS-Kansas: Telecommunications and Information Sciences Laboratory, University of Kansas (`http://www.tisl.ukans.edu`)
- US-ITS: Institute for Telecommunication Sciences, USA government research and engineering laboratory (`http://www.its.bldrdoc.gov/its.html`)
- US-NTIA: National Telecommunications and Information Administration (USA) (`telnet://ntiabbs.ntia.doc.gov`)
- US-NTIA web: National Telecommunications and Information Administration (USA) (`http://sunny.stat-usa.gov/resources/NTIA_info.html`)

Culture

While the Net is composed of hardware, software, and network connections—the most amazing thing about the online world is the cultural and social expressions that take place on it. This section surveys online art, communities, language-related resources, people, and society. You'll find pointers to individual home pages as well as pointers to collections of papers about societal impacts and issues.

Art

- ANIMA: Arts Network for Integrated Media Applications (`http://wimsey.com/anima/ANIMAhomeF.html`)
- Art/images: a collection of art and images in several formats (ASCII, TIFF, GIF, JPEG) (`gopher://cs4sun.cs.ttu.edu/11/Art%20and%20Images`)
- Art/Net: Art on the Net, artists share and create works together on the Internet (`http://www.art.net`)
- ArtSource: a gathering point for networked resources on Art and Architecture (`http://www.uky.edu/Artsource/artsourcehome.html`)
- ASCII Art Bazaar: collection of ASCII art and images, 12 megabytes of information covering an estimated 24,000 art works from more than 3300 contributions classified under 759 subject titles (`gopher://twinbrook.cis.uab.edu/1asciiarc.70`)
- Cyber Art: art from a course at Rensselaer Polytechnic Institute, instructor Kevin Daniel (`http://www.rpi.edu/~daniek2`)
- Cirque de la Mama: to bring works of art to people and to bring people to works of art (`http://lancet.mit.edu/cirque/cirque.html`)

- CIS-AH: Center for Integrative Studies—Arts and Humanities (`http://web.cal.msu.edu`)
- CyberCafe: conference at the Institute of Contemporary Art in London (`http://cybercafe.demon.co.uk`)
- Digital Co-op: a nonhierarchical organization of artists, writers, and computer professionals in Vancouver B.C., a community-oriented body dedicated to the sharing of information, talent, and resources (`http://www.wimsey.com/~jmax/DCO.html`)
- Digital Gallery: Syracuse University's Computer Graphics for the Arts Department (`http://ziris.syr.edu/home.html`)
- Electric Gallery: presents native and primitive art that is unique and famous throughout the world (`http://www.elpress.com/gallery/homepage.html`)
- FineArt Forum: List of Art Related Web Resources (`http://www.willamette.edu/~jpatters/art-resources.html`)
- Free Art: pages and the graphics, by Harlan Wallach (`http://www.mcs.net/~wallach/freeart/buttons.html`)
- ISEA: International Symposium on Electronic Art (`http://www.uiah.fi/isea/index.html`)
- NWHQ: New World Headquarters-free expression and the distribution of artistic ideas, independent artists supporting independent artists (`http://www.wimsey.com/~jmax/index.html`).
- Off the Wall: works of one or more artists, from Global Network Navigator (`http://nearnet.gnn.com/gnn/arcade/gallery/art.html`)

Community

Information

- Civic Networking: WWW Guide to Community Networking, by Catherine Kummer (`http://http2.sils.umich.edu/ILS/community.html`)
- Community Nets/McGee: information about community networks, by Arthur R. McGee (`ftp://ftp.netcom.com/pub/amcgee/community/`)
- CPSR Community Net info: (`http://www.cpsr.org/dox/community.nets.html`)
- Free-Nets Home Page: Free-net information, presented as a public service by Peter Scott, at the University of Saskatchewan Libraries (`http://herald.usask.ca/~scottp/free.html`)

- NPTN: National Public Telecomputing Network (`ftp://nptn.org/pub/`)
- Public/Nets papers: Working Paper Series in Public Access Networks (`http://libertynet.upenn.edu/world/comm-net/papers.html`)

Virtual

Some instances of virtual communities.

- Blacksburg electronic village: (`http://www.bev.net`)
- CIAO!: British Columbia, Canada (`telnet://ciao.trail.bc.ca`)
- Cleveland Free-Net: the world's first community Fee-Net (`telnet://visitor@freenet-in-a.cwru.edu`)
- Digital City: de Digitale Stad, Amsterdam, Netherlands (`telnet://dds.hacktic.nl`)
- Ecafe: the electronic cafe, a communiting of music, art and imagination (`http://www.cyberspace.org/u/ecafe/www/index.html`)
- Silicon Valley: Silicon Valley Public Access Link Community Page (`http://www.svpal.org`)
- Virtual City: Virtual City Network Project (`http://virtual.net/VirtualCity/`)
- WebWorld: people build places and link net resources to a graphical interface, uses Mosaic forms capability for interaction (`http://sailfish.peregrine.com/ww/welcome.html`)

Language

- ACW gopher: Alliance for Computers and Writing gopher (`gopher://logos.daedalus.com/11/Alliance%20for%20Computers%20and%20Writing`)
- ALEX: find and retrieve the full-text of documents on the Internet from such archives as Project Gutenberg, Wiretap, the On-line Book Initiative, the Eris system at Virginia Tech, the English Server at Carnegie Mellon University, and the online Oxford Text Archive (`gopher://rsl.ox.ac.uk/11/lib-corn/hunter`)
- Book Info Center: Internet Book Information Center (IBIC) (`http://sunsite.unc.edu/ibic/IBIC-homepage.html`)
- Computer Jargon search: search the jargon file on WWW (`http://web.cnam.fr/bin.html/By_Searchable_Index?Jargon_File.html`)
- Computing Dictionary (web): The Free On-line Dictionary of Computing (`http://wombat.doc.ic.ac.uk`)

- CMT: The Center for Machine Translation (CMT) at the School of Computer Science at Carnegie Mellon University; advanced research and development in natural language processing, with a focus on multi-lingual machine translation (`http://www.mt.cs.cmu.edu/cmt/CMT-home.html`)

- eText-Caltech: the eText (electronic hypermedia textbooks) group at Caltech (`http://www.etext.caltech.edu`)

- ETC-UV: Electronic Text Center—University of Virginia (`http://www.lib.virginia.edu/etext/ETC.html`)

- Gutenberg Web Page: a project to give away online texts, hundreds of titles (`http://med-amsa.bu.edu/Gutenberg/Welcome.html`)

- Hacker's Dictionary: a searchable index of Hacker's Jargon (`http://iicm.tu-graz.ac.at/Cjargon`)

- Human: human languages page, cataloging human-language resources and making those resources available to the Web community through a concise index (`http://www.willamette.edu/~tjones/Language-Page.html`)

- Internet Glossary: search a collection of Internet terms (`wais://pinus.slu.se:210/Internet-user-glossary?`)

- Internet Wiretap Gopher: electronic books and information (`gopher://wiretap.Spies.COM`)

- ITK: Instituut voor Taal- en Kennistechnologie, Institute for Language Technology and Artificial Intelligence (`http://itkwww.kub.nl:2080/itk/itkhome.html`)

- Natural Language: Natural Language Software Registry, summary of the capabilities and sources of language processing software available to researchers (`http://cl-www.dfki.uni-sb.de/cl/registry/ed_note.html`)

- Smileys (all): all the smileys in the known universe (`gopher://gopher.ora.com/00/feature_articles/universe.smiley`)

- Writer's Resources: Internet Writer Resources, Compiled/Edited/Maintained by L. Detweiler (`ftp://rtfm.mit.edu/pub/usenet/news.answers/writing/resources`)

People

Aspects

- Cognitive/Psychological sources: information sources on the Internet about academic programs, periodicals, network resources, and many other online resources, by Scott Mainwaring (`http://matia.stanford.edu/cogsci.html`)

- GA Tech-Cognitive: Cognitive Science at Georgia Tech (`http://www.gatech.edu/aimosaic/cogsci.html`)

- HCRL-Open U: Human Cognition Research Laboratory, The Open University, Milton Keynes, United Kingdom (`http://hcrl.open.ac.uk`) 4.4.2 Lists - directories, home pages

- BEST N. American: identify and locate researchers by interest and expertise (in North America) similar to your own (`http://best.gdb.org/best.html`)

- CMC People: people interested in the study of CMC, from the CMC studies center (`http://www.rpi.edu/~decemj/cmc/people.html`)

- DA-CLOD People Page: Distributedly Administered Categorical List Of Documents collection of personal home pages (`http://schiller.wustl.edu/DACLOD/daclod?id=00008.dcl`)

- GNN's People: Global Network Navigator's Internet Center Netizen's project, a directory of home pages written by GNN users (`http://nearnet.gnn.com/gnn/meta/internet/netizens/index.html`)

- Houh's People: Henry Houh's List of People on the Web (`http://tns-www.lcs.mit.edu/people/hhh/people.html`)

- Internet People: Who's Who in the Internet, Biographies of IAB, IESG and IRSG Members (`ftp://nic.merit.edu/documents/fyi/fyi_09.txt`)

- UT-Austin Personal Pages: a collection of personal pages worldwide, from the University of Texas at Austin (`http://www.utexas.edu/world/personal/index.html`)

- Who's Who: a collective database of a noncommercial biographies of people on the Net (`http://www.ictp.trieste.it/Canessa/ENTRIES/entries.html`)

- WSPS Personal Pages: Web Self-Publishing System People Pages (`http://sparc57.cs.uiuc.edu:8000/groups/personal_homepages_group.html`)

- Yahoo Personal Pages: Entertainment-People's Home Pages, from Yahoo (`http://akebono.stanford.edu/yahoo/Entertainment/People_s_Home_Pages/`)

Society

- ACM SIGCAS: Association for Computing Machinery (ACM) Special Interest Group on Computers and Society (`gopher://gopher.acm.org/11[the_files.sig_forums.sigcas]`)

- CCH: Centre for Computing in the Humanities (`gopher://alpha.epas.utoronto.ca/11/cch`)

- Coombs Papers: science and humanities papers, bibliographies, directories, theses abstracts and other high-grade research material (`gopher://coombs.anu.edu.au`)

- Culture/Tech: a collection of texts exploring the relationship of technology and culture (`http://english-server.hss.cmu.edu/Cyber.html`)

- Cyber papers/EFF: collection of cyberspace-related papers, from the Electronic Frontier Foundation (`ftp://ftp.eff.org/pub/Publications/CuD/Papers/`)

- Cyberspace: The New Frontier, by The Laboratory for Applied Logic at the University of Idaho (`http://www.cs.uidaho.edu/lal/cyberspace/cyberspace.html`)

- Cyberpunk FAQ: from the Usenet newsgroup alt.cyberpunk (`ftp://rtfm.mit.edu/pub/usenet/news.answers/cyberpunk-faq`)

- Cypherpunk Topics: information pulled off of many sources, mostly sci.crypt and the cypherpunks mailing list (`ftp://ftp.u.washington.edu/public/phantom/cpunk/README.html`)

- Cypherpunks gopher: clipper, DC Nets, digital cash, protocols, other info (`gopher://chaos.bsu.edu`)

- Cypherpunks home page: PGP, remailers, rants, various crypto-tools, newspaper clippings, and a good deal of other things (`ftp://soda.berkeley.edu/pub/cypherpunks/Home.html`)

- MetaNet Gopher: management, organizational change and development, education, the arts and the humanities, the impact of technology on society, the future, law, health, the environment, public policy, reinventing government (`gopher://tmn.com`)

- English Server: examine the possibilities of collaborative, community-run communications (`http://english-server.hss.cmu.edu`)

- Future Culture: information about Net culture, media, virtual communities, cyberpunk, memetics (`http://www.ifi.uio.no/~mariusw/futurec/index.html`)

- Gender/Spertus: Ellen Spertus' Writings on Gender and Science/Engineering (`http://www.ai.mit.edu/people/ellens/gender.html`)

- Global/Women: Global Fund for Women, an international grantmaking organization (`http://www.ai.mit.edu/people/ellens/gfw.html`)

- Hacker Crackdown: text of *The Hacker Crackdown—Law and Disorder on the Electronic Frontier* by Bruce Sterling (`http://www.scrg.cs.tcd.ie/scrg/u/bos/hacker/hacker.html`)

- Internet demographics: a survey by Texas Internet Consulting (`ftp://ftp.tic.com/survey/`)

- McGee collection: Art McGee's collection on culture and society issues—Activism, African, community, development, gender, indigenous, Latin (`ftp://ftp.netcom.com/pub/amcgee/`)

- Net Etiquette Guide: by Arlene H. Rinaldi (`ftp://ftp.lib.berkeley.edu/pub/net.training/FAU/`)

- Netizen Anthology: The Netizens and the Wonderful World of the Net-an anthology, Ronda Hauben, Michael Hauben (`ftp://wuarchive.wustl.edu/doc/misc/acn/netbook`)

- Networking: Networking on the Network, by Phil Agre (`mailto:rre-request@weber.ucsd.edu Subject: archive send network`)

- SeniorNet Profile: (`http://nearnet.gnn.com/gnn/meta/internet/mkt/seniorNet/center.html`)

- UWI Cultural Play: UWI's Web's Edge/UnderWorld Industries' Cultural Playground (`http://kzsu.stanford.edu/uwi.html`)

GLOSSARY

Add-ons General term encompassing viewers, players, and other multimedia additions to Web clients.

Amiga Mosaic Web client program for the Amiga (formerly from Commodore) computer; otherwise known as AMosaic. Unlike the other Mosaics, *not* distributed by NCSA.

Browser More common term for *client*.

Bulleted List List of items on a Web page, separated by large dots.

Cello Popular Web client for Microsoft Windows, distributed through Cornell University's Legal Information Institute.

CERN The European Laboratory for Particle Physics, where the World Wide Web project originated in 1989.

CERN Line Browser The first Web client, distinguished by the use of numbers where most clients show highlighted hyperlinks.

Chimera Web client for X Window systems.

Clickable Map   Unofficial name for *Imagemap,* so called because to access a related URL the user "clicks" the mouse when the on-screen pointer is juxtaposed on a portion of the map (or graphic).

Client   Software that allows users to access and browse the World Wide-Web. Clients can display HTML pages in their desired format. Unofficially termed *browsers.*

DNS   Domain Name System; DNS errors occur when clients cannot determine the site of a requested Web document.

Document   Catch-all term for anything that appears in the main windows of a Web client. More specifically, a Web document is an HTML document that the client displays.

Editor   For the Web, an editor is a program that assists in the authoring of HTML documents. Typically it includes tagging and formatting macros.

Fill-in Forms   Specially designed section of HTML document that accepts input from users; typically used for user feedback, product ordering, or document searching.

Firewall   Areas of a computer file system protected against unwanted access by Web users.

Formatted Text   Text included on a Web page that was formatted by another type of computer program (i.e., is *not* in HTML format), and is displayed by the Web client in that original format.

Forms   Short-form for *fill-in forms.*

FTP   File transfer protocol, a means to exchange files across a network. The set of all resources accessible through publicly-available file transfer protocol sites is sometimes referred to as FTP space.

Gateway   A connecting point that translates different network email protocols, thus enabling them to intercommunicate.

Gopher   A means for disseminating or discovering resources on the Internet through a menu interface. Menu items can be links to other documents, search utilities, or information services. The set of all resources publicly accessible through the Internet Gopher protocol is sometimes referred to as Gopher space.

Graphical Browser   A Web client capable of displaying inline graphics, and which offers a mouse-based point-and-click hypertext interface.

Graphics file   A file in graphics format that can be retrieved through the client's capabilities, but which usually cannot be displayed via the browser itself. Graphics files are typically viewed through an add-on or file viewer associated with the client.

Heading   An emphasized line or section in an HTML document. Several heading styles are available.

Helpers   Macintosh name for add-ons, viewers, and *players.*

Home page   Refers to a designated entry-point for access to a local web. Also refers to a page that a person designates as their own "main page" often presenting personal or professional information.

Hotspot   A region within the display of hypertext that, when selected, links the user to another point in the hypertext or to another (possibly nonhypertext) resource.

HTML   HyperText Markup Language: the coding mechanism used to author Web pages. Web clients display HTML pages according to their coded format.

HTTP   HyperText Transfer Protocol: the Web's primary protocol, HTTP performs the request and retrieve functions necessary to display documents stored on remote computers.

Hyperlink   A *hypertext link* appearing as a number of a highlight in a client's main window.

Hypermedia   An extension of *hypertext* that includes sound, graphics, and video as linking devices.

Hypertext   Term coined by Ted Nelson denoting text linked across a potentially unlimited number of information sources. One link takes the user to another document, which contains links to other documents (and so forth), and these documents can be located on any hypertext-capable system anywhere in the world. Hypertext is the basis of the World Wide Web.

Imagemaps   Formal name for *clickable maps*: imagemaps are graphic elements that have embedded into them two or more hyperlinks, each hyperlink offering an individual jump to a linked document. Frequently imagemaps are in fact maps, but they can appear as any graphic. A medical tutorial, for example, could offer a graphic of the human body as an imagemap; users

clicking on the heart area of the imagemap would be linked to a document or series of documents related to heart issues.

Inline Image   Graphic that appears as part of the Web page: inline images are coded into Web documents through the HTML language, and load with the Web page itself. In most Web clients, inline images can be delayed or toggled off to improve retrieval speed.

Internet   A cooperatively-run, globally-distributed collection of computer networks that exchange information via a common set of rules for exchannging data (the TCP/IP protocol suite).

Jump   The act of retrieving a new document as the result of selecting a hyperlink. The term "jump" is used because the user is often accessing a new computer somewhere in the world, but no actual leaping about takes place, except for a change in URL addresses.

Knowbot   A *robot* that is programmed to acquire specific document references.

Line Browser   Short-form for *CERN Line Browser.*

Link   A reference to another Web document, or another section of the same Web document. Links are typically highlighted when displayed in Web clients.

Lynx   The most capable nongraphical Web client, developed by the University of Kansas and available on many UNIX servers.

MacMosaic   Short-form for *NCSA Mosaic* for the Apple Macintosh.

MacWeb   Web client for the Apple Macintosh, distributed by EINet.

MacWWW   Alternative (and little used) name for the Web client *Samba*.

The Matrix   The set of all networks that can exchange electronic mail either directly or through mail gateways. This term was coined by John S. Quarterman in his book *The Matrix* (Digital Press, 1990).

MidasWWW   X Window System Web client developed by the Stanford Linear Accelerator Center.

Mosaic   Short-form for *NCSA Mosaic* or a licensed version distributed commercially.

Multimedia   Catch-all term for the integration of text, graphics, sound, animation, video, and communications technologies.

Navigation   The act of traversing the Web, or of moving among linked documents on a variety of computers. Navigation is a central topic in discussions of hypertext system, because of the problem of getting "lost in hyperspace." Web clients typically offer navigation histories to help users find their way back along their hyperlink paths.

NCSA   The National Center for Supercomputing Applications, located at the University of Illinois at Urbana-Champaign. Developers and distributors of *NCSA Mosaic*.

NCSA Mosaic   The most popular graphical Web client, available for X Window System, the Apple Macintosh, and Microsoft Windows, and licensed to several companies for commercial release.

The Net   An informal term for the Internet or some subset of *The Matrix,* with its specific meaning defined by the context of use. For example, a computerized conference via email make take place on a BITNET host that has an Internet gateway, making the conference available to anyone on either of these networks. In this case, the developer might say, "Our conference will be available on the Net."

Numbered List   List of items on a Web page, separated by numbers.

Page   HTML document displayed in a client's main window; completely undefined parameters, but typically a Web page is about 40-60 lines in length including inline graphics.

Player   Software program capable of displaying sound or video files retrieved through a Web client. Players are separate programs from clients, with their functions and file associations specified in the client's configuration system.

Robot   Program that automatically traverses the Web looking for URL addresses: the results of the search are typically built as an HTML document. Potentially harmful to Web servers.

Samba   The first graphical client for the Web, developed by CERN and still available. Significantly lacking in features by the standards set by today's graphical clients.

Site   File section of a computer on which Web documents reside. Typically used to refer to the specific organization that controls these documents (e.g., the MIT site, the AT&T site).

Sound File   Computer file containing digitized sound; can be retrieved by a Web client but can be heard only through *player* software associated with the client.

Spider   Program that traverses the Web automatically. Similar to *robot,* a spider creates a database of Web links.

Surfing   The act of navigating the Web, typically used to denote jumping (see "jump") from page to page, using techniques to rapidly process (or disregard most) content in order to locate subjectively-valuable or interesting resources.

Tag   Formatting code item within an HTML document.

Text-Based Browser   Web client used by text terminals, typically UNIX-based.

Title   The author-determined name of a World Wide Web page.

tkWWW   Graphical Web client for the X Window system.

URL   Uniform Resource Locator, the addressing system for Web documents.

Usenet   A system for disseminating asynchronous text discussion among cooperating computer hosts. A Usenet newsgroup is a forum for discussing a particular subject, topic, or subtopic. Usenet is not a network nor is it limited to distribution on the Internet, but is disseminated widely throughout the Matrix and beyond.

Video file   Computer file consisting of digitized video; can be retrieved by a Web client but can only be heard through a player or *viewer* associated with the client.

Viewer   Software program capable of displaying graphics or video files retrieved through a Web client. Viewers are separate programs from clients, their functions and file associations specified in the client's configuration system.

Viola   Graphical Web client for the X Window system, part of an object-oriented programming language.

Wanderer   Program that automatically traverses the Web. Similar to robot, its aim is to measure the growth of the Web.

web   A set of hypertext pages related to a particular topic or which may be located on a single host; a subset of the *Web.*

Web   Common short-form for the World Wide Web.

Web Server   Computer on which Web documents reside, and which runs HTTP software to permit Web transactions.

WinMosaic   Short-form for *NCSA Mosaic* for Microsoft Windows.

WinWeb   Web client for Microsoft Windows, distributed by EINet. It is the Windows version of *MacWeb.*

World Wide Web   Distributed hypermedia system originating at CERN in 1989.

www   Little-used name for the *CERN Line Browser.*

WWW   The *World Wide Web.*

XMosaic   Short-form for *NCSA Mosaic* for the X Window System.

INDEX

Add to Your Sams Library Today with the Best Books for Programming, Operating Systems, and New Technologies

The easiest way to order is to pick up the phone and call

1-800-428-5331

between 9:00 a.m. and 5:00 p.m. EST.

For faster service please have your credit card available.

ISBN	Quantity	Description of Item	Unit Cost	Total Cost
0-672-30519-4		Teach Yourself the Internet: Around the World in 21 Days	$25.00	
0-672-30466-X		The Internet Unleashed	$44.95	
0-672-30485-6		Navigating the Internet, Deluxe Edition	$29.95	
0-672-30520-8		Your Internet Consultant: The FAQs of Life Online	$25.00	
0-672-30530-5		The Internet Business Guide: Riding the Information Superhighway to Profit	$25.00	
0-672-30595-X		Education on the Internet	$25.00	
0-672-30464-3		Teach Yourself UNIX in a Week	$28.00	
0-672-30457-0		Learning UNIX	$39.95	
0-672-30382-5		Understanding Local Area Networks	$26.95	
0-672-30206-3		Networking Windows, NetWare Edition	$24.95	
0-672-30209-8		NetWare Unleashed	$45.00	
0-672-30173-3		Enterprise-Wide Networking	$39.95	
0-672-30501-1		Understanding Data Communications	$29.99	
0-672-30119-9		International Telecommunications	$39.95	
❏ 3 ½" Disk		Shipping and Handling: See information below.		
❏ 5 ¼" Disk		TOTAL		

Shipping and Handling: $4.00 for the first book, and $1.75 for each additional book. Floppy disk: add $1.75 for shipping and handling. If you need to have it NOW, we can ship product to you in 24 hours for an additional charge of approximate $18.00, and you will receive your item overnight or in two days. Overseas shipping and handling adds $2.00 per book and $8.00 for up to three disks. Prices subject to change. Call for availability and pricing information on latest editions.

201 W. 103rd Street, Indianapolis, Indiana 46290

1-800-428-5331 — Orders   1-800-835-3202 — FAX   1-800-858-7674 — Customer Servic

PLUG YOURSELF INTO...

The MCP Internet Site

Free information and vast computer resources from the world's leading computer book publisher—online!

Find the books that are right for you!

A complete online catalog, plus sample chapters and tables of contents give you an in-depth look at *all* our books. The best way to shop or browse!

- ✦ **Stay informed** with the latest computer industry news through discussion groups, an online newsletter, and customized subscription news.
- ✦ **Get fast answers** to your questions about MCP books and software.
- ✦ **Visit** our online bookstore for the latest information and editions!
- ✦ **Communicate** with our expert authors through e-mail and conferences.
- ✦ **Play** in the BradyGame Room with info, demos, shareware, and more!
- ✦ **Download software** from the immense MCP library:
  - Source code and files from MCP books
  - The best shareware, freeware, and demos
- ✦ **Discover hot spots** on other parts of the Internet.
- ✦ **Win books** in ongoing contests and giveaways!

Drop by the new Internet site of Macmillan Computer Publishing!

To plug into MCP:

World Wide Web: http://www.mcp.com/
Gopher: gopher.mcp.com **FTP:** ftp.mcp.com

GOING ONLINE DECEMBER 1994!